Russell Warren Howe is a Washington freelance writer specializing in foreign affairs and defence. He has been a foreign correspondent for the *Washington Post* and the *Baltimore Sun*. The author of many books on global subjects, Russell Warren Howe has won international acclaim for his book *The Power Peddlers*, which investigated foreign-policy lobbying in Washington.

WEAPONS

Russell Warren Howe

WEAPONS

The International Game of Arms, Money and Diplomacy

First published in Great Britain in ABACUS in 1981
by Sphere Books Ltd
30/32 Gray's Inn Road, London WC1X 8JL

Printed and bound in Great Britain by
Cox & Wyman Ltd, Reading

Samuel Cummings: *All weapons are defensive and all spare parts are nonlethal.*

Senator Stuart Symington: *That is a most significant observation.*

. . .

Cummings: *I know of the theoretical desire [of] the American Government to balance [weapons]. In my personal opinion, that is a total mirage and illusion . . . The mere fact that the United States tries, that will encourage the U.S.S.R. just to put the thumb on the balance and throw it out of kilter . . .*

Symington: *Another most significant observation. What you are saying is, as we try to balance it, the Soviets try to unbalance it.*

Cummings: *Exactly. It is a game, if nothing else, and we would do the same in a reverse standpoint.*

. . .

Cummings: *There are wonderful regulations and pronouncements of policy, and white papers, but the plainest print cannot be read through a gold eagle.*

Symington: *That is quite an observation.*

> Hearings: Senate subcommittee on Near Eastern and South Asian Affairs. April 13, 1967.

CONTENTS

PROLOGUE

Shoot to Miss

Things are in the saddle
And ride mankind
EMERSON

I ONCE WENT to Armageddon for the sort of reason reporters go to places with names like that. I went there to be able to use the cypress-studded hill as a dateline for a Baltimore *Sun* article on the chances of peace that year in the Middle East.

Armageddon—Megiddo, in the local Hebrew—overlooks the fertile Plain of Esdraelon and the haunting Valley of Jezreel. Little seems to have changed since it found its way into the Book of Revelation. It could belong in any war. If you built a plywood monastery, you could film the epic World War Two battle of Monte Cassino on its chalky-white abutments; or you could just sit there, as I did, and meditate on arms and men.

It was not far away to the northeast—say, thirty miles, or seventy seconds Mach-2 flight in a Phantom or a MiG-23—that something happened on October 8, 1973. What took place then was just possibly more frightening than anything else that has occurred in global affairs since World War Two—an officer's decision which set a caravan of events in motion that brushed the face of the Armageddon of our minds, like a bird of prey that has dropped a wing clumsily, then regained its normal lift and thrust and peeled away without causing harm.

The scene was the Golan, an Israeli-occupied high plateau which the Syrians were in the process of recapturing in what most of the Middle East calls the Ramadan War.

At 10 P.M. on that October 8, Israel's northern front commander, Major General Yitshak Hoffi, informed his defense minister, Moshe Dayan, that he could not hold out much longer against Syrian armor. A U.S. intelligence report says that shortly after midnight—a seemingly symbolic hour for such decisions—Dayan exacted permission from Prime Minister Golda Meir to arm thirteen Jericho missiles with nuclear warheads. The Jericho is a surface-to-surface weapon jointly developed by France and Israel.

U.S. intelligence analysts have since determined that the warheads were assembled in three days and six hours of feverish activity, in an underground tunnel, at the start of the war, using plutonium from the nuclear energy plant at Dimona in the Negev. They were of 20-kiloton, "Nagasaki" force. The Jericho has a range of roughly three hundred miles, putting Cairo and Damascus within its target ability. Fired from Sharm esh-Sheikh, in the occupied Sinai, a nuclearized Jericho could even have taken out both the new and old Aswan dams, and drowned a million Egyptians. Fitting such warheads to air-to-surface missiles instead of Jerichos would of course have extended the range, and Israel's Phantom fighters could carry such a payload.

The nuclearization of Israel's missiles remained a deep secret until three days later. Then, before dawn on October 12, a U. S. Air Force SR-71 took off from a base on the east coast of the United States. Two hours later, a KC-135 from Rota, Spain, refueled it high above the waters off the Algarve coast. An hour or so later it was on a routine, war-report reconnaissance over Israel, Jordan and Syria.

The aircraft and its crew belonged to the 9th Strategic Reconnaissance Wing, normally based at Beale Air Force Base in California. The plane requires special fuel and maintenance, and a "classified" air-refueling technique. For what a Pentagon source calls "both practical reasons and security," it is easier to operate it out of the United States or Guam than from foreign bases.

Known to laymen as the Blackbird, from its dull black, heat-resistant paint, the Lockheed SR-71 is specifically designed to monitor breaches of the Nuclear Non-Proliferation Treaty. It has "global range": Refueled in flight, it can circumnavigate the world in under a day. It flies exceptionally high and exceptionally fast. (At Mach-3, its optimal speed, it can keep pace with a rifle bullet. In 1974, flying from a field near New York to Farnborough Air Show in southeast England in under two hours, a Blackbird broke the transatlantic speed record.)

The delta-shaped plane roams the stratosphere, a platform of infrared cameras, radiation, radar- and radio-monitoring devices and other sensors surveying 100,000 square miles of the earth per hour. It could map the United States in three passes. SR-71s regularly overfly China, and skirt the Soviet border using "slant" photography. Their high-resolution cameras are of the sort that sold President Eisenhower on the virtues of spy-in-the-sky aviation—by picking out, from 60,000 feet, a golfball lying in the rough at Augusta golf course. Over the Negev Desert, the cameras and perhaps the sensors also (the writer's information on this "classified" incident is inevitably incomplete) began to get the doomsday message. However, this could not be known by either the pilot or the reconnaissance systems officer (RSO) seated at his back, for the secret was sealed in the equipment beneath their cockpit. Both men aboard the SR-71 are pilots and their job is to fly a pre-set route and return to base. They are not even told later if they have scored.

But on a panel, the RSO could see something else: his downward radar had picked up two aircraft climbing: his computer, data-linked to a control plane and to "ground" control—in the event, a U.S. warship—had identified them as Phantoms, and neither was responding to the pulses of the Blackbird's IFF (Identification Friend or Foe).

Seconds before, out in the choppy blue waters of the eastern Mediterranean, the control ship—a communications vessel with codebreaking equipment—was busy intercepting the traffic of all the belligerents. Suddenly, voice communications from two Israeli pilots came through in Hebrew and in clear.

"Affirmative, I have it," said one. "It's a U.S. Blackbird."

The Israeli ground controller's voice cracked back: "Down it!"

Meanwhile, the ship, data-linked in turn to the Hawkeye control plane flying off eastern Cyprus, had passed its first signal, through the Hawkeye, to the Blackbird. Computered words had appeared on a screen, telling the RSO what the control plane's sensors, linked to the ship's computers and analyzing the emitters of the "bogeys" (unfriendly planes), had discovered: that they were Phantoms. In a microsecond, the computer, also from its memory, had described the probable ordnance aboard the Phantoms and their target range. Then came the unusual pickup of Israeli voice communications. Immediately, on a panel by the Blackbird pilot's hand, a button flashed, telling the Blackbird to "break off." This was an order from the Hawkeye. The spyplane at once began nosing up to 85,000 feet—about twice the operational ceiling of a Phantom, and out of its missile range. The two U.S. airmen in the sleek, dark aircraft raced for home, refueling again shortly after Gibraltar—and still not knowing what they had discovered.

The Israelis would shoot down a U. S. Air Force aircraft? Well, possibly—but then again, possibly not in this case. Voice communications aren't needed in such an operation: The Israeli pilot would normally tell his ground controller of "acquisition" by punching a button rather like a typewriter or touchtone key. Identification of the SR-71 would go to him, from ground or air control, not the other way round. His instructions would come when another key—"Destroy"—lit up, along with yet another key commanding the ordnance he should use. The voice communications were presumably meant to be overheard—to get the Blackbird to decamp. This is the writer's assumption, and two separate Pentagon experts agree with it. But it *is* conjecture: After all, in 1967, the

Israelis had gone one further and tried to sink a U.S. communications ship that had uncovered an Israeli disinformation tactic. (Of this, more later.) In the 1973 Blackbird incident, historically speaking, the scenario became less lethal, but even more dramatic.

A meeting of some members of the National Security Council was hastily called in Washington. The meeting faced a contingency of the sort which the Pentagon faces familiarly in the game of nations. This time it was real. If Israel nukes Cairo or Alexandria or Damascus, what happens next? It is an unwritten law of nuclear strategy that every strike calls forth a counterstrike of at least equal force. Presumably, therefore, Russia nukes Tel Aviv or Haifa to give protection to its protégés. Congress boils over, the United States intervenes, and we have World War Three on our hands. The riposte to any Israeli nuclear attack must therefore be "local": It must come from an Arab country, not a superpower, and from moderate Egypt rather than from less moderate Syria.

Neither Israel nor France, its nuclear Svengali, signed the Non-Proliferation Treaty of 1968. The three major nuclear powers that did—America, Russia and Britain—have since sought to plug such loopholes in the treaty as the one that was now occurring. Under Article III of the so-called Accidental Nuclear Warfare Agreement signed by the United States and the U.S.S.R. in Washington on September 30, 1971, each party undertakes to "notify the other immediately in the event of detection by missile warning systems of unidentified objects . . . if such occurrences would create a risk of outbreak of nuclear war between the two countries."

Article VI directs the parties to "make primary use of the Direct Communication Link"—the so-called "hot-line" satellite telex. A further U.S.-Soviet Agreement on Prevention of Nuclear War, signed in Washington on June 23, 1973, says in Article IV that "if relations between countries not Parties to this Agreement appear to involve the risk of nuclear war between the United States and the Union of Soviet Socialist Republics or between either Party and other countries, the [United States] and the [U.S.S.R.] . . . shall immediately enter into urgent consultations with each other and make every effort to avert this risk."

Proxy nuclear wars in the Middle East may not have been uppermost in the minds of Dr. Kissinger and Ambassador Anatoliy Dobrynin at the time these pacts were written into history; but America's treaty obligation was clear once the Blackbird's report reached the NSC.

The hot line ceased exchanging proverbs and pleasantries—the usual hourly activity to keep it open—and a message signed Richard M. Nixon left the 60-foot dish antennas atop a single-story cinderblock building at Fort Detrick, Maryland, informing General Secretary Brezhnev of what the SR-71 had learned. Brezhnev quickly agreed—virtually, to prevent the risk of World War Three—that atomic warheads must be provided for the Russian-made Scud missiles that form a protective ring around Cairo and the new Aswan Dam. U.S. experts think he probably also began seeking confirmatory information over Israel from one of the Soviet Union's own Kosmos "spy" satellites.

The day after the hot-line call—October 13—the Russian warheads were reported by American intelligence to be leaving Nikolaev Naval Base at Odessa. Two days later, the carrying ship (a freighter, because a foreign warship would have had to give seven days' notice to Turkey, under the Montreux Convention) had cleared the Black Sea, the Bosporus and the Sea of Marmara, and was photographed and "sensored" by a Blackbird while cruising through the Dardanelles. By then the tide of war had turned in favor of Israel; when the Soviet ship reached Alexandria, the fear of nuclear weapons being used by Tel Aviv had receded. By October 25, when the warheads were in place on the Egyptian Scuds, there was now a new fear—of their pre-emptive use by the now hard-pressed Egyptians. U.S. electronic surveillance facilities in Turkey also showed that the Russians were moving troops up to their Middle East back door—the borders with Bulgaria, Turkey and Iran. President Nixon called a "world military alert" as a warning against any upgrading of the war—and the rest, as they say, is history.

The Soviet Union almost certainly removed its warheads later. If it did not, Egypt is the only country friendly to the United States which has Russian nuclear warheads with which to defend itself. (It is also, of course, the only nation where NATO-country firms are repairing MiG-21s, Sukhoi-7s and Mi-8 helicopters, and fitting some of the 21s with Rolls-Royce engines.) Meanwhile, Israel's doomsday warheads—estimated to number at least eighteen by 1978—remain stored in hardened underground arsenals in the Negev.

If all this leaves room for thought about the real or projected power of unused weapons—about winning *diplomatic* wars rather than *fighting*, by just having, or appearing to have, the right weaponry—it also points to an adversary's prudent tendency, in cases like this, to assume the worst. But what if Israel had been bluffing? What if Israel *was* bluffing? Nuclear experts agree that it would be easy to fool the high-resolution cameras: a nuclear warhead's shape, its attendant equipment, the sort of security precautions associated with nuclear weapons could be reproduced as easily by the Zahal as by Hollywood. And basically, all the Blackbird's sensors can pick up is the presence of a certain level of radiation, which can exist in other environments beside a bomb.

Some U.S. intelligence officials leaned at the time to the theory of an Israeli bluff. Moreover, a knowledgeable congressional aide believes that at Blackbird heights, radiation sensors are ineffective and that the SR-71 then relies almost entirely on its cameras. He notes, for illustration, that detecting that a missile has been MIRV-ed (fitted with multiple, independently targeted re-entry vehicles) can only be done visually. He, too, suspects an Israeli bluff.

In his second television interview with David Frost, former President Nixon tied the alert solely to Moscow's activation of "two" (actually, seven) Soviet divisions "unilaterally." Although Frost was apparently not briefed to raise the nuclear question, Nixon, picking his way cautiously through the classified minefield of any President's memory, did refer briefly to a "nuclear component" in the altercation with Moscow. He did not implicate Israel; but he did say, ambiguously, that the alert was intended to impress that country with America's resolve.

Was Dayan the first person since Eisenhower (in Korea, in 1953) to contemplate a doomsday strike? Was Golda Meir an inevitable hawk on this as on other things, to prove that the world's rare female leaders are no softer in the crunch than men? Or was it more probably saberrattling, with the apparent bid to shoot down the detector-plane intended to enhance the rattle—a good bluff ("shoot to miss") must appear to go the whole way, to be convincing.

Bluffing apart, the whole October 1973 sequence of events corresponds to everything people fear when talking about arms—the possible use of nuclear weapons, an outbreak of world war. In this respect, the "Blackbird story" is uncharacteristic of the role of arms in the world today. (It could not be repeated now: The latest SR-71s have electronic countermeasures which erase their image from a radarscope.) Nuclear weapons have never been used in war since 1945. Except for the United States in Vietnam—now a closed chapter—the Middle East cockpit has proven to be the only area of the globe where some countries have purchased even sophisticated "conventional" weaponry with a view to actually using it. Fears of a nuclear holocaust in Korea and Taiwan have faded. Even in Europe, where the huge armed forces of NATO and the Warsaw Treaty countries face each other over thousands of miles of potential front, nations go about their business convinced that a major conflict is most unlikely. Some generals and others on both sides still express fears of such a conflict, but NATO's decision not to compete with the Warsaw Pact's huge superiority in tanks is graphic evidence of how little NATO really thinks that a war in Europe is in the offing. With the end of the Vietnam conflict, it is only in the Middle East that anything worse than the world's sempiternal brush-fire wars is seen as a constant possibility. Even there, thanks to the Egypt/Israel peace treaty, a really major war now seems unlikely. Outside of the Middle East, wars are mostly fought with small arms and obsolescent aircraft.

In our era, the major weapons systems have become a feature more of politics, economics and diplomacy than of the battlefield. In weapons politics as in Monopoly, you win according to how rich you become—but by retaining, not spending, the symbols you acquire. Yet in their new role as weapons of finance and diplomacy, arms have strangely become even more indispensable than in the past. They are like the cattle which the Bamangwato of Botswana breed, not to eat or sell, but just to have, to keep up with their neighbors in prestige and power.

To return to the Israeli initiative which triggered the sequence of events in October 1973, the rattling saber is, today, almost every major nation's—including America's—first real line of defense. Yet to give clout to this mythical sword, America, Russia, China and many major and lesser powers spend more on defense than on any other single item in their budgets. A world which has all but renounced, overtly, the notion of conquest continues to produce arms as though conquest was still the ultimate objective. A post-imperial age manufactures far more, and more powerful, weapons than imperial eras ever dreamed of.

In presumed anticipation of future diplomatic failures, our global stockpile of weapons, from the rifle to the intercontinental ballistic missile, is today greater than ever. Arms-limitation agreements notwithstanding, it will be greater tomorrow. Even if you read this book at one sitting, the world's capacity to kill tens of thousands more people will have been added to the global overkill ratio between this paragraph and the last sentence of the final chapter. One country, South Africa, spends nearly half its treasury on arms intended almost exclusively for internal repression. Vice-President Walter Mondale told the UN session on disarmament in New York in 1978 that the world was spending "almost a million dollars a minute for weapons."

But few countries still have officials called ministers of *war*. We find it easier to live with secretaries of *defense*, with ministers of *national security*. In most cases, weapons are genuinely purchased only for defense. Swing-wing supersonic bombers like the proposed B-1, MIRV missiles, nuclear submarines, tanks, even biological-warfare systems are intended as a prophylaxis. For the terror implicit in modern arms has proven to be a potent source of war-avoidance. Just as Churchill spoke of the "nuclear balance of terror" keeping the peace, so many politicians and generals speak more broadly today of the whole pattern of overkill as a lever for preventing war. Just as the world's war ministries have become "defense" departments, so our instruments of assault have become "deterrents."

Most knowledgeable people in Washington believe Israel *does* have nuclear warheads and *did* arm the Jerichos; but a sizable number also believe that Israel would not have used them—because of the quasi-certainty of retribution. The SR-71 incident is a primary illustration of the new use of weapons to avoid war, or in this case to deter defeat, by intimidation. If Brezhnev and Nixon were nervous, and they probably were, it was because Israel is a sometime breaker of the rules, an anti-UN, maverick member of the comity of nations with a romantic approach to politics that most other militarily significant countries have now outgrown.

The simple fact, and the basic theme of this book, is that *weapons are not what they were.* In past centuries, wars were carefully prepared and judiciously announced. Often, it took weeks to translate the declaration to the battlefield. The weaponmakers took orders: swords, customed in length and weight to the physiques and battle styles of each officer, crossbows for the small standing armies, longbows for the arrow-fodder shanghaied in the taverns. After the war, the swords went back into ornate scabbards; the bows and arrows rotted; a peacetime terrorist like Robin Hood had to make his own.

In World War One, despite the extreme brevity of direct U.S. involvement, Woodrow Wilson poured a staggering $28 billion into armaments. Then, after the war, international disarmament on an equally regal scale was seriously attempted. Standing forces became minimal; warships were scuttled or remolded into cooking pots; U.S. military aircraft, few of which had ever seen battle, rusted and fell apart; of 2 million Lee rifles, those that survived the war became hunting guns on both sides of the Atlantic. But since the beginning of World War Two—thanks to Korea, Vietnam, the Mideast imbroglio and various degrees Fahrenheit and Celsius of cold war between the superpowers—the arms industry has become a major factor in U.S. economics. Let us never forget that the market soared after Pearl Harbor, and sank for two years after the Vietnam peace. Columnist Clayton Fritchey, perhaps exaggerating slightly to make a point, has noted that "the ever-rising U.S. defense budget today reflects not so much congressional fear of Russia as fear of unemployment and the closing of costly but needless military installations in their states and districts."

America is not unique. Arms have become the single most important item in the export economies of France and Israel. But the United States is the league leader, with a $32 billion current backlog in arms-export orders; the Soviet Union is not so far behind. Definitively killing the B-1 program would kill thousands of present (and even more thousands of future) jobs in California. Dismantling an ABM site created a ghost city in North Dakota. The most liberal congressman votes faithfully for doomsday dollars when he knows they will end up in the purses and pockets of his constituents.

Hypocritical? Not entirely. The role of weapons has largely changed, even if the vocabulary of those who decry the waste of money on defense —instead of on schools or hospitals—has failed to accommodate to the new ambiguities.

Bowmakers fitted arrowheads with the quasi-certainty that they would be used against human flesh—not stacked and invisibly displayed before a summit conference. Even today, a Sam Cummings, a Gerhard Mertins or a Sarkis Soghanalian can sell carbines and mortars to the brush-fire areas of the world with the thought that they may be used for the purpose for which they were designed. But many modern weapons, like a boxer 12 feet tall, are pragmatically too big for the ring. They are designed to kill, but programmed for other objectives.

The United States is selling F-15 air-superiority fighters to Saudi Arabia and agreed to sell AWACS control aircraft to Iran essentially to recycle petrodollars and keep "leverage" with key nations. Titans stand in their silos in the foothills of Arkansas, not to atomize Moscow but to enable the United States to negotiate with the Kremlin on an at least equal footing.

In short, there seems a reasonable chance that the days of "real" war may be over. When second-league wars break out—in Vietnam, the Mideast, the Indian subcontinent—the death tolls, bad as they are, are modest compared to Korea, World War Two or World War One. In the Mideast, wars are so short that the armed forces involved do not collect enough combat time to qualify for a wartime furlough.

Egypt and Israel have armed not so much to fight each other— although of course they sometimes have—as to threaten each other with what would happen if they did. Metaphorically, each rattling saber has its own throw-weight; the long-range ballistic missiles in Soviet silos and U.S. strategic submarines are the two-fisted rattling sabers of all time; but the relatively modest tactical nuclear missiles with the U. S. Army in Korea have been just as successful in that role.

In other words, in an age when all strategic and tactical (and most heavy conventional) weapons are built principally, not for war, but for finance and diplomacy, the rattling saber is by far the most perfect, sophisticated arm—winning battles without fighting, without killing and without disrupting economies. A recent cartoon showed two designers poring over the blueprints of a massive new weapons system; one asks the other, "But what if we built the thing and they made it a bargaining chip?" The real joke is that the lethality and deadly effectiveness of such a design would be at least as important as a bargaining chip as in war.

Why should South Africa have done everything necessary to produce a usable nuclear warhead except, possibly, testing it? To take on the sprawling village-capital of Lusaka, or the resort-sized ports of Maputo, Beira or Luanda—any of which could be laid flat by old-fashioned high explosives? In an age of nuclear poker, the South African atomic warhead, whether assembled or ready for assembly at a few weeks' notice, is above all else a symbol of ultimate self-sufficiency in armament. The disclosure of Israeli nuclear warheads in 1973 may well have been the discovery of the ultimate uses to which atomic weaponry can now be put.

Nuclear weaponry stands at the opposite end of the "implements of war" spectrum which begins with Armalite rifles for Northern Ireland, or night-vision rifles that silently kill one government critic at a time, after dark, in obscure African republics. America, Russia, Britain, France and China have atomic warfare potentials created by their own technology. Other countries have joined the nuclear club by buying nuclear fuel on the pretense that it was needed for "peaceful" purposes, and acquiring from major countries the sophisticated missiles or aircraft to deliver a nuclear bomb or warhead.

Although even the most modest tactical nuclear weapon has never been used in action, the kill power of the major and secondary nations has increased astronomically since World War Two. Between 1939 and 1945, 434,000 tons of high explosive and incendiary bombs poured down on German cities. Half of this huge tonnage consisted of incendiaries, each weighing little more than a baseball bat. The bombs caused about 500,000 deaths, with 780,000 seriously wounded. Roughly 80,000 acres of built-up areas were devastated, including 3.6 million homes; 7.5 million people became homeless. At war's end, infant mortality in Berlin was 359.4 per 1,000, demonstrating how well bombs alone can disrupt food supplies and cause a total breakdown of sanitation and public health facilities. But more died on battlefields. Total war dead, worldwide, were estimated by Alistair Cooke in his book *America* at 30 million.

Bombing tonnage in the Korean War exceeded all tonnage dropped in the Pacific theaters in the early forties. In a single two-and-a-half-year period, from mid-1965 through the end of 1967, the United States dropped a greater tonnage of bombs on Vietnam than all the Allied air forces dropped on Germany and the whole of enemy-occupied Europe during the six years of World War Two. In the Six-Day War of 1967, two Third World powers, Egypt and Israel, deployed more tanks than were used by the Germans, the Italians, the British and various Allied units in World War Two's largest and most notable armored battle—El Alamein, in 1942.

The Soviet Union lost a billion dollars' worth of arms and equipment in Egypt in the Six-Day War. Much of this booty—worth about $2 billion today—ended up in good condition in Israel's inventory, some of it later scattered around other Third World countries as part of Tel Aviv's own weapons diplomacy. (Naturally, most of the Communist weaponry disposed of in this way ended up in pro-Western, anti-Communist countries, while a small fraction of the $6 billion bonanza in U.S. weapons and equipment left behind in Vietnam at the Thieu debacle has since turned up in the hands of Marxist or Marxist-supported revolutionaries, such as Ethiopia's Eritrean secessionists.)

In recent decades, Congress has appropriated ten times as much money for weapons research as for the peaceful development of nuclear energy. The Russian performance is similar. But nuclear and heavy conventional arms proliferation is modest compared to the proliferation of small arms—the arms most used in the conflicts which actually take place regularly, around the world. George Thayer, probably relying on the computerlike knowledge of privateer-emeritus Sam Cummings, recorded in his 1969 book *The War Business* that there were then 750 million operable military rifles and pistols in the world—one for every adult male alive. These, too, play their role in weapons diplomacy and can often rebound against their diplomatic users: using little more, in most cases, than assault rifles, submachine guns, mortars or tracked cannon, dissidents have overthrown pro-Soviet governments in Ghana, Indonesia and Algeria with Soviet weaponry.

But even produced for simple economic and diplomatic reasons, weapons must have a proven capacity to do what they are designed to do in warfare. Smaller wars make great test beds, whether in the Mideast or Southeast Asia. With nuclear weapons seen as too doomsday to touch, the United States in Vietnam extended the frontiers of war technology beyond high-explosive and incendiary bombs to other systems which loom as factors in terror diplomacy of the future: U.S. planes imposed chemical warfare from the air—an unprecedented assault on forests and agriculture, producing a cumulative total of homeless and displaced persons estimated, in a 1975 report by Senator Edward Kennedy's subcommittee on refugees, at 11,683,000.

As science and technology have improved our capacity for making war, and for making weapons diplomacy more effective, the weapons industry's share of the world economy has increased in staggering ratio. Straight figures can be deceptive, since inflation over the decades has been almost as impressive as the arms race; but in 1976, the prestigious Stockholm International Peace Research Institute (SIPRI) estimated cumulative world military expenditure since the end of World War Two at $4.5 trillion, at 1970 prices. This equaled the combined Gross National Products (GNPs) of the sixty-five independent countries of Africa and Latin America, or total worldwide expenditure on education over three decades, or twice the worldwide expenditure on health during this period.

Scaling all amounts in terms of the 1970 dollar, however, SIPRI noted in 1976 that world military expenditure, even in the light-headed, unsuspecting days of 1908, was already the equivalent of $9 billion. Thirty years later, with war clouds approaching but with many still averting their eyes, it had passed $61 billion. By 1953, the last year of the Korean War, it had reached—still in constant 1970 prices—two and a half times as much. When Kennedy was elected in 1960, it was down, in constant prices, to $130.8 billion. By 1969, a peak period in the Johnson-Nixon buildup in Vietnam, it had soared to almost $213 billion. In 1977, the U. S. Arms Control and Disarmament Agency estimated world military expenditures and arms transfers for 1975 at $345 billion, or 5.5 per cent of a world GNP of $6.2 trillion. SIPRI's 1977 yearbook listed worldwide military spending in 1976 at twenty-five times the total of global foreign aid—despite world "peace." In 1978, the ACDA put the 1977 figure at a round $400 billion in 1975 dollars, 5.8 per cent of GNP, and noted that this was still the equivalent of world spending on education, and 150 per cent more than global disbursements on health, with the biggest imbalance being in the developing countries.

Indeed, the agency, which looked at 142 countries, including 131 of the 149 UN members, said the rate of growth of military spending was actually decelerating in the developed[1] countries while accelerating in

[1] The United States, Canada; Japan, Australia, New Zealand; Britain, France, West Germany, Italy, Holland, Belgium, Luxembourg, Denmark, Norway, Ireland, Iceland, Sweden, Switzerland, Austria, Finland; the Soviet Union, Poland, East Germany, Czechoslovakia, Hungary and Romania. The ACDA list also regards as "developed" Portugal (1975 per capita income in 1974 dollars: $1,420) and South Africa ($1,300) but excludes Israel ($2,940), Greece ($2,310), Spain ($2,430) and Bulgaria ($1,930). Per capita income is not, of course, the only criterion, but most "developed" lists drawn up by economists include Israel and Bulgaria, but exclude Portugal and South Africa.

the underdeveloped world. There had been significant increases in arms budgets in the Middle East, Africa and China.

In the United States, the ACDA said, actual direct military expenditure had dropped, in 1975 dollars, from a peak of $122 billion in 1968 to $88 billion in 1976. In the same period, the Soviet Union's spending on arms had risen from $86 billion to $121 billion. Spending by NATO and Warsaw Treaty countries had also risen, even though NATO forces were down over the decade from 6.6 million to 4.9 million (Warsaw Treaty forces were up from 5.2 million to about 6 million). In the United States, there is actually, now, a military pilot shortage.

By 1978, however, there were 27,000 more U.S. soldiers overseas than the previous year, according to Pentagon figures. The Center for Defense Information estimated that, by then, 70 per cent of U.S. defense spending was for the "defense of allies"—which the CDI doubted were in much danger.

Worldwide arms exports grew 60 per cent in the past decade, according to the ACDA report. Thirty-nine per cent of the total had come from the United States (down from 51 per cent in the sixties) and 28 per cent from the Soviet Union, followed by France with 6 per cent. Only China's arms exports were falling off noticeably, from $549 million in 1972 to $112 million in 1976, the last year for which confirmed figures are available. The principal arms importer—using "arms" to include all imported support services and construction—was Iran, followed by Israel, Iraq, Libya and West Germany.

In short, the biggest arms export market is not the developed but the developing world. Between 1967 and 1976, the ACDA says, Middle East defense spending, in 1975 dollars, rose from $7 billion a year to $24 billion. In Israel, the per capita rise was from $163 to $1,110. In Oman, per capita arms spending over that decade went from zero to $782, in Saudi Arabia from $47 to $257, in Iran from $25 to $203, in Iraq from $47 to $153. For comparison, the East German figure went from $123 to $211.

In Africa, not counting Egypt—seen as part of the Middle East—arms expenditure rose from $2 billion to $6 billion, with South Africa the main spender. African arms imports rose from $180 million to nearly $800 million by 1976. By 1978, the imports figure had reached $3 billion, including nearly $500 million for South Africa. Africa now takes 11 per cent of all arms imports. South Africa's military budget went from $357 million to $1.52 billion over the decade, and is now past $2 billion, not counting military spending disguised in other budgets.

China, on the other hand, with an estimated 1975 population of 934,600,000, spent $32.8 billion on arms that year. This meant a per capita investment in defense of only $32.10, but it represented the beginning of a substantial increase—and over 10 per cent of the country's relatively modest GNP. Defense expenditure in east Asia as a whole, which buys 8 per cent of arms imports, went from $34 billion to $47 billion over the decade surveyed by the ACDA. Latin America now has 6 per cent of the trade, south Asia 4 per cent. Military manpower in the developing countries had risen over the decade from just under 12 million to nearly 16 million. The Third World, which had less than 4 per cent of the world's arms inventories in 1955, now has about 19 per cent. The Middle East share is up from half of 1 per cent to just over 6 per cent. From 1970 through 1978, said a State Department release at the end of that year, "Western and Eastern suppliers made arms-transfer commitments of about $140 billion to developing countries."

As noted in Chapter 2, arms spending in Russia is reckoned to have reached somewhere between 11 and 15 per cent of the GNP, compared to between 5 and 7 per cent in Russia's Warsaw Treaty allies and slightly less in NATO countries. Today, the Soviet Union devotes about half its budget to defense, closely followed by Israel, South Africa, Taiwan, both Koreas and Oman, with only a slightly lower proportion. Indeed, Oman devotes 40 per cent of its entire GNP to military spending, followed in the area by Israel (32 per cent), Saudi Arabia (19 per cent) and Syria (14.7 per cent). Iran, Iraq and North Korea have all devoted more than 10 per cent of their GNPs to defense.

Syria is now spending nearly twice as much of its GNP on arms as it did in 1965, while in Egypt, the percentage went from 5.6 in 1960 to 18 ten years later and 31.4 in 1973. (By 1976, with Cairo shorn of Russian supplies, it fell to 10.5 per cent.) In Israel, the share rose from 6.6 per cent of the GNP in 1960 to 23.6 in 1970 and 32.2 in 1976. In the Middle East, only Jordan, partly from financial necessity, has tempered its hunger for products of the death industry, going from 19.4 per cent of gross domestic product in 1960 to 17.8 per cent in 1970, 14.7 per cent in 1974 and 9.4 per cent in 1976. On the other hand, rich countries with per capita incomes of over $3,000 spending less than 1 per cent of their GNP on arms were Iceland, Japan and the United Arab Emirates. The defense expenditures of the nations of the world average 25.3 per cent of their budgets, according to the ACDA; quoting figures for weapons and support equipment, but not including training, construction, other services and "consumables," the agency said America devoted 24.8 per cent, or about the world average; for comparison, West Germany's proportion was 22.7 per cent, France's 17.6 per cent.

However, filtering through the blizzard of statistics, one discovers that, in recent years, only about 37 per cent of the U.S. military budget has been for weapons and military transportation, and this ratio is falling;

about 11 per cent has gone on research, development and the testing and evaluation of weapons and equipment by the Department of Defense. This figure, however, does not include hundreds of millions of dollars spent annually for the design, development and testing of nuclear warheads—carefully concealed in a little non-military budget silo of their own—or more than 1 billion dollars for "Bids and Proposals" (the expenses incurred by defense contractors or would-be contractors in response to official requests for proposals concerning weaponry and weapons technology). Indeed, about 10 per cent of all worldwide defense expenditure goes on R & D—occupying, according to SIPRI calculations, the energies of over half the world's physicists and engineers.

Thirty per cent of world military expenditures comes from the wallets and purses of Americans. And, 1976 campaign rhetoric notwithstanding, there is no doubt that the defense budget will rise each year, even in constant dollars, under the Carter administration. Carter's five-year projections, in 1978, were only marginally lower than Ford's. The Soviet Union comes a close second to the United States, although the secretive and deliberately deceptive way in which Moscow prices its budget and disguises war expenditure under different budget titles makes anything but round-figure, informed guesstimates impossible for Western analysts —who multiply the official Kremlin figure by what amounts to a factor of five.

The cost of technology addictiveness—"sophistication" in weaponry— is enormous, and gives armaments as great an economic importance as their political and military importance. The Air Force's F-15 Eagle fighter currently costs about $18 million a unit, without spares or weapons, or over three times the cost—even at constant dollars—of the F-4 Phantom which it replaces. Inflation will push the price higher. The cost of producing two prototype YF-16 and YF-17 fighters was over $100 million—although the performance parameters of the prototypes were "deliberately restrained so that [the aircraft selected] will be relatively inexpensive and can therefore be produced in relatively large numbers," a 1976 report noted.

When the Air Force selected the F-16, it won approval for a further $574 million for development, making a total cost of $674 million over six or seven years for the basic fighter of the eighties, before the first wing-service aircraft lines up for takeoff. Although Congress requested the Navy to base its own "low-cost" fighter on the YF-16, the Navy—understandably reluctant to fly single-engined aircraft over the open ocean— preferred the twin-engined YF-17 and ordered a derivative, now the F-18 Hornet. (The prefix "Y" means prototype. "X" stands for experimental. The difference between the two designations is marginal.) Overcoming stiff congressional opposition, the Navy secured approval for $1.4 billion for R & D on the F-18, and won an initial appropriation in the fiscal 1976 budget. The plane went into production in 1978.

Yes, modern arms are expensive—and not just planes. Between 1968 and 1975, the United States spent $129 million developing the AIM-7F Sparrow III air-to-air missile. During the same seven-year period, the World Health Organization spent about two thirds of that sum—$83 million—on a campaign which virtually eradicated smallpox from the world.

Any money saved by congressional cost-cutting on one system is usually diverted to expand the budget for another, and some high-technology weaponry can survive even a governmental thumbs-down. This is not only true in America. In 1975, the French Government canceled the multi-role Super-Mirage F-1 in favor of the less costly, single-engined, delta-wing "2000" interceptor. But Dassault, the Mirage firm, decided to pursue development of the Super-Mirage for export; by 1978, the orders were flowing in from the Middle East, Asia and Latin America. Also in 1975, the British Government, strapped for funds, canceled three missile programs; but British Aircraft Corporation (now British Aerospace) announced that it would continue to develop two of them for export—and then did so with success.

The spinoff from research and development is an important factor in the development of many important domestic products. Television was developed to help win World War Two, and has become the world's leading source of entertainment. The wartime development of plastics cut the costs of millions of postwar domestic products. Nuclear fission may be usable to help build dams and widen canals, as well as bury cities. We eat on plates made of unbreakable material designed for war, our teeth capped by a substance produced for the nose cones of space modules. Our airliners are only built at commercial prices because of the billions spent on their military precursors. Today's most successful airliner, the Boeing-707, is a civilianized version of the KC-135 refueling plane mentioned earlier in the Blackbird story. America has no supersonic airliner yet, because Boeing had no earlier contract to produce a supersonic bomber: The federal subsidy for Boeing which Congress refused would not have been needed if the Rockwell International B-1, or something similar, had been on the drawing boards a decade ago. The economic problems of the Concorde stem from its emergence as a purely civilian aircraft.

But weapons production diverts equity and skills from more productive enterprises; it also depletes a startlingly growing fraction of essential raw materials like bauxite (used to make aluminum) copper, lead, zinc and nickel. The figures are even more impressive for industrially precious materials such as the ultra-light, ultra-strong titanium, the military demand for which has greatly increased with the demand for fighter aircraft that can carry an aggressive payload to greater altitudes and at greater speeds. The F-8s and F-105s of the fifties had airframes composed of about 10 per cent by weight of titanium. For the new F-14 Tomcats and F-15 Eagles, the fraction is between a quarter and a third. The fuselage and wings of the Mach-3, strategic-reconnaissance SR-71—the Blackbird mentioned earlier—are made almost entirely of titanium and titanium alloys. Already by 1972, estimated military requirements for titanium were 4,800 tons, or 40 per cent of total U.S. demand for the metal. The classified figure has since risen further. The growing use of epoxy will diminish world stocks of graphite and boron.

Given all these—sometimes contradictory—facts, is it cynical to consider whether the continual building of arms almost too devastating to use is a source of relative peace, an extension of the pax atomica which has reigned between Moscow and Washington for more than a generation?

Since World War One, toxic gas has been used only twice in warfare—by Italy in Ethiopia in 1935–36, and by Japan in China in the same period. Nuclear weapons have never been used in war since Nagasaki. Part of the reason for these welcome inhibitions is that today's toxic gases are much worse than those that terrified the British and French in 1915, and today's nuclear arsenal infinitely more powerful and accurate, and easier to deliver, than Nagasaki's "Fat Boy."

Reasonable people aver that the very existence of nuclear weapons, killer satellites, toxic and nerve gases or environmental-warfare techniques that could swamp California in a tsunami tidal wave or make Brazil a desert is dangerous enough in itself. Suppose Israel had triggered World War Three six years ago? Suppose a post-Tito Yugoslavia could only fend off a Soviet invasion by nuclearizing the battlefield? Suppose, in a Sino-Soviet conflict, the Chinese felt they had no choice but to preempt with the ultimate weapon, and damn the consequences? Is it cynical to respond that there is probably not much that we can do about it?

There is also an ironic, less reassuring side to the affair; in an age when the superpowers dare not make war on each other, the proxy birds in the cold-war cockpits of the world could still wittingly or unwittingly sweep the superpowers' colors onto the nuclear battlefield. Thus the superpowers, arming themselves with presumably unusable weapons to intimidate or counterbalance—"deter"—each other, must even unite on occasion to restrain or counterbalance the satellites which recent history has conferred on them. The Middle East cockpit—Russia's back yard, and the filling station for Japan, Western Europe and America—is not the only one of its kind; it is merely the most active and the most reported.

The superpower nuclear stalemate has, so far, guaranteed against a third world war. But the nuclear threat has also popularized the pacifistic ideal, which first took shape, in the form of disarmament talks, after the appalling carnage of World War One. Renewed attempts at disarmament resulted from World War Two and the cold-war fear of a nuclear World War Three. But practical obstacles were at once apparent. Although the word "disarmament" still appears in the title of government agencies, private organizations and conferences, we now usually speak, more pragmatically, of arms limitation or "restraint." Disarmament attempts, today, apply only to doomsday weapons, and they have largely failed. The UN has eschewed the task even more than the League of Nations: No country is prepared to surrender its fate to an international body, whether through disarmament or through reliance on a UN international defense force.

Arms limitation is even overtly aimed at preserving superpower stalemate, rather than at achieving disarmament. Moreover, since real disarmament would only mean reducing each superpower's capacity for overkill to, say, the ability to destroy Russia or America twenty or forty times over (instead of sixty or seventy times), arms limitation cannot seriously be seen as a factor in war or peace. If weaponry is more diplomatic than military, arms limitation is essentially an economic question; what is at issue is a more rational deployment of money and skills, with an avoidance of the recessions usually associated with the winding-down of arms industries.

In the past generation, "arms limitation" has taken on greater urgency in our imaginations, and even greater acuity in our international discourse. But arms limitation means what it says—not giving up smoking, but going from three packs a day to four instead of five. This is the world we live in—a world in which many expanded arms industries, representing vastly more investment than all the gold in Fort Knox, cannot conveniently be throttled back or converted to peacetime products as in days of yore. Even if all of President Carter's arms-limitation objectives were achieved—a naive and pious hope at best—the world would still be more heavily armed in 1980 than it was in 1976.

The role of arms in economics and diplomacy has reached a point where arms could no more be removed from the elaborate game whereby governments rule mankind's affairs than the rules of the game could be changed by a decision of the two superpowers alone, or even by a consensus of the main "Western" and "Eastern" powers. The fact that man created arms does not mean that he entirely controls them: They have taken on a life of their own, and man has become, to some degree, their dependent.

Arms predominantly exist to give political power, the tiger whose tail so many are seduced to hold. Arms-industry expansion, or increased defense budgets, do not imply that a war is on, or even near: We live in an age of sophisticated and expensive rattling sabers which determine the balance of power. The bloodless wars we fight are wars without much honor, in which friends and even protégés are fickle, and sometimes vicious.

Israel, as noted, has been an exception to the rule that weapons are no longer conceived to conquer territory, unless it is by intimidation (although even Israel has always managed to muster enough good arguments, at least for an audience with sympathetic preconceptions, to rationalize its policies of expansion in terms of defense, and has always been squeamish enough to do so). In historic terms, Israel has been militarist. It invaded Suez in 1956—to conquer the Sinai, open the Canal to Israeli shipping and please France (a private French company had owned the Canal before Nasser nationalized it) and Britain, then the Canal's principal user. In 1967, Israel invaded Egypt, and subsequently Syria and Jordan, to enlarge its borders, placing them farther away from Israel's main centers of population. South Africa is a maverick power also: it is feasible to imagine that, were world pressure against Pretoria not so strong, South Africa might well use its awesome regional military superiority to occupy the sources of its immigrant labor—countries like Mozambique, Malawi and Lesotho. The former Shah of Iran was generally believed to have expansionist plans.

But the basic fact is that acquisition of territory is out of date. The Vietnam War was a leftover from World War Two, a neocolonial enterprise which America inherited from the clumsy hands of a then weakened, reactionary France—an almost understandable mistake in the light of cold-war realities that existed when the U.S. involvement began. Minor territorial-acquisition wars will of course continue, with minor weapons: Somalia's attempts to recover Somali territory lost in the colonial division of Africa a century ago are a good example.

All this is not to say that global war is unthinkable, or that official explanations for the U.S. strategic forces or the existence of NATO make no sense. Even in his own era, Hitler was an aberration, and aberrations could occur again. A thermonuclear Stalin might well have started something. But the pattern is clearly to use armed forces, and especially the overkill capacity which the superpowers now possess, by not actually using them at all. The aim of the game is no longer to shoot to kill but to shoot to miss, like the shot in the air which enables a policeman to halt a fugitive.

The Industrial Revolution gave control of arms production to the industrialized powers. Modern sophistication, involving heavy capital outlays and technological investment in research and development, has narrowed control even further. The growth of the industry, tied to the growth of the arsenals of the major powers, has itself spurred the growth of the arms-export market. Indeed, the economic significance of the arms trade for a small number of mostly major powers has become the prime spur of the industry.

Britain and France are even prepared to sell arms, today, to Communist nations. We may reasonably deplore our allies' cynicism in this regard, but we cannot deny the truth of what they are implying—that the arms industries are now more of a factor in economics and diplomatic leverage than they are in war, particularly at the great-power level. Major arms sales to China by both France and Britain now seem likely, and even the United States indulges in arms-related sales to both Peking and Moscow—major computers, for example.

In 1974, when world sales peaked, arms-export contracts (to be fulfilled over a number of years) by the three major arms-exporting powers alone—the United States, the Soviet Union and France—totaled nearly $25 billion. The U.S. share of this trade, then as now, in constant 1970 prices, ran around $12 billion. Except for the United States, the U.S.S.R. and China, most arms exporters will sell to virtually anyone not seen as hostile.

As a consequence, it is no secret that the military-industrial complex decried by Eisenhower, himself the most famous general of the century, is big business. Export sales substantially help the balance of payments of some nations. France, now challenging Germany for the economic supremacy of Western Europe, has based its successful trade balance on its successful weapons industry, now its main foreign currency-earner. Arms, as noted earlier, are Israel's main export also. For Britain and even America, exporting weaponry has been a major factor in redressing economic recessions and recycling petrodollars. During its export-booster phase, France was simultaneously selling to both its substantial neocolonial imperium in black Africa and to the area's natural enemy, South Africa, as well as to both Israel and its hostile, immediate neighbors. (The United States, of course, also sells to Israel and its neighbors, but predominantly for reasons of balance.) During 1978, France's role as Pretoria's main supplier was in fact taken over by its erstwhile client, Israel, which begged or bought $4 billion of arms that year from the

United States, while actively promoting global sales of its native arms industry—largely based on pirated French and American technology.

The main exporters are naturally countries with large armed forces of their own. In thirty years, the United States, Russia, France and Britain have put into wing service 76 different types of interceptor, fighter and attack aircraft alone, along with 144 variants. (Another 36 types never went beyond the experimental stage.) As in less lethal industries, variety itself helps bolster world demand.

Popular, anti-arms pressure in the matter has little effect: Arms-sales control is, today, whatever each arms-producing government cares to make it. In most cases, it is based on restricting sophisticated weapons sales to "friendly" markets, and occasionally on "end-use" clauses, forbidding the utilization of the arms purchased for aggression or for resale to third countries without permission. But virtually all America's arms clients, including Britain, France, Germany, Italy, Greece, Israel, Jordan and possibly Turkey, get around U.S. end-use provisions. The U. S. Government never reacts with more than a reprimand. Congress reacts only when some lobby draws attention to a real or imagined violation by a country which the lobby opposes. The most massive violations—Israel's invasion of Egypt in 1967, or its bombings of neutral Lebanon in the seventies—have drawn only formal diplomatic protests, and nary a word from Capitol Hill, since most congressmen either approved or were scared to disapprove openly. Moscow's control is not much better: Did the Soviet Union really want Libya to replace the eleven MiG-21s lost by Uganda in the 1976 Israeli Air Force Entebbe raid? Was Moscow even asked? France, Britain and Israel impose virtually no end-use provisions at all, and Russia does not impose them as part of Soviet legislation.

Recent congressional efforts to limit arms proliferation are largely self-defeating, since for the most part they merely transfer trade to Paris, Tel Aviv, London and Bonn. Even in the measure that they count for something, they come rather late: Iran alone, for instance, now has over 400 supersonic aircraft, including 78 of the latest-generation F-14s, plus 700 military helicopters, at least 1,200 tanks and over 2,000 major missiles. Missile proliferation—with many of the best-selling models being capable of nuclearization—is one reason for galloping concern. So is the enormous spread of naval weaponry, rationalized by the problems of patrolling the new, 200-miles-out territorial frontiers.

The arms industries and the armed forces of the Western powers both argue that the high cost of modern weaponry has made export sales "essential." The United States, unlike most of its competitors, produces aircraft, warships, missiles, armored vehicles and cannon mostly for the use of America's own military. But even America sells weapons systems not only to buy and keep allies and friends, or to bind countries to "spare parts dependency"—and to ensure that countries do not become similarly dependent, instead, on Moscow or other Communist arms producers—but also to make money, and to reduce the unit cost of arms to U.S. forces.

Evidence of the economic importance of arms in international trade was underscored by the recent battle between the United States and France (largely won by the United States) to produce the next-generation NATO all-purpose combat aircraft. This was soon followed by a similar struggle between America and Germany to supply the next-generation NATO main battle tank.

Exporting arms may also reduce the cost of political conflict to the United States. A friendly country armed by the United States is enabled to perform missions that might otherwise fall to U.S. forces; if it does, as noted earlier, the U.S. military, and the American arms industry, also get a free "test bed" for their latest weapons.

To some extent, Washington has been activated to promote sales in Europe by a desire for standardization of NATO weaponry, and by traditional American reluctance to rely on foreign suppliers for any but the most marginal items in the U.S. inventory; the United States counterbalances its economic advantage in these military boardroom battles by co-production arrangements with the more industrialized purchasers, especially NATO countries; but the notion that economic power resides in whoever owns the means of production is one Marxian dictum with which American free enterprise has never quarreled.

People being what and who they are, and things being the way they are, as de Gaulle used to say, payola has entered the picture. Shakedowns of American arms manufacturers, kickbacks—in some cases, outright bribery by the U.S. firms—have hit the headlines in recent years. Japanese and Italian prime ministers and Prince Bernhard of the Netherlands have become figures of disgrace. Some of the middlemen involved have a patrician mold, varying from Teddy Roosevelt's grandson "Kim" to Saudi Arabia's first self-made multimillionaire, Adnan Khashoggi. Names like Northrop and Lockheed and General Electric have moved from the stock tables to embarrassing banner headlines on page one.

The arms trade, along with everything that accompanies it, from portbuilding to installing computers, is a complex one, as sophisticated as the new precision-guided weaponry itself. It involves sometimes parallel, sometimes complementary, sometimes competing roles for government agencies, for major arms firms—and for privateers. Since World War

Two, there have been growing incursions by government into previously private markets; but the areas in which the privateer still reigns supreme are interesting too, and he is still the principal purveyor of surplus or "obsolescent" arms, of which—like used cars—there are always more around than new ones. Any analysis of weapons economics and weapons diplomacy involves a look at the arms-control laws of the United States and the other arms-producing countries, and of how privateers either manipulate or evade these laws.

The privateers account for about a billion dollars of the international arms trade annually. This means just under 5 per cent of the whole bonanza; since Communist countries do not have privateers (although they sometimes use Western privateers to dispose of surplus), the private arms dealers probably take about 8 per cent of the "free world" trade. But this relatively low figure is deceptive in political terms. Most government-to-government sales go to areas of potential, not actual conflict. American F-15s for Saudi Arabia or Soviet MiG-23s for Iraq earn nine-figure sums, but are not expected to be used; a privateer's ten thousand used rifles for Tibet, costing only $200,000, could tie up impressive portions of the Chinese Southern Army for months or even years to come. The "little" hot wars in places like Lebanon, Ulster, Iraq's Kurdistan or the south Moluccas, the insurgencies, coups, secession wars and border conflicts going on in other parts of Africa, Asia and Latin America depend mostly on the privateer—sometimes acting as the middleman for governments.

Much of the privateer's domain is cheap, bulky stuff, like crates of rifles; but a good deal of it is more exotic, especially miniaturized night-vision, laser-beam or eavesdropping equipment and assassination weaponry. These are high-priced items, even when legally obtained—which is almost impossible in the West. Such lethal gadgetry, along with the miniaturization and vulgarization of much more powerful weapons and new explosives, emphasize the need for more control of the colorful world of the privateer, and his role in maintaining the only wars that never cease.

The Communist countries have, on the whole, been more cautious than Washington and the West about supplying their friends with latest-generation weaponry; but in the area where Russia has had the most political impact—anticolonial and similar insurgency—it has been generous with its best guerrilla-warfare weapons, notably its assault rifles and its shoulder-mounted, surface-to-air missile launchers.

The absence of world war since 1945 has not precluded some substantial "world" conflicts fought by proxies. Thayer counted 55 wars of "significant size, duration and intensity throughout the world" between 1945 and 1969, along with approximately 250 smaller conflicts. In 1976, SIPRI recorded an increased tempo since Thayer surveyed the scene; there had been 119 significant conflicts between 1945 and 1975, and the total duration of these conflicts had been over 350 years. The territory of 69 countries and the armed forces of 81 states had been involved. Since Japan's frock-coated ministers signed an end to the war to end all wars on the sun-bleached decks of the *Missouri,* in August 1945, no day has passed without one or several wars going on somewhere. On any average day in the past three decades, according to SIPRI, there have been twelve wars in progress.

Talleyrand said that wars take place when diplomacy fails—when the sabers of weapons diplomacy rattle free from the sheath and glitter in the sun. But even successful weapons diplomacy often involves a "show of force," sometimes incorporating a limited element of violence. Even though the superpowers have never gone to war with each other, their weaponry—not just lying like a threat in conference documents, but flying the skies, sailing the oceans, or rolling on heavy tracks along beaches or city streets—has written a lot of history since World War Two.

A 1977 Brookings study noted that the United States alone had deployed its military forces abroad for political impact "at least 215 times" over 30 years—not including the Korean and Vietnam wars. The Soviet Union had done the same on at least 115 occasions. The study noted that a U.S. show of force by naval, air force or army units usually achieved the political objective desired—in most cases without firing a shot. Success was greatest where U.S. forces were "actually emplaced on foreign soil," or when land-based combat aircraft were involved.

Post-1945 saber-rattling of this sort would constitute a history of its own. As far back as early 1946, President Truman sent the remains of a Turkish ambassador, Mehmet Munir Ertegün, who had died in the United States, home to Istanbul aboard the battleship *Missouri* rather than aboard a freighter; this was in order that the world's largest warship, accompanied by a cruiser and a destroyer, should lie at anchor in the Bosporus and deter a Soviet threat to seize two eastern Anatolian provinces of Turkey and a base in the Dardanelles.

In the late fifties and early sixties, the United States "showed force" in several incidents associated with Berlin—in reaction to Soviet actions. In July 1958, fourteen thousand U.S. troops, spearheaded by Marines, intervened in the Lebanese crisis—successfully, and with little fighting. In May 1961, Kennedy sent a naval task force with Marines to Dominican waters after dictator Trujillo was assassinated; this helped prevent an anticipated left-wing coup d'état. In 1964, a U.S. naval task force stood off Brazil to give its mute but eloquent support to that country's armed forces as they toppled leftist President João Goulart in a coup d'état. When North Korea seized the virtually defenseless electronic-surveillance ship *Pueblo* in 1968, twenty-six ships—including five carriers and three cruisers—were sent to the waters off Wonsan, and Johnson mobilized nearly fifteen thousand air and naval reservists; but the only concession made by Pyongyang was to agree to talks.

Some shows of force had either mixed or even negative results. In 1970, Nixon alerted the Sixth Fleet, the 82nd Airborne and other troops and threatened to land at Amman airport to help counter Palestinian guerrillas (partly for domestic reasons—an off-year election was only weeks away). But Jordan defeated the guerrillas and their Syrian allies unaided, and the only result of the saber-rattle was that the Palestinians angrily blew up four hijacked airliners. Nixon sought unsuccessfully to intimidate India in 1971 by sending ten warships, including the carrier *Enterprise*, to the Bay of Bengal, thus provoking a similar show of Soviet naval force. This encouraged Pakistani depredations in Bangladesh and further alienated India.

President Ford's air and naval action to secure the release from Cambodia of the crew of the freighter *Mayagüez* in 1975 may or may not have helped to liberate the seamen, and proved costly for helicopter pilots and Marines; but it served as a warning to the eccentric new government in Phnom Penh not to overinterpret America's recent humiliation in Southeast Asia. When two U.S. army officers were hacked to death in the demilitarized zone between North and South Korea in 1976, a more classic saber-rattle was ordered—a massive demonstration by U.S. air and naval forces. But not a shot was fired, even "in the air."

Some instances of bloodless gunboat diplomacy have passed unnoticed by the general public: also in 1976, for instance, Uganda's volatile President Amin threatened an invasion of Kenya: just by chance, as it were, a U.S. warship soon moored off Mombasa, and Marines were sent ashore for rest and recreation on the East African Riviera. Like the *Missouri* serving as a freighter for a flag-draped casket, this made it clear which side Washington was on.

The Cuban missile crisis of 1962 and the "Nixon alert" of 1973 were nuclear saber-rattlings. Strategic Air Command—America's airborne long-range nuclear delivery service—has been alerted at least ten times since World War Two, and other strategic nuclear-force units twice as often.

The Brookings study noted that shows of force by the United States rose from an average of five a year in the Truman era to about seven and a half under Eisenhower, as the Communist and non-Communist war-time allies drifted further apart in cold-war animosity and competition. Under Kennedy, the incidence almost doubled to 13.4 a year—more than one a month—scaling down to just under ten during Johnson's reign and to half of that figure under Nixon and Ford. The report found that the greater the U.S. commitment implied by the size of the force committed, the more successful the impact and result.

By any standards, Russian saber-rattling and direct military "diplomacy" have been considerably more aggressive than those of the United States. Soviet military personnel have participated covertly or semi-covertly in four "non-Russian" wars—over the Suez Canal after the Six-Day War, and against civil insurrections in Sudan, Iraq and Ethiopia. But the Russians, as the Brookings study noted, have almost never instigated the crises in which they have intervened since 1968—in the Middle East, "tensions have grown more fundamentally out of local issues."

This was not always true elsewhere, especially under Stalin. In the years following World War Two, Russian troops intervened in Manchuria and North Korea, massed threateningly on the borders of Turkey and Iran, and blockaded Berlin. They intervened in Czechoslovakia, East Germany and Hungary, and regularly harassed air traffic over Austria or along the Berlin corridor. By the sixties, the Russians were flying troops for Congolese rebels, putting missiles into Cuba, skirmishing on the Chinese border, expanding their navies in the Mediterranean and the Indian Ocean.

During the 1967 war in the Middle East, Moscow succeeded in stopping the Israeli advance on the Syrian front by alerting paratroops. After the Egyptians, using a Russian guided missile, had sunk the Israeli destroyer *Eilat*, Moscow prevented Israeli reprisals by sending eight Red Navy ships to Port Said and Alexandria. That November, Soviet air support in Yemen was credited with turning the tide against the royalist forces there. In Czechoslovakia in 1968, Dubček was ousted by 400,000 Soviet troops.

Achieving rough strategic parity with the United States at that time, Moscow seemed to have become emboldened. Soviet forces have been involved in at least thirty-two incidents in the past decade, from Bulgaria to West Africa to India. In 1969, the Russians actually began building a submarine base at Cienfuegos, Cuba. Warned that this was a violation of the 1962 Kennedy-Khrushchev agreements, the Russians stopped construction but continued sending submarines on visits to Cuba.

But the Middle East remained the main center of Soviet operations. In 1973, the Soviet Air Force flew Yemeni troops to Oman to help the Dhofar rebels. When the Ramadan War began later that year, the Soviet

Air Force flew supplies to Egypt and Syria—including Moroccan troops for the Syrian front. Three Soviet airborne divisions were put on alert, and later, as recorded, Moscow nuclearized Egypt's Scuds to meet the apparent threat of Israel's Jerichos.

Soviet soldiers drove tanks from Damascus to the Golan front and helped Egypt by firing conventionally headed Scuds against Israeli forces in Sinai, presumably as a warning that any Israeli escalation would lead to strikes at Israel itself. When the Egyptian Third Army was surrounded east of Suez, Moscow alerted four more divisions—while urging Sadat to accept a cease-fire.

The general U.S. official view is that Moscow showed restraint during the 1973 war, as it had shown a year earlier during the U.S. mining of North Vietnamese harbors—when it limited its reaction to protests and token naval deployments. Washington delayed activating the mines for three days to enable Russian ships to leave the harbors.

Russia's initial stepped-up support to the Marxist MPLA in Angola in 1975 seems to have been at least partly a reaction to increased Chinese, American and Western support for the FNLA and UNITA resistance forces. What seems to have triggered—or excused—the later massive Russo-Cuban intervention was the U.S.-encouraged introduction of South African troops on UNITA's side that August, and the sudden, congressionally enforced collapse of U.S. support for the major Angolan parties. Eventually, fourteen thousand Cuban troops and five hundred Soviet military advisers turned the tide of the war, ushering the minority MPLA into power, driving out the main nationalist forces and crushing secession in the Cabinda enclave. On the other side of Africa, Moscow backed first Somalia, then Ethiopia.

Such largely bloodless weapons diplomacy, sometimes involving limited proxy wars by lesser powers, seems likely to continue.

ON THE CREDIT side, if arms have proliferated and controls are often more rhetorical than real, the very development of war-related sciences has helped to make accidental wars or escalations less likely than in the past. The revolution in communications gave Johnson far more control of Westmoreland in Vietnam than Truman ever had over MacArthur. The daily bombing raids over North Vietnam were controlled from Arlington, Virginia. If forward defense systems were largely ignored in the SALT I talks, it was partly because America's and Russia's first line of defense is not the European glacis but the superpowers' nuclear triads. Foreign bases are less vital than once they were: U.S. nuclear-missile submarines could almost as conveniently be based in American mainland naval ports as in Guam, Rota and Holy Loch.

Nuclear holocausts aside, neither superpower could go to war today with equanimity. U.S. dependency on oil is matched by Russian dependency on food. Twenty-five per cent of Soviet animal protein comes from the sea, making the Russians the second greatest consumers of fish after the Japanese. Moscow's huge Indian Ocean fishing fleet is almost as precious and as vulnerable as the wellheads in the Persian Gulf—so precious to the United States. All in all, of the two superpowers, Russia is clearly the most nervous, and with the best of reasons. Soviet concern with nuclear encirclement, with its extraordinary problems of naval egress into the open oceans, with its shortages of wholly owned foreign naval bases all influence thinking, especially in light of the fact that Russia is a great power only militarily. Economically, it is not in the same league with the United States, and perhaps not even with Japan. This imbalance helps to perpetuate the arms race; but the arms race curiously perpetuates a sort of peace, and pays good dividends, to both stockholders and diplomats. It even provides jobs for the bureaucrats who work, at least theoretically, on how to scale it down.

I

Arms

1

From Flintheads to Warheads

IT WAS A fine spring day in 1977. Outside the windows, the sun glinted brightly on the calm Mediterranean. Samuel Cummings, the world's biggest private arms dealer, sat back in his plush office in Monte Carlo and told this writer: "What I do is like running a casino. When your business depends on human folly, how can you lose?"

Cummings has a point. Fighting is older than man, since it goes back to our animal antecedents. Anthropologists seeking the missing link between earliest man—*Homo habilis*—and his less able primate ancestors look for evidence of chipped stone. The difference between a nonhuman primate and man is that man makes tools. And, despite recent efforts by some researchers to prove that our forebears were peaceful folk, the earliest tools of all were weapons.

Violence is a prehistoric solution to disputes which time and culture have endowed with endless sophistication, but otherwise have left unchanged. The recent centuries of enlightenment and science have merely enabled us to kill more people, more quickly and effectively, than our medieval ancestors or our fellow primates and other mammals.

Ancient Weapons

Most modern weapons still have a distinguishable ancestor. The modern input has been precision in aim, velocity in delivery, and awesomely augmented power.

The earliest weapons were the jawbones of animals, stripped by prehensile fingers to a cutting and a hammer edge. Next came clubs of stone or wood. Spears were initially staves, later embellished with stone tips. Stone daggers were also fashioned. The metal age was slow in adapting itself to weaponry, but swords of bronze—ten parts copper, one part tin—featured in Roman times, and in the Crusades: They were originally an Arab invention whose secret soon passed to Europe. Later, iron swords were preferred to bronze ones; eventually, blades of steel proved the best.

The first serious improvement in assault power in ancient times came from the missile. Initially men, like apes, threw stones—perfecting slings, then catapults called manganels and onagers, for their delivery. Alexander the Great relied heavily on such arms. These, and battering rams, became siege weapons. The infantry threw javelins and spears, while different cultures used throwing hammers, throwing axes or boomerangs. The ancient British, acquiring horses from the Romans, designed chariots with sword blades attached to the wheels—contraptions that looked like Rube Goldberg versions of certain modern harvesters. But for centuries, the main propulsion-missile weapon was the bow and arrow, challenged only by the blowgun and dart in the Americas.

The Encyclopaedia Britannica says that "the origins of the bow are lost in Paleolithic times." Arrows soon acquired a stone head, usually of flint, and a feathered tail. The bow was the primary military weapon in the Mediterranean area from Egyptian times. It spread, east and west, through the Middle Ages. For reasons connected with the Bushido Code, which restricted the use of guns by Japanese to hunting, the bow lasted even longer in the Far East, where some Japanese weapons were eight feet long.

In the West, the best bows were made of yew and required a force of 100 pounds to draw the string. Arrows were about 3 feet in length and a good bowman could send one for 200 yards. From the bow was developed the longbow, which was the principal weapon of Europe's Hundred Years' War, and which held its importance until well into the sixteenth century. It was longbows which won the epic battles of Crécy and Agincourt.

Longbows, which measured about 6 feet, were thought to have originated in either Italy or Wales in the tenth or eleventh centuries. The English longbows of the Middle Ages had a "string" of linen or hemp. Turkish and Arab bows used silk or mohair. Both bow and longbow remained in use long after the invention of the crossbow—a short metal bow fixed transversally on a stock. Using a trigger on a grooved guide, an archer could fire short arrows at great speed, achieving greater accuracy and more deadly penetration. So lethal was the crossbow that the Lateran Council of 1139 outlawed its use against Christians. Sometimes the bowman caught the "string" in a hook at his belt and used his whole body to tense it; but mostly a hand crank was used. The arrows could travel 1,000 feet and could penetrate chain mail.

The crossbow forced the creation of a more opaque suit of armor—the one familiarly seen in plays or movies set in old, haunted mansions. Huge crossbows were built that could hurl boulders into the enemy ranks. But reloading was slow, and the longbow consequently survived. And by the time the crossbow was in wide use, in the fifteenth century, it was overtaken by the invention of the arquebus—the first gun.

The gun was made possible by gunpowder, which was invented and reinvented all over the world. In the thirteenth century, both the Arabs and the Tartars used rockets when their forces invaded Europe; gunpowder, however, was probably first invented in China, but not immediately used in warfare. In the West, the Englishman Roger Bacon (c. 1220–c. 1292) first made gunpowder with niter, charcoal and sulfur.

Berthold Schwarz, a fourteenth-century German monk, was probably the inventor of the cannon. Edward III used crude cannons at Crécy in 1346, and both the English and the French used cannons at Agincourt sixty-nine years later. Early cannons fired arrows, then stones, and eventually metal balls. The cannons frequently burst, to the extreme prejudice of their crews. Bronze or brass cannons were preferred; as cannons improved, so did the gunpowder that went with them.

The arms trade as we know it—still mostly made to order, but often made to order in quantity—began about this time, in the Belgian city of Liège. In the fifteenth century, Charles the Bold issued an edict forbidding the Liégeois to make weapons. The ban was defied, so Charles razed and burned the town, driving out its occupants and slaughtering those that stayed behind. But unrepentant Liège was soon back in the arms business. When the Duke of Alva invaded the Low Countries in 1576, both his Spanish forces and those of the Dutch and Flemish defenders were armed by the weaponsmakers of Liège. By the mid-eighteenth century, Liège was producing 100,000 "pieces" a year. Today, Liège is the home of the Fabrique Nationale d'Armes de Guerre, whose "FN" rifle was the NATO standard weapon for two decades after World War Two, and which now makes the U.S.-designed M-16 which took its place. Every Sunday, while other Belgian cities are holding open fruit and vegetable markets, the modern Liégeois stage a "flea market" of used machine guns, grenades, mines and military pistols which attracts urban guerrillas from as far afield as Lebanon, Italy, Germany and Ireland.

It was in the late sixteenth century that explosive shells or bombs first made their entrance on the field of battle, although efficient shells were not really produced in quantity for nearly three hundred years. The first successful artillery general was the youthful King Gustavus Adolphus of Sweden (1611–32). His cannons fired projectiles weighing 1.5 pounds, which could easily take a trooper's head off. Howitzers fired canisters of grapeshot. By the eighteenth century, muzzle-loading smooth-bore field pieces were used wherever European armies fought each other.

Some early cannons were huge. The Russians made one with a 30-inch bore, and the Turks used even larger ones in the siege of Constantinople. Napoleon used 6.5-inch howitzers weighing more than a ton, and 12-pounder guns weighing twice as much. Wellington used lighter 6-pounders at Waterloo, which gave an advantage in mobility. The recoil of the bigger guns was considerable, and springs were poor; both on land and especially at sea, the sappers held their guns by ropes. All these elementary cannons overheated quickly, fouling the bores; they then had to be left to cool. During the Napoleonic Wars, an Englishman called Henry Shrapnel got his name into the language by inventing a shell that burst, throwing out lead or iron projectiles. By then, the first mortars were also in use, although it was the need for a plunging shell in the trench warfare of World War One that established the mortar's importance.

The Rifle

The basic weapon of war for the past half a millennium has been the musket—now called the rifle because of rifling within the barrel. Early muskets needed two people—one to aim the weapon, the other to fire it. Arquebuses or matchlocks lasted from the fifteenth century through the eighteenth, and longer in Asia. They took their name from the fact that a match was used to ignite the powder. The Spanish developed a matchlock musket that could fire projectiles fast enough—1,000 feet per second —to go through armor. These guns weighed between 15 and 25 pounds and were fired from a forked rest, set in the ground. Because of reloading time, musketeers needed a protective force of pikesmen and swordsmen, much as World War Two fighter planes protected the slow and vulnerable bombers. Heavy rain would put matchlocks out of action.

George Thayer, in his standard work *The War Business*, says:

> Over 100 years were to pass before the matchlock rifle gave way to the wheellock, over 200 before the wheellock gave way to the flintlock and over 100 before the flintlock gave way to the percussion-cap rifle . . . [But] the [bolt-action] Springfield rifle was standard issue to U.S. forces for only 33 years; the [automatic] M-1 Garand for only 21.

Today, the rapid obsolescence of almost all weaponry is guaranteed.

It was the musket's ignition process that was slow to improve. Wheellocks and flintlocks produced less smoke and noise than matchlocks, but they were slower to operate. The wheellock used a serrated wheel which sent off sparks, as in a cigarette lighter. The flintlock was more successful, and became the standard weapon in the late seventeenth century.

Flintlocks wrote the pages of history on the battlefield for fully a century and a half. The bullets were initially narrower than the barrel's bore, to enable the musketeer to cram them in. As a consequence, they ricocheted along the barrel and rarely came out straight. By then, a musketeer could fire from two to four shots a minute, according to his skill and the weather. One time-consuming task was the ramming of a paper "cartridge" on top of the bullet with a ramrod.

Rifling the barrel had already been invented either in Leipzig or Vienna in the last half of the fifteenth century, but in those artisanal times it was a costly process; so for nearly two centuries, rifles were generally used only for patrician sport; the humble trooper still defended himself and the nation with the smooth-bore musket. Initially, rifling was straight, not spiral; the bullet still did not fill the barrel to capacity, but it came out more straightly than before and was "accurate" for targets not more than 150 yards away. The paper cartridge had been replaced by a greasy rag which spread lubrication as it ejected.

Christian IV of Denmark was the first to use the rifle in war—in the early seventeenth century. Bayonets had been invented—presumably, but not certainly, in Bayonne—a few decades earlier. The combination of an accurate musket and a thrusting spear improved infantry morale. Americans used rifles in the Indian wars and the Revolution, leading to adoption of the rifle by the British forces.

The first rifles had been brought to America by German and Swiss immigrants. The earliest model was known as the Pennsylvania or Kentucky gun. With spiral rifling, the bullet swiveled inside the barrel and continued swiveling, outside, toward its target. The gun was now accurate to 300 yards. In the nineteenth century, the French Minié rifle, or some copy of it, was in almost universal use by the world's armies. Standardization of rifle parts had begun a century before.

Besides rifling, the other great development had been the percussion cap, invented in 1805 by a Scottish clergyman, Alexander John Forsyth. Forsyth perfected a compound, in which the crucial ingredient was potassium chlorate, that would explode if struck a hard blow; he patented it in 1807. The British Government gave him a workshop in the Tower of London, and he found a local congregation, dividing his time between prayer and experiments on arms. Forsyth's discovery obviated the need for a separate priming powder; it made possible today's metallic cartridges and the contact fuses used in shells. But nineteenth-century armies were notoriously conservative and romantic. Forsyth's great invention was not used against Napoleon—although it could have been used by the other side if Forsyth had not refused a handsome cash offer of 20,000 pounds from Paris for his patent. It was not until 1842 that the Presbyterian dominie's prayers were finally answered: The U.S. and British forces adopted the cap for military use, and Forsyth was awarded a pension.

Another important time-saving was achieved when the principle of ramming bullets down the barrel was replaced by breech-loading; but once again, progress was slow. The first breech-loaders appeared in the hunt, in the early sixteenth century. It was two hundred years before French and Austrian troops began using them on the battlefield. Some British troops used Ferguson breech-loaders during the American Revolution: these could fire an impressive six shots a minute. In 1817, the United States adopted the Hall rifle, named after John H. Hall of Yarmouth, Maine. It was a breech-loading flintlock with interchangeable parts and was soon copied in Prussia and France, where it was known as the needle gun. The Hall rifle was superseded by the Sharps rifle in 1848, and later by the Springfield and the Krag-Jorgensen. America began to move into the forefront of small-arms innovation. The nineteenth century saw experimental repeating pistols, with anything from two to eighteen barrels. Meanwhile, Samuel Colt's hand pistol, capped by hand, established itself as the basic holster weapon in 1830 and was soon copied all over Europe. Horace Smith and Daniel B. Wesson produced an improved pistol in 1850.

Around the turn of the century, the enormous market in America for hunting guns sparked several improvements in rifles. The Spencer gun, soon renamed the Winchester, was a firm favorite. Around this time the British developed the Enfield and the Germans the Mauser.

Gunpowder had originally been carried in horns, then in bandoliers. The first cartridges—in the late sixteenth century—long preceded the invention of smokeless powder. In the seventeenth and eighteenth centuries, when the cartridge reached the battlefield, soldiers had to bite off the edge of the wad, pour a little of the powder into the flintlock pan and the rest down the barrel, ramming this in with cartridge paper. Britain once had an army problem on its hands in India when its Muslim sepoys were told—an early disinformation tactic—that the grease on the cartridge they had to bite came from the pig, which was of course taboo in the Islamic diet; Hindu sepoys were told—correctly—that it came from the holy cow, making biting it sacrilegious. Both Muslims and Hindus mutinied.

The first truly effective cartridge was produced by Smith and Wesson in 1856. Eventually, brass cartridges became universal.

Faster and More Massive Methods of Destruction

Prior to the French Revolution, armies were small. Historians have tied the growth of armies to the growth of the Industrial Age. Conversely, war subsidized the growth of the industrial era.

Big armies required faster and more massive methods of destruction. Richard Jordan Gatling produced his machine gun in 1882. Another American, Hiram Stevens Maxim, designed an improved version two decades later. By 1900, there was a wide range of rapid repeating rifles, of carbines (which were shorter and lighter and intended for mounted troops), of semi-automatic pistols and revolvers, as well as fully automatic machine guns. The end of the cavalry era was approaching, and with it came the new era of mass slaughter—the trench warfare and long stalemates of World War One. The hideous vulnerability of the soldier in World War One spawned the tank—the modern equivalent of a suit of armor against arrows.

Rifles became lighter and shorter. Virtually all were fed by five-cartridge clips. The bolt-action Mauser was probably the best in World War One: The American Springfield, first produced in 1903, had been a modification of the Mauser. Other World War One rifles were the Lee-Enfield (Anglo-American), the Mannlicher (Austria), the Mosin-Nagant (Russia), the Arisaka (Japan), the Lebel (France) and the Ross (Canada). These were all repeaters, not automatics. The gunner, using the bolt, had to eject and reload. German and French experiments with automatic rifles in World War One were not successful. It was John C. Garand of the United States who finally adapted the Springfield to produce the M-1, the automatic rifle of World War Two and Korea; this used gas pressure from a propellant to reload and cock. U.S. troops in some theaters were supplied with the Johnson gun, designed by Melvin M. Johnson. The German and Russian automatic rifles of World War Two were less successful than the M-1, although the German bullet was bigger and more lethal.

Back at the end of World War One, the machine gun had spawned the lighter submachine gun—a portable weapon for firing pistol-caliber ammunition. American gangsters brought fame to the Thompson or "tommy" gun. By World War Two, the submachine gun had developed into the assault rifle. These were initially much heavier than they are now. The very first was the Lewis gun of World War One, designed by Britain and best remembered for being perched on the fuselage in front of the open cockpits of that war's fighter planes, synchronized to fire through the moving blades of the propeller. Between the wars, the United States developed the Browning in time for use in World War Two. Britain used the Bren, a Czech weapon originally made at Brno but built at Enfield by the British: its name is a composite of both cities. Germany produced a similar weapon, the Schmeisser.

Submachine guns usually fire pistol ammunition at between 450 and 900 rounds per minute. The one patented in 1920 by John T. Thompson, a retired army officer, had a massive revolver chamber. This weapon was finally adopted by the U. S. Army in 1928. In World War Two, GIs mostly used the M-3, known as the "grease gun" because it resembled the lubrication tool used in service stations. The M-3 also saw service in Korea. Its successor today is the 6-pound M-16.

As weaponry diversified, the need for standardized ammunition became apparent. Early bullets were round, like buckshot; but by the nineteenth century the spherical form had given way to the cylindro-conoidal shape which enabled bigger bullets of the same caliber to be used. The Frenchman P. M. E. Vieille discovered smokeless powder in the 1880s, thus clearing battlefields of the acid-smelling fog of earlier centuries and making more accurate ammunition more important. But it was not until 1953 that a standardized cartridge was finally adopted for NATO: this was to be the 7.62mm. for rifles and machine guns; the same caliber was also to be used for the duplex cartridge—in which one bullet spirals around another.

At that time, the United States was using the Garand rifle and Western Europe the Belgian FN. By 1957, NATO forces began adopting the M-14, superseded later that year by the M-15 and in 1960 by the earlier-mentioned M-16, firing 5.56mm. ammunition. The Soviet Union adopted the Avtomat Kalashnikov, or AK-47, and the SKS or Simonov carbine, both using 7.62mm. ammunition. Early NATO ammunition cannot be used in these guns, however, since the NATO bullet is almost half an inch longer.

The recoilless rifle only appeared at the end of World War Two. The Korean War model was a 50-pounder, fired from a bipod or tripod. In 1959, a lighter model was adopted which was effective against tanks: this later evolved into the contemporary Davy Crockett, which can fire a shell or a low-yield nuclear warhead.

Grenades date from the seventeenth century, but were mainly developed in World War One, which also saw the development of mines. These in turn became more varied, with antipersonnel mines requiring only a touch to be detonated, while antitank mines required greater pressure. The Claymore mine, extensively used by the United States in Vietnam, fires slugs as it explodes. Booby traps were a variant of mines. Rockets, beginning with bazookas and antitank weaponry, were the forerunners of today's missiles.

As ammunition improved, so inevitably did armor. But the early World War One tanks were essentially what tanks have remained—mobile gun platforms. The main battle tank of World War Two was the U.S. Sherman, which, with an improved (French) turret, was the tank used by Israel in its 1967 blitzkrieg on Egypt. World War Two saw the development of Armored Personnel Carriers (APCs) and half-tracks—which have wheels in front for greater maneuverability, and tracks on the driving (rear) axle for greater mobility in rough terrain. Another development from the tank was the self-propelling gun. The introduction of diesel engines minimized the dangers of fire inside tanks in battle.

If the tank was nothing but a gun with a suit of armor, naval warships were simply gun platforms afloat. The huge battleships with their enormous, earsplitting cannons lasted until 1945. Missiles helped miniaturize the navy, leaving aircraft carriers as the only really big ships; even these seemed destined for a permanent size reduction with the development of the assault helicopter and the vertical takeoff plane.

The elite weapon of the new twentieth-century navy is the submarine. The German *Unterseeboot*—undersea boat, or U-boat—nearly won World War One, sinking 11 million tons of shipping in the Atlantic. In World War Two, U-boats sank 14 million tons, including two hundred warships, three of them carriers. Today's nuclear-powered submarines are also nuclear-armed, and thanks to their mobility and relative invulnerability would be the first line of NATO's defense and attack in any all-out World War Three.

Aviation and Bombs

Aviation was originally seen, in 1914, as merely an ancillary to ground forces—reconnaissance, or "spotting" targets. But as "recce" planes of both sides met among the clouds, pistol battles ensued. By 1915, machine guns were mounted, then the lighter Lewis guns. By then also, the first bombs were being carried. They were initially thrown out by hand, until a mechanical release gizmo could be adapted to the underside of the fuselage. By war's end, Britain's Vimy bomber, named after a famous battle of the war and made by Vickers, was carrying 2,500 pounds of bombs. The aircraft, which cruised at 80 miles per hour, itself weighed 4 tons. In

June 1919, two British aviators, John Alcock and Arthur Brown, flying a Vimy carrying extra fuel in place of bombs, became the first persons to fly the Atlantic. When the tension wires of the big biplane began to collect ice over the mid-Atlantic, Brown turned up his flying boots, tightened his scarf around his helmet and clambered out onto the lower wing to knock it off, a feat that makes modern astronauts close their eyes in vertigo at the thought.

Perhaps the most offbeat aviation development of World War One was the German Zeppelin, a dirigible or "blimp" powered by hydrogen gas and pusher propellers. But the war ended with the armed forces unsure of the value of their new aviation tools. In the thirties, Brigadier Billy Mitchell had to fight hard to make converts to his prediction that the next war, if there was one, would be fought in the air; but he succeeded, and the U. S. Army Air Corps, and other air forces around the world, began to get a heavier share of defense budgets.

Europe, however, was pressing aviation development more slowly than America. At the beginning of World War Two, the best superiority fighter was Germany's Messerschmitt Bf-109. Its immediate British competitors, the Hawker Hurricane and the Fairey Battle, were slower and less maneuverable. Work in Britain on a new engine, the Merlin, and in America on a new fuel, code-named BAM-100, just managed to get the first Supermarine Spitfires rolling off the assembly lines in time for the Battle of Britain in the spring of 1940. Developed from an aircraft which, in a seaplane mode, had consistently won the Schneider Trophy (for the world's fastest aircraft), the Spitfire-III—the first efficient combat version —weighed 3 tons, which was considered light for an all-metal aircraft. The Merlin generated 1,000 horsepower—1,300 at rich-mixture with BAM-100 fuel—and the Spitfire flew at the same speed as the Bf-109: 360 miles per hour "through the gate." The Germans only introduced a superior aircraft very late in the war, and in small numbers—the jet-propelled, rocket-firing Messerschmitt-262 fighter.

Britain's main contribution to the air war was, however, the introduction of radar—zeroing in on the enemy or bringing one's own planes home by radio waves. America's main achievement was the era's most effective bomber family, beginning with the B-17, known as the Flying Fortress. Originally generating only 3,000 horsepower, it could carry 3 tons of bombs at a top speed of 200 miles per hour, for a range of 600 miles. However, its eventual development, the B-29 or Superfortress, could boast 15,200 horsepower, enabling it to carry 50 tons of bombs; with its bombs away, it could keep pace with fighters at 340 miles per hour. The six machine gunners among its crew of ten could fire from thirteen machine gun positions. On March 9, 1945, 276 B-29s took off from the Marianas and flew 1,400 miles to drop 2,000 tons of bombs on

Tokyo, burning a hole in the city nearly 16 square miles in size and causing 185,000 casualties. All but fourteen planes returned to their island base. On August 6 that year, one Superfortress, the *Enola Gay*, dropped the first atomic bomb on Hiroshima. Three days later, another was dropped on Nagasaki. The Hiroshima bomb had the explosive power of 14 kilotons (14,000 tons) of TNT, the Nagasaki bomb 20 kilotons. The world had entered the age of nuclear fission. In the Hiroshima bomb, part of the uranium-235 was fired into the rest from a gun within the bomb itself. In the Nagasaki bomb, friction between the particles was procured by pressing two parts of the bomb—the so-called "critical mass"—together.

After World War Two, supersonic military aircraft became commonplace. Nuclear warheads became immeasurably lighter. The Hiroshima weapon had weighed 6 tons; only a B-29 could have carried the bomb from the Marianas and returned. By 1970, even light fighter-bombers could deliver a nuclear strike of comparable power. In the direction of gigantism, the hydrogen or thermonuclear bomb was developed: since no critical mass was needed, bomb size and power became virtually unlimited.

The wartime Allied advantage in atomicry had been slim, and the enemy had been ahead in rocketry. German experimentation with jet engines and rockets had produced, by 1944, the pilotless, jet-propelled V-1—a forebear of the cruise missile. In the last year of the war, eight thousand were fired over Britain, along with several V-2s, which were rocketed out of the atmosphere and returned at supersonic speed. It was these Nazi achievements which hailed an era in which rockets and missiles would begin to replace heavy bombers. Had the Germans succeeded in their efforts to produce a nuclear warhead for the V-2, Hitler's fortunes would have changed. It was German technicians captured or recruited by the Russians or the Americans after World War Two who eventually laid the basis for developments in nuclear and rocket science, including space travel. Today, intercontinental ballistic missiles could hit anywhere in the world, and the strategic nuclear balance of power has led to a proliferation of smaller, tactical nuclear weapons.

Chemical and Biological Warfare

If nuclear weaponry has remained, since 1945, wholly in the realm of the rattling saber, chemical warfare—much more within the reach of even modestly developed countries—has never been ruled out.

Weapons with which to burn people or property have been known and used since ancient times: The figures on the ramparts scalding those

below with boiling water have remained favorites of cartoonists. The
Spartans burned wood treated with sulfur and pitch to create a cloud of
poisonous sulfur dioxide. Poisoned daggers often decided medieval politics. Leaving the diseased carcasses of horses in wells or streams, or
poisoning food, were seen as acceptable under the rules of war. As late
as 1914, the Germans overcame the Romanian cavalry by infecting their
mounts with glanders. But one really giant step for inhumanity was
taken on April 22, 1915, when the Germans released chlorine into a Belgian village called Vijfluege, in the Ypres salient. Dr. Robert Jones, writing in *New Scientist* in 1975, describes the event:

> The day was a fine one in the immediate vicinity of Ypres. At 5 P.M.,
> men in forward positions heard a light hissing noise from the direction of
> the German trenches. Within fifteen minutes, no less than 168 tons of
> chlorine had been released along a front extending about four miles. A
> light wind of 3-4 mph bore the wall-like cloud toward trenches manned
> by British, Canadian, French, and Algerian troops. Distant observers
> spoke of a low greenish mist "such as seen over water meadows on a
> frosty night." The deadly gas brought horror into the ranks of the Allies.
> . . .
>
> More chlorine was discharged on an adjoining sector of the front on
> April 24, this time against Canadian troops . . . [As to] the numbers of
> victims, the figures most quoted are 15,000 casualties, of whom 5,000 died
> during or soon after the attacks.

Both sides then began using gas, and started to manufacture masks to
filter out the enemy's toxin. The Germans used gas mostly on the Russian
front, where there were 56,000 deaths and 419,340 non-fatal gas casualties. On the Western Front, 8,109 British soldiers died and 180,607 were
stricken; the French recorded 8,000 deaths, 182,000 other casualties. U.S.
losses were 1,462, plus 71,345 casualties. German deaths numbered 9,000,
with 191,000 casualties.

Late in the war, Germany introduced the more deadly mustard gas,
which Britain perfected and stocked in the twenties. In the buildup to
World War Two, Nazi Germany developed nerve gases which brought
instant death by incapacitating the nervous system.

But public reaction is particularly strong against any weapon which
kills slowly instead of "cleanly," and gas warfare has always generated
extreme emotions. When the United States briefly used an emetic gas in
Vietnam—enabling an enemy position to be taken without inflicting
casualties—there was a strong press reaction against the "indignity" of
making soldiers vomit on the battlefield. This led to a return to something which public opinion could accept more readily, namely, capturing
positions by killing those holding them. The reaction is similar to that

which enables most Americans to approve capital punishment, while considerably fewer would accept a return to some less drastic forms of corporal punishment, since all of these except execution are slow and generally messy.

The Geneva Convention of 1925 outlawed the use of toxic gas in warfare. The only Western country that has used it since is Italy—in Ethiopia, in 1935 and 1936. Germany, of course, used gas to execute concentration-camp prisoners, but its last use on the battlefield was by Japan —in China, in 1936. During World War Two, both sides stocked toxic gases; but they were never employed, although the British intended to use them if German forces ever landed on British beaches. Since then, Mace and similar gases, including tear gas, which incapacitate without usually causing permanent injury, have been used as riot-control weapons by civil forces.

The Germans used flamethrowers in World War One. In the Second World War, the United States mixed gasoline with aluminum soap of naphthenic and palmitic acids to produce napalm. Being thicker than gasoline, it could be propelled farther. Being stickier, it stuck to its target. It burned at a higher temperature than gasoline. Phosphorous bombs were used against both personnel and property. Biological warfare was a feature of the Vietnam conflict, in which massive defoliation was undertaken by the U. S. Air Force—both to uncover forested targets and to sabotage enemy agriculture.

Psychological warfare is as old as conflict. Ancient armies used noisemakers; as late as the Battle of Tunis in World War Two, Scottish Highland regiments advanced to the sound of bagpipes, both to inspire the Scots and demoralize the Afrikakorps. Drums have always been used as much to intimidate the enemy as to keep soldiers in step on the march. Tall headdresses were favored by soldiers of all cultures, from the Romans to the Algonquin Indians. Body paint, especially facial makeup, was a tool of terror. In modern times, "psy-war" is more associated with propaganda and the now highly skilled art of disinformation. World War Two also advanced the art of economic warfare, including embargoes and naval blockades: Economists rather than generals selected most of the targets for the USAAF's Flying Fortresses and the Lancasters of the RAF's Bomber Command.

The Future

The 1975 edition of the Encyclopaedia Britannica noted that "more than three quarters of all infantrymen in the armies of the world carry essentially the same weapons today that their predecessors had before

World War One. Their pistols, rifles and machine guns fire single-projectile rounds in which smokeless powder propels small-diameter bullets from brass cartridge cases and contain percussion primers."

But weapons of the future are countless. Small arms are no longer so mild as the appellation suggests, and are likely to become more deadly in the future. Originally, the U. S. Army defined "small arms" as meaning anything up to 60 caliber. Since then, portable rocket launchers and recoilless rifles, mounted aboard their own mini-armored vehicles, have joined the "small arms" ranks.

Small projectiles of the future may include multiple fléchettes, for instance. The new objective will be to kill with a single shot. At present, soldiers still fire several thousand rounds for each casualty. With automatic (multiple-burst) weapons, the recoil spoils the aim: In this case, only the first shot is relatively accurate; this factor may encourage greater use of rockets, which have no recoil, or—when they are more perfected and less expensive—of laser weapons.

Artillery has moved on from the ballistic shell to the guided missile; but for close combat, the basic artillery weapon may be the self-propelled gun vehicle in which weapon, ammunition and crew are all sealed against nuclear fallout. Field pieces can now be deployed by helicopter. Howitzers—cannons with a multiple choice of trajectories and velocities—have not lost their uses, and mortars continue to improve: The Soviet Union has some that fire a projectile with a diameter of 16.5 inches; these weapons weigh 60 tons and the projectiles nearly a ton apiece: They can reach targets at 20,000 yards.

Missiles come in all sizes. The Viet Cong fired missiles weighing 100 pounds; at the other end of the scale, the American Saturn missile weighed as much as a light cruiser. The range of the latest U.S. Minuteman ICBM is over 8,000 miles. Some missiles are free-fall, but most now are guided. The ballistic missile has brought into existence the Antiballistic Missile (ABM), which can intercept a missile while it is traveling at twenty times the speed of sound. In this field, the United States has the Nike-Zeus, the Russians what NATO terminology calls the Galosh.

Improved range-finding is certainly expected in the near future, whether by heat-seeking systems, wireguides, radar guidance or other "homing" technology. It is not inconceivable that rocket missiles may eventually replace entirely the manned bomber, turning NORAD—the U.S.-Canadian air defense command—and PVO-Strany, the Soviet equivalent, into fleets of robots.

Tactical nuclear weapons as light as 100 pounds with a firepower equal to 100 tons of TNT already exist. On the drawing boards are similar light weapons with a potential firepower of 20,000 tons. Nuclear-powered ships may soon be joined by nuclear-powered aircraft. Of all these wonders, more later.

But the doomsday weapon remains essentially a bee's sting: Its use leads to the death of the aggressor himself. If used against another nuclear power, retaliation would be certain. If used against a non-nuclear power, world reaction would be such that a nuclear adversary could probably retaliate with world opinion on its side. Its use, in other words, would involve a misdirection of the real purpose for which it was built. Today's warhead is not only more sophisticated and powerful than the flinthead of ages past: It is a different, more political weapon altogether.

2

Orders of Battle, Balances of Power

IT WAS A fine day in October 1984. In the five minutes that he had given himself to decide, the President had opted to go aboard the "kneecap"—the National Emergency Airborne Command Post. He had made the short journey from the White House to Andrews Air Force Base in suburban Maryland by helicopter.

During the five minutes of decision, he had oscillated among the options. He could go to Fort Ritchie and fight the war from there, or to Strategic Air Command headquarters in Nebraska, where—in a room four stories high covered with floor-to-ceiling display screens—he could speak to missile silo centers and military command posts across the world, through SAC's primary alerting system. But after the brief moment that had seemed longer than it really was he had decided to take the advice of the Joint Chiefs, who preferred the "bird."

There was something sci-fi and slightly unbelievable about controlling a nation and a nuclear war from a Boeing-747—a plane designed for long-distance tourism. There would be only fifteen staff officers aboard, the highest a colonel, and a twenty-seven-man Air Force crew. Yet there was something chilling, too, about being pinned underground like a bear in a pit. His family was in the redoubt at Fort Ritchie; there were just too many of them to find places in the "kneecap," so he had left them together. As he literally ran from the helicopter to the plane, its engines already warm, his mind was still going over the events of the previous months. If at the meeting with the Soviet ambassador on August 3, or if in the hot-line communication of September 1, instead of . . . or if at the secret meeting in Geneva on the thirteenth . . . Well, it was too late now. At least we knew their intentions and we were now pre-empting. Or did we? Could it be a mistake? As the brakes came off and the jumbo began rolling, the President reflected that they could stay aloft in this thing for three days, if a refueler could be sent up. But from where? Where would not be radiated? Guam? Hawaii? Diego Garcia?

Aloft, once the 25,000-foot transmission antenna had been released, the

President picked up the red secure-line phone. The white phones around went dead. Looking ashen, the lines on his face like barbed-wire scars, he made a half-nod to Colonel Rensellaer of the battle staff, who put down the receiver he had been using.

The President spoke a few words in grim, imperial tones: It was more of an authorization than an instruction—from now on, the war was too serious an affair for anyone not military or technical. The President's authorization became coded words, over the ether, and over the President's signature.

Deep under the Arabian Sea, about 100 miles south of Karachi, a telex machine aboard Trident-II submarine *New Mexico* clattered noisily into life and began unscrambling the President's message, coming in on the new Seafarer communications system. The first word was: FLASH. A watching radio operator stiffened.

"Emergency Action Message," he said. He called a second operator for a mandatory check. By now the message was coming over in three-character cryptic digits.

"Emergency Action Message!" the second operator called.

The first operator tore off the message and took it a few steps to the officer of the deck in the message center. By now the telex machine was repeating the message, again with the preamble FLASH.

All strategic submarines would be getting the same message, but the OOD recognized the code figures for the *New Mexico*. He announced over the intercom system: "Alert One!"

This announcement brought the captain, the executive officer and the navigator to the radio room to check the Alert message. The XO went to a safe, opening it with a memorized code, and took out a sealed envelope, containing a sample EAM. The three officers compared it with the one they had just received.

"Authenticated," the captain said. The eyes in his bearded face took on a look of strain.

"Yep," said the XO.

"That's it," said the navigator, reading the cryptic number groups that spelled out targets. "All twenty-four of them!"

The captain stepped briskly to Launch Control, up a few steps. Leaning down to a microphone, he spoke over the general announcing system: "Man battle stations, missile!" He paused. "Set condition 1-SQ."

When you command a weapon platform that can only be used for strategic nuclear war—the holocaust—and nothing else, this is something you should be prepared for, the captain thought. But it took some thinking.

The 150 members of the crew began preparing for the missile launch.

They had done it all before, many times. But this was for real. Or was it? Was it just another test of readiness, but purposely omitting the reassuring words: "This is a drill"?

The *New Mexico*, snub-nosed, black, 535 feet long, 43 feet tall, was ascending. It stopped with its antennas and its sail—what old submariners used to call the "conning tower"—about 100 feet below the surface.

Just abaft the sail, the twenty-four missiles, each with a range of 6,000 miles, each with fourteen independently targeted, thermonuclear—hydrogen—warheads aimed at military targets and cities sometimes as much as a hundred miles apart, stood, vertically, amidships. Behind were the engines, the nuclear reactor, the engine room staff.

The XO and the navigator had already proceeded to another safe. Again using his top-secret, classified human memory, the XO dialed the code of the door, then stood aside. The other officer similarly gave his fingers a code confined to his memory; he opened up an inner door of the safe. From inside, he took out a batch of envelopes containing keys—one for each missile. These were the firing keys which would start the war.

Three decks below, meanwhile, in Missile Control, the weapons officer snapped to a chief petty officer: "Weapons supervisor, assign Missile One." Then he spun the dial of another safe over his computer console and extracted a key. The XO joined him. Each using a separate key, they opened an inner door of the safe. The weapons officer drew out a trigger, rather like the stock of an old-fashioned Colt pistol, but made of red plastic. He slumped back in his chair, watching the burly weapons supervisor.

The CPO, facing his familiar brown and green display panel, had already punched the Tactical button. The first missile's computer began automatically checking its systems, lighting green blips on the petty officer's panel as each check was completed. As the Tactical button had lit up, he had punched Bypass, closing the bypass mechanism which would have been used for a check not destined to end in firing. The missile guidance systems were now beginning to be spun up. This would take about ten minutes. The CPO punched Interrogate: A computer began checking the launch system.

The green blips were now becoming more numerous. There were, so far, no red lights for malfunctions (which could mean that a missile aimed at a lower-priority target would have to be retargeted), no yellows calling for corrective action. There had better not be. Not today.

The air in the missile tubes was being brought up to the same pressure as the water around the sub. The flood valves were made ready to take the water which would rush in to replace each missile. Compensatory mechanisms were activated to take the added burden of weight on the

18,000-ton submerged vessel—a tube full of water weighs more than a missile. Steam was prepared to launch the missiles. Ignition would be computer-controlled on contact with the air at the surface.

At Launch Control, near the bow, the captain watched a gray panel, about 11 inches by 14, as, one by one, the first among twenty-four banks of red lights began to come on. The navigator had earlier handed him the firing keys. They were red, no bigger than door keys, with distinctive handles. Down below, the weapons officer said, this time more quietly: "Assign Missile Two." The tension mounted.

The minutes seemed long. Had war perhaps begun already? Had Russian sonar found the *New Mexico*? Was "something" already on its way? From the moment when the EAM was first read, it was nearly a quarter of an hour before the first bank of lights on the captain's panel was complete, indicating that all readiness procedures had been carried out for Missile One. The other banks were catching up. On the weapons supervisor's panel, two of the last three lights came on. First: Erection. For once, the CPO didn't smile. Then: 1-SQ. In the navigation center, a switch was thrown. The captain could see that the electrical circuit was complete but for one final step. Now it was up to him.

He inserted his flat red key into a lock rather like that on an elevator panel. Grimly, he turned it.

"Weapons Control, you have permission to fire," he said on the general announcing system. Every member of the crew could hear. The role of a human voice in the final chain of preparations seemed oddly out-of-date, like a last vestige of chivalry. Over the Fire Control announcing system, the XO's equally recognizable voice gave the confirmation: "Weapons Control, you have permission to fire." Then the captain punched a button, and an electrical contact confirmed the voices—on the weapons supervisor's panel, the final light for Missile One came on: Authorized to Fire.

The weapons officer picked up a cable and used it to plug the red trigger into the console of a computer. His mind as empty as he could make it, he squeezed the trigger. It felt as though something heavy had bumped the *New Mexico* from above. The ship shuddered slightly. All the weapons officer could find to say was a short, cloacal expletive. Awe and fear.

Above, the first Trident missile was screaming for the stratosphere, toward an apogee 800 miles from earth.

Fifteen seconds later, the weapons officer fired Missile Two, and fifteen seconds later, a third. It had been an agonizing, tense fifteen minutes leading up to the launch, but in six minutes all 24 missiles were gone, all 336 warheads soon to be diving at many times the speed of sound toward.

336 Soviet missile sites, nuclear storage depots, bomber fields and other targets; each warhead was equal to 50,000 tons of TNT, or more than three times "Hiroshima." Dummy warheads and electronic chaff, discharged also, would be confusing Soviet radar. Nine minutes after the last launch, the first would strike target.

The captain wondered if we had struck first, and by how long. What of the Soviet antiballistic missiles? Oh well, there were forty-some other strategic nuclear submarines in the U. S. Navy still around, half of them at sea. There were the Trident-Is and the Poseidons. The Poseidon missiles had only half as many warheads, the few remaining Polarises less. But even one Poseidon battery could close Russia down, if anything had gone wrong with the *New Mexico* launch. But what if the Russians had interfered with our satellites, deceiving the sub's computers and spoiling the aim, perhaps even falsifying in some way the President's order? Suspicions were endless. The captain wondered how many other "boomers" —strategic submarines—had been ordered to "fire." He thought about fellow captains in the "skimmers"—the surface ships. What were their chances of survival? At all costs, with its missiles gone, the active life of the *New Mexico* was now over, and it had, after all, betrayed its presence twenty-four times, at fifteen-second intervals. Back in his cabin, he looked at a small photograph over his mini-desk: the children he would probably never see again.

Could it happen? The chances are more than 99.9 per cent against. But the chances of winning first prize in a huge sweepstake are also more than 99.9 per cent against, and somebody *does* win first prize. The main thing about strategic and tactical nuclear weaponry, of course, is that it is never *intended* to be used, except in diplomacy. But its diplomatic effectiveness depends on its potential use and effectiveness in "real" war.

Which weapons are needed for this task and which are unnecessary? The question is at least in part academic. New weapons, like all new technology, have a "life" of their own. Funding for research is never seriously questioned—it would be like saying that you didn't want to know all the answers, and that you had confidence that the enemy did not seek them either. And once a system is shown to be workable, it is invariably put into production.

Suppose, for example, an antitank missile (ATM) was in use which was only accurate to within 50 feet of target but which had a warhead so powerful that it could always destroy its target and perhaps other tanks in the vicinity. Then suppose that a new precision-guided ("smart") ATM was developed which always scored a direct hit, but which—

because of the bulk of the sophisticated precision-guidance system—could only pack a lighter warhead that could destroy only the target tank. A congressional committee might argue that the gain—a direct hit—was offset by the weaker firepower. The Army would say that nothing beats a direct hit, and that somewhere down the pike would be a *bigger* precision-guided missile. Congress would give its okay, perhaps reducing the authorization from 1,000 batteries to 800. The real reason for funding and building the PGATM would be *because it was there*—because it had been invented and tested, and it worked. And a workable antitank weapon is a workable diplomatic weapon—at the very least, a bargaining chip in arms-limitation talks.

The Background

America is, with Russia, the world's largest arms producer. Even more than Russia, it is the world's principal arms innovator. But America's addiction to the arms industry is something new. One of the first decisions of the infant United States was to abolish a standing army and navy. With American ships no longer protected by the British Navy, this was to cause a major problem. Clauses in the Constitution forbade the billeting of soldiers on the citizenry, and—to replace a professional army with an instant militia—upheld the rights of Americans to keep and bear arms. Unfortunately, the words "in defense of the United States" were not included, enabling anti-gun-control lobbies in our own time to pretend that the Founding Fathers sought to protect the right to sell mail-order weapons to teenagers.

It was to save the merchant ships of an America about to lose the shield of the Royal Navy that the Continental Congress created the Marines in 1775. The corps, aimed at checking the depredations of pirates out of Barbary, is still an elite and legendary force, but one that could be annihilated *in toto* by a squeeze on the right trigger from the index finger of a chimpanzee. The United States Cavalry was designed solely to maintain internal order. Even for the tiny task of capturing Cuba in 1898, volunteer forces had to be raised, with the officers buying their uniforms and rifles from Abercrombie and Fitch and often paying their troopers' wages out of their own pockets.

A much larger and more professional citizens' army and navy was hastily raised in 1917 to help Britain, France and Italy defeat the Kaiser—and was just as hastily demobilized. In 1939, when "fortress America" sought to evade involvement in World War Two, the soldiers, sailors and

airmen who garrisoned that fortress were less numerous than the standing forces of little Sweden. Soldiers were rarely seen in the streets, although sailors were sometimes spotted on the Pacific coast. Then, at the
urging of a beleaguered Britain, Franklin Delano Roosevelt made the
United States the "arsenal of democracy": In 1941, America entered the
war itself and the arsenal grew; at one assembly shop near Detroit,
Willow Run—a room half a mile long, a quarter mile wide—8,760 planes
a year, or one an hour, were produced. Henry Kaiser, by welding instead
of riveting vessels, managed to produce a "Liberty ship" in four days,
thus creating a supply force for the projected Second Front.

Had Hitler invaded Britain in 1940, in the wake of Dunkirk, without
waiting for his enemy to resuscitate in the Battle of Britain, and had
Europe thus been relegated to nothing more than "resistance warfare," it
is hard to retropredict what would have happened. Would we still be living, from here to eternity, with Swedish-style armed forces? But Hitler's
policies also contained the germ of another, more devastating Hitlerian
error: Among the Jews who fled his burgeoning pogrom in Europe were
Albert Einstein of Germany, Enrico Fermi of Italy and Edward Teller of
Hungary; with the help of Niels Bohr of Denmark and American and
other scientists, notably Robert Oppenheimer, these geniuses of physics
perfected the "atom bomb," working in tarpaper shacks in the desert at
Los Alamos.

The atom bomb did not win World War Two. By the time of its use,
Germany had already surrendered and Japan had no hope of surviving
alone against the world. The Hiroshima and Nagasaki bombs merely hastened a Japanese surrender and saved hundreds of thousands of American and Allied lives. But the nuclear missile—as the diplomatic weapon
it has become today—was decisive in the Korean War: Early in 1953,
shortly after his election, President Eisenhower went to Korea and let it
be known that unless a truce was achieved swiftly, the American-led
United Nations Command would use tactical nuclear arms on North
Korea and China. An armistice was signed a few months later.

Long before Eisenhower's election, the cold war unleashed by Marshal
Stalin and upheld by his then Chinese ally, Mao Tse-tung, had ensured
that the world in general, and America in particular, should never be
able to retreat entirely from the arms race. Hydrogen bombs and atomic
warheads on assorted strategic missiles have dominated the doomsday
end of this competition, and today we face the growth of at least tactical
nuclear weaponry in the arsenals of small powers.

In the long run, then, it is nuclearization rather than simple "militarization" which is the real threat and which has made the world a "smaller" place, subject to menace even by unlikely states.

The Budget Debate

Despite the growth of Western arms, NATO strength is diminishing proportionally to the Warsaw Treaty countries, partly because the United States has held defense expenditure steady. President Eisenhower's first defense budget in fiscal 1955 was $35.6 billion. In 1978 dollars, that would be $120.5 billion. But President Ford's last defense budget was "only" $116.6 billion at 1978 values. Several congressional voices have been raised, especially in the House, about a growing imbalance which could tilt in Moscow's favor. Conservative Republican congressman Jack F. Kemp of Buffalo, New York, has noted that:

> Fiscal 1978 budget outlays are nearly 10 per cent less than constant 1978-dollar outlays in fiscal 1964—a year when military compensation and related personnel costs accounted for only 42 per cent of the defense budget compared to over 50 per cent today.

At constant prices, Soviet military expenditure has been rising at 3 per cent annually since 1964 and surpassed U.S. outlays for the first time in 1971. In 1974, the Soviet military budget was estimated at $93.5 billion, nearly 20 per cent higher than America's. By 1978, the CIA put the discrepancy at 40 per cent. The real difference is greater, since the Russians spend a larger share of these funds on arms and a lower ratio on personnel—salaries, catering, housing, medical care, pensions, etc.—than the United States. Russian spending on the manufacture of offensive strategic weapons, for instance, has exceeded that of the United States for a decade now, and was already 60 per cent higher than similar American spending by 1974. In 1978, the CIA estimated the Soviet weapons budget alone for the previous year at between $72 billion and $79 billion, or nearly twice the U.S. total. The main new growth sectors were seen as frontal aviation, ballistic submarines, and systems directed against China. A breakdown of Soviet military expenditure shows weaponry claiming nearly 80 per cent of the total, of which 35 per cent is for procurement and nearly 20 per cent for research and development (R & D), the rest being accounted for by operation and maintenance (O & M). Soviet expenditure on R & D began to exceed that of the United States in the early seventies, with the margin—according to SIPRI's figures—already widening to about 25 per cent by 1974.

The Library of Congress breakdown of the U.S. figures for 1976 showed a massive 63 per cent for personnel and training, only 37 per cent for procurement, R & D and O & M together. Since then, the disparity has increased. Between 1968 and 1977, the Pentagon payroll rose from $32 billion to $52 billion, despite declining manpower. Federal salaries were raised in 1967 to match wages in private industry: But the military benefited without serious cuts in their subsidized housing and commissaries. A thirty-eight-year-old with twenty years' service can retire on half pay and start a new government or private career with a second pension at the end. A new act sponsored by Congresswoman Patricia Schroeder puts limitations on this practice for admirals and generals, but otherwise "double-dipping" remains undisturbed. Pension payments rose from $1.4 billion in 1965 to $8.4 billion in 1977—six times as much as the B-1 program—according to Congressman Les Aspin of Wisconsin. Aspin, who projects them at $34 billion by the year 2000, called for pension cuts, and a 1978 Brookings report said that a further billion dollars could be saved annually by civilianizing more defense jobs—and by bringing civilian defense salaries down to the level of those of the corporate world.

The Red Army, in contrast, is a great force but hardly a great attraction. The pay is poor—three dollars a month for a private—and the food execrable. Leaves are rare or nonexistent, even for married men. There are no married quarters for enlisted men. Alcoholism is rife—mechanics even pilfer the deicing alcohol from aircraft. The Soviet taxpayer pays for his armed forces to have guns, not butter, and the punishment for desertion is death.

The Carter administration projects a 1983 military budget of $172.7 billion; but by computing long-term current program costs, the Center for Defense Information puts the true figure at about $200 billion. Total procurement costs, over the coming years, of the principal current weapons programs are $119.4 billion. This includes $54.4 billion for fighter programs, $47 billion for ships (of which about $24 billion is for Tridents and Trident missiles) and over $10 billion for the XM-1 tank. Naval aircraft are particularly costly: For $13.2 billion, the Air Force got 746 new planes in fiscal 1978; for over half as much—$7.4 billion—the Navy got only 280.

The following year, a Library of Congress study said the Air Force was getting ten times as many aircraft as the Navy, for two and a half times the money. The Navy's purchase of planes was down from 339 in fiscal 1970 to 131 in fiscal 1979. The average cost of a naval plane rose over the period from $5.9 million to $33.3 million. One result is that squadrons are getting smaller: An A-6 squadron, for instance, now consists of ten planes instead of twelve.

The NATO and Warsaw countries are not alone in excessive spending. In the Third World, Israel, South Africa and probably India and Taiwan are all developing nuclear missiles, and other countries, including Pakistan, Brazil and Yugoslavia, are expected to follow. In 1975, Israel went into production with the Kfir fighter, thus joining the superpowers, France, Britain, China, Japan and Sweden in producing advanced supersonic combat aircraft. In addition, Israel has a diversified army and naval war industry. Also in 1975, with an initial promise of $2 billion—later doubled—from Saudi Arabia and other oil-producing kingdoms, Egypt started setting up the first weapons-plant complex of the Arab Organization for Industrialization (AOI): France and Britain began competing for large licensed-production contracts for fighter aircraft, helicopters and other projects. That year, sophisticated military-aircraft construction plants were also started in Iran, the Philippines, North Korea and Peru. Poverty or relative poverty is no longer a barrier to power.

Debate over U.S. defense policy and the military budget moved into high gear in 1977, following Jimmy Carter's election-campaign promises to cut arms spending—promises which soon became a political embarrassment to the new President. Liberals said that putting ceilings on rising military costs would help détente, and the new Defense Secretary, Harold Brown, claimed the United States had no choice but to negotiate arms reductions with Moscow. But Energy Secretary James Schlesinger —a former Secretary of Defense himself—made it clear that he distrusted détente and the pacts it produced. So did many others, both inside and outside government.

Financially, two issues were paramount: How much should the United States spend on developing new weapons, and how could the cost of training, paying and retiring defense personnel be brought under control? There was talk of a reserve draft, of longer tours of duty between moving troops, of a less generous instructor/trainee ratio, of closing bases, of a new, less generous—but not retroactive—pension plan.

Most hawks and doves agreed that Pentagon spending, overall, should increase. By 1976, defense spending had declined 30 per cent over a decade, in constant dollars, and much of those diminishing funds had been spent fighting in Vietnam, not building up America's global defenses. Brown was thought to favor development of the B-1 strategic bomber, but to be prepared to give up cruise-missile development as a bargaining chip in the ongoing round of SALT—the strategic arms limitation talks. This added a new twist to weapons diplomacy that is characteristic of the age: Even *threatening to build* a weapon still insufficiently researched and developed to be ready for the assembly line is the new, subliminal rattling saber.

The Carter administration did seek, somewhat ineffectively, to lower the rhythm of the arms race in the Middle East. Refusing Israel's request to sell U.S.-engined fighters to Ecuador (a sale partly aimed at diminishing the unit cost of Kfirs to the Israeli Air Force), canceling plans to sell American concussion bombs to Israel and reprimanding Tel Aviv for its wildcatting of Red Sea oil in Sinai (Egyptian) waters made it likely that, with the other hand, the new administration would cancel the Ford White House's plans to sell the supersophisticated, twin-boomed F-18 fighter to Iran. And so it happened.

But the main concentration was on the U.S.-Soviet military balance. Retired Colonel John M. Collins, the Library of Congress' top arms expert, stressed in a 1976 study of that balance for the Senate Armed Services Committee that just being ahead of Moscow in the development of new weaponry was not enough. Said Collins: "What each side *has* is less cogent than what U.S. armed forces can *do* on demand, despite Soviet opposition."

Barry M. Blechman, then Collins' equivalent at the Brookings Institution, took a different view: In a December 1976 *Saturday Review* article, Blechman said: "For years now, critics have been charging that new weapons are needlessly complicated and excessively advanced technologically, and that they are produced through a process that encourages waste and high price tags."

Blechman and others have stressed that decisions about new weapons are often more political and economic than military, based on pressure from manufacturers and labor unions, from Congress members with defense payrolls in their districts at stake, and from military and retired-military groups. These latter in turn complained about overinterference in vital defense policies by unqualified congressional staff.

Schlesinger, former Deputy Defense Secretary Paul Nitze and other so-called hawks start from the premise that America should be ready to fight a limited nuclear war. The partial or total bluff implicit in all cases of weapons diplomacy only works if the threat is real or at least perceived by others to be real. Harold Brown and others have argued in response that it wouldn't take long for limited war to escalate into total war. Indeed, the most popular scenario in Pentagon contingency thinking sees war beginning "conventional"; then the losing side quickly goes "tactical nuclear"; then whoever seems to be losing the tactical war soon goes "strategic." But many doubt if there would be a "conventional"—or even a "tactical"—phase at all.

U.S. plans for defending NATO are now based on three weeks' advance warning of an attack, and this also is criticized by "hawks": Many strategists believe that the Soviet forces, better equipped than the forces of most NATO allies, and half again as numerous as they were a decade ago, could strike at a few days' notice. Even Blechman, now assistant director of the ACDA, says: "Should a crisis unexpectedly develop, as it may in Yugoslavia after Tito dies, the U.S.S.R. could well take an active role. Thus, an expansion of U.S. military capabilities . . . in the European theater seems prudent, [especially] Army and Air Force [weaponry] suitable for the high-speed intense conflicts that the Soviet military is geared to fight."

This is the language of "deterrence," as the reference to the Soviet Union implies. Most defense thinkers believe China is not a foreseeable threat to the United States, and the Carter administration seems committed to reducing U.S. forces in Asia while possibly increasing them in Europe.

On the whole, surprisingly little thought seems to have been given to China's position in the global strategic equation. Arthur Macy Cox, a defense writer who was formerly with the State Department and the CIA, says: "The Press reports estimates of the Soviet defense budget and Soviet strength as though all of that strength is directed against the United States and its Allies. If you reduce that budget by the proportion that is directed against China, you get a budget that is a good deal smaller than that of the United States and its Allies." By late 1978, Russia had 650,000 troops massed on the Chinese border.

Contingency planning, of course, has to allow for the possibility of a resumption of the alliance between the two great Marxist powers. But Cox has a point. He notes CIA reports that Soviet military spending rose in a single year—1975 to 1976—from between 6 and 8 per cent of the Soviet GNP to an estimated 11–13 per cent. (William Perry, Under Secretary of Defense for research and engineering in the Carter administration, has put the figure at 15 per cent.) But Cox points out that the Russian GNP is "less than half America's." This is something of an oversimplification because, given the frugality of Soviet military *manpower* spending, Moscow's weaponry spending is obviously ahead of Washington's; but Cox notes that spending by America's Western European NATO allies is much greater than that of Moscow's Warsaw Treaty allies —although, here again, NATO personnel costs are higher, and not all NATO spending is for the defense of Western Europe. Many European armaments are produced by government for export—for diplomatic and balance-of-payment reasons.

So, of course, is some Soviet spending. Says retired Rear Admiral Gene LaRocque of the Center for Defense Information: "A common worry is that the Soviet Union, while not seeking war, will manage to convert its military power into worldwide political influence and eventually dominance." There has, for instance, been a Soviet naval buildup in the Middle East, where U.S. power—a factor in American mediation of a Mideast peace—is mainly projected by weapons sales, and where sales in turn are partly intended to guarantee oil supplies.

Arms-limitation goals notwithstanding, the U. S. Army is now up to 16 active (i.e., nonreserve) divisions (from 13 in 1974)—but the size of a division is down from an average of 60,200 men to a mean of 49,100. Total Army numbers have been close to 800,000 since 1974. (Sixteen divisions was the norm in 1965, before the Vietnam buildup. In 1968, the Army had almost 20 complete divisions, averaging 79,800 personnel each.) In 1976, the Air Force was allowed to begin expansion from 22 to 26 tactical air wings. The Marine Corps' strength is fixed by law at 3 combat divisions and 3 air wings, plus 1 reserve division and wing.

The NATO/Warsaw Balance

What to add or not add to the American order of battle is largely an echo of the arms balance between the United States and the Soviet Union, a subject that regularly exercises the minds of experts. In 1977, using 1976 figures, John Collins prepared his massive study for Congress of the balance of forces between the two superpowers. It supported the view that the U.S. edge is diminishing, but above all it illustrated the totally different problems facing the two different countries: one lying behind two huge ocean moats, the other surrounded by land and—except for the Eastern European glacis—by enemies. Two contrasting strategies are apparent from a comparison of the armed forces of the two countries.

In numbers, the Soviet Union was vastly superior: Russia had a million military personnel in its strategic nuclear services, for instance; the United States had 163,000. Russia's general-purpose forces outnumbered America's 2,470,000 to 832,000. The U. S. Air Force, however, outnumbered its Soviet counterpart, while the U. S. Navy was almost 25 per cent bigger than Moscow's. Add all Russia's forces together, including 455,000 paramilitary "frontier forces," and the total, according to Collins, was almost 4,900,000 compared to America's 2,100,000. In civilian defense manpower, however, the Pentagon employs nearly a million people, while another 100,000 Americans are in defense-related government jobs, compared to the Kremlin's figure of just over 700,000. (Adding together the civil service, the military, other sectors and 1,100,000 pensioners, nearly 4,500,000 citizens are on the U. S. Government's broad "defense" payroll.)

Russia's armed-forces reserves, because of the long period of military service involved, were immensely more numerous than those of the United States: 6,800,000 in 1976 to America's 1,308,000 that year (down to about 700,000 in 1978). Grouping active, reserve and civilian defense manpower together, the Kremlin commanded 12,424,000 people in 1976. Immediately deployable ground forces were put at 1,737,000 for the Soviet Union, 575,000 for the United States. However, about one third of Soviet forces are deployed against China. All NATO ground forces in Europe totaled 1,205,200 in 1978—of which 224,000 were American. America's NATO allies also had reserves of 1,310,500.

In intercontinental ballistic missiles (ICBMs), Russia's first line of strategic defense, Moscow counted 1,549 launchers to the United States' 1,054. The imbalance was greatest in the field of heavy ICBMs: Russia's SS-7s, SS-8s, SS-9s, SS-18s and SS-19s totaled 559; America's Titan-IIs have numbered only 54 for a decade. The United States had 1,000 Minuteman missiles, while Russia's SS-11s, SS-13s and SS-17s totaled 990. However, in land-based warheads, because of the United States' advanced MIRV technology, America outnumbered the Soviet Union overall by 2,154 to 2,109—the "rough equivalence" to which the Nixon, Ford and Carter administrations have constantly referred.

Beyond this point, the Russian advantage began to go downhill. Moscow had 785 submarine-launched ballistic missiles (SLBMs) to America's 656, but had only 842 warheads, Collins said. (The U.S. total of submarine-launched warheads in 1978 was about 7,000.)

In heavy strategic bombers, the Kremlin was still far behind: the United States had 330 operable B-52s, according to Collins: Moscow's strategic-bombing fleet numbered 135, of which 100 were turboprop Bears. (By 1979, whereas tanker-refuelers made up 60 per cent of the SAC force, they were only 7 per cent of Soviet Long Range Aviation [LRA], stressing the Soviet emphasis on regional rather than transatlantic or transpacific operations.) In the medium strategic aircraft range, Collins found America's 66 FB-111s and Russia's 60 new Backfires to be about equal—although Russia, he said, had reportedly begun building 5 Backfires a month—but the United States' 2,058 strategic airborne missiles vastly outnumbered the Soviet Union's estimated 255.

By 1979, the United States still had a clear advantage. The Soviet Backfire force then totaled 115, with production re-estimated at 30 per year, for a final speculative total of 450. Overall, the United States has about 9,000 independently targetable warheads to Moscow's 4,000, but the latter include a larger number with massive "throw-weights."

How much more of a threat to the Soviet homeland exists than is faced by the North American continent was illustrated by the numbers of strategic defense interceptors: Already by 1976, Russia flew 2,700 of them, while the United States had only 114, plus 243 with the Air National Guard. Similarly, Russia already, by 1976, had 42,000 heavy and medium tanks to America's 6,265, 3,000 light tanks to the United States' 1,570, and 38,000 armored personnel carriers and other armored vehicles to America's 11,245. Soviet cannons outnumbered America's by 19,000 to 4,885, but in antitank guided missiles, the United States had a distinct edge—72,555 to 6,000. Since 1976, the figures have increased, but the proportions remain about the same.

In the tactical (short-range nuclear) air forces, Collins credited the USAF with 1,650 fighter-bombers, including 1,091 F-4 Phantoms, 312 F-111s and 210 close-support A-7s; the Marines had 318 fighter-bombers, including 132 F-4s. The Soviet Union had 680 tactical bombers and 3,350 tactical fighters, including about 500 MiG-23s (some of them the MiG-27 variant), roughly 1,700 MiG-21s and 400 Sukhoi-7s. But Moscow was vastly outgunned in accurate air-to-air and air-to-surface missiles, and the United States was developing new combat planes—the F-15, the F-14 and the F-16 in particular—much more quickly than its adversary.

At sea, U.S. power today is phenomenal: 14 attack carriers, 3 of them nuclear, to Russia's 2 antisubmarine-warfare carriers (and another nearing completion), while the United States has 8 other carriers. Carrier-based fighter attack aircraft numbered 610 in the U.S. fleet in mid-1978, including 274 A-7s, 139 F-4s and 93 F-14s; the Soviet Union had only 25 Ram-G vertical takeoff planes, plus helicopters, on its (then) 1 carrier. Russia's 31 cruisers were roughly equivalent to America's 26 (five of them nuclear), while 99 U.S. destroyers competed with 84 Russian ships. Russia was heavy on frigates—106 to 64—and had 102 lighter craft and 512 shore patrol vessels to America's 8. But, as will be seen later, the Soviet Navy is catching up in many essential areas. That the United States contemplates longer and more difficult supply lines to its allies was reflected in the imbalance of airlift aircraft: The United States had 304 assigned to strategic airlift while Russia had only 80, but only 608 assigned to tactical (short-range) airlift compared to the Soviet Union's 630.

The Carter administration was displeased at the Collins report and, in Presidential Review Memorandum (PRM) 10, offered a more optimistic assessment which noted that many Soviet and Warsaw Treaty divisions were mere "shells." Other voices also questioned the validity of some of Collins' comparison figures. General George Brown, then chairman of the Joint Chiefs of Staff, noted that usually "only eleven per cent" of the Soviet submarine fleet is at sea at any one time, compared to 50 per cent of the U.S. Poseidon/Polaris fleet. Liberals argued that NATO's seven thousand tactical nuclear weapons could meet any Soviet armored blitzkrieg in Europe.

Dr. Jeremy Stone, director of the Federation of American Scientists, admits ruefully that the main inbuilt weakness in U.S. defense is that Soviet militarists are not encumbered by a "free market place of ideas." But he notes that while U.S. missile-firing submarines are currently indestructible by Soviet technology, a sub-launched missile attack on Russia could destroy all Soviet cities and towns with five-figure populations or more—"Perhaps not Plains, but certainly Americus," he told a congressional seminar in 1977. Both sides' land-based missiles are vulnerable, but each would theoretically always have enough second-strike capability left to destroy the other.

Professor Earl Ravenal of the Johns Hopkins School of Advanced International Studies, who thinks all new land-based ICBMs, like the proposed mobile M-X, would be vulnerable to new antiballistic missile systems by the time they go into production, favored both sides scrapping land-based missiles in SALT II; but he thought other cost-cutting should mostly be applied to the general-purpose forces. Observing that the United States has no counterrevolutionary, antinationalist or colonialist ambitions, he saw the conventional forces as purely contingency-oriented: Ravenal has calculated that defending Europe, where the prospect of conflict becomes annually more remote, now costs the American taxpayer an astonishing $55 billion out of the proposed $98 billion general-purpose military budget for 1979. Speaking before the proposed (now uncertain) withdrawals from Korea had come about, but after withdrawal from Vietnam, he said that even Asian defense was costing the United States over $25 billion a year.

But the broad-based Committee on the Present Danger has said that the nuclear balance would tip away from the United States in the eighties by any standard, and that "only prompt and prudent strategic initiatives can restore the adequacy and credibility of our fading second-strike deterrent capability." The Coalition for Peace Through Strength, grouping 149 members of Congress led by GOP senators Robert Dole and Paul Laxalt, Republican congressman Jack Kemp and Democrat Sam Stratton, has sounded a similar note. The Coalition also includes Admiral Thomas Moorer and General Lyman Lemnitzer, both former chairmen of the Joint Chiefs, Major General John Singlaub, the former U. S. Army commander in Korea, and former Treasury Secretary William Simon. GOP freshman senator Harrison H. Schmitt, a former astronaut, has called for a U.S. antiballistic system similar to Moscow's, and for expanding the strategic triad of submarine-, land- and air-based missiles into a "tetrad" through use of defensive satellites in space.

Concern about growing Soviet strength has also been notably expressed by retired Lieutenant General Daniel O. Graham, former head of the Defense Intelligence Agency, and retired Major General George Keegan, Jr., former director of Air Force intelligence. Both men have noted that Warsaw Treaty forces have grown by "130,000" in recent years and that the Russians are now producing an estimated 2,000 tanks a year. General Robert J. Dixon, the recently retired commander of Tactical Air Command, has said the Soviet Union is currently outproducing the United States by two to one in fighter aircraft, six to one in tanks and a massive eight to one in cannons.

But Defense Secretary Brown, in a 1977 statement to Congress, said:

> I believe that for the present and the near-term future the United States and its Allies should be ready to deal effectively with, and hence deter, these four major contingencies: strategic nuclear attacks, attacks in Europe, attacks in northeast Asia, and attempts to close our main lines of communication.
>
> In several areas—Europe, and, in some locations, at sea—our forces would be less sure of success than is desirable. Additional efforts by both the United States and allied nations are therefore clearly in order. But none of these balances has tilted dramatically against us.

Brown admitted only that "the Russians have temporarily stolen a march on us in the realm of relatively short-range antiship missiles." Of the risks of a new Korean conflict, he said that the "ground forces of South Korea are comparable in numbers and capability to those of the North, and should be able to hold defensive positions north of Seoul. However, they might require logistic and tactical air support to ensure a successful forward defense, and hence an assured deterrent . . . A case may also be made for Japan to share more of the burden in protecting the sea lines of communication in northeast Asia." Brown urged increased spending on the U.S. strategic nuclear forces, which now cost about 1 per cent of the nation's GNP.

In late 1977, the White House ordered a major review of contingency plans for nuclear war and an assessment of the Russian civil defense program. The order called for a new list of priority Soviet targets, a determination of the number of missiles needed and consideration of whether "limited" nuclear war was still a contingency. National Security Advisor Zbigniew Brzezinski was known to consider that major targets should include the Soviet Union's precarious food supply and Russian forces in the Far East, whose decimation would encourage a Chinese attack on the U.S.S.R. When this report was leaked to some journalists early in 1978, it concluded that neither superpower could win a strategic nuclear conflict. While generally upbeat about U.S. security, the study called for a strengthening of Western conventional forces in Europe and the Far East. On a global trip that January, Carter promised Europe more U.S. forces. Abandoning his campaign promises of cuts in the defense budget, Carter told his European audiences that he would in fact increase it. Later that year, he offered a fiscal-1979 budget proposal of $126 billion, 1 per cent higher than the previous year's in constant dollars.

President Carter's Defense Spending

But in the first year of his administration, the President had still been hoping for reductions. The debate on the East-West arms balance had in fact been the prelude to the voting, in 1977, of the U.S. arms budget for the next fiscal year. After a great deal of rhetoric, Congress had approved, on June 30, 1977, defense appropriations of $110.6 billion, culling a few R & D items requested by the Carter White House, but restoring some other items which Carter and Brown had pared from the outgoing Ford administration's proposals. On July 19, after Carter had "canceled" the B-1, Congress shaved its figure down to $109.8 billion.

Back in January, Ford's retiring Defense Secretary, Donald Rumsfeld, in a massive report urging that the downward trend in U.S. defense spending, in constant dollars, should be reversed, said that "to a degree unprecedented in its history, the United States has become directly vulnerable to attack." Rumsfeld claimed that military spending would have to rise at least until the early eighties, whatever the incoming President might have said on the campaign trail, and few experts seemed to disagree. Rumsfeld stressed that the Russians still regard nuclear war as "thinkable," and said any U.S. response to a Soviet nuclear attack must be massive enough to ensure that Soviet industrial recovery is slower than America's. He defended Pentagon cost overruns, saying they were proportionally less than those of "the Washington Metro system, the San Francisco Bay Area Transit System and the John Hancock Building in Boston." The arms industry is never short of telling arguments.

Rumsfeld had urged a growth in defense budgets of 6.3 per cent a year, or 3 per cent after inflation, and proposed a fiscal 1978 outlay of $110.1 billion for a total obligated authorization of 122.9 billion (Carter later proposed $120.1 billion, an approximately 2 per cent cut, or about what a Democratic Congress would have stripped from the "Rumsfeld budget" anyway. In 1978, stressing NATO needs, Brown asked for $56 billion in military-budget increases over five years, putting the defense budget, as noted earlier, at $172.7 billion in 1983).

The Ford package for 1978 had included $23.8 billion for new weapons and $11.4 billion for R & D. The new weapons were to include 26 new warships (including 2 Trident submarines for $2.5 billion), nearly 700 aircraft—including 8 B-1s for $2.1 billion and 6 AWACS radar control planes for $529 million—3,000 new tanks and 45,000 missiles. The R & D figure included funding for the M-X missile, for cruise missiles and for outer-space warfare. To sweeten the pot, the Pentagon promised 217,000 new defense-industry jobs, meaning incomes for about a million people. Carter's final fiscal-1978 figure showed a 9 per cent increase over Ford's fiscal-1977 budget, 6 per cent of which represented inflation. Weapons procurement was up $4.3 billion, operation and maintenance by $2.9 billion, R & D by $1.3 billion, pay and pensions by $2.3 billion.

Congress authorized $36.1 billion for weapons procurement; in the Senate, not a single amendment was introduced to cut spending in this area. About half of the $1.5 billion approved by Congress for five production B-1 bombers which Carter canceled was later transferred to other parts of the weapons budget. Overall, final authorizations were up about $51 million over White House requests. The Senate approved, against Carter's wishes, $81.6 million for the engines of a fourth *Nimitz*-class large carrier; the House opposed this, but the House-Senate conference, under Navy lobby pressure, later deferred until 1978 a final decision on whether to go, instead, for the first two of a series of smaller carriers. But the new budget gave weapons only about 32.5 per cent of defense appropriations—strategic weapons about 9 per cent.

Military construction proposals came under some criticism, mostly from congressmen opposed to base closures in their districts, but this section of the defense budget also came through more or less unscathed, at just under $3 billion. Efforts to trim "double-dipping" (retired military personnel on other pensionable government payrolls) or to cut back on the military's commissary privileges were defeated.

The House-Senate conference approved $213.5 million for continued research on antiballistic-missile (ABM) defenses, and $25 million for development of Project Seafarer, the Navy's new proposed communications system. It cut $222 million from intelligence activities (the House had called for a $422 million cut) but the final total figure for that item was left classified. A compromise figure of $6.8 million for chemical warfare development was approved.

Major authorizations included $1.7 billion for two more Trident submarines, $134 million for mobile ICBM research (the M-X missile), $295 million for development of the new XM-1 tank, $165 million for the development of the Advanced Attack (antitank) Helicopter (AAH) and $236 million to build 56 UTTAS (Utility Tactical Transport Aircraft System) troop-carrier helicopters. All conformed to White House requests, except that the AAH request was increased. Congress approved the Administration's request to build 105 more F-16s for $1.5 billion, and increased the number of new F-15s from 78 to 108, for nearly $1.7 billion.

The first year of the Carter administration was, however, the first year of zero-based budgeting, and there were some procurement cuts. The Navy was given $29.3 million for advanced procurement for the F-18 but was told to find an additional $50 million for 2 more R & D F-18s by paring other budgets. The Navy had wanted 36 F-18s, anticipating reduced costs because of an order from Pakistan—later vetoed by Carter—for 110 of them. The Marine Corps request for $198.5 million for Harriers was cut in half under Navy pressure for the Marines to use the A-18 version of the F-18—to assure commonality, and lower unit costs for the Navy. Instead, in place of the new Harriers refused, the Marines got 24 more A-4s. All in all, despite the Navy's commitment to Vertical-and-Short-Takeoff-and-Landing (V-STOL) aircraft for the nineties, research in this area was slowed generally, probably in part because the design is basically a foreign one. Three new squadrons of F-4s for the Marines were also canceled, along with the last 90 F-4J life extensions.

The Texas congressional delegation lobbied hard against the Administration's request to close down Ling-Temco-Vought's A-7 attack plane assembly line; the House-Senate conference authorized the building of twelve more A-7s, after an ex-pilot, Texas Democrat Dale Milford, told the House it was better than the proposed new F-18.

The principal subject of congressional debate was the Navy. Former Ford administration Navy Secretary J. William Middendorf II had written in a recent article in the *Strategic Review*:

> In 1963, Admiral Gorshkov began the oversea deployment of the Soviet Navy. Gradually at first, the Soviet Navy moved away from the defense-oriented, anti-submarine role and began adopting some of the missions traditionally associated with sea power—the interdiction of enemy sea lines of communication and the support of Soviet foreign policy.
>
> . . .
>
> The [U. S.] Navy's solution to this critical issue is a balanced objective force level of 600 active ships in the fleet by the mid-1980s. This active fleet is built around 13 to 15 carriers and 190 to 220 surface combatants.
>
> . . .

The key element in this naval strategy remains the aircraft carrier. As a mobile, forward-deployed base, the carrier remains today that single platform which is capable of carrying out all the missions of the U. S. Navy.

But, as noted, Congress put off the choice between big and small carriers. The proposed fourth *Nimitz*-class ship—the $2.3 billion *Carl Vinson*—would carry nearly 100 fixed-wing planes and helicopters, along with 6,000 crew; it would displace 94,000 tons and require an escort of one or more cruisers and destroyers, plus several submarines and supply vessels. A big carrier with its planes and attendant ships constitutes a cost of about $30 billion and is seen by its critics as a sitting duck for Soviet missiles. The smaller, conventionally powered, $900 million carriers would displace about 60,000 tons—70,000 tons with ship and aviation fuel and reserve boiler water. The smaller ships would not accommodate the new F-14 fighters. The Navy currently has four large carriers—three nuclear-powered and the fifteen-year-old *Long Beach*. (The most recent, the *Dwight D. Eisenhower*, was only commissioned in late 1977.) The White House favors the smaller carriers—called CVVs, or carrier vessels for V-STOL aircraft—while the Navy (and especially Carter's old mentor, Admiral Hyman Rickover) wants the big carriers as well.

The fight over big carriers went to the heart of the discussion over the Navy's future. Even some admirals agree that these ships would be too vulnerable in an environment like the Norway approaches or the Mediterranean. Opponents of the big carriers also say that if slowed down by damage, they lack enough forward speed to enable their aircraft to clear their decks. They argue for a larger number of "platforms," noting that both the Russian and British navies are going over to V-STOL carriers. In short, above all, they favor cheaper, safer ways of providing air power at sea. Some carrier critics simply say that no third world war is likely to last long enough for the Navy to win ocean supremacy or begin moving large reinforcements across the Atlantic. But many naval strategists argue that, even if the war lasted only for a week or two, carrier-based air protection would be needed by the convoys of tankers and freighters going to Western Europe.

Working against carriers in general, especially big ones, is the "Big Momma" concept. Still on the Pentagon's drawing boards, this calls for an aircraft flying on the fringes of the stratosphere to attack enemy surface ships, submarines, bombers and fighters from a single platform which it would be difficult to assail. Big Momma—officially, the Land-based Multipurpose Naval Aircraft (LMNA)—is partly the brainchild of William D. O'Neil, a Pentagon scientist, partly the obvious lesson of one of the roles fulfilled by the Soviet Backfire bomber, now increasingly seen on Atlantic patrol. O'Neil says 180 LMNAs could be produced for about $75 million each. Big Momma would stand off and attack surface ships with long-range missiles and get at subs by dropping listening devices into the ocean and homing air-launched torpedos on the vessels they detected. But this is a project for the eighties, if it develops.

The Navy is, in any event, committed to the small V-STOL carriers for the nineties; but R & D funds for these carriers have to compete today with the development costs of the F-18 and the new version of the British-designed "jump jet" (V-STOL) Harrier itself, plus procurement costs for ships and production aircraft. In fiscal 1977, the Navy procured only 93 new fighter production aircraft—half the number it wanted—and had to make do with conversions and extending the life of existing craft. For fiscal 1978, the Navy finally requested only 56 new fighter and attack planes, saying this was only 30 per cent of what was needed, while only 57 were requested for fiscal 1979. For 1978, the Navy had wanted 44 new F-14s, then 60 in 1979, but was told to share the annual Grumman production run of 72 of the planes with Iran. By late 1977, with only 20 aircraft still to be produced for Iran, the White House called for the Navy's 1978 intake of F-14s to be cut back to 24.

The Navy, like the Air Force, has been plagued by overruns and lemons. In October 1976, Jack Anderson and Les Whitten reported that the first Trident submarines were developing cracks "in more than 100 critical places." The following month, the General Accounting Office said the Navy's new 8-inch gun, on which $76 million had been spent and for which a further $718 million had been requested, was so inaccurate at its range (10–20 miles) that it would use up its ammunition before zeroing in on a target. Thirty of the 40 new guns were due to be fitted on the new *Spruance*-class destroyers, requiring a billion-dollar retrofit.

Also under criticism as too expensive and too sophisticated—even from former Admiral Elmo Zumwalt—were the new *Los Angeles*-class nuclear attack submarines. These are the huge, 7,000-ton, "hunter-killer" subs, displacing as much tonnage as a World War Two light cruiser and costing $370 million each. Three were authorized in 1976, and nine more have been requested by the Navy. The cheapest combat ship in the current five-year naval construction program is a guided-missile frigate; even that costs $166 million.

Delays and overruns in the shipbuilding program, and a torrent of litigation between the Navy and some of the yards, have added to the air of crisis. Desertions have reached record levels: Older vessels mean more maintenance, while the shortage of ships means longer tours at sea; both factors have contributed to declining morale.

The more successful programs have tended to be in the attack submarines mentioned earlier and in relatively small surface vessels. If the days of big carriers are coming to an end, guided-missile destroyers (DDGs) may become the Navy's first-line surface ships. With their surface-to-air Sparrow missiles, antisubmarine rockets and the usual complement of guns, torpedos and nuclear depth charges, they present a far more formidable challenge than the word "destroyer" usually conveys. Some have Harpoon and cruise missiles, and carry an antisubmarine helicopter. With the sophisticated navigation and fire-control systems that all this implies, destroyer crews now sometimes number four hundred.

A visitor to a modern guided-missile destroyer's combat information center is struck with how it resembles the interior of an AWACS plane. Computer consoles data-link the weapons officers to ships and to the control aircraft above. The big hull of the vessel contains the missiles, arranged around a "drum." They are raised to the missile center to be hand-fitted with their "wings"—a twenty-two-second operation. The writer was told by officers that experienced crews, working in tandem, can load up one fresh missile every ten seconds.

With the Harrier, it is the Marines who are keeping the project alive—while facing uncertainty as to the Corps' own future. Then Marine Commandant Louis H. Wilson said in 1977 that Marines would always be needed for brush-fire operations and "on the flanks," but critics contend that the relatively small amphibious force could be absorbed by the Army or Navy. The Marines staged major landing operation exercises in Turkey and Norway in 1977 to demonstrate how they could "anchor" a NATO flank. General George S. Brown, then chairman of the Joint Chiefs, said the "defense guidance" of the sixties had not been revised: This stated that U.S. forces should be prepared to fight major wars in both the Pacific and Atlantic areas and a minor war somewhere else—the two-and-a-half-war strategy; but with Vietnam having proven how many forces could be drained by a single war, thought is now being given to a one-and-a-half-war strategy, which may eventually eliminate the Marines.

General Brown, however, when asked one day by the present writer if he thought the Marines would continue to exist as a separate unit, replied: "That is one I have stayed away from because . . . it would be like stirring a hornet's nest with a stick . . . I feel that the Marines contribute four additional divisions and air wings and I don't care how they paint the airplanes or what uniforms the fellows wear, it's still all tactical air . . . I think the United States has a need for some element of force that is a little lighter, a little more mobile, that can go in, in their terms, projecting power, go ashore for a time and not stay too long. So I think this nation can afford the Marines."

If the Marines survive, they will probably eventually "go ashore for a time" by using one of the Navy's more interesting craft now being developed—a British-invented troop-transport hovercraft, capable of skimming the water surface at 50 knots, driven by four gas-turbine-powered propellers and carrying payloads of up to 75 tons. The vessels themselves weigh 170 tons apiece. The Navy also plans a 2,000-ton hovercraft which will be as fast as light aircraft. Russia already has a 220 mph model that transports 900 men.

Increasing the Navy's financial problems is congressional criticism of ship-leasing: Under this system, the Navy's military sealift command contracts with private investors who in turn contract with shipbuilders, with the Navy agreeing to lease the ship from the investors for the ship's normal "economic life." This has enabled the Navy to use O & M (operations and maintenance) funds, not subject to specific congressional authorization. Senator Edmund Muskie said in 1977 that this procedure had "serious implications for the integrity of the budget process."

Looking toward the future, Navy spokesmen told reporters that year that it would cut its new-ship program by over one third—by between $5 billion and $7 billion over five years—and spend more money on overhauling older ships. The number of new ships would go down from 160 to 101, which would mean that the goal of a 600-ship fleet in the eighties would be shelved for the moment. At present, the U.S. fleet numbers about 460 ships. The Navy said there would be no cuts in submarines, only in ocean escorts and other surface ships.

To increase the financial problems for the services, the cost of R & D guidance now comes out of service budgets. In the past, the services pared down some R & D programs when submitting their recommendations, assuming that the Directorate of Defense Research and Engineering would add their favorite programs and provide funding. In 1977, for instance, the USAF omitted research funding on the Tomahawk air-launched cruise missile, assuming that such a favored White House program would be added anyway. It was—but at USAF expense.

Although many service complaints about budgeting reflect a natural desire to "build everything," there was apparently valid criticism of the short-term nature of much congressional planning—the expensive tendency to drop programs which have already cost a small fortune to the taxpayer. Evans W. Erikson, the president of Sundstrand, a major aerospace subcontractor, has suggested the creation of a board of supervisors for Defense programs, similar to a regulatory agency: Erikson envisages a board of eight to ten persons, appointed by the President with the advice and consent of Congress, serving overlapping terms which would exceed those of the presidency, to avoid total turnovers at the beginning of new administrations. Erikson sees this as making it harder for congressmen to vote for programs solely because they are built in their district or state, and against programs built elsewhere.

The high budget approved in 1977 reflected the fact that both the Carter White House and Capitol Hill are sensitive to reports about growing Soviet power. For the moment, both the executive and legislative branches of government are reluctant, however, to reinstitute the draft—although a "draft reserve" seems a strong possibility for the near future.

Senator Sam Nunn, chairman of the Senate Armed Services manpower subcommittee, has recommended that Congress consider restoring selective service. He cites racial and disciplinary problems in the all-volunteer force, falling recruitment, the effects of France's and Greece's withdrawal from the NATO command structure and Italy's one-third cut in its armed forces. Nunn also pointed out that the draft would help solve unemployment. Senator John Stennis, the full Committee chairman, predicted that a Selective Service Act would be "back on the books in the course of some few years." Meanwhile, General Bernard Rogers, then chief of the Army staff, recommended making Reserve service more attractive to volunteers.

Defenders of the all-volunteer force say recruitment could be brought up by the acceptance of more women, who are already 8 per cent of enlistees—17 per cent in the Air Force. Fears that the U.S. armed forces would be composed almost exclusively of white southern officers and poor black troops have diminished in recent years: Blacks are now down to 17 per cent of the forces—although they still are more than 24 per cent of the Army. Supporters of a return to the draft argue economies; but government figures show that, although draftees would be paid less than regulars, the saving from selective service—with the federal minimum wage now at $3.10 an hour—would be less than $2 billion a year. (*Barron's*, the financial weekly, has estimated such a saving at only $350 million.) In March 1977, Carter said he had no intention "at present" of reinstituting the draft; but two years later, the Joint Chiefs told Congress it would become necessary in the eighties, and urged a registration system for eighteen-year-olds. This now seems unlikely until after the 1980 elections.

Carter's earlier-mentioned 1979 military budget of $126 billion included the costs of going ahead with the M-X mobile ICBM, the Mark 12A warhead and Trident-II missiles, but did not include $2.8 billion for nuclear warhead production, still included in the Energy budget. Carter proposed delaying some strategic programs and even canceling, for the time being, U.S. surface effect ships (hovercraft)—despite the expenditure, already, of $300 million in research and development of them.

In all, the Navy was to get $41.7 billion, the Air Force $35.6 billion, the Army $32.1 billion. Other items were "defense-wide," including Pentagon costs. Personnel costs and pensions would total $38.9 billion, O & M $38.1 billion, weapons and equipment procurement only $32 billion. Research, development, test and evaluation (R, D, T & E) would cost $12.5 billion, military construction and family housing $4.3 billion. The Air Force would get 390 new planes, the Army 223, the Navy and Marine Corps 120—of which, as noted, only 57 would be Navy combat planes. The Army would receive 10,260 new missiles, the Air Force 4,736, the Navy 3,864, along with 1,882 new torpedoes, 15 new ships and 8 conversions. There would be 1,935 new tracked vehicles and 9,407 other weapons.

The House recommended $2.4 billion more—a new, big, conventionally powered carrier, a nuclear cruiser and more F-14s and F-18s for the Navy. It wanted to reactivate the A-7 assembly line, but to delay one Trident submarine for one year, and limit Harrier V-STOL aircraft to the Marines, who would lose their A-4 program altogether. The Trident delay would save $1.2 billion—not including the savings on the cost of its nuclear power plant, and its twenty-four missiles at $10 million each. The Senate recommended a $615 million increase, counterbalancing its demand for a new *nuclear* carrier and more F-14s and F-18s with some cuts. Both houses gave the green light to the F-18, after a spirited defense of the plane by influential Senator Edward Kennedy and Speaker "Tip" O'Neill, both of Massachusetts. (Its General Electric engines are made at Lynn.) Senator Gary Hart of Colorado was easily defeated in his attempt to kill $983 million for F-18s; but funds to restore the full V-STOL program were won on the Senate floor, along with Hart's request for $5.5 million for research on the Navy's future model.

Late in 1978, the departing 95th Congress cleared the fiscal-1979 weapons procurement authorization bill, adding on $1.9 billion for the nuclear-powered fifth big carrier over White House objections—a ten-year program for Tenneco's Newport News Shipbuilding and Dry Dock Company—along with $413 million for more carrier planes and $173 million for Harrier V-STOL research. The latter figure was twice what Secretary Brown had wanted, but Congress had deleted $113 million for more Phantoms to replace crashed Harriers.

In all, the House-Senate conference figure of just under $40 billion was $1.4 billion over Carter's proposals. It included $20.6 million for research on the B-1 and the upgraded B-52 and on improving C-5 and C-141 transports, $80 million for hovercraft, $35.6 million for German guns for the new XM-1 tank, $151.3 million to modify F-111 fighter-bombers as radar jammers, $165 million for Roland missiles, $689 million for 36 more F-14s, $110 million for 12 more A-7s and $146 million for 16 two-place trainer versions of the plane for the Air National Guard, along with $429.5 million for 9 F-18s for the Navy and $20 million for the Seafarer communications program. It cut back on the LAMPS (Light Airborne Multi-Purpose System) helicopter program, where runaway costs had reached $15 million per plane, and deleted $911 million for the eighth Trident submarine because of building delays—with the intention of putting it back in the 1980 program. Congress gave more money than Carter requested for satellite protection and for satellite detection of nuclear explosions. Keeping Ling-Temco-Vought's A-7 production line open was a triumph for the Texas delegation, who were able to note that, for the second year running, an A-7 wing from the 23rd Tactical Air Force had defeated twice as many RAF Jaguars and Buccaneers in the annual air exercises at Lossiemouth in Scotland.

In a conversation shortly before his death, General Brown admired the tenacity of the A-7 lobby—"It has been put in by the Congress every year." He saw it as probably an advantage, since it kept a "warm base" going for production in case of war. In any event, Carter vetoed the bill as inflationary. NATO allies criticized the veto; but after blustering and fuming, and threatening to pass no bill at all until 1979, Congress sustained it. Then, it merely took out the carrier—Carter had promised to include a large, conventionally powered one in 1980—and refused to transfer the funds saved to other projects the White House wanted, such as more TOW (tube-launched, optically tracked, wireguided) antitank missiles, more Maverick and Sparrow missiles, more A-6s and F-15s. It voted only enough funds to cover part of the Navy's back bills to contractors, and later cut $318 million for NATO-related building projects from a military construction bill, saying America's allies should do more.

Testifying in support of the veto, Secretary Brown, in the words of a *Congressional Quarterly* summary, said that "Congress was simply not equipped to analyze how the myriad bits and pieces of the defense budget are related to each other. Without such analysis, Congress might sew together a lot of individual programs, each of which was attractive when taken on its merits, but which would cost more while providing less defense than an administration-coordinated budget." Bob Carr of Michigan, a congressional lightweight who frequently tries to score on defense issues, criticized Brown and said Congress had not intended to cut U.S. defense capabilities. Brown, an often abrasive and immodest figure, cut Carr down in schoolteacherly fashion: "I would hope, if the Soviets invade western Europe, not to have to wave signs saying 'We didn't intend to cut our capability.'"

Shortly before adjournment, Congress voted total defense appropriations of $117.3 billion, $2 billion less than the White House request, plus an energy bill that included $3 billion for nuclear and "neutron" weapons.

The new budget offered $12 billion to the aircraft industry, plus $4 billion for missiles, including $490 million for cruise missiles. Military R & D would provide another $12.7 billion in industry revenues, despite the partial cuts in V-STOL development agreed in the House-Senate conference. NATO-oriented costs were put at about $52 billion. The House-Senate compromise increased immediate weapons-procurement authorizations from $22.9 billion to $25.9 billion, but cut R, D, T & E authorizations from the requested $12.5 billion to $11.8 billion. Carter got a little more than he had asked for—meaning, perhaps as much as he had wanted, with the chance to blame Congress for the budget inflation. Carter's total projected defense budgets through 1983 would now amount to $790.2 billion, or $41.3 billion less than projected by Rumsfeld. But clearly the President had become considerably more "hawkish" since being elected and getting a chance to read intelligence material. In March 1978, he made a strong "defense" speech at Wake Forest University in North Carolina. All in all, Administration and Congress now seemed agreed on maintaining the stress on strategic systems, and increasing it on NATO-related weaponry.

For the period 1978–83, Carter was planning to try to spend 7.8 per cent more than Ford intended on O & M, 4.5 per cent more on military construction, 2.8 per cent more on personnel and pensions, but 20.4 per cent less on procurement, and 2.2 per cent less on R & D. Thus, Carter's small overall saving is on the "lean," rather than on high-cost "fat" areas. The biggest Carter reductions in 1979, compared to the earlier Ford/Rumsfeld projections for that year, were 14.6 per cent on armor, 50.7 per cent on Army missiles, 10.5 per cent on airlift aircraft.

The preliminary 1980 budget, sent to Capitol Hill in February 1979, was for $135.5 billion. In it, Carter reversed himself on the big carrier, over objections from Secretary Brown and Rickover, and announced that only mini-carriers would be built. In an apparent contradiction, he also announced a stoppage of funds during 1980 for AV-8B V-STOL development. The Marines instead would get 27 of the Navy's first 103 A-18s, including 9 of the 15 to be funded in 1980. In short, more swings of policy seemed likely during the remainder of Carter's term.

The tentative 1980 figures allocated $35.4 billion to weapons procurement, $40.9 billion to operation and maintenance, $13.6 billion to research, development, testing and evaluation, and $45.6 billion to personnel, pensions, housing and construction. Aerospace-related funding was about $30 billion, up from $25.76 billion in 1979, and destined to go to $34.4 billion in fiscal 1982. The 1980 aircraft budget was $9.1 billion for the USAF, $4.7 billion for the Navy and $1.24 billion for the Army. The Air Force would get $2.6 billion for missiles, the Navy $1.7 billion, the Army $1.5 billion.

At the end of the year, Carter, swept along by the need to ratify SALT II and by the U.S. "hostage" crisis in Teheran, promised to increase the defense budget annually by about 5 per cent. He put the $2.1 billion carrier back into the 1980 budget, along with a total of $4.6 billion for 13 other ships, including a Trident sub and 2 attack submarines. The expanded 1980 budget included $13.6 billion for 705 new aircraft, $5.1 billion for missiles, $1.7 billion for tanks and other armor, $13.5 billion for R & D and $107 million for civil defense.

One possible future trend may be toward more multipurpose aircraft and other weapons. The U.S. armed forces currently have 31 different aircraft, 25 different missiles, 13 types of ship, 10 types of combat vehicle and 14 other different major weapons in production, with 30 more under development. Over the eight years, to 1983, the Army alone was expecting to spend about $1.4 billion on developing new aircraft, and $1.6 billion on missile research. The Pentagon is as hard to beat as city hall.

In 1978, *Aviation Week* editorialized:

It is a simple fact of our history that only the legislative branch and the career professionals of the military services have sufficient longevity in their positions to insure that their approval of new weapons and changes in concept or employment of forces will be tempered by the discipline of personal retribution should they fail.

In war, as the battlefield becomes more real, the role of civilians inevitably diminishes, even if they happen to be in the White House. And, as noted earlier, even weapons built for diplomatic conflict must be designed for war. The retiring Joint Chiefs chairman, General George Brown, told the author in 1978: "To be effective as a bargaining chip, it has to be effective as a weapon. You can't really design it, build it and acquire it with bargaining in mind, or it loses some of its value. If the other fellow you are negotiating with feels that you are only putting it up there for that purpose, and you had no intention of deploying it and putting it in your forces, it is of far less value in the trade." There had to be, said Brown, either an elementary commitment—or a very good bluff.

U.S. STRATEGIC WEAPONS

Buried in the maze of the Pentagon is the two-story National Military Command Center. To get past the varnished timber door involves presenting a color-coded Joint Chiefs of Staff identification, which armed guards scrutinize under ultraviolet light. Inside, amid the clutter, there is a red phone for direct calls to the White House, a beige one for reaching any U.S. military commander in the world.

On one wall are a series of big, 6-by-8-feet screens on which computers flash the status of U.S. forces; the strategic order of battle lists the nuclear submarines, the ICBMs, the SAC bombers; other screens tell of the number of ships in each U.S. fleet, the divisions poised for battle in Europe, Korea and elsewhere, and other assets.

The first line in the order of battle is strategic weaponry. "Strategic" means capable of reaching Soviet or American territory, shorter-range nuclear weapons being categorized as "tactical." In reality, the distinction is clouded by the existence of "forward systems"—notably, shorter-range NATO weaponry that can hit the Soviet Union from Europe, U.S. weapons in Alaska or Soviet arms that can hit Alaska from the Kamchatka peninsula. Two NATO countries, Norway and Turkey, actually have borders with Russia. West Germany, of course, has borders with two Warsaw Treaty members. Moscow's one attempt at creating a nuclear forward system in the western hemisphere—Cuba, 1962—was defeated by President Kennedy's weapons diplomacy.

The debate over different strategic weapons systems is essentially related to range, firepower and accuracy, along with vulnerability or invulnerability to defense and attack. Since too great a strategic advance can trigger an enemy's pre-emptive strike, the crucial arguments boil down to two: Which weapons make the best rattling sabers to support our diplomacy, and how can we ensure—short of deliberately sharing each other's technology, and boosting the spending race—that neither side gets so far ahead in strategic first-strike and counterforce capability as to scare its adversary into striking first?

Common to all strategic and tactical weapons is the nuclear warhead. Since World War Two, orders for these have been placed, not by the Pentagon, but by the Department of Energy and its predecessors, which have controlled all aspects of nuclear power production. All nuclear warheads and their triggering devices are designed and evaluated at two government installations—the Lawrence Livermore laboratories at Livermore, California, and the more publicly known facilities at Los Alamos in New Mexico. Livermore currently is producing or devising warheads for such news-making weapons as the ground-launched cruise missile, the M-X mobile intercontinental ballistic missile, the enhanced-radiation or "neutron" bomb, and the big B77 bomb. Los Alamos is perfecting the warhead for the Pershing-II surface-to-surface missile, the Mark 12A warhead for the new version of the Minuteman ICBM, and the business end of the Trident-I submarine-launched ballistic missile (SLBM). It will probably get the contract for the Trident-II as well.

The warheads are actually assembled at the production phase, and sometimes mounted on their launchers as well, at a single site—the aging Pantex ordnance plant 23 miles northeast of Amarillo in the Texas Panhandle. The plutonium comes from several plants, and is brought to Pantex in convoys of tractor-trailers; every thirty minutes along the way, the lead driver calls the Department of Energy office at Albuquerque, certifying that there are no breakdowns or hijackings. From Pantex, the assembled warheads are taken to their military "customers" by armored train. When they are about twenty years old, they are shipped back to Pantex and disassembled.

Between design at Livermore or Los Alamos and manufacture at Pantex, there are years of tests; most of the testing is of the rockets and the guidance machinery. The big nuclear weapons, the ICBMs and the SLBMs, are fired (without nuclear warheads, of course) into what was once a paradisic setting, the Kwajalein lagoon about 2,000 miles southwest of Honolulu—with Soviet monitoring ships riding at anchor nearby, and Soviet satellites passing overhead.

Strategic weapons can only be used for an all-out holocaust. They have no other warfare purpose. There are three types of strategic-weapons systems: submarine-launched, land-based and air-launched, known together as the Triad. The relative newcomer to the strategic scene—cruise missiles—can operate in all three modes, as well as from surface ships. Understanding the capabilities and limitations of all the systems also calls for a comprehension of the various antimissile defense programs, including each side's antibomber forces of fighter, interceptor and fighter-bomber aircraft.

When U.S. nuclear war planning was centralized in 1960, it was still under the dominance of Strategic Air Command. Targeting options were —and still are—set by the Joint Strategic Target Planning Staff (JSTPS) in Omaha, under the Air Force general who commands SAC, with a vice-admiral as his deputy. The JSTPS produces and regularly revises the Single Integrated Operational Plan (SIOP), coordinated with NATO. SIOP's computers pass their time war-gaming their estimate of RISOP, the Soviet equivalent.

In 1960, Polaris was in its infancy and Poseidon had not yet surfaced. The main naval role, then, was to strike from carriers. Since 1968, however, aircraft from carriers may only strike at Soviet targets on a "not to interfere" basis with SAC's bombers and ICBMs and with submarine missile operations.

The National Strategic Target List, compiled by the JSTPS, computerizes literally thousands of high-priority nuclear targets in Russia, Eastern Europe and China, along with several hundred thousand lower-priority ones, stored in the Defense Intelligence Agency's Automated Installation File. The highest of high-priority targets are all Soviet military facilities, notably "time-urgent" nuclear-threat targets—Russian missile launchers—whose annihilation would be Nato's first defense consideration. General George Brown, then chairman of the Joint Chiefs of Staff, said in 1977: "We do not target population *per se* any longer." However, Democratic Senator Thomas McIntyre of New Hampshire noted that the target list does call for destroying 70 per cent of the Soviet industry needed for economic recovery after a war, and Brown agreed that "what we are doing now is targeting a war-recovery capability."

The Carter administration is reassessing U.S. nuclear strategy, moving away from the likelihood that limited nuclear war is possible. Defense Secretary Harold Brown has said that "assured destruction is a good deterrent." It is in this context that the submarine-launched missile has primacy.

Submarine-Launched Ballistic Missiles (SLBMs)

The Russians, as Collins noted, have 62 strategic submarines to America's 41, but here again quality rather than quantity—plus the MIRV capability—gives the United States a decided edge.

The Polaris submarine force dates from 1960. Polaris submarines were big for their time—380 feet long, 32 feet in height and breadth, displacing 7,000 tons. The first type had single-warhead missiles with a range of 1,500 miles. The 10 Polaris submarines still in service today carry the final, 2,800-mile-range version of the Polaris missiles—16 per ship, each with 3 re-entry vehicles. These are not independently targeted, but scatter their warheads like doomsday buckshot upon release.

Polaris subs and their 480 warheads are being phased out. Their heavyweight companions in today's SLBM force are 31 Poseidon submarines—435 feet long, 8,500 tons displacement, each carrying 16 Poseidon missiles, each missile having 10 to 14 MIRVs. This means 496 guided and targeted missiles, with as many as 6,944 thermonuclear (hydrogen) warheads of 50 kilotons (about three times "Hiroshima" each) with a range of 2,800 miles. The missiles are 32 feet long, 6 feet in diameter, and weigh 34 tons apiece. Like the Polaris submarines, the Poseidon vessels have a useful life of about twenty-five years.

The main weapon in the U.S. nuclear arsenal of the near future is the Trident missile, to be carried by the Trident submarine and by some adapted Poseidons. Trident subs of the sort described in the dramatized incident which opened this chapter are scheduled for manufacture at a rhythm of 3 every two years. At least 13 are planned so far, but the Navy is talking about needing 27 of them to cover the world, at a price—in fixed 1975 dollars, missiles and power plant included—of over a billion dollars each. Congress has approved funds for 5 thus far, and advance funding for 3 more.

The Trident-I submarine will carry 24 8-MIRV missiles, with a range of 4,600 miles—or 6,900 miles with a reduced explosive payload. The Trident missile is the same length as the Poseidon missile and is a similar three-stage, solid-fuel-propellant projectile with inertial guidance—a "smart" bomb.

This is a big program: about 465 persons at Cape Canaveral are directly involved with Trident, most of them technicians from Lockheed and Lockheed's subcontractors. There are rigid weather limitations because of the proximity of the Trident pad to residential areas. Under certain wind and temperature conditions, a launch accident detonating the missile's solid propellants on the pad would create what Lockheed calls "damaging overpressures" in the town. About two dozen tests took place at Cape Canaveral in 1977–78, firing into the South Atlantic near Ascension Island. Assembly-line production of the missile began shortly afterward. Commencing in 1978, 10 Poseidon subs were retrofitted with Trident missiles, some of them for test firings. Sometime in 1980, the first Trident sub, with Trident missiles, will join the fleet.

Next, according to schedule, will come the Trident-II missile. This will be about 43 feet long and so will only be adaptable to Trident subs. Expected by the early 1980s, it will have a higher throw-weight than its predecessor, thanks to a range with full payload of 6,000 miles. A Trident-II submarine will carry 24 of these monsters, each of them with 14 MIRVs. This means that one ship will be able to fire as many as 336 warheads with a total clout approximately 1,200 times that of "Hiroshima." They should by then have the Mark 500 MARV "Evader" warhead, a sophistication of MIRV capable of evasive maneuvers after re-entry into the atmosphere—though at some cost in accuracy.

The MIRV system is in the missile's final stage, known to the Navy as the "bus." It has its own guidance capability, its own group of directional jets like a space vehicle. It drops off its "passenger" warheads on signals from its computer. Declassified information gives its accuracy as "within a quarter of a mile," but defense literature now estimates that this has been improved, at least to 200 yards, and perhaps under ideal circumstances to less than 100 feet.

The 5 Trident-I subs already ordered will replace the 7 oldest Polaris vessels. The 3 remaining Polarises should remain seaworthy until 1986. The last Poseidons should not be phased out until 1989–92.

Nuclear submarines can cruise indefinitely, until they run out of food for the crew. (On an average Poseidon, according to one interesting Navy statistic, the 150 crew, divided into 3 teams of 50, consume 600 bags of popcorn a week.) The nuclear power plants are virtually inexhaustible, and as well as driving the ship they generate oxygen from seawater by electrolysis. The carbon dioxide of the crew's breath is disposed of by a "scrubber." Carbon oxide, such as tobacco smoke, is "burned" to produce CO_2, then "scrubbed." Computers ensure that the missiles are kept at a constant temperature. Patrols last 70 days, preceded by 30 days of shore preparation, and followed by 100 days of leave and training while another crew take over for a 100-day schedule. The two crews are called Gold and Blue. During shore preparation, 2 missiles are rotated each time. The introduction of the Trident submarine will expand the operating area of American strategic subs from about 2.5 million square miles to about 40 million square miles, which means lengthening patrols.

Today's Poseidons are based, when not in U.S. ports for maintenance, at Holy Loch in Scotland, at the Rota base near Cádiz, Spain, at Guam and at two stateside ports—Charleston, South Carolina, and Bangor, Washington. A new Trident facility at King's Island, Georgia, is under construction.

Life aboard is testing: The crew work a ceaseless schedule of six hours on, twelve hours off, sleeping in three-tier bunks. There is no TV, mail or newspapers—although occasionally four wire antennas are allowed to float to near the surface, attached to a squat, torpedo-shaped "kite," so that the crew can pick up a batch of twenty-word messages from families, transmitted from Cutler, Maine, or North West Cape, Australia, by VLF (Very Low Frequency, capable of penetrating water), backed up by Lockheed C-130 "Tacamo" communications aircraft. The sub never responds, never identifies itself. It rarely uses its IFF (Identification Friend or Foe), since even this would give away its presence.

The crew of a strategic sub have a sense that they are different. Within their cramped living space, there are considerable areas off limits to those with no "need to know." There are the fail-safe security procedures: There are two people for every combination code and every key, but there are no "even pairs": If Officer A and Officer B share keys to Safe 1, then A will share with C for Safe 2, and B will share with C, or someone else, for another key or code. Codes are committed to memory, but replacements for an incapacitated officer will learn their codes by opening a sealed envelope, access to which is again guarded by two keys. If the captain goes berserk, or dies, two officers must agree that he should be replaced, using two combinations to open the captain's safe and procuring—you've guessed it—more sealed envelopes, more keys. When Gold crew relieve Blue, the keys are handed over to opposite numbers with a fitting touch of solemnity.

Life in a nuclear submarine is strangely quiet and restrained for a Navy ship, with little to disturb the peace of the night watches but the creaking of bulkheads as the vessel rises or descends and the outer pressure from the ocean consequently changes. Off duty, crewmen watch movies, play penny-ante poker or study correspondence courses. There are no real "days," no breakfast-lunch-dinner routine, only the eighteen-hour schedule, punctuated by meals. The midnight rations—"midrash"—would be breakfast for the oncoming team, "lunch" for those whom they replace, "dinner" for those coming on at 6 A.M., if they are awake; but no one thinks in those terms. Generous meals and the lack of any real exercise have led to diet programs aboard some Poseidons.

Nuclear submarines are marvels of navigation as well as firepower. Although the present ones occasionally rise close to the surface to take fixes from satellites, or use charted features of the ocean floor to pinpoint position, they mostly, like today's long-haul airliners, use inertial guidance. (The system is called Synergistic Inertial Navigation—SIN.) Inertial navigation was originally designed for missiles, then adapted to planes and submarines. In inertial guidance, gyroscopes basically similar to those that operate the automatic direction finders of most aircraft hold small weights called accelerometers in position. The accelerometers react to movement forward, backward, up, down and sideways, signaling these movements to computers which translate the movement into speed and distance, thereby determining position. Inertial guidance is not only necessary to prevent the sub from getting lost: It is vital to the vessel's ultimate attack mission; for as the vessel's position constantly changes, its computers revise the trajectories of the missiles so that they are continually aimed at their pre-selected targets.

At any one time, the U. S. Navy has about twenty strategic subs at sea, in the Atlantic, the Pacific, the Mediterranean and the Indian Ocean; the Russians field about six or seven, mostly within the Arctic Circle.

In late 1977, the Trident submarine program was a year behind schedule at the Electric Boat Company in Groton, Connecticut, and overruns on the initial vessels were about $400 million—meaning a cost of about $1.2 billion each (without engine or missiles) instead of the original $800 million estimated. This meant the Tridents were currently eating up about three eighths of the entire Navy shipbuilding budget. Rear Admiral Donald P. Hall, co-director of the Trident program, re-estimated the full program at $22 billion for thirteen Tridents, including the cost of further research, test missiles and shore facilities. But the Navy claimed late in 1978 that after initial production problems had been ironed out, the unit cost of the submarine could fall as low as $500 million. As well as cost, there is also a problem about floating the thing: As the first Trident, the *Ohio,* goes down the Thames channel from Groton for sea trials in 1980, it will be only 18 inches from the bottom at high water. (The *Ohio* was launched in April 1979.)

At the Pentagon, some questioned Admiral Rickover's insistence on a 25-knot underwater speed, since this involved a huge nuclear power plant and a longer hull: Since a bigger sub means a bigger profile, and Soviet destroyers and killer subs can do 30 knots, was the expense justified? Admiral Elmo R. Zumwalt, former chief of naval operations, told a reporter pithily: "Designing a ship from the power plant out never has struck me as an ideal procedure." Strategy Experimental—Strat-X— the top-secret Pentagon report which gave birth to Trident, originally called for a smaller, slower vessel with more powerful missiles.

The Trident and the Poseidon, like the British Polarises and France's and Russia's own sixteen-missile strategic submarines, are only as good as their chance of surviving an enemy pre-emptive attack; but in the case of American submarines, these chances today are very good indeed. They are certainly better than those of Russia's nuclear subs. The U. S. Navy's Sound Surveillance Under Sea (SOSUS) system, using microphones anchored to the ocean floor, or towers on the continental shelf or on buoys, can scan the depths for as much as 1,000 miles around, but the Soviet Union is known to be far behind in this technology. Even if detected by chance, through a fortuitous encounter, a Poseidon can fire an "acoustic decoy" which sounds like the sub itself: Then it shuts down some of its systems and waits for the enemy to pursue the decoy, before slipping away in the opposite direction.

However, the American SOSUS system is not "adequate" unless it can pinpoint *all* enemy ballistic-missile submarines and thus enable their elimination. One surviving enemy sub might annihilate America. In this respect, SOSUS, good as it is, is still far from adequate. As sea temperatures change, sound waves passing through the sea are refracted. Scanning all the oceans—most of the world's surface—is impossible, even for futurological scientists. The pattern of sea temperatures changes from year to year, while weather causes changes from day to day, even hour to hour.

One major program to improve underwater communications—the 'Seafarer project—has run into local opposition. Residents of Michigan's Upper Peninsula have objected to the Navy's plan to bury the Seafarer's ELF (Extremely Low Frequency) antennas a few feet below the surface there, because of risks—albeit minimal—of non-iodizing radiation.

But President Carter said in 1977 that Seafarer was essential to U.S. security, and Congress voted $25 million for continuing development studies at a test site at Clam Lake, Wisconsin. At present, transmission goes from arrays of 1,300-foot-high antennas, easily destructible in war, backed up by fourteen TACAMO planes trailing five-and-a-half-mile-long antennas; one of these planes is always airborne over the Atlantic, and another over the Pacific. (In war, only the TACAMOs might remain serviceable. TACAMO stands for "Take Charge and Move Out.") The subs can only receive at a preset time every day, when they slow to five knots and raise their antennas near the surface; for the rest of the day, they are out of touch.

Seafarer will transmit over as much as 4,000 miles to a submarine's trailing antenna-receiver, from a grid of antennas totaling about 2,400 miles in length, each spaced between 1 and 4 miles apart. God and Congress willing, Seafarer should be operational in 1984, providing the Michigan site is finally approved. (Carter scaled down the program in 1979.) Although the radiation danger appears to be as imaginary as that once predicted from the supersonic Concorde, one real danger is apparent for local residents if Seafarer is buried in the Michigan granite—it would make the area a top-priority Soviet target in time of war.

Land-Based Intercontinental Ballistic Missiles

The ICBM program began in 1958. The first American missiles of this type were Atlas and Titan—big, relatively inaccurate, liquid-fueled projectiles with massive warheads, comparable to many contemporary Soviet ICBMs. The Atlas program has been deactivated, and only 54 Titans remain in the U.S. inventory.

Built by Martin Marietta with a General Electric re-entry vehicle, and first produced in 1963, the Titan is thus the biggest land-based warhead in the American arsenal. There are 3 wings of 18 Titan-IIs apiece, based in Arizona, Arkansas and Kansas. Nearly 100 feet long, 10 feet wide, with a 15,000 mph speed and a ceiling of 800 miles, Titans carry over 5 megatons of explosive power for 15,000 miles by inertial guidance.

Boeing produced the first 17-ton Minuteman-I, a more accurate weapon, in 1961. It became operational the following year. The Minuteman-II is a longer missile, with a greater range and payload and a flexible targeting capability: It could fling the equivalent of 2 megatons of TNT toward a target at the same speed as Titan: 450 Minuteman-IIs remain in service.

Minuteman-III—officially called the LGM-30G—introduced a 3-MIRV capability. It was introduced in 1970 and deployed by 1975. By 1977, 550 were in service; 60 more had been approved by the 94th Congress but Carter later tried to reduce the figure to 10, already under construction, for use as "spare parts" only, as a SALT II gesture. The upgrading of Minuteman-II was also "canceled" at the same time.

The Carter cutback on the $317 million program would not have saved much money: In October 1977, the Office of Management and Budget released $105 million for the limited program, and was set to pay $185.5 million in fiscal-1978 funds for closedown costs, much of the construction work on the additional 50 missiles being already in progress. A full restart, if ever ordered, would have been massively expensive: Lieutenant General Alton D. Slay, then deputy chief of the Air Force staff, told a House Appropriations Committee hearing that a restart "could cost as much as $300,000,000"—or half as much if the program was put back on the rails before the end of 1977. In the end, that was what happened: Congress refused to rescind the remaining original funds; in November 1977, Secretary Brown authorized reinstatement of production of "whole missiles." Reactivated deliveries started in mid-1978, at 5 missiles a month.

Both the II and III are solid-propellant, three-stage missiles. The III is 60 feet long, with an 8,000-mile range but less firepower than the II; nevertheless, its 3 thermonuclear warheads each packs the equivalent of between 170 and 200 kilotons of TNT, or about twelve to fourteen times "Hiroshima" apiece, and the new planned Mark 12A warhead for the III will give greater accuracy and more explosive power.

The 2,154 warheads in the ICBM force (versus 1,054 a decade ago) are now in hardened silos. Although many of them would be expected to fall prey to the 64 antiballistic missile sites around Moscow, use of this force would undoubtedly devastate most other Soviet targets.

Computers and associated command and control facilities, including those involving satellites, allow rapid retargeting of missiles prior to launch, and increase their effectiveness in complex attack patterns. Each missile has between 100 and 200 attack plans in its own computer memory. In contrast, the Soviet Union has only just begun to deploy missiles with on-board computers and mid-course flight control.

The annual operating cost of the American ICBM force is less than $300 million for 1978, or not much more than a third of the cost of the strategic submarine force. It is less than a quarter of the cost of the B-52 and FB-111 SAC fleet and its associated tankers: The air tanker fleet alone costs nearly half a billion dollars.

To discourage a successful Soviet attack on their silos, the missiles are deployed over vast areas of the United States. As they are Air Force-controlled, they are grouped in "wings," like manned aircraft. Wing I, for instance, is spread over 18,000 square miles of Montana. Each individual, hardened launch site enjoys 2 or 3 acres. A silo is a hole about 75 feet deep, 12 feet wide, bulging out below the surface to accommodate equipment rooms. Little is visible at the surface but a lamppost, and radar devices to deter intruders: These are so sensitive that even field mice and tumbleweeds set them off. The separate flight launch-control center is about 45 feet down and, on alert, would be manned by two Strategic Air Command officers, usually young lieutenants. Each pair controls 10 sites. Except for exercises, the centers are not manned, but the missile guidance equipment power is left continually on. An exception is North Dakota, where fifteen crews maintain permanent vigilance over 150 silos. This is because the state is the geographic center of the continent, the best-suited area to pick up warning of an attack from any direction. In an emergency, all the launch-control centers could be controlled from "kneecaps"—airborne 747s.

If an order to fire came through, the two officers in a forty-one-by-twenty-six-foot launch center would decode it. Then they would open a small red metal box, using two locks, the code for each being committed to each officer's respective memory. Inside the box are two keys and "authentification documents" that enable the two men to check, again, the genuineness of the coded message.

They feed the "enabling code" transmitted in the firing order into a computer, thus arming the missile. Buttons light up—"Strategic Alert," then "Warhead armed." When an alarm bell rings, indicating that the systems are ready, the men insert the keys of the launcher. The keyholes are 12 feet apart, so that no single officer can operate both. They are marked Off, Set and Launch. The officers turn the keys to Launch simultaneously—within two seconds of each other—and hold them "on" for five seconds against spring pressure. Then a Missile Away light comes on, on the console panel. World War Three has begun.

There are doubts as to Minuteman's vaunted accuracy. Veteran reporter Arthur Hadley noted in the Washington *Star* in 1979 that a cooling fan in the drive system has created its own magnetic field: In firings into Kwajalein lagoon—east to west—this has been compensated for. (The four hundredth Minuteman test launch, from Vandenburg Air Force Base to Kwajalein, took place in July 1979.) But in war, when Minutemen would be fired from west to northeast, would the cooling fan botch the missile's navigation to target?

A more obvious problem is vulnerability. To limit this, each launch site is at least 3 miles from the next, and launch-control centers are at least 5 miles from any launch site. The latest silos are hardened to withstand any enemy missile attack falling farther away than 30 feet. They also, of course, have considerable "offensive" defenses and these are constantly being improved: In 1977, Army Ballistic Missile Defense Command ordered a $100,000 research study to determine if rotary-barrel guns firing depleted-uranium penetrator-rod ammunition—either the 30mm. General Electric GAU-8/A used in the A-10 aircraft, or GE's 20mm. M-61—could be used to destroy incoming ICBM warheads. The following year, Secretary Brown formed "Jason"—a secret panel of forty American scientists—to advise on ICBM protection and other matters. One Jason member proposed that each ICBM site be surrounded by 150 fences, each 2,500 feet long, made of steel reinforcing rods on which incoming nuclear warheads would be impaled, thus preventing fusing. The rods would be 7 feet long, of which 2 feet would be belowground. The plan called for 10 million feet of quarter-inch steel for each fence, or 1.5 billion feet for each site. Another brainstorm was a pebble fan projector which would hurl a barrage of stones or steel balls 1,000 feet into the air to intercept a re-entry vehicle. Alternatively, he proposed using small, half-pound steel darts with rocket engines that would give them a speed of 3,000 feet per second. Each site would require 40,000 darts.

In short, Minuteman is not invulnerable; nor is it as powerful as the Soviet "medium" ICBMs now in development: since 1974, research has been going on in the United States into what is known as M-X (missile experimental). Now well advanced in the research stage, and timed for introduction into service in the mid-eighties, M-X would be a more powerful missile than Minuteman, with 10-MIRV, 200-kiloton capacity, housed in *mobile* silos. The missile would either move at random among a number of covered launch sites or travel by train along 20-mile-long underground trenches, estimated to cost $5 million a mile. A force of 250

M-X missiles might require up to 5,000 miles of trenches. Says the Center
for Defense Information:

> In view of increased public sensitivity and the great difficulty the Penta-
> gon has had in finding suitable land for the [Seafarer] submarine com-
> munications antenna field, it is likely there will be equally great difficulties
> in obtaining territory for the M-X program.

To be put out of action, the M-X system would have to be attacked at
all its possible launching sites. The M-X could also—although this is currently judged unlikely—be put aboard C-5s, militarized 747 jumbo jets or
even helicopters, with its guidance system (Advanced Inertial Reference
System—AIRS) constantly correcting itself by fixes on the NavStar
Global Positioning System satellites. These planes would have to maintain a perpetual airborne alert; by reason of their speed, compared to the
"subway train" of the silo-based variety, they would make for a less accurate missile. Airborne, the M-X would be pulled out of its canister by
parachute and fired by remote control when it was dangling, vertically,
and had ceased to sway from side to side. Former Defense Secretary
Melvin Laird has even suggested putting ICBMs aboard barges at sea.
Defense Under Secretary William J. Perry told a closed-session committee meeting in 1979 that serious consideration was also being given to
basing some M-Xs on barges in the Great Lakes, while some reports
talked of launching them from small coastal submarines.

The M-Xs will be mostly (perhaps all) housed in silos hardened to
withstand pressure of 3,000 pounds per square inch. In all, thirteen silo
concepts have been considered: off-road railroad flatbeds, an inland wa-
terway system, a canal system, a pool system, a combination of both, an
off-road nonrail system, a hard capsule, shelter-basing, a revetted rail system, a covered trench, a buried trench, a soil tunnel and a hard-rock tunnel.

The most likely to be adopted is either a "race track," with spurs to
shelters, or a buried-trench rail system, running between semi-hardened
shelters (able to withstand between 100 and 150 pounds per square inch
of blast overpressure—that is, pressure above average atmospheric pressure of 14.7 pounds per square inch). The shelters would be arranged
around a central station in such a way that no two shelters (or no one
shelter and the central station) could be taken out by a single enemy
warhead; the missile could be moved from the central station to any ran-
domly selected shelter—there would probably be ten or twenty, each
about 6 miles apart and about 10 miles away from the central station—
between the time when warning of an attack is received and the time of
impact of the hostile warhead.

The satellite early-warning system over the eastern hemisphere gives between twenty-five and thirty minutes' warning of a Soviet (or Chinese) ICBM launch, using the Cobra Dane phased-array radar at Shemya Air Force Base on the western tip of the Aleutian Islands, or a "backscatter," over-the-horizon radar now under construction. According to a source in the Joint Chiefs of Staff organization, the Cobra Dane facility can "spot an object as small as a basketball 2,000 miles away." By the time this book appears, the Pave Paws phased-array early-warning radars will also have been completed at Otis Air Force Base in Massachusetts and Beale Air Force Base in California. The earlier, less dependable ballistic-missile early-warning systems such as DEW—the distant early-warning bases at Thule and Sondre Strom Fjord in Greenland—provided only about fifteen minutes' warning. Thus, the transporter/launcher system must move at fairly high speed—probably at least 30 miles an hour (some experts envisage twice that)—with a minimum of jolting.

The M-X, which will be "cold-launched" by low-pressure gas from a canister on the transporter/launcher, then ignited when it is on its way—thus not destroying its launcher like other ICBMs—will weigh about 175,000 pounds, or more than twice as much as Minuteman-III. If the transporter/launcher (which is about 111 feet long), the erector, the canister and the missile are counted together, the system weighs more than 600,000 pounds.

The warheads from the M-X should fall within 300 feet or less of target. Since M-X launchers can be reloaded—and SALT II only limits launchers—there is at present no limit to the number of M-X missiles which the United States could build. (The Soviet Union's equivalent, the SS-20, is similarly unrestricted by SALT.) Secretary Brown has spoken of M-X deployment by 1985.

The M-X has been attacked as a counterforce weapon—one devised for destroying the enemy's defenses—and therefore as "destabilizing"; partly for this reason, President Carter, shortly after taking power in 1977, cut the R & D budget for the M-X in fiscal 1978 from $294 million to $150 million. But the project remained very much alive, and the following year it was given the full-speed-ahead. Deployment centers under consideration are all on federally owned land: China Lake, Fort Irwin, Twentynine Palms, Chocolate Mountain and Blythe, all in California; the Nellis and Fallon ranges, and Ely, all in Nevada; Yuma and Gila Bend in Arizona; White Sands and Fort Bliss in New Mexico; the Hill-Wendover Dugway and the Delta group of military sites in Utah; an area in southern Wyoming; and Saylor Creek in Idaho.

The Air Force originally planned to introduce the M-X into wing service by December 1983; the temporary Carter cutback forced a year's delay, and the program became a controversial item in the SALT II talks. Some reports say it will not be ready, in any case, until 1987. Building 250 M-Xs and putting them into trenches would cost an estimated $30–34 billion, possibly more, so the project has also come under attack because of expense.

Critics have pointed out that the Soviet Union already has a more serious vulnerability problem than the United States. Since most of its nuclear warheads are carried by ICBMs, it has naturally turned, they say, to greater ICBM survivability through a mobile system. U.S. missiles remain more "survivable," and "many years ahead in accuracy," in the words of the CDI. Some see the M-X as intended to persuade Moscow to move away from land-based missiles and toward relatively less powerful missiles in strategic submarines, but this would involve a massive and lengthy restructuring of strategic policy by a notoriously conservative regime.

In his February 8, 1977, press conference, shortly after taking office, President Carter proposed a mutual ban on mobile-launched ICBMs. The SALT agreements depend for enforcement on monitoring the ceilings in missile numbers, and monitoring is currently deemed to be possible only when missiles are deployed in fixed underground silos or in large submarines, the construction of which cannot be kept secret. The Russians have since begun to deploy the SS-20, which moves on a caterpillar tractor. Carter's offer amounted to saying that if the Soviet Union would not deploy the SS-X-16, the United States would not even develop the M-X. But SALT II, finally, did not affect the heavy Soviet ICBM program, and the M-X buried-trench concept may be vulnerable to Moscow's larger warheads. A 25-megaton warhead would give a seismic reading of seven on the Richter scale. Says one Pentagon expert: "This would jolt the internal blast doors inside the trenches off their hinges and render the concept invalid."

Survival, the organ of the International Institute of Strategic Studies, said in 1977: "Two arms-control issues are relevant here. The first is whether deployment of a land-mobile system would stimulate a further arms race. The second . . . concerns the question of verification." The journal suggested leaving the shelters open to satellite reconnaissance, except in conditions of rain or snow.

Survival perceived other headaches:

> There are severe operational problems involved in blanketing a shelter complex with MIRV—specifically, enemy warheads detonated closely in time and space to destroy the shelters simultaneously might destroy each other by "fratricide." It is virtually impossible to program all warheads to

arrive and explode at precisely the same instant. If detonation is not simultaneous, the first warheads to explode will create nuclear radiation, fireballs, shock waves, nuclear winds and clouds of dust, debris and ice crystals that will either destroy other warheads arriving over nearby targets ("fratricide") or grossly reduce their accuracy. Planners must therefore limit themselves to only one or two reentry vehicles per target. Since a second wave of attacking warheads must be withheld until the adverse conditions dissipate, surviving missiles could be launched against the attacker in the interim.

A 1977 Brookings report said M-X would be "the single most important weapons-system decision faced by the Carter administration." Senator McIntyre, chairman of the Senate Armed Services Committee's research subcommittee, said Brown's decision on full-scale M-X development "commits us to the madness of limited nuclear war."

The New Hampshire senator said the proposed M-X force could "wipe out the entire Soviet ICBM force and their command and control centers in thirty minutes. In a period of crisis, the Russians would be faced with the choice of either using their missiles or losing them. This would put a hair trigger on nuclear war. It would give the Russians a military reason to strike first." But the Air Force went ahead with requests to defense contractors to submit M-X designs within forty-five days. In its October 31 issue, *Aviation Week* reported a test firing of an M-X missile first stage by the Thiokol Corporation at its facility near Brigham City, Utah. In November, however, both houses of Congress killed an administration request for an additional $30 million in fiscal 1978 funding for the M-X and Advanced Ballistic Reentry Systems (ABRES) programs, indicating that the survival of the M-X program was still not guaranteed. M-X funding in the fiscal-1979 budget passed Congress, but a 1978 report by the GAO (General Accounting Office) urged delaying M-X development.

Pro-M-X experts argued not only that the weapon was necessary, but needed in large numbers. Fewer than 100 of them, it was claimed, could probably be eliminated by a Soviet first strike; about 300 was said to be the needed final figure. Basic to the argument was the claim by hardliners that the very U.S. approach to SALT II was wrong. Instead of limiting missile launchers, these critics said, the United States should go for limiting weapon capabilities. One Hill expert said improved Soviet accuracy and greater throw-weight were more threatening than improved launchers.

"What's a launcher?" he said. "The United States has defined it as a hole in the ground. It has nothing to do with the missile inside it."

A former director of the Pentagon's Directorate of Defense Research and Engineering, John S. Foster, agreed. He told a House Armed Services Committee hearing: "It seems more appropriate to limit throwweight," which Soviet development is emphasizing—apparently as a firststrike counterforce.

"In risking war," Foster, now a defense contractor, said, "[the Soviet Union] would be risking the lives of millions of Russians, but they would not, in their view, be risking the Soviet Union. [But] we would be risking the United States."

Others believed that by attacking a full American M-X system, the Russians would, as an *Aviation Week* article put it, "exhaust more of their ICBM warhead inventory than they could destroy in the United States."

The M-X program in 1978 included two tests in Arizona, simulating a situation in which Soviet warheads would strike along the length of a trench and detonate almost simultaneously, along with other tests at Luke Air Force Base in Arizona to determine blast and shock effects on two buried trenches and adjacent shelters. The tunnels, 14 feet wide at the widest point, had airblast-attenuating ribs, 5 feet apart. A 64-inchwide floor provided a surface for the huge Boeing/Martin Marietta transporter-launcher vehicles, which are 172 feet long and nearly 11 feet wide.

Meanwhile, the Pentagon was considering mobile basing for the Minuteman-III if this was reconcilable with SALT II MIRV-launcher limits. (This proved to be the case.) The mobile Minuteman-III would use a nonhardened vertical canister, not the buried-trench concept. The vertical shelter would be less expensive to construct, USAF experts said—approximately $18 billion for 4,500 shelters, of which 95 per cent would be empty at any one time. Another plan calls for placing ICBMs in trucks aboard giant C-5s of Strategic Air Command, which would land them at smaller fields, where they would be erected and fired in about an hour. The ultimate land-based missile may be a land-launched Trident; this would mean a slightly lighter payload, but reportedly involving the sacrifice of only one re-entry vehicle. Meanwhile, Defense Under Secretary Perry said that a new antiballistic missile system might also be mobile-based. The 15-feet-long ABM would be targeted only at the enemy warhead aimed at an M-X-occupied silo, and would intercept it in the stratosphere.

But well before the projected wings of M-X or other mobile missiles are ready, if they ever are, a new warhead will have joined the U.S. inventory—the General Electric Mark 12A. This will be a 370-kiloton thermonuclear monster with a perfected terminal homing system—twice as powerful and twice as accurate as the present three-MIRV-ed warheads of the Minuteman-III. Because of the improved accuracy, the 12A is reckoned to be perhaps as much as eight times more deadly than its predecessor. The Mark 12A was rushed through R & D in time to be ready for initial production by March 1976—the cutoff date for new systems set by the Threshold Test Ban Treaty. Flight testing of the prototypes was completed in 1977, with production beginning shortly thereafter, thanks to a go-ahead from President Carter.

Dr. Jeremy Stone, director of the Federation of American Scientists, noted in 1977 that "the Soviets are spending $30 billion, it's estimated, to modernize one missile, the SS-11, and about $15 billion to modernize the SS-9." Before this work was finished, Stone said, both weapons would be "neutralized" by the Mark 12A, for which Stone predicted a minimum of 200 yards accuracy. Stone said the Mark 12A represented a "five-year lead" on Moscow, and warned that it was therefore, like the M-X, a weapon which risked triggering Soviet pre-emption. In 1979, however, a GAO report said the Russians were developing a jammer that would fool the Mark 12A's distance-measuring radar—the device which starts the firing process in the warhead. Meanwhile, work goes on to perfect a revised antiballistic missile system—mobile or not—to be in place, if needed, in the mid-eighties.

Soviet ICBMs are controlled by the Red Army, and the U. S. Army has occasionally tried to wrest the American land-based strategic missile system from the Air Force. Should this ever happen, interservice rivalry would make it less likely that any of the American "triad" of delivery systems would be abandoned. Since ICBMs and air-launched missiles are today both in the Air Force domain, the arguments of some strategists for scrapping one or the other system have some chance of eventual acceptance. Phasing out both in favor of the Navy's Trident program would be resisted by the Air Force.

Strategic Air Command

The third leg of the strategic triad is the nuclear bomber. At present, this means the subsonic B-52 deep-penetration aircraft, armed with bombs and air-to-surface missiles. The future of SAC, at present, appears based on a refurbished B-52 capable of launching cruise missiles—of which more shortly—from a "stand-off position outside enemy airspace. The second string of SAC is the FB-111 variable-geometry ("swing-wing") fighter-bomber.

Scheduled to replace the B-52 was (and perhaps still is) the B-1, a swing-wing Mach-2 bomber which President Carter decided on June 30, 1977, to leave in the "development" stage—despite a House of Representatives vote, two days before, to provide $1.8 billion, partly for further R & D, partly to fund production of the first five wing-service aircraft. The Carter decision surprised Congress and press, and especially the Air Force, which had gathered together thousands of copies of B-1 brochures for distribution on that day.

One SAC squadron of B-52s with "nukes" in place is scrambled—on alert, on SAC runways—at all times. Before 1968, they were scrambled in the air, but this practice was dropped following noted accidents in Greenland and Spain. The squadrons' purpose is attack, but it is directly related to defense. Watch for a possible Soviet attack is maintained constantly by U.S. and Canadian teams at North American Air Defense Command, inside the pink granite of Cheyenne Mountain near Colorado Springs.

Wherever he goes, the President of the United States is escorted by an aide—usually a naval officer—with a black case; this contains the code of the day, or the hour, corresponding to one in a black box aboard the lead plane in the squadron and to the one at SAC headquarters in Omaha. Formerly, the SAC bombers, which can fly 10,000 miles without refueling, headed daily for enemy targets, with orders to turn back unless they received a checked and rechecked war alert. The crews average a seventy-four-hour workweek, including practice, and sleep close to their aircraft. To fire the missiles, as aboard a Poseidon, a Polaris or—tomorrow—a Trident, requires opening a box with two keys, in this case used simultaneously by two officers.

If the President was running a war from a ground headquarters, an airborne battle-staff plane would relay his orders. Such a plane would be a reduced version of the President's "kneecap": a crew of four, plus three radio operators, two maintenance men, a steward and a battle staff of eleven. From a cabin 15 feet by 5, the head of the airborne battle staff can command all bases, submarines and air forces. He can signal the launch of every missile in the inventory. He is intended to be, of course, in direct contact with the President, the chiefs of staff and the National War Command, at all times.

On the port side of the battle-staff bomber sits a red box containing the President's secret orders of the day, which arrive regularly by courier under armed escort. Only two men can open that box, too—the chief of the airborne battle staff, who sits by the box during the flight, and the general officer. They must use their keys simultaneously—so that one cannot wrest the other's key and open the box alone. If alerted, the two men would open the box, break the seal within, decode the President's instructions and check to see that the order corresponded with the orders hidden in the box.

Alistair Cooke, in his book and TV series *America,* showed viewers and readers the inside of a control room at Bellevue, near Omaha, from which such doomsday messages could be sent. Cooke said that all the men who work in the control rooms were psychiatrically tested—"If one of [a pair] breaks down and seems likely to go berserk, it is the duty of the other to shoot him," Cooke explained in his avuncular manner.

The war room in Omaha, covering missiles around the world, is of course under the ultimate supervision of the President. There are forty-six world bases, under parallel control of SAC's underground headquarters. Cooke noted that relay teams control "more than a thousand missiles, any one of which packs the destructive force of all the bombs dropped in the Second World War." If SAC headquarters is atomized, control of the missiles passes to alternative commands, notably a SAC battle-staff lead plane, in the air, as described earlier.

The gas- and radiation-proof underground command post at Bellevue controls both land-based and air-launched missiles. A visitor is led down steel corridors by blue-bereted guards, past doors marked "No Lone Zone." The war room is huge, overlooked by the command balcony where CINCSAC—commander in chief of SAC—would receive the President's orders on the gold phone on his desk and pass them on from the red one that lies alongside. Below him work the battle staff, watching radar displays and operating computer terminals. Dominating everything are six wall panels, each as tall as an average house, which give the current state of play between East and West. The battle staff and other missilemen practice continually, retargeting missiles, fighting simulated warfare.

The late General George Brown, when he was chairman of the Joint Chiefs, reminded the author in 1978 that CINCSAC can always put his bombers in the air, on his own initiative, in a "fail-safe" mode—"They can't go anywhere unless specifically ordered. In other words, they can't go to a target." Ground-based as they are now, the SAC force is not secure "unless we get a warning," the general noted.

SAC's curious role, now that bombers are no longer America's first line of defense, leaves something of a question mark over the future of offensive strategic aviation. Asked at a 1977 Senate hearing what targets could not be attacked by a B-52 "weaponized . . . with as rich and versatile a mix of these advanced bomber weapons as possible," Lieutenant General

Alton D. Slay, then Air Force deputy chief of staff for R & D, said, "You could not attack any defended targets, sir."

America's original force of 600 B-52s—the most recent of which was built in 1962—was down to 349 in 1977. Of these, 165 were B-52Gs and 109 were B-52Hs, of which 19 were inoperable. These are the two models with SRAM (Short-Range Attack Missile) racks that can take either SRAMs or cruise missiles. The 75 remaining B-52Ds cannot be adapted in this way, but all three models of B-52 are undergoing other updatings to improve their penetration capacities. The 66 FB-111s also could carry doomsday weaponry into parts of the Soviet heartland.

The reason for preserving a bomber which would take seven hours to reach its bombing area—the B-1 would take about five hours, flying subsonically most of the way—in an era of ballistic missiles that arrive in minutes lies precisely in the bomber's relative slowness. The strategic bomber, until it goes over to radio silence, can be recalled—allowing time for a few hours of precious hot-line diplomacy. The submarine-launched and land-based missiles, once on their way, could only be stopped in their entirety by an array of highly accurate antiballistic weaponry which neither superpower completely possesses at present.

There are other arguments for preserving the strategic bomber: Bombers can be dispersed, making a hopelessly scattershot target for the enemy. As an attack system, they increase the number of aerial targets at which the enemy must direct his fire. The B-52, operating at about 500 feet in enemy airspace (200 feet on final approach to target, but at only 400 mph), would hit the radar scans—unless detected from above—only when it is 25 or 30 miles away; this means only four or five minutes' warning for the "hostiles." Russia's equivalent of the Air Force's AWACS (Airborne Warning and Control System), a modification of the Ilyushin-76 known to NATO as the Candid, might not see the B-52s amid the ground clutter, except over a desert or a calm sea—at all costs, not over Russia or Eastern Europe. The same positive arguments apply to the B-1, even more convincingly.

Critics of the SAC program say that it cannot strike Soviet ICBMs, which would all be gone long before the bombers arrived. Past its fail-safe point, it is for its final two hours of flight out of contact; by then, as in a movie of a few years back, its mission could only be aborted if Washington cooperated with Moscow in having its own planes shot down. Proponents of the B-1 say it is the answer to the Soviet swing-wing Backfire bomber, but critics say this reasoning is specious, since neither would meet the other in combat. The opponent of each is its enemy's defenses.

Critics also say that Russia has as yet only a few squadrons of Back-

fires, plus 35 Bison strategic bombers and about 100 prop-driven stra-
tegic-range Bears. If the Soviet Union is dropping the manned bomber,
should we not do the same? But against this—even if the new buildup of
Backfires is seen only as defense against China—is the argument that the
two superpowers have different strategic plans, with the U.S.S.R. depending mainly on land-based ICBMs with relatively low accuracy but
huge throw-weights.

Of the two alternative American strategic bombers, the B-52 and the
B-1, the B-1 is unquestionably superior. As a penetration bomber, its
greatly increased speed in the stratosphere, its ability to fly safely at
near-sonic speed at 200 feet—over flat terrain, at 80 feet—and its greatly
reduced radar signature make it considerably less vulnerable to enemy
defenses. (The B-52 would be particularly vulnerable to the Soviet SA-10
missile.) The B-1 could launch cruise missiles or supersonic SRAMs at
distant targets from points inside Soviet airspace that could not be
reached by the vulnerable B-52. Both as a penetration bomber and as a
standoff bomber, it has the advantage of carrying a greater payload of
missiles. It carries 24 SRAMs, air-launched cruise missiles or Advanced
Strategic Air-Launched Missiles (ASALMs) to the B-52's 20, and has a
crew of 4—2 pilots, 2 weapons-systems officers—against 6 for the B-52.
With its 4 engines (against 8 for the B-52) it is more efficient and much
less costly to maintain. It has the merit of being designed for cruise-missile launching, has the latest refinements to deceive enemy defenses and
is hardened against nuclear detonation.

The B-1 is the successor to earlier *high*-altitude bomber programs—the
B-58 and the B-70. (Had the B-70 been built, the United States would almost certainly have developed a civilian supersonic transport.) But the
shooting down of Gary Powers' U-2 over the Soviet Union not only
brought the unmanned spy satellite into prominence: It also switched
U. S. Air Force strategic planning to low-altitude bombing.

The controversial aircraft looks a bit like the Concorde, its civilian
supersonic cousin. The first four sleek, white B-1s have been built; the
fifth development model should be finished in 1979, by which time the
first two will have been retired. Described by friend and critic alike as
the most sophisticated piece of military aviation engineering ever built,
the B-1, if produced in numbers, would cost only twice as much as a
defenseless, unhardened, unarmed Concorde—demonstrating the merits
of mass production. But according to Robert Berman of Brookings, an
entire B-1 program would cost, with operation and maintenance, refueling tankers, auxiliary equipment and armament, during a lifetime of
about thirty years, approximately $91.5 billion in constant dollars.

The main argument used by the White House to shoot down the B-1 was economy. But this is an argument which it is hard for defense observers to take seriously. Originally, the Air Force wanted about 240 B-1s, at an estimated construction cost of $24 billion. Finally, it wanted to settle for 150; but with cost overruns, inflation and support costs, the tab would have been about the same. Refurbishing the B-52s—President Carter's alternative choice—is a massive task: "strengthening the wings," for instance, means building new ones. New engines are required for the B-52Gs. The estimated cost of the refurbishing program is $18 billion. Since both programs were set to take six years, canceling production of the B-1 means an apparent saving of a billion a year—three quarters of 1 per cent of the defense budget through 1983, or one eighth of 1 per cent of the federal budget. But the estimated operation-and-maintenance budget of a four-engined B-1 is $7.5 million annually, while that of the aging, eight-engined B-52 is currently $10.3 million. In short, a fleet of refurbished B-52Gs and B-52Hs would cost nearly half a billion dollars more, yearly, in O & M, than a fleet of new B-1s. (Moreover, canceling Rockwell International's contract cost the taxpayer nearly a billion dollars.)

Another argument put forward for dropping the production phase of the B-1 was that it was a gesture to Moscow, related to SALT. But the Russians fear the cruise missile itself—which is part of both the B-1 and B-52 programs—more than its launcher, and had concentrated their principal fire on the land-based and naval versions. Moreover, by the time of the B-1 decision, Carter had withdrawn President Ford's offer to count cruise bombers as MIRVs, for which the SALT I ceiling was 1,320 (the SALT II ceiling is the same), and proposed instead counting them as missile launchers, for which the ceiling was 2,400. Thus, the United States would not have to trade any MIRVs—a technology in which, as with cruise missiles, Moscow is far behind—for the introduction of air-launched cruise missiles.

Technology, however, undergoes a sea change almost every year, and one of the B-1's outstanding characteristics—its ability to penetrate defenses—may be already shot. The Washington *Post*'s London correspondent, Bernard Nossiter, reported on February 11, 1977, from Copenhagen that the Russians now have a high-powered radio beam which bends with the curvature of the earth. Aircraft like the B-1 or unmanned ones like the cruise missile might no longer be able to fly beneath the radar sweep—and the B-52, of course, even less. According to Bud Nossiter, disruption of Danish routine communications traffic, detected by the country's posts and telegraphs network, led to the discovery of the Russian achievement. Later the beam was also detected in Britain, where engineers dubbed it the "woodpecker," because of its staccato drilling sound—which appeared to come from a site southeast of Minsk. By 1978, the beam appeared to be less in use, having proved its point, and high-frequency communications in northwest Europe were less subject to interference.

Some see a B-1, B-52 or FB-111 crew as almost as anachronistic as Marines—the only human beings who would still *accompany* a missile to Armageddon. But arguments about what the B-1 or the B-52 can or cannot do may even be irrelevant. What would an air force without bombers do with its bomber pilots? Dr. Malcolm Currie, former director of research and engineering at Defense, in one of his typical acts of massive retaliation on the English language, has said that the B-1 is "our best answer to the problems of survivability and penetrativity." The plane's critics have lost some credibility by getting the "kneejerk" support of liberals, whose laudable opposition to the notion of war itself tends often to make them poor strategists and weapons diplomatists, and from sustained Soviet broadsides against the aircraft, which imply that its qualities are real. J. W. R. Taylor, the influential editor of *Jane's All the World's Aircraft,* calls the need for the B-1 bomber "urgent." In a preface to the 1977–78 edition of the famous annual, Taylor said emotionally of Carter's B-1 cancellation: "If our planet is subjected one day to the unimaginable horrors of a third world war, 1977 might be recorded as the year in which the seeds of defeat for the Western powers were sown." Opinion polls, notably by Gallup, seem to show most Americans still in favor of the program. Senator Goldwater, the Senate's main military aviation expert, is a strong advocate of the B-1 because of its "complementary role" with other strategic systems.

But when Carter, in July, had asked Congress to rescind the funds which it had approved for the first production-line B-1s, it was with a sudden surge of support from the Air Force—which, assuming the B-1 program to be dead for the time being, hoped to salvage as much of the money as possible for other programs. The Pentagon even weighed stopping work on the (authorized) fifth development model of the plane, to acquire additional funds.

Rockwell International countered with a proposal to build two of the three proposed production models for fiscal 1978, for the amount already appropriated. This, said Rockwell, would preserve the production force and the network of suppliers, which under the Carter plan were finally dispersed in 1978; otherwise, if Carter revived production—as he was retaining the option of doing—this would be a massive and expensive task. Rockwell said it would cost only $220 million more to complete the two planes than to cancel them. A GAO report estimated that it would cost an additional $100 million to restart the program.

Rockwell International even proposed a slower, nonpenetrating, fixed-wing B-1 which would fire 16 internal and 14 external cruise missiles from a standoff posture. The firm estimated the flyaway costs (i.e., without support equipment) of such a B-1 as "$35,000,000–$43,000,000," against a flyaway cost for the swing-wing B-1 of $56 million.

Meanwhile, the Air Force was talking of reviving the FB-111 production line, terminated in 1974, to provide an alternative penetration bomber. It proposed "modifying" 65 existing FB-111s and adding 100 more, saying this would cost only $7 billion, or less than a third the cost of the proposed B-1 fleet. The FB-111 would have the engines designed for the B-1, extending its range from 4,100 miles to 5,700 miles without refueling. The House Armed Services Committee and Senator McIntyre's subcommittee approved $20 million for the relevant FB-111 studies. This was a windfall for General Dynamics, the sole-source contractor.

By September, the House Defense Committee's appropriations subcommittee had decided to delay action on rescission of the B-1 funds until it had more information on the feasibility of an FB-111 alternative, already styled the FB-111H. Because of the approaching October 4 deadline for rescission, the irritated chairman of the full Committee, George Mahon of Texas, and the ranking Republican on the subcommittee, Jack Edwards of Alabama, brought the rescission before the full Committee September 28; but it was defeated, 34–21.

The proposed "modification" of the 111, as put forward by the Air Force and the manufacturer, General Dynamics, sounded rather like a whole new plane; apart from taking on the B-1's engines, avionics and electronic countermeasures, the adaptation to greater fuel load and a mightier weapons combination—therefore, inevitably, new landing gear —meant that only part of the nose and cockpit, the wingtips and part of the tail would remain unchanged from the existing plans. Could all this be done for only $7 billion? And what had happened to the Administration's argument that penetration bombers were passé? In the corridors of Capitol Hill, the Californians began to bristle, with Rockwell lobbyists feeding them with data.

Republican freshman senator Sam Hayakawa welcomed the House Committee's action in rejecting the White House's rescission request, and noted:

> In recent weeks, the Pentagon has indicated that the President still wants to retain a manned penetrating-bomber option . . . This is indicated by the fact that he has asked the Armed Services Committee to give the

Pentagon another $20 million to initiate a $350 million R & D program to convert the F-111 to the FB-111H.

. . .

The 165 FB-111Hs which the Administration proposes to buy are equivalent, when measured by the number of weapons delivered on target, to only 61 B-1 aircraft. Because of the requirement for extra tankers for the FB-111H, as well as higher maintenance cost, the FB-111H program would cost $17 billion, compared to $11 billion for the B-1 alternative, to provide equal effectiveness.

The Arms Control Association agreed that the FB-111H would indeed have only half the cruise-missile capability of the B-52, and less range. A House study said a B-1 force could deliver 1,032 SRAMs to Soviet targets, while an equivalent FB-111 force would only deliver between 522 and 774. "The cost per SRAM delivered by the B-1 would be $16.1 million versus $29.7 million if delivered by the FB-111H," the report said. An ACA article backed Hayakawa: "A force of 165 FB-111Hs would have a 20-year life-cycle cost of $17 billion compared to an equal alert force of 61 B-1s at $11.5 billion."

The battle of the statistics was on. A Rockwell study said 140 B-1s could be procured, operated and maintained for ten years at a cost of $12.9 billion in 1977 dollars; equivalent cost for 82 Boeing 747s would be $15.5 billion, while 105 McDonnell-Douglas DC-10s would cost $15.6 billion. Because of the B-52's lower "survivability," 377 B-52s would be needed for equivalent effect, the study said, and this would cost $21.2 billion over ten years, while 470 FB-111Hs with 70 supporting KC-135 tankers would cost $30.4 billion. Over a ten-year cycle, the analysis added, the cost of the B-1 would be $10 million for each cruise missile carried, compared to $12 million for the 747, $15 million for the DC-10, $20 million for the B-52 and $30 million for the FB-111H. Air Force sources said that the Rockwell figures were accurate to within "five or six per cent" and that the B-1 manufacturer had actually underestimated the cost of adding EMP (electromagnetic pulse) hardening against radioactivity to commercial transports. Nevertheless, a Congressional Budget Office report the following year recommended $15.6 billion for 75 widebodied jets with 4,800 cruise missiles, while opposing the M-X and "mobile Minuteman" programs and any plans to double the projected size of the Trident fleet.

The Senate finally approved Carter's request for a $20 million study of FB-111 modifications—which Senator Proxmire described as a "down payment" on the building of two 111H prototypes for $380 million. But the House struck the sum out, saying the White House should decide whether it wanted a penetration bomber or not. In 1978, Carter dropped R & D funds for the enlarged FB-111 from the fiscal-1979 budget because its similarity to the B-1 was making it hard to kill the B-1 program.

Meanwhile, the House Appropriations Committee decision had virtually obligated the Office of Management and Budget to spend the funds originally voted for production B-1s. The Senate had rescinded the funds by a 90–0 vote, but the House still refused to do so. The Senate Appropriations Committee decided to add new language to the measure cutting off the money, but the House refused this amendment as well and a House-Senate conference failed to resolve the issue.

The House's B-1 forces had by then taken off in attack formation. John Flynt of Georgia was one of the leaders, pointing out that huge stocks of components for B-1s had already been produced:

> Without exaggerating too much, it would take nearly all the storage facility at a large Air Force base to store these aircraft component parts which are already in production and which are going to be paid for regardless of the outcome of this vote which will come up shortly.
>
> . . .
>
> The newest B-52 will be twenty years old at the time of the planned B-1 Initial Operational Capability . . . The B-52 in combination with the cruise missile cannot penetrate Russian defenses. Operationally, against the Russians, the B-52 must launch the cruise missiles at high altitudes. The Russians can easily detect the launching of the cruise missiles at high altitude and defend themselves by destroying them miles before they reach their target. Russian high-speed fighters have the capability to intercept our cruise missiles. They can overtake, track and destroy the subsonic cruise missile launched at altitude.

Republican freshman Samuel L. Devine of Columbus, Ohio, noted that B-52s were "shot down like flies in Vietnam. We had 750. I guess we have about 260 left." (He was presumably referring to -52Gs and -52Hs only.)

To make the B-52 more "survivable," Defense Secretary Brown and the Joint Chiefs of Staff recommended to the White House that the range of the air-launched cruise missile be extended to 1,800 miles—a sensitive SALT question. This would enable the B-52 to stand off further from Soviet airspace. This raised obvious questions: Would the Russians object? And was there any way of monitoring the range of a cruise missile?

Only in 1978 did the House agree to rescind the money for the B-1s. In a possibly unrelated measure, NASA gave Lockheed, about the same time, a $270,000 contract to study possible development of a liquid hydrogen-fueled supersonic transport capable of carrying 200 passengers, or an equivalent payload, at 4,000 mph.

What will happen to the B-1 program? Deborah Shapley, a perceptive editor at *Science* magazine, makes this comment:

> From a historical perspective, neither Congress nor the President has much say over military weapons options. Which weapons can be built depends on available technology; and he who controls the technology controls the evolution of major weapons systems. In the case of the B-1 bomber, it is the Air Force that exercises that crucial control.

In other words, campaign rhetoric and 1977 slowdown aside, the B-1 will probably be built. Indeed, in 1979, Under Secretary Perry said a revised B-1 was on the drawing boards, to succeed the B-52s in the mid-eighties and early nineties. Later that year, it was revealed that the redesigned B-1 would be a multipurpose bomber and tanker, with the wings being differently positioned according to the aircraft's role. Air Force bomber pilots believe the new B-1 will come none too soon. In July 1979, Arthur T. Hadley recounted in the Washington *Star* his experience of accompanying a simulated bombing exercise in a B-52, flying over Oklahoma, Kansas and New Mexico. The aircraft took off from a Louisiana base, with some difficulty and delay, and with long-recorded defects such as defective gyros and navigation instruments, faulty instrument-panel lights and SRAMs that would not fire. Hadley also noted that B-52 gas tanks are not self-sealing if the plane is hit, since the plane was originally designed for high altitude.

His narrative contained the following passage:

> Suddenly the gyro instruments which show how the plane is flying, whether it is upright or turning, all begin to spin and tumble on both the pilot's and copilot's side. Fortunately, we are not in the clouds. Up pop the heads back into the real world as we keep through the hills and valleys of the New Mexican badlands at 200 feet. Bruce [a pilot] opens his can of juice and drinks it down calmly. "This happens all the time," he says. Next—I am not making this up—he squeezes the can together with his hands and then jumps on it a bit, making of the juice can a truncated "V" with a bubble at one end. He takes out his pocket knife and opens up the instrument panel, revealing the pumps for the worthless gyros. He wedges his sculpted juice can beneath the forward edge of the vacuum pump. He ties the can in there with a bandage from the first-aid kit—[by then] I could use a little oxygen from that kit myself. The gyros spin back to life. Bruce fits the panel back together with his pocket knife. We return to flying the mission.

Looking further ahead, some experts saw Carter's B-1 decision as indicating that the United States is moving slowly toward reliance on a single strategic deterrent, the submarine-launched ballistic missile. SLBMs are the least vulnerable leg of the triad. Submarines, however, have more communications problems than aircraft or land-based missile sites.

Meanwhile, the new star in the defense firmament, at least as far as the front pages were concerned, was the cruise missile.

Cruise Missiles

Early in January 1977, with the Carter White House still waiting in the wings but threatening military budget cuts, the lame-duck Ford Defense Department made a first move of its own in the cruise-missile area. It ordered Boeing and General Dynamics to begin full-scale development —the last step before production—of the air-launched and submarine-launched versions. Two weeks later, the Navy announced that the ship- or submarine-launched Tomahawk cruise missile had flown its first successful test, locating a ship "over the horizon" 188 miles away in the Pacific. On this occasion, the Tomahawk was fired from a Navy A-6 twin-engined Intruder attack plane. Days later, again using an A-6, another cruise missile flew 350 miles in a zigzag pattern to locate its target. Both triumphs were trumpeted to the press.

The cruise missile, current star that it is, is not all that new. In 1915, Dr. Elmer Sperry, the inventor of the directional gyro, interested the Navy in what was variously called an "aerial torpedo" and an "automatic flying bomb." The directional gyro is basic to a number of aircraft instruments, from the turn-and-bank indicator to the automatic pilot or to the equivalent systems in pilotless or remotely piloted aircraft today. The "flying bomb" program was put under the direction of Lawrence Sperry, who incorporated Elmer's gyros into the "Curtis flying bomb." The Navy conducted its first tests in 1917, but it was on March 6, 1918, that an "unmanned flying bomb" was recorded as having made its first successful flight of 1,000 yards at Amityville, New York.

The Army Air Service then sponsored the Kettering Bug aerial torpedo program. The Liberty Eagle, as it was renamed in the euphoria of victory later that year, finally flew at Carlstrom Field in Arcadia, Florida, in August 1919; but funding died with the disarmament of the twenties.

Just over a generation ago, the cruise missile was resurrected as one of the more curious of Hitler's last-gasp weapons. Germany's V-2, which rocketed into the stratosphere and roared back to earth in southern England with what we would today call a powerful "conventional" warhead, was the product of Hitler's brilliant rocket engineers, many of whom went on to father America's and Russia's space programs. But the V-1, or "buzz bomb," seemed like a tactical cul-de-sac. It was an unguided, pilotless aircraft with a decidedly subsonic speed and a meager explosives payload that could just about destroy a cottage. Its fiery tail was the public's first sight of the jet engine. RAF pilots would fly alongside at reduced speed and tip one of its wings with one of theirs, sending it into an obedient, 180-degree turn, and out to sea, like a paper dart hit by a draft.

Both America and Russia began the development of cruise missiles after World War Two. The Northrop Snark was perfected in the late forties and flew from Cape Canaveral to Brazil. With the Navajo came an improved rocket booster and a ramjet engine. The Navy developed the Regulus for firing from the deck of a submarine. In the early sixties, U.S. strategic surface-to-surface CMs were replaced by the new ballistic missiles; but some cruise missiles, such as the 600-mile-range Hound Dog, deployed on B-52s, remained in the U.S. arsenal. In 1962, the Soviets deployed the SS-N-3 Shaddock, a short-range (300-mile) weapon with a kiloton nuclear warhead, and some naval air-to-surface short-range CMs. Today, the Russians have thousands of short-range tactical (nuclear) cruise missiles.

The main advances over the years have been the development of small turbofan engines, especially the Williams Research F-107-100—which measures 30 by 12 inches and weighs only 126 pounds—and of much improved guidance systems. There have been increases in the yield-to-weight ratios of nuclear warheads. The smaller propulsion units—originally designed to fit into a soldier's backpack and lift him out of trouble spots, Batman-style—give more space for the sophisticated guidance system and the warhead.

Western literature does not reveal whether or not the United States knows the firepower of the Soviet 450-mile-range SS-N-12 surface-to-surface naval missile and the 350-mile-range AS-6 air-to-surface missile for the Backfire, nor that of the SS-N-7 40-mile-range naval cruise missile; but there are no reasons for thinking these deceptively tiny winged robots are much less deadly than the 200-kiloton (fourteen times "Hiroshima") air-launched and submarine-launched missiles which Boeing and General Dynamics are developing.

At all costs, the cruise missile's on-again, off-again career is on again, and the buzz bomb has grown up to become, in its air-launched, ship-launched, submarine-launched and land versions, a bargaining chip in SALT, no less. Boeing's air-launched version (ALCM) is a sleek, pilotless baby plane with retracted wings and fold-over elevons and tail. The commonest model—the ALCM-A—is only 14 feet long and flies 1,100 miles. Its 36-inch nose cone contains its bulk memory unit, tape transport, radar altimeter and pre-programmed air-data unit. Another version, the ALCM-B, which is 5 feet longer, packs more fuel and does 1,500 miles. The speed of both versions is subsonic—550 mph.

General Dynamics' sea-launched version (SLCM), the Tomahawk, with a 1,500-mile range that can be extended to 2,000 miles, can be fired not only from surface vessels but also, theoretically, from torpedo tubes. Like Russia's SS-N-3 and its successor the SS-N-12—now deployed on the Soviet mini-carriers *Minsk* and *Kiev*—the Tomahawk is targeted by aircraft or satellite. It is capable of nuclearization. A medium-range (300-mile) version with a conventional warhead, the Harpoon, similar to the Russian SS-N-9, will be used as a "ship killer." It is targeted by helicopter or fixed-wing plane. Its design, down to the terminal guidance system, is the same as the Air Force's, but the airframe is slightly larger. On the drawing board are such variants as a 2,000-mile "strategic" ALCM for the eighties, and a "land" version that can be fired from trucks.

Additionally, there are very-short-range cruise missiles with ranges of less than 25 miles. These are guided to target by radar, and electro-optical and infrared sensors on the launch platform. There are few U.S. missiles in this category, but Russian models include the ship-launched SS-N-2 and SS-N-11, the submarine-launched SS-N-7 and the antisubmarine SS-N-14.

Satellite maps of Soviet territory have been acquired through high-resolution photography in recent years, and something like an airliner's en-route chart can be stored in a cruise missile's computer memory bank. This, along with McDonnell-Douglas' ingenious TERCOM (Terrain Contour Matching), of which the Russians have as yet no equivalent, allows the low-flying buzz bomb of today to avoid hills and finally thud to earth within 30 yards of target. (Declassified material says 200 yards. The Center for Defense Information claims 10. Pentagon sources say 30.)

While in flight, the missile uses its radar periodically to measure altitude and position. If it finds itself off course—for instance, after terrain avoidance—the computer chooses a new compass radial toward the next fixpoint. The inertial guidance system keeps the missile on course between "terrain comparisons." After several course corrections, the tiny computer learns to predict inertial drift and compensates for it through a sort of auto-pilot called a Kalman filter. Drift is rarely more than 100 yards off course per 700 miles.

The Navy and Army versions of the projectile, which start toward their target with no acquired aircraft speed, are boosted by rockets to cruising speed before the air-breathing propulsion unit—turbojet, turbofan or ramjet engine—takes over. By then its control surfaces are extended and it flies at near-constant speed, correcting its course and avoiding land obstacles in the usual way.

When 20 ALCM-As, weighing nearly a ton apiece, are put aboard a B-52, eight Bs will go in the bomb bay—in the rotary launcher designed for the Air Force's Short-Range Attack Missile (SRAM)—while twelve As will be slung from wing pylons. But they could be launched from almost any aircraft heavy enough to haul their weight, such as a C-5 transport—or even, according to William Graham, director of engineering sciences at the RAND Corporation, from a blimp. A Defense report says that a 747 jumbo liner could carry "several dozen of them"; other sources say a 747 could carry "a hundred."

The Boeing company actually modified a 747—principally by installing a door just over 20 feet long and 5 feet high on the starboard side of the fuselage. Using this hatch made pressurization impossible, and crewmen had to wear oxygen masks soon after climb-out and keep them on during launching tests.

Although vulnerable to antiaircraft defenses, especially interceptor aircraft, the small size of cruise missiles makes them difficult to see among the near-ground clutter on an interceptor's downward-looking radar, and almost impossible to spot from ground surveillance, especially as they can hedgehop at 100 feet. Cruise missiles can also be made of materials that reflect radar waves poorly. Captain William Locke, who is in charge of the Navy's Tomahawk and Harpoon programs and also has joint oversight of the air and land versions of the cruise missile, claims the Tomahawk will be "no larger than a seagull" on enemy radar. Moreover, so little heat radiates from its exhaust that infrared, heat-seeking missiles would have difficulty "finding" it, even if radar spotted it. Further cruise missiles may be endowed with electronic countermeasures (ECMs). Sufficiently impressed, the Russians are building radar towers several hundred feet high to "look down" on low-flying U.S. bombers and cruise missiles, along with shorter towers on wheel-driven flatbed vehicles.

Perhaps the most articulate advocate of cruise missiles has been Dr. Malcolm Currie. He told the House Armed Services Committee in 1975 that "cruise missiles, because they are designed for use on existing carrier vehicles and therefore cost relatively little, are potentially very high [diplomatic] leverage systems."

But the cruise missile divides defense experts as no other controversial proposed element in the armory of the eighties has done. To some, it is just a complication to détente. The authoritative, if dovish, *Defense Monitor* said:

At first glance, cruise missiles seem too good to be true . . . More than a hundred cruise missiles for the price of a single B-1! . . . [But] these missiles cannot do anything that cannot be done by existing ballistic missiles. Furthermore, because they can be easily concealed inside ships and airplanes, they complicate the problem of arriving at a verifiable SALT II nuclear-arms limitation agreement.

Since cheapness means deployment in numbers, monitoring them would be "virtually impossible," said the Center for Defense Information, adding that the existence of strategic cruise missiles "makes the negotiation of a meaningful SALT agreement unimaginable," while the threat of a vulgarized version for small nations is a "frightening prospect." (SALT II, as noted later, finally did approve cruise missiles, with limitations.) Dr. Currie, however, stressed his belief that cruise missiles were not "destabilizing" by emphasizing their vulnerability to Russia's newest surface-to-air missiles.

Like many other "smart bombs," the cruise missile is already "battle-tested"—a great help in a weapons-system's survival. Unlike the others, however, Vietnam was not its main testing ground. In 1967, an Egyptian ship, without leaving harbor, fired two Russian Styx cruise missiles at the invaders' nearest naval vessel, the Israeli destroyer *Eilat* 12 miles away, and sank it. In the Indo-Pakistani War of 1971, three Indian patrol craft fired nine Styxes at Pakistani ships, sinking one destroyer and crippling another—both "over the horizon." In 1973, the Israelis sank hostile patrol boats with their 12-mile-range Gabriel cruise missiles; the 25-mile "over the horizon" Styxes also scored several hits, but by 1973 Israeli radar had improved enough for fifty-five Styxes to be intercepted and downed.

As the last sentence indicates, the cruise-missile program is far from perfected anywhere, and in 1977 knowledgeable sources said the United States was about five years from producing a really effective, long-range ALCM arsenal. Robert Hotz, then publisher of *Aviation Week*, said: "It will be well into the eighties before stand-off range permits launch well outside Soviet territory. To achieve maximum range, the cruise missile must fly at the high altitude of turbofan efficiency for much of its penetration and during that period is exposed to even current Soviet air defense."

Air Force pilots, even more concerned with their own "survivability" than the generals, and wanting their risks to be associated with an effective weapon, noted that NATO's Roland and Hawk missiles could intercept air-launched cruise missiles, and that Russian equivalents would do so too. If the surface-to-air missile site was at the target, the cruise missile "will fly right into it," said one. Whatever countermeasures were put aboard the launch aircraft, there would be none for the missile itself, which, as another pilot put it, "can't even tell when it's being attacked, let alone dodge [other] missiles."

Highly placed sources with similar views were getting their message through to two columnists with close contacts with the Pentagon, Rowland Evans and Robert Novak. In late 1977, they wrote that "secret computer studies show that the existing U.S. cruise missiles would not have a chance of penetrating the Soviet Union's sophisticated defense system." The studies, they said, had shown that a U. S. Hawk battery could locate a Tomahawk and shoot it down. The brunt of the column was that, because of these conclusions, a planned "live" test against a Tomahawk scheduled for Nellis Air Force Base on December 6 had been canceled and replaced by a simulated test, involving no actual launch of a Hawk against the cruise missile. The columnists quoted a technical expert as saying: "I'm very much afraid that the cruise missile is about one weapon-generation away from being able to penetrate Soviet defenses."

Successful Tomahawk tests were, however, conducted at Dugway, Utah, in June 1978. Pentagon officials pronounced the Tomahawk to be "survivable," after E-2C Hawkeyes and E-3A AWACS planes had tried and failed to vector F-14s, F-15s, F-4s and F106s to shoot down the missile—whose tiny radar cross section proved to be hard to find on the radar display tubes. The Tomahawk's accuracy was also praised. Said a Pentagon source: "The TERCOM guidance puts the cruise missile within the football field of the target, and the scene-matching area correlator puts it between the goalposts."

A few days later, the Pentagon took the unusual course of holding an exercise involving Tomahawks for the press at White Sands missile range in New Mexico, with Secretary Brown on hand to boost the cruise missile's public image. The missile defied attacks by improved Hawk and Roland missiles, simulating SA-10s. One Tomahawk destroyed a runway with a curtain of "submunitions." By then, contracts with three manufacturers had been renewed to produce wide-body cruise-missile launchers: Boeing was working on the 747 and the YC-14, Lockheed on the L-1011 and the C-5, McDonnell-Douglas on the DC-10 and the YC-15. Improved Soviet SA-X-10 anti-cruise-missile missiles should be ready in the eighties, but the Pentagon said the Kremlin would need 5,000 to 10,000 of them to be effective, at a cost of $30 billion, together with $50 billion to $100 billion for airborne warning aircraft.

The top Pentagon brass, envisaging a fleet of 200 bombers firing 3,000 cruise missiles at a time (at a cost, not mentioned to Congress, of about $2.5 billion for the missiles in this one broadside alone), insisted that an effective force of missiles would get through, and that it would take the

U.S.S.R. "at least eight years" to develop a sufficient defense. Launched from positions at least 300 nautical miles off Russia's north coast, it was argued, Tomahawks could reach virtually every target in the country, if they got through. Cruise-missile ranges could be extended by adding air-breathing propulsion stages, which could fall away as fuel is consumed, so that the missile would present a smaller radar cross section as it approached its target.

Senator Gary Hart even spoke of replacing much of U.S. offensive aviation in Europe by 100,000 long-range cruise missiles, implying a bill of over $50 billion. But "cruises" lack the pinpoint accuracy and the power to destroy major targets—or even, some sources say, to take out major bridges or sprawling targets like railroad marshaling yards.

The Navy estimates the unit cost of the Tomahawk, in 1975 dollars, at $792,000. The Air Force version would cost around $500,000. Since each Minuteman-III costs $5.8 million—and, 3-MIRV-ed, only packs thrice the mischief of one "cruise"—air-launched cruise missiles can theoretically do what Minuteman can do for only about a quarter the cost. But the cruise missile's slowness, and its vulnerability to being shot down—impossible at present, except around Moscow, for the Minuteman—mean that huge numbers of the weapon have to be fired to ensure a hit; and any realistic costing must compute the proportionate cost of the submarine, ship or plane that serves as the cruise missile's platform. Bombers and submarines would have to have retrofit modifications to accept cruise missiles (and, at the time this book was written, all tests of Tomahawks from submarines had failed). Says the CDI: "At a bare minimum, the CM program acquisition costs will likely exceed $5 billion."

Missiles carried by B-52s or adapted airliners will remain high-flyers—as Hotz has noted—vulnerable to detection and interception in a way that would not be true of missiles carried by the low-flying B-1 or the possibly adapted FB-111. This means that, under present plans, as Evans and Novak indicated in their column, relatively few cruise missiles would get through to their targets, so understandably more will be needed than the original figures of 2,328 ALCM-As and -Bs and 1,264 Tomahawks. This makes the "cheap" cruise missile an ardently expensive way of destroying an East German munitions plant compared to, say, an A-10 attack plane, which costs $6.1 million with all support systems, and is recoverable. Splice in the cost of the bombers themselves and their support systems, and strategic submarines and ICBMs begin to look more cost-efficient. By late 1977, Boeing was admitting that the 150 B-52Gs and 90 -52Hs would probably have to be remodified for the longer-range ALCM-Bs and would need improved countermeasures, for a total extra modification cost of at least $700,000 per aircraft.

The main strategic argument for the cruise missile is that almost any heavy aircraft could launch it. A Brookings report speaks of a 747 hurling the equivalent of "about fourteen hundred times" the Hiroshima attack without penetrating Soviet defenses. With a "safe" base, an aircraft bearing CMs could, in theory, return for reloading and a second mission. But 747s would have to stand off from enemy airspace as much as 800 miles, Brookings said, so could only use long-range ALCMs to reach Russian control sites, nuclear storage and naval installations. In any event, SALT II was to limit "cruises" to twenty-eight per aircraft, so that a 747 with eighty-four of them would have to count as *three* strategic bombers.

A total of $400.2 million had been voted in 1977 for the fiscal-1978 U.S. cruise-missile program—almost the same as the figure proposed by the outgoing Ford administration, which planned the Tomahawk for limited naval operations in 1979. With the Carter decision of June 1977 appearing to emphasize the air-launched cruise missile's importance, Congress increased the budget the following month, and for 1979 Carter asked $416.1 million for the Boeing missile alone, along with $74.1 million for the Tomahawk (against $18.7 million the year before).

But the weapon's future is still clouded. Not only is it opposed by those liberals who favor disarmament generally, or who scorn its poor cost-efficiency, but also by those admirals and generals whose own bailiwicks it threatens. It could make not only manned penetration bombers but also aircraft carriers redundant, for instance. However, with a Russian cruise-missile program well advanced, and with its already established role as a bargaining chip in diplomacy, the U.S. cruise-missile program, for all its limitations, will probably survive and prosper.

Indeed, by 1978, to the ALCM and the SLCM—"Alchem" and "Slickem" in Pentagonese—was being added a new ground-launched GLCM ("Glockem") to be based in Germany, possibly with a conventional warhead; and there was even talk of a nuclear-engined Intercontinental Cruise Missile (ICCM) which could reach the Soviet Union from the United States. A total of 167 Glockems is being requested by the White House in fiscal 1980, and 240 the following year.

So far, the Russians have professed to see the American program, with its "smarter" warheads, as destabilizing rather than an attempt to catch up with Moscow.

Because "cruises" are inexpensive in unit cost, and technology for the short-range models easily acquired, smaller powers seem sure to be attracted to them. Mexico could easily afford enough to obliterate every large city in the United States, and Iran could do the same for Russia—in both cases, if defenses could successfully be penetrated. Already, secondary NATO military powers have them, while France has had a ship-to-ship, "conventional" 6o-mile-range version in its inventory since 1956. A more accurate, similarly light-powered cruise missile was jointly developed by France and Italy in 1975. The German Navy is producing an air-to-ship model. Britain developed a surface-to-air version, the Bloodhound, in 1958, and a naval surface-to-air version, the Sea Dart, in 1973. All these have "conventional" warheads.

The American inventory still includes 6 early models: 3 surface-to-surface missiles with ranges of around 600 miles and a choice of nuclear or high-explosive warheads, the Hound Dog nuclear air-to-surface cruise missile, the Bomarc surface-to-air model and the Quail decoy. All were in service or production by 1961. The Soviet armory includes 3 early short-range air-to-surface CMs with NATO code names like Kennel, Kipper and Kangaroo, 2 modest surface-to-surface models called Scrubber and the previously mentioned Shaddock, along with the Genef antiaircraft version. All date from the Khrushchev era. Since the sixties, according to *Aviation Week,* the U.S.S.R. has produced more than 5,000 cruise missiles of varying ranges, deployed aboard about 230 surface and subsurface vessels. The ALCM is the only American *strategic* cruise missile in development, but all the Soviet cruise missiles are believed to be "nuclear-capable" except the SS-N-2 and its successor, the SS-N-11.

Moscow, announcing a major increase in land defense spending, appeared however to be convinced that the cruise missile was—or would be, one day—an effective threat. The Soviet Union's squadron (reportedly, eight aircraft in 1977) of Il-76 Candid transports adopted on Il-112 radar-control planes is not presently capable of operating a barrier defense to intercept cruise-missile-carrier aircraft at long ranges. But improved microcircuitry should make this possible. Meanwhile, Soviet interceptors would keep B-52s sufficiently outside Soviet airspace to limit the accuracy of their targeting.

The inferiority of most of Russia's own cruise missiles, when weighed against America's, comes predominantly from geographical rather than technological ignorance: The Soviet Union lacks accurate terrain contour-matching. This is why Moscow has concentrated on naval missiles, whose sea journey obviates the need for terrain avoidance.

The Russians asked, unsuccessfully, in the SALT II talks, for U.S. assurances that advanced cruise-missile technology would not be transferred to other countries for at least three years; these reports worried America's NATO allies. But both Britain and France were talking of developing their own new-generation cruise missiles, possibly in cooperation with Germany. The British were reportedly interested mainly in submarine-launched nuclear CMs, the French in both nuclear and conventional ones. The Germans seek a short-range, land-based, conventional-warhead model. But for reasons of standardization and possibly cost-cutting, all three countries were said to prefer joint development and research with the United States.

Second in line in the order of battle is the tactical nuclear force.

U.S. TACTICAL AIRCRAFT

Perhaps the best-known elements in the modern U.S. armory are the aircraft normally associated with nonstrategic warfare. The aging McDonnell-Douglas F-4 Phantom and the A-7 Intruder are about to be superseded by a new breed of planes, notably the F-15, the F-16 and the F-14.

Perhaps the best place to see these new aircraft is in Tactical Air Command's (TACOM's) Operation Red Flag program at Nellis Air Force Base in Nevada, where F-15 and F-14 pilots are trained on their aircraft in Russian fighter tactics, flying nine sorties a day, five days a week, to get used to wartime pressures. F-16s will follow. They are pitted against F-5s (in Soviet colors, about which Moscow has officially complained) which imitate MiG-21s and use Soviet Air Force combat techniques. Styrofoam and plywood copies of Russian T-62 tanks and other armor serve as ground targets for the F-15 in its fighter-bomber role, and the desert has blossomed with copies of Altenburg air base and Jüterborg industrial complex in East Germany and other potential targets, as well as surface-to-air missile sites. In all, there are nearly thirty mock targets, complete with supply depots, railheads, tunnels, surface-to-air missile sites and one convoy of old cars and trucks that stretches for 17 miles. Foreign air forces also train there. In its first three years of operation, nine thousand U.S., Canadian, British and German air and ground crews have used Nellis. In the third year, 1977, alone, six thousand trainees flew twenty-three thousand sorties. In 1979, South Korean pilots joined the throng.

Here, in "enemy" territory, it is the Americans or allied flyers who are the "bogeys" or "bandits"—the invaders. Within hours of returning to base, pilots can watch themselves being shot down on videotape, their aircraft locked in on radar. They learn to jink—take evasive action. By 1978, there had been thirteen crashes during low-level jinking, at a cost of nine lives. A look at the planes themselves:

F-15. The new first-line air-superiority fighter—designed, that is, to have "superiority" in the skies over enemy fighters and bombers—is the twin-engined McDonnell-Douglas F-15, described by the Air Force as the "best fighter plane in the world" and appropriately named the Eagle. With an operable Mach speed of 2.5—about 1,750 mph, at altitude—it is designed to fly both close air-support missions and deep interdiction raids.

It was first flown in 1972. In 1974, an unweaponed F-15 with wing fuel tanks flew the 3,063 miles from Loring Air Force Base in Maine to the RAF base at Bentwater for the Farnborough Air Show, without refueling, in 5.4 hours. It captured eight speed records for climbs to 3,000, 6,000, 9,000, 12,000, 15,000, 20,000, 25,000 and 30,000 feet—later losing the last two to the MiG-25 Foxbat.

Fears that the strategic role of the Soviet Backfire bomber may include strikes against the United States have added an increased antibomber role to the Eagle, and the original Air Force order of 749 aircraft may be increased—although Admiral LaRocque says: "Since we have agreed by treaty with the [Russians] not to defend against the more serious missile threat [a reference to limitations on the antiballistic missile], it makes little sense to defend against bombers."

LaRocque's argumentation is, of course, open to dispute; but one of the early acts of the Carter administration was to try to cut the annual output of the plane from 108 to 78. (Congress restored the original figure.) Deliveries of the aircraft began in 1974. With F-15s already in service with the Air Force, including a squadron in Germany and a wing in Britain, any production cuts such as those recommended by the White House would presumably delay deliveries to Israel, Saudi Arabia and Japan.

The total F-15 program cost is set at about $14 billion and the unit cost at $18 million, not including weapons: According to White House plans, sixty will be produced each year in fiscal 1980 and 1981. The inertially navigated plane has nine external positions for Sidewinder and Sparrow missiles, carries a 20mm. six-barrel Gatling gun and has the now standard IFF (Identification Friend or Foe) sensors. It can carry general-purpose or guided bombs, other ordnance, and has electronic warfare pods.

F-16. This lightweight, single-engined, air-superiority or attack fighter built by General Dynamics is America's main new "weapons diplomacy" plane. Its absence of a name reflects the fact that it is a "multinational" fighter, having blanketed out the French Dassault Mirage F-1E, Sweden's SAAB Viggen and fellow-American contestants to become the staple fighter of several air forces speaking different languages.

The overseas base price of the F-16, which will replace F-5s and

F-104s and gradually supersede F-4s in friendly air forces, is $6,091,000; but by the time this book was written the tag for fully equipped F-16s had hit $10 million for the USAF itself and was still rising. The Air Force will get at least 1,388 F-16s, starting with 120 in 1979, for an initially estimated cost of $13.8 billion, and with the initial contract (for 650) set at $5.1 billion. A total of 175 has been requested by the White House for fiscal 1980, and 180 each year for 1981 through 1984. But the Air Force insists it needs over 2,100 in all, and funds made available by President Carter's B-1 cancellation, along with Iran's annulment of an order for 160 F-16s, will probably help increase the USAF inventory of the plane—although a 1978 GAO report calls for a review of the program. Wing-service production began in 1978.

With a 1,000-mile autonomy (500-mile radius), the plane operates at Mach-2, using the same Pratt and Whitney engine and blended wing-body process as the F-15. With a nuclear capacity, the F-16 normally carries four Sidewinder missiles and has five external stations for other weapons, such as the television-guided Maverick antitank missile, 20,000 pounds of conventional bombs, and electronic countermeasures. Its nose-mounted, 20mm. multi-barrel cannon (with thirteen thousand rounds) gives it a close-in dogfighting ability.

Brigadier James Abrahamson, who is in charge of the Air Force's F-16 program, waxes enthusiastic about the plane, in which rudder, elevators and ailerons are controlled by computer, leaving the pilot's hands free for weapons control. This means that the pilot can manually point the aircraft away or down from the target for a better view, leaving the computer to "crab" it onto the desired course direction, not nose-ahead. The pilot can make relatively flat turns, and point the nose up or down without changing power, yet maintain constant altitude. "Sideways" flight has raised new fatigue problems, with pilots calling for lateral constraints to be built into the cockpit around their shoulders.

F-18. This is the Navy superiority fighter from McDonnell-Douglas, now named the Hornet. An attack (A-18) version may also be built, while Northrop, the co-contractor on the prototype, may build an F-18L (for Land) version for foreign air forces and perhaps for the U. S. Air Force. It is still under development, with most of the technical data under wraps; but it is known that the Navy wants a total of 1,366 of both its versions, for an estimated present unit cost of $17.4 million. The Hornet is a twin-engined, Mach-2 fighter. The A-18 will have a longer range.

The F-18 will have nine weapon stations: It can carry Sparrow and Sidewinder air-to-air missiles, antitank missiles in the attack version, and has a 20mm. cannon. Despite lobbying by the Texas and Massachusetts congressional delegations to revive the A-7 (made in Texas) and give it the General Electric engines (made in Massachusetts) intended for the F-18—which would then have been canceled—funding for the first 36 operational F-18s was approved by Congress for fiscal 1979. Eleven of these are development aircraft, however, being tested at Patuxent River naval air station in Maryland in 1979, and 9 of these will be a single-engine version. Production F-18s and A-18s would not have hit carrier decks until May 1980 at the earliest. This year, the Navy and the Marines hope to get 30 of them in all, with 48 the following year, 96 in 1982, 108 in 1983 and 186 in 1984.

F-14. This is one of the most controversial and trouble-ridden of the new generation of fighters, but also one of the most impressive. Apart from the usual complement of heat-seeking, short-range Sidewinders and medium-range (8–12 miles) 500-pound Sparrow missiles, and a 20mm. Vulcan gun firing up to a hundred rounds a second, usually in two-second bursts, this twin-engined Mach-2 fighter, known as the Tomcat, also carries the 100-mile-range, 1,000-pound Phoenix missile. This can hit surface-to-air enemy missiles with its lookdown radar and also reach aircraft well above fighter ceilings—such as the Soviet Foxbat, an armed reconnaissance plane which cruises at about 85,000 feet. Its own top altitude is 50,000 feet. At subsonic speeds, it has a two-hour range, at loitering speeds three hours.

The Tomcat's radar and fire-control systems can track multiple targets at "extreme" ranges and fire six Phoenix standoff missiles simultaneously—for instance, to intercept an incoming missile barrage. To decrease vulnerability, there are eleven separate self-sealing fuel tanks and two separate hydraulic systems, split roughly down the center of the plane, while the tail empennages are built nearly 11 feet apart.

The plane's variable geometry, usually operated automatically, varies the angle of the wings from 28° to 68°, virtually halving the aircraft's profile. When a pilot climbs into the cockpit, puts his hand on his helmet and raises the seat until his hand touches the canopy, the field of vision which he discovers is exceptional.

The Navy calls the Tomcat what the Air Force calls the Eagle—"the world's greatest fighter"—and the crews that fly the F-14 at Oceana naval air base near Virginia Beach are enthusiastic about the aircraft. Most are former Phantom pilots, and clearly the F-14 is a generation ahead of that famous plane, as well as being 40 per cent more economic on fuel; because of its raked nacelles, able to absorb airflow at a high angle of attack, it can perform a vertical climb, which would stall an F-4.

The F-14s are deployed on the carriers *Kennedy, America, Dinitz* and

Eisenhower. Most of the training is done from Oceana, under positive control from nearby Dam Neck, data-linked to E-2C Hawkeye control planes. Pilots describe the Tomcat as "very G-capable," with an excellent rate of climb and "good dash capability." At top speed—Zone-5 afterburner—fuel consumption, however, rises from 8,000 pounds per hour to 2,000 pounds per minute (with drop tanks, maximum fuel is 19,600 pounds).

But the Tomcat, superbly sophisticated as it is, has proven to be mangy with problems. Once an $8.1 billion undertaking in 1969, the program is currently edging $20 billion and the twin-finned bird is still not quite ready for the fray. Unit costs will finally be over $20 million—$25 million with the Phoenix missiles, making it the most expensive fighter plane in history.

Object Lesson

The F-14 is an interesting object lesson in some of the political factors that go into a weapon system's success or failure.

After delays in producing a special engine, the Navy let Grumman build its initial 100 planes (out of about 700 planned) with a modified 1959 Pratt and Whitney engine, the TF-30, which powers the F-111. Shocked by mounting expenses, Congress almost halved the order of planes to 390, and allowed the old engine to go in virtually all of them, while awaiting the troubled new propulsion unit. The order figure was later raised to 403 and—according to Rear Admiral John Alvis, the Navy's F-14 program manager—will probably reach 521.

Faced with reduced orders and other problems, Grumman threatened to go bankrupt and break contract. Then the Nixon administration, including the President himself, intervened, notably with the Iranian deal, which will be described in a later chapter.

The underpowered "old" engine, which had caused eight crashes in F-111s in recent years, began to give trouble in the Tomcat. Excessive vibrations caused a fan disc-blade in the propulsion unit's third stage to wear out—a similar problem to one that has plagued the engines of MiG-23s. The Tomcat became what airmen call a "hangar queen," always under repair and in the hands of "tecreps" (technician representatives) from Grumman.

Three Tomcat engines blew up at sea within weeks of each other in 1975; a fourth malfunctioned, again causing loss of a plane in the ocean. More crashes followed. In September 1976, one engine of an F-14 malfunctioned on the deck of the carrier *John F. Kennedy,* then sailing the icy waters off Scapa Flow, north of Scotland. The pilot was unable to idle the other engine and the Tomcat skewed around, injuring three of the deck crew and reeling into the ocean. The two pilots ejected safely.

A Soviet cruiser hovered a few hundred yards off and a contest began in the inky depths to raise the top-secret plane before the Russians—already angered by the recent defection to Japan of a Foxbat pilot with his top-secret aircraft—could get at it. Worth finding by the Russians in the 1,890-feet-deep water would have been an intact $500,000 Phoenix missile and what Pentagon sources called "devices so sensitive that a friendly nation wouldn't get them if it bought the plane." (Other sources said the devices included gadgetry for coding voice communications and foiling enemy jamming attempts, a computer to angle the plane for the best possible "shooting" position and a data-link system that would enable the mother ship to fly the plane from its own control center.)

After an exciting narrative that occupied front pages on and off for six weeks, a nuclear-powered recovery submarine managed to help two oil rigs get lines to the sunken plane and drag it toward land; it broke in half on the rocky bottom, but the sensitive elements were apparently scavenged successfully.

GOP congressman Bob Wilson of California, a conservative, tongue-lashed Grumman and Pratt and Whitney, noting that the first Tomcats had suffered seventeen crashes in all, killing five crew members—but omitting to blame Congress for its earlier approval of the "old" engine. Wilson, however, claimed that two of the Tomcat's missions—air-to-air combat and close air support—could be done as well, if not better, by the California-made F-18, while its main role (to defend the fleet against antiship missiles by superiority over missile platforms and missiles themselves) seemed, he claimed, beyond its ability with the TF-30 engine. Some Navy brass, including Navy Secretary W. Graham Claytor, argued, however, for scrapping the F-18 program and putting the money saved into more F-14 development and production.

A leitmotiv of congressional criticism in recent years has been that the Navy, now flying twelve models of six different aircraft types, has forced manufacturers into relatively low production schedules and high unit costs. Overshadowing the arguments are those about the future Navy role in warfare and the related disagreement about mini-carriers for V-STOL (Vertical and Short Takeoff and Landing) aircraft. In 1976, in sixteen simulated combats with the Marines' British-designed Harrier (AV-8) V-STOL plane, the F-14 was mauled each time. Since Wilson spoke, more F-14 crashes have taken place, but these apparently have been due to pilot error. Yet the plane remains the only one that can take the Phoenix, and in October 1977, both houses upped F-14 production from 40 to 44 aircraft in 1978 and from 36 to 60 in fiscal 1979; the White House, as noted earlier, later cut the figure to 24, thus extending the production phase by several more years over the previously anticipated five. Present administration plans call for 24 each year through 1984.

At Grumman headquarters in Bethpage, on Long Island, and at the F-14 assembly plant at nearby Calverton, the troubled image of the F-14 is naturally seen differently. Engineer Mike Pehalac, the firm's senior vice-president who was the "father of the F-14," admits the plane's present engine has a "durability problem." But he told the writer in December 1977: "We've put it right and we've had no problems on the present engine for fifteen months." Pehalac then thoughtfully touched wood.

At literally all aerospace establishments, test pilots, engineers and others intimately involved with the local product not only speak with religious faith about their plane but also dump sarcastically on its competitors. The F-14's chief test pilot, Chuck Sewell, is no exception. Like Pehalac, he believes that the F-14 makes the F-15 "irrelevant." Pehalac is critical of the A-7 and, especially, of the A-10, believing the F-14 could also be a more effective attack plane than either, despite its high speed. Grumman Corporation president Joe Gavin, noting that his firm is essentially a Navy contractor, said the Air Force was "just trying to prove something by pushing so hard for the F-15, the B-1 and AWACS"—the aircraft which compete with the Navy's F-14, the new version of the F-111 which the Air Force regards as inferior to the B-1, and the Navy's E-2C. Grumman produces the first and third and is the contractor for the new F-111. Gavin maintained that the F-14 would last "until the end of the century."

The outlook for the new F-14 engine, the people at Grumman think, is that it will be introduced "when we cilop." This is an industry phrase: "Cilop" stands for "conversion in lieu of production," meaning the growing tendency to convert older aircraft (such as the B-52) rather than build a whole new system. "Cilopping" the F-14 is seen as likely in the eighties.

The F-14's fortunes improved in 1979 when the Air Force agreed to consider purchasing it, perhaps starting with some of those rejected by Iran and available at discount prices. The Air Force admitted that the Tomcat's antijamming radar was twice as powerful as the F-15's, and said it was also attracted by the Phoenix missile.

A-10. On the Air Force side, an old mustang, Hellcat or Spitfire pilot looking for the equivalent of World War Two-type flying with today's sophistications would probably not be principally attracted by the new breed of fighters at all—flying, as they do, so fast that they may overtake their own munitions, while aiming their ordnance at an enemy they cannot see. The late General Brown, himself a former Liberator pilot, echoed this point in his final interview before he died. He told the author: "The new generation of pilots do fantastic work, but I still think that unless they get their kicks out of all the technical things, it isn't as much fun." A World War Two or Korean War pilot's first choice in the modern USAF inventory would probably be the A-10, the twin-engined, subsonic, relatively cheap ($4.3 million) plane of which the Air Force has ordered 733 copies.

Designed for army support, the A-10 has a top cruising speed of 368 knots and a never-exceed dive speed of 450. Fairchild experts say it should approach target at between 300 and 325 knots, or about Hellcat and Spitfire speed, and keep below 100 feet over the battlefield. (In early simulated combat training, however, the Air Force keeps its pilots above a 100-feet floor rather than below a 100-feet ceiling.) At forward-airstrip weights, the A-10 can land and take off in about 1,100 feet.

This is certainly not a beautiful plane; but it makes up for what it lacks in looks with the sort of tight-turn maneuverability—less than 1,000 feet of diameter at 150 knots, with flaps—which combat pilots had come to believe was a thing of the past. It also has an exceptional choice of armaments: up to 28 conventional, laser-guided or electro-optically guided bombs, along with laser-guided Maverick antitank missiles, concussion bombs, cluster bombs, retarded and incendiary bombs and flare launchers. Later models will have IIR, the "Imaging Infrared" sensor. But its main weapon is a seven-barrel, 30mm. Gatling gun projecting from its nose, capable of firing 1,350 rounds of armor-penetrating shells at two speeds—2,100 or 4,200 per minute—for a claimed strafing accuracy of 4 mils CEP (meaning 4 feet "Circular Error of Probability" for every 1,000 feet of distance from target). In all, it normally carries about 9,500 pounds of ordnance for a range of 250–300 miles with about two hours' "loitering time." This means that A-10s can hang close to the battle area, and be called in for swift strikes by army commanders. When maximum range is needed, the plane carries only 18 missiles and bombs, but for short ranges it can carry up to 8 tons of ordnance.

The plane was literally designed around the aluminum Gatling gun, made by General Electric, and the nosewheel is set several inches to right of nose center so that its retraction gear will leave room for the 21-foot gun, which fires depleted-uranium, nonradioactive rounds.

The contest for the Air Force contract began in 1970, with six firms competing. The Fairchild plane was finally chosen in 1973 over the semifinalist, the Northrop A-9, in the face of strong opposition from the Texas congressional delegation, which wanted to preserve the A-7—

which has no STOL (Short Take-Off and Landing) characteristics, could not accommodate the same big machine gun as the A-10 (although it could conceivably take the Oerlikon—Swiss—equivalent) and had only one seventh of the "loiter" time.

If a land war ever broke out in Europe, Allied soldiers would probably see more of the A-10 than of any other American aircraft. It is already based at Sembach, Leipheim and Ahlhorn in Germany, and Bentwater in England. Fairchild executives claim an A-10 could eliminate as many as eleven tanks in one sortie, using two-second bursts, or twenty-two stationary, unmanned, nonfiring tanks in a surprise attack, using one-second bursts; but the Air Force thinks about three to five tanks per sortie would be more likely—and eminently satisfactory—at least in Europe. Full delivery of the 733 planes was originally timed through fiscal 1982, but the Carter administration has rescheduled the program to take longer; the first 226 were built in 1977 and 1978.

Tactics worked out by test pilots call for targeting tanks at 6,500 feet (up to 12,000 feet for lightly armored vehicles, at some cost in accuracy) and pulling away 3,000 feet short of the quarry, instead of overflying the target, Vietnam style. The Maverick, a standoff weapon, of course allows for firing from greater distances. The shells for the Gatling gun look enormous beside those for normal 20mm. aviation guns, and a one-second burst sets the federal budget back $1,400. However, considering the A-10's effectiveness in tests against Soviet armor, this is cheap compared to the $21,600 cost of a Maverick, or the $24,800 for a Rockeye missile.

The pilot, perched well forward in a "bowsprit" cockpit, sits in a "bathtub" of armor plate which is 96 per cent titanium; in tests, the plate has survived direct hits from captured Shilka antiaircraft guns, a weapon which wrought havoc in Vietnam and on the Israeli Air Force in 1973. In the test, 839 rounds of Soviet API (Armor-Piercing Incendiary) and HEI (High-Explosive Incendiary) ammunition were used. There are as yet no foreign sales for the A-10, but a German expert has flatteringly called the plane a "flying panzer." The fuselage has only just over 3 square feet of "vulnerable area." The fuel, in a self-sealing, tear-resistant cell, encased in internal and void-filler foam, is said to survive explosion or fire aboard the aircraft.

The engines are extremely quiet: A Phantom can be heard 5 miles away, an A-10 only at a mile. Smokeless—because of an optimal fuel-air mixture and other refinements—and "very cold" by jet standards, A-10s are harder to track and offer less of a lure to heat-seeking missiles, while the aircraft's gray paint is designed to be as insensitive as possible to infrared sensors. As an added aspect of "survivability," the engines are 9 feet apart: By jettisoning remaining ordnance, a pilot can theoretically return home on one—flying "by wire" if all the hydraulics are gone. The twin tail is also rationalized by the fact that one of those is theoretically expendable too. Because of its large profile, it risks being hit more often than, say, the A-7; but its "survivability" is reckoned by pilots to be higher.

The plane pulls apart like a racing car, making repairs or cannibalization rapid in a "high attrition" war. It carries its own auxiliary power unit. In a 1977 test at Gila Bend, Arizona, two A-10s flew thirty-four sorties in eleven hours, delivering 35 tons of bombs and 3,610 Gatling shells. Some Air Force reports talk of eight-minute turnarounds, including reloading. The A-10 can take off from 2,000-feet unimproved strips—4,500 feet at maximum load. Pilots say they can attack with 1.25-mile visibility, under "200-foot ceilings." (For comparison, the A-4 Skyhawk which the A-10 will replace needs 3.5-mile visibility for combat.)

Even though the plane is as yet untested in war, all this is clearly a long way ahead of the performances of World War Two, when it took about twenty-five sorties per tank kill. It is also a vast improvement on the Mideast war of 1973, when few tanks on either side were hit from the air—and when Israeli air losses were eight times those of the USAF in Vietnam, for an equivalent density of air defense. But Fairchild and the Air Force have delved deeply into the only records of airmen against Soviet tanks—those of the Luftwaffe in the early forties—for guidance about Russian tactics. One expert consulted was the most-decorated soldier of the Third Reich, now sixty-two and living in Austria. He "killed" 519 Russian tanks in 2,500 sorties and was shot down about thirty times. His secret: His guns were synchronized to hit at 200 meters instead of the 400 meters of other Stukas, thus calling for a breathtaking, last-minute pullout.

The A-10, for which the full tab, including support costs, is $6.1 million, is primarily designed for the war in Europe: There, tanks would be the first Russian weapon of attack in any conventional war, and poor visibility usually rules out any but low-altitude attacks on armor. The A-10 will be combined with AAHs (Advanced Attack Helicopters): The choppers will "hide behind the trees" with their 20-magnification scopes and concentrate on taking out air defenses before the A-10s go in to kill the tanks. A later refinement to this type of warfare may involve replacing helicopters with side-firing short-takeoff-and-landing planes (the Thai Air Force now effectively uses ungainly, Swiss-designed Pilatus Porters). This would have an added advantage of reducing flying costs from a chopper's $180 of fuel per hour to about $20.

The formidable A-10 is easy to fly. Jet pilots talk of conversion taking "about twenty minutes," and the Air Force programs only three check rides for conversion. The plane will redress itself from a dive, hands off, in 5,000 feet. But combat training on the aircraft is arduous, and its tree-top-height combat zone will undoubtedly lead to a fairly high number of training accidents.

Two A-10s crashed in June 1977—one of them, with Fairchild's chief test pilot Sam Nelson at the controls, at the Paris Air Show. But by and large this is one of the Air Force's most successful programs. There have been no production delays. The 1978 models included FLIR (Forward-Looking Infrared) sensors, new electronic countermeasures and an iner-tial navigation system. Since that year, the A-10 has been deployed by the USAF in Britain, where it has been associated in exercises with Brit-ish, Canadian and Dutch attack helicopters. Some critical observers of these exercises have maintained that the A-10 may need a fighter escort, but the Administration plans to ask for 144 A-10s in the 1980 budget and 88 more the following year.

Meanwhile, General Dynamics, Vought, Northrop, Grumman and North American Rockwell are competing to produce, for the late eight-ies, a lighter, less sophisticated attack plane, provisionally called the Blitzfighter, for a flyaway cost of about $2 million.

AV-8. To the Marines, an aircraft which can take off vertically from any-thing solid—in forest warfare, from a 72-foot-square pad of aluminum matting—then zoom off at supersonic speed sounds like a dream. Brit-ain's AV-8—the $3.4 million Harrier "jump jet"—was the answer. Even with 3,000 pounds of ordnance it can do a jet-assisted (water-injection) takeoff in 800 feet. It has a self-starter like a light aircraft and therefore does not need the normal warplane's auxiliary power unit. In mock com-bat, as noted earlier, the Harrier has repeatedly "shot down" the F-14—something which the Marines' five squadrons of A-4s and twelve squad-rons of F-4s (which they seek to replace with 360 Advanced Harriers) reportedly could not do. The Harrier can avoid the dangers of loitering and refueling in the "NATO environment." It can be called in quickly by any infantry officer, without help from a forward air controller, from a "masked takeoff" in some nearby forest. Two Marine squadrons of the plane—40 aircraft—are now stationed at Cherry Point, North Carolina, while there are single squadrons at Yuma, Arizona, and Iwakuni, Japan; some are aboard the carrier *Roosevelt*.

But that an aircraft so unforgiving at transition—from horizontal to vertical flight, or vice versa—should cause a number of training accidents was inevitable; and that the larger services should object to the Marines having a plane of their own, instead of ordering price-reducing numbers of Navy planes, inevitably threatened the program even more. Accidents have indeed plagued the Harrier as the Corps has converted more and more pilots without helicopter experience. Screaming to a halt in 1,000 yards at treetop height, then setting the Harrier down on its two curious outrigger landing wheels takes considerable skill. It is probably the hardest plane to fly in the U.S. inventory, a fact of which its fliers are understandably proud—"AV-8-er, aviator!" was how one pilot at Cherry Point summed it up for the writer. But by late 1977, 26 of the Corps' 110 Harriers had crashed; 20 had been written off; 10 pilots had been killed. Flight or ordnance delivery at low level—200 feet in daytime, 1,000 feet at night—was canceled until further notice. Training in transition flying was increased from 17 to 31 hours, since 20 of the accidents have been attributed to pilot error (and another 2 to maintenance error). Pilots blamed their problems on deficiencies in the cockpit information-display system.

Captain W. O. Wirt, director of the rotary-wing aircraft-test directorate at the Naval Air Test Center at Patuxent River, Maryland, says transition and hover "in the inkwell environment of horizonless nights, on the open ocean, when you literally can't see the surface from 40 feet," is difficult, because of the absence of external references. "It is roughly akin to driving down the glidescope without benefit of airspeed, angle of attack or stall-warning information," he says. (The glidescope is the runway beacon which tells a landing pilot whether he is above or below the recommended angle of descent, while the angle of attack is the angle between the attitude of the wings and the aircraft's actual descent path.) General Brown, in his final interview, recalled his own experience of flying a twin-place Harrier in Britain with an RAF pilot: "I flew with a young fellow, and he didn't think a thing about going off in weather that would have me think twice about walking to the club. You know, you have a couple of hundred feet [cloud ceiling] and less than a quarter-mile visibility, and the nearest alternate field is 300 miles away." For many new Marine pilots, the Harrier has been a challenge. Yet in spite of all its problems—its radical originality, its accidents and its foreign parentage—it has survived and is now spawning a new generation of American offspring.

Currently under development is an AV-8B, a combined Hawker-Siddeley/McDonnell-Douglas program with an improved performance, delivering 4,000 pounds of ordnance over a range of 600 miles. The British, having decided on mini-carriers, are developing the Harrier as a STOVL (short-takeoff, vertical-landing) plane, mostly to save the high fuel expenditure of vertical lift-off. For this, the AV-8 does away with catapult equipment, taking off from a 9° "ski ramp" on the carrier's bow; a 20° ramp is envisaged for the future.

Secretary Brown still seems to have little faith in the concept, and he has sought a slowdown in V-STOL research and development for both the Navy and the Marines. However, the Marines' aviation commander, Lieutenant General Thomas H. Muller, Jr., has said that most battles "are decided in about thirty minutes" and that the AV-8 could reach the battle "faster than anything else we have." The Marines have asked for 90 of the $5.3 million AV-8Bs over the next five years, but Corps plans call for ultimately seeking 340–360 of them. The Bs are mostly American-built, but include Rolls-Royce engines and other British components. Now a Navy version of this aircraft, called the AV-8B+, is in research.

Other U.S. V-STOL planes on the drawing board or the company-strip runway—both for the Navy and the Marines—include the Rockwell International XFV-12A, a Mach-1.6 aircraft first tested in 1978; the same company's subsonic NA-420; the planning-stage Vought V-530, which will carry a variety of systems and even twenty-five Marine troops; and the McDonnell-Douglas still-undesignated "Type-A V-STOL." In the V-530, over half of which will be made of graphite epoxy, the engines do not tilt. In the McDonnell-Douglas plane, the nozzles alone will tilt down.

A Sikorsky entry for the contest takes off on rotary wings, helicopter style, then goes into level flight on ordinary jets. There are proposed Boeing and Grumman tilt-nacelle planes, a General Dynamics "lift wing" concept, a Boeing four-fan design. In the Grumman design, now in the flying-model stage, the two engines are "tied" so that the fan in a dead engine will continue to move. For NASA, Bell Helicopter is designing a tilt-rotor XV-15.

AAH. The Advanced Attack Helicopter, designed by Hughes, is now in development. Intended for close ground support and antitank missions, in all weathers and at night, the 180 mph, 365-mile-radius chopper costs $6.4 million per unit—and the whole program, potentially, $3.6 billion. The Army wants 536 of them, to come with three quarters of a ton of ordnance, including 16 TOW missiles and a 30mm. chain gun. The AAH is the aircraft sought to back up the A-10 and the AV-8 on the European battlefield.

LAMPS. Another important helicopter program is LAMPS (the Navy's Light Airborne Multi-Purpose System). LAMPS is essentially an antisubmarine aircraft which can be launched from destroyer pads. Boeing Vertol's Model 237, with fiberglass-epoxy rotor blades, beat Britain's Westland Lynx and a navalized version of the Sikorsky VH-60A, which had earlier won the Army's UTTAS (Utility Tactical Transport Aircraft System) contest, in a 1977 flyoff for the Navy contract.

LAMPS choppers lower sound-detecting devices into the ocean, data-linked to Illiac-4 computers which have "memorized" each Soviet submarine's "signature"—the sound of each sub's propeller, like each fingerprint, is different. The planes are also linked to the Sound Surveillance Under Sea (SOSUS) system, which consists of the earlier-mentioned submarine microphones called hydrophones, suspended in oil in drums on the ocean floor. Cross-checking between different hydrophones hearing the same enemy submarine enables U.S. defenses to calculate its position, speed and direction.

STOL Transports. Boeing and McDonnell-Douglas have built two different prototypes of a medium short-takeoff-and-landing transport (AMST), the Boeing YC-14, tested in 1977 on a dirt runway at Edwards Air Force Base in California, and the McDonnell-Douglas YC-15, which was tested at the Yuma Proving Grounds in Arizona. The Air Force, which chose between them in 1978, had called for a plane to carry such armor as the M-60 tank and the 29-ton self-propelling howitzer—plus, eventually, the XM-1 Main Battle Tank—into forward landing strips, landing and taking off with at least 27,000 pounds, over 50-foot obstacles, within 2,000 feet, if need be on only three of its four engines. Both contestants carried the load in and out of strips using only 1,000 feet, and both lifted 50,000-pound flatbed trucks. But finally, in 1978, the Air Force decided it needed 277 wider-bodied aircraft than the present YC-14 or YC-15, in order to accommodate a new "infantry fighting vehicle."

Control Planes

In modern air-to-air warfare, perhaps the most indispensable of all the new aircraft are the command and control planes which direct battles by radar and computer. For the moment, the most command and control in American airspace, at home and abroad, is done by the E-2C, or Hawkeye, a twin-engined turboprop, which costs $17.3 million, or $32.7 million with support items.

The Hawkeye is a sophisticated upgrading of an earlier craft called the Bravo. Its usual task would be to control three pairs of fighters. Those operating out of Oceana usually work with half a dozen F-14s, flying out over the Atlantic about 150 nautical miles to "station," then flying "grids" for up to four hours. Most practice flights are in fact shorter, since fatigue sets in after three hours.

The three officers who sit facing the three television-screen display units have one of the most demanding tasks in modern warfare. They are data-linked both to the aircraft under their control and to a ground computer, by ultra-high-frequency radio.

In the center sits the combat information center officer; to his left is the air control officer, who actually directs the interceptors, while on his right is the radar officer, who is mainly responsible for maritime surveillance.

Aircraft and ships appear on the display screens in the form of blips. In the symbology of the screen, a "raw return" appears as a line, curving slightly at the ends and known to Hawkeye controllers as a "banana." A light-pen is used to illuminate the banana and to provoke an IFF "squawk" from the "unknown"—ship or plane. A starlike flash then appears around a dot on the screen. The black box in friendly aircraft or ships, its pulse train coded to the code of the day, then signals back. The ship or plane, by its own systems, knows that it has been challenged. A correct response puts a slash across the blip. Inability to respond— theoretically indicating a foe—means that no slash appears; but by then the "banana" has taken on more meaningful shape: By radar, an unknown ship appears on the screen as a hollow square, while an unidentified aircraft is a square with the bottom line missing. If the challenge is by IFF, a ship appears as a square with its upper right and lower left corners missing, while a plane is simply the top left corner of a square.

A friendly squawk on the IFF transponder would give a different blip. A friendly aircraft becomes a dot with the top half of a circle above it. A friendly surface ship is a full circle with a dot in the middle. A friendly submarine is a dot with the lower half of a circle around it. A hostile plane appears as a dot capped by the top half of a hollow diamond. A ship is a whole diamond with a dot, a sub the lower half of a diamond with a dot.

The Hawkeye uses four or five different detection systems: the APS-120 radar with ARPS (Advanced Radar Processing System) is most effective over water, covering ships and larger planes for 250 nautical miles, and smaller aircraft for 150. The new APS-125 radar now being fitted will be effective over land, using electronic countermeasures to operate in "jamming environments." At sea, the 125 will even pick up missiles. The other three detectors are the APX-76 IFF transponder, the ALQ-108 IFF, and the ALR-59 Passive Detection System. The new and highly sensitive 108 is still classified, largely because the Soviet Union has no equivalent.

The information from these systems goes to a central computer which feeds it to the display units. Since targeting an invisible enemy obviously depends on the position of the attacking aircraft, the computer is also "fed" by positioning information from the aircraft's own inertial navigation unit. A radar director processor interprets returned pulses from ships and planes and informs the computer, which is data-linked to an "electronic brain" called a Link-11. It is the Link-11 which then refers the information back to the computer, which transforms it into ultra-high-frequency (UHF) or high-frequency (HF) tones for transmittal to the E-2, which receives on five UHF and two HF frequencies. The computer then figures out which is the best target for each aircraft and which missile to employ.

The computer identifies, say, a MiG-23 from two distinguishing characteristics—its radar profile and its emitter; it then also produces from its memory the types of armament normally carried by such a plane. If more than one "bogey"—enemy aircraft—has the same emitter, and two of these have similar profiles, the computer will respond with two identifications. All this information, including the ranges of the "bogey's" guns and missiles, is given to the pilot of the interceptor. The whole operation of identifying the craft as hostile, specifying the type of ship or plane involved, describing its weapons and their ranges and recommending which friendly aircraft and which missile should be used to destroy it is all accomplished in a matter of seconds. Some of the operations take only a microsecond.

The controller in the E-2 virtually supervises the battle and directs the aircraft to "destroy." Picking up blips ("signal watch") is entirely computer-controlled, but emitter identification and "platform" identification are operator-assisted where necessary. The "associated weapons display" comes solely from the computer's memory. The system has data-processing capacity for three hundred "active tracks"—aircraft or ships whose movements are followed constantly—and airmen at Oceana say that over the European and Mediterranean theaters such a forest of blips is not abnormal.

"It's assumed," says an E-2 instructor, "that in the event of war the Russians would attack all our carrier task forces at once and try to sink all the carriers. In such a scenario, we would have three hundred active tracks on our screens for sure."

A weakness in the system has been that, in past exercises, the aircraft simulating "hostiles" have been uncontrolled, therefore at a clear disadvantage. But in 1978, Hawkeyes were beginning to be used to simulate the role of Russia's Ilyushin-112s, making the conflicts more realistic. The U. S. Navy is seeking six E-2Cs a year through 1984.

Gradually superseding the E-2C will be the E-3A, the Air Force's Airborne Warning and Control System (AWACS). This is a Boeing 707 topped by a black and white radar rotodome similar to that of the Hawkeye. The rotodome turns at six revolutions a minute. The big unarmed ship is now entering squadron service: Five arrived in 1977, three in 1978; the Air Force is taking delivery of four more in 1979, and expects three a year thereafter—it may get more because of Iranian cancellations. The AWACS carries computers with 1,410,000-word memories: They can perform up to 740,000 operations a second. There is a crew of seventeen. The plane does long-range (five hours, 2,300-mile) all-weather surveillance of virtually everything large enough that flies within its compass. The nine multi-purpose consoles and two auxiliary display units can be "configured" for surveillance, weapons-direction or battle-staff roles.

The E-3A AWACS, like the Hawkeye, tracks hostile targets and provides overall air control for friendly forces. Its Westinghouse look-down doppler radar sensor has, as yet, no equivalent anywhere in the world, and could be as important to the United States in a war today as was Britain's possession of radar in 1939. The E-3A can detect, track and identify aircraft above and below the radar horizon, and locate electronic countermeasures. The Air Force has ordered thirty-four of these $118.8 million aircraft, with over half of the total $4.1 billion program expenditure going for R & D.

In a November 1976 test at Nellis, an E-3A controlled a force of 132 other "friendly" aircraft—Air Force, Navy, Air National Guard and Air Force Reserve, from 21 bases in 9 states—and it was later claimed that it had successfully enabled them to dominate 274 F-5s flying as MiG-21s. The AWACS "saw" 250,000 square miles—3 million cubic miles—of airspace. None of the "Russian" planes, it was claimed, had succeeded in locating the AWACS aircraft. In another operation code-named Vigilant Overview, an E-3A functioned as the command and control system for the continental United States. Major General Lawrence A. Skantze, the AWACS program officer, claims the plane "equaled or exceeded expectations." Over some parts of North America, E-3As will have mixed U.S.-Canadian crews. But, as will be noted in later chapters, the airplane is not without its critics. Eventually, satellites controlled from the ground seem likely to take over from airborne control planes.

A related aircraft is the E-4B "kneecap," mentioned in the opening anecdote of this chapter—a conversion from the earlier E-4A. Although Carter spoke disparagingly of the $190 million aircraft after flying in one in early 1977, the following year he increased the government's order from four of the planes to six, for delivery in 1980 and 1981. The E-4Bs will replace seventeen of the smaller EC-135 planes currently still in use as airborne command posts.

In a manned-aircraft equivalent of electronic warfare, Grumman is modifying a General Dynamics F-111A airframe to develop the EF-111A —a "multipurpose tactical airborne jamming system." The plane will screen friendly aircraft routes and maneuvers from hostile radars, or will escort bombers or strike aircraft on penetration raids, jamming enemy defense radars. Colonel James McKenna, director of the EF-111A program at Wright-Patterson Air Force Base at Dayton, says the aircraft's systems will counter all known early-warning, height-finder, ground-control intercept and acquisition radars. The plane's development program was expected to be completed in 1979.

Future Tactical Aircraft. The aircraft of the new generation are mostly wonders of titanium. But tactical aircraft of the future are likely to be built, not of metals, but of composites. Parts of the tail assembly of the F-14 and the F-15 are of composite, as is most of the huge brown stabilizer of the B-1. This stabilizer, built by Grumman, weighs 2,000 pounds instead of the 2,500 pounds which it would have weighed if built in aluminum. Grumman's Mike Pehalac says bluntly: "Aircraft of the future will just not be made of metal."

The main present composites are carbons like graphite-epoxy and boron-epoxy. (Epoxy is a kind of resin.) Cheaper composites of the future will include fibers of silicone carbide or aluminum oxide. Tungsten wire in the composite gives the "grain," pointed in the direction taking the most stress. Composites are not only lighter than aluminum; they are also 25 per cent stronger (and 80 per cent lighter) than steel. Boron gives greater strength than graphite but is more expensive: Where virtually no strength is needed—on the leading edge of wings, for example—aircraft of the present already use fiberglass.

Planes of the future will not only be much lighter but also smaller. Militarily, they will therefore have a usefully smaller antiaircraft silhouette. There has even been a comeback of the "flying wing" of the nineteen forties—an aircraft with no distinguishable body. Wings carried well back behind the center of a fuselage may eliminate horizontal tail stabilizers altogether. The Grumman V-STOL prototype, for instance, has such wings and no tail stabilizer. Even the biplane design is back: Some American aircraft now on the drawing board have "canard" wings forward of a main delta wing—like Sweden's already existing Viggen.

All this means research, and research means expense. By the late eighties, it is thought, most major new tactical and strategic aircraft systems will be the product of international consortia, and built for guaranteed international markets.

TACTICAL WEAPONS SYSTEMS

Backing up strategic land-based weaponry are the tactical or "theater" nuclear armaments—the shorter-range missiles and their platforms, and a panorama of nuclear artillery. By late 1977, there were well over 22,000 U.S. "tac-nukes" in the world, including about 11,000 in the United States, 7,000 in Europe, at least 2,500 aboard warships and submarines, and 1,700 in Asia—Korea, Taiwan and the Philippines.

So vast is the number of theater nuclear arms (confined to a single theater of war, such as Europe or the Middle East) that literally hundreds of thousands of Americans, allies, friends—and, of course, enemies—are authorized to handle them. Some of the "tacticals" are so nearly "strategic" as to make little difference. Pershing missiles, for instance, as part of the forward system in Europe, are short-range by definition but could hit the Soviet Union with more power than a "strategic" Poseidon.

Significant in the tactical armory are such nuclear-tipped weapons as the following: the Army's Lance surface-to-air missile, which has a 50-kiloton clout, a 70-mile range, is located in the United States and Europe, and developmental versions of which have neutron and conventional warheads; the Pershing surface-to-surface missile (SSM), which packs 400 kilotons, flies for 450 miles and is located in the United States and Germany; the Honest John surface-to-air missile (SAM—100 kilotons, 25-mile range, stationed in the United States and, for the time being, in Korea; the Sergeant SSM, a NATO weapon now being phased out—100 kilotons, 85-mile range; the Nike-Hercules SAM—5 kilotons, 80-mile range, in place in Korea and Europe and destined to be replaced by a more accurate missile called the Patriot; nuclear howitzers of 115mm. and 203mm. caliber (in the United States, Korea and NATO countries); and Atomic Destruction Munitions (ADMs) of 1 kiloton or less.

The Navy has an estimated one hundred air-to-surface (ASM) or air-to-air (AAM) missiles with tactical nuclear warheads aboard each of its thirteen carriers; yields vary from 1 megaton down to 10 kilotons, the ranges from 400 to 1,100 miles. The Navy also has nuclear depth charges of 1 to 5 kilotons. The Air Force has nuclear air-to-air and air-to-surface weapons.

At least 2,250 NATO tactical aircraft, missile launchers, cannons and land mines are stationed in Western Europe, with a total explosive impact of 460 million tons of TNT, or 35,000 "Hiroshimas," even though there are not enough launchers for all the missiles. These weapons, distributed among Germany, Britain, Italy, Turkey, Greece and Holland, do not include France's own homemade, tactical-nuclear force. Across the glacis are at least 3,500 Soviet tactical nukes, reportedly capable of inflicting 100 million casualties.

All these weapons are theoretically intended to fight "tactical" war—but, as noted earlier, few U.S. strategists believe that a war could be kept limited in this way. So they are essentially first weapons of attack. Since a tactical onslaught of the ferocity which these tonnages suggest would disrupt communications, the resultant uncertainty and fear would probably lead to an early escalation to "strategic" levels. Their existence also poses what Barry Schneider of the CDI calls "peace-time safety dilemmas." Schneider lists such possible dangers as seizure of nukes by allies (for instance, during a coup d'état), "unauthorized" use by a military maverick with official access to the weapons, use by "terrorists" and nuclear accidents. This problem is looked at in the following chapter, on arms control.

One tactical nuclear weapon has attracted especial interest.

On June 6, 1977, veteran investigative reporter Walter Pincus launched a news story in the Washington *Post* that probably stirred up Congress more than anything that year except the Tong Sun Park investigation, yet left people wondering later whether it had all been a nuclear firestorm in a teacup. But the debate offered a chilling glimpse of what "tactical" battlefields might be like for those on the scene.

The story was that the United States was about to begin production of "enhanced-radiation" warheads for 70-mile-range Lance missiles. Later stories showed that similar "tips" were also being built for 8-inch artillery shells, while an air-to-surface version was under consideration.

The enhanced-radiation warhead releases neutrons instead of gamma rays, causing greater radiation of humans and animals but considerably less damage to structures and tanks because it causes less blast and fire. The result of ten years' advanced research, the "neutron" warheads are said to be the only tactical weapon able to kill crews in the new, "hardened" Soviet tanks; they also give shells increased range, have an internal security system missing in nukes and can be loaded and fired more quickly.

It subsequently transpired that at least $10 million for neutron bombs, as the press soon called them (including $650,000 for the neutron shells), was hidden within a $1,466,000,000 nuclear-weapons budget, itself concealed within the $6 billion budget of the Energy Research and Development Agency (ERDA), now part of the Department of Energy. This in turn was part of a $10.2 billion public-works appropriation for 1978, approved by President Ford but re-examined by Congress when it was resubmitted by Carter. (All U.S. nuclear warheads were developed by ERDA and its predecessor agencies.)

Other items in the nuclear-warhead budget were the Mark 12A, mentioned earlier, a delayed-action "full-fuzing option bomb" (FUZO) that allows a low-flying delivery plane to get away from the area after dropping its load, a nuclear warhead for cruise missiles, the warhead for the Trident-II and new warheads for the Harpoon and the Pershing-II. But it was the "neutron bomb" that stirred up Congress and the print media.

Initial work on neutron weaponry began in the late fifties at the University of California's Lawrence Livermore laboratories at Livermore. The work continued while Harold Brown, the present Defense Secretary, was director of the facility, 1960–61. An earlier W-63 enhanced-radiation warhead was replaced by the W-70 Model 3—the model for which funds were sought by Carter, and subsequently approved by Congress. Several classified reports had been supplied to Congress over the years about the weapons.

An Atomic Energy Commission report, for example, had explained exactly what heavy doses of neutrons do to the central nervous system. Either immediately or later, the victims become incapacitated, with spasms and lack of muscle coordination. Death may come at once or take several days. An Army source gave reporters more details, based on tests on monkeys in Nevada. A 1-kiloton neutron missile warhead or artillery projectile would deliver 8,000 "rads" of radiation within about a half-mile radius of the explosion (which takes place aboveground). All living beings within that radius would probably be incapacitated within five minutes and dead within two days.

On the fringes of the half-mile area, radiation would fall off quickly. A dose of 3,000 rads, however, would also incapacitate within five minutes. Then the victims would recover for several minutes—perhaps an hour—then relapse, dying four to six days later after spasms of vomiting, diarrhea and radiation pains. At three quarters of a mile from the point of aerial explosion, only about 650 rads would remain. Incapacitation would take as long as two hours to develop. Some victims would recover, but most would die within a few weeks.

Defense Nuclear Agency (DNA) sources, noting that these figures were for a 1-kiloton radiation shell—less than half the power likely to be used—estimated that a dose of 300 to 450 rads would be delivered about a mile from ground zero. This would be enough to kill about half the persons in the area within two to three months. Persons inside houses might get only 150 rads, but 10 per cent of these would die also. In basements, the dose would fall to 30 or 40 rads, but leukemia and other cancers might develop later in people suffering even this dose. Studies of Marshall Islanders exposed to 14 rads by a nearby hydrogen-bomb test in 1954 show a high incidence of thyroid and other cancers two decades later, while leukemia has occurred in soldiers accidentally exposed to such "low" doses. (A dental X-ray, for comparison, exposes the patient to about 1 rad of radiation.)

With ten times more killing effect on people than a nuclear warhead ten times more powerful—and with ten times less fallout, blast and heat —the weapon is seen by the Pentagon as "getting" enemy tank crews while limiting damage to civilian structures in such potential battlefields of the future as Germany. This is a sensitive subject: Secret NATO orders forbid the use of warheads of over 10 kilotons in Western Europe itself, or above 1 kiloton in West European cities and towns. In Germany, as one expert put it to the author, "the towns are only 2 kilotons apart."

The "neutron bomb" would also, because of its confined impact, and in spite of its greater lethality within the confined area, kill fewer people overall than "ordinary" nuclear weapons. Because of the relatively limited fallout, killing would be more restricted to the military, less to civilians, and—the Pentagon notes—postwar rebuilding problems would be reduced. Proponents also argue that enhanced-radiation warheads could be used as "tac-nukes" with less of the usual fear of escalation to strategic warfare. The radiation would disperse quickly, enabling occupation of the area by "friendly forces" only twenty-four hours later. The Pentagon, which had sought to keep the weapon secret, suggested that its surprise use would catch the Russians unawares and put them back "20 years" in preparing a response.

In two Senate sessions, the first closed, the second open, Republican senator Mark Hatfield of Oregon led opposition to funding the weapon. Hatfield argued that because the neutron weapons would be more accurate, commanders would be more tempted to use them. Leading the administration forces, Chairman John Stennis of the Senate Armed Services

Committee said because it was more accurate, it was a cleaner weapon. Senator Sam Nunn of Georgia said that because it was more likely to be used than a nuclear warhead, it was a more credible deterrent.

The White House declared first that neither Carter nor Defense Secretary Harold Brown had known that funding for the weapon was in the public works budget until they read Pincus' story. Carter asked for funds to be approved, but said he would reserve judgment until later as to whether to use them, hinting that actual deployment of the weapon could become a bargaining chip in SALT—a chip which might be canceled if Moscow canceled deployment of its considerably more lethal SS-20 missile. Congress agreed, but insisted on an impact statement regarding the Lance neutron warhead—the most powerful "neutron bomb" proposed.

Congressional Quarterly Weekly Reports summed up the debate:

> Is a Russian attack on Western Europe better deterred by terror or by tactical efficiency? . . .
> The basic premise of Pentagon strategists has been that a Soviet attack is deterred by the threat of weapons that could be employed by U.S. troops without causing so much damage as to destroy West Germany in order to save it.

Essentially, the neutron bomb was a development of Kennedy's "flexible response" strategy, a reaction to the "massive retaliation" philosophy of John Foster Dulles. News of the development of this relatively old weapon raised predictable opposition in the Soviet Union. It was also opposed by the U. S. Arms Control and Disarmament Agency. The Washington *Post* editorialized against it twice. In a feature article in the *Post*, Alton Frye of the Council on Foreign Relations raised the specter of "walking corpses," in their last hours of lucidity, taking wildly vengeful measures with whatever Soviet weapons were at hand. What Frye failed to point out is that this would be true in any scenario using nuclear weapons, not just "neutron bombs." Most NATO countries cautiously welcomed the enhanced-radiation warhead—albeit with some criticism from West Germany's Social-Democrat opposition and from some other left-wing European parties, which called the weapon "inhuman." By 1978, after the NATO Council condoned the weapon, it was learned that France had developed its own neutron bomb.

Amendments to delay U.S. production were twice defeated by 3-1 majorities in the House, in 1977 and 1978, and the Senate also voted to pursue the program. The President continued, however, to hold up his decision on whether to use the funds voted—although not to do so would probably run up against the "impoundment" measure passed by the 93rd Congress to restrain former President Nixon. In April 1978, Carter said production would not start if Moscow showed "arms restraint," but declined to be specific.

That year, Carter won congressional approval for a "blast bomb" with almost exactly the opposite characteristics of the "neutron bomb." This RRR (Reduced Residual Radiation) weapon destroys buildings and topples small mountains; it would replace the present Atomic Destruction Munitions (ADMs), but with a minimum of fallout and irradiation of the soil. Energy Department experts called it a "clean bomb." Congress also approved funds for the B77, a new nuclear bomb to be carried by strategic penetrating bombers.

Another interesting horror which was in the inventory until recently was the "Daisy Cutter" or "Cheeseburger" of Vietnam fame—the concussion bomb which hit the front pages in 1977 when President Carter twice turned down Israeli requests to add this monster to the Mideast arms race. This is not a nuclear weapon, although the difference is slight. The Vietnam War model, later improved, was the BLU-82/B—11 feet long, 4.5 feet wide, weighing 7.5 tons, and containing over 6 tons of a "gelled aqueous slurry of ammonium nitrate and aluminum powder" with a binding agent. Only a nuclear blast is more powerful, and its explosion sends a mushroom cloud into the sky for 6,000 feet. Light planes as much as 2 miles away have been tipped over in flight by the concussion waves. Floated to the ground by parachute, it is impacted by a 3-foot probe which touches the ground first, exploding the bomb just above the surface, crushing bodies and everything else within a 50-feet perimeter. Then, as air—including the air in people's lungs—rushes in to fill the vacuum within the perimeter, bodies literally explode. All living things, including worms in the ground, are killed for a 775-acre area. Most living things are killed over an area two and a half times as big. It usually leaves no crater, but clears everything animal or vegetable within the impact area. Originally intended to clear helicopter landing sites and minefields, it was used against gun positions and eventually against troops. A 1972 Army film graphically describes the bomb's effects; its use in Vietnam led to international protests. Remaining U.S. stocks of the bomb were destroyed in late 1978 after ten of them exploded mysteriously at a Sierra, California, Army depot, causing $500,000 of damage but no injuries.

Writing in the Baltimore *Sun*, retired general Arthur S. Collins, Jr., a former deputy commander of the U. S. Army in Europe, expressed a cynical view of nuclear restraint:

Ask any U.S. commander what he would do if his units were hit by a few small nuclear weapons. The response would be a request for all the nuclear firepower he could get. Are the Russians likely to be more restrained in similar circumstances?

But in an article in *Retired Officer* magazine, Colonel E. Asa Bates, formerly of the Joint Chiefs staff, wondered whether tactical nuclear or neutron weapons could ever be used by the United States in any case. He wrote:

U.S. Army Field Manual 100-5, published in July 1976, provides a hypothetical chart which shows that it might take up to twenty-four hours to convey the request and release up and down the chain of command to fire a nuclear package of missiles and cannon.

Colonel Bates' point, of course, was that in twenty-four hours the war might already be won by an enemy pre-emptive attack.

CONVENTIONAL WEAPONS

Precision-guided munitions (PGMs) or "smart" weapons have revolutionized the nonnuclear battlefield as well. With the Soviet Union and its allies exceeding NATO in tanks by over four to one, and by 19,000 artillery barrels to about 5,000—and by sheer weight of numbers in the armed forces—quality and efficiency are the key elements in the American conventional armory. By 1978, the United States had 4,000 M-1 tanks and 3,000 new armored personnel carriers on order; but these are easily outmatched, in numbers, by current Soviet production: The United States thus expects—or hopes—that it would win any conflict on the basis of superior technology, and that this gives the West the edge in its weapons diplomacy with Moscow.

In 1972, F-4s destroyed the Thanh Hoa and Paul-Doumer bridges near Hanoi despite cloud cover and massive defenses, thereby launching the era of PGMs. A year later, Egypt destroyed Israel's 190th Armored Brigade in two hours with wireguided Soviet antitank missiles whose NATO code name is Sagger, while Syria cleaned the skies of most hostile aircraft with Soviet SAM-6s. Since then, neither the United States, the Soviet Union nor their allies and friends have looked back.

Major "conventional" missiles in the American armory include the already mentioned Maverick air-to-surface missile with its television-camera nose, and the Hawk surface-to-air missile, which can hit aircraft up to 50,000 feet: Over two thousand of the latter had been sold to Iran, Israel and Jordan by the time this book was written. Also a factor in the

Mideast is the portable Redeye SAM—now being replaced in the United States itself by the Stinger, which incorporates IFF (Identification Friend or Foe) technology, thus enabling it to take evasive measures when it is in danger of being shot down. Other important elements in America's SAM arsenal are the Chaparral and the French- and German-designed Roland, along with the Vulcan antiaircraft gun.

These are just a few of the stars of "smart" technology. The Navy's Harpoon cruise missile continually shifts radar frequencies to avoid jamming. The Russians have similar if less developed capabilities and the technology is spreading. The German Kormoran air-to-sea missile shifts from radar to infrared seekers, while Israel's less sophisticated Gabriel naval missile shifts from radar to television.

Nonnuclear air-to-air missiles (AAMs), most of them now incorporating precision-guided technology, include the Phoenix and the Seek Bat, made by Hughes for the Grumman F-14 Tomcat and destined to shoot down the high-flying MiG-25 Foxbat. The United States now has 1,500 Phoenixes in service and, before the 1978 turmoil, had sold Iran 600 and taken orders for 400 more. The radar-guided Sidewinder air-to-air missile is now being replaced by the Super-Sidewinder AIM-9L, which has a "fire and forget" capacity—the target can be dropped from the sights once the missile is fired. A similar active-radar-seeker is found on the AIM-7F Sparrow, made by Raytheon for the F-15 Eagle and the F-18, and which may be adapted for the F-16, the F-18L and the F-5 now in service in a score of countries. Other current AAMs include the Navy's Brazo and Agile and the Air Force's Falcon and Genie.

Antitank missiles (ATMs) like the Dragon and the wireguided TOW are giving way gradually to the Rockwell International Hellfire—fired, as the name indicates, from a helicopter, and with a "fire and forget" capacity: The target is held by a laser beam from the air or the ground. Nevertheless, the TOW—a 54-pound launcher that can be set up by two men and be ready to fire in less than a minute—is still a key weapon, hitting targets 2 miles away in fifteen seconds. The TOW, which receives targeting signals through its wires, had about 90 per cent accuracy in Vietnam and has since improved. In 1973, the Israelis claimed a 100 per cent "kill ratio" for the weapon.

The U.S. inventory also includes many other "smart" SSMs, ATMs, ShShMs (Ship-to-Ship Missiles), SAMs, SSubMs (Surface-to-Subsurface Missiles), ASMs and AAMs, plus rockets, torpedoes, guns and other "smart" weaponry.

Smart weapons are, of course, prime targets for other smart weapons or for massed fire of any sort, so a crucial technology to develop has been remote firing. Earlier weapons were guided by a "designator"—a precision-guided artilleryman—from the positions whence they were fired. This is true of both early U.S. weapons and of the Sagger. The British Swingfire was the first successful PGM to separate the designator from the missile, which flies the final part of its course on its own, guided by its infrared sensors. Similarly, the American artillery shell called Copperhead rides its own laser beam to target.

Just as inertial-guidance navigation has left airline pilots with a lot less to do than in the past, so PGMs may eventually make the bomber, the tank or the large surface ship redundant. The multilateral environment which serves such a weapon also poses administrative and budget problems. Arthur T. Hadley, then of *New Times* magazine, put it rather well:

> Who pays for the following? A missile that is fired from the ground, guided through the atmosphere by a combination of radio command and magnetic homing, its target a ship that has been located by a combination of satellite photography and long-range aircraft infrared search. Who funds the development of that damn thing? . . . Who is going to pay for the satellite, which has other functions? Who will interpret the pictures and order up the tracking aircraft? And who decide to fire that portion of the nation's wealth at that particular target, perhaps at a time when a great many other deadly targets are presenting themselves with extreme rapidity?

Some of the most significant new weapons are so cheap and so relatively simple that newspapers never mention them. For instance, weapons to distract enemy defenses, such as the so-called Northrop "low-cost expendable harassment vehicle," a 10-foot-wingspan model plane with a 10-horsepower gasoline engine which can fly at 160 knots and reach 5,500 feet. Intended to be released in large numbers to bewilder enemy radar, only its weight—89 pounds—reveals that it is no ordinary model plane.

The Navy is studying the possibility of a ship-launched, remotely piloted plane that would carry an aerial torpedo. Indeed, remotely piloted planes—or vehicles (RPVs), as the military calls them—have come into their own. One of the most sophisticated is Boeing's Compass Cope, built for the Air Force. The handsome, twin-finned bird is an all-weather battlefield support weapon, small enough to be hard to track itself, which can reconnoiter, photograph, track and target tank columns. Launched and recovered from outside the battlefield area, it uses sophisticated high-altitude sensors. It is flown, through a satellite link, by a pilot sitting on the ground, but is capable of automated takeoffs and landings, with the pilot only "getting in the loop when and if something goes wrong," says Donald Jacobs, the program manager for the "vehicle."

Operating at an average altitude of 60,000 feet, outside Europe's dense commercial traffic, it has already performed "strategic reconnaissance."

In war, it could penetrate 250 miles beyond the Allied front lines—well into East Germany, Czechoslovakia and even Poland. With Western Europe under cloud cover 83 per cent of the time, the Compass Cope flies above the weather and pierces the clouds with its "imaging" radar. Its long-range oblique photography would be used to assess damage from Allied missiles. Equipped with multi-channel, single-frequency repeater equipment, the Compass Cope RPV would be the communications link between command and forces when these are separated by vast distances, such as in the Pacific Ocean. Its commonest task would probably be passing target data to the TV screen of a close-support aircraft such as the A-10. Middle East experts note that one reason for the success of the 1973 attack on Israeli-occupied territories was Syria's ability to move two thousand tanks on to the Golan Heights undetected in night fog: Now Egypt has ordered American RPVs.

New refinements on the vehicle-plane will include a small turbofan engine in the nacelle as an emergency power unit. In case of failure of the main power plant—either the Williams engine that drives the air-launched cruise missile or the Teledyne engine of the Harpoon missile—the emergency engine would be cartridge-started, permitting an air-restart on the main engine. Should this still fail, the emergency unit alone would bring the Compass Cope home for up to one hour of flight.

A dual-digit flight-control system and dual automatic takeoff and landing systems will be incorporated through the Air Force's tactical microwave landing gadget, permitting "day and night, all-weather landings in zero-zero conditions," Boeing says. Test flights of this little marvel were suspended in 1977 because research on some of the sensors which it will carry had fallen behind.

In 1979, another RPV under development was a 75-foot-span inflated-wing, with an air-pressure regulator for altitudes; the craft, which could be folded and stored aboard ships, would float if ditched. Intended for ocean surveillance or as a harassment drone, its fabric wing was said to be virtually invisible to radar.

Other RPVs will, like the cruise missile, carry weapons. *Aviation Week* editor Robert Hotz wrote in 1979:

> With the addition of outboard microprocessors to both the vehicle and its munitions and with the introduction of new warhead technology into its munitions, the non-piloted vehicle is finally ready to fulfill its promise as a relatively low-cost, devastating battlefield weapon against key hardened targets.

The fiscal-1979 defense budget included about $12 billion for R, D, T & E (research, development, test and evaluation), about 36 per cent of this sum being for tactical weaponry, compared to 20 per cent for strategic systems—and 21 per cent for theory, management, support and intelligence/communications programs. The Air Force gets the lion's share of R, D, T & E with $4.2 billion or 35 per cent.

The research dollar stresses two main areas—defensive and warning systems, and technologies that synergistically increase force effectiveness. The Directorate of Defense Research and Engineering says it is notably emphasizing research into "beam weapons, lasers and spaceborne sensors," of which more later. Beam weapons are an extension into the weapons field of the linear-accelerator technology of nuclear power plants. Much current work is also directed to finding ways of attacking MIRV-ed enemy ICBMs with tactical or conventional artillery before the separate warheads in the "bus" have left the vehicle.

On the offensive side, concern with the much-improved Soviet ballistic missile defenses has led to research in the area of Maneuverable Re-entry Vehicles (MARVs) and development of the GBU-15 air-to-surface weapon, the "guided flying bomb," with mid-course and terminal guidance options that include television, imaging infrared, laser and DME (distance-measuring equipment). The Navy is developing, for joint service use, the High-Speed Anti-Radiation Missile (HARM).

DARPA is looking into the future of what its spokesmen call "really smart" weapons. In 1977, the Agency's director, Dr. George Heilmeier, told *Air Force* magazine:

> Current smart weapons mostly require clear weather and a man in the loop, vulnerable to counter-action, to accomplish their mission. Ponder the consequences of weapons that seek out and destroy specific targets such as tanks and surface-to-air missile sites without the need for a designator; weapons that can wait for their specific targets to appear; weapons so accurate that conventional warheads could perform some of the tasks reserved today for nuclear weapons.

There is a program, also, to develop the capability to detect aircraft over long range, using only "passive means," thus eliminating the masking effects of countermeasures, while "sanctuary radar" technology should lead to a long-range air-defense radar that does not reveal its presence to approaching enemy aircraft and therefore can be neither jammed nor attacked.

Many of the new systems involve the use of satellites, and the increased importance of the National Reconnaissance Office—which operates satellites and SR-71 aircraft—has led to a major tussle over its control; but the Pentagon, backed by Secretary Brown, national security adviser Zbigniew Brzezinski and, at the time, Budget Director Bert

Lance, retained the reins in a 1977 conflict with CIA Director Stansfield Turner.

The principal "conventional" weapon remains the tank, which is the weapon in which the Russians have invested even more of their trust than they have in aerospace. The U.S. answer to Moscow's T-72 is the XM-1.

Some observers see tanks as obsolete, or nearly so: They point especially to the devastation of Israeli armor by Syria and Egypt in 1973. But if the Russians still believe heavily in the tank—less massively, perhaps, than prior to 1973, but still heavily—the West has little choice but to follow suit.

XM-1. The Chrysler XM-1 (Experimental Main Battle Tank-1) is still highly classified—production models are not due to emerge until 1980. Squat, ugly and usually covered in mud, the "Abrams" attracts less public attention than the beautiful weapons of the skies; but if "conventional" war occurred, any single combat aircraft type in the U.S. inventory might well be more expendable than the Abrams tank.

The XM-1, at $1.5 million per copy, is the most expensive piece of automotive equipment ever devised. The Army order of 7,058 of them will cost (without overruns) $10.4 billion in 1978 dollars over ten years—half of it for R & D. The Abrams will enable a new generation of crews to train at the Fort Knox armored school in Kentucky in the sort of nighttime, blitzkrieg warfare designed by the Kremlin for the conquest of Western Europe, if the test ever comes. Martin R. Hoffman, Army secretary in the Ford administration, told a press conference that the 58-ton, 50 mph Abrams would be "two to two and a half times more effective than the present U.S. battle tank, the M-60." A laser beam and computer will guide its 105mm. gun, and later a 120mm. model. The tank will also have the new Copperhead antitank laser-guided missile.

The contest to produce a U.S. challenger to Russia's T-72 lasted two years. At one point, GM was announced the winner, but a contract was finally awarded to Chrysler, in November 1976, for the tank which is to be named after the former Army chief of staff. Chrysler was awarded $196.2 million to build eleven more prototypes over three years at Warren, Michigan; the rest will emerge from the production lines at Warren and Lima, Ohio.

Competition for Chrysler and GM had come from West Germany, whose Leopard-II tank was admitted by U.S. testers at the Aberdeen proving grounds to be in the same class as the Abrams. For nationalist reasons, both sides of the Atlantic built their own tank, but the Abrams will eventually incorporate the larger German gun—requiring a larger turret—and German tracks. The shells from the German gun will travel a mile a second and penetrate 15 inches of armor. The gun's thermosight permits fire both at night and in fog. It will be armored by a new laminated British steel, known as Chobham steel, after its place of invention. This is divided by air pockets, and was said in 1978 to be able to resist every antitank missile then existing. The Germans would use, in the Leopard, the same Avco Lycoming gas turbine engine as the Abrams, thus ensuring standardization of those items most logistically important on the battlefield—guns, ammunition, tracks, power plants and fuel. The Abrams is also vouched to correspond to the Army's latest orgy of initialese—RAM-D (for reliability, availability, maintainability, and durability).

Visiting the tank-testing grounds at Aberdeen has none of the romance of calling at an Air Force test facility. A huge, flat plain, ending in gray-green marshes, a river and creeks, rolls over into Delaware. A partly open-air museum of rusting rocketry and weapons features such movie-set items as the Anzio railroad gun of World War Two and 17-inch coastal-battery cannons from World War One. A complex visitor's map indicates that much of this humid desolation is target country: Literally millions of shells lie buried in the fetid marshes, to be discovered perhaps a few millennia hence by some new civilization which may assume that Armageddon was fought out here. On the fringes of the 80,000 acres, patrol boats keep sport fishermen from becoming unwitting bomb targets.

The tank was the child of World War One, and most of the workshops at Aberdeen date from that era. Many are built of corrugated metal, bending in the wind. The base housing, only slightly more modern, was a make-work project of Roosevelt's New Deal era. The whole forlorn, underdeveloped effect is that of a Greek or Spanish army camp.

There are American touches. Fallow deer roam the range—the tank range, that is. Delicate herds of bambis stare in wonderment as the XM-1 storms past, putting testing wear on the German treads. The deer live with the constant sound of guns, occasionally wandering from their copses to trigger the ultrasensitive security devices which bring the gates clanging shut in the restricted areas; then, impressive traffic jams occur, as corporals' wives are stymied on their morning drive to the commissary.

Aberdeen is perhaps the least known of the Defense Department's major future-warfare facilities. It has forty-two different sections, testing everything from new army boots to the effects of nuclear radiation on weapons. Close by is Edgewood Arsenal, with its chemical-warfare systems laboratory and the Ballistic Research Laboratory of DARCOM (Development and Readiness Command), which controls these facilities.

Everything that the Army buys and develops is procured by DARCOM. With a few exceptions, Army plants, not private contractors, make all artillery and artillery components of armored vehicles. The exceptions include small arms and such items as Chrysler's recoil machinery for the gun on the M-60 tank.

Aberdeen employs eight hundred civilians and two hundred military. The civilians work for the Materiel Testing Directorate (MTD). The personnel figures are down from three thousand during the Korean War, many thousands more during World War Two. The head of MTD is Harry H. Bechtol, an emaciated, bespectacled, humorous man who works behind a desk marked "Oberhaupt der Munition." He runs a largely civilian world in which you guess at people's ranking only by noting whether they rise or are risen to in the presence of someone else.

The sanctuary of the ultrasecret Abrams is one of the old 1918 buildings. A crudely painted sign over the door says, innocently, "Automotive Facilities Development Shop." It takes a mixture of American euphemism and bureaucratese to reduce the XM-1 to an "automotive facility."

Inside, muzzle breaks and recoil blocks lie around in apparent disorder. The visitor tries to reconstitute tank parts in the mind: Sections are painted black where they mate with other parts; white paint indicates which sections go inside the tank, where everything is white to relieve the gloom. There is a long bath for testing cracks in metal by the magnetic effect: To back up ultrasonic testing for cracks (which the Army euphemistically calls "discontinuities"), the bath is used, because the north-south orientation of molecules in the fluid that flows into cracks contrasts with the molecules of the rest of the item being tested.

Away in one area, an old Russian T-68 lies in exile, dissected. Then suddenly the visitor comes upon a larger tank. It is the XM-1 itself, recognizable by its seven ground wheels. In place of the neat paint, discreet stenciling and squadron signs of the Air Force's latest stable star, the XM-1 has some crudely stenciled letters: "Automotive Test Rig." Nearby, the only other XM-1 in existence when the writer was at Aberdeen was marked "Fire Control Rig." Windshields and other improbable excrescences have been built onto the automotive rig for the convenience of the civilians testing out on the windy plain. The turbine engine of the fire-control (i.e., weapons-test) rig had been taken out, to be run alongside. The aviation-type power plant makes a similar whine to that of a large aircraft: Because of the noise, the workshop supervisor had agreed with the local union that it would be run only once a day, after 4:30 P.M.

The tank-test range looks like a doomsday Disney World: There is a track to test the vehicle's frame, teeth-chattering washboard tracks—a whole shock-and-vibration course which is sometimes used by the manufacturers of civilian vehicles. There's a "Belgian block" course composed of cobblestones with rain-filled hollows. An army truck, driven by a calloused black civilian, is circling this at 15 mph, putting on 3,000 miles—that's two hundred hours of bumpy driving. There is a "dipper" with up to 5 feet of water in it, an open dry ditch with sharp inclines and walls up to 5 feet high for tanks to climb. A few hundred yards away, in the swampland, there is a creek where a tank with snorkel gear can go down into 35 feet of water. As it crosses the bottom, it hits poles which emerge above the surface, thus enabling testers on shore to gauge its speed and maneuverability under water. A bridging device tests the largest gap which a tank can "jump." The M-60 and the M-48 can bridge 8.5 feet. The secret capabilities of the XM-1 are presumably greater.

A few miles away, in a building apart, tank and gun parts and almost everything else are tested for tolerance of temperature and humidity, including the saline effect of traveling on troopship decks, and for sand and dirt: Three years' dust can be blown on an item in a day. In a sealed block, parts are subjected to intensive ultraviolet and infrared radioactivity by a ceiling of bright lights which rise, shine and set like the pattern of the sun.

Out on the gunnery range, the visitor comes across a leathery civilian in his late fifties, obviously a veteran, who is firing 102mm. ammunition from a 105mm. howitzer. His face is covered in gunblack warts. Once in a while he pauses to let the barrel cool and to snatch a drag on a cigarette. He is testing for breechblock endurance; and as he is firing through rings like hoops suspended in the air, the shells are also being checked for velocity in a monitoring hut a mile away. The reporter learns that the current task to which this man drives to work each day to earn his living involves firing no less than 22,500 shells from this particular gun. He has done the whole monotonous detail before, but the Directorate decided to try a different recoil action, so another 22,500 sample firings were demanded. That means approximately $4.5 million worth of shells for the two exercises. He stares into the leaden sky, his ear protectors framing his pitted face, opens the breech, loads the big shell with both hands, slams the breech shut, shuffles back to a small shelter, rings an electric warning bell and fires. There is a roar, smoke, a plunge of the recoil, and another of 45,000 shells goes off into the distant marsh. He says he can fire 12 a minute, but that under battle pressure a team could get off 15. The only variety in the task comes from the fact that this is a howitzer, not a cannon, and he has different velocities and eight different elevations of the barrel to choose from—the Army calls them "zones," because they determine where the shell will land.

An escort officer says that it's been found that some of the civilians at Aberdeen are too expert: Sometimes, problems develop when Army recruits get their hands on a weapon, so now the Pentagon has a program of "interfacing" some of the troops with the new weapons at Aberdeen. Here and there one sees a group of young, fresh-faced soldiers mixed in with the weatherbeaten veterans.

At lunch, Aberdeen officials look suspiciously at the rare press visitor and talk of other special problems. A widow has sued the Army because her husband, a soldier, had been killed by a premature artillery round. With the support of the government's own Occupational Safety and Health Administration (OSHA), she won a $2 million award which the Army is appealing. A soldier who lost his leg because of a faulty gun got $700,000 with OSHA support—another case for appeal.

Such grievances are presumably not encouraged or entertained by the Kremlin. How does the Soviet Union itself stack up against the military-science marvels of the West?

SOVIET MILITARY POWER

About 100 miles northeast of Vladivostok lies the sprawling Soviet air base of Sokolovka. Shortly after breakfast on September 6, 1976, three pilots in gray flying suits jeeped out from their mess to their waiting MiG-25s, their white helmets cushioned in their laps. It was a clear, chilly day. The three men went through their pre-flight external checks, mounted steps to the wings of their respective crafts and climbed into the cockpits. More checks. Ignition. Second engine ignition. Radio chatter came in as each closed his canopy against the Siberian wind. More checks. Soon, the entire flight was ready and began rolling out to the holding point. A minute or so later, all three aircraft with their high, anhedrally (downward) angled wings were climbing like huge birds of prey into the sky for a routine training mission. Because it was not a weapons test, only the cannons were loaded.

Near the Primorsky Kray coast, one of the Foxbats (the NATO code name: F for fighter, two syllables for jet) broke formation, peeling off into a tight turn, then leveling the wings and throttling back slightly for a steep dive. What on earth—or rather, in the sky—was Comrade Belenko doing? By the time he had leveled off 150 feet over the waves of the Sea of Japan—below the Soviet or any other radar angle—his colleagues and their controller had decided it could mean only one thing. They set off in pursuit. But the Foxbats being flown that day lacked downward-looking radar, and trying to spot Belenko's aircraft visually among the whitecaps was impossible. When Belenko was sure he was far enough ahead to risk flying higher, he glanced at his fuel gauges: low-altitude flight is fuel-expensive. It was time to get back to more economical levels for the world's most spectacular high-altitude fighter-reconnaissance plane.

At 20,000 feet, the handsome Ukrainian leveled off again, his avionics guiding him to Hakodate, a civilian airport on Hokkaido, the northernmost of the principal Japanese islands. Off Sapporo, scene of the 1972 Winter Olympics, he was nearly into Japanese airspace. The pursuing Foxbats turned back.

By now, a radar operator of Japan's Air Self-Defense Forces perceived Belenko's blip. Belenko was warned in Russian that he would soon be in Japanese air. Belenko did not reply and did not change course. It took the thoroughly startled Japanese nine minutes to get two Phantoms into the air to find him. By then, Belenko was back at wave-top height, probably with a slight smile of anticipated triumph creasing his features: Phantoms have no downward-looking radar either. Twenty-four minutes later, short on fuel but long on self-satisfaction, the twenty-nine-year-old flyer crossed the coast.

He circled Hakodate twice, not trusting the civilian control tower's limited or nonexistent Russian to give him landing instructions, and noting the traffic pattern and active runway visually. Then he swept in for a short-field landing, releasing two drag chutes. A tire blew out, making the wheel brake on that side inoperable: Using the brakes on the other gear would have meant a ground spin, so he rolled on past the end of the runway, bumping 700 feet into the grass, upending two glidescope locator antennas.

Japanese construction workers looked up in surprise as the unexpected visitor skimmed out of the sky and rolled to a halt in the turf. They ran over in time to see the canopy swing back and Belenko ease himself up and pull his helmet off. In Russian, his only language, he shouted "Get back!" He was brandishing a pistol. "This is top secret!" he said, pointing to his plane. "Please cover it up and take care of it." The construction gang smiled expressionlessly. Because they were Japanese, one of them had a camera and began squeezing off a few frames to show the kids. Belenko fired his gun in the air, apparently unaware that anyone interested had been able to look at the outside of a Foxbat in photographs published in *Jane's All the World's Aircraft*.

American air attachés in Tokyo learned of First Lieutenant Viktor

Ivanovich Belenko's defection with delight. The world's fastest weapons-carrying airplane has reached Mach-3.2—1,852.6 mph—and ceilinged at 118,000 feet: It would be interesting to know why.

The Japanese police obligingly accepted Belenko's surrender and whisked him safely into custody on three charges—entering Japan without a passport, flying without carrying his pilot license and possession of a gun. When the Soviet embassy in Tokyo insisted that the Foxbat be left untouched until one of their air staff could fly it home, the local Japanese police chief smiled politely and said that when anyone entered Japan with a gun in his vehicle, it would be normal to take said vehicle apart to see if other weapons were concealed therein. Japanese foreign ministry officials acknowledged that the plane was Soviet property, and once Belenko was through with Hokodate traffic court's need for it as Exhibit A, the Soviet Government could have it back. Four days later, Belenko, having refused to say anything in a brief confrontation with a Soviet diplomat, and having ignored pleas from back home from his mother, wife and three-year-old daughter, boarded Northwest Orient's Flight 22 for Honolulu and Los Angeles. President Ford had granted him political asylum. He spent the flight in the upper-deck first-class lounge with what a correspondent described as a "bevy of U.S. officials."

Apart from the Russians, also not clearly pleased with the whole performance were the Japanese Air Self-Defense Forces. Hokkaido was supposed to be their most alert area—the closest to the Soviet Union—and the ease with which one pilot, playing things by ear, had invaded Japan was not reassuring. This in turn was good for the United States, since it made a Japanese decision to buy American F-14s, F-15s or F-16s more urgent. On the minus side, since the Foxbat was no longer secret, Moscow could export it to friendly states with less concern. Until then, MiG-25s had gone only to Egypt—in 1971—and then only on the condition that Russians flew and serviced the craft themselves. Now Iraq learned that it could have some, and almost canceled an order for fifty French Mirage-1s.

Belenko's gift turned out to be the Foxbat-A—the interceptor version. Foxbat-Bs—the reconnaissance version—have been seen frequently over the Middle East, easily outflying Israeli and Iranian aircraft: The Shah's decision to buy Phoenix-armed Tomcats had been prompted—as he bluntly told Mike Wallace on television in 1976—by the need for a plane that could shoot down Foxbats.

Inevitably, the accidental American triumph raised sourer points. If the Foxbat was so good, how come we didn't have something like it? Its nearest American equivalent, the YF-12A—an armed Blackbird—was dropped from the inventory after a brief appearance in 1964. Soon, a flow of disparaging comments about the Foxbat flowed from the Pentagon. Its rivets were not flush with the wing surface; manual, arc-, spot- and resistance-seam welding had been used; to a pilot this looks like maybe a loss of 3 or 4 knots; at all costs, it had not prevented it capturing world speed records. It was said at first to be built entirely of steel, not titanium like the slower Blackbird. This, of course, only raised the point as to how the Russian scientists had managed to produce steel that did not melt at Mach-3, thus saving both money and rare metal which is difficult to machine; but a later, classified report talked of "liberal use" of titanium and aluminum structures.

The initial tendency, in other words, was to downplay the aircraft's qualities. An obliging congressman who is also a pilot weighed in. Democrat Robert Carr of Michigan used a full page of a Sunday edition of the Washington *Post* to explain why he found the Foxbat "obsolete and inadequate." He artfully compared the high-altitude interceptor's performance at lower altitudes with American interceptors designed for those lower altitudes and unable to reach the Foxbat in its own environment. He claimed the Blackbird could outpace the Foxbat-B, and noted that it could operate higher than the Foxbat's best altitude—88,000 feet. (Both planes can.) To save weight, Belenko's plane even had no ejection seat, he noted correctly, adding that the Blackbird can sustain supersonic speeds for a longer duration and had "superior . . . navigation and countermeasure equipment." Belenko's plane had "no look-down radar," which was "simply beyond the reach of Soviet technology and will probably remain so for several years." Carr was right on the first point, but proven wrong on the second a few months later, when news of the new Soviet radar development on the reconnaissance-version Foxbat leaked out.

Carr referred to a 1973 statement by the then Air Force Secretary, Dr. Robert Seamans, that the Foxbat was the world's best interceptor and had "a highly capable avionics and missile system": The congressman noted scornfully that "the 'highly capable avionics' are in fact simple vacuum-tube systems we would have considered obsolete ten years ago and unimpressive fifteen years ago."

But by January 1977, U.S. experts were prepared to admit that the Foxbat was much better than that. They were impressed with its radar— more powerful and therefore less vulnerable to jamming by an enemy's electronic devices than anything then in service in the U.S. arsenal. The reason? A top Air Force source said it was the magnetrons or vacuum tubes, which the B-52 still uses and of which Carr had been too hastily derisive in this age of transistors and printed circuits. This source called the Foxbat's automated functions "the most sophisticated ever, in an air-

craft." A New York *Times* article, simplifying slightly, said: "The pilot
has little to do except take off, adjust the throttle, wait for the ground-
controlled interception of an enemy, fire his air-to-air missiles and, on return, put the plane on the ground." But another source noted that there
was an intentional avoidance of "over-design" in the Foxbat. He called
the MiG-25 "unsurpassed in . . . ease of maintenance and servicing."
Such virtues are characteristic of Soviet aircraft design, a field dominated
for years by four great names—Oleg Konstantinovich Antonov, Sergei
Ilyushin, Aleksandr Yacovlev and the late Igor Sikorsky. So well favored
are these four excellent engineers by the Kremlin that they enjoy the almost private-enterprise privilege of giving their names to all their aircraft.

On the sophisticated side, the Foxbat's warning system of sixteen un-
safe conditions—six for malfunctions such as engine fires or low hydraulic pressure, ten concerning aircraft and missile maneuvering limits—activated, not the usual control-panel lights, but voice recordings (a
woman's voice, presumably to be more reassuring).

Now a two-seat variant of the plane, the MiG-25MP, is in development
and should be operational by 1979, taking a systems officer aloft. According to U.S. intelligence sources, it has a more efficient engine, a look-
down radar capable of handling twenty targets and tracking four at a
time, and will fire either AA-2 Atoll or AA-8 Aphid missiles that can
shoot downward and seek targets in ground clutter.

Soviet Advances

That Moscow was closing the gap in military performance seemed un-
questioned. By early 1977, NATO headquarters staff in Brussels were
anxious to tell any visiting correspondent about the West's concern. Particularly worrying was Soviet deployment that year of what had been the
mobile SS-X-20—the 2,700-mile-range, triple-warheaded ICBM, said to
be accurate to within half a mile of target. The SS-20—no longer X-
perimental—was being trucked to "garages" with sliding roofs for
launching. By 1978, three hundred were said to have been deployed. The
Boston *Globe*'s William Beecher revealed that some Soviet short-range
missiles had been made mobile also.

The principal concern among the "hawks" was about the SS-20, which
uses the first two stages of the three-stage SS-16 and the same transporter-launcher. Beecher pointed out in another article that the SS-20
could be "quickly transformed into an uncounted ICBM [for SALT pur-
poses] merely by adding the SS-16's third stage." The reporter noted
that "more than 1,000 SS-20s appear to be contemplated for construction,

far exceeding the number of IRBMs (Intermediate Range Ballistic Missiles) they are to replace."

According to GOP congressman Jack F. Kemp:

> The Soviet Union has initiated deployment of the SS-20, a two-stage mobile missile equipped with [MIRV] with an order of magnitude improvement in the delivery accuracy over its predecessor systems, the SS-4/5 and the variable-range SS-11. Moreover, if the SS-20 is loaded with a single warhead of the U.S. Poseidon type, the SS-20 is capable of intercontinental range when deployed from either the Kola or Kamchatka peninsulas.
>
> . . .
>
> The Soviet Union has initiated deployment of the Delta-III submarine capable of launching MIRV payloads comparable to the Trident-II in range if not in sophistication.
>
> . . .
>
> Evidence continues to mount that the Soviet Union is maintaining a reload capability for some of its intercontinental and intermediate-range ballistic missiles.

Land-based missiles, controlled by the Red Army's Strategic Rocket Forces, remain Moscow's first line of defense and attack. In March 1977, Chinese intelligence informed the United States that SS-20s were being deployed in western Russia in replacement of some of the six hundred SS-4s and SS-5s already there. Peking estimated that the SS-20s would make the Soviet strategic nuclear force against Western Europe four times more powerful than before. But Secretary Vance told the Senate in 1978: "We do not believe that the Soviets have deployed an ICBM in a mobile mode." Said Vance:

> The SS-20 is being deployed to replace older medium and intermediate-range missiles. It is judged to be capable of reaching the Aleutian Islands and western Alaska from its present and likely deployment areas in the eastern U.S.S.R.; however, it cannot reach the contiguous forty-eight states from any of its likely deployment areas in the Soviet Union. While the range capability of any missile system, including the SS-20, can be extended by reducing the total weight of its payload or adding another propulsion system, there is no evidence that the Soviets have made any such modifications to the SS-20. We have confidence that we would detect the necessary intercontinental-range testing of such a modified system.

In 1978, Moscow was reported replacing older ICBMs with the new, more accurate SS-16s, SS-17s, SS-18s and SS-19s, with the SS-18s capable of reloading—an option not yet developed by the United States. The SS-18 has eight to ten re-entry vehicles, the SS-19 six. General Keegan even claimed in 1977 that "every" Soviet intermediate, medium-range and battlefield ballistic missile had a refire capacity, and that ICBM launchers could be used "four times." He went on:

> The [intelligence] community has steadfastly, on emotional grounds in my opinion, refused to treat the refire capability. The Soviets picked up a Boeing design, thanks to [*Aviation Week* editor] Robert Hotz. We didn't want it, so Bob published it. Why not? The Soviets picked it up, proved it, and today there are two types of their silo-based, cold-launch missiles in which the main engine ignition occurs outside the silo and does no damage to the silo. They can lower another missile in a canister and refire it, if not in minutes, in just a very few hours. Now the silos are too hard for us to destroy, so a great many more are going to survive.
>
> . . .
>
> The Soviet Union is twenty years ahead of the United States in its development of a technology which they believe will soon neutralize the ballistic missile weapon as a threat to the Soviet Union.

The Soviet Navy also continued to make important advances. On the eve of the SALT talks in Moscow that month, Moscow fired two un-MIRV-ed SS-N-8 missiles from Delta submarines in the Barents Sea into the Pacific Ocean, about 300 miles northeast of Wake Island, 5,700 nautical miles away; Western sources had previously estimated the range of the SS-N-8 at 4,000 miles, but hypothesized that the test missiles, having no nuclear warhead, might be lighter. In addition to SS-N-8s, Soviet subs also have an experimental naval version of the land-based SS-18, known to NATO as the SS-N-X-18. By December 1977, the Russians had begun firing twin-MIRV-ed SS-N-X-18 missiles from submarines in the White Sea north of Russia into the Pacific 4,600 miles away. Four such tests with dummy warheads were conducted that month. Also that winter, Yankee-class Soviet submarines appeared in the Atlantic and Pacific oceans with MIRV-ed SS-N-8s, using a stellar inertial navigation system. The following year, the authoritative British magazine *Flight International*, citing "U.S. congressional studies," said the SS-N-8 was as accurate as Minuteman-II, as well as being more accurate and longer in range than Trident-I.

NATO sources in Brussels said that in addition to adapting three Delta-III subs for the weapon, the Soviet Union was building a new nuclear submarine that would carry twenty-four of the missiles, whose apparent range—judging from the tests mentioned in the previous paragraph—is 3,200 miles greater than that of the Poseidon. Its MIRV capability (like that of the high throw-weight 18) is of course inferior to the Poseidon's, but with such a long-range weapon, Moscow's strategic submarines could blanket parts of the United States without leaving port.

In 1978, the Soviet strategic-submarine fleet was believed to consist of: 34 Yankee-class subs with 16 missiles each, 18 Delta-Is with 12 missiles, 8 Delta-IIs with 16 missiles each, and 4 Delta-IIIs with 16 or 20 missiles. The antiship SS-N-6 cruise missiles on the Yankees were being replaced by solid-propellant SS-N-X-17s. The Delta-Is and -IIs were being refitted with the long-range SS-N-X-18s, which, along with the new X-8s, will apparently be standard on the Delta-IIIs. According to Japanese intelligence, Delta-IIs with SS-N-X-18s had joined the Pacific fleet by late 1978. Said the Nippon report: "These vessels could launch ballistic missiles from the Okhotsk Sea to New York, Washington and other eastern coastal cities of the United States." Twenty more Deltas were believed to be under construction, and the new Typhoon-class submarine, which is of Trident size, will come into service before the ten-year-old Yankees are due for retirement. In 1979, the first of a new Alpha class of submarines was tested. Intelligence reports claimed it was built of titanium, could do a staggering 40 knots submerged and dive to 2,000 feet; but it was said to be detectably noisy.

Russian heavy-missile experiments continue. Shortly after the 1977 SALT talks collapsed, a 50-kiloton bomb was detonated at Semipalatinsk, causing readings of 5.9 on the Richter scale in Sweden, 5.7 in Norway and 5.1 in the United States. The Carter administration had ordered that there be no U.S. nuclear detonations during the SALT negotiations period, and continued the Ford ban on explosions of over 100 kilotons (the threshold-ban ceiling, still unratified by the Senate, is 150 kilotons, and the Russians have frequently exceeded it).

There was continuing Western concern, too, that two decades after introducing the first Soviet "family" of air-to-air missiles, a more sophisticated breed of these weapons, with semi-active radar homing and passive infrared homing systems, was now deployed—although there still were only four per plane. The Soviet system is to launch these in pairs, at split-second intervals, with the first having an infrared head and the second a radar seeker. The largest of the three new missiles, the AA-6 Acrid, is the armament for the Foxbat interceptor. The AA-7 Apex goes on the MiG-23D and was expected to be fitted on the MiG-21J and possibly on the new Su-19 fighter.

The 1978 edition of *Jane's Weapons Systems* also praised the new Soviet cruise missiles, claiming that either the SS-N-X-13s or -17s could be as good as the U.S. Tomahawk. The claim implied that the Russian cruise missiles could be launched from submerged submarines and carry nuclear or conventional warheads over 2,000 miles to target. By December 1977, a Tu-16 was photographed over the Sea of Japan carrying a new missile about 33 feet long—either a huge "cruise" or some other devastating air-to-surface weapon, probably the new AS-6 Kingfish.

Also in 1977, the Soviet Navy was building a third *Kiev*-class aircraft carrier, probably for the Pacific, while the Red Army began deploying the new T-72 tanks and other new armor, including self-propelled 122mm. and 155mm. guns, as well as new low-altitude surface-to-air missiles and antitank helicopters. In 1978, the Red Army introduced into service the SA-10, a surface-to-air missile which travels at five times the speed of sound and would be a probable defense against Western cruise missiles. In the Soviet Union's 60th Anniversary parade in Moscow, amphibious Soviet armor carried new antitank guided missiles along with the familiar wireguided AT-3 Saggers. The parade also showed off the SA-6, SA-8 and SA-9 surface-to-air missiles and other impressive antiaircraft artillery. Retired Lieutenant General Daniel O. Graham, who formerly headed the Defense Intelligence Agency, has claimed that a "large proportion" of Warsaw Treaty Organization rockets and missiles have toxic-gas tips. During the spring of 1977, NATO troops in Europe began getting decontamination suits, gas masks, other protective equipment and, in some cases, personnel shelters.

NATO sources said that Soviet chemical weapons, which can be fired from planes, cannons, mortars or rockets, were superior to Western equivalents, and included nerve gas, blister gas and a gas which kills blood corpuscles. The Russians, as mentioned earlier, have developed "decontaminated" tanks and armored personnel carriers, thus avoiding the need for masks and suits, and each Soviet regiment has a chemical warfare (CW) defensive company. (As a consequence, the U.S. fiscal-1978 defense budget included just over $100 million for CW equipment to protect America's NATO forces.)

Deciphering Moscow's Strategies

With U.S. emphasis more and more on strategic sea-based warfare, the Soviet Union has inevitably concentrated heavily in recent years on naval development. The partial success of the CIA, using the *Glomar Explorer*, in raising half a Soviet submarine from the depths drew public attention to the rising importance of the Russian Navy; and recent public speeches by congressional defense experts have been peppered with references to Admiral Gorshkov's growing fleet.

As noted earlier, because of Russia's lack of forward bases, it is almost impossible for its submarines to reach the open ocean unobserved. From

Murmansk, the Arctic Fleet—including at least 175 submarines, 90 of them nuclear-powered, and over 50 major surface vessels—must proceed down Norway's Lapland coast, past Spitsbergen, Bear Island, the Faroes and the Orkneys—all bristling with detection gear. From Vladivostok, the Pacific Fleet must head for the open sea either through the 25-mile-wide Soya Strait, past Hokkaido (which, but for General MacArthur's truculent opposition, would have been seized by Stalin after World War Two) or through the Tartar or Korea straits. The Black Sea Fleet must negotiate the Turkish waters of the Bosporus, the Sea of Marmara and the Dardanelles, and from there on through Suez, or past Sicily and Malta and through the Gibraltar Strait. The Baltic Fleet must go through Denmark's Skagerrak and the North Sea or the English Channel. Even at sea, a roving submarine's impulses—its "voice autograph"—can be picked up by the earlier-mentioned SOSUS computers of Allied surface ships and attack submarines, programmed to distinguish between friend and foe.

The Soviet Union, hopelessly far behind in this technology, has sought to catch up through espionage: A Soviet diplomat in New York was expelled and two Soviet UN employees arrested and convicted in 1978 for trying to obtain secrets about three U.S. detection systems: SOSUS, SURTASS (Surveillance Towed Array Sensor System—a multi-hydrophone "convoy" towed by CIA "civilian" trawlers) and TACTASS (Tactical Towed Array Sensor System—a short-range hydrophone system towed by warships).

In defense circles, a debate continues as to what Soviet naval objectives might be. Shortly before he was appointed director of the CIA, Admiral Stansfield Turner published an article in *Foreign Affairs* which noted that during the *Okean* fleet exercise of 1975, the Russians "rehearsed tactics of cutting open-ocean sea lanes." Was such a "long war" strategy intended to deceive? Such questions lead in turn to the debate on whether U.S. naval strategy should be oriented toward "sea control" (defensive) or "power projection" (an offensive mode).

In the summer of 1977, 89 Soviet strategic and attack submarines sailed past Norway into the Atlantic to join the 4 strategic and 3 attack submarines already there. The 96-boat swarm—nearly one third of the whole Soviet submarine fleet, and probably involving every currently operable submarine based at Murmansk—forced NATO to use an unprecedented array of surface ships, reconnaissance aircraft and submarines to back up the underwater sensors normally adequate for monitoring most hostile underwater craft. Forty of the Russian submarines, accompanied by impressive surface ships, including the *Kiev* mini-carrier, and squadrons of Backfire and other long-range planes, "occupied" the area south of Iceland which would be Europe's American lifeline in time of war.

Such a deployment would be expected if war was about to begin—it would be one of the warnings that hostilities were only a week or so away. The Russians announced that no aggressive designs should be deduced from the operation. The huge fleet was only "standing guard over the security of the country, the entire socialist community . . . [and] world peace."

Whether bluffing, or practicing "for real," the Soviet Union certainly goes out of its way to imply preparations for an attack on the West. Almost once a week, a Soviet four-engined Tu-16 Badger reconnaissance plane takes off from a field near Murmansk, which has been described as the world's largest military base, and flies over the ocean to the edge of Norwegian airspace. On orders from a command center buried in Norway's snowy mountains, two Starfighters are routinely scrambled to intercept. One sits on the Badger's tail, the other flies just above and ahead. As Norwegian airspace approaches, the lead Starfighter waggles its wings above the Badger's nose. If the Soviet pilot pushes on, a game of "chicken" begins in the Arctic air, with the lead Starfighter slipping back alongside and just beneath the Badger, raising a wing toward the Badger's, ostensibly to tip the heavy hostile plane into a turn. Contact could well be fatal to both crews, but the Russian pilot knows that if he continues on course, the tailgating Starfighter could blast him out of the sky. The Danish Air Force faces similar challenges, albeit less frequently. At sea, Soviet warships maneuver as close as they dare to the Danish and Norwegian coasts. Intensively patrolling the Skagerrak from May to October, they effectively monitor all entry to, and egress from, the Baltic.

General Alexander Haig, the NATO supreme commander in Europe, said in 1977 that "if you look at the current situation of strategic parity, it's evident that we're not going to be faced in the short term with a major onslaught across the eastern frontiers. We're going to be plagued by those ambiguous situations on the flanks." Haig's superior, General Brown, told the author the following year that he disagreed: "I don't think they would gain much on the flanks. The only thing they gain up in the northern flank is added security for their fleets coming round the Northern Cape. And if they think that is important or not, they might try to neutralize any land base up in that area. I don't think they would gain much in the south either, unless they wanted to make a thrust for the Persian Gulf oil, if they need that or wanted to deprive us of it."

Asked if it wouldn't be easier to take out the wellheads and refineries by missiles, rather than by projecting naval power, Brown said, "I don't know. It is no longer necessary to do a war of attrition at sea, if that's what you're saying. But I would think they would come right through the center [of Europe] with a view to moving hard against the lowlands and right up to the [English] Channel, expecting that NATO would capitulate."

But in support of General Haig's thesis, several times in 1977 naval exercises featuring the *Kiev*, about forty other surface ships and about thirty submarines were held close to Norway, with some of the submarines entering the mouths of Norwegian fjords. On the Kola Peninsula, in full view of western satellites, Soviet forces carry out sophisticated amphibious exercises—a reminder that Moscow has territorial claims on nearly 60,000 square miles of Norway's portion of the Barents Sea, potentially rich in oil and gas.

Spitsbergen, demilitarized in 1920 and placed under Norwegian sovereignty, has had to accept a pseudo-civilian colony of 3,400 Russians—outnumbering the approximately 1,000 Norwegian inhabitants. On the island, the NATO country and Russia spy on each other with the latest electronic equipment, with the Russians jamming Norwegian surveillance of the Kola Peninsula.

Haig's reference to "ambiguous situations on the flanks" extends beyond Europe. Later in 1977, he noted that: "As long as we maintain a viable deterrent in Europe, conflict is more likely to arrive on the periphery, as the Soviet Union exploits targets of opportunity. And these situations will carry the implications of major confrontation. I believe that we must be armed with regional military capabilities which could be employed as deterrent forces to prevent the escalation of Third World dynamics into major conflict." He gave the conflict between Ethiopia and Somalia as an example.

Nor is Russia above twisting the eagle's tail feathers themselves. In August 1976, a Soviet submarine drove through a U.S. naval formation off Greece, colliding with the frigate *Voge* and severely damaging both vessels. The submarine limped away, unable to submerge. In December, a Soviet *Kashin*-class destroyer sailed through an American carrier formation in the western Mediterranean, ignoring warning signals. That U.S. exercise was also monitored by Russian Tu-95 turboprop Bears, which have an 8,000-mile range, operating out of Conakry, Guinea—a facility moved, at Guinea's request, to Angola in 1977. F-14s from the carrier *Franklin D. Roosevelt* chased the Soviet aircraft off. A month later, two Bears from Vladivostok flew to within 50 miles of Guam, the site of major American air and naval bases.

Again, in April 1977, two Bears from Cuba flew within 60 miles of

North Carolina's Outer Banks, directly over the carrier *Saratoga*, a cruiser and two frigates engaged on a training exercise, but withdrew when two Phantoms arrived from Seymour Johnson Air Force Base in North Carolina. The Associated Press quoted U.S. officers as saying that "the episode fits into a pattern of more assertive Soviet naval, air, surface and submarine activity within the past year." Sure enough, in October, two Bears headed for Cuba dogged a U.S. task force led by the carrier *America* and headed for the Mediterranean, unfazed by the appearance of two F-14 escorts. Later that month, F-106s were scrambled from Otis Air Force Base in Massachusetts and from Atlantic City when Bears from Havana flew 1,000 feet over the masts of the new U.S. destroyer *Spruance*, presumably photographing it, and dropped electronic chaff to confuse American radars. In May 1979, two Il-38 antisubmarine aircraft flew at low level across the landing and takeoff paths of the carrier *Midway*, in the Persian Gulf, disrupting operations.

The first Soviet nuclear-powered ballistic-missile submarine was launched in 1963; by 1977, there were forty-four of them. The United States, of course, has almost as many, and they are quieter, better armed and less vulnerable; in addition, Britain has four and France three such craft. But, as noted, Russia's MIRV-ed SS-N-X-18 and SS-N-X-8 entered service that year, ahead of schedule, aboard Delta submarines which began penetrating farther into the Arctic where—under the ice—they are harder to detect. Willy Ostreng of the Norwegian Arctic Research Institute noted that "for the first time, the Russians have direct access to the high seas, even if under ice, without having to go through international straits. From that area, the Delta could shower any part of the United States with nuclear missiles."

Russia's Backfire bomber is also seen by many Pentagon experts as a long-range, supersonic, naval attack aircraft—a formidable one with either AS-4 Kitchen or AS-6 Kingfish air-to-surface missiles and passive and active electronic countermeasures, and to which some experts say the only effective response is the still developmental AV-8B Advanced Harrier V-STOL plane. Both Backfire missiles have speeds approaching Mach-3 and ranges of 150 nautical miles. The AS-6 has an active homing system for terminal guidance and is therefore an ideal antiship weapon, whether conventional or nuclear. Backfires from Kola Peninsula bases near Murmansk are now seen frequently near U.S. maritime-patrol air bases in the Azores islands. Proceeding around the northern Norwegian coast, they are refueled in the air for the return flight. Similarly refueled, they could reach New England, while Pentagon sources say Backfires based at Anadyr on the Bering Strait could overfly states from California to Minnesota.

In the 1977 edition of *Jane's All the World's Aircraft*, editor J. W. R. Taylor, joining the ranks of those who classed the Backfire as a long-range weapon, accorded the Soviet Union a clear lead in military aviation. The Backfire could "bomb targets in the U.S. and then land in Cuba." Added Taylor: "The three immediate requirements for the United States are to recognize that Backfire is a strategic weapon, to build the B-1 bomber as its wholly essential and uniquely flexible counterpart, and to order, as a matter of urgency, replacement for Aerospace Defense Command's time-expired F-106 Delta Dart interceptors."

But as a naval attack plane, how might the Backfires operate? A possible scenario has been suggested by William D. O'Neil in a 1977 issue of the Naval Institute *Proceedings*:

It is the fifth day of World War Three, and a resupply convoy is in mid-ocean on its way from Hampton Roads to Le Havre. Soviet satellites are tracking it. Midway between the Azores and Ireland, the convoy comes under attack from forty Backfires from Murmansk, flying widely dispersed most of the way and relying on inertial and satellite navigation to bring them together just before target.

The Soviet planes, in O'Neil's description, have been successfully escorted past Norway by MiG-23s. As their fuel load decreases, they climb subsonically, dipping to 8,000 feet between Iceland and the Faroes to avoid radar detection, then returning to 30,000 feet. O'Neil estimates that about thirty-six would probably survive to meet at the revised rendezvous point, where they follow the lead plane in applying full afterburner, climbing to 45,000 feet at 1,000 knots. Radio silence is broken when the lead plane sights the convoy on radar, 250 miles off. This alerts the U.S. frigates with their SPS-49 air-search radars, which pick up jamming strobes and no friendly response on IFF. Six minutes later, the range has closed to 150 miles and each Backfire fires its pair of missiles at its selected target.

In O'Neil's words, "the guided-missile frigates among the [convoy] escort belch . . . missiles until their foredecks are burned black, but they can get only a fraction of the AS-6s. More than thirty survive to plunge into convoy ships. Several ships are sunk, and several more have much of their vital cargo destroyed."

A few Backfires remain in the area to make damage assessments, but most turn for home. NATO interceptors from Iceland and Scotland attack the returning force, but long-range Soviet interceptors arrive to escort them; these and the Backfires' electronic countermeasures enable most of the bomber force to return home to Russia safely.

Effective use of AWACS planes would of course change this scenario considerably, and for the better.

The Naval Balance

A considerable debate has been triggered in the past year or so over the relative strengths of the Soviet and American navies. Over the past twelve years, the United States has taken delivery of 20 per cent more surface ships than the Soviet Navy. NATO nations as a whole have received two to three times as many surface ships as Warsaw Treaty nations. But over the same period, the Soviet bloc has brought into service at least 114 new nuclear submarines, compared to 77 for all NATO nations (41 of them American). Russia has 64 of these (plus 19 diesel ballistic submarines—no longer in service in the U. S. Navy), while the other Warsaw countries have built 53 new ballistic-missile nuclear subs, vastly improving their missile armament. The NATO navies have taken delivery of 20 ballistic nuclear submarines, 12 of them for the U. S. Navy. In addition, 13 U.S. Poseidon submarines have been converted. New nonballistic nuclear subs have numbered 55 for the Soviet bloc, 57 for NATO, all but 8 of them American. New Warsaw Treaty nonnuclear subs numbered 28, while NATO vessels in this category totaled 48. To get a clearer picture of the naval balance, however, it has to be recalled that non-NATO nations such as South Korea, Taiwan and Spain also form part of the world's anti-Soviet navies, as of course—at present— does the navy of China, with about 70 submarines.

Nevertheless, the Pentagon's claim that the Soviet Navy is a growing threat has been supported by liberal Democratic senator Gary Hart of Colorado. In a major speech to the Senate in February 1977, Hart said that "driven by the new Tirpitz, Admiral Sergei Gorshkov, the Soviet Union, a nation with no defensive requirement for a blue-water Navy, has built and deployed a worldwide naval presence." (Tirpitz was the famous German admiral who was the scourge of the Allies in World War One. A blue-water navy is one committed to the open ocean.)

Hart claimed that the Soviet Navy now had "335 submarines, about three times as many as the United States," and stressed that "only the Soviet Union today possesses attack submarines which can launch antiship missiles while submerged."

Hart noted that Russia's first anticarrier exercises were conducted in the Mediterranean by submarines based in Albania. Today, as U.S. strategy has moved slowly from the carrier to the submarine, Gorshkov has concentrated on antisubmarine warfare (ASW), Hart said, and was apparently developing the SS-N-X-13 missile as a satellite-guided ASW weapon.

According to declassified literature, the United States detects enemy submarines not only by sonic sensors but also by monitoring anomalies in the earth's magnetic field created by their movement. The Soviet Union is behind in both acoustic and magnetic methods of detection—as the 1978 New York spying case emphasizes—and lacks the worldwide bases for deploying sensors adequately. Yet Admiral Gorshkov declared back in 1975 that the *Okean* exercise had demonstrated that his ships could "repulse and disarm" the threat of U.S. subs. Bluff? American scientists believe Moscow is working on thermal differences (a warm sub in a cold environment) and other "hydrodynamic signatures," such as the tracing (by radar) of dead microorganisms in the atmosphere at the surface— killed by the effect of the vessel's passage on ultraviolet radiation. When the Soviet Kosmos-954 satellite crashed in Canada in 1978, its 1,000-pound nuclear reactor was found to be powering an ocean-scanning radar, probably connected with these experiments. Moscow is now thought to be relying more on satellites and less on ships for detection, planning perhaps to be able to hit U.S. strategic subs with satellite-guided, land-based ballistic missiles.

Submarines are considerably more dangerous now that they are nuclear-powered. World War Two submarines spent most of their time on the surface; submerged, their top speed was 8 knots, with an average speed of only 3 knots—giving a destroyer a ten-to-one speed advantage. A nuclear submarine can sustain its top speed indefinitely and can often outrace a destroyer. With cruise missiles as "standoff" weaponry, firing "over the horizon," the tactical role of subs in a short, sharp war would be devastating. Senator Hart has noted, however, that "since the objective in a crisis confrontation is local and limited, and is defined basically in diplomatic rather than military terms, the Soviet objective is probably more one of deterrence than of actual conflict."

Some Western military analysts think Russia's shortage of home-porting facilities weakens the Soviet Navy's apparent strength. In the Mediterranean and elsewhere, the Soviet Navy spends long days anchored on sandbars. Of 55 Soviet naval ships in the Mediterranean, only 10 are combat vessels, the rest service ships. Of America's 45 ships there, 28 are fighting vessels, including the nuclear-powered carrier *Nimitz*, the world's largest warship, with 100 planes. Sometimes, 2 other U.S. carriers are also in the Mediterranean. Moscow has only the *Kiev* carrier, with its small complement of helicopters and Ram-G V-STOL jump-jet fighters, and its more recently commissioned sister ship, the *Minsk;* but these are rarely on station. (In 1979, Japanese industry completed a dry dock for the *Minsk* at Vladivostok, implying that its station would be the Pacific.) From late 1976 to late 1977, the *Kiev* went to sea only twice, for a total of fifteen days, and remained anchored off Murmansk the rest of the time, its Ram-Gs and Kamov-25 antisubmarine helicopters removed to an air base nearby. (U.S. intelligence theorized that the Ram-Gs were melting the deck plates when they took off, and that the Russians were either ceramizing the takeoff pad or installing ski-jump ramps for conventional takeoff. However, one U.S. aerospace contractor involved in V-STOL development—Joe Gavin, the president of Grumman Corporation—told the writer he found this theory fanciful.)

Overall, the Russians have more military tonnage at sea than the United States. In ships displacing 1,000 tons or more, the Soviet Navy leads America's by 993 vessels to 475; even above 3,000 tons they have a narrow lead; their main deficiency is in carriers, but this reflects the limited "blue water" nature of their defense strategy until recent years. Some of the Russian advantage in smaller ships comes from the fact that the Soviet Navy clears mines by minesweeper; the U. S. Navy uses helicopters—which ties up carriers.

Although the *Kiev* mini-carrier is clearly having teething problems, it should not be underestimated. When it sailed into the Mediterranean in 1977, the first photos (taken from an RAF reconnaissance plane) made startling news that proved that *Jane's All the World's Aircraft*—which is to aviation what Webster's is to the language—had been wrong for once. On board, in place of the slow, snub-nosed Yak-36 VTOL fighters which *Jane's* said shared deckspace on the *Kiev* with attack helicopters, were some MiG-23-shaped V-STOL aircraft. Observation soon showed that they were about as fast and sophisticated as the supersonic Harrier V-STOL of the U. S. Marines. Early evaluation of the Ram-G—the new Soviet plane's Western identification—gave it a defense, close-support, strike, antisubmarine warfare and reconnaissance role. The *Kiev* appeared from the photos to have about twenty-five Ram-Gs and twenty-five helicopters aboard. The Ram-G, developed at Ramenskoye airfield near Moscow, is clearly a great improvement over the earlier Yak-36, and appears to have hit the deck two years ahead of the schedule predicted by U.S. intelligence.

The main theme of Soviet naval strategy seems based on the cruise missile. Military institutes in Marxist-Leninist countries teach warfare on the premise of a maximum-force first strike. Specifically, the naval plan appears to be to use heavy "cruises" in a short, massive surprise attack. In naval terms, this means that surface ships are seen as expendable missile platforms, with submarines and bombers fulfilling the second-strike capacity.

The best Soviet cruise missiles are all-weather weapons, with relatively simple fire-control systems but accurate homing systems. They are mostly aboard small craft which—viewed head on especially—do not make much of a radar blip and are easily lost in the coastal clutter of small boats, buoys and tiny islands. Their disadvantage is the relative ease with which their fire-control radars can be jammed, and the natural answer to this problem is large numbers. The shipborne missile probably eliminates the amphibious assaults of earlier wars, since a concentration of vessels close to batteries would be an easy target—another nail in the coffin of the Marines. Similarly, the traditional naval battles between task forces or fleets, and involving ship-based tactical aircraft, have become outdated now that the objective is not merely to sink a few large enemy vessels. In cruise-missile warfare, every enemy "platform" would have to be destroyed. Says Captain William J. Ruhe, director of marine program development at General Dynamics: "Cruise missiles provide the wherewithal in weapon power and flexibility to cause a lot of Pearl Harbor-type attacks worldwide if this potential for warfare is underrated and not adjusted to." Ruhe noted that this capacity is now potentially "also in the hands of the smallest of navies."

Is Russia Resigned to War?

In Europe, the main confrontation area between NATO and Warsaw forces, most specialists aver that the advantage lies with Moscow. In December 1976, a Congressional Budget Office report authored by G. Philip Hughes criticized NATO planning: Hughes said NATO, compared to the Warsaw Treaty Organization, had too many light divisions, with insufficient firepower. Hughes noted particularly the enormous deployment in Eastern Europe of T-72 Main Battle Tanks—expected to reach seven thousand by 1981.

The Russian equivalent of the Abrams has an automatic loader and so only requires a crew of three to the Abrams' four. It is lower, and so presents a smaller target profile—a result obtained by limiting Soviet tank crews to men under 5 feet 6 inches tall. Its 115mm. weapon outguns, in power and range, the present U.S. 105mm. model, but will be at least equaled by the German gun to be fitted to the Abrams in the eighties. The T-72 is lighter but not faster than the Abrams (which was designed in length and height so that two could fit inside a C-5A transport aircraft).

Soviet military strength played a role in the 1976 election campaign. In a film circulated free to TV stations across the United States by the conservative American Security Council, the Secretary of the Navy, an admiral and two Air Force generals warned, in effect, that the Russians were coming. In a panel discussion for TV, sponsored by the slightly right-of-center American Enterprise Institute for Public Policy Research, former deputy Defense secretary and SALT negotiator Paul Nitze noted that U.S. negotiators at arms talks were under more pressure than their Soviet counterparts to reach an "agreement for agreement's sake"; in the meantime, Soviet military power had increased.

After the election was over, the DoD's retiring research and engineering director, Dr. Malcolm R. Currie, said Russia's strategic-missile development was aimed at "a countersilo capability . . . The Soviet Union has never accepted this theory of assured destruction" (under which each side assumes that it would not be worth fighting a nuclear war because of the massive damage which would be inflicted by both sides). Currie added: "They feel strategic war is kind of inevitable."

Appearing to support Currie's fears was the Soviet civil-defense program, dispersing Russian industrial centers and hardening factories to withstand—reportedly—100 psi (pounds per square inch), making them about twenty times as resistant to attack as a normal brick structure. The Soviet Union is said to employ 100,000 people full time, and to have spent $65 billion in all, on civil defense—compared to $895 million in the United States. Moscow is still believed to be spending 400 million rubles a year in this field, under the direction of four-star general Aleksandr Altunin. A 1978 State Department report says equivalent measures, given American manpower expense, would cost the United States $2 billion a year. Said Currie in 1977: "They're sandbagged. They're postured to survive any war as an industrial power."

Experts have claimed that, because of the extensive Russian population-protection program and the relatively low payloads of U.S. submarine-launched ballistic missiles compared to Russian ICBMs, only 5–8 per cent of Russia's urban population, or 3–4 per cent of the whole population, would be casualties in a full-scale nuclear war. For comparison, a study by a U.S. group including Nitze estimated that a third of the U.S. population might perish in such a conflict. Bardyl Tirana, the head of the Pentagon's Defense Civil Preparedness Agency, goes further: He envisages a U.S. death toll of 145 million. Boeing, in a 1977 study, projected the figure even higher—171 million.

(In 1978, Carter set up a White House civil defense office which proposed a five-year, $1 billion civil-defense program; later, the President signed Presidential Directive 41, approving this, beginning with $91 mil-

lion in 1979 and $140 million in 1980. Carter's move was seen as partly
intended to make SALT II more palatable to Congress. According to
sources close to Defense Secretary Brown, such a program would be expected to cut the projected death toll to 100 million. The White House
decision followed a secret test in which national security adviser Zbigniew Brzezinski and his secretary, playing the roles of President and Mrs.
Carter, tested White House evacuation procedures and found that it took
forty-five minutes to get "President" Brzezinski aboard a "kneecap," ten
minutes' helicopter flight away.)

In an address to the American Security Council, veteran doomsayer
General Keegan went even further:

> The United States today lacks the firepower, the accuracy and the yields
> to overcome the enormous advantage in terms of neutralizing our retalia-
> tory punch which the Soviets have engineered for themselves at great cost
> . . . The nuclear chain of command from the general staff to the lowest
> regiment is now beyond the reach of American retaliatory weapons . . .
> They have put their strategic communications [and] their nuclear weapons
> underground. They have hardened most of their fighting capabilities—
> particularly in the defense area.
>
> The entire industrial population of the Soviet Union, it would seem
> from the evidence which we examined, and the human sources we spoke
> to, are now 100 per cent protected. Every daytime working industrial shift
> in the Soviet Union has within a few feet a vast underground bunker
> hardened to 145 psi. Now unless you get a direct hit against one of these,
> the occupants are going to survive.

A Boeing Aerospace private study in 1977 estimated that Russia's vast
evacuation and shelter program would cut losses in an all-out war to as
low as 10 million to 13 million people. A "sixfold increase in the U.S. surviving arsenal" (after the first Soviet attack) would raise Soviet losses to
20 per cent of the population, or about 56 million people in 1985, the
study said. The State Department's 1978 report said Moscow could shelter 110,000 VIPs, between 10 and 20 per cent of the population, between
an eighth and a quarter of the key work force—more if there were several days' warning of conflict.

These and similar reports became a scare story. The massive Russian
expenditure on civil defense was seen as illustrating Russian resignedness
to the inevitability of World War Three. T. K. Jones of Boeing claims
that if the Soviet Union were to lose "half its population and all its industry," it could still recover its "pre-war GNP" within fifteen years.

But most experts doubt this recovery ability. Paul Warnke, after retiring from his post as chief SALT negotiator, warned the Senate banking
committee in 1979 against the United States' becoming involved in a

"civil defense race." Some Soviet specialists say that if the files and computer tapes in the State Planning Commission in Moscow were destroyed, for instance, the whole Russian economy would have to be replanned from scratch. Blowing the dams of the huge irrigation systems would create millions of acres of desert. Similarly, there is no way that Russian oil refineries could be "hardened" against blast. The *Post's* William Greider and Robert G. Kaiser have written that even a "victorious" Soviet Union could emerge from World War Three weaker than China or Japan. They add: "In the view of many scholars, the most plausible explanation for Soviet civil defense would appear to be the Chinese threat."

For the doves, Congressman Les Aspin said the figures for Russian fatalities did not include later deaths from radioactive fallout, hunger, disease or other "post-attack threats." Aspin, a member of the House Armed Services Committee, called the claims about the extent and effectiveness of Soviet civil defense "exaggerated or unsupported." A year-long study by the Joint Congressional Committee on Defense Production agreed, but since then both the Carter administration and the Congress appear to have taken the scare stories more seriously.

As mentioned briefly earlier, the CIA, in addition to its annual, supersecret national intelligence estimates, decided in 1977 to have a competing group of experts—Team B—make a parallel evaluation. Team B, headed by Harvard's Professor Richard Pipes, a hardlining Sovietologist, found the original NIEs too optimistic and said that "the new official NIEs will record that the Soviet Union appears to be driving more than ever toward military superiority, beyond equality or parity with the United States."

One B team player, Air Force general Keegan, charged that the U.S. intelligence community had consistently underestimated Soviet military growth and that the United States was "superior in only one major area, and that is in its ability to respond quickly and efficiently to a nuclear initiative by the Soviet Union." He reiterated that Soviet strategy was based on Russia's belief that it could successfully survive a nuclear war, and said U.S. intelligence had known this since the days when its principal spy in the Soviet Union had been General Oleg Penkovsky.

The Committee on the Present Danger, which includes a broad political spectrum of figures ranging from Nitze to former Secretary of State Dean Rusk, said the SALT agreements had had no visible effect on the Soviet military buildup. Retired columnist Joseph Alsop wrote in the Washington *Post* that the CIA had known from a highly placed Russian defector in 1975 that the Agency's estimates of the Soviet defense budget had been wrong by 50 per cent.

For the doves, the CDI noted that Dr. Kissinger had said in 1976 that U.S. technology had "always been ahead of the U.S.S.R.'s by at least five years." It quoted General Graham, the former head of the Defense Intelligence Agency, as rationalizing Russia's expansion of its blue-water fleet: "It's a tough thing for the Soviet Navy to come up with a [broad-ocean] capability," Graham had said. "Their seas are landlocked." The Center quoted the Library of Congress study as concluding that "the Soviet Navy . . . is still structured primarily to protect the mother country."

Doves also took heart from the basic inferiority of Soviet troops, a point confirmed by the MiG-25 defector, Viktor Belenko. Belenko said 29 per cent of Soviet forces were composed of minorities not fluent in Russian. Because of low capabilities, most "technicians" knew only one aspect of a given task. Soldiers learned by rote.

Even an elite Soviet force such as pilots are given considerably less initiative than Western pilots. In 1978, General Brown recounted, to the author, Belenko's surprise at how his American equivalents operated: "He just couldn't believe what he saw. We took him around, after they finished interrogating him, to visit some of our units and what-have-you. He was utterly amazed. They just don't operate that way. He was amazed at the degree of reliance we placed on the individual planning initiative of flight leaders, in addition to the [freedom of the] social environment and everything else."

But discipline and health standards were reported high in the Soviet forces—no soldier in armored units wears glasses, for instance; and a CIA report on Soviet defense spending, produced during the election campaign "in the interest of timeliness"—as its preface said—had impressed a large number of policymakers. The report noted that the U.S.S.R.'s Strategic Rocket Forces, which operates land-based strategic missiles, now commanded 14 per cent of the Soviet defense budget, compared to 11 per cent in 1970. The Air Force's share had gone from 17 to 20 per cent, with most of the increase going for Frontal Aviation Command, some for Military Transport Aviation; although spending on Long Range Aviation had increased, it had decreased proportionally. Spending on the Air Defense Forces had fallen.

That Soviet military air transport was being upgraded was demonstrated in late 1977 by the massive Soviet arms airlift to Ethiopia. This was treated as a test exercise, using far more aircraft than were really required—225, according to U.S. intelligence, most of them the big Antonov-22s, some of them empty, under the navigational control of a new reconnaissance satellite, Kosmos-964, launched for the occasion. Several merchant ships were also sent to Ethiopia from the Black Sea, with rail lines closed to routine traffic as part of a war-priorities exercise.

The Army's share of the budget, the CIA report said, had remained steady at about 23 per cent, and the Navy's at 18 per cent, with the major growth item being Backfires for naval aviation. Almost 20 per cent of all spending went on command and support. The implications were that the Russians were planning for an attack situation, using land-based missiles and Backfires, not long-range Air Force planes. They were also said to be pushing ahead with the new Baykal-Amur railroad to the Pacific naval base at Sovetskaya Gavan.

The NATO defense ministers, meeting in Europe in 1977, were given a grimly impressive picture of current and future Soviet military programs in Europe, stressing developments in the fields of missiles, tanks, submarines, carriers and other ships, and chemical and antisatellite warfare. The Russians were said to be producing a new submarine every five weeks, 800 warplanes a year. (In 1978, the Pentagon said that by the following year, the Soviet Union would have as many fighters as the United States and NATO put together.) The NATO report said that in 1976, the Soviet Union had fielded 2,000 new tanks, compared to 400 in the United States, despite the fact that NATO had 50 per cent more manpower than the WTO, and twice the industrial base.

Army Lieutenant General Samuel V. Wilson, the present director of the Defense Intelligence Agency, made additional points about increased Soviet strength in congressional hearings later that year. Columnists Rowland Evans and Robert Novak claimed that Russia was now producing MiG-27s—the improved MiG-23, and Moscow's answer to the F-15—at a rate of 1,000 yearly. *Aviation Week* reported that they were being deployed by the air forces of Hungary, Bulgaria and Czechoslovakia. Government spokesmen said the Soviet Union was developing 3 new aircraft—a MiG-29 multi-role, all-weather fighter which would be better than the F-15, an antitank aircraft equivalent of the A-10 and a supersonic bomber based on the Tu-144—Moscow's equivalent of Concorde—which would be better than the Backfire and more like the politically stalled B-1. This was expected to be operational by 1982. A new submarine, code-named Typhoon by NATO and resembling the Trident-II in satellite shots, was being built at Severomorsk, near Murmansk. The Czechs were outfitting the Warsaw Treaty nations with a rapid and deadly rocket-fired antitank system, the RM-70 Tatra.

Defense Department projections said that the United States currently had 140 per cent more warheads than the Soviet Union, but with 65 per cent less megatonnage. Using the B-52 instead of the B-1 would reduce the superiority in warhead numbers to 26 per cent by 1986 and would produce a 75 per cent inferiority in megatonnage. In throw-weight, the Pentagon said, the Soviet Union is 33 per cent superior to the United States; the B-52 option would make this Soviet superiority 94 per cent by 1986. U.S. accuracy—"hard target kill potential"—was said to be 60 per cent superior to Russia's, but this was projected to give way to a 50 per cent Soviet advantage by 1986.

The claimed imbalance partly comes from the fact that the Soviet Union has the world's most powerful ICBM force—namely, 50 6- or 8-MIRV SS-18s, whose throw-weights are seven times that of the Minuteman-IIIs—and from the fact that Soviet ICBM silos are said to be twice as hardened as U.S. silos.

Defense Secretary Harold Brown told a Washington audience in 1977 that Russia was developing a "fourth generation of ICBMs" at a rate of "100–150 a year." In all, it had "4 new ICBMs" under evaluation. But White House officials agreed that the Russians were not "cheating" on SALT I. They had exercised their right to transfer 200 SS-7 and SS-8 ICBMs to their submarine fleet, thus keeping the land-based ICBM force to the agreed 1,400 warheads, and bringing submarine launchers up from 740 to something close to the SALT I permitted figure of 950. A senior Carter appointee in the State Department said the Russian buildup in Europe was aimed, not at preparation for war, but at Europe's "Finlandization" by intimidation.

The *Times*'s authoritative Drew Middleton raised the question of a Soviet threat to Yugoslavia appearing after the death of President Tito—a question which presidential candidate Jimmy Carter had mishandled during the campaign, implying a green light from Washington to Moscow to invade. Middleton also raised the problem that weapon-grade chrome was mostly imported into the United States from two countries, South Africa and Rhodesia, where representative governments were coming to power with Russian help. A logical conclusion would be that the West in general, and the United States in particular, should throw its support now to the political forces which everyone expected to govern the two countries in the near or fairly near future; but this logic faces the reflex of powers—especially great powers—to support a status quo that is not hostile, and to go down the tube with it.

What is the meaning of the huge Russian missile buildup? Are the Russians stressing unmanned weapons to make up for human deficiencies? Certainly, Soviet Government trust in the Russians themselves is limited in some ways: When a Kosmos-955 electronic Ferret satellite was launched from Plesetsk, on September 20, 1977, Leningrad spectators who noticed the glare in the sky were informed by the local press that it was an "unidentified flying object."

American opinions as to how to interpret all these problems into policy remained sharply divergent. Some were not disturbed by the Soviet buildup. The CDI, for instance—concentrating on cost, and ignoring the diplomatic power of arms—recommended canceling the B-1 bomber, the sea-launched cruise-missile program, large attack submarines, the Army's SAM-D missile and a proposed new jet-engine facility, while delaying a decision on the nuclear strike cruisers and AWACS planes, stopping production of A-7 and A-4 naval attack aircraft, cutting back on every major construction project in the defense budget and gradually withdrawing tactical nukes abroad.

But on the whole, as mentioned earlier, the mood of American thinking about the Soviet threat was moving well to the right of liberal thinking on the subject. A U.S. poll conducted in late 1976 showed hawkishness growing in the American population: In 1972, only 9 per cent of respondents had favored an increase in defense spending, while 37 per cent had wanted a cut; by 1974, 17 per cent had wanted an increase, while those wanting to spend less had fallen slightly to 33 per cent. By 1976, a greater proportion favored an increase—28 per cent, against only 20 per cent seeking defense-budget economies. In 1978, in a similar poll, hawks outnumbered doves by 37 to 16 per cent. Wrote Washington *Post* defense correspondent George C. Wilson:

> Regardless of how the most recent national intelligence estimates on the Soviet threat are interpreted, a broadened constituency favoring higher defense spending faces the Carter administration, according to Pentagon leaders.

There are clearly strong doubts in the minds of most Americans about the reality of détente—doubts stirred by the Soviet military buildup. Whether for politics or war, there seems to be broad acceptance that the rules of the game of weapons cannot be changed by one player alone.

THE NATO FACTOR

The United States has, of course, a stake in the armories of Latin America and Canada, and the latter has "northern tier" NATO responsibilities. But the rest of the Americas have relatively modest armed forces in global terms; reluctant and often resentful pawns in major-power politics, these countries will be looked at in the final chapters of this book, on weapons diplomacy as such. Of much greater enduring concern, for both Washington and Moscow, is Europe.

Under the Atlantic Treaty, an attack on any member state is an attack on all. Europe is thus the only potential war theater where U.S. troops would be automatically committed if an ally was attacked. It is, therefore, the region of the world most in the mind of American planners when armor is discussed.

Rainforested Vietnam was not really tank country, in the way that, say, the Middle East archetypically is—conflicts there are studied with consummate interest in the Kremlin and the Pentagon. The drubbing which Israeli tanks took in 1973 consequently marked a turning point in the thinking of army planners. With new antitank missiles scoring direct hits on their targets 2 miles away, and minefields being sown rapidly in the path of a tank column on the move, was the day of armor ending, just as the knight in armor had disappeared from the battlefield long before the end of horse cavalry itself? Yet, for so long as the remote possibility of conventional war in Europe was a part of the elaborate game of weapons between the superpowers, armored warfare·could not be ignored.

In short, the Chrysler XM-1 Main Battle Tank is not mainly intended to defend the shores of Oregon or New Jersey, but to hold Western Europe. The principal defense debate of recent times has been to decide who would win a presumably short, sharp holocaust across the Atlantic, given the greater strength of the Warsaw Treaty powers in Europe. NATO's contingency planning concerns how to respond to a swift Marxist-Leninist assault on what is, seen from Washington, the soft underbelly of capitalism.

But a nuclear war is even more on the planners' minds. As mentioned earlier, Western Europe is not nuclearly defenseless, even without the U.S. umbrella. Britain has its own nuke warheads on its 64 Polaris A-3 missiles; France has two different models of submarine-launched missile of its own: the M-2, with a 500-kiloton warhead and a nearly 2,000-mile range, and the M-20, which hurls 1 megaton of firepower over one tenth that distance. In production since 1973, there are now over 50 M-2s in the Gallic inventory. Production of the M-20 started in 1975: At the time of writing, production figures were still secret. Both missiles, like their American counterparts, use solid propellants. They have interchangeable second stages. The thermonuclear warhead of the M-20 will eventually become standard on both weapons.

America's principal NATO allies also have exceptional air-to-air missiles, notably the British Taildog and especially the French Matra-Magic R-550. For a while, the German Air Force relied on that country's Viper missile, since scrapped in favor of the U.S. Super-Sidewinder. European technology is closely involved in some basically American-made NATO weaponry, as the cases of the Harrier or the XM-1 tank show. Missiles are an active field for technological cross-fertilization. Britain adapted the Sparrow AIM-7E air-to-air weapon with a monopulse (target) seeker, calling its own version the Skyflash missile. Tried out at the Pacific Missile Test Center, the adapted Sparrow scored eleven hits in twelve firings, six of them contact hits. Its look-down seeker after low-flying targets has since been adapted on the American Sparrow. Northrop has a license agreement with France's Engins Matra which provides the U.S. firm with aerodynamic and control data relating to the Magic missile, mentioned above. This has enabled Northrop to make the Sidewinder more maneuverable, with less drag. The United States is also building the Franco-German Roland missile.

Still more obviously, in aerospace, many European front-line aircraft are comparable in quality to the most sophisticated of U.S. planes, and are their competitors on the global market. A typical example is the Tornado Multi-Role Combat Aircraft (MRCA), which can skim the trees at near-sonic speeds and pass Mach-2 at altitude. It can climb from brakes-off to 30,000 feet in less than two minutes at 90 per cent of rated power. Built mostly by Britain and Germany, with some input from Italy, in a trinational consortium called Panavia, the first twin-place, swing-wing Tornado was flown in 1974: The plane was scheduled to be in wing service by 1979. Britain has ordered 385, Germany 324 and Italy 100, all over a ten-year delivery period. In early 1977, Britain was expecting a total bill of $7.25 billion for the program, Germany $6 billion and Italy $2 billion. At about $19 billion apiece, the Tornado is not a cut-price plane, but the European consortium hopes to reduce this figure by selling as many as 200 more to Belgium, the Netherlands, Denmark and Norway—the purchasers of the American F-16.

With terrain-following radar automatically flying the plane up and down over hills, a Tornado with wings extended could fly under enemy defenses and radars for close ground support and, like the A-10, bomb a battlefield from 100 feet; with wings swept back for high-speed flight, it fulfills a range of other fighter and fighter-bomber functions. Turbo-Union, a company owned 40 per cent by Rolls-Royce, 40 per cent by a West German corporation and 20 per cent by Fiat, will build all the tur-bofan engines in Britain. British Aerospace, Messerschmitt-Bolkow-Blohm and Aeritalia will each build the number of airframes needed by their countries' respective air forces. According to a press release by the consortium, the Tornado project was expected to provide 35,000 jobs in Britain alone, 27,000 in Germany, about 8,000 in Italy.

The economics of weaponry will be examined in a later chapter, but some evidence of how this factor can compete with the efficiency of the NATO war machine was illustrated by an article on the Tornado published in August 1976, in the British journal *Flight International*. This noted that the three producing countries had, at that time, eleven pilots checked out on the Tornado, and added: "Early in the program, the U. S. Defense Department turned down a request that Panavia pilots be permitted some time on F-111s to familiarize them with variable-geometry [swing-wing] handling." The article added that the pilots had fortunately adapted, without accident, but without this help.

Another major European development is the Anglo-French Jaguar attack plane. This twin-engined aircraft is built by British Aerospace and Dassault-Bréguet, with engines by Rolls-Royce and Turboméca. Research began in 1965. The first Jaguars entered service with the French Air Force in 1972 and with the RAF the following year. A bilateral agreement calls for both air forces to take about two hundred of them. In addition, there is a Jaguar International for export, with more powerful engines, which has already been sold to such varied markets as Ecuador and Oman.

All models will do Mach-1.6 a 36,000 feet, Mach-1.1 at sea level. The higher speed than the American A-10 gives them a less impressive short-field performance. The range is 500 miles, or 310 at sea level, but with additional fuel tanks and lighter ordnance this goes up by over 50 per cent. The tactical versions carry two 30mm. single-barrel cannon and up to 6,000 pounds of munitions on four wing pods, including a choice of Sidewinders or Matra-Magics. French Jaguars, which have laser-guided AS-31 air-to-surface missiles, have been used by the French Air Force in support of the governments in two former French colonies—Chad, which faces a Libyan-supported rebellion, and Mauritania, which tried to annex part of former Spanish Sahara and faced a counterinvasion by the Saharan guerrilla army, Polisario.

Another European attack plane in advanced development, as noted later in a discussion of German forces, is the Franco-German Alphajet.

Is NATO Prepared?

Floods of ink have been used in the past two years or so to evaluate the comparative strength of NATO and Warsaw Treaty Organization (WTO) forces. The bulk of NATO strength lies with American weapons and German men. The Bonn Government could mobilize a million men in forty-eight hours and its armed forces are said to be the best-trained in the Alliance, barring none; a congressional seminar was told in 1977 that German forces' combat-readiness surpassed that of American forces. In 1973, the "largest part of the [U. S.] Army's tanks and heavy weapons stockpiled in Germany was shipped to Israel to replace armaments lost in combat," according to General Michael S. Davison, who commanded the U. S. Seventh Army in Germany at the time. As mentioned earlier, the author was told in 1978 by the retiring chairman of the U. S. Joint Chiefs, General George Brown, that the U.S. stockpiles in Europe were still deficient. That year, Congress voted to bar further sales of U.S. stocks in Europe to non-NATO countries unless the President certified that an "international crisis" existed and sent Congress a plan within sixty days for replenishing stocks.

Dr. Kissinger, in a press conference, sought to allay fears about the Alliance's unpreparedness for war. There was parallel pressure for the allies to make up their minds quickly on one key program—to spend an estimated $2.4 billion on twenty-seven European-based AWACS planes to join America's twenty-four. These were to be "NATO property," with NATO (not national) wing and fuselage markings, and the wholly new concept of multi-national crews. There was hesitation (and ultimately refusal) from Britain, which would have had to scrap its own, less expensive Nimrod program. This conflict is looked at in more detail in Chapter 7.

NATO was clearly in disarray—unconvinced of its own abilities, suspicious of the reliability of the American commitment, and resentful of U.S. supremacy in the global arms trade, particularly as it affected Europe itself. To bolster morale, the United States promised lamely to deploy the new F-15 in Germany in the spring of 1977, and to add a further wing of F-111 swing-wing fighter-bombers to its presence in Britain.

The handwringing about NATO brought home strongly its essential dependence on two national forces—those of the United States and Germany. This was emphasized by the "Autumn Forge" NATO exercise conducted in the fall of 1978—to which the Soviet Union and China were invited to send observers. (The 1975 Helsinki agreement requires notification of major military maneuvers by both sides. The Soviet Union notifies but does not always invite observers.) To the Germans would go the heavy task, in the event of a conventional war, of holding the Russians for two days while a diplomatic settlement was sought: If that—or they—failed, most defense analysts seemed agreed, the prospect was for tactical nuclear warfare at least. Norway expressed growing concern in 1977 about the huge concentration of Soviet military power in the Kola Peninsula, near Norway's polar border. Congress, State Department and CIA reports continued to stress the imbalance of numbers between WTO and NATO tanks and tactical aircraft, notably interceptors, and the growth of Soviet and Eastern European defense budgets.

Budget comparisons with the Communist countries are, however, difficult. For simplification, U.S. strategists usually extrapolate a Soviet figure by calculating what it would cost the Russians to produce its forces if they paid American wages and other advantages, and American prices for weapons—in other words, what it would cost for the Pentagon to "buy" Red Army or Soviet Air Force equipment. For comparison, this is not unrealistic, but NATO figures do not similarly inflate the lower costs of, say, German and French forces, which still benefit from the money-saving draft. A table published by the International Institute of Strategic Studies found NATO spending $149.4 billion on defense in 1975, compared to a figure of $132.1 billion for the WTO. (The reader should bear in mind that the Soviet Union can, in Fischer's words, "use manpower rather lavishly," while its technology is relatively expensive—but, conversely, simpler, which cuts operation and maintenance costs.) Of the NATO figure, $89 billion came from the United States, $16.1 billion from Germany, $14 billion from France and $11.1 billion from Britain. U.S. armed forces then totaled 2,087,000, to France's 513,000, Germany's 495,000 and Britain's all-volunteer forces of 344,000. Russia accounted for $124 billion of WTO expenditure—with East Germany a distant second at $2.6 billion. The Soviet Union provided 3,650,000 of Eastern Europe's 4,722,000 forces, according to the IISS study.

In active combat divisions, the Warsaw Pact nations today have an advantage of 58⅓ (24 of them armored) to 28⅓ (8 armored); but NATO divisions are substantially larger than WTO equivalents. In actual manpower, the three central European countries of the WTO (East Germany, Poland and Czechoslovakia) have 925,000 men (564,000 in combat units) of whom about half (455,000) are Russian, to the West's 780,000 (414,000 combat troops) in the central European area; of these, 495,000 are German and 224,000 American. But official U.S. estimates have the WTO mobilizing about 90 divisions in the region in a few weeks. Library of Congress expert Collins thinks immediate reinforcements would be 21 fresh divisions, 18 of them Russian and 14 armored. Fischer sees NATO going from 414,000 combat troops to 589,000 in two weeks and to 660,000 in five weeks; the Eastern European countries, which would presumably have a day or so's head start in any case, would, Fischer thinks, go from 564,000 men to 934,000 in two weeks. Collins sees NATO drawing on 12 or 13 reserve divisions, only 2 of them armored—because of the 3,000 miles separating the United States from its allies.

Warsaw Treaty Organization aircraft in the central European area outnumber NATO aircraft by more than two to one, but ranges and payload generally favor the more sophisticated NATO inventory, which has more accurate weapons and better-trained pilots. But because WTO aircraft are usually simpler, and therefore easier to maintain, they may be able to fly more sorties between maintenance checks than those of the Alliance. Congress was told by Pentagon experts in 1977 that NATO must triple traditional sortie rates "if we are to turn the tide." Charles E. Myers, Jr., assistant director for air warfare of the research and engineering division of Defense, suggested more light all-weather interceptors with a "look-down" and "shoot-down" capability, supplementing expensive F-15s with more F-16s, F-18s, F-5s and Mirages. Since only the more sophisticated, more powerful F-15 can as yet handle AIM-7F and Skyflash missiles, Myers said, a smaller "fire-and-forget AMRAAM" (Advanced Medium-Range Air-to-Air Missile) would have to be developed.

Overall, in central Europe in 1978, WTO had 92 divisions to 71 for NATO, while both had just over 4,000 aircraft. On the northern flank, the East had 9 divisions to NATO's 7, but was outnumbered 300–130 in aircraft. In reserve divisions, WTO had 73 to NATO's 6, and 5,800 aircraft in all to NATO's 4,400.

However, south of the Alps, on NATO's southern flank—Turkey, Italy and Greece—the advantage was clearly to the West: These countries had 540,000 troops committed to NATO, most of them Turkish, facing 395,000 Warsaw Pact forces, or 34 combat divisions to 28; but the Communist countries, according to Collins, had 5 armored divisions with 7,500 tanks to NATO's 2 divisions with 4,000 tanks, and, overall, had 54 divisions to NATO's 47. Warsaw Treaty combat aircraft—625—were outnumbered by 725 NATO planes, although in overall aircraft inventory the Communist countries outnumbered NATO's southern flank 1,720–1,260. The non-U.S. NATO fleet in the area totaled 99 ships, including 32 submarines. The U.S. Sixth Fleet included a classified number of submarines and 19 other vessels. The only opposing fleet is Russian—23 ships, by Collins' count, including about 12 attack submarines. U.S. naval aircraft in the Mediterranean averaged 200 to Russia's 15. Naturally, all these 1978 figures will be slightly out of date by the time this book appears, but they are indicative of the balance of power in Europe.

In a mobilization situation, NATO could muster about 3,450 aircraft—perhaps nearly 6,000 (including the small Canadian component) if defenses in other parts of the world were run down. The Communist countries could be expected to increase their numbers to about 3,700, but to perhaps as much as 6,800 if Russia feared no attack from China. Compared to NATO's advantage in quality of crews, aircraft and weapon accuracy, WTO has stronger ground-to-air defenses, notably the SA-9 and the new, electro-optically tracked SA-8. But thanks to Western advances in the technology of electronic countermeasures, both sides are reckoned equally vulnerable to attacks while on the ground. NATO's deep strike capacity is, in Fischer's view, "considerably superior." He concludes that "the major area of concern about the air balance is the uncertainty about the early period of reinforcement."

In war-games terms, and therefore in terms of the use of armed power in diplomacy, this issue is crucial. To what extent is NATO essentially a desperate holding operation, based on the assumption that the Warsaw Pact could easily win the first stages of any European conventional and tactical-nuclear confrontation, with massive—and, by modern standards, belated—U.S. intervention necessary to reverse the tide?

PRM 10, an early, top-secret Presidential Review Memorandum prepared for President Carter by Zbigniew Brzezinski, noted that "consonant with present NATO strategy, including forward defense, the United States is committed to minimal loss of territory in the event of a WTO conventional attack." The wording seemed ominous when it leaked to Allied defense attachés in Washington, so a later version of the PRM added the words "and ultimately to restore pre-war boundaries."

Defense sources said the Pentagon in fact envisaged the loss of about one third of West Germany in any war, unless unacceptably high increases in the U.S. and other NATO budgets were imposed—including a doubling of NATO combat divisions.

Fourteen NATO defense ministers, including Secretary Brown—but not including those of France and Greece—agreed in 1977 to a 3 per cent increase in defense expenditures; but in Washington the Office of Management and Budget put a 1 per cent ceiling on fiscal 1978. U.S. defense spending did in fact rise by about 3 per cent in 1977, compared to over 4 per cent in the Soviet Union. Among other NATO countries, only Denmark and Belgium increased their military budgets by 3 per cent or more. The North Atlantic Military Committee's report for the 1977 meeting appeared to agree with the CIA figures in saying that Soviet military expenditure was "between 11 and 12 per cent" of GNP (the CIA had said "11 to 13 per cent"), compared to America's 5.5 per cent (of a much larger GNP, of course) and Western Europe's average of 3.5 per cent.

Two senators specializing in defense matters, Democrat Sam Nunn of Georgia and the late Republican Dewey Bartlett of Oklahoma, along with retired Lieutenant General James F. Hollingsworth, made proposals that year for vastly increased NATO spending, involving a 20 per cent increase in manpower. The aim was to meet a surprise Warsaw Pact attack—with only forty-eight hours anticipated warning instead of the previously anticipated three weeks—and aiming at a "rollback" of invading forces in two weeks instead of eight.

Congressman Les Aspin, a dovish House defense expert, estimated the tab for "H.N.B." (as he described the Hollingsworth-Nunn-Bartlett proposals) at $46.4 billion. Aspin's budget included figures for hardened shelters for increased numbers of NATO aircraft, and the cost of buying vast tracts of expensive German real estate to build the new U.S. bases.

The "NATO crisis" is an ongoing debate. Many congressional Democrats join hawks in supporting the pessimistic view of the Library of Congress' senior defense expert, John M. Collins, who is persuaded that the Russians have overwhelming superiority. Several senators and congressmen have claimed White House harassment of the outspoken Collins—including canceling his automatic "step" pay increase in 1977.

Indeed, it looked as though Collins' views were getting home on the Hill itself. In 1977, nearly a quarter-billion dollars was voted by Congress in the military construction authorization bill to improve the combat-readiness of U.S. forces in Europe. Included among the authorized projects in 1978 were new ammunition storage depots, maintenance shops in Europe for U.S. reinforcements in time of crisis, and bomb shelters for U.S. aircraft. In 1979, the Pentagon began transferring about $3 billion of Stateside equipment to Germany—the stockpile for three reinforcement divisions. Since U.S. reserve armor alone is normally intended to be enough for nine divisions, this gives some idea of the staggering shortages caused by claims on NATO stocks by Israel and the Vietnam War—shortages which had been partially made up in the past five years. About 100 miles north of the main U.S. air base at Ramstein, a hardened underground bunker is finally being built at Boerfink to house a wartime joint headquarters for the commander in chief, Allied Forces, Central Europe, and the Allied Air Forces commander for the sector. But many Pentagon experts seemed unsure whether even these measures, and increased spending by NATO allies, would save what they still see as a gravely flawed and ineffective organization.

While boosting the budget to beef up NATO's defenses, the Carter administration is also offering, as part of SALT, to cut U.S. force commitments to Europe. After the President contradictorily agreed to bring some U.S. units in Europe up to full strength, NATO approved a U.S. offer in the SALT talks to withdraw 1,000 nuclear warheads and 29,000 troops in exchange for a proposed Soviet reduction of 5 divisions (55,000 to 75,000 men), including 1,500 to 1,700 tanks, and the setting of manpower ceilings. Senator Nunn has criticized this proposal, saying that it is not manpower *per se*, but specific types of units, that would have to be withdrawn for such a *quid pro quo* to mean anything. He suggested that the Russians would merely remove their most obsolete tanks. And his Republican defense-specialist colleague, Dewey Bartlett, said: "The most significant balance in conventional arms is not in fact between the United States and the Soviet Union but rather between NATO and the Warsaw Pact. The United States provides only 10 per cent of NATO's ground forces, 20 per cent of its naval forces and 25 per cent of its tactical air forces."

The man behind Senator Nunn's thinking is Jeffrey Record, his legislative assistant for military affairs. Writing in the fall 1977 issue of *Survival*, Record found another major weakness in NATO planning. He criticized the "simple and obvious lack of even the most rudimentary preparation for combat on a nuclear battlefield shown by NATO's general-purpose forces."

Record added:

> Despite a strategy which pays lip service to escalation across the nuclear threshold, and despite unceasing official discussion within NATO about the importance of chemical-biological-radiological (CBR) protection, both U.S. and Allied forces stand virtually naked before an adversary who intends and is prepared to use [CBR] weapons.

The Soviet Union, said Record, had made a "comprehensive effort" to insulate its forces from radiation, but

> NATO continues to develop and produce armored fighting vehicles whose crews and occupants would be easy game in a lingering nuclear environment. Even the new American XM-1 Main Battle Tank and the proposed new mechanized infantry combat vehicle lack any system of collective protection. Continued reliance upon fighting vehicles ill-equipped to operate in a CBR environment is nothing short of criminal.

Record suggested relying more on submarine and other offshore platforms and dispersing nuclear artillery and surface-to-surface missile ordnance among a larger number of storage sites. He added: "The U. S. Army, Europe, might consider an alternative to storing over half its theater [tactical] ammunition reserves at a single location."

Alton Frye, a Council on Foreign Relations gadfly, agrees with Jeffrey Record and scores NATO's nuclear forces as "largely an anachronism." He says:

> The temporary U.S. advantage in "tac-nukes" long ago dissolved in the face of matching Soviet deployment—whose principal targets are our own nuclear storage facilities and delivery vehicles in Western Europe.

Frye says that "one or two Poseidon or Trident boats could handle the tactical targets . . . under far superior control to any arrangements for commanding soldiers caught up in the heat of combat. Indeed, if essential, these weapons could be programmed on short notice to attack major tank and infantry concentrations assembling for an advance." But Frye admits that "it may be useful to retain certain nuclear forces on the Continent."

Essentially, since Nixon's time, the United States has been moving from a two-and-a-half-war readiness to a one-and-a-half-war one—probably a war in Europe and a "brush-fire" war, perhaps in the Gulf. There is little emphasis at present on the Pacific theater. The stress in the new Carter defense budget for fiscal 1979 was on support for NATO—notably, doubling the order for Abrams tanks over the next decade. Administration spokesmen talked of an "antiblitzkrieg emphasis."

Secretary Brown told a House hearing: "Currently, within ten days, we could augment our five and two thirds [U.S.] divisions and twenty-eight tactical air squadrons in Europe by little more than one division and forty squadrons. We plan, by 1983, to be able to add five divisions and sixty tactical air squadrons in the same amount of time." This and other defense needs were the rationale for the increase of $56 billion in the budget over five years.

At the 1978 NATO "summit" in Washington, the allies as a whole agreed to spend $80 billion on improving NATO's defenses. Each country promised, once again, to increase defense expenditure by 3 per cent. The United States agreed to develop plans to bring reserves to Europe more quickly in the event of war by the massive use of civil airliners. And in late 1978, Carter was actively considering giving NATO an equivalent of the Soviet Union's 3-MIRV-ed, mobile SS-20 surface-to-surface missile. Deploying the Pershing-II and a ground-launched version of the Tomahawk cruise missile in Europe is being mentioned. The Europeans agreed to build up their reserves and concentrate on the development of antisubmarine warfare, air defenses and electronic warfare capabilities.

The stress on air defenses and electronic warfare is a direct lesson of the 1973 war in the Middle East. Within thirty minutes of the outbreak of hostilities, Egypt, using Warsaw Treaty equipment, had either jammed or destroyed, both from the air and the ground, most of Israel's radar, air-to-surface communications and long-range ground communications. This gave pause to Pentagon planners. The basic unit of NATO combat communications is the FIST (Fire Support Team). This small (six- or seven-man) group directs aircraft, missiles and artillery. Students at West Point are taught a recent "classic" case: In 1974, Turkish forces swiftly occupied enough of Cyprus to protect the Turkish minority from a hostile junta largely thanks to its success in first putting down a FIST, by helicopter, in a Turkish ghetto near Nicosia airport.

This handful of officers and men virtually directed the decisive moves in occupying northern Cyprus. Without secure communications, much of warfare would be left to chance. *New Times* Washington correspondent Arthur T. Hadley asked a USAF pilot in Germany in 1978: "Colonel, do you expect to be talking to the FIST team after the first half hour?" Retorted the pilot: "Hadley, I don't expect to be able to talk to my wing man after the first ten minutes."

At the NATO summit, Belgium, Britain, Canada, Denmark, France, Germany, Holland, Italy and Norway decided to participate in the U.S. Navstar (satellite navigation) program, as a step to protecting one key element of communications. There would also, it was announced, be more flying time for aircrews—USAF units were said to be down to ten hours a month. Special help was promised for economically disadvantaged Portugal and Turkey.

Congress was skeptical. The Senate Armed Services Committee, reversing itself from the year before, rejected an administration request for $373 million for further U.S. military construction in Europe, saying the Europeans should do more themselves. To counterbalance part of the cut, the Committee did, however, recommend increasing the U.S. share of the proposed NATO-wide construction program (shared airfields, fuel dumps, headquarters buildings, etc.) from the $90 million requested by Carter to $150 million. Currently, the United States pays about 27.3 per cent of the NATO infrastructure, but this is due to go down, proportionally. Germany pays 26.5 per cent. Britain comes a poor third at 12 per cent. There are wide variations between what each country pays. Poor countries like Greece and Turkey, despite their apparently modest contributions in financial terms, are actually spending 6.3 per cent and 5.4 per cent of their GNPs, respectively, on defense. The United States, in 1978, spent 5.2 per cent, Britain 4.9 per cent. No one else spent over 4 per cent. Denmark and Italy spent only 2.5 per cent, Canada 2 per cent.

Standardization and Interoperability

A Euro-NATO group is studying comparative training, and RAF, Canadian and German units, as noted, have flown in the Red Flag program —the air-combat war games at Nellis base. But standardization of weapons, and interoperability, are still a long way off. NATO's principal single disadvantage vis-à-vis the Warsaw nations is thought by many specialists to stem from this lack of standardization; it is, after all, an alliance of competing capitalist societies.

The U. S. Army has an International Rationalization Office, and the

Air Force has a similar project, while NATO's Task Force No. 8 also handles the problem. The Senate Armed Services Committee has proposed setting up an Office of Standardization at the Pentagon, while its House equivalent created, in 1978, a subcommittee on NATO standardization, interoperability and readiness. But the Alliance's planes do not yet even have interoperable IFF (Identification Friend or Foe) equipment. It was this that led to forty-four Allied aircraft (half of the patrol planes used) being "shot down," photographically, by "friendly fire" in a 1976 NATO exercise in Europe. Now that Hawkeye and AWACS equipment is sensitive to the "radar reflection signature"—the aircraft's or ship's silhouette —and not solely to IFF, the situation has improved, but nonstandardized IFF is still a problem. (In 1979, the Pentagon announced a $250 million program to enhance and standardize IFF in NATO.) Similar snags exist in voice communications, for which each country uses scramblers whose codes are jealously guarded. This could be solved by outfitting NATO tactical radios and teleprinters with a device that could take an unscrambling printed-circuit board, the code of which could be changed daily— or even twice daily.

NATO operates 39 models of 23 different "families" of tactical aircraft alone; it has 31 different antitank weapons, including 20 different antitank missiles—of which 4 are different types of wireguided missile; there are 18 more antitank weapons under development. There are 7 different Main Battle Tanks, 8 types of armored personnel carrier, about 100 different tactical missiles. The introduction of the XM-1 American tank and the German Leopard tanks will help, especially when they eventually share a common gun.

Dr. Walter LaBerge, the American assistant secretary general of NATO, wrote in the *NATO Review* in 1977 that the Alliance had 41 different types of naval gun above 20mm., 6 different species of recoilless rifle, 36 different types of fire-control radar, 8 different surface-to-air missile systems and 6 different types of anti-surface-ship missile. The "integrated" seven-nation Allied Mobile Force alone uses 7 types of tactical aircraft, 3 different types of mortars, machine guns and rifles, 50 different types of ammunition. Germany, for instance, still uses 7.62mm. machine-gun ammunition, because of its greater range and lethality. Canadian ovens are too small to heat American rations, while Germany (which expects to fight on its own territory) does not use field ovens at all.

LaBerge said in his article:

> Take, for example, the almost classic case of the F-111/MRCA [contest], where two aircraft, one American and the other developed by European partners, have many similar characteristics but have been developed with no standardization apart from the air in the tires and the fuel in the

tanks. Yet both aircraft have essentially the same mission, fly at the same low altitude at the same high speed, have the same aerodynamic configuration of swing wings, and both have two engines, terrain-following radar and similar low-altitude bomb-release systems.

Even more serious, there will be little or no interoperability in the future munitions of the two aircraft; weapons for the F-111 will be different from, and not interchangeable with, those of the MRCA and vice versa. This long-term incompatibility arises because in the initial airframe design neither producer considered the other's market as worth designing for.

That year, the Pentagon was prepared to admit that duplicative R & D was wasting over $11 billion of the $90 billion appropriated annually by NATO members for their NATO commitments. Back in 1974, General Andrew Goodpaster, then NATO's overall commander in Europe, had estimated that the Alliance was losing between 30 and 50 per cent of its capability due to lack of standardization.

In London in May 1977 Carter called for a strengthening of NATO forces and for further standardization. He made no mention of his own campaign promises to cut defense spending. He promised to consult with America's allies on all major arms decisions, and he pledged a "genuine two-way transatlantic trade in defense equipment."

In Brussels that month, Defense Secretary Harold Brown told British Defense Minister Fred Mulley that he had authorized Ford Aerospace and Communications Corporation, a subsidiary of the automobile giant, to share technical information with Britain's Marconi Elliott firm to co-produce a replacement for the Super-Sidewinder air-to-air missile, made by Ford and Raytheon for use with the F-14, F-15 and F-16. Marconi would build the guidance system. Britain responded by ordering 1,709 more of the present Sidewinders for $119 million.

Carter came to office espousing standardization as a cause. He promised sympathetic consideration for the Tornado, the Franco-German MILAN (*missile léger anti-char*) antitank missile and the Franco-German Roland surface-to-air missile. Aides said righteously that the President was hoping that, by providing American markets for European weapons, he would be able to discourage the allies from fueling the Third World arms race.

But the main rationale for standardization remained the simplifying of supply in the field and the coordination of operations. Democratic senator John Culver, recalling the case in which NATO planes were "shot down" by "friendly fire," said there were still differences in coding machinery, while some NATO radar systems interfered with the operation of others. Different air forces use different ordnance, different fuel nozzles, different auxiliary power units; in air refueling, USAF booms are not compatible with the European probe-and-drogue system; such items could, of course, be standardized at the planning stage, even with different aircraft.

NATO's Second Allied Tactical Air Force, containing Belgian, British, Dutch and German units, has eleven types of combat aircraft with different combat radiuses and five different missions, armed with five types of ammunition, six types of napalm container, sixteen different models of auxiliary fuel tanks. The Second ATAF's communications are not completely compatible with those of the Fourth ATAF, comprising U.S., Canadian and German wings. Such problems will be partially—but far from completely—solved by the widespread introduction of the F-16 and the Tornado.

General James H. Polk has noted the problem of rearming aircraft in Europe:

> It is a rare case when the visitor [to a base] from another nation can be rearmed, and then certainly not in the desired configuration. There are some differences in bomb racks and connectors, so that even a fresh load of iron bombs is at times impossible. Also, few national air forces have certified as safe and serviceable the bombs of other nations, and our air force is no exception. For most NATO aircraft, 20mm. cannon are quite common, but, curiously enough, reloading machines are not available at most foreign bases. Our F-4, for instance, cannot reload its cannon at a Belgian base, though the ammunition may be available. With respect to more advanced systems, only the Sidewinder missile is standardized and available, but other missiles and smart bombs cannot be cross-serviced. Thus the Allied fighters are interoperable to a degree; most can be turned around and put in flyable condition but must return to their own national air base for rearming.

Experts say that all this nonstandardization doubles deployment time; by 1978, it was costing NATO about $15 billion yearly that could be spent on additional weapons and equipment. The R & D subcommittee of the Senate Armed Services Committee still estimates that "NATO loses 30 to 40 per cent of its effectiveness because of inadequate standardization."

One problem is that replacement schedules for different nations do not coincide. If an important technological advance is scored by one member, standardization would either mean that others would have to make some of their systems obsolete ahead of time, or the inventor-nation would have to delay introducing the advance into its own inventory until the others were ready.

Initially, when NATO was armed by U.S. charity, standardization was nearly complete. Today, NATO Secretary-General Joseph Luns calls the situation a "nightmare." It is one not suffered by the Warsaw Pact countries.

Interoperability—different guns firing common ammunition, different aircraft carrying common weapons, different communications systems being able to talk to each other—is less difficult to achieve than standardization. LaBerge recommended concentrating on interoperability in five areas—tactical area communications, tactical aircraft rearming, tank gun ammunition, fuels and publications. Ambassador Robert W. Komer, adviser on NATO to Secretary Brown, addressing the 1978 NATO meeting in Brussels, added aircraft cross-servicing, battlefield surveillance and target designation-acquisition systems, as well as components and spare parts generally.

LaBerge thinks much of the absence of standardization and interoperability springs from commercial greed or misunderstood security. In his *NATO Review* article, he said:

> We occasionally appear to deny each other knowledge of analyses and test data, using the security blanket to achieve a delay for industrial or government exploitation within the discovering country. The result could be that unnecessary tests and trials are reproduced by several countries.
>
> . . .
>
> It may be true that some cases are justified on security grounds and others in order to make the free enterprise system work. However, on a government-to-government basis, I believe we should find a way of licensing inventions while maintaining security, so as to protect industrial positions while reducing the waste of multiple effort.

Opposition to standardization came from U.S. manufacturers, their congressmen and big labor. The Maremont Company of Saco, Maine, with five hundred workers, two senators and two congressmen, fought long and hard in 1976 against the Army's purchase of 14,000 Mag-58 machine guns for $30 million. Maremont protested that its M-60 was cheaper, challenged the Army's claim that the Belgian gun was more efficient and said the Belgian purchase had been part of the deal whereby Belgium agreed to buy the F-16 fighter. A court granted a preliminary injunction pending a GAO study, but this favored the Mag-58 and the Belgian import is now coming in. Congressmen William S. Cohen and David F. Emery, both Republicans, tried to delete funds for the foreign weapon from the fiscal-1977 defense appropriations; but in the final version of the weapons procurement authorization bill, Congress settled for an amendment by Maine's Democratic senator William D. Hathaway requiring Defense to report to Congress all NATO agreements calling for U.S. procurement of non-U.S. military equipment. Cohen's feistier defense of local interests later helped him defeat Hathaway for the Senate in 1978. Co-production, while often essential to winning an export contract, also involves the problem of selling technology to friendly countries which are, at the same time, commercial rivals; this, too, often arouses congressional ire.

On the other hand, Nunn and others have argued forcefully *for* standardization. A 1975 Nunn amendment to the defense-budget bill obliges the Pentagon to report, every six months, a "specific assessment of the costs and possible loss of nonnuclear combat effectiveness" resulting from nonstandardization within NATO. Amendments by Nunn and Culver in 1976 and 1977 require equipment procured for U.S. forces stationed in Europe to be standardized and operationally compatible with the equipment of NATO allies—but it will be a long time before this is so.

Competing with Nunn-Culver is the Buy America Act, which requires items purchased for "public use" to be "manufactured in the United States, substantially all from articles, materials or supplies mined, produced or manufactured in the United States" except where this is inconsistent with the "public interest." Since 1972, defense appropriation acts have included language inserted by South Carolina Republican Strom Thurmond banning non-American specialty metals, such as titanium, certain steels and other high-stress, heat-resistant alloys. The Buy America Act even bars the purchase of foreign-made uniforms or other textiles for "public use."

In 1976, the Ford administration requested language permitting the purchase of specialty metals where needed to satisfy offset agreements or to achieve NATO standardization. In the Ways and Means Committee, Republican Bill Frenzel of Minnesota and Democrat Sam Gibbons of Florida opposed this, saying legislative provisions could not be tacked onto an appropriations bill. The Senate went along with the White House request, but the House-Senate conference removed the provision. *Congressional Quarterly* noted that "no member of the appropriations committee of either house has embraced NATO standardization as a cause." Since 1975, while NATO has made progress at standardizing combat procedures, fuel and ammunition, Congress has criticized the high cost of making the Roland missile acceptable to Pentagon standards, and in 1976 the House Armed Services Committee directed the Army to develop an improved Chaparral as an alternative weapon.

There has unquestionably been some progress toward commonality. The U. S. Navy and Raytheon waived license fees and the recoupment of R & D costs to get the AIM-9L Super-Sidewinder missiles co-produced for local air forces in Germany, Britain and Norway. A similar arrangement will enable Germany to produce the USAF's Forward-Looking Infrared (FLIR) sensors, while AWACS is being offered to Allied air forces for a price that includes only 4 per cent recoupment of R & D.

To help standardization, the United States is jointly developing with Britain the latter's JP-233, a weapon designed to destroy enemy runways and "deny personnel access to the runways for repair." But this is a small program: The USAF has invested only $2 million in joint development. Another British system being developed in conjunction with the United States is the BL-755, an "antiarmor cluster-munitions family" for aircraft. Britain's Marconi Elliott, as well as its role in the new Super-Sidewinder, has a share in the development of America's earlier-mentioned AMRAAM missile; and if the AV-8B program is not killed off, Rolls-Royce and Hawker-Siddeley will receive $600 million in subcontracts from McDonnell-Douglas—engine and fuselage work—on this basically American improvement on the British jump-jet design. All such projects are meant to ensure that at least two Allied forces share the same weapon.

The Western fighter of the nineties may be a joint product of Grumman, British Aerospace and Messerschmitt-Bolkow-Blohm, or of some similar U.S.-European consortium. As well as helping standardization, this will also avoid duplication of R & D, and firms like Grumman claim that it will even cut production costs, although this is a much-contested point. Germany, Britain, Italy and the United States are cooperating on a joint ground rocket defense system, with the American half of the work being done by Boeing and Vought: The minimum aim is interoperability —different launchers firing the same projectiles. In 1978, the U. S. Navy and NATO began standardizing communications in rescue helicopters. The bulk of R & D funds for tactical warfare in the current U.S. military budget is NATO-oriented, and some of this will contribute toward standardization.

At the Washington NATO summit of 1978, the Alliance agreed to more "two-way standardization" and adopted fifteen cooperative weapon projects (air-to-air, ship-to-ship and antitank missiles, and communications systems). It agreed to a joint training system—in the United States—for some Allied aircrews. Among the new weapons systems which will receive joint logistical support will be the F-16, the British Lynx helicopter (to be used by Britain, Norway and Holland), the British Swingfire missile (shared by Britain and Belgium) and the Mark 46 torpedo, to be deployed by West Germany, Denmark and Holland.

Inflation as much as common sense is helping standardization, since high costs encourage shared research. American protectionism is breaking down, and a few guarded exceptions to the Buy America Act became possible in 1978, thanks largely to the earlier-mentioned legislative action by Senators Culver and Nunn. For fiscal 1979, the United States considered purchase of French, Italian and German aircraft bombs and missiles, German, Swiss, Swedish, Belgian and Italian guns, Belgian munitions and Norwegian surface-to-surface missiles and bomb fuses. In May 1978, the USAF in Britain went over to JP-8 kerosene-based fuel, which the RAF and other European air forces use, and which is rated safer and more efficient; this meant dropping JP-4, the naphtha-based fuel used by American military aviation. U.S. aircraft in continental Europe were to adapt to JP-8 later.

Standardization plans within Europe are affected by the tendency of the French to make end runs of their own. In 1968, all European members of NATO except Iceland, Portugal and France constituted Eurogroup, to cut costs and push for arms standardization; but it was not until 1975 that a European Program Group, composed of Eurogroup plus France, was set up—outside NATO. French egocentrism is breaking down only slowly. A 1977 study of Eurogroup and the EPG by the International Institute of Strategic Studies said the two groups had increased strains with the United States and had had only limited success. But Eurogroup is growing and spawning subgroups such as Euronad (Eurogroup National Armaments Director), Eurolongterm (planning) and Eurocom (tactical communications systems).

If proposals were solutions, the problems would have been solved long ago, for there has been no shortage of experts to make them. Robert A. Basil, the former assistant director for international programs in the Directorate of Defense Research and Engineering, has called for Europe and the United States to establish a fuller industrial partnership. He has said the United States should "NATOize the U.S. system-acquisition process" and ask that America's allies NATOize their own. He suggested going faster on interoperability initially, and more slowly on standardization. Basil favored "sustaining the American technological leadership" but resisting "the compulsion to have U.S. hardware always selected," noting that "it is difficult for the United States to choose even a European machine gun."

LaBerge similarly pointed out that "co-development of weapons is something that has seldom taken place on a transatlantic basis." Defense Secretary Brown pointed out that in spite of the eight-to-one ratio (of European spending on U.S. systems as opposed to American spending on European systems), Europe still had a dollar-flow advantage because of U.S. forces based there; but LaBerge pointed to the airborne warning and control system program as one into which few incentives for European participation had been structured. In a 1977 interview with *Avia-*

tion Week, he said the United States would have to provide a greater degree of offset to "get the program moving." The General Research Corporation, in an evaluation ordered by NATO, suggested a NATO common defense market. The corporation's report looked at the problem of military and patent security and said firms licensed to produce systems were often unable to distinguish legitimate national-security concerns from the industrial-competitive concerns of licensor firms, especially when these are American. It said this was an area requiring "high-priority attention." In late 1978, Deputy Secretary of State Warren Christopher told the House subcommittee on standardization: "The job before us is to see if we can work out with our allies adjustments in our modes of arms cooperation that will satisfy the vital security and economic interests we have in common, while helping the competitive commercial interests within the acceptable bounds of creative free enterprise . . . We plan to intensify our discussions with the Congress and with U.S. industry and labor." This would also mean, Christopher said, allowing Allied co-producers of U.S. weapons the right to "third-country sales that we would be prepared to make ourselves."

But the "Carter guidelines" on arms sales, virtually precluding some exports of co-produced U.S. weapons by NATO allies to third countries, seemed to contradict Christopher. If these guidelines threatened NATO standardization, this was already under criticism from the allies. At a NATO meeting in Tarabya, Turkey, attended by this writer shortly before the guidelines were announced, chairmen and members of the armed services committees of the parliaments of Germany, Britain and Norway complained that such arrangements were not working out equitably in any case.

France, a nonmilitary member of NATO, sought a memorandum of understanding from the United States similar to the one signed in 1975 by then Defense Secretary Schlesinger with Britain's Defense Minister Roy Mason, which exempts Britain from the higher costs of meeting the provisions of the Buy America Act and from import duties. Another sore point with its other European NATO partners is that Britain has a Treaty of Secrecy with the United States, as does Canada, allowing these two countries to participate in the high technology of purely U.S. defense hardware, a privilege denied to other NATO members.

Meanwhile, Belgium, Holland and Denmark had a problem with their fellow members of the European Common Market because they were being obliged to pay duties on U.S. components for the F-16. (Norway, the fourth European purchaser of the plane, is not a Common Market member.) The European Commission had ruled that exemptions for defense articles must be approved by all nine (now ten) member-nations;

but the three countries said exemptions had been automatic for larger European countries. They noted that American components for the Panavia Tornado aircraft had not been taxed, although no request for exemption was submitted to the Commission. Paul Vanden Boeynants, Belgium's Defense Minister, complained: "It is hard for me to understand why a measure which is regarded as being right for three large countries [Britain, Germany and Italy] would not be acceptable for three small countries." One hundred million dollars was at stake, and with it a threat to buy lower numbers of the aircraft. The Common Market implied that it would waive the duties only if the United States bought more European military hardware.

With Europe purchasing eight dollars' worth of U.S. arms for every dollar's worth of European weaponry sold to the United States, the allies were still complaining that standardization was not the two-way street that they had asked for—nor was it cutting their costs. Meanwhile, Senators Nunn and Bartlett, and others on Capitol Hill, had begun to articulate European-inspired expressions of concern. The two senators said in effect that an unstandardized NATO would be ineffective, however greatly its present forces are expanded. Some other military analysts, however, felt that standardization was perhaps not all that it was cracked up to be: Writing in *National Defense,* a conservative monthly, Californian management consultant John K. Daniels has said:

> There is good reason to believe that the U.S.S.R. would welcome an arms race based on homogenous equipment. Soviet technological innovation is no match for the West's . . .
>
> A NATO commitment to uniformity—with the one possible exception of communications—would emasculate the potential for shocking surprise that is latent in any diversified force . . .
>
> The Warsaw Pact military planning job would be much simpler if NATO would standardize on only one weapon.

General James H. Polk sees other problems in standardization. He notes that what standardization exists is often more apparent than real. In a paper for the American Enterprise Institute, he says:

> Our U.S.-developed Hawk missiles and much of the supporting hardware are not interchangeable with the Hawk systems built in Europe under U.S. license. Similarly, the U.S.-built version of the Franco-German Roland air defense system will have only slight compatibility with the European-made system; in fact, it will have an entirely different chassis of American design.

As Polk says, the Hawk and the Roland are often cited as shining examples of standardization, whereas "in reality, very limited cross-servicing of spare parts is possible, particularly of the more sophisticated and essential items." Polk also questions whether standardization really saves money. He says:

> Contrary to general belief, international R & D has turned out to be very costly in both time and money, undoubtedly more than R & D sponsored by a single nation. The four-nation Multi-Role Combat Aircraft (MRCA) project took more than a decade to develop with attendant large cost overruns. The German-American MBT-70 tank was priced out of the market, and the millions of dollars it cost were in no way recovered. One German industrialist [quoted by the House International Relations Committee] figured out that bilateral development programs implied 40 per cent higher costs and trilateral ones as much as 73 per cent higher costs, thereby certainly casting some doubt on the money to be saved by some form of international R & D. The Roland air-defense system, already mentioned, for which we paid the Europeans a $30 million license fee, has already doubled original estimates in both time and money before fielding to combat units, and the system is still in trouble.

Polk also doubts if standardized parts will be more readily available than unstandardized ones:

> Down time for combat aircraft in Vietnam for repair of minor battle damage averaged over thirty days, primarily as a result of the lack of the appropriate spare part. The normal order and ship time today for a part not stocked (or possibly not identified or located) in Europe is also about thirty days.

Polk, former commander in chief of the U. S. Army in Europe, urged standardization simply of petroleum, oil, lubricants—known in armed-services jargon as POL—and of ammunition, and greater cooperation in handling casualties and in feeding. He concludes:

> We do *not* want to adopt an international logistic system [since this would not be] workable, efficient or cost-effective . . . The services and supplies needed would actually require another layer of management and facilities, with attendant delays and mark-up fees . . . The whole effort at standardization or interoperability or, better yet, cross-servicing, should in fact be concentrated almost exclusively in the area of POL and ammunition . . . Not only should we have standard calibers (and similar rounds and bombs) but also we should have similar racks, fuses, loading machines, propellant charges, firing tables, magazines, link belts and the like. All of these should be NATO standard and totally interchangeable. We should be able to cross-service with essential expendables our combat aircraft, tanks, cannon and guns with professional confidence and speed, anywhere across the central European front. We should even try to make our missiles interchangeable on common launch rails or tubes. On this basis, it should be acceptable to let each nation build and service its own weapons

systems around a common fuel and ammunition program. Each nation would be free to build the fighter, tank or rifle that suits its own national requirements. Then, when and if one nation "builds a better mousetrap," the other armies and air forces should buy it directly from the sole-source producer.

Asked about standardization in 1978, the late General Brown told the present writer: "NATO will be working on standardizations forever. There is some progress, but it's slow, even on simple things . . . The basic thing is it means dollars and pounds and deutschmarks. Research and development lead to a concept and a weapon and usually it's only after the thing is pretty well developed that everybody else gets interested in seeing what piece of the game they can get. That's what [Defense Under Secretary for Research] Bill Perry is working on—how to get everybody into it early enough."

British Forces

Britain is currently spending over $5.4 billion to update its air defenses with new aircraft, missiles and hardened bases. Despite International Monetary Fund pressure to reduce spending, Britain devoted nearly 5 per cent of its gross domestic product to defense in fiscal 1978–79—$13.5 billion, of which 40 per cent is for weapons and parts—and planned a further 3 per cent increase in 1979–80. The Air Force gets the largest share, followed by the Navy. As host to both U.S. and British bases— mostly in East Anglia—which contain 40 per cent of NATO's combat aircraft and the main staging facilities for U.S. troop reinforcements, the RAF, with only five interceptor squadrons, is currently weak in response to any attack by Soviet Backfires or Sukhoi-19 Fencer attack aircraft. British forces are also below their NATO commitments in men and tanks, partly because of Northern Ireland, partly because of fairly massive early retirements by young officers. So serious is the British position in NATO that the British Army in Germany was reported in 1978 to be working seventy-hour weeks (with, of course, no overtime pay), a factor in the desire of many officers to return to civilian life.

One major recent British expenditure, apart from the purchase of more Anglo-French Jaguar attack aircraft (based in Germany) and Anglo-Italo-German Tornado MRCAs, has been the retrofitting of eleven military Comet four-engined jets (Comets were the world's first jet airliners, in the fifties) as improved Nimrod airborne early-warning and command craft to cover the northeast Atlantic on a round-the-clock basis. In the interest of NATO standardization, the Nimrod will probably incorporate some Grumman Hawkeye avionics, such as the General Electric APS-15 radar, and thus will be able to sense targets better than at present. Thirty-eight other, less sophisticated Nimrods will also remain in service.

The RAF chose Nimrod over AWACS largely for economic reasons, notably about seven thousand British jobs; but at $800 million, the eleven-plane program will be almost as expensive as AWACS purchases would have been. However, Nimrod is less effective than AWACS over land, although it is claimed to be superior over sea—a key consideration to air-defense planners in an island nation. It also uses a much smaller crew—a tactical air-control officer, three air-direction officers, a communications officer, an electronic-signal-monitoring operator, a navigator and two pilots.

Britain's Polaris submarine force—four ships—will be ready for the breaker's yard by about 1993, and is at present only a "last resort" segment of NATO strategic defense: Britain cannot afford to expend missiles on counterforce targets, to exhaust enemy defenses, as can the superpowers. The United States will phase out Polaris subs in the mid-eighties, so that parts will then become scarce for both the boats and missiles—although Britain does make its own re-entry vehicles and nuclear warheads.

There is discussion in Britain of building at least five new nuclear submarines with missiles similar to Poseidon or Trident, or a larger sub fleet with cruise missiles. However, if the United States and the Soviet Union agree to stop nuclear testing, Britain—which uses U.S. sites for this—would seem to have little option but to follow suit; while the possibility that SALT III will eventually prohibit long-range cruise missiles would make that option redundant also. The likelihood was that Britain would cease to be a naval strategic power.

French Forces

France remains a more autonomous and ambitious military power than Britain. The principal new French aircraft is the Dassault-Bréguet single-engined delta-wing Mirage-2000, due for delivery from 1979 onward. Production should reach 48 a year by 1983. The French Air Force is scheduled to receive 400 by the nineties, half of them for defense—armed with 4 Matra missiles and with dogfight and ground-attack cannons—half for long-range, low-altitude interdiction and reconnaissance. In all, the plane has 5 weapons stations and can carry about 11,000 pounds of ordnance.

Eventually, the total French Air Force inventory of this aircraft may reach 600. Five prototypes were being built when this book was written, 4 of them for the French Air Force, including a 2-seat trainer, and 1 for the manufacturer, with a simplified weapons system, as an export demonstrator. The first 2 prototypes flew in 1978.

General Maurice Saint-Cricq, the French Air Force chief of staff, says the Mirage-2000 will have 50 per cent more range than the Mirage-III which it will replace, and twice the climb rate. The approach speed is down from 190 knots to 150 knots, making it operational into slightly shorter fields; but the plane still has a reputation for poor stability on approach. It will have an operational ceiling of 60,000 feet, at a speed of "at least" Mach-2.2, and a look-down doppler radar. Saint-Cricq calls it "infinitely superior," especially in high-speed maneuverability, to the F-16, even though it was the French Air Force's second choice—selected for economic reasons—after the proposed twin-engined Dassault-Bréguet F-1 ACF (initialese for "future combat aircraft"). A twin-engined Mirage-4000 is on the drawing boards.

The French Air Force has also converted 12 of its Mirage-IV fighter-bombers into strategic-intelligence reconnaissance aircraft, with their nuclear arms replaced by infrared cameras and sensors. The 40 remaining IV bombers will be replaced in the mid-eighties, probably by cruise missiles. Since France, like other Western European countries, does not need counterforce weaponry, it is considering dropping its strategic air arm of the "triad" altogether.

New French missiles include the M-4 submarine-launched ballistic missile, the laser-guided AS-30 M-1 air-to-surface missile, the Thomson-Brandt Walloby, which carries 4 "sub-bombs," and more missiles in the Exocet series, including the AM (air-to-ship) -39 and the MM (ship-to-ship) -38. France's wireguided HOT antitank missile, the equivalent of the American TOW, claimed a 100 per cent target impact ratio in test firing in late 1978.

France was scheduled to have added a fifth strategic submarine to its fleet in 1979 or 1980, and is planning a new version for the nineties.

German Forces

Germany no longer leads Europe in military aviation, although it is Britain's and Italy's partner in the Tornado and is building its own anti-tank assault helicopter, the Messerschmitt-Bolkow-Blohm BO-105M (NATO code-digits PAH-1), of which the German Army will begin taking delivery in late 1979. It is also the co-producer, with France, of the Dassault-Bréguet/Dornier Alphajet, which joined the Luftwaffe as a ground-attack plane in 1978, but which the French Air Force will use only as an advanced trainer. A wholly German "tactical combat fighter" is on the drawing boards.

But Germany's main military construction achievements are the Leopard tank and the Marder armored combat vehicle, said by many to be the two best weapons in their class. The Germans have 3,700 tanks, half of them Leopard-Is; their American M-48s are due to be replaced by Leopard-IIs. The Bundeswehr also has 4,000 Marders, and Franco-German Milan antitank missiles are used by German, French and British forces.

West Germany can—and has to—mobilize faster than any other NATO power. Its total active-duty forces—including draftees—of 495,000 personnel would be augmented in case of war by about 800,000 reservists and behind-the-lines home-guard forces. At all times, about 30,000 key reservists are on call at a few hours' notice.

The Washington *Post*'s West German correspondent Michael Getler noted in 1977 that "the West Germans are very proud of their teeth-to-tail ratio—a high percentage of actual combat troops to those in support." Partly this is because, unlike U.S. forces, the Germans do not anticipate a war on foreign territory and can therefore rely on civilian facilities such as gasoline dumps and hospitals.

Turkey and NATO

The next most crucial territory in NATO after West Germany is Turkey, whose four-year, billion-dollar purchase of U.S. armaments on credit was long delayed in Congress by the Greek lobby. A 1977 report by the Congressional Research Service stressed the irreplaceability of most of the Turkish facilities closed to the United States following the 1975 arms embargo—obtained by the lobby to try to pressure Ankara over the Cyprus issue.

These facilities included intelligence-collection sites at Sinop and Samsun on the Black Sea coast, Belbasi near Ankara, Diyarbakir in the southeast and Karamürsel on the Sea of Marmara, a U. S. Navy station at Kargabarun, Inçirlik air base near Adana, supply depots near the Syrian border, Ankara and Izmir air stations, Çigli air base on the Aegean and fourteen NATO early-warning sites.

The key intelligence sites were Sinop, a radar monitoring and communications facility run by the Army's component of the National Security Agency, and Karamürsel, manned by U. S. Air Force Security personnel of the NSA. Sinop collected data on Soviet air and naval activity in the Black Sea area and missile-testing activities. Karamürsel monitored Soviet naval traffic in the western Black Sea and the Straits. The long-range radar complex at Diyarbakir, which can survey as far as the Soviet test center at Tyura Tam, east of the Aral Sea, tracked Soviet missile launches from several testing sites. Belbasi monitored Soviet nuclear tests. Samsun mostly monitored communications. In 1967, monitors there overheard Colonel Komarov, whose Soyuz spacecraft had gone out of control, receiving a personal call from Premier Kosygin and saying farewell to his wife and child before being incinerated on re-entry into the atmosphere.

Inçirlik was the major tactical fighter base, accommodating squadrons rotated from Spain and Italy. U.S. fighters at Inçirlik were the most forward-deployed, land-based American aircraft for a tactical nuclear strike in the event of war. Izmir is NATO's South East land headquarters and the command center for the Sixth Allied Tactical Air Force.

Most of these facilities were set up by a then-secret Military Facilities Agreement in June 1954. In 1969, a Defense Cooperation Agreement homogenized and revised this and several other accords reached over the years. The 1969 pact, which was classified, was declared by Ankara to have lost its "legal validity" after the 1975 congressional embargo. All installations in Turkey used by the United States were then placed under the control of the Turkish armed forces. Inçirlik could continue to be used, but only for NATO purposes. Intelligence-gathering activities at Sinop, Karamürsel, Diyarbakir and Belbasi ceased. The other facilities were kept semi-operational, in case of war.

In an effort to get around the embargo, the Ford administration signed a new Defense Cooperation Agreement with Turkey in March 1976, which stipulated that "the extent of the defense cooperation envisaged . . . shall be limited to obligations arising out of the North Atlantic Treaty." The implication of this apparently innocuous clause is that Inçirlik could not be used in connection with resupplying Israel in time of war or for other activities related to the Middle East. All activities at U.S. installations had to be authorized by Turkey.

Future operations and maintenance would be a joint U.S.-Turkish affair, with Turkey having the right to supply up to 50 per cent of personnel at the facilities. This pact was also held in abeyance, pending ratification by the Senate, because of Greek lobby pressure.

The Library of Congress report examined and rejected, for practical or political reasons, the alternatives to bases in Turkey; Syria and Egypt were held unlikely to accept U.S. facilities; Lebanon and Israel were too vulnerable, and the notion of American bases in Israel was seen as counterproductive to U.S. diplomacy in the Mideast conflict, since it would mean committing U.S. forces to a country in the area which is hostile to all the others. Cyprus was inadequate, especially in airfields, and—with a 40 per cent Communist electorate in the Greek sector—thought unlikely to accept U.S. bases. (Indeed, realistic forward planning would have to encompass the possibility that Greek Cyprus may eventually be a Warsaw Pact country.) Greece could accept some of the naval and fighter installations and a few of the intelligence-gathering activities, but was thought unlikely to want to. Like France, it is no longer a "military" member of NATO. Much of Iran was "topographically unsuitable." Some important data relating to Soviet observance of the ABM and SALT agreements could not be obtained except from Turkey, the report said, even if additional satellite inspections were undertaken.

By late 1977, Turkey, still hamstrung for arms supplies, was openly debating whether to wind down its commitments to NATO. At the 1978 NATO "summit" in Washington, all the NATO allies except Greece called forcefully for repeal of the U.S. arms embargo—which Carter also opposed as strongly as Ford had. Carter agreed to make repeal his highest foreign-policy priority, and this was finally achieved in mid-1978. Ankara then authorized the reopening of Sinop, Samsun, Diyarbakir, Belbasi and Kargaburun. Karamürsel was turned over to Turkish forces. When turmoil in Iran that year reduced U.S. surveillance there to a single site, and later to no sites at all, the Turkish posts became more crucial than before. They are currently being "upgraded." But in 1979, Turkey, shocked at the size of the Israeli and Egyptian arms packages following signature of the peace treaty, and especially by news of a $500 million U.S. arms transfer to North Yemen, quietly informed Washington that the posts would be closed down again if the United States did not greatly increase military and economic aid to Ankara, including writing off a $437 million debt. Ankara also declined to authorize U-2 flights, to monitor SALT II, since Moscow was opposed to them.

At the core of the crisis with Washington lay the fact that Turkey, with the second largest NATO ground forces after those of the United States, had intensely antiquated weapons systems. Its best tanks were M-48s of Korean War vintage; its air force still flew F-100s and F-86s; its fleet was even older. As the rest of NATO prepared to go over from the TOW to the Hellfire antitank missile, Ankara did not even have TOWs. Greece's entry into the European Community in 1979 weakened Turkey's influence with its European NATO allies, while within the country political discontent fanned by poverty and other economic troubles both threatened Turkey's democratic system and made neutralism more of an attraction. Moscow played its hand carefully, courting Ankara with economic aid.

Whether Turkey will remain a full member of NATO seems uncertain: Political opinion in Washington is divided on this subject, but on one point most area specialists agree—it will depend on U.S. policy toward Turkey.

Greece, however, having lost the "lever" of the arms embargo, became more cooperative with NATO, and took part in the 1978 "Autumn Forge" exercises.

Spain

Outside of NATO, the United States has something close to a military alliance with Spain; a new 1976 treaty between the two countries was essentially a landlord-tenant accord, giving Madrid nearly $1.25 billion of military aid in return for restricted use of four Spanish bases. This followed $4 billion of aid over the previous two decades, about half of it spent to build and rent the bases in question.

Critics opposed the new treaty as overly expensive, as well as for making the broad assumptions that Spain would continue to move toward democracy and not revert to dictatorship. NATO allies, more sanguine on this matter, continued to refuse Spain as a NATO member. But U.S. support for Madrid, even rebuffed, has been useful to the Spanish Government. Says Senator Thomas Eagleton of Missouri: "There are many in both Europe and the United States today who hold our government responsible for Franco's long and stultifying reign."

No U.S. flag flies over the "American" bases. No new units can be introduced into them, nor units relocated between them, and their use was forbidden to Washington for resupply of Israel during the 1973 conflict. With their 12,000 American dependents, the bases' principal usefulness to Spain would appear to be less strategic than economic and political, according Madrid a measure of respectability, even in Franco's time.

The bases at Torrejón, Morón and Zaragoza are training and transit airfields for U.S. military aircraft stationed elsewhere in Europe or in the United States. Morón, near Seville, has been on standby status since 1970, when Zaragoza—on standby since 1965—was partially reopened. The best-known base is the U.S. naval station at Rota, near Cádiz, which is home port to 9 strategic Poseidon submarines—with, between them, over 1,400 SLBMs—and to part of an EA-3B air reconnaissance squadron. But the submarines were due to be rebased in the United States from 1979 on.

The new money seems intended to bring Spain's antiquated forces up to NATO standards, with a view to eventual membership. Opposing the treaty, the Center for Defense Information said: "The original rationale for the Spanish bases was gone by the time they were completed," noting that all C-5 cargo aircraft are now "routinely refuelable in flight."

The CDI continued:

> Upgrading our military ties with the government of King Juan Carlos is the . . . U.S. response to the political and military changes elsewhere in southern Europe—the Portuguese revolution and the uncertain future of bases in the Azores, the restrictions on U.S. bases in Turkey, the collapse of the Navy's home-porting scheme in Greece and the perennial political crises and leftward shifting in Italy.

To these points could be added the uncertain political "Eurocommunist" future in France. When the U.S. bases in Spain were first planned, the CDI noted, they "were beyond range of Soviet attack, and it was thought that Spain might be a sanctuary where U.S. air power and supplies could be marshaled for movement to central Europe."

Nuclear submarines, critics say, could have been based (with the others) at Holy Loch in Scotland, or at Sigonella in Sicily. In any event, the new treaty bans them from Spain from 1979, along with any other "nuclear devices or their components on Spanish soil."

To quote from the CDI report again:

> No one has seriously suggested that the Spanish armed forces are needed in NATO or would make any significant contribution to "defense of the West." The Spanish Army's 220,000 men—mostly conscripts—lack mobility, firepower and modern armor (all but 20 of its 530 tanks are of World War Two vintage) . . . The Spanish Air Force's fighter aircraft and miscellaneous light transports are adequate for purely local tasks, but not larger ones. One half the Spanish Navy is obsolete by any standards; its largest ship—a cruiser—was commissioned in 1936.

The implication of the CDI's comments is that the Spanish treaty was an achievement of the U.S. arms industry:

> The $600 million in military credits and guaranteed loans will be spent entirely on U.S. military products having built-in repeat-sales potential and generating additional requirements for companion cash sales.
>
> A prime example is the treaty's offer to sell Spain 72 advanced F-16 fighters that will tie the Spanish Air Force to U.S. production lines and spare parts.

The ultimate aim of the industry would be to bring Spain into NATO, and Dr. Kissinger has spoken of an American "moral commitment" to defend Spanish territory. The CDI complained that the 1976 treaty made a defense commitment to Spain "unavoidable," and declared: "American bases in Spain are not essential for the defense of NATO or the United States."

Sweden and Switzerland

Spain is an underdeveloped country, but two European nations not associated with NATO—Sweden and Switzerland—are considerably better able to defend themselves. Sweden is largely self-supporting in arms and in 1977 voted a defense budget of nearly $3 billion, partly to convert its air force fighter wings and reconnaissance squadrons from the SAAB J-35 Draken (Dragon) to the SAAB JA-37 Viggen (Thunderbolt), both entirely Swedish-designed and -built. The Viggen is, in effect, a biplane, with high-stability "canard" wings up front giving greater lift and maneuverability to the delta wing behind. The SF-37 reconnaissance version of the Viggen will carry nine cameras, capable of taking seventy-five photos a second. When this book was written, the Swedish Air Force had six squadrons of Viggen fighters and planned to add eight more.

About a third of the 1977 budget was for the Swedish Air Force, and of this $850 million was for equipment, including nearly $400 million for JA-37s. A further $60 million was for developing Swedish air-to-air missiles—primarily SAAB 372s—for these aircraft, and there was an additional $320 million for other R & D.

Experts are long on praise for Sweden's Bofors guns, notably the new BOFI 40mm. antiaircraft system, which has a laser range finder, night-vision capacity and computerized fire control, and compares with U.S. and Soviet weapons.

Switzerland does not design its own combat aircraft, but the Oerlikon artillery industry is comparable to Bofors in Sweden. The new Oerlikon-Contraves twin-35mm. Guépard antiaircraft system, for instance, is built to fire Raytheon's Sparrow missiles.

Yugoslavia

As underdeveloped as Spain, but better armed, is Yugoslavia, NATO's fence-straddling Communist friend. In anticipation of threats and possible invasion from Soviet forces after the death of Marshal Tito—eighty-seven years old in 1979—Belgrade has augmented its 200,000-strong forces with a territorial militia of 600,000. It has also sought to diminish its dependence on Soviet weaponry by developing with Romania a twin-engined interceptor-attack plane, the Orao (Eagle), and by sounding out Washington over the possible purchase of antitank missiles and other sophisticated American defense systems. The arms-sales relationship with the United States is briefly looked at in Chapter 7.

Yugoslavia's Air Force has eight squadrons of slightly outdated MiG-21s, some Yugoslav-produced aircraft, adapted, Chinese-fashion, from Soviet models, and fifteen American F-84s. The Yugoslavs believe Moscow seeks to encourage irredentism by Croats and Slovenes, who compose two of the six Yugoslav federated republics; the Croats and Slovenes have never been happy under Serb rule and are under-represented in the armed forces, especially the officer corps. Russia would see an independent Croatia or Slovenia as offering Moscow access to an Adriatic port, such as Rijeka (formerly Fiume, under Mussolini) or Pula, in Istria, which the Italians built into the major naval port of Pola. Yugoslavia also has other discontented minorities—Muslims, Albanians, Macedonians, Montenegrins and Hungarians.

In an interview which stimulated great interest at the CIA, Colonel General Ivan Kukoč of the Yugoslav planning staff said in 1977 that his country was considering the development of nuclear weapons.

In 1975, *Borba*, the official Belgrade daily, had already said that "our armed forces are prepared for long-duration, successful warfare under the most contemporary conditions, which means even nuclear war." Kukoč, questioned in the weekly magazine *Nin*, was more blunt. Asked "Do you think that an armed attack on Yugoslavia would in fact be an overture to a new great world conflict?" he answered: "Most probably."

The questioner, clearly putting staged questions, later asked: "Do we possess an atomic bomb? Is a Yugoslav A-bomb being considered?"

Said Kukoč:

> We do not have an atomic bomb; that is perfectly well known . . . [But] it depends the least upon us whether Yugoslavia will be obliged to consider her A-bomb or . . . . begin production. It is known that we are and remain resolute champions of the policy of disarmament, but of disarmament for all . . . [But] factually, contemporary wars, such as the latest wars in the Middle East, have shown that the success of a country which does not have basic sources of its [own] armament, and even success in a war which it is conducting, are conditioned by the behavior of the country on which it relies for its armament.

What Kukoč appeared to be saying was that Yugoslavia's inability to rely on either Washington or Moscow for its defense might force it to adopt a nuclear "deterrent."

ASIA AND THE INDIAN OCEAN

Asia appears a more volatile and therefore potentially more conflict-prone area of American interests than Europe. The Soviet Union and the United States are only a few miles apart at the Alaskan border, and the United States is still, because of Hawaii, Guam and its Pacific trustee-ships, even more of a Pacific than an Atlantic power. Japan is America's leading trading partner—more important than West Germany and Britain combined. With the world's third largest economy after those of the superpowers, it seems likely even to overtake Russia in that area in a few decades, and perhaps become a superpower itself.

As mentioned earlier, among the many mutual defense treaties signed by the United States, only one—the North Atlantic Treaty—commits U.S. forces to war automatically if a member-state is attacked. In all other cases, both America and the treaty partner are "committed" to the support of each other, but not necessarily by direct intervention. By the wording of these treaties, in the case of the United States a final decision would rest with Congress.

But when new arms-sales guidelines were drawn up in 1977 by the incoming Carter administration, three other countries besides the NATO allies were exempted from the restrictions: Japan, Australia and New Zealand. The latter two once seriously feared invasion by China, and would still regard Peking as their main potential enemy; but the inclusion of Canberra and Wellington as privileged capitals for arms sales probably mainly reflects official American empathy with two English-speaking democracies which can afford sophisticated weapons and which are trusted not to engage in aggressive policies. Japan, however, could be dispassionately regarded as America's single most important ally, and it would be virtually unthinkable, today, that America might not go to war if Japan was invaded.

Japan

Japan's 113 million people have no draft, and the so-called Self-Defense Forces total only 235,000; defense expenditure is pegged at not more than 1 per cent of a $550 billion economy, and since World War

Two Tokyo has been reluctant to assume its full military responsibilities. The Japanese economic miracle has been partly dependent on Japan's relative freedom from defense spending.

Japan's army of 153,000 includes little armor—only 1 mechanized division, 1 tank brigade and 1 composite brigade. Its armored force—750 tanks, 500 armored personnel carriers—would be outmatched by, say, Syria's. A defense-oriented navy and naval air arm includes 39,000 men and 16 submarines. An air force of 43,000 men flies 448 combat aircraft, with the best being 6 squadrons (170 planes) of F-104Js and 3 squadrons (80 aircraft) of F-4EJ Phantoms. (More modern types are on order.) Japan's Base Defense Ground Environment, containing 28 control and warning units, is probably not the world's most ready for a surprise attack, judging from Lieutenant Belenko's caper. Thus, Japanese concern at America's decision, in 1977, to withdraw ground forces (and about 1,000 tactical missiles) from South Korea surpassed that of the most hawkish elements in the U.S. military. But the proposed withdrawal helped bolster Washington's insistence that the Japanese do more than in the postwar past to guarantee their own defense.

Even with the phased, five-year withdrawal of three quarters of the 40,000 Americans stationed in Korea, the U.S. presence in the area will remain significant. In late 1977, the U.S. presence in the Pacific and Asian region totaled 170,000. By 1982, it should remain at about 140,000, with 7,000 Air Force personnel and a small unit of the Seventh Fleet remaining in Korea itself. (The USAF in Korea consists of 3 tactical fighter squadrons, an air support squadron, and command and control units.) There are 78,000 American military personnel in Japan and on Okinawa. The full Seventh Fleet includes 2 aircraft carriers with escort attack submarines, several wings of tactical aircraft, strategic bombers (on Guam) and nearly a full Marine division.

Although Japan's major weaponry is almost exclusively American, the Japanese war industry is beginning to become more self-sufficient. The first production version of the Mitsubishi F-1 close-support supersonic fighter rolled out of the manufacturer's Komaki plant early in 1977, and test flying began in May. By the end of the year, the Air Self-Defense Force took over the testing program of the twin Rolls-Royce-engined plane, which will carry Japan's own, new ASM-1 antishipping missiles. Japan's Kawasaki Heavy Industries has teamed up with Germany's Messerschmitt-Bolkow-Blohm to produce the BK-117 utility helicopter, and a Mach-2 Tansam surface-to-air missile with an infrared seeker is being developed for use against eventual low-flying supersonic intruders. As noted in a later chapter, Japan is also buying or co-producing 100

McDonnell-Douglas F-15s, along with Lockheed P-3s and advanced American helicopters.

Japan's 1979–80 military budget was set at $9.5 billion, a 10 per cent increase over the previous year, and included a more ambitious satellite program. But the total included only $597 million for aircraft procurement—71 planes.

North Korea

Japan's immediate concern, like South Korea's, lies less with China or the Soviet Union than with unpredictable North Korea, which has frequently sought to provoke the United States itself into conflict. The rigidly authoritarian state has only 17 million population, but imposes a draft of up to seven years to maintain armed forces of nearly 700,000—the world's fifth largest—costing about a quarter of the country's GNP. A well-trained, highly motivated, 41-division army of about 600,000 with 2,600 tanks—over twice as many as South Korea—is supported by a navy of 20,000 with mostly light, defense-oriented shipping, but including at least 8 submarines. An air force of 45,000 personnel and about 655 combat aircraft, a paramilitary force of some 40,000 and a militia of 1.8 million reservists complete the picture.

South Korea

In the event of war with South Korea, North Korea would be dependent on substantial and immediate assistance from Russia or China and perhaps the direct intervention of such friendly forces. South Korea's forces number about 642,000. It has twice North Korea's population, about five times its GNP and spends about twice as much on defense. Over a third of its present 580,000 soldiers are Vietnam veterans. This army of 25 large divisions is backed by reserves of about a million. In the north, it is equipped with Korean-designed surface-to-surface missiles which could reach Pyongyang, the North Korean capital, and a better, two-stage tactical missile is under design. South Korea's navy of 32,000 includes an offensive capability—70 amphibious craft—and 120 American Harpoon missiles are on order; but it has no submarines. Naval reserves total 33,000.

South Korea's Air Force is smaller than North Korea's—30,000 men, 276 combat aircraft—but it is more up-to-date than that of its adversary, whose best planes are 150 MiG-21s and a squadron of Sukhoi-7s. South Korea has 72 of the latest-model Phantoms, capable of accommodating nuclear-tipped missiles, and 160 F-5s; there is an air force reserve of 55,000 men. Paramilitary forces total over 750,000 men, and according to Senator McGovern there are also an impressive 300,000 men and women in the Korean intelligence services, including substantial contingents in Japan and the United States.

Although both the United States, on the one hand, and Russia and China, on the other, have intentionally limited the capacity of their protégés in the peninsula to launch offensive war, the presence of U.S. forces in South Korea has led to North Korea's having greater firepower than the more numerous forces of its southern neighbor. When Major General John Singlaub, chief of staff of the U.S. forces in Korea, reacted sharply to the 1977 plan to withdraw U.S. soldiers—a reaction which led to his being relieved of his command—one of his main points was North Korea's distinct superiority in armor. Over the previous year, North Korea had increased its number of tanks from 500 to 1,995, about twice the South Korean figure. North Korea's Navy also outnumbers and out-guns South Korea's, and Pyongyang has about twice as many combat air-craft as Seoul. Both sides have an indigenous arms industry mostly lim-ited to small arms and armored vehicles, although North Korea also builds submarines, while the South assembles Hughes helicopters and air defense systems. The franchise to manufacture the M-16, the NATO as-sault rifle, in South Korea belongs to a firm headed by the Reverend Sun Myung Moon, the colorful leader of the "Moonies" Unification Church.

Even with present plans to compensate South Korea for the U.S. pullout (on which President Carter put an at least temporary stay in July 1979), the Pentagon is doubtful whether the South could resist a Com-munist invasion in five years' time, and it is generally accepted that the South Korean Air Force will still be inadequate. Testifying before Congress, General George Brown, then chairman of the Joint Chiefs, and General Bernard Rogers, the Army chief of staff, confirmed that they had recommended that only about one quarter of U.S. combat troops be withdrawn, in order not to heighten the risk of hostilities. It had been the President's decision to withdraw all ground forces.

At the time of the withdrawal decision, there were over 40,000 U.S. military in South Korea, including 33,000 soldiers, 8,300 airmen and about 200 Marines and naval personnel. Nearly half the soldiers were members of the 2nd Infantry Division, stationed in the mountainous area between Seoul, the 7.3-million-population capital, and the demilitarized zone (DMZ) 25 miles to the north—one of the two most probable inva-sion routes. Two Korean divisions will replace the departing American one, and ten other Korean divisions are also in this area. American troops no longer patrol the DMZ itself. Other U.S. combat troops are stationed near the eastern end of the DMZ—the other obvious invasion route. U.S.

ground forces include an air-defense artillery brigade and a signal brigade.

PRM 10, which recommended the withdrawal of U.S. ground forces— currently in a tripwire position near the border, sure to be involved in any conflict and therefore sure to provoke the intervention of other U.S. forces—implies that South Korea could not be expected to hold Seoul from a surprise attack. Withdrawal was recommended in order to give Washington flexibility as to whether or not to intervene under the 1954 Mutual Defense Treaty, in case of war. South Korea, the PRM said, could win a sustained combat—but only with American assistance. In reality, since 6,000 lightly armed American troops supervising the armistice have to remain, and would presumably be slaughtered in any North Korean blitzkrieg, the tripwire situation probably remains.

Both the U.S. Administration and its critics seem agreed that South Korea's forces will have to be substantially built up to deter an attack from Pyongyang, despite the continued presence of the U. S. Air Force and Navy. Critics of U.S. troop withdrawal like General Richard Stillwell, a former commander in Korea, note that Russian and Chinese reinforcements could arrive over the North Korean frontier much more quickly than U.S. forces could be reintroduced in time of war. Given the North Korean infiltration raids, tunnels under the Demilitarized Zone and other activities, few doubt that North Korean Premier Kim Il Sung still wants to invade the South—despite his 1979 offer of talks with Seoul. Both China and the Soviet Union have mutual defense treaties with Pyongyang, as the United States has with Seoul—but China has never requested a U.S. troop withdrawal from Korea in recent years, seeing the Eighth Army and the Seventh Fleet as a deterrent to Russia, and having no desire to cooperate with Moscow in another Korean peninsula war.

However, faced with the pessimistic predictions about South Korean strength and uncertainty about a continued American commitment, especially following the Tong Sun Park lobbying scandal in Washington, South Korea—although a signatory to the Non-Proliferation Treaty—has warned that it may develop nuclear weapons of its own. Indeed, given the high degree of technology available in South Korea, this might well have been inevitable in any case.

Taiwan

Taiwan, with a similar size of population to North Korea's but with a GNP almost equal to South Korea's (in other words, with nearly twice

South Korea's per-capita income) spends about 6.5 per cent of its GNP on defense, or roughly a billion dollars yearly. The armed forces of 470,000 include about 330,000 soldiers. There is also a militia of 100,000. The Army has Hawk and Nike-Hercules missiles. Eighty thousand troops are deployed on Quemoy and Ma-tsu islands, within swimming distance of China's Amoy harbor. Army reserves total about 1 million.

A Navy of 35,000 personnel includes only 2 submarines and 50 landing craft. Naval reserves number 45,000. Two divisions of Marines total 35,000 men. There is an Air Force of 70,000 men (with 90,000 reservists), but only about half the 500 planes are combat aircraft. Until recently, the most modern aircraft were 60 F-104s and about twice as many F-100s; but F-5s are now being co-produced, under a contract which expires in 1980. However, given the antiquity of China's own aviation, Taiwan could probably inflict heavy punishment on a mainland invader. The two wings of Mach-1.6 F-5Es existing in 1978, with Sidewinder and Super-Sidewinder missiles, are replacing the two wings of F-100s. They include active squadrons on five-minute alert. Whereas Chinese mainland planes never come closer to Taiwan than 50 miles, the feisty Taiwanese pilots often fly to within 15 miles of the mainland shore.

Taiwan's problems in acquiring new American or other aircraft are described in Part III of this book, on weapons diplomacy. The United States has carefully deprived Taiwan of any offensive power: There are no bombers, and Taiwan had to go to Israel in 1977 to buy surface-to-surface missiles—a still secret number of Gabriels. Since then, as will be noted in Chapter 9, the Israeli role has much increased.

As part of the Shanghai agreement signed with Mao Tse-tung, President Nixon promised to phase out U.S. diplomatic ties to Taipei, and to remove the 1,400 American armed-forces staff that were still on the island. President Carter promised to do the same, but not at the expense of the "independence and freedom" of Taiwan. At the end of 1978, however, when the United States extended full recognition to Peking, Carter gave the required twelve-month notice for canceling the U.S. defense treaty with Taipei. But disengaging from Taiwan is not as simple as it sounds.

The United States has private investment of $2.5 billion there, along with nearly $1.6 billion in outstanding ExImBank loans. American trade with the island grew from $1.5 billion in 1971 to $4.8 billion in 1976 (Taiwan's exports are so successful that imports and exports that year totaled more than the GNP). Most important of all is the fact that, except for three brief years from 1945 to 1948, Taiwan has not been governed by China since the nineteenth century: A Japanese colony from 1900 to 1945, it has been a de facto nation since Chiang Kai-shek was driven there from the mainland in 1948. The Taiwanese, mistreated by Chinese emperors, insular by nature and immeasurably more successful as a nation than the mainlanders, would strongly resist any attempt to impose Peking control—though some nationalist leaders say they might accept a sort of "commonwealth" link to save China's face, and to benefit from being a free-enterprise "window" for the great Communist republic.

Since Nixon's trip to China, Taiwan's defensive forces have been steadily built up—partly with an infusion of half a billion dollars' worth of U.S. military aid in two years. In 1978, Taiwan ordered a Hughes semi-automatic air defense system that can track multiple, low-level, high-speed targets in the Taiwan Strait. When the bombshell of Peking recognition broke, Taiwan announced increased defense expenditures, and U.S. sources talked of selling $800 million of weapons to Taipei in the next few years—despite initial reports that Peking was actually moving forces away from the Taiwan Strait area to its Russian border. Meanwhile, the Kuomintang government of General Chiang Ching-kuo, the Generalissimo's son, who was "elected" president that year, had already turned to a nuclear initiative to deter Peking. This embryonic development is described in a later chapter.

India

India, the world's second largest nation and by far its largest democracy, has an all-volunteer Army, Navy and Air Force totaling, in 1978, 1,055,500 persons, plus reserves and militia totaling 240,000. The country spends roughly $3 billion a year on defense or about 3.3 per cent of its GNP. Its Army of 913,000 is composed of roughly 30 divisions, of which 10 are "mountain divisions" solely concerned with defense against China —which has seized Indian territory in the past. The only other conceivable enemy, for the moment, is Pakistan: Although a challenge from that direction seems improbable, unless it was supported by Peking, India maintains a fairly large Air Force conceived largely to do battle over the subcontinent with its Muslim neighbor.

With 100,000 men and 950 combat aircraft, India's Air Force is something of a showpiece for Soviet aviation, albeit of an earlier, less expensive generation of planes. But in addition to Sukhoi-7s, MiG-21s and Mi-4 helicopters, New Delhi has also acquired a mixed bag of earlier French and British fixed- and rotary-wing aircraft, including Alouette-IIIs, and has developed a native arms industry. Six of its 13 tactical support squadrons fly 135 Marut-1As, and its 250 Gnat naval interceptors from Britain are being joined by 100 more made in India and named the

Ajeet, along with 90 locally made Iskras. The country is also developing a twin-engined helicopter gunship. From the United States, India still hopes to buy A-4s. By 1980, the Indian Air Force will number nearly 1,300 combat aircraft. It also operates 20 surface-to-air missile sites, using Soviet SA-2s.

A relatively small Navy—42,500 personnel, including a naval air arm—has a mix of Soviet submarines, a formerly British aircraft carrier (with partly French aviation), along with other Russian, British and French craft. These include 8 Soviet *Osa*-class missile boats firing Styx missiles; 8 more are on order. Naval aviation includes 2 fixed-wing squadrons flying rather venerable British Sea Hawks, French Alizés and other French craft, and 4 helicopter squadrons using French and British equipment. Alouette-IIIs are used by the Army, the Navy and the Air Force, and all services use at least some Indian-made planes.

Pakistan

With about one tenth of India's population, Pakistan has armed forces nearly half as big as its neighbor's, thanks to a two-year draft. It only spends about a quarter as much as India on defense, however—just over $800 million, or about 10 per cent of its GNP. As these figures suggest, Pakistan is heavy on army, weak on aviation and ships.

Its total forces of 428,000 men include 400,000 soldiers, plus 500,000 reservists. The French have sold successfully to both sides in the Indo-Pakistani conflict, and Pakistan's purchases include Alouette-IIIs and Super-Frélons, Mirage fighters and *Daphné*-class submarines (3 are already delivered, 3 were due for delivery by 1979). Sixteen of its 17 patrol boats are Chinese. Otherwise, the Navy is mostly of British origin. The Air Force includes American F-86s, C-130s, trainers, and even B-57s, 50 Swedish (SAAB Supporter) trainers, and 80 MiG-19s from a different era of its diplomacy.

Southeast Asia

Other substantial forces exist in Indonesia and, of course, Vietnam. With 140 million people, Indonesia has forces of 247,000. The Army uses mostly French and British equipment; but the Navy, which includes 3 submarines, has almost exclusively Soviet matériel. Its antiquated Air Force is mostly American.

Vietnam's exclusively Soviet-armed forces are thought to number about 615,000—mostly army. Its most modern aircraft are the MiG-21 and the Su-7; but it has inherited, as noted earlier, about $6 billion of equipment from the United States, for most of which it apparently has little use itself. According to General Alexander M. Haig, the supreme NATO commander in Europe, Camranh Bay, for instance, is now a "Soviet air and naval facility." The whole question of U.S. surplus in Vietnam is looked at in broader detail in Chapter 8.

Singapore and the Philippines still have only limited forces.

South Africa

Also in the Indian Ocean area, and by far the most heavily armed country in black Africa, is South Africa.

Despite an arms embargo imposed by the UN in 1963, the country has —in addition to the beginnings of nuclear weaponry—also managed to establish a sufficient arsenal for a sizable regional war or massive internal repression. Some of the arms buildup came from Britain's decision to complete arms contracts already signed before the embargo was imposed, some from minor slippage in the U.S. embargo; but mostly supplies came from France and in more recent times from Israel, with France finally imposing a 1975 "embargo"—but contingent on so many exceptions that it was virtually meaningless. SIPRI estimates that during the decade preceding 1975, South Africa imported approximately a billion dollars' worth of foreign arms, in addition to its own indigenous production of small and medium weapons, which include surface-to-air missile systems of French design and close-support combat aircraft based on largely Italian types.

A great deal of secrecy has surrounded the South African buildup. The International Institute of Strategic Studies listed South Africa's helicopter force at 92 in 1977; but Aviation Advisory Services noted that year that 90 French Alouette-III helicopters had been delivered in 1975 alone, and 25 more the following year. *The Almanac of World Military Power* says 16 French Super-Frélon heavy assault helicopters are mysteriously unlisted by the IISS (although their sale was announced in the French press). Defense Marketing Services of Connecticut records the sale of 40 Pumas and 25 Bell-205A helicopters made in Italy, plus 17 Westland Wasp and two Gazelle helicopters supplied by Britain in spite of the embargo. Thus, the minimum size of South Africa's chief weapon of internal repression in 1977 was 215 military helicopters.

In 1978, the IISS still mysteriously listed South African helicopters at 91.

American intelligence figures also suggest that other IISS statistics about South Africa are so badly underestimated as to suggest infiltration of that prestigious organization. For instance, the IISS listed South African combat aircraft in 1977 at 133: Classified documents from South Africa's own Defense Ministry show the figure to be 625—of French, British, Italian and American origin. (In 1978, the Institute revised the figure, but only to 362.) Tanks, listed by the IISS at 170, actually number 525, including 150 British-made Centurions, modernized in Israel. It has 1,600 French-designed armored cars, manufactured locally.

Armored cars totaled 1,630 instead of the 1,050 listed, and armored personnel carriers 960 instead of 250—errors largely corrected in the Institute's 1978 figures. The U.S. intelligence sources also report 380 pieces of medium and light artillery, and 294 self-propelled guns (an item for which the IISS has no listing at all). These revelations came before the more sobering—but not unexpected—news of South Africa's secret nuclear experiments, and Premier Pieter W. Botha's 1979 announcement that his country had now designed its own air-to-air and air-to-surface missiles.

The surface Navy is mostly of British origin, but the submarines are French. The 41,000-man Army uses the old 7.62mm. NATO rifle: Both gun and ammunition are manufactured in South Africa.

Diego Garcia

One reason for the U. S. Navy's voracious new appetite for funds is Russia's increasing presence in the Indian Ocean—the pretext for the creation of an Anglo-American air and naval facility on the atoll of Diego Garcia. In November 1974, as a countershow of force to the Soviet Union, American and four Allied fleets carried out the largest naval exercises ever conducted in the Indian Ocean, with the 80,000-ton U.S. carrier *Constellation* as the flagship. Since then, the United States has kept either a cruiser or a carrier task force in the region, in addition to the three ships based at Bahrain.

About a decade before, Britain detached Diego Garcia and the rest of the Chagos archipelago from its Mauritius and Seychelles colonies, just prior to the independence of Mauritius, and created the British Indian Ocean Territory. In December 1966, Britain agreed to "share military purposes" on the archipelago with the United States, which contributed $14 million to the $30 million purchase price paid to the small colonies (Washington paid London by waiving R & D costs on Britain's Polaris program, and London in turn paid the Mauritians and the Seychellois.) Admiral John McCain, former commander in chief of the Pacific Fleet, said shortly afterward that "as Malta is to the Mediterranean, so Diego Garcia is to the Indian Ocean." Despite strong objections from India and other riverine countries, which wanted to demilitarize the ocean into a "sea of peace," the region is now regularly visited by U.S. ballistic submarines, using the Navy's communications facility at North West Cape in Australia.

Dr. Kissinger has said privately that creating Diego Garcia to counter "growing" Soviet naval force in the region was a needless, extravagant provocation, based on a self-fulfilling prophecy. Former CIA director William Colby has concurred with this view. But in 1975, Admiral Elmo Zumwalt, then chief of naval operations, called India's "ocean of peace" concept for these waters "very dangerous."

Among his scattershot détente proposals shortly after election, President Carter suggested to Moscow a "complete demilitarization" of the Indian Ocean. This implied not only the closure of Diego Garcia and the larger Soviet facilities then existing in Somalia, but also ending USAF and RAF refueling rights at Masirah Island off Oman, and the token U.S. naval presence—two destroyers and an "office ship"—at Bahrain. Assuming this package is not attractive to Moscow, it can surely be only a question of time before strategic U.S. submarines base in the Indian Ocean, which at present they only visit: U.S. officials say there are, as yet, no plans for support facilities at Diego Garcia for ballistic missiles, but such facilities did reportedly exist at the Soviet complex at Berbera.

In late 1977, Paul Warnke, the director of the Arms Control and Disarmament Agency, proposed to the Russians that both sides freeze their naval activity in the Indian Ocean. Pentagon sources said this meant confining the U.S. presence to the three permanent ships based at Bahrain and occasional task forces of five or six vessels, while on the Soviet side it would mean about twenty vessels, less than half armed and including only one submarine. Meanwhile, plans went ahead to lengthen the Diego Garcia runway, expand the anchorage and build new facilities onto the 640,000-barrel jet-fuel farm.

Since development of Diego Garcia began in March 1971, military personnel from Britain and the United States there have grown to about 5,000. The single 8,000-foot runway is used by long-range P-3 naval patrol aircraft and cargo planes. The natural harbor contained by the atoll has been dredged. Sophisticated aviation and radar facilities have been built, at a cost of nearly $200 million. Although Defense Secretary Schlesinger said in 1974 that the Navy had no intention of creating an Indian Ocean Fleet, Admiral Zumwalt, then chief of naval operations, said later that the value of Diego Garcia was that it enabled more ships to be maintained in that ocean. Justification for the increased U.S. presence was related to protecting the "oil lifelines" which might be threatened in a long war; but a Center for Defense Information report argued that Diego Garcia and the increased U.S. presence in the area were rationalized by "exaggerating" Soviet naval strength there. Although the Soviet Navy accumulated three times as many ship-days in the ocean as the U. S. Navy, it accomplished only one tenth of the port calls; the Russian ships spend long periods at open-sea anchorages, accomplishing little for "weapons diplomacy."

The study noted that the Soviet Union "has important nonmilitary maritime interests in the Indian Ocean." It quotes George Vest, then director of the Politico-Military Affairs Bureau of the State Department, as saying that "it is the natural trade route for them, being largely landlocked; this is their natural transit point." Nearly one fifth of all merchant ships traversing the Indian Ocean are now Russian. In addition, a third of the Soviet fishing catch is acquired in that ocean. The CDI report notes numerous Soviet civilian oceanographic, hydrographic and space and missile test support ships there. Some of the merchant shipping is bound from Black Sea ports to ports in Asian Russia, or vice versa, this being an all-weather route. Cautioning against a too-hawkish interpretation of the "Soviet naval buildup," the CDI says: "The lack of seaborne fixed-wing aircraft to provide protection and the lack of aircraft for reconnaissance severely constrains the flexibility of Soviet naval forces in the Indian Ocean . . . Western powers control most of the egress and ingress points to the . . . ocean."

Strategists point out that the "oil lifeline" argument counts for little. In time of war, oil is more likely to be cut off at the wellhead than by blockade, and the open ocean would be a ridiculously large goalmouth for the Soviet Navy to try to close. Russia's own concern for oil is probably greater, at least in the area. Its facilities at Berbera and Kismayu, in Somalia—the existence of which was jeopardized, probably fatally, in 1977, by President Siad Barre's decision to expel the Soviet military mission—stored 170,000 barrels of oil, compared to a projected 700,000-barrel capacity for the United States and Britain on Diego Garcia. Thirty-six Indian Ocean ports bunker U.S. military vessels in the area—more than offer these facilities to the Soviet Navy. In India as in Somalia, dependence on such supply points is, of course, related to possibly unreliable political relationships. The Soviet Navy still has no nuclear-powered surface vessels, compared to America's fourteen—three of them supercarriers: There seems little likelihood that open-ocean blockades are part of future Soviet planning. Nor is it likely that the Soviet Navy could hope, through friendly riverine countries, to close such straits as the entrance to the Arabian Gulf. A CIA report says these straits are too deep to be blocked by sunken ships, and that coastal artillery would need naval and air support to close such a wide channel. Nevertheless, after the revolution in Iran, plans for a U.S. "fifth fleet" in the Indian Ocean surfaced once again, and in 1979 the Pentagon began producing contingency plans for a U.S. force of 100,000 men, including 40,000 combat troops, for the Middle East. The object of such a force would be to fight a war of up to sixty days to "anchor" U.S. oil supplies. But predominant Pentagon thinking was that such an intervention would probably be counterproductive: wells and refineries might be burned in a "scorch-earth" defense strategy, and there could be superpower confrontation.

ISRAEL AND ITS NEIGHBORS

The balance of forces in the Middle East is one of eternal fascination to military observers. It is a story of constant growth, especially in firepower, by one of the world's most efficient fighting systems—the Zahal, or Israeli Defense Forces (IDF)—and of response to that firepower. Israel's armor is equal to about 60 per cent of all NATO's. Ze'ev Schiff, military correspondent of *Ha'aretz*, noted in the American magazine *Air Force* in 1976 that the Israeli Air Force (IAF) then "outnumbered in equipment" the military aviations of Britain, France or Germany. By 1978, it equaled in size any two of those three countries' air forces put together. Indeed, research on the Israeli inventory that year revealed 1,212 aircraft, of which 104 were trainers—most of these even usable in a ground-attack mode. To the 1,108 combat and transport aircraft could be added 90 new frontline fighters promised by the United States in 1978, and at least 60 more Kfirs in production. The fact that more and more of the planes were of Israeli manufacture helped to explain why Israel was challenging Britain for third place in non-Communist arms sales abroad, after the United States and France.

Although the IDF as a whole have a good reputation, it is the IAF which has enabled Israel to survive.

It all began in late 1947 with Nazi Messerschmitts bought from Czechoslovakia, which also sold pilot training. The Israeli Bf-109s first saw action the following year, against Egyptian Spitfires over the Mediterranean. First blood was drawn on January 7, 1949, when a squadron of Israeli Messerschmitts flying close support for Israeli troops of the Haganah, which was invading the Sinai, shot down five RAF Spitfires protecting the Suez Canal.

The 109 had been one of the best fighters of World War Two, but as a chosen superiority-fighter for a new air force it had a problem: Hitler had been defeated and spare parts were no longer produced. The nascent IAF switched to surplus American Mustangs, and even bought Spitfires itself, along with ex-RAF Mosquitoes (lightweight, all-wood, low-altitude bombers). In 1953, it bought its first jets—British Meteors.

When the war of independence broke out in Algeria the following year, France went through a catatonic era of anti-Arabism which made the French the best friends of the Israelis. Kennett Love, in *Suez: The Twice-Fought War*, recounts how from 1954 to 1956 France began to ship arms to Israel in violation of the 1950 tripartite arms-control agreement signed by France, the United States and Britain. In 1955, France began modernizing the IAF with Ouragans and Mystères. Israel's most stunning military victory—the "Six-Day" surprise-attack war of 1967, largely won by the Air Force—was an almost exclusively French affair, from the point of view of equipment. But Israel's role as the aggressor caused President de Gaulle to embargo all further arms for that country, including 50 Mirages which Tel Aviv had already paid for. The IAF then consisted principally of Mirages, Super-Mystères, Mystères and Vautours, along with the three-engined Super-Frélon assault helicopters and Nord-Atlas transport planes. (French jets had already made their presence known in the brief Sinai War of 1956, when France and Britain helped Israel conquer territory from which the United States and the UN later insisted on all three countries withdrawing.)

Washington took over completely from Paris after the 1967 war, supplying first A-4 Skyhawks, then, the following year, the first Phantoms. One of America's rationalizations for becoming Israel's main arms supplier was that the area, like Vietnam, was a superb weapons laboratory. The IAF, like the USAF in Vietnam, had a purely offensive role, and a high quality of pilot. Israeli flyers claim that standards were initially set so high that in 1960, only one flight cadet graduated: The others were flunked.

Israel's blitzkrieg advantage in 1967 was not a great test of equipment or even skills, but the so-called war of attrition that followed, with dogfights over the Canal and Israeli terror raids near Cairo, certainly was an excellent testbed for U.S. and Russian planes and missiles. In one year, from mid-1969 through mid-1970, the Israelis shot down 113 Egyptian MiGs and 26 Syrian aircraft, and destroyed 12 SA-2 missile batteries inside Egypt.

Israeli raids forced the Russians to increase arms deliveries, especially to the Egyptians. This enabled the world to judge the excellence of the new SA-3 surface-to-air missiles and the radar-guided ZSU-23 antiaircraft artillery. Then, on July 30, 1970, the Soviet Air Force went back into action for the first time in 25 years, when eight Russian pilots, flying MiG-21s, met eight Phantom F-4s of the IAF. Not surprisingly, the battle-tested Israelis won, downing five for no losses. But by then the SA-3s and ZSU-23s were taking their toll, and Egyptians were taking heart from Phantom heaps along the road from Cairo to Ismailia.

In the war of October 1973, according to Israeli claims, over a thousand Arab planes were involved; squadrons from Iraq, Algeria, Libya, Saudi Arabia and Kuwait participated, and a few North Korean pilots reportedly flew under Arab colors. The Israelis lost 102 aircraft—about 40 per cent of all front-line combat planes—of which a huge number were brought down by surface missiles. Egypt had 146 of the new SA-6 batteries, including 62 on the Suez front. Noting that defenders will usually score better than attackers, Schiff records that 73 Egyptian, Syrian and Iraqi planes were shot down in the first forty-eight hours. The final claim was for 265 Egyptian and 131 Syrian planes, including 42 Egyptian troop-carrier helicopters.

The war marked a new advance for electronic countermeasures on both sides. First used to mask the movement of invading armies and air forces into Czechoslovakia in 1968, ECMs were a major asset—or disadvantage—to both Egypt and Israel in 1973. Israel also made extensive use of metal or plastic chaff to clutter hostile radar screens.

Since 1973, Israel has copied Egypt in emphasizing missiles even more than aircraft, buying Hawks and Chaparrals and Vulcan 20mm. antiaircraft artillery from the United States and installing ZSU-23s captured from Israel's neighbors. The Lance surface-to-surface missile, which can be nuclear-tipped, was requested: Washington was still weighing a response in 1979. Israel has also bought Hawkeye radar planes, Cobra attack helicopters and some of the new, sophisticated F-15s. But the F-15 order was cut back by Washington as Israel boosted to 200 its production run of its own Kfir fighter. On the negative side, Israel was now the only country in the world which had to *draft* pilots—ordering some sufficiently healthy recruits to go to flying school even though they had not volunteered. Volunteer pilots, Schiff admitted in 1976, were being accepted even with slight physical defects that would disqualify them as airline pilots. The positive development had been the growth of Israel's own armaments industry, and here the star was the Kfir—actually an improved French Mirage-III, the plans of which had been pilfered in Switzerland. Although Jericho missiles could deliver Israel's atomic warheads to Cairo and Damascus, most current doomsday scenarios call for Israel to prefer a mobile platform—probably the Kfir.

If history was just, the Kfir (Lion Cub) would be named the Frauenknecht, after a non-Jewish Swiss engineer who helped Israel out of idealism and who now lives in disgrace near Zurich. Alfred Frauenknecht worked for the Swiss firm of Pulzer, which had a contract to make 100 Mirage-IIIs, under license, for the Swiss Air Force. Costs skyrocketed, the burghers of the legislature clucked and the assembly line was halted at 53 aircraft, although the parts themselves for the remaining 47 had all been made. In December 1967, under embargo by France, Israel offered a cash sum, plus battle-tested Israeli technology for Switzerland's own Mirages, in return for the 47 unassembled planes. Paris shook its head, and Berne said no. It was then that the crewcut Mr. Frauenknecht, who had a soft spot for Israel from personal knowledge of Nazi Germany, had an idea.

He told his superior that storing the plans for the canceled Mirage line was occupying space and costing a large sum of money. He offered to microfilm the plans and destroy the originals. The proposal was approved. In cooperation with an Israeli spy, Frauenknecht and his brother took the originals to a garage, from whence they took other boxes of old plans to the city incinerator. Frauenknecht then took the Mirage plans over the border to Germany, whence they were flown by Israeli agents to Brindisi, Italy, and Lod, Israel. In weekly shipments, the whole operation took fifty weeks—which gives some idea of the many thousands of blueprints involved in the manufacture of a single aircraft. But the Israeli agent in Switzerland left a few plans behind that the Swiss police discovered, and Frauenknecht was caught. He was sentenced to four and a half years' hard labor for high treason. Israeli agents had promised him $200,000 as "insurance" if he was caught, and this he apparently received. But Tel Aviv washed its hands of him, and today he is reportedly unemployable.

Since 1973, the Israeli arsenal has greatly expanded, including standoff missiles and precision-guided munitions, laser-guided bombs, and pilotless decoy aircraft, used to confuse a radar defense as an electronic countermeasure, or even to carry up to 1,000 pounds of ordnance. The Egyptians, for their part, have acquired the French-made Martel standoff missile, which has a 35-mile range—and, as will be noted later, have ordered a great many other weapons.

In an important study written in 1976 for the American Enterprise Institute, Robert J. Pranger and Dale R. Tahtinen predicted: "The next round of fighting in the Middle East will involve efforts by one side or the other to deliver a pre-emptive 'knockout' blow to enemy forces in relatively quick order by focusing on rear-echelon military and infrastructure targets." The danger is that "the best support for an unstable military position might appear to be a nuclear doomsday weapon in the

Middle East . . . There will be a tendency to move nuclear weapons out of the deterrent realm into the attack strategy itself."

Pranger and Tahtinen noted the proliferation of Israeli and Arab surface-to-surface missiles, as well as Israel's acquisition from the United States of four Hawkeye control planes which "will significantly increase Israel's capability to operate in a hostile, electronically cluttered environment."

In 1978, after deliveries of the first 25 F-15s, Israel's air inventory consisted additionally of approximately 200 Phantoms, 235 Skyhawks, 110 aging Mirage-IIIs, about 80 remaining Super-Mystères, Mystères, Ouragans and Vautours, and about 140 Kfirs (which could cannibalize some of the older French planes for parts). A total of 200 Kfirs were expected to go into squadron service by 1979. Additionally, Israel has 12 high-flying RF-4E reconnaissance aircraft, 2 other reconnaissance aircraft, 4 E-2Cs, 186 helicopters, 125 troop transports, 2 aerial tanker-refuelers (with 5 more on order), 104 trainers and 67 other planes.

Egypt, having twice been invaded by Israel, had built up the second largest air force in the region, with a total of about 500 combat aircraft (not all serviceable) of the MiG, Sukhoi, Tupolev and Ilyushin families. About a quarter of all aircraft were outdated MiG-17s and MiG-15s, while 250 were MiG-21s. The number of MiG-23s, the Russian equivalent of the Phantom, was still small—24 in 1978, not all of them serviceable.

Total Arab air forces in the region posed to defend themselves from— or to attack—Israel now slightly outnumbered Israel's own military aviation, if Iraq, Saudi Arabia and Lebanon were all counted; but these forces remained inferior to the IAF in overall quality and preparedness. Syria, with 45 MiG-23s, 250 MiG-21s and 45 Su-7 fighter-bombers, and a total combat aviation of about 400 planes, was as well equipped as Egypt, with about 350. Iraq had nearly 400 planes, including MiG-23s, but more were on order. Libya's 160 planes, including 92 Mirages, some of them Mirage-III/5s, were a factor only if they were loaned or given to a more effective air force, which seemed unlikely. For the time being, Saudi Arabia's Air Force, still in its training stages, was negligible, and Jordan's was expected to remain so.

Israel's force of helicopters has doubled since 1976. Only Egypt's inventory of 192 helicopters is comparable, since this includes about 40 large Mi-6s and Mi-8s; but Iraq had 135 rotary-wing aircraft, including 16 Mi-6s, which can carry 65 troops, and 30 Mi-8s, which carry about 30 soldiers apiece.

Israel today can muster trained ground forces of 400,000 or about as much as Egypt and Syria put together, and has nearly 3,000 tanks—

against about 2,000 in Egypt, about 2,600 in Syria and 520 in Jordan. The proportions of armored personnel carriers is similar, with Israel's 4,000 including captured Soviet equipment. Israel, however, has a decided advantage in other armor, as well as in antitank missiles, wireguided and otherwise, and precision-guided munitions.

Israel's 75-ship Navy is of the "light and fast" type, except for 5 submarines. Egypt's 110 ships include 12 submarines and 5 destroyers. Syria's Navy is negligible.

A key problem is the risk of a nuclear first strike. Both sides have considerable nuclear delivery platforms. Each side has three fighters—the Phantom, the Kfir and the F-15 (and soon the F-16), versus the MiG-23s and -21s and the Sukhoi-7 fighter-bombers. Israel's neighbors also have the Il-28 light bomber and the Tu-16 medium bomber. Israel has two nuclear-capable surface-to-surface missiles, the Jericho and—probably any moment now—the Lance. Its neighbors have the Scud and the Frog-7. Both sides have nuclear-capable howitzers.

As Pranger and Tahtinen noted as far back as 1976, the agreed concept of retaliation which has given the superpowers the balance of terror might not be clear to conflicting countries in the Middle East. Israel has two reactor centers—the Nahal Soreq Research Center near Tel Aviv, purchased under the U.S. "Atoms for Peace" program in 1955, and the better-equipped Dimona center. Western experts have concluded that Dimona can produce enough plutonium for at least one 19-kiloton bomb annually. Dimona was first identified as a nuclear-weapon facility by Egyptian intelligence as far back as 1960: Cairo passed the information to Washington, and U.S. spyplanes confirmed it. It had been suspect from the start because of the secrecy surrounding the installation and its budget, and because of its ownership by the Ministry of Defense in Tel Aviv.

When ordering its first fifty Phantoms in 1968, Israel stipulated that they should have pylons for nuclear bombs. Israel has not signed the Non-Proliferation Treaty. (Egypt has signed it but says it will not ratify until Israel does.) A physicist with the Ministry of Defense in Tel Aviv, Isaiah Nebenzahl, and Menaham Levin of Tel Aviv University have described a laser process for enriching uranium isotopes, and if this is currently being used successfully, nuclear-warhead production would be much faster than one bomb a year.

Egypt's small, Russian-built reactor at Inshass would take eight years to produce a bomb, according to the American Enterprise Institute study. Dr. Kissinger promised an American reactor, which would take about eight years to build. When Congress wavered over this, France offered to build one in America's place: Experts say a French reactor would take even longer to reach a productive stage. This is what arms-controllers call an "unstable" situation, because it seems that the law of retaliation falls on the Soviet Union. In 1973, stability was achieved—thanks to the discoveries of one American aircraft—by Moscow arming Egyptian Scuds; but, given less warning, the Russians might feel they had to respond to any Israeli "strategic" initiative themselves, with dangerous implications.

Distances have always been short in the immediate conflict area—the arms-control terms "strategic" and "tactical" can both mean the same in certain circumstances, and this is one of them. Even with the older generation of aircraft, Damascus was as close to Israeli sites as Philadelphia was to Washington; Cairo was not much farther from Tel Aviv than Washington was from New York, and was barely a hop, skip and a jump from Israeli-occupied Sinai. Poorly defended Saudi Arabia is equally close to two Israeli air bases in Sinai—called by the Israelis Ofira and Etzion. The latter was being used by the United States as an occasional base for high-altitude reconnaissance over the gulf and adjacent areas. (In 1978, President Carter, at Camp David, sought assurances that Etzion would be handed over to Egypt in a peace agreement undamaged, so that the USAF could continue to use the base. Theoretically, however, the 1979 peace precluded any military use of Etzion.)

The Egypt/Israel peace treaty, if it endures, makes war in the Middle East less likely. But a future war might well spread beyond the territories of conflict of the past. The F-15 not only puts Israel within striking distance of all of Egypt but also parts of Libya. The F-16 is almost equally capable. Israel's acquisition of KC-130 aerial tankers puts both fighters within reach of gulf oil fields. Similarly, Saudi Arabia's F-15s could reach Israel from bases safely back from Israel's border—or even bomb parts of socialist Syria and pro-Soviet Iraq. Since Saudi Arabia also has aerial tankers, the range—using F-5s—could be approximately doubled.

Just short of the nuclear threat was Israel's request for CBUs (Concussion Bomb Units), to be fired in clusters from Lance missiles; but, as noted earlier, this request, approved by Ford, was refused by Carter in 1977. Even the presence of nuclear capable artillery, such as Israel's American howitzers and the Soviet 8-inch cannons of the Muslim states, could be—as Pranger and Tahtinen have pointed out—more provocative than deterrent in a Mideast context. Various war-games scenarios in Europe suggest strikes at secondary targets as "warnings" which need not provoke escalation. But there seems little hope for such sophisticated brinkmanship in the Middle East. President Sadat, for instance, has said that an Israeli attack on the towns being rebuilt along the Suez Canal would be met by strikes at major Israeli cities.

Tahtinen and Pranger conclude:

> Any pre-emptive strike against airfields in today's Middle East, with the purpose of producing the same complete effect achieved by Israel against Egypt's Air Force in the 1967 war, would require enormous explosive power to destroy the kind of sheltering that now protects aircraft on the ground, even if ones attack plan could solve the wide-dispersal, quick-alert and antiaircraft protection afforded today's Middle East air forces. Using nuclear weapons pre-emptively, out of fear that ones opponent will attack first and one will somehow be left inferior, or that ones enemy might retaliate with his own unconventional means, would, for all practical purposes, constitute engaging in a surprise atomic attack.
>
> Any pre-emptive use of nuclear weapons would not only bring world condemnation but probably retaliation of some sort from one or both superpowers.

Israel is now designing and building all but the most sophisticated components of its armory, or nearly 70 per cent of all weapons. Its indigenous Kfir fighters—and its American-made Phantoms—are currently being fitted with locally made Luz-1 440-pound air-to-surface missiles, predominantly designed to destroy Russian-built SA-6 installations and other antiaircraft defenses. Said to be "jamming-proof," the Luz, like the Shafrir air-to-air missile, is designed by Rafael, the official state arms industry, and built by Israeli Aircraft Industries. It has a range of 50 miles and is replacing the 27-mile-range U.S. Maverick; Egypt's, Syria's and Iraq's SA-6s have a range of 35 miles, so that the implication of the change is that the Luz will permit standoff bombing. Israel's new Arieh (Lion) multi-role attack plane will be available in the eighties.

In a study of the Mideast balance in 1977, veteran defense writer Drew Middleton said in the *Times:* "Israel still enjoys an overall qualitative military superiority over any combination of Arab states, even when forces from Saudi Arabia, Kuwait and Libya are added to those of Egypt, Syria, Iraq and Jordan—the participants in the [1967] war." But Middleton said this superiority "could be eroded in the next eighteen months."

However, columnists Rowland Evans and Robert Novak, who often reflect the views of Pentagon experts, noted around the same time that "[Premier] Begin has a $3 billion U.S. military pipeline, the payoff for Israel's modest 1974 pullback from the Suez Canal and the Syrian plain. President Carter has pledged there will be no interruption of those weapons, guaranteeing Israel military superiority over the Arabs far into the future, unless Moscow starts a major rearming program."

The columnists also quoted Begin as telling Senator Jacob Javits, "a leading member of the pro-Israel bloc in Congress," not to worry that Israeli intransigence in peace, or success in war, might affect U.S. oil supplies as it did in 1973. Begin was reported to have shocked the New York Republican by offering to capture an oil-producing country such as Libya.

By late 1977, Middleton had also concluded that Israel's superiority was guaranteed far into the future. He wrote in the *Times* that Israel had increased its weapons stocks by 60 per cent since 1973 and its manpower by 40 per cent. He added:

> Israel's military power is considered so strong today and that of the Arabs so weak that the prospect that the United Nations Security Council or an individual member could influence Israeli military policy in a crisis seems increasingly remote.
>
> . . .
>
> Israel's reliance on [American] weapons, most sources agreed, would not prevent Israel from fighting a short, successful war even if the American Administration decided at the outbreak of war to halt all arms shipments. The consensus is that the Israelis would require at the most three weeks to defeat the Arabs, and that, given the present temper of the Israeli Government, the Army would not be restrained by American pressure from seeking a complete victory.
>
> . . .
>
> Israel would emerge from a war of three weeks or less still qualitatively superior to its Arab foes in personnel, armor and aircraft, the analysts say.

Later, most observers attributed President Sadat's spectacular and controversial visit to Jerusalem at least partly to his country's military weakness. Some Egyptian fighter pilots were reported to be flying only four hours a month, because of the shortage of spare parts for Russian aircraft and the slowness of French and British deliveries. Pentagon analysts said it would take Egypt and Syria until 1979 to reach their strength of 1973, and that by then Israel would be nearly twice as strong as it was at that time. Egypt in particular was said to be at least five years behind Israel in technology. Today, with Egypt apparently "neutral," at least for the time being, the balance of power is so strongly in favor of Israel as to be even more destabilizing in the sense to which Pranger and Tahtinen referred. Although a third of the $3 billion of additional U.S. military aid to Israel, promised as a reward for the peace agreement with Egypt, will go to rebuild air bases in the Negev which Israel already had in Sinai, one result of the peace treaty will be to increase Israel's arms superiority in the area. The extra $1.5 billion of arms for Egypt would only counterbalance this partially, if the peace treaty "failed."

Najeeb Halaby, the former administrator of the Federal Aviation Administration, and father-in-law of King Hussein, notes that more and more Arab countries are buying from Japan and Western Europe the sort of military technology which Israel acquired by copying French and American models. But the Arab countries were well behind in arms self-sufficiency, pending the development of their own arms complexes in Cairo and Saudi Arabia. Moreover, Cairo's role in this sector is now uncertain, because of Saudi and other Arab reaction to the Cairo/Tel Aviv treaty. The complexes are run by the earlier-mentioned Arab Organization for Industrialization (AOI). An *Aviation Week* report in 1978 remarked on the AOI's growing efficiency and good security. But AOI general manager Yousif al-Turki said production costs would be higher than for direct purchase of foreign weapons; he said the acquisition of technology—and independence—justified the higher cost. If the main plants are now removed from Helwan—except for assembly lines supplying Egypt alone—the delays and higher costs in developing these industries will be even greater, and their effective role in the Middle East balance of power more uncertain.

The AOI is run by a Higher Council, consisting of the defense ministers of the four participating states, and a twelve-man board of directors (three from each state). The Organization is not bound by the customs or labor laws of any of the participating states. Strikes are forbidden. Most of the 15,000 employees are currently Egyptian, drawn from the four existing Egyptian arms plants.

The Egyptian plants were intended to do most of the work requiring large numbers of workers. Saudi Arabia was to manufacture electronic components. There are now some 2,500 AOI trainees overseas, including some management students at the Harvard Business School. The AOI is 70 per cent aerospace-oriented, and the United States, Canada, Britain and France are also providing assistance for Cairo's Arab Institute of Aerospace Technology: The Western role in the AOI is examined in a later chapter.

Until the peace treaty with Israel gave Cairo a breathing space, Egypt was the Mideast country with the most military problems. Its aircraft cannot range farther afield than Israel, and then only if airfields near the Suez Canal are used. By trying to replace its dependence on Moscow with dependence on Paris, London and Washington, Egypt lost both momentum and the advantage of standardization. In 1977, Egypt sent about half its 210 MiG-21s to Russia for repairs and time-overhauls; the

Russians began returning them, later, only in "drop-counter" quantities. But for the moment, with only one partly hostile neighbor—Libya— Egypt's relatively weak defenses were of less immediate concern.

The arms buildup—and collapse—in Iran, the beginnings of an arms buildup in Saudi Arabia and the development of the area's smaller air and other forces are described later in this book.

CHINA

The Middle East is not the only non-NATO, non-Warsaw Pact part of the world which could upset global peace. China, which believes in a global Marxist revolution, is a nascent superpower, a threat to the Soviet Union and—despite its current courtship of Moscow's foes—a potential threat to the West and others.

China has a population of about 1 billion people and maintains regular armed forces of approximately 4,025,000. Draftees serve from four to six years in the Navy, from three to five years in the Air Force and from two to four years in the ground forces. In 1978, the Chinese defense budget was put at $30 billion (up from $17 billion four years before) or 10 per cent of the GNP. This is low for a militarized underdeveloped country, and presumably reflects the modest salaries and living conditions of Chinese troops and the somewhat artisanal nature of much of China's war industry. No major increase was expected before 1980, because of the cost of current plans to reform industry, agriculture and education, but China's ambitious military plans for the future are becoming clear.

China was estimated by the International Institute of Strategic Studies in 1977 to have between 20 and 30 multi-stage, 3,500-mile-range intercontinental ballistic missiles, and between 30 and 50 medium-range missiles. These, plus "about 65" Tupolev-16 medium strategic bombers, put a wide range of Russian population centers and major military targets within strategic reach, if defenses could be penetrated. China's Army numbers about 3.5 million men and women. Its Navy of 275,000 includes 28,000 Marines and a Naval air force of 30,000, all shore-based. The Air Force of 250,000 personnel has about 4,250 combat aircraft, mostly outdated, short-range interceptors, and includes the (nuclear) Strategic Forces. There are about 2,000 MiG-19s, and a slightly smaller number of MiG-21s.

Summing it up succinctly, the IISS said that year: "Chinese defense policy operates at the two extremes of nuclear deterrence and People's War." A deployment of 200 or 300 fission and fusion tactical nukes, both surface- and air-launched, could support the strategic armory and the

2,000-mile-radius Tu-16 bomber to ensure saturation of Russian targets—once again, in the unlikely event that any Chinese aircraft reached their targets. The medium-range ballistic missiles, with a range of 600 or 700 miles, were being replaced in 1979 with intermediate-range CSS-1 ballistic missiles with a range of up to 1,100 miles. A CSS-X-4, 6,800–8,000-mile-range intercontinental ballistic missile, with a reported 3-megaton warhead which could take out Moscow (or Los Angeles), is under development. China has one G-class submarine with missile-launcher tubes, but does not yet appear to have perfected missiles for it. All China's present missiles use liquid fuel, but solid propellants are being developed. In any nuclear conflict with Russia at present, China would be literally obliterated, and Peking has stated that it will not use nuclear weapons "first."

John H. Barton and Lawrence D. Weiler, in their book *International Arms Control: Issues and Agreements*, have noted:

> It is often said, almost disparagingly, that the Chinese want nuclear weapons for political as well as military reasons. This is precisely why any country wants such weapons—to gain the political leverage that can come from advanced military power. Nevertheless, China's nuclear strategy differs from that of other nations. Its cultural background is different from that of the other nuclear powers. It is not, like the United States and the Soviet Union, locked into a bilateral strategic relationship that dominates other nuclear balances. Neither is it, like Great Britain or France, aligned with one of the nuclear superpowers, so that its strategy must be analyzed in relation to that superpower's nuclear guarantees. Rather, the People's Republic of China seeks to guarantee its security in part by attempting to use the position of one superpower to constrain the other.

Barton and Weiler recall that the Soviet Union provided China with a reactor in 1955, and trained a number of Chinese scientists at Dubna. In 1957, in association with the Soviet Union, the Chinese established an Institute of Atomic Energy. China's best-known weapons expert, Ch'ien Hsueh-sen, was, however, trained in the United States.

The 1957 agreement called for Moscow to supply Peking with advanced information on nuclear weapons, but the Soviet Union abrogated the pact in 1959. According to Barton and Weiler, China has invested between 2 and 3 per cent of its GNP in nuclear weaponry. Between 1964 and 1975, the Chinese exploded seventeen nuclear devices. On November 17, 1976, a hydrogen bomb in the 3- to 4-megaton range was detonated.

China has built its own (F-6) version of the MiG-19 and designed the Shenyang fighter, which Western reference books record as the F-9—a Mach-2 aircraft derived from the MiG-19 and the MiG-21. The delta-winged F-12, under development, will be an advanced, twin-engined version, using Rolls-Royce Spey engines built in China under license. The country has old Russian or modern Chinese models of the SA-2 surface-to-air missile, and T-34 and T-60 amphibious tanks. There are also tanks and armored personnel carriers of Chinese design, notably the T-59. A 1977 CIA report said China had built one nuclear submarine, but otherwise the Navy is diesel-powered.

China has a thirty-year Treaty of Alliance and Friendship with the Soviet Union which expires in 1980; but in recent years this has been a dead letter. All experts seem to agree that China genuinely fears attack from Russia, and Peking has invested heavily in rather crude civil-defense projects. The Pentagon said in 1978 that two thirds of China's 121 infantry divisions, or about a million troops, were on the Soviet border, along with 7 tank divisions. About 10 divisions, of 120,000 troops, faced Taiwan—a decline of 30 per cent since 1972. (More of these were removed in 1979.) About 14 divisions (170,000 troops) faced India. The Soviet Union, in contrast, understandably seems to fear Peking less than Peking fears Moscow. It has 7 tank and 34 mechanized infantry divisions on the Sino-Soviet border, less than half at full strength—about 650,000 troops in all; but these have 7,000 armored vehicles and 45,000 tanks to China's 4,000 and 10,000 respectively, and a very substantial part of Moscow's strategic defenses is aimed at China.

China's artillery and heavy mortars equal Russia's in numbers if not in quality, but Moscow's 2,500 helicopters are more than six times as numerous as Peking's. China has French Super-Frélons, one of the best heavy military helicopters in the world—but only 13 of them, so far.

China's Air Force—which should have improved thanks to the British-assisted program to develop Rolls-Royce Spey engines locally, in remote Sian, for the F-12—is heavily defense-oriented, as is its Navy, the world's third largest: Its 1,245-ship fleet (including 300 "brown water" or river ships) gets its cutting edge from 63 big vessels and, at last report, 67 attack submarines—barely a quarter as many as in Russia's 470-ship fleet. But the Chinese fleet is outdated and could achieve little more than a rearguard action. In war, its main attack posture is expected to be to try to close the Straits of Malacca to the Soviet fleet.

The *Times*'s Drew Middleton visited China at the end of 1976 to make an evaluation of China's military strength, based on some elite units which he was allowed to see, and on interviews with several Chinese commanders, including Wu Hsiu-chan, deputy chief of the Army general staff. Middleton called the weaponry he saw "obsolescent or obsolete," "ten to fifteen years out of date," and Chinese strategy "anachronistic." The Chinese apparently hoped the Russians would stretch themselves thin by huge infantry incursions. Middleton confirmed that Chinese combat aircraft were no match for Soviet equivalents and said Chinese guns could not pierce Soviet armor. Chinese armor was of poor steel: Improvements would depend on trade with Japan. In another article some months later, Middleton reported that the Chinese lacked remotely controlled weapons and said "antiaircraft guns have only the most rudimentary radar guidance, while the infrared and laser sights for antitank weapons, now standard in NATO and Warsaw Pact armies, are unknown in China." He also found China lacking in command-and-control systems: "Warning of the approach of hostile aircraft toward Shanghai, the largest city in China, would come over the regular telephone system." A CIA report noted that year that Chinese underdevelopment was related to stagnation in the growth of the economy, the result of earthquakes and political upheaval.

Nevertheless, there are now clear signs that China is moving into a more modern military age, and its interest in arms and arms-related purchases in the West is examined in a later chapter. In preparation for its new posture, five military reconnaissance satellites were launched in 1975 and 1976, and China's whole satellite program has since taken on—with U.S. help—a far more ambitious stature.

FUTURISTIC WEAPONS OF THE PRESENT

Any reader of defense literature today is impressed with the profusion of contracts awarded each year to literally hundreds of firms for research and development into modern warfare's more frankly science-fiction world. Strange forces of power are being tapped. Almost anything that can be "proved" on paper is being tried.

The best-known, and most expensive, science-fiction weapons are satellites.

Military Satellites

The first universal use of satellites was for communications. Both the United States and the Soviet Union have fired nearly a thousand satellites into "space"—which begins about 100 miles up—and of these a few score orbiting at any one time are military communications satellites. They were first used in the Vietnam War not only for communications, but also for weather prediction and naval bombardment guidance. Reconnaissance satellites, however, have attracted more attention.

Initially, all reconnaissance was done by aircraft, notably the U-2—a powered-glider design put forward in 1954, without there being a previous government or company request for it, by Clarence L. Johnson, who incorporated revolutionary photographic techniques devised by Edwin Land of Polaroid fame. U-2 flights for the CIA began in June 1956, with aircraft based in Turkey, Pakistan and, later, Cyprus, but were stopped after Soviet protests. The age of the "spy" satellite then began.

In America, the overall spy-in-the-sky program was called MIDAS (Missile Defense Alarm System) and the satellites themselves were termed Satellite Data Systems (SDS). America's first "Big Bird" satellite, SDS-1, was launched in March 1971, using a Titan-3B rocket, into an orbit about 100 miles from earth; it had a life of fifty-two days. SDS-2 was sent up in 1973 and SDS-3 in 1975, followed by three more that year. The first two 1975 launchings were essentially experimental, although they provided communication links to SAC bombers in polar regions, but SDS-3 began monitoring signals from Soviet Molniya satellites. Its main function, however, was to spot the fiery plume of a ballistic missile as soon as it was launched and flash the signal to the Worldwide Military Command and Control System inside Cheyenne Mountain in Colorado. Like all the early Big Birds, it often failed to distinguish between a missile's plume and sunlight reflecting on high-altitude clouds.

The first real Russian early-warning satellite was probably the Kosmos-775, sent up in 1975: It was placed in geosynchronous orbit over the Atlantic, where it could observe any American submarine launch of a ballistic missile. Each year now, the Russians launch about thirty short-life (twelve- to thirteen-day) reconnaissance satellites, the majority of them being—like their U.S. equivalents—close-look vehicles with high-resolution camera systems, and the others having wide-area surveillance missions. Since 1973, the Russians have also used ocean-surveillance satellites, in pairs, while about half a dozen electrical reconnaissance satellites are launched each year from Plesetsk. China, as noted earlier, began launching satellites in 1975.

By that time, U.S. reconnaissance satellites were in orbit for about 150 days at a time. The four American reconnaissance satellites launched that year were two very large Big Birds, capable of reaching 50,000 miles into space, and two close-look and ocean-surveillance satellites. From then on, some of the Big Birds carried into orbit octagonal electronic "satellite satellites" weighing only 130 pounds; these have independent, nearly circular orbits.

By mid-1976, the United States was devoting a growing portion of its military and civilian space program to satellites, and 60 per cent of all U.S. and Soviet satellites were by then military—navigation, communications and reconnaissance. By then, Big Birds had become virtually 11-ton television cameras, with high-powered lights: No longer just recording the existence of a missile's plume, but actually showing what the missile looked like, they ejected film cartridges by parachutes which were caught by Y-shaped hooks projected by C-130s, flying just north of Hawaii, and swiftly processed on the ground. If a hook missed, the cartridges floated, emitting radio and sonar signals, and were recovered by frogmen. The Russians are only just evolving this technique: For the moment, their entire reconnaissance spacecraft must return to earth before its images are recovered.

America's new, supersecret KH-11 satellite, with extra fuel, and rockets for evasive tactics, is even more sophisticated, developing the film on board and transmitting it direct to TV screens. It flies orbits that bring it between 111 and 180 miles from earth, with occasional rocket firings to bring it up to 250 miles to prevent it sinking into the atmosphere and burning up. This gives it a "life" of about 220 days, so that only two launchings a year are necessary.

The Keyhole satellites do three different types of photography: ordinary, high-resolution photography concentrates on visible features like launch sites; infrared photography is used to detect temperature differences, thereby revealing the presence of a heated underground silo in cold earth, or "seeing" things at night, such as a tank column on the move; multi-spectral photography "pierces" camouflage, distinguishing for instance between false vegetation and a real forest.

Some of the wonders of spy-in-the-sky satellites and reconnaissance aircraft are, however, considerably simpler. How, the present writer asked an expert, do we count the number of re-entry vehicles in a MIRV-ed warhead? The answer: by counting the number of splashes in the ocean.

Until 1974, all military satellites were low-altitude, orbiting the earth from 500 to 1,650 miles up, or about 100 to 150 minutes per orbit. Now two other altitudes are also used, 8,000 to 12,000 miles (8-to-12-hour orbits) and geosynchronous 24-hour orbits of 13,000 to 30,000 miles elevation. (Geosynchronous means orbiting at the same speed as the earth revolves; thus the satellites are kept in the same overland position.)

Perhaps the best-publicized recent satellite project is the NavStar Global Positioning System, since this involves a $100 million order to firms for receiving sets for aircraft, ships and ground forces throughout the world. The little-known Defense Systems Acquisition Review Council met for the second time in early 1979 and decided to move into full-scale development of the NavStar system. Ultimately, any suitably equipped user will be able to use NavStar to locate position with mind-boggling accuracy, and nuclear sensors aboard will supplement the coverage of early-warning satellites, increasing the detection capacity and reducing the system's vulnerability to Russian "killer satellites."

Air Force aircraft which will initially use the equipment include the F-16, the Boeing B-52, Lockheed C-141 transports and Sikorsky HH-53 helicopters, along with the Navy's Lockheed P-3C patrol planes, A-6s and Sikorsky RH-53D choppers, carriers, attack submarines, frigates and minesweepers. General Lew Allen, commander of Air Force Systems Command, calls NavStar "possibly the greatest technical advance applicable to theater war"—but there is a danger that the Soviet Union may plug into it also.

The Army will begin equipping UH-60A and Cobra helicopters, and Grumman OV-1B observation aircraft, along with various tanks and trucks, for NavStar. Eventually, some foot soldiers with the right backpacks will be able to take their bearings on these artificial stars, while NavStar satellites will also guide missiles. The receiving equipment will weigh between 8.8 and 26.4 pounds, not including—on aircraft and ships —the inertial measuring units, inertial navigators, doppler sensors and other complementary equipment.

The Naval Research Laboratory sent up its first navigation technology satellite in June 1977. Rockwell launched the first of five developmental satellites, with General Dynamics Atlas-F boosters, from Vandenburg Air Force Base in California in September; three more were launched from Vandenburg in 1978. Phase Two of the $4 billion, ten-year program will involve the launching of eight more satellites, partly for the Air Force, while between fourteen and twenty more will be sent up in Phase Three.

When fully operational, the NavStar Global Positioning System will consist of three groups of eight satellites each, in three separate, overlapping, twelve-hour, circular, synchronous orbital planes, giving continuous global coverage from an altitude of 12,500 miles. The Air Force will not call the twenty-four a wing or a squadron, but a constellation, no less. Most users will have receivers that can lock on to four satellites, but some supersonic aircraft will carry five-channel receivers to ensure that at least four are always available for navigational cross-references. A navigator would get continuous tri-dimensional position fixes, based on determination of his speed to within 10 centimeters (4 inches) a second.

Air Force magazine said in 1976 that NavStar signals would "permit an unlimited number of properly equipped users to determine their position and velocity in three dimensions anywhere in the world, day or night, under all weather conditions, with an estimated accuracy of about 30 feet." But tests on the inverted range (that is, with the satellite system on the ground, and the plane above) at Yuma showed even more accuracy than projected: Errors were from 11 to 14 feet laterally and 12 feet in altitude. While navigation will be NavStar's most constant task, its potentially most important function is the targeting of missiles. The system should be operational, worldwide, by 1985 and, like communications satellites, could be standardized within NATO, which already had three communications satellites of its own in orbit by 1978. The last of the current series of NATO communications satellites, each with seven-year lifetimes, was launched early in 1979, and when this system ceases to be operational in 1983 or 1984 a new and more sophisticated system should be ready. Already, the 125-pound Ferret electronic-intelligence satellite monitors radar and radio transmissions—even telephone conversations.

The Air Force also seeks to make its space programs less dependent on ground terminals. The Space and Missile Systems Organization (SAMSO) hopes by 1980 to have a small, satellite-borne autonomous navigation system enabling satellites to locate themselves without recourse to external ground computers or tracking systems. Meanwhile, IBM is developing simplified processing stations for the Air Force's early-warning satellites, mostly housed in a widespread array of 40-foot trailers.

The new Defense Communications Agency satellites, which should be ready by 1979 or 1980, will have a life of ten years. Their transponders will receive signals for retransmission to SAC aircraft, protected from enemy jamming by three new multiple-beam array antennas in addition to the more conventional horn radiators that illuminate an entire face of the earth.

Satellites will eventually be used to locate and track enemy aircraft and cruise missiles, to complement the triad of synchronous early-warning satellites—whose main task, as noted earlier, is to detect Russian and Chinese ICBM and SLBM launches by sensing the short-wavelength infrared emissions in their burning booster propellants. Because radiation from jet-engine exhausts is weaker than that of ballistic missiles, and because of background clutter and the masking effect of the earth's atmosphere, aircraft or cruise-missile engines are difficult to spot from outer space; but here as elsewhere technology is constantly improving, using mosaic infrared detectors, lightweight optics and what are called acousto-optical filters. As their name implies these are wavelength-tunable optical filters sensitive to (high-frequency) sound (or, as the manuals picturesquely describe sound, "acoustical excitation"). Defense Advanced Research Projects Agency (DARPA) sources say "thousands" of mosaic infrared detectors could be fabricated on a single chip.

As most readers of serious newspapers know, the CIA is not the only "spy agency" in the United States, nor is it the biggest. The National Security Agency, specializing in communications, has the largest staff and the largest budget—about $1.5 billion annually, compared to about $800 million for the CIA, out of a total intelligence budget estimated by informed sources at $7 billion. A lesser-known intelligence institution than the NSA, but one growing enormously in importance from these satellite developments is the USAF's National Reconnaissance Office (NRO). This, as noted earlier, has so far resisted Admiral Stansfield Turner's bid to make it hand over to the CIA its management of satellite and SR-2 interception of Soviet and Chinese communications.

The reason why the military regard knowledge of all data obtained by the NRO as crucial is not far to seek, for the next step in the "star wars" battlefield is killer satellites, which will hunt and perhaps destroy hostile satellites and—in wartime—ballistic missiles. Already, from the ground, the Soviet Galosh antiballistic missile (ABM) could be used against American satellites, just as the U.S. Titan-IIs could be used against Soviet constellations. Now, in America, Ling-Temco-Vought, TRW, Hughes and Lockheed all have defense contracts tied to the U.S. killer-satellite program.

Before dawn on February 6, 1977, residents of Cape Canaveral heard a huge roar: Those who went to their windows saw the orange glow of a Titan-IIIC launch rocket shimmering into the sky. The Air Force simply called it a "classified launch." It was the first U.S. killer satellite, going up to investigate one already sent up by the Soviet Union.

Information on these killer satellites is understandably classified, but experts believe they would be sent in considerable numbers as far as 60,000 miles from earth, there to roam in orbit until needed. When a Russian or Chinese satellite that might be dangerous is picked up, the killer satellite will be called down to the "suspect's" level and will slip into orbit with it, "inspecting" it with its infrared sensors and sending its findings back to earth. Then, if needed, it will destroy the enemy satellite with conventional or nuclear warheads or laser beams. Although a 1967 agreement banned weapons of mass destruction from space, and the 1972 ABM treaty said neither side would sabotage the other's arms-limitation surveillance methods, both sides are in fact working against the clock today on a devastating variety of killer satellites (the Soviet Union had already space-tested at least sixteen of them by late 1978, ten of which were classed by U.S. sources as "probably successful") as well as on countermeasures to render the enemy's "Asats" ineffective. On the reassuring side, North American Air Defense Command (NORAD) also uses satellites to plot the position of the 3,000-plus man-made objects in space, including rocket debris, to ensure that they do not trigger an unneeded—armed—automatic response.

The program to match Moscow's offensive—antisatellite—techniques is extensive. General Dynamics and Vought are developing a small, unmanned "homing" device: A number of these would be carried aboard a spacecraft "bus" or launched from earth: Fired at the Soviet vehicle, they would home in by radar and a long-wavelength infrared seeker; but this technology was said in 1979 to be about two years away.

About $10 million was spent in fiscal 1978 and twice as much the following year to enhance the "survivability" of U.S. satellites against Soviet antisatellite measures, as well as against inadvertent interference and natural disasters. "To counter the potential prospect of laser threats," *Aviation Week* reported in 1977, "the USAF has been exploring laser warning sensors similar to [those deployed by] the Navy on . . . aircraft." If a satellite is illuminated by laser energy, the sensors would react, triggering a shutter to protect sensitive cameras or other optical sensors. Already by then, various firms were working on devices to counter laser jamming and other laser effects, while another Air Force contract calls for an "electro-optical terminal threat warning sensor." This would provide an electro-optical flash warning of a detonation similar to that given by the infrared tail-alert receivers on aircraft which warn the pilot that a missile is on the way. A receiver that warns of radar energy impinging on a satellite already exists, but work continues on devices that would enable the satellite to take evasive maneuvers or to eject a decoy. IT&T is working on electronic countermeasures for satellites, while other contracts call for "reducing satellite observability." *Aviation Week* reported that to get replacement satellites into orbit more quickly, boosters may be based aboard wide-bodied aircraft or in Titan silos. This would reduce the payload, sacrificing capacity but reducing "observability," and making it harder for the enemy to locate and track such a so-called "dark satellite" as it moves into orbit.

The Vought Corporation is building fruit-can-sized explosive projectiles which will rush an enemy killer satellite in clusters. Suicide "decoy" satellites are also on the drawing boards, and consideration has been given to using the freight bay of the space shuttle to snatch hostile satellites out of space. Another system uses pellets. The simplest way suggested for knocking out an enemy satellite is sprinkling gravel in its path, creating a collision between the slowing gravel and the 10,000-miles-an-hour satellite, and thus totaling it. By the time the "accident" occurred, the satellite discharging the gravel would be on the other side of the earth. In November 1977, the Pentagon announced that it was developing high-energy laser technology for possible use against hostile satellites: of this, more later.

More satellites will be placed in orbit by the U.S. space shuttle, after

1980, and the Russians see the shuttle itself as part of a killer-satellite program. Soviet satellite launches exceed American ones, but their vehicles usually have shorter lives. The Soviet launches include an experimental Fractional Orbital Bombardment System (FOBS)—a partially orbited ICBM, using a four-stage, bottle-shaped SS-9 (Scarp) rocket, which could strike virtually any target in the mainland United States. President Carter proposed in 1977 that space vehicles be demilitarized. For the moment, they are simply not nuclearized. In 1978, Moscow and Washington began secretly discussing, in Helsinki, a "killer-satellite limitation agreement," to curb satellite warfare preparations.

Since the January 1967 Outer Space Treaty, basing of space-based weapons, whether for attack or deterrence, has been prohibited, but as both East and West maintain early-warning, communications, geodetic, navigation and reconnaissance satellites, these remain vulnerable to jamming and outright attack. Both superpowers employ satellites for command and control as well as surveillance. Neither arms-control verification nor crisis management is possible without these systems. In 1975, when a U.S. early-warning satellite was "blinded" by the flash of a gas pipeline fire in western Russia, the incident was initially attributed to Soviet lasers. (Some experts still disbelieve the "pipeline fire" explanation.)

Satellite interceptors have a long developmental history. In June 1960, after Gary Powers' U-2 was shot down, Chairman Khrushchev warned that reconnaissance satellites could also be "paralyzed." Two years later, a Soviet defense writer, G. P. Zadorozhnyi, iterated the Soviet right to "destroy a satellite spy and in general every space device whatsoever interfering with the security of this state." Soviet journals frequently asserted that America was developing space weaponry and that Moscow could therefore do the same. In his *Soviet Military Strategy*, V. D. Sokolowsky alleged that the United States had embarked on a fifteen-year space-weapon program involving "bombardment satellites," militarization of the moon and "antispace" lasers. Sokolowsky said reconnaissance and other satellites could be used as weapons platforms.

The Russians themselves have the largest air-defense network in the world: There are about 6,000 radar installations from Murmansk to Vladivostok, and about 12,000 surface-to-air missiles at over a thousand sites. Backing these up by satellite-based missiles might well be seen as one way of making the Soviet Union invincible.

After the Outer Space Treaty, Soviet journals ceased to refer to the *Protivo Kosmicheskaya Oborona*—the "antispace" unit of the PVO-Strany (the air defense command); but Soviet tests of interceptor satellites long preceded those of their early-warning vehicles. They began in October of 1967, when U.S. monitors on Kwajalein Atoll followed Kosmos-185 as it maneuvered and docked in space with Kosmos-186 and -188. Another experiment the following April failed, and the interceptor was brought back to earth; but in October 1968, Kosmos-248, launched from Tyura Tam, was joined the following day by Kosmos-249, which exploded at an altitude of about 300 miles. Twelve days later, Kosmos-252 went into elliptical orbit, also came close to -248 and exploded. Soviet press releases said the experiments had been "successful." In 1970, Kosmos-373, in a circular orbit 300 miles up, was joined on different dates by -374 and -375 in elliptical orbits. The two elliptical-orbit satellites both exploded.

The explosions were caused in each case by self-destruct mechanisms on the interceptors—similar to those used on satellites which have failed, to prevent them falling into U.S. hands; the "success" of the operations was the ability of the interceptors to join another satellite in space. They were not actually used for a "kill," presumably because of the 1967 treaty.

Until 1971, both targets and hunters were launched from Tyura Tam, using heavy 10,000-pound payload rockets. Then, with the transfer of operations to Plesetsk, target satellites were launched by 1,200-pound payload rockets; only the "hunter" satellites continued to use the heavy F-1M rocket. Further tests stopped in 1972 during negotiations for the SALT I agreement, partly—Western observers thought—to discourage development of America's own antisatellite capability.

Kosmos-758, an apparent satellite interceptor, was launched from Plesetsk in 1975 on an unusual 67° orbit; it exploded—or was "self-destructed"—after four days in orbit. When Soviet killer-satellite tests resumed openly in 1976, it was with mixed results. The new Soviet vehicles are 78 feet long and weigh 2.5 tons at launch. Kosmos-404 and -804 co-orbited with the target satellites, allowing time for close inspection. Others swooped in on the target at 400 meters per second in an elliptical orbit, giving little if any time for inspection but enough time to destroy. A typical case occurred in May 1977, when NORAD radar in the Aleutians picked up killer satellite Kosmos-910 as it closed in on its target, Kosmos-909. On October 27 that year, in a seventh killer-satellite test, a Kosmos launched from the Baikonur pad at Leninsk in Kazakstan passed within lethal range of Kosmos-959, launched six days earlier from Plesetsk. The target satellite was in an orbit varying between 91 and 526 miles from earth. The killer, with a circular orbit of between 78 and 188 miles, had to rendezvous with its victim when the latter's elliptical orbit brought it close to earth. An eighth successful killer-satellite intercept was achieved in early 1978, and a target vehicle, Kosmos-1,006, was launched later that year; the program showed every sign of continuing, as did other satellite projects. In late summer, a new reconnaissance satellite, Kosmos-1,028, was launched and stayed up for a month—double the time of its predecessors. Covering the world every ninety minutes, it had a view of China, Western Europe and the United States. About this time, fresh emphasis was given to the Soviet space program when a Russian spacecraft, Soyuz-31, with a Soviet and an East German astronaut aboard, beat Russia's own world manned-flight space record by staying up over four months. In September, Kosmos-1,031 was launched from Plesetsk: This was a close-look satellite sent up to report on NATO exercises in the Shetland Islands north of Scotland.

Some Soviet killer satellites have approached within 100 feet of the passive target satellite and have demonstrated "quite complex maneuvers," according to the International Institute of Strategic Studies; none, however, has seemed able to follow a maneuvering target or to take on more than one target per flight. None of the interceptions was carried out at the very high, geosynchronous altitudes used by American early-warning or communications satellites. From launch to interception has taken only one to three hours, compared to the six hours which would be needed to reach targets in geosynchronous orbits. (Such a longer time frame would facilitate both evasive maneuvers and diplomatic action.) No target satellite has been destroyed, although this could have been achieved during the close docking by exploding the interceptor. Western strategists believe the Russians are unwilling to display space weapons: Once the docking technique is mastered, arming the interceptors is a relatively simple task.

Meanwhile, the Soviet Union continues to launch electronic ocean-surveillance, early-warning, navigation, communications, weather and geodetic satellites, the latter having importance for military targeting. By late 1978, the U.S.S.R. had launched 325 "military" satellites, compared to an unclassified U.S. figure of 48. That year, a Soviet "space crane" satellite, Kosmos-929, that could be used for building a space station, was finally destroyed by its controller over the Pacific, having changed orbits successfully at least five times. Earlier that year, considerable alarm was caused when Kosmos-954, a Soviet ocean-reconnaissance satellite, crashed in northern Canada, scattering radioactive debris. Two more ocean-reconnaissance satellites, Kosmos-1,075 and Kosmos-1,077, were launched in early 1979. In all, the Kosmos program involved 99 launchings in 1976, 98 in 1977 and 88 in 1978, for a total of 1,069. The 1978 figure included 35 reconnaissance vehicles and 2 early-warning satellites, Kosmos-1,024 and Kosmos-1,030.

Concern that an attack could "blind" reconnaissance satellites necessary for monitoring arms-control agreements led to inclusion of a clause in SALT I under which each superpower consented not to "interfere" with the "national technical means of verification of the other"; but satellites broadcasting Western television programs are still vulnerable under the treaty. China, which had launched only seven space vehicles by the end of 1977, is well behind in its own satellite programs, but it is possible that the Soviet interceptor program is destined mainly against such a Chinese development, and only secondarily against the United States. China launched a military reconnaissance spacecraft in 1978 and, it was learned, had plans to launch two communications satellites into geo-synchronous orbit by 1980, using a liquid-hydrogen/liquid-oxygen upper stage.

Just how sensitive is the space contest was stressed in 1978 when a junior ex-CIA officer, twenty-three-year-old William P. Kampiles, was arrested for selling a manual on the KH-11 satellite to a Soviet agent in Athens for $3,000. Revealing the secret characteristics of this improvement on the Big Bird was considered so serious that it was said at the time that it could affect the SALT II talks, since it could help the Russians to deceive America's most advanced verification system.

The Pentagon's space budget for fiscal 1978 reached a record $2.8 billion, but the following year Carter requested and obtained nearly $3.4 billion for space programs. America, Russia and China are not alone: France and India both have predominantly military space programs involved with reconnaissance and targeting. After earlier failures, Britain's communications satellite Skynet-2B was launched from Cape Canaveral in 1977, with an approximately three-year life. Stationed over the Seychelles, it provides communications for an area bordered by Norway, the Antarctic, western Australia and the eastern Atlantic. In Japan, Mitsubishi is building a maritime observation satellite in cooperation with West Germany's Messerschmitt-Bolkow-Blohm.

But because of blind spots in satellite coverage, $10.2 million of the 1979 U.S. budget for strategic reconnaissance is being spent on bringing back the U-2 of Gary Powers fame. Tactical Air Command is planning to buy twenty-five TR-1s—an improved, larger version of the U-2—for $8.5 million each, mainly for battlefield coverage: Production will begin in 1980. The Tr-1 will fly outside enemy airspace and "see" for 300 miles.

Strategic Air Command's SR-71 assembly line has, however, closed, with its dies being broken and melted down for security reasons.

Lasers

The earlier-mentioned use of lasers in space would only be an additional task for a weapon already well into development and limited deployment. Advances in the fanciful world of earth-based laser-beam weapons are preparing the way for some of the possible stellar battlefields of tomorrow. Both America and the Soviet Union are now close to producing weapons of awesome power through laser technology, and a 1977 Library of Congress report urged that the Pentagon be required to send Congress arms-control impact statements on high-energy laser research and other futuristic weaponry.

The laser program is known to the Department of Defense by the code name "Eighth Card." The Air Force's antisatellite laser-development project, noted a few pages back, is part of the work of the Air Force Weapons Laboratory of the Defense Advanced Research Projects Agency (DARPA) at Kirtland Air Force Base near Albuquerque, New Mexico. The tests themselves will be conducted from a nearby mountaintop. (The Department of Energy's laser-fusion program for nuclear power is also under military control, despite some Carter administration misgivings, and because of security considerations.)

Laser stands for Light Amplification by Stimulated Emission of Radiation. Lasers use concentrated beams of light particles called photons, traveling at 186,000 miles per second, through a device which projects the light along a pinpoint-narrow optical wave band—instead of diffusely, as with normal light radiation. The speed, enabling aim to be *at*—not a calculated distance in front of—a target, ensures an extraordinary concentration of heat with deadly accuracy over enormous distances. Virtually anything in its path would melt, including unfriendly missiles. Laser guns are planned for many contemporary weapons, including the F-15, and were intended for the B-1.

The first laser was developed by Dr. Theodore Maiman of the Hughes Aircraft Company in 1960. Now, Superman- or Buck Rogers-type American lasers exist which could destroy aircraft, missiles or even satellites—which would merely have to be nudged by a laser beam to start tumbling, fouling their radio-antenna communications with earth. DARPA, as noted, admitted in 1977 that it was developing high-energy chemical lasers using hydrogen fluoride, for possible deployment against hostile spacecraft—probably by burning holes in their solar panels. Meanwhile, the Russians were testing a new hydrogen-fluoride high-energy laser at Krasnaya Pakhra, near Moscow—"probably for space-basing," according to a report.

A ground-based laser beam can even determine what optics and what film are stored within a satellite, and can probe almost anything else. The USAF is seeking active and passive techniques for hardening America's own supersonic aircraft and missiles against laser radiation. This will probably be achieved by ejecting particles or chemicals into the windstream which would either shield the structure or would ionize to produce plasma, blocking the laser beam. In three U.S. satellites, vulnerable external solar panels have been replaced by shielded, internal nuclear generators. This may well be the pattern of the future.

Not all military lasers are directly destructive. Lasers are used for target acquisition by other weapons, and DARPA director George H. Heilmeier says an infrared laser radar has already been developed which could track an object in space. For the other side, U.S. intelligence learned in 1977 that a Soviet laser station for range-finding tests with spacecraft had become operational near the Cuban seaport of Santiago de Cuba.

The developments in the laser field—including peaceful uses, such as energy—have revolutionized science; but the number of different types of potential laser weapon is almost unlimited. Laser-guided missiles have proved easier to operate than precision-guided munitions. Laser designators, like infrared seekers and electro-optical systems, are already accurate to 30 feet—much better than most radar-guided systems. In 1978, the USAF ordered the designing of a new low-level laser-guided bomb to replace the first-generation weapons developed during the Vietnam War. The new-generation weapon would require no external assistance. Lasers may be used to guide the multiple warheads of ballistic missiles. And at the other end of the scale, there is even talk of testing, soon, a light, hand-held laser gun which would vaporize an enemy soldier.

According to Captain G. R. Villar, former director of British naval intelligence, the Russians already have an "antiballistic laser missile." Writing in *Jane's Weapons Systems*, Villar claimed that on five occasions the Russians had "illuminated United States satellites for periods of up to four hours with powers of up to 1,000 times that seen in a forest fire or an ICBM launching." In 1975, as noted earlier, the "blinding" of an American early-warning satellite, caused by the flash of a gas-pipeline fire in western Russia, was mistakenly attributed to a laser beam.

For fiscal 1979, Congress voted $184 million for military laser research, a 24 per cent increase over the previous year. Shortly before, laser weapons from Kirtland had destroyed two TOW antitank missiles in a Navy test at the San Juan Capistrano facility of TRW Inc. This was the fastest target hit yet—formerly, lasers had only been tested against fixed and rotary-wing aircraft. Production by 1980 was under consideration, with a weapon to be developed for carrier defense at China Lake. In addition, McDonnell-Douglas were developing laser weapons for ground-based air defense and for installation in fighters, while Hughes Aircraft, McDonnell-Douglas and General Electric were working on a laser ballistic-missile defense. Basic research is being conducted by the University of Texas Center for Electromechanics at Austin.

Particle-Beam Weapons

Also in 1977, it was learned that the Russians were ahead in experiments with charged-particle beams—aiming a stream of subatomic particles called electrons, protons or neutrons at a target through the use of precisely tuned electromagnets, which drive the particles to velocities approaching the speed of light. These would literally dissolve everything in sight. Electron and proton beams were said to be most effective in the atmosphere, and neutron beams in space. Military intelligence officials claimed that the Soviet particle-beam project was "comparable in size to the Manhattan Project" (which produced the first atomic bombs in World War Two). In prospect, it could be virtually as terrifying as the first stages of nuclear power were then, if one superpower acquired particle-beam weapons first; but a balance of PBWs might eliminate—or replace—nuclear terror.

The first research work on particle-beam weapons was performed by Nikola Tesla, of what is now Yugoslavia, as far back as the 1890s. Tesla demonstrated his discoveries to a scientists' meeting in Colorado Springs in 1899, producing artificial lightning. The U. S. Patent Office refused Tesla a patent in 1915, presumably refusing to take him seriously. Since then, comparatively little research has been done in this area until recent times, although British scientists did explore the concept in the late forties.

To make particle beams effective, a portion of the atmosphere must be pre-heated, perhaps with a laser beam, which would literally bore a hole in the atmosphere. Particle beams are less accurate over immense distances than laser beams, but they could destroy nuclear missiles rapidly by melting the plutonium explosive, thus neutralizing it before it could be detonated over a target. Meanwhile, according to a *Times* story, Swiss scientists have discovered yet another new force in nature—composed of transmuted atomic particles—which is stronger than gravity.

But principal attention went to the particle-beam "death ray," as it soon became known in the press, which Defense experts said would drastically change the military balance—by neutralizing American ICBMs. The reported Russian achievement was first made public—to some skepticism—by testy Major General George Keegan, Jr., shortly after his retirement as head of Air Force intelligence. Keegan said he estimated that a Soviet charged-particle-beam weapon would be operative by 1980 "if they don't blow themselves up—and they may."

Reporters learned that the intelligence debate was focused on mysterious buildings, 35 miles south of Semipalatinsk in Soviet Central Asia. The buildings were protected by several fences and included what one source called the "world's largest crane." This source estimated the cost of the complex at "between $10 and $15 billion" and agreed that charged-particle-beam research might be its purpose.

The full story finally broke in an article by Clarence A. Robinson, Jr., in the May 2, 1977, issue of *Aviation Week*. Robinson said Keegan's intelligence services had concluded that the Semipalatinsk facility was involved with particle-beam research, and gave their reasons: The detection of "large amounts" of gaseous hydrogen with traces of tritium in the upper atmosphere; the ground testing of a small hydrogen-fluoride high-energy laser, and the detection of preparations to launch the device aboard a spacecraft; finally, the "test of a new, far more powerful, fusion-pulsed magnetohydrodynamic (MHD) generator to provide power for a charged-particle-beam system at Azgir in Kazakstan near the Caspian Sea." MHD generators use superheated gases or plasmas to deliver far more power than electric generators.

Wrote Robinson: "The experiment took place late last year [1976] in an underground chamber in an area of natural salt dome formations in the desert near Azgir, and was monitored by [an American] early-warning satellite stationed over the Indian Ocean." The new test site at Azgir had been placed under the direct control of Marshal P. F. Batitskiy's national air defense force (PVO-Strany)—indicating a "near-term weapons application for these experiments," Robinson said.

There were also classified revelations by a Soviet scientist, Leonid I. Rudakov, during a visit to the Lawrence Livermore laboratories in California. Rudakov claimed that the Soviet Union could convert electron-beam energy to compress fusionable material to release maximum fusion energy.

The cost of the Soviet research facility at Azgir was put by *Aviation Week*'s sources at the more modest figure of $3 billion. The magazine article said:

The U.S. used high-resolution photographic reconnaissance satellites to watch as the Soviet technicians had four holes dug through solid granite formations not far from the main large building at the facility. Mineheads were constructed over each opening, and frames were built over the holes. As tons of rock were removed, a large underground chamber was built deep inside the rock formation.

In a nearby building, huge, extremely thick steel gores were manufactured. The building has since been removed. These steel segments were part of a large sphere estimated to be about 18 meters in diameter. Enough gores for two complete spheres were constructed. U.S. officials believe the spheres are needed to capture and store energy from nuclear-driven explosives or pulse-power generators . . . The components were moved to the nearby mineheads and lowered into the chamber.

Some other U.S. physicists believe the steel gores are designed for underground storage of unused nuclear fuel for a magnetohydrodynamic or closed-cycle gas-core fission process needed to power beam weapons or for storing waste products from the fission process . . .

Initially, some U.S. physicists believed there was no method the Russians could use to weld together the steel gores of the spheres to provide a vessel strong enough to withstand pressures likely to occur in the nuclear-explosion fission process, particularly when the steel to be welded was extremely thick. U.S. officials later discovered that the Russians [had] invented a process called flux welding and had been using it for years in producing pressure spheres. The flux-welding process, according to some U.S. officials, makes the bonded material weld as strong[ly] as, or [more strongly] than, the steel walls.

While the CIA, skeptical about the significance of the Azgir facility, referred to it as URDF-3 (Unidentified Research and Development Facility 3), General Keegan's Air Force intelligence named it PNUT—Possible Nuclear Underground Test.

Earlier, U.S. scientists at DARPA had attempted unsuccessfully to develop a charged-particle beam device—Project Seesaw. But *Aviation Week* asserted that "explosive generation" had been "solved in the U.S.S.R. by Soviet academicians Andrei Terletsky, who was once a KGB agent in Sweden, and Andrei Sakharov, who was instrumental in developing the Soviet hydrogen bomb and [who] is now a dissident." One of the magazine's sources said the Livermore physicists regarded Keegan's interpretation of what was taking place at Azgir as "pure Buck Rogers"; but *Aviation Week* claimed that "U.S. scientists since have been able to confirm that Soviet high-energy institutes long ago solved problems of electron injection that placed them years ahead of U.S. technology." This had peaceful applications, the magazine said, and such Soviet equipment, produced at the Institute of High-Energy Physics at Novosibirsk, was even being exported commercially to the United States.

Robinson said that in 1975 Keegan had informed CIA director William Colby of his conclusions about Azgir; Colby had briefly informed Dr. Kissinger, just before the arms-limitation talks that year, that there was "a facility related to nuclear functions that are unknown but which might have high scientific application." Otherwise, the discovery was withheld from the White House and the NSC, Robinson said. Physicist Edward Teller later told the U. S. Senate that, "despite some exaggeration," Keegan's analysis was correct.

Pragmatically, how useful would such a weapon be to the Soviet Union? Said *Aviation Week:*

> Precise pointing and tracking may not be required, an official said. "All that is needed," he explained, "is for the Soviet long-range precision radars now deployed in violation of the ABM agreement to detect avenues or windows for re-entry-vehicle trajectories against targets in the U.S.S.R. By aiming rapidly pulsed proton beams into these windows, ICBMs and SLBMs could be quickly saturated and destroyed.
>
> The windows would be located from 1,000 to 2,000 nautical miles out in space. "With this method, many acquisition and tracking problems could be overcome. By using the window concept to scatter the beam over a wide area through which warheads must transit, it is believed that not many beam-weapon devices would be required to protect the U.S.S.R. from a U.S. retaliatory strike," the official said.
>
> There are at least 150 of these silos that the United States is now overlooking by accepting the Soviet definition for their use, as command and control centers.

Observers noted that low-flying weapons like the B-1 bomber and the cruise missile would be invulnerable to beam weapons during their final approach to target, and saw the strong Soviet objections to such weapons as possibly confirming the views of USAF intelligence. In the fiscal-1978 budget, the U. S. Navy acquired $6 million for what was called the Chair Heritage program—the exploratory development of American beam weapons. The program is conducted at the Lawrence Livermore laboratories in California.

In the Senate, after the 1977 revelations, Democrat William Proxmire of Wisconsin called hearings of his Joint Committee on Defense Production to investigate the *Aviation Week* story; but in the weeks leading up to possible new SALT II talks, the hearings were put off at CIA director Stansfield Turner's request—for what a Committee staffer called "classified reasons." Defense Secretary Harold Brown ordered the Defense Investigative Service to find out who had "leaked" to *Aviation Week*.

Meanwhile, Admiral B. R. Inman, acting director of the Defense Intelligence Agency, answered in the negative three questions from Proxmire: whether Moscow was developing a beam-weapon antiballistic missile; whether it was preparing to test a space-borne hydrogen-fluoride high-energy laser as a satellite killer; and whether Soviet long-range perimeter radars had been deployed in violation of the ABM treaty. Inman found it "doubtful" if Russia could have a prototype beam weapon by 1978 and an operational one by 1980, and doubtful if (ABM) perimeter radars could be used in conjunction with beam weapons to destroy incoming American warheads.

Asked "Could collective accelerators be fitted vertically inside silos that the U.S.S.R. now claims are for command, control and communications?" Inman said: "There is no data base in the West upon which to base an estimate, since such an accelerator is only now in its conceptual stages. Our assessment is that the Russians are no further ahead than we in this technology."

Questioned by the senator as to whether the magazine had correctly described the Semipalatinsk facility and its construction schedule, Inman said any response would have to be classified, and offered to give Proxmire's Committee a classified briefing. Proxmire said he wanted to stay away from classified briefings if possible.

Defense Secretary Harold Brown told a National Press Club luncheon: "The evidence does not support the view that the Russians have made such a breakthrough or indeed that they are very far along in such a direction . . . I'm convinced that we and they can't expect to have such a weapons system in the foreseeable future."

But in late 1977, a Swedish scientific study reported that on five occasions in early 1976, airborne short-lived radio-nuclides of unknown origin had been detected in southern Sweden. The Swedish National Defense Research Institute report said:

> As the observed events cannot be readily accounted for in terms of any known source, the observations and speculation concerning charged-particle beam experiments at Semipalatinsk in the Soviet Union raise an interesting possibility.

The study said nuclides from the Semipalatinsk area could have been carried into southern Sweden by the wind. Since the Semipalatinsk experiments had reportedly started at that time, the study concluded that they were probably the source of the nuclides. By late 1978, the Russians had reportedly conducted eight tests at Azgir. They were also reported to have two ground-based electron-beam accelerators at Sarova, near Gorki, a facility directed by a well-known Soviet scientist, M. S. Rabinovich of Moscow's Lebedev Institute; other Soviet scientists were doing joint work with France, using a Russian accelerator on French Eridan sounding rockets, launched from France's Kerguelen Islands.

A leading American physicist, Dr. Richard L. Garwin, later pointed out one of the problems of making beam weapons effective: since the charged-particle beam is bent substantially by the earth's magnetic field, it cannot be aimed directly at its target; but Garwin conceptualized basing the beam on a satellite to avoid the problems posed in the atmosphere, and destroying unfriendly warheads during the boost phase, which lasts for about five minutes from lift-off, before they have released their MIRVs. Said Garwin: "This has the advantage for the defense that there is only one object to attack rather than the large number of re-entry vehicles and decoys which might otherwise be the case. Also, the rocket in boost phase is far less durable than the re-entry vehicles once they have been deployed, and it is also much more visible since it is radiating a large amount of light and heat from its rocket exhaust."

Other sources have suggested that a hydrogen-atom beam, being uncharged, could cross the earth's magnetic field without being bent; but Garwin said that a "nuclear explosion smaller than the present warhead on any of our ICBMs or SLBMs would suffice to render ineffective a Soviet hydrogen-atom beam device." He concluded that "the system's problems are such that the future looks dim for a charged-particle beam ABM system to be effective against the ballistic missile force of the United States or the Soviet Union." But no one seemed quite sure.

Indeed, in 1978, this writer was told that an antisatellite and antiballistic-missile charged-particle beam weapon called Sipapu was within three years of testing at a U. S. Army facility in Los Alamos, for later basing at the China Lake Naval Weapons Center. Sipapu—apparently an Amerindian word for "sacred fire"—is part of a $12 million segment of the fiscal 1979 defense budget allotted to charged-particle beam weapons. But the House Armed Services Committee has recommended that the Chair Heritage program be transferred from Navy control to DARPA. The Navy wants PBWs for carrier defense, while the Air Force wants them for antiballistic-missile warfare against ICBMs, submarine-launched ballistic missiles and antisatellite satellites. Carter in 1978 set up a survey team to centralize PBW research, after an intramural administration squabble as to whether this would irritate the Russians and therefore complicate the SALT negotiations. At last word, U.S. particle-beam and advanced laser weapons were not expected to enter the inventory until the late eighties, and a 1979 report by a research team at the Massachusetts Institute of

Technology thought that even that date was optimistic. A Pentagon report later that year admitted that the Soviet Union was probably "five to seven years" ahead of the United States in particle-beam research.

Meanwhile, some experts said that Soviet ability to send false instructions to American space vehicles might be more of a problem than attacking them with Buck Rogers weapons. One noted that "lasers can't penetrate fog, cloud or rain. The right kind of radio signal can go through anything." On the other hand, their use in space—above cloud and fog—is obvious, and particle-beam weapons were reported to be able to penetrate cloud and dust and other obstacles.

The Automated Battlefield

The Vietnam War played a seminal role in developing sci-fi weaponry. Some of the first "smart weapons" of that war have already been mentioned. It was in Vietnam that U.S. forces first dropped battery-operated sensors behind enemy lines to detect the movement of troops or vehicles. These sensors were sensitive to metal, heat, sound and even the smell of urine. (Their antennas were disguised as young palm trees—and still are, which might be a bit of a giveaway on a snowy day in Eastern Europe.) Pilotless drones at high altitude relayed the signals from the sensors to a control center code-named Igloo White, where computers analyzed them and proposed targets. Pilots then took off and handed over climb, speed and navigation to the planes' computers and dropped bombs guided by computer. Defense writer Phil Stanford of the CDI recalls an officer saying: "We've got the Ho Chi Minh Trail wired like a pinball machine, and we plug it in every night."

Just as underwater sensors, relaying signals through Norway, Iceland and Canada to a control center in Norfolk, Virginia, have greatly improved, so the plane-dropped ground sensors of the Vietnam War have moved on to REMBASS (Remotely Monitored Battlefield Sensor System)—virtually, an automated battlefield.

In Vietnam, the computers often failed or worked imperfectly, but the groundwork was laid for future wars that could be fought by planes without pilots, or between armies which would never see more of the enemy than blips on a screen. Even antitank projectiles now find their way to targets over the horizon. Sensor-programmed guns, including SIAMs (self-initiated antiaircraft munitions), will select their own targets. Some SIAMs will be dropped near enemy airfields, and will wait until planes there take off, then fire themselves. Some missiles, as noted earlier, already read maps. Encapsulated torpedoes, called "captors," on the ocean floor, will spring into action when their sensors pick up the signals of an unfriendly submarine. (Captors can be nuclearized and their role in war would be to "interdict" the North Sea between Iceland and Norway.) Another naval weapon, dropped from subs, will float to the surface, also firing its missile when it picks up unfriendly frequencies. A naval automatic antimissile gun called Phalanx may eventually be put aboard every ship to catch incoming warheads faster than human thought. The sensors of this were not yet perfect, however, at last report: a Phalanx identified one of the Santa Barbara Islands as an incoming missile and blew a crater in it.

The TOW (tube-launched, optically tracked, wireguided) missile, also mentioned earlier, is guided by signals transmitted along a thin wire that the missile plays out as it travels. The operator simply keeps his sights on the target, enabling electrical impulses to travel along the wire and adjust the missile's course. TOWs and their Russian equivalents were as accurate in the October 1973 war in the Middle East as were the well-known, infrared, heat-seeking missiles thrown at aircraft. For the moment, the U. S. Army's experimental 155mm. laser-guided artillery shell is operated by a soldier with a 30-pound pack. But eventually, a drone with laser designators—so far, only effective in daylight—will fire that too. We may not be far from the day when wars could be fought entirely with weapons whose every projectile, unless shot down or deflected, will be "right on" target. This in turn emphasizes the importance of electronic countermeasures—jamming, lasers, other light systems, even artificial fog. These are a far cry from decoy fires and camouflage—although even camouflage can deceive weapons fired by electro-optical contrast seekers.

Pilotless aircraft with wingspans barely greater than the height of their operator, and light enough—200 pounds or less—to be lifted by one strong person, have been mentioned earlier in this chapter. Their multiple roles will increase. Some will merely fly in huge numbers toward the enemy to fool his radar. Others will have downward-looking TV cameras and laser designators: When a target is spotted, the operator, seeing it on his display panel, activates the laser beam, locking it onto target, while his buddy launches a laser-guided shell. As far back as 1971, in a California test, a remotely guided, pilotless plane engaged a manned fighter and, in simulated missile-firing, "shot it down." Needless to say, the drone's pilot, sitting comfortable back at base, was cooler and more foolproof in his "flying" than the pilot actually flying the other plane from the cockpit. In a real battle situation, where the real pilot would fear for his life, while the armchair pilot would not, the latter's advantage would be even greater. Even manned planes are taken over by robots. The F-111 and the Tornado now come equipped with similar terrain contour-matching guidance to that of the cruise missile. Locked on—for instance, at night—the microminiaturized electronic circuit system literally jerks the controls against pilot pressure to avoid hills he cannot see.

Much of the sci-fi weaponry requires generous budgets and sterling skills, but much of it does not. The original Colt revolver with interchangeable parts took weaponry out of the artisanal field and gave Everyman the possibility of shooting someone. Much of the new weaponry enhances the potential kill power of Everynation. In an article, "Tomorrow's Wars," published by the London *Economist* in December 1976, a writer called some sci-fi weapons the "great equalizers." The *Economist* noted that a skilled society like Singapore could not afford a large air force, but could build enough pilotless "nuke" bombers to conquer, by surprise, its neighbor Indonesia, which has about one hundred times Singapore's population. With one purchased submarine, some (initially conventional) missiles, a few hired nuclear scientists and weapons technicians, Libya could "take out" Israel, while Malawi could raze the main cities of South Africa.

Chemical, Biological and Environmental Warfare

One still more obvious means of mass destruction for less-developed nations is chemical warfare. Currently, the United States—against strong congressional opposition—is expanding work on binary weapons and protection from them, to counter a much bigger Soviet program. The U. S. Army Chemical Corps now includes about 3,000 men, while the Red Army has 80,000 "CW" troops. According to a Pentagon source, "Warsaw Pact military planners consider chemical weapons to be an integral part of the future tactical scheme."

Binary weapons are so called because two different chemicals are involved, stored apart. Toxic-tipped shells contain only one of the chemicals. The other is added just before use. In flight, the two chemicals combine to produce a nerve gas which, released on impact with the target, attacks the nervous system of all in the target area. Uncontrollable muscle spasms follow and death comes quickly. According to Charles W. Corddry of the Baltimore *Sun*, the United States has two such binary gases—GB, or sarin, which disperses quickly, and VX, which lasts for days, or even weeks in a windless or almost windless environment.

The U.S. "binary" bomb, the Weteye, is stored in relatively small quantities in Bavaria, but NATO countries have objected to having them on their territories. War planning calls for bringing 3 million of them to Europe over two weeks if an emergency seems imminent.

CW, as chemical warfare is known, gets around certain clauses in the 1925 Geneva Convention. There is virtually no country on earth so small or so underdeveloped that it could not produce toxic gases or chemicals, or the means to deliver them to an enemy. In the Vietnam War, after all, probably 10 per cent of the entire country, or 4,250,000 acres, was covered with plant-killer. (Vietnam, says SIPRI, was the first war in which "the biosphere was systematically assailed for military purposes.")

One of the grim factors about chemical warfare is that, unlike most other modern warfare methods, it can be conducted covertly. Less covert, but at least as dangerous—and also related to CW—are what are disarmingly referred to as environmental modification techniques (EMT). Starting with the useful purpose of making rain in drought-dry farm areas, EMT figures as one of the most awesome of the futuristic weapons. The Senate Foreign Relations Committee held hearings on "military weather modification" in 1972 and passed a "sense of the Senate" motion calling for an international ban on environmental or geophysical modification "or any research or experimentation with respect thereto." After further hearings in 1976, the Committee produced a draft international convention to ban these activities.

The 1976 hearings learned that the Pentagon was practicing cold-fog dispersal at military airfields (notably Elmendorf in Alaska, Fairchild in Washington State, and Hahn air base, Germany) and also testing warm-fog and cloud-dispersal techniques. These, of course, are efforts related to navigation safety. But Democratic Senator Claiborne Pell of Rhode Island read a letter to the Committee from Bernard A. Power, president of Weather Engineering Corporation, who is suing the United States for patent infringement in the Vietnam War, and who claimed that U.S. forces had "seeded typhoons extensively over North Vietnam and the South China Sea." Power claimed weather warfare was being developed at the Naval Weapons Center at China Lake, California.

Weather warfare has several uses. Rain can be produced, increased or decreased by seeding clouds with chemicals: In Southeast Asia, silver and lead iodide were used to increase monsoon rainfalls. Cloud seeding in mountainous areas could dump snow on armies. It is also possible to produce, increase or decrease fog, hail, electric storms and hurricanes. By transferring heat from the sea to the atmosphere and diminishing sea evaporation by laying a thin film of oil on the surface together with cloud seeding, a hurricane can be hurled against an extensive coastline, destroying coastal defenses. Other climate modifications can be brought about by similar manipulations of the radiative and thermal budget of the atmosphere.

Much of EMT is still experimental and even theoretical, but the possibility of destroying an enemy's agriculture has already raised it to the level of a strategic weapon. If certain gases, notably ozone, were removed from the atmosphere—either by an ozone-reactive chemical or a nuclear explosion—there would be increased ultraviolet, electromagnetic radiation on shortwave bands, killing or inhibiting plant life and even causing skin cancer.

A series of phased—presumably nuclear—explosions under water or along the base of a large ice sheet (causing cliffs or mountains of rock or ice to slide into the sea) would create tsunamis—huge tidal waves. If the strain pattern in a region of the earth's crust is accurately known, it may be possible to release the strain and cause an earthquake by remote, phased or timed explosions. Gordon J. F. MacDonald of the Council on Environmental Quality thinks, however, that no one possesses this technology today.

However, if Very Low Frequency (VLF) radiation waves were bounced from earth off the ionosphere (which starts about 30 miles up), the interaction of the radiation and the electrical activity of the brain could alter the VLF (about five or ten cycles per second) electrical activity of the brain—the so-called "alpha rhythms"—and thus alter human behavior. An obvious target would be to turn an enemy army into babylike idiots. Dr. MacDonald *does* see this as within our capacities already.

A reminder that the Frankenstein world may not be all that far off came in February 1977, when a Princeton science junior, John Aristotle Phillips, designed (in eighteen weeks and thirty-four typescript pages) a $2,000 bomb which could trigger a "half-Hiroshima" nuclear warhead—as an extracurricular project to earn an "A" from his professor. The 15,000 pounds of plutonium which would have been required would have cost a further $100,000–$150,000—a fairly cheap price for, say, "taking out" Cleveland. French and Pakistani diplomats hounded him for the design, which was classified and handed over to defense authorities after Phillips wrote to Wisconsin Democratic senator William Proxmire. Proxmire revealed that the Pakistanis had dutifully called the Energy Research and Development Agency, which had advised them to go to Phillips directly. The French had gone to him directly after reading a story about Phillips' project in the New York *Times*. Experts said that although the component suggested by Phillips to create a critical mass and trigger the warhead was outdated by modern technology, it was in advance of the one devised in 1945 by the Manhattan Project.

Sci-War For Everyman

Finally, with the role of assassinations in history in mind, some attention should be paid to frankly individualistic sci-fi weaponry. This is by no means a new development, as readers of spy novels know. World War Two produced a crop of them—some with a double use as last-chance suicide weapons for agents about to be captured and tortured for information. "Stingers" were probably the smallest actual weapons—guns that could be fired only once. The best-known Allied version was built to resemble a cigarette lighter: One German type clipped onto a belt, like a buckle.

The Office of Strategic Services used deadly, tiny crossbows called William Tells for dealing with sentries. They fired steel-tipped darts at a velocity of 180 feet per second and made virtually no sound. The OSS pen gun, which resembled a fountain pen (and could be used for writing) did make a noise, but the bullet left no traces within the weapon, which could be filled with a fountain-pen inksack until needed again to write someone off. There was a whole range of so-called "Woolworth" weapons which similarly left no mark; they had to be reloaded after each firing, and after "about fifty uses," one former operative recalls, they were worn out. Some OSS weapons have survived: In Vietnam, the William Tell was replaced by Little Joe, an even smaller crossbow firing a 24-gram (less than an ounce) dart that would penetrate a body with enough force to emerge on the other side. (John Wayne's actors used them in *The Green Berets.*) A 45-caliber automatic was also adapted to fire an almost-silent heavy dart.

For government and antigovernment terrorists alike, there is a great range of explosives: Some are packaged to resemble baseballs (the Beano), or balls of flour (the Aunt Jemima) or even turtle eggs. In World War Two, retarded incendiary explosive devices were attached to bats released from planes flying offshore over the Sea of Japan; the bats flew off into the lofts of Japanese buildings, causing unexplained explosions attributed to omnipresent human agents. Since then, as fiction readers and moviegoers know, larger magnetic bombs have been devised to be carried to enemy ships by porpoises.

A retarded-action bomb triggered by the pressure needle can be attached by underground agents to the altimeters of aircraft, causing explosions at a pre-determined altitude. A bomb triggered by darkness can be attached to trains so that they blow up on entering tunnels, thus blocking the tunnel as well.

One World War Two underground weapon still in use is the British Welrod—originally made, like the Welman (one-man submarine) and the Welbike (miniaturized motorscooter for agents parachuted behind enemy lines) in the city of Welwyn. The British had earlier developed a sound suppressor (then called a silencer) for their Sten gun, as had the Americans for the M-3 "grease gun"; but the production of a silencer for a weapon so small that it could be tucked up an agent's sleeve, while still big enough to fire 32 ACP or 9mm. ammunition (seen in the movie *Taxi Driver*), was a great breakthrough for the time. Designed by a Major Dolphin, the Welrod is just over a foot long and can hold three cartridges—or in the "sleeve" version, only one.

The Welrod is still in the CIA arsenal. It was used in Korea and Vietnam—for which it was remanufactured by the legendary Mitch WerBell of Powder Springs, Georgia. It has appeared more recently with the British Special Air Services—the equivalent of the Green Berets—in Northern Ireland.

Other concealed weapons of modern times include an attaché-case gun, triggered from the handle and fired through a vinyl-covered hole in one side of the case. Such an arm was used to try to kill President Park Chung Hee of South Korea in 1973 and cost the life of his wife.

The modern CIA and KGB armory includes a motley assortment of different poisons and poisonous gases. A West German technician went to Moscow in the sixties to "debug" his country's embassy there, doing such a good job that he was invited to "clean" the U. S. Embassy as well. Disapproving local law-enforcement officials later zapped a near-lethal dart of mustard gas into his leg while he was praying in a church near Moscow, thus discouraging him from returning to service his customers again.

In 1978, a Bulgarian defector called Georgi Markov was killed in London by a poison pellet injected when he was stabbed by an umbrella while waiting for a bus. Another Bulgarian defector, Vladimir Kostov, was similarly hit that year while mounting an escalator in the Paris subway: the pellet was removed and he survived. A third Bulgarian exile from communism narrowly escaped a similar fate in London shortly after. The pellets which killed Markov and nearly killed Kostov proved, in both cases, to be 90 per cent platinum, 10 per cent iridium. They were only one fifteenth of an inch in diameter, and left no puncture trace. Two minute holes in the pellets, each one sixtieth of an inch deep, contained the poison.

The Russians have also developed a prussic acid vapor which contracts the target's blood vessels, causing instant cardiac arrest; a few minutes later, the vessels of the corpse return to normal, making his heart attack look the same. Our own side has produced a new poison-dart gun in which the dart is as fine as a human hair. It would be hard to detect, even if the forensic surgeon knew what he was looking for and in what part of the body it was embedded. Prime users of this sort of exotic weaponry include the dirty-tricks branch of the French equivalent of the CIA and the overseas hit men (Mivtzam Elohim—"Wrath of God") of the Mossad (Israeli intelligence). The CIA—and especially the OSS—used them in the past.

Allied agents have used stink bombs (made from the same hydrochloric acid used to clean swimming pools) to disrupt meetings and clear crowds, and ammonium nitrate laughing gas to put the kibosh on serious political rallies. There are different lethal bombs for individuals, buildings or cars. The "Mafia"-style bomb attached to the ignition or foot brake of automobiles is regarded as sloppy by professional spooks, since it may maim instead of killing and since the target may be a passenger who is not already in the car when the chauffeur switches on: More thorough assassins prefer attaching a fuse to the exhaust manifold; the fuse ignites when the engine has run long enough to make the manifold red-hot; this not only causes an explosion but a crash as well. The heat of the exhaust manifold is also used with castor oil to create a pall of black smoke for getaways. But remote-control explosions are now used more often for assassinations—as in the Washington slaying of former Chilean ambassador Orlando Letelier.

Tiny spy submarines are on the market. And for lethal after-dark operations, the modern undercover agent comes equipped with night-vision devices—some using infrared rays, some light-intensification. For protection, there is—as mentioned in the section on the Abrams tank—a steel which is impenetrable by anything but radiation.

Just as the various types of "spy" gun are almost endless, so are the various "knockout drops" or Mickey Finns which can be slipped into drinks: One of the most popular remains a gram of chloral hydrate, mixed with saccharine to counteract its suspicious bitterness; but nicotine, made from snuff, is also used, while nicotine made from soaking cigarette butts in water has been used by captured agents to commit suicide. In recent years, mind-altering drugs have been put in drinks and food to remove enemy agents' inhibitions and persuade them to talk.

Miniaturized electronic arson devices, miniaturized explosives and miniaturized bugging equipment reflect the trend toward easier concealment for spy weapons; electronic micro-miniaturization has produced circuits which can be seen only under a microscope, as owners of digital watches know. Miniaturized equipment is now standard for the CIA, the KGB and their equivalents in China, Britain, France and many other countries, and are even used by domestic forces such as the U. S. Drug Enforcement Agency. Their vulgarization emphasizes the need for more control of the colorful world of the arms privateer. Relatively small weapons intended for the battlefield—such as shoulder-fired missiles—have made it possible for an individual, working alone, to create the sort of havoc once associated with a motorized platoon. As with nuclear weapons, the trend in clandestine weaponry is toward the theme that small is beautiful—and more deadly than ever before.

3

"Disarmament":
More Poker Than Stripping

DISARMAMENT HAS PROVEN, thus far, to be a pious dream. Talk of mutual force reductions refers only to redeployment. Arms limitation, such as it is, refers only to nuclear weaponry—and arms control essentially only means the restraints which nuclear powers impose on themselves in selling arms to the smaller fry, in particular by not selling them nuclear weapons at all. Attempts at conventional (i.e., non-nuclear) arms limitation have been few, solely related to sales, and mostly restricted to largely unsuccessful embargoes.

In 1973, the UN General Assembly overwhelmingly approved a Soviet resolution calling for a 10 per cent reduction of the military budgets of all five permanent members of the Security Council, and the allocation of a portion of the savings to development assistance. Such a proposal was, of course, sure of Third World support; but China labeled the resolution an exercise in Soviet propaganda, while the United States abstained, stating that there was no common standard for measuring a country's military budget and no system for verifying budget cuts. America also opposed linkage between defense cuts and aid.

The most public concern has been over the role which arms limitation might conceivably play in preventing a *nuclear* showdown. This limits the issue to a very small number of countries, so far. This number will grow. Perhaps the main practical fear is of the spread of sophisticated, low-yield, *tactical* nuclear weaponry. Even in China, deployment of this type of arm to its field armies seemed unlikely before the eighties— partly because of the absence of roads, through most of the country, suitable for transporting heavy equipment.

Anyone looking at the question of arms limitation or control today finds a vast fresco of unfinished or patched-up designs scattered across a crazy-quilt political landscape, littered with good intentions and a few bruised national egos. There are broad headline-catching efforts connected with "détente," and others that seem to presume hopefully that détente is already there and that the superpowers have a duty to keep the frenetic junior powers in line if they can.

Like laws to prohibit alcohol, control lobbying or impose taxes, arms control is an exercise in questionable implementation and ingenious evasion. When Britain, France, Germany and Belgium—the powers with African possessions—signed the self-serving Brussels Act of 1890, to keep arms out of their empires (except of course those of their own security forces), independent Ethiopia refused to sign; it thus became an important "black market" for bootleg arms in the region, notably to Arabia. In 1906, a further attempt was made by the senior powers—thirteen countries, including the United States—to repress illicit arms trafficking: This was the Treaty of Algeciras. In 1908, the Hague Convention was signed, outlawing the use of poison gas. Most of these pacts were targeted at the arms privateers, who then controlled the weapons market. Their main effect was to drive up prices—itself a limited form of control. But like speed-limit laws, anything like widespread respect for these agreements would have astonished their authors.

In the twenties, the legendary "merchants of death" still controlled the war industry. Also in 1925, and once again in Geneva, a number of them met for the privately sponsored International Conference of Gunmakers and drew up an understanding which advocated reliance on existing laws and treaties rather than international control to regulate munitions exports. Six years before, there had been a tentative League of Nations plan for the "licensing and publicizing of arms sales." The 1918 Convention of St.-Germain-en-Laye was signed by twenty-six nations. The United States, in a mood of postwar isolationism, did not ratify it and the convention lapsed.

After poison gas was used, in defiance of the Hague Convention, in World War One, the Geneva Protocol of 1925, outlawing all chemical warfare, was ratified by thirty-three nations. (The U. S. Congress, however, balked.) But, in the words of a 1977 Stanford Arms Control Group study, "the Geneva Protocol is essentially a no-first-use agreement, and in no way prevents the development of chemical weapons as deterrents against possible use by an enemy." In other words, it is like a law which prohibits the use of guns, but allows everybody to buy one to use against anyone who breaks the law. Before and during World War Two, both sides developed nerve gases and biological agents but never used them, with the exception of Japan in the China theater. After the war, producing countries, notably Britain, sold nerve gas for riot control all over the world.

The 1925 Geneva Protocol was finally ratified by the United States in

1935, but with the provision that the ratification would only become effective if Belgium, Czechoslovakia, France, Germany, Britain, Italy, Japan, Sweden and the Soviet Union also ratified. By then, it was already obvious that the Axis powers—Germany, Italy and Japan—would never ratify such a pact. Germany had quit the Geneva Disarmament Conference in 1933.

All that survived of these abortive inter-war agreements was a Statistical Yearbook of the Trade in Arms and Ammunition, produced by the League.

Unilateral attempts at arms control have been limited. In Britain, Charles II sealed a Tonnages and Poundages Act in 1660 which regulated the sale of weapons. The law was updated in 1755, 1825, 1833 and 1845. In 1898, the President of the United States was authorized to embargo certain arms exports. The 1922 Arms Embargo Act prohibited American exporters from shipping arms to China; but in 1929, arms for Chiang Kai-shek were sanctioned by executive decree. By this time, Du Pont was supplying competing Chinese warlords, including the regime in Mukden.

In 1933, Belgium introduced arms-sales licensing. A Senate investigation of weapons trading led to similar legislation in the United States in 1935. Holland and Sweden followed suit the same year, France in 1939. America's Neutrality Act of 1935 was an example of negative arms control: It hurt Ethiopia, with no arms industry of its own, infinitely more than the aggressor, Fascist Italy.

After World War Two, with the privateers mostly restricted to selling surplus, and the war industry passing more and more completely into government hands—the Soviet and Chinese side, of course, placed it entirely under such control—the pacts multiplied. Not all of them were ineffective. Several treaties, for instance, successfully limited arms for the buffer states of Finland and Austria. These restricted the size of forces in those countries, the number of aircraft, the number of Finnish warships (Austria has no coast). Finland was forbidden atomic weapons, missiles, heavy bombers, sea mines, submarines, even motor torpedo boats and assault craft. It could only fit its warships with old-fashioned torpedoes of the sort that had to make contact with a target to explode. The quadripartite 1955 peace treaty which ended the four-power occupation of Austria forbade the importation or construction in that country of guided weapons. (This has since been interpreted, however, as not forbidding guided antitank missiles.) Earlier, the then "Big Four" (the superpowers, plus France and Britain) had imposed similar limitations in the peace treaty with Italy; but some of these were lifted in 1951, and all or most of the rest of them the following year. Italy introduced licensing for arms sales in 1956; Germany followed suit in 1961. Seven years earlier, Germany had accepted restrictions on the types of weapons which it could build.

After the 1948–49 war in Palestine, America, Britain and France signed a tripartite agreement embargoing arms shipments to the Middle East. Even before French contraventions made the agreement inoperative in 1953, Italy, a nonsignatory, had sold Syria thirty surplus British Vampire fighter-bombers; these were later transferred to Egypt.

The German arms law of 1961 was forced by another Near East conflict, the independence war in Algeria. In September 1960, the 3,000-ton German freighter *Las Palmas* was stopped by the French Navy off the Algerian coast and taken to Mers el-Kebir. Its cargo of flamethrowers—of a type which had been rejected by the German Army —was destined for Casablanca in Morocco, a sanctuary for Algeria's National Liberation Front.

The German Foreign Minister, von Brentano, told the Bundestag there was no law to prevent such sales between dealers. The Foreign Trade Act and the Weapons Control Act, both passed in 1961, set out to regulate both the manufacture and export of arms and their transportation in German ships or aircraft, even if such ships or planes never called at German ports or airports.

In Britain, even a crossbow is a weapon under the statutes, but most countries exclude ancient weapons from control. In America, this means anything made before 1898; in Sweden, before 1860. Most laws have loopholes for equipment which is normally "peaceful"; for instance, early in the Biafran War, the Swedes sold MF1-9B light aircraft to Biafra, where they were fitted with rockets. In 1969, Swedish law was amended to cover virtually all aircraft.

Some recipients of U.S. military aid have mutual aid agreements among themselves which may conflict with end-use agreements. Turkey and Iran supplied Pakistan during the Kashmir War, with Turkey furnishing about $5 million worth of small arms and ammunition, mostly of Turkish manufacture to NATO specifications. India urged U.S. pressure to stop the flow, but with little effect. In contrast, in July 1966, Britain refused to supply the United States with certain air-to-air missiles (Firestreak and Red Top), claiming it was unable to produce those items at that time: The Johnson administration saw this as a thinly veiled attempt by London not to compromise Britain's position as co-chairman of the 1954 Geneva Conference on Indochina, should this be reconvened in the search for a peace settlement in Vietnam.

Some governments break their own laws. In 1967, France allowed spare parts to continue to go to Israel in spite of the embargo. Some "spares" were actually end-items. A flotilla of motor torpedo boats was simply sailed away from a French port, one Christmas morning, theoretically by Israeli privateers who avoided Cherbourg port guards; the subterfuge was thin. France selectively broke its embargo for other Mideast countries, in an only partly successful deal to sell Iraq $124 million of Mirage-III and -III/5 aircraft, armored cars and tanks, in exchange for oil concessions. But France did block delivery of fifty Mirage-III/5s to Israel, holding on to the approximately $60 million deposited by the purchaser.

Arms Embargoes and Africa

Economic and diplomatic factors—looked at in finer detail in later chapters—tend to overcome control restrictions. The Security Council took three years to pass (in 1963) a measure embargoing arms for Portuguese repression in Africa; to get it through, member-states had to be left free to provide arms to Lisbon for use outside Africa; there was no provision for verification of end-use. Portugal's NATO allies—especially the United States, which had base rights in the Portuguese Azores islands—only halfheartedly attempted to keep arms out of the Portuguese African campaign. In 1961, the United States had ostensibly placed an end-use obligation on Portugal not to transfer U.S. equipment to Africa. But Portugal continued to transfer equipment received before 1961, including Lockheed Harpon tactical bombers supplied for a nominal price in 1960, North American Harvard T-6 trainer planes adapted for tactical support and Republic Thunderjet F-84 tactical-support aircraft. Lockheed Neptune long-range reconnaissance aircraft based at Montijo patrolled the African Atlantic. Portugal regularly used NATO napalm and bombs against African resistance forces.

In 1964, France gave Portugal $125 million in credits to cover the building of four frigates and four Daphné-class submarines in French yards. Two years later, Paris signed a twelve-year agreement with Lisbon for a French missile-tracking station in the Azores. This gave Portugal the same "hold" over France which it already had over Washington: In 1968, France sold Portugal the most deadly of all antiguerrilla weapons in a tropical context—twelve Alouette-III gunships. Pearton and Stanley, in their evaluation of the Portuguese "arms embargo," estimate that only

Sweden among well-known arms-producing countries actually observed the boycott faithfully.

Another Security Council embargo dating from 1963 required "all states to cease forthwith the sale of arms, ammunition of all types and military vehicles to South Africa." The scope of the measure was expanded the following year to include "equipment and materials for the manufacture and maintenance of arms and ammunition." Nine days after the settler revolt against Britain in Rhodesia, in November 1965, the Security Council embargoed arms for that country also.

However, by 1964, South Africa was self-sufficient in weaponry for the enforcement of apartheid and the repression of popular resistance—light aircraft, explosives, small arms, vehicles, tear gas, etc. The former NATO FN assault rifle, along with French Panhard tanks and armored cars, were being manufactured under license there, as was the Aermacchi 326 jet trainer—ideal for close army support. Before the embargo, France had sold South Africa Alouette-II and -III helicopters; after the embargo, France sold Pretoria Mirage fighters with Nord air-to-surface missiles, Transall transports and Super-Frélon helicopters. When French-African leaders mildly protested, Jacques Foccart, the head of French intelligence for Africa, had a superb tongue-in-cheek response: The Sydney Greenstreet lookalike said profits on arms sales to South Africa enabled France to subsidize French-African budgets. Observers noted, however, that as France's arms exports grew, its aid to Africa fell. But Foccart's incredible argument worked so well that it was not until 1968 that the Organization of African Unity got around to criticizing South Africa's main arms supplier. Later, Presidents Pompidou and Giscard d'Estaing modified their arms-sales policies regarding South Africa, but always on terms which cost neither supplier nor purchaser anything: Spare parts for past sales were guaranteed, and important sales were replaced by franchise agreements which were more economically favorable to South Africa: From 1971 onward, for instance, South Africa built its own Mirage-III and F-1 fighters under license.

Britain theoretically supported the South African embargo—a little more forcefully after Labour was elected in 1964. But even Labour allowed existing contracts to be fulfilled, including a major one for sixteen Buccaneer S-50 fighter-bombers. The excuse was that the Buccaneer was *designed* for naval use—which merely meant that it had a long range. On the same basis, in 1967 the British Government authorized Decca to create a navigational aid system for the country which could determine the position of ships 240 miles from the coast with 25-yard accuracy. Britain continued to supply spare parts for Canberras, Buccaneers,

Shackleton long-range bomber-reconnaissance aircraft and Vampire jet trainer-ground attack planes. Re-elected in 1970, the Conservatives raised the "Cape sea lane" bogey as a reason for supporting South African "defense."

Rhodesia depended mostly on South Africa to circumvent the UN embargo. In seeking direct supplies, it was less successful: In 1966, a well-known British arms dealer, Major William Turp, was approached with a request for arms for "Pakistan": From the items listed, he deduced that the purchaser must actually be Rhodesia, which might use them against British troops. He rejected the deal, and made it harder for others to take it over by giving the story to the London *Daily Mirror*. But the South African Air Force loaned Buccaneers and napalm bombs to Rhodesia and supplied spare parts for Canberras, Vampires and Alouettes.

The U.S. record was better. In 1966, Washington prevented a company from selling ostensibly civil French jet aircraft to South Africa because they were powered by engines built under American license.

The West sought to impose an embargo on both sides in the Nigerian civil war—mainly to keep out Soviet weapons. The embargo, instead, opened a hitherto closed market to the Russians, who wanted the use of Lagos harbor—and may even have hoped to buy Biafran oil after a Nigerian reconquest of the country. Russian technicians extended Calabar and Kaduna airports, heading off offers of Chinese assistance.

Nigeria, however, never got all the weapons it wanted from Moscow, which sought to prolong the conflict and Nigeria's consequent dependence. In particular, it deprived Lagos of night-fighting equipment, thereby allowing the heroic Biafran airlift to continue. Moscow's support of Lagos drove Peking to support Biafra with light weapons.

France sold armored cars, cannon and ammunition to Nigeria before the war and during its early stages. By mid-1968, however, Foccart was directing that the embargo be broken in favor of Biafra—light weaponry, but including mortars and antitank weapons. Like China, France "processed" its supplies through African nations which recognized Biafra: While China used Tanzania, France used Gabon and the Ivory Coast. To confuse control, France also sold Biafra Mauser rifles from Czechoslovakia. Since the same air-charter firm brought in arms to Biafra from both South Africa and France, observers hypothesized that Paris might also be using Pretoria as a "processing" point. Later in the war, France also supplied mercenaries.

Like Moscow, Paris sought a weakening of the Commonwealth; but Paris also sought a weakening of Nigeria itself. The Foccart policy caused friction with the French Foreign Ministry, but Foccart's influence with President de Gaulle was unchallengeable.

Despite the embargo, Britain supplied Lagos throughout the war. Her reasons were obvious enough: When Israel invaded Egypt in 1967, Britain realized that, with Suez cut, it would be dependent on Nigeria for a quarter of its imported oil. The Biafran conflict began one month after the Six-Day War.

The Mideast and Arms Control

Mideast arms embargoes have been equally unconvincing. The area imported only $2 billion of arms between 1945 and 1955. Over the next decade, with embargoes in existence, the figure rose to $9 billion, and for 1965 to 1975 to over $30 billion. Most arms sales are now government-to-government—"highlighting the axiom," note Pearton and Stanley, "that as a nation's interests extend, so its capacity for self-denial diminishes." Sweden and Switzerland, with limited foreign interests, have embargoed arms for the Middle East since 1955, as has Germany since 1965. Italy and Holland have been only modest suppliers. Mostly, Mideast wars have made money for Americans, Frenchmen and Britons, and indirectly for Russians.

In a sense, a certain embargo prevails, for except in the Anglo-French Suez fiasco of 1956, when London and Paris sought an outright conquest of territory by Tel Aviv, neither East nor West has sought total victory for their protégés. Moscow on the one hand, Washington, Paris and London on the other, have sought to counterbalance "enemy" forces and discourage confrontation.

The Tripartite Declaration of May 1950, opposing an "arms race between the Arab states and Israel," worked fairly successfully for the first five years, while the three arms-producing countries enjoyed a monopoly. The United States, involved in Korea, shunned the area. It was the 1955 Soviet arms deal with Egypt, operating through Czechoslovakia, that is usually credited by Western spokesmen with starting the Mideast arms race. In February 1956, Secretary Dulles told the Senate Foreign Relations Committee that Israel should seek protection from the UN, not the United States. Britain, with a close association with Iraq, a major oil supplier, was also unanxious to be identified with Israel; it was France that stepped into the breach, motivated by anti-Algerian passions of the moment and by Egyptian support of Algeria.

As an exercise in arms embargoes and arms control, the Mideast well illustrates the point that the value of diplomatic leverage and economic gain for the arms suppliers will always outweigh any ethical concern which suppliers may have about war among the purchasers. France, Britain and the Soviet Union were the main entrepreneurs, and their successes soon broke down American principles. From that point on, talk of restraint was merely that.

Arms Control and Latin America

The United States also sought to limit arms for Latin America, where there had been only one prolonged international conflict in this century—the 1932–35 "Chaco War" between Bolivia and Paraguay. The Nazis had been active in Argentina before and during World War Two. German military aircraft had been built there under license. Mussolini had been active in Ecuador and Bolivia. For this reason, Washington exempted some Latin American countries from the Neutrality Act, and sent $400 million of Lend-Lease military assistance into the region during World War Two. Except for Argentina and Chile, Latin American countries broke relations with the Axis powers after America entered the war.

After the peace, Washington signed a number of bilateral military-assistance agreements with Latin nations, but sought to contain the arms trade. Between 1944 and 1945, Latin America acquired 255 military jets from Britain, only 32 from the United States. By 1955, however, there were more U.S. jets in Latin America than in all the Mideast and South Asia combined. Over the following decade, the United States supplied 323 jets to Britain's 108. Kennedy sought to cap the developing arms race, but in 1962 supersonic jets entered the picture—Cuba received MiG-21s.

Washington remained reluctant to send in more than counterinsurgency weapons systems. In 1967, the United States vetoed the British sale of six Canberras to Peru because the aircraft had been partly funded by the Mutual Defense Assistance Program. The United States said Peru was too poor to buy such aircraft. But Ecuador and Venezuela already had Canberras, so Britain found six Canberras not paid for by MDA funds and Peru made the purchase.

However, London agreed with Washington about the ban on supersonics and refused Peru's request for Lightnings. This gave France its opportunity: It offered the Mirage-III/5. The State Department then allowed Latin American countries to purchase F-5s; but Peru went ahead with the acquisition of twelve Mirage-III/5 fighter-bombers and two Mirage-III trainers for over $20 million. In a bid to head off the race, Massachusetts congressman Sylvio Conte put through an amendment in

1967 whereby aid to an underdeveloped country would be reduced by a sum equal to that spent by the recipient nation on sophisticated weapons; excepted were Greece, Turkey, Iran, Israel, Taiwan, the Philippines and South Korea—and these countries, together, easily outnumbered the countries "punished" under the amendment.

Existing Controls and Loopholes

Arms embargoes are of course overtly intended to control conflicts, but they are usually as ineffective as international arms-limitation treaties. In the case of South Africa and the earlier case of Israel, they spawned impressive native arms industries. Frank, in his important work, observed that "tighter end-use controls over weapons without effective controls over the spread of technical information concerning their manufacture would probably increase the number of arms-producing nations while reducing the number of 'over the counter' sales."

There are other conflict-control options beside embargoes, but these rarely work once fighting starts. A 1967 study by the U. S. Arms Control and Disarmament Agency (ACDA) noted that "of 400 instances in which these measures could have been used in 8 interstate and 6 internal wars occurring since 1944, 149 appeared in the pre-conflict phase. Once hostilities had begun, the possibilities of conflict control declined through succeeding phases of the conflict itself."

On the positive side, governments now exercise more power than ever before over armorers.

French Government control over the country's arms industry is almost total. An exporter cannot even sign a contract with a purchaser until he has obtained authorization to do so from the Ministerial Delegation for Armament of the Armed Forces Ministry. If a proposed sales contract is controversial, the application will be referred to the Interministerial Commission for the Study of War Materials Exports, on which the Delegation and the Foreign and Finance ministries are all represented. The chairman is a Defense official. The decision must be unanimous. Disagreements are referred to the three ministers concerned—a factor which makes for compromise and consensus at the lower level.

Once the writing of a contract is authorized, the contract itself must be submitted to the Delegation for approval, along with an application for an export license. This is mainly to ensure that production schedules do not conflict with those for the French armed forces, and to supervise technical standards.

In Britain, the potential supplier draws up a contract, then applies for an export license, which must be approved by the export-licensing branch of the Ministry of Trade and Industry. Disputed cases go to an interministerial Arms Working Party. Government sales are not covered: They are treated as diplomacy.

In Belgium, export licenses are issued by the Ministry of Economic Affairs, in Sweden by the War Materials Inspectorate of the Department of Trade, in Switzerland by the Federal Military Department of the Defense Ministry. The controls on European arms exports are further explained in Chapter 9.

The main agency for controlling the spread of U.S. weapons and technology is the Office of Munitions Control (OMC), a State Department unit mostly staffed by Foreign Service officers with the requisite area experience. Part of the Department's Bureau of Politico-Military Affairs, the OMC supervises commercial sales of arms, ammunition, "implements of war," and the technical data involved. Set up under Section 414 of the 1954 Mutual Security Act, it implements the International Traffic in Arms Regulations (ITAR) and a constantly changing Munitions List, prescribed by State. It does not cover items directly exported by Defense, but it does control the re-export of munitions or other war implements which transit the United States, even if they are being returned (for instance, after repair) to the country of ownership.

As well as arms, ammunition, tanks, aircraft etc., OMC also regards as implements of war propellants, explosives, protective gear, toxic agents, helium gas and a host of other articles, including military versions of civil equipment—for instance, trucks. Anybody resident in the United States engaged in making, exporting or importing articles on the Munitions List must register with OMC: About 1,100 persons were listed in 1978.

The Arms Traffic Division of OMC processes about thirty-thousand applications a year. As in Britain, contracts are drawn up first, then submitted along with export-license applications. Some cases are referred to the State Department/Defense Department Coordinating Committee, which meets at State: Its top members are the director of the Bureau of Politico-Military Affairs and his Pentagon counterpart for "International Security Affairs for International Sales Negotiations." The State/Pentagon Coordinating Committee was set up by President Johnson, with Jeffrey Kitchen representing State and Henry Kuss the Defense Department. AID and the Arms Control and Disarmament Agency have a voice in decisions, while the Treasury is consulted on credit terms and balance-of-payments considerations. In the past, AID has sometimes opposed sales to underdeveloped countries: In 1966, for instance, it caused the sale of F-4s to Iran to be reduced to thirty aircraft. Other relevant agencies, such as the Energy Department and NASA, may also be consulted in certain cases.

Countries are rated on a secret points system, with NATO allies at the top of the list, and a country of uncertain international allegiance—say, Mozambique—at the bottom. OMC channels views based on current U.S. political and economic policies, and approval or disapproval may take anything from hours to months. Where different agencies of government disagree about the handling of an application, the first "appeal" goes to the director of OMC, who can refer it up to the director of Politico-Military Affairs, who can pass the buck up to the Under Secretary of State for Political Affairs—the Department's Number 3 person and the highest post occupied by a career Foreign Service officer.

The OMC director or his nominee represents the State Department on the National Disclosure Policy Committee, which classifies military information and is chaired by the representative of the Defense Department. OMC supplies the chairman of the State Department's "Gray Area Committee," which deals with the export of "commodities with dual commercial and military use," such as light civil aircraft to South Africa—which uses them for counterinsurgency spotting and light bomb attacks. The Office can investigate breaches of the ITAR and recommend prosecutions.

Licenses can be revoked—as when the United States and other Western countries embargoed arms for India and Pakistan in 1965, and for Israel and the Arab countries in June 1967. Exporters are informed. When the Dutch Government embargoed arms for Nigeria in June 1968, the Staatsbedrijf Artillerie-Inrichtingen was obliged to surrender its license. When France embargoed Israel in 1967, the government also informed the customs authorities. Britain informs manufacturers and sometimes customs also. Germany pays compensation to manufacturers affected by embargoes.

End-use and resale provisions offer perhaps the greatest scope for ingenious evasion. These say that the importer—who signs—is purchasing the weapons for his own use and will not transfer them without the supplier-country's consent. All U.S. sales contracts say the purchaser "shall not transfer title to or possession of the items furnished under this sales agreement to any person or organization or other government, unless the consent of the Government of the United States has first been obtained."

France requires from the exporter a percentage-deposit on the sale, which is held until French consular authorities at the destination confirm arrival. On expensive major systems, the deposit may be 10 per cent, but for small arms it may go as high as 100 per cent. However, France and Britain rarely insist on end-use certificates, so that once the approved country has taken delivery, resale is usually unrestricted. France placed end-use restrictions on its Mirages for Libya, but merely complained when these were not observed. In 1969, Britain similarly placed end-use restrictions on Centurion tanks for that country. The United States is stricter, but contraventions are legion. In 1977, Washington offered arms to Somalia, whose forces were over 100 miles inside Ethiopia, on the oddly ambivalent condition that they be used only for the defense of Somali territory. Later, the offer was withdrawn.

The Soviet Union usually makes no restrictions about resale, but sends technicians to the recipient country with the weapons. Egypt gave Soviet arms to Nigeria secretly, while Greece, in the late sixties, sold NATO weaponry secretly to both Nigeria and Morocco. Similar end-use breaches are related in a later chapter.

Since licensing and co-production agreements constitute a form of export, these are also subject to restrictions. In the United States, OMC must approve, and the United States maintains control over export by the licensee country. The United States forbids South Korea, for instance, to export its locally made M-16s. France forbids Belgium to sell locally made Mirage parts to third countries without French permission —notably vetoing airframe parts for the Mirage-III/5 when Israel sought to buy these in Brussels in 1969.

The absence of end-use restrictions has frequently caused political embarrassment. In 1964, Aeronautica Macchi of Italy sold the South African Air Force MB-326 jets with Bristol Siddeley engines made by Piaggio under British license. In 1966, France sold nine Transalls to South Africa with Rolls-Royce "Tyne" engines made by Hispano-Suiza in France and Maschinenfabrik Augsburg-Nürnberg AG in Germany, thus embarrassing both Britain and Germany, which largely respected the UN embargo. In the case of the Transall, the tail planes and parts of the fuselage were also made in Germany, but bought by France under a separate contract not overtly related to the South African sale.

In the case of Anglo-French co-production of the Jaguar attack plane, clauses in the co-production contracts say each country may only export with the approval of the other. The United States imposes strict restrictions on the sale of items co-produced in Europe such as the Hawk missile, the F-16, the F-104 Starfighter, the J-79 turbojet engine and the Bullpup and Sidewinder missiles. The U.S. veto on the sale of Israeli Kfirs to Latin America because of their American engines made headlines. Less noticed was a similar veto, in 1978, on the sale of Swedish Viggen fighters to India because the Viggen's Volvo-Flygmotor engine is an adaptation of the Pratt and Whitney JT8D and because the plane also uses the Singer-Kearfott navigation and target control system.

Obsolescent weapons are the hardest to control, since an outdated arm can continue to be useful in war for decades, and purchasers of new systems need to sell old ones to raise purchase cash. The Biafrans used Czech Mauser rifles made in 1924. Some weapons were sold off as scrap, then rebuilt. Sam Cummings told the Senate hearings in 1967 that a Patton tank was worth $2,000 as scrap, $32,000 rebuilt. At the time, he estimated that there were about seven thousand Pattons (M-47s and -48s) in Europe. "Scrapping" on the scale that followed World War Two is rare today, but the rules still apply that dealers will do almost anything to make a buck. Said Cummings with his boy-scout smile: "There are wonderful regulations and pronouncements of policy, and white papers, but the plainest print cannot be read through a gold eagle."

Safer than scrapping, from an arms-control point of view, is demilitarization. Tanks, for instance, can be turned into tractors, or rifles into sporting rifles; but even this is no guarantee against "remilitarization." Under a 1968 act, surplus rifles cannot be imported into the United States to compete with American-made sporting guns. All formerly military aircraft such as the C-45, the C-46, the C-47 and the C-54 are subject to OMC controls for export.

U.S. economics, as well as those of purchaser countries, can also overcome U.S. end-use restrictions. In 1962, Germany agreed to buy $1.3 billion of U.S. arms to offset the cost of keeping U.S. forces in Germany. To ease the financial burden, Washington offered to help Germany sell older U.S. equipment in the German inventory by canceling the end-use clause. Since the equipment had been sold to Germany at its scrap value of $75 million, this concession was important. Washington merely required Bonn to inform it of sales, so that pressure could be brought to bear if a sale was deemed particularly unsuitable.

However, when Germany began replacing M-47 tanks with its own Leopards in 1965, and had 400 M-47s to sell, Washington forbade Sam Cummings, a prospective middleman, to sell any to Pakistan. Italy, however, sold 100 M-47s to Pakistan in 1968. With France replacing the M-47 by its own AMX-30 tank, Belgium and Norway by the Leopard and Italy by the American M-60, and with more of these older models of Patton for sale in Portugal, Turkey and Greece, Jeff Kitchen estimated at the time that 7,000—twice all the tanks used in the 1967 Mideast war—were then in the market. Most were eventually sold for scrap.

U.S. end-use provisions also limit the way in which American-made weapons can be employed. As noted elsewhere, numerous client-countries have breached these agreements.

Jimmy Carter came to office promising that the United States would cease to be the world's largest arms dealer. He sought cooperation from allies and especially from the Soviet Union for restricting transfers to developing countries. U.S.-Soviet talks on this point were held in Washington in December 1977, and continued in Geneva.

But for petrodollar and geopolitical reasons, the Administration went ahead with major sales to Saudi Arabia, Iran, Israel and South Korea, and opposed a proposal from Democratic senator Frank Church of Idaho for a one-year moratorium on sales to Iran. The Congressional Research Service published a study concluding that the Administration had made no serious cuts in arms transfers; Senator Proxmire, in a floor statement, said: "Based on the evidence now available, I must reluctantly conclude that President Carter's arms-sales restraint plan appears to be a flop." (Carter's six-point plan for sales—and U.S. "unilateral" restraints in general—will be looked at in Chapter 7.)

Carter did ban some sales to less significant dictatorial regimes, notably in Latin America, and gave U.S. support to a mandatory UN arms embargo on South Africa. But with South Africa already heavily armed, and—with French and Israeli assistance—75 per cent self-sufficient in weapons production, the gesture was essentially symbolic.

Treaties Galore

If treaties meant as much as their authors presumably hope, preventing the arms race would be about as easy as preventing crime. Which is perhaps the case. Probably the most-abused among modern pacts aimed at eliminating disastrous conflicts is the Treaty on the Non-Proliferation of Nuclear Weapons (NPT), signed in Washington, London and Moscow on July 1, 1968. It entered into force on March 5, 1970, and has been honored largely in the breach.

The earlier Partial Test Ban Treaty of 1963 was followed up in 1967 by the "Outer Space Treaty"—on "principles governing the activities of states in the exploration and use of outer space, including the moon and other celestial bodies." This prohibited "placing in orbit or on celestial bodies any weapons, military bases or fortifications, or the conducting of tests or military maneuvers there." This was a pact drafted by the United Nations, and signed by most UN members. In 1977, Moscow accused

Washington of developing killer satellites in contravention of the treaty. The charge was true; but the American tests, as noted in the previous chapter, were in reaction to antisatellite experiments begun by the Russians almost before the ink was dry on the 1967 pact, and highlighted by four closely observed intercept tests in 1976.

In 1972 came the biological warfare (BW) convention. The full title is the Convention on the Prohibition of the Development, Production and Stockpiling of Bacteriological and Toxic Weapons and on Their Destruction. Under the treaty, such weapons had to be destroyed or converted to peaceful use within nine months. The United States stated at the time that all its BW materials had already been destroyed, and former BW facilities had been converted to peaceful purposes. The British delegate said Britain had no BW stocks and that it was a criminal offense to produce them in the United Kingdom. Russia claimed to have no "weapons as defined in the treaty." No verification procedures were envisaged in the pact. In 1975, American press reports said that President Nixon's directive to destroy biological weapons had been disobeyed and that the Soviet Union was building new BW facilities. As noted in the previous chapter, the United States continues to make binary gases.

This pact is clearly of only limited significance. In 1973, as mentioned earlier, the U. S. Senate called for an international treaty banning research and experimentation and the use of "environmental and geophysical modification activity as a weapon of war." The matter was taken up at the 1974 Nixon-Brezhnev talks, and later that year Moscow proposed, at the UN, a draft convention banning ecowarfare, including climate modification. The Soviet draft listed virtually all possible methods, some of them decidedly futuristic. In 1975, both superpowers submitted identical draft conventions—on less ambitious lines than the Soviet UN document—to the Conference on the Committee on Disarmament (CCD); on May 18, 1977, thirty-three nations, including the two superpowers, signed the Convention in Geneva.

Except in an old League of Nations pact, chemical warfare is less well covered. Already by fiscal 1976, the U.S. chemical-warfare budget totaled just over $95 million, of which all but $3 million was for the Army. Approximately two thirds was for R & D.

Since chemical weapons are easier to produce, hide and use than any other major warfare systems, Senator Lowell Weicker of Connecticut and Congressman Richard T. Schulze of Pennsylvania, both Republicans, proposed a concurrent congressional resolution in 1977 calling for tighter chemical-weapons control, the destruction of CW stockpiles and the banning of future production on a worldwide scale. Weicker and Schulze suggested a unilateral three-year American moratorium on production, the destruction of 3,000 tons of "lethal chemical mustard agents" in U.S. stockpiles and an appeal by the President to Moscow to follow suit. The resolution also asked Third World nations not to "introduce chemical weapons into their arsenals." The senator and the congressman said the President should seek an international treaty banning production, destroying stocks and providing for verification. (Britain had proposed such a treaty at Geneva the previous August.)

Meanwhile, partly in fear of Soviet exploitation of America's old Indian wars, the United States, by 1979, had still not ratified the four-decades-old international Genocide Convention.

In his annual report on the work of the UN, its Secretary-General recommended at the end of 1975 that the General Assembly set up an ad hoc committee to review the UN's role in disarmament. The first meeting, in 1976, grouped representatives of Austria, Grenada, New Zealand, the Philippines, Romania, Sri Lanka, Sweden, Tunisia and Venezuela. One basic problem that this and other parleys have faced is how to define a weapons system. In war colleges, it is taught that a weapons system comprises a weapon, the means of locating and identifying a target and the means of controlling both the engagement as a whole and at least a part of the sequence of operations which brings the weapon to the target. But a Soviet delegate, addressing the UN General Assembly recently, described weapons systems—not unreasonably—as including gene engineering and environmental-modification techniques.

DÉTENTE AND SALT

Meanwhile, partly impelled by Russia's fear of Nixon's opening to China, détente was born in the early seventies and took its first cautious steps. In 1973, a conference on "security and cooperation in Europe" opened in Helsinki. It adjourned to Geneva that September, and moved back to Helsinki two years later to adopt a final act on August 1 that year. All European states except Albania participated, along with Canada and the United States. The final act contained a "document on confidence-building measures and certain aspects of security and disarmament." It specifically mentioned prior notification of major military maneuvers, along with the exchange of observers, and prior notification of major military movements. In January 1976, the Soviet Union invited

NATO observers to its maneuvers for the first time, following similar invitations by NATO powers to Eastern European states.

Some bilateral Soviet-American agreements go back to the Kennedy era, such as the so-called Hot Line Agreement of 1963, establishing a direct telex link between the White House and the Kremlin; a Hot Line Modernization Agreement in 1971 added two additional circuits using satellite communications systems; a Nuclear Accidents Agreement that year provided for immediate notification in the event of an accidental, unauthorized incident involving possible detonation of a nuclear weapon; and a 1972 agreement on the prevention of incidents on and over the high seas included rules of conduct for ships launching or landing aircraft or engaged in the surveillance of other ships.

Strategic Arms Limitation Talks (SALT) were held in Moscow in 1972 and resulted in the SALT ABM (antiballistic missile) treaty. This prohibited the deployment of ABM systems for the defense of the whole territory of the United States or the Soviet Union or of an individual region—a confidence-building, détente measure. ABMs would be limited to the two capital cities and one ICBM concentration in each country. No more than 100 ABM launchers and 100 ABM missiles could be used in each deployment area. There were qualitative and quantitative restrictions on ABM radars.

SALT I, as the talks were known, also produced the so-called SALT Interim Agreement of May 1972, to limit strategic weapons. This provided for a freeze of up to five years on the aggregate number of fixed land-based intercontinental ballistic missile (ICBM) launchers and of submarine-launched ballistic missile (SLBM) launchers. Both parties could choose the "mix," but there was a prohibition on converting light or older ICBM launchers into land-based launchers of modern heavy ICBMs. Verification was to be by "national technical means"—meaning satellites. Neither party would interfere with the "national technical means" of the other. There would be no "deliberate concealment measures." Six months' notice had to be given if either party wished to withdraw.

A protocol to the agreement specified that the United States could have no more than 710 ballistic missile launchers on submarines and no more than 44 modern ballistic submarines, while the Soviet Union could have no more than 950 ballistic missile launchers on submarines and no more than 62 modern ballistic missile submarines. Up to those levels, additional SLBMs could become operational as replacements for equal numbers of pre-1964 ballistic missile launchers or launchers on older subs.

In July 1974, two more documents were signed in Moscow. One was a protocol to the SALT ABM treaty, reducing the two possible ABM areas in both countries to one. Both parties could dismantle or destroy an ABM site and build one in the permitted alternative area, provided that notification was given between October 3, 1977, and October 2, 1978, or during any year which commences at five-year intervals thereafter, when the treaty comes up for review. This right may be exercised only once.

The other document was the (earlier-mentioned) so-called Threshold Test Ban Treaty, prohibiting nuclear weapons tests of more than 150 kilotons after March 31, 1976. At Moscow's insistence, peaceful nuclear explosions were exempt: An agreement on those was concluded later.

In November that year, President Ford flew to Vladivostok in Russian Manchuria to sign an agreement on strategic offensive arms for the period up to October 1977. Mr. Ford told a press conference on December 2 that Russia and the United States had agreed to a ceiling of 2,400 ICBMs, SLBMs and heavy bomber-borne missiles each, of which not more than 1,320 could be MIRV-ed. All delivery aircraft with a range of more than 360 miles could be classed as strategic, but NATO forces, U.S. aircraft in Europe and other "forward systems" were not counted. The United States understood that only high-trajectory ballistic missiles were covered, but the Russians afterward contended that air-breathing, low-altitude missiles, guided through to target, were included too. Thus began the cruise-missile debate.

Critics of Vladivostok claim that it merely allowed both sides to do what they planned to do in any case. The New York-based Institute for World Order, in an analysis of Vladivostok, noted that the agreement did not arrest development of America's Trident-II submarine or Trident-II missile; since Vladivostok, the report noted, R & D had continued on the MARV re-entry vehicle, the bigger-yield Minuteman, the M-X, mobile ICBM launchers, the cruise missile, the B-1, the Command Data Buffer System for retargeting ICBMs en route, a new aerial tanker, new precision-guided munitions, and on NavStar. It said that "advocates of weapons innovations" claim these provide the United States with bargaining chips at arms-limitation talks, and added: "Since the Soviet Union has sought no less than equality in armaments, at least since World War Two . . . the bargaining-chip strategy [is unlikely] to work."

Also critical of Vladivostok was the new national security assistant to President Carter, Zbigniew Brzezinski. He said shortly before his appointment in 1977 that lower missile levels should be negotiated, either before the current agreement expired in October 1977, or in the later SALT III talks.

There have been yet other international agreements related to arms. In 1973, a protocol to the High Seas Agreement was signed in Washington forbidding simulated attacks on nonmilitary ships or the dropping of "any objects" near such vessels "in such a manner as to be hazardous . . . or to constitute a hazard to navigation."

Later that year, an Agreement on the Prevention of Nuclear War was signed, also in Washington. The United States and the Soviet Union agreed to refrain from the use or threat of force against the other, its allies or other countries. Where there is a risk of nuclear war between the superpowers, even if the cause is "relations between countries not parties to this Agreement," the parties would hold urgent consultations and "make every effort to avert this risk." This, as related earlier, proved a blessing only weeks later.

At the UN level, resolutions about arms are endless. There were thirty-four in November and December 1975 alone, reflecting huge majorities for a ban on all nuclear-weapon tests, calling for reduced military budgets, for the removal of military bases from colonial territories, for making Africa and Asia nuke-free zones and for banning chemical, biological and environmental warfare.

Carter and Arms Limitation

The 1976 election campaign shifted the arms-limitation debate into high gear. Jimmy Carter railed against the arms race and promised to do something about it. Shortly before he took office, a United Nations Association panel, which included future Secretary of State Cyrus Vance and future Geneva arms negotiator Paul Warnke, produced a Rockefeller Foundation-funded report which recommended that the U. S. Government "explore" the possibility of a 5–10 per cent cut in the defense budget—with the understanding that the Soviet Union do likewise, and with UN members reporting their military budgets to the international organization in "standardized form." It called for international control of the development of long-range cruise missiles. The report also suggested a freeze on the conventional arms race, especially general-purpose naval forces, noting that nonnuclear weaponry, including personnel and other support costs, gorged three quarters of both American and Soviet defense spending. It all sounded like a rehash of the headline-catching Soviet proposals at the UN in 1963—or a calling of the Soviet bluff.

The panel also recommended the dismantling of both the U.S.-British base of Diego Garcia and the Russian base at Berbera, Somalia—in apparent response to Secretary-General Leonid Brezhnev's 1976 challenge to the United States to join in "demilitarizing" the Indian Ocean. The report described U.S. tactical forces in Europe as obsolete and provocative. It called for denuclearizing South Korea and gradually withdrawing U.S. forces there.

Before such a pacifist barrage, observers could almost see the stockades go up at the Pentagon. Less controversial were suggestions that in future wars, the bombing of cities, nuclear reactors and dams be proscribed, and that all U.S. precision-guided munitions in foreign countries be equipped with Permissive Action Link (PAL) procedures "to prevent their unauthorized use." PAL is a remote digital-code lock system on nuclear weapons that ensures that a bomb or warhead accidentally dropped or discharged does not detonate—although some release of radiation is usually unavoidable.

In a short and otherwise unexciting inauguration speech, Carter called for an end to all nuclear testing and eventual total nuclear disarmament. During the campaign, he had proposed the evacuation of tactical nuclear weaponry from South Korea and a withdrawal of U.S. forces there over four or five years. This had quickly stimulated a response from President Park that such a program would force Korea to go nuclear itself— precisely the development which the presence of U.S. nukes was meant to render unnecessary.

Carter ordered an NSC review to prepare for renewed SALT II talks in the spring. By February, he was explaining that to get SALT II, he was prepared to "set aside" the increasingly controversial issue of Moscow's new Backfire bomber if Moscow would do the same about the cruise missile. White House sources told reporters that Carter was not attracted by the long-range naval cruise missile—the one the Russians feared most—and Defense Secretary Brown told the Senate Armed Services Committee that "the sea-launched cruise missile is an inefficient weapon for attacking shore targets."

Cruise missiles were clearly a possible "bargaining chip" at the talks. Some Pentagon experts suggested the United States limit cruise-missile production if the Russians put a ceiling on Backfires. This reflected the "bargaining-chip" syndrome within the U.S. military itself: Some SAC bomber commanders were lukewarm about the air-launched cruise missile, seeing it as signaling the end of their deep-penetration wings; while naval surface-ship commanders feared the submarine-launched cruise missile meant that the "subbies" would soon have the Navy to them-

selves. Kremlinologist Victor Zorza felt there was a good chance of halting new systems and urged "a pause in the development of the cruise
missile." Britain and Germany strongly opposed such a pause, saying
they needed long-range cruise missiles well back from the first areas of
eventual combat to counterbalance the Soviet SS-20 and other missiles,
and to attack Backfire bases which threatened Europe but were out of
range of Allied tactical weapons.

In March, Carter became more specific: He would seek agreement on
those issues on which the differences were not too wide: These could include an agreement not to arm satellites and to discontinue the killer-satellite program, a comprehensive nuclear test ban and prior notification
of test missile firings. He would try for "complete demilitarization" of the
Indian Ocean, a concept clearly capable of a score of different inter-
pretations.

To veteran observers of the arms-talks scene, it looked as though the
ultra-religious President was still letting his mouth precede his thought,
preacher-style. Said columnist Charles Bartlett: "Carter's repeated professions of eagerness to negotiate nuclear disarmament will build pressure on him to deliver a treaty. This pressure can become bargaining leverage for the Soviet negotiators."

When Evans and Novak said in a column that Carter had ordered
General George Brown, head of the Joint Chiefs of Staff, to study the
possibility of cutting back American submarine-launched ballistic missiles to "200-250," White House press secretary Jody Powell denied it,
saying the President had asked Brown only to determine what constituted "minimum deterrence," and that he intended that any cutbacks
should be matched by the Soviet Union. But a fortnight later, the columnists again asserted that Carter himself had suggested the "200-250"
figure. They said the new Defense Secretary, Harold Brown—who had
formerly been the scientific member of the U.S. delegation to the Geneva
arms-limitation talks—had now turned in the report from his chiefs of
staff, who all opposed any cutbacks in American strategic missiles. Defense sources began telling reporters that any rundown of nuclear forces
would mean a costly American buildup of conventional forces to match
those of the huge Red Army—a buildup which they doubted Congress
would approve. Earlier, White House sources had said that the President
had proposed various formulas for cutting nuclear forces to Soviet ambassador Anatoly Dobrynin. There were widespread doubts that ex-
nuclear-submariner Carter would abandon the "blue-water option"—
which says, in effect, that whatever else is bargained away in strategic
arms talks, anything to do with the submarine-launched ballistic missile
must be the last.

In part, Carter's quasi-Wilsonian commitment to open covenants fairly openly arrived at was clearly genuine; but the new chief executive was obviously having to face up to the handicaps of negotiating with a closed society on the other side—and with no prior reason for expecting that he would encounter any less of a cold douche than Eisenhower had met with his "open skies" proposal. If both sides were as "open" as the United States, negotiations would obviously be easier. If both sides were as secretive and as uncontrolled by public opinion as the Soviet Union, meaningful negotiations would probably be impossible, and World War Three would presumably have taken place years ago, if only by mistake. The availability of quasi-total information about the U.S. inventory is probably the vital factor giving the Russians the confidence to negotiate from their position of relative strategic weakness.

What loomed as a major pressure on Carter not to give too much away in arms talks with Moscow was his controversial decision to appoint a major "dove," attorney Paul Warnke, as head of the U. S. Arms Control and Disarmament Agency (ACDA) and as ambassador to head the U.S. arms negotiating team.

The Warnke Debate

Warnke had frequently criticized the Nixon and Ford administrations' agreements with the Soviet Union for being too "permissive" to both sides. In a controversial 1975 article in *Foreign Policy* magazine, he had suggested the United States tell Moscow that it would hold off on the development of certain weapons systems for six months, then review Soviet response.

Warnke supporters felt outgoing ACDA director Fred C. Ikle had too hawkishly opposed Dr. Kissinger's attempts at cutbacks in U.S. defense spending—sought by the Secretary of State as levers to encourage the Russians to pursue détente. Conservatives thought Warnke's prognosis that U.S. constraint would encourage Soviet constraint was naive. Columnists Evans and Novak said that when the United States had showed constraint by ceasing support for the majority parties in Angola in 1975, the Soviet Union "immediately took decisive advantage of the American back-out" by throwing in a Cuban division which thrust a small splinter party into power. The comment, clearly inspired by Pentagon sources, showed the scattershot nature of the opposition: The "back-out" in Angola had been the fault of Congress, with its ignorance of a local situation, not a calculated administration decision, with Moscow being expected to show parallel restraint.

In the liberal-leaning Senate Foreign Relations Committee, President Johnson's former Assistant Secretary of Defense for international security affairs seemed assured of confirmation. There, the principal opposition to Warnke came from Democratic senator Henry Jackson of Washington—a hawk who had been largely responsible, in 1973, for separating the functions of arms negotiator from those of ACDA director (two functions which Carter's nomination of Warnke recombined). As Congress' principal spokesman for Israel, Jackson also probably entertained doubts as to Warnke's potential views on the Mideast arms balance.

An anonymous memorandum attacking Warnke's dovish views had been prepared by Josh Moravchik, with some assistance from Penn Kemble, both of the Coalition for a Democratic Majority, a month before, when the nomination was first bruited (initially, Warnke was mentioned as a possible Secretary of Defense). It was circulated to columnists and on the Hill by Moravchik, then a temporary aide to freshman Democratic senator Daniel "Pat" Moynihan of New York. Moravchik, a former Young Socialist, had broken with the new liberals of the McGovern campaign in 1972 and had helped form the Coalition with the support of Senators Jackson and Humphrey and others who were liberals on domestic issues but hardliners on Soviet affairs and critical of McGovern's liberalism in foreign policy. Most opposition to Warnke, however, came from the Republican wing of politics—notably the American Security Council and the American Conservative Union, as well as from the Committee on the Present Danger, a 141-member cross-party group which included several pro-Israeli Democrats; the Committee was formed in 1976 to lobby about the Soviet arms buildup.

Mark Lockman of the ultra-right Liberty Lobby summed up the hawks' view of Warnke when he told the Foreign Relations Committee that the Washington lawyer's selection had been "like choosing a boll weevil to head the Department of Agriculture." Conservative direct mail specialist Richard A. Viguerie sent out half a million mailings, asking recipients to sign an enclosed card opposing the Warnke nomination and mail it to a senator. Another half-million pieces of mail were launched into countrywide orbit by other campaigners: Senators' offices were reported swamped.

During the Foreign Relations Committee hearings, Missouri Republican John C. Danforth asked that former Deputy Secretary of Defense Paul Nitze be called to testify. Nitze rejected Warnke's views and opposed the attorney for both posts, recommending instead his own formula for arms limitation: Both superpowers should scrap their current land-based ICBMs in favor of 5,000 smaller, non-MIRV-ed long-range missiles each, while retaining their SLBMs.

Warnke was closely questioned as to whether he had anything to do with the Pentagon Papers leak in 1974. Warnke said he never knew that RAND Corporation official Daniel Ellsberg had requested access to his (Warnke's) copy of the notorious report on Vietnam policy; but he agreed that when he had left the Johnson administration, he had sent his copy to RAND for safekeeping because he no longer had any classified storage facilities himself. Morton Halperin—later a strong critic of Vietnam policy—Leslie Gelb and Warnke himself had access to this copy, Warnke said, and any two of the three could authorize access for another person with the right Defense clearance. Warnke said Halperin and Gelb—until recently, director of the State Department's Bureau of Politico-Military Affairs—had given Ellsberg the authorization. Warnke added that "the security requirements were not inadequate, they were [simply] not abided by."

Warnke insisted that he did not support unilateral disarmament; he said his downplaying, in 1972, at the time of SALT I, of the Soviet numerical advantage in missiles was "because . . . the Soviet Union . . . had not yet developed multiple independently targeted warheads." He added bluntly: "Neither one of us could gain strategic nuclear superiority unless the other allowed it." He reiterated his position that nuclear arsenals could not be used as international bargaining chips, noting that "no sane American President will start a nuclear war to gain a political advantage in a non-crucial confrontation with the Soviet Union."

Warnke's main supporter, Minnesota Democrat Hubert Humphrey, reminded the hawks that "no agreement is worth the paper it is written on unless it is mutually beneficial. Agreements are not kept, nor should they be kept, unless they are beneficial."

The Foreign Relations Committee cleared Warnke 14–1 to head ACDA and 14–2 as SALT ambassador. Danforth opposed both appointments. Michigan Republican Robert Griffin opposed the second.

In the Armed Services Committee hearings, Warnke came under heavier pressure. Critics charged that he had opposed nearly every major U.S. strategic weapons development of the past decade. But it was Warnke's frequent changes of position on specific weapons and nuclear strategy in general which came in for the most criticism. In one inconsistency, Warnke had opposed, a year before, improvements in missile-guidance precision to enable exclusively *military* Soviet targets to be taken out—a "counterforce" capability—saying that if both nations developed such a capability, the risk of nuclear war would be increased by the strong temptation to pre-empt. Now Warnke told the Committee he was in favor of a counterforce capability because, if the Russians had one, the United States would have to have one too. The nomination was finally cleared by the Committee.

In a floor vote, Warnke was approved for both positions by the full Senate, 58–40—less than the two-thirds majority that would be needed to ratify any agreement the new ambassador might bring home from Geneva, after which he planned to resign.

The Salt II Talks

The proposed SALT II talks of 1977 were initially to be based on the Vladivostok guidelines, which did not seriously limit the nuclear arms race quantitatively. SIPRI's annual report for 1976 noted that: "If planned deployments are carried through, the strategic nuclear arsenals of the two powers will about double, to a total of about 17,000 nuclear warheads or missiles alone. Several thousand more nuclear warheads will be carried on strategic bombers." SIPRI added that "the quality of nuclear delivery systems will be improved." Circular Error Probability (CEP) of American ICBMs would be reduced from 350 meters to 30 meters. No "hardening" would resist this, SIPRI said. Land-based ICBMs would either become obsolete or would have to be made mobile or provided with launch-on-warning ability to fire the missiles before the enemy struck—"the decision to initiate nuclear war would in the latter case then pass from man to machine."

Many in both parties claimed SALT II would be a waste of time; but no bilateral force reductions were likely without it, and putting it off would be a threat to the momentum of détente, as well as authorizing resumed development of anything which both sides chose. A Senate staffer experienced in arms-control agreements told the writer: "The ABM treaty and other international agreements, including the Threshold Test Ban and the existence of the Standing Consultative Commission, are all at risk if SALT I dies with nothing to replace it." Critics urged the inclusion of chemical and biological warfare in the talks, following widespread use of biological warfare in the Vietnam conflict.

But the Carter administration was taking a fresh look; it insisted it was not impressed with Vladivostok. Vice-President Walter Mondale had remarked earlier: "It looked like both sides took their weapons programs, stapled them together and called the result a breakthrough." Criticisms made at the time of Vladivostok by Brzezinski and others were mentioned earlier. But veteran doomsayer Victor Zorza still thought there was a chance of a breakthrough at SALT II. He noted the appointment by Moscow of a less hawkish new chief of staff, General Nikolai

Ogarkov, a member of the Central Committee of the Communist Party who had been the deputy head of the Soviet delegation at the SALT I talks, and a major increase in consumer-goods production in the current Soviet five-year plan. Zorza said these were "grounds for expecting a breakthrough which could lead to major advances in arms control, and even reduction—provided that the politicians in both countries don't muff it, as they have muffed it so often before."

Other experts in Sovietology were also optimistic. Former ambassador to Moscow Averell Harriman told a February 1977 seminar that he had spoken to Brezhnev for six hours, a few months before, while on a private trip to Russia from which he reported back to Carter. "The leaders of the Soviet Union don't want to have a nuclear war," Harriman said. "I think this idea of us going ahead with the nuclear arms races is absolute insanity."

Richard J. Barnet, co-director of the Institute for Policy Studies, warned the gathering about Carter's talk of linking human rights in the Soviet Union to arms talks; Barnet accused the United States of being "self-righteous," adding: "If we looked around the world, and particularly if we looked . . . at some governments [with which] the United States is not only having friendly relationships . . . but is supporting and in some cases actually abetting . . . we would find people experiencing things on a level of repression, and in the number of political prisoners, which far exceeds what you have now in the Soviet Union."

Most Democrats wanted to keep détente alive. Professor Walter Clemons of the Kennan Institute for Advanced Russian Studies said: "It is ridiculous for someone like Solzhenitsyn to come to Washington and talk down détente. He wouldn't be outside the Soviet Union were it not for détente." Of the upcoming talks, Clemons said: "We have to make sure that there is something in this for the Kremlin. What they particularly want is more trade, and some kind of long-term credits, and some kind of a deal on arms control."

Earlier, columnist Marquis Childs had warned about the "military-industrial-political complex," attacking seventy-five-year-old Senate Armed Services Committee chairman John Stennis of Mississippi as a "gentle patsy for the Pentagon," and Senator Henry Jackson of Washington, who expects to succeed Stennis. Said Childs: "Jackson fought the SALT I nuclear arms agreement, harassing witness after witness who had worked to negotiate abolition of the antiballistic missile and a freeze on offensive nuclear weapons." He noted how, when Jackson was bested in hearings by Air Force Lieutenant General Royal B. Allison, an expert delegate at Geneva, the senator spitefully blocked Allison's promotion and forced his premature retirement.

Ex-CIA and State Department official Arthur Macy Cox said in a book, *The Dynamics of Détente,* that "the arms race will end when the United States decides to end it." But the urge to produce new weapons a generation ahead of the Soviet arsenal lay partly in the urge not to forgo the right of pre-emption—a right equally jealously guarded or sought by Moscow. The only way to deal with the biggest bully on the block—or whoever was perceived to play that role—was to hit him from behind in the dark; and neither side wanted to exclude that opportunity.

New York Republican Jack F. Kemp, one of the House's experts on defense, reminded Congress of the complexity of roles for which the new weapons systems were designed, noting wryly that, with a new administration, "important policy positions will be filled by individuals without the two-edged sword of years of direct experience with strategic-arms limitation policymaking." Meanwhile, "the Vladivostok guidelines . . . embodied the most dangerous elements of the SALT I accords without any redeeming reductions in the most threatening Soviet systems." Kemp attributed this to "misplaced zeal to conclude an early agreement" and said: "The limitation of strategic arms should not be made to bear the burden of all of our efforts to reduce the risk of nuclear war."

In a new study, veteran defense writer Lewis Allen Frank looked at the arms race from the point of view of a Soviet Defense Ministry planner and came up with a recommendation to his hypothetical superiors that the Soviet Union should push ahead with new systems. In effect, Frank predicted that Moscow would have "seven to ten new weapons by 1985," adding: "Such a move would triple the number of arms now in the Soviet inventory."

Hawks were concerned that if nuclear disarmament were ever achieved—and if potential war became "conventional" again—the Soviet Union would be able to take over Western Europe by tank battles and high-explosive bombing, with the United States merely fighting a rearguard action with its own and its allies' forces, helped by some American reinforcements based in the United States but earmarked for NATO. On the other hand, the United States itself would remain invulnerable to invasion, and vulnerable only to "standoff" conventional bombing. Knowledge of American "invulnerability" would create fear on the part of the Soviet Union, since it might—along with Western European vulnerability—encourage a pre-emptive American strike. This fear, in turn, could lead to Russian first-strike pre-emption.

One such hawk was Dr. Fred Ikle, director of the Arms Control and Disarmament Agency in the Ford administration. His last ACDA report said:

It is a mistake to think that the principal purpose of arms control is to save money . . . Even if we were to give up our weapons, it would not put an end to war between other nations . . . Unbalanced, unilateral reduction of armaments can be a prescription for war, not peace.

The report noted that for almost three years, from 1958 to 1961, the United States, Britain and the Soviet Union suspended nuclear testing in an effort toward a nuclear test ban treaty. France failed to follow suit, and the voluntary ban lapsed. Moreover,

even if all existing stocks of nuclear weapons could be eliminated, as long as men know the secret of their manufacture, another global war would probably witness their reintroduction . . . One of the basic techniques of arms control, paradoxically, is to improve the military forces . . . by making them less vulnerable to attack . . . Another major task for arms control is to reduce the danger of accidents or miscalculations that could lead to war.

The report went on: "Our most fundamental objective is to reduce the likelihood of nuclear war by improving the stability of the strategic balance." The study stressed the problems of arms-limitation verification, and added:

As we begin to look beyond the immediate task of limiting arms competition and [as we] contemplate an eventual reduction of military forces, we must remember that the risk that treaty requirements will be evaded may increase as the advantages of evasion become greater. At the same time, the verification of agreements is likely to become more difficult . . . Marked improvement—perhaps bold innovation—in our verification methods may be needed.

As the talks approached, it was confirmed that the main Russian concerns were about the range of American cruise missiles and the number of launchers that could carry them. This posed a typical problem of verification. Not only do cruise missiles normally fly a zigzag pattern, but in tests they could even be programmed to fly in circles. Moreover, the speed, flying altitude, warhead size, engine efficiency and fuel consumption could all be altered to extend range without changing the missile's length or shape.

Two Center for Defense Information experts, Barry R. Schneider and Stefan H. Leader, writing in 1976, had seen the problem complicated by the importance attached to Soviet missiles' throw-weight—the weight of that part of a missile above the last-boost stage. In an article, Schneider and Leader had noted that:

Several smaller nuclear weapons can accomplish the same destruction as one very large weapon. Five 1-megaton explosives can inflict damage equivalent to one 25-megaton explosive; four 1-megaton bombs equal one 16-megaton bomb, and so on. By this measure, the U.S. and Soviet arsenals contain roughly the same explosive power . . .

The most important question in assessing the nuclear forces of each side is not "Who is number one?" but rather "Does each side have sufficient forces to perform this essential mission?" The answer is "Yes." As Secretary Schlesinger has stated: "We have a good second-strike deterrent, but so does the Soviet Union. Although the two forces differ in a number of respects, no one doubts that they are in approximate balance."

But at the Arms Control Association meeting in 1977, the doves were in full cry. Strategic limitation expert Herbert "Pete" Scoville called for a 10 per cent cut in the Vladivostok ceilings, the banning of submarine-launched cruise missiles with a range of over 375 miles and the reclassifying of air-launched cruise missiles as MIRVs—as Moscow wanted. The Backfire bomber, said Scoville, should not be treated as a strategic-delivery vehicle unless modified to take cruise missiles. Scoville called for "reciprocal unilateral restraint," recalling that this had led to a mutual withdrawal of troops from Europe in 1963 and to the biological warfare convention. He advised against developing counterforce weaponry and proposed canceling the Mark 12A Minuteman-warhead program and the M-X program, if Moscow, in exchange, would "scale off" its development of MIRVs. (Later, Scoville said in an article that counterforce weapons "weaken the strategic deterrent balance . . . To match in advance a future ephemeral capability will only ensure that the Soviets eventually acquire such weapons.") Jim Leonard, then head of the UN Association in the United States and later deputy permanent head of the U.S. mission to the UN, told the ACA conference there was a need for "new thinking" on arms which probably would not come from the present disenchanted generation which "knows so many reasons why this or that solution won't work."

Challenged on his views on Backfire, Scoville later told this writer that the Soviet bomber could only reach the U.S. coastline and return if it was refueled and flew subsonically. Without refueling, it would have to be a "kamikaze" mission. He agreed, however, that the Backfire crew could avoid self-immolation by landing in Cuba.

One Senate expert told the writer he feared that if the United States insisted that Backfire was strategic, the Russians would counterinsist on discussing NATO "forward systems"—Western Europe's nuclear-strike capability against Russia. He thought Backfire was essentially Russia's anti-China weapon, and "if we are to give up some of our bargaining chips for Soviet concessions, it should be for something more relevant to U.S. defense than Backfire." Backfire would have to fly high, subsonic and "without course deviations" to reach U.S. soil, thus making it vulnerable to the F-111. The Senate staffer felt disarmament was a dead issue, and arms limitation the most one could hope for: "The doves realize that there is a threat, and the hawks realize that you can't have everything." He echoed a growing view that there should be more stress on conventional-arms limitation.

But no one sought to minimize nuclear risks. The Senate expert quoted Edward Teller as saying that between 100,000 and 1 million people now knew how to make a nuclear bomb. "And any country could build nuclear warheads much more cheaply," the staffer—an author of much recent arms legislation—added, "if they were prepared to take a few risks on safety procedures, and prepared to accept a few radiation deaths among scientists and workers." He agreed, however, that even *more* countries could produce toxic gases, and that the almost total decision not to use gas in warfare since World War One might ensure that nuclear capabilities, similarly, might never be employed, "except perhaps by minor powers." One of his main fears was that deception techniques like mobile missiles would make verification so difficult as to create dangerous fears, leading to a pre-emptive strike: He wondered aloud if the Russians might not find some way to strike all silos and strategic-bomber bases at once, plus perhaps all submarine launchers by "penetrating the opacity of water."

These were a few of the hail of problems out of which the new administration sought to make a "breakthrough" on arms limitations. The views of allies also had to be considered. Sounding the European view, General Georges Buis, the former chief of staff of the French Army, said:

> The essential fact remains that neither of the two superpowers can attack the other without signing its own death warrant. The Americans have at their disposal forty nuclear warheads for each Soviet city of 100,000 or more. In comparison, the Russians have only fifteen. But one warhead is enough to do the job. That is why the two superpowers are more partners than adversaries. And that's why Europe is alarmed about a de facto equilibrium in which European territory is a possible theater of nuclear operations without jeopardizing the homeland "sanctuary" of its protector.

Richard Burt, then with the London-based International Institute of Strategic Studies, sounded a similar alarm on the op-ed page of the Washington *Post*. Noting that the Soviet Union had "gained a commanding edge in Eurostrategic capabilities" in recent years, Burt said that "if the [Carter] administration is unwilling or unable to use SALT as a mechanism for limiting Soviet Eurostrategic power, then the United States could feel pressure from allies to augment its own Eurostrategic capabilities. In fact, this pressure already exists: The transfer of eighty-four nuclear-capable F-111 aircraft from the United States to Britain last fall was clearly designed to demonstrate U.S. concern over the maintenance of regional nuclear deterrence in Europe."

Burt said the deployment of Russia's mobile SS-20 could push Western Europe to develop a more independent nuclear capability. "Eventually . . . it will be necessary to devise a way of bringing the SS-20, the British and French nuclear forces and other Eurostrategic weapons into the arms-control arena . . . It is to be hoped that the Soviet leadership . . . will follow Carter's advice on the SS-20."

One of the most lucid of the doves, Earl C. Ravenal, wrote in 1977 on SALT:

> I would opt for eliminating our fixed land-based missiles, moving to a dyad of highly secure forces consisting of submarine-based missiles and standoff bombers armed with air-launched cruise missiles. This would have the additional advantage of extending the life of our B-52s and obviating the "need" for the B-1 . . . We [should] also adopt the longer-range Trident-I . . . missile, and install it in our present Poseidon submarines.

Ravenal argued against matching the planned mobile Soviet ICBM, saying strategic stability

> might be enhanced by a shift to movable land-based missiles [in the Soviet Union]. They would achieve the analogy of our "putting missiles to sea" by using their expansive "land ocean" to base their movable missiles. An American move to sea and a corresponding Soviet shift to movable land-based missiles would restore stability at lower levels of arms, not by "strengthening deterrence" but by eliminating incentives on both sides to strike at the adversary's force . . . [thus] reducing the chance that an adversary would attack our missiles and thus precipitate our second strike.

The International Institute of Strategic Studies, in one of its monthly Adelphi Papers, pushed for a new round of Mutual and Balanced Force Reductions (MBFR) talks, aiming for a pullback of a Soviet tank army —1,700 tanks, 68,000 ground-force personnel in five divisions—and of 29,000 American ground-force personnel in the area of reductions (the Benelux countries, West Germany, Poland, Czechoslovakia and East Germany). Under this proposal, the United States would also remove 1,000 nuclear warheads, 36 Pershing surface-to-surface missile launchers and 54 nuclear-capable Phantom aircraft, followed by reductions of forces by both sides to parity at about 700,000 ground troops and 200,000 aviation forces each. The IISS noted that "such an American-Soviet reduction would somewhat improve NATO's M-day position" (i.e., position on the first day of World War III). Later, Carter adopted a version of this proposal and offered it to Moscow for negotiation.

Russia at first suggested a 17 per cent across-the-board reduction on both sides, then agreed to consider the U.S. proposals. It claimed, however, that the Warsaw Treaty armies totaled only 805,000, not 950,000 as claimed by the West—thus reducing the numbers of withdrawals it was agreeing to consider.

Peacetime Safety Dilemmas

James Willis, a former American diplomat who is now with the CDI, has urged more peaceful uses of space, including merchant-marine and other civilian use of NavStar and other "military" satellites. He noted that reconnaissance and early-warning satellites are a destabilizing factor because they are also used for pinpointing targets. Although SALT I called for each side not to interfere in the other's verification technology, "the Outer Space Treaty, though designed as an arms-control agreement for space, does not cover any of the military space activities, including the development of space weapons, now under way or being planned . . .

"NavStar is an example of advanced military technology that is fueling the nuclear arms competition and will potentially destabilize superpower relations."

CDI's Barry Schneider, like many others, thought insufficient attention was being paid to tactical and conventional war risks. In a position paper, Schneider cited four possible "peacetime safety dilemmas" involving tactical nuclear weapons.

The first was danger from nongovernmental movements, such as the IRA:

> One of the hundreds of tactical nuclear bombs in the 1-megaton range, if exploded on Manhattan island, would inflict casualties exceeding the combined totals of the [battlefield] dead from the American Revolution, the War of 1812, the Mexican War, the U.S. Civil War, the Spanish-American War, World Wars One and Two, the Korean War and the Vietnam War.

The Congressional Office of Technological Assessment's secret report on nuclear proliferation in 1977 also spoke of the continuing dangers of

militant groups stealing a bomb, even in the United States, and holding
governments to ransom—even if they were incapable of detonating it.
Radioactive isotopes could also be stolen from "hospitals, universities,
research institutions and industrial facilities," the report said, noting that
"plutonium dispersed in the form of powder through a building's air-con-
ditioning system or through the open air of a crowded city could be ten
times more fatal than an equivalent amount of nerve gas." On the thirti-
eth anniversary of Hiroshima, two thousand American members of the
Union of Concerned Scientists had sent a "declaration on nuclear power"
to Carter, warning of the "grave risk you and other Americans face from
nuclear radiation accidents."

Barry Schneider's second scenario had supposed seizure of an American "tac-nuke" by one of America's allies or clients which has them on its
soil—Germany, Greece, Holland, Spain, Britain, Turkey, Belgium, Portugal, Italy, the Phillippines, Iceland, South Korea and possibly Taiwan
(from whence they may have been removed in 1975).

Schneider noted that

> many of the host countries that permit U.S. nuclear bases are dictatorships
> with oppressive regimes that spark dissent. Some countries that permit
> U.S. nuclear weapons already have domestic insurrections on their hands.
> The Philippines and the United Kingdom are current examples. In Greece
> and Portugal, recent government overthrows have changed the complex-
> ion of the ruling groups . . . Korea might seize U.S. weapons to defend it-
> self from—or possibly attack—its antagonists.

Schneider's third possibility would be unauthorized use of nukes by
Americans—a "Twilight's Last Gleaming" scenario—while the fourth
threat lay in accidents. Known as "broken arrows" in Pentagon terminology, there has been about one American nuclear accident a year since
1945.

The most dangerous probably occurred at Goldsboro, North Carolina,
in 1961, when a B-52 jettisoned a 24-megaton bomb. Five of the six interlocking safety devices were set off by the fall. Only a single switch
prevented an explosion 1,800 times more powerful than Hiroshima.

Three years earlier, a B-47 accidentally dropped a 1-megaton bomb
over Mars Bluff, South Carolina. The trigger detonated, leaving a wide
crater, but no nuclear explosion occurred and no one was killed.

In 1966, a B-52 based in Spain, and carrying four thermonuclear
bombs, collided with a KC-135 tanker-plane over Palomares. There were
some conventional explosions and some radiation leakage, but the bombs
were recovered after a land and sea search.

Two years later, a B-52 crash-landed and burned on the ice approaching Thule Air Force Base in Greenland. Four nuclear missiles detonated,

contaminating the whole area. In 1959, a fire at McGuire base in New Jersey caused the explosion of a Bomarc atomic missile and "a certain amount" of radioactive leakage.

The View from Moscow and Peking

The Washington *Post* ran a long series on the arms race in 1977, noting that at the time of the 1962 Cuban missile crisis, the United States had about 7,000 warheads compared to about 300 for the Russians. The paper quoted then ACA director Tom Halstead as saying that the Russians "have pretty much caught up, and it's a difficult psychological thing for the [American] public to live with parity." The *Post* noted that "the Pentagon has rarely been turned down on a major new weapons system by Congress." But looking at it from a Soviet point of view, former Moscow correspondent Robert G. Kaiser described the threatening array of arms around Russia's borders—from Western Europe, Greece, Turkey, Iran and China—and compared it with a hypothetical situation in which the United States had Mexico and Canada as nuclear-armed enemies.

Kaiser felt that part of the desire of Moscow to catch up was prompted by the "Cuban" humiliation of 1962. Economically, Kaiser said, Russia was still far behind America: "The Soviets may now agree that there are two superpowers, but they also see that only one of the two goes to the other to buy computers, steel foundries, oil drilling equipment, wheat, corn and thousands of other products." Kaiser saw the current Soviet arms buildup as a desperate race to compete. Kaiser's successor in Moscow, Peter Osnos, wrote that Soviet saber-rattling had disappeared from Russian journals and speeches, adding:

> Middle East and southern African flashpoints are presented as serious but residual, while scores of recent agreements with the United States and other Western countries are endlessly praised as contributions to the relaxation of tensions . . .
>
> While Soviet generals and party leaders doubtless study every contingency, the sort of frightening scenarii of Red Army troops reaching the Rhine in forty-eight hours that appear periodically in the West, attributed to NATO or the Pentagon, have no real public counterpart here.

The ACA noted early in 1977: "Up to now, very inadequate attention has been given to the Soviet-China conflict as it relates to the arms race." A few months before, Soviet Foreign Minister Andrei Gromyko had said in a memorandum to the UN General Assembly: "It is inconceivable that some nuclear powers should be moving ahead toward eliminating their nuclear weapons while others are stockpiling and perfecting them . . .

The prohibition of all tests of nuclear weapons will put an end to their qualitative improvement, and prevent the emergence of new types of such weapons." France, China and Israel were all nuclear-weapon powers which had not acceded to the Non-Proliferation Treaty—"and one of them, China, still continues to carry out nuclear test explosions in the atmosphere."

Said the ACA newsletter:

> China has made its opposition to détente abundantly clear. Every American who goes to Peking hears the same thing. The Chinese are opposed to relaxation of tensions between the United States and the U.S.S.R. because they believe that the Soviets will divert more of their power against China if the threat from the West is reduced. The Chinese are years behind the Soviets in strategic weapons and are unwilling to give up nuclear testing and development of nuclear weapons until they have had a chance to catch up . . .
>
> The Soviet Union for its part considers China the major enemy . . . How can the Chinese be brought to the negotiating table to participate in ending the arms race? . . . Some U.S. observers, claiming that continuing Sino-Soviet hostility is advantageous to U.S. security, have urged that the United States provide advanced weapons systems to the Chinese. Such action would obliterate all prospects for ending the U.S.-Soviet arms race . . . For the time being, the United States and the U.S.S.R. should nevertheless move ahead to end the arms race between them. They are both decades ahead of China from a strategic standpoint, and can make substantial cuts in existing forces without fear of being threatened by China.

Former Nixon White House aide H. R. Haldeman said in his memoirs in 1978 that in 1969, during Nixon's first year, the Russians had moved nuclear-armed divisions to within two miles of the Chinese border. He said the megatonnage of weaponry involved was so great that, apart from the effect on China, it was possible that their use would have meant that "every man, woman and child in Japan would have died," while some of the 250,000 U.S. troops in Korea and the Pacific would also have been affected.

Haldeman said Major General George Keegan, Jr., then the Air Force chief of intelligence, sent a message from Honolulu to the Secretary of Defense—purposely "in clear" so that the Russians would intercept it—saying the United States had 1,300 nuclear weapons airborne, and naming Soviet targets. The former White House chief of staff quoted an unnamed Middle East general who was visiting Khrushchev at the time as seeing the Soviet leader get news of Keegan's message, and trying to use four phones at once. The Russian threat to China, Haldeman said, was called off. He attributed this U.S. assistance to Peking as being partly responsible for Mao's invitation to Nixon in 1972.

The Geneva Fiasco

But by 1977, U.S.-Soviet relations faced other problems. When Secretary of State Cyrus Vance met the Russians in Geneva in late March that year, the air had been considerably charged with static by Carter's public comments about the state of human rights in the Soviet Union. Many columnists were critical of Carter for jeopardizing the chances of SALT II by what looked like linkage to domestic reforms in Russia.

Others were critical of the new President's tendency to promise too much. Columnist Joseph Kraft wrote:

> Carter has proposed that the Indian Ocean be completely demilitarized—a virtual impossibility given the depth of Soviet and American commitments already, but a position sure to worry friendly leaders in Iran, Saudi Arabia and Pakistan. Carter also wants to withdraw all troops from South Korea, a position that complicates life (though they cannot say so) for the governments of Japan, Taiwan and, I believe, China . . .
> The President is needlessly making big mistakes for which later on we will all have to pay.

Initially, the State Department had wanted to wrap up SALT II quickly by basing it on the Vladivostok figures. But two weeks after the Inaugural, Senator Jackson had breakfasted with Carter and urged cuts in Soviet heavy missiles and land-based MIRVs. Jackson followed up this discussion with a twenty-three-page memorandum drafted by Richard Perle.

In March, Brzezinski had chaired a meeting of the Cabinet-level Special Coordination Committee in the White House basement situation room. It was there that the decision was taken to try to limit Soviet programs in return for not developing some U.S. weapons still in the blueprint stage.

The broad, underlying principle of the proposals which Secretary Vance finally took to Geneva was nuclear parity. Given the different nuclear strategies of both powers, parity is something which inevitably means different things in Moscow and Washington. Former Secretary Rumsfeld's final report had given the United States 8,500 warheads to Russia's 3,650. In megatonnage, however, Russia surpassed 9,000, while the U.S. figure was only about one third of that. Forty-seven per cent of U.S. warheads were in submarines, 30 per cent in bombers, 23 per cent in land-based missiles. For the Soviet Union, 75 per cent were land-based, 16 per cent bomber-launched, only 9 per cent aboard submarines.

Vance arrived in Geneva with two alternative proposals: keeping the Vladivostok "limits" and deferring the Backfire, cruise-missile and modification-of-strategic-warheads issues to SALT III; or a reform package. The points in this package were: a cutback from Vladivostok's 2,400 delivery vehicles to 1,800–2,000, of which 1,100–1,200 (instead of 1,320) could be MIRV-ed; MIRV-ed ICBMs would be limited to 550 on each side, instead of 584 for the United States and 670 for the Soviet Union; Soviet monster ICBMs would be reduced from 308 to 150; modification of ICBMs would be banned, as would mobile ICBMs; cruise missiles with ranges of over 2,500 kilometers (1,550 miles) would be proscribed, and the Russians would accept "strategic" restrictions on the Backfire; flight testing of ballistic missiles would be limited to six a year each, to cover both land-based ICBMs and submarine-launched ballistic missiles.

The Russians reacted as though Vance had desecrated Lenin's Tomb. *Pravda* later commented: "These proposals . . . are aimed . . . at undermining the principle of equality." The combination of attention-seeking public diplomacy, the rhetoric about human rights and the unprepared major changes from Vladivostok were too much for the conservative Kremlin. In a couple of days, Geneva was over, postponed until May. Meanwhile, bilateral working groups were set up to study various aspects of SALT.

There was a flood of critical comment in America. In the Washington *Post*, Richard Burt of the IISS admitted that Russia's new MIRV-ed SS-17s, -18s and -19s might be capable of destroying all or most of the U.S. Minutemen and Titans; but he noted that ICBMs play a more important role in Soviet than in American defense. Burt also pointed out that U.S. superiority in submarine-launched ballistic missiles was even greater than appeared, since half the Poseidon/Polaris fleet is always at sea, compared to 15 per cent of the Soviet equivalents. The United States seemed, in its proposals, to be coaxing the Soviet Union toward greater reliance on submarine strategic warfare, with Brzezinski probably reckoning (Burt felt) that the very undetectability of submarines could induce both sides not to risk a first strike.

The new national-security adviser appeared surprised by the rigor of the Soviet reaction. He saw substantial U.S. concessions in offering to abandon plans for mobile ICBMs, and said the reduced ceiling for Soviet ICBMs would mean an increase on their present stocks with no increase in U.S. stocks, which had lower throw-weights.

Columnist William Safire reported that Vance had offered to restrict the ranges of cruise missiles on light bombers and asked how any range restrictions on cruise missiles could be verified. By May, Vance was telling reporters that perhaps on-site inspection would be necessary—a Russian no-no, thus far.

At the resumed talks in May, the Russians proposed accepting the Backfire production restrictions—but with a ceiling that some Pentagon critics claimed was "higher than the Russians can possibly achieve"—in return for a moratorium on cruise-missile development. They spoke of a possible ban on all nuclear-weapon testing by both nations for eighteen to twenty-four months, to see if China would join in. At the State Department, the ACDA favored a longer ban, and said Britain was prepared to join. Experts at Los Alamos and at the Livermore laboratories in California noted that the Russians could evade detection on testing below about 20 kilotons, especially in soft earth. A total ban would mean a loss of skilled technicians in the United States, and would forbid testing of the 350-kiloton Mark 12A warhead or the Almendro triggering device for the M-X. Testing was necessary, the experts said, because the stockpile of U-235 was diminishing, and the designers were experimenting with U-238.

Aviation Week said that a cruise-missile moratorium would mean U.S. agreement not to deploy its planned long-range missiles, while Russia could still launch cruise missiles from *Echo*-class submarines "off New York City at the 100-fathom line, about 95 miles from the coast." Guided Shaddock cruise missiles had a 250-mile range, or 500 miles without the guidance machinery.

Nevertheless, Vance spoke with reporters of putting a moratorium on long-range U.S. sea-launched and ground-launched cruise missiles, while continuing development of air-launched cruise missiles. Carter confirmed this in vague terms at a news conference at the end of May. Vladivostok launcher ceilings, reporters were told, might be reduced by 10 per cent instead of the President's hoped-for 25 per cent.

That spring, former New York *Times* reporter Leslie Gelb, then director of State's Politico-Military Affairs Bureau, and the NSC's William Hyland had a three-hour lunch at which both men drew columns of figures on a paper napkin. These related possible new proposals to "Vladivostok" guidelines, but added in trade-offs between U.S. cruise-missile ranges and proposed new Soviet ICBMs, along with an outline for SALT III.

Gelb later wrote, and leaked to selected reporters, a memorandum which suggested further U.S. concessions in the form of "parallel decisions" which would not require congressional approval. The United States, Gelb had proposed, would not count 120 disputed Soviet silos and would limit the number of cruise missiles which B-52s or other aircraft could carry. When Soviet Foreign Minister Andrei Gromyko met Vance in Geneva in May, he seemed reasonably happy with the Gelb proposals, and Gelb's was the line followed in September, when Gromyko came to Washington, with the United States agreeing to continue to respect SALT I ceilings if the Soviet Union did the same. Earlier, when Australian Prime Minister Malcolm Fraser had come to Washington in June, Carter had backed down on demilitarization of the Indian Ocean and agreed instead to a "freeze" of current installations there.

Meanwhile, the Russians raised a host of last-minute problems, such as concern about neutron bombs and about a high school speech given in Frankfurt by a four-star general, Donn A. Starry, predicting war between Russia and China—with the United States getting involved to oppose absolute control over the bulk of the Asian land mass by one or the other.

Congress still seemed concerned that Carter might be giving away too much. When voting the Arms Control and Disarmament Agency's $16.6 million budget for fiscal 1978, Congress demanded improved verification techniques. This followed a critical House International Relations Committee report. The budget act also called for impact statements on non-weapons technology such as breeder reactors and high-energy lasers, and "programs of a 'seminal' nature, such as major philosophical or doctrinal changes in defense posture." Later that summer, Democratic senator Claiborne Pell of Rhode Island forced an impact statement out of the ACDA on the proposed neutron warhead for the Lance missile—a statement which the Ford administration had refused to give the year before.

John F. Lehman, the former deputy director of the ACDA, said in 1977: "The single most critical requirement for the future progress of arms control is adequate verification." Restraints on the Backfire, he said, would be meaningless if refueling or Arctic basing were not forbidden, since "the difference between theater attack, which is the Soviets' declared intention for use of the Backfire, and strategic attack, is a difference only of miles of ocean." Lehman conceded that on-site inspection would have to be achieved.

In Geneva, verification had become the major negotiating battlefield. The U.S. team was particularly concerned about two Soviet ICBM fields near Derezhnya and Pervomaisk in the Ukraine. "D & P," as U.S. memos referred to them, contained 180 launcher silos, one third of them housing MIRV-ed SS-19s, two thirds of them older SS-11s. Only a domed antenna distinguished the SS-19 holes from those for the single-warhead missiles. The Russians, in response, noted that both MIRV-ed and unMIRV-ed Minutemen at Malmstrom Air Force Base in Montana were completely indistinguishable.

When Gromyko came to Washington, these preoccupations about uncertainty in verification were still encouraging the Russians to oppose a sub-ceiling for MIRV-ed ICBMs. After a sterile first session, Vance took Gromyko into his private office, with interpreters but no advisers, and suggested that the Russian's planned meeting with Carter the following day would be canceled if he could not be more forthcoming. Gromyko's expressionless eyes glinted slightly: The Soviet Government, he conceded, might "respond favorably" after all to sub-ceiling proposals.

After walking Gromyko to his car, Vance headed back upstairs and called Brzezinski. A hasty meeting between the two of them and Carter was set up, and the decision made to go for a maximum of 1,200 MIRVs of which no more than 800 could be land-based. In return, the United States would agree to count SAC bombers with single-warhead cruise missiles as MIRV launchers. These would constitute the difference between the 1,200 limit and the 1,320 Vladivostok ceiling. More than 120 long-range bombers could only be introduced at the expense of sacrificing other MIRV missiles.

The Gromyko-Carter meeting went well, with Gromyko offering to convey these new proposals to his colleagues in Moscow. While at the UN in New York the following day, Gromyko got new instructions and said he wanted to see Carter again. Hyland predicted that Moscow would accept the American figures if these were slightly increased.

Gromyko and his advisers met Carter, Vance, Brzezinski, Vice-President Mondale, chief White House aide Hamilton Jordan and Hyland in the cabinet room. Hyland's prediction turned out right. While waiting for the interpreter, Viktor Sukhodrev, to translate for his minister, Carter and the others were watching Brzezinski and Hyland, who understood Russian. As Brzezinski's thin lips creased into a smile, the President knew that Hyland had been right. Jordan, seated next to Hyland, impatiently asked him what Gromyko was saying; Hyland, a hand to his ear, remained impassively silent, but the expectant tension in the room began to relax. Weeks later, in Geneva, the Soviet delegation agreed to cancel development of the SS-16, and Carter began telling audiences that SALT II was in sight. Inspired comments appeared in the press about SALT III.

SALT III, Lehman had suggested, should eventually tackle "gray area" subjects so far ignored, such as French and British strategic submarines, French intermediate-range ballistic missiles and Mirage attack bombers, US F-111s and, eventually, air-launched cruise missiles in Europe, and the potential strategic role of Soviet submarines, medium-range ballistic missiles and medium bombers, including Backfire.

Seymour Weiss, one of Gelb's predecessors as director of Politico-Military Affairs, offered a note of warning on the euphoria: "We probably are not going to save money through SALT agreements, at least for any foreseeable time," he said. He noted, however, that "we spend 8 per cent of our defense budget and less than 1 per cent of our GNP on the direct costs of strategic forces. This is not a large burden to bear as a price for peace."

Weiss thought that the Russians would have come out better, overall, from Carter's package proposals in March 1977, and was surprised that they disagreed. But he noted that a "feature frequently ignored by American observers but not, I believe, by the Soviets, is the effect on the three-sided U.S.-Soviet-Chinese relationship of SALT agreements."

On balance, while the mood of the country seemed to be growing more hawkish, or at least more conservative, the bulk of published opinions were "dovish." Soviet expert George Kennan even wrote in a 1977 book that "both sides could afford to give up four fifths [of their nuclear weapons] tomorrow [and still have enough] to serve all useful purposes."

The problem, of course, was getting both sides to agree on this simultaneously. In an earlier book, Alva Myrdal, economist Gunnar Myrdal's daughter and a former Swedish Minister of Disarmament, saw a "consensus" between the two superpowers concerning "the game of disarmament." Reviewing the book, the ACA newsletter said:

> With its amendment to the Arms Control and Disarmament Act, the Congress (with some significant exceptions) seems to be getting the cart before the horse or at least to be looking at the verification problem myopically. There is a danger that the present concern about the adequacy of verification capabilities may divert us from more serious problems with respect to future agreements, and it may lead to our not concluding agreements that would be advantageous. As we look to the future, it is worth bearing in mind three main points:
>
> We have missed at least one opportunity, and possibly more, to improve our security because of excessive concern or misplaced emphasis on verification;
>
> There appear to have been no instances where we have agreed to anything and had reason to be sorry later because of a failure of verification (although there has been dissatisfaction for other reasons with agreements concluded);
>
> We have had agreements which have been widely seen as desirable when verification capabilities were nil or nearly so.

As Senator Humphrey had said, countries will only sign agreements that suit their interests. They would also only adhere to them for so long as their interests did not change. An arms-control case in point is the Montreux Convention restriction on the type of warships which Russia may sail through the Turkish straits. Moscow broke the law in 1976 when it took the light carrier *Kiev* through to the Mediterranean, broke it once more in 1979 with the *Kiev*'s sister ship, the *Minsk*, and clearly intends to break it again, since it is building another carrier in this class in the Black Sea. A Soviet writer, Captain V. Serkov, has argued in a Russian publication that any Black Sea state vessel can transit the Bosporus and the Dardanelles, perhaps preparing Western opinion for eventual open passage by a submarine

In the past, the Red Navy is known to have brought submarines through by hiding them under freighters, but that Moscow was aware that the *Kiev* was breaking international law was apparent from its having informed the Turkish authorities that the vessel was a "submarine-intercepting cruiser"—it happens to have the bows of a cruiser. Turkish Radio and the Anatolia Agency, however, announced on July 18, 1976, that "the aircraft carrier *Kiev*" had entered the Bosporus at six that morning, and noted that it was just two days before the fortieth anniversary of the Montreux Convention.

Barry Buzan of the IISS has commented that "a mere protest would be an academic exercise . . . since the Soviet Union is hardly likely to suspend construction of the remaining ships of the class." Instead, he suggested sending "signals" to the Soviet government:

> These might take the form of policy statements on the matter by key NATO governments, or by the Alliance as a whole; or of an increased NATO naval presence in the Black Sea. Salami tactics can be used in reverse, and as a nonsignatory to the Convention the United States is in a good position to exercise this option. For example, much more powerful warships within the "light surface vessels" category might be sent into the Black Sea in response to exits by *Kiev*-class ships, and explicit violations by Soviet aircraft carriers might be matched in kind by American capital ships. A carefully measured use of such warning tactics might deter the Soviet Government from further erosion of the Convention, if indeed that is its intention.

In 1978, the United States did in fact send warships for a cruise in Turkish Black Sea waters.

Outline of an Agreement

As the end of 1977 approached, with SALT I expiring on October 3, the Administration expressed optimism about getting, not only a new

SALT agreement, but also other accords—a comprehensive nuclear test ban, limitations on theater nuclear weapons, agreement on advance notification of missile launchings, a Mutual and Balanced Force Reductions (MBFR) pact and new conventions on chemical and satellite warfare. There was muted optimism about an agreement to prevent the proliferation of nuclear arms, but admitted pessimism about any agreement to limit conventional arms transfers.

In August, the Russians had firmed up an earlier proposal to ban particle-beam, radiological, electromagnetic-radiation and acoustic-radiation weapons. But the Russians were reluctant to make serious concessions about their major weapons, and the Joint Chiefs in Washington, deprived of the B-1 penetrating bomber, opposed limitations on cruise-missile range for its standoff replacements.

There were leaks in the fall that both sides were close to agreement on an eight-year pact. Carter and Brezhnev met in Washington, smiling for history, and the President told the UN General Assembly in October that a SALT II agreement was "in sight." But congressional opposition was developing, fanned by Senator Jackson's office and Paul Nitze, despite the existence of twenty-five senators and fourteen representatives in a congressional advisory group for the U.S. negotiating team. Washington was apparently ready to give up M-X development for three years in return for Moscow canceling all deployment of its SS-16 and SS-20 during that period. This was seen as a critical area, since SALT I only limited launchers, and some Soviet mobile launchers can be reloaded. Brezhnev was reportedly offering not to increase Backfire production and to deploy the aircraft only in the European and Asian theaters.

There was concern, however, over Soviet violations of SALT I—the testing of antiballistic radar systems, the upgrading of the SA-5 antiaircraft missile as an antimissile missile, the attempted concealment of strategic submarine construction and of some SS-16 and SS-20 production, and killer-satellite testing. The Russians, in turn, were said to be still unhappy over U.S. refusals to include European forward-based systems—seen in Washington as a more suitable subject for SALT III.

The Russian complaints were not all unreasonable. In October 1977, both sides had again seemed close to an agreement on freezing superpower military developments in the Indian Ocean, including a ceiling on ship-days there. But when Somalia expelled the Russians from their Somali bases, Moscow lost a bargaining chip, as a result of which the United States—mindful of Australia's concerns—refused a Soviet proposal to close the Indian Ocean to all nuclear-armed ships.

In May 1978, Gromyko was back in Washington with a novel proposal: The Soviet Union would produce no new ICBM if the United

States would accept a seven-year ban on M-X. This was seen as significant, since Moscow had never before offered to scrap a major weapon system already well into development. But Carter, mindful of the hawks, did not offer to scrap M-X, the replacement for the growingly vulnerable Minuteman. He could only offer to delay deployment to 1985: For Gromyko, this was not good enough. Back in Geneva, both sides began to talk in terms of an ICBM ban with mutual exceptions. Moscow would freeze MIRV warhead totals for each particular missile at the number already tested if the United States would count a B-52 with twenty cruise missiles as one launcher, or a 747 with eighty "cruises" as the equivalent of four single-warhead Minutemen. Considerable haggling went on over the "twenty" figure, with the United States arguing for thirty-five.

On June 2, the *Post,* from State Department sources, reported that Carter—under hawk pressure—had decided virtually to "freeze" the SALT talks. The next day, Carter angrily denied this. But the *Post* insisted that the U.S. negotiators had rejected Gromyko's latest proposals for strategic-weapons cuts without making a counteroffer. A Mutt-and-Jeff act seemed to be in progress for Moscow's benefit, with "hawkish" Brzezinski and "moderate" Vance symbolizing the two trends.

Meanwhile, while pushing for MBFR in Vienna, Carter had promised earlier that year to bring U.S. units in Europe up to strength. Germany revived the proposal that the Soviet Union withdraw a tank army from Europe by detaching armored units from several divisions; in return, Bonn suggested, the United States could withdraw 1,000 tac-nukes and Germany would reduce its standing forces. Washington hawks again saw the proposal as "cosmetic," allowing the Russians to withdraw only obsolete elements in their forces and armory.

Finally, Western Europe was in arms about Carter's apparent willingness to discuss restrictions on the transfer of cruise-missile technology. Secretaries Vance and Brown went to Europe to reassure America's allies, and the subject was a major cause of disagreement at the year's-end meeting of NATO in Brussels.

The SALT II talks droned on in the highly formal atmosphere of Geneva, with chief Soviet delegate Vladimir Semyonov, who had held the post since 1969, talking in imperfect German, which chief U.S. delegate Paul Warnke understood, and Warnke responding in simplified English for Semyonov's benefit. Most of the other delegates used interpreters.

Warnke assured the Senate Foreign Relations Committee that agreement was close on a treaty, along the lines leaked earlier, and which would last until 1985, as well as on a protocol to last until September 1980, temporarily limiting air-launched cruise missiles to a range of 1,550 miles, and sea- and land-based "cruises"—which the United States could deploy in Europe—to 370 miles. There would be limits on new types of ballistic missiles and a ban on the deployment and testing of mobile ICBMs, along with agreement on the "principles and guidelines" for SALT III, which would go into the "gray areas." There would be a sublimit of between 1,200 and 1,320 on MIRV-ed ICBMs and submarine-launched ballistic missiles, a ceiling on aircraft equipped with long-range cruise missiles and a sublimit of 820 MIRV-ed ICBM launchers.

Both sides would be able to deploy one new submarine-launched ballistic missile—the U.S. Trident-I, and the SS-N-18 on Russia's Delta-IIIs. This would presumably mean a ban on the planned upgrading of Moscow's earlier Delta submarines. It was, Warnke said, understood that each side could deploy another new ballistic missile later—the U.S. Trident-II, and the missile which the Russians were developing for their new *Typhoon*-class submarine. Submarine-launched missiles were now seen as less destabilizing than land-based missiles as they are not a good "counterforce" weapon: They are not accurate enough to hit enemy silos with certainty.

The Russians were still expressing concern about possible U.S. use of wide-bodied jets for cruise missiles. The Senate Armed Services Committee had voted funds for this program, but the House Committee had turned it down. Pentagon sources said that if U.S. cruise missiles were deployed in Europe, the Russians were expected to deploy submarine-launched cruise missiles at Cienfuegos in Cuba.

The United States was still seeking restrictions on the deployment, refueling and training procedures on the Backfire bomber, especially after intelligence reports said in 1978 that Moscow was developing a long-range, precision-guided "standoff" weapon for the plane, bringing U.S. targets into reach without the bomber having to reach U.S. airspace. Late that year, at the suggestion of Democratic congressmen Thomas Downey and Robert Carr, the United States suggested a mutual ban on low-trajectory submarine-launched ballistic missiles: These climb at an angle of only 6 degrees and are harder to spot on radar until it is too late. A SAC base, for instance, would be destroyed within five minutes of getting its missile alert. This is a weapon still in the developmental stage on both sides.

Discussion on Russia's killer satellites also gave the Soviet Union an excellent bargaining chip which was prolonging the negotiation. This was possibly the main U.S. cause of anxiety, because Soviet capabilities in this area could render satellite verification of SALT II itself meaningless.

Ratification and Verification

By now, Carter's main SALT problems were not in Moscow, but in the Senate. Whether SALT II could win ratification that year or the next seemed doubtful. Senators were concerned, once more, about numerous reports of Soviet violations of SALT I. By the time Warnke had spoken, some Pentagon reports had estimated that the Russians had at least 71 strategic submarines, or 9 more than the SALT I limit, with 986 launchers—36 over the limit.

The National Security Council's Verification Panel insisted that all Soviet violations of the agreement had been minor, detected and corrected by Moscow. The Arms Control and Disarmament Agency hinted that the United States was more adept at verification than the Russians thought. The Agency said: "The deterrent value of verification depends to a considerable extent on a potential violator being ignorant of the exact capability of the intelligence techniques used to monitor his compliance with an agreement"—but also added that "verification contributes to mutual trust among the parties." Verification is crucial to any arms-limitation program. As noted earlier, when ex-CIA officer William Kampiles was arrested in 1978 for selling a manual on the U.S. KH-11 ("Keyhole") reconnaissance satellite to a Soviet agent, it was suggested that SALT II might be in jeopardy. The Russians had apparently classed the KH-11 as a nonphotographic satellite and consequently had not concealed such sensitive activity as deployment of the SS-20 missile when a Keyhole passed overhead. Secretary Brown had told Congress that the SS-20 was not deployed—in order to keep the Russians in ignorance of the Keyhole's capabilities. In December 1978, a CIA report claimed that Russia's huge SS-18 missiles were now being fitted with twelve to fourteen MIRVs instead of ten, implying plans to "violate SALT II" when and if it was signed.

H. R. Haldeman's book that year contributed to hawks' fears by telling of a 1976 discovery by the Ballistic Missile Early Warning System that the Russians had been developing a system for attacking "all twenty-one American nuclear command headquarters" from Cuba, "before starting their main attack over the [North] Pole." The targets would have included the White House, the Pentagon, NORAD in Colorado Springs, Atlantic Fleet headquarters in Norfolk and SAC headquarters near

Omaha. This, Haldeman said, would have inhibited the U.S. power to counterstrike. But the author could find no one to confirm this story.

Verification is predominantly by satellites. Soviet medium- and inter-mediate-range ballistic missiles, including targets for antiballistic missiles (and for the interceptor missiles launched 1,200 nautical miles away near Sary Shagan, west of Lake Balkhash), are all sent up from Kapustin Yar, north of the Caspian, as are longer-range cruise missiles. Most of the Kapustin Yar launchings land near Sary Shagan, but long-range IRBMs fall near Lake Baikal. ICBMs and space vehicles are launched from Tyura Tam, east of the Aral Sea, or from Plesetsk, and "impact" on the Kamchatka peninsula or in the Pacific. Submarine-launched missiles are developed at Kapustin Yar and Tyura Tam, but fired from submarines in the White Sea, landing, according to range, either in continental Russia, or at Kamchatka, or in the Pacific.

Kamchatka and the Pacific impact zone are monitored by the United States from Shemya, in the Aleutians, or from planes and ships. The ac-tual firings are monitored by satellite and from the NSA monitoring sta-tions in Turkey and, until recently, Iran. These land bases are principally useful for monitoring the telemetry—the signals from a missile's systems which indicate performance and failure.

In the United States, the debate over SALT II was fanned by the ex-treme activism of the hawk minority on the Hill; Senator Jackson's aide Dick Perle played a key role by leaking to the press secret information from executive sessions which bolstered the hawks' arguments, thus bringing constituent pressure on doves. Democratic senator John C. Culver of Iowa took the unusual step for a member of the Senate "club" of publicly suggesting that SALT should be removed from the power of a Jackson subcommittee—leading Jackson to express "deep regret" over "leaks to the Evans and Novak column." The Washington *Post* said it had received, but not used, a similar leak from Perle—who had earlier been accused of being principally responsible for Carter's disastrous March 1977 SALT II stance in Moscow. Perle was said to have threat-ened to muster opposition to an agreement if it was not based on his own more aggressive proposals than those originally sketched out by the State Department.

National security advisor Brzezinski, now the main White House hawk, had said publicly in May that the United States would link SALT to Russian and Cuban activities in Africa—implying that the United States would not sign SALT II unless Soviet and Cuban forces in Ethiopia, Cuban forces in Portuguese-speaking Africa and Cuban advisers to southern African guerrillas were withdrawn. Cuba was also accused by the CIA and the White House of being involved in a tribal rising in the Shaba (Katanga) province of Zaire, but this apparently referred to military training given to some of the Katangese when they were members of the Angolan forces, some years before.

Secretary Vance denied that "linkage" was U.S. policy, but observers noted that linkage existed, psychologically, in congressional minds. Vance told the Senate Foreign Relations Committee that the United States expected Moscow to "respond" in some way to Carter's unilateral decision to suspend neutron-bomb production. The United States still wanted a total nuclear test ban, of whatever duration.

At a UN special session on disarmament that summer—the first real international conference on disarmament since 1932—Soviet Foreign Minister Andrei Gromyko called rhetorically for deeper mutual cuts in superpower strategic weapons. This contrasted—presumably intentionally—with the flurry of hawkish denunciations of the Soviet Union then flowing from the White House. Meanwhile, Canadian Premier Pierre Elliott Trudeau said his country had "withdrawn from any nuclear role by Canada's forces in Europe" and would replace all nuclear weapons on Canadian aircraft in North America by conventional weapons.

By 1979, difficulties were still expected in getting the Senate to ratify a SALT II agreement, especially if this included a freeze on testing American mobile missiles in the eighties—when development is planned—or if, in return for the United States being allowed to deploy the M-X, Moscow was allowed to deploy a new ICBM. Carter considered submitting the treaty as an executive agreement, requiring a simple majority in both Houses rather than ratification by two thirds in the Senate—then changed his mind after protests by Senate Democrats. He did, however, say later that he would abide by the terms of the future treaty, even if the Senate did not ratify it. Congress obligingly voted $18.4 million for the Arms Control and Disarmament Agency budget in fiscal 1979—$2 million more than the Agency requested—and earmarked $1 million of it for the U.S. delegation in Geneva.

By then, NATO allies were predominantly concerned with what would be the guidelines for SALT III, which will cover "theater weapons" in Europe. These negotiations were expected to stretch until 1985. Meanwhile, the 149-nation UN "disarmament" session, which brought in China and France—which were not members of the Conference of the Committee on Disarmament (CCD) in Geneva—was essentially a cockpit for rhetoric; in addition to the Soviet antinuclear proposals, it also heard American suggestions for curbing international arms sales. Indicative of the small hopes in the session were the absence of President Carter and

Chairman Brezhnev, even from the opening day. France's President Giscard d'Estaing attended, however, and proposed that the UN have its own arms verification satellites. France also agreed in 1978 to join the CCD in Geneva, while China finally sent observers.

Another weakness of the New York conference was that important arms-producing or military powers like Switzerland, Taiwan and the two Koreas are not UN members. Yet another was that several well-armed or potentially well-armed UN member-states showed no interest in the proceedings: These included Israel, Vietnam, Saudi Arabia, South Africa and Portugal.

Then a disagreement arose over the Soviet practice of "encrypting" (encoding) their telemetry—the signals whereby the components of a missile, each on its own frequency, record their performance for controllers. Out of about fifty channels in use, the Russians were encrypting the data on all but four. Moscow agreed not to encrypt those channels which were necessary for SALT verification, but critics noted that this left the choice to them as to which those were. Doubters further noted that the Russians could also evade U.S. monitoring by using low-powered transmitters or by ceasing transmission altogether and recording the information in an on-board "black box."

The disagreement had already existed secretly as far back as July 1978, when encryption was first detected. In December that year, Brzezinski persuaded Carter to order Vance to tell Gromyko in Geneva that if encryption did not cease, SALT II was off. Vance called Brzezinski, back in Washington, in protest, but Brzezinski later called Vance again confirming the President's order. Vance was at the Soviet mission in Geneva when the call came through and had to converse with the national security adviser on an obviously bugged line. The two men referred to "that matter we discussed earlier" and Brzezinski said the matter was, in the President's view, "critical for [Senate] ratification." As Vance had expected, Gromyko was abrasive and noncommittal. After calling Brezhnev, Gromyko said the planned Brezhnev-Carter summit in Washington would not take place unless all SALT issues were resolved first. This conflict, and the planned visit to Washington of China's Deng Xiao-ping, did in fact lead to a cancellation of the meeting.

With events in Iran and Ethiopia in the background, Hill conservatives found the question of encryption an added reason to be restive. Six GOP senators—minority leader Howard Baker, Sam Hayakawa, John Danforth, John Tower, Jake Garn and Malcolm Wallop—returned from a Moscow visit in early 1979 expressing renewed skepticism. Baker said that Soviet enthusiasm for a treaty was suspicious enough in itself. In the House, the Armed Services Committee recommended against approving the treaty. In response, the Administration suscitated a lobby group, "Americans for SALT," which included many left-of-center Democrats, and which insisted in its manifesto that "all provisions of the agreement would be verifiable by intelligence means at our disposal."

Meanwhile, Warnke had resigned, conscious of his problems with Congress; he was replaced, in a recess appointment just after the 1978 elections, by Lieutenant General George M. Seignious at the ACDA and by Warnke's deputy, Ralph Earle II, at the talks. Warnke's old adversary, Ambassador Vladimir Semyonov, was appointed to Bonn. After successful tests in which MiG-25s with look-down radar hit simulated cruise missiles flying 200 feet above the trees at Vladimirovka, on the Caspian coast, Gromyko told the U.S. delegation in Geneva one day, with a smile: "You can fly your air-launched cruise missiles around the world if you like!" Pentagon research director William J. Perry riposted later that the Caspian exercise had been a lucky fluke, and said the Soviet Union would need "a thousand planes" with the new look-down radar to replace "ten thousand ground stations." This, he said, would cost $50 billion. By the time they were built, the United States would have cruise missiles which were harder to track and able to take evasive action. Moscow, however, seemed suddenly to be confidently accommodating, and also consented to M-X development—while insisting that B-52s in the workshops for extensive revision, and the five R & D B-1s, should be counted against the U.S. strategic-launcher total. Earlier, during the Vance talks in Moscow in October 1978, Gromyko had even agreed to attend a conference with the United States in Venezuela to study the banning of antisatellite weapons.

Planning for SALT III had already begun under a young RAND official, Fritz Ermath; but the chorus of American opposition to SALT continued, and the Mutual and Balanced Force Reductions (MBFR) talks were bogged down in Vienna over NATO's disbelief of the Warsaw Treaty's published force figures.

The SALT II Agreement

The final weeks of the SALT II negotiations were mostly conducted by Vance and Ambassador Dobrynin in Washington, in Vance's study next to his formal office. In April the Soviet envoy accepted new limitations on any upgrading of existing Russian missiles by increasing the number of warheads. In return, Vance agreed not to increase Minuteman warheads from three to seven—an increase which, though possible, was not intended anyway. He also agreed to remove new Minuteman shelters at

Malmstrom which Dobrynin claimed "blinded" Soviet verification satellites.

All the bargaining chips had been spent: SALT II was announced to be ready, and a tottering Brezhnev agreed to meet with Carter in Vienna to sign it.

The new pact, not ratified when this book was written, covers over a hundred pages—a preamble, nineteen articles and a three-year protocol. It recognizes the U.S. MIRV-ed missile-launcher total at 2,283 and the Soviet equivalent at 2,504. The United States admits to 656 launchers for mostly MIRV-ed SLBMs, and 1,054 launchers for ICBMs, over half of which are MIRV-ed. There are 573 SAC bombers—the figure claimed by Moscow, including a number of "hangar queens." The Soviet Union admits to 950 launchers for SLBMs, of which only 144 are for MIRV-ed missiles, and 1,398 launchers for ICBMs, about half MIRV-ed. The Soviet Air Force has 156 strategic bombers. All missiles are presumed to be MIRV-ed to the maximum for which they are capable. To prevent the rapid reloading of launchers, storage of excess missiles at launch sites is prohibited.

By 1981, both sides can have 2,400 launchers—an increase for the United States, a decrease for Moscow. By 1985, this figure will decrease to 2,250 each, only 1,320 of which can launch MIRV-ed missiles. There can, by then, be no more than 1,200 ICBMs, of which only 820 can be MIRV-ed, and no more than 1,320 ICBMs and SLBMs together, of which no more than 1,200 can be MIRV-ed. The maximum MIRV capability for ICBMs is put at 10, with 14 for SLBMs. The final limit on cruise missiles per bomber is set at 28—meaning that a wide-bodied jet carrying 84 of them would count as 3 strategic launchers. Ground-launched and sea-launched cruise missiles with ranges of over 500 kilometers (about 300 miles) can be tested but not deployed for three years. There are to be no new land-missile sites, but each side can develop one new land-based missile and any number of new SLBMs: For the United States, this means the M-X, expected to be deployed in 1982, after a three-year ban on deployment ceases, and the submarine-launched Trident-Is and -IIs. For Moscow, the new missiles will be the improved SS-19, whose exact throw-weight has never been revealed by Russia, and the submarine-launched Typhoon SLBM. The Soviet Union will thus not deploy the SS-16, at least until 1985.

As a sidebar to the treaty, Brzezinski wrote Carter a letter promising to keep Backfire production at 30 annually, and to restrict the plane to medium-range activities, with no in-flight refueling.

Both sides agreed to work toward a Comprehensive Nuclear Test Ban, an improved Non-Proliferation Treaty, a Mutual and Balanced Force Reduction pact, an antisatellite warfare treaty and agreements to limit conventional arms sales in the world.

Groups like the American Defense Preparedness Association and the Committee for the Present Danger began claiming that the treaty still left the Soviet Union with a massive throw-weight advantage, and did not solve verification problems: *Aviation Week* claimed that the Russians were now taping their telemetry aboard some missiles and parachuting it to earth, thus making it unverifiable by the United States.

The National Defense Clearinghouse and other liberal organizations joined the Joint Chiefs in supporting the treaty, and Norway cautiously offered to try to replace some of the Iranian verification sites, and the uncertain sites in Turkey.

NATO allies were assured that the three-year ban on cruise-missile ranges would not be renewed—so that Washington will presumably have to find new bargaining chips, before then, to restrain Soviet qualitative improvements on its heavier missiles.

THE NUCLEAR FACTOR

Overlaying the whole arms-control debate at the major-power level has been the question of how to get the toothpaste of nuclear fission itself back into the tube. Probably few Americans or Europeans (of East or West) actually think a Third World War is likely, or that the sophisticated weaponry developed by both sides will ever be used except for diplomacy and economics. But the dangers of "brush fires" between secondary powers becoming nuclear is very real, and even this eventuality could lead to nuclear fatalities in the supernations, or in Europe and Japan.

The Nuclear Non-Proliferation Treaty (NPT) prohibits the transfer by nuclear-weaponed (NW) states, to any recipient anywhere, of nuclear arms or other nuclear explosive devices, including "peaceful" ones, or control over nuclear weaponry belonging to NW states. States not then possessing nuclear arms were prohibited from receiving, manufacturing or otherwise acquiring them. Non-NW states which signed the treaty agreed to conclude safeguard agreements with the International Atomic Energy Authority (IAEA) to prevent the diversion of nuclear energy from peaceful uses. The task is formidable: The IAEA estimates that by 1985 a fifth of the world's electrical energy will come from nuclear plants.

The NW states also agreed to share their peaceful nuclear technology with non-NW states that signed the treaty. The signatories undertook to pursue negotiations to end the nuclear arms race, to ensure nuclear disarmament and eventual "complete disarmament." But under the treaty, a non-NW signatory state could "legally" make all the preparations necessary for a nuclear weapon, so long as it did not actually assemble the warhead—a quasi-uncontrollable loophole through which more and more countries pass each year.

A review conference of NPT was held five years after it came into force—that is, in May 1975, in Geneva. A SIPRI report noted that "although NPT was considered the most important multilateral arms-control treaty ever concluded, attendance was poor." Only fifty-eight of the ninety-six signatory powers came. Seven of the fifteen states which had signed, but not ratified, participated, without taking part in decisions. These included Japan, Switzerland and Turkey. Seven nonsignatories had observer status: Algeria, Argentina, Brazil, Cuba, Israel, South Africa and Spain.

Of major concern was the spread of plutonium-separation facilities, giving countries access to weapons-grade material. The United States, which had fifty-five reactors at the time, has no commercial reprocessing plants; spent fuel is simply stored. Sweden suggested that peaceful nuclear explosions be discontinued, drawing support from other Western countries, including the United States, where peaceful nuclear-explosion experiments have been disappointing. But the U.S.S.R. still favored them. Experts later agreed that it was impossible to develop nuclear devices capable only of peaceful applications. Moreover, excavatory explosions could release radiation, which could cross frontiers. Any restrictions on underground nuclear testing, it was recommended, should apply also to "peaceful" nuclear explosions, since peaceful programs could be used to obtain weapon-related information.

The conference did agree to permit contained thermonuclear microexplosions produced in tiny pellets of fissionable or fusionable material by laser or particle beams. The energy rapidly released is nondestructively contained within a suitable vessel. Twenty small states, mostly in Africa and Latin America, but including Romania, Yugoslavia, Syria, Lebanon, Nepal and the Philippines, wanted the United States, the U.S.S.R. and Britain to suspend underground tests for ten years when NPT ratifications reached one hundred, extended by three years for every five new signatures acquired. The moratorium would become permanent if all NW states became party to it. The same group minus the Philippines wanted the strategic ceilings agreed to by Moscow and Washington at Vladivostok, the previous year, to be halved when NPT ratifications reached one hundred, with further 10 per cent decreases for every ten new NPT members. The NW states angrily rejected this "link-age" proposal.

The Soviet Union and some of its satellites brought up a 1972 UN General Assembly resolution renouncing force and the use of nuclear weapons. The United States complained that this resolution presumed a link between the nonuse of force and the nonuse of "nukes"; it thus condemned the first-use of nuclear weapons by a nation in response to a nonnuclear attack. American spokesmen have always argued that renunciation of the option of first-use of nuclear weapons would amount to a "self-denying ordinance that weakens deterrence." The United States is officially prepared to use nukes if "faced with serious aggression likely to result in defeat in any area of very great importance to the United States in terms of foreign policy." Theater (tactical) nuclear weapons stored by the United States in Korea and Europe attest to this.

The predominantly Third World delegates at the NPT review conference were less worried about the dangers of sharing the nuclear technology of the major powers. The following month, Germany signed an agreement with Brazil for cooperation in the peaceful uses of nuclear energy. Brazil undertook not to make weapons or other nuclear explosive devices; but few expect that country's authoritarian government to keep its word. The only serious discouragement to small nations to "go nuclear," militarily, is a 1968 UN Security Council resolution stating that nonnuclear states which renounce nuclear weapons in observing NPT would receive "immediate assistance" under the UN Charter if they became "a victim of an act or an object of a threat of aggression in which nuclear weapons are used"; but it is of course far from clear how this resolution would be applied. Would a major power hoist the UN flag and fire a nuclear ballistic missile at the culprit country's capital? In July 1975, the Sixth Islamic Conference of Foreign Ministers, meeting at Jidda, adopted a proposal asking NW states to undertake not to use or threaten to use nuclear weaponry against non-NW states "which are not protected against nuclear threat or attack by treaty guarantees from a nuclear power." China, a non-NPT signatory, is the only NW power to have declared that it will never make first-use of nuclear weaponry.

Other states which now already possess nuclear weapons but which have not signed the treaty are France, Israel, India and almost certainly South Africa. Nonsignatories expected to be "nuclear" soon, or with everything completed except warhead assembly, include Argentina, Brazil, Pakistan, Taiwan and Spain. South Korea, as noted earlier, has said it will produce nukes if the American nuclear shield is withdrawn, and Iran once said it would build the bomb if any of its neighbors did. Both are NPT signatories. In Libya, the unpredictable President

Muammar al-Qaddafi has said he expects that eventually all nations will have nuclear arms.

Under U.S. pressure, Seoul agreed not to buy a French plutonium-processing plant in 1977; but the UN Special Committee on Apartheid was less successful in dissuading Germany and Israel from supplying technology (and Iran from supplying part of the funds) for the South African nuclear-bomb project—for which the fuel, as mentioned earlier, comes from the United States. Germany, as will be noted later, also went through with a huge sale of nuclear plants to Brazil.

Nuclear power stations are not necessary to manufacture nuclear explosives. These could be produced, for instance, from a research reactor using natural uranium and heavy water. It is, in fact, easier to process fuel and extract plutonium in a research reactor than to process fuel strongly irradiated from a power reactor.

In short, the problems remain not only immense, but more immense each year. SIPRI noted in 1977 that the NW powers consider NPT as "an end in itself" while other parties to the treaty see it as a transitional stage toward a hypothetical nuclear disarmament. The Stockholm institution noted of the 1975 talks: "The conference succeeded in not breaking down. But it failed in solving the problems [whose solution is] essential for the survival of the treaty."

Besides NPT, there are many other "nuclear" treaties. The 1959 Antarctic Treaty established a demilitarized and denuclearized zone in that region, freezing territorial claims in the area and providing a framework for international peaceful scientific cooperation. At a consultative meeting on this treaty in 1975 it was decided to reaffirm the treaty's prohibition of burying nuclear waste in the ice sheet. A further consultative meeting was held in London in 1977.

The 1963 Partial Test Ban Treaty prohibits nuclear weapons tests in and beyond the atmosphere, including outer space and under water, or in any other environment if such an explosion causes radioactive debris to cross frontiers. In 1975, France unilaterally committed itself to underground explosions, and had two that year (to America's sixteen, Russia's fourteen, China's one). But hopes that all nuclear explosions would remain underground were shattered by China in 1976. Five of the U.S. tests in 1975 and seven in 1976 were in the 200–1,000-kiloton range, implying warheads with yields exceeding the 150-kiloton ceiling agreed to by the U.S.-Soviet Threshold Test Ban Treaty of 1974, which, along with the Peaceful Nuclear Explosions Treaty of 1976, was still unratified by the Senate when this book was written. Ford, as noted, later placed a 100-kiloton ceiling on tests, which Carter continued.

Also in 1967, the Treaty of Tlatelolco made Latin America a nuclear-weapon-free zone. In an additional protocol, France, Britain, Holland and the United States agreed to apply the treaty to their western-hemisphere colonies, but France and America exempted the French West Indies, the Virgin Islands and Puerto Rico, because they are not officially colonies. In another protocol, NW powers agreed not to use or threaten the use of nuclear weapons in Latin America. The Bahamas, Cuba, Guyana and Surinam did not sign the treaty. Argentina signed but did not ratify. Brazil and Chile ratified, but not as "full parties"—meaning that they rejected key provisions.

The 1971 Sea Bed Treaty prohibited nuclear warheads from the sea bed, the ocean floor and "the subsoil thereof" outside the 12-mile zone. There was a review conference in 1977 at which no breaches were reported.

In 1974, at Finland's suggestion, the UN General Assembly ordered a comprehensive study of nuclear weapon-free zones by an ad hoc committee of government experts under the auspices of the Conference of the Committee on Disarmament (CCD). This group met for two months in 1975 but reached a consensus on what SIPRI later described as "only a few rather trivial, self-evident principles."

It was noted that states which do not accept the concept that *all* nuclear explosives have a war potential had refused to sign NPT. The Treaty of Tlatelolco is even more ambiguous: "An instrument that may be used for the transport or propulsion of the [nuclear explosive] device is not included in [the] definition if it is separable from the device and not an indivisible part thereof."

The boundaries of nuclear-free zones are not always clear. In signing the second additional protocol at Tlatelolco, France, Britain and the United States said that nothing in the protocol would be observed if it contravened the law of the sea. Russia refused to sign the protocol at all, ostensibly because of its "high seas" aspects. Broadly speaking, what this means is that nuclear powers refuse to limit the freedom of their navies in international waters. SIPRI comments: "The experience of Japan, visited for years by U.S. vessels carrying nuclear weapons without the Japanese Government being aware, or wanting to be aware, of it, shows the dimensions of the problem."

Control of nonconversion of peaceful nuclear facilities to weapons use had been vested in the IAEA, but this body could clearly not monitor the importation of weapons. The conferees agreed broadly that more verification measures were needed.

Britain and the United States said they would reconsider their Tlatelolco obligations if a nonnuclear state committed aggression "with the support or assistance" of a nuclear power—a presumed reference to Cuba. Russia said the same, only more strongly, referring to any Latin American country's aggression, irrespective of whether it had the support of a NW power.

Finally, Senate ratification is still awaited on the Peaceful Nuclear Explosions Treaty (PNET), signed in Moscow in May 1976. With the United States having concluded its own peaceful nuclear-explosion program, this will merely permit American inspectors, in their own seismic-monitoring vans, to witness Russia's tests—such as those to be associated with diverting the Pechora River in the Urals to raise the level of the Caspian Sea. Duplicating sets of recording equipment would be used at each firing; then, "by an agreed process of chance," the host side will choose which set of recording equipment to take away.

Thus, if the inspecting side wanted to cheat by concealing spy equipment in their instruments, they would run a fifty-fifty chance of being found out. But can the Russians cheat, also? Although the inspectors can supply the calibration equipment to measure the hydrostatic shock waves, the side carrying out the explosion will lower the equipment into the ground. Photographs taken by the inspectors must be of the Polaroid type, so that there can be an immediate check that no unauthorized subjects have been filmed. As with the Threshold Test Ban Treaty, there is a 150-kiloton limit on individual explosions.

Five months after signature of the treaty—that is, in October 1976—reports circulated that two Soviet explosions on August 27, 1976, had exceeded the limit. Moscow denied this. Both explosions were thought to be weapons tests, not peaceful tests, because they took place at two nuclear-weapon test sites—one at Semipalatinsk in central Russia, the other at Novaya Zemlya in the Arctic.

In January 1977, America got a new President who was a physicist and a former nuclear submariner. He held strong views on proliferation, some of which seemed at times to be more idealistic than pragmatic. John O'Leary, Jimmy Carter's new Federal Energy Administration head, announced that he would be "cautious" about U.S.-aided nuclear-power development across the world because of the danger of nuclear-weapon proliferation, using plutonium waste from power plants. Before the election, Carter had told the Arms Control Association in an interview: "We should refuse to sell nuclear power plants to nations [which] do not become party to the Non-Proliferation Treaty or [which] do not adhere to

. . . international safeguards . . . or [which] refuse to refrain from . . . nuclear reprocessing." He left "international safeguards" unclear.

In his first press interview, with wire-service reporters, the President again called for a comprehensive nuclear test ban; but the immediate aim was more modest—a week later, the new State Department spokesman said that the Carter administration would seek congressional approval of the Threshold Test Ban Treaty and the Peaceful Nuclear Explosions Agreement.

In November came Brezhnev's headline-hunting proposal that all nations halt production of nuclear weapons and reduce stockpiles. It was a safe proposal to make, since Peking was sure to reject it, but Secretary Vance saw it as a "major step" toward a comprehensive ban. Earlier, Moscow had suggested an eighteen-month moratorium on all nuclear explosions, including peaceful ones, by the United States, Russia and Britain, to be extended if other countries joined the ban.

When the 1977 session of the Geneva talks began, both superpowers were apparently agreed in principle on banning all nuclear testing, but Moscow said it would not observe such a ban until France and China did also. Aviation Week's Clarence A. Robinson, Jr., reported exclusively on February 21 that the Carter administration was moving toward a unilateral cessation of American nuclear-weapons testing, "to maneuver the Russians into a bilateral agreement to halt [such] tests." In Washington, this was hotly opposed by Energy Secretary John Schlesinger, the Carter Cabinet's only Republican, who said testing was vital for weapons research. But the Carter commitment seemed to work. In 1978, Moscow withdrew its proviso about China and France, accepted on-site inspection and expressed willingness to sign a five-year comprehensive test-ban treaty.

Earlier, in an effort to head off nuclear-weapon proliferation, fifteen supplier-nations reached agreement in London on "comprehensive controls" over nuclear exports. In truth, the controls agreed to after thirty months of talks were very limited. The fifteen countries were: the United States, Canada, Britain, France, West Germany, Holland, Italy, Belgium, Sweden, Switzerland, the Soviet Union, Poland, East Germany and Czechoslovakia. China did not sign.

Under pressure from France, West Germany and the Soviet Union, the conferees at first failed to agree on pledging nuclear-importing countries not to detonate atomic devices, even for peaceful purposes—although an accord on this point was reached later. It was only with reluctance that France and Germany finally accepted inspection safeguards meant to prevent the secret manufacture of nuclear weapons.

The London meeting was followed by a thirty-five-nation International Fuel Cycle Evaluation Conference in Washington, aimed at checking the spread of nuclear arms. South Africa, Taiwan and Pakistan boycotted the gathering. To discourage the growth of breeder reactors and reassure nuclear fuel-importing countries about continuity of supplies, the Carter administration proposed setting up an international nuclear-fuel bank. The United States also offered to absorb and dispose of the world's nuclear waste, for a nonprofit fee.

In 1978, the U. S. Congress passed its own nuclear-exports law, setting stricter criteria. The Nuclear Non-Proliferation Act directs the President to negotiate with other countries to set up the nuclear fuel bank. No supplies would go to any country not accepting "international nonproliferation standards" within eighteen months of the signing of the act.

But many questions remained unanswered, including the issue of whether American separation facilities would be nationalized. Meanwhile, many different nuclear production systems were being developed, worldwide.

How Nuclear Weapons Are Produced

Nuclear power originates from nuclear fission or thermonuclear fusion. In fission, heavy uranium or plutonium isotopes are bombarded by neutrons; they split into atoms of lighter elements and emit two or more neutrons for each atom that splits, releasing about 10 million times as much energy—atom for atom—as is obtainable from ordinary chemical combustion. One pound of fissionable material releases as much energy as 8 kilotons of high explosive.

In fusion, a less expensive process, the hydrogen isotopes deuterium and tritium are heated to tens of millions of degrees Fahrenheit; they then combine—fuse—to form heavier elements, releasing in the process six times as many fast neutrons as in fission, and a great deal of energy (less, atom for atom, than in fission; but, since lighter atoms are involved, a pound of thermonuclear fuel releases as much energy as 25 kilotons of high explosive).

Only a fraction of fissionable atomic nuclei are fissile—that is, fissionable by both fast and slow neutrons. Weapons can only be made without great difficulty from fissile materials like uranium-233 (U-233), uranium-235, plutonium-239 (Pu-239), a combination of these, or (by high-energy neutrons) uranium-239 or thorium-232.

When small amounts of fissle material are used, too many neutrons escape to cause fission in other nuclei. The minimum amount of material necessary to sustain a chain reaction is called the critical mass—which can vary from about 20 to over 100 pounds, according to the fissile material used, or less if the nuclear core is compressed.

Either a gun or an implosion device is used to start the chain reaction. The Hiroshima bomb used U-235 and a gun, yielding a 14-kiloton explosion; the Nagasaki bomb used Pu-239 and an implosion method and yielded a 20-kiloton explosion. Both bombs weighed about 5 tons. The Nagasaki weapon—"Fat Boy"—was 5 feet in diameter, with a baseball-sized plutonium core, the rest being tamper and high explosive.

U-235 is found in nature, mixed with U-238 in the proportion of roughly seven parts per thousand; U-235 is produced in nuclear reactors from thorium-232; Pu-239 is similarly produced from U-238. The mixture of U-235 and U-238 is "enriched" to produce a blend that is 90 per cent U-235. A weapon could still be made from an equal mix of 235 and 238, but the critical mass would need to be about three times as great.

The plutonium produced in light-water reactors is only about 60 per cent Pu-239; in other words, it is not "weapons-grade"; separating 239 from Pu-240 and heavier isotopes is more difficult and hazardous than uranium enrichment, but a less efficient weapon could in fact be made from reactor-grade plutonium. U-233 is rarely used in nuclear weapons at present, but because of the abundance of thorium-232 in nature its military use seems likely to grow. If a country or organization lacked the skill to process uranium or plutonium in metal form, a less efficient weapon could be made from the oxide compounds of U-235, U-233 or Pu-239.

Thus, nuclear weapons are usually composed of plutonium, "reprocessed" or "separated out" from spent fuel rods in nuclear reactors. In a nuclear bomb of very modest efficiency, 10 per cent of the plutonium is detonated to give a yield of about 20,000 tons (20 kilotons) of TNT for 12 kilograms (about 26 pounds) of plutonium. Reactors can be expensive, and take time to produce electricity; but the fabrication of weapons is relatively cheap and quick—as the now notorious Princeton student's 1976 term paper demonstrated, at least theoretically. Normally, it takes a grapefruit-sized sphere of plutonium weighing about 33 pounds to serve as the core of a bomb with a similar destructive capacity to the one exploded over Hiroshima. Even a modest heavy-water reactor with a power of 120 million watts thermal (40 million watts electrical) would produce about 20 kilograms (44 pounds) of plutonium-239 a year—more than enough for two 20-kiloton bombs.

The so-called breeder reactors are designed to produce large amounts of residual plutonium from the irradiated fuel, which is recovered and recycled. A breeder reactor, in fact, as the name indicates, produces more fissile material than it consumes.

Enriched uranium and thorium are converted into an oxide or a carbide for use as reactor fuel; plutonium is converted into an oxide. Uranium-oxide pellets are stacked in tubes, creating "fuel rods." Plutonium-oxide powder is mixed with uranium-oxide powder to make plutonium pellets. If the Clinch River, Tennessee, breeder reactor is built—based on research being currently conducted at Barnwell, South Carolina—it will be the world's first full-scale reprocessing facility for uranium oxide (as opposed to uranium metal) fuels. After removal from a reactor core, spent fuel is stored for about six months to allow radioactivity to decline to manageable levels, before reprocessing.

Several countries are undertaking reprocessing to fuel breeder reactors to supplant fossil fuels in the future. At least twenty countries now have nuclear-power reactors, and at least six have advanced breeder-reactor programs. Nuclear accidents are consequently becoming commoner—worldwide, about one every ten weeks. Already by 1978, there had been ninety-seven in the United States alone, of which twenty-seven were major.

In 1977, President Carter proposed "deferring" the reprocessing of plutonium in the United States—possibly placing it under international control—with emphasis being put on research into nuclear-fuel cycles not involving weapons-usable materials. He called for other countries to follow suit. The United States has never exported uranium-enrichment facilities or reprocessing plants, as they are not presently safeguardable, but it has been the leading country in exporting nuclear materials and technology. Under pressure from Washington, France and Germany made public assurances in 1977 that they would cease the export of reprocessing technology in the future.

Most reactors use light or heavy water. Fast-breeder reactors—in use in Russia, France and Britain, and planned for the United States, Japan and West Germany—mostly use liquid metal; high-temperature gas reactors are also under development. Light-water reactors are the commonest around the world, but if enriched fuel is imported, and spent fuel is not reprocessed, such a reactor would not produce weapons-grade material. With pressurized heavy-water reactors, however, natural—not enriched—uranium could be used to produce material for a weapon. Reprocessing would give plutonium, and weapons-grade U-233 could be produced from even low-quality plutonium.

Between 1953 and 1974, the United States cheaply and unrestrictedly exported, under the "Atoms for Peace" program inaugurated by President Eisenhower, the enriched fuel for reactors from which is created the plutonium on which the current fear of nuclear-weapons proliferation is based. Reprocessing plants, as noted, have not been exported, and have been seen as difficult and expensive for nations to build from scratch: A simplified reprocessing plant, economizing by using less stringent safety standards, could cost as little as $10 million—but, without experienced assistance, might take as much as seven years to build. Enrichment is either by gaseous diffusion, the "gas centrifuge process," an "aerodynamic process" developed by Professor Erwin Becker in West Germany or a slightly different aerodynamic process evolved in South Africa. The last two are simpler and less expensive than the others, because they require fewer stages, and they are ideal for small-scale weapons manufacture. Brazil will use the "Becker nozzle" process. When enrichment by lasers, now being developed in Israel, the United States and elsewhere, is achieved in the future, simpler, still less expensive plants could produce weapons-grade plutonium for bombs of up to Hiroshima power without bothering to build power reactors at all.

Russia has substantial uranium deposits, as have the United States, Canada, Australia, South Africa and Namibia. Smaller deposits exist in many countries, including Zaire and the former French colonies of Gabon and Niger, as well as Spain, Portugal and Argentina. Without "breeders," there will, however, probably be a uranium shortage by the end of this century; but huge thorium reserves exist in the United States, Canada, Australia, India, Norway and Brazil.

Proliferation

A standard-sized nuclear-power plant produces enough plutonium for a bomb in about two weeks. Seeing that states without nuclear weapons (non-NW states) do not do so is the task of the IAEA, which has a budget of less than $7 million and a staff of less than a hundred inspectors, relying on about two thousand remote cameras. Any country with a reprocessing plant could expel inspectors and start bomb production in a few days—or weeks at most. The temptation to countries like Germany and France to export reprocessing plants has come from the soaring cost of building their domestic nuclear-power programs. It was when the United States decided, in 1974, that it could no longer export enriched uranium that a $12 billion, twelve-reactor deal between Westinghouse and Brazil collapsed and Brazil turned to Germany—which offered not only reactors and fuel but also an enrichment facility and a small reprocessing plant as well, all to be situated at Angra dos Reis, 120 miles southwest of Rio de Janeiro. U.S. opposition to the German deal soured relations between Washington and Brasília, and in late 1977 the State Department relented and recommended that a license to export American nuclear fuel to Brazil be granted. This was one of thirty-two long-pending licenses involving Brazil and twelve other countries—Belgium, France, West Germany, Sweden, Holland, Switzerland, Spain, Yugoslavia, Japan, Mexico, India and South Korea.

It was shortly after the German-Brazilian arrangement was announced that France negotiated the sale of reprocessing plants to Iran, Pakistan and South Korea. Later, the French admitted that they were also providing Iraq with a two-year supply of 93 per cent-enriched uranium for the Osiris research reactor which French technicians are building in that country. America opposed these sales also, but the French noted that the United States was still selling power reactors and nuclear fuel, under existing contracts, to more than a score of countries—many of them not signatories to NPT.

In 1976, Congress cut off aid to countries that purchase enrichment or reprocessing plants unless they place all these facilities under international inspection. As mentioned earlier, Washington pressured South Korea into not buying the facilities offered by France, while Iran was dissuaded from going into reprocessing when canceling these plans was made a condition of Teheran's right to purchase, from the United States, virtually any non-nuclear weapons which it desired. Dr. Kissinger suggested at the time that an "international agency," possibly situated in Iran, could produce plutonium for Iran. France, however, went ahead with the building of two billion-dollar nuclear reactors on the Karun River in Iran, and had hoped, before the turmoil of 1978, to build two more. West Germany was building two nuclear power plants near the Iranian port of Bushire—another $2 billion deal—and had also planned to build two more.

Pakistan held out longer, despite heavy pressure on Paris by President Ford and Dr. Kissinger, who offered Pakistan A-7s if it would forgo the deal. Although neither France nor Pakistan is among the 109 signatories to NPT, President Giscard d'Estaing stated finally that France would be prepared to take part in an international effort to limit the spread of nuclear technology, but said France would honor its commitment to Pakistan. Subsequently, the French did impose delays on blueprint deliveries because of Bhutto's overthrow and the country's apparent political instability. Then, in late 1978, Carter triumphantly announced that France had agreed to cancel the sale altogether. Earlier, France had not protested when the South Korean deal, which was similar to Pakistan's, had been canceled by Seoul itself under U.S. pressure. Meanwhile, Third

World governments attacked the U.S. push for nuclear restraints, seeing it as depriving poor countries of cheap energy. Also in 1978, President Giscard d'Estaing began discussions with President Carter about nuclear proliferation in general, and long-term arms-sales limitations to the Middle East. The German-Brazilian deal, however, went through, with Bonn agreeing that it would be the "last" such export.

Pakistan responded to the Paris action by openly starting to build its own uranium-enrichment facility. But the country was much further along toward bomb production than the abortive deal with France had indicated. In 1979, in Stockholm, SIPRI reported that the contract of the previous year whereby the French firm Saint-Gobain Techniques-Nouvelles would supply most of a plutonium-reprocessing plant to Islamabad, for $540,000, was actually a "blind." The purchase of this plant, under IAEA safeguards, was intended, SIPRI said, to indicate that Pakistan was unable to reprocess plutonium in any other way. SIPRI said that Pakistan was actually using domestic uranium, officially mined for its 137-megawatt Canadian electric-power reactor near Karachi and for two research reactors in the Islamabad area.

British press reports revealed shortly afterward that President Bhutto had decided to make plutonium from this domestic uranium, by the centrifuge method, at the Pakistani Institute of Science and Technology at Nellore, an Islamabad suburb. To buy centrifuge equipment without raising suspicion, said the London reports, Pakistan set up front companies in Swansea, Wales, in Switzerland and in Germany. Many of these firms made only a single order, ostensibly intended for a textile plant, but the total orders were over $11 million.

The buying strategy was reportedly coordinated by Ikram ul-Haq Khan of the Pakistan Ordnance Service, using an office just outside Bonn. The orders were fulfilled by the Swindon, England, subsidiary of Emerson Electric Industrial Controls, by two German firms—Aluminum-Walzwerke Singen of Singen and Leyboed Heraens of Hannen—as well as by two Dutch concerns, Van Doorne Transmissie of Tilburg and Leifeld of Ahlen.

Alerted by the SIPRI report, which went unnoticed in the U.S. press, British reporters stumbled on the whole story after Frank Allaun, a Labour member of Parliament, intervened in a labor dispute at the Swindon firm and was told by striking workers about the "Pakistan Special Project." Allaun became suspicious, and urged a government investigation. To prod Whitehall, Allaun spoke to reporters, and the U.S. embassy in London also launched its own inquiries. According to the British reporters, the CIA uncovered the Nellore project in March 1979, learning that a small atomic explosion had taken place, shortly before, at Mulatan, over 250 miles to the south.

The following month, President Carter took action against Pakistan by ordering that fifty F-5s, which the United States had agreed to sell to that country, must now be paid for in cash—a virtual impossibility for the impoverished state. Washington also canceled all U.S. economic aid.

Shortly before Bhutto was executed by his successor, following a "show" trial for allegedly ordering the killing of a minor rival, he smuggled a two-hundred-page report from his cell, apparently admitting that Pakistan was working toward a bomb. In the report, Bhutto said:

> We know that Israel and South Africa have full nuclear capability. The Christian, Jewish and Communist powers all possess it. Only the Islamic civilization is without it. But that position is about to change.

The British reporters theorized that Pakistan had been encouraged by its financial benefactor, Saudi Arabia, seen to be seeking an Arab counterbalance to Israel's nuclear power—and one not dependent on Moscow.

By the time this book appears, probably thirty-five nations will be handling plutonium, and in a decade they will be producing more of it each year than currently exists, worldwide. According to Dr. Vinay Meckomi, an Indian chemical engineer with the IAEA, there will then be about 400 tons of it in storage. Already by the end of 1980, it is estimated that the world's nuclear reactors will have stockpiled about 250,000 kilograms (550,000 pounds) of plutonium and be producing 100,000 pounds of it annually. It is big business. In 1978, Gulf Oil Corporation pleaded no contest to charges of helping form an international uranium cartel that boosted the price of the mineral from $6.00 a pound to $41 in the early seventies. Gulf was fined $40,000. This started a spate of lawsuits by purchasers.

The Office of Technological Assessment of the U. S. Congress has estimated that "a dozen" good scientists are all a country needs to make a bomb. India, with some help from the Vitro Corporation, an American firm, exploded its bomb in 1974, thus becoming the world's sixth openly admitted nuclear-weapon power. This was done with fuel from a $12.5 million power reactor—called CIR for Canadian-Indian Reactor—supplied free by a Canadian aid program in 1963 to encourage "research in nuclear physics" and as a showcase for Canadian technology in the Third World. The United States supplied 21 tons of heavy water—the first such export under Eisenhower's Atoms for Peace program, and CIR became CIRUS. Partly to compete with Canada, the Johnson administration, in December 1963, authorized a $71.8 million loan to India to

cover purchase of a power plant from General Electric. The loan terms—
three quarters of 1 per cent interest over thirty years—amounted to a $58
million gift (in saved interest) from the American taxpayer. Part of the
loan went to pay for the training of four Indian scientists at the then-
secret plutonium-reprocessing facility in Hanford, Washington.

The Indian technicians were not an isolated case. Between 1958 and
1972, the United States trained 169 foreign scientists at Hanford and
three other Atomic Energy Commission laboratories, including 29 Japanese, 24 Indians, 12 Germans, 11 Pakistanis, 9 Taiwanese, 8 South Africans, 7 Brazilians and 5 Israelis.

In 1965, India built a plutonium-reprocessing plant at Prererai alongside the Canadian reactor. The Canadians raised some objections, pointing to the safeguards in their agreement, so the Indians returned the Canadian fuel without reprocessing it. Instead, they used plutonium made
from Indian uranium in a research reactor, and informed Ottawa that the
safeguards therefore no longer applied. It was this that led then Pakistani Prime Minister Zulfikar Ali Bhutto to tell reporters that his country
would eventually have the bomb "even if we have to eat grass."

However, India's decision to make a nuclear weapon of its own did not
come until 1971, during the Bangladesh crisis. The United States and
Canada then refused to provide more heavy water, and France stepped
into the breach. The bomb exploded May 18, 1974, making a crater 39
feet deep and 252 feet wide in the Rajasthan desert. The following year,
France agreed to sell Pakistan a $150 million plutonium-reprocessing
plant; as noted earlier, this was eventually canceled.

India's experimental nuclear explosion created a furor in the West, and
especially in the United States. All through 1975 and 1976, Congress and
federal energy authorities were wrapped up in a debate over whether to
sell further American nuclear fuel to the new reprocessing facility at
Tarapur, just north of Bombay. The Edlow nuclear-transport firm in
Washington, which would handle the shipping, lobbied Congress for
India. Washington insisted that India return its 400 kilograms of spent
fuel to the United States as a condition for further supplies; India responded that the United States must therefore supply fuel at one eighth
of normal prices, to compensate for the savings India would be prevented from achieving by reprocessing fuel at Tarapur. The Indian argument illustrated some of the growing difficulties in control. Washington
shelved its request that India resell the spent fuel to the United States.

However, following the defeat of the Indira Gandhi Government at
the polls in 1977, the Carter administration continued with exports of nuclear fuel to New Delhi, with the new Indian Government initially accepting international safeguards. It was understood that India had also

agreed to forgo further explosions, although experts agreed that there was almost no way of preventing India from storing weapons-grade fuel for future use. A license for the export of 27,000 pounds of uranium was approved that year by the Nuclear Regulatory Commission, which said that future supplies for Tarapur would be cut off if India exploded any more nuclear devices. When the NRC refused an export license for a further 8 tons of enriched uranium in 1978, Carter overruled the Commission by executive order. Later that year, however, Indian Premier Morarji Desai, while in Washington, said his country would only accept international safeguards for nuclear facilities other than Tarapur if countries with "military reactors" civilianized them and opened them to inspection. Since the nuclear nonproliferation law passed by Congress in 1977 forbids U.S. nuclear exports after 1980 to countries not accepting "international safeguards," a new conflict with India seems likely then. After Desai's visit, there was a congressional move to block further uranium sales to India, but this was rejected. Later, India, in a move welcomed by the U. S. Government, suggested the setting up of an international commission to examine the safeguards question.

The U.S.-built Tarapur reactor is an important factor in India's future electricity supplies. Under the accord that created Tarapur, India agreed to buy its fuel only from the United States. Officials had argued in 1976, before Mrs. Gandhi's defeat, that for the United States to renege on its supply agreement would leave India at liberty to buy its fuel elsewhere, or to reprocess freely. In 1976, the Soviet Union agreed to sell India 200 tons of heavy water. By then, India was estimated to have enough material for between forty and eighty bombs. That year, India and Turkey—an odd alliance—announced an agreement to cooperate bilaterally on the use of nuclear power for "peaceful purposes." As well as Tarapur, Prererai and the four research reactors at Trombay, near Bombay, India has a fuel-fabrication plant at Hyderabad.

The attention of U.S. opponents of nuclear proliferation centered largely on France. Already by the mid-sixties, France had the largest non-Communist plutonium-reprocessing plant in the world—at La Hague, on the Norman coast. This plant was expected to produce 400 tons of nuclear fuel in 1978. The fact that a 33-pound container of plutonium (or of highly enriched uranium) costs almost $500,000 helps explain the degree of self-discipline that would be necessary in fuel-starved countries like France not to proceed with breeder reactors.

Japan is a similar case. It was in late 1976 that Tokyo contracted with Britain and France to reprocess American-origin Japanese fuel at what were described at the time as "bargain prices." Japan would invest $1 billion over the years in the two countries to build the facilities. American practice has been to supply nuclear fuel under bilateral agreements which give the United States the right to determine where fuel could be moved, and where and whether the plutonium produced could be reprocessed. In October 1976, Ford ordered a moratorium on the reprocessing of U.S.-origin fuel; but in December he relented, permitting Japan, Switzerland and Spain to send such fuel to France and Britain. One reason for relenting was that it was known that by May 1977, Japan would have its own plutonium-reprocessing plant at Tokai Mura, near Tokyo. Carter later continued the Ford policy. Some of the fuel reprocessed in Britain and France may be sold to Germany, which is building a breeder reactor. Not surprisingly, Carter's 1977 offer to stop reprocessing in the United States and defer the construction of breeder reactors—to encourage other nations to do likewise—ran into immediate objections from Japan, Spain and Germany, not to speak of the congressional delegation of Tennessee, site of the proposed American breeder.

In 1978, Britain decided to go ahead with reprocessing nuclear waste for a wide spectrum of foreign clients, at Windscale, on the northwest coast. Local press critics complained that the country was becoming a "nuclear garbage dump." Hardly encouraging was the belated confirmation, that year, that a gigantic explosion had taken place in 1957 at a Soviet nuclear waste-disposal facility at Kyshtym in the southern Urals: Kept secret for a generation, the accident had killed hundreds of thousands—some immediately, some over ensuing months and years— and contaminated food over hundreds of square miles. The area had been closed for nine months, after which trucks were allowed to drive through at high speed. All topsoil had had to be burned, and pregnant women in the area aborted.

Taiwan, a country faced with a possible invasion threat from a nuclear power, China, is known to be secretly reprocessing spent uranium fuel to produce weapons-grade plutonium at the local Atomic Energy Council's Institute of Nuclear Energy Research, just southwest of Taipei. The Institute uses a 40-megawatt Canadian-supplied reactor and a hot-cell reprocessing plant, initially placed under international safeguards. It was in 1976 that U.S. officials first told reporters that secret reprocessing was going on. The Arms Control and Disarmament Agency in Washington was then delaying approval for the export of two additional nuclear power plants to Taipei. Four others were exported from the United States in 1972 and 1974 as part of a program to produce half the country's electricity from nuclear power by 1985. Although Taiwan has signed the nonproliferation agreement and officially accepted International

Atomic Energy Administration inspection, it was ousted as an IAEA member in 1971, thus creating an anomalous situation.

Canada broke relations with Taipei in 1970, thus losing all leverage there; but since the inception of the Atoms for Peace program, 713 Taiwanese physicists have studied nuclear technology in the United States. One of them, Dr. Chung Woo, only finished his one year's study in reprocessing at the Argonne laboratory of the Energy Research and Development Administration in Chicago as late as mid-1976. Taiwan is now supplied with uranium by South Africa, which refuses to register its exports with the IAEA. Taipei—which has no native oil resources or other fossil fuels of any significance—is also able to buy reactor fuel from the United States.

India's and Taiwan's development of a nuclear weapon is characteristic of a Third World trend, particularly in Asia and the Indian Ocean. Brazil, followed by other leading Latin American nations, is clearly working toward a nuclear bomb, and the Indian mushroom cloud itself—the first Third World bomb—was a by-product of the threat of China's, and also partly of the eventual threat of South Africa introducing this level of weaponry into the Indian Ocean area. Most leaders of the industrialized countries appear to believe today that the main threat to peace comes less from the nuclear and conventional stalemate between the NATO and Warsaw Treaty powers than from the spread of nuclear technology to client states of militaristic bent, such as Pakistan or South Korea. These could thus place their major- or super-power protectors in jeopardy, breaking the rules of some local nuclear balance of terror.

Muammar al-Qaddafi, the maverick President of Libya, was probably devastatingly accurate when he remarked in 1976 that "atomic weapons will be like traditional ones, possessed by every state according to its potential. We will have our share of this new weapon."

The vulgarization of nuclear knowledge has been awesome. By early 1976, 168 nuclear-power reactors in nineteen countries were producing a total of about 73,000 megawatts of electricity (MWe). At full production, their capacity would be over 17 million MWe. By 1980, twenty-nine countries should have reactors producing 219,300 MWe, or about eleven times the production figure of 1970. The anticipated production figure for the year 2000—3.6 million MWe—is over sixteen times the projected figure for 1980.

The step from peaceful nuclear production to nuclear-weapon technology is, as noted, not all that great—although it is often a slow and tedious step for underdeveloped scientists. The real problem is that many of the countries acquiring nuclear power are nonsignatories to the Nuclear

Non-Proliferation Treaty; some have signed the pact but their legislatures have not ratified it. This is notably true in the Middle East, where the danger lies not only in the risk of destruction of large local areas of civilian population—appalling as that would be, especially in highly populated Egypt—but also in the risk of superpower confrontation. In one of their AEI studies, Pranger and Tahtinen have written:

> A bilateral code for regulating nuclear defense has developed. Whether a given period in Russo-American relations is called détente or cold war, both sides assume that a sense of nuclear equilibrium, together with balanced thinking on military matters, will be maintained.

The Middle East, however, presents certain anarchic dangers. Although Pranger and Tahtinen were writing before President Sadat's Jerusalem initiative, most of what they said then still holds true:

> In the Middle East no significant formal or informal relationships between the Arab governments and Israel exist, to say nothing of a code for nuclear conduct should such weapons be introduced into this tumultuous setting . . . It may well be that nuclear weapons will be used in the Middle East in the near future . . . If so, this will occur in the complete absence of diplomatic relations for crisis management between Jerusalem and the Arab capitals and between Jerusalem and Moscow.

How long can the Third World nuclear option be put off? Admiral LaRocque estimates that the United States, in the past decade, has given away or sold about 19,000 missiles, ships or aircraft capable of launching a nuclear warhead; he says: "It's now within the capacity of almost every nation to develop or obtain nuclear weapons to go with these missiles, ships or aircraft." Carter administration decisions to limit sales to strict needs, to American security interests and not to considerations of "balance" come rather late, and would in any case be difficult to apply without massive exceptions. Moreover, not considering balance could be a formula for war.

However, since the 1973 Nixon-Brezhnev summit meeting in Washington, the superpowers have agreed to warn each other of the risk of use of nuclear weapons by third parties—and, as we have seen, the hot line was put to just such use shortly after, specifically in the context of the Middle East. Pranger and Tahtinen believe Iran, Egypt and Iraq all have the potential for acquiring nuclear-weapon capability.

The Soviet-built nuclear reactor at Inshass, in Egypt, has only a 2-megawatt capacity, compared to the 24 megawatts of Dimona, in Israel; so Egypt's nuclear capability would probably have to be imported. France has offered to build Cairo a reactor if the one promised by Dr. Kissinger—which has since become a political football in Congress—is not delivered, but it would take a decade for such a facility to become productive of weapons-grade material. Thus the nuclear perspective in the area is overshadowed by the implication of superpower involvement.

The only Arab country known to have built its own surface-to-surface missiles is Egypt; but to have an equivalent to the Jericho, or even more the Pershing, Egypt and Syria would need the Soviet Union's SS-12 Scaleboard, which, like the Pershing, is essentially a nuclear projectile, and which can be fired from the same launcher-vehicles as Egypt's Scuds. If Egypt's submarines acquired the naval version of the Soviet Shaddock missile, which has a range of nearly 100 nautical miles, it could not only attack Israeli ships but also, and more probably, cities and land-based military targets. Waiting well offshore in preparation for war, the nuclear-capable Shaddock would be a sufficient response to the nuclear-capable Jericho. The Egypt-Israel peace treaty makes this less of an apparent threat, but other Middle East countries fearing Israel—such as Libya, Syria or Iraq—might acquire submarines.

Pranger and Tahtinen say:

> The chief danger posed for American interests by nuclear war in the Middle East is the possible erosion and rupture in the U.S.-U.S.S.R. nuclear equilibrium.

And they recommend:

> As a bilateral measure with the Soviet Union, the United States should propose an agreement of finite duration that would prohibit introduction into the Middle East of any launch vehicle that has not been totally stripped of special devices for use with nuclear ordnance. In addition, both superpowers should watch closely technological exchanges (including technical manuals and briefings) that might yield valuable information on how to construct nuclear arming devices for certain systems. Ordnance, such as "smart bombs," that could be converted to tactical nuclear use should also be carefully controlled through bilateral agreements.

All this is seen from the statesmanlike view of those who wish to harness conflict. Unfortunately, the U.S. military who advise Israel and other states in the Middle East often view weaponry solely through the prism of effectiveness.

In the light of congressional indignation about India's acquisition of nuclear-weapon capacity, Dr. Kissinger's offer of reactors to Israel and Egypt seemed a contradictory gesture on America's part. The Israelis were anxious that the promise to Egypt should not be kept, maintaining that Egypt's dependence on outside sources of energy (at the time, Mideast oil) was less of a problem than Israel's (which involved dependence on Iranian oil and South African coal). But the Ford administration, already embarrassed at obliging Cairo to continue to depend on Russia for arms, feared pushing President Sadat into nuclear dependence on Moscow also.

The obvious fear of Congress was that the reactors could be used for military purposes. Dr. Kissinger's probable reasoning for making the offer was that Israel was already producing nukes; Sadat had long ago publicly stated that he would match any Israeli nuclear-weapon industry, either by producing weapons of his own or procuring them. And Egypt had already had nuclear warheads set to Scud missiles in 1973. A delegation of twelve senators led by Democrat Abraham Ribicoff of Connecticut visited the area in late 1976 and later recommended that the United States export nuclear fuel to Egypt, Israel and Iran, even though only Iran had signed and ratified NPT. The party was not allowed to visit the Israeli facility at Dimona, yet eleven of the senators (the exception being Democrat John Glenn of Ohio) recommended against conditioning export to Israel on the whole Dimona complex being placed under international controls.

Congress, at White House request, placed stricter controls on the export of nuclear fuel and technology in its Nuclear Non-Proliferation Act of 1977. But all this comes too late to make much difference: The nearly 30 tons of "special strategic nuclear material" which the United States has permitted Edlow International and Transnuclear Inc.—the other U.S. nuclear transportation firm—to ship across the world over the past quarter century is at the base of much of the hundreds of thousands of tons of recycled fuel which will emerge from plants in three dozen nations in the eighties.

At the IAEA, officials have come to the conclusion that setting international safeguards may be politically impossible. Theoretically, if an IAEA inspector notices weapons-grade material missing from a country's nuclear stocks, he informs his director general, Dr. Sigvard Arne Eklund of Sweden, who must report it to the UN Security Council. Since only a few weeks, at most, are needed to produce a bomb, it is unlikely that even a massive international effort could head such a development off. The sixty-four signatory countries to the Non-Proliferation Treaty allow IAEA inspectors to put seals on their plutonium containers, and detection would amount to seeing that seals had been removed. The inspectors also examine security measures to verify if these are observed—for instance, to prevent theft. But any report by an inspector "against" a country must, by agreement, be kept secret, and there is no provision for a penalty. Moreover, as noted earlier, after China's admission to the UN in 1973, Third World countries put together the votes to expel Taiwan from the IAEA, thus liberating that sophisticated, nuclear-capable country from international restraints.

Dr. Meckomi proposes some form of international nuclear-fuel storage facility, perhaps at one of the poles. In Washington, the ACDA has experts working on a technique to adulterate plutonium with some element that would inhibit the fast chain reaction necessary for a strong explosion; but so far none have been found that cannot be removed fairly easily. However, in 1978, France announced the discovery of a new lightweight reactor fuel, nicknamed "caramel," that was only enriched by 8 per cent—well below the 20 per cent threshold regarded as minimal for weapons-grade fuel.

In mid-1976, Carter appointed Ambassador Gerard C. Smith, the former arms-control chief in the Nixon administration, to a roving assignment—an effort to get international agreement to cap the nuclear bottle. Smith is charged with renegotiating U.S. nuclear-fuel supply contracts with no less than thirty countries. But there is little support for the U.S. stand except from Britain, where a Labour minister, Lord Goronwy-Roberts, told the Geneva disarmament conference that summer that in the fourteen years since the partial test-ban treaty there had been over five hundred underground nuclear tests, as well as the atmospheric tests by France and China.

Articulating the opposition in the United States itself to Carter's policy, Democratic senator Frank Church of Idaho—chairman of the Senate's energy research and development subcommittee—told an audience at MIT:

> However well-intentioned, I am convinced that the Administration's nuclear-energy policy is a formula for nuclear isolationism. It will reduce, not enhance, U.S. influence in shaping worldwide nuclear policy. Thus, instead of advancing the control of nuclear-weapons proliferation, our self-imposed restraint runs the grave risk of leaving an international vacuum, which is an invitation to nuclear anarchy.
>
> I believe the administration proposal is flawed for at least two reasons:
>
> First, it does not take sufficient account of the energy vulnerability of countries lacking our resource base . . .
>
> The second flaw . . . is that it fails to offer a satisfactory substitute for the world's diminishing supply of oil.

Not making the President's task much easier was the news, in July 1977, that in order to fulfill the weapons programs approved by Congress, the Pentagon would need substantially greater production of American plutonium. Major General Joseph K. Bratton, director of the Military Applications Division of the Energy Research and Development Administration, told a congressional subcommittee that year that the additional plutonium would be needed for several warheads. These were the new W78s for the improved Minuteman-II missile, the W79s for the neutron artillery projectile (to be fitted to 450 8-inch cannons in Europe), the W70-3 Lance missile neutron warheads, the W80s for cruise missiles and SRAM-B short-range attack missiles (of which a greater number may now be necessary because of Carter's emphasis on the cruise missile), the B61 bombs for tactical fighter-bombers, the B77 bombs to go in the bays of the B-52, the FB-111, perhaps eventually the B-1 and some other Air Force and Navy fighter-bombers, as well as for the Trident-II missile warheads and the twelve-to-fourteen thermo-nuclear warheads on each of the proposed M-X mobile land-based mis-siles. In all, Congress authorized $2.6 billion for nuclear warheads and bombs in fiscal 1978, to add to the existing stocks.

In May, a Soviet delegate to an international nuclear power conference in Salzburg, Vladimir Schmidt, had said his country would not forgo plu-tonium production. So far, Russia is the country most advanced in build-ing breeder reactors. French, Belgian, Japanese and even British dele-gates all said there was no hope of replacing plutonium entirely by thorium in the foreseeable future.

In Washington, Congress was deeply divided over whether to build the "demonstration model" American breeder reactor at Clinch River, Tennessee. Initiated by Nixon in 1971, the $2 billion project was due for completion in 1984. Carter asked Congress to reduce fiscal-1978 funding from $150 million to $30 million—just enough to finish design work and "mothball" the project for the time being. In June 1977, the House Sci-ence Committee, just back from a tour of plutonium-eager Europe, recommended approval for the full $150 million. The main spokesman for plutonium in the House was Democrat Olin Teague of Texas; in the Senate, the main voice was Church.

In June, Washington *Star* reporter John Fialka revealed the existence of a four-year-old memorandum by Burns and Roe, a firm with a $175 million design contract for Clinch River, saying the site was "one of the worst . . . ever selected for a nuclear power plant based on its topogra-phy and rock conditions." The report was also critical of other aspects of the plan and predicted delays and mounting costs if Clinch River was chosen. Burns and Roe at once issued a statement saying all the difficul-ties detected in 1973 had been resolved.

The GAO said that any attempt by ERDA to stop awarding subcon-tracts for Clinch River would be a violation of the Impoundment Control Act of 1974, an anti-Nixon measure that will haunt all future Presidents. In July, the Senate adopted a compromise delaying construction for a year, but providing $75 million to keep the technicians involved on the payroll and to continue research. In September, the House knocked this down by 277 votes to 129 and voted, 246–162, the full $150 million needed to proceed with the project on schedule. The House-Senate conference (followed by both houses) finally voted to require the Administration to spend $80 million on the Clinch River program. Carter successfully vetoed the measure—as he did again in 1978.

In the fall of 1978, Carter agreed to spend just over $1.5 billion over three years on research connected with the liquid-metal fast breeder reactor program, as a quid pro quo for Senate approval of his measure to deregulate the price of natural gas: But he made no commitment to build such a reactor at Clinch River. The "comprehensive nuclear test ban" seemed further away than ever, mostly because of continuing strong opposition within the American scientific community, and Carter ceased raising the question of such a treaty with the Russians.

France, whose domestic reserves and virtual control of uranium in Gabon and Niger give Paris access to 10 per cent of known world reserves, and whose Phénix breeder, in service since 1973, is the world's oldest, would still like to sell breeders abroad, possibly in cooperation with West Germany, and Clinch River would help release Paris from its commitments to Washington in this regard. The French Government faces relatively little public opposition to nuclear proliferation. Although public opinion forced a Dutch firm to withdraw from the South African reactor program, France went ahead there on a "business is business" basis. France claims to be well advanced in "safeguard technology," and to have written strong safeguards into the proposed deals with South Korea and Pakistan.

The Germans went ahead with approving export licenses for the blueprints of the uranium-enrichment and reprocessing plants sold to Brazil. German spokesmen talked of building eight plants in Brazil in all, for a total of about $5 billion.

Earlier in 1977, Canada had halted uranium shipments to Euratom, the European Community's joint nuclear program, because of inadequate safeguards, raising strong protests in Germany and Britain; but shipments on an interim basis were resumed in the summer. The United States imposed a partial embargo on nuclear fuel to France and West Germany until, in 1978, both countries agreed to bring their American supply agreements into line with the congressional nuclear nonproliferation act—which forbids the reprocessing into plutonium of American enriched uranium.

Under U.S. pressure, Japan delayed going ahead with plutonium production and a plutonium-fueled experimental reactor, but clearly a compromise was in sight. Japan had imported 2,200 pounds of enriched uranium from the United States in 1976, and is a major U.S. customer. It signed NPT in 1976 and has renounced not only nuclear weapons but also war itself in its "MacArthur constitution." However, although it forbids the presence of nuclear weapons on Japanese soil, it has tolerated visits by American ships bearing such weapons and the presence of tactical missiles with U. S. Air Force squadrons.

Because of the Hiroshima-Nagasaki legacy, popular opposition to nuclear proliferation is strong in Japan, and there have been violent demonstrations against the siting of nuclear reactors. But with a $170 million, French-built plant at stake, a compromise on safeguards was soon worked out.

Almost the only positive news Carter heard in his first two years in office was an optimistic joint call by Iran and Egypt in April 1977 for the "early establishment of a nuclear-weapon-free zone in the Middle East."

Japan's neighbor China, of course, already has nuclear warheads, so after a euphoric visit to Peking by Dr. Brzezinski in 1978, the White House approved the sale to that country, by France, of two Westinghouse-designed nuclear power plants.

Nuclear Smuggling

Canada's concern about the inadequacy of European safeguards, and Iran's and Egypt's about proliferation in their area were amply justified by a fascinating story about nuclear smuggling which finally emerged in 1977.

The story went back to November 17, 1968, when a small (1,790 tons) German-built freighter of Liberian registry, the *Scheersberg A*, left Antwerp in a misty dawn with 560 drums of "yellowcake" uranium oxide weighing 200 tons and worth 190 million Belgian francs—then just over $4 million. The drums were marked "plumbat"—a lead derivative The cargo's declared destination was a paint company called SAICA (Società Anonima Italiana Colori e Affini) in Genoa. Paul Leventhal, a former U. S. Senate staffer, told the Salzburg nuclear conference in April 1977 that the vessel turned up a few weeks later with "a new name, a new registry, a new crew but no uranium" (Leventhal was wrong on the minor points: Investigations show that the name and the registry remained the same.) The yellowcake had been smuggled to Israel's Dimona reactor in the Negev desert by agents of Mossad, Israel's CIA, which secretly owned the *Scheersberg A*.

Two months after the freighter left Antwerp, Euratom checked with the SAICA company to see if the shipment had arrived. On getting a negative response, Euratom initiated an investigation, code-named Plumbat. Having no police powers, Euratom recruited the help of European police and security services. In Germany, the investigation was abruptly and mysteriously ordered stopped by the government in 1969. The security director and the supply chief of Euratom had, by then, been replaced.

The exporter had been a small German petrochemical firm called Asmara Chemie, with no previous record of buying uranium, but which had originally purchased the uranium from Belgium's Société Générale des Minerais in Zaire. When reporters began asking questions in 1977, the two owners of the then-defunct Asmara company pleaded the involvement of "secret service agencies" to avoid responding. Earlier, when the official liquidator had arrived at Asmara's offices after a bankruptcy ruling, he had found that the offices had been burgled and some of the files removed.

Initially, Asmara—run by a former Nazi officer called Herbert Scharf and a younger partner, Herbert Schulzen, a former Luftwaffe pilot, and named in honor of Scharf's happy memories of Eritrea—had told the Société Générale that it was buying the uranium oxide in behalf of Chimagar, a seaweed-processing firm in Casablanca. Chimagar exported algins for use in dyes: Asmara was its German agent. When Euratom posed difficulties about exporting the uranium outside the Common Market area, Chimagar's name was replaced on the Asmara-Société Générale contract by SAICA, which, it was stipulated, would mix the oxide with other elements and return it to Asmara. SAICA was paid an advance of $20,000 for agreeing to perform this unspecified process. Then, shortly after the ship left Antwerp, Asmara called SAICA to say the vessel had been lost at sea and that SAICA could keep the advance payment.

Two months before the departure from the Belgian port, the ship—then called simply the *Scheersberg*—had been purchased for $160,000 by a brass-plate company in Monrovia from a Hamburg shipping broker, with the help of a mysterious Turkish shipping executive, Burham Yarisal, who pretended to own the ship himself. The Liberian firm, Biscayne Traders Shipping Corporation, was incorporated a month earlier —in August 1968—at about the same time that Asmara signed with Société Générale for the uranium.

Biscayne Traders Shipping was a front for the Mossad. The firm's president, Dan Ert, was convicted of murder in Norway in 1973 for his involvement in the killing of a Moroccan immigrant waiter, Ahmed

Bouchiki, who his group mistakenly thought was a Palestinian militant involved in the seizure of Israeli athletes during the Munich Olympic Games (an incident in which eleven persons died in crossfire between the Palestinians and the German police). The actual murder was carried out by an English Israeli called Jonathan Englesberg and an Israeli woman called Tamara; Ert was the organizer of the six-person hit team sent to Norway for the purpose, and of which the most striking member was a South African model, Sylvia Raphael.

The day after his arrest in Norway, Ert, a joint Danish and Israeli citizen who has since changed his name to Aerbel, broke down and told the whole story, eventually winning early release from a Norwegian prison in 1975. Ert revealed his Mossad identity (and helped to prove it to his interrogator by giving him a secret Mossad headquarters telephone number in Tel Aviv); he told police lieutenant Steinar Ravlo in detail about the Mossad's "hit" network in Western Europe. Finally, he told Norway's then chief prosecutor, Haakan Wiker, about the *Scheersberg A* caper, admitting that he owned the ship and specifying—according to Wiker—that the amount of yellowcake was sufficient for "forty-two nuclear weapons."

Ert revealed that he had persuaded his German friend Schulzen to buy the yellowcake; Schulzen had brought in, first Chimagar, then SAICA, run by Schulzen's friend Francesco Sertorio. On November 15, 1968, Yarisal had told the largely Spanish crew that the ship had been sold again and that they were no longer needed. The next day, an Israeli crew boarded—causing some attention in Antwerp, where a dilapidated freighter with all-white deckhands is unusual—and the loading of the yellowcake began.

Of the Israeli crew, who had false identities and passports (the young captain was listed as Peter Barrow, and he claimed to have been born in Wales), only one was finally traced—in the Ivory Coast. This man confirmed Ert's story to Ravlo and Wiker that the ship had sailed direct from Antwerp to a point off the southeast Turkish coastal city of Iskenderun. In darkness, the *Scheersberg A* was met by an Israeli ship which winched the drums aboard while two Israeli gunboats stood guard. The freight arrived at Haifa the next day, and the *Scheersberg A* sailed for Iskenderun, where it arrived empty on December 2. Three days later, it was at Palermo, Sicily, and Yarisal—pretending to have bought the ship back—cabled the old crew to rejoin the vessel. When they did, they found that two and a half weeks of the ship's log had been ripped out.

The secretly Mossad-owned ship then went about normal freight activities in the Mediterranean and the Atlantic; but after a year, the crew were told on November 17, 1969, that the ship had been sold again. Now the overt owners were Ert and a Danish friend, the much-convicted owner of a Copenhagen massage parlor where Ert was a regular customer. The crew was dismissed. Again, a crew of Mossad spooks came aboard—this time at Almería, Spain—and sailed the vessel through the Gibraltar Strait. At the time, France was refusing, under the 1967 Mideast arms embargo, to deliver five missile and torpedo boats ordered from a Cherbourg shipyard and already paid for by Israel. France had strengthened its embargo after the Israeli raid of December 28, 1968, on Beirut airport, in which thirteen Middle East Airlines Caravelles, worth $60 million, had been destroyed. De Gaulle had been especially miffed because Israel had used French-supplied helicopters to destroy French-built planes of an airline in which Air France was a major stockholder.

In connivance with a Norwegian oil-exploration company, which pretended to buy the seized 40-knot vessels as "supply boats" for its rigs, Mossad agents smuggled the boats out of Cherbourg on Christmas Day, rendezvousing with the *Scheersberg A* in the Bay of Biscay for refueling. Five days later, the *Scheersberg A* was sold in West Germany to a Greek Cypriot company, Pidalion Three. According to the Lefka, Cyprus, *News Bulletin,* it is now registered on the island under the name *Kerkyra;* its old name *Scheersberg A* is still legible, however, in a photograph seen by the writer. Its main run these days is reportedly into Benghazi, Libya.

The revelation of the *Scheersberg A* affair stressed the need for greater nuclear safeguards. When Dr. Kissinger promised reactors to both Israel and Egypt in 1974 as part of the Sinai agreement, Israel said it would accept supervision for the new reactor, but not for reactors already in operation. Israel's President, Ephraim Katzir, joked with reporters that year about the Israeli bomb, saying: "Let the world worry about it." General Moshe Dayan, later Israel's Foreign Minister, said that Israel had gone "about as far as we can go" with reliance on conventional weapons. In November 1976, as noted earlier, visiting U.S. senators were barred from Dimona.

Later in 1977, it was revealed that 280 pounds of enriched weapons-grade uranium—possibly enough for as many as twenty warheads—was missing from a private nuclear plant at Apollo, Pennsylvania, now owned by the Babcock and Wilcox corporation, which bought it from Atlantic Richfield in 1971. Atlantic Richfield had purchased it a year before from a small corporation called Nuclear Materials and Equipment Corporation (NUMEC) under whose stewardship the fuel was lost, most of it in 1967.

House Interior Committee chairman Morris Udall launched an investigation of NUMEC and its founder-owner, Zalman M. Shapiro, a former

AEC chemist and subordinate of Admiral Rickover's at the Bettis laboratory in nearby Shippingport, which makes nuclear submarine reactors. NUMEC made fuel for the Bettis lab, for Westinghouse and for nine foreign firms, including two Israeli organizations.

In November 1965, the AEC discovered that 382 pounds of enriched uranium was unaccounted for at NUMEC. Shapiro hired Jack R. Newman, chief counsel of the Joint Congressional Committee on Atomic Energy, as NUMEC's chief attorney. Some of the losses were explained as being "lost in the pipes," but 206 pounds remained unaccounted for, and Shapiro had to pay $929,000 to the AEC to cover the loss, borrowing the money from a Pittsburgh bank. He sold the firm in 1967 and went to work for Westinghouse, where in 1978 he was manager of a fusion-reactor program.

A former CIA technical expert, Carl Duckett, who was involved with the investigation of Shapiro, says he discussed the case with then CIA director Richard Helms, who spoke to President Johnson, who ordered the Agency to drop the case. Then, following a British intelligence report, Shapiro was investigated by the FBI as a possible Israeli undercover agent involved in what the British described as "black market sales in Europe" of enriched uranium. Ramsey Clark, then Attorney General, authorized electronic surveillance of Shapiro over several weeks.

The FBI learned of a meeting at Shapiro's home in Pittsburgh at which a suspected Israeli intelligence official asked Shapiro and other American scientists to obtain specific information for Israel.

CIA officers told the Udall investigation that the Agency had concluded that Shapiro helped smuggle the missing Apollo fuel to Israel. Kenneth R. Chapman, former head of the Nuclear Regulatory Commission's safeguards section, says this was the conclusion of Duckett—then the CIA's third-ranking officer—when he spoke to an NRC meeting in 1976. J. Edgar Hoover, head of the FBI, was reportedly miffed. When he testified to the NRC, Duckett said the CIA was now sure that Israel had nuclear weapons. He related an A-4 bombing practice in Israel in which the aircraft took the evasive action that spares the plane from being destroyed by a nuclear explosion.

The NRC reviewed the case again in 1976 and President Ford ordered another FBI probe. The House Commerce Committee's energy subcommittee received an AEC report which said that investigations had shown that twenty-six NUMEC ledgers dealing with foreign contracts were "incomplete, inaccurate or missing." Some House staffers theorized that, because of the taut situation in the Middle East in 1967, lower-echelon CIA officers may have cooperated with NUMEC in making the smuggling to Israel possible. Indeed, it later emerged that some of the technology needed by Israel to produce nuclear weapons had been made available to that country by a CIA agent.

The investigations were complicated by the necessity to penetrate foreign groups, including Israeli Isotopes and Radiation Enterprises Ltd. (ISORAD), a company which was half owned by the Israeli Atomic Energy Commission. Under the Freedom of Information Act, the Department of Energy made available to the press in late 1977 about three thousand documents relating to the case. One showed that NUMEC was "technical consultant" and "training and procurement agency" in the United States for Israel's AEC; but Shapiro was apparently never asked to register under the Foreign Agents Registration Act.

A CIA report said that enough enriched-uranium waste was detected at Dimona by the Agency (probably by use of a mass spectrometer) to imply the possible production of "several nuclear bombs." CIA files also showed that Shapiro used a scrambling device on his telephone when talking to Israeli officials.

At the time this book was being written, Shapiro was still under investigation for possible breaches of Section 222 of the U. S. Atomic Energy Act, which prescribes the death penalty for persons violating AEC regulations "with intent to secure an advantage to any foreign nation." Shapiro has persistently denied any wrongdoing.

In October 1977, Barbara Newman of National Public Radio and Howard Kohn of *Rolling Stone* said in an article in that paper that Israel had purchased enough "stolen" enriched uranium in the late sixties to make as many as 150 nuclear bombs. Newman and Kohn said that four hijackings of uranium shipments were staged in France, Britain and Germany by Israeli commandos in the 1968–69 period, after suspicion fell on Shapiro and supplies from NUMEC dried up. The reporters gave as their sources a Pentagon consultant and a former official of the National Security Agency, and said confirmation had come from CIA, White House and other sources.

One of the "hijackings" referred to was the *Scheersberg A* affair. In the other cases, truck drivers in France and Britain had been disabled by tear gas and their vehicles and nuclear cargoes stolen and flown to Dimona, allegedly in connivance with corrupt French and British officials.

The most conservative estimate is that Israel has produced at least one nuclear warhead a year since 1963, when Western intelligence first detected an underground test. The Newman-Kohn revelations, of course, suggest a much higher figure. That the Jewish state should be in the forefront of this military science is hardly surprising, given the key role of refugee Jewish scientists in the Manhattan Project, which produced the American nuclear weapon of World War Two. Chaim Weizmann, Israel's first President, a scientist himself, encouraged nuclear research. Already by 1953, Israeli scientists were engaged in advanced experiments with heavy water and Negev phosphate. Israel gave the results to France, which in return allowed Israeli experts to participate in the Sahara bomb tests. In 1957, France gave Israel its first reactor and helped design the Dimona facilities.

Dimona's reactor began functioning in 1964, and Defense Intelligence Agency data imply that research work on nuclear weaponry began at once. However, some usually reliable Israeli sources believe the separation plant for producing the sort of fissionable material needed for a weapons-level explosion was only built in 1967, following the Israeli invasion of Egypt. Until then, these sources say, Israel concentrated on theory—notably on how to foreshorten the time needed to produce nuclear weapons.

The Dimona nukes have already claimed 109 lives, not counting any accidents that may have occurred at the plant itself: The unarmed Libyan airliner shot down by Israeli Phantoms in 1973, after accidentally straying past Cairo in sandstorm conditions, was apparently attacked because it was accidentally approaching—albeit still from a considerable distance—Dimona airspace; 108 of the 113 aboard, including the French captain, perished. In 1967, an Israeli Mirage strayed into the area and was shot down by "friendly" surface-to-air missiles.

The NUMEC case drew attention to the problem of safeguards. The House energy subcommittee concerned with this issue, under the chairmanship of Democrat John Dingell of Michigan, was told in 1977 by Robert W. Fri, then acting administrator of the Energy Resources and Development Agency, that a further 16 tons of weapons-grade uranium was missing from warhead plants at Oak Ridge, Tennessee, and Portsmouth, Ohio—in addition to "about 80 pounds" of the material "bound up" in the pipes at both installations after twenty years of operations. Later, retired Air Force general Alfred Starbird quoted Theodore Shackley, former CIA deputy director for "intelligence collection tasking," as saying that samples of highly enriched uranium procured from Israel bore the chemical "signature" of material "lost" from Portsmouth.

The South African Bomb

Fortunately, atomic security is an area where the two superpowers have collaborated constructively. The usefulness of U.S.-Soviet cooperation in nuclear control was stressed once again in mid-1977 by the confirmation of the existence of a South African nuclear weapon.

With mostly American fuel and mostly French and American technical assistance, South Africa had been developing nuclear power which will make it less dependent on world oil supplies—and thereby, ironically, diminish European and American political leverage on Pretoria. By 1977, with Israeli technical assistance, it had produced at least one (possibly then unassembled) nuclear bomb at a secret site in the Kalahari Desert. It was prevented by U.S. and French pressure—and to some extent by the outrage expressed by nations all over the world—from testing the bomb that year, but was presumed to be going ahead with production of warhead elements, and simulating tests by computer.

The United States supplied both enriched uranium and scientists for the pilot nuclear plant at Valindaba, near Pretoria: This produces fuel of weapons grade. The smaller, research reactor at nearby Pelindaba is also American-designed, and resembles the one at Oak Ridge, Tennessee. Like Valindaba, it is fueled by enriched uranium from the United States. Two French-supplied, 922-megawatt nuclear generators now being installed at Koeberg, in Cape Province, will produce fuel which the United States has contracted to enrich for three years, from 1981 through 1984—after which Koeberg's own enrichment facility should be functioning.

An unabashedly fascist state, governed by zealots, some of whom were jailed for their Nazi beliefs in the thirties, and who are convinced that the Afrikaners are a "chosen people," South Africa has three nuclear objectives: to create a $500 million-a-year enriched-uranium export industry; to be independent in energy needs; and to have a nuclear-weapons capacity, either as a diplomatic or a battlefield tactic.

A uranium producer itself, with 17 per cent of the world's known uranium deposits, South Africa has earned $1.5 billion in raw uranium exports over the past quarter century. Its main customers have been Britain and the United States. It was in return for these supplies that the United States helped set up Valindaba and Pelindaba, supplying 112 pounds of weapons-grade uranium to Pelindaba in 1975 alone.

South Africa first began using nuclear science as a diplomatic weapon in 1970, when it let it be known that it had perfected a cheaper process for enriching nuclear fuel. Pretoria said it would share this knowledge in return for "better understanding" from Washington, notably at the United Nations, and for a guaranteed sugar quota in the United States. Pelindaba was actually exploiting a slight variation of the earlier-mentioned "stationary wall centrifuge" process, developed by Germany's Erwin Becker, and already known and tried in the United States. This is suitable for countries with hydroelectric resources. Germany had in fact supplied some of South Africa's uranium-enrichment equipment—in conjunction with fuel, computers and training supplied by the United States. But it was not until 1976 that the outside world got a hint of just how dangerous was the West's South African connection.

The first reports appeared in the Soviet press. Pretoria issued bland denials; but Soviet then-President Nikolai Podgorny told a public gathering in Maputo, Mozambique, that year that his government had evidence of South African preparations for nuclear-weapon production. Israeli ambassador to Pretoria Itzhak D. Unna denied that Israeli scientists were helping the South Africans; but an agreement on scientific and technical cooperation between South Africa and Israel was signed during Premier Balthazar Johannes Vorster's visit to Israel in 1976. That year, American intelligence sources confirmed that Israeli nuclear scientists were working in South Africa, and the United States finally got around to banning the export of nuclear machinery to the country.

Early in 1977, Washington *Post* correspondent Jim Hoagland reported from South Africa that the Afrikaner Republic was only two to four years away, "at the outside," from nuclear weapons manufacture, and that a crash program could reduce production time to "a matter of months." In Paris, French Premier Raymond Barre confirmed that South Africa "already has nuclear military capability."

Later that year, confirmation came from Soviet high-altitude photography. On Saturday, August 6, the acting head of the Soviet chancery in Washington, Vladilien Vasev, called at the White House with an urgent message from Leonid Brezhnev for President Carter: Soviet intelligence —presumably by satellite—had detected preparations for a nuclear explosion in the Kalahari. Brezhnev suggested that Russia and the United States cooperate to stop it. Vasev was received by William G. Hyland, the NSC duty officer that day, who speaks Russian. Hyland took notes on Vesev's summary statement, read the Brezhnev message, and promised to call Carter at once at Plains.

After Vasev left, Hyland first contacted his boss, Brzezinski, then on vacation in Maine, then called Plains, where he spoke to press secretary Jody Powell. Next he called Deputy Secretary of State Warren Christopher, who was replacing Secretary Vance, then in the Middle East; then CIA director Stansfield Turner, who at once ordered a low-orbit satellite inspection and a meeting of experts on the Monday to evaluate the results.

The infrared pictures showed a cluster of huts and other buildings around a tower, with a more solid structure some distance away. The experts agreed with the Soviet analysis—it was an atomic-explosion testing site. What the world feared most of all about nuclear-weapon proliferation—the "banana republic" scenario—was coming true.

As Vasev had announced, Brezhnev informed French President Giscard d'Estaing of the Soviet discovery on the Sunday, British Premier Jim Callaghan on the Monday, and West German Foreign Minister Hans-Dietrich Genscher the following day. On the Monday evening, also as Vasev had stated, Tass carried the story, noting that South Africa had had help from NATO countries and Israel in developing its atomic program. The United States, Britain, France and Germany agreed to make parallel efforts to head the South Africans off from the test. The Soviet Union, which has no diplomatic relations with Pretoria, would be kept informed. Propagandawise, there was little time to lose: A conference on apartheid was due to open in Lagos, Nigeria, later in the month.

In London, on August 11, Vance saw South African Foreign Minister Roelof Botha, mainly on the Rhodesian question, but did not raise the nuclear issue. He did, however, inform Callaghan and Foreign Secretary David Owen that the U.S. assessment of the Kalahari site matched that of the Russians. On August 15, Carter sent a message to Brezhnev confirming the Soviet suspicions and agreeing with him about the international consequences.

Ambassador Gerard Smith was summoned from vacation and sent to Paris with the U.S. satellite photographs. France, as the supplier of South Africa's two new reactors, agreed to threaten to cancel its nuclear contracts with Pretoria and to warn South Africa of a possible break in diplomatic relations if the test was not halted. On August 21, South African Premier Balthazar Johannes Vorster gave President Carter the assurance that there would be no nuclear test. Carter announced the whole story and its apparently successful conclusion on the twenty-third.

South Africa then claimed that no explosive test had actually been planned, but White House officials told reporters candidly that this was a lie; some CIA officials, however, hypothesized that the tower and its surrounding huts might have been an elaborate bluff. Abandoning nuclear-explosive tests did not of course prevent South Africa continuing with research and development, and a bomb could always be assembled at short notice without a test.

In October, Vorster said on the American television program "Issues and Answers" that he had given no undertakings to the United States. The State Department said Vorster was dissembling, and that "formal assurances" had been given. The United States suspended nuclear-fuel supplies to South Africa and threatened a total ban. America backed the United Nations arms embargo on South Africa, voted later that year, adding "gray area" items (civil exports with possible military uses) to its own embargo list. In December, Washington said it would not supply further nuclear fuel to Pretoria until South Africa signed NPT and accepted international safeguards and inspection. Only in May 1978 was the Kalahari facility finally dismantled, and a few weeks later South Africa agreed to sign NPT. Washington released a blocked shipment of 57 pounds of weapons-grade uranium for Pelindaba and a supply of slightly enriched uranium hexafluoride. But less than two years later—September 22, 1979—U.S. and foreign monitoring facilities picked up traces of a 3-kiloton nuclear explosion in the atmosphere south or southwest of South Africa. Although Pretoria denied responsibility, hinting that the explosion might be Chinese, Soviet or Israeli, Washington remained strongly suspicious that the bomb test was South African. The Soviet Union does not conduct atmospheric tests.

There have been substantial delays in approving U.S. export licenses for nuclear fuel for Pakistan, Bangladesh, Malaysia, the Philippines, China, Bolivia, Mexico, Yugoslavia, Iran and of course India and Taiwan.

Observers thought the search for security, however illusory, by smaller nations would make the spread of nuclear weaponry almost inevitable, whatever the superpowers wanted. Law professor John Gorham Palfrey of Columbia University told a group of Woodrow Wilson Scholars at the Smithsonian: "Absolute security for one nation means absolute insecurity for all the others . . . So the Third World wants the Bomb."

The 1978 military-aid bill passed by Congress forbade sales of nuclear fuel or technology to any country, other than France, which has not signed NPT. South African ratification of NPT would satisfy this clause, but Israel is now banned from U.S. supplies. The special 1978 UN session on "disarmament" discussed such restrictions by nuclear-fuel-producing countries. By 1978, Carter, as noted, was theoretically still interested in a five-year comprehensive nuclear test ban, if verification could be assured. The Union of Concerned Scientists wrote the President urging him to persevere in this effort.

But how secure is "security" in the already nuclear-weaponed countries? In the light of the Apollo and Portsmouth cases, how good is security in the United States? In 1978, Cox Newspapers reporter Joseph Albright, posing as a bidder on nuclear-systems construction contracts, visited two Air Force nuclear-weapons depots and discovered all sorts of missing safeguards. As "credentials," all Albright produced were a D.C. driver's license, a credit card and a yellow hard hat. At only one of the depots was his briefcase opened. He legally purchased, for $5.30, fifty-three government plans showing the layout of the weapons compounds, the alert areas where B-52s are loaded for nuclear missions, and the existing security systems, along with three hundred pages of technical specifications for the contracts.

"One blueprint disclosed a method of knocking out the alarm system," Albright wrote. "Another diagram showed two unguarded gates through the innermost security fence." A Pentagon spokesman said his report was useful.

But not useful enough, apparently. A few weeks later, despite having published his story and revealed that he was not a genuine contractor, Albright received seventeen revised blueprints through the mail, including a new wiring chart for the solenoid locking system for the B-52 alert area.

The reporter also obtained an unclassified Pentagon order dated December 20, 1972, that listed unpopulated areas of the world where nuclear weapons could be jettisoned. He revealed that the Pentagon still stored about ten thousand obsolescent nuclear weapons without PAL—the Permissive Action Link which requires knowledge of a six-figure code to detonate a nuclear device. He said funds were still awaited for a self-destruct feature for nuclear warheads, which could be remotely operated if these were seized.

In February 1979, David L. Dale, a temporary worker for a General Electric subcontractor, was arrested in Wilmington, North Carolina, and charged with stealing 150 pounds of "brown powder" containing 3 per cent by weight of U-235 and demanding $100,000 for its return. The FBI said that Dale had threatened, if not paid, to mail some of the powder to President Carter, newspaper editors, congressional leaders and public-advocacy figures like Ralph Nader, and to disperse some of it through various large American cities.

II

Money

Undershaft: What on earth is the true faith
of an Armorer? To give arms to all men
who offer an honest price for them, without respect of persons or principles: to
aristocrat and republican, to Nihilist
and Tsar, to Capitalist and Socialist, to
Protestant and Catholic, to burglar and
policeman, to black man, white man and
yellow man, to all sorts and conditions,
all nationalities, all faiths, all follies, all
causes and all crimes.

GEORGE BERNARD SHAW
Major Barbara

4

The Doomsday Dollar

WEAPONS, LIKE TIME, are money, and nothing has been so good for the industry as the vulgarization of warfare.

Time was when it was an exclusive pastime: The historic battlefield of Marathon pitted about 5,000 Greeks against a like number of Medes and Persians. At the height of his power, Alexander the Great never commanded more than 40,000 men in his bid to "conquer the world." In 1066, the victory of 7,000 Norsemen at Hastings over 4,000 fellow foreigners from Saxony opened Britain to the "Norman" conquest. About 82,000 men met at the decisive Battle of Crécy, between England and France, in 1346. Cromwell's New Model Army—Britain's first junta—numbered only 20,000. At Yorktown, 9,000 Americans and 7,000 Frenchmen defeated 7,000 British soldiers under Cornwallis. Only 16,000 Americans fought at Bunker Hill. The first United States standing army was composed of 80 men.

By the early 1800s, the French Revolution had created great coalition armies against France: In response, Napoleon was soon marching six-figure armies across Europe. By 1870, almost 1 million Prussians invaded France. In World War One, approximately 66 million men fought on all sides.

Wars had always broken budgets, but the budgets were relatively modest. By the nineteenth century, conflict had become astronomically expensive. Not only were armies larger, requiring more weapons, but weapons themselves became deadlier, and costlier to produce. Americans saw only about five months of warfare in World War One, but Congress appropriated over $12 billion for the conflict—about half of all the moneys appropriated during the preceding 141 years of independence, including the costs of the Civil War. The United States actually ended up spending or lending more than twice the $12 billion figure. Putting more printed money into circulation in 1918 gave America its first serious dose of inflation.

But the arms industry had come to stay. That industry and Hollywood were almost the only ones to sail through the Depression years virtually unaffected. Nor did the war industry help only arms manufacturers. Putting shoes on 2 million men and women in uniform, in World War Two, required the skins of 4,462,500 steers for soles and 3,750,000 cows for uppers. Even cowboys prospered.

An organized trade in arms and munitions in the Western world dates from the Middle Ages, when gunpowder—mostly Moroccan saltpeter—was first imported into Europe, thus gradually rendering the artisanal crossbow out-of-date. Initially, firearms were custom-made. Since the profession of bearing arms was usually regarded as an honorable one, it was hard to deny such a status to the manufacturers of weapons, and many distinguished persons were attracted to the craft. Michelangelo was the engineer in chief of the fortifications of Florence. Leonardo da Vinci designed all sorts of weapons. In England, there had been a Master of the King's Ordnance since 1414, with an office in the Tower of London: Other great European centers of the arms trade were Belgium, Spain, Italy and some cities in central Europe. The industry grew up around coal and iron deposits, near rivers deep enough for heavy transport.

In the United States, the arms industry was started with French finance, when the gunpowder firm of E. I. du Pont de Nemours was founded in 1902. Irénée du Pont was a personal friend of Jefferson's, and his business expanded greatly during the War of 1812.

Earlier, in 1797, Robert Fulton had founded the Fulton Nautilus Company to sell his invention—the first submarine, which predated the first steamboat. It submerged by taking on water, and surfaced by pumping it out. In Paris, the Directoire expressed interest, but finally the French Navy proved too conservative. Fulton also met with a rebuff in England.

By 1914, the arms industries were more widely spread. A significant industry had developed in Switzerland, which sold to all sides during the first world conflict, marking crates with false titles and shipping matériel over the frontiers by devious routes.

By this century, arms had become not only good business but also good politics. The politico-military-industrial complex had been born. Arms merchants controlled newspapers and used them to drum up business. In France, Schneider of the Le Creusot arms fortune owned *Le Journal des Débats,* which carried the message of the "menace of Germany" and the "danger of disarmament." Arms merchants even sold weapons to their country's enemies to improve the chances of greater domestic sales. In 1933, a British aircraft company accepted an order for sixty aircraft from the new Hitler regime in Germany, and would have fulfilled it if the Air Ministry had not intervened. Earlier, after World

War One, Vickers had paid royalties to Krupp of Germany for having used Krupp-patented fuses in British grenades and shells during the conflict.

In a 1934 study, *Merchants of Death,* H. C. Engelbrecht and F. C. Hanighen said that "it is well to acknowledge that the arms industry did not create the war system. On the contrary, the war system created the arms industry." But many were not so sure, for the weapons industry had acquired a niche of its own in the economies of major nations. Engelbrecht and Hanighen also noted that "the world at present apparently wants both the war system and peace; it believes that 'national safety' lies in preparedness, and it denounces the arms industry."

Krupp

The most legendary arms industry of all time was indubitably that of Krupp in Germany. The Kruppwerk was a four-centuries-long dynasty—a firm that remained in the same family until Bertha Krupp's marriage at the turn of this century to a diplomat, Gustav von Bohlen und Halbach, who was given the name Krupp by Kaiser Wilhelm to preserve dynastic appearances. The last in the link was Alfried—who was condemned at Nuremberg to jail and confiscation of his property for his use of slave labor during World War Two. But Alfried was pardoned by High Commissioner John McCloy in 1950, after the outbreak of the Korean War, and re-established his empire for a while.

Krupp's traces back to Arndt Krupp, a late-sixteenth-century artisan of substance. Although arms—especially swords—were produced at the Kruppwerk from time to time, until the mid-nineteenth century the factory's main output was, of all things, spoons. It was then that the works were inherited by Alfred Krupp (who had anglicized the spelling of his first name while studying in England).

Alfred was the sickly son of an unsuccessful father, and the enterprise was in danger of going under when he took over. But he had been fascinated by Leonardo da Vinci's plans for a breech-loading cannon—plans never realized because the metallurgy of da Vinci's day was inadequate. Alfred financed the research and development of cannons from the enormous profits he made by selling steel railroad ties to American railroads, then in full expansion.

At that time, virtually only bronze cannons existed, but Alfred's confidence was in steel. However, the crowned and helmeted heads of Europe proved to be skittish about putting their trust in arms of steel, and slow in paying for the few they bought. Alfred's first satisfied and satisfying customer was the Khedive of Egypt, who settled his bills on time. But finally a sort of politico-military alliance developed between the Kruppwerk and Kaiser Wilhelm von Hohenzollern; Krupp became the armorer of Prussia. The apogee of Alfred's rise to eminence was the Franco-Prussian War of 1870–71, when Germans avenged themselves for countless French invasions over the centuries, and asserted Prussia as a nation to be reckoned with. But except during the war itself, Alfred continued to sell more steel to the Tsar in St. Petersburg than to his own government in Potsdam.

The war of 1870 was a modern one in more ways than the new material it used for cannons. It was a conflict noted for ingenuity. Besieged French leaders escaped from Paris by balloon, floating over the heads of the enemy—who occasionally brought balloons down by lobbing hand grenades into their gondolas as they passed by. Another aspect of the "air war" was the use by the French of carrier pigeons—and by the Germans of hawks to down them.

Krupp emerged from the war a richer and also a tougher man. The once sickly spoonmaker had become self-confident. Engelbrecht and Hanighen say of him: "Krupp had now learned a technique. When he wanted something from the government, he must speak of his patriotism and include a veiled threat that he might sell his guns to other nations." He made his armor plate—then easily the best in the world—available to all countries, either through purchase or through local manufacture at a royalty of $45 a ton.

Alfred Nobel's invention of smokeless powder in the nineties cleared battlefields of their normal fog, making accurate fire more possible. Krupp developed cannons with long, graceful bores which could take advantage of the situation, after Nobel had sold his powder formula to the gunmaker. Later, Rudolf Diesel brought Gustav the plans of his oil-burning engine.

Krupp was an inventor himself. His KPz—Krupp patent fuse—was the one used on both sides during World War One, and for which Britain later paid him a substantial part of the seven and a half cents per fuse to which the Kruppwerk was entitled by contract. But naturally most of his arms genius went to his own country during that war, and historians have suggested that without U.S. intervention—officially in 1917, although it was 1918 before American troops entered combat—Krupp would have won the war for Berlin.

Essen, the home of the Kruppwerk, was occupied by French troops after 1918. It was a vengeful, often unimaginative occupation, and friction in the city reached tinder proportions when a French platoon shot down some unarmed Krupp workers at a meeting. Gustav Krupp von Bohlen could easily have become unpopular himself, since he was obliged to collaborate with the occupation authorities; but fortunately for him he was held responsible for the alleged riotous actions of his employees and sentenced to fifteen years imprisonment by a French court. He handled himself well at his trial and became an instant hero. As the German economy collapsed and inflation became rampant, he was not there to be pointed out as a comfortable capitalist. After a few years, he emerged from prison, his reputation intact, and began finding work for his employees by investing in the infant Soviet Union. The Kruppwerk was forbidden to produce arms, but secretly did so anyway, providing weapons for the nascent National Socialist party. Krupp also acquired three newspapers, the *Rheinisch-Westfälische Zeitung*, the *Tägliche Rundschau* of Berlin and the *Neuests Nachrichten*.

Gustav threw in his lot totally with Hitler, winning all sorts of Nazi decorations. By 1939, having worked himself into old age by the time he was sixty-nine, he handed over de facto control of the Kruppwerk to his son Alfried, then in his twenties, and later passed over power to him completely. Came the war. Although Alfried later argued at his trial that he had had no choice but to use the labor of concentration-camp victims, there was evidence that he did so willingly: He had even established a factory next to the Auschwitz camp to use its inmates.

Released from imprisonment in 1950, Alfried built up a huge conglomerate based on steel, selling particularly heavily to the Third World. At his palatial home, the Villa Hugel, he received distinguished foreign guests, including the Emperor Haile Selassie of Ethiopia and President Modibo Keita of Mali. His father Gustav, who had been too paralyzed to stand trial in the forties, finally died in 1950, the year of Alfried's release; but his widow Bertha, who had given her name to the biggest cannon in World War One, lived on in *grande dame* style for a few more years.

According to William Manchester, the biographer of the Krupps, Alfried was for a while the richest man in the European Common Market. But he overextended his firm, and his life was unhappy: He had two marriages, both of which failed, and a playboy son who it was clear would never be able to take over the huge enterprise. Affairs were left in the hands of a free-spending general manager. With the four-centuries-old firm threatened with bankruptcy, Krupp—who like all his forebears had been the "sole owner"—handed it over to a limited stock corporation. He died in 1968, at the age of fifty-five.

American Armorers

America's first great arms fortune had a different story and enjoys a prosperous present, although the firm makes no weapons now. Éleuthère Irénée du Pont emigrated to America around 1800, a modestly wealthy, young, radical intellectual. He discovered that gunpowder was more expensive in the United States than in Europe, and of poorer quality. Irénée had done chemistry at Essonne, and one of his father's closest friends had been Lavoisier, who as well as being the greatest French scientist of his day was also supervisor of gunpowder manufacture for the French Government. Lavoisier had helped Irénée with his studies.

Since England was then the world's main exporter of gunpowder, Napoleon supplied investment capital for the du Pont enterprise in the United States. French Government draftsmen made the plans for the plant at Wilmington, Delaware, and government arsenals manufactured the machinery. Operations began in 1802, under the trade name of Du Pont de Nemours Père et Fils et Cie. Later the name was anglicized to E. I. du Pont de Nemours and Company.

Through his father's circle of moderate revolutionaries, who had favored the overthrow of the monarchy but had opposed the execution of Louis XVI, the young man had come to know many intellectuals in America, including Thomas Jefferson, who encouraged the Wilmington project. Correspondence between the two men still exists, including a complaining letter written in 1809 by the Frenchman: "Although Secretary Dearborn said du Pont powder was the best, orders so far have amounted to only $30,000." But in the second war with Britain, in 1812, du Pont virtually cornered the market.

The plant burned down, was rebuilt and soon expanded. Du Pont sold powder both to Spain and to South American colonies striving to break with Spain; but he refused to sell to South Carolina secessionists, although they wanted a massive 125,000 pounds of powder and offered $24,000 in cash. He opposed the U.S. decision to go to war with Mexico, seeing it as a thinly disguised plan to increase the number of slave states; but when the opportunity occurred in 1846 to sell powder to Mexico—with the order disguised as being for Cuba—he refused. When the Crimean War broke out in 1854, however, du Pont supplied powder both to Britain and its allies Turkey and France, and to their enemy, Russia. By then, according to Engelbrecht and Hanighen, "several hundred descendants of French Revolutionary soldiers served as employees, like serfs for a medieval baronial family, and the president had his office in a mere shack on the grounds." He refused to use the railroad, and rode to town on a mule.

In the Civil War, he supplied the Union, creating a relationship with Washington similar to Krupp's with Potsdam a few years later. In 1873, the company perfected hexagonal powder, and exported 2,000 pounds of it to Britain. The firm had by then passed to Irénée's son, who went, at the request of the U. S. Government, to Belgium and Germany to learn the secret of the new brown, prismatic, smokeless powder.

When the government, in 1899, set up its own gunpowder plant in Dover, Delaware, with a congressional appropriation of $167,000, the Du Pont company gave government officials access to its own facilities and helped with the blueprints of the new factory.

But du Pont and other powder manufacturers were not simply philanthropic patriots. Theirs was an industry which had to expand in time of war, then undergo grave conversion problems afterward, especially if peace broke out suddenly. In 1872, the seven largest powder companies had formed the Gunpowder Trade Association of the United States with the express object of rigging the market, underselling the independents initially, in order to bankrupt them or take them over. In 1897, European and American manufacturers agreed to cartelize the world market. Neither group would establish plants in the territories of the other. If a government sought bids from foreign powdermakers, these should first ascertain the prices charged by domestic plants and refrain from underbidding them. The American firms were to have, beside the United States, control of the markets in Canada, Central America, Colombia and Venezuela. Most of the rest of the world "belonged" to the European manufacturers, with a few countries listed as being of "free access."

Du Pont went from strength to strength. Between 1903 and 1907, the firm bought up over a hundred competitors, closing down sixty-four of them. By 1905, Du Pont had a monopoly on all government orders and was able to establish "national" prices. But the Congress had passed the Sherman Antitrust Act in 1890, and in 1907 the government brought suit against du Pont de Nemours. By then, it was impossible to restore the *status quo ante* because Du Pont had closed so many former competitors and broken others up; but an upshot of the case was that two independent firms were established to compete with Du Pont.

In World War One, Du Pont supplied 40 per cent of all the powder used by the Allies. Since then, Du Pont has diversified into many chemical fields and is no longer principally known as a gunpowder company.

Throughout the nineteenth century, United States arms manufacturers, as such, concentrated on small arms. The famous three musketeers were Colt, Winchester and Remington, whose hunting guns were a sensation at the World's Fair in London in 1851. For two decades, the governments of Britain, Russia, Prussia, Spain, Turkey, Sweden, Egypt and Denmark bought their machinery for the manufacture of small arms in America. As the century wore on, competition developed, but American machinery still went into new plants in Japan and Latin America.

Eli Whitney, the inventor of the cotton gin, had proposed making guns with interchangeable parts. The U. S. Army had scoffed, but the idea had eventually won acceptance. Whitney's muskets were used in the War of 1812. Samuel Colt mass-produced them. Colt also produced a torpedo, but failed to impress the Navy, and he patented the first American percussion-cap revolver in 1835. He set up a $250,000 plant at Paterson, New Jersey, to make the revolvers, offering them to the government for $25 apiece. But a committee of Army officers decided unanimously that revolvers were "unsuited" to military use. By 1842, with Colts selling for $200 apiece to Texas Rangers who needed a weapon that could be fired from the saddle, the company went bankrupt. But General Zachary Taylor had been impressed, and asked the War Department to order Colts; the Department called for a thousand at $24 each. Colt started up again, building a plant in Connecticut.

This time, he became wealthy. Like Du Pont, he sold to both sides in the Crimean War. His Connecticut mansion, Armsmear, was soon filled with eye-catching gifts from the Tsar of Russia, the Sultan of Turkey and the King of Siam, as well as from equally famous if less establishment figures like Garibaldi and Louis Kossuth. The Civil War helped, by "proving" weapons, to sell Colts, Winchesters and Remingtons to Europe, Turkey, Egypt, Japan and Latin America.

The Winchester rifle won fame when it was used to effect by Don Benito Juárez's rebels against the Emperor Maximilian in Mexico in the 1860s. The Winchester Repeating Arms Company was run by "Colonel" Tom Addis, who welcomed the Mexican sale but was doubtful if the rebels would pay; he decided to carry the guns to Juárez himself and insist on cash on delivery. He took a thousand rifles and half a million rounds of ammunition to Brownsville, Texas, on the Mexican border, and waited for one of Juárez' people to arrive with the money. Two months went by, then Juárez ordered the munitions brought to Monterrey. Addis decided to take the risk.

He made the 240-mile journey by oxcart, and on arrival he put the weapons in storage, with an American flag flying over a makeshift warehouse. Juárez kept asking for the guns, but there was still no sign of money. Addis waited on, in the heat and flies, for four months. Then Maximilian heard about the cache—presumably thanks to a discreet indiscretion by Addis—and offered ready cash for the Winchesters. Addis passed the news of this offer to the guerrillero leader, and said if he did not receive money at once he would accept the emperor's bid. "Almost immediately," he notes in his memoirs, "keg after keg of silver coin arrived." He handed over the arms to Juárez' envoys.

The problem of returning safely to the United States still remained. Addis had little doubt that Juárez' army would be lying in wait to relieve him of the small fortune. The dealer loaded the coin in a stagecoach and set off. Once outside the town, he leapt on the Mexican driver and tied him up, with the luckless man's bound hands attached to a noose around his neck which tightened if he tried to break loose. Then Addis left the main trail for Brownsville and made his way home by back paths. Nine months after leaving the Winchester factory, he finally reached U.S. soil with his silver.

Another famous American gun fortune was that of Eliphalet Remington. This enterprise really began in 1816, when Eli, then in his teens, was refused a gun by his father. The teenager went to work and made his own, taking it to a neighboring town to have it rifled. The artisan admired the boy's handiwork and soon many citizens had heard of it. Eli was asked to make guns for the customs trade.

Two years later, in 1818, business began to flourish with the outbreak of the Mexican War, and from then on he never looked back. He finally collapsed and died from overwork during the Civil War.

The firm continued. In 1867 came its biggest peacetime order—12,000 rifles for the U. S. Navy. Then Spain ordered 85,000. The next year, Sweden purchased 30,000, the Khedive of Egypt 50,000. More huge orders followed—145,000 for France, 130,000 more for Spain, another 55,000 for Egypt, 89,000 for Cuba. Even the New York State police ordered 21,000. In 1868 and 1869, Remington exported 616,000 rifles. But the biggest nineteenth-century order for Remingtons got away: The staid company refused to pay bakshish for a 400,000-gun order from the Sultan of Turkey, and the contract was placed elsewhere.

Remington diversified into typewriters, sewing machines and farm implements, but in the nineteenth century guns were still the firm's main item. The Chinese War Minister Li Hung-chang ordered Remingtons for his army—then defending itself from a French colonial bid—after Remington's man, dressed in Chinese clothes, managed to reach Peking, the "forbidden city," with a Remington catalogue specially printed in Chinese. At the time, the French Army had not yet adopted the repeating rifle, and Li's forces drove out the invaders.

When Russia invaded Turkey's Balkan provinces in 1879, both sides had Remingtons, and the Turkish order for 210 million rounds of ammunition was, at the time, the largest ever placed in the United States. Both Russia and Turkey sent inspectors to the Bridgeport factory to appraise each shipment for quality, and the company's history notes that the two enemy officers "treated each other with formal courtesy."

Just how gentlemanly the officer class could be in those days was shown after the Turkish order had been finished. Cuba, then at war with Spain, had bought a large stock of Remingtons; the Spanish, seeing how deadly accurate they were, ordered Remingtons also. But the firm was still busily fulfilling the Russian order. However, Remington executives reasoned that it would be unfair for them to keep Spain waiting when the Cuban order had already been fulfilled. They talked it over with the Tsar's man, General Gorloff, who agreed to reject a shipment for St. Petersburg as "faulty" so that the company could sell it to Spain instead.

Engelbrecht and Hanighen note that "in one case . . . Colombia and Venezuela were at war with each other while a separate insurrection was proceeding in each country; all four of the warring bodies . . . used Remington rifles and ammunition."

During the Franco-Prussian War of 1870–71, France had made Remington's their arms-purchasing agent in the United States, starting with the purchase of 37,000 U. S. Army surplus Springfields. But there were only 3 million rounds of surplus ammunition, so the U. S. Government obligingly agreed to have 14 million more rounds of new ammunition made and declared "surplus." (Under the neutrality doctrine imposed by Congress, the government could not sell new weapons to a belligerent.) Later, 10,000 more Springfields under manufacture for the U. S. Navy were declared "defective" so that they could be sold to France. German Americans protested at the subterfuge, and a Senate committee, including their spokesman Carl Schurz, held hearings but exonerated Remington's. Schurz angrily denounced both the firm and the committee on the Senate floor. Meanwhile, during the siege of Paris, a balloon sailed out of the city and over the German lines one night, with two anxious men aboard. One, Gambetta, was out to rally the country to continue resistance, even if Paris fell. His companion, W. W. Reynolds, was Remington's agent, getting the latest order out. Du Pont acquired Remington's in 1933.

Some weapons labeled defective really were just that. In 1893, the Navy rejected some naval armor made by Carnegie, Phipps. When it was "replaced," Navy inspectors discovered that they had been sent the same plates, which had been reannealed and tempered secretly at night. The government rejected the armor and assessed a fine of 15 per cent of the bill. No word of this reached the press at the time; but rather than pay $288,000, Andrew Carnegie stalked into the White House and had a long chat with President Cleveland. Not only was the fine reduced to 10 per cent, but the total on which it was to be assessed was lowered. The cadaverous little Scot finally only paid $140,484.94. Eventually, the story leaked, and Carnegie was "condemned" in a congressional report.

Other successful firms included Bethlehem Steel, which printed catalogues in English, French and Spanish, and sold heavy guns and armor to Russia, Greece, Italy, Belgium, France, Argentina, Chile, Cuba and Guatemala, as well as to the U. S. Navy.

As the arms trade prospered in the nineteenth century, so did that of the arms dealer. The first major practitioner of the art in the United States was the firm of Francis Bannerman and Sons, founded in 1865. The company's founder traded in used weapons only, and got his start with the end of the Civil War. Bannerman kept his arsenal in a fake Scottish castle on the Hudson near West Point. Like Sam Cummings today, he bought huge "job lots" and cornered the market. His clientele was eclectic: He sold arms to governments and individuals, antique weapons to museums and collectors, uniforms to theatrical costumiers.

His catalogue listed a cannon that could be mounted on a camel's back. He claimed to have converted a passenger ship into a warship in a single week, for a "South American government." When 20,220 Mausers were captured in the Cuban War by Teddy Roosevelt's Rough Riders, Bannerman bought 18,200 of them at an auction, later selling them to the Panamanians for their T.R.-supported revolution against Colombia.

With the superb gall of his calling, Bannerman's catalogue noted: "The Good Book says that in the millennium days, swords shall be turned into plowshares and spears into pruning hooks. We are helping to hasten the glad time by selling cannon balls to heal the sick."

Earlier, John Pierpont Morgan had made money selling used arms *during* the Civil War. A few years previously, the Army had condemned a large quantity of Hall carbines, and Morgan had purchased 5,000 of them at $3.00 apiece. When war began, he offered them at $22 each to General Frémont at St. Louis, for a profit of $95,000. Many soldiers lost their thumbs firing them, and the government refused to pay. Morgan sued, and was offered $13.31 per carbine, but he persisted and won a full settlement.

Perhaps the most internationally known arms name to emerge from the United States in the last century was that of Hiram Maxim, whose machine gun outstripped all competitors. Maxim became a British subject and was knighted for his invention. His brother Hudson Maxim improved on Nobel's smokeless powder with a concoction of his own, while Hiram's son, Hiram Percy Maxim, became the inventor of the silencer.

Sir Hiram's own inventions were legion. He devised the hair curling iron, riveting machines, headlights for locomotives, fire extinguishers. He made a better gaslight, and when this became out-of-date he made a better electric bulb. He introduced improvements for aircraft. But weapons were really where he made his name, and he went on developing better machine guns and more effective cartridges all his life. An agnostic in an age when this was thought to be unseemly, he would state his religion as "Protestant," mumbling to his staff that he did so because "I protest against the whole damn idea of religion."

Several machine guns existed before Maxim came along, notably the Gardner gun, the Gatling gun and the Nordenfelt weapon. All used a crank to wind the ammunition into the firing chamber. If the gunner became nervous under fire and turned the crank too quickly, the gun would jam. It was in 1884 that Maxim perfected a gun in which the cartridge belt was moved by each successive recoil. The Maxim fired an astonishing 666 bullets a minute. He patented it in Britain, giving displays of the weapon for royalty and government. The Prince of Wales—the future Edward VII—tried his hand at the trigger. Maxim also gave demonstrations in his native country, but American generals declined to buy.

Later, the British were about to pay Krupp 35,000 pounds for the formula for his slow-burning "cocoa powder," which was adjudged safer to use than ordinary gunpowder. The crafty Maxim took the Krupp sample back to his laboratory, successfully analyzed it and informed the British Government that they could turn Krupp's offer for patent rights down. Maxim could make the powder himself.

Although his first loyalty was to his adopted country, Britain, Maxim sold to most of Britain's enemies or potential enemies—the Germans, the Russians, the Chinese. In the Boer War, Maxim sold both to his own government and to the Boers, who gave the Maxim gun a name which later became its nickname in the British Army also—the Pom Pom Gun.

Maxim traveled across Europe, giving successful trials in Versailles, in Switzerland and in Italy. While in Spezia, Maxim met the Russian consul to that city, Nicolas de Kabath, who soon began moonlighting as the local agent for the gun. Among European nations, only in Germany were there hesitations about buying, but the Prince of Wales persuaded his cousin the Kaiser to change his mind and buy. St. Petersburg purchased Maxims in time for the war with Japan—but not enough of them to win. The Tsar, however, was sufficiently impressed with the weapon to invite Maxim to the Winter Palace to be decorated.

When Li Hung-chang arrived in London from Peking, his first words were reputed to be: "I wish to see Hiram Maxim." The manufacturer put on a demonstration for the Chinese minister at Eynsford.

"How much does it cost to fire this gun?" Li asked afterward.

"One hundred and thirty pounds a minute," said Maxim.

"This gun fires too fast for China," said Li sadly.

The Danish King also remarked that the Maxim gun "would bankrupt my little country in about two hours."

But most military establishments bought happily, and worried about the bills later. Poor countries like Turkey and Portugal were avid buyers, and the Sultan, in Istanbul, presented Maxim with a decoration and a beautiful concubine. In Spain, Maxim set up a plant to build the gun locally.

The Maxim gun played a signal role in Britain's Victorian drive for empire, carving a barbarous swath through the unwashed of two continents. Churchill recounted its use at his first battle—Omdurman, in the Sudan. But perhaps the most famous anecdote associated with the Maxim gun was the "Vienna story." This will be recounted in the next chapter, since it tells more about Maxim's future colleague, Basil Zaharoff—the most famous arms trader of all time—than about Maxim or his gun themselves.

The Twentieth Century

Stories of Zaharoff's wiles brought public attention to the incredible corruption of the trade in arms. The British press, less "controlled" than that of France, recounted how the Coventry Ordnance Company had secured orders to build eight naval cruisers in 1909 by publishing false figures about the size of the German Navy. Bribes, shakedowns and kickbacks were the stock-in-trade of the death industry. Even the sober Japanese were not immune: When Rear Admiral Fujii of Japan came to Britain in 1910, he collected bribes from—or shook down—all the companies with which he placed orders, including famous names like Vickers and the Barrow shipyards.

But it was not until the thirties that politicians were pushed into making serious investigations of some of the fortunes on which they often depended for campaign funds. The U. S. Senate's investigation by the famous Nye Committee lasted from 1935 until the following year. In 1936, a Royal Commission on the Private Manufacture of and Trading in Arms heard witnesses in London. Both committees discovered massive evidence of bribery, collusive bidding, profiteering, violations of arms embargoes, illegal financial transactions, the production of shoddy equipment which cost the lives of the purchasing country's own soldiers and those of their allies, sales to the enemy, and sabotage of competing products. They also found that the ineffable gall of a Zaharoff was not unique. Retired Admiral Sir Reginald Bacon told the Royal Commission that it had been a good thing that British troops at Gallipoli had been fired at with British ammunition, because British ammunition was inferior to German bullets.

Inferior or superior, the "Great War" brought equally great refinements to armaments and encouraged deathly inventiveness. It was a testing ground for new ideas in weaponry, opening up new markets. The tank, an American and French invention, was first used by the British. The war had virtually given the world aviation—until then, an experimental toy—and the submarine. A French firm, and Vickers in Britain, even produced submarine aircraft carriers. The single seaplane, with folding pairs of wings, was concealed inside the conning tower—the projection which in modern submarines is called the sail. It was catapulted into the air.

Part of the growth—and invulnerability to reform—of the arms industry stemmed from the role of major banks, and ownership of media by arms corporations. Engelbrecht and Hanighen noted in 1934 that Du Pont then owned all the dailies in Delaware. Morgan owned magazines and part of Crowell Publishing. Krupp owned three major German dailies and had a piece of the burgeoning German film industry. His fellow German arms tycoon Hugo Stinnes owned or controlled nineteen newspapers in Germany, Austria, Hungary and Norway. The French press was notoriously buyable.

Military attachés were already, in the thirties, salesmen for their countries' arms manufacturers, and the links between government and the industry were already apparent. The Kaiser had been a stockholder in two large German arms concerns, including Krupp. In Britain, ministers and parliamentarians in both houses of Parliament had substantial arms holdings. Vickers shareholders even included the bishops of Adelaide, Chester and Hexham and Dean Inge of St. Paul's. Leading politicians like Neville Chamberlain and Sir John Simon later had substantial stock in Imperial Chemical Industries, which produced poison gas.

When the armistice was signed, there were 21,000 new American millionaires. Du Pont stock had gone from $20 to $1,000. J. P. Morgan had made more money in America's nineteen months of war than his wealthy father had made in a lifetime. France and Britain, by 1918, were spending $10 million a day in the United States on munitions alone. Foreign demand created shortages at home and raised prices, but the United States paid off its debts and became a creditor nation for the first time, thanks to the arms trade of World War One.

The year 1916 had been America's most prosperous year since the inception of the Republic. But when Wilson had declared war in 1917, stocks had risen further. During those next nineteen months, the government poured $22.6 billion into industry and loaned $9.5 billion to its allies. Winchester sold more than 2 billion "units"—guns, bayonets, shells and 700 million cartridges. American industry produced 63 types of poison gas: 810 tons of it were manufactured *weekly* at a small plant at Edgewood, Maryland—twice Britain's or France's entire production for the whole war. The U. S. Government had appropriated an astonishing $100 million for chemical warfare and intended to expand the industry to 48,000 employees when the armistice called a halt to plans.

When the war started, experiments on improving the Springfield rifle were not complete, so the British ordered Lee-Enfields—British Enfield rifles with a bolt action designed and patented by an American, James P. Lee. Britain had purchased 700,000 by the time America entered the war. Although the Springfield was by then in production, Remington and Winchester had most of their space devoted to producing Lee-Enfields. Since there was not enough time to reconvert, American doughboys got the inferior Lee-Enfield, not the Springfield. In all, the United States produced 2 million Lee-Enfields during the four-year war.

Much of the huge fortune spent in government money was wasted. President Harding said in a letter to Congress in 1921 that the United States had expended nearly $6 billion on aircraft and artillery, but that only about two hundred American planes and a similar number of cannons had seen action. Another report said that over $1 billion had been spent on aviation alone, but that "not one American-built pursuit or combat or bombing plane reached the front." Harding admitted that less than 1 per cent of the ammunition used by American artillery had been of American manufacture. A total of $3.5 billion had been appropriated for shipping, but only one American ship had carried U.S. troops to Europe—the *Liberty,* which took fifty men in October 1917. But used or not, all these implements of war were made, at a bully profit.

Between the wars, armed forces became progressively smaller and more powerful. Surface ships became lighter, submarines bigger. It was a time for consolidation in the arms industry. Vickers had swallowed Armstrong, English Steel and Metropolitan-Cammell-Laird; it had an aviation subsidiary, and overseas subsidiaries in Canada, New Zealand, Spain and Ireland—where the Vickers plant supplied both sides in the "troubles." With Creusot, it owned subsidiaries in Romania and Poland, and had shares in Brown-Boveri of Switzerland, as well as in Termi— which supplied Mussolini—and in the Bank of Romania and Japanese Steel. Krupp partly owned Bofors, the big Swedish producer with—like Krupp—its own company town. Creusot acquired Skoda in 1920, building it up to the point where 10 per cent of all Czech exports were arms.

The Versailles Treaty forbade Germany from importing or exporting weapons; but by 1930, twenty-two countries cited Germany as their main or second source of munitions supplies. Both Krupp and Thyssen backed Hitler from the start. Only in the United States was there a brake on arms production. To evade control, the gangsters of the thirties ordered most of their famous "tommy guns" from a Belgian franchise-holder. There was no American equivalent of Vickers or Creusot. Du Pont and Bethlehem Steel had diversified. By the thirties, only 2 per cent of Du Pont products were military, although in 1933 Du Pont did acquire a majority interest in Remington Arms. Bethlehem Steel made armor and warships. At the time, U.S. arms exports totaled only $15 million annually—half of Czechoslovakia's, a third of Britain's, a quarter of France's. But the United States was also not importing much, since the local weapons industry produced 96 per cent of American arms needs.

A rare American exporter of serious military hardware was Curtiss-Hawk: Thanks to a convincing salesman—Major James H. Doolittle—the C-H plant in Buffalo sold thirty-six pursuit planes to Chiang Kai-shek. Colonel John B. Jouett led the first team of twelve pilot instructors and four mechanics to China to set up a school which graduated fifty pilots every eight months. Nanking decided to buy at least sixty C-H planes a year, and the company built a plant in Hangchow.

In Europe, there were again calls for arms nationalization. Cupidity by private manufacturers was seen as the chief obstacle to peace. But others noted that the nationalization of the industry in Japan had not prevented war. Nonproducing countries saw nationalization, and all disarmament pressures, as a restriction on their right to buy. Engelbrecht and Hanighen noted that:

> The international sale of arms has far deeper roots than the "consciousless [*sic*] greed" of the arms makers. If all private arms makers decided to discontinue their international trade tomorrow, a worldwide protest of governments would not permit them to do it. As long as war is a possibility, nations will demand arms. The world economical situation makes it difficult or impossible for most, if not all, of them to manufacture all the types of armaments which they demand. Hence it is laid down and affirmed in solemn international treaties that arms must at all times be sold freely, even in times of war.

Things have not changed all that much since then.

World War Two gave a boost to the arms industries, especially in the United States, from which they have never seriously looked back. Already by 1940, export and production figures were beginning to look like nothing which anyone had ever seen before. By the fall of France, Britain had already received 951 Douglas A-20 Boston light bombers, and during the next four years received 455 more, diverting 387 to Russia; another 2,530 went directly to the U.S.S.R. The RAF also took delivery of 340 Republic P-47 Thunderbolts and 1,800 North American P-51 Mustang long-range escort fighters. During the war, the United States produced 150,000 combat aircraft, over 2.5 million caliber-45 pistols, over 3 million Springfields, over 1.5 million tommy guns, over 6 million of the M-1, M-2 and M-3 carbines and nearly as many Garands—the 9-pound rifle which was soon to be replaced by the 5-pound M-16. America's entry into the war solved the remains of the Depression more rapidly than anything the Roosevelt brain trust could have devised.

Selling Weapons Today

Is arms business legitimate business? Are the professions of manufacturing and selling arms less honorable than the occupation of soldiering? The public image, as George Thayer noted in *The Arms Business,* is fickle: It accepts the idea of the Pentagon selling arms for the companies more readily than it accepts the idea of a GE, a Northrop, a Chrysler—or even a Remington or a Colt—selling arms directly.

In consciousness of this, companies, where possible, scatter their defense contracts across a broad spectrum of subsidiaries—although this scarcely helps either efficiency or profits. This was already evident a decade ago: GM did nearly $2.5 billion worth of work for Defense in 1969, but made no mention of this in its report to stockholders. The work included development of a potential Main Battle Tank (the MBT-70) and production of jet engines and even M-16A rifles. Thayer quoted a company spokesman as saying: "We want to be known as a car and appliance manufacturer, not as a merchant of war."

Some arms manufacturers argue that although war creates jobs, it no longer greatly increases a corporation's profitability, which comes more from "peacetime" articles with a well-calculated markup and aimed at a carefully researched market, and less from plant conversions to relatively short-term increases in arms production. Nevertheless, many smaller firms still stand to profit greatly from localized wars which drive up the demand for replacement parts for "last-generation" weaponry. There are companies that "guarantee" to supply, say, any mechanical, electrical or hydraulic part for any combat or tactical vehicle made in the United States since 1940, or any airframe, air engine or avionics replacement of American manufacture produced since World War Two. As well as merchants for the huge American war surplus that went on the market in

1945, there are plants still turning out M-1 and M-2 carbines and other World War Two-era matériel—for antiriot work, counterinsurgency and rabbit-hunting—and many of these enterprises gross annually in seven figures. In Europe and elsewhere, the war surplus of Allied, German, Italian and Japanese equipment also generated an industry which still sometimes manufactures World War Two weaponry.

The earlier-mentioned Defense Marketing Services, based in a leafy residential section of Greenwich, Connecticut, is one of the more successful of several "service industries" answering a need by helping potential arms manufacturers find purchasers. Founded in Los Angeles in 1959, DMS is an employee-owned firm which prefigures requirements—"demand analysis"—for governments all over the world, whether in tanks, planes, electronic systems or maintenance equipment. A 10-year world warship forecast, for instance, details the related missile, ordnance, propulsion and electronic items which the navies of 43 countries will probably need. About 4,500 subscribers buy one or more of the 16 $425-a-year ring-folder publications which are updated monthly or of the 12 that are updated yearly. Some of the publications are regional, while others are specialized in such areas as military aircraft, missiles and rockets, or antisubmarine warfare. In all, DMS identifies current and future requirements in military hardware for 78 countries. DMS also publishes *Deadline Data on World Affairs* for schools, libraries and small-town papers. A slim, 4-page newsletter costs $90 a year.

The president of DMS, a one-armed, bespectacled former science and aviation reporter for the New York *World-Telegram,* Richard E. Slawsky, says most of the information comes from published sources, but that the Pentagon often calls to ask if certain material is still classified. If DMS has already published it, or is about to, there is no point in restricting it.

Not that DMS is for everybody. Individuals may not subscribe and the only Communist government whose check was accepted was Yugoslavia's. Peking, for instance, was turned down. Defense contractors, organizations and friendly governments make up the bulk of readers. A research force monitors over 300 publications, but the entire staff numbers only 75. They keep a file of 25,000 defense-related code names and print an annual code-name handbook listing 10,000 active words—acronyms, project titles, model names and so on.

The principal aim is to record every contract signed for most defense-related equipment. The best-known DMS publication is probably the *World Aircraft Forecast,* which gives aerospace firms a picture of the military aviation market for each of the ten years ahead. It runs to three volumes and over one thousand pages. Some governments use the *Fore-*

cast to help plan their budgets. Many smaller organizations—some spin-offs from DMS by former employees—are more specialized.

Major producers of war equipment employ fleets of salesmen overseas; they usually draw a salary plus a sales commission of up to 5 per cent. The "average" salesman is a native of the country in which he operates—usually an ex-officer with access to decisionmakers in military purchasing. Big arms exporters, notably aircraft firms like Northrop, General Dynamics, Lockheed or Grumman, normally have Americans in charge of their permanent offices in such key locations as Riyadh, London or Tokyo. These offices frankly lobby and entertain, collect data on local defense needs and help procure credit finance for their foreign clients. The American directors of these operations are invariably former officers of general or equivalent rank, or specialized ex-officials from the departments of Defense or State. The huge sums involved have led to shakedowns and kickbacks, with often devastating results for all involved.

Perhaps the messiest case was that of a decade ago, in Japan, when Hughes Aircraft bribed a Japanese Air Force technical specialist to leak them data that would ensure that they won a helicopter supply contract. The top functionary in the Japanese Defense Agency's procurement office put his neck under the wheels of an express train to protest this unofficerly behavior by his subordinate; the general commanding the air defense staff offered to resign, and when this was not accepted he shot himself. Usually, however, tales of graft involve little more than temporary front-page exposure: Congressional rhetoric to the contrary, there is probably no way that a U.S. citizen can be convicted in U.S. courts for having been shaken down abroad, or even for voluntarily giving kickbacks or bribes. This phenomenon will be looked at in detail in Chapter 6.

The incestuous relations between industry and the military had already begun to come to light in the Eisenhower era. In 1959, a House Armed Services Committee investigation revealed that 72 U.S. defense contractors were then employing 1,426 ex-officers, including 251 of general or flag rank. Lockheed and General Dynamics each had 27 admirals or generals on their payroll. As will be seen later, the situation remains unchanged for "double dippers"—officers who retire on a military pension, then get a military-related job at higher pay than they earned when they were in uniform.

Arms contracts with the government of the arms-producing country are in many cases only profitable, or seriously so, if exports to other governments can be developed. Cost overruns are the rule rather than the exception; but they are, in most cases, compensation for additional work required by the contracting agency, or for delaying problems encountered at R & D. Unlike business relations in the ordinary market, arms manufacturers can be held up to opprobrium if their product proves costlier than Defense Department spokesmen had originally suggested in order to win congressional approval for a program; not unnaturally, many manufacturers are adept at finding ways to score back. In the sixties, for instance, with Colt Industries producing 25,000 M-16s a week for Vietnam, Defense contracted to buy the entire output. Colt soon found its profit margin eroded by salary inflation and other factors and increased production to 32,000 a week; but the Pentagon, despite the contract, refused to buy more than 25,000. Left with growing stocks of the assault rifle on its hands, Colt sold 20,000 to Singapore. The Pentagon's international security assistance bureaucracy objected, then gave way, permitting the sale. But later, the Pentagon punished Colt by giving a $56 million contract, for 240,000 more M-16s, to GM instead of Colt. Since GM had to tool up for the order, its bid was about twice Colt's, but Pentagon honor was satisfied.

Almost as attractive as foreign sales—in a few cases, more attractive—are foreign co-production arrangements. Virtually every large U.S. arms maker, whether producing aircraft, missiles, armored vehicles, engines or ammunition, has licensing arrangements across the world, especially in Europe. European firms have similar arrangements, especially in other European countries. The Hawker Harrier V-STOL jump jet used by the U. S. Marines, for instance, was originally not made for the Marines in Britain, but in the United States under license. The licensing of foreign producers heads off the "danger" presented by potentially competing technologies. Sophisticated countries like those of Western Europe or Japan must either persuade the United States to lift its embargoes on certain weapons or on "ABC" (atomic, bacteriological and chemical) technologies, for instance, or generate their own programs. American firms would naturally prefer that the embargoes be breached.

But co-production raises costs. The first twenty-nine Japanese-built F-18s cost the Japanese Defense Agency $32 million each (support costs included), or over twice the then price of F-18s made in the United States. To save money and diminish American complaints about Japan's hugely favorable trade balance with America, Tokyo decided in 1978 to import more of the planes and build less locally.

European firms are potentially and often actually as active in promoting arms sales as American firms. France is the best-known example, but Belgium's famed FN (Fabrique Nationale) was exporting 98 per cent of its production when its 7.62mm. rifle was NATO's standard weapon.

When the United States went over to the .223-caliber cartridge, FN produced this too, along with a competing model of the M-16, and copies of the Israeli Uzi submachine gun; FN successfully relied on its ability to undercut U.S. manufacturers on price.

In the neutral nations, Bofors, SAAB, Fortsvarets Fabriksverk (all Swedish), Maschinenfabrik Oerlikon and Schweizerische Industrie-Gesellschaft (both Swiss) underwrite most of their R & D themselves. They develop their own, mostly overseas markets, and only seek government approval to export when contracts are signed. Bofors' small board of directors includes Sven Hammarskjöld, an appeal judge and cousin to the late Nobel Peace Prize winner, Dag. Annual reports for Oerlikon—now a Brown-Boveri subsidiary—do not refer to defense production, however, and SIG's are almost equally discreet.

Weapons and Economics

Weapons are now enmeshed in the economics web to a degree unthinkable in the thirties, when guns were merely, as Field Marshal Göring accurately if cynically said, an alternative to butter in national development. The deals today are endless. The United States, as will be described later, enabled Britain to buy F-111s by handing its NATO client-state a market in Saudi Arabia, which Washington encouraged to buy British Lightnings instead of an American plane. Because Germany lacks bombing ranges—plentiful in America's desertic Southwest—the Luftwaffe paid the United States $63 million to train pilots and maintenance personnel for Starfighters, even though the plane was built in Germany itself under Lockheed license.

Until 1975, the country most proportionally reliant on arms exports was France, where the *dirigiste* system, in existence since the Popular Front came to power in 1936, favors an efficient, well-capitalized arms industry. Initially largely dependent on the Israeli and South African markets, France diversified after 1967, with impressive results for the country's global influence and balance of trade. French arms exports were 7.3 per cent of all exports in 1970, outpacing tourism as the main foreign exchange earner; in very recent years, the average has oscillated around 6 per cent, which is still slightly higher than the U.S. figure, and considerably higher than the arms percentage of foreign sales in Britain. But the leading arms salesman in the world today is unquestionably Uncle Sam.

One reason for growing American arms-exports successes is the size of American production lines and the excellence of government-funded

R & D; long production lines are not only more economical, but "teach" more: The "learning curve" rises especially with production in the case of aircraft, with their multiple technologies. In terms of cost, Stanley and Pearton estimate that if the first unit assembled takes 1,000 man-hours, assembling 2 units would average 800 hours, with 640 hours per unit for 3: This constant 20 per cent drop means that 100 units will average only 22 man-hours each. The United States initially ordered 3,000 F-4 Phantoms, whereas Germany and Britain ordered only 400 each of their locally produced MRCA (Multiple Role Combat Aircraft), while Italy ordered 100. The United States frankly hoped that the MRCA consortium would fail, or at least incorporate the Pratt and Whitney JTF-16 engine in its plane.

Another reason for American excellence is America's lead in computerization, enabling parts to be delivered on time to countries often too inefficient to do more than order them after the planes have been grounded for a month or so. But yet another reason was hinted at in Eisenhower's famous parting remarks about the military-industrial complex —the U.S. arms industry is becoming more and more a seminationalized, *dirigiste* sector, just like those of most Western European countries.

John Kenneth Galbraith, the economist, told hearings of the congressional Joint Economic Committee in 1969:

> Where a corporation does all or nearly all its business with the Department of Defense; uses much plant owned by the government; gets its working capital in the form of progress payments from the government; does not need to worry about competitors because it is the sole source of supply; accepts extensive guidance from the Pentagon on its management; is subject to detailed rules as to its accounting; and is extensively staffed by former [armed] service personnel, only the remarkable flexibility of the English language allows us to call it private enterprise.

Even if arms exports divert funds from social policy in purchaser countries, they may underwrite social policy at home, since they create employment and generate taxes, both on salaries and on corporate profits overseas. The arms industry has indubitably brought employment to depressed areas, notably in the southern fiefs of some congressional committee chairmen. This is true in other countries also: The Italian Government insists that 30 per cent of defense contracts be executed in the Mezzogiorno—the poor south of the country. In Sweden, nearly all the more than 40,000 population of Karlskoga depend on Bofors. Three eighths of the working population of Barrow-in-Furness, in Britain, work for Vickers' shipyards.

The spin-off from certain branches of arms research, especially in aerospace, has been tremendous—radar, transistors, new light metals, the ultrahard nose cone "glass" from space vehicles. The reheat system for jet engines is now used in the building industry. Many airliners have a "military transport" ancestor. Most of these "civil" advantages have been the product of American R & D. But American overseas sales would undoubtedly be higher if the United States itself was not so rigidly protectionist in defense matériel. The AFL-CIO understandably looks with suspicion on co-production arrangements, and lobbies for protectionism. The long battle to help British shipyards and other arms industries of NATO allies overcome the Buy America Act and penetrate the U.S. market was recounted in Chapter 2.

The importance of defense spending in economics—in the world in general, and the United States in particular—is hard to overestimate. Expenditure is only part of the story; manpower is another, and manpower doesn't only mean the armed forces totals given each year in *The Military Balance*. Reservists and civilian staff need to be counted as well. Barton and Weiler, in their study of international arms control in 1976, estimated that 50 million people were employed in the world's military economy. Much of the money involved is directed toward research and development of new weapons and instruments of war. In a 1970 survey, the United Nations estimated that the world was then already spending about $60 billion annually on R & D, of which about $25 billion was for military R & D. Military research has had, of course, as noted earlier, a massive impact on civilian technology.

Theoretically, the United States spends just under 6 per cent of its GNP on defense—about the world average, and roughly half the Soviet percentage. Over 3.5 million jobs in U.S. industry are defense-related. If this figure is added to the 3.2 million (civilian and military) defense-related federal employees and the 1.1 million Pentagon pensioners, it would appear that one American salary or pension earner in every ten feeds off the defense budget. Private-industry defense jobs are not shared out all over the country. Like a majority of U.S. armed-forces bases, they are concentrated in the South, the Southwest and—where industry is concerned—the West Coast.

Over two thirds of prime defense contracts go to about a hundred large contractors. In many cases, as Galbraith noted, the government provides the plant, the equipment and the working capital for the prime contractor. Much of the work is passed on to subcontractors. The defense industry employs a high ratio of skilled and semiskilled workers and technicians, fewer managers and far fewer sales and service personnel than most industries. Experts have found defense industries to be not particularly labor-intensive, and reformers have noted that government expenditure on health care and education creates more jobs than defense.

The Center for Defense Information complains that the country now has a strong "pro-military constituency as concerned about jobs and income as national defense" and which believes that military spending is good for the economy. But the CDI maintains that "military spending as an economic stimulant is wasteful and inefficient. As a job-creator, it is among the least effective kinds of federal spending."

According to these arguments, the growing defense budgets are contributing massively to the continuing high federal deficits, while government reluctance to raise taxes to pay the bills ensures continuing inflation. Says the CDI bluntly: "The evidence suggests that defense dollars may be more inflationary than others." The CDI *Monitor* sums up this Galbraith-like point of view:

> Over the years, the special characteristics of defense contracting have created an industry which violates all the principles of competitive efficiency. It maximizes costs, employs the most talented and highest-paid scientists and engineers, and by providing easy income for many of the nation's largest firms, debilitates and destroys the innovativeness and adaptability to changing demands which in earlier eras made American consumer-goods manufacturers among the most efficient in the world . . .
>
> Schoolchildren who are taught that advanced industrial nations import raw materials and export finished products are surprised to learn that the United States is an exporter of wheat and an importer of automobiles, television sets, motorcycles and cameras.

The argument is impressive, but it remains a minority one. The Defense Security Agency estimates that each $1 billion in foreign arms sales creates 50,000 new jobs and maintains 50,000 existing ones. The arms industry itself puts the figures at 31,000 and 60,000 respectively. The Congressional Budget Office estimates that $1 billion in overseas arms sales saves $70 million on the budget, of which nearly 29 per cent is in R & D recoupment.

Only about 10 per cent of the total business of the country's twenty-five top defense contractors is military, however, partly because defense contracts yield an estimated 4.7 per cent profit (4 per cent on aircraft), compared to 17 per cent on civilian products. Manufacturers argue that the importance of foreign military sales is crucial to the industry. A Council on Economic Priorities report in late 1977 estimated that just over 30 per cent of the production of the ten largest U.S. defense contractors was for export.

The Fat in the Budget

The issue of weapons economics is one over which reasonable people may disagree. Barton and Weiler sum it up well when they say that "military spending has often been said to be beneficial to the U.S. economy; in contrast, the relative absence of defense spending has often been said to be beneficial to the Japanese economy."

One sure way to make money out of the defense economy is to drop out of it altogether: Of nearly $112 billion appropriated for defense by Congress in 1977, $9.1 billion was for retirement benefits, an increase of about 11 per cent over the year before. This compared to $9.4 billion for the U.S. strategic forces. The retirement fund is expected to cost $12.1 billion by 1982. This, however, is not because old soldiers are happily living longer, but in most cases because they never grew old—or even middle-aged—in soldiering. After twenty years in service, a serviceman is entitled to a pension equivalent to 50 per cent of his salary, with annual adjustments for the cost of living. These men—and a few women—then begin new careers, and some do not even drop out of defense. In 1977, of 141,817 military retirees working for the federal government, 78,000 were working for defense; 8,000 of these "veterans" were under forty. That year, the U. S. Senate killed a clause in the defense appropriations bill which would have banned military retirees from drawing their pensions if they were receiving another federal salary. The clause was not well thought out—it would merely have ensured that military retirees took nonfederal jobs—but its rejection was in any case not surprising: 38 of the military pensioners were receiving a federal salary as members of Congress. In 1978, however, Congress did restrict "double-dipping" for retired senior generals and admirals.

As in the rest of the federal civil service, defense employees only qualify for a full pension (75 per cent) after 30 years' service. Most private pension systems are, of course, considerably less generous than those of the U. S. Government. Several politicians, including Ronald Reagan and Representative Les Aspin of Wisconsin, a congressional defense expert who formerly worked in the Pentagon, have suggested various reforms; one of the more practical came from the Defense Manpower Commission, which proposed scaling pensions according to length of combat duty. Clearly, special allowance has been made for the military because the risks to life and limb are greater than in the average federal civil service job; equally clearly, some take more risks than others. Congress, in its 1977 vote, eliminated the 1 per cent "kicker" on cost-of-living increases for federal pensioners, but continued subsidies for the commissaries which are open to active servicemen and retired officers alike.

The April 1977 congressional debate on the defense authorization bill produced a loquacious discussion of an amendment from Aspin to put the military on congressional retirement rules. Congress pays pensions at the age of sixty-two, or with reduced benefits at fifty-five. Military pensions, as noted earlier, can be picked up after twenty years' service, which, in the case of most enlisted men, means between the ages of thirty-seven and forty-two. The average officer retires at forty-six. Congressman Downey, supporting Aspin, sputtered: "We send men to the moon who are older than forty-six!"

Congressional pensions are based on the average salary for the last three years, military pensions on the last paycheck—which may reflect a last-minute promotion. To sweeten the blow to the armed forces contained in his proposal, Aspin pointed out that congressional pensions are payable after as little as five years' service (but deferred to age fifty-five or sixty-two). This would mean that soldiers would not be forced to remain in for twenty years in order not to lose pension rights, while failures would not be re-enlisted after fourteen or fifteen years' service to save those rights. Conversely, better soldiers, with no prospect of actually drawing the money until fifty-five or sixty-two, would not be tempted to drop out after twenty years' service.

Representative Bill Nichols of Alabama pointed out that congressional contributions were higher and might be too high for enlisted men. An E-6 (sergeant) with twelve years' service might have to contribute about a thousand dollars out of his annual base pay of $12,000.

The floor manager of the bill, Charles E. Bennett of Florida, raised the question of disability retirees. Early retirement, he said, was normal in life-risk services like the armed forces, the CIA, the Secret Service and fire departments. Bennett said the Pentagon had been made a scapegoat because retirement pensions came out of the defense budget: Retirement pensions for other parts of the federal service did not come out of their departmental budgets.

Said Bennett: "If we pass this amendment, we will strike one of the worst blows at the American military and the defense of our country since I have been in Congress." Aspin went down to defeat 247–148.

Since the traumatic Vietnam debacle, a number of factors have kept Congress from being more than nominally disarmamentist: The Soviet arms buildup is one—even though this seems partly a counterbalance to China's. Growing Soviet influence in Africa is another element—even though Congress muffed its one opportunity to do something about this, in Angola, and was caught by its (and the White House's) hesitations over Somalia two years later. But mostly, Congress remains traditionally reluctant to try to second-guess the Pentagon on national security. In 1976 and 1977, both houses rejected, by large majorities, several relatively small proposed arms-budget cuts. They approved all nuclear-defense programs, including (in 1976) development of the Maneuverable Re-entry Vehicle (MARV). The decision on whether to replace the maturing B-52 force with 244 Rockwell International B-1s at a cost of $22.6 billion was put off, in 1976, to the next President, and defended strongly against the Carter suspension in 1977. Only the Navy lost a few programs, partly because of in-house disagreement as to what sort of new ships it needed. The only villain for the arms industry was the Pentagon itself, which reached mid-1976 with a $34.5 billion carry-over of unobligated funds instead of the anticipated $18 billion—thus contributing to unemployment in an election year. Some of the shortfalls were in foreign military sales programs, under which the Department of Defense places orders and is reimbursed by foreign governments.

Except in relative terms, the figures mean little. Inflation and the realities of quality control virtually mean that sophisticated weapons have a budgetary life of their own. In its mandatory quarterly report to Congress, Defense revealed in 1976, for instance, that for the second quarter of that year alone, projected costs for all major weapons systems then in development or production had risen by $4.8 billion.

The biggest increase in defense costs came at the end of the Ford administration, when concern about Russian defense spending was at its highest. The Pentagon projected an increase of $18.5 billion in previously estimated costs for 45 major weapons systems for the final quarter of 1976, of which only $11.7 billion was accounted for by inflation. An order to General Dynamics for 1,388 F-16s instead of 650 (some, of course, for delivery to foreign customers) increased the projected bill for those from $6.3 billion to $13.8 billion. General Dynamics and its subcontractors would also get $21.4 billion instead of $18.9 billion for building 13 Trident submarines instead of 11. The Navy's decision to have 74 guided-missile frigates instead of 50 pushed that tab up from $8.9 billion to $13.7 billion. Grumman was asked to supply 521 F-14s for $10.6 billion instead of 403 for $8.8 billion. Lockheed was called upon to produce 275 P-3C antisubmarine aircraft instead of 234, and because of added support costs this was expected to push the item from $3.6 billion to $4.9 billion. There had been a saving of about $2 billion because of cancellation of the nuclear carrier, and Vought would lose $862 million because the order for 578 A-7E attack planes had been stopped at 464, leaving the company with a completed order now worth only $2.3 billion.

In the following quarter, the jump in costs for the 45 systems rose only $3.35 billion, or 1.7 per cent, to $201 billion. Some projections later fell. But overall, by late 1977, 32 weapons systems begun since 1970 had overruns of 50 per cent or more, for a total additional bill of about $61 billion.

Summing up the situation, the CDI laid the blame principally on lack of competition, flaws in the contract system and poor management. The Center said 45 per cent of cost overruns were attributable to quantity, schedule and requirement changes by the Pentagon, 25 per cent to estimating errors and only 30 per cent truly to inflation.

Investigating the 1975 budget in late 1976, the Center had found that only 30 per cent of military procurement dollars were awarded through price competition of any sort. Only in less than 10 per cent of Defense purchases are contract bids sought and the lowest realistic bid accepted.

Most increases in original estimates result either from what is called "buying in" or from "gold-plating." Contractors buy into a contract by making a bid they know to be too low. Once work has started, it is not usually difficult to get the Pentagon to agree to reassess costs. Sometimes the higher cost is provided by giving a contract for additional production —not at a lower cost, as would be realistic, but for a higher unit figure. In 1975, for instance, almost 20 per cent of military contracts were "follow-ons." A classic example of "buying in" was Lockheed's contract to build the first C-5A transport—the world's largest—for $1.9 billion, undercutting Boeing and McDonnell-Douglas. The final cost was $3.9 billion.

"Gold-plating" is the Pentagon's habit of hanging every imaginable piece of arms or avionics gewgaw onto equipment already ordered—not always in the interest of combat efficiency but always against the interests of economy. According to former Deputy Defense Secretary David Packard, had everything been put on the MBT-70 Main Battle Tank that the military requested, the tanks would have cost over a million dollars each—the equivalent of about $2 million in 1978 dollars. The development program of the MBT-70 was canceled in 1972 after nearly a quarter-billion dollars had been spent. The search for sophistication has doubled the unit price of combat aircraft every four years. In 1975 dollars, World War Two aircraft averaged $300,000 apiece. Today, the average unit price is about $10 million, also in 1975 dollars.

To fudge the quarterly Selected Acquisition Report (SAR) to Congress on the cost status of major weapons systems, the Defense Department resorts to all sorts of tricks, such as changing the list of systems reported, including systems under different categories, and altering the cost categories it uses. Billions of dollars in overruns have been successfully hidden: But the GAO found "errors" of about $3 billion in 1972 and two years later "errors" totaling over $4 billion. The 1976 SAR, for instance, later undercosted the F-16 fighter program by $260 million.

Revealed overruns are, of course, impressive themselves. In addition to those already mentioned, the Army's program to build 481 advanced attack helicopters (AAHs) had gained just over 100 per cent, or $1.66 billion, by 1977; the XM-1 tank program had risen 63 per cent in four years, or $1.9 billion. The Air Force had added $1.7 billion—69 per cent—to the cost of 733 A-10s, while the B-1 had doubled in cost in seven years, adding about $11 billion to the development and pre-production tab. The cost of 34 AWACS aircraft went from an initial $2.6 billion to $4.1 billion; the original 650 F-16s went from $2.5 billion to $5.1 billion, while 749 F-15s went from $7.1 billion to $10.9 billion.

The Trident submarine, with a 51.6 per cent increase in two years (about $6 billion) and the SSN-688 nuclear attack submarine program, with a gain of $3.9 billion (68.6 per cent) were startling enough, but costs for the FFG-7 guided-missile frigate rose 177.8 per cent in two years. The Navy had to reduce its orders by 12 ships, but the taxpayer will still pay an extra $6 billion for the frigates. Other Navy overruns include an increase of at least $2 billion on the original estimate of $7.8 billion for 800 F-18s.

Avionics—aviation electronics—add enormously to an aircraft's price. These navigational, communications, defensive and fire-control aids average about a quarter of the entire aircraft's unit price, and sometimes more.

The House Armed Services Committee's nineteen professional staffers, and the Senate Armed Services Committee's sixteen, cannot possibly deal adequately with the intricacies of a $120 billion defense program, containing scores of major programs. Congressmen and senators have to rely on their expertise, however—which often is provided to the aides by the defense contractors themselves.

Liberal congressman Michael Harrington noted:

> By the time a weapons program reaches the stage at which it becomes a prominent issue for debate in the Congress, the battle is already lost. The Defense Department's near-monopoly of relevant information, together with the vested bureaucratic and economic interests which propel the high-budget, high-prestige weapons programs, conspire to give such programs an all but unstoppable momentum.

Says David T. Johnson, the CDI's director of research: "What the Pentagon wants, the Pentagon gets." This is of course nothing new in history, nor is it unique to the United States. But Congress has been remiss in not demanding more realistic price estimates from the Pentagon, partly because it is easier to vote relatively smaller sums, then additional funds in later years. No one is really fooling anybody—except the public.

The Office of Management and Budget did introduce what seemed like a useful reform in 1976. Cost-plus-fixed-fee (CPFF) contracts—which guaranteed profits, which increased proportionally with overruns—were abolished. Contracts must now detail "mission needs"—the tasks a weapon is to perform; thus, it is the contractor who lists the specifications, not the armed service seeking the item, and profits are related inversely to costs. Contractors must also now list "life-cycle costs" where possible. For instance, the F-14 and Phoenix program will total at least $23.6 billion; fifteen-year life-cycle costs will add another estimated $21.2 billion. The $10 billion-plus F-18 program will require at least $13 billion more over fifteen years. The A-10 with its armaments, totaling $4.3 billion at acquisition, will cost another $9.8 billion. To the $14 billion for F-15s and all their systems must be added an estimated $11.4 billion. Life-cycle costs for the F-16 were put at $10.5 billion. The proposed $118.8 billion AWACS program will require at least $27 billion more over fifteen years, and life-cycle costs for the AAH and its systems will be higher than the cost of the production program. However, even these figures, as Northrop's chairman Thomas V. Jones has pointed out, have no guaranteed reality—nor under present contract regulations can they be enforced.

Robert J. Art of Brandeis University, the author of a book on former Defense Secretary Robert McNamara, has recommended other reforms in defense contracting, which he says should reduce cost overruns to 20 per cent. These include: avoiding crash programs wherever possible; regarding a contractor's capital investment in a project as an important criterion for awarding contracts; offering "incentive" contracts, but with tight controls on changes in contract orders; putting greater emphasis on development and testing before a commitment is made to pre- and full-scale production. In programs that demand major technological advance, says Art, avoid "total package procurement."

Problems will surely continue. J. Kenneth Galbraith has said that "big, specialized defense contractors . . . combine all the comforts, including all the classic inefficiencies of socialism, with all the rewards and immunities of private enterprise." Galbraith proposed nationalizing firms which, over a five-year period, do more than three quarters of their business with the government. Another economist, former Assistant Treasury

Secretary Murray Weidenbaum, has recommended conversely that the government sell its own defense plants and equipment and award all contracts on a strictly competitive basis. The CDI's conclusion on this issue was: "Weapons procurement should not be used as an artificial device to create profits and jobs, or to increase the GNP."

Are Systems Cost-Effective?

Apart from the Trident and attack-submarine programs, most of the high runaway costs concern tactical air force craft, for all four arms. A persistent critic of much spending in this area has been retired colonel Robert W. Whitaker, who notes that the air-superiority tactics on which most programs are based are outdated by new, effective, relatively cheap surface-to-air missiles.

General John W. Vogt, Jr., former USAF commander in Europe, appears to agree. He has written in the *International Defense Review* that the air situation near the battle line "pretty much determines the outcome of what's happening on the ground."

Yet two thirds of the new fighters whose construction has been approved by Congress—the Air Force's F-15s and F-16s and the Navy's F-14s and F-18s—are designed for deep-penetration missions.

Says Whitaker: "Although the Air Force claims its F-15 and F-16 fighters are for multipurpose use, they are clearly designed for air-superiority tasks. Their ground-attack capability is an expensive afterthought.

"Multimission aircraft sound attractive, but using a $14.6 million aircraft such as the F-15 in close air-support missions is not cost-effective."

Whitaker notes that "Congress approved the F-15 program without fully understanding that this fighter's vaunted advantage over Soviet aircraft was partly dependent on the controversial AWACS. The Air Force was slow to tell Congress that without AWACS, the F-15's long-range radar and Sparrow missiles would be wasted: They cannot discriminate between friend and foe without the help of [airborne] air controllers. This forces the F-15 into visual-range engagements . . . Consequently, there's a high-risk factor in the AWACS and F-15 programs—or, to put it another way, a $15 billion gamble."

Whitaker is also critical of aircraft-carrier warfare, which he sees as a leftover from the "gunboat" war of Southeast Asia, but vulnerable and obsolete in a conflict with a superpower. He sees the F-14, for which carriers are designed to be a platform, as "needlessly overdesigned and unnecessarily costly." He thinks the role of the F-18, as designed, is too limited, necessitating attack-aircraft programs like the A-18 and the proposed F-18L. If war lasts long enough for surface ships to be needed, Whitaker believes, the Navy's role will be to control vital sea lanes, with little land-strike capability needed.

Like other cost-cutters, Whitaker would like to abolish the Marines as a separate corps and save another $4 billion or so there. As light infantry with its own close air support, the Corps, he says, could be absorbed by the Army. Its existence as a separate corps, its critics say, invites extravagance: For instance, the Navy almost forced the Marines to buy four squadrons of F-14s, to cut unit costs; the Marines spent $6.1 million on F-14 pilot training, then balked and decided to stay with F-4s after all.

Whitaker also questions whether the Army really needs 481 new advanced attack helicopters (AAHs) and 600 new gunships, which he sees as outdated in the European war environment for which they are designed. "The Army," says Whitaker, "can justify the helicopter gunship in low-threat environments like Southeast Asia, but even there it lost 2,282 helicopters to small-arms fire."

Other Cost Factors

One hard-to-estimate factor in rising costs was the boom in special minerals. Cobalt is used in high-temperature superalloys for gas-turbine engines. One General Electric CF-6 turbofan engine uses 900 pounds of it. The rare metal is mostly produced in Zaire—which has almost half of world exports, and provides 70 per cent of U.S. needs. Cobalt's price went from $2.45 a pound in 1972 to $5.40 in 1976. Secessionist warfare in Shaba (formerly Katanga), where most cobalt is produced, aided the inflationary trend by impeding transportation. When this reoccurred in 1978, the price jumped to $8.50, rising 24 per cent in a week. By the following year, the figure was an astounding $40, later easing off to $25. While Zaire provides four times as much cobalt as Australia, the world's second source of the metal, and five times as much as Canada, Rhodesia—long wracked by a settler rebellion against Britain, and native resistance to that rebellion, and the object of trade sanctions by the UN—is a main source of high-grade chrome. The price of pure (99.3 per cent or better) electrolytic chromium was $1.15 per pound in 1970, $2.63 in 1977—when Union Carbide and other firms began building a three-year stockpile of the metal, bought from South Africa, Turkey, India and Brazil.

Nickel, another superalloy base used in the hot, high-stress sections of jet engines, such as turbine blades, and for which America depends on Canada for about two thirds of its needs, went from $1.53 per pound in

1972 to $2.41 in 1976. Similarly tungsten, which only melts at 3,410° centigrade, rose from $39.59 per short ton in 1972 to $106 in 1976, then jumped another 30 per cent in February 1977. Interestingly enough, this is a metal in which the United States is self-sufficient.

Molybdenum, a high-temperature metal famous since the days of the Spitfire—and as molybdenum disulfide in lubricants—went up 119 per cent in the seventies. Here again, the United States is self-supplying, with 40 per cent of known world reserves. Columbium, for which the United States depends on Brazil for 78 per cent of its supplies, rose 176 per cent in price between 1969 and 1976. Tantalum, used in electronic components and imported from Canada and Brazil, rose 106 per cent. Tantalum pentoxide—tantalite—rose nearly 200 per cent.

Vanadium, largely imported from South Africa and Chile in pentoxide form, went from $1.50 per pound in 1972 to $2.90 in 1976. Titanium, used extensively in both air engines and airframes, more than doubled in price to $2.70 per pound. Australia is the main supplier. Beryllium, used by the aerospace industry and for nuclear reactors, and mostly purchased from Brazil, also rose about 25 per cent in the seventies and was expected to rise dramatically because of the high cost of safety measures for workers handling the carcinogenic substance. High-quality beryllium alreadys fetches $1,000 a pound. Some of the new technologies, however, have saved money. GE, by using "powder metallurgy," is producing turbofans for aviation engines for 60 per cent less than two years ago. Pratt and Whitney is developing a superalloy that will enable a turbine blade to operate at a 100° Fahrenheit higher temperature, thus extending its life. Boeing is working on fiber optic systems which transmit information by means of encoded light beams instead of by electronic signals carried by metallic conductors.

Richard E. Donnelly, the Pentagon's director of materials policy, has recommended building up three-year stockpiles of ninety-three "critical" metals. This plan, originally proposed in the Ford administration but rejected by the House of Representatives, was approved by the Senate in 1978. Lead, rubber and zinc were said to be in particularly short supply. That year, the current U.S. stockpile was estimated at $8.6 billion. Stockpiling further would of course drive prices still higher.

Another cost factor is waste. The Senate Armed Services Committee said in a 1977 report that the Defense Department was duplicating too much academic research and thereby slowing results. The Committee cited "ten years to develop a sono-buoy, fifteen to twenty years to develop an amphibious assault vehicle, eighteen years to develop the Patriot"—an advanced surface-to-air missile. Private research, said the report, achieved results in less than half the time.

The GAO reported that the Navy could economize $865,000 a year of its $1.2 million budget for the Naval Weapons Support Center in Crane, Illinois, just by reducing its nineteen officers there to one, and its forty-nine enlisted men to two, and replacing the departing sailors by a smaller number of civilians.

Arms Lobbies

With so much money at stake, lobbying for defense contracts is naturally intense, especially when a major program is involved. In 1976, when the foreign-aid bill set limitations on arms sales abroad, the lobby of the Aerospace Industries Association succeeded in persuading President Ford to veto the measure. The bill sought to follow up on earlier legislation (which obliged all arms sales of more than $25 million—$7 million in some cases—and all sales commissions to be reported to Congress for approval) by slapping a ceiling of $9 billion on overall annual military exports.

Early in 1976, the lobbyists circulated on Capitol Hill a hundred-page report with no letterhead, noting that arms sales overseas had given the United States a favorable trade balance and claiming that arms exports provided 1.8 million of the arms industry's 3.2 million jobs. The lobbyists' report argued that the proposed ceiling would merely pass all these jobs and exports to European firms. A grass-roots lobby campaign was generated among defense-plant workers, who were urged to write, cable or call their congressman or senator.

Senator Humphrey, sponsor of the bill, angrily told James McCartney, Knight Newspapers bureau chief in Washington, after the veto: "I can play hard ball too. I happen to be chairman of a subcommittee that handles every kind of military and economic assistance in the book . . . Well, I can be a very busy man when they want something. I have lots of things to do that would keep me from taking up their business. Yessir, more than one can take up that hard-ball game."

But by the following month, the "ceiling" had been removed from the bill's provisions, along with Congress' proposed veto rights on commercial sales. Congress did, however, insist on all sales of over $25 million being "handled" by government, even when they were "commercial," and banned military aid or arms sales to Chile. The $5.1 billion bill, nonetheless, did include $1.235 billion in military grants and $500 million in military credits for Israel, a cause which Humphrey strongly supported and which had rewarded him handsomely in the past.

In 1979, General Electric lobbyist George C. Troutman, working largely through the office of Congressman Joseph P. Addabbo of New York, launched a brisk campaign to have the Pratt and Whitney TF-30 engine in the F-14 and that same company's F-100 power plant in the F-16 replaced by a GE engine derived from that designed for the "canceled" B-1. Pratt and Whitney were battling equally feistily back, their lobby force led by local congressman Robert N. Giaimo of Hartford, Connecticut, and Clark MacGregor for United Technologies—owner of Pratt and Whitney. MacGregor is the former chairman of President Nixon's 1972 election campaign. Involved was a long-term order worth $16 billion.

Rockwell International directed a massive campaign at Congress in 1976 and 1977 to keep the B-1 flying, informing as many members as possible about the 70,000 jobs—and additional work for another 120,000 Americans—that the swing-wing wonder would provide across the nation. The Ohio delegation, for instance, was naturally informed that General Electric would build the engines at a plant near Cincinnati.

In September 1976, Jerry Wurf, president of the American Federation of State, County and Municipal Employees, took a page in *Time* magazine to reply. Headed "One of these could educate every kid in Cincinnati," it showed a B-1 taking off; the caption referred to the fact that the plane's then estimated unit cost, $87 million (it later rose to $102 million), was the equal of the city's public education budget.

But fellow labor leaders in the AFL-CIO and the United Auto Workers saw it differently, and their lobbyists plied the Hill along with industry's, buttonholing aides in the offices of opponents of the strategic bomber. Labor and other lobbyists for the B-1 were supplied with a target list of Congress members: Beside each name were the names of companies with subcontracts on the B-1. Since the program had over 500 subcontractors and suppliers in forty-eight states, the ammunition was impressive. Republican senator Clifford Case was told about the $400,000 contract for Bendix in New Jersey. Democratic congressman Louis Stokes was informed that the Cleveland Pneumatic Company had a $227,000 share of the pie. New York Democrat Jonathan Bingham, a B-1 doubter, doubted less when he learned of his district's share in a $2.3 billion, 45,000-job part of the contract. According to the Washington *Post*, Rockwell contributed to the 1976 election campaign of no less than eighteen members of the House Armed Services and Appropriations Committees.

Retired Air Force brass on the board of Rockwell and major subcontractors tackled their old Pentagon colleagues, inviting them to Rockwell's now famous Maryland hunting lodge. Malcolm R. Currie, then the director of defense research and engineering at the Pentagon, was fined a month's pay and received a reprimand letter from Secretary Rumsfeld for accepting an invitation to stay on Bimini, in the Bahamas, with Rockwell's president, Robert Anderson. He took along a lady friend and his thirteen-year-old daughter.

Anderson asked his 119,000 employees to write their congressman about the B-1, supplying stationery and stamps for the purpose. A Rockwell film on the B-1 went out on the college and civic-organization circuit, and to independent TV stations.

Rockwell and Currie have had other problems. Late in 1976, an investigating subcommittee of the Joint Congressional Committee on Defense Production produced a 193-page report on the shenanigans involved in keeping the firm's $500 million Condor missile program alive. In 1974, the Condor, an air-launched cruise missile with conventional or nuclear warheads, was rejected by Leonard Sullivan, the Pentagon official then responsible for investigating excess costs. Like the Sparrow, the Condor was found lacking in the all-weather capability claimed, and too expensive.

Sullivan's negative memo fell into Rockwell's hands and a lobbying strategy was devised to meet it, mostly aimed at the Senate, the Navy and Secretary Schlesinger. A Rockwell vice-president, J. F. Reagan, soon won over Currie, who agreed to help Rockwell lean on the late Senator John McClellan, then chairman of Senate Appropriations. However, Schlesinger decided to put the Condor program on ice and requested only $3.7 million from Congress to complete tests. According to the investigating subcommittee, Currie, Navy Secretary J. William Middendorf II and other Navy brass then persuaded Pentagon controller T. E. McClary to write McClellan requesting $19 million for pre-production. McClellan's committee obliged. Since the House had rejected the program altogether, Rockwell finally got $5.7 million in conference.

To restore the full program, Reagan put out another game plan, aimed at friendly members of the House Defense Appropriations subcommittee. The targets for the missile this time were Chairman George H. Mahon of Texas and fellow Democrats Robert L. F. Sikes of Florida, Daniel Flood of Pennsylvania, John M. Slack of West Virginia and John J. McFall of California. (Sikes was reprimanded by the House for conflict-of-interest voting in 1976, and lost his seat that year. McFall lost his whip post in 1977 and his seat in 1978 because of involvement in the Tong Sun Park Korean scandal. Flood's trial for alleged campaign improprieties initially ended in a hung jury.) At the Pentagon, Currie and his deputy, Robert Parker, now recruited Navy Under Secretary David S. Potter and Vice-Admiral Thomas Hayward, director of the Navy's program planning office, to neutralize Sullivan. In February 1975, Schlesinger asked Congress for

$103 million for Condor in fiscal 1976—$1 million for development tests, the rest for production. Another $45 million would be required in fiscal 1977, he said.

The investigating subcommittee's report said Currie, the Navy and Rockwell worked together to conceal the cruise missile's defects. But the Office of Management and Budget, primed by Sullivan (whose office was later abolished), ruled against Condor. Rockwell and Currie fought back, this time with the assistance of Deputy Secretary of Defense William P. Clements, a former congressman, who wrote his former colleague, President Ford, on November 26, 1975, asking him to overrule OMB. Ford obliged. Clements wrote to the Senate the following June, certifying that the Condor was "ready for initial production." But the House subcommittee rejected the program again, and soon the joint investigating subcommittee's report was in Senate hands. In conference, Condor was finally deep-sixed. Senator Eagleton called for the dismissal of Currie and Parker, saying that they had been working for Rockwell, rather than for the nation.

Currie wrote the Joint Committee on Defense Production: "In fulfilling my responsibilities, I have always had an open-door policy with top executives of Defense Department contractors . . . [But] I have been involved in absolutely no conflict of interest in any program, including Condor."

In 1977, Currie returned to his old company, Hughes Aircraft, as vice-president of the missile systems group, for a salary and fringe benefits reported to total $180,000 a year. Senator Proxmire of Wisconsin said Hughes had received $826.3 million in Pentagon contracts during Currie's tenure, including a subcontract on Condor. Proxmire questioned the efficiency of the attack helicopter which Hughes will build, and called a Hughes program to modify a European missile (the Roland) for $487 million a waste of money. At the Pentagon, Currie had been instrumental in giving Hughes the Roland contract—originally budgeted at $104 million. Other Hughes missile systems which Currie managed at Defense and would now manage at Hughes itself included the Phoenix air-to-air weapon, the air-to-ground Maverick and the TOW antitank system.

The Currie affair raised strong sentiments in Congress. Gary A. Myers, a Pennsylvania Republican, finally withdrew an amendment to the appropriations bill which would have obliged Defense officials and armed-forces officers with decision-making functions in contract handling to reveal conflict-of-interest links to the defense industry, because the Post Office and Civil Service Committee's subcommittee on employee ethics and utilization was drawing up broad-brush legislation to cover all federal employees in this way. The House passed an amendment by New

Jersey Democrat William J. Hughes forbidding officers of the rank of colonel or naval captain and up from taking private employment, within three years of retirement, with firms producing systems in which they were involved less than twelve months before retirement. (The Senate cut the limit to two years after retirement—in which form it passed in conference in 1978—although some senators favored a lifetime ban. The Hughes measure was slightly easier for civilian officials, setting the base rank for restrictions at GS-16—the equivalent of major general.)

Hughes quoted from a Common Cause study showing that during the four-year period from 1969 to 1973, 1,406 Defense officials and officers left the Department to work for Defense contractors: 379 went to contractors they had dealt with while in office. He quoted Senator Proxmire as saying that in 1975 alone, the figure for officers had been 620, and for 1976, 1,044—while "large numbers" of civilian Defense employees had also moved to private defense jobs, often with contractors with whom they had been dealing. Said Hughes: "This is a situation which must inevitably undermine the faith of the American people in the process through which Defense contracts are awarded to private industry."

The Center for Defense Information agrees with many congressmen that widespread conflicts of interest have undermined public confidence in the Pentagon's willingness to make reforms. The lure of post-retirement jobs makes Pentagon program officers go easy on contractors who may be the source of post-service careers. Even before the 1977 reforms, there was already a legal provision prohibiting retired officers from selling materials to their former branch of the armed services, but it has never been enforced. For three years after retirement, an officer was supposed—even before 1977—to file a yearly employment statement, available for public inspection. The Pentagon is supposed to make regular reports on these. But the officer reporting requirement is not enforced, and the Council on Economic Priorities estimates that nearly half of all retired officers omit to file.

The CEP found that of the 1,406 ex-officers who filed reports in the early seventies, 27 per cent were open to charges of conflict of interest. Presumably the percentage for those omitting to file was much higher. Eighteen per cent of the 1,406 who filed were hired by the top twenty-five defense contractors. All prime contractors were found to have on their staff at least some former Defense Department officials or officers whose previous tasks had been to evaluate the work of their present employers. Between 1974 and 1975, the number of former senior Pentagon officials working in the defense industry increased from 433 to 715.

In many cases, defense industry executives go to work for the Pentagon for a few years, then return to their corporations. Roy Ash, the former director of the White House's powerful Office of Management and Budget, had been the president of Litton Industries, a major defense contractor. David Packard, a co-founder of Hewlett-Packard, a defense contractor, became Deputy Secretary of Defense under Nixon, then returned to his firm. The case of Malcolm Currie of Hughes Aircraft being director of the Pentagon's R & D office has just been mentioned. Many of his deputy directors at Defense were from industry also.

In 1979, ethics legislation was toughened, restricting ex-employees of government from "personal appearance" lobbying before their agency of previous employment. Mail and telephone lobbying remain unrestricted, however.

Incest does not only take place between industry and the Pentagon but also with the Hill itself. A former top Boeing technician, Peter Hughes, was working, when this book was being written, for the investigations subcommittee of the House Armed Services Committee. Boeing built the Minuteman ICBM and is competing with Martin Marietta for the M-X contract. His wife, Mary Rose Hughes, a former legislative aide to Congressman Jack Kemp of Buffalo, a conservative defense expert, does Hill work for Boeing's Washington office.

Harold Rosenbaum left Avco, which builds warheads, to work for a year with House Armed Services, 1975–76, returned to Avco, then set up a Washington consulting firm with the Committee as a client. How advantageous this will be to Avco remains to be seen. But when Bill Spell, an aide to Senate Armed Services Committee chairman John Stennis, left that office to become the Washington representative of Beech Aircraft, it was not long before the Navy received a letter from the senator saying, in effect, that if it planned to order CTX utility planes from any other manufacturer than the Wichita firm, it might take some time, because his committee would want to "review the matter." The Navy took the hint, and Beech got the $21 million contract.

Contractors may design their systems so as to give work to the electoral fiefs of powerful members of Congress. Dale Milford, the former professional pilot and TV weathercaster who represented the Dallas district, where many people work for the troubled Vought Corporation, put up a steady fight to get the Navy to keep the A-7 attack plane in production, calling it "the best light attack fighter-bomber in the world today." But his struggle seemed hopeless until Vought hit on the idea of converting the A-7 to a twin-engine plane and replacing the Allison turbofan with two General Electric power plants built in Lynn, Massachusetts. This not only gave the proposed aircraft some appeal for senators Kennedy and Brooke but also and more importantly for Speaker "Tip"

O'Neill. Vought's main problem was that the aircraft whose production would have been cut back to make room for the new A-7s in the inventory was the A-18, also powered by GE engines from Lynn. Any cuts in the F-18 or A-18 programs, built by McDonnell-Douglas and Northrop, would annoy the Californian delegation. Vought recruited Marine Corps support by suggesting that McDonnell-Douglas could be "compensated" by approval of the developmental AV-8B jump jet, which the Marines want more than anything else in the proposed inventory of the eighties, and which McDonnell-Douglas would build under British license.

Aerospace lobbying is conducted by individual companies like McDonnell-Douglas, Grumman, Northrop, Lockheed, Hughes, Boeing, Rockwell International, Raytheon, General Dynamics and Fairchild, and also by organizations. The Aerospace Industries Association groups forty-eight companies, including nineteen of the top twenty-five U.S. arms exporters. A major force in the AIA is the earlier-mentioned Nixon crony Clark MacGregor, top lobbyist for United Technologies Corporation, formerly known as United Aircraft. Other active groups include the Defense Supply Association and the American Defense Preparedness Association, which is heavy with retired officers, but which told the writer in 1979 that it is precluded from direct lobbying by its charter.

The new boy—or girl—on the block is "Lisa," the American League for International Security Assistance, which is predominantly concerned with helping arms exports, mostly in aerospace. "Lisa" is run in Washington by tough-talking Joe Karth and his partner, Bob Best. The two men and a secretary coordinated activities for thirty-one firms and labor groups in 1977, including Westinghouse, UTC, Northrop, Martin Marietta, Hughes, Boeing, Raytheon, Control Data (computers), Vought, Singer, Aerojet, Goodyear, Rockwell, Sundstrand, General Dynamics and Lockheed, and such unions as the United Brotherhood of Carpenters, the Teamsters and the National Marine Engineers Beneficial Association. Most of the members resubscribed in 1978, including all three labor groups.

Karth says "Lisa" favors all sales "which do not endanger our country's security, which are not the latest technology and which are defensive rather than offensive systems." But pressed for a sale which "Lisa" had not supported, or for a hypothetical sale which the group would oppose, Karth could not think of one.

"Basically, we ask the question: If it's not supplied by us, will it be supplied by someone else?" says Karth. "What influence and leverage will we get on their [foreign client-state] foreign policy by supplying?"

Karth would not name any Senate or House office which he regards as friendly because, he said: "No matter how good your intentions are, some sonofabitch will cut your head off."

Much is at stake in the lobbying. Carter's suspension, at all costs for the time being, of the B-1 program was perhaps the most significant recent example of the important economic repercussions which defense-budget decisions can have. In past centuries, war industries adapted to the production of civilian goods fairly easily; but this is not always possible now. To what do you transform a Minuteman assembly line? What civilian work is available for some of its technicians?

A B-1 critic, New York Democrat Thomas J. Downey, called the B-1 a "military-industrial welfare program rather than an efficient weapon." In *supporting* the B-1, the AFL-CIO executive council was not necessarily disagreeing with Downey.

Shortly after the President's announcement on June 30, 1977, Bastian Hello, head of Rockwell's B-1 division in Los Angeles, called the news a "major shock" that would necessitate "major layoffs" both by Rockwell and its subcontractors, notably Vought and Cutler-Hammer, integrator of the defensive avionics system, which involved twenty-eight subcontracts in all. Evidence of Rockwell's hard times came the following year, when the firm sold a 75-acre plant and office complex on the Imperial Highway near Los Angeles International Airport to Northrop. By then, it had become a shell of largely empty sheds and offices and silent equipment.

Some subcontractors—such as General Electric, Boeing, Goodyear Aerospace, Texas Instruments, Bendix, Singer, Sanders Associates and Sundstrand—were able to absorb most of their B-1 workers elsewhere. But Rockwell eventually fired 8,000 of its 13,000 B-1 workers and announced plans to phase out 2,000 more. Some B-1 avionics programs were continued as part of plans to upgrade the B-52s. But Vought, the Dallas firm which had already apparently lost the Navy fight with McDonnell-Douglas and had had to concede the Tomahawk missile program to General Dynamics, laid off nearly half its 11,800 workers during 1977. Vought also lucked out when President Carter blocked their sale of 110 A-7 attack planes to Pakistan, despite the best efforts of Texan Congress members. Later, Vought lost again from a Carter administration decision not to build the non-nuclear version of the Lance missile.

But the big apparent loser was Rockwell. On the New York Stock Exchange, trading in Rockwell shares, which had opened that day at 36⅞—close to the 37¼ high for the year—was halted for nearly four hours. When trading resumed, it was at 32, and it closed for the day at 32⅜. Total volume for the day was 160,300 shares. At 37, with earnings for the second quarter of 1977 at $36.2 million (against $32.1 million for the same period in 1976), the price-earnings ratio had been 10. Rockwell, however, still had a backlog of $7.3 billion in funded and unfunded aerospace and commercial orders; but the B-1 decision was hailed as a disaster by Californians in Congress, especially Senator Sam Hayakawa and conservative congressman Robert K. Dornan, whose district was the most affected.

The Wall Street Journal said the cancellation would contribute to an expected decline in aerospace earnings from the sale high of $29.3 billion in 1976. Even this high largely reflected inflation. The Aerospace Industries Association said that, measured in 1972 dollars, sales had been $35 billion in 1968, $23 billion in 1971 and $22 billion in 1976. Many in the industry, however, saw the B-1 cancellation as liberating up to $25 billion in defense money for other projects over the coming five years.

Grumman officials told the writer in 1977 that government cutbacks in the F-14 program would cost 3,000 jobs (out of a 28,000 total) to Long Island's principal employer by 1980, and "thousands" of other jobs to subcontractor firms. Later, Speaker Thomas P. "Tip" O'Neill admitted that he had used his influence to get the F-14 program cut back—to help sales of the F-18, the General Electric engines for which are made in his electoral district.

The nervousness at Grumman was compounded by Carter administration plans to prune some defense programs while also reducing arms sales overseas. In the defense debate that year, Texas Democrat Dale Milford, a pilot, noted that this policy would not only affect "2 million American jobs" and pass markets to foreign competitors, but would also affect the country's civil aviation industry. Said Milford in a letter to President Carter:

> The economics of civil air transport production are dependent upon military sales in the world market, and vice versa . . . This nation could not have maintained [its] prior pre-eminent status in civil aircraft sales without the benefit of foreign military aircraft sales . . . There is no doubt that a plan to reduce world armament is a lofty goal, but *only* if we have an ironclad agreement, including validation, with our foreign competitors wherein they would also cease military aircraft sales.

Regional Arms Economics

The regional economic impact of the arms industry is a major political consideration in the approval or rejection of weapons programs. The regions of concentration of the industry have varied slightly over the years. In 1952, almost 25 per cent of U.S. defense purchases were made in the

East and the north-central part of the country. By 1962, this area had only a 15 per cent share of the bounty. In contrast, the Pacific area was over 21 per cent. Viewed the other way around, defense industries accounted for just over 35 per cent of out-of-state income for the Pacific states in 1952, and this figure did not change much over the years.

Of all U.S. defense purchases, California already came first in 1952 with over 12 per cent. New York State was second with nearly 11 per cent. Four years later, California was still first with over 16 per cent. New York was still second, but with only 9 per cent. By 1962, California had climbed to a nearly 18 per cent share, with New York down to about 8 per cent. By 1964, according to the Stanley-Pearton study, California was getting 28 per cent of all prime Pentagon and NASA contracts. In 1968, California was employing 600,000 of the nation's 1.5 million aerospace industry workers, and aerospace now contributed 37 per cent of all manufacturing in that state. By 1970, however, partly because of the phasing out of the space program, California was down to 20 per cent of prime Pentagon/NASA contracts, but still of course leading the nation. This figure has since remained roughly constant.

Texas, with 5 per cent of defense purchases a quarter century ago, had already climbed from fourth place in the nation to third by 1962, overtaking Pennsylvania. Washington State, despite its small population and remoteness, already had over 3 per cent of the pie by then. Indeed, many saw the Boeing B-52's and the Boeing cruise missile's victory over the B-1 as being first and foremost a concession by Carter to appease Senator Henry Jackson of Washington State, a hawk opposed to Carter's views on détente and disarmament, a supporter of the Israeli hard line on Mideast peace and familiarly known on the Hill as the "senator from the Pentagon," the "senator from Israel" and the "senator from Boeing"—that corporation being his state's main single employer, and a strong supporter of Jackson's re-election campaigns. Jackson became chairman of the Senate Armed Services Committee in 1979.

Boeing scored hugely from the B-1 decision, notably where the B-52 is concerned. The plane is destined to need at least $100 million in new electronic countermeasures and a much larger sum for new wings. Boeing also scored on the cruise missile, on which it had only a thousand people working before the decision. Many of the B-1 avionics subcontracts which Boeing held continued—for fitting into the upgraded B-52. Boeing also profited outside of Washington: Boeing-Wichita increased its work force from 5,900 to about 10,000 over the final months of 1977, and the firm hired 8,000 new workers in 1978.

The later Carter administration decision—linked to SALT—to continue with the Minuteman upgrading program also helped Boeing, which is the prime contractor—although here some major subcontracts are held by Rockwell for the control and guidance system, as well as by Aerojet General, General Electric and Bell. The Jackson-Boeing relationship was also seen at the time as ensuring that the Shah of Iran would be able to go through with the controversial purchase of seven AWACS control planes—which are adapted Boeing 747s.

(Ironically, when Carter canceled production of the B-1, he also tried to cancel a Boeing program—fifty more Minuteman-IIIs. But since this would have cost the taxpayer almost as much in contract-breach penalties as it would have cost to build them, Boeing would not have suffered. Later, the Minuteman-III program was restored.)

Rockwell International, the prime contractor for the B-1, is a California firm: Neither of the Californian senators—Democrat Alan Cranston and freshman Republican Sam Hayakawa, who both opposed Carter's decision—is on Armed Services or on the defense or military construction subcommittees of Appropriations. Rockwell had also suffered in 1969 by losing the F-15 contract to McDonnell-Douglas of St. Louis: six thousand Californian engineers, or 10 per cent of the Rockwell work force, were fired. California also lost when F-111 subcontracts from General Dynamics were cut, and when the Lockheed C-5A program was ended.

Already by 1962, defense industries were meeting nearly 15 per cent ($2.8 billion) of New York State's payroll, over 23 per cent ($1.9 billion) of that of Texas, and a third of the payroll in Washington State (also $1.9 billion). These percentages have remained roughly constant since in the latter two states. Texas' Dallas-Fort Worth area lost out on Vought's fading fortunes, but the state has picked up 35 per cent of the work on the current, huge, long-term F-16 program.

States whose economic growth in the sixties was more than 20 per cent attributable to defense contracts included California, Utah, Arizona, New Mexico, Colorado, Kansas, Mississippi and New Hampshire. Military payrolls, as a percentage of state payrolls, have averaged 15 per cent in California in recent years, and are high in Texas, Virginia and Florida. Defense Department civil salaries provided another 15 per cent of the Californian payroll, and are considerable in Pennsylvania, Maryland, Texas and New York.

R. E. Bolton, in a Brookings study, notes that after the Korean War, states with Air Force training centers and other large air bases benefited from the increasing emphasis on air and missile warfare. After the post-Korea cutback in forces, the Air Force began to grow relatively more quickly than the other services. "Expansion of bases to suit new aircraft, the conversion of some to ICBM bases, and construction of new missile bases all favored the Southwest, Mountain and Pacific regions," Bolton wrote. "Some states in those areas also increased both their shares of procurement and their shares of military payrolls." He cites Kansas, Nebraska, Oklahoma, Montana, Idaho and Nevada.

Stratford, Connecticut, picked up 1,800 jobs and $60 million a year when Chrysler won the Main Battle Tank contract in 1976, because the local Avco plant is making the engine. Also good for Stratford was the Pentagon's decision on December 23, 1976, to award the local Sikorsky helicopter plant the $60 million, 2,000-job contract to build UTTAS (Utility Tactical Transport Aircraft System). Gerald Tobias, the president of Sikorsky, a subsidiary of United Technologies, predicted that the money the contract would pump into the local economy would create at least two more new jobs for every existing job at Sikorsky.

Beaten in the UTTAS contest was Boeing's Vertol subsidiary at Ridley Township, Pennsylvania, where the December 23 Christmas party "turned into a wake," according to a participant. Both competing firms had lost heavily from the Vietnam peace. Vertol had gone from 13,900 workers and production of 30 aircraft a month to 5,500 employees and only 2 choppers monthly. Sikorsky had slid from 11,000 workers to 6,200 and its plant was at only 22 per cent capacity. Local unemployment was already 12 per cent at Ridley and 10 per cent in Stratford.

While Sikorsky workers, assured of ten years' work, went on a spending spree, President Howard Stuverude at Vertol announced in a shaking voice that there would be further layoffs. A few months later, things looked even worse at Ridley Township when Vertol lost the LAMPS (Light Airborne Multipurpose System) helicopter contract also. By late 1978, however, Boeing-Vertol was recovering, having entered an entirely new manufacturing field—streetcars.

As mentioned earlier, Vought Corporation of Dallas was hit by the cuts in the A-7 program and by the veto of the nonnuclear Lance. Since the latter was to have been made at Vought's aerospace division in Sterling Heights, Michigan, Senator Robert Griffin, who is not a member of the Armed Services Committee and no expert on defense, took to the Senate floor in February 1977 to argue against cancellation of the $140 million, two-year program—which President Ford, if re-elected, would probably have saved for his old friend and fellow Michiganer. Extolling the merits of the weapon his electors had hoped to build, Griffin called the cancellation "madness." For only 10 per cent of the cost of the Lance nuclear program, he argued, the six battalions (2,500 men) equipped with Lances would be able to "deter a conventional Warsaw Pact attack on Europe" if they had Lances with conventional warheads as well. At present, he said, the men "would sit idly by on their hands until the conflict escalates into a nuclear war."

Some towns expand to accommodate a defense industry, then face problems if it is phased out. In 1970, a farm field at Langdon, North Dakota, was chosen as the first site for a Safeguard antiballistic missile (ABM). Over $5 billion was expended on the project. Langdon's population rose from 2,300 to 4,500 in five years. The village of Nekoma, near the site, went from 84 people to 450. The school population doubled in three years. Fifteen new businesses arrived.

In 1975, at SALT I, the ABM was sacrificed to détente. By 1977, the Langdon population was down to 2,800, Nekoma's to 125. The school population was off by 40 per cent and 10 of the 30 local teachers had been fired. Annual local revenues were down by $30 million. The departure of the Morrison-Knudson and Boeing project left behind $7 million of town improvements; while the new parks and Nekoma's first paved road were worthwhile, some improvements became a financial liability—a new hospital wing, new classrooms and fire trucks, and more water and electricity plant than Langdon could use—not to mention a huge radar-guidance tower, a furnished office building and a four-floor apartment complex in the middle of what had become nowhere again, along with empty houses, squash courts, a sauna, a playpark and 197 empty houses.

But the United Nations Association of the United States has argued in a recent report that "in the long term, a reduction of defense expenditures would produce a healthier economy less dependent on fluctuating military programs. Moreover, it would release capital and manpower for the production of goods and services which would benefit the general public."

The UNA stresses the argument that defense is not manpower-intensive. Whatever share it plays in a state's income, defense industry does not employ "more than 4 per cent" of workers in any of America's four regions, the UNA claims. (This argument, of course, ignores the role that defense jobs play in creating other jobs by the money these programs put into the economy.)

Says the UNA:

> An [East-West] agreement to reduce tank inventories would have its greatest impact in the east north-central area, which supplies . . . about two thirds of [U.S.] tank and automotive needs. The Pacific region, on the other hand, produces almost one half of the U.S. military missile and space systems as well as one third of the electronics and communications equipment. The regional impact of a cutback in the procurement of aircraft or ships would depend primarily on the specific weapon systems affected, since production is distributed among several regions.

The report says local leaders have an "exaggerated perception" of the importance of military facilities to the health of local economies, since military personnel spend "relatively small amounts" outside of base, and since most supplies and construction materials are procured elsewhere. (This, of course, only means that the effects of a shutdown are more widespread.)

The U. S. Office of Economic Adjustment has managed to generate almost two civilian jobs for every one lost in areas affected by defense realignments, the UNA claims, citing figures for the years 1962–73. Thirty-five bases had become colleges or vocational institutes, with more than fifty thousand students. The report adds:

> A recent OEA analysis of twenty-two communities which successfully adjusted to base closings shows that the former military bases now fulfill a variety of functions for the local communities. All but one of the bases are being used by private industry, eighteen have educational institutions, fifteen provide airports or other aviation facilities, eleven have recreational facilities, eleven still perform some functions for federal, state or local governments; nine provide housing, two are partially used for agriculture and two provide medical facilities.

A more sanguine picture was painted by a 1978 report by the American Enterprise Institute, which said that for every payroll dollar lost because of base closings, three more were lost in reduced sales and other business receipts.

The AEI report focused partly on base closings between 1971 and 1974, whose medium-term effects were now apparent. It found that 124,000 defense jobs had been lost. Of 51,000 persons who had lost jobs from base closings between October 1973 and October 1975, only half had found new employment by the end of the period. The communities involved still suffered from depressed real estate markets, high unemployment and low retail sales two years after the closings. The report quoted an Air Force environmental impact statement regarding the proposed closure of a bombing wing: The area affected would lose 20 per cent of its population, and one community 65 per cent. There would be a sales loss of 6.5 per cent, involving a sales tax loss of $346,000 a year. Housing vacancies would rise from 3 to 14.5 per cent and unemployment from 12.2 to 22 per cent. These losses would not be recoverable by litigation against the government.

Some questioned whether the closures were always economic for the general taxpayer. Massachusetts Democrat Silvio Conte says that when the Navy closed the Boston shipyard in 1973, it estimated a saving of $20 million. Instead, Conte says, the closing cost the Treasury $25 million.

The Office of Economic Adjustment has operated on limited funds. In 1973, it spent $28.4 million helping communities in several states adjust to base closures. In 1974, the figure was $71.1 million. Allowing for inflation, the expenditure was about the same the following year—$85.2 million. The figure was $114.1 million for 1976 but fell (if inflation is considered) to $61.7 million for the first half of 1977.

Other legislation has been passed or proposed to ease the burden. The Military Construction Appropriation Act of 1977 set a number of restrictions on the use of its funds, all aimed at easing the burden of base closures. Congress had to be notified in advance of projected closures and would have sixty days in which to impose a veto. Pending when this book was written were bills originally introduced by the two Michigan senators, Robert Griffin (who was defeated in 1978) and Donald Riegle, and by Michigan GOP congressman Philip Ruppe requiring the Secretary of Defense to establish a grant program for local governments economically harmed by base closures. These measures would be called the Defense Economic Adjustment and Recovery Act.

Opponents of such measures argued that, as the AEI report put it, "the primary purpose of military forces should be to defend the nation and not to cater to self-serving local economic interests." The Pentagon, critics said, is not the most appropriate government agency to handle welfare. Putting social expenditures into the defense budget would diminish funds for real defense programs. One reason for closing bases, it was pointed out, was to save and thereby provide more funds for weapons procurement and research.

The "Social" Argument

"Social" critics of military spending have noted the negative effect of the arms race on solving human problems across the world, where they are magnified—especially in comparison to the United States, where living on welfare compares to, say, middle-class life in India. Ruth Leger Sivard, who publishes an annual *World Military and Social Expenditures*, noted in her 1977 report that global military spending had already surpassed $350 billion and that a "huge backlog of arms is two to three times the size of present deliveries." She added:

> Economic progress is affected on a broad front. The large diversion of resources to nonproductive use impedes growth, fuels inflation, contributes to unemployment, and squanders resources in short supply. The economic burden is exceeded only by the looming threat to world survival . . .
> Heavy military spending generates a stream of buying power without

producing an equivalent supply of economically useful goods for the civilian market. The excess of disposable income over available supply steadily builds up a generated pressure on prices. In time, that excess becomes a prescription for permanent inflation.

Sivard produces a mass of impressive "comparison" figures: For instance, the world's military budget equals the annual income of nearly 2 billion people in thirty-six tropical countries; "through public budgets, the world community carries more insurance against deliberate military attack than against illness, disease and all natural disasters"; the world's nuclear arsenal is now "several million times" more powerful than the Hiroshima bomb; "at present levels of military spending, the average person can expect to give up three to four years' income to the arms race." If Sivard's figures are looked at differently, one can also calculate that the cost of a Trident submarine would educate a million Asian, African or Latin American children from kindergarten through college.

Sivard estimates that the world has 32 million people in uniform, another 24 million in reserves, perhaps 30 million civilians in defense jobs. Of the $25 billion expended annually for military and space research, $12 billion is spent by the United States, compared to only $6.8 billion spent in America on "civilian" research, such as medicine. (In contrast, in the nine European Community nations, $10.3 billion is spent on civil research, only $3.6 billion on military and space R & D.)

The $80 billion which the world spends annually on weapons alone is now over twice the total of all the health and education budgets of all developing countries. The United States, Sivard calculated, had taken orders for $29 billion worth of arms from developing countries alone, over the previous decade. In addition, a quarter of the developing countries, her research indicated, can now assemble major weapons systems themselves.

A third of the world's population is of school age, by Sivard's rather broad definition (ages five through nineteen), but less is spent on education than on defense. Schooling children, worldwide, costs $230 annually per student; military expenditures average $14,800 annually per soldier. Expenditures on UN peace-keeping operations equal three hours of the total of the world's defense budgets for a year.

The United States ranks 1st in military expenditures among 138 countries listed by Sivard, but ranks only 13th in the number of teachers per thousand children, 17th in the number of doctors (30th in the number of hospital beds) per 1,000 patients. It ranks only 18th in life expectancy and in resisting infant mortality.

The Soviet Union ranks 2nd in defense expenditure (and 1st in the ratio of doctors to patients), but is only 27th in both per capita income and life expectancy and 30th in getting school-age children to school. China ranks 4th (after Germany) in military spending while being 103rd in per capita income, 100th in per capita public expenditure and 118th in availability of hospital beds.

Britain comes 6th among military spenders, but ranks 14th in literacy levels—well behind Japan and barely ahead of China. Iran, until 1978, ranked 7th in defense costs while being 91st out of 138 in getting children to school, 109th in providing hospital beds, 82nd in life expectancy and 106th in resisting infant mortality. Israel ranks 10th in military expenditures while ranking 36th in literacy and in getting children into school and 38th in providing hospital beds.

Japan—1st in literacy, 3rd in resisting infant mortality, 5th in life expectancy—ranks only 9th in military spending.

Arguing against the theory that defense expenditures are a shot in the arm economically, Sivard estimates that while the United States, from 1960 through 1973, devoted 8.1 per cent of its output to military spending, leaving investment at 13.6 per cent, and productivity growth (in man-hour terms) at 3.3 per cent, Britain, with "only" 5.6 per cent on military expenditures, devoted 15.6 per cent to investment and had a productivity growth of 4 per cent. France's figures were better, while Germany, with only 3.9 per cent on military spending, had 20 per cent for investment. Japan, with 0.9 per cent on defense spending, devoted 29 per cent to investment and had a productivity growth rate of 10.5 per cent.

Sivard sees overspending on overkill as diminishing aid to underdeveloped countries, thus ensuring that in the past decade the per capita incomes of developed countries have increased ten times as fast as those of tropical states. Major donors now give about 0.3 per cent of their GNPs to aid, or a third of what they agreed to give, a decade ago, in a UN resolution.

The 1977 Sivard report recommended diverting 5 per cent of world military budgets, or $17.5 billion, to social spending. She suggested devoting $4 billion to supplementary feeding for 200 million starving children, $1.5 billion for supplementary feeding for 60 million malnourished pregnant or lactating women, and $3 billion to improving food-growing in the Third World.

In education, Sivard would have the world spend an additional $3.2 billion on 100 million new primary-school places, to attract some of the over 50 per cent of children in tropical countries who do not attend school, and $1.2 billion to teach literacy to adults (a quarter of the world's adult population can't read or write). Another $3 billion would give clean, hygienic water to "all humanity by 1990," while $600 million would pay for a vaccination program for the 95 per cent of tropical children not reached by present programs. A quarter billion dollars would train medical auxiliaries, and three quarters of a billion would go for homes for the poor, including self-help construction projects.

Congress and Cuts

Sivard's proposals are attractive, but defense spending is more likely to rise than fall. The original objective of expanding the U. S. Navy to 600 ships would have added anything from $60 billion to $100 billion to naval budgets over the next ten years. The $381 million estimated in 1975 for equipping three new Army combat divisions was expected to work out at something like $2.5 billion by 1979. The proposed cuts in the three land divisions, three tactical air wings and three carrier task forces which the United States maintains in Asia might or might not provide some saving: At present, their mission costs alone exceed $20 billion. But the cost of U.S. forces in Europe is well over twice as much, or more than the total military budget of any NATO ally.

The Center for Defense Information, seeking flab in the Carter defense budget, noted that the armed forces were still spending $10 billion on training and transfers, and asserted that "some blue-collar workers are paid 35 per cent more than their counterparts in the private sector." The average rank of both military and civilian personnel is higher today than ten years ago—a "grade creep" that was "costly but reversible." The CDI supported the call for deferring retirement pay for those who left the military with under thirty years of service. It called for cutting the armed forces by the numbers involved in withdrawals from Korea, and reducing the Marine Corps from 192,000 to zero by attrition, since the Corps "has no clearly defined mission today." It proposed cuts of 100,000 military and 50,000 civilian places soon, beginning with 7,000 in the Navy in fiscal 1978.

But the House debate in April 1977 on the defense authorization bill was one of the most lackluster in years. Cost-cutting bills mostly fell by the wayside—such as a Ronald Dellums amendment to save nearly a billion dollars by slashing 50,000 troops from the payroll and bringing home 17,000 personnel stationed overseas, or a Patricia Schroeder measure to delay procurement on three AWACS aircraft until America's NATO allies took a decision on procurement, and to hold back funds for advanced AWACS procurement: This would have saved about a quarter billion dollars.

But when Representative Cornwell proposed that the Committee's recommendation for a 1.5 per cent maximum increase in civilian personnel be changed to 3 per cent, this sailed through handily. Cornwell's Indiana district includes the Naval Weapons Support Center at Crane, which is working on the Trident program. Said Cornwell: "Clearly we are dealing with highly skilled and motivated government workers who are performing vital defense functions."

An amendment to limit chemical and biological warfare and one forbidding the use of public funds to advertise the amnesty program on television were almost the only cost-cutting measures passed. Altogether, as mentioned earlier, the act, passed by 347 votes to 43, represented a small *increase* over Carter's request, and involved a transfer of three quarters of a billion dollars from R & D to weapons procurement. The Senate later made a few other small cuts. In 1978, this scenario was repeated, with only slight variations.

Another area for possible economies is in defense transportation. In a report for the American Enterprise Institute, Professor Clinton Whitehurst has urged that the Defense Department dispose of its parallel capabilities and let the private sector do the job. Traditionally disbanded in peacetime, naval transportation competes with a depressed U.S. merchant marine, while Military Airlift Command maintains costly bases and fleets to do what commercial cargo planes could accomplish for less, in competition with each other. Whitehurst recommends that such defense transportation facilities as are preserved should be consolidated into a single service.

A more obvious field for thrift is space. Of the nearly $90 billion spent on space programs since 1959, about a third has been related to the militarization of the outer ether. Some spending is still to be found in the $2 billion or $3 billion requested for this purpose each year, but many more hundreds of millions of dollars are disguised under other titles, such as "missile procurement." Defense space budgets itemize costs for navigation, communications, mapping, early-warning and weather satellites, but the funding for surveillance and killer satellites is believed to be hidden throughout the budget. Experts estimated the military space budget back in 1976 at $3.2 billion, including nearly a billion dollars "concealed." Life-cycle costs, over ten years, of the NavStar program alone are estimated to be "at least $2.7 billion."

Renegotiation

The much-amended Renegotiation Act of 1951 came up for review again in 1978. It officially expired on September 30, 1976, but because of the backlog of cases the five-member Renegotiation Board, appointed by the President and approved by the Senate, had remained very much in action.

The Board, created during the Korean War, examined true costs, reducing contract prices where applicable, and adding to them where necessary to give a contractor a fair profit. All defense contractors whose total sales to government surpassed $1 million in any year were covered. Losses could be carried forward for up to five years to diminish taxable profits. Contractors aggrieved by Renegotiation Board decisions could appeal to the U. S. Court of Claims and from there to the Supreme Court. "Reasonable" profits were assessed, taking into account such factors as the volume of production.

In 1976, there were 3,067 requests for renegotiation, and 552 cases were assigned to regional boards for investigation. Excess profits of $40,086,556 were assessed, but 24 cases involving alleged excesses of $35,717,528 were appealed to the courts, where cases may take several years. If all were successful, what would be left would not cover the $5,555,678 the Board cost that year—a figure which included $4,839,759 in salaries. Congressmen from defense-contractor states, led by liberal Republican "Pete" McCloskey of California, had long used this as an argument for trying to kill the Renegotiation Board altogether.

Many big contractors voluntarily make refunds when their costs turn out to be lower than projected; but in a quarter century, 466 of the Board's 765 orders have been appealed. By mid-1978, about 150 cases were still *sub judice*, and the Court of Claims was averaging only about 30 judgments a year.

Star plaintiffs were private yards building for the Navy. Some orders may now go to the Navy's own yards, following massive disputes over costs.

One major controversy was over the Trident strategic submarine (SSBN), the tag for which was originally estimated at $800 million, only to rise by 1978 to $1.2 billion. The builders, Electric Boat of Groton, Connecticut, a subsidiary of General Dynamics, claimed, however, to be none too solvent. They laid off 3,000 workers in 1977 and suggested that they might not be able to finish either the SSBN contract or another to build 18 nuclear attack submarines if the Navy did not pay off $544 million, which Electric Boat said was owing on the first 11 attack submarines because of cost increases. These were mainly due, the company said, to "35,000 revisions" of Navy specifications. The corporation claimed it was losing $15 million a month, instead of making a profit.

The Navy urged settlement of the debt, but crusty Admiral Rickover insisted the claim was "fraudulent" and that settling it out of hand would excite the attention of the Newport News shipyard, which claimed millions of dollars in overruns on nuclear-powered cruisers and aircraft carriers.

Eventually, in 1978, Electric Boat stopped work for a while on the attack submarines until a compromise was worked out. By then, Electric Boat was projecting an overrun cost of $843 million on the attack subs; the compromise was that the Navy would pay $484 million and Electric Boat would "absorb" the remaining $359 million. The division declared a loss for 1977. The Navy agreed to pay for any inflation beyond the 7 per cent for labor and 6 per cent for materials on which the $843 million figure was based. The White House began considering a cut from 13 to 7 Tridents, replacing the others originally planned with smaller subs that could handle Trident missiles. But no decision was likely until SALT II was signed and ratified.

Meanwhile, Newport News Shipbuilding and Drydock Company, a subsidiary of Tenneco, and Ingalls, a subsidiary of Litton Industries, were indeed, as Rickover had said, also fighting the Navy over past contracts. The case was similar to Electric Boat's—but was retroactive. Newport News claimed the Navy owed over $2 billion on past orders, and in 1978 both shipbuilding firms continued some contracts only because they were under court order to do so. Their complaint was that the Navy had ordered changes in programs but only paid later; they objected to funding the changes from their own resources. Eventually, an Alexandria, Virginia, court dismissed the Navy's allegations that Litton had overcharged by $37 million on three nuclear submarines. A circuit court of appeals overturned the decision; but in the initial euphoria in the industry, GE won a much better contract from Defense for the Trident sub: The Navy agreed to pay for inflationary cost overruns not covered by inflation projections.

In late 1978, the Pentagon proposed paying off most of the shipbuilders' claims against the Navy, suggesting about half a billion dollars more than the Navy's original offers. In the Senate Armed Services Committee, Democratic senator William Proxmire called the Pentagon proposal "back-door welfare" for the corporations. Under pressure from Rickover, the Navy had suggested limited payments of $125 million to Electric Boat, $312 million to Ingalls. The new figures would be $484 million and $447 million. The Newport News company was then claiming $741.6 million in back bills.

Under a new Renegotiation Board bill, proposed in 1978, only excess profits, not losses, would be renegotiated—a factor which the House sponsor, Joseph Minish, a New Jersey Democrat, said could bring in $1 billion a year. Although Minish envisaged exceptions for firms with less

than $10 million of business, opponents argued that the prospect of un-
limited losses but restricted profits might reduce the incentive for contractors to undertake "iffy" projects. Partisans of the new act said the
very existence of the Renegotiation Board had a deterrent effect and had
resulted in over $1 billion of voluntary refunds over the years.

Arguing for the new bill, Renegotiation Board chairman Goodwin
Chase said that Lockheed, which had $2.6 billion of "renegotiable" cases
for the year 1971, had made profits of 246 per cent, 131 per cent, 95.6 per
cent and 141 per cent in four divisions, but had been allowed to offset
these against losses on the C-5A, on shipbuilding and on work done by
the Lockheed Propulsion Company. He claimed that the shipbuilding division had billed for 21 million pounds too much of steel for the building
of amphibious docks—which was hotly denied by Lockheed chairman
Robert W. Haack. Later, Chase alleged that the steel "fraud" amounted
to 117.4 million pounds, worth $10.2 million. He said that, according to
his investigation, Lockheed had built seven of the docks and charged for
"enough steel for sixteen."

One of Chase's investigators, T. E. Driscoll, told Chairman Proxmire at
Senate Banking Committee hearings that two people who could furnish
useful information were H. P. McLaughlin, president of the predecessor
corporation of the Lockheed subsidiary when the contract was first negotiated, who was in South America and "not available," and Robert N.
Waters, a former executive vice-president of the Lockheed subsidiary and
a former vice-president of Lockheed Aircraft: In 1975, when Proxmire
first challenged the costs—in which a $250 million government-guaran-
teed loan was involved—Waters shot himself three days before he was
due to testify at hearings. Lockheed, however, won the case, and its
innocence was upheld by a GAO report.

This defeat, rightly or wrongly, contributed to the Board's reputation
for ineptitude. Proxmire got the bill for a new Renegotiation Act through
the Senate, but it was defeated in the House—leaving delighted defense
contractors with no "watchdog agency" at all.

Costs and Strategy

Morton Halperin, a former assistant secretary of defense for international security affairs, has written of the complexities of defense budgeting and warned that merely correcting inefficiencies and political-indus-
trial corruption will not solve all the problems, which are often related to
defense planning itself. Writing in *Foreign Policy* in 1972, Halperin said
that although the NATO allies based their procurement on the assumption that a conventional war in Europe would last only a few days, U.S.

ammunition procurement for NATO purposes assumed a war of up to ninety days, while some naval and land weapons systems were procured "as if a war in Europe might go on indefinitely." For instance, Halperin said, an army division of 16,000 men was assumed to need 48,000 men and their arms. Requirements also depended on whether NATO planned to check a Soviet invasion at the German border or farther west. In the latter case, fewer forces would be required initially, but more later for recapturing lost territory. He foresaw "large reductions in the need for general-purpose [nonnuclear] forces" if the accent was simply on deterrence.

Strategically, Halperin recommended relying on submarine-launched ballistic missiles "as the backbone of the American deterrent, while maintaining the other two systems [of the triad] without spending substantial sums on their modernization or improvement." But Halperin warned that the saving on land-based missiles would be "wiped out" by increased spending on strategic bombers. If there was reliance solely on strategic subs, expenditure on these and on antisubmarine warfare would probably counterbalance savings on the other two arms of the triad.

Halperin concluded that "cancellation of specific weapons programs does not lead automatically to reductions in the defense budget." It would be hard to argue with that.

5

Some Privateers

It is time to look more closely at those weapons traders who are not —or only marginally—weaponmakers themselves, but who are sometimes as important to the arms industries as designers, investment banks and governments. Undoubtedly the most famous, or infamous, of all time was the late Sir Basil Zaharoff, a man of uncertain origins and fragile allegiance, whose life was enveloped in intrigue and secrecy to a rare degree, even for practitioners of his morbid craft.

Basil Zaharoff

Mystery surrounded Zaharoff from his birth, and his death did little to dissipate it. His most painstaking biographer, Donald McCormick, cleared away some of the smoke, but his investigations also raised more question marks. Zaharoff's life is worth looking into in some detail because it offers a profile of the emergence of weapons politics and the sophisticated arms-trade mentality we know today.

It is not even clear where and when Zaharoff was born, or what, in consequence, was his first nationality. McCormick concluded that the birth certificate which Zaharoff habitually used, showing that he was born on October 6, 1849, at Mouchliou in Anatolia (Asian Turkey), and baptized in the rites of the Greek Orthodox Church, was a forgery. The real birthday may have been in 1849, 1850 or 1851, and the place either Tatavla—then the Greek quarter of Istanbul—or Odessa, a Russian city. The likeliest evidence indicates that he was initially a Russian subject of Jewish faith, born in Tatavla and raised in Odessa, who fled back to Tatavla in early youth to avoid military service under the Tsar. At what he insisted was his first marriage, he claimed to be the son of a Tsarist officer.

Researchers have found evidence that although his Russian was faultless, he spoke Greek with a slight accent. Although he changed his nationality twice, he never chose Greek citizenship. But throughout his adult life, he stressed his claim to a Greek-Christian origin—possibly so that anti-Jewish prejudices should not inhibit his business opportunities —and in later years he even demonstrated a romantic patriotism for Greece. In this latter period, he confused the issue even further: He told a biographer, Rosita Forbes, that he had been born in Anatolia to a father of Polish origin. In yet another departure, he described his mother as having been "French with a Levantine strain." But he said he had attended a Greek school in Turkey—at the time, under the sultanate, a normal education for anyone claiming to be Christian, regardless of his *milliet*, or ethnic nationality. Engelbrecht and Hanighen, in their classic work *Merchants of Death*, sought to trace Zaharoff to a Greek-Anatolian family called Zacharias which fled to Odessa after Greece became independent and the Ottomans retaliated against local Greeks. In Russia, these authors say, Zacharias was Russianized to Zaharoff; but they claim that "Basileios" was born after the family's return to Turkey.

In his own very thorough study, Donald McCormick says he thinks Zaharoff spent part of his childhood, as well as his youth, in Tatavla— now the Kurtulus section of Istanbul. Tatavla was, among other things, the whorehouse district of the city, and the young Zaharoff was a hustler and brothel tout, a member of the feared *tulumbadschi*, or firemen's guild—which set fires, then demanded a price for fighting them, thoughtfully looting the burning buildings in the process. In 1865, Zaharoff was the prime suspect when fire gutted a large warehouse from which a safe was later reported missing. He disappeared, turning up in England, where he told people he was an alumnus of Rugby, the elite private institution of *Tom Brown's Schooldays*.

By the following year, then probably aged about seventeen, Zaharoff was back in Istanbul; two years later, he took a job with his "maternal uncle" Sevastopoulos, a cloth merchant in Galata, the port area of the then Turkish capital. This was at a time when many non-Muslims in European Turkey took Greek names. In 1870, the twenty-one-year-old decided to disappear once more, taking a chunk of his uncle's money with him. Apparently, he went first to Izmir—known to the Greek community there as Smyrna—and then to France, Belgium and England, where he now called himself Prince Gortzacoff. He had become a "Russian nobleman" in search of business commissions—and a wealthy wife.

In 1872, he settled for Emily Ann Burrows, whose father owned a small construction company. It was an Anglican wedding, and on his marriage certificate the groom describes himself as Basilius Gortzacoff, General de Kieff. Some other documents of around that time describe him as Prince Basilius Zacharoff. The wedding made the papers, and his uncle caught up with him.

Zaharoff then claimed that the money he had taken was his by right; but he was worried enough about his situation to flee to Belgium with his startled bride. Arrested in Brussels and extradited, he was arraigned in London's Mansion House Police Court for stealing "securities worth about 70,000 pounds"—then roughly $350,000. When McCormick researched the trial, he could find only press accounts: All transcripts of the process had been removed from London's Public Records Office.

The prosecution claimed that, during his brief sojourn in Izmir, after fleeing Galata, Zaharoff had proposed marriage to a British woman there and had later married her in Paris, under the "Prince Basilius Gortzacoff" description. This civil ceremony had preceded the English religious wedding. Did Emily Ann marry a bigamist, or was he divorced? We may never know, for all records of his British marriage have disappeared from Somerset House (where records of births, marriages and deaths are kept) and have presumably been destroyed. Records of the reported earlier, Paris marriage were never found.

The London *Times* of January 17, 1873, gives his age at indictment as twenty-two. The angry "uncle" now has a different name—Manuel Hiphestides. Zaharoff was remanded without bail, and when he went to trial on February 3, he pleaded guilty. Prosecuting counsel said the plaintiff was "now prepared to put the most favorable construction on the prisoner's conduct." The reason, McCormick says, was that Zaharoff, using his wife's money, had agreed to repay his uncle and to defray the latter's legal costs.

Basil and Emily Ann then followed a common practice of the middle class when smeared by a court case in Victorian times—they left the country, settling in Cyprus. There, Zaharoff, apparently in return for performing intelligence services for the British, was issued with a United Kingdom passport in the name of Z. Z. Williamson, a name which some researchers say he copied from a billboard over a general store in Nicosia. On his frequent trips to Athens, he used other names, Zaharoff being one of them. With his wife left behind on Cyprus, he began to cut a figure in Athens society, until news of his London trial circulated. Meanwhile, his wife grew sick and had to return to London, where she lived in virtual penury.

Dogged by his past, our hero now decided it was time to "bury" Zaharoff and become someone else. The *Mika Ephimeris* of Athens published a story saying Zaharoff had been shot and killed while trying to escape from the Athens jail. It later transpired that the body was not Zaharoff's, nor had the killing taken place in prison: The victim was a

Canadian, surprised while burgling an Austrian steamer. McCormick, in his handling of this incident, hints that the Canadian may have been set up to provide a corpse to which the name of Zaharoff could be attached. Stephanos Xenos, the reporter who wrote the story, said later that he got his information from an underworld character who had just been released from prison, where he had been serving time for theft. Xenos came to the conclusion that the story had been "planted" on him at Zaharoff's direction, and later claimed that the thief had subsequently admitted that Zaharoff had paid him to plant the story. But while the story of Zaharoff's death held up, Zaharoff, still in Athens, became "Williamson" again. By the time he rejoined Emily Ann in London in 1876 or 1877, however, he became once more Zaharoff—while his wife still used the title of Princess Gortzacoff. The couple separated shortly afterward.

Sometime in 1877, back in Athens, Zaharoff took a room at the prestigious Hotel Grande-Bretagne, then owned by a friend called Lampsas. There, he began to improve his relations in the business world: He became the Athens agent for Nordenfelt Guns and Ammunition, an Anglo-Swedish company. He was to receive five pounds sterling per week, plus commissions. Greece, recently pushed into independence to suit the expansionist designs of Orthodox Russia, was then arming to invade the Ottoman heartland of its former ruler. Athens was therefore a good place for selling guns. The handsome young businessman worked a twenty-hour day and entertained as lavishly as his salary permitted. By then, he spoke, in addition to his childhood Russian, Greek and Turkish, a number of other languages—English, French, Spanish, Italian, German and some Balkan tongues. He also spoke the Levantine language of the pocketbook, getting orders for Nordenfelt by bribing Greek officers.

The dealer, who Rosita Forbes said had a gift for almost total recall, even in old age, told his biographer: "I made wars so that I could sell arms to both sides. I must have sold more arms than anyone in the world. I made my first hundreds (of pounds sterling) gunrunning for savages." He was apparently referring to his participation, as supplier to both sides, in an African tribal war. Zaharoff had other talents: He even designed a submarine, building a model with his own hands and demonstrating it in his bathtub at the Grande-Bretagne. Nordenfelt bought the patent and began to build subs. The first, not surprisingly, was sold to Greece, through the designer—who then hurried to Istanbul to inform the Sultan's divan of what their enemies were up to. Turkey then ordered *two* submarines, for which Zaharoff charged a higher unit price. By 1880, he had sold four submarines to the Tsar and had gone to America to look for orders there.

Shortly afterward, the Burrows family learned through the press that their erstwhile in-law had married an American with a dowry of $200,000. When the honeymooners disembarked from the transatlantic liner at Southampton, who should be waiting by the gangplank but Emily Ann and her indignant brother. Zaharoff brazenly told his bigamous bride that he had never seen Emily before. But the Burrows pair called the police, and Immigration put the American "wife" back on the ship. While this tearful scene was being enacted, Zaharoff slipped away. Cinderella "Gortzacoff" never saw her prince again.

Zaharoff's most sellable item was not, of course, that exotic and expensive novelty the submarine, but the Nordenfelt machine gun. This was threatened by the masterpiece of Hiram Stevens Maxim, which could be fired by one soldier—the Nordenfelt required four. The Maxim was also faster and more accurate. Both Nordenfelt, through Zaharoff, and Maxim —through himself—sought the clientele of the Austro-Hungarian Empire. The Emperor Franz Josef and his field-marshal son, the Archduke Wilhelm, agreed to watch a demonstration of the two weapons on a range near Vienna. The contrast between the two weapons was enormous, and Maxim, firing his own gun, ended by drilling the Emperor's initials onto the target. Zaharoff circulated along the press seats, saying how remarkable the Nordenfelt gun was. Puzzled reporters said they thought the one-man weapon was the Maxim. Oh no, said Zaharoff. So the press carried the story the wrong way round, thus enabling the Austrian War Ministry to justify ordering Nordenfelts (and only 150 Maxims) in return for handsome bakshish from Zaharoff. Zaharoff had quietly told them the Maxim gun was too sophisticated, could not be copied and required precision manufacture to within one hundredth of a millimeter. It was "a conjuring trick, a circus attraction." Only Maxim himself, or an "army of Boston philosophical instrument makers," could fire it. The deception later came to light—but somehow the papers relating the Austrian investigation disappeared after World War One, when Zaharoff just happened to find himself in freshly defeated Vienna.

The unfortunate Maxim fought back and managed to get a larger order for a new version of his gun made to Austrian specifications. At the demonstration, the new gun jammed. Maxim found that Zaharoff had visited his (Maxim's) workshop in England and taken his foreman out to lunch, getting him drunk. The befuddled artisan had then been financially persuaded to sabotage the weapon that was about to be sent to Vienna. Maxim reported his findings to the Austrian War Ministry, but the papers relating to the investigation that followed also disappeared in the wake of World War One. Zaharoff, however, admitted to the caper in his recollections with Forbes. He also claimed that his commonest trick was to sell to men through their wives or mistresses, who were alert to his elaborate courtesies and Edwardian manners. There seems little doubt, however, that he had only contempt for women—with the solitary exception of the Duchess of Villafranca.

Zaharoff probably first saw the little duchess when she was seventeen and on honeymoon at the Grande-Bretagne. Her husband, the brutal Don Francisco, was one of the sons of the Infant (crown prince) Sebastian, and a homosexual. Another story was that Zaharoff had first met her on the Orient Express. This story has the teenage duchess fleeing down the Tiffany-lighted corridor to escape the duke, bellowing angrily behind. Zaharoff opens the door to his *wagon-lit* and suavely invites her to come inside and hide. Zaharoff's own story of their first encounter, however, places it at a reception at the Escurial—the royal palace in Madrid. The meeting apparently did take place, but was probably not their first encounter. The dreadful duke was twisting the arm of his weeping spouse, and the gallant arms dealer stepped forward and struck him. A duel was, of course, inevitable. The arms trader's blow went wide—to have damaged a member of the royal family with a Nordenfelt sword would clearly have been bad for business. The duke's own thrust landed in Zaharoff's shoulder. Heavily bandaged, the bearded cavalier was taken to a hospital, where he was frequently visited by a young, dark-veiled woman of the duchess' height and build.

The duke himself said he had challenged Zaharoff because the dealer was cuckolding him. Certainly, Zaharoff was in love. Over the years, he never forgot to order flowers for the duchess' birthday. The duke ended his days in an asylum, but the duchess couldn't divorce under Catholic law. But if she was frustrated, her lover at least found compensations: Through her, he is believed to have received 30 million pounds' worth (about $150 million) of orders from Spain. At the other end of the continent, Zaharoff courted the ballerina mistress of a Russian grand duke, to get orders from St. Petersburg.

Only his links with the Tsarist court saved Zaharoff from arrest in that city. According to Tsarist police (Ochrana) records—absorbed into those of the Soviet police, after the revolution—"Basilius Zacharias" was wanted by the Tsar's police for "desertion, theft and revolutionary activities." These documents, copies of which were made available to the Turkish Government in 1924 by the Soviet embassy in Ankara, agree that Basilius was born in Tatavla on October 20, 1849; but they say he was the son of "one Sahar, a Jew, of Odessa," who had returned to his native city with his family. The records add that Zaharoff, to avoid military service, had later gone back to Istanbul and lived there with relatives.

By 1890, we find him living at Number 54 of the fashionable rue de la Bienfaisance in Paris and keeping a suite at the Hotel Grande-Bretagne in Athens. That year, Nordenfelt sold out to Zaharoff and his old rival, Maxim, and the two became partners. Maxim, a former weaver, bartender and boxer, had no taste for salesmanship; he had decided that his inventiveness, allied to Zaharoff's unscrupulous business talents, would make a good match. Two years later, still fleeing the shadows of his past, Zaharoff persuaded the Archimandrite Makharios to provide him with the Mouchliou birth certificate mentioned earlier.

Latin America now attracted his attention. In 1894, war broke out between Paraguay and Bolivia. Paraguay refused him a visa, so he went to Bolivia, the weaker power. On his advice, the Bolivians made peace, ceding territory to Paraguay. This gave Zaharoff two months to ship in arms, after which they declared war again and won. When the USS *Maine* blew up in Havana harbor four years later, provoking war between Spain and the United States, Zaharoff was blamed—probably wrongly.

The arms manufacturers of Western Europe began to draw together. Maxim-Nordenfelt, under Maxim and Zaharoff, the Barrow Shipbuilding Company and the growing arms industry of Britain's Tom Vickers formed an alliance, with Lord Rothschild injecting capital, and Zaharoff spreading the cartel to include Germany's Alfred Krupp and Sigmund Loewe, the Nobel Dynamite Trust, French and Italian firms and Bethlehem Steel.

The key figures in this rogues' gallery were Krupp and Tom Vickers. The Vickers engineering works dated from the early nineteenth century. Alfred Krupp had studied with them during his English phase. In Zaharoff's time, the heir, young Thomas E. Vickers, had served an apprenticeship at Essen. Vickers had established itself making railroad cars and other heavy steel products. In the sixties, the firm had gravitated into arms by making gun barrels and armor plate. When Zaharoff came aboard in the nineties, Vickers began absorbing firms in Britain and elsewhere. Only in South America and the Far East did Vickers' principal competitor, Armstrong-Whitworth, hold sway. In Latin America, Armstrong-Whitworth's agent, R. L. Thompson, found a cheaper way of controlling the news than Zaharoff's, Schneider-Creusot's and Krupp's method of buying newspapers: He got himself the job of London *Times* correspondent in the area.

By the turn of the century, Zaharoff was also using his wiles to fight the pernicious influence of the pacifist movement. A central figure was Lloyd George. The Welshman, a rising star of British Liberal Party politics, had notably accused Cecil Rhodes, the swashbuckler in southern Africa who was still a British hero, of having staged the famous Jameson

Raid on South Africa to secure a huge profit on the arms sales involved. In December 1900, Lloyd George intended to attack the rearmament policy of the Prime Minister, Joseph Chamberlain, by alleging similar venality in a speech in the Premier's own constituency, Birmingham, a center of the British arms industry. Zaharoff got there first and, according to Birmingham police, "stirred up" the arms workers with a speech telling them Lloyd George wanted to kill their jobs. The workers subsequently rioted at the Lloyd George speech, and police had to rescue the fiery orator from the meeting hall.

In 1901, Zaharoff's partner Maxim was knighted and sent to The Hague to try to buy off the Boers. If they would stop their war with the British in South Africa, and allow gold mining to restart, the Boer leaders would receive $100,000. The ploy failed. Meanwhile, Maxim's partner Zaharoff, who was supplying arms to both sides in the selfsame war, bought a house that year in the most expensive street in Paris, the Avenue Hoche, and took to driving a three-horse, Russian-style troika in the Bois de Boulogne. The multinational arms merger was now complete, and Vickers paid the expenses of maintaining the mansion. They also paid Zaharoff 34,000 pounds in commissions in 1902, 35,000 pounds the following year, 40,000 pounds in 1904. Zaharoff sold arms to both sides in the Russo-Japanese War (which Japan won) and received 80,000 pounds from Vickers in 1905. One notable Zaharoff sale in Tokyo was of the battle cruiser *Kongo*, a sale which involved bribing Admiral Fujii and others to the tune of over $500,000.

To spread the gospel of rearmament, he bought the Paris newspaper *Excelsior* and urged his agents in Germany to become military correspondents of German papers. While whetting the war spirits of both countries, Zaharoff deftly appeared as a friend of Germany and as a loyal citizen of the Triple Alliance (Britain, France and Russia). He placed articles in *Le Figaro*, *Le Matin* and the *Echo de Paris* praising the merits of French machine guns, carefully drawing the articles to the attention of a Prussian legislator called Schmidt who was a pawn for Krupp and other heavy industrialists. Schmidt duly asked the Chancellor what Germany was doing to respond to this threat of French belligerence. Funds were voted for more machine guns. Zaharoff also began to buy into the Banque de l'Union Parisienne, a subsidiary of the French arms giant, Schneider-Creusot. His hope was to acquire enough stock to sit on the French firm's board. By then, he was aiming for French citizenship: He had founded a home for French seamen and been rewarded with a knighthood in the Legion of Honor. But Schneider-Creusot was, for a while, his enemy—and particularly the enemy of Zaharoff's partner Tom Vickers.

Schneider-Creusot was the largest arms manufacturer in France. The firm still belonged to the Schneider family, and owed its hyphenated name to the city of Le Creusot where the company works were situated. The founding Schneider had been an eighteenth-century bank clerk with an interest in engineering, who had moved into business and supplied arms to Louis XIV. For a song, he bought up companies which were failing or had failed, then restored them. Later, in 1833, he acquired some workshops at Le Creusot from the bankruptcy court.

Like the Japanese of the early twentieth century, he was not innovative—he appropriated the techniques of other countries. But his talents and those of his son and heir were uneven; by 1850 the founder's son was himself facing bankruptcy when he had the wit—or the luck—to back Louis Napoleon's coup d'état, which was to lead, two years later, to his enthronement as Emperor. Napoleon III made Joseph-Eugène Schneider the official government armorer. And just as Alfred Krupp made his fortune from Prussia's victory over France in 1871, so Joseph-Eugène made his from France's costly defeat. Armorers, like lawyers, cannot lose. Joseph-Eugène completed his castle, the Chateau de la Verrerie, on a hilltop overlooking his smokestacks, much like Krupp's at Essen.

His political position was, however, weakened by the advent of the republic which followed the defeat at Sedan. But he was too rich and too essential to the nation's defense to be ignored, and the government lent him troops to shoot down Communist strikers in the eighties. His son, Eugène, restored the family prestige, and sat in the Chamber of Deputies from 1900 to 1925.

In the early 1900s, Schneider and Krupp fought each other for the burgeoning new Latin American markets, created by frequent wars, in a campaign marked by every imaginable foul play. Krupp usually won. Then, Schneider extended his empire by advancing in a different direction—the East. Beginning in 1909, Schneider set his sights ambitiously on Russia.

Using the press, Schneider and a Tsarist agent in Paris, Arthur Raffalovitch—who himself bought the Agence Havas, the main news agency—raised huge Russian loans on the Paris stock exchange to pay for Schneider's development of the Putiloff works in St. Petersburg, Russia's main arms industry. Schneider also hoped to build French 75mm. cannon at Perm, in the Urals, where the firm acquired land. But Zaharoff, funded by the Société Générale, a rival bank to Schneider's Union Parisienne, built the Tsaritsyn factory on the Volga for Vickers and Vickers' partners, instead.

The Tsar, however, still favored Schneider, and proposed extending Putiloff by the creation of new Baltic shipyards. But the Union Pari-

sienne was overextended in Russia, and Russian bonds were beginning to
fall. Schneider chirpily tried to get funds from the Société Générale;
when that failed, he turned brazenly to Krupp. Zaharoff's press told the
story of how Schneider was becoming a "front for Krupp"; Schneider's
papers denied it. Krupp, through cartel arrangements with Skoda of Austro-Hungary, got the money for Schneider from Skoda's bank, the Kredi-
tanstalt of Vienna, enabling the French firm to cover 25 per cent of a
new issue of stock. But this financing was still inadequate, and Zaharoff
saw his chance: Vickers, backed by the Société Générale, tried to buy in.
Schneider's papers, rather than complain about British competition,
trumpeted falsely that the Tsar was about to sell out to Krupp—who was
of course Schneider's own partner, but a buzz word for "enemy" to most
Frenchmen. Public opinion ran high: The perfidious Tsar had been
"given" an arms industry by France, only to turn to the Prussians! In St.
Petersburg, the Russians fed a false story to the London *Times* correspondent, saying that they were thinking of turning to Berlin. Patriotic
Frenchmen hastened to oversubscribe the new Russian loan and keep the
good French company Schneider on the Neva. Virtually every French
bank of importance contributed.

French journalists were bribed not to report the growing scandals,
naval mutinies and incipient revolution in Russia. Russian royalty visited
Paris and the French Prime Minister went in some state to St. Petersburg. An angry Vickers was urged by the Société Générale to blow wide
open Schneider's links to Krupp, but Zaharoff's counsel prevailed: Today's enemies are tomorrow's friends, he reminded them, and if the Russian bond issue collapsed, the Société Générale would be among the
losers. When the Russian revolution came a few years later, Schneider—
and French investors in Russian bonds—lost everything.

Schneider was luckier in Bulgaria. By bribing the King, and getting
the French Government to threaten to refuse a loan if the Sobranje (the
Bulgarian parliament) did not approve the huge order for Schneider
weapons which the King had made, Eugène made a killing. But in July
1914, when the Turkish Navy Minister visited Le Creusot and ordered
cannons, to be paid for by a French loan, things worked out differently.
War broke out as the minister was on his way home, so the Turk stopped
off in Essen, deposited the French loan there and ordered from Krupp.

Only partially successful in Russia, Zaharoff helped Vickers establish
themselves in Turkey—one result of which was that when British troops
landed for their ill-fated expedition in the Dardanelles, in World War
One, Colonel Mustapha Kemal—later, Kemal Atatürk—mowed them
down with British guns sold by Zaharoff. When this story emerged,
Zaharoff had a ready counter: He had been bribing the Ottomans to

break their alliance with Germany, which would have brought them into the war on the Allies' side, but had been outbribed by the Germans.

When war broke out, leaders on all sides said it would be over soon. Zaharoff said it would last about four years, and he was right: As he was to explain much later, it would have been ruinous for the arms industries of Britain, France, Germany and Russia to gear up to maximum production and then see the market collapse overnight.

Somehow, at the height of his financial successes, Zaharoff's checkered early past always kept popping up. In 1911, one Haim Manelewitsch Sahar, a Russian Jew who had settled in Birmingham, England, claimed that Zaharoff was his long-lost father, whom he had been seeking since he was seventeen. His story seems to fit in with the Russian records now in Turkey, but Haim's story was more complex, and original: He said the arms dealer's name was Manel Sahar, that he came from Wilkomir in Russia and had been married to Haje Elka Karolinska, a fellow Jew, but had later deserted her. Zaharoff, then preparing for French citizenship —which he acquired in 1913—and armed with the archimandrite's false birth certificate, naturally denied everything. The French, however, had been suspicious all along about this document, tracing the millionaire to Mouchliou in Anatolia. Jean Jaurès, the French socialist leader opposed to the arms manufacturers, urged the French authorities to contact the Tsar's government to check the Birmingham claim. The French Government sent an agent called Nadel to check out Haim Sahar's story.

Nadel was selected for his linguistic abilities—he was of Russian Jewish origin. Zaharoff got wind of the Nadel mission and contacted Nadel before he left, checkbook in hand: Nadel, of course, found the Mouchliou certificate was perfectly kosher. Nadel, it later transpired, had a background remarkably similar to Zaharoff's: He was a native of Odessa who had gone to live in Tatavla to avoid Tsarist military service and had, like Zaharoff, become a brothel tout. In Paris, he had followed various professions—pimp, interpreter, police informer and finally agent of the Sûreté.

In the last year or two before World War One, Zaharoff's business machinations become progressively more involved. We find him arming Greece against Turkey, Turkey against Serbia, Serbia against Austria. Through Vickers, he is expanding the Turkish armed forces and ensuring that Vickers is paid by securing a contract which stipulated that the money should come from tax collection in the province of Sivas—with collection entrusted, not to the Turkish authorities, but to a private institution headed by Sir Vincent Caillard, who was on the Vickers board and was an old friend of Zaharoff's. The Turkish deal enabled Zaharoff to increase arms orders from the fearful Russians, whom he helped to raise another loan in France. Always noted for being "one war ahead" of the generals, Zaharoff was also investing in aircraft and submarine development, and correctly foreseeing that the key to modern war would be oil.

Zaharoff's main enemy at the time was the "pacifist" Lloyd George, and more was needed to bring the Welshman around than stirring arms workers to occasional riot. Enter a new Zaharoff ally, Ignaz Trebitch, a Hungarian Jew who had immigrated to Britain, where he had changed his name to Timothy Lincoln and become a Church of England clergyman thanks to a mysterious theological diploma from Canada. Lincoln, while curate of Appledore, ran for Parliament from Darlington with support from Lloyd George and won.

Lincoln was presumed to be a protégé of the Prime Minister. Actually, he was soon in the pay of Zaharoff, after the latter had informed the new Member of Parliament that he knew (correctly) that Lincoln was a German spy. Lincoln's Zaharoff-appointed task was to spy on Lloyd George's notoriously variegated love life, and he soon came up with a story that was almost too good to be true. One of Lloyd George's mistresses had been none other than Emily Ann Burrows, who had resumed her maiden name when she had finally divorced Prince Gortzacoff alias Zaharoff. In those days, when even one extramarital affair would have ruined a British politician if it had become known, Lincoln discovered several. As well as informing his German masters, he also informed Zaharoff, who passed the information to his arms agent for Latin America, Michel Clemenceau, who informed his father Georges Clemenceau, the French Prime Minister—who hated Lloyd George and was thus able, McCormick theorizes, to blackmail him into not opposing rearmament. Lloyd George, who became Prime Minister in 1916, would soon have to make war as well as love.

Next Zaharoff acquired oil rights in Algeria and sought a way to make this new industry pay off. He passed word through Lincoln of the Algerian petroleum finds to Lloyd George, who was persuaded to go to North Africa, ostensibly for a vacation. Zaharoff then informed the French that the British leader was really in Algeria because the British hoped to make a killing in oil in the French colony. Zaharoff thus triggered a contest for oil between France and Britain—although neither Clemenceau nor Lloyd George really understood the true importance of petroleum—and Zaharoff's investment soared.

Zaharoff now had stock in an arms empire that stretched from Spain to Russia, from Italy to Japan, from Turkey to Canada. He was on the board of the French firm Le Nickel and, at long last, of the French arms-maker Schneider-Creusot. He may even, according to some biographers, have ordered the assassination of Jean Jaurès on July 31, 1914—the same day Zaharoff was promoted to commander in the Legion of Honor. He dominated a powerful portion of the French press scene.

When war broke out, orders mounted from the Triple Alliance—Britain, France and Russia—but Zaharoff ensured that orders from Germany and Turkey were fulfilled also; these back orders were not completed until 1915. In late 1914, a Norwegian ship carrying nickel to Hamburg from the mines of Le Nickel in New Caledonia (a firm in which Zaharoff, as noted, had an interest) was captured by the French warship *Dupetit-Thouars* and brought into Brest. Zaharoff secured its release, and ship and cargo continued their voyage to the enemy port.

It was, indeed, a Zaharoff war, with British ships built by Vickers sunk by mines provided by Zaharoff, and with German arms plants in which Zaharoff had an interest ruled off limits to Allied bombers. In fact, virtually no arms plants on either side were attacked. At the outbreak of war, the French were mysteriously ordered to retreat 22 kilometers from their early capture of Thionville—just over the German border in Lorraine— so that a factory there, partly owned by Zaharoff, should not lie within the range of French artillery—and so that the Thionville plant could continue to be supplied by the blast furnaces at Briey, nearby in France, which the retreat allowed the Germans to capture. Through high French officials, Zaharoff ensured that Thionville was never attacked, nor Briey retaken. When the French War Minister ordered Briey bombed, the orders were mysteriously countermanded by a subordinate. The French government later explained that if they had bombed Briey, the Germans would have bombed Dombasle, France's chief source of iron ore. Thus, each side protected the other's profits, thereby prolonging the war, and declined to bomb some of the enemy's strong points—while executing their own deserters and even conscientious objectors.

Meanwhile, the British became the first to use a dirigible for naval reconnaissance, thanks to Zaharoff's purchase of a German zeppelin a year before the war. Germany had also sold airships to Russia and Japan. For it was not only a Zaharoff war but a Krupp war too. Germans invading Russia faced Krupp cannons, while their Austro-Hungarian allies were raked by Skoda fire. French troops pressing into Bulgaria faced the French "75s" which the Sobranje had been forced to buy. The Belgian and Italian armies had been largely armed by Germany. Most of the world's navies used Krupp armor. On the other side, most of the Central Powers' units had British Maxims or copies of them. The British, through Zaharoff, had built Austro-Hungary's torpedo plant at Fiume (now Rijeka, Yugoslavia). The Nobel Dynamite Trust was Anglo-German: At the outbreak of war, the trust was dissolved and the stock distributed among British and German stockholders, instead of each country confiscating the other's stock.

Both sides bought or salvaged fats from which to extract glycerine for explosives. The Allies allowed the Germans to import vegetable oils and oil cake through neutral Denmark, with some of it arriving in British ships from Britain's Far East possessions. The British naval attaché to Scandinavia during the war revealed later that American copper was allowed to reach Germany through Norway, Sweden, Denmark and Switzerland.

The French company Le Nickel, which largely belonged to the French Rothschild banking company, included on its board not only Basil Zaharoff but also two Germans, representing Krupp and the Frankfurter Metallgesellschaft, of which the Kaiser himself was a director. Total German demand for nickel from 1900 to 1910 was 3,000 tons a year. Between 1910 and 1914, Krupp alone imported and stockpiled 20,000 tons. After the incident with the Norwegian freighter, the Rothschild concern continued supplying nickel to Germany from France's Pacific colony. Other nickel from New Caledonia reached Germany by freighter submarine via the American Metals Company, which was linked with the Metallgesellschaft: On its outward trip, the sub carried German chemicals to the United States. The Spanish firm of Penarroya, controlled by the Rothschilds since 1883, continued fulfilling a Metallgesellschaft contract until the end of 1916.

A German senator called Possehl owned Russian factories and continued operating them through the war. He was charged with treason, and replied that if he had not kept his Russian plant going, it would have been confiscated. He was acquitted, and the Kaiser congratulated Possehl on the verdict. During the war, the Germans sent France 150,000 tons of iron and steel each month, through Switzerland. France sent back bauxite and chemicals needed for explosives. The German firms faced treason trials but won acquittal simply by pleading that they were fulfilling legal contracts. The French bauxite appeared as aluminum in German U-boats. The British imported Zeiss lenses through Holland, but lacked German craftsmen to adapt them to artillery sights; so Zeiss sent some of its workers to Vickers, in order not to lose the contract. During the crucial battle of Verdun, Germans advancing on Fort Douaumont were halted by a forest of barbed wire manufactured by the Magdeburger Draht und Kabelwerke, which had been shipped to France through Switzerland only two months before.

All this has to be set against the slaughter which prolongation of the war imposed: By 1918, an average of 3,680 officers and 75,500 enlisted men were being killed—on both sides—each month. The average life expectancy of an officer at the front was five months.

But these arrangements were covered by discretion and hypocrisy. When the Cleveland Automatic Machine Company took space in the May 6, 1915, issue of the *American Machinist*, to advertise a shrapnel shell that released poison gas, the details were too explicit for German taste. The advertisement said: "Fragments become coated with the two acids in exploding, and wounds caused by them mean death in terrible agony within four hours if not attended to immediately." The advertisement went on to explain that immediate attention was not available in trench warfare, and that there was no antidote. Affected limbs had to be amputated. The advertisement was discussed indignantly in the Reichstag, and the American minister in Berlin had to apologize.

Zaharoff later told the Greek politician Venizelos—whom he financed for the ill-fated attack on postwar Turkey—that "I could have shown the Allies three points at which, had they struck, the enemy's armament potential could have been utterly destroyed. But that would have ruined the business built up over more than a century, and nothing would have been settled. The world would have been ripe for revolution. Our policy was to control the Central Powers, then to achieve victory without permitting industrial chaos in Europe." The German official war memoirs agreed: If the Allies had penetrated 12 kilometers into Lorraine at the onset of war, Germany "would have been defeated in six months."

Shortly after the nickel-cargo incident, Zaharoff's country house in France was captured by the advancing Germans. But Zaharoff had been tipped of the enemy's plans and was able to evacuate his staff, his valuables and of course himself.

In 1916, he was sent to the United States to buy arms for Britain. This time, the Germans were less friendly—and were also well informed. A U-boat stopped the passenger liner on which he was sailing, and a German officer boarded and asked for Zaharoff, whom he intended to take prisoner. But the wily dealer had prepared for such an eventuality and had taken with him a man of similar height with the same shape of beard, posing as his secretary. This man gave himself up and was taken aboard the submarine. Zaharoff took great pleasure in stunning his fellow passengers when he joined the captain's table for dinner that night.

In March 1917, Zaharoff's agents informed him of the content of a letter sent by the Emperor Charles of Austria to his brother-in-law, Prince Sixte de Bourbon, an officer in the (enemy) Belgian army. It was apparently a reply to a letter from the Belgian prince suggesting that Austria relax its war on the Western Front and press east. Zaharoff saw the possibility of creating new arms markets in Eastern Europe, including Greece. Making Britain's and France's small operations in the oil countries of the Middle East more difficult would also increase arms demands by those Allied armies in Arab countries. Zaharoff informed Lloyd George of the correspondence and urged him to communicate with the Emperor on the same lines. He won over Lloyd George, but the British leader was unable to convince his allies, France and Italy.

In 1918, the intrepid dealer set off for Germany, disguised as a Bulgarian army doctor. The Bulgarian had been kidnapped in Switzerland by Nadel and brought to Britain, where Zaharoff interrogated him closely, in order to be able to assume his identity completely. The Bulgarian was promised his freedom and a large sum of money for his cooperation. After the interrogation, however, he was poisoned and the money recovered from his pockets. The disguised Zaharoff went straight to see his old friend Krupp, urging him to force the Kaiser to make peace: Zaharoff genuinely feared a spread of the Communist revolution from Russia, and warned Krupp that a Communist Germany would expropriate him. Talking from his intelligence reports, Zaharoff told Krupp of Moscow's plans to found the Comintern—the Communist International—and to move the capital of "world communism" to Berlin. He also recounted Russian plans to stir up the Arab world, to evict France and Britain from the Middle East. He correctly predicted the Communist revolutions that were soon to start in the eastern provinces of Germany and the one that was to be led by Béla Kun in Hungary. If peace could be obtained through an armistice, he said, Germany would not be invaded, and the arms factories would be left intact. Krupp was cooperative, and an armistice was finally reached that year. Krupp then revealed that he had, through Switzerland, sold Britain 123 million shrapnel fuses during the war, with the Krupp marking—KPz 9604— unchanged. Krupp, as mentioned earlier, charged Britain for the patent on his fuses, demanding the equivalent of 7½ cents for each of the millions of shells fired: With Zaharoff's help, he received partial payment.

After the war, Zaharoff persuaded Lloyd George to drop plans to nationalize the arms industry in Britain. Perhaps, who knows, he strengthened his hand by asking indiscreetly about Emily Ann . . . By then, Zaharoff was engaged in the one war he almost entirely financed himself, for romantic reasons—that of the Greek Republicans against Turkey. Always ahead of his time, he bought radio stations to spread propaganda about Turkish treatment of Greeks in Turkey. The Athens prefect of police claimed later that Zaharoff had had "160 agents" in the city, listing them as including "27 convicted thieves, 21 professional gamblers, 20 white-slavers, 10 smugglers and 8 suspected murderers." Zaharoff was also busy farther east, investing more deeply into oil and opposing Arab nationalism.

By then Zaharoff had expanded his own intelligence service, which was run by Arthur Maundy Gregory. The son of a Southampton vicar, Gregory, an Oxford University dropout who had been a teacher, actor and unsuccessful theater producer, had been set up in a detective agency by Zaharoff. The agency was a cover for the arms dealer's espionage network; during the war, it had been incorporated into the British intelligence system. Gregory participated in the setting up of the propaganda radio network which helped bring about Greece's war with Turkey, and which was earlier credited with bringing about the collapse of Bulgaria. He went to prison in 1926 for selling peerages and other honors, on a commission basis, for Britain's Tory government.

Still in search of more respectability, Zaharoff founded a chair of aviation studies at the Sorbonne and one of French literature at Oxford; he endowed a French literary prize which still exists—the Prix Balzac. He was rewarded with a Grand Cross of the Legion of Honor and with an honorary doctorate at Oxford. He had already acquired British citizenship and been knighted, in 1918. Zaharoff then set seriously about the task of fighting Bolshevism: Shortly after he arrived in Germany for his first postwar visit, Karl Liebknecht and Rosa Luxemburg, two vocal German Communists who had proposed disbanding the arms industries, were murdered and their bodies thrown into a canal. At the same time, Zaharoff was acting as a go-between for Lloyd George with the new Bolshevik government in Moscow. When Sir Basil Thomson, the head of the Special Branch (counterespionage) at Scotland Yard, learned of Zaharoff's contacts and "revealed" them to the Prime Minister, he was unceremoniously fired for his "interference." Zaharoff opposed the League of Nations because of its disarmamentist character, and encouraged American isolationism in order to keep American firms out of Mideast oil.

After his friend Venizelos failed in his attack on Turkey, he became expendable to Zaharoff, who responded to a request from Queen Marie of Romania—one of Queen Victoria's granddaughters—and used his influence to help the restoration of the Greek monarchy. But the Greek defeat by Kemal Atatürk cost Lloyd George his leadership of Britain, since on Zaharoff's advice he had aided the losing side.

Now seventy-three, Zaharoff saw monarchies as the answer to communism. At his instructions, Gregory placed an advertisement in the London *Times,* asking for an "English country gentleman" who would be prepared to be Mpret (king) of Albania. Harry Sinclair, the American oil

tycoon, volunteered, but finally the Italians imposed an Albanian nobleman, Zog. Zaharoff, annoyed by the Sinclair bid, used his Agence Radio
to accuse Standard Oil of fomenting the war then going on in Ireland.

Still, like a blocked toilet that will not flush, the old man's scruffy past
kept re-emerging. His alleged son Haim Sahar, who had changed his
name to Hyman Barnett Zaharoff, invited the press to his daughter
Yvonne's wedding, and the London *Daily Sketch* captioned its picture by
describing her as the "granddaughter of the well-known philanthropist
Sir Basil Zaharoff." Once more denying any link to Sahar, Zaharoff told reporters he had not been born in Odessa, nor even in Mouchliou, as his
"birth certificate" stated, but in Istanbul. This was probably true, but he
now claimed to have been born in that city's fashionable Phanar section.

Sir Basil Thomson, still fuming over his treatment by Zaharoff and
Lloyd George, decided that maybe Sahar could help him bring the arms
dealer down. He contacted one of his old Special Branch agents, Clérisse
Thirza, in France, and asked her to come to Britain and interview Sahar.
But Zaharoff was one step ahead, and persuaded the British police that
Thirza—who had risked her life as a spy for the British and French—
was actually a German agent; as a consequence, she was not allowed off
the boat at Dover.

In retirement in Tangier, Thirza told McCormick that she had known
the ubiquitous Nadel when he had been working for the French Sûreté
and moonlighting for Zaharoff: Nadel had told her Zaharoff was a Bulgarian who had pretended to be Greek because it sounded more cul-
tured. During World War One, Nadel had become a physiognomist at
Monte Carlo casino: When Zaharoff later bought the casino, Nadel was
soon found dead. The Monaco police obligingly said he had committed
suicide because of gambling debts, but when his will was read it was
found that he was a millionaire.

In 1924, at the age of seventy-five, Zaharoff finally married the love of
his life. He had been corresponding and clandestinely meeting with the
Duchess of Villafranca for about forty years, and she was now well into
her fifties. Her husband had died in his asylum in 1923. The marriage
took place at the city hall of suburban Arronville near Paris. The
certificate describes the couple as Zacharie Basil Zaharoff and Marie del
Pilar Antonia-Angela-Patroncinio-Simona de Muguiro y Beruete. The
groom was made a Spanish duke, but never used the title, preferring "Sir
Basil." The couple resided mainly at Monte Carlo or at Zaharoff's chateau, the Villa Balincourt, once the home of Baroness Vaughan, the
morganatic wife of King Leopold of the Belgians.

The duchess lived for only eighteen months after the wedding. These were hard times for Zaharoff. The arms trade was in a slump. But the casino—euphemistically titled the Société de Bains de Mer—flourished, after Zaharoff doubled the minimum stake. In 1925, it paid a 100 per cent dividend to its shareholders. Zaharoff ultimately sold the casino to the French banking house of Daniel Dreyfus, but he retained ownership of Monaco's Hôtel de Paris, where he lived for most of his widowerhood. He maintained elegant private brothels in Paris and on the Riviera, entertaining generals and visiting politicians. To ease the pain of Marie's passing, he had a string of affairs, but maintained his detachment from his mistresses by always having two at a time.

He developed some senile quirks. He would, for instance, send a girl a doll, stuffed to appear pregnant, as an announcement of his intentions. When courting an English debutante who was infatuated with Venice, he flooded the cellar of a house with water and floated a gondola-shaped bed in it. To all his women, he wrote passionate love letters. His most intriguing old-age relationship was with an Algerian girl called Zora, whom he taught to read and write. In 1928, at the age of seventy-nine, he had a passionate affair with Lady Edmée Owen, who wrote an equally passionate memoir about the experience.

Zaharoff began preparing for the end, seeking once more to cover himself in mystery. He sold his arms, banking and mining interests, and set a fire in his Paris apartment to destroy diaries and documents. He also made sure the destruction of the documents was reported—presumably meaning that some had been "saved." Researchers believe he had caught a servant trying to sell some of his papers to a French journal and feared that all of them might fall into editors' hands when he died.

Still as wily as ever, in 1932—he was eighty-three—he planted a story in *Excelsior* saying he had had arms talks with President Hoover aboard the presidential yacht *Corsair*, in Washington. The U.S. press soon revealed that the *Corsair* was under repair in New York, so the talks could not have taken place. Zaharoff thus skillfully concealed the fact that he actually *had* had talks with Hoover—but at the White House. His aim was to urge the United States not to back the Disarmament Conference.

Another apparently false report which appeared in the press the following year was that Zaharoff was going to raise the British cruiser *Hampshire*—sunk off the Orkneys in 1916 while on its way to Russia with Lord Kitchener, the British army commander in France, and 2 million pounds sterling in bullion aboard. The reports said that the American locksmith Charles Courtney had been engaged to crack the *Hampshire*'s safe. (When Zaharoff died, Courtney did get the job of opening the arms dealer's safe in the Avenue Hoche.)

Whether Zaharoff intended raising the *Hampshire* for the bullion remains a secret; but later Otto Stormer, then the director of the Abwehr (German intelligence), claimed that Zaharoff had offered him 2 million pounds for all German records on his World War One activities, which were incriminating both for Zaharoff and Krupp. This story, however, seems implausible, since the Abwehr could easily have photographed the documents before selling them.

Zaharoff threw his ideological support to the fascists in Germany and Spain. Though no longer involved in arms directly, he tried to stage-manage the cartelization of a number of heavy industries in France, Luxembourg, Belgium and Germany. His principal opponents were Prince Radziwill (who had earlier lost out in a bid to buy the Monte Carlo casino, and nursed a grudge against Zaharoff) along with a rich metallurgist called Mayrich in Luxembourg and a Belgian tycoon called Alfred Lowenstein. Lowenstein mysteriously fell from his own plane into the English Channel. Mayrich died in a car accident on a lonely road, with no witnesses. Radziwill died of poisoning and the woman who killed him was declared insane.

Zaharoff spent his last days in Monaco, being pushed in a wheelchair along the promenade. Still mischievously crafty, he planted stories in popular papers saying that he was dead, and that the figure in the wheelchair was a double—then read his obituaries. His intelligence network, though smaller, remained effective: In 1934, he told a French politician which Germans would betray Hitler if war came, naming several who subsequently became involved in the plots to kill the Führer.

He died on November 28, 1936, and was buried, with his 298 decorations from 31 nations, beside his duchess in the grounds at Balincourt. Armed guards continued their twenty-four-hour duty, keeping all but his two stepdaughters from the funeral. But two months later, thieves broke into the duchess' casket, probably seeking her jewelry.

Mysterious to the end, his fortune was never found. Officially, his French estate was worth less than $5 million, his British holdings less than $700,000. The wills were only contested by two alleged cousins, Iphigenia and Melpomene Zaharoff, living in penury in a village on the shores of the Sea of Marmara; they were presumably bought off by the heirs—the two stepdaughters—because the case never came to court.

Sam Cummings

Most arms transfers take place today on a "government to government" basis; but about 5 per cent of total global transactions—worth perhaps $2.5 billion or more—still goes through the modern descendants of Bannerman and Zaharoff. This is especially true of the trade in used weapons, which have a useful life much longer than that of, say, a used toaster or a secondhand automobile. Even aircraft, whose worn parts are constantly replaced, have an almost indefinite life, although the "1938 C-47" that you purchase for $15,000 may have little that is 1938 about it except chunks of the fuselage and the registration number. There is a good market for yesterday's weaponry, especially but not exclusively in "backward" countries—and it is used weapons, or weapons overtaken by the "state of the art," not the engineering marvels that grace the pages of *Aviation Week* and the *International Defense Review*, that are used to fight most of the dozen or so wars going on somewhere in the world each day.

A massive uncontrolled arms market, largely helped along by privateers, flourished during Algeria's war for independence, from 1954 to 1962. In its attempts to blockade the traffic in the last years of the war, the French actually sank at least three merchant ships carrying weapons from Germany and Belgium, and stopped a score of other German freighters; they seized seventeen Yugoslav gunrunning vessels and a Czech ship, the *Lidice,* said to be carrying "enough arms to outfit a division."

Short-term demand is the specialty of the privateer. Frederick Forsyth, in his novel *The Dogs of War,* paints a good picture of small-arms dealers and how they operate. Lewis Frank, in his study *The Arms Trade in International Relations,* notes that "private arms dealers such as Interarms have a slight edge over governments in the short term—although it operates only by official sanction. Private dealers can eliminate red tape and offer recent-model weapons at attractive 'no-strings-attached' prices which governments, even if willing, take a much longer time to do. At times, governments prefer the use of private channels for small consignments of arms where overt aid is not feasible." Dealers can sometimes deliver within forty-eight hours, drawing on their own stocks of surplus or phased-out weaponry. Moreover, Frank, writing in the late sixties, noted that "Interarms and others have taken out insurance against [a] temporary decrease in used-weapon demand by becoming regional sales agents for new weapons."

What is Interarms? Interarms is really one lone, improbable Pennsylvanian, a chubby, nonsmoking, nondrinking—even nonhunting—scoutmasterish-looking fellow called Samuel Cummings, who appears to be at least a decade younger than his fifty-two years. He lives in Monte Carlo, a stone's throw from the Hôtel de Paris where Zaharoff died, his old-world apartment-office looking out on the casino Zaharoff once owned. His American office at Alexandria, across the Potomac from Washington, includes the second largest depot of small arms anywhere in the world. The largest is Cummings' depot in Manchester, England. Between them they hold more small arms than the combined arsenals of America, Germany, France and Britain. In addition, there's an Interarms depot in Singapore, run in conjunction with the local Ministry of Defense, and sales offices in Panama, Nassau and Buenos Aires.

Every address has a reason: Monte Carlo, for instance, has no income tax; this doesn't reduce tax on corporation profits but does relieve Cummings of any personal tax obligations. When American law was changed to make all U.S. citizens abroad taxable in the United States on all of their earnings surpassing a fixed modest figure (currently, $20,000 a year), Cummings took British citizenship. The Alexandria complex is aimed mostly at the hunting trade: Through the offices there come 85 per cent or more of all small foreign weapons imported into the United States. Panama and Nassau are tax havens, while Buenos Aires is the center of the flourishing South American trade—just as Singapore is an island of safety for foreign businessmen in the East.

Of Philadelphia Main Line stock, Cummings was born to a family with "safe" investments and began life with governesses. But the stock market crash wiped out his father's fortune, forcing Cummings Sr. to take a small job. Then, when Sam was eight, his father died. Working for a real estate firm, his mother managed to keep him in private schooling—specifically, the local Episcopal academy, whose motto *Esse Quam Videri* (To be rather than to seem) is emblazoned on the Interarms logo. At the age of five, someone gave him a World War One Maxim machine gun, purchased at an American Legion fundraiser, and he thinks it was then that the nickel dropped and character began to form.

A brief stint in the infantry at the end of World War Two, during which he became a sergeant weapons instructor, was followed by studies at the capital's George Washington University, interrupted by a tour through France, where he came across a sight that would not have stirred thoughts of fortune in most of us: In the Falaise Gap of Normandy, where American forces had trapped ten divisions three years earlier, he saw skeletons of German soldiers clutching weapons, and other weapons, helmets and paraphernalia strewn around. The French had not cleared the area for fear of booby traps. Cummings reckoned that anyone who would do the clearing would get the weapons cheaply, and be able to sell them at a handsome profit. Since he only had a GI Bill grant of $65 a month, he wrote to the Western Arms Corporation in Los Angeles, offering his services as a scout.

WAC was no ordinary business firm. When the OSS was disbanded after World War Two, the Research and Analysis Division was absorbed by the State Department and became the Bureau of Intelligence and Research (INR); the rest was absorbed by the War Department as the Strategic Services Unit, which in 1947 became the CIA. An early CIA decision was to bring war surplus in Europe to the United States, rather than let it fall into the hands of left-wing movements. Some of the guns would also, it was reasoned, be useful as "sterile" weapons (foreign-made and untraceable to the United States) to be provided secretly to foreign friends. Two firms were set up to handle this trade: one was WAC, headed by Hollywood promoter Leo Lippe.

But WAC hesitated over Cummings' offer to join the firm, and he finished his studies instead. During this period, Cummings spent a semester at Oxford and became addicted to British life. Back in the United States, he bought a stock of German helmets for 50 cents each from a junkyard at Richmond and drove them to Aberdeen, Maryland, where he sold them to the Proving Grounds Museum for $4.00 apiece. The Museum resold them to movie studios and theatrical costumiers. Cummings also began buying and selling antique guns.

Then the Korean War broke out and he served a stint at the CIA, identifying Korean weaponry. Finally, WAC took him on for $5,600 a year, plus one eighth of 1 per cent commission. By then, Lippe's British salesman Arthur Cecil Jackson had bought Lippe out and it was Jackson who hired Cummings. The Philadelphian managed to save $25,000 in two years, and launched Interarmco—as the corporation was originally known, until Armco Steel, acting through the courts, forced a change in 1967. While with WAC, Cummings had seen Jackson quarrel with his American partner, Seymour Ziebert, who had then founded the Golden State Arms Corporation and the Pasadena Firearms Corporation—two firms which subsequently went bankrupt trying to compete with Cummings.

In 1962, Cummings admitted to *The Saturday Evening Post* that initially, in his correspondence, he had referred to himself in the third person, "so people wouldn't suspect that Interarmco's entire staff was me." He registered with the Treasury Department and the State Department's Office of Munitions Control (OMC), and made his initial purchases and sales in Latin America, including grossing $3.5 million from the Dominican Republic for twenty-six British-built Vampire jet fighters, acquired from Sweden, reportedly for $650,000. He became a close friend of Dominican President Rafael Trujillo Molina. He sold to both sides in the Cuban civil war, as he had done earlier in the Costa Rican conflict; he began to collect a staff, along with the first of his Alexandria warehouses

—where he originally dressed his employees in surplus uniforms, Allied and enemy.

When Germany had begun rearming, it had bought from Cummings a stock of MG-42 light machine guns which Cummings had purchased earlier in Holland as Wehrmacht "scrap." He bought 300,000 mostly Russian weapons from Finland and sold them to Americans. Other early clients included the Austrian and Kenyan police forces. The Liberian Frontier Force bought 2,000 Springfields with extra-long bayonets, chromed to withstand humidity. The Irish sold him tommy guns confiscated from the IRA. Argentina sold him 144 cavalry lances, which he resold to newly independent Sudan for its camel corps. In 1956, according to George Thayer in *The War Business*, Israel sold him Russian weapons captured from Egypt that year.

The secret, he soon decided, was to acquire huge stocks, both to be able to satisfy demand quickly and to corner the market. As countries rejuvenated their arsenals, Cummings or an agent of his would arrive with a handsome silver pistol for the Minister of Defense and an offer to buy everything—lock, stock and barrel, in the true meaning of that phrase.

Cummings acted as a conduit for "CIA" weapons to President Jacobo Arbenz Guzmán of Guatemala; then, learning that Arbenz was about to resume arms shipments from Czechoslovakia, the dealer armed an invasion and coup by anti-Arbenz elements, once again under CIA guidance. In 1959, Cummings bought a million dollars' worth of Spanish surplus—600,000 weapons. In partnership with others, he paid a similar sum to Britain for nearly a million Lee-Enfield rifles, thus emphasizing the advantage of buying in bulk. The rifles, renovated and "sporterized," brought about $9 million at wholesale. A year or so later, he had sold them all. Looking to the day when "surplus" might grow thin, he also acquired franchises to sell the new small arms produced by the nationalized arms plants of Holland, Sweden and Finland.

Cummings profited greatly from the switch in U.S. policy from military grant aid to sales. Once free arms were no longer so easily available, buying them from Interarms often seemed simpler than government-to-government purchases. The firm unscrambles the red tape, delivers quickly and has access to a greater range of small weaponry than governments—sometimes including arms originally produced by the purchaser country itself.

Cummings also relies for a heavy part of his income on the sports gun trade, which is nearly insatiable in America. His prices frequently undercut those of his competitors by 50 per cent or more. The Alexandria operation is mostly directed toward that market. He also sells rare guns and antiques and custom-made weapons, and sells or rents out guns and other military paraphernalia to film producers. To develop the customs trade, Cummings has, at various times, controlled seven British sporting-weapon firms: Churchill, Hercules, Grant and Lang, Henry Atkin Ltd., F. Beesley Ltd., Harrison and Hussey, and Charles Harris and Sons. For five years, Cummings also owned a controlling interest in Cogswell and Harrison: In 1963, he sold the name and the retail store while keeping the inventory and the warehouse facilities. Before he became British, he was the only foreigner ever elected a member of the British gunsmiths' guild—the Worshipful Company of Gunmakers.

In the sixties, Cummings banded together importers of foreign surplus rifles to hold off threatened legislation intended to protect domestic U.S. hunting-gun manufacturers, led by Remington and Winchester. The domestic producers used the Kennedy assassination in their campaign against the availability of cheap foreign rifles and carbines, and in 1968 the Gun Control Act finally passed. In Monaco in 1976, the head of Interarms told the writer the 1968 measure was "the act to drive Sam Cummings out of business."

It had been a profitable business, promoted by shrewd business tactics. When a stock of redundant weapons was about to come on the market, Cummings, through his subordinates, often passed the word around the world that his warehouses were already overstocked with such material. If the story were true, Interarms could drive the price down if anyone bought the new supply and tried to unload it. If not true, it could still drive bids for the new stock of weapons down—enabling Interarms to outbid competitors more easily and secure the stock on highly profitable terms. If Interarms stocks of a weapon were genuinely high, Cummings could hold the trove from the market until the price rose again. Around 1960, Cummings bought 5,000 Bulgarian Lugers through Austria, for about $9.00 apiece. Cummings informed OMC of their Bulgarian source, but as they were German-origin weapons an import license was readily granted. A Finnish freighter brought them from Hamburg to Alexandria, where they were cleaned up and sold for $700 each to collectors.

Also in 1960, Czechoslovakia's Omnipol offered Cummings a load of Mausers. Cummings accepted the Mausers, to test OMC policy on "Communist" weapons. The import license was refused, so the Czechs shipped the arms to freedom fighters in Angola—carefully forgetting to remove the "Interarms" stenciling put on the crates at the time of the abortive Cummings purchase bid.

Interarms once imported 50,000 Danish grenades to extract the gunpowder. Thayer tells the story: The crates split open during the Atlantic passage and "dozens of loose . . . potato-masher grenades" were found by the frightened Alexandria dockers. Thayer recounts that "eventually, at Cummings' expense, the lot was dumped into the sea off . . . Georgia by the Coast Guard."

During the late fifties and early sixties, Interarms operated a revolving purchasing fund. Interarms (Canada) Ltd. was based in Monaco, which at that time had a favorable corporate tax rate of 1 per cent; the Canadian corporation had its account with the Banque Commerciale in Geneva. Revenue from sales would go into the account, virtually untaxed, and be used to purchase more weapons—and at favorable rates, since Cummings paid cash. This manner of doing business is easiest when there is only one owner, not answerable to stockholders who want some of the money distributed, at fiscal-year end, as dividends. It is especially possible with a company owner whose own money needs are slight. During this period, Cummings allowed himself about $10,000 a year as salary.

Before the 1968 act, rifles—the main stock-in-trade of the sporting-gun industry—could be imported into the United States at the GATT (General Agreement on Tariffs and Trade) rate if they cost less than $5.00 apiece. The GATT rate was 75 cents plus 22.5 per cent *ad valorem*. So, Interarms (U.K.) might buy Lee-Enfields at $1.50 and resell to Interarms (Canada) for $1.65, thus covering handling costs and yielding a small—taxable—profit. The Canadian corporation would pay the U.K. corporation, which would then pay the British Government. The Canadian subsidiary would then sell to Alexandria for $4.95 and bank the proceeds—over 200 per cent profit—in Geneva. Interarms would add $1.87 tax, clean up the guns for the market and sell at another substantial (but this time, taxable) profit.

The British turned to selling in small batches to help smaller bidders, who were often prepared to pay more and settle for lower profits, and who made the buyers' market more competitive. But in 1976, Cummings told the writer that he still bought nearly 90 per cent of all surplus British small arms, through his British firm.

Cummings first blow came in 1958, when the domestic arms industry got section 414 of the 1954 Mutual Security Act amended to ban the reimportation of American arms exported as lend-lease or military assistance. The next came the same year when Defense banned the sale of U.S. military surplus firearms in the United States. Then de Gaulle cracked down on Monaco, forcing the nominally independent principality to raise its corporate tax from 1 to 25 per cent, then later to 35 per cent. Another blow was the successful drive by the Internal Revenue Service in Washington to tax Americans not living in the United States. Yet another was the 1968 act, which transferred control of arms imports from OMC to the

Alcohol, Tobacco and Firearms division of Treasury. But Monaco is still without income tax, so today Cummings can run down taxable corporate profits by paying himself a mammoth, tax-free salary. When this too was threatened, he gave up citizenship. Already, in 1962, he told John Kohler: "I'm an economic exile. I don't prefer life abroad, but in America today nobody starting from scratch can accumulate capital any more. It's an immoral situation. What the IRS doesn't take, you have to sink into new stock."

But if Cummings still thrives it is also because he runs his business efficiently. Often he owns the entire stock of some rare weapons. These he can sell at a high price through Hunter's Lodge, the Alexandria sporting-weapon enterprise. For twenty years, Interarms has also sold through chain stores—Monty's, Sears, Macy's, Gamble, Gimbels. An excellent private intelligence system usually spots surplus just before it comes onto the market, and Cummings has nearly two hundred agents spread throughout the non-Communist world. For many years, his Iranian agent was a personal friend of the Shah's. His Finnish agent was a hero of the Karelia campaign during World War Two. In Indonesia, when Sukarno was in power, Cummings' agent was Sukarno's cousin. When Suharto took power, the agent was replaced by a classmate of Suharto's. But agents who embarrass Cummings are quickly fired. In 1961, Hans-Joachim Seidenschnür of Germany was dismissed after he and two arms smugglers were found to be involved in helping the Algerian independence movement; Cummings, living in Monaco, enclaved by France, could not afford French official enmity. Seidenschnür was jailed later that year on smuggling and swindling charges.

The little boy who tried to take a Maxim apart at five has inevitably become an authority on small arms. When Cummings testified to the Senate Foreign Relations Committee, in executive (closed) session, in 1967, he recalled how the Pentagon had rejected the Armalite-10—designed by Eugene Stoner of Fairchild Engine and Airplane Corporation—in favor of Stoner's lighter AR-15, now known as the M-16 assault rifle. (Mr. and Mrs. Stoner get a royalty of 50 cents each on every M-16 sold.) This, Cummings asserted forcefully, was a real goof. The following exchange took place:

Cummings: I am not personally an enthusiast of the M-16.
Senator Stuart Symington: In Vietnam they are enthusiastic because of the weight.
Cummings: The World War Two carbine was a useless weapon . . . Everybody loved it because it was light, but it was a dog.
Symington: Why is it a dog?
Cummings: Ballistically. You can have a hatful of the cartridges in your stomach and still live long enough to blast the man who fired at you.

At this point, an extremely rare kind of interruption occurred, and one that was probably only tolerated because it was a secret session. The stenotypist suddenly raised his head and cried: "He's right! He's right! I was in the Battle of the Bulge and I shot a German six times with a carbine and he was able to shoot me!"

Cummings revealed what soon became common knowledge—that Americans in Vietnam were using, whenever possible, Russian AK-47s taken from dead "Congs."

Several sources told the present writer that Interarms was a CIA front. Cummings scoffs at the notion. Thayer, who did a thorough investigation of the dealer, agreed that there was "no indication" of any direct link. A staffer at Alexandria attributes the rumor to a Drew Pearson column in 1961 which claimed that Interarms was owned and "financed" by the CIA. Thayer thinks Pearson or his informant may have been led astray by Cummings' sense of humor: His real estate in Alexandria is owned by Cummings Investment Associates and another holding company is called Cummings International Associates—both of course share the CIA's initials.

However, Interarms and the CIA have often collaborated, with Interarms being used as an arms conduit, and the intelligence unit benefiting from Cummings' private, resourceful intelligence network. The CIA also uses Interarms to buy Communist weapons for evaluation and for familiarization training for the Green Berets and others. Later, Cummings may be used to resell these weapons to clandestine, pro-American movements abroad. The Kurds in Iraq, for instance, used Communist weapons supplied by the United States. Thayer called Interarms "a convenient buffer between the government and the critics of the arms trade." The firm sometimes barters foreign small arms to the government for American weapons. Interarms also collaborates with AID (the U.S. Agency for International Development), which acquires police weapons and other riot-control equipment from Cummings for delivery to friendly countries. In 1960 and 1961, the CIA bought rifles from Interarms to distribute to anti-Castro Cubans: Some of this weaponry ended up on the beach at the Bay of Pigs. But often OMC and the Pentagon have frustrated Cummings from getting into a used-weapon market, even though this inhibition has given Washington less control over the ultimate destination of the arms involved. In April 1967, not long after the Indo-Pakistani War, Cummings told the Senate Near East and South Asia subcommittee: "It drives my Scotch-Irish nature crazy to see this trading going on through every nogoodnik and his brother, which we would not be able to do, and which we *could* do if we could get an accord from our country. It is our own material!"

Cummings has been denounced by Moscow's semiofficial daily *Pravda*, by Germany's sensation-hunting *Der Spiegel* and by Switzerland's sober *Tribune de Genève* as a modern Zaharoff. In 1974, the Soviet features agency Novosti said that this "merchant of death" controlled "90 per cent" of world trade in small arms—which Cummings says is true, within a percentile or two. But Jeanne Kubler, in her 1963 study *Traffic in Arms* for the Editorial Research Reports of *Congressional Quarterly*, noted that "[Interarms] transactions are aboveboard and lawful." Today, with his involvement in heavier weapons—submarines, aircraft, tanks, stocks of napalm—limited to occasional brokerage deals, this is probably even more incontrovertible. Put simply, Cummings would be a fool to make a fortune dishonestly when this would prejudice his ability to go on making an even larger one honestly. The dealer also notes that privateers without respectability in the corridors of power in the West often meet untimely ends. Several of Seidenschnür's friends in the Algerian arms trade, such as Paul Stauffer of Zurich and Georg Püchert of Hamburg, were gunned down by hit men of the French "Red Hand." Cummings carries no side arm to defend himself, and apparently feels safe.

John Kobler, who profiled "The Man with the Crocodile Briefcase" for *The Saturday Evening Post* in 1962, noted Cummings' Mayfair manners, his expletive-free language peppered with no term stronger than "Rubbish!" or "Baloney!" He only goes to the famous casino near his office when foreign visitors insist on it. Thayer noted that his strongest drink is a sip of champagne for a toast. French food is wasted on him. ("I guess I have a puritan streak in me," he told Kobler.) All reporters have ascribed part of his success to his constant travel, delegating little final authority —he even carries his own magnet, to test the composition of cartridges— and his habit of always going to the top to seal a deal.

He employs a correspondence code, and also sends playful postcards to friends signed by such names as Rasputin or Strangelove. His agents also shelter in similar high school humor, calling themselves such things as "your friendly neighborhood merchant of death," according to a Thayer anecdote. Before settling in Monte Carlo, Cummings ran Interarms from Salzburg, Copenhagen and Geneva, where he met his present Swiss wife, Irma. (His first spouse, a German, never accommodated to his quasi-permanent, globetrotting absences.)

Kobler interviewed Cummings in 1962, Thayer about six years later. When the present writer saw him in late 1976, little had changed. He was then forty-nine, but appeared to be in his thirties. He remains bluff, jovial, cordial, still without creature vices. Over an indifferent lunch at the local tennis club, his only excess was to drink a full liter of mineral water.

His office-home is one floor of the Building L'Armorial at Number 2 of the rue des Giroflées. His permanent headquarters staff appears to consist of a single secretary, and he frequently answers the phone himself. The high-ceilinged room in which he has his office is decorated by engravings and a few ancient arms—sabers and pistols. The bookshelves are lined with military histories and arms manuals. The U. S. Army map of the world which Thayer saw is no longer there, but the sixteenth-century suit of German armor still faces what looks like a typical French bank manager's desk. The most unusual furnishing is a British 2-pounder from the Napoleonic wars. There was a cat sleeping under it, and it was still there, snoozing peacefully, when we returned from lunch.

Cummings counted his blessings and problems, beginning with twin fourteen-year-old daughters who currently risked becoming stateless. After sixteen years in Monaco, Cummings still enjoyed the climate— "Nice airport is never fogged in"—but was lobbying against a U.S. law which says that children with only one American parent must spend two years in America between the ages of fourteen and twenty-six. The girls cannot have dual nationality, because Monégasque citizenship is the exclusive gift of Prince Rainier; ten years' residence is required, and even then he rarely consents to make the gift. The children cannot be Swiss because under Swiss law only a father can confer citizenship. If he loses his case, Cummings will send them to America for two of their college years. Cummings himself acquired British citizenship under the "grandfather clause"—his own was born in Padstow, Cornwall.

Cummings admitted in 1976 that he still occasionally bought Eastern European weaponry. They had, he said, more surplus to dispose of than ever before. Bulgaria was particularly active, although Hungary had also sold weapons to Interarms. East Germany had sold Hitler-period police weapons to Bulgaria, which had resold to Interarms for the rare-weapons buffs. Earlier, Cummings explained, East Germany had given its redundant weaponry to Africa, but now it had to give African nations new arms, to compete with those offered by Western suppliers. Romania now traded with the West in new weapons. Russia and Albania refused to deal with private firms: Partly as a consequence, the Soviet Union was still giving old weaponry to new allies; Cummings cited transfers of Russian T-34 tanks to Angola—and noted that the United States no longer had any Second World War armor. The Soviet action had persuaded Cuba to pass on to Angola some of its own out-of-date Soviet weaponry, presumably in the hope of getting "new" replacements from Moscow.

Cummings said that only truly industrialized countries, East or West, disposed of surplus. Rich but still developing nations now tended to hold on to their last-generation weaponry as part of their galaxy of power and prestige symbols. (And when they sell, it could be added, they usually have the company furnishing new weapons, particularly aircraft, find authorized buyers for the old.)

In a letter later, I asked Cummings if he was in the market for the billions of dollars of American arms abandoned in Vietnam at the time of the debacle, and whether he thought that the United States was seeking to buy them back as a form of "aid" to Hanoi—thus getting them out of the revolutionary arms circuit. Cummings replied:

> [Regarding] the VN surplus, this is and will remain the Sword of Damocles over the commercial arms market until it is disposed of and/or deteriorates into scrap, the latter being unlikely to happen in our view. While I do not have personal knowledge of the role this may be playing in current contacts between Hanoi and the USG, I do not have the impression from our own sources that the USG is emphasizing this surplus issue in our own Hanoi approaches, but I may be entirely wrong here. We have not had any luck in obtaining any of this nor, to the best of our knowledge, has anyone else to date, and this includes governments, East and West. Here again, we may be wrong, but this is our current view up to the present date. We would love to buy all this material and are, in fact, prepared to do so and move it to our own "neutral country" for sorting, rebuilding and licensed disposal, but this remains a pipedream so far.

A pipedream, indeed. The abandoned weaponry, which theoretically makes Vietnam the world's third most powerful nation—after the superpowers and ahead of China—includes nearly 800,000 M-16s. Vietnam has released film of some (presumably damaged) armor being melted down, but this has only raised suspicions about what might happen to more sellable weapons. Meanwhile, many like Cummings have their eyes open for this weaponry—which is easily traceable: If the serial numbers are erased, FBI and CIA gadgetry can restore their trace in the molecules of the metal itself. Some limited arms transfers from Vietnam are looked at in Chapter 8.

Cummings said in Monaco that nearly all his firm's work was now in light arms, including some light artillery. He occasionally acted as broker for the sale of armor—noting that the cost of actually handling and transporting such equipment was "astronomical." In the future, however, he noted, he could park tanks and armored vehicles and transport them on the 347 acres which he now possessed at Warrenton, Virginia, where his new gun factory had its own rail spur.

Following his split with his old German partner, Gerhard Mertins, Cummings did not buy arms from Germany for some time, but he said he was now beginning to buy again from Walther and Mauser. He denied, less convincingly, any "serious" involvement in the Lebanese conflict, then in full spate: He said the Lebanese rightists bought through "agencies" and Israel, adding protectively: "The only serious arms business today, legal or illegal, is governmental." He said a "conservative" estimate of the arms trade in 1976 was $50 billion, yet "Interarms has never yet had a hundred-million-dollar [profit] year."

Although Interarms had never been able to buy from the Soviet Union, Cummings said he had sold Kalashnikovs (AK-47s) "all over," as well as Ghalils—Israeli-made Kalashnikovs adapted to take (NATO) .223 ammunition. Czechoslovakia was selling .762 ammunition to NATO countries, while the West European Tornado MRCA (Multirole Combat Aircraft) used titanium imported from Russia.

Cummings said U.S. legislation would make it impractical for him to warehouse arms in America as he did in Manchester, England, and in most cases impossible even to bring it in, in the first place, although apart from sports weapons he did warehouse ammunition in the United States. He described his warehousing arrangement in Singapore as a "management expertise" contract with the Singaporean Ministry of Defense, "somewhat like a Hilton hotel contract."

Cummings' fame brings him some strange callers. In 1969, a Libyan colonel called him from Rome and asked if he could come over and talk business. The colonel said he had seen a film on Italian television which featured Interarms, and that Cummings "seemed to be the only non-Jew in the business." Cummings did not encourage him. He agreed to be interviewed by Russian television in 1975 on condition that nothing he said would be edited out, but he says the Russians did not keep their word. Later, the *Russian Military Review* referred to Interarms, in November 1976, as a CIA outfit, "not quite as important as IT&T but ahead of United Fruit."

The following year, his phone rang and a bass, accented voice at the other end said: "I want to speak to Samuel Cummings."

"This is I," said Cummings.

The deep voice said: "You don't know me, but I know you."

"I don't know you, but if you tell me your name, then I will," said the dealer.

"I am President Amin," came the rejoinder. "I want to send you my private jet, and I want you to come down and give us a modernization program for our army."

Cummings said cautiously that he couldn't make the trip to Kampala just then. He'd need U.S. and British approval to ship arms to him from

Manchester. Amin said that nevertheless he needed a set of Cummings' catalogues at once. How could he get them? Cummings said French postal workers were on strike that week, adding with tongue in cheek that if Amin would send his plane, a messenger would bring the catalogues to the airport. To Cummings' amused astonishment, Amin's personal Gulf-stream swooped into Nice the following day to pick up the books; but Cummings was under no illusions that OMC would authorize sales to Uganda at that time. Amin later sent a delegation to Monte Carlo, but the Ugandan brass left empty-handed. The African leader got his arms instead from Moscow, paid for by Libya.

A week before the writer's visit in 1976, the Washington office of Tong-Sun Park had called to ask if Cummings could go to see the wealthy Korean wheeler-dealer at the Dorchester Hotel in London, where he was in exile from the FBI investigation into his free-spending activities on Capitol Hill and elsewhere. Cummings replied that he would be in London soon; he later called the Dorchester, only to be told that "there is no one of that name here."

The author tried the same call, in London, the following day, and suggested that the hotel clerk give "TS" a message asking him to call back. The clerk insisted that the Korean was not there and that he was not expected. Cummings found resources for getting past this security and wrote the author later that "I had a cordial visit with Tong Sun Park last week in London and he is as you described him; we discussed several matters but I do not see any current active projects with his country for us . . ." As a congressional investigation later discovered, what the wily Korean wanted Cummings to do was to sell Korean-made M-16s on the international market—in contravention of U.S. law. Park was clearly trying to restore himself, with Cummings' aid, in the good graces of the presidential Blue House in Seoul. The M-16, along with two other U.S.-designed weapons, the Vulcan gun and the M-79 grenade-launcher, is made in Korea under license by Tong Il Industries Company, whose president is the Reverend Sun Myung Moon, head of the "Moonies" church.

Cummings bears no resemblance, in personality or style, to Zaharoff, but he admits to a little nostalgia for his predecessor in Monte Carlo. He says he once asked the Hôtel de Paris for some articles of memorabilia of Zaharoff, such as one of the dealer's monthly bills, but he was told that hotel papers that old had all been destroyed years before. He excuses his occupation more disarmingly than Zaharoff probably would have done. In 1962, he told Kobler: "I feel no more responsibility for what people do with the weapons I sell them than an automobile manufacturer feels for traffic deaths. I won't turn down any profitable trade I can get a license for. It's not my job to be a moral judge of humanity." Then he paradoxically quoted from Kipling and Tolstoi to say that his own moral code was based on man's responsibility for his fellows.

He told the present writer: "If you believe dealing in arms is evil, then to be logical you should refuse to pay your income tax because the government spends two thirds of it on weapons!" Years before, he had given David Brinkley the same argument, and noted that distilleries were not held responsible for alcoholism. Thayer noted: "Nor does he believe that selling to two countries which later go to war with each other is immoral; all large American firms, from Coca-Cola to Standard Oil, he says, sell to both sides." Perhaps his best argument would be that the United States and other governments all sell far more death-dealing equipment than Cummings can ever hope to do.

In August 1976, Cummings inaugurated, at Midland, Virginia, an arms manufacturing plant that by 1981 will cover 50,000 square feet and employ up to 300 persons. GOP congressman Kenneth J. Robinson and local officials were present. Production began on handguns, at a tempo of 20,000 a year, and by the time this book appears sporting rifles and shotguns will also be manufactured. Cummings told local Rotarians that month that if handguns were outlawed—which he thought unlikely—his Colts would become percussion weapons. He estimated that there were already 50 million privately owned guns in the United States. Writing that month in the Fauquier *Democrat*, Cummings said his Manchester warehouse now measured 200,000 square feet. Ninety-nine per cent of Interarms' exports came from there. But high taxes and the laziness of his 150 British workers made it less of a successful operation than it should have been. At Midland, Cummings said, they would build Colts for 42 per cent less than the cost of production in Switzerland, and Mausers and Walthers for 30 per cent less than in Germany—"the Germans will be buying their own pistols back from us."

In a later article, Cummings said one reason why he acquired so much surplus was because most countries wouldn't allow their own people to buy it. He stoutly defended America's predilection for the privately owned weapon, noting that in Sweden and Switzerland all males up to middle age—in Switzerland, until the age of sixty—had to keep a gun in their home to serve in an emergency, and that in Switzerland it could even be a machine gun.

Cummings was back in Virginia at the time to open his new plant and pay one of his six-monthly visits to his American staff, headed by Dick Winter, a stocky, gray, handsome, tough-looking Virginian a few years

Cummings' junior. Winter usually sits in a huge, low-ceilinged office with his desk at the far end. A zebra skin with the head pointing toward the desk adds to the long perspective. It must be an awesome office for an eighteen-year-old typist to enter. Arms, as samples or as decorations, or turned into lamps, seem to be everywhere. From Winter's window, part of the dockside complex can be seen, next to Old Alexandria's yacht marina.

Winter stresses the largely sports-weapon character of Interarms in America. With fifty salesmen, coast to coast, backed up by fifty headquarters staff, he boasts of still holding 90 per cent of the sports-weapon import market in the United States, mostly with European arms. The American firm also exports weapons, but only about 10 per cent of exports from Alexandria are military, Winter says. These include armored personnel carriers and antiaircraft artillery, but not missiles. Winter talked to the writer of a recent sale of "a whole battery of 155mm. howitzers." Cummings' vice-president won't give sales figures but, as Cummings was to do later, said there was still a target profit figure of $100 million.

Winter defends Interarms from charges of contributing to American crime statistics. Interviewed by the magazine *The Shooting Industry* in 1970, after citing the recent (1968) Newark and Detroit riots, and arms confiscated in Miami, Winter said less than 6 per cent of guns seized were military surplus. Winter emphasized Interarms' increased sales to law-enforcement agencies.

Since Cummings began importing Mannlicher-Carcano rifles and carbines in 1957—beginning with 70,000 that year at 75 cents purchase price each—the point inevitably arose as to whether Cummings imported the weapon that killed President Kennedy. Thayer, who researched the question, noted that Interarms imported mostly short-barreled, hunting-type Terni 7.35mm. carbines, selling them at $14.95 retail, and concluded that Lee Harvey Oswald's 6.5-caliber Model 91/38, serial number C2766, was an import of Adam Consolidated Industries Inc., of New York City.

Thayer says Adam Consolidated paid an average of $3.10 per weapon, which was considered high. He hypothesizes that Interarms drove up the price by spreading rumors of being prepared to outbid everybody. Thayer adds $1.72 for refurbishing, shipping costs from Italy and within both countries, import duties of $2.00 plus 22.5 per cent *ad-valorem*, and storage fees for twenty-eight months at Harborside Terminal in Jersey City. He thinks Klein's—the mail-order house patronized by Lee Harvey Oswald—bought for $8.60, which probably presented a loss for Adam.

Thayer says Adam ordered 570,745 Mannlicher-Carcanos but had only brought in 125,000 when one was used in the assassination, after which the market dried up. He assumes the rest of the order was unloaded at little or no profit. Thayer also reports that when Adam's goods were on the high seas, in September 1961, Cummings dropped his own price for Mannlicher-Carcanos to $9.95, "a price at which he could turn a profit but which his competitor could not match." Hence, the long sojourn for the shipment at Jersey City.

Gerhard Mertins

"So if you've talked to Cummings, who was a sergeant in your Army, why do you need to talk to me? I was only a general in the German Army!"

The rasping, accented voice on the telephone sounds more plaintive than angry. An American inevitably thinks of the Red Baron. Gerhard Georg Mertins was once the principal arms dealer in his country—the NATO nation with the most surplus to dispose of. He was, for three prosperous years, his government's "official" broker for such trading, dealing with the Verwertung für Bundeseigenes Vermögen (VEBEG). For twenty months, he was Cummings' agent in Germany, and Interarms was the representative of Merex AG, Mertins' company, in the United States. The biggest profits were in salvageable scrap. An M-47 tank, bought as scrap metal for $2,000, could, after reconditioning expenses, yield between 1,500 and 3,000 per cent profit.

Today, at fifty-eight, Mertins sounds like a broken man. He says he only contravened a few laws because his government had told him to. He nearly went to jail for it, trapped in the whiplash between Germany's two main parties. His real offense is obvious enough: He got caught.

Merex AG was founded in 1963. Mertins—who was a paratroop major, not a general—served in World War Two under Otto Skorzeny, the dashing SS commando officer who once rescued Mussolini. After the war, Mertins held an administrative job with Volkswagen, then operated his own buses between Bremen and Berlin. Next, he was in Egypt with the German military assistance group for four years, forming parachute units. His team left when the first Russians came. He then tried to rejoin the German Army. Recalling this period for the writer, Mertins said that "the screening committee included a German who had spent the war in London and another who had spent the war in Moscow. I decided the odds were stacked against me, so I withdrew my application."

Mertins had already conceived a hearty dislike for Germany's Social Democrats, whom he rates as little different from Communists. Refused for the Army, he moved to Boston. Two years later, adventure beckoned again: He was offered the task of training paratroops in Saudi Arabia; he accepted, taking with him an Egyptian team. After that, banker Herbert Quandt gave him the task of setting up the Mercedes-Benz assembly line in Saudi Arabia.

Back in Germany, he founded Merex. In 1965, it was through Merex that Cummings obtained about fifty-four unused F-86 fighters, plus another twenty from Luftwaffe service, and sold the lot to Venezuela. Interarms/Merex bought for a reported $46,400 per unit. Even allowing for handling and transportation, the sale price of $141,000 each must have shown a healthy profit. Delivery of the seventy-four jets was completed in 1966.

Until that year, Mertins worked hand in glove with the Bonn Defense Ministry. Bonn shipped Bundeswehr surplus to the Middle East and Africa through Merex. But that year, according to a prosecution case which took nearly a decade to come to trial, Merex sent eighty-nine F-86s and a huge quantity of ammunition to Iran, on a purchase order from General Toufanian, then Iran's G-4 (top procurement officer). This was done, according to the prosecution, "without waiting for U.S. end-use approval"—and while knowing that the load would end up in Pakistan, then (with India) under a NATO arms embargo because of the Indo-Pakistani War.

The Saberjets were the remnants of a 225-unit force bought by Bonn from Canada in 1957. Bonn wanted to unload them, to move up to the Starfighter. When the redoubtable Toufanian—later reckoned the second most powerful Iranian to the Shah himself—came to Bonn to buy, he was accompanied by Colonel Hussein Zaidi of the Pakistani forces. Merex, which had acquired the F-86s for $6,750,000, sold them to "Iran" for $10 million, of which $300,000 was extorted by "Iranian middlemen" (presumably including Toufanian), according to Mertins' then partner Sam Cummings. Merex received another $7.6 million for the airplanes' ammunition. The records show that both Canada and the United States had okayed the German deal.

Mertins pointed out feistily that the fighters were delivered to Iran by Luftwaffe pilots in civilian clothes, so that the deal clearly had government support—and implied that Bonn knew perfectly well where the planes were really going. Of this, there seems no doubt. The Luftwaffe fliers returned with souvenir cups presented to them by the Shah. Iran pretended to send the planes on to Pakistan "for repair." When their presence in Pakistan was announced in the Indian press, some of the planes returned briefly to Iran, to try to preserve the subterfuge.

At the time, Iran had a total air force of 110 planes and had ordered

F-4s. The pretense that it would also buy a load of aging Saberjets was for public consumption, and clearly did not fool Ottawa or Washington —which may even have suggested that Pakistan "go through" Teheran. Senator Stuart Symington told the Senate the following spring: "Our own intelligence services knew exactly at the time that these F-86s were meant for Pakistan." Deputy Assistant Defense Secretary Townsend "Tim" Hoopes revealed that there had been no end-use inspections by American military officials in either Pakistan or India for the past two years. Sam Cummings told the hearings that "thousands of rounds of tank gun and artillery ammunition had been shipped out of Germany and France to Iran for Pakistan." Cummings added archly: "I thought the United States knew."

Around the same time, Mertins handled a sale of twenty-eight British Seahawk naval fighter-bombers to India, and of $5.5 million worth of tanks, rockets, mines and parts to Saudi Arabia, then rearming for the potential conflict triggered a few months later when Israel invaded Egypt. The Indian order dated from August 1965 and had been ready for execution when the war with Pakistan broke out.

In June 1966, Mertins was authorized to sell the Seahawks to a Naples firm, Tirenna, with a prohibition on resale outside Italy. Merex reportedly had bought the planes for $625,000, with a resale tag of $875,000. The aircraft were loaded at Nordenham onto the Merex-leased freighter *Billetal*, which sailed for Italian waters—then, without touching shore, switched course for Kotchin, India. En route, the *Billetal* overtook its sister ship, the *Werretal*, also on lease to the tanks-and-guns package. Saudi Arabia then had no relations with Bonn and had presumably ordered, like Pakistan, through Iran. Another Merex arms shipment allegedly went to India that year, after a charade of being unloaded, then reloaded, at London.

Also that year, Mertins bought a large house in Bethesda, Maryland, and installed Gerhard Bauch as his U.S. agent, thus precipitating the break with Cummings. Bauch had an interesting past. He had earlier been the Cairo agent of Hamburg banker Quandt. In 1965, Bauch, his associate Sigmund Lotz and others were arrested as Israeli spies. Lotz was specifically charged with terrorizing German rocket and aircraft engineers working for the infant Egyptian air industry at Helwan—and of sending, to rocket expert Wolfgang Pilz, a letter bomb which had blinded Pilz's secretary. Lotz got life imprisonment, the others lesser terms. Bauch was acquitted. Mertins met Bauch through Quandt.

By 1969, when Thayer reported on the firm, Merex, although capitalized at only $27,000, still employed sixty-four people and grossed a respectable $7.5 million. But the salad days were over, and Bonn now sold

its surplus through Werkszeugaussenhandel (WAH), a $5,000 corpora-
tion founded in 1966 by ex-lieutenant general Gerhard Engel, Hitler's
former adjutant. WAH and Interarms became each other's agents the following year.

Rumblings of Mertins' funny sales in Asia kept surfacing in the German press, but only in 1974 was a prosecution announced. It was a
highly political case—an intentional embarrassment for former Christian
Democrat Chancellor Ludwig Erhard and his state secretary and close
friend Ludger Westick. Social Democrats saw it as a "retaliation" case
for the spy scandal which had involved a close friend of their own ex-
Chancellor, Willy Brandt.

Lothar Bungurtz, the Cologne attorney, charged that the ministry and
the national public radio had connived to "use" Mertins and to disguise
his deals, since the radio had reported the false destinations for the arms
cargoes.

The case brought in prominent German corporations, including a bank
and a shipping company. But Mertins had covered his tracks too well—
or too badly. He had omitted to show his profits on the covert sales in his
tax returns, the prosecution said. Mertins was charged with falsification
of documents and tax evasion. He claimed both acts were committed out
of loyalty to the republic and to national security.

Mertins is now a tired, tousled figure. The nine-year, on-again, off-
again case has taken its toll. He was acquitted in November 1975, but
only a year later did the prosecution drop plans to try him again. He
talks with an aggressive Berlin accent, watching a visiting reporter carefully through his one good eye—the left one was pierced and blinded by
a rose thorn while he was helping clear a site for a city children's project.

He chain-smokes, as does his slight, Armenian-Egyptian assistant, who
sits in witness to all Mertins says. The dealer is voluble as he unburdens
himself about Cummings, who he thinks played a disloyal role in his un-
doing. Just as Cummings hands out Xeroxes of London *Sunday Times*
and *Der Spiegel* clips with the Mertins indictment, so Mertins chides visitors for even talking to the Philadelphian:

"I know him. He's Cassius Clay—the greatest! 'We have enough
supplies in store to furnish two divisions!' I've heard it all! He's a *scrap
dealer!* He keeps files the way he learned as a corporal. Merex is not on
the level of scrap!" Later, he mentions that his family is related to the
Dulles family, and Gerhard himself has a similar cold-war philosophy to
the late Foster's. He sees current American criticism of the CIA as
"teleguided" by Moscow, which he also thinks was behind the draft-
evasion movements. "How much are they behind the peace movement
today?" he asks rhetorically, referring to détente. He also sees Soviet

provocation in gun-control measures: "No one is producing a rifle to shoot someone down!" he exclaims. "It is for security, for protection!"

He sees a Soviet military buildup all around the world, citing "$10 billion" of Soviet military aid for Iraq ("without discounts, that means $20 billion!") and "twice as much" for Libya. The East Germans are getting "hundreds" of the new T-72 tanks and RPG-7 antitank missiles, while Peru is buying MiG-23s and MiG-21s. The Russians are spending "15 per cent" of their GNP on the military budget. And so he goes on.

When the author saw Mertins at the end of 1976, he was planning to return to Germany to recover his fiscal fines and overtaxation, following the dropping of the case against him. While there, he hoped to found a German equivalent of Washington's Committee on the Present Danger. Then he was going to take an early partial retirement in the United States, where he has two married daughters.

He still has a firm—Merex-U.S. Mertins says it is capitalized at $200,000 and has an annual gross of $2 million. The corporation is a "mostly nonmilitary" German procurement agency and imports "peaceful" German products into the United States—along with ammunition, "a few weapons" and military spare parts. Merex is not registered under the Foreign Agents Registration Act, so presumably does no promotion. The firm has two offices in Germany, plus others in Quito, Athens, Riyadh and the Trucial States. There are agencies in Ankara, Teheran, Bangkok, Santiago and other places—forty-seven offices in all. Mertins regrets that he cannot sell Leopard tanks and Marder APC's to Saudi Arabia because Bonn has classed the Mideast as an "area of tension."

Then he explodes. "Why do you ask all these questions? Why do you ask about the Western arms trade? Investigate Omnipol! Investigate Yugoexport!" He calms, and his brown teeth smile. Later, he escorts the caller cordially to the elevator, where he even becomes ingratiating. "Do you want a scoop? The Shah of Iran has offered to mediate between Peking and Taipei! He's acceptable to Taipei, and I understand that he's acceptable to Peking also!"

Kim Roosevelt

Often significant in arms sales are highly placed middlemen who sell their contacts and high-level access. When the Senate subcommittee on multinational corporations investigated Northrop in 1975, a key figure who emerged was Kermit Roosevelt, President Theodore Roosevelt's Harvard-educated grandson, who served in the OSS and the CIA. With arms-purchase decisions often running into the hundreds of millions of dollars, a six-figure commission to someone like "Kim" Roosevelt, a personal friend of the Shah of Iran, King Hussein of Jordan and several Saudi princes, made sense. The Los Angeles-based aircraft firm, which produces the F-5 Freedom Fighter—the world's most exported military plane to date—hires several such "consultants," notably recently retired generals and recently defeated senior politicians, and has admitted (as noted in more detail in the next chapter) that it sometimes had to give kickbacks to foreign dignitaries. It had been revealed, shortly before, that Northrop had passed $450,000 to Saudi agent Adnan Khashoggi to "buy" the present and former heads of the Saudi Air Force. After the revelation, Khashoggi loyally "covered" the generals by saying he had pocketed the money himself.

Northrop executive John R. Hunt told an auditor that the firm had to employ agents in foreign countries, and added frankly: "The role of the agent is primarily that of the influence peddler—that is, he knows who to talk to and whose pockets to line in a particular country to get the job done . . . Agents are an expensive and necessary evil of doing business in a foreign country." Corporate officials "don't know and don't want to know where the money paid to agents goes," Hunt said.

Northrop president Thomas V. Jones told the auditor—whose report later went to the Senate subcommittee—that Kim Roosevelt, now sixty, is "perhaps the key figure in establishing the very high level of activity Northrop now has in the Middle East, with contract values in this area in the past seven to eight years running close to a billion dollars."

Nothing in the subcommittee report showed that Roosevelt, who set up Kermit Roosevelt and Associates—"international business consultants" —in 1962, ever was involved in passing bribes or kickbacks, or being shaken down for Northrop, himself. When congressional inquiries revealed that middlemen were entitled to $6 million of commissions on the contested 1975 sale of Hawk surface-to-air missiles to Jordan, Roosevelt refused to take his own $600,000, and his colleagues followed suit.

In Iran, Roosevelt's main contacts were the court minister, Assadollah Alam, and later, his old CIA boss, erstwhile U.S. ambassador Richard Helms. But the role of Roosevelt and his old partner Miles Copeland in restoring the monarchy to Iran didn't do Roosevelt any harm.

In 1973, Roosevelt was the linchpin for a projected deal whereby Northrop would build an F-5 plant in Iran to serve both Iran and three other countries—Saudi Arabia, Kuwait and Sudan. Some of the financing would be Saudi, and Egypt would also benefit by sending its pilots to Iran for F-5 conversion.

For a while, the deal seemed in doubt. In late November that year, we find a Northrop vice-president, M. G. Gonsalez, writing to Roosevelt that U.S. ambassador James A. Akins in Riyadh wanted the lawyer to get Saudi middleman Adnan Khashoggi to "speed up" Prince Sultan abd-el Aziz, the Defense Minister, on buying F-5s. Khashoggi, with a 5 per cent commission riding on the $756 million sale, tried to do just that.

However, a few weeks earlier, Northrop had authorized Khashoggi to represent Britain in Saudi Arabia for the sale of Anglo-French nuclear-capable Jaguar fighter-bombers for "resale or redelivery" to Egypt. The upshot of this was that eventually the Arab countries decided that French and British aircraft and helicopter plants in Egypt would be preferable to financing Iran as a center for Middle Eastern aerospace industry. Roosevelt reported back Arab suspicions that Zionist lobby control of the U. S. Congress would make a deal with the United States "unreliable."

Interviewed in his Connecticut Avenue office in Washington, the ailing Roosevelt said he had clients in "just about every state from Algeria to Pakistan, except of course Israel."

Roosevelt began his Mideast service in Cairo, in 1943, partly with the OSS, partly working for Dean Acheson at the State Department. In 1944, he was moved to Italy. After the war he went back to Cairo to write a book and a *Reader's Digest* article on Palestine called "Arabs Live There Too." In Iran for the CIA from 1951 to 1953, he and Miles Copeland were credited with overthrowing the left-wing government of Mohammed Mossadegh and restoring the monarchy. He left CIA service in 1958 and joined Gulf Oil. He says he disagreed with Gulf over the firm's "huge transfers of funds" to officials in the Middle East and Korea; he claims Gulf canceled his contract because they feared he would report back to government on the practice.

Copeland was an early associate of Roosevelt in the Washington practice, but now his top aide is his son, Kermit Roosevelt, Jr. Roosevelt formerly represented Raytheon, a top missile-maker, as well as Northrop, but he gave up the contract to avoid a conflict of interest. The bulk of Roosevelt's consultancies are not connected to arms. Among other firms, he represents Page Communications, Kaiser and Fleetwood.

Roosevelt says he thinks the Pentagon is "completely capable" of handling government-to-government sales, but he says foreign clients "feel the need for intermediaries, especially local agents, who are used to dealing with their American counterparts." Intermediaries are also needed to help dispose of "trade-in" weaponry when countries move up to more sophisticated wares. The Pentagon refuses to say which countries are eligible to buy which items, so agents sometimes handle the task of making requests for the selling governments. Roosevelt thinks the current congressional desire to have the last word in all foreign policy decisionmaking, including arms sales, leads it to put the worst interpretation on everything; he believes Congress will gradually have to curb its own power.

"No other arms producers are so hamstrung on sales as those of the United States," Roosevelt says. "Other countries will just pick up sales which the United States would have gotten." American sales survive, in spite of the handicaps, he thinks, because clients get far less for their dollar in Europe, and above all less follow-up service. Soviet weapons, Roosevelt says, are the cheapest on the market and are usually of good quality, but there are political handicaps to accepting them and the follow-up operation is poor. But he believes Hussein would have gone through with his threat to buy Soviet missiles if Congress had vetoed the Hawks sale, providing the Jordanian King could have persuaded puritanical Saudi Arabia—which was financing the deal—to spend money in Communist Moscow. Roosevelt sees a chance, through arms sales, to bring Syria completely into the Western camp.

Arms for Lebanon

The Lebanese civil war, which began in 1975, proved a "field day" for big and small privateers. Although Cummings claimed to the writer in 1976 that he would "never have anything to do with the warfare in Lebanon," he was named in the press as the main single supplier of weapons to Christians and other right-wing forces there the previous year. In July 1975, M-16s, machine guns, mortars and ammunition with an estimated value of $2.5 million were landed at Christian ports in North Lebanon, following a deal said to have been made by Cummings in Monte Carlo with Omnigroup, a Paris firm, and paid for by a draft on the Banque de Paris et des Pays-Bas in Geneva. Omnigroup was headed by a Lebanese Christian. Cummings was reportedly competing at the time—for $10 million of orders—with dealers, some of them backed by their governments, in France, Belgium, West Germany and Portugal. In most cases, the reports said, bills of lading indicated that the arms were for the Lebanese Army. Often the freighters, it was alleged, off-loaded their cargoes onto lighters and yachts just outside Lebanese territorial waters.

The well-informed but intensely anti-Arab Parisian satirical weekly Le Canard Enchaîné accused Samir Souki and his wealthy Saudi Arabian business associate, Adnan Khashoggi, of selling arms to the rightists through Khashoggi's Paris office. The French Government, carefully balancing its support of the Palestinians with its need to stroke oil interests in the Middle East, apparently closed its eyes to these sales—while Gaullist Premier Maurice Couve de Murville was blandly offering himself to "mediate" the Lebanese conflict.

The war was also fueled by supplies to the rightists—for obvious political reasons—by Jordan and Iran, and by Israel to increase the turmoil. Intelligence sources identified some material used by the Falangists as Soviet weaponry captured by Israel from Egypt and Syria in 1967. Israeli sources said at the time that the arms had been given by Israel to Biafra in 1969, then sold later by the victorious central government forces in Nigeria to a Lebanese merchant in Ghana. But the smoke screen was thin: After the Nigerian civil war, Nigeria did not reduce its forces but expanded them, and observers thought it highly improbable that it would have disposed of the sort of standard Soviet weaponry that is used by the armed forces of the Lagos regime. In 1976, Israel made its arms support of the Falangists open. The Israeli Government's arms trade in Lebanon in more recent times is described in Chapter 9.

Heavily involved in the Lebanese conflict, with its windfall profits for dealers, was the Beirut representative of Colt Arms Industries, Sarkis Soghanalian of Buffalo, an Armenian who has lived in the United States since 1958. Soghanalian was unwillingly drawn into the limelight in 1976 when OMC—because of the spreading violence in Lebanon—canceled his license, issued that year, to export three thousand revolvers and pistols, with ammunition.

A stocky, olive-complexioned, genial figure, Soghanalian works out of two small offices—one in Miami, one on the sixth floor of a Beirut building. The brass nameplate in Beirut bears the anonymous name of his company—United Industries, Inc.—but visitors are scrutinized through a peephole in the door and watched carefully by two bodyguards.

Soghanalian told a reporter that year that Lebanese law forbids foreign arms sales to any purchaser except the government, and "I don't break laws." Later, he grinned and said: "Maybe we bend them a little."

Soghanalian said he had acted as broker in sales of patrol boats and aircraft, and like most "small" dealers he does a profitable sideline in intelligence equipment. He told Washington *Post* reporter Jim Hoagland that he collected a commission of only 20 per cent, but estimated his profits at about $1 million a year, all from the Middle East.

At the height of the fighting, Soghanalian was bringing in arms in his own plane—a 707 whose Pan Am livery had been poorly painted over but which still had a PA registration. This helped persuade Pan Am to suspend its own flights into Beirut for several weeks, fearing they might be shot down by Palestinians or other "leftist" units with shoulder-mounted SA-7 heat-seeking missile launchers. Soghanalian told Hoagland that his plane had been sold by Pan Am to Yugoslavia in 1970 and that he had purchased it there; but he did not explain the registration number and livery marks.

Subsequently, Soghanalian admitted that his Colt order for the "Lebanese Army" did not correspond to any procurement made by that force. Later reports said half the three thousand guns were acquired by ex-President Camille Chamoun's right-wing National Liberal Party. The Soghanalian plane, with 20 tons of Portuguese weapons aboard—also for the "Lebanese Army"—was briefly grounded at Lisbon that year for unpaid repair bills, but released when a Lebanese businessman in Madrid paid the maintenance tab.

Soghanalian said it "takes a special type of character" to deal in arms, combining patience with a willingness to take risks and occasionally to lose money. "Trust and reputation mean everything in this business," he said solemnly.

One American pilot in Beirut that year told a reporter he had been kidnapped by leftists and interrogated about his cargo. After that, he had refused to fly in cargoes of medical supplies because the hold also contained unmarked boxes.

Money to pay for rightist weapons was supplied by members of the movements themselves, or from assets in Maronite monasteries, or by contributions from overseas Lebanese in Europe, the United States, South America, Australia and West Africa. More money was often raised by resale to nervous Beirut residents seeking protection, and occasionally even to opposing groups. The M-16s, priced at $175, could be resold for about $1,000, thus refinancing purchase of five times as many as those disposed of in this way. Soghanalian's Colts were soon available on the "street" for $600; he had charged only $135. The "black" price of mortars reached $10,000.

Arms for Ireland

The "Irish Question," as it used to be called, has provided a useful market for privateers in recent years, with Ulster under siege by its inhabitants of both factions of Christendom, and Belfast a drab modern equivalent of some lawless frontier city of yesteryear. As Sarah Hays Trott and this writer recounted in *The Power Peddlers*, almost all the money to buy weapons for the Irish Republican Army "Provisionals"— the Catholic side—is raised in the United States within the Irish "ethnic" community, most especially (according to the Irish Government) by the Irish Northern Aid Committee, based in Queens, New York. The explosives used by the "Provos" are usually stolen from quarries in the Irish Republic, but most of the weaponry is purchased on the East Coast of the United States.

Until several discoveries were made, it was smuggled in, in suitcases, aboard ocean liners, often with the complicity of longshoremen. Now, usually, small ships are used: A trawler, the *Claudia*, was accosted in 1971 as it entered Irish waters carrying arms from Libya and with an IRA leader aboard. That year, a Yonkers, New York, gunshop owner, Edward Agromante, was convicted of supplying weapons to the Irish guerrillas. Five men were sentenced in Baltimore in 1974 for gunrunning 158 Armalite semiautomatic rifles, but the principal charge was reversed on appeal in 1976. In 1975, former mayor Herbert Quinn of Concord, New Hampshire, was jailed for contempt of court for refusing to answer questions about gunrunning to Northern Ireland. The Ulster Defense Force, a Protestant counterterrorist group, gets some of its weapons from former compatriots in Canada.

Although the IRA cause against the governments of Ireland and Britain is a good deal narrower and more obscure than that of the Palestinians against Israel, the IRA manages to kill more compatriots than the Palestinians kill Israelis. Over a ten-year period from 1968, the comparative scores were 1,860 to 185. The Irish factions use a variety of weapons. The Provos use automatic and semiautomatic (one shot at a time) assault rifles, usually in their civilianized versions, along with the shorter (under 24-inch) carbines, submachine guns and some mortars and RPG-7 rocket launchers. Their handgun collection includes .375 and .38 magnums—the favorite weapons of many law-enforcement agencies in the United States. Fans of "Kojak" and other TV series would recognize them, as they require two hands to hold the gun steady when firing.

Initially, the M-1 Garand World War Two semiautomatic rifle was the commonest gun, but this has been replaced on the streets of 'Derry and Belfast more and more by the Armalite-15 (made by Colt) and the preferred Armalite-180—made in Costa Mesa, California. These are the "sporterized" versions of the standard NATO M-16 assault rifle. The weapon has little recoil—which helps accuracy—and a detachable stock, which is good for concealment. AR-180s with tungsten-tipped bullets can pierce armor and are accurate to 300 yards or more. The "elite" weapon, possessed by relatively few, is the Soviet AK-47, or Kalashnikov. Provos sometimes tinker with Armalites and Kalashnikovs to make them fully automatic, and some still use the automatic "grease gun"—the M-3 of World War Two.

In contrast, although the Loyalists have been known to make their own mortars, their armory has a dingy ring—mostly bolt-action rifles and an assortment of revolvers and pistols. Compared to the 3,285 feet per second of the Armalite's .223 American bullet, the .303 Lee-Enfield's projectile does only 2,240 feet per second: Reporters in Ulster often distinguish who is firing by the sound—the Armalite's bullet makes a sharp crack as it breaks the sound barrier on leaving the barrel; the Lee-Enfield's .303 is subsonic. The Loyalists also have some submachine guns and have been known to use crossbows, said by experts to be "lethal at 50 yards." Intelligence reports note, however, that the Protestants also have a vast array of *legal* weapons—in 1976, 78,000 Protestants had 101,000 licensed guns.

In recent years, AR-180s and AR-15s have been selling for about $200 legally, and $300 illicitly, in America. (The M-16 costs about $85.) Although advertised as "sporterized," the Armalite-180 may come with a bayonet fitting, a flash eliminator (for firing at night without making the gunner himself a target) and a big, thirty-shot magazine.

The IRA has a good reputation for paying promptly, thanks to their ample American financing. The organization is respected on the international guerrilla circuit as representing a heartfelt cause. Some arms have come in, not only from Libya, but from Eastern Europe and even Uganda. In the international coterie of dedicated crusaders, Provos spread the word that the (Protestant) Loyalists are fascists—which is often true—that the IRA "Officials" are Stalinists (also broadly accurate) and that the Dublin Government is composed of quislings, which is of course something of an exaggeration.

Today's armed crusaders, whether in Ireland, the Basque country of Spain, Palestine, Eritrea or Kurdistan, tend to share the same suppliers, catholic in their objectivity toward the causes from which they profit. In 1975, an arms-running group was uncovered in Belgium, centered on the cities of Liège and Bastogne; caches of explosives, guns, rockets, grenades and other bombs were seized, and a number of possible intended markets mentioned in press reports; in Paris, *Le Monde* theorized that the cache was assembled by "the emissaries of Mr. Claustre," a Frenchman whose anthropologist wife was then a prisoner of an insurgent group in Chad.

Privateers Galore

In a Vietnamese restaurant in Georgetown, Washington's Latin Quarter, a swarthy, intense, voluble man talks in muted tones of the vast degree of stealth and duplicity which still accompanies the arms trade, especially where privateers and their erstwhile allies in secretive government agencies are involved. He talks of how arms are described as fruit or other commodities on ships' manifests; of how—as in the famous Merex cases—the port destination that appears on the manifest may bear no relation to the truth; of how private arms exporters will ask the companies from which they lease ships for particular captains who have a reputation either for asking no questions or for already knowing the answers and maintaining discretion.

Governments set the example in this fraudulent behavior. France, for example, sent arms, including aircraft, to Israel in 1952 in preparation for the Suez invasion by consigning them to Naples, as though intended for the Italian armed forces. In Naples, the crates were stenciled "Achaba"—the Italian spelling for Akaba, Jordan—with manifests to match. Many carriers of contraband arms do not know the nature of their cargo.

Much NATO military matériel reached revolutionary movements through the Italian Communist Party (PCI), the Georgetown informant —a former official of AID's own "economic warfare department"—recalled. He saw this as a prime reason why the Party, already with prospects of sharing power in Rome, favors Italy remaining in NATO and in the European Community. He quoted a friend in the PCI as telling him about a potential take-over of power by the Communists in Italy: "Today is too soon for us, tomorrow will be too late for you." This ex-official saw widespread problems relating to the covert transfer of NATO weaponry if, as widely predicted, some Mediterranean countries acquire Eurocommunist regimes—notably Spain, Portugal, Greece and Italy.

The United States Government often has channeled arms, through allies or friendly governments, to subversive movements which it favors, or to countries where Washington seeks a low profile. The Georgetowner recalled the CIA using Israel to ship arms to Kenya, adding with a grin: "End-use is whatever you want it to be."

Neutrals are also in the trade. Some Swiss firms and Swedish companies go through dealers to evade their governments' restrictions on selling arms to so-called areas of tension. Needless to say, Communist countries also use covert methods. Frank recounts how Peking used a retired Polish major to purchase 300,000 surplus German Mauser rifles in the fifties. The weapons had originally been consigned to King Farouk of Egypt, but left in storage in Switzerland after his 1952 ouster.

Some weapons fell into Communist hands because they were supplied to friendly countries by the West so cheaply that they could be resold. In 1967, Britain sold a consignment of arms to Saudi Arabia at such low prices that the Saudis resold them profitably to dealers who sold them again, at a handsome profit to themselves. At this point, "end-use"—never a strong point with the British in any case—is meaningless.

Says Frank: "The Russians and the Red Chinese were able to obtain late-model U.S. and British small arms and . . . radar sets through the use of a Franco-Swiss cover firm until 1958, when its operator mysteriously 'disappeared.'"

Blueprints of Western weapons are of course sought by Communist countries, and sometimes dealers are more adept at brokering these than the often amateur spies who steal them. Alternatively, a sample may be even better than a blueprint. In late 1967, a Luftwaffe pilot pre-flighting his F-104G stared in amazement: One of his German-made Sidewinder heat-seeking missiles was missing; the case was never cracked. The traffic, of course, works both ways. The first MiG-21 to be taken apart in the West was one flown by an Iraqi pilot to Israel in 1966. Two more were flown to Jordan that year. A decade later came the famous flight by a Soviet pilot in Siberia to Japan with a MiG-25 Foxbat.

Resistance movements themselves are less adept at smuggling arms; but back in 1947, foreign Jewish supporters of the Haganah underground army in Palestine created a bogus airline—the Líneas Aéreas de Panamá S.A., based at Tocumen airport in Panama, and using surplus C-46 transports. Canadian and British pilots flew the C-46s to airfields in Czechoslovakia, where they took on surplus Nazi weaponry, including dismantled Messerschmitt Bf-109s, which they then flew on to Palestine.

Free ports like Rotterdam and free airports like Basel are much used for the traffic. Under a consular agreement dating from 1920, government authorities cannot step in during a transshipment process in such ports unless they *know* they will find, say, arms or drugs. Unless they find what they say they are looking for, they have no case.

Not all weapons of war are arms. Control applies to strategic minerals, which are often smuggled too. Take the case of "ferro-molly": Molybdenum is used to harden steel in most weaponry, and on the international black market can command a much higher price than is quoted on commodity exchanges. Similarly, during the Vietnam War, AID sent silver nitrate to Saigon for medical use. Local Chinese merchants would buy the supplies illicitly and extract the silver, which they could sell for overvalued piasters to nervous hoarders. This left a nitric-acid explosive so sensitive that it frequently killed its handlers—urban Viet Cong guerrillas. The ex-AID official said blithely: "Everyone knows that Qaddafi is shopping everywhere for plutonium." And well he might, as the 1962 case of 200 tons of weapons-grade nuclear fuel for Israel shows. In the global corridors of power, the assumption is that if Israel ever used "the

Bomb," the nuclear response would come, directly or indirectly, from the Soviet Union—but in these days of détente, how can Qaddafi be sure?

In 1976, the Senate subcommittee on internal security uncovered a case dating from the previous year, when 700 pounds of U. S. Army plastic explosive were found aboard a ship outbound in New Orleans harbor, in boxes marked "Olive Oil." The boxes bore stenciled AID markings, with the familiar clasped hands and the "Gift of the American People" wording. The destination is classified, but subcommittee sources say it was "somewhere in Europe." These sources said other cases were under investigation, as some involving "10,000–20,000 pounds" of explosive, similarly auctioned off by the Pentagon, and that the inquiry revealed "a minimum of control over disposition" by the Treasury's Bureau of Alcohol, Tobacco and Firearms.

Three scrap-dealer millionaires in Rochester, New York, Bernard, Stanley and Jerome Bachman, came to public notice in 1960 when they were charged with supplying arms and ammunition to Fidel Castro. Castro came to power that year, and seemed at first to be an improvement on Fulgencio Batista, even from the U.S. point of view; so the charges against the brothers—known to the Rochester press as "the amazing Bachmans," because of their capacity for turning scrap into "gold"—were reduced to a misdemeanor. Stanley was fined $500 and placed on probation for a year. Stanbern Aeronautics Corporation, one of their companies, was fined $2,500 and given three years' corporate probation. Although the Agency was never mentioned, subsequent revelations about CIA support to Castro suggest that the operation was probably masterminded from Langley.

In 1965, the Bachmans, along with their landlord Morris Diamond, were in difficulties again. This time it was for supplying parts for B-29 World War Two bombers to four CIA agents.* Three of these were charged under the Neutrality Act with illegally exporting seven of the Superfortresses to Portugal, for use against independence movements in Angola and Mozambique, which in turn were being assisted by another faction within the Agency—which may explain how the operation came to light. The Bachmans, who became state witnesses, were not charged.

According to the prosecution, the man in charge of breaking the U. S. Government ban on supplying Portugal with weapons for use in Africa was Gregory R. Board, an Australian-born American pilot who operated Aero Associates Inc., an aircraft-leasing firm in Tucson, Arizona. Board slipped away to Kingston when his three accomplices were arrested in

---

* The term "agent" applies to nonmembers of CIA staff working for the Agency. Regular employees are called "officers."

Tucson, and the government made no attempt to extradite him from Jamaica, where he had a house. Eventually, the cases against John R. Hawke, a twenty-eight-year-old, bearded ex-RAF pilot from Fort Lauderdale, Count Henri de Montarin, a fifty-eight-year-old French aircraft broker, and Woodrow W. Roderick, a forty-seven-year-old Canadian, were withdrawn after their lawyer announced plans to subpoena some ex-CIA officers.

The seven B-29s all made the transatlantic trip to a Portuguese air base near Lisbon, refueling en route at St. John's, Newfoundland, an out-of-the-way jumping-off place for Europe-bound planes less closely watched than Gander. The Bachmans, who gave evidence, admitted supplying long-range tanks, Norden bombsights, machine-gun parts, bomb racks, gun mounts, ammunition boxes and other Fortress parts, along with B-29 maintenance and operating manuals, but claimed that as the parts were "antiques" they did not think they were liable to arms control.

Jerome Bachman told the prosecuting attorney that he had never heard of the Munitions Control Act. Asked "Are Norden bombsights used by private aircraft?" he said: "People buy them for the parts." His sales manager, Jack Bachman, said they had sold bombsights before, and had even sold some to the USAF. A Page Airways employee at Rochester who had helped Hawke fit a long-range tank on a B-29 said he had asked him what he was doing with such an unusual plane. "He said it was being taken to Montreal for conversion to an executive aircraft," the employee added.

A C-46 that took on some of the Bachman parts was impounded at Tucson in September 1965, and the three defendants were arrested at that time. A Californian aircraft mechanic, Kent Griggers, who had flown with one of the bombers to Canada and Portugal, and seen Hawke arrive in Portugal with each of the seven, was the government's chief witness.

Rochester Airport employees told the Rochester *Democrat and Chronicle* that the Bachmans, who operate the Bachman Wholesale Company and "Surplus World," had helped outfit two of the B-29s and two C-46s at the field. These employees recognized Hawke and de Montarin and identified Board from photographs. Defense lawyer David Tumin of Miami said the aircraft transfer was authorized by the government, whether OMC had given a license or not, and that the recipient country was an ally—all of which was true.

A year later, Bernard and Jerome Bachman announced a new line— reconditioned armored cars for $3,000–$4,000. They said there was a flourishing market for the vehicles, especially in South America, for riot control. The Bachmans, who have a Washington office under the name

Mutual Defense, registered in 1976 as U.S. representatives of the French nationalized arms industry.

The world of the small international arms dealer is vast. A onetime Leo Lippe associate, Haywood Henry "Hy" Hunter, and his friend George W. Rose operated West Coast arms firms in the sixties, exploiting their links to Germany. Both men had pornography convictions dating from the fifties. Rose's Seaport Traders Inc. sold Lee Harvey Oswald the Smith and Wesson .38 with which he killed Patrolman J. D. Tippit shortly after assassinating President Kennedy. Hunter operated five corporations, most of them involved in arms. Rose built up a considerable business in cheap foreign pistols. He had the barrels unscrewed and replaced with solid barrels for firing blanks, thus qualifying for the lower duty on starter pistols. The normal barrels were imported as parts. When customs law was changed to plug this loophole, the ingenious Rose found it profitable to have his guns completely dismantled abroad and imported as parts—which also cut shipping rates since they ceased to be dangerous cargo.

West Indian-born Colonel Hubert Fauntleroy Julian, the "Black Eagle" who flew for Haile Selassie in Ethiopia against the Italians in 1935, went into the arms business after World War Two, in which he served as a sergeant (his colonel rank came from Ethiopia). A naturalized American, Julian says he supplied "everything from Swiss antitank guns to flak vests" to Guatemala. A 1953 shipment of 25,000 Italian antiaircraft shells for the Arbenz regime was seized in New York harbor. In 1962, he was arrested in Katanga carrying arms samples for the secessionist Tshombe regime, and spent four months in a Congolese jail. Earlier, he had been linked as an arms supplier to dictator Rafael Trujillo of the Dominican Republic, and he later became an arms agent for President "Papa Doc" Duvalier of Haiti.

Some Americans have exported, not arms, but fellow Americans to fire them. Robert Bufkin appeared in both Angola and Rhodesia in the seventies, proclaiming himself both a mercenary recruiter and a CIA agent. In Colorado, Robert K. Brown publishes *Soldier of Fortune,* which contains a sort of "Help Wanted" and "Situations Wanted" column for modern-day legionnaires.

Several arms dealers, both Canadian and American, are based in Canada. Montreal and Toronto are main centers. Their "turf" is largely Latin America, but Ian Smith's rebel settler regime in Rhodesia imported weapons from privateers in Buffalo and Toronto, two cities divided by a porous frontier. Levy Industries of Toronto supplied surplus U.S. M-47 tanks from the German Army to Pakistan during the embargo, ostensibly selling the armor to Iran's General Hassan Toufanian. According to Thayer, another Canadian privateer was Andrew McNaughton, a former squadron leader (major) in the RAF and the son of a former Canadian governor-general.

In the United States, the arms trade is mostly concentrated in or near major ports; a noted watering hole for privateers was the old Brasserie restaurant in Washington, now a Vietnamese eating place.

In Latin America, Roberto M. Arias and his wife, British ballerina Margot Fonteyn, were allegedly caught trying to smuggle arms into Arias' native Panama, where a coup d'état was planned. The clutter of different suppliers to both governments and dissident groups in Latin America creates a difficult "standardization" problem. Castro, during his rebel period, bought not only from Interarms and the Bachman brothers but also from a spectrum of suppliers, some based in Georgia and Florida. Castro imported in numerous small quantities so as to disguise the strength of his arms buildup from Batista spies. The absence of standardization in Castro's forces was not seriously cured, Thayer believes, until large supplies of M-1 rifles were captured from Batista's forces.

The courageous but naive Biafrans paid top dollar for equally unstandardized equipment from Portugal, South Africa, France, Gabon, Ivory Coast, Communist China and Tanzania. Earlier the Katangese secessionists had received an almost equally varied selection of weaponry from Rhodesia's federal Premier Sir Roy Welensky and from illicit Belgian sources, as well as Uzi submachine guns from Israel.

The CIA has used numerous different channels to cover its role in supplying arms. When Chiang Kai-shek fled to Taiwan in 1948, he left the 55th Kuomintang Regiment behind in Yunnan. The twelve thousand men crossed into Burma, where for thirteen years they were supplied by the CIA through various fronts and dealers, with the Agency's own Air America flying in the weapons and other goods. They occasionally staged raids into China, but eventually concentrated more and more on raising opium, becoming known as the "opium army." About six thousand of them were moved to Taiwan in recent years, but the rest—the numbers are now tripled by population growth—have remained in the "Golden Triangle."

Through the RAND Corporation and academic-sounding front and fringe groups, the CIA and its NATO equivalents have tried to keep track of worldwide underground movements. The most headline-seeking front group, in recent years, has been London's Institute for the Study of Conflict, which now has a nascent American equivalent. The ISC has attracted a nest of far-right journalists, huddled around their guru, Brian Crozier, the biographer of Chiang Kai-shek, Franco and Charles de

Gaulle. The guerrilla movements studied by these latter-day Commie-hunters are among the most regular markets for private arms dealers.

West Europe is the main center for small arms merchants—many of whom are only small in comparison with Sam Cummings. The main gunrunning port is probably Hamburg; but Antwerp, Marseille, Rotterdam, Genoa and even Barcelona are competitors. Some of the trade is centered in respectable Switzerland's capital, Berne, and the main Swiss business center of Zurich. One Swiss firm lost its Boeing franchise and was graylisted by OMC for supplying aircraft to the Smith regime in Rhodesia. From all these great centers of trade go crates marked "water pumps," "engine parts," "porcelain" or whatever title will seem to justify the weight. Often, humor dictates the choice of nomenclature. West German flamethrowers were discovered on their way to the Algerian resistance movement, the FLN, in crates marked "crop sprayers."

Perhaps the most colorful French sale of "munitions of war" in recent times was that made in 1976 of fake Smith and Wesson Startron night-vision devices to Libya. The Startron, used in Vietnam, and by the Israelis in the 1973 war, magnifies stray rays of light 65,000 times and enables tanks and other targets to be spotted over 600 yards. France, Sweden, Switzerland and the Soviet Union produce similar devices. The Smith and Wesson model is on the U.S. munitions list and cannot be exported without U.S. approval.

However, in 1975, two Frenchmen, Georges Starkmann and Claude Dumont, trading as "Régie Monceau," sold Libya 110 genuine Startrons for about $7,000 each. At the time, France, not a member of NATO's integrated command, was not applying the U.S. ban. Régie Monceau "laundered" the order through a company with a post office box address in Panama. However, when trying to complete Libya's original order for 300 of the devices, the exporters ran afoul of the ban. By then, President Qaddafi had increased his order to 3,000—presumably for use with his huge new orders of tanks—for a price of $15,282,000.

Stymied by the embargo, Starkmann and Dumont asked an optical-instruments manufacturer in the Paris suburb of Asnières to make 3,000 optical instruments that would resemble the Startron in appearance and packaging, for $96,000. French customs heard about the order and visited the plant, then cleared the devices for export because they were obviously not "classified" munitions.

The black tubes were shipped to Madrid, where a Libyan military inspector cleared the shipment and approved release of the over $15 million to Dumont and Starkmann's account with the Bank of America in Zurich. Then the tubes were flown back to Paris for not being "in conformity with the specifications." French police theorized that a Thomson-CSF executive, J. Abbatucci, who had introduced Libyan officials to the Monceau pair—and who resigned when the fraud was discovered—had advised the two men to tell Libya that the French had discovered and banned the shipment and confiscated the goods. Thus the tubes were left in the theoretical ownership of Libya—thereby leaving Tripoli with no financial claim against Starkmann and Dumont.

The duo apparently had another deal in the works with Libya—for nonexistent American-designed 155mm. and 175mm. cannons—which would reportedly have earned them another $151 million. One report said Libya had already deposited $60 million as part payment for the artillery into the Zurich account.

Major British traders include Cogswell and Harrison of London and Parker-Hale of Birmingham. Cogswell and Harrison was founded in the nineteenth century. It is now run by a quiet, rather bland man, E. H. "Ted" Holden, who is reputed to drive a hard bargain. He claims to have as much as a million dollars' worth of small arms in his warehouses at any time. Holden enjoys close relationships with Omnipol, the Czech export agency which sells arms for any currency except Czechoslovakia's. Holden's office is above his gunshop in Piccadilly. Parker-Hale is run by John Le Breton, who also has dealings with Omnipol.

More colorful than these bowler-hatted businessmen is John Dawson-Ellis, who was born Ellis Jacob Jacobs. He reportedly has a flourishing trade in the Middle East; in a British Government report published in 1956 he was named as one of the people behind the covert sale in 1951 of $434,000 worth of Valentine tanks to Egypt. Thayer named as another globetrotting arms salesman one Dominick de Fekte von Altbach und Nagyratoth, "formerly of the Royal Hungarian Horse Artillery."

Major William Robert Turp and his less well-known partner Thomas Clement Borrie founded Intor, Ltd., after World War Two in a London suburb called Bexleyheath. The firm called itself "gun reconditioners." According to Thayer, Turp received an order, in 1963, from Sheikh Ibrahim Zahid of Saudi Arabia, for ten thousand Lee-Enfields with bayonets, scabbards, pull-throughs and oil bottles. London's Board of Trade refused the export license, so Turp, according to Thayer, told Zahid to order from a Belgian company, Transma. Finally, Zahid ordered twenty thousand rifles from Transma, which legally bought them from Intor, which had legally exported them to Britain's ally, Belgium. They were for Yemeni royalist forces. Thayer quoted Turp and Borrie, whose partnership broke up in 1967, as saying that Dawson-Ellis had arranged the deal. (Beside Transma, another Belgian corporation that has been involved in international arms deals is Siden International, run by a French-born American citizen called Jacques S. Michault.)

In 1966, Turp became the unwitting party for an arms deal with Biafra. The cache of small American and British arms in question had been acquired in 1960 by Paul Favier, a former French police officer, from Holland, which had been given them in 1945. By 1966, Favier still had 3,600 British Manchester and U.S. Thompson submachine guns left, stored in a Dutch warehouse. The Biafrans, about to be forced into secession, offered to buy.

Favier, anxious not to arouse the suspicions of Dutch customs, contacted Turp, who had already reconditioned 500 Browning machine guns for Favier, and who had re-exported them with genuine British export licenses with no difficulty. Turp got an import license for the 3,600 tommy guns, which made Favier's Dutch export license easy. The Englishman never heard from the Frenchman again.

Favier had contacted Henry Warton, an American pilot with an elderly DC-4, who agreed to fly the weapons to Biafra in four flights for $14,000 plus flight costs. On October 9, 1966, Warton arrived at Zestienhoven airport, Rotterdam, and took the first consignment. Since Warton was known as an "arms pilot," the Dutch were suspicious, but his papers were in order. He filed a flight plan for Birmingham, England.

Late that afternoon, Warton's DC-4 entered the Birmingham control zone, where he canceled the flight plan, saying the owners had ordered him to Palma de Mallorca, where he landed that night and slept over. The following day, he crossed the Sahara, refueling and spending the night at the oil town of Hessi Messaoud in Algeria.

On the eleventh, he lost his way to a refueling stop at Fort-Lamy (now N'Djamena) in Chad. He landed instead on a riverbank near Garoua in Kamerun. The aircraft broke, the cargo scattered and an injured Warton was arrested, fined and spent a month in an African jail.

Turp's success in foiling a bid by Rhodesia to get British arms in spite of an embargo was recounted in Chapter 3.

Sharpness is a condition of survival in the arms trade, and bribery a fact of life. Thayer records that in Sukarno's Indonesia, 15 per cent had to be added to all sales prices to pay kickbacks to officers, bureaucrats and politicians. Even in Europe, political parties frequently shake down foreign arms suppliers. The system helps the survival of the privateer, who can more easily find unaccounted-for cash to grease palms than governments can. When Venezuela wanted F-86s in 1965, it could have obtained them more cheaply from the German Government than from Merex, but Merex could pay kickbacks. In the late sixties, Thayer records, Thailand wanted to buy M-16s from Colt Industries, but Colt refused to pay the negotiators. When the deal fell through, dealers tried to revive it. Then the U.S. embassy offered to undercut the dealers, since Thailand was a recipient of American aid and the United States did not want to see money wasted on corrupt officials. The indignant Thais bought Armalite-180s instead, from Japanese dealers, and at a price higher than any mentioned by Colt, American dealers or, of course, the embassy. In Indonesia, rascally air force generals opened a "Widows and Orphans Fund" in Singapore to receive kickbacks.

Arms dealing, as Cummings noted, can be dangerous. The Red Hand, a Corsican Mafia said to be more ruthless than the better-known Sicilian one, dealt harshly with German suppliers to the Algerian FLN. In addition to those dealers whose murders were recalled by Cummings, Georg Püchert was bombed to death in his car, and Wilhelm Beisner severely injured when a shrapnel weapon blew him through the roof of his; Ernst-Wilhelm Springer also nearly died from a bomb in his auto, while Marcel Leopold was slain by a poisoned arrow in his Geneva hotel lobby.

Just as political causes need lobbyists, and governments need middlemen, so arms dealers frequently require the services of munitions manipulators—called MMs. If OMC refuses an export license, an MM may try to get arms to his client through AID or the CIA. Many arms are initially exported to Britain, where export controls are relatively lax, and many MMs are British ex-officers. A well-known American MM is Mitchell Livingston WerBell of Powder Springs, Georgia, a Hemingwayian figure with a Guards mustache, a monocle and a shoulder holster, who frequently also sports a Tyrolean jacket, sometimes bearing his old paratroop insignia. WerBell, who has links with Latin America through the fruit trade, is the inventor of the world's best sound suppressor, or "silencer." His son, Geoffrey, is also a noted arms dealer. There will be more about this family later.

Still further down the scale comes a plethora of small privateers who may either make the quarter-million-dollar killing of which they have always dreamed, or get killed themselves, financially or truly. In 1976, Scotland Yard discovered that the South African Government was getting British arms, in spite of the embargo, through a firm in the semi-autonomous Channel Islands. The corporation was sending tank and armored-car spares in crates marked "Machinery—Spare Parts," and defied a Defense Ministry order to reveal the destination of its goods.

British intelligence sources say a close watch is kept on a former Defense Ministry explosives expert who lives on the Isle of Man in the Irish Sea. The semi-self-governing island is a tax haven, and also includes small ports into which "trawlers" can sail without drawing attention. A chemist by training, he was dropped into France during World War Two and blew up railroads and other targets. This man (who has never been charged with any offense) is also employed by a security agency, which protects VIPs and which belongs to a radio and communications equipment company.

A British "Middle East expert" who was formerly with the Foreign Office and who has close links with Israel told the author in 1976 that he had been approached that year by a Kurdish agent who wanted antitank weaponry but had only $60,000 to spend. The Kurds, once supported in their secession movement against Iraq by Iran and the CIA, now found themselves politically isolated. He suggested to the agent that he ask the British Ministry of Defense for covert aid. The Kurd reportedly received satisfaction.

He also reported Vietnam surplus turning up among guerrilla movements in obscure parts of the world where American arms would not be expected. Sometimes when arms come from unexpected sources, sabotage may be involved. The British have covertly sold damaged weapons to the IRA, just as Britons of a previous generation sold such guns to earlier Irish rebels.

In 1977, the U. S. Justice Department began investigating sales by Colt Industries of New York, and by Winchester International, to countries and agents acting as fronts for South Africa, which is, as noted earlier, under a U.S. arms embargo. The original story was broken by the New Haven *Advocate*. Third-party countries initially named included Zambia, Botswana, the Canary Islands, Mozambique and West Germany. Evidence showed that exports to the Canaries by the two companies rose from $52,000 in 1973 to $406,000 the following year. Colt blamed an employee, Walter S. Plowman, who pleaded guilty to falsifying OMC applications—thus saving his employers from having to give evidence—and was sentenced to twelve months' imprisonment. He claimed the State Department had acquiesced in the sales. A government attorney denied this.

The Olin Corporation of Stamford, Connecticut—parent firm of Winchester International—also blamed employees, who it said had been fired following an in-house investigation in 1976. But in March 1978, a New Haven, Connecticut, grand jury indicted Olin on twenty counts of falsifying documents and one of conspiracy.

The corporation was said to have knowingly sold 3,200 guns and 20 million rounds of ammunition, over a four-year period, to a South African dealer through the Canary Islands, Austria, Greece and Mozambique. Olin, pleading *nolo contendere*, admitted the sales, which it put at $1.2 million, but again blamed the former employees. The court imposed the maximum fine of $510,000, which was ordered to be paid to local charities; but the Treasury the following month agreed not to lift the firm's permit to manufacture, and trade in, arms.

In a consent decree signed in March 1979, Smith and Wesson agreed to pay a civil penalty of $120,000 for the unauthorized sale of 283 night rifle sights to Libya.

But South Africa remained the main target for investigations of this sort. A BBC TV special claimed that "millions of dollars" of U.S. howitzers, APCs, shells and helicopters had reached the apartheid regime illegally, starting in the Nixon era. Michael T. Klare of the Institute for Policy Studies, who conducted his own inquiry, said all sales were "private"—i.e., commercial.

The most documented concerned the Space Research Corporation of North Troy, Vermont, a town which straddles the Canadian border. SRC was a prime subject of the BBC film. What was learned was that SRC was shipping howitzer shells to the tiny West Indian republic of Antigua for "testing"; the company maintained an artillery range on the island, but Pentagon sources said SRC's license to test howitzer shells specified that the firm use the White Sands, New Mexico, range. In reality, the shells were merely transshipped from St. Johns, Antigua, to South Africa.

Klare found that between March and May 1977, two shipments of the shells went to Antigua from the similarly named port of St. John, New Brunswick. In Antigua, they were reloaded onto the *Tugelaland*, a German-registry freighter owned by South African Marine Ltd., which sailed for Durban. In May 1978, Klare said, 4,500 shells were trucked from North Troy to Canaveral, Florida, with a manifest ostensibly showing they came from the Army Proving Grounds in Aberdeen. At Canaveral, Klare related, the cargo was reloaded onto two military freight vessels, the *Inagun Cloud* and the *Star Trek*, which brought them to Antigua, whence they were transshipped to South Africa. Two months before, according to Klare, 21,000 shells had been consigned from Antigua to Barcelona but had turned up in Durban in the Dutch ship *Breezand*. According to reporters David C. Martin and John Walcott of *Newsweek*, 55,000 shells in all were sent, against the wishes of the State Department's Office of Munitions Control.

The whole story began to come to light on August 25, 1977, when a crane on the dockside at St. Johns, Antigua, fell into the hold of the *Tugelaland*, smashing open boxes of supposed "metal forgings." Howitzer shells spilled out. Martin and Walcott say U.S. customs agent Gordon Monroe got no cooperation from Antiguan authorities when he was assigned to the affair; but a later report by one of his colleagues, Barry

Greiner, alleged that SRC had sent at least five shiploads of shells to South Africa in 1977 and at least two in 1978.

On July 12, 1978, John Eddy, the chargé d'affaires of the U.S. embassy in Barbados, which has diplomatic jurisdiction for Antigua, met Antiguan Premier V. C. Bird and found him unwilling to crack down on the traffic. Eddy's classified report to the State Department said that, while at Antigua's airport waiting to return to Barbados, he was told threateningly to "back off" the SRC investigation by an expatriate American brandishing a revolver. Later, he reported that a Barbadan-born SRC employee had called on him at the embassy and also had taken a threatening tone about the investigation.

Two months later, U.S. ambassador Frank V. Ortiz reported from Barbados that Barbadan Premier Tom Adams had claimed that SRC was connected to the CIA. Adams named two of Ortiz's staff as CIA officers. U.S. sources say both of the men were actually ordinary Foreign Service officers, but that one of them, Charles Bass, was so depressed by the false accusation that he committed suicide.

Klare says SRC helped South Africa develop its own howitzer ammunition, the G-5, but not before it had provided Pretoria with special long-range shells made in the United States. Author Anthony Sampson has reported that such arms are routinely bought with a secret fund of Armscor, the South African arms industry.

Klare says the whole traffic was facilitated by a 1968 agreement permitting SRC to operate its own customs post on the North Troy site. The Rutland, Vermont, *Herald* quotes a "former SRC employee" as saying that U.S. customs officials were told not to inspect this private customs facility because its operations were "secret."

John Stockwell, the former CIA station chief in Angola who wrote *In Search of Enemies*, says the CIA asked SRC, using a Belgian manufacturer, to procure the special long-range 155mm. howitzer shells for South Africa, to counter Cuba's Soviet-made 122mm. shells in Angola.

When this book was written, a grand jury was meeting once every three weeks in Rutland, and the case seemed likely to take some time.

In 1978, Ethiopia and Somalia, embroiled in war, became meccas for small and large privateers. Ethiopia made some arms purchases for coffee, worth top dollar on the U.S. market. A German dealer selling parts and ammunition for Ethiopia's American equipment said that year in Addis Ababa: "This war was made for the middleman, because both sides have been cut off from traditional suppliers." He said he had a contract worth "a hundred million dollars."

A Frenchman who also desired anonymity said in Mogadishu, the

Somali capital: "This is going to be a very profitable little war." He had a six-month, $11.5 million contract for ammunition and spare parts for Soviet tanks. "The demand is strong," he said, "and the profits are high."

The Somalis were also in the market for parts for American equipment captured from the Ethiopians—mostly tanks and field guns. But Michael Parks of the Baltimore *Sun* reported that they did not need U.S. ammunition, having seized "tens of millions of dollars of shells, mines, rockets, grenades and antitank weapons." But Somali troops and the bands of irredentist Somali irregulars in Ethiopia's Ogaden and Haud districts had some difficulty with the new weapons, to which they were unaccustomed: Somalia was offering to trade some of the captured booty, through privateers, for Soviet equivalents.

A British dealer said that year: "Certainly there are countries which would like very much to get American weapons and would be happy to work out a deal with payments in Soviet arms."

German dealers, with the apparent approval of the Bonn Government —grateful for Mogadishu's assistance in foiling a major hijack case in 1977—were trying to buy ten American C-130s from Vietnam for Somalia, which had been promised parts for the planes by Iran and Saudi Arabia. Meanwhile, an Italian dealer supplied Mogadishu with $2.1 million of Pakistani-made uniforms and boots.

Communist Ethiopia, which buys its uniforms in anti-Communist South Korea, was getting F-5 parts and armament from the Israeli Government. With Soviet aid to the Addis Ababa junta already put at roughly $1 billion, Arab countries were reported to have put up a similar sum for Somalia, including $600 million from Saudi Arabia.

In 1977 and 1978, Mogadishu's airport was regularly closed for several hours each day to enable arms and other essential supplies to come in. An informant told the writer of seeing mysterious transports from Luxembourg, Belgium, Britain, Iran, Saudi Arabia and Pakistan arriving within a few hours one afternoon.

New Twists

A modern twist to "small" arms privateering is the link between gunrunning and drugs. As well as the Shan states, the Mediterranean is an area where weapons are traded for dope. The Franco-Dutch island of St. Martin in the Caribbean is rated by the FBI as a headquarters of the Corsican Mafia—the people who gave you *The French Connection*. When El Salvador's ex-chief of staff was arrested in New York in 1975, attempting to smuggle out ten thousand submachine guns, police said it

was a "drug-related" case. The general had been paid $75,000 for certify-
ing that the hoard was needed for his country's armed forces—which
number five thousand men in all.

The following year, it was revealed that drug smugglers in the northern Mexican city of Culiacán—20,000 of whose 300,000 inhabitants were
said to make their living in the drug trade—were selling their goods for
arms from the United States and from crime chieftains in Hong Kong. A
Mexican Army raid on a nearby mountain hamlet with a population of
240—all over the age of ten were said to be drug traffickers—produced
Chinese-made AK-47s, along with 74 M-16 automatic rifles (possibly
procured from Vietnam by the Hong Kong traffickers), 27 pistols, 2,000
rounds of ammunition, a hidden airstrip, 2 planes and 16 new pickup
trucks. The Kalashnikovs are known locally as "goat's horns," because of
the shape of the clip. (In Vietnam, grunts called them "bananas" for the
same reason.)

Mexican police said that in Mafia-style battles between rival drug
gangs, about a thousand Culiacanos had died in 1975. AP called
Culiacán, about 450 miles south of the U.S. border, high above the
Pacific, Mexico's "drug capital."

The profits of the drug trade drive up weapon values. Experts pointed
out that used AK-47s and M-16s could be picked up in Southeast Asia
and the Middle East for less than $200 apiece; in Bangkok, M-16s from
Vietnam sell in stores—illegally—for as little as $50. M-16s were selling
for $1,000 illegally in Mexico, and Kalashnikovs for twice as much. Yet
marijuana, then more important than heroin in the Mexican drug trade,
was selling for only $10 a pound in the mountains, making an AK-47
worth a ton of "grass."

The likely small trade of the future, however, is in more exotic weaponry than fully automatic assault rifles; and often the exotic stuff comes
more cheaply. The M-11, for instance, was designed by the father of
arms dealer Geoffrey WerBell of Powder Springs, Georgia, and is listed
at $80. A hand-held machine gun, it fires thirty-two gas-propelled rounds
in 1.7 seconds, without sound, flash or smoke. The M-11 comes in two
pieces, each about 9 inches long, easily carried in a raincoat pocket, and
weighs about 7 pounds in all. About fourteen thousand copies of the gun
—including an earlier M-10 model—are now on the market. Some M-10s
were sold at $5.00 apiece to licensed dealers at a 1976 bankruptcy auc-
tion in Marietta, Georgia.

Moving on apace, Russia's SA-7 Strela ("Arrow") and America's Redeye surface-to-air missiles are heat-seeking, precision-guided, shoulder-
fired, and can hit a plane up to altitudes of about 6,000 feet. Weighing

less than 30 pounds, neither is a difficult weapon to use. The gunner of the Redeye tracks the plane in an optical sight, while pressing a button to energize the guidance system. A buzzer in the gripstock of the launcher, near the gunner's ear, goes off when the guidance system is ready. The gunner then fires. A booster charge takes the missile out of the tube; when it is far enough away to protect the gunner from blast effect—about 20 feet—the main rocket ignites. Cruciform tail fins stabilize the missile in flight and the guidance system steers the weapon through two movable mini-wings near the warhead.

The cost of the Redeye, made by General Dynamics (the launcher is a use-once-only throwaway) is $9,000. The Strela is similar and of course costs less. Comparable weapons are the more sophisticated American Stinger, the British Blowpipe and the Swedish RBS-70. In the case of the British weapon, no guerrilla has to wait for the buzzer before firing and perhaps jam the weapon through impatience. One trigger works both guidance-energizer and launcher, and the missile emerges about one second after squeezing the trigger. But the Blowpipe is heavier than its American cousins and the gunner has to control it in flight like an electronic toy aircraft, sighting in on the missile's flares. When the infrared sensors of the missile either reach the target's engine or are about to pass close by it, a proximity fuse explodes the warhead. The Swedish weapon is bulkier and more complicated.

Strelas have been used in Angola, Mozambique, Palestine, Eritrea, former Portuguese Guinea and Spanish Sahara. Among nonguerrilla armies with Strelas in their armory are South Yemen, North Korea, India and Egypt. It was a Strela that Italian police found in 1973 in the hands of Palestinians about to down an El Al 707 as it made its final approach to Rome's Leonardo da Vinci Airport. Redeyes have gone to Sweden, Australia, Israel and Jordan. Vietnam, needless to say, has both Strelas and Redeyes in abundance.

But perhaps the ideal weapon of this sort for a lonely activist would be the 14-pound, 31-inch-long, 3-inch-wide, German-made Armbrust-300, a throwaway antitank weapon which can be carried, three at a time, by an infantryman. Produced since 1970 by Messerschmitt-Bolkow-Blohm Ottobrunn of Munich, the Armbrust (German for "crossbow") has a range of 300 meters, reaching target in 1.7 seconds, and an armor-piercing capacity (with a 2.6-inch-diameter shell) of about a foot.

Recoilless, with no report or blast (the noise, at the ear, is a bearable 135 decibels), the weapon has neither muzzle- nor rear-flash, gives off no smoke and has no infrared signature. It can fire fragmentation and flare shells. Not surprisingly, given its close range, it is not guided. There is a reflex sight, notch and bead; a pistol trigger and cocking lever with safety catch add to the weapon's simplicity. With a rear safety area of 10 meters (3 meters minimum) it can be fired from a window without scorching the furniture in the room. In 1979, Israel introduced a 30-inch, 13-pound copy of the Armbrust called the Picket. The Picket has a gyroscopic corrector to handle a crosswind component, and fires supersonic shells.

U.S. intelligence sources say weapons of the near future will include "one-man MIRVs" and "multishot, shoulder-fired, squirtless flamethrowers."

In 1975 hearings, the Senate internal security subcommittee investigated worldwide sales of weapons to "terrorists," and heard evidence from the London-based Institute for the Study of Conflict that possible guerrilla activity of the future might include attacks on nuclear power stations, the theft of nuclear, chemical-warfare or biological-warfare materials, the poisoning of water supplies of large cities, the hijacking of oil tankers or passenger liners and the sabotage of oil refineries, offshore oil rigs, communications centers and railroad installations. Agents of the Bureau of Alcohol, Tobacco and Firearms gave similar testimony the following year, and in 1977 began a drive against explosives stealing, with TV advertisements starring Chuck Connors. One Senate hearing looked into arms trafficking by and for the American Indian Movement (AIM). Numerous magazine and newspaper articles have stressed the danger inherent in the profuse spread of nuclear power stations throughout the world—not only the possible misuse of nuclear waste, but attacks on the stations themselves. A group seizing a station, it has been theorized, would be able to make extravagant demands.

In April 1977, a Georgetown-based "security" group called Forum announced an "Arab terrorist spectacular" for "early summer," using Japanese Red Army militants from Libya. The target was said to be Arab-Israeli meetings, then taking place between senior Israeli and PLO envoys in France. It never transpired, but this of course did not necessarily disprove the veracity of the report.

Meanwhile, the spread of exotic weaponry of a mostly miniature sort has gone on apace already. The Senate learned in 1975 that Colonel Lucien Conein, a colorful, burly, three-fingered veteran of the CIA in Vietnam—and in youth, he claims, of the French Foreign Legion—was showing an interest in assassination devices: These included telephones that blow up in your ear when the voice at the other end of the line says "hello," flashlight guns, camera guns, and so on. The fear of some members of Congress was that Conein, director of special operations at the Drug Enforcement Agency in Washington, might be considering dealing with heroin traffickers by their own methods, improved by modern technology.

A World War Two OSS operative, and a member, since then, of the Corsican Brotherhood—which was active in the French resistance—"Luigi" Conein was sent behind Japanese lines in Southeast Asia and befriended Ho Chi Minh and Nguyen Giap, then America's allies against Hirohito. Conein and other CIA officers were at Dien Bien Phu, where France was defeated in 1954; he was one of those who managed to escape. In 1963, as part of General Edward Lansdale's covert team, he was the Agency's liaison with Vietnamese leaders who plotted against—and finally assassinated—President Diem. Aided by Daniel Ellsberg, Conein helped organize General Lansdale's guerrilla army of Meo mountain people—after a brief period of banishment to Washington for allegedly exceeding instructions.

Leaving the CIA under yet another cloud in 1968, he started a dealership in Vietnam surplus weaponry, which enabled him to return once more to Saigon, his Eurasian wife's home. By 1970, the business had gone broke because—as he told Taylor Branch of *Esquire*—"my Vietnamese friends charged me more under the table than I would have made in profit." Back in America, he was recruited by Howard Hunt to help destabilize Ellsberg, who had by then leaked the Pentagon Papers. George Crile III, in a Washington *Post* article, claimed he was unsuccessful in this but he says he drew the attention of Hunt's White House colleague Charles Colson when Conein gave an NBC interview in which he blamed President Kennedy for Diem's assassination. He was transferred out of the White House shortly after Watergate, and into what became his Drug Enforcement job.

Both Crile and Branch quote the late former CIA station chief Peer da Silva as saying that "you've got to start with the premise that Lou Conein is crazy. He worked for me in Vietnam, if work is the word. He was certifiable at that point, I think." But another former Saigon station chief told the present writer that "you have to have Lou Coneins in intelligence work," and Conein himself, in his favorite Washington bar—the Class Reunion, next door to his office—claims his reputation is exaggerated, partly because of his own imaginative raconteur style when he is drinking. Free-lance reporter Stanley Karnow even claims that Conein was never even in the Foreign Legion—but Conein certainly attends the annual Washington reunion of Legion veterans.

Conein does not deny holding human life cheaply. He says jokingly that he should have drowned Ellsberg in Vietnam while on river patrol. On the assassination-devices story brought to light by Senator Lowell Weicker of Connecticut, he admits seeing the weapons in a CIA safe house on Washington's Connecticut Avenue, near the Mayflower Hotel. He claims he and his assistant, Searl (Bud) Frank, had gone there to see other equipment and were surprised to be shown the lethal toys by Barbara Fox, widow of the famous Bernie Spindell—of whom more later. Mrs. Fox apparently worked out of the safe house—actually, an apartment—and had a business association at the time with Mitchell Livingston WerBell III.

WerBell—whom his onetime business associate Conein dismisses as "an unreliable informant"—is best-known for his perfection of the sound suppressor. He has also built a cigar that fires a single bullet when you chump on it with your teeth (Conein describes the recoil as "sickening") and a swagger stick that launches a small rocket. WerBell, who first met Conein in the OSS, was—according to aides to the Senate permanent investigations subcommittee—involved with Conein in business as recently as 1974. WerBell told Crile that he had supplied assassination devices to Conein's DEA office through Barbara Fox. In 1974, WerBell was refused an export license to sell two thousand silenced machine guns to Robert Vesco, the now fugitive swindler, in Costa Rica; he later reportedly decided to build an Ingram submachine gun plant in that country in association with Vesco.

According to Senate sources, the DEA stifled an investigation into Vesco's possible connection with the heroin trade, "lost" most of Vesco's file and sent DEA wiretap specialists to Vesco's New Jersey home to sweep it for listening devices. A 1974 drug-smuggling case against WerBell never came to trial. The sources say plans by the permanent investigations subcommittee staff to call Conein, his DEA boss George Belk and others to testify about all this were called off without explanation by subcommittee chairman Senator Henry ("Scoop") Jackson of Washington, after the subpoenas had been issued. The plot thickens and is unlikely to thin out quickly: The Number 2 man on the DEA's inspection division, Bud Frank, is also Conein's deputy; and DEA, after all, is a part of Justice. It seems fair to assume that if assassination devices have not been used yet by American operatives in suppressing drug traffickers, they have probably been used by friendly agents in less squeamish countries.

Visitors to the sort of exhibitions put on each year for police chiefs from the United States and foreign countries are treated to a display of extraordinary weapons, and a plethora of "security-systems" manufacturers will give catalogues to almost anyone. A monthly magazine, *The Police Chief*, published in Gaithersburg, Maryland, is a mine of information.

Clients for some of the weaponry include services that protect VIPs and their families from assassination or kidnapping, or which provide private intelligence networks. This is big business in Europe, especially Italy, and it is a spreading industry in America, Asia, the Middle East and even Africa. Pinkerton's, Wackenhut, and the William J. Burns International Security Services firm have all increased their overseas operations, recruiting former CIA and FBI officers.

A London-based firm, Argen Information Services, initially set up to deal with industrial espionage, has devised protection systems for many scores of clients, from Latin America to South Africa, from New York to Hong Kong. Run by two former British intelligence officers, John Fairer-Smith and John Savage, AIS has six offices around the world and charges up to $120,000 for its services; but Fairer-Smith claims they have never lost a client (to assassination) and says insurance premiums are reduced for AIS clients.

Fairer-Smith, who is forty-two, grew up in Rhodesia and joined Britain's colonial intelligence service. He has lived in London since 1967. Most of AIS's British clients are IRA targets; but Fairer-Smith, a thin-lipped, steely eyed man, claims the PLO also has a "hit list," and that some are on that. Thirty per cent of Argen's clients are American corporations or their executives. Fairer-Smith said in late 1977 that business was booming—well into seven figures, with about 75 regular clients and about 120 "one-off jobs" every year. He said Argen employed 28 persons "with backgrounds in management consulting and spying."

Savage, who devised security for Malawi's eccentric President Hastings Kamuzu Banda, says America's secret service is the most efficient and Israel's equivalent the most successful, but that there is plenty of room in the industry for privateers. Fairer-Smith and Savage stress prevention, especially bugging and debugging equipment; but they smilingly admit that more lethal defensive weaponry is readily available. One man who guards the life of a neighbor President to Banda talks more freely. His story comes next.

Marshall Soghoian

On the evening of August 28, 1973, a posse of "about ten" FBI agents burst into rooms 825/826 of Washington's plush Embassy Row Hotel with search and arrest warrants in the name of the tenant, Marshall Soghoian (pronounced S'hoyan). They found their man nonchalantly watching TV, stripped to the waist and munching watermelon. They forced him to open his briefcase (lock code: 007) and went through the rooms in fine detail. The Feds came away from the search with a miniature TV tube "exclusively" built for the CIA, a $90,000 wide-range radio receiver, a video display analyzer (standard tool of code breakers), a frequency counter stabilizer and files of classified documents belonging to the African republic of Zambia. From Soghoian's petty-cash box, they seized $405,000.

They also seized evidence that Soghoian had not been taken entirely by surprise—a matchbook on which he had scribbled "Dan Mahan—McDermot head." Mahan was the FBI agent in charge of his case, and Jack McDermot was then head of the FBI's Washington field office.

Soghoian was hauled off to McDermot's headquarters in the city's Old Post Office Building and cuffed to a desk. The forensic photographer was asked to take twenty mug shots, then sent off for color film to take twenty more.

The arrest had been carried out under United States Code 951, an antiquated legal joke which requires foreign agents to register with the State Department: It is the catchall under which Soviet master spy Rudolf Abel, and others of that ilk, were first booked. But the Feds had other statutes in mind—notably USC 753 (Espionage).

Actually, Soghoian is an expert in miniaturized and other "CIA-type" weaponry and in electronic eavesdropping, and perhaps the smartest operator of them all in these fields. As a colorful case study, he is worth a closer look, for his story gives a real-life picture of how privateers involved in today's world of minor wars, terrorism and counterterrorism work.

By the time the bare facts of Soghoian's arrest broke in the local press, which thereafter dropped the story, Soghoian had spent a night as a celebrity at the D.C. jail, being looked after by other prisoners. Still, the brief jail episode came as an icy shock to a man used to working in a presidential palace, and washing down his Oysters Rockefeller with Chivas Regal.

His prison physical included a crude check to see if anything was concealed in the alimentary canal. He was fingerprinted. He shared a cell with two other men and no mattresses; but sleep was impossible in any case "because of the yelling and drunks throwing up." Unshaven, he was cuffed to another prisoner in the morning and taken to court. Convinced it had a major spy case on its hands, the United States asked bail of $1 million. Finally, bail was reduced to $100,000—a $35,000 security bond and his mother's house in Richmond, Virginia; 9,000 miles away in Zambia, the parliament met and passed a motion protesting his arrest.

Judgment for Soghoian—"Technical Director Adviser" to the President of Zambia—did not come until the following April. The grand jurors—which in Washington means a heavy sprinkling of janitors and cleaning ladies in retirement—found the evidence highly technical. Some actually went to sleep.

The United States weighed various charges: possessing secret NATO suppliers catalogues (Soghoian said the most sensitive pages had been removed before he got them); channeling Zambian-bought devices to third countries; and trying to suborn government cryptographers. But the prosecution was also worried about overinvestigating. Said a government source: "We were on a tightwire because of Watergate. Here was a 'bugger' who had worked for Nixon. Did he work for the CIA?" Zambia's President Kenneth Kaunda, nervous about his government's ability to break the army codes of Zambia's hostile white-ruled southern neighbors becoming known—and bothered by the prospect of press reports revealing that he was bugging his ministers and closest friends, as well as visiting presidents—won the State Department's support in keeping "Zambian internal matters" out of court. The Justice Department, however, held on to the seized Zambian official files until Zambia, on Soghoian's advice, quietly reminded the United States that it had three vulnerable embassy warehouses in the Zambian capital of Lusaka. The collapse of the "Zambian evidence" and fear of the defense dragging in the CIA left Justice without much meat. After an expensive tour of the arms-trafficking, eavesdropping underworld, the U. S. Attorney's office decided that most of the witnesses that emerged from it were too flaky or too vulnerable to take the stand.

After considerable bargaining, Soghoian reluctantly pleaded guilty to a D.C. Code misdemeanor—"*attempting* to possess a device primarily designed for the surreptitious interception of oral communications." He was fined $1,000. He claimed the whole episode cost him $200,000 in court and legal fees. The IRS then hit him with a jeopardy assessment of $360,000 in back taxes for the first nine months of 1963, but later settled for about a quarter of that sum.

A year later, on August 28, 1974, a group of friends gathered in the living room of Soghoian's tasteful apartment in the Fairfax Hotel—across the street from his old quarters in the Embassy Row—to celebrate the first anniversary of his arrest. The author and a co-writer were invited to witness the triumphal scene.

Soghoian was a playful forty-eight at the time. He wore a white suit and maroon ascot. Haunted eyes twinkled under simian brows. His gaunt face was framed in a graying bush of hair. One side of his Mexican mustache was shaved slimmer than the other. He looked like a friendly movie villain.

Undaunted by his brush with the law, the Richmond-born Armenian-American spent most of the evening indulging his favorite pastime of blinding his friends with science of a decidedly James Bondish turn. From a drawer, he pulled out the flat battery of a Polaroid color film pack and explained how it could be employed to detonate a letter bomb. He talked about his invention which opens letter bombs in safety. The mention of bombs led him to produce a plaque of translucent armor, made for presidential sedans. Into it, he had pumped bullets of several different calibers.

"We could if we wished," he announced like a happy child, "go down to the basement here and tap the phones of virtually every embassy on Massachusetts Avenue." To keep his guests amused after topping off their glasses with vintage Mumm, he showed them the now-recovered $12,000 "CIA" TV tube 4 inches long, the cigarette pack-sized camera into which it fitted, and an eight-hour tape recorder which is even smaller. Finally, he told his rapt audience, point by point, all the mistakes that James McCord made at Watergate, and how the job could have been done more efficiently without ever entering the building.

Today's specialists in sophisticated small arms and other "munitions of war" gadgetry have to be much more science-minded than the arms barons of the past. A Sam Cummings knows his Kalashnikovs and his M-16s, but it needs more than a gift for tinkering with infantry weapons to move expertly in the field of assassination and counterassassination equipment.

Soghoian's two worst enemies—one claimed that the Armenian had stolen a $2 million contract from him, while the other unsuccessfully sued him for a paltry $3,000—both used the words "electronics genius" to describe their foe to the author and his fellow writer. Another man, who lost an $80,000 deal because of Soghoian's fancy footwork, said admiringly: "He can absorb a service manual in a single reading." Soghoian once worked for eavesdrop-equipment inventor emeritus the late Bernie Spindell, who—along with his legendary martini-olive bug—made *Life*'s cover in 1966, and who is thought to have been the model for Harry Caul in the film *The Conversation*. (The earlier-mentioned Barbara Fox is Spindell's widow.)

Today, Soghoian is Harry Caul. His former associate, Michael Doud Gill, Mamie Eisenhower's nephew, called him "one of the most insidious, dangerous men I have ever met."

His main task in Lusaka was and remains the security of President Kaunda—from coups or assassinations. This meant bugging a lot of people, and spending "$20 million to $50 million a year"—as he boastfully admitted—on all sorts of other CIA-type gadgetry. "There won't be a coup in Zambia," he bragged. "That's my job. If there's a coup, it will be my fault." The local American embassy reported in 1970 that he had bugged the accommodations of all the Non-Aligned Conference delegates—mostly presidents and ministers—and the attendant press, including the present writer. But Soghoian noted that bugging was "only a quarter of my operation." Weapons and other munitions of war were the other three quarters.

Soghoian told the writer about "tearing down the walls" inside Zambia's State House—the former colonial governor's palace—to make "safe rooms" for Kaunda; he boasted of night-vision devices used to patrol the State House grounds, of bore-sighted laser pistols with a "99 per cent kill rating" to shoot at targets that only the goggled, laser-wielding guard can see, of official cars with tires that cannot be shot out (solid tires fit inside the pneumatic ones) and of silent automatic weapons fired from within unopened attaché cases (as noted in Chapter 2, Mrs. Park Chung Hee, wife of South Korea's President, was felled by one in 1974).

Soghoian broke the Portuguese Army codes, to help Zambia in its cold war with the then-Portuguese colony of Mozambique, and forecast the 1974 Portuguese revolution six months in advance. But cryptography, he admitted later, was not his real specialty: Trying to hire a U. S. Government specialist to help him with this was probably the main cause of his arrest.

The $1,000-fine case against Soghoian cost the taxpayer at least a hundred times as much. The FBI, convinced that it had laid hands on a melon-munching Rudolf Abel from Africa, carried out more than two hundred investigations—virtually everyone in Soghoian's address book or on his telephone bills, including the teenage brother of his current girl friend, who had used his phone to call the youth in Alaska.

The hotel room search had been expected to yield much more—vocoders (voice scrambling devices), a spectrum analyzer (for testing or trying to break vocoders) and cryptological materials from the National Security Agency. They expected to find bugs—rendered illegal under the 1968 Omnibus Crime Act. A key grand-jury witness, Tom Blazek, who testified that he had made a "latest generation" bug to Soghoian's specifications (after secretly getting permission from the FBI), said the United States really botched the case. One of the four unindicted co-conspirators claimed the Embassy Row rooms had earlier been full of "illegal devices."

Soghoian thought the whole thing was political, despite his earlier services to the United Citizens for Nixon-Agnew Committee in 1968 (where he worked with Charles Rhyne, later the lawyer for Nixon's secretary, Rose Mary Woods) and his loan of special phone equipment to the White House in 1972. He blamed Henry Kissinger's and the State

Department's sympathies for pre-revolution Portugal, South Africa and Rhodesia—Zambia's neighbors—for his arrest. He told the author: "They needed a hammer. They wanted to take me out of circulation."

To some extent, they succeeded. Salesmen of security devices became wary of him for a while. Export-license officers at the office of Munitions Control formed up in defensive squares whenever the author and his co-writer on the Soghoian investigation called. Soghoian was bitter about the whole "rotten fink supplier" world.

But no one was much surprised that Soghoian ended up in trouble. To begin with, there was what Soghoian's attorney, John Risher, Jr.—later the D.C. corporation lawyer—called the "Catch-22" situation surrounding certain "implements of war": You can (with licenses) export them—but not possess them. But in any case, Soghoian, like others in his trade, incurred suspicion by his modus operandi: He used his own name (or a pseudonym), not Zambia's, and paid in cash, not by check (he said this was to protect Zambia's security, and not tip off Rhodesians and others to what Zambia was buying). As a consequence, he always paid partly in advance.

Said his prosecutor, William J. Hardy: "He was the candy man with bags of money, always putting half up front." And, unlike many members of the tight-lipped community of dealers in implements of war, Soghoian was a talker.

Like others in the arms trafficking world, Soghoian had a tormented background. A Lou Conein or a WerBell, like a Zaharoff, is not an "ordinary" person. Even a Philadelphia Main-Liner like Sam Cummings remembers being orphaned and faced with the threat of poverty. Most smaller arms dealers are tortured folk, often living on—or over—the fringes of legitimacy, and only at ease in a similarly marginal world.

In Soghoian's case, it all went back to his childhood in the cathouse and penitentiary district of Richmond, where, in Mike Gill's words, "the only thing lower than a nigger was an Armenian." Because he was constantly beaten up by rednecks, his father bought him chemistry sets to keep him amused at home. (At college, he majored in both chemistry and physics.) An old acquaintance told the writer: "His ambition is to go back and buy Richmond, to show them for what they did to him."

Washington TV theater critic Roy Meachum, who worked with Soghoian for the Armed Forces Network in boxer Max Schmeling's old house in Berlin after World War Two, described him as "an electronics genius at nineteen." After military service, he founded a store, the Research Instruments Corporation, in Richmond. The front-door trade was buying high fidelity; but already there was a back door, where fidelity meant little. Soghoian got a $25,000 subcontract from arch-bugger Spindell. In 1968, he was McCord's predecessor, responsible for keeping Nixon's campaign headquarters in Washington eavesdrop-free.

But arms privateers, like gangsters, envy what used to be called the jet-set life. It was in 1968 that Soghoian first met apparently wealthy Mike Gill—in a former employee's words, "a spoiled brat who was in and out of the back door of the Eisenhower White House." Gill was then living on his $200,000 houseboat, moored at Miami's Doral Beach Hotel. Gill's friends included airline stewardesses who descended from the sky to bathe naked in swimming pools with see-through walls, and dudes who had see-through mirrors in their bedrooms.

A mutual friend introduced Soghoian to Gill—naturally, as an "electronics genius." That year Gill, as co-chairman of Citizens for Nixon-Agnew, took Soghoian on as his unpaid electronics specialist and jack of all trades. Soghoian organized a worldwide conference call, a telecast, even the Inaugural Ball—everything from the sound equipment to ticketing and accountancy.

Gill, a Texan, had recently bought a house just off Massachusetts Avenue and refurbished it to sell off as a diplomatic chancery: But a new zoning law made it usable only as a residence. Before this was known, Zambia's then ambassador, Rupiah Banda, showed interest. Gill and Banda became friends, so Soghoian met Banda too and dazzled him with his electronic wizardry. The two Americans were invited to Lusaka by President Kaunda. Gill was asked to use his presumed "Ike" connections with the Nixon White House to lure investment to Zambia. As a part of Gill and Associates, Soghoian was to install a communications grid throughout Zambia, and linking the country to its diplomatic missions in New York, Washington, London and Bonn. It was to have independent power, secret transmission characteristics, and should "remain operational during a coup."

Soghoian's initial Zambian years, if recounted in detail, would read like a lurid paperback with an exotic setting. It was a story of claims and counterclaims, of mysterious deaths—including that of the country's police commissioner—of J. C. Penney dimestore heiresses Gay and Joan Fletcher living with Gill in a $280,000 villa (Joan came away from a Zambian police "interrogation" with a paralyzed arm). Gill and Soghoian accused each other of padding the communications contract proposal, and finally the Gill and Associates job was given to Soghoian alone. Gill's dream—to make $2 million, and use it to campaign for a Texas seat in Congress—disappeared into the clear blue skies of Africa.

While electronics specialists recruited by Soghoian in the Washington area darted around the wastescapes of Zambia's Barotseland in a light plane and a Mercedes, setting up antennas, Soghoian commuted between Lusaka and the United States, taking "classified" equipment out or bringing it back to America for maintenance. He carried with him everywhere a reputation as a rampant stud, a Hemingway-class drinker and a pal of Greek millionaires and mysterious African diplomats. Into the crowded scenario go stories of impounded passports, of Communist Chinese railroad engineers and of shadowy Britons on the lam from Scotland Yard or selling Jaguars as a cover for intelligence work. In Hyattsville, a Washington suburb, Soghoian was then running a diplomatic-seal warehouse for his gadgetry, secured from burglary by a motion detector which "sees" through walls. Tardy suppliers and the warehouse caretaker lived in fear of Soghoian's exuberant threats.

As government sources recounted the Soghoian saga, he had been under scrutiny since 1968, when—with Citizens for Nixon-Agnew—he tangled with the Secret Service over Nixon campaign-headquarters security. In 1969, Gill reported nervously to the State Department on Soghoian's bugging activities in Zambia. From then on, he was never completely without surveillance.

Within months of taking the Kaunda appointment, he had built up a nationwide network of suppliers and other contacts in the United States. Between 1969 and 1974, he chartered eleven DC-8s and 707s, at $60,000 to $95,000 a time, to shift loads of equipment to Zambia weighing 20,000 tons or more. OMC officials became intrigued by the diplomatically sealed crates, and sources there referred to Soghoian's "air force" of "great huge flying pouches." Soghoian, always living at a feverish pace, reveled in his new importance. He sent long, detailed, secret reports to Kaunda in officialese, but peppered with exclamation marks and excited comments like: "At that price, it's practically stealing the stuff!"

By 1970, he was interested in sophisticated "A to D" cryptography, which converts voice from analogue to digital characteristics and back—one of the forms of what laymen call scrambling and unscrambling. A "co-conspirator," William Timothy Gales, a hard-drinking, tallow-complexioned, drooping figure in green glasses, offered to act as go-between in finding both equipment and a code expert who would sell his skills to Zambia. Gales actually produced a retired Air Force general and a retired Army Department cryptographer, but Soghoian dismissed them both as incompetent.

That year, the scene shifted to Baltimore, where Gales lived in funereal mystery. Still looking for his 5 per cent of the Soghoian action, Gales conducted his search for bugging equipment through a gallery of Runyonesque characters. At the long bar of the former Belvedere Hotel, he sought out cherub-faced Colonel C. Cole (Colonel was his given name), who used a barstool as his office and drank the rent he saved: An FBI report described Cole's profession as "fixer." Cole wore white suits and Stetsons, and talked—like Gales—in a cultivated, Rooseveltian accent. When the author and his fellow reporter found him, he was operating out of the Governors Club in Baltimore. He told us he had done nothing more than interrupt a friendly game of cards to help his friend Gales meet some suppliers, and expected nothing in return. Then he asked hopefully: "But did the deal come off?" It didn't.

One Jewish potential supplier produced by Cole, and who recalled meeting Soghoian under a pseudonym (Marshall Graves—with women, he sometimes used Marshall Love or Marshall Dear), became leery. He told the FBI that Soghoian had originally hinted that the deal was for a "Near East country" and had thrown Yiddish words into the conversation. The supplier had assumed the project was for Israel. As his doubts grew, his enthusiasm waned.

The Belvedere incident is typical. "Implements of war" is a field where the underworld and IT&T share the turf, and it is full of unskilled parasites like Bill Gales who must lose nine times out of ten. But Gales, the hanger-on, hung on. In 1972, when Soghoian began shopping for night-vision targeting devices capable of magnifying light 100,000 times, Gales acted as middleman for Baird Atomic, a Medford, Massachusetts, firm. Gales drew up a contract with Baird, guaranteeing Gales 5 per cent of a $6 million deal, "Project Marshall." Soghoian refused to buy from Baird. Gales later brought a $300,000 suit against Soghoian; even when he offered to settle for $3,000, he lost the case.

But Gales just would not go away. He told Soghoian he had pledged one third ($100,000) of his prospective Baird Atomic "cut" to a Mafioso for a quick $10,000 loan and was about to be eliminated for nonpayment. He said Soghoian's life was in danger too. He begged Soghoian to okay the Baird deal and to talk to the Mafia man. Soghoian tartly suggested a meeting the next day at FBI headquarters. The supposed Mafioso, John Giadono, never turned up anywhere; but at the time, Soghoian was sufficiently scared to record a telephone conversation with Gales, to change his room at the Embassy Row and to take on a major Washington lawyer, Charles Donnenfeld—whose firm later undertook Soghoian's defense.

Soghoian decided to call Gales's bluff by telling him to tell Giadono to kill him soon, because he was "leaving the following day"—August 29—for Zambia. Gales then precipitated Soghoian's arrest by passing on this false information to the FBI, which was thus forced to act before it had a case. Four hours after the tip, President Kaunda's Technical Director Adviser was tossed in jail.

Nearly a year before, Soghoian said, he had been warned by "two State Department guys" that he should watch his step. In the fall of 1972, military night-vision device salesmen William W. Bonds and C. M. "Woody" Wood had found OMC worried about Soghoian's strange working ways and cash payments, his growingly more sophisticated purchases for Zambia. Wood and Bonds (who was with IT&T) brought two OMC licensing officers, Robert H. Meyer and John A. Sandford, to the Embassy Row to meet Soghoian. Over lunch, they told Soghoian they were principally worried about Chinese involvement in Zambia.

Justice sources agreed later that Soghoian was seen at the time of his arrest as a "shady guy involved with a Third World country which had the Chinese building a railroad." (Curiously, the railroad—which Zambia clearly needed to escape dependence on hostile countries to the south, and which it had only turned to the East to build when the West refused—seems to have worried government officials more than the presence of Chinese setting up Zambia's short-wave, long-range, propaganda broadcasting facility.)

But the long lunch apparently went off well, and afterward Meyer and Sandford went up to Soghoian's room for further drinks, while the two salesmen waited downstairs in the lobby. Soghoian recounted later that both officials drank a great deal, and accepted gifts. Wood and Bonds agreed that when the two came downstairs, each was carrying a rare Makonde wooden sculpture from Soghoian's collection, and Sandford a bottle of cherry brandy. Soghoian's delayed authorization to export night-vision devices, and parts for these, was cleared in short order the following day.

At subsequent interviews, both officials were clearly worried about the incident. At first Meyer, who admitted to receiving the gifts, was even too frightened to reveal his first name to visiting reporters. But most of Soghoian's professional colleagues made fun of Meyer and Sandford. Because Sandford is black, the arms-dealer mafia referred to them as "Sandford and Son." OMC officials do not rate highly in the eyes of arms dealers, generally. One, Frank Terpel—a Beirut-based former CIA officer who in 1973 bugged the Algiers Non-Aligned Summit Conference for President Houari Boumedienne—said: "They're the sort of people who eat egg sandwiches all week until we hit town. Then they eat Chateaubriand."

By 1973, the net was closing around Soghoian, who was talking to too many of what State Department officials called "classified people." Terpel had put the dealer in touch with Ed Morris, a debugging expert whose job was to "sanitize" President Nixon's accommodations whenever the Chief Executive traveled abroad. For such an officer to have resigned and gone to work for Zambia for the $35,000 which Soghoian was offering would have been a breach of his secrecy bond with Treasury. Terpel also approached a CIA cryptanalyst, without success. A good man, it was clear, would be hard to get, therefore expensive. But the OMC warnings to Soghoian seem not to have sunken in.

At this point, an electronics engineer, Tom Blazek, entered the picture. He had an industrial-secrets Defense clearance and made bugs for the CIA and the FBI. Blazek offered to use his official clearance to recruit someone from the NSA—America's largest intelligence agency and the one that specializes in cryptology. Blazek soon claimed to have found a cryptanalyst there who was prepared to go to Zambia for about a year and teach Soghoian and his assistants the requisite skills, for $250,000. Soghoian later told the grand jury he only wanted the skills, not U.S. code secrets. He said Blazek asked for $25,000 for the man's name and received $20,000.

By then, Blazek was not only singing to the FBI but acting as a walking transmitter as well. He and three other future witnesses were protecting their precious "secret" clearances by also talking to OMC.

In the bugging field, Soghoian was now into LSI—large-scale integration. In October 1972, Blazek had gone to the FBI with an illegal, miniaturized bugging device which he said Soghoian had asked him to copy in a "subcarrier" version that would fit into an electric wall socket. This was to be the basis for the indictment for possessing and transporting a bug: Grand-jury witnesses from another U.S. firm admitted making the original device to Soghoian's specifications. After hesitations, the FBI told Blazek in January 1973 to go ahead and build the subcarrier version. During testing at the Hyattsville warehouse, Blazek's prototype burned out. Soghoian claimed he never touched the device so did not "possess" it. Blazek made three versions of the bug in all.

Two weeks before Soghoian's arrest, Blazek went to Assistant U. S. Attorney William J. Hardy's office with two FBI agents, Daniel C. Mahan and Michael L. King, and consented to make a taped telephone call to Soghoian at the Embassy Row. He put off Soghoian's suggestion for a dinner with Blazek and the cryptanalyst, but offered to come by the hotel "if you got 'em and if we can be alone for a few minutes." The "'em" presumably referred to Soghoian's handy packages of $100 bills. Blazek then went off to the hotel, wired for sound—two microphones were taped to his shoulder blades and a recorder was taped to his back. He was there for about half an hour.

The FBI transcript shows Soghoian dickering over the cryptanalyst's fee, offering $150,000, and suggesting that the man travel through London to allay Agency suspicions. He wanted to test the man's skills first. The conversation turned to nocturnal sharpshooting night-vision devices, which Blazek seemed anxious to sell. Soghoian agreed to take two hundred of them, at $3,000 each, paid in cash.

Blazek then returned to Hardy's office and a third telephone conversation was taped. He said the cryptanalyst would accept $150,000; for the decoding test, the man needed an "adequate sample." Soghoian offered to provide it the following day. The FBI turned a transcript of the tapes over to the NSA.

After the arrest was made, most of Soghoian's "friends" were summoned to the FBI and the grand jury. Terpel filled Soghoian in on the evidence, with both men talking to the shrubbery in the Zambian embassy yard, to ensure that no passing spook was reading their lips through binoculars.

Two months after Soghoian's arrest, Blazek made yet another taped call from Hardy's office, this time to a Zambian diplomat, Joseph Mmembe. Blazek offered to return the carrier current transmitter "which Marshall made" and which he had wanted Blazek to miniaturize. Mmembe bridled at Blazek's request that he write a letter asking for it. Mmembe went on to say that, if Blazek was subpoenaed, he need only point out that he was "returning the item." Blazek interjected: "Except that the device is illegal in this country!" Mmembe continued to hedge. Protected by diplomatic immunity, he became an unindicted co-conspirator.

This profile of a wealthy, successful, unknown privateer in the world of sophisticated "implements of war" helps to show that the novels of Frederick Forsyth and Robin Moore are not farfetched.

The author and his colleague, when concluding their investigation of Soghoian, met him socially at a nightclub with a few of his friends. He crowned the women present with $20 bills torn into paperchains, then watched as they burned the chains on a candle. It was a demonstration of wealth by a man who still felt the need to demonstrate it. Like the Harry Caul of *The Conversation*, he was obviously insecure, the victim of his own suspicions, which the arms-trafficking and bugging industries themselves create. Soghoian was worried because Zambia had been embarrassed by the whole affair. But he knew too much about President Kaunda's affairs to be easily put out to pasture; and when the author had lunch with him two years later—with Soghoian still insisting on paying, and still tipping 100 per cent of the bill—he reported that Kaunda had given him "another raise." But an FBI source noted, while this book was being written, that "the Soghoian file is still open. This is an ongoing case." The Justice Department and OMC said the same. It is not an easy life.

6

The Boardroom Bombers

A DECADE AGO, even with the Vietnam War in full swing, defense-cost figures looked substantially different from today. By the standards of the eighties, the Southeast Asia conflict was fought at discount prices. Since then, competitive sophistication has become more intense, the Pentagon more and more exacting. The profits and the risks are greater: Some companies have lost fortunes of their own on R & D alone.

Joe Gavin, the president of the Grumman Corporation, spoke to the writer over a beef-sandwich-and-apple-pie lunch at his desk, shortly after returning from a lobbying expedition to Washington. Gavin, a spare, handsome, MIT-trained engineer with a Boston accent, complained that it was becoming harder to produce a new weapons system in America.

"You have to open many gates," he said. "If one is closed, it's no go."

Gavin, who is regarded as one of the industry's most articulate spokesmen, insisted that congressional precautions on procurement "inevitably result in inertia . . . Delays undo the advantage of the novel idea. By the time a system is approved, it has been plagiarized by everybody. If there's no risk in producing a certain weapon, then it's probably not worth producing. It's probably too old already."

Gavin blamed overruns on intentional Pentagon underestimates, designed to get initial appropriations from Congress, and on congressional hypocrisy in pretending to believe such figures; but he agreed that contractors also indulged in intentional underestimates to help both themselves and the Pentagon—and indirectly Congress. The U. S. Government, said Gavin, "gets the contractors to lean out of the window, to see who'll lean out furthest." Gavin also complained that Congress' geographic approach to defense contracting—favoring or opposing systems according to the state and district in which they are built—"doesn't serve the best interests of the armed forces." This, he noted, was a problem Moscow didn't share.

Grumman's boss is particularly hard on the Air Force, noting that three major combat aircraft of the sixties and seventies—the legendary

F-4, the A-7 and Grumman's own F-14—had all been developed by the Navy, even though the F-14 was the first aircraft able to take both Sparrow and Sidewinder missiles. The Air Force had only taken the strategic F-111, Grumman said, because it was "foisted on them by the Pentagon."

So much is involved in the military aerospace market—billions of dollars, thousands of jobs, more thousands of stockholders, constituent issues —that the arms industry has inevitably become flavored with corruption. In past eras, the corruption of politicians and others by the arms trade was largely the work of dealers and middlemen. Today, the economic importance of the arms industry is so great that manufacturers themselves get into the act more. The best-known scapegoat name in recent years has been Lockheed Aircraft.

The Lockheed Saga

Lockheed is probably no more corrupt than any other large firm engaged in trade abroad—and in the case of arms sales most corruption is in fact a shakedown by the purchasing country. But Lockheed's expensive problems in the area have become well-known.

The largely California- and Georgia-based company was, for some time, the world's largest defense contractor, slipping to second place in 1976. It nourishes 60,000 employees and their 200,000 dependents. It also feeds nearly 60,000 stockholders. By 1977, although hit by the scandal investigations, its net earnings held steady at about $12 million a quarter, despite decreased sales.

But the various investigations in the United States and abroad had revealed that Lockheed was certainly being heavily shaken down. Congress inevitably asked whether any of the $250 million loan to the firm which the government had guaranteed in 1970 had been used for "bribes." By 1977, the firm was clearly in disgrace: A $1.3 billion contract in Japan had been canceled, and others were in jeopardy. Chairman Daniel Jeremiah Haughton, a self-made Alabama country boy, had been forced to retire (on an annual pension of $750,000), as had the firm's seven-year president, A. Carl Kotchian. Haughton's successor, Robert W. Haacke, a former chairman of the New York Stock Exchange put in to inspire bankers' confidence, was succeeded in 1977 by Roy A. Henderson in a further shuffle.

Lockheed's troubles date back to the sixties, when several defense contracts fell through, while the decade before the firm's latest civil airliner, the Electra, had been plagued by crashes. (The aircraft later became a success, and was even copied by the Russians as the Ilyushin-18.) A 1964 defense contract to build the C-5A Galaxy, a transport aircraft with four times the capacity of a C-130, had become a nightmare. The contract had been obtained with the strong support of Senator Richard Russell of Georgia, then chairman of the Senate Armed Services Committee, since the 20,000 Lockheed employees at Marietta would do most of the work.

Like all aircraft breaking new ground, some of the C-5A's development costs were unpredictable. Like all contracts that have to be approved by Congress, the C-5 program carried the lowest believable price tag, to get it started. By 1970, the winged mammoth was foundering in a sea of red ink, and the Galaxy had become a political football. A Pentagon official, Ernest Fitzgerald, won newspaper fame for "blowing the whistle" on his department's attempts to shield the public from the full details of a "$2 billion overrun." Essentially, Lockheed was the scapegoat for pent-up public reaction against the Vietnam War and the military-political-industrial complex which was widely seen as supporting its continuance. Professor John Kenneth Galbraith had even, as noted, recommended nationalization of the arms industry. More pragmatically, Lockheed needed defense sales, and especially foreign defense sales, to keep the firm going.

It was shortly after Fitzgerald's revelations that stories began to emerge about Lockheed and its competitors paying kickbacks overseas. Part of the U.S. reaction was traditional American primness, but part of it sprang from the assumption that Americans—stockholders, taxpayers—must be footing the bill for venal foreign fat cats.

In Germany, it was discovered that a Lockheed representative, Ernest Hauser, had passed on $12 million to the right-wing Christian Social Union leader Franz-Josef Strauss, when he was Defense Minister, to encourage him to choose F-104 Starfighters for the German Air Force. When the Germans started to investigate, following the crash of 174 of the 900 F-104s purchased (and of 60 of the 230 bought by Japan), the pertinent Defense Ministry files were found to be missing.

The story goes back to the mid-fifties, when Strauss wanted Germany included in the nuclear strike force, for which the Luftwaffe's then F-85s and F-86s were not suitable. After studying three aircraft with similar assault, attack, support, reconnaissance and bombing capacities, similar climb, speed and range, Germany rejected France's Mirage-III and Northrop's F-5 in favor of Lockheed's lighter, competitively priced F-104. A contract was signed in 1959 calling for Germany to produce 250 F-104s—a figure extended the following year to 700 and later to 964, with a tag of over $2 billion. With Lockheed's happy acquiescence, the Germans then decided to "gold-plate" it—to hang every imaginable system on the light fighter, thus changing its weight distribution and handling characteristics to the point where the Starfighter became a very un-forgiving plane which pilots were reluctant to fly. By the time the first hundred had crashed, the German press had dubbed the aircraft the "Widowmaker."

Chairman Kurt-Georg Kiesinger of the Bonn parliament's foreign affairs committee and Speaker Kai-Uwe von Hassel, who later became Defense Minister, defended themselves by complaining that Lockheed had understated the dangers of the weighty extra equipment. Moreover, problems developed in the radar systems and the Starfighter proved in-adequate at night or in poor visibility: It was not the all-weather plane which is the first requirement in Europe. Problems also developed in the bomb dispenser and—worst of all for morale and public relations—in the ejection-seat release. So complicated was the highly modified plane that it took the full eighteen months of a draftee's service for a mechanic to finish his F-104 courses.

The Luftwaffe had ordered no spare avionics, so that repairs led to in-creased "down time" and idle pilots. Germany's small airspace, crowded with commercial aviation, proved too confined for combat training, and, as noted earlier, an expensive Luftwaffe Air Defense School had to be set up at Fort Bliss, Texas.

By 1966, the three highest-ranking generals in the Luftwaffe had been forced to resign because of press and parliamentary complaints about the Starfighter, which was partly blamed for a budgetary crisis, which in turn led to the fall of the Erhard government. Corruption was also found to have been involved in Lockheed's sale of antisubmarine warfare air-craft, through another agent—party-giving German socialite Christian Steinrucke.

In Holland, the prince consort, Bernhard, was found to have accepted $1 million from Lockheed's Dutch-born agent Fred Meuser for pushing the F-104. He had reportedly also been offered $40 million by German Defense Minister Helmut Schmidt for the same services, since Dutch or-ders would help to justify German ones. The Dutch press, it turned out, had been sitting for some time on what became the story behind the story: Bernhard, married for life to one of the world's less glamorous women, Queen Juliana, had consoled himself with a number of more delectable creatures, many of whom had untidily and expensively pro-duced children who could not be succored adequately on the relative pit-tance allowed to Bernhard for regal representation expenses. The best-known "secret" mistress of Bernhard was a Parisian whom he called Poupette ("Little Doll") and who had borne him a daughter. Although nothing was ever quite spelled out, the implications were that Lockheed's million—offered after Haughton had vetoed the brazen proposal to give the prince a million-dollar Jetstar of his own—had gone to secure the future of "Little Doll" and her baby.

The money was paid in three roughly equal installments to a Swiss bank account—thus evading Dutch taxes—through the agency of Bernhard's elderly mother's patriarchal lover, a retired Tsarist colonel.

Later, Lockheed sought to slip Bernhard another $100,000 for trying to sell his country on the P-3C Orion antisubmarine plane. When the project was revived and seemed to have been approved, Bernhard wrote in his own hand two rather crude letters, which later emerged, asking for "4 to 6 million," but quickly cut his demands back to a single million. The cut-rate prince complained bitterly when the two farm boys back in Burbank, Haughton of Alabama and Kotchian of North Dakota, bridled at paying an agent who had failed, simply because his successor had apparently been more successful. Then the sale of the four P-3Cs was shelved, and the kickback became moot.

In his dunning letter, Bernhard said he had worked hard for Lockheed; but a subsequent Dutch official investigation concluded that he had not done much, and that he had concealed from Burbank the fact that he was also on the take from Northrop—that he had, in effect, lied to Haughton in an effort at extortion. The Dutch Government report deplored the prince's activities: He had "shown himself open to dishonorable requests and offers" and "allowed himself to be tempted to take initiatives which were completely unacceptable."

Bernhard was removed as inspector general of the armed forces and forced to resign his seat on several prestigious boards, such as KLM. He gave up his post as the head of the World Wildlife Fund. But a television poll taken two days after the government report appeared in the press showed that 71 per cent of the Dutch people still had a "favorable" opinion of him. Neither parliament nor press objected when his salary was raised in 1977 to $335,400, an increase of about 17 per cent. When the socialist Premier, Joop den Uyl, ruled out a criminal investigation of the prince, only 2 of the 143 members of the national legislature challenged the decision. Bernhard now submits virtually all his proposed activities to the Premier for approval. But in 1977, he was voted "Man of the Year" by the Netherlands Export Association.

Other Lockheed stories cropped up around the world. In 1976, the Italian parliament sent an investigating mission to Burbank, following reports that the sale of fourteen C-130s to the Italian Air Force in the sixties had involved kickbacks to three former ministers and possibly to a former Premier. The targets of the investigation were ex-Foreign Minister Mariano Rumor and former Defense Ministers Mario Tanassi and

Luigi Gui. (In 1979, Tanassi was sentenced to twenty-eight months in prison and five others also received prison terms. Gui and four others were acquitted.) The $60 million deal was also linked in Lockheed communications to "Antelope Cobbler"—Lockheed code for "Prime Minister of Italy." In all, the Lockheed communications refer to transfers of $1,680,000 to Christian Democrats through attorney Ovidio Lefebvre, using accounts in Liechtenstein, Panama and Switzerland.

In Japan, Lockheed went through Tokyo's equivalent of the *capo di tutti capi*. This was Japan's most famous gangster chieftain, Yoshio Kodama, who admitted at his 1976 trial that Burbank had paid him $45,000 a year from 1958 through 1969 and $150,000 a year thereafter. Lockheed records showed that in fact he received $1 million over four years, 1969 through 1972, and another million over the next two years.

Kodama had also distributed $8 million of Lockheed money to Japanese political figures and all Nippon Airlines executives for military and civil sales. Ex-Premier Kakuei Tanaka, who collected half a billion yen personally, and seventeen other politicians were indicted.

Kodama, a right-wing political figure and onetime CIA agent well known in the drug and prostitution industries, was a natural choice for Lockheed: In 1958, he had persuaded the Defense Minister to make General Minoru Genda of Pearl Harbor fame head of the Japanese Air Force; his friend Genda had then gone to California, flown the 104, and returned to push enthusiastically for the purchase of two hundred of them—even though this involved calling off an almost completed deal for Grumman F-11s.

In a later deal, when Japan canceled plans to build a locally designed antisubmarine warfare plane and bought Orions instead, much of the $8.3 million of Lockheed shakedown money passed through Kodama's hands (1,720,000,000 yen out of 2,330,000,000 yen)—roughly half of it through Hong Kong and half through Switzerland. Courier Hoze Aramiya, a Spanish-born Japanese citizen who had formerly been Father José Gardeano of the Catholic Church, and other henchmen for Kodama carried nearly a quarter of a ton of 10,000-yen notes—packed, 9,300 at a time, into 28-pound bags—from Deak and Company's Hong Kong currency-exchange office to Tokyo, making several trips. A substantial nonpolitical beneficiary of this largesse was Lockheed's correspondent company in Japan, the Marubeni Corporation, which collected $2.9 million.

Kodama, a beady-eyed, expressionless hunk of a man who had made his first fortune as head of the Japanese war industry in occupied China, and who spent three years in jail after World War Two, finally came to court accused of evading $6.5 million in taxes and obtaining $3.6 million in foreign currency unlawfully. In addition to Tanaka, he was said to have been the patron of two other Japanese Premiers, Ichiro Hatayama and Nobusuke Kishi, whom he had met in prison.

Lockheed officials had little difficulty explaining their willingness to be shaken down: The French and the Germans had started the game, they said, and it was the only game in town if you wanted to sell aircraft abroad. Moreover, the money came, not from the pockets of the corporation, but from the purchasing country, since the bill was padded to cover native venality. Moreover, the Lockheed markup was made on the final figure, so that the more corrupt the customers, the more money Lockheed stockholders made.

Nowhere was this more evident than in Saudi Arabia, where middleman Adnan Khashoggi, as principal commission agent, reportedly often took from 5 to 16 per cent on sales, instead of the more usual 2 per cent. Between 1970 and 1975, he accepted $106 million from Lockheed. Like Bernhard, he also helped Northrop, who claimed later to have paid him another $100 million. Khashoggi kicked some of this cash back to Nixon's 1972 campaign.

Theoretically, Riyadh outlawed fees to agents "within the country." Before signing an arms contract, the producer firm's representative would be asked if any such fee had been paid. Khashoggi would always arrange to be out of Saudi Arabia at the time, so that the American's negative response should be truthful, after a fashion.

To ensure that Khashoggi's bill-padding did not enrich the IRS too much, the young entrepreneur would bill Burbank, which would bill its Swiss subsidiary, which would conclude the sale. The maximum Swiss corporation tax is 15 per cent, versus 48 per cent in the United States.

The California-educated Khashoggi came aboard for Lockheed in 1964, when he was only twenty-six. With his two brothers, he founded the Triad Corporation—a Liechtenstein company based in Geneva. A portly figure who travels worldwide in a personal 727, adapted as an apartment and office, Khashoggi still claims he is "indispensable" to sales in Saudi Arabia.

In Turkey, Lockheed paid Nezih M. Dural $5,000 a month for "intelligence" and $876,000 for various Starfighter deals. When the Greek lobby in Washington brought off the Turkish arms embargo, which came into force early in 1975, Dural bought two squadrons of 104s produced in Italy, collecting $240,000 on that alone. In 1976, despite the U.S. embargo, Turkey spent $2 billion on defense, buying from Iran, Italy, Germany, Libya and other countries.

During the Ankara-Athens imbroglio, Washington discovered that one reason why Greece could not oppose the Turkish intervention in Cyprus was that a great deal of NATO hardware in Greece had been illegally resold to African countries, notably Nigeria. The lesson was not lost on Lockheed and other U.S. arms producers: During 1976, U.S. arms sales to black Africa rose 800 per cent.

One of the attractions of black Africa and of some other Third World buyers is that local governments would themselves ask manufacturers to increase their prices so as to justify a fatter kickback. Some Southeast Asian cases were cited in Chapter 5. In Nigeria, ministers and generals opened their own individual numbered accounts in Switzerland.

Another underdeveloped country with generals on the take was Spain. In late 1976, Brigadier Luis Rey Rodriguez and Colonel Carlos Grandal Segade, both sixty-one, were suspended for shaking down Lockheed in a $50 million C-130 deal. The officers had just collected $295,000 each, but fifteen more people were involved for a total of $1,350,000. King Juan Carlos asked Washington to "keep a lid" on the scandal until his new transition government was more securely in the saddle. The Information Ministry tried to stop Cambio-16 from publishing the story, and the editor of another Spanish magazine, Sábado Gráfico, was tried by a military court for publishing the list of the officials implicated in the Lockheed case.

Earlier in the year, the police had arrested Fernando Herce, manager of the Spanish firm Avionica—Lockheed's correspondent firm in Spain—as the conduit for the payoffs. Herce confessed to transferring at least $600,000 to Switzerland.

The U. S. Senate hearings learned about business in Europe and the Third World, and heard U.S. and foreign firms blaming each other for letting the system continue. Dr. Kissinger warned against the international damage which the investigation would do by embarrassing highly placed foreign friends, and pointed out that to be shaken down abroad—or even to bribe—was not an offense under U.S. law. Eventually, the congressional investigation was called off; but the IRS started going through Lockheed's books, and a grand jury was empaneled at Burbank.

In April 1977, a GAO report found that Lockheed was doing what it could to eliminate "questionable payments," but noted that this practice could not be ruled out altogether. Commission payments are permitted under foreign military sales regulations provided they are "reasonable and . . . disclosed." Tightening up its own practices had led Lockheed to face suits from dissatisfied agents around the world.

The same year, Lockheed published its own report, based on an in-house investigation. It admitted that there had been "questionable payments" of "$30 million–$38 million"—an increase on the figure of $24 million admitted the previous year to the Senate multinationals subcommittee. At home, between $372,000 and $432,000 had been spent entertaining "sensitive individuals" between 1970 and 1975, but no tax deductions had been taken for these expenses.

Overseas, the report said, there had been "political contributions, bribes, payments to customers' employees and payments to persons of influence seeking to extort money from the company." Payments to about 150 sales consultants in about 50 countries had totaled $165 million in commissions and "other fees," which the firm calculated meant an average of 6.4 per cent on sales of $2.6 billion. The heaviest payments had been in Saudi Arabia. Haughton and Kotchian had been "willing to distort such a primary principle as integrity for short-term expediency, in order to aid . . . the company's financial survival."

At sixty-two, Kotchian was bitter. He reminded a reporter that he had been thirty-five years with Lockheed and had brought the corporation back from the brink of collapse.

"My experience has some of the elements of Watergate," he said shortly after the ouster. "A lot of the things that came out in Watergate were going on previously—and all of a sudden there's a different set of standards . . . Lockheed has become the scapegoat for three hundred companies that the SEC said were doing the same thing, and Haughton and I are scapegoats for the scapegoat." In some instances, he said, Lockheed had lost business because the Russians or the West Europeans paid even higher bribes.

With the help of a Japanese reporter, Kotchian recounted the story of Lockheed in Japan in a book published in Tokyo which sold over fifty thousand copies.

The Grumman Story

Next to Lockheed, the second best-known scapegoat had been Grumman. Grumman's sale of the F-14 Tomcat to Iran saved Long Island's main employer from extinction or take-over. Its victory in Teheran and its subsequent defeat over a NATO radar-aircraft contract illustrate perhaps better than any other case how interwoven are the economic interests of corporations, branches of the armed services, U.S. senators and even, in this case, the White House.

At Senate hearings in 1976, former Grumman International president Thomas P. Cheetham, Jr., told how a Nixon White House aide, Richard V. Allen, had asked him for a million-dollar contribution to the President's re-election campaign, in exchange for White House assistance in selling the E-2C Hawkeye radar control plane to Iran. Cheetham had turned the brash NSC official down. Peter Oram, Grumman International's current president, told the hearings how the late Kenny O'Donnell, who had been President Kennedy's appointments secretary, had introduced him to two friends in 1974 and persuaded him to make the friends Grumman's agents in Teheran, to help sell the F-14, and how they subsequently drew $2.9 million in commissions from the Long Island firm. Grumman had also paid $3.1 million to Iranian agents. When the Shah later insisted that the cost of commissions be deducted from his bill for the planes, Grumman agreed to pay the fees out of profits—even though some of the money paid was reportedly kicked back to some of the Shah's officials. In 1978, in settlement of this and other litigation with Iran over commission payments, Grumman agreed to give the country $24 million of F-14 spare parts, free, over three years.

By the early seventies, Grumman had been yet another example of a great defense manufacturer facing hard times. Founded in 1931, Grumman Aerospace—the parent company of Grumman International—had employed 25,000 people during World War Two and built 17,000 planes, mostly Hellcat and Wildcat fighters and the sturdy Harvard—as its name indicates, a trainer. (Every World War Two RAF pilot won his wings on Harvards.) Seven different Grumman types flew in Vietnam. But Grumman would have gone bankrupt had it not been for the Shah's decision to buy 80 F-14s—with missiles and support costs, a bill for over $2 billion, of which $1.3 billion went to Grumman.

At the time, Grumman was losing money on a "fixed-price" contract for F-14s for the U. S. Navy, agreed to in 1969 by company co-founder E. Clinton Towl. Unit cost of the aircraft had gone from the 1969 figure of $7.3 million to about $11 million, and was destined to rise higher both from inflation and from a Congress-imposed Navy decision to order fewer than the 300 planes originally stipulated (the lower the production run, the higher the unit cost). Grumman was even considering closing down without completing the Navy order. Congress made difficulties about renegotiation of the Navy contract and vetoed a Navy loan: The renegotiation achieved still left Grumman with a $235 million loss on the first 134 aircraft. Over 1971 and 1972, Grumman lost $88 million. With renegotiation, Grumman made a modest $28 million profit in 1973 on sales of $1.1 billion. The real reason for the turnaround in the corporation's fortunes was the Shah.

The ruler had followed the development of the F-14 Tomcat, the work of one of the world's most brilliant aircraft designers, Michael Pehalac in the pages of Aviation Week. On a visit to the United States, he was the object of an intense sales drive by Grumman officials. The Navy lent the firm a pilot to demonstrate the plane for the Shah. Grumman International's president, Peter Oram, presented the prospective customer with a tailor-made flying suit bearing the royal arms.

Riza Pahlevi was principally attracted to the plane because of the six Phoenix missiles it carried. Although the F-14 operated at about 40,000 feet, its Phoenixes could reach the MiG-25s overflying his country at twice that altitude. Passing through Teheran on his way back from Moscow in 1972, Nixon agreed to let Iran buy any conventional weaponry it wanted. Officially, the quid pro quo was that Iran would agree not to "go nuclear"; almost certainly there was also a royal contribution to Nixon's re-election campaign that year, although this has never been proven.

The decision to let Iran have F-14s with Phoenixes raised problems about which no one in the Pentagon had been consulted—such as providing "classified" information on the state-of-the-art Phoenix to a friendly but not allied power, and the need to send thousands of American technicians and dependents for an extended period (at least five years) to Iran, where they would be hostages in the event of conflict. Moreover, the "population buildup" of middle- and lower-echelon Americans in Iran was already creating social strains, especially outside of Teheran. At conservative Isfahan, a major air base for F-14s and helicopters, one hundred Bell Helicopter instructors went on strike in August 1975, as a protest against conditions; sixty were subsequently fired. The flight instructors complained of being too restricted to base. Thereafter, efforts were made to ensure that "at least 90 per cent" of instructors should be married and accompanied by their families.

The murder of three Rockwell International technicians in Teheran in 1976 helped draw public attention to the problem. It was estimated that by 1980 about sixty thousand American civilian weaponry advisers would be serving in Iran. Similar situations were developing in other Middle East countries, and elsewhere. Hughes, with sales contracts to supply helicopters and TOW missiles to twenty countries, had training missions in twelve of them by 1977. But the U.S. firm with the largest number of personnel in Iran was Grumman.

Grumman's F-14 sales campaign in Iran had begun early in 1972, before the Nixon visit. The company had hired Houshang Lavi, a Long Island-based Iranian, to lobby top Teheran officials for an F-14 contract. There is substantial disagreement as to how much commission was promised; Grumman says about $30 million. Lavi says much more. The commission was to be 3.75 per cent—presumably a compromise between 5 per cent asked and 2.5 per cent offered. When the Shah and his Vice-Minister of War, General Hassan Toufanian—the redoubtable former G-4 —objected to Lavi and his company (consisting of his three brothers) being part of the deal, and Grumman thereupon agreed to pay Lavi out of profits, the percentage went down to 2 per cent.

It was at this point that Lavi was "persuaded" to sell his contract with Grumman to O'Donnell's friends, notably a retired U. S. Army colonel with an Iranian service background, Albert J. Fuge. The Iranian said his price was the first $1 million and 35 per cent of the rest of the commission. Lavi says Grumman were forced to pressure him to sell out by the insistence of Toufanian and the then chief of the Iranian Air Force staff, the late General Muhammad Khatami, the Shah's brother-in-law, both of whom—according to Lavi—were cut in on Fuge's fees. Grumman, as noted earlier, say they paid $2.9 million to Fuge's group, $3.1 million to the Lavis.

That a middleman may have been more necessary than the Shah seemed prepared to admit was indicated by Grumman's extraordinary success in increasing the original Iranian order, which had been for thirty Tomcats. The Iranian Air Force then planned to buy fifty McDonnell-Douglas F-15s. Grumman's man in Teheran, L. M. "Butch" Satterfield, had pointed out to the Iranians that buying two air-superiority fighters would be more expensive and make maintenance more difficult. Somehow or other, the point was successfully made: Iran would buy eighty Tomcats, and no F-15s, and would lend Grumman $75 million from the Shah's personal Meli Bank; this loan made it easier for Grumman to raise an additional $125 million back home.

To bring off the full deal, Grumman, Satterfield and Lavi had not only had to fight off McDonnell-Douglas—who were much more experienced in Iran than Grumman—but also the U. S. Air Force, which had made the F-15 its top fighter for the eighties and had not ordered the F-14. USAF unit costs for the F-15 would be reduced by F-15 foreign sales, and USAF officers already training Iranian crews and ground staffs were naturally pro-F-15. On Capitol Hill, senators Stuart Symington and Thomas Eagleton of Missouri—the McDonnell-Douglas state—had clamored for the F-14 production line to be closed altogether, to leave the field open to the F-15. The F-15 protagonists could even argue that their bird was cheaper. The final overseas-delivery tab on the Tomcat was already around $20 million per copy, including support costs, but the Shah didn't blink; he merely increased the price of oil.

Oram and Joseph G. Gavin, the president of Grumman Aerospace, told the Senate that Toufanian was dunning them for $28 million in "illegally paid" commissions and threatening to deduct that sum from their payment. The Pentagon advised Teheran against this, pointing out that under the Foreign Military Sales contract, Iran would pay the Department of Defense, which would then owe Grumman the originally stipulated sum. Eventually, as noted earlier, Grumman agreed to lop $24 million off its bill, recognizing that it was saving that much by the new terms for Houshang Lavi. Lavi then began a long suit against the Bethpage firm for $14.6 million. In spite of all the shenanigans, the Shah seemed happy. In 1975, he told a visiting British reporter: "The strength that we have now in the Persian Gulf is ten times, twenty times more than the British ever had."

Congressional and liberal criticism of the arms deals in Iran continued, however. In September 1976, Congressman Wilson asked why F-14s had been sold to Iran before the U. S. Navy had mastered the new aircraft's problems. He related the plane's seventeen crashes up to that date. Recalling how important the sale had been to Grumman, Wilson said:

> The decision to bail out [Grumman] was no doubt eased by the fact that the former chairman of CREEP, Clark MacGregor, had just signed on as vice-president of United Technologies, a company which stood to lose at least a billion dollars' worth of business had the F-14 project been discontinued. Not so coincidentally, two close Nixon associates, W. P. Clements and J. Fred Buzhardt, were members of the government negotiating committee. Formerly head of the Texas Committee to Re-Elect the President, Mr. Clements was, as he is now, the Deputy Secretary of Defense; Mr. Buzhardt was a general counsel for the Office of the Secretary of Defense. Recent evidence of then-President Richard Nixon's personal interest in the lifesaving sale of F-14s to Iran is only another example of a remarkable relationship.

Wilson went on:

> Official U.S. objections to the sale, anticipated by more rational men, never surfaced. It was Nixon himself who removed any obstacles to the transaction with his infamous visit to the Shah in 1972. The State and Defense departments remained unconsulted by a deranged administration and a desperate firm out to save itself.
>
> We live today with the deformed fruits of this misguided policy—large increases in sales to Iran exempted from the normal interagency review, and an escalating arms race in the most volatile region of the world.

Despite all this, and the row about commissions between General Toufanian and Grumman, the last of the eighty F-14s with Phoenix missiles were delivered in 1978. The total cost of the program had reached about $2.5 billion, including training, maintenance and other support costs. Iran's five F-14 squadrons, at two bases, employed an air and ground staff of 6,500 people, of whom 2,650 had received or were receiving F-14-oriented training.

In 1976, Grumman borrowed another $160 million from U.S. banks and paid off the Iranian loan, putting up—as security—all its subsidiaries except Grumman American. The company's 1977 sales reached a record $1.56 billion, with profits of $34.4 million. By mid-1978, Grumman stock had risen markedly, and nine banks gave the corporation a $175 million unsecured loan. The Shah had apparently saved the day for the company, and Grumman seemed secure.

The next goal for Grumman would logically have been to sell NATO on the E-2C Hawkeye. The Long Island firm had been beaten out on this one by Boeing in Iran, with the Shah preferring the more expensive AWACS—conscious that this purchase would have the powerful Hill backing of the "senator from Boeing," Henry Jackson, whose mettlesome defense of the corporation was briefly mentioned in Chapter 4. Now Jackson was to unsaddle Grumman again for the NATO contract—with the net result that *neither* American plane would land more than a diminished sale.

By 1977, when the pressure from the White House and the Pentagon to standardize around U.S. wares was gathering speed, Grumman badly needed new business again. In 1976, it had laid off a thousand people. Grumman's chairman John Bierwirth was convinced that the firm's future lay in foreign sales, and in less dependence on the U. S. Navy.

On the face of it, the Hawkeye would have served Iran's purpose at least as well as the more sophisticated AWACS. The same was true in Europe—less concerned with the defense of huge ocean areas than the United States. The E-2C, after all, could "control" 3 million cubic miles of airspace. Apart from an Israeli purchase of four Hawkeyes, only Japan loomed at the time as a potential overseas customer for the Grumman plane. Yet early in 1977, Bierwirth told a New York brokerage house that the plane was "sold out until 1982" and that no new orders could be taken. The reason: The Pentagon had ordered Grumman not to sell in Europe, or else. The reason: Jackson had cautioned the Pentagon to salvage Boeing, or else.

Boeing's troubles went back to 1970, when the Minuteman line closed down. The B-52 line was already closed. There was widespread unemployment and a recurrent sick joke ran: "Will the last person to leave Seattle please turn off the lights?" Jackson saved Boeing's bacon by persuading the Air Force to adapt 747 airliners for military use as AWACS, and as special emergency ("Kneecap") wartime command centers. The senator got the R & D money out of Congress in 1971. The ABM treaty the following year partly outdated the AWACS concept in America, but possibly not in Europe. Meanwhile, the Hawkeye had gone into squadron service in 1971, just as AWACS made its first landing on the drawing board. Everybody using the plane seemed to like the Hawkeye: There had been no serious cost overruns; it had been produced on time. At Bethpage, it gave employment to two thousand people with about seven thousand dependents.

There were other strikes against AWACS: A former British air marshal named Sir Peter Fletcher now ran Hawker-Siddeley, and had started production of the British equivalent aircraft, the Nimrod. The United States had argued for an integrated system, with integrated crews. NATO, as noted in Chapter 2, wanted a system which worked with a ground-control center, which Hawkeye does. To pay more for a fully independent aircraft like AWACS did not appeal to Europe.

Clearly, if the Pentagon generals were not to be put across Scoop Jackson's knee, they would have to rig the game. Both the Hawkeye and AWACS were presented to the allies for a demonstration. The Grumman plane came straight from duty over the Atlantic. The 747 was incomplete, so its ultimate specifications had to be spelled out in print. Admiral Gene LaRocque quipped at the time: "In a contest between a plane and the specifications for a plane, the specifications will generally win."

Instead of sending F-4s or F-5s flitting low in the ground clutter, to imitate MiGs, the Air Force provided huge B-52s—so that AWACS would be sure to find them. Later, in 1976, when AWACS was used in war games at Nellis Air Force Base, it was able to find F-5s—but experts said it would probably not have been able to find MiG-21s and -23s, with their more advanced radar countermeasures. The "enemy" planes were flown by the usual Nellis "MiG" team, not by the crack USAF "MiG" team, based at Alconbury in Britain. No NATO observers were invited to watch the AWACS performance.

None of this went unreported by NATO defense attachés in Washington. In London in 1977, Carter tried and failed to sell AWACS to NATO. Britain, miffed by U.S. cancellation of Skyflash and concerned about seven thousand Hawker-Siddeley jobs, decided to build eleven improved Nimrods. Manfred Woerner, chairman of the defense committee in the Bundestag, and Geoffrey Pattie, a Conservative defense spokesman in the House of Commons, told the present writer at a NATO meeting shortly before the "Carter summit" that an "integrated" system might have been built around Hawkeye, but not around AWACS.

An angry Peter Oram had earlier decided to hold a press conference in London to protest the squelching of Hawkeye in favor of the apparently doomed AWACS campaign in NATO. At the last minute, he canceled it on orders from his board at Bethpage. By mid-1977, New York senators Jacob Javits and Daniel Moynihan were advising Bethpage that they could not fight Jackson over this. The local congressman, Thomas Downey, inserted a favorable statement about the Hawkeye in the Congressional Record, and that was that. Final negotiations were for limited AWACS sales, based—as noted in Chapter 2—on a compromise deal involving U.S. purchase of European equipment. The AWACS issue is looked at in more detail in the following chapter.

For the moment, Grumman's fortunes depend principally on continued sales of the F-14 to the Navy—since made more difficult by the availability of used Iranian Tomcats at discount prices. In December 1977, Carter reduced the size of the annual order, spinning out deliveries over a longer period of time. By then, only 20 of the Iranian order remained to be completed. These—identical with the Navy version except for the desert camouflage paint and Farsi decals, even down to the same heavy landing gear intended for carriers—shared the assembly line at Calverton when the writer called that month. Officials were anxious to sound optimistic.

Oram told the author that he hoped the Navy would extend its order for 521 Tomcats, and that Iran would also order more. The F-14 was competing for the "new Canadian fighter" program, and there were hopes of sales to Australia. Japan had stayed with McDonnell-Douglas, going from the F-4 to the F-15, and he thought that West Germany would do the same. Oram believed Europe might be a better market for F-14s in the mid-eighties, when there could be rethinking about whether Mirages and Tornadoes can perform all the missions assigned to them.

Where will Grumman sell the E-2C next? "Japan probably," said Oram. "Perhaps Saudi Arabia. Israel will get the first two of its four next month [January 1978]. Its crews are in training at Bethpage now. The E-2 is ideal for small countries with sophisticated surveillance problems, even for larger countries like Australia." He thought China was a market possibility, although perhaps only for civil aircraft in the immediate future. He agreed with Bierwirth that "the future of Grumman breaks on international business," but he thought "international business" now predominantly meant joint production plans in Europe and Japan.

In this regard, it may be noted that European aerospace already uses a great deal of U.S. technology, especially in major programs, partly because of joint ownership. Pratt and Whitney, for instance, owns 10 per cent of France's (government-controlled) SNECMA aerospace firm. Its parent, United Technologies (formerly United Aircraft), has 26 per cent of Vereinigte Flugtechnische Werke (VFW)—only 3 per cent less than Krupp—and 20 per cent of France's Précilec. Until 1978, when it pulled out, Boeing owned 25 per cent of Bolkow, while Northrop owns 20 per cent of Fokker; Lockheed has 20 per cent of Aermacchi and Raytheon has a 45 per cent holding in Italy's Selenia. GE controls Machines Bull, a French computer firm, while Bendix owns 50 per cent of the German electronics corporation Teldix.

Britain's updated Rapier missile, the laser-seeking Sabre, uses a Martin Marietta system. The British Hawk, the Franco-German Alphajet, the trinational Tornado and Swedish aircraft will all be users of the Sabre, which has been suggested for the F-16, the A-10, the F-5 and the F-18L, as well as for attack helicopters. Some European arms are jointly produced with U.S. firms: Both Raytheon and General Dynamics have teamed with Switzerland's Oerlikon to make antiaircraft artillery, while Ford has joined Bofors of Sweden to make surface-to-air missiles for the U.S. forces. General Dynamics is combining with firms in Germany, Denmark, Norway, Italy and Holland for an antiship missile defense system, geared for 1979 production.

Grumman and British Aerospace already do joint R & D, and Grumman was one of three hundred American subcontractors on the A-300 Airbus. Honeywell is making laser range finders under contract from Britain's Ferrari firm. There are close contractual arrangements between Hughes Aircraft and SAAB, between Pratt and Whitney and Svenska Flygmotor, and between Allison and Rolls-Royce. Noting that "no industry uses more different scientific disciplines than aerospace," Oram, in his interview, said that more technological transfers were necessary in the interests of standardization and interoperability. He pointed out that the wing pivot of the F-14 was that designed for France's Avion de Combat Futur (the "F-1"), and that all the HUDs (head-up displays) in Grumman cockpits were by British Marconi, while Grumman's ejection seats, by Martin Baker, were British as well. The F-14 also incorporates British fire-prevention devices which seal off the gas tanks if lightning strikes.

Trade magazines also report a great number of ventures linking U.S. and French avionics. France's Thomson-CSF is producing its cathode-ray tube flight displays in cooperation with Bendix and its Atlis laser target-designation system with Martin Marietta. It licenses Motorola to make integrated circuits. SFENA (Société Française d'Équipements pour la Navigation Aérienne) co-designs equipment with Jet Electronics and Technology Inc. of Grand Rapids. Crouzet Aéronautique has a similar arrangement with Boeing. TRT, a Paris firm which has designed a digital radio altimeter, is developing it with the Kohlmann Instrument Company of the United States and with British Aerospace. France's SODERN (Société Anonyme d'Études et Réalisations Nucléaires) works closely with McDonnell-Douglas. Within Europe itself, a great deal of technology is exchanged, and not only between France, Britain and Germany; in

1978, Sweden and Italy were negotiating to design and produce, together, a new light attack aircraft.

Oram said the AFL-CIO was opposed to international cooperation, but that the United Auto Workers and the International Association of Machinists were not; he noted that these two unions were members of the American League for International Security Assistance ("Lisa") lobby. Looking to the future, Oram expected Euro-American cooperation on a civilian supersonic transport. He also mocked the campaign against Concorde, noting that "F-14s have been flying supersonically over Long Island for years." U.S.-European and U.S.-Japanese jointly *designed* and built products are clearly a thing of the future—and another great way of evading any Washington-imposed restraints.

Because of administration pressures against promoting arms sales overseas, nearly all U.S. aerospace companies decided not to appear at the Farnborough Air Show in 1978. Apart from air-defense radar systems, and a single Boeing-Vertol CH-47 Chinook helicopter, for which the Defense Department refused an army maintenance team, the major exception was Fairchild, which showed off the A-10 in a static display. Grumman had planned to appear, and would have had to lease a demonstration F-14 from the Navy, which owns them all—including the Iranian units, which were delivered to the Navy for consignment to Iran. (The planes were flown out in Iranian desert camouflage paint but with USN markings.) The White House was urging American warplane makers not to look for sales outside NATO, Japan and Australasia. Both Oram and Joe Gavin, president of the Grumman parent corporation, tried to console themselves with the thought that "air shows don't sell military aircraft, in any case." But like institutional advertising, they are a necessary showcase, a calling card to the global market.

Gavin thought the industry was handicapped by the government's arms policy, which was to "build toward a stalemate" and avoid tipping the balance toward the West, while preventing it tipping the other way. This raised the questions of counterforce, destabilization and pre-emption; but Gavin said that "I don't think the balloon will go up just because you've created instability." He saw a more real need for balance in certain regions, such as the Middle East, because total victory for either side would be destabilizing. In 1978, Grumman and its subcontractors continued the fight against cutting F-14 production to two a month and won the support of the House Armed Services Committee; an angry Defense Secretary Brown ordered the Defense Audit Agency to investigate whether military contract funds were used for lobbying. The probe drew a blank. An internal audit in 1979 also cleared Grumman of charges that

its representatives had made payoffs to ensure E-2C sales in Japan: But
the audit found payoffs for sales of civilian aircraft overseas, and re-
buked Bierwirth for covering them up.

Northrop Sales

Northrop, run since 1960 by gentlemanly Thomas V. Jones, followed
modestly in the steps of Lockheed. Northrop's export-only F-5 had been
an immense success, but Jones decided the company could do better.
Through a Paris lawyer, he laundered contributions to American politicians—about a million dollars through the sixties. He became friendly
with Lockheed's erstwhile Dutch agent, Prince Bernhard. When Lockheed turned down an offer to buy into Fokker, Jones decided that
Northrop would take a 20 per cent share, thus making him a fellow
director with the prince.

In Paris, when General Paul Stehlin retired as chief of French Air
Force staff, Jones contracted with him, for $7,500 a year, to provide
arms-trade intelligence. Stehlin, who had an American wife, improved
his usefulness by getting elected to the French parliament, where he became deputy speaker.

In Germany, Northrop worked through an American lawyer, Frank de
Francis, who initially earned $100,000 a year, but later was paid between
.5 and 1.5 per cent of all foreign sales.

On Capitol Hill, Jones, working through a member of the staff of
House Armed Services Committee chairman Mendel Rivers of South
Carolina, obtained a $28 million R & D contract to upgrade the F-5 into
the even more successful F-5E, over 1,500 copies of which were sold to
about 25 countries. In nearby Maryland, a Northrop duck-hunting lodge
was used to entertain Pentagon brass and Hill figures. Author Anthony
Sampson says that 144 such parties cost Northrop only a modest $37,000.
(Not far away, on Wye Island, Rockwell had a similar establishment.)

Northrop also had a minority share in the F-18, with McDonnell-
Douglas, but in the mid-seventies it concentrated on trying to make the
land version—the F-18L—an export-only plane, like the F-5. In October
1976, after Iran had ordered the F-18L, Northrop asked the Pentagon if
it would object to a $6.7 million feasibility study on the projected plane
being paid for by the Shah. It would be the first time that a foreign government had invested in the development of an American weapons system not being made for the U.S. forces. With the Navy ordering 800 of
the original version, on which the prime contractor was McDonnell-

Douglas, Northrop was naturally eager to build the 250 F-18Ls wanted by the Shah (for an overall figure, including support costs, estimated at nearly $4 billion) as a lever to getting further orders and to firming up those from Japan and Australia. (To keep the twin-engined F-18L competitive with the single-engined F-16, Northrop, as the prime contractor for the F-18L, in December announced a "flat price" of $6 million for its plane.) Also enthusiastic about the proposed Iranian sale of F-18Ls was the U. S. Navy, because the Shah's willingness to pay some of the development costs would reduce the bill for the Navy's 800 Hornets by a cool $240 million.

In September, Toufanian had written to Defense Secretary Donald Rumsfeld, asking for the plane and offering to pay the $240 million toward development. When the Pentagon's Defense Systems Acquisition Review Committee considered the request in October, it took into account the staggering cost (on top of Iran's existing bills for U.S. arms, including the nearly $2.5 billion for the F-14s and the prospective $3.9 billion for 160 F-16s).

By offering to pay $6.7 million for an initial feasibility study, Teheran hoped to get around the requirement that Congress approve any "individual" sale of an item surpassing $7 million. But Lee Hamilton of Indiana, chairman of the House subcommittee for Europe and the Near East, wrote Secretary Kissinger, in the closing days of the Ford administration, urging re-examination of the F-18L-for-Iran project and more consultation with Congress. Hamilton told the House: "Our entire arms policy of sales to Iran and the Persian Gulf needs scrutiny and definition." In a reply sent the following month, State Department lobbyist Kempton B. Jenkins promised: "No action which might be construed as a U. S. Government commitment to the proposed sale will be taken before Congress convenes in January."

On March 5, 1977, shortly after Carter took office, U.S. officials flew to Teheran with a letter of offer to sell Iran the 160 F-16s. Robert Hotz, editor of the Shah's favorite publication, *Aviation Week*, boldly sent the ruler a tactical message by announcing the trip and adding in boldface: "If the Government of Iran signs the offer, it may lose any opportunity to procure eventually the Northrop-McDonnell-Douglas F-18L Cobra." The brief story said the Shah "may use the F-16 offer as leverage for the F-18L." Permission for the $6.7 million feasibility study was being held up "by a senior official in the Pentagon," the journal said, noting that the Iranian order would "open the production line and place the F-18L on the world market."

Hotz, however, also warned his imperial fan that "if the Shah balks at the F-16 offer until he gets an indication that he may get the F-18L, he could lose his place in the F-16 line, U.S. officials said." But Hotz quoted one such official as saying: "If the Shah holds up the letter of offer for the F-16 until he is assured of the F-18L study agreement and possible procurement, General Dynamics and the [four-nation NATO] consortium could find themselves in the unique position of having to ask the U. S. Government to release the letter of offer for the F-18L, a competitor." (This would be because Iranian purchases of the F-16 would increase the co-production work on—and revenues from—the aircraft by the consortium.)

Having thus signaled the Shah on the canniest ways to get what we wanted, *Aviation Week* then added what looked like a reminder to the White House that if it nixed an American sale, a European firm would replace Northrop: "If the Shah opts for the F-16 [but] is . . . unable to get the F-18L or another F-18 variant, Iran is expected to look to France for the Dassault-Bréguet Mirage-2000."

However, in June, a week after canceling the offer to sell A-7s to Pakistan, the White House decided against the F-18L sale also.

Even the deal for the single-engine F-16s came under attack and was the subject of congressional hearings in September 1976. But when the letter of offer went off to Teheran the following March, Air Force officers who went along offered the Shah a special pricing mechanism: The more F-16s were sold worldwide, the lower the price would become. However, the Shah and Toufanian had read *Aviation Week* attentively, and Mr. Hotz's pupils dutifully crossed their arms and stuck out their chins. Instead of eagerly signing the letter of offer as the U.S. mission had expected, they merely agreed to pay $41 million for some items produced in the earliest stages of procurement; this money would be forfeit if they later decided not to purchase, but through the payment Iran—learning another of Mr. Hotz's careful lessons—kept "its place in the line."

Iran, in any case, wanted 300, not 160 F-16s, and both the Air Force and General Dynamics postulated foreign sales of at least a thousand planes in estimating unit prices. Achieving that export figure was important both to the Air Force, as purchasers of at least 1,388 planes, and to the four European countries, as co-producers of these and of their own 348. Israel had now asked for 250 and Spain for 72 of the aircraft.

However, when Carter killed the F-18L project—at least for the time being—Toufanian signed for the F-16s, whereupon the friendly U. S. Air Force sprang a surprise: They successfully insisted on delays in deliveries so as not to slow introduction of the aircraft into U.S. service. Former deputy defense secretary Robert Ellsworth had approved an accelerated program for the Iranian F-16s, delivering some to Iranian officers for training in the United States in March 1979. Secretary Brown now put this date back to January 1980. Deliveries of F-16s to Iran itself would still begin in July 1980, at a rate of four a month. In the end, of course, a revolutionary Iran later refused the planes altogether.

At the heart of Iran's F-18L problem was a Carter administration decision against any export-only warplanes; but in Washington, no political decisions are forever. Jones spoke of selling two thousand F-18Ls, beginning with Iran. The Pentagon was not slow to see that, with about 90 per cent commonality of parts with the F-18, such sales would cut F-18 unit costs for the United States, notably in regard to the identical engines. The F-18L's attraction was a better performance than the Navy model, which has heavy landing gear, folding wings and other structural requirements for carrier landings and basing.

Meanwhile, the F-5E continued to sell well, and Northrop earnings went up in 1976, 1977 and 1978. The company, which Sampson calls in *The Arms Bazaar* the "most aggressive" arms exporter, made record sales and profits both years. Northrop chairman Jones reported in February 1977 that the fourth quarter net had been $14.5 million, or $2.20 a share, compared to $7.3 million, or $1.26 a share, for the last quarter of 1975. Sales for all of 1976 netted $35 million, or $5.70 a share, for a gross of $1.25 billion, up from $24.7 million ($4.32 a share) on sales of $988.1 million in 1975. Orders fell off in 1977, but actual sales climbed, and in 1978 things were even better. By the third quarter of that year, company profits reached a new record level of $22.2 million, an increase of 31 per cent over the $16.9 million earned in the same quarter of 1977.

The Carter decision to veto the sale of F-18Ls to Iran was a disappointment to both Northrop and McDonnell-Douglas; but Australia, Japan, Canada and Spain were still interested. Jones told stockholders in 1977 that the firm, then the nation's third largest defense contractor, was currently selling about half its production overseas, and that authorization to fulfill all potential F-18 orders would "double the company's size" by 1984. The F-5, Jones predicted, would sell "well into the eighties." The U. S. Navy's orders of 811 of the naval version of the F-18, which cost $1.4 billion to develop, went 60 per cent to McDonnell-Douglas. But in 1977, Northrop finished the first of three inertial-guidance units for the experimental M-X missile—a $28 million contract —and in 1978 it was well into electronic countermeasures development, including a surface-launched "harassment drone" that behaves, in Jones's words, "like a flock of bees" with enemy radar.

Northrop, however, remained hurt by the 1976 report of the headline-hunting Church subcommittee, which had launched several thunderbolts and even published the firm's link to former French deputy speaker Paul Stehlin. Stehlin had also done a little unpaid work for General Dynamics, writing President Giscard d'Estaing that France should choose the F-16 rather than the Mirage F-1, since this was only being produced at the expense of the French taxpayer. On his own initiative, Stehlin sent copies of his letter to leading defense officials in Holland, Belgium, Norway and Denmark—NATO's "northern tier," which was evaluating the GD plane. A Belgian official leaked the letter back to Stehlin's fellow deputy and fellow officer General de Bénouville, who was also the chief executive officer of Dassault. It was in the furor that followed that Stehlin had been obliged to give up his deputy speakership.

GD appears to have brought off its F-16 sale to the northern tier of NATO without being shaken down. The F-16 had the support of then-Defense Secretary Schlesinger, who favored standardization and who saw the F-16 as the F-4 of the future. Unlike the F-104, it had the merit of having been already selected by the USAF. Schlesinger had finally convinced the holdout country, Belgium, by a $30 million U.S. purchase of Belgian machine guns.

Rockwell International's Problems

Another aerospace giant, Rockwell International, invested deeply and unwisely in an Iranian deal only partially concerned with aviation. The secret project became generally known on August 28, 1976, when three Rockwell employees were gunned down by Polish submachine guns in Teheran, after a red Volkswagen had blocked their car and a mini-bus had rammed them from behind.

The project was called Ibex, after the mountain goat. It was a border surveillance system, payments for which were cloaked in secrecy for security reasons. With CIA cooperation, Rockwell were to build eleven ground monitoring posts, some mobile ground units and six airborne control planes with long-range cameras.

Teheran had once again insisted that there be "no middlemen"; but the previous January, Rockwell had signed an agent's contract with Universal Aero Services Company (UASCO), of Box 1179, Bermuda. UASCO —run by an Iranian, Abolfath Mahvi—was to get from 5 to 10 per cent of the Ibex payments. Mahvi thoughtfully put a clause in the contract saying it could not be terminated for five years.

Rockwell won the contract in February 1975, and fifteen CIA and NSA men were sent out to help set up the program. By July, the redoubtable

General Toufanian had found out about Mahvi's role and exploded. The UASCO contract was terminated in September—leaving Mahvi to sue Rockwell for $4,526,758.

The financing of the project was curious. Iran opened an account with the Riggs Bank in Washington, starting with a transfer of $5 million for William Owens and Henry Plastee, both CIA officers. Eventually, over $47 million was deposited at Riggs through Touche, Ross—a local auditors, who made payments to Hewlett-Packard, Watkins-Johnston and other Ibex subcontractors. Donald Patterson, an ex-CIA hand, was paid 5 per cent ($55,000) to authorize payments of $1.1 million to Touche, Ross —whose sole job was to pay contractors secretly.

However, Iran soon began to suspect corruption and incompetence. The Westinghouse radars were not up to par. The cameras were inoperative after dark or through cloud. The sophisticated computer turned out to be a lemon. In July 1976, Ambassador Richard Helms, formerly head of the CIA, told his successor George Bush at Langley that a senior CIA official should be sent out to investigate Ibex. Meanwhile he, Helms, was "washing my hands of the whole affair."

Toufanian had made a similar complaint to Defense Secretary Donald Rumsfeld, using the U.S. embassy pouch for greater secrecy. As far back as 1973, Schlesinger had sent Richard Hallock, a former paratroop colonel with a Silver Star, to Teheran to monitor everyone—the embassy, the CIA and the contractors. Hallock eventually set up a small consultative defense firm called Intrec Inc. His task was to advise General Toufanian and others, independently of the arms firms and their boosters in the military office of the embassy—and to report back directly to the Secretary or a few close Pentagon officials.

A Senate report later said that "it was apparently Schlesinger's hope that Hallock's advice to the Shah might serve as a counterweight to the hard-sales tactics of industry and, on occasion, the services.

"Hallock operated outside of the DoD chain of command, in part because he and the Secretary suspected that some DoD [officials might] be functioning primarily as salesmen rather than advisers."

Out of Hallock's close relationship with the Shah and Toufanian came "a high sense of confidence in Hallock's advice," the Senate report added. But when Defense weighed sending an *official* representative as well, the Teheran embassy objected, and Schlesinger decided against the move. After Schlesinger's departure from the Pentagon, however, Erich von Marbod was sent out in that role in September 1975, for a year. By then, Hallock had left his temporary U. S. Government service and was working directly for General Toufanian.

Both the Shah and Toufanian took a dislike to Erich von Marbod, now the chief Pentagon man in Teheran; but Hallock was very much in their graces. The Shah asked for Marbod's recall, but Marbod—an old hunting-lodge habitué of the great defense corporations—stayed on. Ibex continued. Until the revolution, its Iranian operatives were being trained at Rockwell headquarters in Anaheim, California, and were housed in a wing of the Anaheim Hilton.

The persistent American troubles in Iran led to a Pentagon leak to the Washington *Post* in 1977 that the U. S. Navy was abolishing America's most exclusive spy network, which was heavily involved in Iranian defense contracts. A small network of seventy-five agents with commercial cover, backed up by an equal number of Stateside officials and secretaries, this was the group that first confirmed the nuclearizing of Egypt's Scud missiles in 1973. The leak to the *Post* said the spy network had become corrupt. One member, who had earlier sold an intelligence-gathering ship to Iran as a "scientific research vessel" for $350,000, was under investigation for allegedly selling detonators and other explosive devices to Libya.

Whether this network was actually abolished is, of course, open to speculation.

Box 1179 in Hamilton cropped up again when the Iranian Air Force signed a contract with Management and Technical Consultants (MTC), of that address, to advise on supply and logistics systems for the Imperial Air Force. There were two agreements, assuring MTC of payments of about $7.7 million, half in dollars, half in rials. The money for MTC was sent to the Chase Manhattan Bank in the rue du Rhône in Geneva, in care of Olivier Turretini, a bank officer. What was especially curious about the contracts was that Iran's Air Force *already had* a management contract for such a system—Peace Log—with the USAF, for $16 million, signed earlier with General Jack F. Catton, then commander of the USAF Logistics Command; Catton had since resigned to work for Lockheed—which got the Peace Log contract.

Business As Usual

By 1977, the moneyed battle to sell U.S. weapons abroad continued, especially among the aerospace companies. The coup of the year was a McDonnell-Douglas sale of F-15s to Japan's Air Self-Defense Force, to back up that country's own Mitsubishi F-1—which, in spite of its "F" (for fighter) designation, is really a close-support aircraft. The F-15s would replace the luckless Starfighters. USAF officers in Japan helped McDonnell-Douglas beat out the competition—F-14s and F-16s. The Japanese sales would help reduce F-15 costs on the USAF's own 729 ordered copies.

Although the F-15 costs just under $20 million in America, it will cost about $27 million co-produced in Japan—$35 million apiece with parts. The main contractor is Mitsubishi, with engines by Ishikawajima. The planes should become operational in 1982.

McDonnell-Douglas finally won out in a slick campaign of audio-visual presentations, handsome brochures, test flights and champagne parties against its last remaining competitor, the F-16, which advertised that it had "96 per cent of the F-15's performance for 60 per cent of the cost." The F-14 was handicapped by congressional discussion of its engine problems, but both GD and Grumman hinted darkly to reporters about corruption by McDonnell-Douglas. Lockheed, still lurching from the Kodama scandal, was having difficulty holding on to its $300 million Japanese contract for Orions.

When G. William Miller, chairman of Textron, was nominated to be head of the Federal Reserve Board in 1978, congressional investigators questioned a $2.9 million payment by Textron's Bell Helicopter subsidiary, in 1973, to a sales agency secretly owned by the late General Mohammad Khatami, then head of the Iranian Air Force. Khatami, before being killed in a hang-gliding accident, had been forced to withdraw as a stockholder in the Iranian Aircraft Corporation, partly owned by Northrop. Bell's payment to Khatami's agency, Air Taxi, was said to have been instrumental in landing Bell's $500 million order for helicopters in Iran. Miller's nomination was approved, after he told hearings chaired by Senator William Proxmire that he had not known of General Khatami's link to the agency. He also pleaded ignorance of a $300,000 shakedown by a Ghanaian official in 1971, in connection with the $1,668,000 sale of two Bell-212 helicopters.

Another important nation largely dependent on U.S. military assistance was Indonesia, the world's largest Muslim nation, where there were frequent reports of corruption involved with arms and similar deals. In 1977, officials of the General Telephone and Electronics Corporation accused Hughes Aircraft of paying "20 per cent" bribes on a $160 million satellite communications contract which GTE had sought. Hughes built the system, with the ExImBank granting $50 million in loans to Jakarta for the project. The GTE accusation implied that some ExImBank money might have been involved. The Securities and Exchange Commission was reported looking into the kickbacks question generally in overseas contracts. Hughes Aircraft denied all the charges.

One aerospace major which seemed little affected by allegations of impropriety was Boeing, which netted $39.9 million for the third quarter of 1977, compared to $22.7 million during the same period the previous year. Sales were up 12 per cent (from $799 million to $891 million), earnings 76 per cent. The earnings per share for the first nine months of the year were up even more, from $1.54 to $2.93, on sales of $2.9 billion. But in March 1978, the SEC authorized court action against Boeing regarding "payments made in connection with foreign sales." The Federal Trade Commission had by then started a probe to see if Boeing had engaged in "unfair competition, or unfair or deceptive acts or practices." Charges of making $33 million of questionable payments to foreign officials in connection with plane sales, notably in Iran, followed, and an investigation was under way when this book was written.

U.S. aerospace companies and the International Chamber of Commerce set about producing an ethics code to outlaw "shakedowns in the sheikhdoms" and bribery; but a U.S. bid to interest the UN in such a crusade met strong opposition from Third World countries: A proposed international pact was soon bogged down in a committee.

In late 1977, Congress passed an act forbidding corporate bribery abroad, setting a fine of $1 million—twice the maximum fine for price-fixing—and making corporate officers liable to up to five years in prison. There were no disclosure requirements: Investigation was left to Justice and the SEC. Most Republicans opposed the law, preferring disclosure to retribution. Jurists regarded it as probably unenforceable, since it involved an activity committed abroad, probably by a foreign national, which could only be investigated with foreign cooperation, which was unlikely to be given. But some corporations welcomed the law, seeing it as a way of perhaps avoiding shakedowns in cases where they were confident that they did not face serious foreign competition. A Gulf Oil lobbyist said he wished it had been passed earlier. But Senator Javits said the bribery problem was "absolutely insoluble" without international agreement.

However, the various revelations *had* had international repercussions, rocking governments from Rome to Tokyo, and thrones in Holland and Spain. Senator Church had milked the last ounce of "page one" out of his hearings, before being chastened into silence by a nervous Senate itself. He had certainly impressed the world media. Sampson, recounting the hearings in *The Arms Bazaar*, recalled:

The committee room was besieged by foreign journalists, led by scores of Japanese, who flew over in task forces from Tokyo, occupying the whole committee room until they were removed by the police and the tables carefully allocated. Japanese, Dutch and Italian journalists pursued the Senate staff and the Lockheed executives, waiting at their houses and jamming their telephones.

The French appeared amused by the American penchant for revelation, and continued with business as usual. Having lost the battle for Europe to the F-16, Dassault pushed F-1 sales elsewhere, even selling at least fifty—and possibly seventy-two—of them to Iraq. But France's scandal was coming.

The Vathaire Affair

In July 1976, eighty-four-year-old Marcel Dassault's mournful, gray personal accountant, Hervé de Vathaire, who had been looking more and more depressed since his wife's recent suicide, suddenly drew $1.6 million from the firm's account at the Banque de Paris et des Pays-Bas and disappeared. For two months, Dassault mysteriously said nothing, until finally *France-Soir* broke the story.

It transpired that Vathaire was sharing a young and exotic mistress with an ex-convict, Jean Kay, to whom he had shown some secret Dassault papers. Kay, who had been a soldier of fortune in Algeria, Yemen, Biafra and Lebanon, had filched the papers and had begun to extort money from Vathaire. Kay had come to public attention earlier, in 1971, when he had unsuccessfully tried to hijack a Pakistan International Airlines plane and demanded 20 tons of medicines for Bangladesh. Now Kay was demanding the equivalent of $1.6 million. When Vathaire produced the money, Kay refused to hand over the papers. When the scandal broke, someone claiming to be Kay telephoned French TV to explain that he had given the money to Lebanese rightists to buy arms. Then, Vathaire, who had been in hiding on Corfu, flew in from Athens and gave himself up. The French Government began planning for a partial nationalization of the Dassault empire.

Eventually, the dossier stolen by Kay emerged; this showed that Marcel Dassault (who had changed his name from Bloch to Dassault—meaning, roughly, "of the assault team"—while in the French Resistance) had milked subsidiary companies for his own personal profit. False payroll records had been used to dun purchasers, including the French Air Force, for jacked-up prices for Dassault planes. Dassault had bought control of a newspaper, and had two government tax inspectors under his control. A secret Finance Ministry report, criticizing corruption by French aerospace industries abroad, was leaked to the press, and the National Assembly voted an investigation of the industry. Full nationalization loomed. However, the following year, Dassault, by then eighty-six, was re-elected to Parliament, and his company made record profits on record sales—and record exports.

But in the seedy Paris atmosphere of 1976, violence blossomed. A small Lebanese arms dealer called Antoine Kanoh vanished on the streets of Paris. An Adnan Khashoggi aide, Samir Trabulsi, was shot, wounded and robbed on a boulevard. The Prince de Broglie was gunned down on a Paris avenue, reportedly by the Mivtzam Elohim ("Wrath of God") hit team of the Mossad for his secret arms deals with Arab countries.

In the Third World, who could trust anyone? Many countries hedged their bets: Kuwait bought A-4s from the United States, F-1s from France, Chieftain tanks from Britain, other equipment from the Soviet Union. In the heady atmosphere, as noted earlier, a fly-by-night Paris company sold three thousand fake Startron night-vision devices to Libya.

All this was the economics of arms gone wild. But arms remained a major weapon of diplomacy; and overall, profits continued to mount.

Yet some companies were in difficulties. Starting in late 1976, the Defense Department began to ease the regime under which contracts are awarded. In most contracts signed after October 1 that year, companies are allowed to charge the government for the interest on money loaned to buy or lease plant and equipment. Former Defense Secretary Robert McNamara used to oblige contractors to set a fixed price for development and production; under this system, as noted earlier, Lockheed lost millions on the C-5A transport plane, as did Grumman on the F-14. Now the Pentagon covers development costs, with a small, guaranteed profit. Fixed-price bids are only required for production extensions, when costs can usually be accurately estimated.

Northrop chairman Thomas V. Jones stressed to the congressional Joint Committee on Defense Production in 1977 that not all cost growth in defense was attributable to inflation. Companies made unrealistic bids to win contracts, Jones reminded the Committee, and government often changed the orders. Jones, with his firm's successful T-38 and F-5 programs behind him, argued that a company should make a "firm and binding contractual commitment which it is prepared to meet." This would mean Defense deciding exactly what it wanted and assuring itself that the firm could fulfill. This in turn would permit the reintroduction of fixed-price contracts.

Because R & D now costs more, the Pentagon is tempted to order larger numbers of a weapon, thus giving income stability to manufacturers, often for years ahead. The Abrams tank may stay in production for the rest of this century, and the nearly $5 billion, ten-year order given to Chrysler by the United States in November 1976 will be the seed of perhaps even larger earnings abroad—a godsend to a troubled company going through troubled times. But the race is to the swift; says *Business Week:* "Industry 'haves' such as McDonnell-Douglas, blessed with two big fighter programs [the F-15 and the F-18], will be sitting pretty for the long pull. But such 'have-nots' as LTV Vought Corporation . . . which has no major new prime contracts in view, may be forced to work as subcontractors, to merge or to drop out of the business altogether."

Profits Soar

Yet the arms-orders figures of the companies were dazzlingly high. For comparison, for the four-year period 1962–66, General Dynamics headed the list of U.S. arms manufacturers with a total procurement of $1.1 billion, mostly for F-111As. Lockheed—which later became first in the league table—was second with $960 million over the four years, over half of which was for F-104s. Third was McDonnell-Douglas with $703 million for Phantoms; fourth came Lockheed and General Dynamics together, for a joint-production venture on Polaris missiles, which yielded $427 million.

But in fiscal 1976 alone, the hundred top defense contractors collected $28.9 billion—69 per cent of all prime contracts. McDonnell-Douglas came first with $2.465 billion. Also over the $1 billion mark were Lockheed, Northrop, General Electric, United Technologies, Boeing and General Dynamics. After them came Grumman, Litton Industries, Rockwell International, Hughes Aircraft and Raytheon. Chrysler was only sixteenth, but had orders totaling $468,540,000; GM came twentieth, at $345,179,000. Ling-Temco-Vought, at twenty-third, earned $315,838,000. Ford, placing twenty-seventh, picked up $285,417,000, while Martin Marietta, in thirty-second position, earned a respectable $248,666,000. Even in fortieth position, Bendix received $161,768,000.

The wide contrast in these figures indicates the chanciness of the defense business, with colossal windfalls for those firms producing what is currently wanted, while other giants earn comparatively little. They indicate why a knowledgeable former head of the State Department's Bureau of Politico-Military affairs thinks arms sales abroad are now even more economic than diplomatic or strategic. Some big firms employing thousands would face bankruptcy without the growth of the overseas market indicated by some of the bigger Pentagon procurement orders.

In 1977, McDonnell-Douglas remained first in the contest for defense orders with $2.6 billion, and Lockheed remained second. For the first quarter of 1977, McDonnell-Douglas posted an 11 per cent gain in income, while AVCO, which is building the Chrysler tank engine and had major subcontracts on the B-1 and the C-5, expected to double its Pentagon income by 1981. Although Northrop fell from third place to tenth, with $986,239,000, its total sales reached $1.6 billion, an increase of 27 per cent over 1976, while its income nearly doubled—from $36.3 million to $66.2 million. Its sales for the fourth quarter rose over 28 per cent from $351.5 million to $451.8 million. The firm had a backlog of orders worth nearly $1.9 billion.

In the 1977 list, United Technologies moved from fifth place to third, Boeing from sixth to fourth, Rockwell International from tenth to sixth, Grumman from eighth to seventh, Hughes from eleventh to ninth, Raytheon from twelfth to eleventh. Also in the top twelve were General Electric (fifth) and General Dynamics (eighth). Litton Industries slipped from ninth place to sixteenth, but still grossed over $609 million from the Pentagon. Singer of sewing-machine fame made over $350 million selling weapons systems, while IBM made $547 million and AT&T $457 million.

In actual receipts for defense contracts that year, Rockwell came first, followed by GE, GD, McDonnell-Douglas and Boeing, all with about half a billion dollars. They were followed by Lockheed Missiles, Hughes, Raytheon and Martin Marietta. IBM was eleventh, Chrysler fourteenth, Lockheed Aircraft eighteenth, Northrop twenty-first, Grumman twenty-third. Full figures for 1978 were not available when this book was written, but Lockheed earnings rose from $55.4 million in 1977 to $64 million in 1978, Fairchild's from $7.6 million to $24.5 million. Fairchild's fourth-quarter profits soared from $3.5 million to $7.3 million; shares paid $5.11, up from $2.05. The company's actual revenues were up from $399 million to $544 million, with sales of A-10s up from 56 to 89. There was a billion-dollar backlog of orders.

At the bottom end of the race, only seven yards were still building naval ships by 1978, against fifteen a decade before. The number of missile builders had also shrunk from fifteen to twelve. A contract awarded to Hughes Helicopter early that year to build the AH-64 attack helicopter was that firm's first Pentagon production contract since 1969 and, in *Business Week*'s words, "probably saved it as a defense contractor." The earlier-mentioned award to Sikorsky to build a troop transport copter put the Vertol subsidiary of Boeing, Sikorsky's competitor, in danger of closure for a while.

The race is not only to the swift but to the rich. It is estimated that the aerospace industry's working capital was $5.9 billion in 1976, but that $8.8 billion will be needed in 1980 and perhaps $15 billion by 1985. At the same time, the growth of the European sophisticated-weapons industries, partly fanned by intramural NATO quarrels, will be cutting into the overseas profits of U.S. firms. Overseas orders of $12 billion in 1975 dropped to about $9 billion in 1976, and the rise since (partly because of Carter's arms-sales limitations to Third World countries) has barely kept pace with inflation. Congressional control of governmental arms sales may spike even some foreign orders which the White House approves. However, although an export figure of only $8 billion was initially projected for 1977, the actual total that year was over $13 billion, thanks largely to the Middle East.

What seems *unlikely* to affect the industry's order books is President Carter's promises to cut back on defense spending. The cuts, if achieved, seem most likely to apply to less overseas stationing of troops, or to be achieved by such accountancy tricks as spreading procurement budgets over future years. General Dynamics was forecasting $7 billion in revenues out of its role as prime contractor for the F-16, and $13 billion from its share of the Trident submarine. But an industry source predicted that if GD could sell 2,000 F-16s abroad, this export factor alone would create 900,000 U.S. jobs, improve the U.S. balance of payments by $9 billion, put $6 billion of taxes into the Treasury and allow the firm to recoup an additional $470 million of its R & D costs on the plane. GD also produces the Tomahawk cruise missile, the future of which is, however, still uncertain.

Fairchild expects to collect $4.4 billion over the next four years for building the A-10 close-support plane. McDonnell-Douglas hopes to bring in $11 billion from the F-15 program and, together with Northrop, $10 billion from the F-18. For Northrop, which has now sold over three thousand F-5s around the world, the F-18 was the pump-priming operation. Raytheon's growing fortunes are helped by the Hawk missile—a Saudi Arabian order alone was worth $1.1 billion—and by the Patriot surface-to-air missile, which should yield $5.6 billion in American orders alone.

Grumman is still hungry for a new program to replace the F-14, for which domestic sales will be completed, even with the reduced rate of production ordered by the Carter administration, by 1984. Lockheed is building the Trident missile, worth at least $7 billion in orders, and the

P-3 sub-chaser aircraft. General Electric is building the engines for the F-18 and the B-1 (a program still in the balance) and is competing with Pratt and Whitney for the contract to make a more powerful engine for the F-14 and the F-16. Boeing, still an ailing giant, stands to profit greatly from B-52 conversion and cruise-missile manufacture, and is competing with McDonnell-Douglas for the $6.3 billion contract to replace the C-130 Hercules transport craft and, with other contractors, for an $8 billion contract for a tanker-cargo plane: Boeing's entry for the contest is a version of the 747 jumbo jet.

Business Week, in a 1977 study, noted: "The defense industry's return on sales, currently around 5 per cent before taxes, is admittedly low. But the figure is not a fair yardstick because much of the industry's plant and equipment is owned by the government and risk is often less than in commercial business." The industry had averaged 15.1 per cent profit on equity back in 1965, during the Vietnam "boom," and was expected to climb back to around 11 per cent, largely thanks to back orders from overseas.

R & D contracts usually involve less risk, but by and large it is clearly true that they do involve less profit. Rockwell, for instance, made only 4 per cent on B-1 development but had projected an 8 per cent profit on B-1 production. Challenging the industry's broad dissatisfaction, Northrop's maverick chairman Thomas V. Jones has called for defense contractors not only to work on fixed-price contracts but also to own all their own plant. He says jauntily: "If you manage well, you get rewarded."

But the industry was predicting more mergers, because of the huge capital investments now needed in the weapons industry. The McDonnell-Douglas venture with Northrop on the F-18 was seen as a bellwether. Hughes teamed up with thirteen other firms for the AH-64 attack helicopter program. The stress on customer co-production by NATO allies and by Japan and Israel means more international mergers. America once sold its NATO allies ten times more arms than it imported; but with co-production of some parts of systems, this ratio has fallen to 8:1 in recent years and is expected to fall further. The loss of overseas earnings will probably be compensated by an aggressive sales drive in the Third World; but this is not as easy a market as Europe and the Middle East: Orders are usually small, some purchaser countries have difficulty raising finance and both the White House and large segments of the Congress are in an anti-arms sales phase at present.

However, a look at the military-industrial-political complex still finds government and industry scratching each other's backs cozily. Members of Congress reacted angrily in 1976 when it was found that the Air Force and the Navy were allowing Raytheon to do paid evaluation studies on a new model of its own Sparrow air-to-air missile. It was found that Defense had not certified that the new missile was ready for production. Then Defense Secretary Donald Rumsfeld retroactively confirmed that the Sparrow was "combat-effective," in a letter to the relevant congressional committees; but the Pentagon later admitted that this evaluation was based on Raytheon's own study. Congressional investigators reported that the missile's radar had difficulty picking out low-flying planes and, when faced with two enemy fighters—most fighters fly in pairs—had difficulty distinguishing its target and would fly between them. (This was an early problem with Soviet surface-to-air missiles: Israeli pilots told the author in 1968 that when Egypt-based SAMs were launched at one of their Mirages or Skyhawks, a wing man would zoom in and fly parallel, forcing the other side's missile to fly between.) In the shemozzle over Raytheon that followed on Capitol Hill, payments on the $82.1 million evaluation contract were suspended—for a while.

III

Diplomacy

Diplomacy without armaments is like
music without instruments

FREDERICK THE GREAT

7

In the Name of the Free World

THE SOVIET UNION and the United States dominate the weapons-diplomacy world largely because they are the only countries that can produce economies of scale from supplies to their vast domestic markets. Although France, Britain, Germany and Israel all have arms-export industries in the billion-dollars-plus range annually, these industries were created initially more to ensure arms independence than for profit. Countries like Egypt, Israel and South Africa have established local arms industries which they could not afford without massive damage to their social economies because foreign suppliers were uncertain. Sweden and Switzerland need their own arms industries as an underpinning for their neutrality, but both countries export for economic reasons—notably, to reduce unit costs for their own armed services.

The sophistication of modern weaponry creates technical dependence on the supplier nation, just as its complexity creates continuing spare-parts dependence. In-country advisory teams from the supplier country, where they exist, inevitably exercise some control, however tacit, over weapons deployment and use. In some cases, this control is spelled out: For instance, the Honest John tactical nuclear missile was sold to NATO countries only on condition that its use be subject to U.S. decision. In addition, by bringing officers and technicians from client countries to the United States, the Soviet Union, or other supplier countries for training on the weapons systems sold to client-states, the supplier country creates a network of friendly officers in key nations. Most technical training is accompanied by orientation training—in other words, ideological indoctrination. For NATO and the Warsaw Treaty Organization—which has been more successful than NATO in this regard—superpower sales also help toward the goal of weapons standardization within an alliance.

Arms are also sold or given for base rights, or for staging or overflight privileges, thus creating two-way diplomatic power. Portugal took U.S. arms in return for the Azores base facilities, and then forced the United States to ease up in its criticism of Lisbon's colonial policies. In return for U.S. submarine and air bases, Spain wrung extensive military aid and credit facilities out of Washington, covering aircraft, armor, artillery and warships. Similarly, the British bought their base rights in Oman and on Masirah island with gifts of arms. The Russians purchased base rights at Kismayu and Berbera in Somalia with weapons, and naval facilities in India with bargain-price submarines and other naval vessels. There are, in short, many ways of interpreting Mao's expression that political power grows out of the barrel of a gun.

U.S. sales go not only to forward-defense-program countries such as those in NATO, and to base-rights countries, but also to remoter nations, to forestall Soviet sales and influence. The first sale of F-104s to Jordan in 1966 was a "pre-emptive" sale—Jordan had been offered MiGs. Iran got Phantoms for the first time after signing a military and economic aid agreement with Moscow. Already by 1970, 70 per cent of U.S. arms sales were estimated to be "government-generated." This was the case, of course, for 100 per cent of arms transfers by the Communist world, and for a major part of sales by France and Britain, following nationalization of arms industries in those countries. Some U. S. Government-generated covert sales go through private dealers.

In their study, Stanley and Pearton say arms sales are the "most significant diplomatic currency of all." They define four reasons for the pressure to sell arms: to bolster an ally; to cut procurement costs for domestic forces; to help in the balance of payments; and as diplomatic leverage. The first and the last, which are clearly linked, are obviously the most important; the second and third are useful arguments to cover the diplomatic imperative.

Lieutenant General Howard M. Fish, the former Air Force navigator and World War Two prisoner, who until 1978 headed arms exports at the Pentagon, has elaborated on these principles. He has written:

> Favorable aspects of our foreign military sales program include standardization of equipment, doctrine and training; development of close U.S. and foreign military relations and cooperation; assistance with the maintenance of U.S. base and overflight rights; maintenance of U.S. production and technological base; aiding the U.S. balance of payments; providing a broader U.S. logistics support base through cooperative logistics arrangements and the facilitation of combined operations or joint use of facilities when necessary.

> Perhaps most important of all is the fact that the military capability provided by security assistance can reduce the likelihood of U.S. military involvement, and provides the President and the Secretary of State with an effective tool for the conduct of U.S. foreign policy.

U.S. Policy

America, as noted in Chapter 2, only became the "arsenal of democracy" in the 1940s. Like nineteenth-century Prussia or twentieth-century Israel, America's love affair with machines of death is at least partly a reaction to earlier military impotence. The weeks following Pearl Harbor were the nadir of American strength. But in short order, America became not only the exemplar of military might but also the fount of weaponed assertiveness for a score of allies. The postwar commitment to opposing Communist imperialism inevitably led to equally unrepresentative and repressive regimes around the world wrapping themselves in the banner of anti-communism; in this guise, they expected—and usually received—American arms aid.

Saving the world from aggression was not initially America's responsibility: Article 43 of the UN Charter called for member states to commit their forces to that body when required, to solve international disputes; but the series of bilateral agreements which this called for were never negotiated, and the UN only solved one international conflict—in Korea —because the United States flew the UN flag.

Following World War Two, most American arms transfers were gifts— what the government calls "grant aid." These grew out of the Lend-Lease program initiated in 1941, and the special military aid programs for Greece and Turkey in 1947. Grant aid was finally formalized by the Mutual Defense Assistance Act of October 6, 1949, which inaugurated the Military Assistance Program (MAP).

From 1952 to 1956, U.S. military equipment was given away at a rate of $2.2 billion a year—taking inflation into account, almost as important as U.S. arms transfers in the seventies of about $10 billion a year, most of which are now sales. Huge World War Two and Korean War surpluses were disposed of around the world.

Congressional concern about an arms race led to grant aid being phased out in the sixties and replaced by an emphasis on sales; but between 1950 and 1965, the United States provided $32.4 billion to foreign countries as military gifts, including $26 billion for weapons systems. Of $8 billion in sales in that period, $7 billion went to the western hemisphere and Europe.

With the new emphasis on sales in the sixties, the Pentagon sales office was given the high-sounding name "International Logistics Negotiations" (ILN). Credit was arranged through the Military Export Committee of the Defense Industry Advisory Council. During the decade from 1952 through 1961, only $4.5 billion out of $22 billion of weapons transfers had been sales; but during the following decade, 1962 through 1971, sales easily reached the $15 billion target set by ILN director Henry Kuss; indeed, by 1970, the total had hit $17.5 billion, out of overall transfers of $24.5 billion. The graph is clear enough:

Fiscal years 1952 through 1956: aid, $11 billion; sales, $1 billion.
FY 1957–61: aid, $6.5 billion; sales, $3.5 billion.
FY 1962–66: aid, $4.5 billion; sales, $8.5 billion.
FY 1967–70 (four years): aid, $2.5 billion; sales, $9 billion.

As free aid was reduced, Export-Import Bank credits were made available for military purchases, starting in 1963. These were to be limited to large industrialized countries—euphemistic shorthand for "white" nations, since Japan's purchases were still restricted by Tokyo's unwillingness to invest in heavy arms spending.

However, there were still many ways in which countries that were neither large nor particularly industrialized could get all the weapons they wanted—or at least all that the Pentagon wanted to see them get, which was often much the same. The Department of Defense could control "Country X" ExIm loans—of which more later—to virtually any friendly state. Turkey, Greece, and Israel are still listed today as "underdeveloped" countries, and were certainly so listed then, but all received considerable arms. In the first two cases, this was to fulfill NATO requirements; arms for Israel were the result of a change in U.S. foreign policy following Israel's war with its neighbors in 1967. The arms race fueled technological growth; a new generation of weapons systems began to appear, and recipient countries had to be allowed to "trade in" last-generation, sophisticated weaponry to countries not formerly seen as needing it—in order that the sellers could afford to buy the new systems.

Another consideration for arms transfers was to steal a market—and a "friend"—from the other side. A famous example of how this works occurred in Cyprus in 1963, when Greek Cypriot extremists seeking union of the island with Greece staged the infamous "Christmas pogrom" on Turkish Cypriots, while the Makarios government carefully looked the other way. Persuaded with difficulty by its NATO allies not to intervene with land forces in Cyprus under the Treaty of Guarantee, Turkey exerted pressure on the Cypriot terrorists by some retaliatory air strikes against the strongholds of the extremists. Since Turkey was a NATO country, whereas the Makarios regime was "nonaligned," Moscow in 1964 took sides in the conflict by supplying Nicosia with tanks, patrol boats and antiaircraft artillery; it persuaded Egypt to send Cyprus surface-to-air missiles—ironically, since Turkey's is a "Muslim" air force.

Greece later supplied Makarios with NATO weaponry. This was against the terms of the U.S. Foreign Military Sales Act, but may well have been done with Pentagon knowledge and therefore connivance, to counterbalance Soviet weapons diplomacy. In 1974, when Cyprus flared up again, but with the fascistic colonels in power in Athens, Moscow supported Turkey. More recently, in a different game of musical chairs brought about by a Bolshevik-style revolution in Addis Ababa, Moscow threw its support to Ethiopia, a U.S. protégé, while Washington switched its support to Somalia, a Marxist country armed by Moscow.

Countries under arms embargoes for reasons of underdevelopment or politics have often found the leverage to overcome them, at least partially—weapons diplomacy in reverse. South Africa used the Simonstown agreement, giving Britain naval privileges in the Cape, to continue to receive some arms from the United Kingdom, even though internal repression was their only apparent purpose. When the Labour government finally severed Pretoria from the British trough, France, as noted earlier, stepped into the breach for a mixture of financial and political reasons.

France was similarly persuaded to breach the Western arms embargo in the Middle East by supplying most of the weapons enabling Israel to win the 1967 war. This drew the Soviet Union more deeply into the area as the protector of Egypt and Syria; this in turn persuaded Washington, under massive lobby pressure, to invest heavily in the sort of Israeli arms buildup which earlier American caution had sought to discourage.

Substantial arms supplies from abroad bring with them a useful course in technology, in the long run breeding self-sufficient domestic arms industries, thus weakening the leverage of supplier countries. South Africa and Israel are examples of high-defense-budget countries which now have impressive weapons industries of their own, culled from purchased or pirated technology. Many other countries are in the process of building up such industries.

Economic considerations played an important role in increasing U.S. arms sales to Germany, where the aim was to offset the costs of maintaining American troops in that country. In 1964, when Henry Kuss, the director of ILN, became Deputy Assistant Secretary of Defense responsible for military sales, Kuss's "white team" sought sales to Bonn of $755 million a year. They were completely successful, boosting sales to Germany by 600 per cent. German discontent at this drain on foreign exchange helped cause the fall of the Erhard government—and also helped to persuade Germany to breach "end-use" regulations, selling its "trade-in" weaponry wherever it could.

France and Britain, also seeking smaller "offset" payments from Germany by selling arms, complained of being "snowed" by Kuss's salesforce officers. (Twenty-one in all, they were grouped in teams called white, gray, blue and red, with different geographic responsibilities.) A 1967 Senate Foreign Relations Committee staff study on "Arms Sales and Foreign Policy" recorded discontent in NATO's ranks and referred to "resentful pygmies and an affable giant." But Kuss had told the Foreign Military Sales Pricing Conference the previous year: "The sales tool has become increasingly a major tool of government diplomacy in the area of international security."

Financing Arms Sales

Both the superpowers and other producer countries tailor weapons—and sometimes prices—to foreign needs. The Russians sell the MiG-21 well below cost. France's Mirage-III/5 is a Mirage-III simplified for export. America's export-only F-5 is a simplified F-4. Most successful aircraft types can be adapted to different roles—as interceptors, ground-attack aircraft, bombers, reconnaissance planes. This was notably true of the export-only Starfighter and is characteristic of many contemporary planes—Sweden's Viggen-37, the Mirage-III and the -III/5, the Anglo-French Jaguar and the new Anglo-Italo-German Tornado MRCA.

Major arms sales today usually comprise a whole weapons package. The purchasing country, often with some help from the prospective supplier country, outlines its objectives, and the supplier country then designs all the logistics. An allied country may then be asked not to bid on a particular weapon contract if it would cut across an extensive "package deal"—which may include everything from a new naval port to English-language classes. The United States has been the pioneer of this sort of polyvalent international deal.

The plasma of all this is money. Many Chinese loans are at 0 per cent. Russian rates vary, usually, between 2 and 2.5 per cent, with repayment over ten or twelve years. French rates are variable, with loans rarely extending beyond seven years. In the United States, ExImBank and Pentagon credits have never been for more than ten years; ExIm loans are in fact usually for five to seven years at the going rate of interest; the Pentagon sets its own rates and in the past has occasionally gone down to 0 per cent. Often, purchases of American weapons systems are made through a combination of ExIm, Pentagon and private-bank loans, at different rates. Because of the dangers of default through economic collapse or a change of regime in the client-state, the U. S. Government guarantees private loans.

The Pentagon's Military Assistance Credit Account was made a revolving account under the 1961 Foreign Assistance Act. It was a stunning system: Repayments went back into the ever-growing kitty. Under a 1964 amendment, the account could also be used to guarantee private credit finance by placing 25 per cent of the cash involved in escrow. This made the arrangement even better. In 1966, for instance, the Pentagon used $300 million from repayments over previous years to guarantee $1.2 billion in private bank loans to foreign arms customers.

In other words, the ILN could quadruple its budget by guaranteeing bank loans instead of making loans itself. To avoid congressional criticism of arms sales to Third World countries in greater need of schools and clinics, the ExImBank paid money into "Country-X Loan Accounts" on which the Pentagon could draw at its own discretion, with the ExImBank not knowing which countries actually received which parts of the funds. These ExIm loans, in turn, were guaranteed by the Military Assistance Credit Account. Country-X loans worth $684 million were made available by the ExImBank in fiscal 1966 and 1967 alone, with the beneficiaries including Argentina, Brazil, Chile, India, Iran, Israel, Jordan, Malaysia, Morocco, Peru, Saudi Arabia, Taiwan and Venezuela.

The fund was only discovered when Congress investigated Phantom sales to Iran in 1967. Already by 1964, *half* of the $8 billion which Third World countries were spending on arms was actually going on debt service, putting the instruments of death in the same category as the family home. It was largely this that brought demands for limitations on Pentagon credit. In 1967, Democratic senator Frank Church offered an amendment to that year's Foreign Assistance Act abolishing the Military Assistance Credit Account. Sixteen Democrat and six Republican senators met in Majority Leader Mike Mansfield's office to review the question. With them were Deputy Defense Secretary Paul Nitze, an unregenerate hawk, Under Secretary of State Nicholas deB. Katzenbach, AID administrator William S. Gaud and several arms lobbyists. The aim of the officials, the lobbyists and some of the senators was to restore funds cut by the Senate Foreign Relations Committee and reinstate the existing arms-credit authority. They might well have succeeded, had one senator not been too slick for his own good.

Henry Jackson of Washington, a cat's-paw for the Pentagon, suggested an amendment in terms which seemed to restore the status quo but which actually gave the Pentagon access to additional funds by allowing it to purchase promissory notes given to U.S. firms by foreign governments, and to discount them at the ExImBank. Kuss, who had drafted the amendment for Jackson, remembers his dismay when an indiscreet lobbyist actually referred to these additional funds. There was an uproar, he recalls, with senators using terms like "hoodwinked" and "duped."

Jackson lost seven of his senatorial supporters at the meeting, including six from his own party. On the floor, the amendment lost 50–43. Then, conservative Republican senator John Tower tried to restore the status quo, but even this was narrowly defeated, 46–45. The Church amendment passed.

Military Assistance Credit Account assets were transferred to the Treasury, which received all future repayments. After that, annual appropriations for arms aid were voted, but with no "revolving fund" aspect. Under the Foreign Military Sales Act of 1968, the ExImBank was precluded from lending to "underdeveloped" countries and could no longer rely on Pentagon credit guarantees. With "Country-X" accounts abolished, the Pentagon was allowed to continue to guarantee private-bank loans, but under congressionally imposed ceilings.

Bid to Control Weapons Diplomacy

The 1967 Senate staff study led to some cautious reforms. The Office of Munitions Control began to make more frequent reports on arms transfers to Congress. Congress began to receive a more accurate account of how ExIm funds were used. Implementation of the 1961 Foreign Assistance Act was tightened; there was an attempt to create regional zones within which only relatively minor weaponry would be sold—but this inevitably depended on the success or failure of U.S. efforts to persuade other arms-producing countries, including Communist countries, to go along. A "human rights" provision—502B—already existed in the 1961 statute, but this continued to count for little; so did measures calling for weapons to be loaned to countries in need, then returned, and for the United States to be reimbursed when grant-aid weaponry was sold by its recipient. Such clauses did little more than enable Congress to pretend that it was limiting the arms trade.

The 1961 Act has nevertheless been revised regularly, with the aim of plugging loopholes. Amendments introduced in 1968, 1972, 1973 and 1974 had various effects: One, for instance, stopped arms transfers to countries that seized American fishing ships for fishing inside contested limits, with the President preserving the power to waive such a provision if he "determined it to be important to the security of the United States" or if he received "reasonable assurances" that such seizures would not be repeated. No arms transfers were ever banned under this law.

Another reform, briefly referred to in Chapter 3, forbade credit sales of "sophisticated weapon systems, such as missile systems and [military] jet aircraft to any underdeveloped country except Greece, Turkey, Iran, Israel, Taiwan, the Philippines and [South] Korea" unless the President determined that such a credit sale was important to the national security of the United States. Credit could not exceed ten years after delivery. Interest was set at the "current average interest rate"—giving a distinct competitive advantage to other arms-producing countries, especially the Communist states; but once again this was unless the Chief Executive certified that a soft loan was in the "national interest." The Government was authorized to insure corporations against nonpayment of loans or on sales. The 1974 amendments set a credit maximum for 1975 of $872.5 million, of which $300 million was successfully earmarked by the Israeli lobby for their principal—with $100 million of that written off in advance as a nonrecuperable debt.

In addition to quarterly reports of sales, the executive branch also had to inform Congress of all sales of over $25 million with Congress getting twenty working days to ignore or reject. This measure has since been tightened to include all sales totaling more than $50 million in a fiscal year and in some cases all individual sales of more than $7 million. In 1977, there was an unsuccessful bid in Congress to increase its period of reflection to forty-five days. The President can only override a congressional rejection by certifying "that an emergency exists that requires such sale in the national security interest of the United States."

Another amendment required that "no battleship, aircraft carrier, cruiser, destroyer, or submarine of the Navy may be sold, transferred, or otherwise disposed of, unless the Chief of Naval Operations certifies that it is not essential to the defense of the United States . . . No naval vessel in excess of 2,000 tons or less than twenty years of age may be sold, leased, granted, loaned, bartered, transferred, or otherwise disposed of to another nation unless the disposition thereof has been approved by law enacted after such date of enactment."

Parallel with all this spate of congressional attempts to control, or appear to control, the spread of the implements of war was the congressional override—on November 7, 1973—of President Nixon's veto of the War Powers Resolution. This resolution said that unless there was a declaration of war (there has not been one by the United States since World War Two), the President could not introduce U.S. forces, or expand those already present, in a foreign area without giving an explanation of his acts to Congress within forty-eight hours.

In the arms buildup of the sixties, little if any thought was given to the huge supply of "trade-in" weaponry created by the advent of new weapons. It was seen as "war surplus"—toys for poor nations. Today, as the current new generation of state-of-the-art weaponry enters squadron, flotilla and battalion service, this problem is about to become more acute. But symbolic of how these matters were regarded in the sixties, when arms sales became a major priority in American diplomacy, was

the result of Iran's first purchase of Phantoms. Iran kept its small stock of
two-place F-5B trainers, but wanted to get rid of 120 F-5A fighters—
about 100 of which were airworthy. Eight had been direct purchases;
40 were grant-aid and were therefore still U.S.-owned. These 40 were
shipped to Vietnam in C-5s to satisfy a "head count" for Congress; not
all were flyable. The nearly 80 remaining, flyable F-5s were sold to
Jordan, Morocco and Ethiopia. The Moroccans were interested because
they faced an eighteen-month delay on their order of F-5E fighters and
F-5F trainers; when these arrived, the ex-Iranian F-5As entered the
"used-plane" market again. The Northrop F-5, designed solely for
export, relatively easy to fly and maintain, occurs frequently in this
sort of transaction: A high U. S. Government specialist described it airily
to the writer as "not too effective, not too destabilizing."

As noted in the previous chapter, the role of corporations like
Northrop in pushing this sort of hardware came under Senate scrutiny in
1975 and 1976, when the Church subcommittee was examining multina-
tionals. But the true-believer tone of the subcommittee's staff, especially
top investigator Jack Blum, irritated many senators; and when the subcommittee began to lock horns with the arms industry, it was annihilated, with low-key, patriarchal Hubert Humphrey absorbing arms-sales
investigations into the work of his foreign-assistance subcommittee. Blum
was not long on the unemployment rolls, however. He became, of all
things, an oil lobbyist.

Populist senator William Proxmire led a move in 1977 to disallow
defense-industry lobby expenses as a tax deduction. The Condor missile
scandal was partly responsible for this reaction to huge companies lobbying at the taxpayer's expense, especially as the lobbying budgets of these
firms came at least in part from Defense Department advances for
research and development of new weapons systems. Proxmire told his
colleagues: "There is enough favoritism and behind-the-scenes influence
on large defense contracts without the added insult of having the taxpayer pay the bill." The Defense Contract Audit Agency subsequently
recommended to new Defense Secretary Harold Brown that lobbying
efforts were of no benefit to Government and could well be "inimical to
Defense Department policies as well as program determination."

The Growth in Sales

On the international scene, a number of defense or defense-related
pacts have pushed in the opposite direction from controlling sales. In the
hemisphere, the Inter-American Treaty of Reciprocal Assistance was
signed in Rio in 1947 and ratified by the United States the following

year; the so-called Cuban Resolution (of Congress) of 1962 was followed by the Resolution on Communist Subversion in the western hemisphere in 1965.

America's main defense pact is the North Atlantic Treaty. This, as noted in Chapter 2, states that an "armed attack on one Member" is to be treated as an armed attack on them all. All the other defense agreements of the United States call on the parties to "act in accordance with their constitutional processes"—meaning, in America's case, that Congress should have the last word. In reality, the forty-eight hours of executive privilege in the War Powers Resolution could make it extremely difficult for Congress to withdraw from a war if American forces were already engaged. It would clearly be contradictory for the United States not to supply arms to countries to which America's own forces are or might well be committed.

The other defense treaties in question are: The Mutual Defense Treaty between the United States and the Philippines, 1951; the Security Treaty between Australia, New Zealand and the United States, 1951; the Mutual Defense Treaty with South Korea, 1953; the Southeast Asia Collective Defense Treaty, 1954 (this treaty, between Australia, France, New Zealand, the Philippines, Thailand, the United Kingdom and the United States, has a protocol saying that attacks on Cambodia, Laos and South Vietnam should be regarded as attacks on member states); the Mutual Defense Treaty between the United States and the Republic of China, 1954—which defines "China" as being Taiwan and the Pescadores Islands (this was unilaterally abrogated by the United States in 1979); and the Treaty of Mutual Cooperation and Security between the United States and Japan, 1960. The so-called Tonkin Gulf Resolution, expanding President Johnson's warmaking powers, was passed on August 10, 1964, but repealed on February 2, 1971, in the rising tide of resentment against Nixon's escalation of the Southeast Asian conflict.

The Philippines, Southeast Asia and Taiwan treaties were described as being of "indefinite" duration. All, however, could be terminated by any party giving one year's notice—as happened with Taiwan The South Korean and Japanese treaties include provisions for U.S. bases.

Writing in an in-house Pentagon periodical in 1973, then Deputy Defense Secretary William P. Clements, Jr.—whose duties included the arms-sales program—stressed the importance of arming friends in U.S. efforts to rescue détente. "I emphasize," he said, "the crucial importance to successful negotiations of being in a position to lead from strength. Our power to persuade at the conference table flows largely from the military balance created by the combined military might and solidarity of the Free World." Clements argued that year for Congress to eliminate, or at least raise to $150 million, the ceiling on arms sales to Latin

America, to extend credit terms from ten to twenty years, to abolish the requirement for foreign recipients to deposit 10 per cent of the cost of their orders, and to approve President Nixon's budget requests: $652 million of grant military aid, $525 million of foreign military sales credits, $33 million for training friendly forces in the United States, and the right to sell off $555 million of U.S. military surplus overseas.

Several hearings on arms-sales issues were conducted in 1975 by Senator Hubert Humphrey's foreign assistance subcommittee. While Rear Admiral Gene LaRocque, the director of the Center for Defense Studies, lobbied against arms sales, most witnesses lobbied for. Prominent among the hawks who testified were Dr. Kissinger, Lieutenant General Howard Fish—then the head of the Defense Security Assistance Agency—and ethnic foreign-interest groups. Israeli lobbyists Morris J. Amitay and Ken Wollach, along with their group's "research director" Aaron David Rosenbaum, testified for arms for Israel—and against arms for everyone else in the Middle East. Top Cypriot lobbyist Gene Rossides and William Chargotis, supreme president of the American Hellenic Educational and Progressive Association, called emotionally for more arms for Greece and none at all for Turkey. In such a climate, productive hearings were difficult: Serious study of the diplomatic and economic implications of the arms trade have been largely left to think tanks and to academe. One of the most articulate witnesses at the Humphrey hearings was Dr. Dale Tahtinen, who was later the deputy director of foreign and defense policy studies at the American Enterprise Institute.

Tahtinen played down the threats by potential purchaser-nations of sophisticated systems that they would "go elsewhere," if refused weapons. He said: "There are certain weapons systems [which have] no real equivalents in any other nation—the F-14 being the prime example." This was a dig at Iran's massive arms purchases in America. Tahtinen went on:

> Second, there is the question of the balance-of-payments justification [for arms sales]. We need to sell the weapons because, the argument runs, with the high price of oil, we have to do something about the tremendous imbalance of payments which has resulted. I would submit that there is a strong body of evidence to indicate that our sale of weapons is indeed connected to the price of oil. For example, let us go back to October 1973, when the "Arab oil embargo" was applied. It was not the Arab countries but rather the non-Arab countries, led by Iran, that were in the forefront of the price increases and fought the battle within OPEC—oil-producing exporting countries—after the embargo was lifted to keep those prices at a high level.

But arms-exporting countries are as much pushers as sellers. An aspect of the diplomatic game is to get the client hooked. The name of this aspect is "spare parts dependency." Holding back parts, or replacements for destroyed weaponry, is a part of the clout acquired by being a supplier. In the aftermath of the Arab-Israeli War of 1967, Moscow denied Egypt medium-range surface-to-surface missiles while France, as noted earlier, stopped delivery of fifty Mirage-III/5s which Israel had already paid for. (So that the customer would not look for another store, the money went into an interest-bearing escrow account.) Keeping new customers waiting is another ploy. Henry Kuss told the Senate hearings that year that Washington had been refusing more arms orders from developing countries than it had accepted; at that time, only 10 per cent of U.S. arms were being sold to developing countries.

Today, public opinion is clearly rising against arms sales—while favoring higher U.S. defense expenditures. Even Russian and Chinese arms sales to Marxist or pro-Marxist groups in Africa have been restricted by the attitude of the Organization of African Unity: There are OAU "systems ceilings" on arms for resistance movements in southern Africa, for instance, while arms for Marxist rebels against African governments are restricted even further—and Moscow often gives Western weapons to confuse its critics. But the pressure from the State Department—and, naturally, the arms industry—is for sales. In the United States, as grant aid was phased out, momentum has gathered behind sales, with co-production as the sweetener for major purchasing countries.

Co-production was, however, not introduced in the sixties. Canada began producing F-86Es under license from North American Aviation as far back as 1949. Fiat of Italy began assembling F-86Ks in 1953, as did Japan's Mitsubishi the following year. By 1959, the Raytheon Hawk missile was being produced in Belgium, France, West Germany, Italy and Holland. The General Electric J-79 turbojet engine for the Starfighter, the Bullpup air-to-surface missile and the Sidewinder air-to-air missile were co-produced in several countries. Thayer says that "co-production was the transition point between the United States Government's policy of giving away its military equipment and its policy of selling it." Defense Secretary McNamara also saw it as helping achieve standardization.

The Kuss Era

The key figure in this transition period was Kuss, a burly former naval commander from World War Two who had been a supply officer with

NATO in Paris and had later been involved with the problem of offsetting the costs of maintaining U.S. forces in Germany. During his tenure at the Pentagon, he was credited with selling $2 billion worth of American weaponry which otherwise would have been given away.

In fiscal 1953, liberal senator Eugene McCarthy of Minnesota noted bitterly that $500,000 of defense funds had been programmed for "sales promotion." Questioned on this, Kuss told Thayer: "We follow the principle that you should 'let your light so shine before men that they may see your good works.'"

The Military Export Guide then listed forty-one branches or subbranches of government with an interest in arms sales. The main ones were the White House, the NSC, the Secretary of State, the State Department's country desks, the State/Defense Senior Interdepartmental Group, the Defense/State Coordinating Committee (headed by Kuss and his State Department equivalent, Jeffrey Kitchen, and known as the "Kuss Kitchen Cabinet"). There was a fledgling ACDA, while Defense had its own arms-control office.

Then the Guide listed the Office of Munitions Control, the MAAGs (Military Advice and Assistance Groups) in the embassies, as well as the ambassadors themselves—fervent advocates of arms sales in order to please the local ruler and ensure access to him. Back in Washington were the three service Departments which, in their heyday in the mid-sixties, were sending 11,000 officer-salesmen overseas. Then there were the Unified Commands (which handled procurement for foreign governments), the Advanced Research Projects Agency of the Pentagon—giving technical assistance to underdeveloped countries on arms procurement—the Defense Industrial Security Clearance Office and, to help ILN sales, the Defense Contract Audit Agency. In addition to MAAGs were the military attachés of embassies, plus military missions and military staffs attached to NATO, SEATO, the Inter-American Defense Board, and similar treaty organizations.

The Treasury welcomed sales; the ExImBank encouraged them; commercial banks made money from financing them, while the Commerce Department encouraged arms manufacturers to participate in trade fairs. Even the United States Information Agency reaped "propaganda" benefits from America's modernization of each client-country's local forces.

Where arms go, some military presence is never far behind. Vietnam finally tipped the balance: By 1974, the United States had 523,000 troops in more than thirty foreign countries, compared to 320,000 Russian forces abroad—virtually all in countries close to Russia. Even MAAG groups were imprisoned in the implications of their size—at the time, for instance, there were 431 U.S. military advisers with the Korean forces, 253 in Thailand, more than a hundred each in Iran, Taiwan, Turkey, Saudi Arabia and Ethiopia, for a world total of 2,227.

Sales were and are encouraged by bringing foreign officers to the United States for training on the equipment which America hopes to sell. By the end of 1973, the United States had trained 428,000 foreign troops, here and abroad, notably at U.S. schools in Panama. The training included insurgency, counter-insurgency, jungle warfare, intelligence and interrogation techniques. Six months later, the figure totaled 512,000, including nearly 70,000 Cambodians, nearly 49,000 Laotians, a similar number of Koreans, over 25,000 Vietnamese (not including those trained under other Defense Department programs,) over 15,000 Filipinos, nearly 20,000 Turks and over 15,000 Greeks, between 5,000 and 10,000 each from Spain, Brazil, Peru, Chile, Columbia, Venezuela and Nicaragua, and about 3,000 each from Ethiopia, Portugal and Morocco. The predominance of frankly fascist governments, such as those of Spain and Portugal, or of similarly authoritarian regimes, is uncomfortably impressive. Many of the officers trained in these programs later seized power in their countries by coups d'état. In Vietnam, graduates operated the Phoenix program, which assassinated 26,369 civilians, and arrested and imprisoned 33,358 more.

Documents unearthed by Senator James Abourezk in 1973 showed that 163 policemen, mostly from Third World countries, had received (at the U. S. Border Patrol Academy at Los Fresnos, Texas, and at the International Police Academy in Washington, D.C.) training in homemade bomb design, booby traps and assassination weaponry, at a cost (borne by AID) of $1,750 per student. The largest numbers of students came from Colombia, Guatemala, Uruguay, Thailand, Saudi Arabia, Zambia, El Salvador and Brazil.

At Los Fresnos, the CIA supplied instructors, after Defense had nervously refused the task. The aim was officially counter-insurgency, but graduates went on to become members of vigilante assassination squads like La Mano Blanca and Ojo por Ojo in Guatemala, La Banda in Dominican Republic and the better-known "death squads" in Brazil and Uruguay. The Brazilian squads claimed at least 1,500, often-mutilated victims, operating with military, police and junta approval. After twenty persons were killed in revenge for the murder of a São Paulo police officer, a score of police officers were arrested and convicted of murder and terrorist activities.

Far greater numbers were trained in the U. S. Public Safety Program, established by President Kennedy for police trainees from "friendly" developing countries, and built on a smaller project originated by Eisenhower. In East Asia, 352 U.S. instructors trained 1,600 people at a cost of over $212 million, including 561 in Thailand and 439 in South Vietnam. In the Middle East and South Asia, 731 were trained, including 218 in Iran and 125 in Pakistan. In Africa, the figure was 983, including 139 in Zaire, 125 in Somalia, 118 in Tunisia, 116 in Ethiopia, 113 in Liberia. In Latin America, an impressive 4,170 operatives were given training, including 654 in Brazil, 583 in Venezuela, 446 in Colombia, 373 in Guatemala, 336 in Panama, 229 in Ecuador. The total was over 7,500 foreign officers. CIA agents or officers were infiltrated with the returnees. Local training programs went further: AID admitted to Abourezk that training had reached over 100,000 federal and state policemen in Brazil.

Why so much U.S. help for Brazil? To grasp the strategic significance of Brazil in the western hemisphere, it is not enough to take note of its massive size as a nation; turning a world map to the left, so that "West" is the bottom of the page, shows the importance of Brazil as a naval nation, especially now that the new 200-mile territorial sea is added to its coast-guard responsibilities.

Thanks to Senator Abourezk's discoveries, Congress phased out all programs except those at the International Police Academy in Washington; even these were reduced. But the United States still trains antidrug police in Mexico and elsewhere, and many local police units have been labeled as "anti-narcotics units" in order to qualify for direct assistance and for the highly lethal weaponry that goes with it. Commercial weapon sales to foreign police forces have increased as governmental transfers have been phased out, and were estimated in 1977 at over $200 million a year, with the main dealers being Polak, Winters & Company, Fargo International, and the Jonas Aircraft and Arms Company.

But the bulk of "weapons diplomacy" training programs were frankly military, rather than "police," in nature. Technical manuals were given away liberally. So was hospitality. Thayer reported that the Pentagon spent more than $750,000 on participation in the biennial Paris Air Show of 1967, while private U.S. firms spent another $2,250,000. The embassy in Paris played host to about six thousand aviation specialists from all over the world. Since then, every year, until the Carter administration, similar shows have suscitated similar efforts.

AID and the CIA helped arms sales, while NASA, the Federal Aviation Administration and the Atomic Energy Commission exported technology. The Small Business Administration still lends money to help small-arms manufacturers expand into the overseas market, sometimes with technical help from the Bureau of the Budget or the General Accounting Office. If the foreign country wants to barter its farm produce for weapons, the USDA will helpfully get in on the act, finding a U.S. market.

In the sixties, collusion between agencies tended to help sales, with Kuss orchestrating the whole scene from his podium at Defense. This remains largely true today. State is a poor brother to the Pentagon which—even in the sixties—had a budget about two hundred times the size of appropriations for foreign affairs. (Senator McCarthy noted that Defense ran its own network of children's schools, its own slick public relations and propaganda machine, its own diplomatic corps, and through the PX had the "world's largest retail distribution operation.")

Small wonder that, in all this, the Foreign Military Sales Act offered a wall of often only paper armor to combined assault. Similar arms were often sold to competing sides. In 1965, Pakistan's Patton tanks from the United States battled India's Sherman tanks, also American-made. In 1967, American tanks in the inventories of Israel and Jordan fought against each other in West Jordan. In Greece and all over Latin America, juntas seized power with U.S. weapons, often ousting pro-American regimes. Whatever the FMSA said, client countries agreeing to buy F-4s, F-104s, F-111s or F-5s were obliged to sell F-80s, F-84s for F-86s of Korean War vintage to foot the bill. To buy the Hercules missile meant selling Ajax. To buy the new main battle tank meant finding a purchaser for your aging M-47s and M-48s.

Following U.S. arms sales from year to year is often made intentionally difficult for the researcher. Defense data are often purposely obfuscating. Different aircraft may be listed separately one year, then clustered together the next—to conceal increased exports of a particular plane. For instance, F-5s may be listed apart, then listed along with T-38s as "jet trainers"—although the F-5 is bought by most countries as a combat plane. For grant aid, sometimes the quantity of weapons is given, sometimes the cost—which may or may not include spare parts or life-cycle costs. Much is listed as "general defense equipment."

The Seventies

By the mid-seventies, the policy conflict was the same, but the stakes had grown. In Stockholm, SIPRI reported in 1977 that "of all aspects of world armaments, the arms trade with the Third World is probably the most dangerous at the present time." Orders totaling $13.7 billion had been received from OPEC countries alone. However, "statements that the export of arms constituted a carefully controlled instrument of foreign policy fell on increasingly skeptical ears in many countries," the Institute noted hopefully.

By then, many Third World countries were demanding the latest technology across a wide spectrum of conventional arms and equipment, and suppliers were responding. Israel had taken the lead, forcing Egypt and Syria into competition; this had led to other countries in the region feeling obliged to follow suit. In the Far East, it was the same story with the two Koreas. Supplies included training, technical support, maintenance and repair facilities in purchasing countries, and construction projects. The foreign military sales program in Iran and Arabia included communications networks, command centers and naval facilities.

Orders, of course, are spread over a number of years: a "$5.4 billion order" may add only an average of $600 million to the total each year for nine years. But the annual totals were becoming huge: already by 1974, with U.S. sales at over $11 billion, Defense estimated export sales by France, Britain, Germany and Italy at a further $4.5 billion.

The "best" argument for American sales to NATO countries is standardization, and in 1975, when four European countries chose the F-16 over its main competitors—the French Mirage F-1E and the Swedish Viggen—McDonnell-Douglas had to agree to a $6,091,000 "basic" unit cost, even though two more years of development work remained to be done. Purchaser countries were to receive contracts to manufacture components equal to 40 per cent of the aircraft they bought for their own air forces, 10 per cent of the aircraft sold to the USAF and 15 per cent of the aircraft purchased by third countries. Observers calculated at the time that if Belgium in fact built its contractual share of the 1,700 F-16s then expected to reach the world market, it would earn the cost of its own 102 units of the plane, although some third-country buyers, such as Israel, which initially wanted 400 (but finally settled for 125), and Iran, which wanted 300, also wanted co-production—which Carter later forbade for Third World countries.

The F-16 deal was not atypical, except in size, and those purchaser countries which qualify are becoming more and more demanding about co-production contracts, with some using such deals as a base to create an arms—especially aircraft—industry not yet existent. As SIPRI notes: "Manufacturers have little choice but to comply."

Congressional moralists limited sales of "sophisticated" weapons to Latin America, but only for a while—just the time needed to secure a bonanza for France (mostly aircraft), Britain (surface ships and submarines) and Germany (subs). Then, the U.S. "embargo" was lifted. The Greek lobby-inspired U.S. embargo on arms for America's NATO ally, Turkey, not only opened up new markets for German tanks and French and British weapons but even for Soviet arms credit. France and Britain agreed to help Turkey build its own weapons industry; and while Turkey was short of F-4s, Italy profited by selling Ankara some of its redundant F-104 Starfighters. Libya sold F-5s. For such sales, only State Department (OMC) approval was necessary. To quote SIPRI: "The view that unilateral restraints on arms exports are politically useless and economically costly has gained increasing support in recent years."

In 1971, CBS shook up a great many Americans with a one-hour special entitled "The Selling of the Pentagon," a study in military PR. Two things especially shocked the CBS researchers—the extent and cost of the operation on the one hand, and the message on the other. Commentator Roger Mudd told Americans that the budget of the public-relations division of the Pentagon had gone from $3 million to $30 million in ten years, and that when costs of other divisions (used from time to time for promotion purposes) were added, the true figure might be $190 million. For comparison, the combined ABC, NBC and CBS budgets in 1971 were $146 million. CBS found that 1962-era films about monolithic communism, and attacking "peaceful coexistence" as Communist propaganda, were still being circulated in 1971 as representing U.S. policy.

Many famous names of journalism and the screen had done commentaries for Defense movies, starting in and just after World War Two with Edward R. Murrow, Lowell Thomas and John Daly, and continuing with James Cagney, Chet Huntley, Bob Stack, Jack Webb, Walter Cronkite and John Wayne. Some of these people were embarrassed to learn that their earlier gung-ho scripts were still hitting the Podunk circuit.

The CBS program followed Defense displays for the public, including a $2 million firepower spectacular, ending with a "mad minute" when everything is fired—followed by thoughtful shots of children playing with weapons and armor. It recounted the lecture tour of a team of colonels, using Defense transportation, to 163 cities that year, reaching audiences of 180,000 people, and the special tours arranged for American industrialists, bankers, teachers, publishers and others. With a $12 million budget for moviemaking alone, the Pentagon was reaching audiences of 52 million in a decade. By helping Hollywood with war movies, it was getting its message indirectly to even more. Each year, CBS found, 12,000 radio and television tapes are sent to nearly 3,000 hometown radio stations and over 500 TV stations, telling of the achievements of local sons and occasionally daughters.

If the public was principally concerned, as CBS was, with the promotion of arms sales within the United States, Congress concentrated its fire on the use of arms in diplomacy abroad. By 1976, as already noted, it finally got around to limiting direct commercial sales overseas when orders involved more than $25 million. Large sales would normally be "government to government." Exception was made for sales to NATO countries, and in 1977 Japan, Australia and New Zealand were added to the exemption list, while Israel was put in a special category. The congressional moves constituted the final reversal of the 1960s policy of encouraging foreign nations to purchase directly from corporations, not through the Department of Defense, once the Pentagon had decided that the purchaser-nation needed and could afford the weaponry, and that the sale was in the interest of the United States. ("Commercial" orders, however, have always involved going through diplomatic channels, and the letter of offer—Defense Department form 1513—stipulating the terms and conditions of sale is always issued by the appropriate bureau of the Pentagon.)

An exhaustive 1974 report to Congress by the Arms Control and Disarmament Agency on the "International Transfer of Conventional Arms" had produced interesting data about the growth of the global arms-export business in the sixties: The volume of the world arms trade had expanded from $2.4 billion in 1961 to $6.2 billion ten years later, with the United States then accounting for $3.4 billion and the Soviet Union for about $1.5 billion. Over the decade, America had exported $22.8 billion worth of weaponry, mostly to NATO (one third), Southeast Asia (one quarter) and the Middle East, with recipients in order of importance being Vietnam, West Germany, South Korea, Turkey, Taiwan and Britain. Russia also reserved a third of its exports for its European allies, with a quarter going to the Middle East, and with recipients in order of importance being Egypt, North Vietnam, East Germany, Poland and India. The fifty-four other arms exporters, after the superpowers, were headed (in order) by France, Britain, Poland, Czechoslovakia, China, East Germany and Canada.

Western Europe exported $5.6 billion worth of arms during the decade, with France and Britain accounting for just under a third each. France became the world's leading exporter of submarines. Arms imports by underdeveloped countries rose from $1.2 billion in 1961 to $4.5 billion a decade later.

By 1977, Congress was startled to learn that American overseas weapons sales for the year ending June 30, 1976, had amounted to a record $12.7 billion. For the fifteen-month period from July 1, 1976, to September 30, 1977—when fiscal 1978 began—Reuters Agency estimated U.S. arms exports at about $15 billion, up from well under $3 billion a year a decade before. Fiscal 1978 sales were projected by the Pentagon at $13.2 billion, and $13.5 billion for fiscal 1979.

According to U.S. intelligence calculations, Communist sales for the fifteen-year period 1961 through 1975 had totaled: Soviet Union, $26.5 billion; China, $2.3 billion; Czechoslovakia, $1.7 billion; Poland, $1.6 billion. Exports of arms from all other countries totaled about $5 billion.

Few other countries—and no other major countries—publish military statistics as freely as the United States. Up to 1976 (the Pentagon revealed in 1977) U.S. foreign military credit sales had totaled $10.6 billion, of which all except $2.45 billion for Israel had been or was being repaid. By the fall of 1977, the total was approximately $14 billion, with Israel's un-reimbursed part amounting to $3.5 billion. Apart from Israel, other major credit purchasers had included Taiwan, Korea and Greece, for about a half billion dollars each, and Turkey and Saudi Arabia for about a quarter billion dollars apiece. Cash sales for the quarter century to 1976 had totaled $57 billion. The best customer had been Iran ($12.8 billion), followed by Saudi Arabia ($12.1 billion), Germany and Israel ($5.9 billion each) and Britain ($2.2 billion). Most were government-to-government sales. The largest company sales during the sixties and early seventies were to Canada, Germany and Japan—about a half billion dollars each.

By the late seventies, pressure against the arms race had spread from Congress, the media and the public to the Executive Branch. In its 1976 report, the ACDA listed the "disadvantages and risks" of arms exports as follows:

> There is no guarantee that forces equipped by the United States will always be used in ways favorable to U.S. interests and objectives. Regimes friendly today may become hostile in the future.
>
> The supply of arms to Third World countries may increase the likelihood of conflict between neighboring countries and lead to confrontation between supplier states.
>
> Arms may be transferred from a friendly recipient to a country with policies inimical to U.S. interests, or may fall into the hands of terrorist groups. Third Country transfers of arms supplied are, however, subject to U. S. Government approval.
>
> Pressures from recipient countries for rapid deliveries could lower U.S. military preparedness if arms are supplied from current inventories, or if foreign recipients are given priority over U.S. forces for short-supply items.
>
> Some transfers could involve sensitive technologies which the recipient may exploit for industrial gain or which may fall into the hands of hostile states. This risk arises particularly when the recipient country obtains an indigenous repair and manufacturing capability as a part of the overall supply package.

The last two paragraphs clearly referred in particular to the massive arms transfers to Israel; but in 1977, at the request of the House International Relations Committee's subcommittee on international security and scientific affairs, the Congressional Research Service of the Library of Congress published a review sounding a similar warning about technology transfers and scientific cooperation between the United States and, of all countries, the Soviet Union itself. This point will be looked at later in this chapter.

Arguments over the merits and demerits of the various aspects of weapons diplomacy have been intense. Richard Burt, then assistant director of the International Institute of Strategic Studies, and now with the New York *Times,* said in 1976 that, except in the Middle East, insufficient attention had been given to its implications for conflict. Burt admitted that military supplies gave supplier states leverage in crisis and conflict management, but noted that these supplier states cannot choose their customers entirely freely: "Nations with greater resources and technical sophistication will be the first to acquire the new weapons. An obvious example is Iran, which has deployed new aircraft from the United States before their deployment in Europe." Burt went on:

> It has been argued that the United States has been able to guard against a pre-emptive South Korean invasion of the North by denying Seoul a large, modern tactical air force [and that the United States] can exert some pressure on Israeli policy by manipulating arms supplies. However, the reverse is also true: The increasing reliance of major powers on clients for the performance of vital functions (in Iran's case, policing oil transit routes in the Gulf and the Indian Ocean) may place a weapons supplier in a dependent position.

The Israeli and Iranian cases are related. In one of the Carter-Ford television debates of 1976, the Democratic candidate blasted Ford for injuring Israel by arms sales to Arab countries, and mentioned specifically sales to Iran, possibly believing then that Iran was an Arab country. In defending his policy, Ford omitted to point out that Israel, almost entirely dependent on Iran for its most crucial import, oil, did not object to the Shah's military buildup.

President Carter defended his decision to sell more warplanes to Egypt, Saudi Arabia and Israel in 1978 by citing commitments by previous administrations (against which he had railed in his presidential campaign). In contrast, at the same time, the United States and the Soviet Union issued a joint statement saying the two countries would confer regularly on steps to cut arms sales to developing countries.

Burt in his 1976 report talked of the emergence of a "buyers' market" for advanced armament, the result of a growing number of alternative suppliers and the emergence of "newly affluent recipients." He noted that

Saudi Arabia could buy advanced systems for front-line Arab states, while Pakistan could service and fly sophisticated aircraft in the Gulf—"perhaps in return for some claim on these systems in the event of war in the subcontinent."

In an IISS study on "New Weapons Technologies," Burt said that the "capacity of a small state with a relatively sophisticated force of missile-equipped ships or submarines to disrupt traffic in such congested areas as the Mediterranean, the North Sea or the Sea of Japan would be considerable." He said this concern had persuaded Britain, in May 1975, not to sell six submarines to Libya. But the limits of arms refusal are also finite: A month after the decision to which Burt refers, President Park Chung-Hee of Korea said that if the U.S. nuclear umbrella were to be removed from his country, "we would have to start developing our nuclear capability to save ourselves."

Sounding another note of warning, Professor Donald A. Sylvan of Ohio State University wrote in the *Journal of Conflict Resolution* in 1976 that

> sharp increases in military assistance . . . heighten the likelihood of the recipient country being involved in increased international conflict relative to cooperation . . . Abruptly increased military capabilities . . . seem to overshadow any mitigating factors in creating this more conflictual and less cooperative behavior. This conversion from capability to behavior is reflected most dramatically beginning two years after a sharp increase in military assistance.

Sylvan clearly had Israel most in mind. Back in 1974, Defense Secretary James R. Schlesinger agreed that "the vast bulk of our military assistance and foreign sales programs recommended for fiscal 1975 [is] aimed at two of the more unstable parts of the world—the Middle East and Asia. More than 80 per cent of our proposed grant and sales programs [is] directed to the countries of these two areas." But he noted that one objective in providing military assistance was "continuing an uninterrupted access to bases and facilities important to the worldwide U.S. military posture." The Turkish arms embargo a few months later, leading to the closure of over a score of U.S. facilities and bases in Turkey, emphasized his point. In a 1979 report, Max Holland of the Center for International Policy said U.S. arms exports to the Third World would have increased 85 per cent during Carter's first term.

The Carter Era

When President Carter arrived in the White House, he found a great deal already in the pipeline. A month after taking office, he confirmed $2 billion of new exports already approved by President Ford, subtracting very few items—the most important being concussion bombs ordered by Israel. About half of the $2 billion list was for NATO, therefore noncontroversial. (Indeed, Carter was soon to be urging the NATO allies to increase their defense budgets.) About half a billion dollars was for Saudi Arabia, but for noncontroversial items, notably a military hospital and barracks. Most of the rest was for construction items and other "nonlethal" material. Another $3 billion of orders remained stuck in the pipeline, but most of these were subsequently released—one of the rare vetoes being on Pakistan's order for 110 A-7 attack aircraft. In all, Carter had found $32 billion of congressionally approved orders stacked up, some of which would not be completely fulfilled until 1983.

In 1977, Congress finally approved credit sales for fiscal 1978 of $2.1 billion, almost as much as the Administration asked for, including $1 billion for Israel, $275 million for Korea, $175 million for Turkey, $140 million for Greece, $120 million for Spain and $75 million for Jordan. Controversial credit sales that were approved included $45 million for Morocco, then engaged in annexing former Spanish Sahara by military force and against the wishes of its inhabitants (these sales were later suspended by the White House), and $30 million for the exuberantly corrupt Mobutu regime in Zaire.

A distinction needs to be drawn between credit sales and security support assistance. The Office of Management and Budget informed the House International Relations Committee in late 1977 that credit military sales to Israel for the period 1974–78 totaled $4.3 billion, with $265.5 million for Jordan and none for Egypt and Syria. But the Middle East was receiving 78.6 per cent of security support assistance—$2.7 billion to Israel, $2.5 billion to Egypt, $426 million for Jordan and $265 million for Syria. For 1978, Congress authorized $3.2 billion of security assistance, of which $1.3 billion was for Israel, $750 million for Egypt, and just under $100 million each for Jordan, Syria and the confrontation states in southern Africa. For contrast, Congress did not approve much more—only $3.8 billion—for *economic* aid.

The $100 million (later reduced to $80 million in conference) of security assistance for black southern Africa was slipped in by House liberals. Malawi and Zaire were specifically excluded. By an amendment offered by right-wing Democrat Richard H. Ichord, a supporter of the white settlers, the President was called upon to justify whatever portion of the funds went to Mozambique, Angola, Zambia and Tanzania; only Botswana was to receive funds freely. Another amendment forbade the conversion of American assistance funds in Zaire to anything remotely military, unless the President sent a justification to Congress explaining how this would be "in the national interest of the United States." For human-rights reasons, military aid was forbidden by Congress to Argentina, Brazil, El Salvador, Guatemala, Cuba, Vietnam, Laos, Cambodia, Uganda and Ethiopia.

Grant military aid, which had totaled $6.6 billion in 1952, during the Korean War (the equivalent, with inflation, of about $20 billion today), was "officially" down for fiscal 1978 to $284 million, including $55 million for Jordan, $48 million for Turkey, $33 million for Greece and $25 million for Portugal—in each case, almost as much as the White House asked. But Congress managed to contradict itself without losing face by saying that half the billion-dollar "credit" for Israel could be written off as a bad debt from the start—thus tripling the official grant-aid budget.

However, even with the semantical Israeli clause, grant aid was down steeply. Over the previous quarter century, a survey showed that Korea had received $4.9 billion in military gifts, Vietnam $4.8 billion, France $4 billion. Other substantial recipients had been: Turkey, $3.1 billion; Taiwan, $2.5 billion; and Italy, $2.2 billion. Except for Israel, this era seemed over—but not quite: Gifts of U.S. surplus in recipient countries from which U.S. troops had pulled out over the period had amounted to $6.6 billion, including nearly a billion dollars' worth apiece to Taiwan, Korea and Turkey, over a billion dollars' worth to Vietnam, and a half billion dollars' worth to Greece. This particular "grant aid" policy seemed likely to continue, despite congressional efforts.

Congress in 1977 put a ceiling of $225 million on the amount of American defense stocks which could be held in Korea. This followed the news that Washington was giving over $42 million of ammunition to Thailand. But when Carter decided on the withdrawal of U.S. forces from Korea that year, the U.S. arsenal to be handed over somehow totaled $800 million officially, and over $1 billion by unofficial estimates—not including USAF weapons and equipment which would remain in Korea in American hands. Congress upped the "ceiling" accordingly.

The following year, Congress approved U.S. military economic support for fiscal 1979 at $785 million for Israel and $750 million for Egypt (two thirds of each sum to be gifts), along with $93 million for Jordan, $90 million for Syria, $50 million for Turkey, $60 million for southern Africa and $15 million for Cyprus. An amendment to the defense authorization bill prohibited sales to non-NATO countries of U.S. equipment stored in Europe—a measure largely aimed at Israel—while another strengthened human-rights provisions. But a Senate provision listing ten principles to be observed in arms sales to Third World countries was dropped in conference, as was an amendment which would have extended the congressional period of evaluation of arms sales from thirty days to sixty if two thirds of the members of both Houses requested it.

As noted earlier, only about half of U.S. military aid is composed of weapons, ammunition and spare parts. For fiscal 1975, for instance, Pentagon figures showed that 8 per cent of the military assistance program went on support equipment (such as tankers, trucks and communications gear) while about 36 per cent went on supply services, such as construction, training and administration. In the Southeast Asia program, 18 per cent went to support equipment, over 29 per cent to supply services. In the Middle East, especially Saudi Arabia, non-weapons costs are the predominant feature of all military sales, except those to Israel. Training, hitherto the prerogative of MAAGs, is now mostly contracted out to private U.S. concerns, competing with each other in bidding—and staffed mostly by ex-officers and ex-NCOs, many of them ex-MAAG. The Ninety-fourth Congress, as mentioned, had ordered the phase-out of MAAGs in 1976, but in 1977 Congress continued them on a year-at-a-time basis in Greece, Portugal, Spain, Turkey, Jordan, Indonesia, the Philippines, Thailand, South Korea and Panama. The total MAAG force was not to exceed four hundred people, and there were to be no more than six military attachés per embassy.

What have been the hot items most in demand from American plants? A Pentagon study released at the end of 1976 showed sales, since 1950, of 728 A-4 attack planes and 908 F-4 Phantoms; another 18 had been given away. A total of 647 F-5s had been sold, another 926 donated. Already, 348 F-16s were on order. These figures hardly compared with the give-away of 2,804 F-86 Saberjets in cold-war days, along with sales of a further 375; 394 F-104s had also become gifts for friends and allies, while another 1,500 had been sold—over 1,100 to Germany and Japan alone. The huge and monumentally expensive C-130 Hercules transport plane had been given away 52 times and another 211 had been paid for. The smaller C-119 had been grant-aided in 339 copies, while 137 had been sold. Earlier, countries had received, as aid, 702 C-47s—the workhorses of World War Two and the Berlin Airlift—and had bought a further 119. Impressive figures for U.S. trainer aircraft included the gift of 1,099 T-6s and the sale of 691, the grant of 1,323 T-33 jet trainers and the sale of 334. Thanks mainly to the Vietnam War, 1,628 UH-1 helicopters had been given away; another 383 had been sold.

On the Navy side, America had sold 108 destroyers and given away 41, sold 183 landing craft and given away 1,827, and had sold 53 submarines and distributed 24—to cite only three items in a thirty-item Navy Department list. Other popular crutches of weapons diplomacy included tanks (6,351 sold, 24,428 given), armored personnel carriers (17,254 sold, 7,587 given), and howitzers (1,052 sold, 11,332 given). The most popular American missiles included the TOW antitank projectile (38,385 sold, 5,620 given), the Sidewinder (14,223 sold, 14,008 donated), the Dragon (4,982 sold, 1,440 given), along with roughly 5,000 each of Hawks, Mavericks, Rockeyes and Redeyes.

THE MIDDLE EAST

In recent years, the principal single market for American weapons has been the Middle East. In the mid-sixties, the aim of arms supplies to the area was balance. The United States, Britain and France would determine each country's needs. Britain and France would be the main suppliers, with the United States helping out on finance. The area was seen as a Franco-British sphere of influence. After the 1967 war, "balance" became a race, with Iran getting much greater supplies than before, partly as a friendly, non-Arab, Muslim counterbalance to the growing force of Israel, Syria and Iraq.

If disarmament ever became a tangible issue, the superpowers might well direct their first efforts to this volatile area. Just as U.S. economic aid to Vietnam may one day take the form of buying back some of the huge U.S. arms surplus left in that country, so economic aid to bankrupt nations like Egypt and Israel might take the form of buying their huge offensive capabilities, either as weapons or rare-metal scrap. But this is a vision for the future, and not the immediate future at that.

Meanwhile, the wheel has merely gone full circle; France, Britain and Germany were quietly called on to fulfill America's moral commitment to supply arms to Egypt, a commitment created by President Sadat's expulsion of Russian military advisers in 1972 and by the lead he took in Mideast peace efforts in 1977. The European allies can either sell their own production, which they are only too happy to do, or pass on American-made "trade-in" weapons: This would require approval from the Office of Munitions Control, but Congress would not catch up with the deal for three months, by which time it would probably be too late to block it. With the signing of the peace treaty, the United States will now be selling arms to Egypt also, but Western Europe is likely to remain the major source.

The interlocking of economics and diplomacy in the arms trade makes for a self-perpetuating situation. For instance, in the seventies, the oil-producing countries faced a situation familiar to most Third World states: The raw materials they exported earned no more than they had done two decades before, while the finished goods they imported from the West and Japan had soared in cost.

To correct this imbalance completely would have required going back over the books for twenty years, deciding what fair prices for oil would have been in, say, 1959 or 1966, and setting a new price that would enable the Western World's total exploitation of these developing countries to be reimbursed over a given period. This was, roughly, the program which the more militant leaders of the Organization of Petroleum Exporting Countries (OPEC), Iran, Venezuela and Nigeria, wanted to undertake. But the more moderate producers—those in the Arab countries —sought only a limited price increase, and they forced a less radical compromise. This was merely to index—more or less—the current oil price to the then increase in prices on refrigerators, cars, heavy machinery, etc., which they bought from the industrial nations. This jump in oil prices was hard enough to absorb as it was, but it was met by industrial-nation resolutions to make energy economies. These were welcomed by the then four leading sources of foreign oil in the United States—Canada, Nigeria, Venezuela and Iran—because all these countries knew that their oil deposits were finite and that, except in Canada, it would take decades to create a sufficient industrial or other base with which to replace entirely the oil bonanza.

These sentiments were shared by the Arab countries in OPEC also, because their often desertic, underdeveloped conditions made the absorption of huge sums of capital difficult, and the necessity to extract oil more slowly even more significant than elsewhere.

In 1970, as today, the largest Arab source of oil for the United States was Saudi Arabia, which then fulfilled 0.9 per cent of U.S. oil needs. The assumption then was that oil economies would reduce the Saudi ratio to, say, .75 per cent, but that Saudi revenues would of course increase because of the new pricing. Instead, U.S. purchases increased, and with them pressure on Saudi Arabia to raise its rate of extraction. In 1977 and 1978, Arabia supplied about 4.6 per cent of U.S. oil needs, and found itself flooded with "petrodollars" which had not been planned for, and not all of which could be used up by providing free schooling and medical care in a country of less than 7 million people.

Each oil-purchasing country sought a "recycling" of petrodollars—in effect, a balance of trade, whereby the billions spent by, say, Italy to buy oil would be sent back to Italy to buy cars, shoes or government bonds. Some of this money was duly invested in the customer on a long-term basis. Most Arab investment in the United States, for instance, is in the money market itself, or in minuscule holdings in large firms. In Britain, friendly sheikhs indulged in a splurge of real-estate buying, much of it for huge white-elephant mansions which only the very wealthy could keep up. But the United States, noting that wealthy nations—including newly wealthy nations—need more defense against predators than poor ones, encouraged arms sales as a way of recovering mountains of petro-dollars, as well as of buying alliances.

The main problem was not simply that, by using Arabian or Iranian or Kuwaiti money to provide American jobs, these countries were failing to invest enough in their own economies, because to some degree this was an inevitable consequence of global economics; the main problem was that the whole "Mideast" area was ripe for the sort of wars that would be much more devastating if no longer fought with bolt-action rifles.

Oil-rich, socialist, pro-Moscow Iraq has border claims on Iran and Ku-wait—which it briefly invaded in 1973—and also faces Kurdish secession (encouraged, for several years, by Iran and the West). There is a dis-pute with Syria over the uses of the Euphrates River.

Equally oil-rich Iran is a non-Arabic-speaking nation in an Arab sea, and with a thousand-mile border with Russia to boot. With 35 million people, it has the money and numbers to achieve one day, should it so desire, the former Shah's ambition of being the dominant military power in the area. It has seized islands from the Trucial States, sent troops, arms and other help to Oman and the United Arab Emirates to put down Moscow-supported revolts, and to the Kurds to oppose Iraq. It has sup-ported Kuwait against Iraq, and promised—unsuccessfully—$2 billion of aid to Afghanistan to keep out Soviet influence there. In the days of the Shah, it frequently played both sides, superpower-fashion: It supported Muslim Pakistan against India, while being a major supplier of oil to India; it supported Egypt and the Palestinians against Israel po-litically, and provided economic aid to Egypt, while being Israel's second most important prop after the United States as the source, at one point, of over 80 per cent of Israel's oil. It exported Iranian technicians to small kingdoms, thus providing a future pretext for intervention to protect them. It bought F-14s with Phoenix missiles to shoot down Soviet MiG-25s, a David-like glove of challenge to the Soviet Goliath which even Is-rael has feared to throw down. Iran, since its partly religious, partly left-wing revolution, will clearly now seek a lower profile, but for how long?

Oil-rich Saudi Arabia has been, with Egypt and, until 1979, Iran, one of the three linchpins of America's long-term Mideast policy. Saudi Arabia has been the most easily manageable of the three, but it has sub-stantial reasons for opposing Israel, notably Israeli seizure of Muslim Holy Places in Jerusalem in 1967 and of Saudi islands in the Gulf of Aqaba that year, and has strongly opposed the Egypt/Israel peace treaty. Arabia opposes its Marxist neighbors, Iraq and South Yemen, and supports Oman against Marxist guerrillas aided by those countries; Oman has faced a Communist rebellion in Dhofar province for eleven years, and despite hopes of a merger between the two Yemens in 1979, South Yemen is expected to remain a thorn in Arabia's side.

Tiny, oil-rich Kuwait is not recognized by Iraq, which seeks two Kuwaiti islands which stand off Iraq's Umm Qasr port. The seven conservative, oil-rich states which compose the United Arab Emirates have territorial disputes with their neighbors, Iran and Saudi Arabia. Poor, junta-governed, left-leaning Afghanistan has sought help from everywhere, but principally—at least, until now—from Moscow; strategically placed, it is an obvious battlefield for local and superpower ambitions. Pakistan, a military dictatorship, still seethes from its 1971 defeat by India over Bangladesh, and has a long-standing dispute with India over Kashmir.

Throughout the area, oil wealth itself could be a source of conflict, especially when wells are drilled in contested territories. This is already evident in the Persian Gulf (which Arabian peninsula countries call the Arabian Gulf) where there is friction between Persians and Arabs, and in the Gulf of Suez, where the Israelis have been wildcatting. Except for pro-Western Egypt and Lebanon, pro-Moscow Iraq and South Yemen and fence-straddling Syria, all the regimes in the area are monarchies, therefore subject—as Iran has shown—to violent overthrow one day. These revolutions will cause neighbors to take sides. Many borders are untraced in the desert, and nomads move across them at will, creating the sort of "new facts" out of which violent disputes may arise.

Saudi Arabia, which is slowly overcoming its military weakness, has conducted joint air exercises with Syria. If Israel provokes war by making West Bank Jewish settlements "permanent," Saudi Arabia might conceivably join in, if only indirectly. Lobby-generated opposition, in the U. S. Congress, to Arab economic warfare against Israel—the "Arab boycott"—may also help persuade Israel's neighbors to undertake less gentle methods of dealing with the "foreign body" in their midst. In such a war, arms transfers—whether "legal" or not—would be likely, for instance, to ensure the protection of Jordan and even Egypt. The sort of long-range weaponry acquired by Iran would permit Iranian intervention farther afield—for instance, to protect Pakistan—when its military recovers from the recent turmoil. Given the degree of sophistication in arms acquired by such countries as Iran, Saudi Arabia and Kuwait, and Israel's possession of nuclear warheads, a nuclear capability for at least a few other Mideast states seems likely in the near future. The doomsday scenarios are not lacking.

If you turn the map upside down, as a pilot does when flying on a

southerly course, and you place yourself in Moscow, the Middle East—
from the Dardanelles to the Khyber Pass—presents a daunting threat
and an obstacle to movement. Moscow would be oddly lacking in fore-
sight if it did not seek allies in the area and use arms transfers both to
"buy" them and to make them useful.

Flick the map over again and look at it from the familiar viewpoint of
the United States and you can see the Hormuz Straits, at the foot of the
Gulf, as an obviously vulnerable "choke point" for America's, Western
Europe's and Japan's huge oil demands. Economic, diplomatic and military considerations are such that it would be incomprehensible if Washington did not also seek to "buy," and arm, friends in the area. Iran received some aircraft, including advanced attack helicopters (AAHs),
before these even entered wing service in the United States. Thus, as a
survey by the United Nations Association of Iowa has pointed out, an
added rationale for U.S. arms sales has been created—foreign financing
for American weapons *development,* and even using the area as a test-
bed for new U.S. weapons not battle-tested in Vietnam. The commitment
of American technical personnel to major arms buyers represents a tacit
commitment of sorts to help these customers wage war if and when they
decide or are forced to do so.

Not all the Middle East's reasons for buying arms are unreasonable.
Egypt, as well as needing defense against Israel, has seen arms as a
measure of national independence and as part of its bid to lead the Arab
world. Starving the armed forces of new weapons systems would breed
coup d'états. Syria arms not only to recover the Golan Heights but
against internal instability; in three decades, Syria has undergone eight
successful coups and several attempts. Jordan is under pressure to oppose Israel, and now has territory to recover, but also arms itself to protect the monarchy (the armed forces are predominantly Bedouin)
against Palestinian republicanism. Lebanon, neutral by desire, has been
forced to arm because of Palestinian guerrilla power within the country
and Israeli air and land raids from without. Israel has armed not only to
seize territories identified with ancient Israel, but also to discourage attack.

Nor are the aims of the suppliers monolithic. The United States and
the Soviet Union seek "balance" and counterbalance; both Communist
and non-Communist suppliers seek leverage, while all Western suppliers
seek economic gain. Soviet aims were initially to weaken French and
British neocolonial influence; however, the more Moscow succeeded, the
more it attracted a formidable rival influence into the region, that of

Washington—just as, the more Washington backed Israel, the more Moscow was drawn into support of the Muslim states.

Initially, the area was more coveted by Britain and France than by the United States or even Russia, and direct warfare was not ruled out. Shortly before the Suez operation of October 1956, France supplied Israel with 100 AMX-13 tanks, 100 Super Shermans, Nord SS-10 antitank missiles, 30 Ouragan jet fighter-bombers and a squadron of Mystère-IVA jet interceptors.

Egypt had 40 Il-28 jet bombers, but not enough pilots were trained to fly them so 30 of the bombers were evacuated to Saudi Arabia when Israel invaded. The remaining 10 were destroyed on the ground. Egypt's 150 MiG-15s had no ejector seats, making pilots cautious; in any event, about 100 of these were also destroyed on the ground.

Britain followed France, with British Prime Minister Anthony Eden motivated by hatred of President Nasser, whom he had not forgiven for the 1952 revolution and the more recent nationalization of the Suez Canal. At the UN, the United States and Canada forced the three invaders to withdraw.

It seems fair to say, however, that the chicken that came before the egg in the Mideast arms race as we know it today was Russian, even if today Moscow is exercising more caution than Washington. Within six months of the end of the 1956 war, Moscow had replaced the 100 lost MiG-15s with MiG-17s with ejector seats. In the sixties, the United States made efforts to slow down the race by delaying negotiations and deliveries. In September 1962, for instance, it agreed to sell Hawk missiles to Israel but postponed signature of the contract until May 1963. First deliveries were to begin in 1965. After protracted negotiations, America agreed in February 1966 to sell A-4s to Israel. Deliveries were to start in December 1967 but because of the Six-Day War did not arrive until the following February. Moscow, at the time, was more openhanded with weaponry, accepting soft-currency payments and offering soft loans.

Deprived until recently of serious Mediterranean access, Russia could only watch while America displayed gunboat diplomacy in Jordan and Syria in 1957 and sent the Marines ashore in Lebanon the following year. When Vietnam distracted American attention and made involvements elsewhere unlikely to win congressional approval, Moscow became more ambitious. However, when Israel invaded Egypt in 1967, starting the Six-Day War, the White House was relieved by a hot-line communication from the Kremlin proposing that both superpowers keep their naval vessels at an agreed distance from the scenes of conflict—a proposal which the White House accepted. Russia then delayed aid to the Arab countries. The White House, as we have seen, responded in 1973 with its own hot-line communication to avert a possible nuclear war, to be initiated by Israel.

For other countries, the market was just too good for any embargo to resist. France sold Mystères to Israel to counterbalance the MiG-15s and -17s, then Super-Mystères to match MiG-19s. In the supersonic early sixties, Mirage-IIICs matched MiG-21s, while Tu-16 medium bombers, with a 3,000-mile range and a bombload of nearly 20,000 pounds, were neutralized in Israel by Mirage interceptors and by Hawk missile batteries from the United States. By 1967, Iraq, Syria and Algeria also had -21s; only Jordan, dependent on Britain, was left weak. In actual planes, the Arab countries had a four to one advantage; but Israel needed less aircraft because of its limited airspace, and its pilots were better. The 1967 Israeli victory, however, was due as much to surprise as to skill.

On the ground, the embargo was similarly breached by a standoff between Centurion and M-48 Patton tanks in Israel (and Jordan) and the equally fast Russian T-54s in Iraq, Syria and Egypt.

But after Algerian independence in 1962, France had moved slowly toward what became a 180-degree switch in Near East alliances; Israel's aggression against Egypt in 1967 provided Paris with the excuse it sought. Moscow had continued its arms buildup steadily since 1956, but purchasing patterns changed generally after 1967, with the Israelis still planning for a blitzkrieg on their neighbors, while the neighbors were thinking more in terms of a protracted "war of attrition." MiG-23s and Su-7 fighter-bombers were added to the MiG-21s in the Arab air forces. The remaining T-34 tanks were replaced by T-54s and the newer -55s. To match the Hawk batteries, Egypt in 1970 began receiving SAM-3s.

Now America was breaching the embargo openly, providing Israel with A-4s and the first fifty F-4s, which gradually replaced the Mirages for which France was now refusing parts. Jordan acquired improved Centurions from Britain and F-104s from the United States. France sold one hundred Mirages to Libya. By then, Israel was developing its own armor, light warship and aircraft industries, building the Arava STOL transport, assembling the Magister trainer under French license, and designing the Kfir from the Mirage. The nuclear breakthrough was still a secret, but by 1975 Jerusalem could claim to be "70 per cent self-sufficient" in weaponry.

The 1973 war was a reminder that Israel would probably have been defeated in 1956 had it not been for the intervention of France and Britain. But clearly, American arms leverage is not absolute, both because of the power of the Israeli lobby in Washington and the ingenuity of Israel's arms industry. Similarly, Moscow has found its own local satellites almost equally hard to discipline.

Short of a general peace in the region—presumably implying the implementation of UN Resolution 242 and Arab recognition of Israel—it is hard to see how the arms race in the Middle East can be stopped; at best, the rising graph might be attenuated. Two major problems are the current imbalance of weapons—Israel still is more powerful than its neighbors, especially now that it has a peace pact with Egypt—and the willingness of Western Europe to sell arms to almost anyone. Israel has assumed that being the first Mideast territory to go nuclear, it has a unique saber to rattle—for instance, to try to hold on to occupied lands. But its first rattle led to the nuclear arming—under Russian control—of Egypt, and in the long run it is hard to see how Israel's secret atomic "city" of Dimona can fail to create wider nuclearization. A balance of rattling sabers.

The only momentarily effective attempt at arms restraint in the area had been the Tripartite (U.S.-U.K.-French) Declaration of 1951, abandoned when Nasser bought Soviet arms through Czechoslovakia in 1955. The French embargo on Israel as the 1967 aggressor merely stimulated the U.S. involvement. Moscow's proposal for demilitarizing the area in 1956 was linked to the withdrawal of British and French bases and troops, and was unacceptable to Baghdad Pact members. Since then, Moscow's line has been that it would support arms-supply limitations to the area only in exchange for Israeli withdrawal from foreign territories. At the superpower level, however, there is an unwritten agreement to hold down arms sophistication in the region—up to a point. Israel's nuclear initiative has rendered much of this superpower effort moot. The UN Association of Iowa study concluded that "to put a lid on a spiraling Middle East arms race, two developments are essential. First, there must be Soviet-American agreement on mutual military policies and on the political and military terms for an Arab-Israeli general settlement. And only then, when a political settlement either is negotiated or imposed on the Arabs and Israelis, will there be regional arms control."

Thus, the major league of American arms purchasers in recent times has been composed of three or four countries in the Middle East, where for thirty years the last dramatic legacy of World War Two—depriving the Palestinians of a country, and replacing them by settlers from many nations, ruled by Europeans—has created a conflict, the consequences of which have affected virtually every nation in the world. Yet, as a 1977 study of the Arab-Israeli conflict by the International Institute of Strategic Studies noted, "the interests and policies of the two great powers have been characterized by ambivalence, partiality and only marginal success in resolving the central issues of the dispute." Most newspaper stories on the Middle East are based only on the most recent developments at the time of writing, and are inevitably condensed and simplified. These stories in turn are interpreted by readers according to preconceptions of one sort or another, influenced by anti-Jewish or anti-Arab prejudice, or even by the supersimplified conceptions of cartoonists. So intertwined are weapons, economics and diplomacy in this area of superpower confrontation by proxy that a brief summary of the main stages of the conflict may be helpful.

Background

Fighting began, of course, with the founding of the nation of Israel, recognized in 1948 by the UN and the major powers. The Jewish immigrants took advantage of the 1947–48 conflict to advance the borders given them, occupying West Jerusalem and the Negev. An uneasy peace followed. Nasser's nationalization of the Suez Canal in 1956 was the pretext for the war that year, which ended when the Security Council ordered France, Britain and Israel out, with the United States voting against its European allies. If the upshot was humiliation for Israel and its supportive powers, the lesson learned from the brief clash was that the new Israeli military forces were superior to those of Egypt—though not, at the time, to all their adversaries combined. For a decade, as Israel's power increased, Israel's neighbors—while brandishing rhetorical threats of their own—lived in fear of a fresh assault, which finally came in 1967.

On the Arab side, there had been pressure for a resumption of hostilities when Israel diverted Galilee waters to irrigate the Negev. But the disheartened Palestinian refugees had still been an uncertain force, heavily controlled in Egypt, not yet a cogent whole in Lebanon. The PLO did not exist. It was Syria which became the main ally of the Palestinians; in Cairo, Nasser held out strongly against attacking Israel.

In 1964, he stated: "We will tell you the truth . . . We cannot use force today; our circumstances do not allow us; be patient with us . . . for I would lead you to disaster if I were to proclaim that I would fight at a time when I was unable to do so. I would not lead my country to disaster and would not gamble with its destiny."

The Palestinians decided, with Syria's support, on resistance-type operations against Israel; they calculated that if these lured Israel into open hostilities, Nasser would have to fight. Syria launched a water-diversion program of its own—which the Israelis bombed and destroyed. Syria responded by shelling Israeli villages. When the left-wing Ba'ath coup took place in Syria, in February 1966, the hand of the Palestinians was strengthened in that key country.

Israel began to plan for war. In April 1967, when a squadron of Syrian MiG-21s skirted the Israeli border, the Israelis took off in their French fighters and shot down six—a quarter of Syria's combat aviation. Just as the Palestinians sought to provoke the Israelis and create a war, so Israel, confident of victory, sought to provoke the Arabs. Egypt still wanted peace, and Syria was nervous about where a war might lead. What was expected was an Israeli parachute attack on Damascus, with the aim of overthrowing the Ba'ath government and installing a right-wing regime led by Syrian exiles in Jordan.

On May 13, according to U. S. Government records, Moscow warned Damascus and Cairo that Israel planned to launch an invasion of their countries on the seventeenth, using thirteen brigades. This was an untrue report, transmitted through Sami Sheraf, the head of the KGB in Cairo, and intended to make Nasser feel more dependent on Moscow. Nasser ordered two divisions into the Sinai. On the sixteenth, with the Israeli attack apparently imminent, Nasser ordered United Nations forces in Sinai to withdraw from patrols to their two base camps. UN Secretary General U Thant said that if his expeditionary force could not carry out its assigned duties, he would withdraw it altogether. Nasser was shocked, but dared not back down. By the nineteenth, war had still not come, and Egyptian and Israeli units faced each other across the border. Egyptian troops had also taken over Sharm esh-Sheikh, at the Red Sea entrance, from UN troops, closing the Strait of Tiran. This was of little consequence, since few Israeli freighters used Eilath, Israel's southern port, but it provided Tel Aviv with a *casus belli* of sorts.

Jordan and Iraq signed mutual defense pacts with Egypt. Washington urged Israel not to launch a war, but to little avail. On June 2, the United States ambassador in Cairo warned Nasser to expect an Israeli attack "within three days." But Nasser, preferring to face an Israeli onslaught on his fortified positions to armored combat in the open desert—Israel's forte—did not preempt. Indeed, while wishing to give the maximum impression of strength and pan-Arab support, especially in his public rhetoric, he still hoped to avoid conflict. He sent his Prime Minister to New York to agree to reopen the Tiran strait at Sharm esh-Sheikh and to negotiate for the return of the UN force. With the fragile *casus belli* about to be removed, Israel decided to invade before the Egyptian Premier could address the UN. This was the famous "preemptive attack."

Meanwhile, Moscow had been busy urging restraint on Israel and insisting that Egypt and Syria hold the Palestinians in leash. The Soviet Union agreed to support any Arab countries that were attacked, but not to back a "holy war" against Israel. Moscow did not support the closure of the Tiran Strait, being unanxious to jeopardize, by a precedent, its own need of Turkish and Danish straits to reach open waters. The United States opposed the Tiran blockade more vociferously, by diplomatic notes and in two weeks of debate at the United Nations.

Israel's Foreign Minister, Abba Eban, came to Washington but was kept waiting for twenty-four hours before being seen by President Johnson and Secretary Rusk. Both men told him firmly that if Israel initiated hostilities, the United States would not intervene on Israel's side. By then, both Johnson and Premier Kosygin were sending joint notes to Egypt and Israel, urging restraint all round. The fall of Nasser would have been welcomed in Washington, but not at the hands of Israel. In Paris, de Gaulle proposed a four-power conference, which Moscow rejected, and warned Israel that the consequences of aggression would be the loss of "the friendship of France." Israel ignored the warning and launched the war on June 5, using French aircraft and largely French armor. It was a Pearl Harbor-style operation, destroying the Egyptian Air Force on the ground.

The IISS study summarizes:

> President Johnson himself never made it absolutely plain to Israel that the United States would oppose it if it moved first—as de Gaulle [did] and as Eisenhower had done in October 1956. Washington's efforts were confined to the single issue of the blockade, which affected Israeli interests and American guarantees, while omitting a solution to Arab grievances; and yet the United States lost control over even this issue by failing to make clear to Israel the American position on the consequences of aggression.

The Liberty Incident

The United States soon paid a personal price for one aspect of Jerusalem's strategy—a successful plan to lure Jordan into the war. It learned thereby the fragile value that weapons diplomacy can have with a "friend" who is not an ally.

The Blackbird incident related in the first chapter of this book illustrates how swiftly the "friendship" of another country may become redundant when secrets about weapons may be betrayed. It will be recalled that on that occasion in 1973 the Israelis were apparently prepared to kill two American pilots rather than have the existence of their nuclear warheads confirmed, and their apparent preparedness to use them revealed. (Or, if Israel was bluffing about the warheads, as some Washington experts persist in believing, then Jerusalem had to be sure that the warheads' "presence" was detected, while being prepared to sacrifice the two U.S. strategic-reconnaissance officers, if they didn't decamp in time, to maintain the bluff of protecting nuclear secrecy.)

But in the 1967 war, a much more bloody reversal-of-alliance incident had occurred, when an American communications ship was repeatedly strafed and nearly sunk by Israeli fighters and surface ships for having learned of the existence of a sophisticated Israeli "weapon"—the means to interrupt, and doctor, radio traffic so rapidly as to confuse two of its adversaries. The *Liberty* incident has since divided U.S. policymakers deeply, and inevitably undermined Israel's image at the Pentagon.

After the fighting began, the United States had sought assurances that Israel's sole objective would be Egypt, and that the war would not affect Syria or America's friend, Jordan. If these countries were forced, for appearances, to join the war, Israel undertook not to occupy any Jordanian territory. Hussein of Jordan, like Nasser, had been informed by the United States of Israel's intention to attack Egypt. The fulcrum of communications on the American side was Jim Angleton, then the head of CIA covert activities.

Angleton was sentimentally sure that he could believe in the promises of Jerusalem; but as a check on Israeli good faith, and for information generally, the National Security Agency had asked the U. S. Navy to move the communications ship *Liberty* from West Africa (where it had been monitoring the opening stages of what became the Nigerian civil war) into the eastern Mediterranean, to cover Arab and Israeli traffic. NSA surveillance to see if Israel would keep to all aspects of the agreement was necessary because of a weakness in the CIA's logistics. In some countries, the agency has few officers of its own, no American station chief, and few "agents" (native spies); it relies on the (naturally selective, occasionally even disinformative) data which it receives from the friendly local intelligence organization. Two countries of importance in intelligence terms where the United States suffered this limitation at the time were South Africa and Israel—where, largely on Angleton's insistence, reliance had been placed on the Mossad, Israel's own CIA.

The *Liberty*, a former merchant ship based at Norfolk, Virginia, belonged to Joint Reconnaissance Command, part of the Joint Chiefs of Staff organization. (A similar ship to the *Liberty*, the *Pueblo*, made headlines the following year when it was captured by North Korea.) The *Liberty* had a complement of 19 officers and 295 men, about 100 of them "communications technicians."

The ship's listening devices were tuned to all major government frequencies in the area. Below its decks, Hebrew and Arabic speakers were poised with pencils, headsets on, amid a clutter of cigarette butts doused in coffee grounds in Styrofoam cups. NSA technicians manned decoding equipment. Two hundred feet below the ship, on a parallel course, was its "shadow"—the Polaris strategic submarine *Andrew Jackson,* whose job was to take out all Israeli long-range missile sites in the Negev if Tel Aviv decided to attack Cairo, Damascus or Baghdad. This was in order that Moscow should not have to perform this task itself and thus trigger World War Three.

The first important thing that the NSA monitors learned was that the Israelis had cracked the Egyptian and Jordanian codes. From a relay station inside the swiftly captured northern region of Sinai, Israel was interrupting and retransmitting Cairo's messages to Amman. In spite of world reporting of the Israeli successes, soon to be backed up by television film, Cairo appeared to be telling Amman that the tide of war had turned. Three quarters of Israel's air force, the Israelis made the "Egyptian" messages say, had been destroyed. The three hundred aircraft on Jordan's radars were Egyptian airplanes raiding Israel—not, as was really the case, Israeli planes returning unscathed from raids on Egypt. Cairo's anxious appeals to Jordan for help were transformed into an invitation to join in an assured victory and recapture West Jerusalem. Jordan's consequent participation in the war enabled Tel Aviv to seize East Jerusalem and the West Bank.

On June 7, Under Secretary of State Eugene Rostow called in Israeli ambassador Avraham Harman and warned him that Israel must cease its invasion of Egypt and Jordan, and must not attack Syria. Harman pleaded that Israel was "resisting aggression." Rostow snapped back that the United States knew that Tel Aviv had lured Hussein into the conflict by cooking his communications. Harman drove away from the State Department troubled. He returned to the embassy and called his country. By then, it was night in Tel Aviv, but within hours the Israeli ministry of defense there had ordered aircraft to seek out the U.S. communications ship.

American intelligence analysts now believe that the Israeli intention was complete destruction—a sinking with all hands. This could then be blamed on the Egyptians or the Russians, not only destroying a wartime nuisance, but also making Americans more sympathetic to Israel's cause. The *Liberty's* only defenses were two sets of machine guns, for and aft.

Like the pilots of the Blackbird, Captain William L. McGonagle and his officers on the *Liberty* followed route patterns but knew nothing of the successes or failures of what was going on belowdecks. The amidships quarters near the water line, where the computers, spectrum analyzers and other decoding equipment were stored, were off limits to

McGonagle and his crew. The intercepted traffic or the belligerents went to NSA headquarters at Fort Meade, in Maryland.

The blow by blow details of the martyrdom of the *Liberty* have been told in Anthony Pearson's book. In brief, after several reconnaissance flights by other aircraft to identify the ship, three Mirage-IIIs attacked *Liberty* on June 8 with seventy-two rockets, napalm and withering machine-gun fire, blowing up the boiler room and wrecking the deck-house. McGonagle was among the over a hundred wounded, while eight men, including the Executive Officer, the Operations Officer and a senior helmsman, were killed. Shortly afterward, three French-built missile torpedo boats attacked with guns and torpedos, destroying all the NSA equipment, and raising the death toll to 34 and the number of wounded to 171. McGonagle was hit again, and his second helmsman killed, along with the chief NSA officer, Allen M. Blue, and one of Blue's deputies. The entire action was filmed by the *Andrew Jackson* through its periscope (McGonagle managed to take still photographs) but the submarine was helpless to do anything else. The mangled skipper refused to let a boarding party from one of the Israeli MTBs on his ship; two helicopter loads of Israeli troops hovered overhead—then departed as two wings of A-4s from U.S. carriers began approaching in response to the captain's "Mayday" message: The Skyhawks had crossed over Egypt to reach the spot—with permission obtained from the White House through Moscow. Earlier, President Johnson had countermanded a retaliatory Skyhawk strike ordered by the Joint Chiefs of Staff against the Israeli MTB base at Haifa.

The badly wounded McGonagle steered the crippled, listing ship by stellar navigation and six days later reached Malta, where inspection showed 821 holes in its sides and extensive fire and fragmentation damage. A Court of Inquiry held initially in London, then on board at Valletta, under Admiral Isaac Kidd, heard an elaborate Israeli explanation: This was that the attackers had thought the *Liberty*—festooned with antennas, flying Old Glory, and with a huge "N" number on the side—was actually an equally defenseless Egyptian supply ship, the *Al Quseir*, which is only half the *Liberty*'s length and a quarter of its size. McGonagle testified that the jamming of his transmissions had been on American, not Egyptian frequencies, indicating further that the Israelis well knew the nationality of the ship.

In its findings—later confirmed by the U. S. Navy commander in Europe, Admiral John S. McCain—the court dismissed the "mistaken identity" defense as unbelievable, but accepted Israel's apology. To avoid embarrassment, the final McCain report referred to the attacking craft as "foreign" boats and planes, omitting mention of their nationality. After more than a year, Israel finally agreed to pay $3,325,000 in compensation to the next-of-kin of the thirty-four men killed, but only $3,566,457 for the wounded—$26,224 per casualty—after an expensive court case in which legal fees reduced the effective compensation by about half. But no money actually arrived, and the U. S. Government paid the sums. Israel refused to pay a U. S. Navy bill for $7,644,146 for damage to the ship, which was pronounced irreparable. The action had been the Navy's largest casualty loss in a single action since Korea.

Washington let the matter drop. Had Israel been called to account, it could have riposted—as the Johnson White House knew—by revealing U.S. connivance with Israel in various plots to overthrow Nasser.

McGonagle received the Congressional Medal of Honor. There were 5 Silver and 2 Bronze Stars, and 171 Purple Hearts, many of the decorations being posthumous.

CIA reports at the time—released in 1977, under the Freedom of Information Act, to one of the writer's sources—quote one Israeli official as confirming that Israel knew the nationality of the *Liberty*, and another as saying that General Dayan himself had ordered the sinking, over the protests of another Israeli general and an admiral (whose names are deleted). The Turkish military attaché in Tel Aviv during the 1967 war reported getting similar confirmations. But attempts by three congressmen to get a fuller accounting of the attack on the *Liberty* were to no avail. The full story was first unearthed in the British press. For his book, Pearson interviewed one of the three Mirage pilots, a Baltimore-born American who had immigrated to Israel in 1966. Pearson learned that one of the other two pilots who attacked *Liberty* had also been a U.S. Vietnam veteran. The matter remains sensitive. Pearson recounts that during his investigation, his private office in London was burgled and some of his *Liberty* files taken. The London *Sunday Times* believes that the murder, in Cairo, in December 1977, of its chief foreign correspondent, David Holden, may have been a Mossad job, with Holden being mistaken for Pearson—a similar mix-up to the "Plumbat" murder in Norway.

The attempted or simulated attack on the Blackbird in 1973 showed that either weapons secrecy (or, if the bluff hypothesis is followed, overt preservation of fictitious secrecy) can outweigh considerations of diplomatic friendship, or even of the importance to Israel of its main arms supplier. The *Liberty* incident portrayed how outright bluff (in this case, not of world opinion, but simply of Jordan) constitutes a weapon equally as worth preserving as technology—even at a heavy cost in friendly American lives.

It also served as a reminder that the United States, like the Soviet

Union, has no allies—no mutual defense treaties—in the Middle East, an unusual factor in the light of both superpowers' arms supplies to the region. An ally—such as Japan, South Korea or a NATO country—would not have attacked either the *Liberty* or the SR-2.

Finally, it emphasized the peculiar relationship between Washington and Tel Aviv. British diplomats believe that in a similar predicament Britain would break relations with a nation that tried to sink one of its warships. French diplomats say that, in a similar situation, France would probably have conducted a retaliatory strike.

The U. S. Naval Institute *Proceedings* summed it up:

> If there is a timeless lesson to be relearned from the savage violation of the *Liberty*, it is that nations do not have friends, only interests.

In short, whatever might be said publicly, the United States would never trust Israel again—or no more than any other Mideast state— and this factor later contributed to Washington's courtship of President Sadat, and his break with Moscow.

Post 1967

By the time the *Liberty* reached Malta, the war had been over for three days. When Qeneitra, on the Golan Heights, had fallen on June 9, Kosygin had called Johnson and said that if Israel pressed further toward Damascus, the Soviet Union might have to take independent action, and this action might include military operations. Johnson passed on the message to Israel, advising that it be taken seriously, and this effectively ended the war. In reality, then White House aides said, Johnson himself believed that Moscow was bluffing. The IISS study says: "The United States chose to intervene 'on Moscow's behalf' . . . because of the fear that a complete Israeli military victory would be so destabilizing as to destroy the prospect for political settlement." The analysis also notes that "Israel's defiance of four UN ceasefire proposals was reminiscent of its indifference to the UN's peace-keeping efforts during the first two Arab-Israeli wars."

Moscow broke relations with Israel and agreed to rebuild the Syrian and Egyptian armed forces. A triumphant Israel insisted that a permanent peace could only come from direct talks with the Arabs—but then added that Israel would not talk with the Palestinians, the Arabs about whom the conflict was fought. Israel's aim was not to solve the Palestinian conflict but to secure recognition by neighboring Arab states. The Arab countries refused talks until after a withdrawal from the now

occupied Sinai, West Jordan, Gaza and Golan. War reparations were
also called for. When the United States was unable to pressure Israel,
a partial Arab oil embargo was instituted.

On November 22, the Security Council passed Resolution 242, calling
for the withdrawal of Israeli forces from the occupied territories (the
English translation omitted the word "the," but the preamble, rejecting
the acquisition of territory by force, makes it clear that full withdrawal
was envisaged), an end to belligerency, the right of all states to peace,
security and territorial integrity, freedom of navigation, a "just settlement" for the Palestinians, and the appointment of a UN Special Representative as mediator for a settlement. Egypt accepted 242; Israel did
not, and later hounded the UN Representative, Dr. Gunnar Jarring, from
his post. After a year of bickering, Egypt began the "war of attrition" in
the Suez Canal area on October 15, 1968, with an artillery bombardment.

This was a period of intense diplomatic activity. Moscow and Washington agreed that neither had interests in the region vital enough to
cause war between them; both sought to pressure the capitals under
their influence. Israel's diplomatic position was deteriorating, and Nasser
felt confident enough to offer to take part in indirect talks. But Israel decided to escalate the war, with deep-penetration attacks on Egypt, and
rejected the so-called First Rogers Peace Plan—put forward by the new
U.S. Secretary of State, William Rogers. The Israeli attacks were successful: Substantial casualties were inflicted on Egyptian forces in the
Canal area, and a million civilians had to be evacuated. After successive
pleas and a visit to Moscow, Nasser received 150 MiG-21Js, some with
Soviet pilots, and SA-2 and SA-3 missiles. The missiles had some success,
and Soviet air patrols of the Nile Valley dissuaded Israel from further
penetration raids. However, Israeli fighter probes of Egypt's defenses occasionally led to combat with Soviet pilots, and this persuaded the Russians that they had nothing to lose diplomatically from bringing their
planes into the Red Sea and Canal area. Several dogfights between Israelis and Russians ensued, with casualties on both sides. Early in 1970,
Kosygin wrote to Nixon that if the United States could not restrain Israel, Soviet defensive armament to Egypt would be increased. Finally,
following greater SA-2 and SA-3 successes against Israeli planes, Israeli
Premier Golda Meir agreed to accept UN Resolution 242, and indirect
talks. Nasser, in an American TV interview, offered to recognize Israel in
return for implementation of 242. Hitherto, in the Arab world, only President Bourguiba of Tunisia had endorsed the principle of recognizing Israel.

In June, Rogers went on tour in the Middle East with his Second Plan.
This called for a ninety-day in-place cease-fire supervised by the United

States, and informal talks between Egypt, Jordan and Israel. This time, Moscow gave lukewarm support, leading to Egyptian acceptance of the plan. Before actually ordering a cease-fire, the Israelis deliberately baited a squadron of MiG-21s flown by Russians and shot down four, ending the "war of attrition" on a successful note. But the Russians soon took advantage of the cease-fire greatly to strengthen air defenses along the Canal. A British intelligence report later called it "the most formidable air defense complex in the history of air power."

The IISS analysis of the conflict sees at this point "a new Israeli sensitivity about negotiating procedures that affected substantive interests of the great powers. When its military options were inhibited, Israel [used] procedural limitations to limit Egyptian bargaining latitude to the same extent as it could do by . . . military superiority. The syndrome of imposing a bargaining straitjacket gradually became the underpinning for Israeli negotiating strategy." This was later to characterize the "Kissinger" talks that followed the next Arab-Israeli war, as well as the Camp David and Blair House talks of 1978, all of which the present writer covered as a reporter.

Nasser's death and the coming to power of Anwar as-Sadat, however, brought greater sophistication to the Egyptian negotiating posture. By February 1971, Sadat was sufficiently confident to express willingness to accept a final peace agreement with Israel if an interim accord worked out. This would involve a partial Israeli withdrawal leaving Sharm esh-Sheikh temporarily in Israeli hands. By May, Rogers was busy trying to sell his Third Peace Plan, but this mission ended in a stormy and unsuccessful session with Mrs. Meir. Assistant Secretary Joseph Sisco tried again in July and was again repulsed by Israel, which asked for a fresh delivery of 48 F-4s. Ultimately, to have leverage with Israel, the United States agreed to further aircraft deliveries and to the licensing of Israel's parastatal industries to produce spare parts for U.S. weaponry.

Meanwhile, Moscow was rebuilding Egypt's shattered forces, but under sharp constraints. The key word about deliveries was "adequacy." Moscow sought to deny Egypt the means to go on the offensive. Egypt received some medium-range bombers and some bridging equipment and amphibious craft, but was denied "air superiority" so that these arms were essentially cosmetic. Brookings and IISS reports agree that the United States was less restrained in its buildup of Israel. But Washington was beginning to have signal success in winning Sadat's friendship, and in 1972 he suddenly expelled Soviet military advisers, complaining that the Soviet Union had failed to restore Egypt to fighting strength. This delighted the West; it also soon forced Moscow to increase arms supplies to Cairo, including Scud surface-to-surface missiles and enough weaponry for a Canal-crossing attack on occupied Sinai. Sadat in turn agreed to limit such an attack to just enough territory to permit reopening the Canal.

Preparations continued for a war of liberation—a partial enforcement of Resolution 242. Syria accepted two contingents of Moroccan troops in 1973, and Russia greatly increased Syria's air defenses: About fifty new surface-to-air missile batteries were installed to protect Damascus, along with reinforcements of T-62 tanks. As D-Day approached, secrecy was clamped down. In October, Palestinian radio stations in Syria and Egypt were closed. The Soviet Union was only informed of the impending war on October 2, just in time to evacuate Soviet dependents from Damascus.

For once, Israel's intelligence network was well below par. On September 13, an Israeli squadron even flew a provocative penetration course into Syrian ocean airspace near Latakia, drawing the Syrians into combat and shooting down thirteen planes with only one Israeli loss. Egypt and Syria began the "Ramadan War" on October 4, with Egyptian forces crossing the Canal and barreling through the famed Bar-Lev Line. Once again, the United States suffered from being heavily dependent on Israeli intelligence. Over Defense Secretary Schlesinger's protests, Dr. Kissinger delayed an airlift of resupplies to Israel, and commercial carriers refused to participate. Spain, Greece, Turkey and other NATO countries refused refueling rights for the resupply, and the C-5s finally had to break their journey in the Portuguese Azores. On October 20—with Kissinger in Moscow—Egypt and Israel, with the blessing of the superpowers, accepted UN cease-fire Resolution 338, which called for negotiations between the parties "under appropriate auspices."

On October 23, Israel broke the armistice, completing the encirclement of the Egyptian Third Army on the East Bank of the Canal and occupying Suez City on the West Bank. Egypt managed to hold the Cairo road, but Israel, while losing huge numbers of tanks to Egyptian missiles, had knocked out most of Sadat's air defense system. Moscow, which had been dubious and unencouraging about the Egyptian offensive from the start, was slow to take military precautions. But, as related in the Prologue of this book, Washington's warning of a possible Israeli nuclear initiative had led the Soviet Union to place several airborne divisions on alert and to send nuclear warheads to Egypt for the Scuds. A resupply of Egypt competed with America's resupply of Israel, and no less than forty Soviet warships were soon in the Mediterranean, mostly at choke points like Gibraltar, the Strait of Messina and the Aegean, despite delays caused by the Montreux Convention's clause which required Russia to give Turkey a week's notice of any intended passage of the Dardanelles by a Soviet warship.

Israel reaccepted the cease-fire on October 24 but refused to return to its October 22 lines, as UN Resolution 338 demanded. Talks got under way at Kilometer 101 on the Cairo Road. Under fierce pressure from the Zionist lobby in Washington, Congress voted a $2.2 billion special military resupply of Israel—despite Pentagon and CIA assurances that this was more than Israel could absorb. The Arab oil countries declared their oil embargo of the West, followed later by large increases in oil prices. Moscow did not support the boycott, and even took advantage of it to sell more oil.

By the night of the twenty-fourth, there were eighty-five Soviet warships in the Mediterranean, and Kosygin was informing President Nixon that either the great powers must act together to stop Israeli violations or Moscow would act "unilaterally." This was the overt pretext for the "Nixon alert"—placing all American forces under a "Defense Condition Three." Of this measure, the IISS study says that it "caused more consternation in NATO capitals and among the American public than it probably did in Moscow." Meanwhile, Nixon threatened to supply food, water and medicine to the Egyptian Third Army and beleaguered Egyptian civilians, after which Israel let through a convoy of 125 Egyptian trucks. Kissinger began his shuttle diplomacy, resulting in January 1974 in Israel's agreement to an initial withdrawal, Egypt's reoccupation of the Canal and the introduction of UN buffer forces. U.S. aircraft and satellites were to monitor the limitations on forces on both sides of the new frontier in occupied Sinai. Later, a smaller disengagement was negotiated for the Syrian border. Egypt resumed full diplomatic relations with the United States.

Kissinger's second disengagement operation, resulting in the return to Egypt of the Abu Rodeis oil fields, took much longer, and the intervening decision of the Rabat summit, in the fall of 1974, denying Hussein the right to speak for the Palestinians, was seen as a setback for American diplomacy—especially when Arafat was invited to address the UN, following a savage Israeli air raid on Lebanon in which scores of women and children were killed. But by now, Washington was at least an accepted interlocutor on both sides, and even U.S. relations with Syria were beginning to heal.

However, there were inhibitions. Despite a series of reports by the Red Cross, Amnesty International and others about Israeli repression, and the torture of political prisoners on the occupied West Bank of Jordan, Washington remained pressured by the Israeli lobby not to slacken its support for the Jerusalem government and not to replace Russia as Egypt's armorer. The lobby wanted Egypt to remain wholly dependent on Moscow, so that Sadat should not compete with Israel for America's political affections; but the White House had little difficulty persuading Sadat to turn to Paris and London for arms, and these capitals were glad to respond. Egypt's initial long-term deal with France alone was estimated at $2 billion.

In 1975, Egypt accelerated the construction of the Canal cities—seen internationally as a pledge not to go to war again—and both Sadat and King Faisal of Saudi Arabia told President Ford that they would recognize "Israel's existence" in return for implementation of Resolution 242. The second Sinai disengagement finally took place that year, with Congress agreeing to send two hundred American technicians to live in the no-man's-land of the Mitla and Gidi passes to monitor the truce. The United States agreed to support Israel in a number of ways, including guaranteeing its oil supplies—although how it would do this was not spelled out. There was renewed talk of arranging, through a Geneva conference, joint U.S.-Soviet guarantees of all borders in the confrontation area.

The IISS analysis notes:

> The United States had long sought to establish reliable ties with Arab states, but failed because Israeli intransigence prevented it from reciprocating Arab concessions . . .
> Of the local actors, Egypt in particular has clearly been the quickest to apply the lessons of previous experience . . .
> Israel, on the other hand, has probably learned the least. After nearly thirty years of intermittent war, it remains unable to convert its military strength into diplomatic initiative. It has been politically incapable of visualizing a comprehensive formula for peace and has become increasingly dependent on a single external protector for its ultimate security . . . During each war, Israel has sought enhanced security by extending its borders, and each war has resulted in external intervention.

What had emerged in Israel was

> a consensus that national survival was dependent upon Israeli military prowess. But Israel drew the wrong inferences from these lessons. The siege mentality that inevitably accompanies a constant state of vigilance can be counterproductive: confidence in self-defense often nurtures isolation, first from the outside world, then from reality . . .
> Israelis believe they will survive as they did before, living Jewish life on the margin of other societies, and indeed enjoying not being integrated into regional structures or entities. But living on the margin of Middle

Eastern life is too risky until Israel defines more precisely her terms for accommodation with her Arab citizens and neighbors.

The main lessons of the last war are that renewed fighting can buy Israel only a limited respite, not security; that time is not on its side; and
that the credibility of guarantees must be reassessed.

These comments seem particularly perspicacious in the light of the
Sadat peace initiative of November 1977, the subsequent disappointments, and the fragile peace treaty painfully achieved.

In a 1976 study of the implications of the Arab-Israeli military status,
two senior members of the American Enterprise Institute, Robert J.
Pranger and Dale R. Tahtinen, noted that:

> The guidelines for U.S. arms policy in the Arab-Israeli conflict are basi-
> cally political, as are the guidelines for the Soviet Union's policy. Neither
> Moscow nor Washington seems really capable of saying "no" to its clients,
> even though at times there is delay in supply and even bad feeling be-
> tween client and superpowers.

Pranger and Tahtinen suggested closer cooperation with Moscow to
keep more advanced military technologies from the area, including a nuclear ban, and a better "crisis management machinery in the Middle
East, with the Soviet Union and regional parties."

Like most Middle East observers, Pranger and Tahtinen expect a future area conflict to be much more murderous, noting Israel's nuclear capacity and desire for the Pershing missile, which would bring in the Russian Scaleboard on the other side. (Some U. S. Senate experts told the
writer they saw the Pershing request as merely a "saber rattle." Others
thought it implied that the Jericho was not reliable.) The AEI specialists
also foresaw a temptation for Israel to use chemical or biological weapons, which would be expected to draw a similar response. Israel's Gabriel
and the Arab countries' Styx missiles have improved, with the expectation that naval warfare will be more destructive than before. Israel also
has the air-launched Gabriel and the U.S. air-launched Harpoon. Syria
and Iraq have similar weaponry, and long-range forecasts have to include the possibility of Egypt re-entering the fray. Israel has laser-
guided bombs, and drones for use as electronic countermeasures or as
missiles or both. SIPRI estimates that Israel has the "technological infrastructure in electronics, airframes and jet engines to produce long-range
cruise missiles." Should these be produced, it can be assumed that Arab
countries will acquire similar weapons. In short, Israel, in its technological superiority over its neighbors, faces the same problem as the United
States in its technological superiority over the Soviet Union—the danger
that, by producing new advanced weapons, it so destabilizes the situa-

tion as to invite a first strike. This would be dependent on Soviet weapons diplomacy among its clients, and U.S. weapons diplomacy to friendly Arab states. Israel, by its technological excellence, is slowly escaping from Washington leverage.

The Mideast Cockpit Today

A Hill aide closely connected with defense questions says the U.S. military tends to recommend to any country what U.S. forces would themselves require to defend such a territory. Just as Israel bases its weapons requests on a "worst-case" scenario, so do U.S. advisers to other neighboring nations, the aide thinks. U.S. advisers also usually suggest buying more aircraft than will be needed, because Third World pilots are expected to "bend" more of them than U.S. pilots do—which means that delivery figures are more impressive than the operational reality. Sophisticated systems multiply, and with them the risk of spreading technological secrets. But there is also, the aide thinks, a natural desire on the part of American officers to deplete the U.S. armory of weapons approaching obsolescence, since this heightens the pace of introducing state-of-the-art weaponry into the U.S. inventory. He also attributed the growth of some arms-sale programs, such as those in Saudi Arabia and Iran, to the desire of the military to serve overseas. Modern weaponry sales require heavy contingents of U.S. technicians.

A Jewish aide said he thought many Arab weapons purchases were made to buy leverage in the United States. Speaking in 1975, he welcomed Egypt's then continued dependence on the Soviet Union, since it created suspicion in Congress of Egypt; if Egypt had to buy weapons in the West, he preferred that they should be bought from Western Europe; he noted that Egypt already had Mirages, so already possessed Mirage parts and ground crews trained to maintain such equipment. He saw the principal enemy as being the U.S. arms contractors and their lobbying, and said that there had been a growth of lobbying by potential subcontractors on each system, at the behest of the prime contractor.

But whether the main spur for sales was economic or political, supplier countries were tending to sell, more and more, state-of-the-art weaponry. In many cases—America's F-14 and F-15, Russia's MiG-23 and MiG-27—there was no or little delay between production and delivery. Already, by the beginning of 1976, of the 2,300 combat jets in the area, well over half were late-model MiG-23s, MiG-21s, F-5Es, F-4s, A-4s and Mirage-IIIs. Half the tanks were as modern—Russia's T-62s, America's M-60s, France's AMX-30s and British Chieftains, all battle-tested weapons. Now, F-14s,

F-15s, F-16s, F-1s—and perhaps, soon, the Jaguar, the Tornado or the MiG-29—enlarge the picture.

As a sign of the times, Israel, Saudi Arabia and Iran have refueling tanker planes. All three countries have large helicopter forces. Israel has bought four Grumman E-2C Hawkeye command planes. Iran ordered —but canceled, after its revolution—seven AWACS. Israel, Iran and Saudi Arabia all have teleguided and laser-guided air-to-surface missiles. Israel has electronic countermeasures and counter-countermeasure systems, and both Egypt and Israel possess remotely piloted air vehicles (RPVs). About the only important aviation system which the Pentagon seems to have successfully opposed Israel acquiring is the ALQ-119 aircraft-mounted radar-jamming pods and advanced digital processors. These are for the rapid tuning and directing of jammers against multiple or frequency-hopping radars. Nearly fifteen years of research is involved, and U.S. specialists are understandably unwilling to see this dissipated. The fear is less that a downed plane will yield secrets to the Russians than that Israel will pirate—"modify"—the system, and market it at a lower price under the name of Israel Aircraft Industries.

On the other side, Egypt seems destined, despite Arab opposition to Cairo's treaty with Israel, to become the main center of the Arab states' military industrial organization (AOI)—essentially, a vast aerospace assembly and repair complex. The second complex will go to Arabia.

Farther east, the main buyer of U.S. arms, Iran, had—until 1978— found ways to get the United States deeply involved. The SIPRI Yearbook published in late 1976 said: "In Iran, virtually every major weapons deal in recent years has included the establishment of an appropriate maintenance and repair facility and the training of Iranian personnel in the relevant skills." SIPRI quoted the F-14 Tomcat fighter, the AH-1J attack helicopter, the B.214A utility helicopter, and the Phoenix long-range air-to-air missile as examples, and noted that Iran had also asked for coproduction facilities with Britain on at least 1,200 Chieftain tanks.

In a 1976 Senate Foreign Relations Committee report, it was noted that 50,000 to 60,000 American "civilian" military technicians would be needed by Iran, by 1980, to maintain and operate the $10.4 billion worth of arms which that country had purchased since 1972. At the revolution, most Americans were evacuated; but Iran could not go to war without U.S support on a virtually day-to-day basis. Tens of thousands of Americans will soon be needed in Saudi Arabia to serve the thousands of laser-guided "smart bombs," Maverick air-to-surface missiles, TOW antitank missiles and sophisticated aircraft which have pushed recent U.S. sales to that country close to the figures for Iran before the fall of the Shah.

The Senate report said that "the F-14 system is so complicated that the

U. S. Navy is having major difficulty keeping it operational. Iran's *Spruance*-class destroyers will be even more sophisticated than those being procured by the U. S. Navy." A *U.S. News* article, noting that the United States was politically obliged by domestic pressures to keep Israel ahead of the Arab states in firepower, and that "the United States cannot hope to dislodge the Russians and expand American influence in the Arab world unless it can guarantee delivery of essential military supplies," posed two dilemmas:

> Should Washington in a conflict involving its arms customers let its technicians remain and participate in the hostilities? Or should the United States renege on commitments to keep sophisticated weapons in full operation?
>
> In another Arab-Israeli war, should the United States mount a large-scale resupply operation for American clients on either or both sides? Or should it allow them to run out of essential supplies?

Although the air and tank buildup in the Middle East tends to attract the most attention, naval developments are also impressive. In 1977, Israel received three coastal submarines with Blowpipe short-range surface-to-air missiles, while Iran began taking delivery of the first of six oceangoing (West German) submarines, the four 7,800-ton *Spruance*-class destroyers referred to by the Senate, twelve missile patrol boats, and two 2,500-ton logistical support ships. Delivery was awaited on a 11,000-ton fleet-replenishment vessel. Iran was also building a naval base at Chah Bahar. Saudi Arabia was building two naval bases and had ordered nineteen American vessels, including destroyers, frigates and missile-armed boats.

Meanwhile, the air power of the region continued to grow and grow. In 1978, despite promising moves toward peace generated by President Sadat, Israel ordered F-16s and more F-15s, and counterbalancing, if token, supplies of F-5s were made to Egypt; orders were taken for F-15s for Saudi Arabia, which also ordered F-1s from France. Egypt planned to co-produce the Mirage-2000.

Clearly, while both Washington and Moscow were talking of the need for a diplomatic solution, Israel was putting its faith in a military one and—prior to the Sadat initiative of November 1977—had convinced its neighbors that they had little choice but to follow suit. At the central command of Egyptian armed forces in early 1977, generals spoke of Israel's basic weakness—its unwillingness to accept heavy casualties for several weeks or months. Egypt's forces were therefore being trained so that, if Israel refused to budge from occupied territory, and conflict became inevitable, the Egyptians would hope to make a deep thrust into

the Sinai with a view to causing maximal casualties to the occupants.
The Egyptians would then fall back before the counterthrust to fortified
positions and inflict maximal casualties and destruction of tanks and
planes from a defensive posture.

Even if Egyptian losses in soldiers were vastly greater than Israel's,
this was expected to have its effect on the enemy, both because of its
relatively limited population and the emotional reaction at home to
heavy losses. Egypt would, according to plans, make relatively little use
of its 350-or-so flyable combat aircraft but would rely mostly on its
nearly 5,000 surface-to-air missiles and antitank weapons.

Egypt is now theoretically out of contention, but Israel's other potential enemies see the situation similarly. Syria, geographically more vulnerable, also saw war as a question of engaging Israeli troops against
fortified positions, and hoped that if Damascus was threatened, pressure
from Moscow and Washington would interdict an Israeli onslaught. Both
Syria and, at the time, Egypt counted on support from Saudi Arabia,
Libya, perhaps Iraq and above all Jordan, whose involvement would
draw Israeli forces away from the Golan front and tie up Israeli armor in
the desert. For this reason, the 1977 news was of Syrian courtship of
King Hussein and of a military cooperation agreement between the two
countries. Also in 1977, Syria became deeply involved in the Lebanese
factional fighting, with President Assad fearing that a leftist Lebanon
might lure Israel into occupying that country and creating a new front
for Syria—and one harder to defend than the mountainous Golan country. Israel's 1978 invasion of southern Lebanon, using a small Palestinian
commando raid on the Israeli coast as a pretext for "retaliation," seemed
to confirm Syria's fears: Israel, however, had far less success fighting hit-
and-run guerrillas than fighting Egyptian armor or Soviet planes. Later
that year, Syria began mending its bridges with Iraq, and even signed a
military pact with Baghdad.

Israel, meanwhile, in 1977, appeared to be planning a war directed at
economic and civilian targets, to break morale. Conscious that this
would draw universal opprobrium, Israel was stockpiling offensive
weapons and delivery systems to make it possible to bring off a three-
week blitzkrieg before global pressure became too great. Conscious, also,
that only the Israeli lobby in Washington could save Israel, in such a
war, from American reaction, and that a backlash was developing
against the lobby's heavy-handed ways, Israel chose as its main aim to
build up a self-sufficient arms industry of its own. The lobby's 1978
defeat over the Saudi arms-sales issue confirmed Israel's fears. The
armed forces had been reorganized back in 1976 into separate northern,
southern and central commands, with highly mobile reserves; since then,

the new Begin government has shown every sign of wanting to hold on to the West Bank, partly seen as a *glacis* for Israeli defense.

In 1977, well-informed sources in Amman, Damascus, Cairo and Jerusalem were all telling reporters that they "hoped" diplomacy would work, but that it probably would not. War was thought likely to break out again. Only Sadat's initiative changed the climate.

Syria and Egypt briefly came much closer together in 1977, until Sadat's journey to Jerusalem in November. Saudi Arabia emerged as their military banker. Arabia even managed to impose a cease-fire, for a while, on the Syrians and Palestinians in Lebanon, and later summoned Syrian, Palestinian and Egyptian leaders to Riyadh for two meetings. The conventional American wisdom soon became that the wealthy Saudis had taken over control of Arab strategy, and that Jordan—which was not invited to Riyadh, apparently to satisfy the Palestinian leader, Yasir Arafat—was the loser. But in the Middle East as elsewhere, things are rarely what they seem. Just as the United States has been unable to control tumultuous Israel, and Moscow has failed to dictate policy to Syria, Iraq, Egypt or the Palestinians, so it is far from sure that Arabia controls military strategy in the Arab world—or that Jordan, if Hussein survives, is no more than a pawn. The Egypt/Israel peace treaty brought Syria and Iraq much closer together, and brought about a rapprochement between King Hussein and Arafat.

In 1978, U.S. weapons diplomacy in the Middle East increased apace. The sale of sixty F-15s to Saudi Arabia was particularly welcomed by the aerospace industry as a "watershed in U.S. foreign policy"—the words of the industry's magazine, *Aviation Week*. Carter, said the magazine, had clearly given up naive hopes of peace through disarmament, and the United States was no longer "blindly following" Israeli policy when that conflicted with American policy. Senate approval of the sale had been a "decided defeat" for the Israeli lobby, which "attempted to elevate the interests of Israel above those of the United States." The new turn in weapons for the region, in other words, was expected to be better than ever for weapons economics.

The Israeli Connection

U.S. arms relations with Israel are a case apart, for as well as satisfying the normal diplomatic aims of leverage, counterbalance to Soviet friends in the area, and so on, and the normal economic aim of increasing production lines and decreasing unit costs in the United States, these sales

are also a pawn in domestic politics and even a weapon in presidential
elections. Yet as a client state, Israel presented one obvious problem: Of
America's three major arms clients in the Middle East, the only one with
a record of actually using weapons in war is the Jewish state. Whereas
arms for Saudi Arabia and Iran are thought unlikely to be used except
as rattling sabers—unless Israel forces them into war—military assistance
for Israel is seen as even more likely to be employed than the arsenals of
NATO allies. This gives the Pentagon the "test-bed" asset, but also
means that Israel's arms are not exclusively deterrents—the main "military" function that they fulfill elsewhere. Given Israel's formidable
efficiency in the use of weapons and brilliance in the conduct of war,
arms supplies to that country in the late seventies have been staggering.

The United States, it will be recalled, became Israel's main supplier a
decade ago, after the 1967 war. In hearings that year, after the fighting,
Stuart Symington had questioned the State Department's Jeffrey Kitchen
as to why Washington had allowed Israel to rely on Paris for its air force,
since the money came from American Jews:

> *Symington:* There has . . . been talk about a lot of private money going
> from this country to Israel. Most of that money then went from Israel to
> France. General de Gaulle is today the greatest practical enemy of the
> United States—his raid on our gold supply is but one illustration. Why
> should not State let the Israelis buy these planes from us?
> *Kitchen:* . . . The overriding consideration was for the United States not
> to be identified as a heavy or principal supplier to either of the antagonists
> in a potential conflict. Second, we wanted to maintain as much suasion as
> we could in the Arab countries. We felt that would have been decreased if
> we had become a large single-source supplier to Israel.

From then on, as we have seen, there was a steady buildup in supplies
of F-4s, A-4s and U.S. missiles, with Israel's inventory reaching major-
power levels in the late seventies. For the fiscal period from July 1, 1975,
to October 1, 1977, U.S. arms transfers to Israel totaled $4.4 billion, of
which $1.5 billion were gifts from the U.S. taxpayer, the rest "soft"
credit. For the fiscal year beginning in the fall of 1977, Israel requested a
further $2.3 billion and actually received approval for about $1.8 billion.
The total figure for fiscal 1978 was, however, about $3 billion. In fiscal
1979, U.S. arms and economic assistance to Israel, both credits and gifts,
will approach $4 billion.

Shortly after taking office, Secretary Vance told Israeli reporters during a Mideast swing that three criteria would guide the Carter administration in Mideast arms sales: the recipient country's national-security
needs, the arms balance between Israel and the Muslim countries, and
whether the arms transfer would "facilitate peace." The second criterion

is of course the decisive one; the first and third criteria allow this second criterion to be applied for more intangible and "moral" reasons.

The "balance" is a hard problem for any computer. In 1976, Israel, with 250 F-4E Phantoms and 287 A-4 Skyhawks, took delivery of 25 F-15 Eagles, with Sparrow and Sidewinder air-to-air missiles. It was thus the first foreign country to receive the 3,500-mile-range, $24 million planes (the unit cost to Israel), the top fighters in the U.S. inventory. F-15s and F-16s are eventually intended to replace F-4s and A-4s in the Israeli air force inventory. Israel's aim was originally to have 400 F-15s, with most of them produced locally—a project scuttled by the Carter co-production guidelines of 1977. Israel's order for 400 of the lighter, single-engined F-16s, armed with Sparrows and Mavericks (for a ground-attack role) was placed in 1975. The full number was supposed to be reached by 1981, once again using co-production.

In February 1977, all interested agencies in the Pentagon except Defense Security Assistance recommended against co-production of the F-16 in Israel. By then, Israel had scaled its demands down from 400 to 250; the Pentagon recommendation was for 125, all made in America. When then-Premier Yitshak Rabin was in Washington in March, President Carter told him that he would scotch the co-production deal and would limit sales to 125; the main reason, Pentagon sources say, was that co-production of the F-16 would enable Israel's military aircraft industry to achieve a sufficient level of sophistication to be entirely independent of foreign aircraft supplies in the eighties. But Carter's F-16 decision was not revealed at the time, so as not to hurt the Labor government's chances in the Israeli general election, then only a few weeks off.

In June, the Carter administration refused Israel co-production rights (with an affiliate of Sylvania) on a military communications system, and also turned down co-production of the F-15. Approval was however given for Israel to use $107 million of U.S. aid to produce Israel's own Merkavah (Chariot) tank, and to buy two 40-mph, 94-ton Flagstaff Mk. 2 hydrofoil boats. Sales to Israel of missiles, armored personnel carriers and other weapons worth $115 million were also authorized. At the new Begin government's request, Pentagon sources say, the news was withheld that the Merkavah would only get 750 hp. American engines, not the 1,500 hp. engines requested.

There were other disappointments for the Israeli defense ministry in Tel Aviv. Later in 1977, the United States ceased paying the costs of the 202-man Israeli arms-purchasing mission in New York—a larger mission than the Israeli embassy in Washington—following revelations about the American funding in the Washington Post. General Fish admitted that the communications, market research and travel costs, plus computer and legal fees of the mission, had cost American taxpayers $2.8 million over sixteen months.

Shortly after taking office, Carter had vetoed the sale to Israel of CBU-72 concussion bombs, a weapon not previously exported anywhere and which had been refused to Canada, a NATO country, by the Ford administration. The weapon, described in Chapter 2, had not even been ordered by the U. S. Air Force. Israel had promised President Ford, when he had originally approved the sale in October 1976, that it would use the CBU only to clear minefields or against hardened SAM sites and concrete aircraft revetements. It would not be used against nonmilitary targets, and not be used at all unless Israel was fighting on more than one front. Israel agreed to the same conditions for cluster bombs—then used them in 1978 against civilian "targets" in Lebanon. To support Carter's veto of CBUs in a way calculated to diminish the anticipated Israeli lobby arguments in favor of the sale, Pentagon spokesmen stressed to reporters that since the bomb descended by parachute and was liable to be blown off target, it was too inaccurate to export. The State Department had earlier recommended against its sale to any foreign country.

Ford's decision to sell the CBU had been a clear pre-election bid to meet the rhetoric of Carter, who—while declaiming against U.S. arms sales in general—had asserted that the Ford administration had not provided enough arms for Israel. Taking advantage of the fact that Congress had recessed for the election and so—unless it reconvened in emergency session—could not exercise its right to discuss arms sales of over $25 million, Ford had also agreed to a whole raft of other advanced weaponry for Israel. These transfers, it was learned, were to have included laser-guided bombs and missiles, missile-armed helicopters, electronic countermeasures, more TOW wire-guided antitank missiles, 120 M-60 heavy tanks—of which U.S. forces were then in short supply—and, most controversial of all, a supply of forward-looking infrared (FLIR) heat-sensitive night-targeting equipment. FLIR, which cannot be jammed by countermeasures, was still classified and not yet available to NATO; if captured in a Mideast war and made available to the Soviet Union for study, it would enable Moscow to overtake a five-year American advance in technology, experts claimed. The State Department opposed the White House sale decision as destabilizing—meaning that it would give such an advantage to Israel as to encourage Israel to launch a war. (Carter at first banned FLIR, then released it for delivery to Israel in the early eighties, as a gesture to sweeten Premier Begin's otherwise fruitless Washington visit of March 1978.)

Ford's original FLIR decision had pleased the Israeli Government, which would have preferred to see him re-elected, but created a dilemma for the pro-Israeli lobby: Most American Jews favored Carter. Washingtonologists knew that the weapons promised could be indefinitely delayed in delivery; but Ford, at the time, had used a visit by Israeli Foreign Minister Yigal Allon to announce the news through a White House press conference, at which Allon appeared and pronounced himself well satisfied. A year before, as the American price for obtaining Israeli assent to the second Sinai withdrawal, Dr. Kissinger had agreed to supply Israel with a vast stock of advanced weaponry, including the previously mentioned CBUs and the F-16s, as well as (noted earlier) guaranteeing Israel's oil supplies.

While the argument over co-production went on in 1977, Israel was quietly building up its own armaments industry, notably in planes and missiles. Designed in 1968, the $4.4 million Kfir has been in production since 1974. By 1978, most of the two hundred ordered by the Israeli Air Force were in squadron service, and production had reached six a month. When Carter vetoed sale of the American-engined plane to Ecuador, Israel complained that the U.S. decision to ban Kfirs in Latin America would cost it $3 billion over the years to come: Israeli co-production arrangements were then being negotiated with Peru, Venezuela and South Africa—but these would now clearly have to involve a non-American power plant.

Following the Carter arms-sales guidelines announcement in May, a massive Israeli lobby offensive was launched on the White House. Morris Amitay, chief lobbyist for the powerful American Israel Public Affairs Committee, sent top Carter aide Hamilton Jordan a long chapter of grievances. He complained, for instance, that the President's remarks about visiting Syrian President Hafaz al-Assad, a key figure in U.S. Mideast policy, had been "too praising." Senators Henry Jackson and Clifford Case, the leading non-Jewish, pro-Israeli Democrat and Republican, respectively, in the upper house, called on Carter, who later met with over thirty Jewish leaders, members of the Conference of Presidents of Major American Jewish Organizations which, in consultation with the Israeli embassy, dictates the guidelines of AIPAC. The conference's leader, Rabbi Schindler, then flew off to Tel Aviv. Carter responded with a public statement affirming America's "special security responsibilities" to Israel.

Earlier, Richard Stone of Florida, a Jewish senator with a strongly Jewish electorate, especially in the Miami area, had presented National Security Adviser Zbigniew Brzezinski in March with a "hit list" of Pentagon officials he wanted removed because they had been critical of Israeli arms demands. Leaks to the press helped Brzezinski resist this unusual move by the new chairman of the Senate Foreign Relations Committee's

Near East subcommittee; many Jewish voices were raised on the other side by people who saw the new Israeli Government's inflexibility as endangering for Israel, and "weapons pressure" on Israel from Washington as a force for common sense. Writing in the *Breira* newsletter for pro-Israeli doves, Washington *Post* editorial writer Stephen S. Rosenfeld said: "I believe that Israel's best chance of securing from the United States the immense help it needs in order to get political concessions from the Arabs, is to make itself ready for large-scale territorial concessions. By large-scale, I mean all the territory taken in 1967."

When Senator Charles Percy of Illinois introduced his far-reaching Nuclear Non-Proliferation bill in 1977, one reason he cited for the measure was Israel's nuclear-weapon capacity; Senator John Glenn of Ohio spoke of the desires of President Sadat of Egypt and the Shah of Iran to see the Middle East made militarily nuclear-free. Senator Percy, whose problems with the Jewish lobby in Illinois were described in *The Power Peddlers*, co-authored by the present writer, on this occasion took the precaution of having two Jewish co-sponsors, Abraham Ribicoff of Connecticut and Jacob Javits of New York.

By 1978, Foreign Minister Moshe Dayan could boast that Israel already had "more planes than Italy or Germany or France." But it was requesting 25 more F-15s and trying for 130 more F-16s, with a view to expanding its air force from "550" combat aircraft to "750"—larger than any air force in Europe except Russia's. Actually, counting troop transports and offensive helicopters, Israeli combat aviation, as noted earlier, totaled about 1,100 units in 1978, compared to 550 aircraft in France, a similar number in Britain, and about 500 in West Germany. Defense Minister Ezer Weizmann told reporters in Washington in March 1978, that Israel wanted to buy 175 more American aircraft by 1983.

In May 1978, Congress approved the sale of 75 F-16s and 15 more F-15s to Israel, as part of the controversial Saudi-Egyptian-Israeli "package." The F-16s were for delivery between late 1981 and late 1983, the F-15s for delivery in the 1981–82 period. To ease passage, Carter promised 20 more F-15s in 1983 and after. In reality, although Congress failed apparently to notice it, these further F-15s had already been promised earlier, as had 75 additional F-16s, as part of Ford commitments which Carter was implementing. A few weeks later, the White House approved the sale to Israel of 30 Hughes Defender helicopters with TOW missiles, for delivery beginning in mid-1979.

But Israel had become the principal problem-client for U.S. arms, so far as end-use was concerned. Between August 1976 and April 1978 the State Department informed Congress of five breaches in the Arms Export

Control Law, four of them by Israel. The four were the sale of the Gabriel missiles with U.S. components to South Africa, the sale of Mystères with U.S. engines to Honduras, the general use by Israel of U.S. weapons in Lebanon in 1977 and 1978, and the use of cluster bombs against civilians. (The fifth breach was Yugoslavia's sale of U.S. tanks to Communist Ethiopia.) Israel's arms-export industry is looked at in some detail in Chapter 9.

In May 1978, the National Association of Arab Americans brought suit to try to block U.S. arms deliveries to Israel until the use of these arms in Lebanon had been "corrected"—that is, until Israeli troops withdrew from the country, which they subsequently did. The Egypt/Israel peace treaty of 1978 reopened the whole question, with its implications that Israel's defense needs would now be less. The Begin government, however, said it needed a further "$800 million" of weapons to defend its foreshortened territory; and as part of the treaty, the United States agreed to build two new airfields in the Negev, at an estimated cost of $800 million–$1 billion. In all, U.S. military aid to Israel connected with the treaty was later estimated at $3 billion, of which $800 million was to be in the form of gifts. Sales of F-16s were to be speeded up, and new equipment would include air-to-surface and air-to-air missiles, tanks, armored personnel carriers, and an elaborate early-warning system for the Negev. Over the decade ahead, however, General Ezer Weizmann, Israel's defense minister, said that purchases would be 25 per cent lower than those estimated before the treaty.

In June 1979, Israel illegally used six F-15s and all four of its E-2C Hawkeye control planes in a successful battle with Syrian MiG-21s in Lebanese airspace. To mollify the angry Washington reaction, Tel Aviv offered the Pentagon information on this use of F-15s and E-2s in actual battle conditions. The Israeli report said the Hawkeyes detected the MiGs during their takeoff roll in Syria and that they vectored the F-15s to them. The report claimed the missiles used were all Israeli-made Shafrirs. Five Syrian aircraft were shot down. Republican congressman Paul Findley of Illinois later introduced a token motion to block five further proposed military sales to Israel, including one for two more E-2Cs.

By then, U.S. reports said Israel was planning for a total tactical fighter force of six hundred aircraft, possibly replacing its McDonnell-Douglas F-4s and A-4s with that firm's F/A-18s or, if Carter relented on his export ban, F-18Ls. Aviation Week said Israel would get some of the F-16s refused by Iran, and would thus get earlier delivery of them than anticipated—despite the end-use infringements of the F-15s over Lebanon. The magazine said Israel would continue to buy 90 per cent of its imported arms and 98 per cent of its military aircraft in the United

States, and hoped for more helicopters, to be co-produced by the local
MATA plant, along with more TOW and Dragon antitank missiles. But
there would, *Aviation Week* said, be no need for further imports of remotely piloted vehicles (RPVs) because Israel's own new Scout RPV
could reach 10,000 feet and had an autonomy of 4.5 hours. The Scout is
launched by a truck and recovered by a net.

U.S./Egypt

The linchpin of America's efforts to procure a peace between Israel
and supporters of the dispossessed Palestinians has been Egypt, the larg-
est and most important—and one of the poorest—of the countries in the
Middle East. Egypt depended militarily for nearly two decades on the
Soviet Union, which considered Egyptian soldiers the best in the area.
The breach with the Kremlin in 1972, the role of the Israeli lobby in
Washington in largely scuttling White House plans to replace Russia as
Egypt's armorer, Sadat's consequent continuing uneasy arms relationship
with Moscow, and Cairo's dependence on Saudi financial assistance all
combined with catastrophic economic crises to make Egypt's efforts to
keep its armed forces at credible strength after 1973 a tangled skein of
weapons diplomacy.

In April 1975, as mentioned earlier, Egypt was selected as the first site
for a joint Arab arms industry, with initial—largely Saudi—funding of $1
billion over five years. Beside Saudi Arabia, the partners were Qatar and
the United Arab Emirates. First production was to be of antitank missiles, with aircraft planned for a later stage. Some reports indicated
planned production of chemical and nerve-gas warheads. The Helwan
program firmed up in 1978. It predominantly involved European arms
designs, and so will be looked at in Chapter 9. U.S. involvement was limited to the franchised production of Jeeps for bearing antitank weapons.

When a group of thirteen U.S. senators, led by Democrat Abe Ribicoff
and Republican Howard Baker, visited Cairo in November 1976 to study
safeguards for potential U.S. nuclear reactors in Egypt, Iran and Israel,
Sadat appealed to them to authorize American arms for Egypt.
He noted that Israel had received a massive resupply from America, and
Syria from the Soviet Union, and added: "I think it's an obligation now. I
have proved myself to you." He offered to recognize Israel if Israel
would "adhere to the principles of international law."

In April 1977, preliminary negotiations were completed for the sale of
200 Northrop F-5Es and F-5s (two-seat trainers) to Egypt, and the proposed transfer went to Carter's desk for approval. Northrop said the ne-

gotiations had been on a government-to-government level. The F-5s, which are secondary defense systems in the Mideast context, not front-line fighters, would replace about 200 MiG-21s and MiG-17s and some Su-7 fighter-bombers which had gone out of service for shortage of parts since 1973, and were not intended to balance out Israel's 550 frontline combat aircraft; balancing those remained essentially the task of the air-craft which France was offering Egypt in co-production, and of the remaining MiG-23s. The F-5 sale was recommended largely to set a precedent—of U.S. sales of combat aircraft to Egypt—and to help Sadat show his officers and people that in putting almost all his eggs in the Washington basket he had not been taken for a ride by the Americans. The Egyptians, in short, saw the sale as "political" and precedent-setting, not as doing much for Egyptian defense.

As if emphasizing Egypt's difficult relationship with Moscow, in February the Soviet Union returned only 25 of 175 MiG-21 engines which had been sent to Russia for overhaul, along with an equally small number of other aviation and marine engines. Sadat then canceled his military pact with the Soviet Union, annulling Soviet naval rights. He also "canceled" his debt of $4 billion to Moscow, thus easing a burden on the Egyptian defense budget—until then nearly one third of the entire budget.

Later, Carter won congressional approval to sell 14 additional C-130s to Egypt for $184.4 million (6 had been sold earlier) and 12 pilotless, C-130-launched Teledyne Ryan 124-R Firebee reconnaissance drones with cameras, for Sinai monitoring, at a cost of $66.5 million. Congress also approved $100,000 for Egyptian aircrew training. But the F-5 order was reduced from 200 to 120—with 50 for immediate delivery (a sale approved by Congress in May 1978 as part of the controversial "package" of warplanes for Saudi Arabia, Israel and Egypt). The first 8 came from stocks originally promised to Ethiopia.

The previous year, China had supplied Egypt with some "Soviet" spare parts, and in 1979 Sadat announced that Peking had promised more aid Later in 1977, the Carter administration, in a straight "weapons-diplomacy" bid to help the Egyptian Air Force, authorized General Electric and Lockheed, in cooperation with Rolls-Royce, to repair the airframes and Tumansky engines of the MiG-21s in Europe, notably in Britain, where Rolls-Royce had experience of the Tumansky. This device was meant to evade congressional interference, but a Hill battle soon ensued.

The Israeli embassy had stopped Jewish lobbying against the C-130s and the drones, but the lobby was encouraged to protest against the MiG deal: Senators Humphrey, Case, Church and Stone sent a letter to

Vance. Prompted by the embassy, lobbyists said U.S. know-how of MiGs had been obtained from Israel; but General Fish said the U.S. contractors would be working from manuals provided by Egypt, to which country they had been supplied by the Soviet Union. Under pressure, Lockheed and GE said they would return the MiGs to their original condition, not upgrade them. The White House held firm, but Egypt, mistrustful of the vicissitudes of Congress, finally gave the contract exclusively to Rolls-Royce. Sadat was, however, weighing purchase of American HUD (head-up display) weapons-aiming systems for his MiG-21s: This would immensely improve the destructive power of the aircraft.

With the signature of the peace treaty, Egypt was approved by the White House to receive F-4s, but no F-16s "for the moment." In all, Cairo was initially promised about $1.5 billion in additional arms aid, along with $500 million of extra economic support. New U.S. equipment for Egypt, beside the Phantoms, was to include Hawk surface-to-air missile batteries, four destroyers, submarines, tanks and armored personnel carriers.

But when Saudi Arabia later withdrew all financing for the F-5s and all investment in the AOI, the United States agreed to supply the fighters on credit and to help finance an all-Egyptian version of the arms complex. A twenty-man U.S. mission went to Cairo in August 1979 to look at the Helwan plant, which held on to equipment already supplied at Riyadh's expense.

U.S./Jordan

Jordan, which has never veered from the American sphere of influence since Britain's withdrawal from "east of Suez" responsibilities, finally began taking delivery, in 1977, of the 14 Hawk surface-to-air missile batteries, 300 General Dynamics Redeye shoulder-fired missiles and 100 Vulcan antiaircraft guns which had been the center of an Israeli-lobby controversy in 1975. Agreement to deliver came after Soviet Air Marshal Pavel Kutakhov flew into Amman and offered Hussein Soviet surface-to-air missiles, MiG-23s and T-62 tanks, and after Amman agreed to make the Hawk batteries permanently "nonmobile" (which is not possible). By then, Saudi Arabia had agreed on an increased price for the American package—$540 million. The strongest Israeli lobby opposition came to the $5 million order for Redeyes, which can be used to defend against low-flying attacks on military and civilian targets.

In late 1976 and early 1977, both Egypt and Syria announced support for a Palestinian solution that would virtually absorb "Palestine" (meaning the West Bank and the Gaza Strip) into Jordan, thus enhancing Jordan's Western acceptance and bargaining power. But later Syria wavered, and Jordan remained a minor-league country, militarily, in the area. Its air force has taken no important deliveries since the arrival of 30 F-5Es, with Sidewinders, in 1975. These were supplied, at a unit cost of $2.7 million, under the final phases of the Military Assistance Program. The Army, which took delivery of 100 M-60 main battle tanks in 1972, ordered 50 more in 1975. In April 1977, Carter talked with Hussein in Washington and agreed to sell $64 million of additional antiaircraft defenses to Jordan. But after Jordan opposed the Camp David accords of 1978, and the subsequent Egypt/Israel peace treaty, there was no further talk of U.S. military sales to Amman.

U.S./Iran

Iran, which has taken delivery of over $10 billion of arms from the United States in recent years—and was awaiting further deliveries for about the same sum when the revolution of 1978 began—while receiving by no means negligible amounts of military supplies from Western Europe, stands in marked contrast. Iran has been neither as loyal nor as long-term a friend as Jordan, but it is bigger, richer, geographically more strategic, and a source of oil. After the retaliatory closure of CIA listening posts in Turkey in 1975, those in Iran became more crucial. Although Muslim, Iran has not been challenged by Israeli expansion in the way Jordan has been and continues to be; and Iran, being non-Arab, managed to remain Israel's almost exclusive supplier of foreign oil—thus appearing, at the time, to give Teheran an interesting bargaining-chip in a final Palestine settlement. Finally, Iran was governed by a Shah who, despite his abysmal record on human rights, seemed in the eyes of the State Department and the Pentagon to be of statesmanlike stature.

The U.S. relationship with Iran went back to the restoration of the Shah after the overthrow of the Mossadegh regime. Kermit Roosevelt, Miles Copeland, Brigadier H. Norman Schwarzkopf—famous twenty years earlier as the New Jersey state police officer who investigated the Lindbergh kidnapping—managed this spectacular affair with the help of three other CIA officers and seven Iranian secret agents. They replaced Mossadegh with a regime headed by General Fazollah Zahedi—whose son later became a famous ambassador in Washington. The general at once concluded a secret agreement with an oil consortium highly favorable to U.S. companies. Britain lost its oil monopoly in Iran; Gulf and

Standard Oil of New Jersey got 40 per cent of the fields. It was the start of a wider expansion of U.S. interests. By 1967, U.S. firms which before World War Two had controlled 10 per cent of Mideast oil revenues now controlled 59 per cent of them.

Later nationalizations, in Iran and elsewhere in the area, passed overt control of oil to local governments, but left extraction policy and marketing in the hands of the U.S. technicians. The increased oil wealth of the oil-producing countries, especially Iran, was to a large measure spent on arms, mostly American.

By 1975, well over half the U.S. orders for $4.3 billion of arms for countries on the Persian Gulf came from Iran. The previous year, orders from Iran and Saudi Arabia had totaled nearly $6.5 billion. In 1976, further projected Iranian arms orders from the United States alone were estimated at $5 billion, slightly higher for 1977. Defense budgets in the Gulf rose from a total of $1.6 billion in 1971 to about $18 billion in 1976. Iran's annual military budget, which was $217 million in 1965, and reached $10 billion a decade later, was expected, before the country's political troubles of 1978, to reach $20 billion by 1985.

The ambitious Shah first asked for F-4s in 1966, when they were the hottest thing in the Mideast sky. Even Israel did not have them, then. Characteristically, Iran already had F-5s. The 1967 Senate hearings on Mideast arms sales, following the "Six-Day War," questioned the wisdom of selling to "non-Allies." Henry Kuss defended his sales program energetically, saying of the Shah: "He has expressed his desire to meet his military requirements from the United States, but he has made it abundantly clear also that if the United States is unwilling or unable to meet his major military requirements, he is determined to go elsewhere to acquire what he needs."

Indeed, the Shah had made motions toward buying Soviet missiles, ostensibly for a defense against an attack by Nasser. The United States had dissuaded him by agreeing to sell F-4s, even though there was a shortage of F-4s in Vietnam at the time. The Shah did in fact buy some military items from Moscow—starting with a not insignificant order for $110 million—and Moscow also agreed to build him a $280 million steel mill. Iran paid the Soviet Union in natural gas, a recently discovered fortune which had previously been flared off, delivered to the Soviet border by a British-built pipeline; but the Senate in 1967 was even more exercised about Iran's role in the West German conspiracy to supply planes to Pakistan in defiance of the U.S.-led Western arms embargo.

At times, the exchanges in the hearings were acrimonious, presaging many more such debates to come. The State Department's Jeffrey Kitchen came under fire:

Kitchen: I think it is our intention and our policy to try to limit, as we have been trying to do in the past, the amount of equipment that we provide to the area, and limit the amount that any one country purchases from the United States.

Sen. Symington: How can you say we have been trying to limit arms sales when in five years it has grown from $300 million a year to $1.7 billion a year?

Kitchen insisted that although the United States sought to sell as many arms as possible to developed countries, sales would go to underdeveloped countries "only to the extent that we feel it doesn't impinge on their economies or create local situations of tension."

In spite of the dramatic buildup of arms for Israel that followed the 1967 Senate hearings, Iran remained the principal customer in the area. In May 1972, as noted in Chapter 6, President Nixon agreed to sell the Shah any nonnuclear weapons system he wanted, and instructed State and the Pentagon accordingly. The same year, Teheran ordered 6 P-3F Orions, a singularly sophisticated antisubmarine warfare system for the area, for $98 million. These were delivered in 1975 with Harpoon missiles; by this time, Iran was negotiating to buy 2 more of the aircraft. In 1973, it was finally allowed to order 140 F-4Es for $450 million. A two-year delivery schedule started the following year. The same year, Iran ordered 141 more F-5Es at a cost of $1,160,000 each, with Sidewinder missiles; deliveries of these also began the following year.

That fall, war broke out between Egypt/Syria and Israel, although not for reasons related to U.S. sales. The unspoken argument in favor of arms "for petrodollars" for Iran and Saudi Arabia had been that, if Israeli superiority reached a point where Israeli forces might, say, attack Cairo, the "balance" would be maintained by these two noncombatant Muslim countries making sufficient weapons transfers to the victim to save it. Moreover, Saudi Arabia could conceivably intervene directly in the Negev. With Iran, through oil, as Israel's second crutch after the United States, Jerusalem, as noted earlier, was hard put to lobby against Teheran.

In 1974, Iran ordered 80 F-14s, the U. S. Navy's front-rank fighter, with over 400 Phoenix missiles. (Deliveries began in 1976, before the plane was in wing service with U.S. forces, and were completed in 1978.) It was also in 1974 that Iran ordered the 6 *Spruance*-class destroyers for over $700 million—an order later reduced to 4. The 7,800-ton ships would have over 200 of the new, improved Harpoon missiles.

That year, Richard R. Violette, director of Sales Negotiations at the Pentagon, told senior U.S. officers:

Iran is the largest purchaser of defense equipment from the U. S. Government under Foreign Military Sales . . . Iran continues to modernize its armed services on a long-term basis in order to meet its defense requirements well into the 1980s . . . the United States maintains a MAAG of 200 persons to supervise and administer these programs.

Iran's military requirements are based on Iran's concern for the security of its northern border with the USSR and its western border with Iraq. Although relations with the USSR are cordial, Iran feels it must, on a contingency basis, consider how it would defend itself in the event of a global or local conflict. Iran also feels it must be prepared to deter any aggression from Iraq and, if deterrence fails, defend its airspace and territory.

However, Robert Berman, a defense analyst at Brookings, wrote in 1976 that:

As the Soviet-Iranian détente has moved forward, the deployment of Iranian military forces has been altered to reflect the new international situation and Iranian ambitions. In the late 1960s, Iranian army units were moved from the northern border area to southwest of Teheran. The Iranian Navy moved its headquarters to Shiraz in the south. Three fourths of the F-14s that Iran has ordered from the United States will be based in the central southern parts of the country. This pattern suggests that Iran is much more concerned with dominating the politics of the Gulf than it is with the Soviet threat.

By 1976, the spending spree of the Shah and his Vice Minister of War, Air Force General Hassan Toufanian, had eased down a few notches; but that year still found them seeking (unsuccessfully) 1,000 Leopard-II main battle tanks from Germany, for delivery in 1978, and then buying British Chieftains instead.

A 1975 survey of "Arms in the Persian Gulf" by Dale Tahtinen found the Iranian Air Force distinctly superior to the air forces of its enemy, Iraq, and rival, Saudi Arabia, combined. Its air defenses, including 37 improved Hawk batteries, were also better. Moreover, Teheran was by then hoping—under the Nixon "blank check"—to buy 50 F-15s (which the U. S. Air Force wanted him to buy to reduce its own per-unit procurement costs) and was beginning to show an interest in the F-18. Iran's helicopter fleet of 108 planes was to be augmented by 535 more on order from the United States (the following year, a further 312 were ordered from Italy); Iraq, at the time, had only 69 choppers, Arabia 30. Iran's order included 202 AH-1J assault helicopters with a multisensor fire-control system for night attacks.

Iran's slight inferiority in tanks—920, including only 460 M-60s and 60 Chieftains, compared to Iraq's 1,065 (including 900 T-54s and -55s and possibly a few T-62s)—was soon to be offset by the Shah's order for 740 more Chieftains from Britain. By 1976, the order was increased, first to 1,250, then to 2,250, to London's delight. Iran was already ahead in armored personnel carriers, and in naval craft. As well as the 4 new American destroyers on order, the Shah had decided to buy 3 U.S. submarines, and 31 missile patrol boats from the United States and France.

Iran was also ahead in local production facilities, including Iran Aircraft Industries, jointly owned by the local government and Northrop.

In recent years, Iran had seized islands in the Persian Gulf which belonged to two of the Trucial States (but were much closer to the Iranian coast) and there had been speculation that its export of skilled workers to small states in the Arabian peninsula presaged future claims. But any intervention in Arabia was expected to draw a pan-Arab response. More possible is Iranian intervention in Afghanistan and India—both countries are within the reach of Iran's Phantoms, F-5s and Orions, all of which are refuelable in flight.

Tahtinen echoed concern about the inflow of thousands of U.S. military and civilian advisers into Iran and Saudi Arabia—24,000 already, by early 1976. (A 1976 Senate Foreign Relations Committee report spoke of "problems . . . due to the presence of large numbers of young, single American male civilians without adequate recreational outlet . . . especially in more traditional cities such as Isfahan"—presumably a reference to the Bell pilots' strike.) An alternative was more Iranian training in the United States. By 1976, 11,000 Iranian officers had been trained in America, and the numbers grew yearly.

This was apparently a sensitive question. In 1978, when the writer visited Oceana Naval Air Station, where Iranian pilots are trained, he was shown how to operate some of the ultrasophisticated command systems of an E-2C but not allowed to see or speak to Iranian trainees. By then, most of the eighty F-14s had been delivered to Iran, and Iranian pilots and weapons officers were being trained at Oceana in batches of four or five at a time. These were courses of five or six months' duration (depending on the weather), giving pilots between thirty and fifty hours in the air.

Thus, a complex picture of American weapons diplomacy in Iran emerges—understandably, considering the huge sums of money, the complexity of systems and the serried legions of advisers and their dependents involved. The arms firms sought sales; the embassy sought to keep the Shah happy by getting him the weapons he wanted; Defense sought the advantages of extending the production lines by selling to Iran; Pentagon representative Erich von Marbod, an object of obvious suspicion to all, was there to be the honest broker, counterbalanced by the earlier-mentioned Colonel Hallock—Schlesinger's man—who was now in the pay of the Shah.

In 1976, a drop in demand for Iranian crude forced an oil-price cut and a temporary cash shortage in Teheran. When Henry Kissinger arrived at the Niavaran Palace in August, the Shah offered him a barter deal: He would pay for his arms purchases and the newly ordered U.S. nuclear reactors with oil. Ford, then campaigning for re-election on a flagging record of seeking less dependence on foreign sources of energy, later rejected the plan. When the Shah said grimly that he might have to raise oil prices later that year to pay his arms bills—which were also rising constantly with inflation—the lame-duck Ford White House briefly discussed threatening to cut arms to Iran. But it was not hard to see that armorer and client had each other by the hair. Eventually, the Shah ordered Toufanian to make some economies in arms-purchasing himself, muttering one day: "Hassan, it is better to be defeated than bankrupt!"

When the new U.S. Defense Secretary, Dr. Harold Brown, took over in 1977, he sent a Washington lawyer, R. Kenly Webster, to Teheran to fill von Marbod's old job for three months and make a report. One of von Marbod's last acts was to recommend deferral of building the Chah Bahar air-naval base in southeast Iran. This was to be the base for the Shah's Indian Ocean fleet, led by the *Spruance*-class destroyers. Construction was in fact slowed but not deferred.

One obvious problem for the Shah was the new emphasis on human rights, and growing—sometimes violent—opposition within the country. *The New York Review of Books* published a lengthy article in October 1976 by Reza Baraheni, an exiled Iranian writer, claiming that an average of 1,500 people were arrested for political reasons every month. Amnesty International alleged that year that the total number of political prisoners held in Iran in 1975 was "anything from 25,000 to 100,000." Amnesty said Iran had "the highest rate of death penalties in the world, no valid system of civilian courts and a history of torture which is beyond belief."

Baraheni, who graphically described the tools and methods of torture, asserted that as many as 5,000 people had sometimes been rounded up in a day by SAVAK strongmen. He said that "95 per cent of all the available press in the country is in the hands of two families who take their orders from the Shah and the police." A Turkish-speaking Azerbaijani, Baraheni claimed his people numbered 10 million out of the country's 35 million people but said they were not allowed to be educated or to write in Turkish. Only Farsi is permitted—although Baraheni said the Shah himself spoke Farsi badly, preferring English and French. He claimed

similar repression of the Kurds, Arabs, Baluchis and religious minorities
—Christians, Jews, Bahais and Zoroastrians.

In February 1977, Democratic senators John Culver of Iowa and
Thomas Eagleton of Missouri returned from Teheran with a statement
criticizing an "authoritarian nation whose internal policies often appear
antithetical to American values." The statement mentioned "serious allegations of repression, violations of human rights, and even torture." The
United States should not appear to "support or strengthen these un-
desirable practices." The senators called for an "arm's-length relationship,
based only upon cold calculations of national interests and without hypocritical declarations of warm friendship."

In May, however, Secretary Vance told reporters in Iran that Washington could continue to be Iran's main arms supplier without linking the
sales to human-rights considerations. The Administration approved an
Iranian order for 160 F-16s, with Sparrow missiles, at the same flyaway
price and virtually the same R & D recoupment cost as for NATO countries. Vance admitted the human-rights question had come up in discussions with the Shah at the Niavaran Palace, but reporters apparently did
not ask him who raised it. Only in 1978, in the face of mounting riots, did
the Shah release most political prisoners and agree to a wide program of
democratic concessions.

The month before Vance's 1977 visit, Carter had approved the sale of
7 of the 9 AWACS planes requested by Iran for $112.4 million each,
including support costs, and agreed to consider the request for an
additional 140 F-16s. As with the victory of the B-52 and the air-
launched cruise missile over the B-1, the AWACS sale, despite some opposition on Capitol Hill, seemed safe because it was a Boeing project and
therefore "protected" by powerful Senator Henry Jackson of Washington.
This, as noted in the previous chapter, was probably what dictated the
Shah's choice of it over the $30 million Grumman E-2C Hawkeye, a sys-
tem already in proven USAF service. (Israel, with less problems in
Congress, and no problems with Jackson at all, had ordered 4 Hawkeyes.) U.S. experts had earlier rejected a $15 billion plan for 40 Seek
Sentry mountaintop radar stations as more vulnerable, less effective,
and five times more expensive than radar planes. Work went ahead, how-
ever, with the Ibex listening posts to supplement or replace those lost in
Turkey through the Turkish arms embargo.

The AWACS sale went through, but not without opposition. Senators
Culver, Proxmire, Eagleton, Mathias and Nelson ordered a GAO report
which was largely unfavorable to the transfer. The GAO relied heavily
on testimony from CIA director Stansfield Turner that U.S. security

might be jeopardized if an Iranian AWACS crew defected to Russia. But Turner did not come down against the sale. He noted that secret encoding equipment would not be included on the Iranian models and said that Iranian security had proven, so far, as good as NATO's. Other state-of-the-art equipment in the AWACS was no more advanced than Iran had already acquired by the purchase of F-14s and Phoenix missiles, he said. The Pentagon said that the chances of all crew members of such a plane (from seventeen to twenty-three people) defecting at the same time was remote. No one seriously believed, then, that virtually the entire Air Force might collapse under the strains of a civil rising.

Culver, backed by fifteen other senators, mostly Democrats, kept up his opposition to the sale, as did Congressman Gerry Studds of Cape Cod in the House. Testifying for the Administration, Secretary Vance gave seven reasons for the transfer: Iran was a strong and friendly power; it was a source of stability in a volatile region and had "no territorial claim against its neighbors"; Iran played a constructive role in the Middle East and had not participated in the oil embargo; it was a major oil supplier to western Europe and Japan; it had ratified the nuclear nonproliferation treaty; Iran was cooperating with the United States in "sensitive areas . . . very important to our national security"; and Iran was strategic.

Culver tried a blocking resolution, noting that the Russians were offering $4 million to any West German who would deliver an F-4 to the Soviet Union. He asked: "If a twenty-year-old aircraft with ten-year-old radar is worth $4 million, what would they offer for an AWACS?" Congress, however, began to feel the White House pressure. Carter delayed resubmitting the sale for thirty days to assure passage. Iran weighed in, angrily "withdrawing" its offer to buy.

Finally, a compromise was hammered out, involving increased Iranian security measures, no AWACS overflights of Iran's neighbors, all training to be carried out in the United States, and talk of a possible reduction in future sales of fighters to Iran because of their increased effectiveness with AWACS. No U.S. citizens were to serve in the plane over Iran. On examination, none of these provisions seemed, in the long term, to be more than congressional face-saving. To save face further, Congress delayed the sale until October 1, when fiscal 1978 began, so as to keep 1977 sales figures overtly lower. But a bid by Democratic senator Frank Church of Idaho to place a one-year moratorium on sales of advanced military equipment to Iran was defeated in the Senate Foreign Relations Committee. Significantly, when Iran collapsed in turmoil in 1978, U.S. security concerns became a major issue. The Pentagon at once readied plans to remove all 77 F-14s still in flying condition, along with classified equipment removed from 3 damaged or destroyed in crashes, and to remove sensitive components from Ibex listening posts. None of the AWACS planes had been delivered.

In the same period, Carter approved 31 additional F-4s for Iran, to replace some lost in training. But the President delayed submitting the sale to Capitol Hill until the following year, when McDonnell-Douglas' plan to close the F-4 assembly line made it urgent. With Sidewinder, Sparrow and improved Maverick missiles, needed for Iran's F-14s and F-5s, the tab came to $370 million. That year, the White House approved a further $225 million of sales of artillery and trucks to Iran; this was to bring total deliveries of U.S. military equipment to Iran for fiscal 1979 to nearly $3 billion.

The Administration was still officially committed to an arms-sale ceiling of $8.6 billion for 1978 to areas outside Japan, Australasia and NATO —and this ceiling was intended to cover, as well, large sales to Israel and South Korea. But the Shah was not discouraged. He had about $10 billion of further U.S. orders waiting on his arms shopping list, for the eighties.

In short, the Shah's U.S. relationship, until the 1978 riots, seemed secure. The monarch held himself ready to mediate in the Middle East. Iranian forces served with the UN on the Golan Heights and in Lebanon. The Shah was a major U.S. oil supplier, and a host to important U.S. surveillance facilities. When the Shah came to Washington shortly before the end of 1977, he requested 3 more AWACS, the other 140 F-16s, the 250 F-18Ls refused earlier, 100 more transport aircraft and 6 navy patrol ships. The F-18Ls were eventually to replace Iran's 221 F-4s; Pentagon officials naturally suggested he buy F-15s, the U. S. Air Force's top fighter, instead of the F-18Ls, but he was not convinced. The following year, Iran expanded its contract with Bell Helicopter, changing the original co-production plan from 400 single-engine Bell 214A troop transports to 50 214As and 350 twin-turbine, 19-passenger Bell 214STs. This raised the contract price from $500 million to over $600 million. The plant was due to be finished in 1979, with production running from 1980 through 1985. Bell and Iran were developing a new version of the 214ST and hoping to sell 4,000 worldwide. The Shah seemed about to go into weapons diplomacy himself. But the program was suspended in December 1978, when Iran defaulted on a quarterly payment: 170 instructors at Isfahan quit, and 137 said they would not renew contracts. Bell and Iran began discussing a stretched-out program, but the following month the embattled Shah canceled the program altogether.

In late 1978, the ruler, due for his 31 Phantom replacements, now asked for the latest, single-engined "Wild Weasel" (F-4G) version (which uses the same engine as the F-18) with Sparrow missiles, special countermeasures, and similar radar to the F-16. Carter turned him down, against Pentagon advice. Instead, he offered standard F-4Es with 1,000 Shrike missiles. The price for fighters and missiles had risen to $455 million. Iran accepted the missiles, despite their lack of a "radar-blinding" capability, but hesitated over the Phantoms, hoping to find more updated equipment elsewhere. But with the Phantom assembly line due to close in 1981, the Shah was thought likely to take the aircraft offered if he could pay in oil. In January, as troubles mounted, the Shah canceled the Shrike order and decided against the F-4 purchase.

Despite hints, earlier, that the Shah would cut back on defense spending and devote more money to social programs, Iran's shopping list for the years beginning in fiscal 1980 had included 150 more C-130 transports (100 more than originally asked), the 70 more F-14s (for a total of 150), the 140 more F-16s (making 300 in all), 11 RF-4 reconnaissance planes, 6 P-3 antisubmarine warfare aircraft, 12 Boeing-707 refuelers, and the 3 additional AWACS planes.

One other interesting order was for new naval vessels. To keep under the U.S. sales ceiling for Third World countries, the Shah was encouraged by General Fish and U.S. ambassador William H. Sullivan to buy 8 guided-missile frigates in Dutch and West German shipyards instead of in America, and to buy in the United States only the sophisticated weaponry for the ships—needed as escorts for the U.S.-made *Spruance*-class destroyers which the Shah has ordered. Several members of Congress found the device absurd, as it meant passing a $2 billion order to Europe and keeping only a $350 million one for America, without limiting the arms race. But the Shah accepted the advice—and decided to buy 12 frigates instead of 8.

Said leading Republican congressman Paul Findley: "Simply put, the armaments we have agreed to sell cost less money and therefore fit within an arbitrary and meaningless gross dollar ceiling on arms sales the Administration has set. Therefore, this country finds itself in the ludicrous position of selling the armament or 'lethal' components to Iran while it refuses to sell the 'nonlethal' ships merely because the former are cheaper than the latter."

In 1978, a religious riot in which fanatics burned a provincial movie theater, killing several people, blossomed with amazing speed into a revolution, led from a Paris suburb by an obscure divine, the *ayatollah* (teacher) Khomeini, with a direct-dial telephone to his followers in Iran. The country's left-wing and moderate discontented joined a nationwide rising against the Shah, who fled into exile.

The revolutionary regime at first seemed intent on canceling all the Shah's military orders. But many were already partly or fully paid for, and cancellation of others involved contractual compensations. For about $12 billion of orders already "in the pipeline," Iran had already paid—or would have to pay to cancel—a total of about $9 billion. Nevertheless, most orders were in fact annulled.

The 7 AWACS planes, on which few funds had yet been engaged, were dropped, thus increasing their unit price for NATO and renewing Washington pressure on France to buy a couple; but France was still considering the Hawkeye, the British Nimrod, or increased purchases of its own Dassault-Bréguet Atlantique, while other NATO countries considered either reducing their order to compensate for the increased price, or reviving the plan to build AWACS out of the European Airbus instead of the Boeing 747.

The additional 140 F-16s were canceled without difficulty, but the 160 already "in the pipeline" were also refused. Saudi Arabia, Turkey, Greece, South Korea, Canada, Australia and other countries were interested in buying some, but the USAF seemed the most likely gainer, asking for—and expecting to get—the 55 already on the assembly line. General Dynamics said that, with diverted sales and cancellation fees, the company would not suffer.

The $600 million Bell helicopter plant at Isfahan was abandoned in the building stage, leaving the company with only a reduced training program for pilots and engineers. The Chah Bahar naval base project was scaled down. The order for 4 (originally 6) *Spruance*-class destroyers was reduced to 2, with the U. S. Navy anxious to purchase the other couple.

TOW antitank missiles and Mavericks on order were expected to be delivered, it was said in 1979, but plans for co-producing others in Iran were canceled. Teheran dropped its space program. The 31 F-4 replacements were refused, and 16 of them, already on the assembly line, were offered to Egypt. The order for 1,000 Shrike missiles was canceled.

There was a great deal of excitement over the fate of the supersecret equipment in the F-14s and the Phoenix missiles. Egypt offered sanctuary for the 77 remaining F-14s (2 had crashed, while another was under repair in the United States), and Grumman even prepared plans for seizing the planes with the help of U.S. civilian pilots and defecting Iranian airmen. When that project fizzled, Saudi Arabia offered to buy the 78 aircraft and their missiles; Iran first decided to keep them, then tentatively offered them to the U. S. Navy for $10 million–$13 million each, or half the original purchase price. The order for 70 more F-14s and 400 more Phoenixes, which would have had trouble in Congress in any case, was canceled. The U. S. Navy bought the Phoenixes, but the cancellation of the Tomcats—plus the prospect of the Navy's buying used planes instead of new ones—was a blow to Grumman.

Other cancellations of U.S. equipment included 360 Hawk surface-to-air missiles, 200 Harpoon antiship missiles—at once requested by the U. S. Navy—and 400 torpedoes.

In July 1979, a GAO report, "Financial and Legal Implications of Iran's Cancellation of Arms Purchase Agreements," said that the Pentagon's failure to require foreign countries to maintain sufficient funds in escrow to cover possible cancellation penalties meant that the U. S. Treasury would be $800 million out of pocket because of Iran's potential "disarmament" policy. The Pentagon denied the charge, saying Iranian funds in the United States, along with replacement sales to other countries and to the U.S. military of the "Iranian" weapons, would cover or render unnecessary the penalties.

Arms-sale critics pointed to Iran as evidence of the dangers of transferring sophisticated equipment, much of it secret, to Third World countries. For all one knows, voices may have been raised in the Kremlin, in 1972, as to whether the Soviet Union should have delivered all that expensive weaponry to Egypt. But the Russians went on to run similar risks to the Egyptian one, in Ethiopia a few years later, and it seems unlikely that the Iranian experience will be much more chastening to Washington than the Egyptian experience was for Moscow.

U.S./Saudi Arabia

Saudi Arabia, because of its huge orders for military infrastructure—80 per cent or more of its arms purchases—had been America's second-best arms customer, but moved into first place in 1978. It is both an enemy of the third—Israel—and was a rival of the first, Iran. Arabian enmity is long-standing with the Aryan Iranians, who are Shi'a Muslims, because of the almost "papal" role among Sunnis of Arabia's ruling house of Saud. This was founded by Abdul Aziz ibn-Saud after the capture of Riyadh in 1902. He made political marriages with more than a dozen daughters of prominent chieftains, sired over forty sons and numerous daughters, and today has an estimated seven thousand "royal family" descendants who have a finger in every pie. If the Iranians won out to become the chief military power in the Gulf area, it was not because of oil —Arabia possessed even more—but because of Iran's greater education and sophistication, in twentieth-century terms.

Not surprisingly, in view of Saudi Arabia's importance as an oil supplier and as a force for conservative moderation in the area, the decision to build up the Saudi forces was as much American as Saudi. Early in 1974, plans were revealed in Washington to sell the Saudis half a billion dollars worth of F-5s and naval equipment. Reporters were told that F-4s had also been offered to replace British Lightnings, but that the Saudis were hesitant about the cost; at the time, no other Arab country had the Phantom.

In November that year, Assistant Defense Secretary Ellsworth and George Vest, then director of the State Department's politico-military bureau, flew to Riyadh with recommendations that the Saudi Government spend billions of dollars over the next ten years on more aircraft, 440 helicopters, 26 new ships, tanks, other armor, and equipment to create a paratroop brigade. These weapons, said the Pentagon survey, would give the country the capabilities to "deter aggression and defeat an enemy." That year, Arabia ordered 300 improved Hawk missile batteries, for delivery in the 1976–79 period, at a cost of $270 million.

If Riyadh was coy about buying F-4s, it was because France had already offered an apparently better deal: 38 Mirage III/5 fighter-bombers for a package price, including missiles, of $860 million, with delivery between 1975 and 1978. In 1976, Saudi Araba placed a tentative order for 48 of Dassault's latest F-1s in an "arms for oil" barter contract. But in 1975, the Saudis had increased their order for F-5s to 110, for $756 million. The figure included funding for R & D on special equipment for these F-5s, to enable the aircraft to carry Maverick air-to-surface missiles. The Saudi Air Force bought both French air-to-air missiles—Matra Magics—and American Sidewinders.

During this period, the United States was also building up the Saudi National Guard, a Bedouin force fiercely loyal to the house of Saud and used mainly to guard oil lines and installations. A United States Military Training Mission arrived in the country in 1974. But the principal defense contribution to Arabia from the United States came in the form of construction of airfields, ports, roads and buildings. By 1974, there were over a hundred members of the U. S. Corps of Engineers in the country. By 1976, when sales agreements with Riyadh were signed for a total of $2.5 billion, over $1.9 billion of this was for "supporting services" and $229 million for "supporting equipment." That particular year, only $247 million—10 per cent—was for weapons and ammunition and $84 million for spare parts.

Arabia, as the main defender of the Muslim faith, had taken vociferous objection from the start to the implanting of a European settler government in Palestine. It was particularly opposed to Israeli occupation, since 1967, of the Muslim Holy Places of Jerusalem, a city as symbolic to Islam as to Christianity and Judaism. But since 1948 it had not engaged directly in operations to oppose Israeli expansion. Its immense religious and financial power enabled Saudi leaders to handle the Palestine conflict differently from the confrontation states, where leaders dared not sound too "reasonable" for fear of emotional public reactions among their people.

Israel, however, feared Arabia's sophisticated handling of U.S. relations probably more than Syria's alignment with Moscow or even Sadat's disconcerting swing into the American camp. Saudi Arabia, by sea, is as close to Israel as France is to Britain. The Israeli lobby in Washington, led by AIPAC, lobbied furiously over the years against arms for Riyadh. King Faisal, and later King Khalid, almost ignored the campaign. Both publicly expressed their willingness to recognize the existence of Israel after the latter's eventual withdrawal to its 1967 borders; and Arabia's oil minister, Ahmed Yaki Zamani, saved U.S. industry billions each month by keeping a cap on Mideast oil prices, by also keeping prices pegged to the failing dollar, and by increasing production to meet U.S. needs.

Nevertheless, the Israeli lobby had its way with Congress. Morris Amitay, its chief lobbyist, boasted that "we've never lost on a major issue." The 1975 Saudi order for 2,000 Sidewinder AIM-9J air-to-air missiles and for 1,500 Maverick air-to-surface missiles (reduced from an original order of 5,000 and 2,880 respectively) was whittled down by late 1976 to, first, 1,500, then 1,000, then 850 Sidewinders, and to, first, 1,000, then 650 Mavericks. In a September 15, 1976, editorial, "Missile Madness," *Near East Report*, AIPAC's gung-ho newsletter, noted that the Arabians already had 1,024 Mavericks on order and said Saudi "arms" orders for 1976 totaled over $7.5 billion; it said "the Arabs" had a potential three to one advantage over Israel in both weapons and firepower, but did not spell out the arithmetic.

That month, Hubert Humphrey, who over the years had earned larger fees from addressing Jewish audiences than any other member of Congress, and who was chairman of the Senate foreign assistance subcommittee, held public hearings on arms sales to Saudi Arabia. Senator Clifford Case, ranking Republican on the Senate Foreign Relations Committee, whose aide Steve Bryen was a major figure in the Israeli Capitol Hill lobby, offered a resolution of disapproval to block the sale of the Mavericks altogether. But the Senate voted to recommit the measure back to the committee. Only five senators were on the floor at the time—Foreign Relations Committee chairman John Sparkman, Arab-American senator Jim Abourezk, Israeli lobby critic Robert Griffin of Michigan—then the Senate's second-ranking Republican—Democrat James Allen of Alabama and one then pro-Israeli figure, Senator Robert Byrd of West

Virginia. The lobby had been defeated by procedure. Kissinger then managed to get the committee to bury the resolution.

In the House committee, New York's Ben Rosenthal, supported by Drinan and Dodd, proposed a similar disapproval resolution, but a quorum failed to show up for the committee meeting after the White House asked Republicans not to attend. This footwork by Ford's forces got the sale past the thirty-day deadline for congressional approval. Days later, the Congress had adjourned to the hustings.

Rosenthal, nevertheless, had made some interesting points:

> We are selling the A model of the Maverick, which cost us under $20,000 apiece, to the Saudis for B model prices, about $46,000 apiece, apparently in order to develop and procure the C model. This type of back-door financing avoids the congressional authorization process and provides the Pentagon with an additional source of revenue. It amounts to an incentive to unload unwanted or unneeded equipment on a country that may not need it but has money to burn.

He also raised the question of transfers:

> Jordan already has its own F-5 force and its pilots would have no trouble taking over the Saudis' planes and they would need little training to handle the Mavericks. Moreover, Egypt's highly trained Air Force also could easily take over these planes, which were designed for easy operation and maintenance by Third World customers. In fact, intelligence sources report Egyptian pilots already have been getting "orientation" or, if you will, "training" flights on Saudi F-5s.
>
> The Saudis transferred a squadron of Bell 205 Iroquois helicopters to Egypt during the [1973] war, according to intelligence sources. That was in violation of the transfer clause in the purchase agreement with the United States, but this government did nothing about it.

Rosenthal estimated major (multiyear) orders from Saudi Arabia that year as $5 billion for construction and training and $2.5 billion for "hardware," including $1.4 billion in commercial sales. The Administration had also recommended a sale of 1,000 laser-guided bombs for Riyadh, but notification of this had not yet reached the Congress.

In the Senate committee, Democrats Joseph Biden of Delaware and Dick Clark of Iowa had proposed blocking literally all arms sales to Saudi Arabia, Iran and Kuwait—partly in order not to single out the most important "ally" of the three for special punishment. This was easily defeated. The Case bill became the test. The Hill's senior Jewish legislator, Senator "Jack" Javits of New York, had opposed Case "with tears in my heart" because its adoption would mean reneging on the reduced figures for Saudi missiles agreed with the Administration. Senator

McGovern—who had been the first major Hill figure to propose talks with the Palestinians—had backed Javits. Charles Percy of Illinois, under fire for his criticism of the Zionist lobby, had cautiously voted with Case.

Profiled behind the fight was the main point suggested in Rosenthal's statement: That U.S. arms which could not be shipped to such close friends as Egypt or even Jordan because of Jewish lobby pressure could be "stocked" in Saudi Arabia for transfer to confrontation states in time of war, if not used directly by the Arabians themselves. But with a land mass of 927,000 square miles—just over a quarter the size of the United States—and formidably long, sometimes hostile borders, Riyadh (and the Pentagon) could always make a good case for Saudi Arabia's needing substantial defensive systems.

Frost & Sullivan, a New York market-analysis firm, estimated in January 1977 that Arabia would buy between $2.5 billion and $3 billion more arms and equipment from the United States over the next five years, and would probably order either F-14s, -15s or -16s for the Air Force. To its 21 C-130 transports, needed because of the country's vastness and communications problems, 38 more were expected to be added, at a cost of about $300 million, by 1979.

By March, with the Carter White House shaken down, the Israeli lobby was back at work. Carter agreed to "review" the sale, for $1.06 billion, of 580 more Hawk missiles for Saudi Arabia, which would bring the Saudi Hawk arsenal to nearly 900. The contract had been signed just before enactment of a new aid bill in 1976, so Congress had not had an opportunity to oppose or consent. But the President okayed the deal in late April.

Rosenthal wrote the President, reminding him of his campaign rhetoric aimed at Jewish voters:

> On September 30, 1976, while a proposal by the Ford administration to sell Saudi Arabia 650 Maverick missiles was pending before the Congress, you stated: "There is no reason to think these missiles will increase security and stability in the Middle East. There is no reason to think they can be used only for defense. There are only reasons to fear that we will increase the chance of conflict. No administration which was sensitive to the climate in the Middle East would let the sale go forward."

Rosenthal also wrote:

> I believe your firm stand in the campaign against profligate U.S. arms sales was a significant contributing factor in your election. Unfortunately, after looking over notices for many billions in arms transfers delivered to the Congress in recent weeks, it appears to me that this country's policy continues to be "business as usual."

Later, Carter approved 45 F-15s and 15 F-15 trainers for Saudi Arabia, at a cost of $1.5 billion. These were intended to replace the original 45 British Lightnings, of which 38 had survived and of which only about 20 were regularly flyable. Later, he approved more Hawk batteries, C-130s and construction contracts.

By late 1977, Arabia also had 114 F-5s; even with Hawk missile defenses, these were clearly inadequate against Iraq's MiG-23s. The Administration, worried by Jewish pressures, proposed that, rather than buy F-15s, Arabia buy a larger quantity of the less sophisticated F-16. Israeli lobbyists argued that technology was less secure in Arabia than in Iran, because of the large Palestinian population in Arabia; but the major difference between the two countries, from Israel's point of view, was Israel's dependence on Iranian oil.

In 1978, one of the fiercest Capitol Hill lobby fights of all time developed around Carter's decision to sell Saudi Arabia the 60 F-15s which his administration had approved. The deal was worth $2.5 billion, with deliveries promised between 1981 and 1984. Carter "packaged" the sale with one to Israel of 15 more F-15s (out of 25 requested) and 75 F-16s (out of 150 requested), for a total of $1.5 billion, and one to Egypt (mentioned earlier) for the first 50 F-5s (out of 200 requested and 120 approved by Carter), for $400 million. Congress had to approve sales for all three countries or face a veto. The Saudis would be paying about $45 million per unit for the F-15s, because of training and logistic support, compared to the USAF price of $18 million to $20 million.

The Israeli lobby argued that the Saudis could use the F-15 in a ground-attack role which would be devastating for Israel, while Israel itself denied newspaper reports that it had used its own F-15s in that fashion in Lebanon. The Saudis and the Pentagon said the Saudi planes were required for defense. Their only armament—4 Sidewinders, 4 Sparrows and a 20mm. gun—were all air-to-air. Neither Riyadh nor Arlington could say that "defense" mainly meant defense against Israel; so both the Saudis and the Administration spoke airily of possible threats from Iraq, South Yemen and Ethiopia. The Saudis said that if they were denied F-15s they would buy more French F-1s—which have a greater ground-attack capacity.

The Israelis also argued that the Saudis would not be able to use the F-15 at all, for lack of skills, but in the event of a new Mideast war would turn them over to Jordan or Egypt. Pentagon sources, however, doubted that the Saudis would part with their best aircraft in time of war, and said that since neither Egyptians nor Jordanians had any experience on the complex plane, and none of the requisite command and control equipment, such a transfer would be highly unlikely. Saudi

Arabia could, however, transfer Mirages to Egypt, and F-5s to both Egypt and Jordan.

Defense Secretary Brown, in closed White House discussions, proposed reducing the Israeli part of the package to 40 F-16s, then later restoring it to 75 as a compromise to get the Saudi and Egyptian sales approved; but the Administration decided to stay with the "75" figure, prepared if necessary to see this go higher to clear the whole package. In the event, as noted, Carter confirmed his earlier promise of more F-15s for Israel later, and persuaded Saudi Arabia to agree to some "conditions" which involved no concessions on Riyadh's part. For instance, the Saudis agreed not to ask for additional ordnance wing-pylons which they did not want. They agreed not to transfer the F-15s to other countries without Washington's permission—which, under the Offer of Sale which all foreign buyers of U.S. weapons sign, was a condition they had already accepted a year before. And they agreed not to "acquire any combat aircraft from other countries while . . . preparing for, and receiving, the F-15s." This also changed nothing. Although the Saudis are buying French F-1s, the limited skilled-manpower resources of the Royal Saudi Air Force make it impossible for it to absorb two totally different systems at once. The F-1s were to be delivered later.

The F-15s, in 6 squadrons, were to be based at Taif, Dhahran (the oil-field area) and Khamis Mushait. The vulnerable airfield at Tabuk, near Israel, was to have only F-5s. To increase the range of the F-5s, Riyadh has purchased 4 KC-130 tanker-refueler planes, but these could not be used with the F-15s. Also recently delivered had been 24 C-130 troop-transports, with 11 more on order.

After an emotional debate, the Senate easily approved the Saudi-Egyptian-Israeli package. The Israeli lobby had finally lost on a "major issue."

Saudi weapons orders—"futures"—from the United States were, however, slightly on the decline. From $1.4 billion in 1975 and $2.5 billion in 1976, they fell to $700 million in 1977 and $900 million in 1978, not including a $1.5 billion order to Litton Industries for a countrywide command, control and communications system. Over the past four years, as noted in Chapter 9, Riyadh has also signed weapons orders for about a billion dollars each in France and Britain. A 1978 GAO report said U.S. foreign military sales agreements with Saudi Arabia from fiscal 1950 through fiscal 1976 totaled $12.1 billion, but that only $1.6 billion—13 per cent—had actually been delivered thus far. The report revealed, however, that 912 Defense Department personnel and 2,961 U.S. corporate personnel were already in Arabia providing support, management and training A current three-year U.S. support program of $1.5 billion includes $1.3 billion for air force support and $220 million for training, management and spare parts for the Saudi national guard. Counting all "military" sales beside weapons, Riyadh was due to spend $4.9 billion on defense in the United States in 1978, offsetting much of the $6.4 billion which America expected to pay for Arabian oil. After the fall of the Iranian regime, the United States also gave Riyadh assurances that it would intervene militarily if Saudi Arabia was threatened. This was revealed to the (newly renamed) House Foreign Affairs Committee by Assistant Secretary of State Harold Saunders in 1979.

One congressional problem with sophisticated sales to countries less able to use the weaponry than some of their allies or friends is that resales only require OMC approval. In 1977, a House amendment to the military aid bill required congressional review whenever the OMC approved arms transfers from a U.S. client to a third country. This passed the Senate. But OMC only reports every three months, and it is even doubtful how Congress could affect such an OMC decision abroad, since the resale contract is one between foreign sovereign states and therefore regards executive branches, not legislatures.

U.S./Syria

Syria, which began counterbalancing its arms dependence on Moscow by buying French and German aircraft in 1977, bought two L-100 and two C-130 transports from the United States in 1978. Damascus also expressed an interest in buying U.S. helicopters made in Italy—eighteen Agosta-Bell AB-212s (twelve for antisubmarine warfare, six for air-sea rescue work), along with twelve Agosta-Sikorsky SH-3D Seahawk antisubmarine craft and six Agosta-Boeing CH-47 Chinook transports. These requests were still under consideration when this book was being written. Because of the small sums involved, they would require only OMC, not congressional, approval, but Syria's opposition to "Camp David" made sales to Damascus seem unlikely in the near future. In 1978, Congress disapproved $90 million of security assistance for Syria.

U.S./Gulf States

Kuwait began modernization of its armed forces after its Parliament authorized, in 1973, expenditure of $1.4 billion for this purpose over seven years. The little oil state, with at the time the world's highest per capita income, enclaved by Arabia and Iraq, decided to divide orders between the United States, Britain and France; but initially, there was only a small ($30 million) American order for jeeps, pilot training and language classes, plus an expression of interest in air-defense systems. By and large, Kuwait is mainly dependent for arms on both Western and Eastern Europe.

Apart from C-130s to Abu Dhabi and some armor and helicopter sales to Oman, U.S. sales have been light to the other, smaller countries in the Gulf area; but overall the United States is by far the most important armorer in the region, Kuwait excepted. Robert Berman of Brookings says the Gulf nations prefer American equipment to that of the Soviet Union, France or Britain, because of the delays in getting spare parts from those nations. In a Brookings report, he notes:

> U.S. arms dealers offer a complete package to the recipient country. The United States will survey the needs of a country, provide a list of U.S. weapons available to fulfill those needs, send a demonstration team, possibly offer joint production, train pilots as well as others, and provide replacements needed—even, when required, from the active U.S. inventory. Beside being able to provide a wide variety, the United States offers equipment with more military capability. This is so especially in aircraft.

This overstates the case: Moscow can supply from its inventory or its stockpile even more rapidly, in most cases, than Washington.

U.S./North Yemen

Congressman Lee H. Hamilton, chairman of the Europe and Near East subcommittee of the House International Relations Committee, revealed in late 1977 that the United States had authorized Saudi Arabia to transfer 4 F-5B trainers to North Yemen. He said the State Department had admitted that this made it likely that it would approve of a request from the former Soviet protégé for 12 F-5Es. These were to be paid for by Saudi Arabia. The Yemeni sales package soon swelled to $390 million, and in 1979, when border warfare with South Yemen reoccurred, to $500 million—ordered by the White House, under "emergency" procedures, without congressional review, as a gesture to mollify Saudi Arabia, then disturbed by U.S. inaction in Iran.

Sana'a was to buy—at Saudi expense—the 12 F-5Es, along with 2 C-130s, 64 M-60 tanks and 100 armored personnel carriers. Some of the tanks and half of the APCs would come from Saudi Arabia, and a few of the tanks from Jordan, with those countries later getting replacements. The package also included 1,500 Dragon antitank missiles, 12 TOW antitank launchers, 200 grenade-launchers and some 155mm. howitzers.

What seemed to be under way was a complete Americanization of the Yemeni forces, then reliant on some outdated MiG-19s, a few Il-28 bombers, and some obsolete Soviet and British armor. South Yemen had only slightly better Soviet equipment, along with a reported 1,000 Russian and 800 Cuban advisers. Under the package, North Yemen would get 90 U.S. advisers, with 200 more to follow, but pilot training and most maintenance on the F-5 would be provided by Taiwanese, paid by Saudi Arabia.

United States/Sudan/Lebanon/North Africa

In May 1977, President Gaafar al-Nimeri of the formerly anti-Western Sudan expelled the 70-man Soviet military team working with his 53,000-man forces and ordered the Soviet embassy's staff cut by 50 per cent. When Ambassador Andrew Young, the U.S. envoy to United Nations, called at Khartoum that month, Nimeri asked him for U.S. military aid. Egypt and Arabia urged Washington to take on the Sudan, and the Saudis offered to pay $250 million for new American arms for the country.

In August, the Pentagon sent a team to the Sudanese capital to study Sudan's "legitimate defense needs." The sale of six C-130s went through quickly (with Arabia paying the $50 million bill), and Nimeri's Foreign Minister came to Washington to ask for F-5Es and surface-to-air missiles. He proposed that his country be helped to assume the role so often predicted for it in the past—that of "breadbasket" for the Middle East.

Sudan's fear of Soviet-supported Ethiopia and especially of Libya, which had mismanaged a coup against Nimeri in 1976, was clearly genuine, and a new U.S. arms customer seemed to be aborning.

Following the start of factional warfare in Lebanon, President Carter asked Congress in 1977 to approve $100 million in military credits for that country, to establish a new armed force of between three and four thousand men. Lebanon later said it would need about three times that sum in weaponry and support equipment.

The last U.S. base facility in Morocco, at Qeneitra, was closed down in 1978. Moroccan bases had been intended to replace those in Spain if Madrid went "left," and the kingdom has been a regular customer for U.S. arms since France, the colonial power, withdrew in 1954. In late 1966, King Hassan came to Washington to plead for a free gift of $100 million of arms to offset Algeria's Soviet equipment. He made the mistake, for a man pleading poverty, of bringing a retinue of 136 persons. Washington gave him $15 million of weaponry—but on the understanding that none of it be used in border conflicts with Spain, Mauritania or Algeria. This understanding has since been very substantially broken.

Nevertheless, in 1977, Carter agreed to sell Rabat $200 million worth of aircraft—twenty-four Rockwell International OV-10 "Bronco" armed reconnaissance aircraft and twenty-four Bell Cobra helicopters, sought by Morocco for its bid to annex Spanish Sahara. Under congressional pressure, however, the White House pulled back the following year. Morocco was reminded that the United States bans the use of the arms it sells outside Morocco's borders, except for defense, and that Washington does not recognize Morocco's seizure of ex-Spanish Sahara. Carter, however, left open a $45 million yearly military credit for Morocco, and when Hassan came to Washington at the end of 1978, the Cobra helicopter deal was once again approved, along with six Italian-built Chinook troop-carrying helicopters, providing the aircraft were not used in the Saharan war—a condition which Hassan told reporters he would not accept. (Carter reproposed the sale of Cobras and Broncos in 1979.)

Also in 1978, a Northrop subsidiary began lobbying for permission to sell Morocco, through "commercial" channels, a $200 million underground-sensor surveillance network for the annexed Saharan territory, reportedly to be paid for by Saudi Arabia; OMC opposed the project, code-named "Westwind," but the State Department's Moroccan desk insisted that "Westwind" could be classed as "mostly civilian" technology. With Congress adjourned for the elections, the deal slipped through, apparently emphasizing a significant loophole in the 1977 Arms Export Control Act: This permits commercial sales of items not classed as major weaponry—the latter being, in the words of the act, "any item of significant combat equipment having a nonrecurring research and development cost of more than $50 million or a total production cost of more than $200 million."

Tunisia has continued to be a modest U.S. arms customer, as was Libya before the revolution. Libya, indeed, continues to get some U.S. military equipment. Although an order for eight C-130s which Tripoli had already paid for was rejected by Washington in 1978, along with a spare-parts order for C-130s already in the Libyan inventory, President Qaddafi was allowed to buy four hundred army-type trucks. He had earlier procured Boeing-Vertol Chinook helicopters through Italy.

In the long run, however, Marxist Algeria seemed likely to become the next major Arab arms client of the United States. Algeria has offered

America half of its natural gas production for the next few decades, or about 1.2 trillion cubic feet a year. Technical problems delayed the deal, but in 1978 the El Paso Natural Gas Company and Distrigas began importing about a third of that quantity on a regular basis, using a new terminal at Cove Point, near Baltimore. By 1977, the United States had already become Algeria's main customer for oil, taking about half the country's production, or 1.1 million barrels a day.

BLACK AFRICA

A newly developing arms-export scene is black Africa, notably southern and eastern Africa and Nigeria.

The first early signs that African arms purchases would grow came in 1974 when South Africa, the renegade state on the tip of the continent, imported $210 million of weaponry, compared to $28 million the year before. The rest of black Africa imported $295 million that year, against $116 million in 1973. In the south, two and possibly three wars burgeon —South Africa, Rhodesia, and perhaps Namibia. Nigeria, relatively rich on oil exports, appears to entertain West African ambitions similar to those which the Shah had for Iran in the Gulf area. After its civil war, arms imports continued at almost the wartime level, or about five times what they had been before the conflict. In east Africa, when Libya replaced Ugandan MiGs, lost in the famous Israeli raid on Entebbe in 1976, by sending twenty French-made Mirage fighters, Kenya—one of Uganda's neighbors and enemies—turned to America for arms, buying twelve F-5s. Zaire also sought more American weapons. That year, U.S. sales to black Africa went up 800 per cent. Uganda also bought counter-insurgency and radio-jamming equipment from Britain. In 1977, the Carter administration said it was considering arms sales to Chad, opposed by secessionist forces backed by Libya, and $300,000 worth of military equipment to Upper Volta, Mali and Rwanda.

U.S. arms sales to black Africa had been minimal until that year. Ethiopia and to a limited degree Zaire (formerly the Congo) had been the only modest exceptions. It was something of a watershed when Dr. Kissinger told a National Urban League audience in Boston, in August 1976, that arms requests from friendly African nations such as Kenya and Zaire should receive serious consideration. But many liberal voices saw arms aid less as genuine help than as a means of buying allies, or buying into trouble. Reluctantly approving the sale of the twelve F-5s for $70.6 million to Kenya, Senator Kennedy warned in a Senate speech that month that what was needed was an African policy "under which military issues and any arms sales will be clearly and firmly subordinated."

In May 1977, as noted earlier in this chapter, the House approved, by four votes, $100 million of security aid for frontline black nations surrounding Rhodesia and South Africa—to protect the recipient countries not only from armed incursions by the settler forces in Rhodesia, and also to help them withstand the economic effects of not trading with the settler states. The Senate, as noted, later reduced the figure to $80 million.

The London-based International Institute for Strategic Studies estimated that sub-Sahara Africa would take delivery of $5.6 billion of military equipment in 1978, of which $1.9 billion would be by South Africa and $159 million by Rhodesia. The expenditure of $3.7 billion by black-governed countries, including $2.4 billion by Nigeria, was an increase of 300 per cent over three years, and did not include an estimated billion-dollar gift of arms to Ethiopia by the Soviet Union. Over the three-year period, the IISS estimated that black African forces had gone from 475,000 to 600,000, over a third of them being Nigerian. Zambia had increased its annual military expenditures from $79 million to $309.4 million. Some sort of an arms race was clearly on, and the United States was sure to be involved.

United States/Somalia/Ethiopia

As Russian support for Somalia—which seeks to recover its lost Somali provinces of Djibouti, southeastern Ethiopia and northern Kenya—shifted in 1977 to Addis Ababa, Mogadishu at first received offers of military sales from America, Britain and France. Saudi Arabia offered to foot the proposed $300 million bill—later increased to a reported $600 million. The United States subsequently reneged, giving as its rationale that Somalia was engaged in "aggression"; but U.S. weapons, including M-48 tanks from Iran, reached Somalia from different parts of the Middle East. The role of privateers in this development was recounted in Chapter 5.

In October 1977, the Soviet embassy in Addis Ababa made its change of "alliance" formal. It announced that it was halting all military supplies to Somalia, and "backing" Ethiopia in its war to hold on to its Somali provinces and to put down Eritrean secession in the north. Earlier that month, Somalia had won Western gratitude by helping foil the spectacular hijacking of a Lufthansa airliner. But as the Kremlin had presumably anticipated, Washington, under its own new arms guidelines, had no idea how to handle the "gift" of Somalia. It finally offered defensive arms if Somalia would publicly renounce its irredentist claims—something which neither President Siad Barre or any other Somali leader could do and still survive politically.

In Ethiopia itself, long a U.S. protégé, the picture remained equally blurred. Although all U.S. aid had been halted, Israel had supplied technicians—finally expelled in 1978—to repair American F-5s for the Ethiopian Air Force, and had also provided napalm and cluster bombs from the Israeli inventory, while Cubans were restoring MiGs. The Israeli rationale appeared to be simply tribal—the Somalis are Muslims and members of the Arab League—but the Israeli presence was probably encouraged by Washington for intelligence reasons. In 1978, Ethiopia was allowed to purchase spare parts for its American weapons, including F-5s, through commercial channels. Here again, the role of privateers was explored in Chapter 5.

United States/South Africa/Rhodesia

South Africa, with perhaps the greatest potential for conflict in black Africa, continues to receive U.S. equipment for military purposes, as the court convictions in the Olin and Colt gun cases stressed. About a quarter of all South African Air Force planes are American. Some of the 178 U.S. aircraft—notably the F-86s—were delivered before the 1963 embargo. C-130 troop transports were delivered by Kennedy shortly after the embargo. More recent aircraft deliveries include 15 Lockheed L-100s —civilianized C-130s which South Africa uses as troop carriers, adding a paratroop door—and 7 Swearingen Merlin-IV transports. Pretoria has also "militarized" its Cessna-185s and Helio Couriers for counter-insurgency work, and has purchased 19 P-166 Albatross coastal patrol aircraft made under license by Piaggio in Italy. Several other utility or light aircraft of U.S. design or with U.S. engines, including the AM-3C and the C-4M, are also in the SAAF inventory. In 1979, the Administration ordered an inquiry into the alleged sale to the South African police, by Control Data, of computer equipment, said to have been ordered and installed by International Computers Ltd., of Britain. The "privateer" sale of 155mm. howitzer shells to Pretoria was reported in Chapter 5

In December 1978 *Armies and Weapons* magazine reported from

Monaco that Pretoria had acquired a "sizable batch" of American M-113 APCs and M-109 155mm. self-propelling howitzers, all made by OTO-Melara of Italy. South Africa was also reported to have obtained U.S. ocean-surveillance systems.

Rhodesia has purchased 20 militarized Cessna F-337s from France, through a Spanish fishing firm in the Canary Islands. The militarized version has bomb racks and a short takeoff capability; it was used by the USAF in Vietnam, where it was known as the O-2. In 1978, 11 Bell "Huey" troop-carrying gunships appeared in the Rhodesian inventory; adapted "civilian" 205As, they had been supplied, as is recounted in Chapter 9, by Israel. A Washington *Post* report said 25 other Italian-made Hueys reached South Africa in 1974 or 1975, possibly for Rhodesia.

LATIN AMERICA

One reason for relatively heavy arms buying in Africa is the prevalence of military governments. The same is true of Latin America, where there is, on average, one coup d'état a year. As in such diverse countries as Egypt, Ethiopia and Greece, in Latin America the military career is perhaps the best route to "success" for the lowly born. U.S. attempts to quarantine weaponry levels in Latin America have failed before the aggressive sales patterns of European suppliers, notably France, and of Soviet and Israeli initiatives. The dictatorships of Argentina and Brazil have arms budgets of well over a billion dollars a year, constituting together nearly half the continental total; Peru and Cuba are not far behind. Nevertheless, the area as a whole spends only 2 per cent of its GNP on defense, and Latin America accounts for only 3 per cent of U.S. arms sales abroad.

To hedge the threat of civil and international wars and guerrilla campaigns, various high-sounding agreements have, with U.S. encouragement, been concluded between Latin American countries. The 1945 Act of Chapultepec, signed by twenty countries, ruled that an attack on any signatory state would be an attack on all and would be met with a collective response. The 1947 Treaty of Rio reaffirmed collective self-defense and set up machinery for dispute resolution. Twenty-five countries signed, in 1948, the Charter of the Organization of American States. In 1965, El Salvador, Guatemala, Honduras and Nicaragua formed a bloc against potential Communist aggression. In 1975, ten countries signed the Declaration of Ayacucho on arms limitations.

U.S. arms relations with its western-hemisphere neighbors have been more paternal but scarcely less fractious than with Europe or Canada. American-led attempts to put a ceiling on arms for Latin America were recounted in Chapter 3. After screening Latin America from the European and Communist weapons trade for many years after World War Two, Washington finally agreed, in October 1965, to sell 50 A-4B Skyhawk attack aircraft to Argentina. Because of Vietnam demands, the order was later scaled down to 25, but by then Chile had asked for a counterforce. The United States offered 16 A-4Bs and 16 Korean War-vintage F-86s, for a total tag of $5.5 million, but the Chileans wanted F-5s, then a system which Washington refused to transfer to Latin America.

Chile then turned to Europe and ordered 21 British Hawker Hunters for $20 million, which prompted Peru to ask the United States for fighters. Washington offered F-86s, but the deal bogged down over Peru's inability to pay. Because of the Canberra's American engines, the United States was also to block the sale of 6 of those British bombers to Peru for $2.5 million; so Peru then turned to France, which sold 12 Mirage-III/5 fighter-bombers for $20 million. The Peruvian pilots thus ended up with a more sophisticated plane than the F-5s forbidden to Peru's hostile neighbor Chile.

It was at this point that Venezuela consummated the deal with Gerhard Mertins of Merex, mentioned in an earlier chapter, for 74 F-86s from the Luftwaffe inventory. This persuaded Brazil to enlarge its Air Force and to bypass the United States, purchasing 100 early-model Mirages from Germany.

Meanwhile, the United States had agreed to sell 50 M-41 tanks to Argentina. Deliveries were suspended when a junta seized power in mid-1966, so Buenos Aires bought 50 AMX-30 tanks from France for $200,000 apiece—once again getting a more advanced weapon than the American one. The upshot of all this was the decision by Washington to "release" the F-5 to Latin America.

In more recent times, the United States has eased off on weapons sales to Brazil because of that country's decision to go ahead with nuclear-power development and the overt talk in Brasilia of a nuclear military option. U.S.-Brazilian talks on nuclear restraint in Rio, in March 1977, came to an abrupt halt after twenty-four hours, with the Brazilians rejecting American requests either to put their atomic facilities under international control or to let the United States process nuclear fuel for them.

Two months earlier, West German Chancellor Helmut Schmidt had told Vice-President Mondale that Bonn would honor its agreement to build the Brazilian nuclear power stations. Both Brazil and Argentina scored low figures in the State Department's "human rights" report and in 1977 were banned from further U.S. arms sales. However, minor exceptions to the ban have since been made.

Some restraints on U.S. sales in Latin America, imposed in 1966, were lifted by Congress in 1973, since they were merely serving to promote European, Israeli and Soviet sales. By 1979, the United States had only 10 per cent of a market where it had held a 70 per cent share in the years following World War Two, putting America in fourth place behind West Germany, France and the Soviet Union. Military *aid*, however, is being phased out, in Latin America as in most areas, and the region falls within President Carter's "Third World" restrictions. The U.S. military presence —769 in 1968—was expected to be down to 100 in 1979, with Panama getting the largest share. There are today fewer U.S. military advisers in Latin America than the Soviet Union has in Peru alone. However, the outlook was for Latin America to be a burgeoning sales market for U.S. weaponry in the years to come. In 1977, U.S. military sales to the area totaled $320 million, of which $103 million was commercial. In 1978, the State Department approved $220 million of sales of guns and Chaparral surface-to-air missiles to Ecuador alone, to offset Soviet supplies to Peru, and it was announced that Venezuela would get 16 OV-10 counter-insurgency planes. But the Administration confirmed that it would sell no aircraft more advanced than the A-4 or the F-5 for the time being. Also banned were ballistic missiles or rockets, "smart" bombs, cluster bombs, delayed-action munitions, radiological weapons, napalm, flamethrowers, along with several other implements of war, from large warships to sound suppressors.

ASIA AND AUSTRALASIA

Still more of a tinderbox is Asia. China fears Russia, but itself threatens Mongolia and Vietnam and, through a local insurrection, Thailand. Malaysia fears similar insurgency. Along with Singapore and Indonesia, it looks to Australia and New Zealand for help, just as South Korea, Taiwan and the Philippines look to Washington. Laos, Cambodia and Vietnam, as much as China, threaten the independence of Thailand, the next domino in line. Vietnam, supported by Moscow, invaded Cambodia—supported by Peking—early in 1979, and imposed a new government. Tiny, oil-rich Brunei, which has spent over a billion dollars on arms and support facilities in the past decade, or almost as much as New Zealand, looks to Britain. Japan is precluded from possessing arms capable of aggression, but is expected to expand its forces to something commensurate to France's or Germany's.

India, Pakistan, Bangladesh, Sri Lanka and Indonesia are all theoretically neutral countries, but India and Pakistan arm against each other and India arms against China. Wealthy, neutral Singapore is likely to be attracted to concentrated defense power. Afghanistan has claims on Pushtunistan in Pakistan. Neutral Burma fears China, with which it shares a 1,200-mile border. Following India's absorption of Sikkim, fears of similar expansion exist in Bhutan and Nepal.

In 1967, Indonesia, Singapore, Malaysia, Thailand and the Philippines formed the Association of Southeast Asian Nations (ASEAN), a neutral zone ostensibly free of wider defense entanglements. The idea was to extend ASEAN to the (then) two Vietnams, Laos, Cambodia and Burma. But none of the original five have been willing, thus far, to free themselves of existing defense pacts or to set up machinery for conflict resolution among themselves.

United States/Korea

The greatest potential areas for conflict in the region are still thought to be the two Koreas and Taiwan.

The South Koreans say the 17 million North Koreans (less than half as numerous as the population of the South) receive about $100 million of military aid annually from Moscow and Peking, but this translates into considerably more power than the figure suggests. North Korean leader Kim Il Sung has often promised to reunify the peninsula by war, although he has no aircraft more advanced than MiG-21s.

By 1977, South Korea had received a total of $6.5 billion in U.S. military aid and $5.6 billion in economic aid, including $2 billion of special weapons assistance since the earlier withdrawal of 20,000 American troops in 1971. Since no peace has ever been signed with North Korea—only a truce, monitored by a UN command now entirely composed of Americans—Seoul has become ineluctably dependent on the United States, and more and more Americanized. Significantly, the Christian population now numbers 4 million, three quarters of them Protestants.

In 1977, when Carter announced the graduated, five-year withdrawal of U.S. land forces from South Korea, over the protests of General John K. Singlaub and others, reporters were reminded that several Korean officials, starting with the late President Park, had said that if this ever happened, Seoul would have to develop its own nuclear option. Although this point was not advertised, the American withdrawal was to include the removal of the over one thousand tactical missiles in Korea, reporters were told at the time. Despite strong public (and overt congressional) disapproval of the various scandals in which the Korean lobby in Washington had become involved—notably wide-ranging bribery by Korean intelligence agents and diplomats, and by an enthusiastic amateur, rice broker Tongsun Park—several official statements were made to the effect that Korea would get even more U.S. arms assistance than in the past. This was to enable it to defend itself, along Nixon-doctrine lines, without U.S. troops (but not without continued U.S. air support). In Seoul, then Under Secretary Philip C. Habib said publicly that Washington had a clear "continuing commitment" to South Korea's survival—an apparent reference to the mutual defense treaty, which requires both countries to consult with their legislatures before obligating themselves to the wartime defense of the other.

But the South Korean scandals in Washington had weakened congressional willingness to aid the country. Although a complete U.S. withdrawal from aid commitments was out of the question, there were even strong congressional objections to leaving all U.S. nonnuclear materiel behind as the troops withdrew.

By 1978, Carter faced opposition to transferring U.S. equipment in Korea to the Koreans themselves on two fronts: Conservatives opposed the transfer in the hope of stopping the U.S. troop withdrawal, while liberals opposed it on arms-race and human-rights grounds. The Pentagon opposed withdrawals if the arms-aid package was not assured.

The upgrading of Korean forces was initially expected to cost $5 billion over five years, including about a billion dollars in grant aid—the equipment which the departing American forces would leave behind. But in late 1977, a Pentagon task force put the total figure at nearer $8 billion. Korea, as noted in Chapter 2, co-produces a range of U.S. light and medium weaponry; but the task force report spoke of Korea's need for 250 new fighters, including 90 F-16s, plus hundreds of helicopters and radar control planes, a missile maintenance depot and improved aircraft maintenance facilities. The Army needed more missiles and cannon, and the Navy needed 6 more destroyers, the study said. Among the equipment which U.S. forces would leave in Korea would be the Honest John missile, which now has a conventional warhead but is nuclear-capable.

At the end of 1977, Seoul ordered $470 million of U.S. weaponry, including F-4s, Bell UH-1 helicopters and Maverick missiles. During the year, Korea's armed forces took deliveries of more F-4s, F-5s, Cessna A-37s, Fairchild C-123s and Bell AH-1J helicopters. From the U.S. forces in Korea, they acquired the first of the Honest Johns and some Nike-Hercules missile batteries. The Pentagon scaled down its recommendation of

F-16s to 60, at a cost of $1.2 billion, for delivery from 1982 on. But Carter vetoed the sale as it would have introduced a "significant new weapons technology" into the region. He had earlier rejected co-production of the planes in Korea.

United States/Taiwan

In Taiwan, a repressed population awaits independence from the mainlander oligarchy and fears a restoration of government by Peking— a situation which the island has not known since 1900, except for the brief period 1945–48. The United States has kept Taiwan on a short leash for weapons since Nixon's first visit to China and the Shanghai Declaration, wherein the United States virtually recognized Peking's claim to the island. Taiwan's dealings with other suppliers are recounted in Chapter 9. In 1976, Hughes was able to sell a $34 million radar air-defense system, coordinating Taiwan's F-5s and the Hawks; Raytheon, for $85 million, upgraded the island's 24 Hawk batteries and provided more, improved Hawks; a $95 million deal with Northrop had permitted the production on Taiwan of 60 more F-5Es, in addition to the 120 built there earlier. The Taiwanese complained that the Hawks only defended about one fifth of the island. The short-range F-5 had no all-weather capacity and could only carry a 2,000-pound bomb-load or two Sidewinders.

In 1978, Saudi Arabia—Taiwan's main source of oil—dissuaded Taipei from buying 60 Israeli Kfir fighters for $525 million, and Taiwan once again turned to Washington for planes to replace its aging F-100s and F-104s. Washington had approved the sale of the U.S-engined Kfirs, knowing Riyadh would forbid it, but made it clear that F-15s, F-14s and even F-16s were out of the question, in order not to offend Peking.

The United States was prepared to consider F-4s, but once again Peking was opposed to Taiwan receiving an aircraft with a sufficient range to launch air-to-ground attacks in China. Moreover, the F-4 assembly line was about to close. Under Peking pressure, Carter specifically refused Taipei the updated "Wild Weasel" F-4 which Iran had also requested in vain, as well as the updated F-5G. This left Taipei with a choice of either buying American F-4s from European air forces, as these moved up to the F-16 and the Tornado (always supposing that they would risk the ire of China) or of getting an extension, beyond 1980, of its F-5 production line: This seemed likely to be the ultimate solution, after Carter, at the end of 1978, on the eve of extending full recognition to Peking, offered Taiwan 48 F-5Es, in co-production, upgraded to take

500 Maverick air-to-surface missiles with the new laser designators, as well as the usual Sidewinders for fighter warfare. Co-production of the aircraft's J-85 engine was, however, turned down; but if Taiwan wished to pirate production of F-5s in the eighties, it could do so by cannibalizing the J-85 engines of its old F-104s.

One obvious solution to Taipei's problems would have been to buy what some considered the best fighter produced in Europe—Sweden's Viggen. But a Swedish Air Force general told the author: "Because of its American engines, we knew after what happened in India that we would never get approval from Washington."

The establishment of full U.S. relations with Peking in December 1978 increased Taipei's concern for its defense, although the Chinese leadership made conciliatory noises about its Taiwan policy to help the Carter administration fend off conservative criticism. Carter converted the Taipei embassy to an "American Institute" staffed by State Department officials "on leave," and agreed to a twelve-month moratorium on new arms sales to Taiwan in 1979, but he said orders in train—expected to total nearly $1 billion that year—would go through as promised. A varied group of senators, including conservatives like Barry Goldwater, Robert Dole, Jesse Helms and Democrat Robert Byrd, along with liberals like Edward Kennedy and Alan Cranston, and middle-of-the-roaders like John Glenn and Frank Church, put through a motion committing the United States to protect Taiwan's security, and proposing the sale of F-16s. The NSA continued to monitor Chinese mainland communications from the Shu Lin Kou hill station outside Taipei.

In the United States, the Taiwanese embassy became the Coordination Council for North American Affairs, with "branches" instead of consulates in New York City, Houston, Atlanta, Chicago, Los Angeles, Seattle and Honolulu. The Coordination Council was headed by a former Air Force pilot, retired Colonel Konsin Shah. His air attaché, Major General Jude Pao, said that in 1980 Taipei would be ordering at least five hundred more Mavericks and one hundred launchers, for $25 million, $62 million worth of improvements for existing Mavericks and $50 million of aircraft spares.

United States/Japan/Australia/Singapore

America's main ally in Asia remained Japan, which produced its own F-104s under a co-production license two decades ago and was moving into more ambitious co-production arrangements in the late seventies and the eighties.

Both the Pentagon and the U. S. General Accounting Office have pushed for an increased Japanese defense budget, partly to offset the permanent U.S. trade deficit with Tokyo, partly to diminish the U.S. military presence in Japan—where, according to the GAO, the Japanese-personnel payroll of American forces alone now runs to $400 million a year, with pension liabilities approaching $300 million.

By national policy, Japan's defense budget is limited to no more than 1 per cent of the nation's GNP. It was about $5 billion in 1976, slightly higher in 1977 and 1978. Japan offsets few U.S. military costs. It pays land rental for areas occupied by U.S. forces, constructs replacement facilities and subsidizes communities living near U.S. bases (for road damage and noise pollution). Rents average $112 million a year, community subsidies $163 million. The Pentagon estimates the cost of maintaining about 47,000 U.S. personnel in Japan at nearly $1 billion annually, not including the cost of the U. S. Navy patrolling Japan's sea lanes. The annual $600 million cost of U.S. forces in Korea is also partly justified by the needs of Japanese defense. The United States is pressing for Japan to take part in more joint defense projects, notably in air defense and airborne early-warning systems—Tokyo is buying 6 Grumman Hawkeyes for about $36 million each—and in antisubmarine warfare, for which the Japanese are purchasing 45 Lockheed P-3C Orions (a $1.7 billion Lockheed/Kawasaki co-production deal, with deliveries beginning in 1981). The P-3s—with acoustic torpedoes that home in on the sound of submarines—are to be deployed at Hachinoe, in the north; Atsugi, near Tokyo; Konoya, on Kyushu island; and on Okinawa.

In addition, Japan was authorized to co-produce 100 of its 125 F-15s, at a cost of $3.3 billion with deliveries starting in 1980. This order may later be increased by 20 or so—probably bought discreetly from America, to reduce the cost—but it has already caused debate in the Diet, where socialists and others have called the aircraft "offensive," since it has bomb racks and a refueling (long-range) capacity. There was also opposition to sending Japan's F-4 and F-15 pilots for training in the United States, as Japanese law prohibits taking Japanese military equipment to foreign countries. Japan is limited by its constitution to use its armed forces for defense only. Tokyo, however, was also considering other U.S. purchases, including shoulder-fired Redeye antiaircraft missiles.

Japan already has 125 submarines, 50 of them nuclear-powered. Also on order by Japan in 1978 were several squadrons of helicopters. There seems little doubt that Japanese public opinion would support some increase in defense spending: A 1978 poll found that only 19 per cent of

Japanese believed the United States would defend Japan in an emergency, compared to 37 per cent nine years before.

During 1976, the Japanese Air Self-Defense Force, whose 400 combat
aircraft face 2,000 Soviet planes in the North Pacific area, scrambled 459
times in response to penetrations of Japanese airspace by Soviet aircraft,
compared to 281 times the previous year. A Japanese defense study also
noted the ease with which a defecting Soviet Foxbat landed in Japan in
1976. Japanese defense experts were considering purchase of the Raytheon Patriot surface-to-air missile system.

Australia has traditionally been a British arms market, with substantial
production or co-production within the country of its own weapons systems; but in 1978, Canberra made a tentative order for 41 A-10 close-
support aircraft from the United States. Australia was also interested in
the F-18L and the F-16. It is already a customer for P-3Cs.

Singapore, an oriental Switzerland, has ordered 21 F-5Es with 200
Sidewinder missiles, for a total tag of $118 million.

United States/India

With India, the only other democracy in Asia beside Japan, Washington has followed a zigzag weapons-diplomacy course, as it has with dictatorial Pakistan—which has followed a largely pro-Western policy in
fear of India's might. Bans imposed on arms exports to both countries
during their war over Bangladesh were meaningless, because of the brevity of the conflict. However, there has been concern in Washington over
India's possible nuclear-weapon capacity.

But in December 1976, the Office of Munitions Control, under White
House guidance, cleared McDonnell-Douglas to give information to
India on the A-4 Skyhawk fighter-bomber, normally the first step toward
an authorized sale. India was thought to be in the market for about 300
such aircraft, including about 30 for its single aircraft-carrier; but when
this book was written, the deal was still under discussion.

United States/Pakistan

Pakistan had once asked for a similar attack capacity, and the Pentagon had recommended sale of 110 A-7 light attack aircraft. With a 7-ton
offensive payload and a radius of 600 miles, the A-7 would permit Pakistan to reach most of India. The State Department left a final decision on

both sales over to the incoming administration. The new White House declared itself committed, in principle, to the demilitarization of the Indian Ocean, although it began its term by sending a carrier force—the *Enterprise*, the *Long Beach* and the *Truxtun*—into that ocean for the first time since 1965.

In June 1977, the Carter administration vetoed the A-7 sale, but indicated it would be prepared to sell shorter-range offensive aircraft, such as the A-4, or purely defensive systems such as the F-5. Texan members of Congress, led by Senator Lloyd Bentsen, at once objected to the loss of business by Ling-Temco-Vought, makers of the A-7. Bentsen predicted that all the decision would mean would be a sale of French Mirages to Pakistan. Pakistani Premier Zulfikar Ali Bhutto was by then on poor terms with Washington. He was overthrown in July. In 1976, Dr. Kissinger had rationalized the recommended A-7 sale as being the price to pay to persuade Pakistan not to buy nuclear reactors from France. When this book was being written, U.S. arms sales to Pakistan were under the same cloud as U.S. sales to India, and in 1979, Bentsen's forecast came true: Pakistan bought 32 Mirages—a mix of IIIs and III/5s—for $330 million. Following discovery of Pakistan's nuclear-bomb plans, Washington ruled in 1979 that all arms sales to Islamabad would have to be in cash.

United States/Southeast Asia

Since the Vietnam War, the United States has been only marginally involved in Southeast Asia. Carter approved the sale of 18 F-5s to Thailand in 1978, just as Northrop was announcing plans to "cilop" the plane with a new engine, a new wing design and advanced avionics. Thailand also got 32 Rockwell OV-10 armed-reconnaissance or counter-insurgency planes. Then, in 1979, the Thai Premier came to Washington with a $400 million shopping order for air-to-air and antitank missiles, tanks and artillery—equal in value to all the country's military purchases in the United States over the previous thirty-eight years. Indonesia was approved, in 1978, for purchase of 16 OV-10s.

EUROPE

Basic to the bid to sell U.S. weapons in Europe is the question of standardization, mentioned in detail in Chapter 2. This is a NATO problem where not only do diplomacy and strategy meet at the highest level, but where economics is paramount. America's arms-transfer links to Europe have come a long way from the days when F-80s, fifteen years old, were sold from the Air National Guard inventory for from $1,000 to $15,000 apiece. Even the massive sale of the export-only F-5s was couched in modest figures compared to the multibillion-dollar wrangle in 1977 over the proposed AWACS sale. The biggest contest of recent times for a NATO market was that in which the General Dynamics F-16 competed with Northrop's F-17, France's Mirage F-1 and Sweden's Viggen. This epic air battle began in 1974. Only the Viggen had little or no real chance of gaining favor—more because of Sweden's neutral foreign policy than because of any shortcomings in the plane.

The F-16 Issue

The choice of the F-16 by Denmark (which took 58), Norway (72) and the Netherlands (102) on June 7, 1975 (and by Belgium—for 116 units—later) buried the F-17 program and made the French and Swedish aircraft purely "home air force" planes, so far as Europe was concerned. The four competing aircraft were about equal in performance. The difference in cost between each, with "basic" equipment, was initially small. The battle was mainly over credit terms, offset costs and co-production arrangements; all three contestants were prepared to farm out, in different formulas, 80 per cent of production work to customer-countries.

When the F-16 began to win out, the marketing problems for the GD plane were not over. In April 1977, the Danish Defense Minister, Orla Moeller, said he would delay signing the purchase contract because of increased program costs, a shortfall in the promised offset work for Danish industry, and criticism of the F-16 in a recent GAO report. Similar dissatisfactions were expressed by Norway, and initially by Belgium and Holland.

The GAO report to which the Danes alluded had revealed that the European-produced components would be more costly than when manufactured in the United States; but this would be offset, from a USAF procurement point of view, by the savings achieved through enlarging the production line. Specifically, the GAO said, co-production would add $241 million to the U.S. cost of the F-16 system, but Europe alone would reimburse $200 million to the United States in R & D expenses. The report said ominously, however, that there was "no common understanding" of what the not-to-exceed unit price of $6,091,000 meant for the European F-16s.

As noted in Chapter 2, there was also dissatisfaction over how co-production of the plane was working out in practice. Said Robert F. Hunt, chairman of the Dowty Group, in 1978:

> We in the United Kingdom do not regard the production of F-16s in Europe as an outstanding example of project sharing. This particular program appears to be too much of a benefit game for the U.S. industry and economy without equal technological rewards for Europe and NATO coming down the eastbound lane of the two-way street.

By the following year, these criticisms were mounting. The share of the work promised to the European partners—for American, European and third-country planes—totaled an estimated "58 per cent offset." Actually, by 1979, it had already equalled 52 per cent offset, despite slow initial sales to third-country markets, as well as the cancellation of the big Iranian order for 160 planes and of the planned future Iranian purchase of another 140. Holland, with an aircraft industry of its own, was actually surpassing 58 per cent offset, according to General Dynamics, while Belgium, with the contracts for the engines and other key items, seemed likely to get what it expected. But Denmark and Norway were well behind.

Nevertheless, even some of the Scandinavian carping seemed unfair. According to which F-16 contracts a country was allotted, the transfer of technology was uneven; but this was inevitable, and was presumably foreseen. There were also complaints, as the GAO had noted earlier, that the "not to exceed" price of $6,091,000 had proven unrealistic. But this was essentially a "sticker" price, based on the prototype. Some gold-plating by individual air forces was inevitable, and particular improvements had been requested by purchaser-countries from the start. By 1979, if the average F-16 was costing $11 million in Europe, it was costing about $10 million in the United States. The higher European price was because of the built-in expense of international co-production.

More serious were the complaints that the aircraft was not sufficiently "all-weather"—a basic requirement for Europe. But European air forces knew this from the start, also. Public opinion in Europe was unaware of the plane's limitations because European parliaments are less geared than the U. S. Congress to obtaining expert information, and because the European press largely lacks specialist reporters. Nor was the European press able to fall back on the U.S. press in this case, for the fact that a plane that light cannot carry all-weather missiles for an extended range had not been examined in the United States either.

The plane had been chosen because it was "cheap." Europe, with its constant poor weather, may arguably need a more expensive plane which, given the unlikelihood of a war in Europe, the European governments were reluctant to buy. The F-16, as the Shah recognized, was ideal for the Middle East, where visibility is generally magnificent, or for Australia. Moreover, it was designed as a light "air superiority" plane, intended to shoot down other planes. The close-support (antitank) capacity was added at the request of the Europeans, thus marring its overall performance.

The best plane of the four competitors was probably the Viggen. But for NATO to rely on a "neutral," in the unlikely but possible event of a conventional war in Europe, in which neutral Sweden would be invaded by the Russians if it supplied NATO, was unthinkable from the start. France would have been acceptable as a supplier to Belgium; but its restricted membership in NATO made France unacceptable to Holland and even more so to Denmark and Norway. Thus, once the decision to share a common plane was made, it had to be one of the American candidates—the F-17 or the F-16. The choice between these two was largely based on co-production and offset offers, in which GD was more imaginative than Northrop.

The only serious defect of the F-16 lies in its F-100 engine, which has a tendency to flare out under certain conditions. This is the fault of Congress, which consistently refused funds for an improved power plant. Europe had no choice but to take the only engine available. Some critics have suggested that a twin-engined plane, such as the Mirage F-1, would have made more sense. But whereas navies habitually choose twin-engined planes—like the F-14—because pilots are reluctant to operate constantly over the open ocean on "one fan," tactical air forces traditionally go for warplane quantity, and therefore rely on more economic craft. This is particularly true in Europe, where World War Three would be largely fought over land. The fact that a twin-engined aircraft can get home if one engine fails is, in any event, essentially a peacetime consideration. In war, a crippled plane is a sitting duck.

To sum up, a single-engine interceptor is adequate for European air forces, providing it is powerful enough to carry all-weather ordnance for a reasonable distance. The F-16 was chosen not because GD's hard-sell was any harder than Dassault's, nor because of U.S. pressure, which was minimal, but because GD offered better terms than Northrop, both in terms of price and "offset," and because a French or a Swedish aircraft was politically unacceptable.

Despite all the controversy, the F-16 has unquestionably become the major current American weapon program in Europe. Significantly, no less than 302 U.S. military and civil-service officials staff the F-16 program offices there—adding 2 per cent to the cost of the system. The first

European-made F-16, a two-place trainer, flew at Schiphol airport, Amsterdam, in May 1979; it was piloted by Fokker-VFW test pilot Henk Themmen and Dave Palmer of General Dynamics.

The AWACS Sale

Other major U.S. sales in Europe currently include thirteen P-3s for Holland, for $300 million—chosen against French and British competition because of lower prices and faster delivery schedules—TOW missiles for Britain's Lynx gunships, Sidewinders for the RAF's Phantoms and Tornados, Harpoon submarine-to-surface cruise missiles for the Royal Navy, Tomahawk cruise missiles for several NATO countries, and Raytheon Patriot surface-to-air missiles for the Luftwaffe in the 1980s. The $1.2 billion Patriot order would strengthen Germany's existing Hawk system by replacing the Nike-Hercules batteries acquired from the United States earlier. Britain was also expected to buy A-10s, while Britain's purchase of thirty-three Chinook helicopters, for $242 million and for delivery in 1980–81, was described by Boeing-Vertol as the largest export sale in the company's history.

But the greatest controversy swirled around the bid, partly narrated in Chapters 4 and 6, to sell the Boeing E-3A AWACS radar-control plane to NATO, as a "NATO-owned," multinational plane. With the British decision to build eleven of its own Nimrod radar planes, the United States was still trying to sell eighteen E-3As, notably to Germany and France. One of the selling points to Britain had been that the integrated AWACS fleet would be based in Britain; but Britain's Nimrod decision made it less likely that other countries would buy if the nonbuying country still remained the base country for the system. There was a contest between Portugal and West Germany to provide an alternative base.

When Vice-President Mondale had gone to Brussels for NATO talks in January 1977, Bonn was still smarting from the Pentagon's decision to award to Chrysler rather than to Germany what looked like becoming a $4.7 billion commitment for the new main battle tank. Bonn was only partially mollified by the agreement to include—eventually—the German turret and 120mm. smooth-bore gun, and to build an American gas-turbine engine that would be standardized on that of Germany's Leopard tank. When, earlier, the Army had leaked results of tests on the Leopard tank, conducted at the Army Proving Grounds at Aberdeen, Maryland, showing the Leopard "inferior" to the Chrysler "Abrams" competitor, Bonn scented that the ground was being prepared to renege on the engine/turret pact; German Government spokesmen let it be known that, if this happened, Germany would no longer put up its share of the $2.6 billion costs for an integrated European AWACS program. At the Pentagon, it was reasoned that Germany might both buy AWACS and go along with British basing if the United States adopted the German gun and helped Bonn sell Leopard-II tanks elsewhere.

Mondale's task was not made easier by his instructions to urge Germany to forego the earlier-mentioned, nearly $5 billion contract to build, in Brazil—a nonsignatory to the Nuclear Non-Proliferation Treaty—eight nuclear power stations and a nuclear-fuel processing and reprocessing facility, while at the same time pressing Germany to expand its economic growth and defense budget. The Brazilian deal meant ten thousand German jobs, and Chancellor Helmut Schmidt said that Germany hoped to recoup, from the profits, some of the $7 billion which his country had invested in nuclear research; moreover, he did not think France would renounce a similar nuclear deal with Pakistan, despite Kissinger's promise to sell Islamabad A-7s if it would give up the nuclear project. (In any case, as noted earlier, the Carter administration later canceled the A-7 offer.)

The other major problem in selling AWACS was with Britain. The British felt that they had "paid" for not buying the E-3A by America's cancellation of its intended purchase of the Skyflash missile. The Pentagon denied that the decision not to buy Skyflash was related to Britain's choice of Nimrod, saying that the United States had only agreed initially to buy five hundred Skyflashes for testing, at a unit cost of $100,000—a $50 million order; this, it was pointed out, was not comparable to a British purchase of eleven AWACS, which would cost twenty-six times as much. But in Congress, Democrat Thomas Downey of New York remained incredulous; at hearings, he asked Charles E. Myers Jr., the chief of air warfare in the Pentagon's research and development directorate, why the USAF didn't choose a less expensive system than the E-3A, such as the Grumman Hawkeye or the Nimrod. Said Myers: "Would you mind if I backed away from that question?"

Belgium and Germany seemed the most likely European customers for the E-3A, but another alternative being proposed by Europe was to mount the sophisticated AWACS gear, not on a Boeing 707—the E-3A formula—but on the Franco-German Airbus. At stake was a deal for well over $2 billion, involving mixed manning by integrated NATO crews, with the United States prepared to cover one third of the cost and Canada 10 per cent. Germany was talking of committing $550 million, but impoverished Italy only wanted to put up a token $1 million. Meanwhile, the British were still hoping to sell Nimrods to European allies, to recoup some of the development costs; and Grumman's E-2C Hawkeye, the only well-tested system of the three, remained in the background, with—as noted in Chapter 6—the salesmen from Bethpage, Long Island, waiting to pounce.

Germany, whose Motoren-und-Turbinen Union firm hoped to build the Pratt & Whitney engines for the European AWACS planes, was now linking its decision to buy to its bid to sell the United States half a billion dollars of utility vehicles. In the familiar language of the late seventies, Bonn was insisting that the United States prove that NATO defense industries were a "two-way street," as Carter had promised. The Germans claimed that $330 million of "offset" costs for the proposed AWACS deal remained to be covered, and pointed out that they would only get a $50 million license fee out of adoption of the Rheinmetall gun on the Chrysler tank, plus another $50 million license fee on U.S. production of the Franco-German Roland missile. They proposed that the U. S. Army buy or lease (for fifteen years, at $600 million) the Gepard 35mm. antiaircraft gun, pending development of the U.S. equivalent. In all, Bonn finally negotiated $420 million of offset, to which would be added the financial advantages of the German basing of the plane.

France was considering buying two or three AWACS planes, or purchasing AWACS and Nimrod data through the NADGE data-link system, for a fee of about $20 million a year to the United States.

One of the other problems of selling AWACS was, as noted in the Grumman section of Chapter 6, that the European countries did not want to make command and control entirely airborne. The E-2C, as mentioned earlier, would have been easier to sell. But some sort of airborne early-warning capability was needed to counter low-level penetration by enemy raiders, flying beneath the radar horizon to attack NATO airfields and other targets. In 1977, General David C. Jones, then USAF chief of staff, showed a radarscope photo taken from an E-3A flying near Norfolk, Virginia; the hundreds of radar "returns"—aircraft—displayed on the scope ran from the southern tip of South Carolina to upstate New York, over 700 miles away. Jones contended that there was therefore no doubt that a single E-3A could cover the entire 500-mile gap between Scotland and Iceland. This, he inferred, the plane's competitors could not do.

Commenting on the AWACS issue, *Aviation Week*'s Clarence A. Robinson, Jr., wrote from NATO headquarters in Brussels that an initial buy of about a dozen planes was under consideration. He added:

> One of the principal issues involved . . . is modification of ground-based radar stations to interface with the joint tactical information distribution system data link on the E-3A. That link also will be on the Nimrod and the E-2C. Officials here estimate that establishing terminals for ground

radar sites would cost about $100 million, but that . . . would ensure that the E-3As could be moved to any area of crisis within the coalition and be used effectively. Otherwise, some members of the alliance, particularly those on the flanks, might be reluctant to participate in funding the procurement, believing that the small force of ten to twelve AWACS would be held for use in the central region of NATO where the perceived air threat is now greatest.

The present early-warning system in western Europe, NADGE—NATO air-defense ground environment—is a linkup of eighty-four radar sites in the nine NATO countries. NADGE transmits electronic data to controlled interceptor aircraft and surface-to-air missiles. All NADGE sites have difficulty with low-flying aircraft. Only thirty-four have a data-processing capability. Some are on hilltops and are highly vulnerable to attack. British Shackletons and American Lockheed EC-121s based in Iceland give partial coverage from the air, which will be improved when the EC-121s are replaced by USAF E-3As, based in Iceland and Scotland. There is no NADGE link to Iceland, where the long-range radar has been inoperable for several years. U.S.-Icelandic relations are poor and there would be objections on the island to bringing in more American personnel to man radar sites. Said *Aviation Week:*

> Use of either the E-3A or the E-2C or the British Nimrod would provide early warning without political problems in the area. Norway is reluctant to have U.S. or NATO forces based in that country. With the capability of remaining on station as long as six hours, one thousand nautical miles from its base, the E-3A is optimal for coverage of Iceland and [the] North Atlantic approaches, particularly in the Greenland-Iceland-United Kingdom gap. It will require a force of five E-3As to maintain a continuous alert on station for thirty days within 450 nautical miles from Iceland.

The commitment to buy the F-16 and costly U.S. missile systems had helped sour European governments toward buying the E-3A, despite the apparently expansive offset proposals. Germany, in particular, was reluctant to make a decision until the final French attitude was known. Although a French military evaluation committee reported favorably on AWACS, French political and public opinion was embittered by American reluctance to buy the civilian Airbus (only a few have been sold in the United States) and particularly by the curious New York campaign against the supersonic Concorde. Such factors apparently helped to dictate the statement by General Maurice Saint-Cricq, the French Air Force chief of staff, that the E-3A was too expensive and "vulnerable."

Germany, however, remained apparently convinced of the technical qualities of AWACS, especially after a reportedly successful 1978 exercise using the aircraft in Europe; and at a NATO Defense Ministers meeting in Brussels in May that year, a decision in principle was made to buy the planes—probably, eighteen of them—for main basing at Geilenkirchen in Germany and forward basing in Turkey. Flyaway cost of the program was put at $1.2 billion, with $600 million for initial support costs. Life-cycle operations-and-maintenance costs were now estimated at about $4 billion—an over 50 per cent increase on the original figure; but the substantial offset arrangements meant that, in the end, only a fraction of this bonanza would accrue to Boeing, the subcontractors and the United States. The United States was to pay an initial $770 million toward the program, Germany $550 million, Canada $175 million and other countries $320 million, with poorer members like Turkey, Portugal or Greece paying only $18 million each. The AWACS would cover land and sea areas, Nimrods ocean areas alone. But by 1979, when cancellation of the Iranian AWACS purchase raised the unit price of the planes, the European sale came under harsh scrutiny again.

United States/Germany

America's arms relations with Germany, the frontline NATO country with the second-best forces to those of the United States, have been marked by a series of disagreements, going back to the F-104 affair.

Long before the Starfighter fandango had reached full frenzy, Erhard, back in 1961, had written to Kennedy's Deputy Secretary of Defense Roswell Kilpatric promising to offset the costs of U.S. troops in Germany by buying $1.3 billion of U.S. equipment every two years. This purchasing program necessitated the sale of Germany's more obsolescent weapons systems, so the year before—with secret U.S. approval—Chancellor Adenauer had clandestinely met with Israel's Premier, David Ben Gurion, and offered to sell him $80 million of arms. This too was to lead to problems for Bonn.

In June 1964, Erhard asked Washington to take over Bonn's controversial commitment to Israel, but Johnson refused. Part of the Bundeswehr surplus sold to Tel Aviv that year consisted of two hundred American tanks. This made it impossible for the United States to deny that it had given its approval for the German sale, and news of the earlier U.S.-approved German transfers then surfaced.

Germany tried to excuse the sale as part of a "moral debt" to Israel, but in Cairo crowds stormed the German embassy and burned down the Kennedy Memorial Library. Nasser invited East German leader Walter Ulbricht to visit him. Within months, Germany had stopped aid to Israel.

Nassar did not cancel the Ulbricht invitation, so Germany stopped aid to Egypt as well. By then, Israel was angry at Germany too; Bonn, seeking to mollify Tel Aviv, agreed to exchange ambassadors. Ten Arab states then broke relations with Germany and began threatening to recognize East Germany. It was at this point that Paris announced that it would resume arms sales to Arab countries for the first time in a decade. Germany saw itself as left in the lurch by the United States, and taken advantage of by another ally, France.

Washington then agreed to take over German military aid to Israel—but covertly, counterbalancing this with a supply of Patton tanks to Jordan. Not until May 1966 did Johnson admit to having promised to provide Israel with attack aircraft.

With Germany still edgy from the F-104 fiasco and the collapse of its Mideast policy, Defense Secretary McNamara told von Hassel, by then his German opposite number, that if German offset purchases in the United States failed to meet the now inflated costs of the U.S. forces in Germany, these would be proportionately reduced. The exchange followed a German protest about the transfer of fifteen thousand American soldiers from Germany to Vietnam. Since the German constitution forbids deficit budgets, Erhard came to Washington to discuss a compromise, but failed to budge Johnson, Rusk and McNamara. On his return, he was forced to propose tax increases. The Free Democrats, his coalition partners, resigned over this, and Erhard's government fell.

Perhaps the most positive element in Washington's weapons diplomacy with Bonn has been the Fort Bliss arrangement. Between 1966 and 1976, twenty thousand German pilots and missile crews graduated from the school. By 1977, Germany was paying $5 million a year for the missile training system and other facilities on the Rhode Island-sized base, and $2.1 million for use of the airfield, while the German trainees and their dependents were spending between $8 million and $10 million a year in the El Paso economy. There was even a German school for the children. When the Anglo-Italo-German Tornado aircraft enters squadron service in Europe, training on this may be carried out in Fort Bliss's uncluttered skies, which have also attracted air and missile cadets from Kuwait, Saudi Arabia and Israel.

United States/Britain

Germany's defense problems with Washington are not an isolated case. America's relations with Britain have reflected similar intra-NATO disagreements over weapons. In 1960, Eisenhower and Premier Harold

Macmillan agreed at Camp David that Britain would scrap its Blue Streak nuclear-capable air-to-surface missile program; in return, the United States would supply the RAF with Skybolt missiles, with the United States paying for all R & D. Macmillan saw Skybolt as at least prolonging the life of Britain's "V-Bomber" force and giving Britain the autonomous nuclear strike capability it sought.

But Skybolt never got beyond the research stage and was scrapped in November 1962. The Macmillan government was rocked by this and the British press fulminated. Ike and Macmillan met again—this time in Nassau, in the British Bahamas colony, to enhance the British leader's prestige—and Ike promised to supply Britain with Polaris missiles for Britain's nuclear submarine fleet, then being built. Britain would supply its own atomic warheads. The V-Bomber force was scrapped.

America later had a similar shock, described earlier, when Washington helped engineer the sale of British Lightnings to Saudi Arabia—although their limited range made them unsuitable—to help Britain pay for Polaris and the F-111 fighter-bomber, in return for which Britain had canceled the TSR-2 plane; the following January, Britain, as part of thrift measures accompanying sterling devaluation, reneged on the F-111 order.

Britain's original commitment to the swing-wing F-111 was made in 1967, with deliveries to start in 1970. The order was for fifty. To offset the $1 billion, twelve-year cost, McNamara and Kuss agreed to help Britain export at least $240 million of military equipment by 1977, while at the same time procuring $325 million of British arms for the United States. Washington also agreed to waive terms of the Buy America Act (which said foreign suppliers had to be at least 50 per cent cheaper) to enable London to bid on an $80 million contract to build minesweepers for the U. S. Navy. Then, in September 1967, Republican John W. Byrnes of Wisconsin put through a House amendment to the defense appropriations bill, stipulating that all U.S. naval vessels must be built in American yards. Britain complained that it was bound to a contract which the United States was evading through congressional action. Said the London *Times* in an editorial: "It is not clear why Britain should sign contracts while the United States only agrees to understandings." American officials assured London that other means would be found to enable Britain to pay for the F-111s. The "other means" was the Saudi Arabian deal.

Britain was also angered by the U.S. decision to co-produce the proposed MBT-70 (Main Battle Tank of the seventies) with Germany. London argued that its Chieftain was already the best tank in Western forces, that its R & D costs had long since been amortized and that it was battle-tested (largely by Israel). But by then, Washington was sensitive to Germany's financial problems, which it had earlier played down as poor-mouthing. Later, of course, Germany was scarcely less unhappy than Britain over the final MBT decision. Europeans argued that it was the United States that had proposed the creation of a Defense Common Market, but by its own refusal to be dependent on a foreign arms supplier it had crippled the project from the start. But Britain remained, with Germany, one of America's two main arms customers in Europe, and in 1979 even decided to buy Trident missiles for its planned five new strategic submarines.

Other NATO Allies

NATO Allies' sensitivities about dependence on imported weapons systems were illustrated in 1974 when deliveries of F-104s to Greece were held up after the Cyprus coup. U.S. pilots making deliveries were ordered to stop over in Spain. Greece withdrew its forces from NATO command. The following year, Turkey was even more furious when huge defense orders for its forces were suspended, not to prevent their being used to support a coup d'état, nor for economic reasons, but to satisfy the small but noisily effective Greek lobby on the U.S. domestic scene— amplified by a picturesque Armenian lobby protesting about a massacre of secessionist Armenians in Turkey's monarchic past, nearly sixty years before. Both lobbies blatantly denied Turkey's legitimate right to intervene in Cyprus under the 1960 Treaty of Guarantee—the overt reason for the embargo—and to use U.S. weapons under the terms of a regional defense pact. When the Greek lobby won and the embargo was imposed, Turkey riposted by closing U.S. bases and electronic surveillance facilities.

Although the embargo on arms for Turkey was later partially lifted, the Greek lobby kept up its overt and arcane offensives, conscious that Ankara's disagreements with Athens sprang not only from Greece's sponsoring of the Cyprus coup but also from other acts of the Athens government. These include closure of Aegean airspace to all aircraft approaching or leaving Istanbul, the Greek Government's territorial claim to seabed rights for the whole Aegean, virtually up to the Turkish shore, and Greece's militarization of the Dodecanese islands in breach of two international treaties.

Teleguided by the lobby, Rhode Island senator Claiborne Pell complained in September 1976 that Turkey had moved "second-generation Pershing" missiles from the Soviet border to emplacements opposite the

Dodecanese. Deputy Defense Secretary Robert Ellsworth explained that Turkey had no Pershings, and said the Pentagon had no knowledge of redeployment of other missiles. Undaunted by getting misinformation from a lobbyist—usually a no-no on Capitol Hill—Pell pressed on; Ellsworth replied this time that no missile-equipped units had been redeployed in Turkey, period.

In 1977, Congress refused Carter's request to sell, on a government-to-government basis, F-4s already ordered by Turkey before the Cyprus coup. Faced with the possibility of having to pay expensive commercial-credit terms, Turkey began talking of playing down its NATO role and perhaps even of leaving NATO. It bought U.S. aircraft from Italy and Libya and other equipment from NATO's North Atlantic Maintenance and Supply Agency (NAMSA) in Europe.

In March 1978, Carter proposed repeal of the Turkish arms embargo. This won support in the House International Relations Committee but was rejected by its Senate counterpart. Congressional floor battles loomed; but when Turkish Premier Bulent Ecevit came to Washington at the end of May to chair the NATO summit, he spoke with both Hill committees and at the National Press Club against the embargo, which was hotly opposed by America's and Turkey's NATO allies; Congress, as noted in Chapter 2, repealed the embargo in the summer. After apparently deciding against buying French Mirages, Turkey expressed interest in the F-16 and, if it could afford it, the F-15.

A shakier NATO ally than Turkey or Greece—Portugal—had no difficulty getting over $30 million of grant-aid military assistance in 1977. The measure was pushed through the Senate by Republican Edward Brooke of Massachusetts—which with Rhode Island includes most of the Portuguese-American population. The measure also breezed through the House.

More controversial was an agreement by the Carter administration to set up a combined military coordinating and planning staff with Spain, to ease that country—gingerly emerging from dictatorship—into NATO membership; this was followed by a decision in May 1977 to sell Madrid F-16s and 270 Sparrow air-to-air missiles. The arrangements were made possible by congressional approval, the year before, of a U.S.-Spanish agreement—mentioned in Chapter 2—whereby the U.S. taxpayer would offer $1.22 billion in loans and gifts to Madrid, over five years, in exchange for limited use of three air bases, only one of them active, and a naval station. The fact that the squadron of Poseidon submarines currently based at Rota was to be withdrawn by 1979 to a new base at King's Bay, Georgia, did not improve the argument for Spain.

But at year's end, Spain was balking at buying 72 F-16s, for $1.5 billion, unless components were manufactured in Spain. France was offering 31 F-1s, for $136 million in flyaway costs, with co-production. Spain already had both U.S. and French aircraft in its inventory, so that either plane was acceptable. The United States said that unless Spain signed a letter of offer for the F-16s quickly, GD would not be able to guarantee delivery by 1982, nor maintain the offer price. France's chances for taking the sale away from the United States seemed good; but in 1979, Madrid was said to be still in the market for about a hundred U.S. planes, and to be still looking at F-16s, F-15s and F-18s.

United States/Sweden/Yugoslavia

Less controversial but more amusing was the 1976 revelation that, seven years before—while Sweden was officially and vociferously attacking U.S. policies in Vietnam—it had started secretly buying American equipment to listen in to Soviet military communications. So nervous had the "neutral" government of Olof Palme been of revealing its links with American intelligence—which of course benefited from the information secured through the devices—that Sweden had made the payments, not to the manufacturers (who were not informed who the customer was) nor to the U. S. Government, but in cash. Under the arrangement, then Defense Minister Sven Andersson sent cases of $100 bills to Major General Rockly Triantafellu, then chief of USAF intelligence. The bounty totaled $276,900.

The story surfaced in *Folket i Bild*, a Maoist biweekly, and was written by Jan Guillou, sentenced to a year in jail in 1974 for reporting that Swedish intelligence had links to the CIA and to Israel's Mossad. Swedish chief of staff Stig Synnergren said in 1977 that deliveries were continuing and "we will use the same method of payment . . . no matter what you write." Guillou's 1974 article had also alleged that Swedish agents had staged amphibious landings in Finland with American agents, and in 1973 had burglarized the Egyptian embassy in Stockholm to steal papers for Israel.

The U.S. arms supply relationship with Communist Yugoslavia, initiated to bolster Tito against Stalin, ended in 1961; but Belgrade had continued to spend an annual average of half a million dollars in the United States on spare parts. In 1977, it sought to restore the full relationship, specifically asking for laser-guided antitank weapons; talks began with an initial visit to Belgrade by Defense Secretary Brown. Any deal seemed likely to be controversial in Congress, especially as Yugoslavia, earlier that year, had violated U.S. foreign military sales regulations by giving American M-47 tanks from its inventory to the Marxist junta in Ethiopia.

In Belgrade, however, Brown agreed to expand military ties, with greater cooperation between the defense staffs of both countries and a U.S. training program for Yugoslav officers. Among new weapons to be supplied would be TOW antitank missiles and antiaircraft radar. But sales for fiscal 1978 did not surpass a tokenistic $1.5 million.

United States/Canada

Co-production and cooperation seemed to be working better with Canada. When the Royal Canadian Air Force agreed to buy eighteen Lockheed CP-140 Aurora maritime surveillance aircraft, Lockheed and about thirty subcontractors undertook to give about a billion dollars' worth of work to Canadian industry over eighteen years (1977–95)— roughly equivalent to the cost of the eighteen planes. The subcontractors alone agreed to offset $119 million of work over the first four years of the program. Lockheed also agreed to help Canadair and the Dettar Company of Canada market its products throughout the world.

Canada was to build parts for the CP-140 (the "C" is for Canadian) and for the P-3C Orion from which it is derived, and build complete P-3s for the non-American market (including ten for Australia) except where co-production arrangements precluded this—as they did with Japan. Lockheed called the Canadian offset deal "the largest major tooling move in modern history."

The arrangement called for $414 million in offset work, subject to time penalties. There would be $168 million in contracts for the manufacture of parts for perhaps as many as 150 P-3Cs, including Canadair's own 18–150 being the estimated total production of the plane, the infrared nose sensors of which can even analyze some cargos in merchantmen. Another $350 million of work was promised for the 1981–99 period, with Lockheed considering possible Canadian partnership in future U.S. naval contracts.

When the Canadian deal was announced in the spring of 1977, the Canadian Government also began seeking bids from six American and European manufacturers for the RCAF's multipurpose fighter of the eighties—a contract worth $2.3 billion over ten years. General Paul Manson, the Canadian former fighter pilot who was in charge of evaluating the competing aircraft, said he wanted "at least" 150 per cent offset, spread around Canadian industry. *Aviation Week* said the "industrial benefits list" would be "more comprehensive" than for the CP-140 program. The fighter order would be for 36 aircraft for Canadian defense, 54 for Canada's NATO commitments in Europe, from 12 to 24 aircraft for "northern flank of NATO" work, and 30 for training and attrition. Grumman was offering 44 used U. S. Navy F-14s as part of the deal, with deliveries to start at once, bringing total costs down to $1.6 billion, or $1.8 billion with all-new aircraft. The F-16, also well under the $2 billion ceiling, was to be offered with the new Sparrow missiles. Other contestants were the F-15, the F-18, the Panavia Tornado and the Dassault-Bréguet F-1E. In late 1978, Canadian Defense Secretary Barnett J. Danson narrowed the choice to the single-engined F-16, seen as the most economic over the long run, and the twin-engined F-18— the Canadian pilots' choice. He rejected suggestions that Canada take a mix of the two, and the F-18 seemed likely to win out.

A final and decisive set began to decide the match. General Dynamics was offering 142 F-16s, at $10.8 million each, including support costs. Canada said GD must "improve the quality of its offsets." GD was now offering to create 19,000 Canadian jobs by 1991, involving avionics, engine components, flight simulators and F-16 components for third-countries. Other GD contracts, involving not only aircraft but also ships, were promised as well, and Canada would receive the latest U.S. technology in composites, such as epoxy. There would be "direct investment" in Canadian jobs by GD, Pratt & Whitney, and Westinghouse, and "assistance to the Canadian Government in marketing Canadian products."

McDonnell-Douglas was now offering 127 F-18s at $17.7 million each but was told the RCAF must have "at least 140" aircraft for its $2 billion ceiling. However, the proposed offsets for the F-18 were especially attractive: 22,000 Canadian jobs by the early nineties, with 8,400 guaranteed by 1983–84; offset production work for Canada would include the guidance mechanism for the Tomahawk sea-launched cruise missile and for the air-launched version, contracts on the space shuttle, and construction in Canadian yards of methane tankers. McDonnell-Douglas and its subcontractors would buy Canadian technology in the solar energy, microwave, aluminum-plating and vacuum grain-drying fields.

Canada's R & D share on the F-16 would be $640,000 per unit, and $1,208,000 per unit for the F-18; but the United States was expected to waive these recoupments if necessary.

Out of the six competitors, Canadian sources said, the F-16 rated only fifth out of six on offsets, fourth out of six on the plane itself. The F-18 rated second in both categories. These sources said that, if money had been no concern, the F-15 would have been chosen, but the RCAF could only have bought 117 F-15s, and its operating costs—between $35 million, and $50 million per year—were also too high for Canada.

Industry experts said that a major part of the Canadian fighter agreement would be more closely defining offset work and compensatory Canadian exports. Canadian officials still talked hopefully of "150 per cent offset." Then a new factor intervened—the offer of cheap, used Iranian F-14s—which led to Ottawa putting off a final decision until late 1979.

The new aircraft will replace all fighter and strike planes in the Canadian inventory—103 CF-104s, 59 McDonnell-Douglas CF-101s belonging to North American Aerospace Defense Command, and 103 Canadair-made CF-5s. The F-5s will be kept as advanced trainers; everything else will go to the "trade-in" market.

Canada has probably been the most successful country in encouraging American offset, but other allies have also benefited. When the United States sold Phantoms to Germany in 1968, 25 per cent of the contract was offset. Britain got a slightly more generous deal when buying the F-111, but received no direct offset when buying Polaris submarines, Phantoms or C-130s. In recent years, Australia has insisted on offset arrangements. Under a 1973 pact, Defense agreed to buy Australian products equal to 25 per cent of the value of U.S. arms orders; U.S. firms "benefiting substantially from an Australian order" would "carry the initial and primary burden of offset implementation"; if U.S. contractors or subcontractors failed to fulfill offset objectives, Defense would allow Australian industry to bid on U. S. Government contracts or would select other Australian defense equipment. The agreement contained clauses about the quality and fair pricing of Australian products.

A June 1975 sale of eight P-3C aircraft for $113 million was offset by Lockheed buying Australian manufactures for a total of 30 per cent of the deal. In 1976, sales to Australia of two patrol frigates for $300 million and twelve transport aircraft for $90 million were conditional on offset. When the F-16 comes on stream, Australia is expected to replace its Mirage fighter fleet at a cost of about $500 million, of which $125 million will have to be offset. Australia was also considering the F/A-18, having decided against the Mirage-2000. Offset has not been offered to the less wealthy countries.

Co-Production and Technology Flight

The anxieties of arms-control reformers about the implications of co-production arrangements can only grow. The limitations set on co-

production in Israel come rather late, with many major projects already
under way. Northrop is helping Taiwan build its own F-5s, and is a partner with the Iranian Government in Iran Aircraft Industries. Bell, as
noted earlier, was helping Iran develop a domestic helicopter industry,
before the 1978 crisis.

Co-production in developed countries can also lead to third-country
spread of the weapons involved; there are already cases of this. Aeritalia,
under an agreement with Lockheed, quietly supplied F-104s to the
Turkish Air Force, thus saving Turkey from buying these out of its 1977
$175 million purchase ceiling from the United States. Turkey is a NATO
country, and the Aeritalia deal probably pleased the White House; but
of more concern to the United States were the activities of another Italian firm, Aeronautica Macchi, a Lockheed affiliate, which has sold some
of the Lockheed AL-60 transport planes which it has produced under license to the South African and Rhodesian air forces—both under arms
embargoes by the United States. As noted earlier, other "Italian" American aircraft have reached South Africa, while the Rhodesian forces have
acquired Bell 205A helicopters. Costruzioni Aeronautiche Giovanni
Agosta, initially suspect in the Bell sale, has in fact sold its Boeing CH-47
Chinook troop-carrying helicopters to the Libyan Air Force. Israel's attempts to export Israeli copies of French aircraft powered by American
engines to Latin America, and its controversial sales of weapons involving U.S. equipment to South Africa, raised similar Washington protests.

A 1976 GAO report spoke of Pentagon-approved co-production agreements valued at "$9.8 billion." Agreements valued at $2.1 billion were, it
said, under consideration. These agreements involved the production of
such diversified defense items as armored personnel carriers, howitzers,
tanks, rifles, machine guns, ammunition, helicopters, antitank rockets, aircraft and vessels.

The GAO report also mentioned 387 private licensing arrangements,
about three quarters of them related to aircraft parts; others were related
to complete aircraft, missiles, ammunition, armor, radar, sonar, gyroscopes and electronics. The report added:

> Co-production and licensing arrangements contain clauses which restrict
> third-country transfers of U.S. defense items. However, as in the case of
> direct sales of defense articles, no formal procedures or mechanisms exist
> to insure that transfers to third countries are not made without the prior
> approval of the President. According to Defense and State officials, U.S.
> Military Assistance advisory groups, defense missions and intelligence
> agencies do monitor end item use and disposition to a degree.

Even when transfers are held in check, co-production countries could use the defense information and technology acquired to produce their own arms for export, as in the notable case of Israel. The GAO added:

> Moreover, there is a large difference between the restrictions on third-country transfers of defense articles contained in the Foreign Military Sales Act and restrictions on commercial sales included in the International Traffic in Arms Regulations. Under the provisions of the . . . Act, the President cannot consent to the transfer unless the United States itself would transfer the defense article to the country. No such restraint exists on the granting of U.S. approval to a transfer under the Arms Regulations.

Technology is also spread through the generous distribution of classified manuals by U.S. firms to *prospective* clients. This is a genuine problem—no decision to buy is likely to be made by a potential purchaser without study of these materials; but there is virtually nothing to prevent a purchaser later deciding to buy, instead, from another country, including a Communist one, and secretly offering photocopies of the American manuals as a reason for getting a discount price.

The GAO report quotes Defense officials as saying that "to estimate the potential impact of an export of technology is much more difficult than to assess the importance of exporting a finished product." It adds:

> Where a piece of hardware is concerned, the U. S. Government usually has a fair chance of determining that it went to its intended destination. Should diversion be detected, the value can be reduced by shutting off follow-on spares and refusing to ship similar equipment. The damage to U.S. security tends to be limited, if only because machines and equipment have a finite utility and finite useful life. This is not so with technology. The United States cannot be assured of the uses to which its end products will be put; the United States cannot recall them, nor are they necessarily wasting assets.
>
> A further complication is the fact that the transfer of technology takes place in many ways and that the amount of significant information which can be transferred varies in each case. At one end of the scale is simple visual inspection of, or access to, an item of hardware. At the other end is the transfer of a complete production facility. Between these extremes are other means, such as oral communications, descriptive documents, engineering and manufacturing drawings, training of personnel, technical and management assistance, specialized tooling, and test equipment.

The report ends this section on a slightly contradictory note:

> According to Defense officials, any country with the know-how, the resources, and the will to do so can, over time, acquire any weapon or military capability it chooses. There is little the United States can do to prevent this, and to make such an attempt would be wholly unrealistic . . . Thus, delay is the measure of success.

A plethora of reports has followed. In 1978, the White House submitted its own, and the Congressional Research Service offered a critique. Clement Zablocki, chairman of the House International Relations Committee, commenting on these, said there was a "need for the executive branch to formulate a coherent, comprehensive policy on technology transfer. The need for such a policy is especially important to the long-term success of the President's efforts to restrain the proliferation of conventional armaments, limit the proliferation of nuclear-weapons capability, and promote social and economic development in the developing nations."

U.S. Weapons Technology for Communist Countries

The clear risk is that by selling or even attempting to sell American weapons systems and other products overseas, U.S. technology with defense implications may end up in unfriendly hands. At a little-noticed conference on arms transfers held at West Point in 1976, Dr. John F. Lehman, Jr., then deputy director of the Arms Control and Disarmament Agency, took the question of technology spread further, raising the point as to whether *direct* transfer of technology to Communist nations was not getting out of hand.

General Daniel Graham, the former director of the Defense Intelligence Agency, had complained earlier about sales, since 1972, by the Bryant Chucking Grinder Company to the Soviet Union of 164 Centalign-B precision-grinding machines for making ball bearings. Graham charged that this had enabled the Russians to produce MIRVed missiles, a capacity which they had not possessed before. The defense of the sale had been that other Western countries were offering competing equipment. In 1979, the Washington *Star* reported that Soviet computers built with Centalign-B machines were being used for ICBM guidance, improving target accuracy for some missiles to "600 feet." In 1974, according to Lehman, a sale of eavesdropping equipment by U.S. firms to the Soviet Union was stopped at the last minute, following congressional objections.

Years before, the sale by Britain to Moscow of fifty-five Rolls-Royce jet engines had enabled the Russians to produce their own version for the family of MiG fighter planes, beginning with the MiG-15—which explains why Rolls-Royce has had no difficulty overhauling the Tumansky engines of Egypt's MiGs. Lehman claimed that "of the forty-nine marine diesel engine designs used by the Soviets today in their merchant fleet, forty-two are of Western origin." Others have criticized U.S. sales of

TOW antitank missiles to Yugoslavia, a country which some feel may have a less friendly political orientation now that Tito is dead. In 1977, the Carter administration announced that it was reviewing the policy of exporting technology to Communist nations.

Much technology is believed to reach these countries at second hand. At West Point, Lehman proposed that the United States should only release to neutral countries such technology as it was prepared to transfer directly to the Communist countries. He opposed the sale of the F-14 and the E-2C to non-Allies. He thought F-16 and F-18 sales would spread a "technology that is unnecessary in many areas" and which could end up in the storehouse of Soviet knowledge. Disarmamentists tend to stress the point that sophisticated weapons sold abroad at least become obsolete one day, but that advances in technology, once parted with, cannot be recalled.

In 1978, Carter approved the sale to the Soviet Union, by Dresser Industries of Dallas, of a $144 million plant to make oil drilling bits, against the advice of national security adviser Zbigbiew Brzezinski and Energy Secretary James Schlesinger. A panel headed by J. Fred Bucy, president of Texas Instruments and a hardliner against détente, had also recommended against the sale. Opponents argued that any upgrading of Soviet oil technology could help a future war effort. But the exportation of the plant had the support of Secretary of State Cyrus Vance and Commerce Secretary Juanita Kreps—and of course of the U.S. business community. A particularly controversial part of the Dresser deal was the sale of a $1 million electron-beam welding machine. Defending the sale, Dresser pointed out that Japan had already sold Moscow $6 million of drill bits that year.

The most controversial issue is the direct sale of technology related to major arms systems to the Chinese and the Russians, a development highlighted by the Bryant company's order. The sale of two computers to China and one to the Soviet Union in 1976 raised a congressional storm; electronic and other "sensitive" machinery has also disappeared behind the Iron Curtain, with the blessing of the Department of Commerce.

David Rosenbaum, a Senate staffer, told the wire services in 1975: "The Russians have advanced their capability to make war on an international level from two to ten years with our aid—most of it from money-hungry corporations. Our own aircraft might be destroyed by Soviet missiles that could not have been built without U.S. technology. Pure greed is putting our know-how in the hands of our enemies."

Sales to the Communist countries need approval from the Commerce Department. Veteran Washington *Star* reporter Henry S. Bradsher has noted that the Department is "caught in the middle between industry's desire to sell, the Pentagon's wariness of letting the Soviets acquire potentially useful technology, and the State Department's desire to get along with other countries."

A GAO report said a U.S. export agency had ordered strategic electronic components by mail and shipped them to Holland, where they were resold to East Germany. A GAO source was quoted on the wires as saying: "The electronic components were fully adaptable to radar and communications systems of a military nature. There's no question [but] that the East Germans used them for military communications." Classified machine tools were also said by the GAO to have gone from the United States to Eastern Europe through West Germany, while a French firm producing integrated circuits for missile guidance and fire (targeting) control under American license was said to have sent to Poland a whole turnkey plant for manufacturing the same circuits used in the Minuteman ICBM.

When the news leaked out, Bucy, then still a senior Pentagon official, said: "We didn't have any way of stopping the sale. From Poland, the details of the circuit went right to the Kremlin. We have an informal agreement with our NATO allies prohibiting the export of [classified] technology to the Soviet Union and its bloc nations. But France and other nations are ignoring this agreement because they feel they can make money selling U.S. technology to the Communists."

By far the single biggest controversy of all has developed around the desire of giant American computer firms to sell their products.

In October 1976, Computer Data Corporation was authorized by the Ford administration to sell two Cyber-172 computers, costing between $4 million and $5 million apiece, to Peking, and a more advanced computer to Moscow. The Chinese said they wanted theirs for oil exploration, while the Russians said theirs was for weather research; but experts claimed that in their military mode the Chinese C-172s could be used for nuclear-weapon calculations, for antiballistic missile systems, or for radar to track hostile missiles.

Initially, an interagency task force and the Energy Research and Development Administration (ERDA) both counseled against sending anything with military possibilities to either country; but officials said Dr. Kissinger later changed his mind after Rolls-Royce sold Spey engines to China. The Pentagon withdrew its objection to the sale to China after the State Department forced China to accept permanent supervision by a Control Data supervisor; but critics maintained that he could not keep watch twenty-four hours a day, every day of the year.

James Bowe, director of corporate relations at Control Data, said the "172" had a "relatively small core memory. It has been around since 1974

and we have sold upwards of seventy of them, many of them overseas."
The sale was to be handled through Control Data's French subsidiary,
Compagnie Générale Géophysique. The sale to China was later approved by Cocom, the U.S.-NATO-Japanese commission which monitors
strategic sales to Communist countries. The Soviet sale, although tentatively approved by the Ford administration, was held over for subsequent confirmation by the incoming president.

Early in 1977, computer expert Miles Costick, writing in a publication
of the Georgetown University Center for Strategic and International
Studies, said the Russians were to get a Cyber-7300—"a large scientific
computer ideal for military applications and about fifteen years ahead of
current Soviet computer capability."

Arguing strongly against the sale, Costick said:

> All technologies revolutionizing warfare, such as giros, lasers, avionics,
> nucleonics, propulsion and computers themselves, are dependent on com-
> puters.
>
> For example, the world's most advanced computers (ILLIAC IV, CDC
> STAR-100, Texas Instruments' ASC and Goodyear's STARAN IV) were
> built with the aid of several large computers . . .
>
> The United States enjoys now and is expected to maintain a ten- or
> twelve-year advantage in computer technology, provided there are no ill-
> considered exports to the Soviet Union and other Communist countries.

Costick said the big Cybers were "high-speed, large-volume scientific
computers, suitable for military and intelligence operations. Only twelve
such installations exist in the world, and they belong to such organizations as the Atomic Energy Commission, the USAF, NASA and the
NSA."

In a later article, Costick said the Russians might instead be getting
the Cyber-76, the "world's largest strategic computer," which he said
could "process a phenomenal 100 million instructions per second" and
had "a memory storage capacity at least fifteen years ahead of anything
that a Communist computer maker is able to construct."

The conservative periodical *Human Events* also reported that the Russians might get the "76", which it described as "the world's largest and
most sophisticated computer." The journal said: "Control Data has
closed a tentative deal with Moscow, and the application for an export
license is pending before the Commerce Department. But Commerce
won't give the go-ahead unless Brzezinski gives a nod of approval."

In the House of Representatives, Democratic congressman Christopher Dodd of Connecticut complained that, "once in Soviet hands, this
computer could be used for almost any purpose—including navigation,

weapons guidance, surveillance, antiballistic missile defenses, submarines, et cetera . . . We must assure ourselves that we are not providing foreign countries with the seeds of our own destruction for the sake of alleviating the deficit in our deteriorating balance of trade." In all, sixty-five congressmen wrote to Carter opposing the sale.

In one of his Georgetown articles, Costick complained that Control Data had sold forty computer systems to Communist countries, and established a "joint operation with Romania" to penetrate Third World markets. It was seeking a co-production agreement with Moscow on "100-megabit disk memory units."

Costick added:

> The granddaddy of computer companies, IBM, has frequently sold advanced computers to the Soviet Union and its satellites. It sold the USSR what is believed to be the largest industrial computer in the world for use at the Kama River truck plant, and in 1974 it sold Hungary the advanced 370-155 . . .
>
> IBM has several other impending computer orders from the Soviet Union, including a triplex 36065 computer system for Soviet air traffic control, which would have obvious military uses.
>
> Other firms selling computer equipment, know-how or manufacturing capability to the Soviet bloc include Singer, Dataproducts and Willi Passer.

Costick quoted former Deputy Defense Secretary William Clements as admitting that "there have been some significant losses of advanced technology to the Communist countries, particularly in electronic and very exotic, sophisticated machine tools."

One result of U.S. help in building the Kama River truck-assembly plant at Naberezhnye Chelny was given to the House Armed Services Committee in 1979 by Hans Heymann, CIA national intelligence officer for political and economic affairs. Heymann said some of the 50,000 diesel engines produced at the plant in 1978 had gone into military trucks. He noted that the complex was scheduled eventually to produce 150,000 trucks and 250,000 engines annually, and that 30 per cent of its equipment came from U.S. sources, notably IBM, Swindell-Dressler of Pittsburgh and Ingersoll-Rand of Rockford, Illinois.

In reaction, Rick Burt of the New York *Times* quoted a Pentagon official as saying: "In approving the U.S. sales, our basic consideration was that if we did not make them, other Western nations would."

In 1976, Ford had vetoed an extension of the Export Administration Act which controlled strategic exports to Bloc countries. In its place, under an executive order, he imposed his personal authority over exports under the War Powers Act. For all intents and purposes, this gave technical authority to the NSC, which would only be likely to advise against a sale if it was to an enemy country. China is no longer considered hostile to the United States.

Congressman Robert Bauman, a conservative Maryland Republican, told his colleagues that "companies like IBM have peddled technologically advanced computers and air-traffic control equipment which the Soviets are using on their observation units at Russian military bases. IBM is not alone. Many other American-based multinational corporations have been less American than multinational in their pursuit of dollars in the market of a totalitarian society dedicated to the principle that . . . America must and will be destroyed."

Bauman also claimed that other, more obvious exports were dangerous. He recalled that when the Russians invaded Czechoslovakia, "they came in great numbers. They came in such large numbers, in fact, that there were not enough troop-transport carriers to bring them into Czechoslovakia, and *Life* and *Time* magazines of that fateful week reported instances of Russians traveling on bicycles and in milk wagons in order to bring off their strategic offensive. With the construction of Ford and Mack truck plants in the Soviet Union, invading Russian troops will not be burdened by such logistical problems in the future."

His equally conservative colleague, Robert Dornan of California, said: "It is as if these men had never learned that socialist dictatorships are inherently parasitic and can survive only by borrowing or buying from the free world. Lenin once said: 'The imperialists are so hungry for profits that they will sell us the rope with which to hang them.' He would be pleasantly surprised to see that not only are we selling the rope but we are doing it at bargain prices."

There were hints that Moscow might be prepared to go to desperate lengths to get the "76". The original story of the proposed computer sale was broken by Jeff Kamen, a reporter for WPIX-TV in New York, who passed the information on to Jack Anderson's associate Les Whitten. Fairfax County, Virginia, police said later that one of Kamen's sources had been attacked in his home while talking to Kamen on the telephone about the story. Someone fired or threw something through the source's window, covering him with shards of glass. Fairfax police records of the incident later mysteriously disappeared. After Kamen went on camera with the story, his father, a disabled, acute-care heart patient in Florida, received the first of what Kamen called "a series of obscene, harassing phone calls from an anonymous man who ended each call: 'Your son is spreading misinformation.'"

KGB agent? Passionate anti-Communist acting as *agent provocateur*? In June, Carter vetoed the Russian computer sale. Control Data complained at the time that the 1977 decision was "essentially political." The reasons given by the Administration were "very narrow" and would not stand up to close examination, the corporation said. The firm later gave its side of the issue to a closed hearing of the House subcommittee on international economic policy. In 1978, Carter vetoed the export of another American computer—ordered by the Tass news agency for the 1980 Olympics—ostensibly as a retaliation for "slander" trials in Moscow of two American correspondents, and "purge" trials of Soviet-Jewish dissidents. The Administration urged Britain, France, West Germany and Japan not to take over the Tass sale, noting that the $13 million Sperry Univac model requested had not been cleared for sale to Communist countries by COCOM. But the indications were that America's allies were hotly competing against each other for the contract, and in 1979 Paris announced that Tass was to get an Iris-80 computer in place of the Sperry Univac.

Presidential Review Memorandum 24, which had earlier advised Carter against the "76" sale to Moscow, also criticized sales of arms or sensitive technologies to China, saying these would endanger détente with the Soviet Union. This was essentially a State Department view. Other government experts involved with PRM-24, notably those from the CIA and the NSC, along with former Defense Secretary James Schlesinger, favored arming China to give the United States leverage over Russia in the SALT talks.

The Arms Control Association agreed with the State Department, noting in its newsletter that "such sales [to China] could further retard the already slow progress of Soviet-American arms negotiations," but remarking also that the Chinese see these negotiations "as an effort to deny China its nuclear place in the world."

The official Chinese press has called for the import of American weapons systems, and China has invited to Peking members of congressional committees with arms-sale oversight powers. Some experts noted that those Chinese leaders who had favored arms modernization in the past, and sometimes suffered politically for their ideas, were now in power; these experts thought the decision to invite Western observers like Schlesinger and New York *Times* writer Drew Middleton had been made in the (correct) supposition that they would write disparagingly of China's outdated equipment—thus strengthening the argument for more modern weapons. Washington sources said the Chinese were in the market for aircraft, including C-130s and helicopters, avionics, wire-guided antitank missiles, antisubmarine warfare equipment, laser range finders, Itek satellite cameras, nuclear reactors, more computers, and communications equipment. But at the time this book was written, no formal Chinese request had ever been made.

In Peking, Teng Hsiao-ping, the senior Deputy Prime Minister, told a visiting group of retired Japanese military officers that China was prepared to import arms to insure the modernization of its forces. General Stig Synnergren, the commander of Sweden's armed forces, was invited to Peking in 1977, and a Chinese military mission toured French army installations that year.

The Chinese have acquired a few American surface-to-air missiles and antitank missiles captured by Vietnam, along with Soviet models from Egypt; but they apparently lack the technology to copy them effectively. The Chinese have habitually purchased only limited numbers of foreign weapons systems—usually Russian, in the past—and simply pirated the technology, adapting the systems for Chinese use.

Defense Secretary Brown, in his policy statement on the export of U.S. technology, says that:

> Defense will normally recommend approval of sales of end products to potential adversaries in those instances where (1) the product's technology content is either difficult, impractical or economically infeasible to extract, (2) the end product in question will not of itself significantly enhance the recipient's military or warmaking capability, either by virtue of its technology content or because of the quantity to be sold, and (3) the product cannot be so analyzed as to reveal U.S. system characteristics and thereby contribute to the development of countermeasures to equivalent U.S. equipment.

After Zbigniew Brzezinski's visit to China in the summer of 1978, the White House lifted a ban on selling to China an airborne infrared scanning system for oil prospection with possible military applications. The $2.8 million order from Daedalus Enterprises of Ann Arbor, Michigan, detects infrared heat and focuses it onto a television screen with curved mirrors. (Its export to the Soviet Union remained forbidden.) Peking was delighted by Carter's approval, and responded by inviting Pennzoil, Exxon, Phillips and Union Oil to prospect in China.

U.S. officials were also considering a Peking request to buy an array processor for seabed exploration which could also be used for antisubmarine warfare; but the administration continued to oppose the sale to China of Japanese computers containing U.S. technology. China had made the deal attractive to Tokyo by offering to pay in oil.

Discussions began that year on the sale and launch by the United States of a communications satellite for China. A Chinese team arrived in the United States to buy ground stations and other associated "Landsat" equipment, and the deal—$10–15 million in construction costs, about $15 million for launching, and $200 million a year to NASA for receiving data from U.S. satellites—received official White House approval. Contracts were signed in December. Officially, the satellite would be to aid Chinese scientific, industrial and agricultural abilities, but experts agreed that the space unit could also have defense uses.

At the Fermi National Laboratories near Chicago, groups of Chinese nuclear physicists are spending six months at a time studying the high-energy "atom-smasher" accelerator. The number of ordinary Communist Chinese students in U.S. universities, mostly doing science and engineering, increased from five to about five hundred in the fall of 1978, and top officials from twenty-five American colleges were summoned to Washington to discuss admitting ten thousand in the fall of 1979.

China has already bought French Super-Frélon helicopters and German Messerschmitt-Bolkow-Blohm Bo-105 helicopters, as well as large quantities of aluminum—possibly for copying them.

Some American experts argued against sales to China as posing a threat to Taiwan; but the majority viewed Chinese military modernization as mainly aimed at the threat from Russia, which directs about 30 per cent of its defense budget to the eastern frontier. The Russians, similarly concerned about China, only signed a trade agreement with Britain in 1975 after the British agreed not to sell China Harrier V-STOL aircraft for the time being. But London, as is noted in Chapter 9, later offered Harriers to China.

Although U.S. arms sales to China were still banned after the establishment of full Washington-Peking relations in December 1978, it seemed inevitable that increased U.S. exports of equipment with defense applications would flow from the new relationship, and China decided in late 1979 to standardize its weaponry on Western systems.

Meanwhile, also in December 1978, the Commerce Department fined the Geo Space Corporation of Texas $36,000 and suspended its right to export controlled technology for fifteen months, for selling array transform processor (ATP) equipment to the Soviet Union and China. Commerce noted that ATPs could be used for antisubmarine warfare detection.

ARMS SALES POLICY

U.S. military assistance officers overseas work from a five-page set of guidelines originally issued by General Fish's office in the Pentagon.

These prohibit soliciting trade: "Sales offers will be made only in response to a valid request at a foreign country's initiative," the first guideline says.

Further injunctions are:

> Sales will be made only if it [sic] serves our national interest and it [sic] meets a valid military requirement.
>
> Sales will not be encouraged or promoted except as specifically authorized by the Assistant Secretary of Defense (International Security Assistance).

Until Congress reversed the trend, another instruction read:

> Where practicable, foreign countries will be encouraged to purchase directly from U.S. commercial sources rather than from the DoD on a government-to-government basis.

There is a warning against too much U.S. involvement:

> It is your responsibility to encourage the host [country] to lessen dependence on the administrative "crutch" which is provided by the Military Assistance Program in such areas as programming, communications, military technical assistance and transportation of equipment . . . Ideally, the administrative assistance provided to the host country should decrease in proportion to the phaseout of MAP.

There is a reminder that arms sales are economic:

> Direct sales are preferred to co-production arrangements unless there is a clear contribution to U.S. national interests to be gained by [co-production].

Officers are asked to plan weapons-modernization programs realistically far in advance, and to recommend "the least sophisticated equipment [for] the mission. This often can be furnished from inventories or from production lines with relatively short lead time."

Support functions should be left as far as possible to private contractors "to limit requirements for DoD skilled manpower and to reduce the obvious U.S. military presence in the country involved."

The instructions continue:

> The factors which should be considered before recommending any action which would impact upon U.S. forces include:
>
> a. The relationship of the recipient nation's defense capability to U.S. security interests;
>
> b. Whether force levels projected by the host are realistic, based upon what is needed, what the country can sustain, and what can be provided by the Defense Department;

  c. Economic and political considerations within the country; and

  d. The scope and phasing of actions leading to achievement of planned military capabilities (i.e., to what degree can current forces accomplish missions, and what equipment is needed and when to improve capabilities significantly?).

  It is not the responsibility of the MAAG/MilGroup to encourage or promote sales. The MAAG/MilGroup does have a responsibility to facilitate sales by providing assistance to U.S. industry in making sales directly to foreign governments to meet valid requirements. Also, in performance of their advisory duties, the MAAG/MilGroups will undoubtedly be requested to express an opinion on the relative merits of equipment or services under consideration for purchase by their host country.

Finally come some warnings about the potentially sensitive nature of relations between the Pentagon and industry:

  a. MAAGs/MilGroups will receive from time to time proprietary information from companies. There is an obligation to keep this information in confidence and not pass it to competing companies.

  b. All relations with industry must be strictly at "arm's length." All dealings with private firms must be evenhanded. What you do for one, you must be willing to do for all.

  c. Rules on social activities, receipt of gifts, etc., are set forth [above]. However, some situations cannot be covered by rules alone and take a keen sense of judgment. It is better to "err on the side of caution."

  d. U.S. companies are expert in the field of marketing and are the most knowledgeable as concerns their product and its potential. Thus, it is not only their obligation but also their opportunity to do the selling. Ideally, the U.S. company should gather its own sales leads and make any necessary financing through the private sector. It should also do its own follow-up on the sales and carry out its own training and servicing program.

The fact that firms must now pass their major sales to the Pentagon to complete does not change this. As regards financing, three types of credit assistance are available to purchasers of U.S. arms. The 1976 GAO report listed these as: private guaranteed credit, with the U. S. Government guaranteeing repayment (the Government charges a fee for this service of .25 per cent); ExImBank credit, for developed countries; FMS direct credit, under which the Government directly finances the procurement of defense articles for credit sales, with funds appropriated annually by the Congress (Government policy confines this type of financing to less-developed countries; interest is usually charged at the current average interest rate).

The report said that congressional concern over excessive credit financing had led to certain restrictions. There was an annual ceiling, and regional ceilings for African countries, South Korea and India; "sophisticated weapons systems" could not be financed for "any underdeveloped country other than Greece, Turkey, Iran, Israel, [Taiwan], the Philippines and [South] Korea, unless the President finds that such financing is important to U.S. national security and reports such determination to the Congress within thirty days." There are other safeguards, notably taking into account the "purchasing country's financial condition and need for credit." The ACDA also reviews the propriety of the transfer from an arms-control standpoint.

The Pentagon administers the FMS program, pricing articles and services, including packing, handling, transportation, administrative charges and training. Discount or higher prices may be charged in appropriate cases. The Defense Department can, in the case of state-of-the-art equipment, recoup from foreign purchasers a fair share of the research and development costs charged by the manufacturer to the U. S. Government.

The GAO found ten cases of "inadequate recovery by Defense of all costs associated with articles and services." Mostly these cases referred to failure to recover contract administration costs, the costs of Government-owned assets, transportation and training costs, or adequate R & D and production costs.

Since the days of Secretary McNamara's red, gray, white and blue defense-sales "teams," the Pentagon has been deeply involved with arms sales. Former Deputy Defense Secretary William P. Clements, Jr., said in 1976 that foreign military sales would be such a "high priority mission" until the late eighties that more officers should be "pulled off" other programs to support the sales drive. When the Lockheed bribe scandal in Japan surfaced later that year, the Pentagon rescued the sale of Lockheed P-3Cs by taking it over as a government-to-government deal. Foreign governments usually feel safer dealing with U. S. Government officials than with businessmen, partly because complaints can be directed to the embassy. Handling the FMS program also increases the U.S. diplomatic leverage acquired from sales. Dr. Kissinger, for instance, as noted earlier, promised A-7s to Pakistan (later vetoed by the Carter administration) to persuade then President Bhutto not to purchase nuclear-reprocessing technology from France.

At the head of Pentagon sales until recently was Air Force Lieutenant General Howard Fish, a boyish, gray, tough-mannered Patton-style officer who wore his uniform to the office, which was decorated with models of warplane prototypes. While talking, Fish—who is now vice-president/international affairs of the Vought Corporation—occasionally turned to an impressive eighteen-digit calculator beside his desk to provide a statistic. Fish claimed that U.S. military missions overseas did not push sales as hard as their British and French equivalents. He noted that 60 per cent of sales (80 per cent in the case of Saudi Arabia) were infrastructure, not weapons. The then Deputy Defense Secretary, Robert Ellsworth, stressed the same point in 1976 House testimony, noting that the same was not true of Soviet arms sales. Ellsworth quoted SIPRI as estimating actual Soviet weapons transfers from 1950 to 1974 as being 12 per cent higher than those of the United States.

Are U.S. arms sales too high? Fish said in an interview that, since passing the Nelson amendment—assuring congressional review of all sales surpassing $25 million—Congress had never actually vetoed a sale not subject to an embargo. U.S. arms sales today, Fish claimed, are encouraged mainly in the interests of rationalization and standardization within NATO. He said the United States recognizes that European arms industries, relieving European dependence on U.S. supplies, are important to national independence—hence the push for co-production of American systems in Europe.

Fish said America has frequently let its Allies pick up Third World sales, partly because they were under less of a probing searchlight—less legislative and public pressure opposed to sales. He denied that there had been many serious end-use contraventions of the Foreign Military Sales regulations, noted that the Arms Export Control Act called for sanctions only in the case of "significant breaches," and said that in his opinion neither Turkey nor Greece breached the Act in Cyprus in 1974—or not enough to matter. He said there was a breach by Libya concerning Turkey, when Tripoli transferred F-5s to Ankara in 1976. The principal FMS breaches that Fish recalled were by France, Britain and Israel at Suez in 1956 (under earlier legislation) and by Israel in 1967. Fish also denied that much Vietnam surplus was reaching world markets. Most of it, he said, lacked spare parts (although, given the war situation under which it was provided, the spare-parts inventories were in fact probably huge; and if the matériel is likely to "rot," as Fish maintained, this would be all the more reason for the Vietnamese to sell it reasonably soon).

As the Pentagon's top arms salesman, Fish naturally stressed the value of arms sales as a policy tool. The 1976 GAO study agreed that the sales program was a "useful and highly effective instrument of foreign policy."

But if recipients are dependent on suppliers, a powerful customer can exert reverse power, as noted earlier. Arms exports alone employ about 5 per cent of all American workers. The importance of these jobs to members of Congress and even to the White House gives major arms purchasers considerable leverage to get what they want. The fact that the Shah, for instance, bought more British Chieftains than the British Army made him more important to the manufacturer than the British Minister of Defense.

Weapons and Wealth

E. F. Schumacher, the British economist who wrote *Small Is Beautiful*, claimed that since corruption seems to increase with a country's size, aid is least effective when conducted on a major scale. One of his most quoted comments is: "The poor people in rich countries pay to the rich in poor countries."

This principle applies to arms aid, where what is at issue is less corruption (although that of course exists) than its "honest" corollary—exuberance. More money is wasted on oversophisticated arms when supplier and recipient are biggest, or at least wealthiest.

However, the evidence seems convincing that the Soviet Union has genuinely sought arms restraint in the Middle East in recent years, and that it is U.S. supplies which have mostly fueled the current race. In Russia, only one element in society can argue for arms transfers—the government. In America, industry itself gets into the act, as do the lobbies. But the United States at least seeks hard-currency sales, which itself imposes some restraint. Russia, seeking only political advantage, not solvency for industries, accepts soft-currency and barter deals, and offers loans at dream interest rates.

Disarmamentists argue for a joint NATO-Warsaw Pact agreement to limit conventional sales in the same way that nuclear arms sales have been tightly restricted. The ACA points out, for instance, that more than 85 per cent of conventional arms are still sold by the United States, the Soviet Union, France and Britain. Persuading France, Britain—and Germany—to accept sales restraint would probably involve the difficult task of getting Congress to allow the Pentagon to take up some of the European sales slack by the United States buying more European weaponry. The bottom-line problem is that each country wants flexibility, to use its arms industry as a tool in its sovereign foreign policy. In Europe, only Germany, which in 1975 refused to supply Leopard tanks to Iran (Britain at once offered Chieftains) or eight hundred Marder armored personnel carriers requested by Saudi Arabia, has been susceptible to arms-control arguments—although Sweden and Switzerland, of course, employ self-restraint as a matter of neutrality. German, Swedish and Swiss self-restraint also reflects their wealth.

An alternative to America's buying more weapons from European and other friendly countries would be "offset"—buying more of something else. The United States has agreed to offset arrangements with five countries so far; the Canadian and Australian examples have been mentioned earlier. The system was also undertaken by a European country, Germany, to help cover U.S. costs of stationing troops there, and there have been other, more recent cases of Bonn offering offset arrangements to client-states. But other arms-selling countries with balance-of-payments deficits, such as Britain, have been reluctant to accept such quid pro quo arrangements.

Weapons Diplomacy and the 1976 Election

President Carter's vague additional sales limitations of 1977 built on the International Security Assistance and Arms Export Control Act signed (after the veto of a more far-reaching measure) by President Ford the year before. The 1976 Act did several things: It required the phaseout of the MAAG program and military assistance by September 30, 1977, unless authorized by Congress on a case-by-case basis; it made the 1976 arms-sales figure a ceiling for the future; transfers of over $25 million of arms became a government-to-government concern; the Act called for an annual presidential, country-by-country report on arms sales and an arms-control impact statement; it limited agents' fees (large fees encourage irresponsible sales), theoretically forbade kickbacks, and prohibited drawdowns on U.S. forces' stocks except in special cases certified by the President; the Act denied military and economic assistance to countries supplying or receiving nuclear-enrichment or reprocessing equipment without appropriate International Atomic Energy Agency safeguards. Strictly speaking, the latter provision would preclude Israel from arms sales, but will certainly not do so; like most laws on arms, the style surpasses the substance.

Most importantly, the Ford measure already limited sales of missiles and jet warplanes to most developing countries, except in certain emergencies, and called on the President to take the lead in initiating multilateral discussions on arms-sales restraints, including convening a conference of major suppliers and purchasers. Section 301 of the Act signed by Ford already included human-rights provisions which Carter later made his own. No assistance would be offered to any country discriminating against defense suppliers on the "basis of race, religion, natural origin or sex," if the supplier was a "United States person," or to countries which grant sanctuary to "international terrorists," who were not defined. There were the usual provisions enabling the President to seek congressional approval for exceptions.

It is with the thought of all the exceptions in mind that the ACA wants stricter unilateral arms-control policies by the United States. The ACA supports the UNA report calling for a moratorium on the transfer by the United States to Third World countries, especially in the Middle East, of fighter-bombers, surface-to-surface missiles with "city-busting capabilities" and of nuclear-capable missiles, and restricting the transfer of arms-manufacturing equipment and technology to developing countries. The arms-transfer conference at West Point in 1976 added to the proposed freeze all city-busting weapons and long-range attack aircraft. The UNA wants a U.S.-Soviet freeze, particularly, on the delivery of "very advanced arms" to the Arab states and Israel, consultation between the two superpowers before any major arms shipments to the area, a coordinated NATO arms-sales policy in the Third World, and a Security Council ruling on the "shipment of armaments to regions of high tension."

Some aspects of restraint are feasible, but as they stand, the UNA recommendations would involve withdrawal of some assistance already in place—an unlikely development—and above all they would conflict with Israel's (and tomorrow perhaps other countries') sophisticated ability to produce its own region-destabilizing systems. For instance, Israel's neighbors need a response to the Jericho surface-to-surface missile, if war is to be discouraged.

The Arms Control and Disarmament Agency favors banning sales of long-range interdiction aircraft and cheap precision-guided munitions. At the West Point conference, a questioner asked Dr. John F. Lehman, Jr., then deputy director of ACDA, whether his agency was merely offered a "cut" in administration arms developments as a sop to its beliefs. Lehman gave the following interesting answer:

> Well, let me put it this way: In this year's budget request there are three items, which I will not identify, that we opposed. We felt that these developments were adverse to the U.S. national interest on arms-control grounds. Eventually, we argued our case at the senior level of the White House, at an SRG meeting. On those three items we were overruled. On two items, we are participating in a study that, in effect, vindicates our original criticism. Nevertheless, I will testify in support of those three, and I will continue to be treated as a member of the deliberative body within the Executive Branch that makes those decisions. If I tell the Congress that I have a crisis of conscience or that the Agency opposes these three items, I can probably kill those three programs this year. You might say that is in the national interest. But it [would] be the last year ACDA ever [participated] in Executive deliberation.

The West Point conference recommended submitting all arms transfers to eleven guidelines. The transfer in question should be "limited to mutual security objectives," nonnuclear, "relatively humane," and "geographically suitable." It should be defensive, "nonprovocative" and "incapable of overwhelming destruction in a short war." It should also be "not redundant," recipient-maintainable, technologically secure and industrially competitive. The conference noted that "certain types of weapons would consistently not pass the test; for example, surface-to-surface missiles, long-range attack aircraft and city-busting weapons."

Barry R. Schneider of Brookings offered a checklist of twenty-seven questions which he suggested should be answered before any arms transfer was made. These included such questions as the U.S. interest, including leverage and "quid pro quo," arms balance, whether the technology was new for the region, or secret, and whether alternative suppliers were in competition. Schneider also considered the balance of payments, human rights, and the customer-state's ability to pay without damaging its economy. Schneider's Question 19—"Whose idea was this arms transfer?"—raises the question of the legitimacy of lobbies in this area.

There is obviously a strong liberal bias to all these attitudes and questions. Answering most of Schneider's questions truthfully would have made it hard to approve any arms transfers to Iran, Israel or Saudi Arabia.

The experts at West Point and at similar seminars in Washington and elsewhere seem agreed that the high cost of American and other modern weaponry has had relatively little impact on oil prices in the purchaser-nations; but they seem equally agreed that rapid increases in arms supplies to any area frequently lead to conflict. Many experts say cynically that the most effective arms control at present appears to be slow and delayed deliveries. Middle East wars, it is noted, are usually short and sharp and largely limited to military targets, with Israeli attacks on civilian targets in Lebanon the main exception: The objective is to win quickly before the superpowers impose peace to avoid escalation. If U.S. defense attachés abroad turn down an arms purchaser's request—as they frequently do, to the annoyance of U.S. arms manufacturers—the potential purchasing country will usually go over their heads to Washington; however, if the local American officers say "yes," Washington invariably agrees.

Countries like prerevolutionary Iran have an added leverage—base rights. Spain has used this to advantage also, although not a NATO country and not, until recently, an acceptable country politically. The disaster of the Greek lobby's success in cutting off arms to Turkey showed the importance of the base-rights factor. Had Congress known that Turkey would honor its threat to retaliate by closing the bases, it would have been more susceptible to White House counterlobbying. An effective arms-restraint policy would be dependent on the ultimate removal of superpower forces from all countries not linked to them by defensive alliance—and this is presumably the point toward which the Carter policy is tentatively moving.

Indeed, the most expressed fear of the disarmamentists is of the potential growth of firepower in small states and even revolutionary groups. The cheap, city-busting cruise missile attracts most of the attention, along with the concomitant spread of nuclear technology; but light, relatively cheap naval craft also cause anxiety. Professor Kemp says, for example, that

> the trend in naval procurement is toward smaller . . . vessels armed with increasingly lethal weapons, such as the French . . . missile Exocet and the U.S. Harpoon. [This] means that small states which cannot afford modern capital ships can nonetheless purchase naval weapons which, in certain limited cases, can pose military problems for the maritime powers.
>
> . . .
>
> For example, Malaysia, armed with its Exocets . . . or mines could make it impossible for an oil tanker bound for Japan to negotiate the Strait of Malacca. Or . . . either Mozambique or Madagascar could interfere with shipping traffic in the Mozambique Channel.

The daunting problem for Malaysia or Madagascar as to what to do next, in these cases, is perhaps reason for not worrying too much about such potential acts; but what would happen if a future Marxist Malaysia used its Exocets, not to provoke a big-power attack on Malaysia in the way Kemp indirectly suggests, but to "take out" pieces of Singapore?

The 1976 election campaign brought arms sales into public focus and generated a flood of rhetoric. In written interrogatories with *Arms Control Today*, the ACA newsletter, Ford and Carter expressed their views:

Ford: Any attempt to curtail arms sales will probably be unsuccessful unless all nations involved . . . agree. [I am] unwilling to create a situation in which the more responsible nations are forced to sit by, having agreed to cease arms sales abroad, while the less scrupulous nations [which] opt not to join the agreement are allowed to be the sole suppliers to the ever-increasing market. Such a unilateral curtailment would do little to restrict the traffic in arms.

Carter: We cannot be both the world's leading champion of peace and the world's leading supplier of weapons of war . . . We must assess every arms sale . . . to ensure that the only sales we make are those that promote peace in the regions and carry out our committed foreign policy. At the same time, . . . certain arms sales programs . . . are necessary so that Israel can pursue peace from a position of strength and security. Our diplomacy in this area should be based on a four-part approach: (*a*) an international conference of suppliers and consumers to put the issue to the forefront of the world's arms-control agenda, (*b*) greater U.S. self-restraint, (*c*) working with Western suppliers and the Soviets to dampen down arms-sale promotion, and (*d*) support for regional efforts to limit the arms buildup.

In the televised foreign-affairs debate, Ford took Carter to task for his promise to cut, first "$15 billion," then "$8 or $9 billion," then "$5 or $7 billion" from the defense budget. As noted earlier, post-electoral realities were to result in Carter approving a higher fiscal-1978 defense budget than Ford's 1977 total, and in his making only about $2 billion of cuts in the 1978 budget proposed by outgoing Republican Secretary of Defense Rumsfeld—or about the amount that a Democratic Congress might have cut anyway.

Carter in turn roasted Ford on international arms control. "Mr. Ford's been in office two years and there has been absolutely no progress made toward a new SALT agreement," he told 40 million American viewers in the incumbent's presence. He reiterated a plan for "a complete moratorium on the testing of all nuclear devices . . . [and] that we not ship any more atomic fuel to a country that refuses to comply with strict controls over the waste, which can be reprocessed into explosives." America should "stop the sale" of reprocessing plants to Pakistan by France and to Brazil by Germany.

On arms sales, Carter said he would "never let [our] friendship with the People's Republic of China stand in the way of the preservation of the independence and freedom of the people of Taiwan." But he excoriated sales to Mideast countries other than Israel, saying these other sales were based on oil blackmail. He went on:

> If the Arab countries ever again declare an embargo against our nation on oil I would consider that an economic declaration of war and I would respond instantly and in kind. I would not ship that Arab country anything—no weapons, no spare parts for weapons, no oil-drilling rigs, no oil pipe, no nothing.

A moment later, he said:

> If you include Iran in our present shipment of weapons to the Middle East, only 20 per cent goes to Israel . . . Iran is going to get eighty F-14s before we even meet our own Air Force order for F-14s. And the shipment of *Spruance*-class destroyers to Iran are [*sic*] much more highly sophisticated than the *Spruance*-class destroyers that at present are being delivered to our own Navy. This is ridiculous and it ought to be changed.

Ford failed to point out that the USAF has not ordered F-14s. But he did say that

> we have made available to the Israelis over 45 per cent of the [world-wide] total economic and military aid since the establishment of Israel twenty-seven years ago . . .
>
> The Soviet Union and the Communist-dominated government of Iraq are neighbors of Iran . . . The history of our relationship with Iran goes back to the days of President Truman when he decided that it was vitally necessary for our own security as well as that of Iran that we should help that country. And Iran has been a good ally.

Ford noted that Iran had not participated in the 1973 oil embargo, and added: "I believe that it's in our interest, and in the interest of Israel and Iran and Saudi Arabia, for the United States to sell arms to those countries." Less than two years later, Carter had come around to Ford's ideas.

Speaking during the campaign to the Commonwealth Club of California, vice-presidential candidate Walter Mondale said: "I believe there should be a presumption against arms sales which should be overcome only if the sale advances American security, foreign policy, or world peace." Needless to say, including "foreign policy" as a guideline would probably make virtually any arms sale justifiable.

Carter's nuclear-moratorium proposals were the only "front-page" material in an otherwise lackluster inaugural speech the following January. But on coming to office, the new President found a series of far-reaching arms-sales restraint proposals ordered by Ford. The State Department's position papers called for a temporary *halt* in worldwide arms sales and a major shift in sales policies. GOP Defense Secretary Rumsfeld had also prepared a similar review. Many of the proposals later emerged as Carter administration policy.

The State Department suggestions, authored by William B. Robinson, the OMC director, called for a major tightening of the International Traffic in Arms Regulations, blocking "brochuremanship" sales ploys by U.S. arms suppliers without prior State Department approval, regardless of the advantages that this might give to France, Britain and other competitors. Government assistance for U.S. participation in arms shows was withdrawn. At the Farnborough Air Show in Britain in 1978, as noted in the previous chapter, the Fairchild A-10 and a Chinook helicopter were the only American military aircraft on display. McDonnell-Douglas was forbidden to exhibit the Harpoon missile. It had been allowed to display it at a British naval exhibition at Greenwich a few weeks earlier but was refused permission to show it at a similar naval occasion in Rotterdam—so as not to encourage non-NATO prospective purchasers. (Later, however, the new Pentagon arms-sales director, Lieutenant General Ernest

Graves, announced that Carter would probably relax restrictions on U.S. participation in the equivalent Paris air show of 1979.)

Other State Department proposals were: No new weaponry should be sold abroad until it had been in U.S. military service for at least two years (apparently aimed at the F-18L for Iran); a ban on selling any missile with a range of more than 75 miles or "weapons especially suitable [to] terrorists" such as shoulder-fired missiles; a ceiling on U.S. weapon technicians sent abroad with exported systems, and the establishment of an Arms Export Control Board, to be chaired by the Under Secretary of State for Security Assistance, which would review all sales of over $25 million. The only exceptions to the export limitations would be for Europe and Japan.

In his first press interview after taking office, Carter told wire-service reporters that he had "asked that all . . . arms sales, for a change, be submitted to [the Oval Office] directly before the recommendation goes to Congress."

Perhaps the most strident commitment on weapons exports in his campaign had been Carter's religious insistence on not supplying arms to regimes which violate human rights. Shortly after he took office, the State Department had released its 1976 report showing that only twenty-three of the eighty-two countries receiving U.S. aid respected human rights with any adequacy. In two of the twenty-three, these rights were not respected completely, the report said, singling out Britain's behavior in northern Ireland and Israel's in the occupied territories for criticism. The juntas of Brazil, Argentina, Guatemala, El Salvador and Uruguay, which were among the governments condemned in the report, all huffily announced that they would refuse aid already offered. Brazil canceled its twenty-five-year-old military assistance treaty with the United States. A year earlier, Dr. Kissinger had refused to comply with a congressional demand for a human-rights report, saying that it would annoy friendly countries without achieving reforms.

Fifty-eight senators wrote Carter a letter on March 23, 1977, approving the President's international human-rights concerns. It was not a difficult letter to sign, and the signatories included conservatives like James Allen of Alabama and Herman Talmadge of Georgia, along with right-wing Republicans like Strom Thurmond of South Carolina, Jesse Helms of North Carolina and newly elected Sam Hayakawa of California. But the State Department had already recommended, in a classified report, that military aid should continue to go, for political reasons, to "violators" like Argentina, Haiti, Indonesia, Iran, Peru, the Philippines and South Korea; and the new Secretary of State, Cyrus Vance, had warned that the human-rights question must be handled "pragmatically" and take into account American security interests. In hearings, "human rights" restrictions on arms transfers were even opposed by Patricia Derian, a Mississippi civil-rights leader who is the Carter-appointed coordinator for human rights in the State Department, and by Ambassador Terence Todman, Assistant Secretary of State for Inter-American Affairs, a black career diplomat.

By the time Carter had reached London in May for the economic summit, his aides were telling reporters that he was easing up on human rights. A day after the inauguration, the President had responded to a letter from Soviet dissident Andrei Sakharov. Later, Russian ire at some of Carter's positions had helped torpedo the first SALT-II talks in Moscow. In May, the aides revealed that he had received a second letter from Sakharov a few weeks before and had decided not even to acknowledge it. Carter had come to agree with Kissinger that, except in flagrant cases with no strategic or important foreign-policy connotations like South Africa or Uganda, quiet diplomatic pressure would be more effective than anything that looked like headline-hunting. However, human rights remained officially one of the factors when considering U.S. arms transfers. In short, withholding arms is a form of weapons diplomacy, and violations of human rights could be one reason for withholding them.

The Carter Guidelines

Possibly the new President's most revolutionary move on arms-transfer control was his appointment of a woman as Under Secretary of State for Security Assistance and chairman of the new Arms Export Control Board, with oversight on arms sales and nuclear proliferation. His appointee for the fifth-ranking State Department job was Lucy Benson, a former president of the League of Women Voters. This nomination compared in significance with Ford's decision to make a woman—Anne Armstrong—ambassador to London.

Some of the State Department's proposed reforms were soon adopted, reinforced by the ideas of Leslie Gelb, a former New York *Times* diplomatic reporter who became the Department's new director of the bureau of politico-military affairs. Central to Gelb's philosophy was that sales in the past had been more of a reaction to events abroad than reflective of consistency. Of $93 million of arms supplied to Africa between 1950 and 1976, for instance, $63 million had been sold in the final year alone. In three years, Iran's arms orders had totaled nearly $15 billion. Gelb's presidential review memorandum—PRM 12—warned Carter, however, that there could be no dramatic changes or drastic reductions in the sale of military equipment to Allies or friends, and in fact all or most of the $32 billion backlog of arms orders which Carter found in 1977 was to be left undisturbed by the new President.

But four months after taking office, Carter announced new arms-sales guidelines, most of which, he stated, would not apply to the NATO countries, or to Japan, New Zealand or Australia. A careful examination of them shows countless loopholes. Firstly, the "burden of persuasion would be on those who favor a particular arms sale, rather than those who oppose it," and the "transfer must contribute to national security interests." This seemed to be the sort of semantics with which even Richard Nixon could have lived happily.

Secondly, the President said, the dollar volume of sales would be reduced below the fiscal 1977 level—thought to be $8.9 billion. (This promise was made on the Pentagon's assumption that a reduction would be sure to occur in any case, as sales were then declining, following what looked like a bonanza period. The 1976 figure, originally adopted by the Ford administration as the proposed high-water mark, was dropped by Carter after the Pentagon's prediction of an $8.2 billion total proved wrong—the final figure was $12.7 billion, breaking the $11.4 billion record established in fiscal 1974.) The President retained the right to adjust the ceiling for inflation. If there are problems, the ceiling can be respected by manufacturers spinning out deliveries—which they would sometimes prefer to do, since this stabilizes the feast-or-famine cycle of the arms industries, especially aerospace.

Thirdly, sales, or agreements to produce U.S. weapons abroad, would not be made until the arms were operationally deployed with U.S. forces, so that foreign sales would not be sought to reduce U.S. unit costs. This, of course, would not preclude foreign-power undertakings to purchase or co-produce later, once such weaponry was in U.S. wing, flotilla or battalion service; and foreign sales, even unguaranteed ones, would obviously still be a factor in computing costs.

Fourth, Carter insisted that no advanced weapons would be produced solely for exportation. This seemed aimed at the Northrop/McDonnell-Douglas offer of F-18Ls to Iran; but if these export-only items were to be sold, as expected, to Japan and Australia, through their exception to the guidelines, it would have been difficult for the Administration not to make an exception for Iran, then its single most important arms purchaser.

Fifth, advanced U.S. weapons co-produced by NATO and other privileged countries could not be re-exported to third countries, where co-production itself would be prohibited. If this prevented the privileged co-producers in Europe from exporting to friendly markets, it would make many of those co-production arrangements (which are essentially the price America pays for NATO standardization) of far less interest to the Europeans. Here again, exceptions seemed inevitable.

Sixth, Carter said the United States would not be the first supplier of new advanced weapons to any region. This would seem to have little effect on sales to the Middle East, since Israel has virtually all advanced weaponry, including state-of-the-art countermeasures, and since Carter has promised to make special exceptions, short of "Allied" treatment, for Israel in the future. Hawk missiles for Jordan, for instance, which Carter criticized in the campaign, would go through today because Israel already has them, and because Egypt has had roughly equivalent Soviet surface-to-air missiles for nearly a decade. Any Soviet supply of advanced weapons to Syria or Iraq—such as Iraq's forty MiG-23s and Syria's fifty, along with twenty MiG-25s, probably flown by Russians—would justify equivalent U.S. weaponry for Israel, Jordan, Saudi Arabia, Iran, Kuwait and, now, Egypt. Similarly, Israel's order for F-15s would justify virtually any advanced fighter or fighter-bomber for Iran and Saudi Arabia—as Americans soon learned—or even for Jordan and Kuwait.

Kissinger's offer of A-7s to Pakistan had been made, as noted, to persuade Islamabad to drop plans for nuclear reprocessing. In 1977, only the shorter-range A-4s were being offered, because that was all India was scheduled to get. But while India can cover Pakistan with a short-range attack plane's radius, a Pakistani A-4 could not fly to Calcutta and return. So the Franco-Pakistani nuclear deal seemed, in effect, to be authorized—and then, if India later bought Sukhoi bombers from Moscow, Pakistan would presumably be entitled to A-7s after all. Moreover, observers wondered, what could South Korea request that North Korea's possession of equivalents would not justify? Short of nukes, not much.

Seventh, the President said that future sales agreements would bar resales to third countries altogether, instead of simply making them dependent on OMC (and now congressional) approval. As interpreted by Carter aides, this would even apply to NATO buyers. Given the role of trade-in weaponry in acquiring new systems, this would only seem to be workable if the United States itself agreed to repurchase obsolete systems from its clients—and then, presumably, sold them again.

Finally, State Department approval would be a precondition before arms firms could make a sales pitch. U.S. armed-services officers would be precluded from "hawking" weaponry at all. This latter point, on the face of it, looked a hard or impossible ruling to enforce. All sales surpassing $25 million, Carter had ruled earlier, were to be on a "government-to-government" basis, virtually putting the generals in the salesman's seat.

In case any of these loopholes should be insufficient, the President naturally reserved the right to break his own rules in "extraordinary circumstances" or to "maintain a regional balance"—a concept he had rejected earlier. This would seem to insure that "safe" Muslim countries like Saudi Arabia could expect any "destabilizing" weaponry that went to Israel (whose initial disinterest in the F-18L may explain why this was the only major export weapon which Carter considered banning from the area). Had an exception been made to enable Israel to co-produce the F-16, this could have been used to justify similar facilities in Iran.

Tom Halstead, now ACDA spokesman but then executive director of the Arms Control Association, noted that the 1977 ceiling covered both hardware and personnel and support facilities. He told the writer: "You could go higher than present levels [on hardware] and be under the ceiling . . . The $32 billion in the pipeline means that it will be four or five years before anything changes, if then. Exceptions are going to be invoked all too often. Isn't AWACS a new system?"

Some reports had suggested that the President would choose an option put forward in Presidential Review Memorandum 12 and order a 40 per cent cut in arms exports. This, and a Pentagon-inspired prediction in the Evans and Novak column, a month before, that the new guidelines would involve a 25 per cent cut seemed to fall flat in the face of reality; the New York *Times* wittily referred to Carter, in an editorial, as "the world's leading reluctant arms dealer." To most observers of the defense scene, it had seemed that the U. S. Government was attempting to close a stable door after the horse had gone; now it became clear that the door could probably not be closed anyway, only given a printed sign directed at the horse and marked, optimistically, "Do not open."

Senate aides on relevant committees complained that it was, in any case, technically and logistically impossible to study in detail the avalanche of arms-sale notices from the Executive Branch within the thirty-day limit. Senate Majority Leader Robert Byrd took up this theme in a floor speech on October 7.

"Since August 5," he said, "Congress has received notifications of proposed arms sales totaling more than $3 billion." He said there had been twenty-nine separate proposals involving fifteen countries.

Byrd went on: "An even more incongruous situation developed last year when Congress received notifications of thirty-seven [sales to] eleven countries, totaling $6 billion, in the waning days of the . . . session."

Byrd said notifications were often sent to Congress during or just be-

fore congressional recesses, so that all or most of the thirty-day reflection
period was lost. He supported Senator Nelson's proposal to increase the
period to forty-five days.

The senator added:

> Most of these proposed sales involve delivery at some future date—
> months if not years away. This is a doubly important factor. Because
> many of the sales will involve delivery at some future date, plus services
> and maintenance at even later dates, the long-term implications of these
> agreements are considerable. Therefore, this is all the more reason that the
> Executive can and should provide Congress with ample advance informa-
> tion and opportunity for consideration of major sales.

Byrd called on Carter to submit no major proposals to Congress just
before or during the upcoming adjournment, unless they were of an
emergency nature. He suggested that more thought be devoted to the
cumulative impact of arms sales, and added:

> Consideration should be given to requiring explicit congressional ap-
> proval—rather than a resolution of disapproval—for major arms sales; for
> example, sales or a combination of sales to one nation valued at more
> than $200 million.
>
> Finally, in the case if Iran, to which we have made sales of more than
> $18 billion in recent years, I would suggest a moratorium on further sales
> in the near future.

Byrd entered in the *Congressional Record* a letter from General Fish
predicting that total sales to Iran for fiscal 1977 would, as noted earlier,
be nearly $5.5 billion.

A GAO report published shortly before had confirmed that foreign
sales had posed problems for America's own arms inventory. The situation had improved lately but "a world of localized crisis could reverse
this trend." Drawing down U.S. stocks for Israel in 1973, "and more
recently diversion of additional vehicles to Morocco" had meant that the
U.S. inventory had not fully recovered until 1977. (Later, as noted in
Chapter 2, the retiring chairman of the Joint Chiefs of Staff, General
George Brown, told the writer that the inventory in Europe was still
short.)

The report also noted the beneficial effects of weapons sales: In one
case, of 34,000 M-113A1 armored personnel carriers produced, 23,000, or
68 per cent, had been exported. This had enabled the manufacturer to
remain in operation. Increased foreign demand for Maverick missiles had
"kept existing production lines open and maintained employment during
the recent economic turndown, and the costs, for inventory modernization have been reduced through recoupment of $5.6 million in R & D

costs." The Air Force was selling Model A Mavericks from its inventory, and replacing them with the new Model Bs.

"If the Air Force is successful in maintaining the sales level for another twenty-two months," the report said, "the Model C will be ready for production, and the Air Force expects to avoid about $97.6 million in closedown and startup costs."

Foreign sales of TOW missiles had lowered the cost of launchers by 15 per cent, the GAO said, but "diversions of production . . . have perpetuated the shortage of spare and repair parts and have delayed scheduled U.S. deployments." There had been a similar problem due to foreign sales of the Raytheon Dragon missile.

Aviation Week, the authoritative aerospace industry organ, said at the time that the impact of the Carter guidelines would be "small" and quoted its industrial sources as thinking that any resultant unemployment would be "manageable"; there would be no substantial effect on the U.S. balance of payments. Nevertheless, Britain and France were expected to take over some markets rejected by Washington, as they had already done—with Washington's blessing—in Egypt. Another country likely to be attracted by hard-currency markets disdained by the United States was, of course, the Soviet Union, which had already profited in this way from American hesitations in Peru and Kuwait. This suggested obvious reasons for future exceptions "in the national security interest." Two of America's then top three clients—Iran and Saudi Arabia—were thought unlikely to listen to Carter's pleas for self-restraint if the third, Israel, continued to arm to the teeth. In the measure that the guidelines would work at all, their most likely effect was expected to be to slow down NATO standardization, and encourage Europe's preference for intra-European projects. Concluded *Aviation Week*'s knowledgeable Cecil Brownlow: "Whatever impact the Carter restrictions will have on the aerospace industry probably will not be felt until the early 1980s." Indeed, in January 1979, the magazine listed U.S. aerospace sales in 1978 as $37 billion, of which $16 billion was military aviation and space vehicles, and projected a 1979 figure of $43 billion, of which $17.6 billion would be military, and $9.5 billion earned from exports. The Commerce Department later predicted $47 billion of U.S. aerospace sales in 1979. The industry's backlog of orders was put at $51 billion.

Ironically, the Carter 1977 guidelines had been announced just as the Paris International Air and Space Salon was getting under way, with massive U.S., European and Communist-nation participation. A National Security Council Study noted that other arms-producing countries were unlikely to follow Carter's example in trying to reduce arms sales. A CIA analysis said it was likely that any markets refused by Washington would be picked up by France, Britain, Israel, Germany, Italy, Belgium, Sweden and the Soviet Union. Already, the Soviet Union, Britain and Italy were ahead of the United States in arms sales to Latin America, the study said. By 1978, the general prediction was coming true. That year, France's, Britain's, Germany's and Israel's sales, together, almost equalled U.S. sales to countries outside the "privileged" list (Japan, Australia, New Zealand and the NATO group). Defending Carter's self-restraint policy, then-Senator Dick Clark said: "Nothing seems to grate upon the sensitivities of Americans more than the suspicion that others are benefiting by breaking the rules when we are playing fair."

But Carter's best chances of being able to point to an achievement by 1980 came from inevitability. Arms orders by Third World countries had fallen from $21 billion in 1974 to $17 billion in 1975, and $14 billion in 1976. They would level off at about $10 billion by 1980, the CIA predicted. Sated, the market was ready for a temporary diet of sorts.

Meanwhile, the Pentagon sales force was being informed that it should prepare to add two new foreign countries to its client list each year from 1981 on, notably for the F-16. Here, Washington was under pressure from its NATO co-production allies, who would profit. Holland, Belgium, Norway and Denmark were delighted about the 125 promised to Israel, the 72 for Spain, and the anticipated orders from Japan, Saudi Arabia, Greece and Turkey.

Also being pushed was the A-10 attack plane, whose reputation was not diminished by the fatal crash of one of them during low-altitude aerobatics in Paris by the Fairchild chief test pilot, Sam Nelson. West Germany, Holland, Britain, Israel, Thailand and Korea were all interested in the aircraft. And Carter had begun to relent on the F-18L, authorizing export discussions with Canada, Britain, Germany, Italy, France, Australia and Japan.

Some corporations began to complain that a pinch was being felt. Boeing, having sold over 1,500 C-130s to 45 countries, grumbled that it was being forbidden too many markets. A sale of 8 more of the planes to Libya had been vetoed. Boeing had suggested that Libya order the civilian version, the L-100, for "Libyan Airlines" and adapt it, but a sale on these lines was turned down by the U. S. Commerce Department, which also forbade Boeing to sell 10 L-100s to Iraq and two to Madagascar. Libya then turned to Aeritalia and ordered 20 G-222 transport planes, but the OMC objected because of the planes' General Electric T-64 turboprop engines. When this book was being written, Aeritalia had turned to Rolls-Royce to re-engine the planes Libya wanted, thus proving Boeing's point that the veto was ineffective. Boeing complained that the congressional right of veto on orders of more than $25 million might effectively make it impossible for them to sell more than 2 C-130s at a time to Third World countries, even if OMC and the White House approved.

In May 1979, at an FAA meeting in Miami, U.S. aerospace representatives passed a motion ˙asking the Administration to "remove or amend" bans on sales for human-rights reasons. *Aviation Week* quoted a "sales executive" as calling the human-rights policy a "foreign aid program" for overseas aerospace firms. Alexander Gallard of Technical International Corporation scored inconsistencies in arms-sales restraint policy: "Sales are allowed to Israel which sells to everyone else [on the human-rights blacklist]." Aerospace consultant George C. Pritt was quoted in the magazine as opposing bans on Beech, Cessna and Lockheed sales to Libya: He said paying Libya annually, for oil, $4 billion, with which Libya could buy planes in Europe, was no different—except for the balance of payments—from bartering U.S. planes to Libya for oil.

By 1978, numerous congressional restraints existed which theoretically would have made it easier for a President seeking excuses to refuse sales. Beside the 1976 International Security Assistance and Arms Export Control Act and the 1977 International Security Assistance Act (prohibiting assistance for military operations by Zaire), there is the Foreign Assistance Act of 1961 limiting covert military operations by the CIA. There are numerous more recent measures limiting or forbidding arms for several countries in Latin America and Africa, the "Brooke amendment" forbidding assistance to countries more than a year behind in their U.S. debts (which once again affects Zaire) and another amendment prohibiting the President from adding countries to the foreign assistance list after the annual act is passed.

But by 1978, Jimmy Carter's policy in the field of weapons diplomacy was in disarray. The Congressional Research Service published a critical report. Sales for fiscal 1977 had turned out to be $11.5 billion, not the $8.9 billion earlier announced. Of the total, $9.3 billion had been for sales to countries outside the privileged NATO-Japan-Australasia area.

The reason for the higher figure was an accountancy change that now includes add-ons to previously approved sales in the year of the add-on rather than the year of the original sale; but few journalists or readers realized that. General Fish took the blame off the White House's shoulders. He was, in any event, about to hand over his Pentagon office to Major General Ernest Graves, Jr., Deputy Chief of the U. S. Army Engineers.

The only real importance of the higher 1977 figure was that it made it easier for the White House to achieve some sort of reduction in 1978, which perhaps explained the accountancy change. While ways were sought to achieve this, several other cosmetic changes were made. The Defense Department came up with a new manpower accounting system that would make it possible for the U. S. Government to charge more than 2 per cent for handling foreign military sales for the manufacturing corporations and the purchaser countries. The Pentagon also drew up new controls for the export of U.S. technology; Robert A. Basil, then assistant director for international programs of the Directorate of Defense Research and Engineering, called it "the first major, zero-base, total review of the export-control system since its inception" after World War Two.

Defense also requested legislation making R & D recoupment money from foreign purchasers payable to the Treasury, to "quell criticisms that the military services might be encouraging arms transfers to augment their own budgets," as General Fish put it. The law would also restrict the use of government-owned aircraft and other weapons for sales promotion purposes, such as participation in international shows. The State Department notified U.S. embassies that they were "not to encourage foreign interest in U.S. defense equipment, services or co-production as a means of improving political relations." Congress passed legislation obliging the ExImBank to take extreme abuse of human rights into account when making loans to foreign governments.

But reducing 1978 sales below 1977's only finally became possible by excising arms-related sales, such as military construction, that had been included in previous years. An NSC staffer suggested to the writer that by changing the accountancy system in this way it might be possible to lop off a billion dollars. There was not a lot of leeway, however: The 1978 cost of spare parts, ammunition and support services for weapons already sold came to about $4 billion. Korea was expecting about $1 billion in "abandoned" weaponry. The *Times*'s Rick Burt quoted a congressional aide as saying: "The ceiling just cannot last. Everyone knows that as soon as there is war in the Middle East or somewhere else, it will fly out the window."

Administration spokesmen said confidentially that they would be satisfied if they could merely *not exceed* the 1977 figure, thanks to the new math. Finally, the total for arms transfers that year to nonprivileged countries—$9.3 billion—was used, and Carter announced that the 1978 ceiling for nonprivileged nations would be $8.6 billion, a cut of 8 per cent. The Administration managed to keep to this figure—with about 80 per cent going to the Middle East. Under Secretary Benson said in 1978 that $1 billion in sales to sixty-seven countries, forty-eight of them regular U.S. customers, had been turned down.[1] Because weapons-related sales, and sales to NATO, Japan, Australia and New Zealand (about $1.9 billion for weapons alone) would not count in this ceiling, total sales would be up $2 billion over 1977, to about $13.3 billion. Sales of weapons-related equipment and services would be up from $900 million to about $3 billion. Even so, these figures were only achieved by allowing some countries, such as Saudi Arabia, to use commercial sales, and by sliding some 1978 sales back to 1979.

The Administration blamed its poor showing on the impossibility of getting a multilateral consensus. Neither Soviet, Western nor Israeli arms salesmen seemed anxious to be self-restrictive; if anything, the prospects of some limited unilateral self-restriction by the United States had merely whetted their appetites. France officially rejected multilateral control arrangements. Britain said, tongue in cheek, that it would accept them if the Soviet Union did. Curiously, the Soviet Union did make a gesture at the end of the year: The State Department's director of politico-military affairs, Leslie Gelb, told the House Armed Services Committee that Moscow had agreed to hold regular bilateral discussions on the control of arms transfers. Purchaser nations hotly opposed restraints, seeing them as yet another example of big-power imperialism.

There was some evidence of tighter implementation of end-use provisions and human-rights provisos. Delays imposed on the delivery of a Swearingen bizjet to the Argentinian forces seemed unreasonable since the plane was intended to be used as a flying ambulance; while the veto of the Viggen sale to India—according to *Aviation Week*—merely induced Sweden's Saab firm to consider fitting the aircraft with the same Turbo-Union RB199 engine as the Tornado, instead of the present U.S. power plant. (A high Swedish official source told the author, however, that this proposal had been rejected as infeasible.) The most visible sign of Carter's wish to cut back on sales was the almost total absence of U.S. equipment at the 1978 Farnborough Air Show; but this policy, as mentioned earlier, was due to be diluted for the 1979 Paris spectacular.

A 1978 Brookings report said the Carter administration had a "questionable record" of reducing military sales. Major deals, like the "Mideast arms package," were being subdivided into annual contracts, spread over several years, to give an appearance of sales cutting. Most of the effects of the Carter guidelines were felt by countries of minor or relatively minor military importance like Pakistan, Mexico, Guatemala or Taiwan.

For 1979, Carter set a ceiling of $8.434 billion which, with inflation, represented a potential cut of 8–10 per cent over the previous year.

[1] See note on pp. 633–34.

The "commercial sale" remains one of the most effective ways of countering arms-sales restrictions. This is done by borrowing from the Treasury-funded, Treasury-managed Federal Financing Bank, an institution little known to the general public, and whose moneys are not subject to congressional appropriations and authorizations. The soft-loan FFB was set up in 1973 to take over from the ExImBank those arms sales which Congress, that year, forbade the ExIm to finance.

Officially, the FFB appropriated $740 million for fiscal 1977 to guarantee foreign military sales programs, but it actually used a further $2.6 billion. During the first four months of 1977, this even included $41 million for 54 Pentagon, noncommercial transactions. Although the Foreign Assistance Act of 1977 denies funds "to provide military assistance, international military education and training or foreign military credit to the government of Uruguay," which is on the "human rights" blacklist, the Military Audit Project says Uruguay in fact got $1,294,000 from the FFB that year. The funds were related to U.S. commitments made before fiscal 1977, which presumably makes them legal. Spider Burbank of the Military Audit Project, which is foundation-funded, and which made a special study of the 1977 figures, says some agreements were hastily made a few days before that fiscal year began. Burbank points out that none of the Carter guidelines provide for disclosure of small- or relatively-small-arms transfers. These are, of course, the weapons most used in most actual contemporary conflicts.

"Commercial sales," notes Burbank, "are explicitly exempted from Carter's ceiling."

The Center for Defense Information called for an end to co-production arrangements with developing countries and an end to financing other nations' arms purchases with U. S. Government-guaranteed credit programs. Democratic senator Bill Proxmire of Wisconsin had already optimistically introduced a bill to cut sales, mandatorily, to $8 billion in 1978, $6 billion in 1979 and $4 billion in 1980. But not even his supporters seemed to take the proposal seriously.

NOTE

1. Benson's statement drew some incredulity. But in 1978, the number of U.S. weapons refused appeared to be even higher. A partial list shows even some favored friends being turned down, to wit:
Australia: Sidewinder and Stinger missiles.
Japan: XM-1 tanks and Sidewinders.
West Germany: C-5As and Stingers.
Belgium: Chaparral missiles.
Spain: F-18Ls, Sparrow, Chaparral and Stinger missiles.
Switzerland: Chaparrals and Stingers.

Sweden: F-18Ls and Sidewinders.

Greece: F-16s and E-2Cs.

Portugal: Chinooks, Chaparrals and laser-guided bombs.

Iceland and Luxembourg: Mavericks and Rockeyes.

South Korea: F-15s, F-18Ls, A-7s, Chinook helicopters, Sparrow, Lance, Dragon, Stinger and U.S.-made Roland missiles, the secret AN-ASQ-14 sonar radar, and defoliants.

Taiwan: F-16s, F-18Ls, Maverick, Sidewinder, Harpoon, Chaparral, Dragon and U.S.-made Roland missiles, 175mm. guns and AN-ASQ-14 radars.

Philippines: A-10s, A-7s, Harpoons, Redeyes and other missiles, armored personnel carriers and 105mm. howitzers.

Yugoslavia: Harpoons, Mavericks and Vulcan antiaircraft guns.

Further afield, Bell-206 helicopters with TOW missiles were refused for Botswana, Cameroon, Gabon, Ghana, Ivory Coast, Kenya, Liberia, Malawi, Morocco, Nigeria, Senegal, Sudan, Tanzania, Zaire, Zambia, Egypt, Kuwait, Oman and Pakistan.

Ecuador was refused F-5s, F-104s, A-10s and A-7s, as well as Kfirs and Hawk missiles. A-10s were also refused to Sudan, Tunisia, Malaysia and Indonesia. A-7s were refused for Peru, which was also banned from buying A-4s, TOWs and armored personnel carriers. Honduras was not allowed to purchase A-6s and Argentina was denied Cobra helicopters. Benin was refused Bell-205s, while Botswana, South Africa, Hong Kong and Nepal were denied Hughes-500s. Ghana, Zaire, Somalia, Burma, Malaysia, Singapore and Thailand were not allowed to receive Chinooks. Zaire was also refused AH-15 helicopters, along with M-16 rifles and armored personnel carriers. Chad was denied some unspecified fighter-bombers.

Missile refusals included Sidewinders for Argentina and Brazil, naval and air missiles for Ethiopia, Redeyes and Stingers (and helicopter machine guns) for Morocco, TOWs for Peru, Chaparrals for Tunisia and Thailand, which also got turned down for Mavericks.

APCs were also denied to Bolivia, Guatemala and Peru. Algeria was forbidden an air defense system. The Ivory Coast was disqualified for 105mm. howitzers, and laser-guided bombs were not sold to Kenya and Singapore.

Night-vision equipment was denied to Chad, Mauritania, Senegal, Somalia, El Salvador, Guatemala, Paraguay and Argentina, while Gabon was refused code-breaking equipment. AN-ASQ-14 radars were not sold to Thailand, Panama and Peru.

Ethiopia was denied F-5 parts and South Africa C-130 parts. South Africa was also refused mobile assault bridging equipment. Uruguay was denied hydrofoils, while Libya could not even purchase maps and navigation charts.

The Middle East and its environs was a fruitful area for refusals. F-15s and F-4 "Wild Weasels" were refused for Iran, A-10s for Iran, Egypt, Kuwait, Israel and Pakistan, F-16s for Jordan, F-5s for Bahrein, A-4s to Abu Dhabi, Dubai, Egypt, India and Pakistan, A-7s for Iran and Pakistan, F-104s for Bangladesh and KC-135s for Israel.

Among missiles, Iran and Israel were refused additional Sidewinders, while Iran, Israel and Jordan were denied additional Mavericks; Iran was turned down for Chaparrals, Copperheads and submarine-launched Harpoons. Ordinary Harpoons were also denied to Bahrein and Kuwait; TOWs were refused for Bahrein, Jordan, Kuwait, Israel, Saudi Arabia and North Yemen.

Israel was refused concussion bombs, Jordan was turned down for M-60 tanks, and Egypt and Israel were not authorized to buy additional APCs.

Needless to say, the equivalents of these weapons would not be turned down, in almost all cases, if the purchasers turned to Europe—as in many cases they did.

8

In the Name of Karl Marx

RUSSIA'S ROLE as an armorer goes back to the nineteenth century and the links between Tsarist arms industries and the armorers of Germany, Britain and France. The new Soviet state re-entered the arms-export business in 1921, when it supplied arms to Russia's old rival Turkey to help turn back a Greek invasion sponsored by Britain. It helped rearm Germany in the twenties and thirties, still hoping for a Communist revolution there. It sent arms to foment revolution in the Yemen in 1928. Moscow later helped arm the Loyalists against fascist Spain. In 1948, acting through Czechoslovakia, the USSR supplied arms to the Israelis, working through the predominantly Russian leadership of the Haganah.

Today, the indications are that although Moscow will support most colonial liberation struggles, or similar situations, it no longer thinks in terms of a worldwide Communist revolution. Russia, in effect, no longer expects communism, in Khrushchev's words, to bury capitalism: It expects capitalism to bury itself.

During World War Two, the Soviet arms industry produced over 100,000 combat aircraft. The figure is staggering, when one considers that neither the United States nor the Soviet Union today has as many as 6,000 military aircraft. Between 1949, when the industry got back to full production again, and 1967, Russia produced 40,000 MiG-15s, -17s, -19s and -21s, while 1,400 more MiGs were produced under license in Czechoslovakia, China and India. (Since then, China has managed to pirate copies both of these MiGs and, with less success, of later Soviet models.) During the two decades following World War Two, Russia also manufactured 3,500 Il-28 jet bombers, along with thousands of missiles.

Between 1950 and 1968, the Soviet Union had built enough naval combat vessels to sell or give away 550 of them to foreign countries, along with the export of 20,000 medium tanks. The Russians have also been consistently good in the production of small arms. The Mosin-Nagant, a Russo-Belgian design adopted by the Imperial Army before World War

One, remained in continuous production for fifty-three years and was the basic weapon supplied to Eastern-bloc armies after World War Two. In its heyday it had been co-produced under license in France, the United States, Switzerland and Finland. It had been the favorite weapon of the Spanish loyalists, Tito's guerrillas and Mao's Long March.

Before World War One, the Russians had also made the Danish Madsen machine gun and, after 1905, the Vickers-Maxim model. Both remained in the Red Army inventory until the end of World War Two. The famed AK-47 Kalashnikov assault rifle has been in production since 1950. Lewis Frank, in his book on the arms trade, hypothesized that it "may hold the all-time record for production of a single weapon."

But in the days when the United States was distributing weaponry free, Soviet arms transfers were well behind those of America. Between 1955 and 1969, total Soviet transfers were estimated at $7 billion, or about a quarter of the American figure. But whereas most U.S. arms exports have been support items or construction, most Soviet arms exports are actual weapons. In the fifties and sixties, Moscow was concentrating on rebuilding its own forces and helping the Bloc, so other clients received obsolescent arms. Between 1955 and 1960, the concentrated export effort was on the Middle East—notably, Egypt, Syria and Iraq—and on Sukarno's Indonesia. After 1960, Russia began supplying a larger number of Third World countries, including the nationalists of anticolonialist revolutions, and furnishing better weaponry in some areas. By then, the Moscow leadership had discovered—as had Stalin, during the war in Russia itself—that nationalism had a stronger appeal for most of the world than ideologies.

Soviet efforts then began to focus on the whole southern hemisphere, where the cold war was fought by proxy. But unlike the Chinese, then more inflexible and provocative, Moscow usually sought to give just enough aid to "destabilize" without provoking a confrontation with the West. This was notably characterized by Moscow's basically cautious Mideast policy. Angola, in 1975, became a rare exception to this rule—because the Kremlin saw the signal from the U. S. Congress that it could act freely and set up its own satellite government.

So intent were the Russians on keeping a low profile that Moscow worked for many years mainly through Bulgaria, East Germany, Poland and Czechoslovakia. The latter country, where the Skoda arms industry accounted for 10 per cent of all the country's exports before 1939, had pride of place—through its arms agency, Omnipol. The Czechs were used notably as a conduit for Syria and Guatemala, where the 1954 arms deal wriggled through the Monroe Doctrine thanks to the Prague return address. Guinea's first Communist arms came from Czechoslovakia in 1959, shortly after Guinea's independence, with a Czech general being posted to Conakry to oversee the operation. Earlier, the first deliveries of Soviet arms to Castro came from Czechoslovakia. Omnipol participates regularly in the Paris and Farnborough air shows. It has even exhibited sporting guns in the United States—some of them civilianized versions of guns which Poland was supplying to the Viet Cong. Before the Russian invasion in 1968, Omnipol even sold Delfin trainers to Western countries—notably at the Paris air show of 1967. Some of its agents have an old-fashioned sniff of Zaharoff about them: Their Indian agent used a successful sale in Pakistan to get an order from New Delhi.

The revolution on Zanzibar was armed by East Germany. The Viet Cong got its Russian arms through Poland for many years; the Yemenis and the Eritreans received Soviet weapons from Bulgaria. If there was risk of confrontation with the West, Moscow could always disown any interest or responsibility.

Russia and its European satellites have also done some clandestine importing. A French firm imported $80,000 worth of C-47 parts which it transshipped to Poland. Some Rolls-Royce ship engines, sold to France as "damaged beyond repair," for cannibalizing, appeared in 1962 in Czechoslovakia, where the canny Czechs repaired them. Perhaps the easiest "military" smuggling from the West has taken the form of technical manuals.

Even in Angola, Ethiopia and elsewhere, Moscow has gone carefully. At various times and in various trouble spots, the Soviet Union used Ghana (in Nkrumah's time), Algeria, Cuba or Egypt (until the 1972 breach) to pass on weapons. In Angola, just as the United States used "moderate" Zaire, so Russia used "radical" African states and—when armed intervention could be undertaken without risk—Cubans. (Similarly, the United States, as noted earlier, used West Germany to supply arms to Israel in 1965, and France and Britain to supply Egypt in the seventies.) In Ethiopia, more recently, Moscow "used" Cuban armed forces again—although clearly the Cubans were more than eager to go.

Czechoslovakia, with its large arms industries in Moravia, Slovakia and Bohemia, remains Moscow's most active intermediary. The Lenin (formerly Skoda) works at Pilsen and the Czech Armaments Works at Brno and Prague had been major armorers since the days of the Austro-Hungarian Empire. In 1939, Czech arms exports were 15 per cent of the world total—second only to Britain's 17 per cent. After the Communist coup d'état of 1948, new die tools were brought in from Russia, and production of Soviet-designed weapons began. Czechoslovakia remains today the most self-sufficient Warsaw Pact nation in weapons production, after Russia.

Since each Comecon nation is obliged to specialize in only certain export fields—in weaponry as in almost everything else—no other country comes as close to self-sufficiency or to escaping dependence on Moscow as Czechoslovakia. But while the Czechs were independent in arms, they were dependent on Moscow for other essentials in the economy. Today, virtually all the satellites are gradually acquiring more freedom of action.

All Soviet arms transfer policies are determined by the Politburo. Operational control then passes to the Komitet Gosudarstvennoy Bezopasnosti (KGB), the Committee for State Security—earlier known as the Cheka, the GPU, the OGPU, the NKVD and the MGB. Before World War Two, such transfers were handled by the GRU (Glavnoye Razvedovatelnoye Upravleniye, or Chief Intelligence Directorate). This is Russia's equivalent of the Pentagon's Defense Intelligence Agency (DIA). As a consequence, the cold war dictated many of the deals—to Morocco in 1961, to hasten the closure of America's Strategic Air Command bases at Nouaceur; to Nkrumah to undercut Britain (and China); to Iran in 1967 to undercut the West in general; to the Algerian resistance party for ideological reasons, but partly to undermine France (and once again to try to head off Peking). Most of Moscow's arms recipients in Africa—insurgent movements in the Congo and Portuguese Africa, for instance—were anti-Western. In 1964, just after Makarios' pogrom against the Turks in Cyprus, Moscow, as noted earlier, gave him the arms supply which the West was withholding.

In a study, Robert Berman of Brookings has written:

> A typical Soviet arms package may include a squadron of MiG-21s at very low prices. Along with these will come air-to-air missiles. But more than likely there will not be an abundance of spare parts that would be needed for major operations. These would come later at high prices or in exchange for political leverage. Weapons from the Soviet Union characteristically are defensive in nature, with the emphasis on quantity over quality.

Not all recipients of Soviet arms are Communist, or even "left." Moscow has supplied the right-wing regimes of pre-coup d'état Afghanistan and of Marshal Abboud in the Sudan, and provided arms to the initially conservative regime of Prince Norodom Sihanouk of Cambodia. Nasser got arms from Moscow while continuing to persecute the Egyptian Communist Party. After Moscow's friend Sukarno was overthrown in Indonesia, the successor regime continued to receive weapons from the Soviet Union, and soon used them to massacre the local Communist Party. At this point, Moscow's ardor cooled, with $3 billion of weapons (by U.S. estimates) "down the drain." There have been occasions when non-Bloc customers have had priority for deliveries over European satellites. By and large, less radical leaders seem to give Moscow less problems than true believers, and have been rewarded in consequence.

Soviet credit is unbeatable—except by China. Interest rates until recently had usually been 2 or 2.5 per cent. Repayment may be over ten or twelve years, usually beginning with a grace period. There is little grant aid, but local produce has often been accepted in barter, thus mortgaging this production to Moscow and diminishing trade with the West. But Russia, inexperienced in some of the markets which barter deals may involve, sometimes unloads, for instance, copra or camel skins at below world prices, thus skidding the rate and annoying the customer country which produced them. A notable case was Zanzibar, the world's largest producer of cloves, which found that Eastern Europe's ignorance of the cloves market had severely depressed the price.

Soviet Union/Middle East

Russia's biggest weapons-diplomacy effort has been in the Middle East, largely profiting from Western mistakes and inhibitions. This has been especially true of recent years. According to a CIA analysis, of the $15.5 billion of weapons supplied by Moscow to over forty countries, 1967 through 1976, the bulk have been received by the following ten countries, in order of importance: North Vietnam, Egypt, Syria, Iraq, India, Libya, Iran, North Korea, Cuba and Algeria. Before Angola, the biggest opening made to Moscow by Western error was in Egypt—by a series of blunders culminating in the Anglo-Franco-Israeli Suez operation. Nasser was a charismatic ally for Russia; moreover, he had reason to be suspicious of the West, and to share Moscow's opposition to CENTO. He felt that one of the lessons of Bandung—where he had been a star attraction—was to take arms from both cold-war sides.

In September 1955, Cairo and Moscow announced a two-year, over-$200 million arms deal, to be paid for in Egyptian cotton, fruit and other commodities. The supply started two months later. In a relatively short time, 150 MiG-17s and -15s, 40 Il-28 bombers, 300 T-34 heavy tanks, a destroyer, 6 submarines and considerable small arms arrived; but when Egypt was invaded at the end of the following year, the Israelis captured or destroyed about half of this equipment. Israel, at the time essentially the pawn of Paris and London in the affair, rationalized its aggression by the presence of these hostile weapons. France and Britain sought to recapture the Canal, and to cause Nasser's overthrow. Moscow did nothing to encourage a war, and even withdrew most of its

Il-28s when it started—both for the safety of the aircraft and to prevent any escalation of the action; but the conflict helped drive Nasser further into the Soviet embrace; and the fact that London and Paris had exposed themselves to a worldwide pillorying for overt neocolonialism accidentally helped the Russians in another way—it gave them the opportunity to suppress the counterrevolution in Hungary shortly afterward, with no risk of more than a minor war of words with critics.

Russia at once set about both replenishing Nasser's arsenal and upgrading his inventory. MiG-17s replaced the -15s, while -19s replaced the -17s. Egypt got W class submarines, better destroyers, the latest small arms for the infantry. But the Soviet Union insisted on rigid control of the uses to which these weapons could be put. Not surprisingly, there were persistent quarrels between Cairo and Moscow, with Egypt starting to reorder some weapons from the West in 1960. West German technicians went to Helwan, Cairo's industrial suburb, to build Egypt's illstarred, homemade HA-300 fighter.

By 1963, Moscow agreed once again to upgrade Egyptian arms supplies, providing the MiG-21, then the front-rank Soviet fighter, TU-16 medium bombers and SA-2 and SA-3 surface-to-air missiles. The Russians also sold Egypt a nuclear reactor and helped finance a munitions plant. By June of 1967, with war about to break out again, the Soviet Union had sold Egypt the then considerable sum of a billion dollars' worth of weapons. Nasser sold off his MiG-17s and the remaining -15s to help pay for the new aircraft; these trade-ins and other outdated Russian weaponry now appeared in the inventories of several radical states, mostly African, and (except for the aircraft) with revolutionary movements. Algeria played a similar role in dispersing obsolescent Soviet weaponry.

The Israeli invasion of 1967 once again depleted Nasser's stocks, with most of his air force caught by surprise on the ground. Egypt lost over half its armor in six days—700 out of 1,200 tanks—along with 356 out of 716 aircraft. All the SA-2 "Guideline" missile batteries in Sinai were destroyed or captured. The infantry lost enough equipment for a 15,000-man division. Moscow at once began a massive resupply, delivering 130 fighters within three weeks. By 1969, the Soviet Union had supplied $700 million worth of aircraft, tanks and other new equipment. By then, every Egyptian air and naval base, every military training and maintenance depot had its team of Soviet advisers. The "war of attrition" was under way. When the Israelis made several deep-penetration raids into Egypt, Moscow, as recounted earlier, shipped in a full-scale air defense system. A more extensive network of SA-3 surface-to-air missile sites was established, especially along the Canal. Egypt was now the only non-Communist nation to have received the SA-3. It also had Frog surface-to-surface missiles—and, later, Scuds—and ZSU-23-4 radar-controlled antiaircraft cannon for use against low-flying planes; at the time, some of the Eastern European nations still did not have this weapon. By March 1970, the number of Soviet missile crewmen was reported at 1,500. Improved MiG-21s—the "21Js"—were delivered to key air bases, where they remained virtually under Soviet control. Soviet pilots flew MiG-21J defensive patrols over the Egyptian interior, successfully persuading Israel to cease the deep-penetration attacks—but only after a final engagement on July 30 in which the Israeli Air Force claimed to have downed four of the Russian aircraft. By June that year there were, in all, 15,000 Soviet military advisers in Egypt.

In return, Moscow secured naval-base rights and shore support for its Mediterranean squadron; these included a large dry dock, two floating docks, repair yards at Alexandria and other supply and repair facilities. The Russians took over the old British naval base at Port Said and began developing a deep-water port at Mersa Matruh for the exclusive use of the Soviet Navy. They were also allowed to base naval patrol aircraft in Egypt, and to fly them in Egyptian markings. Finally, in May 1971, Cairo and Moscow signed a friendship treaty committing each country not to join alliances hostile to the other. But Egypt remained undersupplied in comparison with Israel, and fourteen months later, friction grew between the Egyptian and Soviet military. Finally, President Sadat—encouraged by offers of financial assistance from Saudi Arabia to buy weapons from the non-Communist West—expelled 21,000 Russian military advisers. Sadat made an exception for those Russians manning or instructing at the air-defense sites; but the Kremlin, in anger, ordered those out also. Sadat then ordered the removal of the Soviet naval-reconnaissance planes.

The Russians, however, handed over most of the actual air-defense equipment to Egypt but took with them four MiG-25 high-altitude reconnaissance aircraft. By the end of the year, only seven hundred Soviet instructors remained in Egypt. Some spare parts and replacement equipment continued to arrive from Russia, but it was not until the October 1973 war that serious arms transfers were renewed. By then, however, Moscow was insisting on hard-currency payments, so some of the Saudi aid money presumably ended up in Russia.

Kissinger and Saudi diplomacy had its effect, and in April 1974 Sadat announced that Egypt would no longer rely exclusively on Russian arms. Moscow at once froze delivery of spare parts, except for two small shipments that August. With the Ford White House hamstrung by Capitol Hill's Israeli lobby from taking full advantage of the situation, Sadat was advised to turn to France and Britain, and did so in January 1975. In reaction, Soviet Foreign Minister Andrei Gromyko flew to Cairo the following month for talks.

Some serious Soviet arms deliveries resumed. "Blocked" spare parts were delivered for a while. The first six of an additional twenty-four MiG-23s arrived. These, however, would not be as effective as those delivered to Iraq, since Moscow withheld deliveries of Tu-114s—Russia's equivalent of AWACS. Several Egyptian fighter squadrons and SAM sites remained inoperative for need of parts, notably the turboblade for the MiG-21's Tumansky engine, which has a life of only 150 hours. Flight time for Egyptian pilots was cut from twenty to fifteen hours a month. No new missiles were delivered, according to official Egyptian sources, and no new detonators for cannon.

Egypt also faced serious economic problems. It was unable to meet its ruble debts, which were eating up 75 per cent of Egyptian exports. Sadat requested a moratorium on the debts, following a report in *The Economist* that Syria had been accorded such a breathing space.

Disillusioned with the Russians—who were equally disillusioned with Sadat—the Egyptian leader looked to more intra-Arab support. Out of this grew, in May 1975, the $1 billion Arab Organization for (Military) Industrialization—AOI—mentioned elsewhere.

Relations between Cairo and Moscow worsened. Soviet ships were denied berthing at Mersa Matruh and use of a mooring in the Gulf of Sollum. Captains of Soviet ships using the repair facility at Alexandria reported harassment by Egyptian officials. But—despite an estimated "loss" of $5 billion in arms aid—the Soviet Union could not completely turn its back on Egypt, the principal nation in the Middle East and the most important link in Arab defenses against Israeli territorial encroachment. Soviet hopes now centered on replacing Sadat with a leader in Cairo more to their liking.

Soviet arms links with Syria began in 1955, when Moscow began replacing Italy and Britain. The first Soviet deliveries were twenty-five MiG-15s and six MiG-15 trainers. After the 1956 Suez War, Syria's losses were replaced by sixty MiG-17s. Pilot training in the Soviet Union began. Later, Syria received MiG-21Fs and some Il-28 bombers, as well as heavy transports.

The still more important link with Iraq started in 1958, when General Abdul Karem Kassem overthrew the pro-Western government of Nuri as-Said and took Baghdad out of the pro-Western Baghdad Pact.

MiG-15s arrived in Iraq that year, along with a large Soviet training mission. By the early sixties, Iraq was getting MiG-21s and -17s, transports, helicopters and trainers. Early in 1963, the Iraqi Communist Party tried a coup d'état and failed. In the fighting, they were severely beaten by Ba'ath forces which themselves seized power later in the year, assassinating Kassem. Friction with Moscow soon developed over the Kurdish question. Since the Kurds sought autonomy not only from Iraq but also from Iran, they had received Soviet support. Moscow had insisted that arms provided to Iraq should not be used against Kurdish dissidents. For a while, Russia even held back arms deliveries to make the point, and Iraq agreed to reduce its anti-Kurdish operations. Then, late in 1963, a junta took over power from the Ba'ath party, released jailed Iraqi Communists and made a temporary peace with the Kurds. Soviet-Iraqi relations improved greatly.

But in 1965, repression of the Kurds recommenced. This time, Moscow decided to tolerate the operations and new weapons deliveries went through on schedule: Iraq got a complete SA-2 air defense grid, three more squadrons of MiG-21 interceptors and its first Tu-16 medium bombers. A not insignificant factor in all this was oil-rich Iraq's ability to pay in hard currency.

In the 1967 war, Syria, like Egypt, lost half its tanks, and also lost nearly two thirds of its aircraft—32 MiG-21s, 23 MiG-17s and -15s, 2 Il-28 bombers and 3 helicopters. Iraqi losses were 9 MiG-21s, 5 Hawker Hunters, 1 Tu-16 and 2 transports. All these losses were replaced—and upgraded—by Moscow within a year.

The tab for Soviet resupply to its three main Arab friends was put by Western analysts at about a billion dollars, bringing all Soviet aid for Egypt, Syria and Iraq for the period 1955–69 to $2.5 billion, or over one third of all the global Soviet military aid program. MiG-21s were now nearly half of both countries' air forces—a better ratio than in any Bloc country except the Soviet Union itself.

Resupply to Egypt was detailed earlier. Syria, which received $300 million of new equipment, got 120 aircraft to replace the 60 it had lost. As well as MiG-21s, the Syrians received the new Sukhoi-7s. Syria also took delivery of 400 tanks—and over a thousand advisers. Naval port developments were started by the Russians at Latakia and Tartus, and Soviet naval visits began the following year. But once again, the cautious Russians retained control over the use of the new-generation aircraft.

The control of weaponry was needed, for Egypt, Syria and Iraq evaded *political* control. The Syrians, in particular, were gung-ho for another war with Israel, more confident of victory than their Russian advisers. In 1968, in an effort to force the Soviet hand, a Syrian military delegation went to Paris to shop for arms. Moscow then agreed to step up arms supplies. The following year, a similar mission was sent, for similar reasons, to Peking—which declined to provide surface-to-air missiles but agreed to supply small arms for the Palestinian guerrillas based in Syria.

By mid-1970, the Syrian Air Force was three times its 1967 size. There were now 175 late-model MiG-21 fighters and Su-7 fighter-bombers, along with 85 MiG-17s. The country was commanded by a former fighter pilot, President Hafaz al-Assad. A further 300 tanks had been delivered to the Army, along with 100 armored personnel carriers, 400 field guns, mobile rocket launchers and 40 more SA-2 missile sites. The Navy had received 2 Soviet minesweepers, 6 missile-carrying patrol boats and a dozen missile/torpedo boats.

In Syria, Soviet military advisers now totaled nearly three thousand; they controlled not only training, but planning, and logistics down to brigade level. However, eight coups d'état in two decades had left their mark on the ancient empire: Efficiency was rated poor (although the authoritative *Air International* now rates Syrians the best of Arab military pilots). Moscow believed that Egypt—where there were already fifteen thousand advisers—could eventually be strong enough to take on Israel; the Syrians, while more eager for battle, were seen as less prepared—and some of the eagerness of the Syrian leadership for war was not shared by the enlisted men.

But the buildup went on, to meet the colossal buildup in Israel. In 1971, Syria received thirty-five more fighters and the first giant MI-9 troop-carrying helicopters to appear outside Europe—twenty-two of them. In 1972, Syria rejected a Soviet-Syrian friendship treaty but signed a new arms accord which gave the country its first SA-2 batteries.

By then, Soviet-Egyptian friction was at its height, and when Sadat expelled the Russians, Syria took advantage to prod the Russians for more arms.

The Russians were glad to respond, to prove they still had good relations with a key Arab country with which Egypt had long been associated. That fall, twenty AN-12 transport aircraft and a small fleet of merchant ships began regular trips to Syria with more MiG-21s, new SA-3 batteries and T-62 tanks, along with 150 more advisers, mostly for the missiles. Soon came the first new SA-6 sites. In return, the Soviet Navy got new facilities at Latakia and Tartus. During the winter, more arms rolled into Syria—some in the huge AN-22 transports, which can carry over 100 tons. Fighters lost in dogfights with the Israelis were replaced, and more MiG-21s added.

During the first six months of 1973, Russian arms to Syria were estimated at $185 million, putting total Soviet military assistance to that country since 1956 at $1.5 billion. When the Israelis flew their ill-advised "provocation" mission toward Latakia in September, shooting down eight

"21s" for the loss of only one aircraft, Assad asked Soviet ambassador Mukhitdinov for MiG-23s and more Soviet SAM battery crews. MiG-27s (advanced -23s) and Su-20s—both swing-wing fighters—were already in the pipeline. But Mukhitdinov said these would only be available at once if Syria signed a friendship treaty. Assad responded angrily by restricting the movements of Russian officials within the country. In a conversation with a member of his staff picked up by Western surveillance, Mukhitdinov remarked: "These accursed Syrians will take anything—except advice."

Iraq had signed a friendship treaty with Moscow in 1972. Kosygin had visited Baghdad. Later, SA-3 and SA-6 batteries were installed in the country, and in 1973 Iraq received the first Tu-22, 1,400-mile-range supersonic bombers deployed outside Europe. At the time, the delivery was seen as a "lesson" to recalcitrant Syria as to what might be available. Later, the bombers were seen by Western analysts as a planned fallback weapon, in case war between Israel and its neighbors broke out that year—as it did, of course—and Cairo or Damascus were seriously threatened. In the Ramadan war, however, the Tu-22s were never used.

In that war, Egypt deployed forty-six SA-6 batteries, each with four launchers with three missiles apiece. Syria deployed thirty-two. Over a thousand missiles were estimated to have been fired in the first three days, giving heart to the Arab forces and excellent practice for the Russians. Some Western air force experts said it constituted the densest concentration of surface-to-air missiles anywhere in the world, including the Soviet Union.

Syria, however, lost 155 aircraft, or about half of its military aviation, along with 1,100 tanks—nearly half its major armor—and 17 SAM batteries. Two thirds of the aircraft were replaced from Warsaw Treaty inventories before the war ended, the rest shortly afterward.

After the war, Sadat plunged into Kissinger diplomacy, which regained him parts of Sinai but inevitably lost him most of his now limited Soviet support. Once again, Syria profited. By August 1974, Israeli Defense Minister Shimon Peres complained that, once again, Moscow had ensured that the Syrian Air Force should be stronger than before a war. Damascus was now estimated to have nearly four hundred combat aircraft (including some in storage) and 20 per cent more SAM sites than a year before. There were thirty Scud surface-to-surface missiles with a 180-mile range that could pass over the Golan Heights, along with over one hundred Frog shorter-range tactical missiles, vehicle-mounted SA-7s and 180mm. howitzers. The tanks had all been replaced, mostly by the new T-62s. Syria was now reported to have over three thousand Soviet advisers.

Total Soviet military aid to Syria was now put at $2.1 billion. Some alarmist Israeli generals even estimated that Syria could stage an attack on Israel on its own, although the Pentagon noted that Israel still outgunned Egypt and Syria put together—or any other credible combination of Arab countries. Many of Syria's aircraft were said to be short of parts, and still more were short of pilots.

In 1974, Iraq also got Scuds, with Soviet crews, and twelve MiG-23s—principally for defense against the biggest buyer of military equipment in the area, Iran. By then, Soviet military aid to Iraq was estimated by U.S. sources to have reached $1.6 billion. Also in 1974, Iraq persuaded Moscow, at least temporarily, to drop its protection of the Kurds. A Tu-22 with a Russian crew even went on a bombing operation against the hardy dissidents, staying at a high altitude to avoid the embarrassing possibility of being shot down.

But by the following year, friction with Baghdad had developed again: The Russians had bought some Iraqi crude and resold it at a profit. When Iran occupied two Arabian islands in the Gulf that year, Moscow did not back up Baghdad's protest. The Soviet Union also began to have second—or third—thoughts about the Kurds, and ceased supporting Iraqi operations against them.

This seemed all the more incomprehensible to the Iraqis: Iran and the CIA—seeing that most Kurds lived in Iraq—had begun to support their dissidence; Iranian Kurds were being promised autonomy. But when Baghdad made a test order for more Soviet artillery weapons for use against the mountain rebels, Moscow said no. Iraq then bought a small amount of arms from Western countries. The year before, it had bought thirty-one counterinsurgency Alouette-III helicopters from France, arming them with Soviet SS-11 antitank missiles, along with a thousand 6omm. French mortars, sixty thousand rounds of artillery ammunition, and laser rangefinders for armored cars. This order had totaled $70 million. The 1975 order was smaller, but it was enough to alarm Moscow again.

Later that year, Iraq signed border agreements with Iran and Saudi Arabia. Iran withdrew its support from the Kurds, who were soon quashed by Baghdad. To cap it all, Iraq even signed an economic aid agreement with Jordan. Japanese and West European firms were given the job of enlarging the Iraqi port of Umm Qasr.

But Moscow looked like remaining Iraq's protecting power for some time; although Moscow did not welcome Syria's decision to resume diplomatic relations with the United States, or its intervention in Lebanon, it did not cut off Syrian military supplies. In 1976, Moscow even supplied Syria with MiG-25s—probably with Soviet pilots, and presumably only intended in a reconnaissance role—as well as small quantities of still more -21s and -23s.

Iraq, responding to the huge arms buildup in Iran, had by 1976 become Moscow's single main weapons customer, ordering $1 billion of armaments from the Soviet Union that year. It took delivery of more MiG-21s and -23s and a few more -25s, as well as of T-62 tanks, armored vehicles, surface-to-air missiles and radar.

Jordan, financed by Saudi Arabia, turned down the offer of a comparatively inexpensive Soviet air-defense system and bought U.S. Hawks instead; but conservative Kuwait ordered Russian SA-7 missiles.

Moscow was still keeping Egypt on a short leash, but aircraft engines and other spare parts were allowed to reach Egyptian ports from Yugoslavia, Czechoslovakia and North Korea. China also supplied some Chinese-made MiG parts, and in return—according to one U.S. intelligence source—received a single MiG-23, presumably for copying. By early 1977, Egypt had managed to keep forty-eight MiG-23s airworthy, flying half of them as fighters, half as ground support aircraft. Egypt's tank force was creeping slowly back to its 1973 strength—partly from Soviet spare parts, partly from Western supplies.

Farther down the Mediterranean, a major hard-currency buyer of Soviet arms was Libya, which by 1976 ranked closely behind Egypt, Syria and Iraq as a Russian client in the area.

Since the overthrow of the monarchy in 1969, President Mu'ammar al-Qaddafi has had a cautious relationship with Moscow, balancing his opposition to "atheist" communism against his shared opposition to Western imperialism. When Qaddafi forced the United States and Britain to evacuate their air bases in Libya in 1970, he automatically qualified for increased Soviet assistance. But republican Libya's first major arms order was for 110 Mirages from France. Since Libya had no jet pilots at the time, these were presumably intended as a backup for Nasser, more than for Libyan defense.

Tripoli did transfer arms and send financial assistance for arms-purchasing to Egypt during the 1973 war, notably buying seventy replacement MiG-21s for Egypt at a cost of nearly half a billion dollars. Qaddafi also helped Syria. Some of Libya's Mirages, on loan to Egypt, participated in the fighting. These were flown by Egyptians, as Libya still had only twenty-five pilots checked out on the aircraft.

But Sadat's willingness to negotiate with Israel, through Kissinger, lost him Libyan support. Some Egyptian technicians were expelled from

Libya, and Egypt itself withdrew others—including pilot instructors. Cairo also withdrew two ships and some SAM sites which it had placed in Libya, and ceased work on the air defense system it had been building around Libyan bases at Tobruk, Benghazi and Tripoli. In place of Egyptian technicians, six hundred Pakistanis arrived, including about thirty pilot instructors. France, Italy and Yugoslavia also supplied technical assistance.

Premier Jalloud sought military purchases in Western countries; but Qaddafi's support for all sorts of causes, from Uganda's President Amin to the IRA, from Eritrea to the Philippines, had given him a record as a dangerous maverick, and Libya was soon forced to turn to Moscow. In May 1974, Jalloud signed a trade agreement in the Russian capital. This included a barter of Soviet SAM batteries for Libyan oil.

Moscow welcomed the new customer, since arms for Qaddafi could be used to teach Sadat a lesson—just as arms for Iraq had been used to impress Syria. In December, Russia agreed to supply Tu-22 supersonic bombers, MiG-23s, the big MI-8 troopcarrier helicopters, SA-3 and SA-6 batteries, T-62 tanks and antitank missiles. Nearly five hundred Soviet advisers were brought in.

In April 1975, Britain refused to sell Libya six submarines and thirty-eight Jaguar advanced strike aircraft. The order had been part of a $1.4 billion shopping list for British armorers, and London remained anxious to sell less destabilizing equipment which Libya had also requested—transport aircraft, frigates, tank transports, ammunition and support equipment. For Qaddafi, at the time, it was all or nothing, so once more he turned to Moscow.

Kosygin arrived in Tripoli the following month, just preceded by the first MiG-23s. Shortly afterward, a new arms agreement was signed. The Cairo newspaper *Al Ahram* claimed it totaled $4 billion, and included Soviet access to Libyan military bases. Perhaps carried away, President Sadat later told columnist Georgie-Anne Geyer that the deal was worth $12 billion. Both Moscow and Tripoli denied the report about bases—which Pentagon sources said probably meant that the Soviet Navy had acquired simple repair and refueling rights—and Libya claimed the value of the new deal was about $800 million. The usual "Western" figure is $1 billion.

Apparently included was an order for 400 more T-62s (Libya already had 600) and 6 F-class diesel submarines, along with submarine support facilities at Tobruk and Benghazi. About a hundred Libyan naval personnel went to Russia for training. Soviet advisers in Libya were estimated by 1977 to have reached 800, and Libyan trainees in Russia 1,100.

Also in 1975, Russia agreed to build a small nuclear reactor for Libya, but Western experts agreed that a ten-megawatt facility could never be used to produce enough plutonium for a nuclear weapon. If the object of all this was to unsettle Sadat, the latter laughed off the idea by saying that, from the experience of Egyptian technicians in Libya, he estimated it would take "twenty to fifty years" to train Libyans to operate their new armaments.

In 1976, Libya took more MiG-23s, Tu-22 bombers, Scud surface-to-surface missiles, antiaircraft missiles and other land equipment under its agreements. It received replacements for MiG-21s sent to Uganda to replace those destroyed in the Israeli raid on Entebbe to free hostages. A CIA study said Libya's armed forces were now more strongly equipped than Algeria's or Morocco's.

One advantage of Moscow's Libyan connection was that Qaddafi seemed to head a more stable regime than many of his fellow Arab leaders. By spending $20 billion on a welfare state for his 2.5 million people, and by living an austere, uncorrupt existence, he had made himself truly popular. With oil revenues of $8 billion a year, he was clearly a power to be reckoned with, and his loyal support of the Palestinians made him seem less of an opportunist than more important leaders. But of all Moscow's Arab friends, Qaddafi looked like being the most difficult to control.

By 1977, Libya had, according to British sources, a total of two thousand tanks of all types, a substantial air force, air-defense, and surface missile systems. Much of the smaller weaponry was still finding its way abroad—to Lebanon (for the Muslims against the Christians), to the Polisario resistance in Western Sahara (as part of Qaddafi's bid to destroy Morocco's King Hassan), to Malta (to keep the island free of dependence on Britain), to separatists in Sicily, Corsica and Crete, to the Turkish part of Cyprus (for Islamic reasons), to Northern Ireland (to oppose Britain, and to prove—as in Malta—that a pious Muslim can support Roman Catholic causes), to the Muslim Eritrean secessionists (who are opposed by the Ethiopian Government with other Soviet weapons), even briefly—until President Marcos' attractive wife, Imelda, called on him—to Muslim dissidents in the Philippines.

Russia had had its problems coming to terms with Africa's preference for nationalism over ideology; in Libya, it had to accept the notion of an ally—of sorts—who was a traditional Muslim fire-raiser, a classical fundamentalist leader of a holy war. As the United States had found in Israel, few friends are less responsive to their benefactors than those of the Levant. Largesse was accepted, but with grudging thanks, and with no willingness to be "influenced." Ambassador Mukhitdinov had said it well when he spoke of the Syrians: "They'll take anything—except advice."

Indeed, in 1979, the CIA noted that MiG-23s now existed in the air forces of Iraq, Syria, Egypt and Libya—as well as Ethiopia and Cuba—but were still found in only two Warsaw Treaty inventories, those of Czechoslovakia and Bulgaria. T-62 tanks had appeared in the Middle East before they had appeared in Europe at all. In 1979, some were sold to North Yemen, along with six MiG-21s, to counter earlier U.S. sales, while Jordan was reported considering the purchase of the larger T-72s.

Soviet Union/Southeast Asia

North Vietnam relied more on Moscow than on Peking in its bid to conquer South Vietnam and unify the country. Relations between the Chinese and the Indochinese had never been good, since time immemorial. Before 1961, for geographic sphere-of-influence reasons, the Russians had been prepared to concede to the Chinese the primary Communist responsibility for Southeast Asia; but after the Sino-Soviet split it competed openly and aggressively for the loyalty of area Communist forces. In the spring of 1961, the Russians began airlifting military equipment to Hanoi and to Laotian insurgents, but still cooperated with China: Heavy weapons equipment came over the Trans-Siberian Railroad to Harbin and Mukden in Manchuria, then to Peking and Hanoi, to reach the Viet Cong in South Vietnam via trails. Other supplies came by ship from Odessa on the Black Sea or from Stettin on the Baltic direct to Hanoi and Haiphong. China, supplying small arms by coastal junk, and obsolete models of MiGs directly over the border, could not compete seriously as an armorer with Russia.

In 1965, Moscow reacted to the "Johnson buildup" with one of its own. North Vietnam's SA-2 and SA-3 batteries were increased 700 per cent. The latest Soviet and Czech antiaircraft artillery began to arrive. Every soldier now had an AK-47—recognized by Americans and South Vietnamese alike as more deadly than the M-16. With these came a mountain of light mortars and bazookas, electronic equipment, medicine, motorcycles and bicycles. China in its turn began to supply huge quantities of rice, medicine, bicycles, small arms and ammunition. The Russians valued their 1965 supply at $555 million and said Eastern European countries and "others" (China) had supplied another $450 million worth.

The same year, Russia refused a Chinese request for arms, so the Chinese refused Moscow permission to build staging bases in northwest and southern China for Vietnam supply. Soviet goods could continue to transship through China, but subject to Chinese inspection. There were consequent interminable delays, adding to those already created by two gauge-changes on the railroad. Chinese railbeds and rolling stock were poor. Soon, Moscow accused Peking of sabotaging deliveries to North Vietnam and the Viet Cong, then of stealing weapons and replacing them with inferior ones. Some Russian arms crates were relabeled. The Chinese said it was to simplify handling by Chinese transport workers, but the Russians said it was to make Russian supplies look like supplies from China.

In some cases, the Chinese did not steal the latest Russian weapons, but merely "borrowed" them to learn to make copies. Some of these "borrowed" weapons were clumsily reassembled and later proved fatal to their Vietnamese handlers. At this point, Russia was able to blame virtually all delivery delays or faulty weaponry on perfidious Peking, and did so. By April 1967, the scandal had become so great that China agreed to let the North Vietnamese take title to the Soviet goods at the Chinese border and be responsible for their transit through China—a task which the Vietnamese found extremely difficult when the Cultural Revolution broke out that year. North Vietnamese and Viet Cong officers were arrested as imperialist spies. Eventually, the Russians decided to ship almost everything by sea. From that year on, at least one Soviet supply ship arrived each day in Haiphong.

By 1968, 80 per cent of all supplies were coming in by sea, with the fastest route being from Vladivostok, at the head of the Trans-Siberian Railroad. The Chinese were hoping this would provoke the United States into blockading and raiding Haiphong, thus causing a rupture in relations between Washington and Moscow, and a resultant Russian fear to export weapons in case this triggered war with the West; this would mean a consequent greater Vietnamese dependence on China. U.S. bombing, however, merely led to a search for a greater variety of supply routes, of which the most famous was the Ho Chi Minh Trail (most of which was invisible—although not undetectable—from the air). This ran from Sihanoukville, Cambodia, through southern Laos; it could only handle small arms, ammunition, food and fuel. A typical convoy might include forty riverboats, then sixty trucks, then two thousand bicycles and thousands of coolies. The Russians used the route more than the Chinese did for their own supplies. Most Pentagon sources believe that if the Viet Cong and North Vietnam had been reliant only on Chinese supplies, they would have been defeated.

In weapons diplomacy as in defense, Moscow fought on two fronts. Soviet aid to Indonesia and India was aimed at undercutting China. Between 1958 and 1964, Russia was estimated to have sold a billion dollars' worth of arms to Sukarno, whose country dominated the choke point of the Malacca Strait. The Indonesian Communist Party, the largest in the nonaligned world, was programmed by Peking, so Moscow sought to strengthen the relatively right-wing Indonesian military and crush the Communists. Supplying Sukarno was made more respectable for Moscow by the fact that he was not only fighting Communist revolts, but others as well—at least one of them armed by the CIA.

Most of the vast arms order arrived in the 1961–63 period—MiG-21s, Tu-16s, a heavy cruiser, eight destroyers, twelve submarines, at least one hundred other naval craft, along with helicopters, tanks, antiaircraft artillery, field artillery, SAMs and small arms. Sukarno used the arms to drive the Dutch from West Irian and also to supply insurgents in Malaysia. After Sukarno's fall, an inflexibly anti-Communist Indonesian Army then slaughtered the Indonesian Communist Party with Soviet weapons in one of the biggest bloodbaths of the century.

Meanwhile, Washington policy steered New Delhi into Moscow's hands. Finding authoritarian Pakistan more pliable to direction than democratic India, the Kennedy administration followed Eisenhower in strengthening Islamabad. Soviet military aid to India began in 1960, with just over $30 million worth of transport aircraft, helicopters and communications equipment. In return, Moscow received limited naval facilities at Vishakapatnam, in southern India.

Then, China attacked India in 1962 and annexed territory, thus making India still more of a client of Moscow, which began upgrading its deliveries, notably in the field of aviation. In 1964, Russia added a $42 million SA-2 missile complex, more aircraft and armor, and started a co-production arrangement for MiG-21s. The United States had briefly sought a balance in 1962, selling some weapons only for use against "Communist forces"—meaning China. India later used some of this weaponry on Pakistan in 1965. Today, as noted in Chapter 2, India has an aviation of mixed origin, but the hard core is Soviet, and this is true of land forces also. In 1978, India already had the big Soviet T-72 tanks: None of the "Warsaw" or Middle East countries had them. In 1979, when India launched its second spacecraft—an earth resources/meteorology vehicle —it was from a Soviet site, with a Russian booster.

In all, Moscow responded with more understanding to the basic requirement of India—already a nation of nearly half a billion people—to have a native industrial base for armaments; and it accepted soft-currency (Indian rupee) payments or barter deals. However, an attempt in 1977 to lease, for $1 million a year, the former British air base on Gan, in the Maldive Islands, a republic in the Indian Ocean strongly under the influence of New Delhi, was turned down by the local President, Ibrahim Nasir. Gan, about two hundred miles north of the U.S.-British base on Diego Garcia, was leased by the RAF for twenty years shortly after the Maldives became independent in 1965, but abandoned in 1974 as part of Britain's decision to reduce its military presence east of Suez. It has an 8,700-foot runway. The Maldive Government said it wanted to lease the island to a "commercial" interest.

Soviet Union/North Korea

The Soviet Union's arms support of North Korea has been extensive, yet noticeable by its restraint. Pyongyang's over-two-thousand tanks— possibly more, according to a 1979 CIA report—easily outnumber those of South Korea, but most are reportedly T-54s and T-55s, not the more modern T-62. Moscow's provision of artillery has been considerable, but here again the accent appears to have been the familiar one of Soviet weapons diplomacy: quantity rather than quality.

Of 632 Soviet-supplied combat aircraft, the best are 130 MiG-21s, 20 Sukhoi-7 close-support planes, and 80 Il-28 light bombers. Although MiG-23s have been supplied to Third World countries and to two European allies, Moscow has been reluctant to give them to Pyongyang— although, here again, the 1979 report talked of MiG-23 deliveries. South Korea's aviation is leaner and, on the whole, meaner.

Moscow has downplayed Korean affairs for a number of years, apparently continuing to give North Korea a sound defense, but unanxious to see the peninsula become an arena for superpower conflict by proxy again. South Korea's fear of North Korean aggression is real enough, but North Korea's fear of its neighbor appears to be just as great. Major General George J. Keegan, Jr., the former Air Force Chief of Intelligence, has reported that virtually every military installation around the 38th Parallel—the border area—has been hardened against blast, along with most aircraft and submarine bases throughout the country. There are extensive, Soviet-directed civil-defense preparations for the population.

Soviet Union/Turkey/Afghanistan/Iran/Pakistan

Russia sees itself as vulnerable on its southern flank from the Black Sea to Tibet, with the principal problems being Turkey, perhaps still Iran and—until 1978—Afghanistan. Because the Turks are more anti-Russian than anti-Communist, Moscow has had no success so far in turning Tur-

key into a buffer state; but with the help of the anti-Turkish Greek lobby
on Capitol Hill, it is not impossible that Moscow may eventually succeed
in persuading Ankara to be nonaligned, on the lines of Yugoslavia. The
Soviet Union has already opened an arms credit for Turkey and supplied
other economic assistance: the $650 million package in 1975 followed an
earlier $500 million program. Besides a steel plant, other Soviet industrial
projects with military implications completed in Turkey include an aluminum plant, a plywood mill and a sulfuric acid plant.

Because the Turks fear Russian designs on the Bosporus, the United
States originally supplied Jupiter missiles. These were removed by Kennedy as a quid pro quo for the removal of Russian ballistic missiles from
Cuba: Khrushchev knew at the time that the Jupiters had been made obsolete by the deployment of the Polaris submarine fleet; but overtly he
was glad to announce the withdrawal of the Jupiters as a "victory"—
which Washington discreetly did not contest.

Afghanistan, traditionally a buffer state between British India and the
Tsar, was one of the first countries to receive Russian aid after World
War Two—partly as a counter to CENTO and SEATO aid to Pakistan.
Moscow also backed Afghanistan's claim to Pushtunistan in Pakistan. Between 1955 and 1960, Kabul received the considerable sum of $100 mil-
lion of arms from Moscow, including MiG-17s, and -15s and sufficient
armor for two divisions. Russian engineers built roads and airports and
river harbors, and kept two semiarmored divisions on Afghanistan's
border, ready to drive through that country and Pakistan to link up with
India for an eventual war with China. Afghanistan, wishing to remain a
buffer state, also obtained aid for a while from America and other
Western countries; but a coup in 1978 brought a frankly Marxist military
junta into power.

Iran posed more of a problem. Both Tsarist and Communist Russia
have coveted Iranian provinces west of the Caspian. During World War
Two, Stalin occupied all of Iran north of the capital, Teheran; as the war
drew to a close, he made a bid to seize the whole country. In the early
fifties, Moscow backed the "anti-imperialist" government of Mohammed
Mossadecq.

It was a naked power struggle, couched in purely cold-war terms.
When Kim Roosevelt, Miles Copeland and the CIA restored the Shah in
1953, Moscow had lost. The grateful Shah aligned his country on the
West, joining CENTO in 1955. Nevertheless, as mentioned earlier, the
Shah took military equipment from Moscow in 1967, mostly to pressure
the United States for better weapons and terms. Russia built a steel mill
at Isfahan, and later expanded it, with production reaching 1.9 million
tons in 1978 and scheduled for 8 million tons a decade later. By 1975,

Moscow had already invested half a billion dollars in the plant, and also offered to give Teheran a subway—a project later secured by France—build pipelines, and help exploit Iranian natural gas and oil.

Later, even Pakistan bought some Soviet arms. The pattern has been for Turkey, Iran and Pakistan to make relatively small purchases from the Soviet Union, mostly to prod Washington.

Soviet Union/Latin America

Moscow's principal client in Latin America has been Cuba, a beachhead for Marxist-Leninist revolution and government in the western hemisphere. The Soviet Union has provided Cuba with armament out of all proportion to the little nation's size; despite bargain-basement prices, Cuba spends more than 5 per cent of its GNP on military expenses—the highest in the hemisphere. Cuba today has the second largest armed forces south of the border after Brazil's, and indubitably the best—well-trained, motivated, and skilled in the use of their equipment.

With a population of just over ten million—about the same as Chile's—Cuba has a long reputation of fighting. Its war of independence against Spain simmered on and off for thirty years, until Theodore Roosevelt's Rough Riders finally intervened in 1898 and propelled the island into freedom. This left a legacy of dependence on the United States, along with exploitation and suspicion.

Under Fidel Castro, a poor, undereducated population, heavily of slave origin, intellectually weakened by the departure of 700,000 of the middle class to the United States, has gradually evolved into a relatively efficient nation. While still not comparable in skills to countries like Chile or Uruguay, it has proved to be probably the Soviet Union's best Third World success.

All of Cuba's largely legitimate grievances against the United States have been well exploited by Moscow. A country the size of Tennessee has over 600 tanks, or more than its former colonial power, Spain. It has a light blue-water navy of about 100 Soviet-made vessels, some with the "smart" Styx missiles, and an air force of 210 combat aircraft, to which Moscow, in 1978, began adding a squadron of MiG-23s and a squadron of MiG-27s, theoretically capable of reaching U.S. targets and returning. U.S. officials said these might be in breach of the 1962 Kennedy-Khrushchev agreement, and RF-71s were sent over Cuba to check out the ordnance pylons on the -27s. But, unlike the case of the Cienfuegos submarine pens of a decade before, the White House decided not to make an issue of the long-range MiGs. Cuba now has sufficient fighter and interceptor squadrons to take on, say, Italy's on about equal terms.

But since the days of the 1962 "missile crisis," Moscow has been as cautious with Cuba as it has been with North Korea. Cuba has been denied all real ground-attack capacity, except for MiG-17s for internal suppression, and the new -27s.

By transporting, and partly financing, Cuba's interventions in Angola and Ethiopia, and its guerrilla training missions in southern and other parts of Africa, Moscow has eased faster growth of the Cuban forces. By 1978, in addition to about 200,000 armed forces at home, Havana was believed to have about 45,000 troops—almost all except officers being reservists—in Africa.

In South America proper, where the Soviet Union, by the mid-seventies, had a trade deficit climbing toward a billion dollars, Moscow's major breakthrough has been Peru. The country seemed a suitable case for Soviet assistance, since it was on bad terms with two neighbors, Bolivia and Chile—and Chile, in particular, was an American protégé and a witless dictatorship to boot. The fact that Peru was busy arming for a possible war with this permanent enemy worried landlocked Bolivia, which has borders with both countries. Brazil, which supports Bolivia's claim to a sea outlet (lost to Chile in the nineteenth century) has said it would intervene to protect Bolivia in the event of war. Argentina supports Peru, notably against Ecuador.

In 1973, Peru ordered 200 Soviet T-55 tanks, following Chile's purchase of 15 F-5Es and 12 A-27s from the United States. But Peru's air force had still been "Western"—French Mirages, British Canberra bombers and American A-36s—and it continued to order a selection of U.S., French and British planes. Then, in August 1976, it was learned that Peru would buy, for $250 million, two squadrons—36 aircraft—of late-model Su-22s. These are short-range (260 miles) Mach-2 fighter-bombers. The Su-22—an export version of the Sukhoi-17—was so state-of-the-art that *Jane's* did not even include a mention of it that year. The government of President Francisco Morales Bermúdez would have ten years' credit at 2 per cent, with a year's grace. In 1977, Morales ordered 36 more Su-22s, also at a cost of a quarter billion dollars.

Morales admitted the first Soviet sale in November 1976. The United States, as noted earlier, had offered F-5s, and eventually A-4s, but on purely "commercial"—expensive—credit terms. Before going to Moscow, Morales had also turned to Paris and London, but these proposed deals fell through—partly because Britain was selling Peru's other unfriendly neighbor, Ecuador, the Jaguar.

At about $7 million apiece, the Sukhoi was certainly a good buy, and Foreign Minister José de la Puente told reporters blithely that "airplanes have no ideology." Western diplomats quickly pointed out that technicians to train the pilots and the maintenance men would be less neutral.

By late 1977, it became clear that Moscow—now far and away Lima's most important arms supplier—was also selling Peru 30 big MI-8 helicopters, a SA-3 system, 200 T-55 tanks, and 122mm. and 130mm. artillery, protected by batteries of SZU-23, four-barrel, 60mm. radar-guided antiaircraft guns. Pentagon experts began saying that Peru was the first South American nation to have a real "offensive" capability. By early 1978, its fleet of T-55 and T-54 tanks was said to number 400.

In 1976, Moscow made arms proposals to Colombia and Argentina—a right-wing regime which in 1977 was blacklisted for U.S. arms because of human-rights violations. More curiously, Russia also made offers of military sales to Ecuador, which lost a third of its territory to Peru in a 1941 war and has not forgotten its grievance.

Total Soviet arms sales to Latin America in 1977 were estimated by the CIA at $400 million, surpassing those of the United States.

But during Secretary Vance's October 1978 trip to Moscow, the Russians agreed to hold a bilateral conference with the United States in Mexico City in December to discuss limiting arms sales to Latin America. Other bilateral superpower agreements to restrict arms sales were also discussed in Moscow. But when the talks were held, they soon foundered over a quarrel between the National Security Council and the State Department.

Secretary Vance and Foreign Minister Gromyko had agreed to restrict the talks to Latin America and Africa. Then, Moscow suggested also including Iran, the Koreas and China. Dr. Brzezinski said no, but the State Department's Leslie Gelb, who was to lead the U.S. delegation, argued in favor of the Soviet-suggested expansion of the agenda. Brzezinski held firm, and Gelb was obliged to inform his Soviet opposite number, Ambassador Lev Mendelevich, that if these additional areas were introduced into the talks, he was under instructions to walk out. Gelb later described Mendelevich as incredulous; but the Soviet diplomat responded by offering to discuss the Indian Ocean question.

Gelb referred back to Washington, and once again Brzezinski said no. Vance, out of the country on a mission to South Africa, could offer no help, so Gelb fought back alone, unsuccessfully, and nearly resigned as the tempers mounted. Vance later vindicated Gelb, but the damage to

the talks was done. The whole story was later leaked to defense reporters
—to mollify the puzzled Russians.

The Communist Arms Trade in Africa

For obvious geographical reasons, the Russians have consistently
sought repair and refueling facilities for ships and aircraft all over the
world, with a view to transforming these, wherever possible, into bases
for air espionage and arms re-export—even perhaps into future strategic
bases. In the 1962 Cuba crisis, Conakry airport in Guinea was crucial for
a while as a refueling point for Soviet aircraft supplying Havana. It
remains useful as an African arms-export base for Russia and Czechoslovakia and for Atlantic patrols, but these are now mostly based in
Luanda, Angola. Until recently, Moscow enjoyed similar staging rights at
Khartoum and at Sana'a in Yemen, and docking rights at North African
ports like Alexandria and Port Said; it still has such rights in Aden and at
Mers-el-Kebir, the former French submarine base in Algeria; it has ship-
repair rights in Yugoslavia and flyover rights from more than a score of
African and Near East countries.

Not all Soviet gunrunning is to legitimate states or legitimate Communist revolutions like Vietnam's. In 1964, some mysterious crates arrived at
Nairobi airport. Luo strongmen loyal to Home Affairs Minister Oginga
Odinga collected them in the name of the minister, refusing to submit
them to customs examination. President Jomo Kenyatta bided his time;
then, in April 1965, his police raided Odinga's office, carting away some
of the crates, which contained machine guns, small arms and ammunition. Arrested aides were soon singing, and two more caches were uncovered, some containing grenades. A week later, the Soviet freighter
Fizik Lebedev docked at Mombasa, Kenya's main port: Heavy weapons—World War Two tanks and howitzers—were on board, addressed
to a seventeen-man team of Soviet advisers. But where was the team?
Was it already part of the Soviet embassy? No Kenyan politician could
be found who would admit to having invited such a team, anyway.
Kenyatta ordered the boat out of Kenyan waters, expelled seventeen
Soviet diplomats and abrogated his trade agreement with Moscow.

In the early sixties, seeking to help a "Marxist" dissidence in Cam-
eroon, China had sent arms through Syria in crates marked "almond
nuts." An American freight line had innocently flown the "nuts" from
Damascus to Zurich, whence a British line had taken them to Las
Palmas, getting permission en route to refuel at the small RAF base at
Gibraltar. When two Spanish workers at Las Palmas found the crates too

heavy, they complained, and the British aircraft captain ordered a crate opened. It contained six brand-new Chinese mortars. In all, in place of 12,000 pounds of almonds, there were three hundred mortars, along with hundreds of mortar bombs and grenades. Communist Europe used Las Palmas as a way station for weapons for Cuba, Angola, Mozambique and Algeria. Many of these shipments were also consigned as "nuts." The fifty-one surplus British Valentine tanks which Nasser received from Belgium in 1955 (a sale recorded in Chapter 5) were in crates marked "tractors."

In August 1966, Bulgaria sent "duty-free goods" to a Bulgarian food-importing firm in Addis Ababa. Again, suspicions were aroused and the crates were found to contain machine guns for the Eritrean dissidents. (Similarly, in late 1965, crates marked "sewing machines," unloaded from a Bulgarian freighter at Beirut, had broken on the dockside, spilling out guns. Other crates aboard for discharge at Beirut, and marked "mechanical spare parts," were found to contain 1,500 automatic weapons.)

Russia openly supported the rebel Gizenga government in Stanleyville (now Kisangani), during the anarchy that followed independence in the Congo. When Egypt, in a disagreement with Dag Hammarskjöld, withdrew its 512-man contingent from the Congo in February 1961, it left behind 67 tons of military equipment, at Moscow's request. Moscow also used the Egyptians to funnel money to Gizenga and even sent him a printing press to forge Congolese money. This saved him paying his people in gold stolen from a local mine. When the "Simba" rebellion broke out in the mid-sixties, Moscow supplied aid to that at well, to destabilize the pro-American government in Kinshasa.

Just over the border, a reporter did not have to look far to see why Russia was helping these unideological and inefficient rebels. America was not the only cause. The Chinese were there in full strength with abnormally large embassies in Brazzaville and Bujumbura, the capital of Burundi. By April 1965, the Chinese embassy in tiny Brazzaville numbered 210 people, including 180 military attachés. This has been compared to China sending "52,631 diplomats to Washington." China was supplying aid to the "Simba" leaders—"General" Nicolas Olenga, Gaston Soumialot and Pierre Mulele. But China's supply routes were circuitous: Russia's airlift from Kiev flew smoothly via Cairo, Khartoum and Juba, then went by truck. Some material was shipped to Algeria, where dockers, partly paid in American PL 480 food, unloaded it for air-freighting to Khartoum.

But the Russians also committed more bloopers than the Chinese. In 1959, it sent snowplows to Guinea to clear the roads after heavy rain: Instead of flattening the earth as a grader does, they left a wall of mud beside the road. Although forested Guinea is unsuitable for armored warfare and none of its neighbors have tanks, it received mobile antitank guns. Forested Indonesia and mountainous Yemen also got tanks, which —at least in Indonesia's case—would have needed wings to go to war. Soviet guns sold to Morocco were turned on Moscow's friend in the area, Algeria, and used to threaten Mauritania with annexation, although both Russia and Algeria supported Mauritania's right to a separate independence.

In short, despite its superpower status, the Soviet Union has no great record for efficiency in its Third World program. In 1968, the present writer went into Rhodesia with a platoon of Zimbabwean guerrillas, to cover their operations for a few days; our quartermaster's last task before departure was to collect six sacks of flour from the Soviet embassy in Lusaka; when chow time came that night, inside enemy territory, and the guerrilla assigned to cooking began to prepare to make bread, it was discovered that all six sacks contained salt, which had to be perilously traded to villagers, thus betraying our presence.

In 1963, Moscow sold 12 MiG-15 fighters to Somalia, a country with no qualified pilots or aircraft mechanics and only about a hundred university graduates. Over the following years, the relationship grew sixfold until Somalia became the main beneficiary of Soviet arms and economic aid in sub-Sahara Africa. By 1977, Somalia was reputed to be the most effective military force in black Africa after South Africa, with the third largest military inventory in the area after South Africa and Nigeria. Its 56 MiG fighters included a squadron of 12 MiG-21s; it had 12 Il-28 bombers. It also had 300 Soviet medium tanks, an impressive array of artillery, and antiaircraft weaponry including SA-2s and SA-3s. There were reportedly 3,000 Russian advisers—along with 3,000 dependents—helping the 32,000-strong Somali forces.

But in 1977, as Soviet support for the Marxist junta in Ethiopia, Somalia's principal enemy, became more blatant, Somali President Siad Barre—at Saudi Arabia's and Egypt's urging—appealed to the United States for arms, drawing an initially encouraging response. Most of the Soviet military and civilian advisory team began flying out of Somalia's capital, Mogadishu. Moscow was abandoning a major airport, and naval and missile-storage facilities at Berbera, plus other naval facilities at Kismayu. Saudi Arabia promised to provide, first $300 million, then reportedly $600 million in aid, for military purchases from non-Communist sources, as a gesture to an Arab League country at war with a Moscow-assisted nation. Then Washington reversed course on arms supply. British and French arms salesmen, as noted in Chapter 5, were at once reported active; and China, which like the United States had supported the Ethiopian junta earlier—when Moscow was supporting Somalia—soon offered spare parts for Somalia's Soviet equipment, notably T-45 tanks and MiG-17s.

Moscow's initial attraction to Somalia, with its Indian Ocean frontage, was obvious enough. Its just-cause war, and Washington's support of Ethiopia, rationalized Soviet support of Mogadishu. But equally obvious was the attraction, for the Kremlin, of the Bolshevik-style revolution in Addis Ababa and the chance to replace the United States in what had been, until the fall of Haile Selassie, America's principal protégé south of the Sahara. In the late seventies, with Washington's policy vacillating, it presumably hoped for the sort of peaceful settlement of the Ethio-Somali conflict for which Washington was working, after which it could reasonably hope to have both countries within its orbit. During 1977 and early 1978, the Soviet Union provided an estimated $1 billion of military assistance to Ethiopia, including 450 T-34 and T-54 tanks, enabling Addis Ababa to repel the Somali invasion and recommence the conquest of secessionist Eritrea. (At a Brussels conference in June 1978, the NATO commander, General Alexander Haig, put the figure at $4 billion, but did not elaborate.) Ethiopia increased its own arms budget for 1978 to $103.4 million to absorb the new equipment and expand its forces from 41,000 to 50,000, backed by a militia of about 75,000. Crucial to Ethiopian and Soviet successes in the fighting was the role of a division of Cuban troops and Cuban air support, and the overall direction of about 500 Russian advisers, reportedly including 3 generals. The Cubans, like the Russians, had formerly backed the Somalis and the Eritreans, and Havana clearly had migivings about being too involved in repressing the Eritreans.

When Somalia expelled all Soviet and Cuban advisers in 1977, and broke relations with Havana, it allowed half the Soviet embassy to remain and kept half its own mission in Moscow. The Soviet Union, as noted above, presumably hopes to resume friendly relations with Somalia after the end of the fighting in Ethiopia, and has proposed that Ethiopia grant autonomy to its Somali and Eritrean provinces as a gesture. Even if the Soviet Union does not completely recover its former position in Somalia, it is not without replacement facilities—notably air and naval rights at Aden, naval use of the Ethiopian ports of Assab and Massawa (threatened by the Eritrean dissidence), and anchorages at or near Socotra island, Mahé island and the Chagos Archipelago, plus naval privileges not far away at the Iraqi ports of Umm Qasr and Al Basrah on the Persian Gulf. Saudi Arabia began, in 1978, offering financial inducements to South Yemen if it would not grant an expansion of Soviet facilities at Aden.

Angola's minority MPLA party came to power in 1975 with massive Soviet and Cuban help. The Angolan Government then signed a twenty-year friendship treaty with Moscow which included the promise of more military aid; more fighters, tanks and guided surface-to-air missiles were delivered. Although the equipment was modest by world standards, and much of it had already been used by the Cuban forces, it had impact in the region and helped the MPLA withstand—with substantial Cuban troop support—a continuing civil war against the country's two majority parties.

Throughout 1977 and 1978, the Kremlin also increased weapons aid to southern African resistance movements, using established African countries as conduits. Moscow supplied the Zimbabwe African Peoples Union (ZAPU) guerrillas in Rhodesia through Zambia and Angola—while China supplied the Zimbabwe African National Union (ZANU) through Mozambique. (Moscow supported Mozambique itself with 150 T-34 and T-54 tanks and 47 MiG-21s.) Both Moscow and Peking supported South West African People's Organization (SWAPO) guerrillas in Namibia. Elsewhere in the dark continent, Mali also received its first MiG-21s. Moscow's friend Cuba was training ZAPU guerrillas in Zambia and Angola, and even training ZAPU pilots on MiG-21s in Cuba. Despite Havana's links with Moscow, and its anti-Peking rhetoric, it was allowed to compete with China in training ZANU guerrillas in Mozambique.

Even in southern Africa, however, where it would have been senseless for Moscow not to join the winning side—since the Chinese were sure to do so, and the West is hamstrung with its own ambiguous inhibitions—the Kremlin remained cautious. The Soviet Union is conscious of the fragility of Third World friendships. Former protégés like Nkrumah in Africa—or Sukarno in Asia—were not only toppled by Soviet arms, but by Soviet arms in the hands of Soviet-trained elite troops. The Russians would like to be sure that their arms will not steer into power, south of the Zambesi regimes favorable to Washington or Peking. The big question, in 1978, was how far Moscow—and Peking—would go toward stimulating a revolution in South Africa.

Meanwhile, non-Soviet Eastern European arms deliveries—$75 million in 1976, according to a late-1977 CIA estimate—were at their lowest level since 1970.

Chinese Weapons Diplomacy

For a while, China provided arms not only to undercut Washington and Moscow, but also to provoke civil wars and, it hoped, worldwide "revolution." Today, Peking, like Moscow, is cautious. Nevertheless, China is still the preferred supplier of the really radical movements, and leftist luminaries like Sheikh Abdul Rahman "Babu" Mohammed of Zanzibar, the late Alphonse Massemba-Débat of Congo-Brazzaville, President Samora Machel of Mozambique and the earlier-mentioned Oginga Odinga have been proud to call themselves "Maoists"; Mao himself (like Guevara) predicted that Africa would be the first continent to fulfill the Communist revolution.

China suffered initially from its heavy-handedness, plotting against established African nationalist governments in Zambia, Malawi, Cameroon and Burundi—where its embassy armed the monarchist Batutsi, plotted assassinations, and was finally expelled in 1965. In Centrafrican Republic, China helped to bring down the presidency of David Dacko. The Chinese were slower than the Russians to realize that ideology had less attraction for Africans than nationalism. Where the Chinese advocated war, the Russians stressed material improvement. But the Chinese, unlike the Russians, could also score points by appealing to African resentment against "whites."

In a more sophisticated situation, the underdeveloped Chinese war industry would have lost out in competition with Moscow, as it did in North Vietnam. But in Africa, where military demands were mostly rudimentary, the Chinese won admiration for their selfless service. Once they had learned not to plot against existing African governments, they became "safer" sources of technical aid than anyone—even safer than the Canadians and the Swedes, and much safer and less demanding than the Russians, the French, the Americans or the British. Tazara—the Tanzania-Zambia Railway—was their monument, and Peking followed this up by offering arms (pirated Russian designs, of course) at even more generous terms than Moscow's, namely interest-free credit. Recipient countries soon found that Peking and Moscow could be played off against each other, just as West and East had been played against each other before. Offers of interest-free Chinese credit would draw counterproposals of larger interest-free credit from Moscow, and vice versa. In such a competition, the more ambitious states usually turned to Moscow in the end, because Soviet arms were better and more versatile. But the military caste which benefits from new Soviet or Chinese weapons is invariably fascistic, rather than Marxist; and the risk remains that these fickle beneficiaries may use the Communist weaponry to seize power, and reward local believers in the socialist revolution with the firing squad or long years in dank, tropic prisons.

Until recently, China could spare relatively few items of major equipment, except in a pinch—in 1966, it "resupplied" Pakistan with Chinese-made copies of the Soviet T-59 tank, the MiG-19 fighter and the Il-28 bomber. But by 1977, China was estimated to have about sixty aerospace plants producing MiG-21s, MiG-17 trainers and MiG-19s—the latter being the mainstay of its essentially backward military aviation. The main plant, at Mukden, can produce one aircraft a day. China could therefore afford to sell some aircraft abroad. The Mukden complex also produces enough small and medium arms, and armor, to have a small excedent for export. Army trucks, produced at Changchun, have now appeared in Mozambique, while small submarines built at Dairen and surface craft from the yards at the inland port of Shanghai, or from those downriver at Canton and Wuchang, were reportedly offered to Tanzania in 1978.

Chinese military aid to less-developed countries—mostly in Africa—reached $100 million in 1976, about $25 million higher than ever before. Chinese economic aid, however—also $100 million—was down by 75 per cent. Some of the increase in military assistance went to Tanzania, where it was partly intended for southern African resistance movements. China also supplied MiG parts and components for Soviet tank engines to Egypt.

China's most important military sales project to date has been in Egypt. After a token—but free—resupply of weapons and spare parts in the mid-seventies, Peking moved on to straight sales in June 1979, when Sadat announced in a speech to troops in the Suez Canal area that China would sell substantial quantities of weapons. Washington *Post* correspondent Thomas W. Lippman quoted Western sources as saying that "several squadrons of MiG-19s—possibly as many as sixty planes" would be involved.

Economics and Communist Weapons Diplomacy

Perhaps the most interesting development in the Communist arms trade in recent years has been Moscow's tendency to copy the "Undershaft" arms philosophies of France, Britain and Israel: Namely, to be prepared to sell to any country not frankly hostile, in return for hard currency. In early 1977, the Kremlin appears to have taken a conscientious decision to push arms sales, as well as other exports, to solve its hard-currency deficits, following massive grain imports from the United States and Canada. Moscow had a global imbalance of trade of $6.4 billion in 1975; by 1977, experts were predicting a continued hard-currency shortage until at least 1980, but a favorable balance was achieved in 1978. By then, weapons were about 10 per cent of all Soviet exports.

By 1975, Moscow's debts to Western commercial banks alone already totaled $4 billion. By 1977, government-backed credits extended to Russia solely by Japan and Canada totaled $11 billion, of which about half were not tied to specific projects. In 1976, the Soviet Union boosted its exports by 27 per cent, to nearly $10 billion, while holding the increase on imports to only 4 per cent; but these still cost nearly $15 billion. The deficit was only a billion dollars less than the year before. In a characteristic, sell-to-anyone deal, the following year the Kremlin sold the Emir of Kuwait SA-7 surface-to-air missiles and tactical surface-to-surface and antitank missiles. The dollar figure was kept secret, but an agreement was signed under which the U.S.S.R. undertook to supply other weaponry to the conservative sheikdom. Defense Minister Sheikh Saad Abdullah Sabah said Kuwait was also interested in buying Soviet artillery and tanks. The Moscow relationship gave Kuwait a hedge against its potential enemy, Moscow-supported Iraq. Pro-Western Iran had made regular purchases, and already had significant numbers of SA-7 and SA-9 antiaircraft missiles and Soviet armored personnel carriers in its inventory.

So hard-pushed was the Soviet financial picture that Moscow unloaded huge quantities of gold—a billion dollars' worth in 1976—thus unwillingly helping the United States to bring the gold price down. (Russia, of course, is—along with France and South Africa—one of the few countries that wants to preserve gold as an international currency, and therefore favors a high price.) In 1976, the CIA estimated arms sales by the Soviet Union to hard-currency areas to equal about another billion dollars, or nearly a third of all Soviet arms sales; in 1977, hard currencies accounted for about $1.5 billion out of total orders of $3.9 billion: Deliveries were $3.3 billion. Intelligence analysts predicted over $2 billion in sales in hard currencies by 1980, with the Middle East and Africa continuing to be the main markets.

Moscow also began considering raising its oil prices to Eastern Europe to the level of those practiced by OPEC. Some Soviet prices are generous indeed: Cuba, for instance, pays for Russian oil at only one sixth of the world price. The Kremlin could partly justify an increase in oil prices by the discovery that its own oil needs were outstripping supply and that it could soon be a net importer of petroleum products. An obvious solution, for a country interested in barter, would be "arms for oil," a trade already proposed by Saudi Arabia and Iran (without success) to the United States, and accepted by France. If grain harvests fall again, Russia may offer "arms for food," at least outside of NATO—and perhaps within it, for instance to Turkey.

In 1975, Russia exported 130 million tons of crude oil and petroleum products—about 60 per cent to Communist countries and 40 per cent elsewhere, including 39 million tons (for $3.2 billion) to hard-currency Western Europe, an increase over the year before of 8 million tons; because "world prices" were charged, Russia benefited considerably from the 1973 OPEC markup. But with oil production in the Soviet Union expected to peak in the 1980s, the tendency to want to swap arms and other Soviet industrial products for oil will probably become irresistible. (At least, that's how the CIA sees it: Commerce Department reports presuppose drastic measures to curb energy waste, making Russia less dependent on foreign oil.)

Russia's financial problems will limit Soviet economic aid, which has never been very high in dollar terms—a total of about $11 billion since 1954, 80 per cent of it on the southern flank, from the Mideast to China. Even more than in the past, Soviet aid will probably be tied to purchase of Soviet equipment.

By 1975, according to CIA sources, while sales of Soviet arms abroad were not tailing off, overall, they were falling much further behind Western transfers. That year, they were only 10 per cent of all arms orders placed by Third World countries, and deliveries (dating from past orders) were only 22 per cent. Since U.S. programs include much greater infrastructural costs than Soviet programs, the difference in actual *weapons* transfers is, of course, less.

Soviet sales have gone mostly to Moscow's area of first concern—the Middle East. Even there, they have been falling in recent years. Soviet arms transfers to the area, which reached nearly $2.7 billion in 1973, were down to $830 million in 1976, according to House testimony in 1977 by the new CIA director, Admiral Stansfield Turner. He added that Soviet deliveries "are considerably behind their commitments." Intelligence analysts see one major reason for a decrease in sales within the Mideast itself as Saudi opposition to Communist influence; these analysts think the main reason why Sadat expelled the Russians in 1972 was because Saudi financing for arms was dependent on its not being spent in "atheist" Russia. Was our intelligence establishment worried about U.S. advanced-technology sales to Iran in view of that country's continuing purchases of some Soviet weapons? Apparently not. The CIA view was that the Soviet Union already possesses the technical data contained in such advanced weaponry as the Phoenix missile or AWACS, at least in the versions supplied to Iran.

The principal single reason for the relative decline in the importance of Soviet arms sales is the rupture with Egypt—which was and is unlikely, for the indefinite future, to be able to pay its Soviet arms debts, in any case. (In 1977, as noted earlier, Sadat simply "canceled" his $4 billion debt to Moscow.) Increased arms for Angola and Ethiopia (conservatively estimated, as mentioned, at $1 billion in 1977) barely makes up the difference, if inflation is taken into account, and the promise of more arms for Afghanistan is not expected to mean much, in annual dollar volume. Total Soviet arms supplies to underdeveloped countries of $2.5 billion in 1976 (plus another $2.5 billion of orders) compare to $2.3 billion (and $3.5 billion of orders) in 1974. The 1976 figure included $900 million of arms-aid gifts.

These CIA reports also pointed out that Soviet arms sales to developing countries in 1976 surpassed Soviet economic aid to the Third World ($1.5 billion—down half a billion dollars over 1975) and said Moscow had a reputation for making "fast deliveries" of arms when it wanted to. Other CIA sources expected Third World arms sales in 1978 to turn out to be more than double those of 1976. Economic aid fell further to $392 million (mostly to India) in 1977—less than the $438 million supplied by Eastern Europe.

Moscow was now more generous with sophisticated weapons, including MiG-23s and T-62 tanks and a broad spectrum of air-to-air, surface-to-air, antitank and Frog and Scud surface-to-surface missiles. A NSC report released by the White House in 1977 said that the Soviet Union was "still the leading supplier worldwide of artillery, supersonic combat aircraft and surface-to-air missiles." This comparison is of course based on unit figures, not firepower. A 1979 analysis estimated that Russian sales still were surpassing America's in the field of tanks and artillery and roughly equaling America's in supersonic aircraft and missiles.

Some German intelligence sources, however, saw Soviet arms sales as *rising* in 1976 and 1977. One such source claimed that during those years Soviet arms transfers surpassed those of America; he ascribed the belief that Soviet arms transfers were smaller to Russia's "political prices"—charging the purchaser country only what it could afford to pay. But no American sources detected that Moscow's sales might actually be surpassing Washington's.

Of 8,090 Soviet and East European military technicians already in recipient countries in 1975, the CIA estimated there were 5,450 in the Near

East and South Asia, and 2,605 in Africa (as opposed to China's 1,140 in Africa, 70 in the Near East and South Asia, none elsewhere). The main increases in this field had been in Syria, Iraq, Somalia, Algeria and Afghanistan, in that order. Somalia already had about a thousand Soviet technicians then, but had tripled that figure—plus dependents—by 1977, shortly before their expulsion. CIA reports that year noted that the greater sophistication of new Soviet arms deliveries had resulted in a 20 per cent increase in the number of military advisers accompanying new weapons systems in Syria, Libya, Uganda and Mozambique.

Of the 17,785 Soviet "economic" technicians (some of whom might be "military") in the Third World in 1975, nearly half were in Egypt, Iran, Turkey and Iraq. The Near East and South Asia total was 11,500, with 5,930 in Africa and 330 in Latin America. Eastern Europe had 10,290 in Africa, 3,370 in the Mideast and South Asia, 255 elsewhere. China had 21,325 in Africa, 70 in Malta and 105 in the rest of the world. China does not charge for support services, only for administrative help and the technicians' (low) salaries, with easy credit available.

By 1978, there were over a thousand Soviet military in Ethiopia, including three generals. By then, the overall overseas Communist military presence had grown to 11,700 Russians and other East Europeans, plus over 50,000 Cubans (civilians included). Most of the latter were in Angola and Ethiopia. The Russian and satellite military specialists in Algeria included instructors for Polisario, the Spanish Saharan resistance movement against Morocco and Mauritania. Most of the Chinese military instructors were in Tanzania, predominantly for training Zimbabwean (Rhodesian) resistance forces.

As arms sales apparently fell, overall, there was a sharp increase in another form of Soviet weapons diplomacy—the training of foreign officers and specialists in the Soviet Union. Here the Communist emphasis was on Africa. Already by 1975, Russia had 2,325 trainees from Africa, 1,200 from the Near East and South Asia; Eastern Europe had about 100 trainees from each area. China was thought to have about 600 from Africa, and a handful from elsewhere. The bulk of the African soldiers in training in Russia came from Libya, Somalia and Tanzania. Now the main country of origin for military students is Ethiopia. The latest estimates in 1978 showed 2,500 Third World trainees in Russia, three quarters of them coming from Ethiopia, Iraq, Syria, Afghanistan, Libya and Peru. Most were learning to operate or maintain aircraft or air-defense systems.

In addition, according to intelligence analysts, nearly 30,000 Third World students attend Communist higher-learning institutions every year —two thirds of them in Russia—at a bargain-basement cost of only $70 million to all Communist countries involved. Of over 27,000 students estimated by the CIA to be undergoing such training or education in 1975, nearly 15,000 were already from Africa (principally Algeria, the Sudan and Nigeria), over 9,000 from Europe and Asia (notably from Syria, Bangladesh and Cyprus), and nearly 3,000 from Latin America, the largest contingent being from Colombia. By 1977, the figures had reached a total of over 30,000 students.

While Russia was extending economic credits to Afghanistan, Turkey, Cyprus, Argentina and Indonesia, Iran was offering credits to Russia (for a paper plant), Poland and Bulgaria. Of the $1.3 billion of Soviet credits announced in 1975, half ($650 million) went to Turkey, and $437 million to Afghanistan. In Turkey, Moscow expanded Soviet-built steel and aluminum plants, with the steel mill at Iskenderun due to produce a million tons a year. Both steel and aluminum are important in arms production. Smaller credits went to Somalia, Sri Lanka and Bangladesh. East European economic aid is in sharp decline, with Algeria, Brazil, the Philippines and Tunisia the main recipients in recent years. Africa was the main beneficiary of Chinese economic assistance, but Nepal was the main single beneficiary country.

As well as arms sales and gifts, Soviet weapons diplomacy may also be obliged to use more "gunboat" methods. The Soviet Navy stood off Libya during Qaddafi's overthrow of King Idris, and monopolized Angolan waters during the final stages of the MPLA takeover. Colorado's Senator Gary Hart, in his 1977 speech on the Soviet Navy, noted that

> the Soviet capability to use naval forces as tools of crisis management and political influence has increased markedly, and must give us concern. It is not clear that the Soviets could not achieve their political objectives in a crisis confrontation with U.S. naval forces, either as a result of an actual naval engagement or, more probably, by deterring U.S. actions against third powers. Areas in which this could occur include the eastern Mediterranean.

Russia's boldest move in 1977 was its attempt to gain permanent, official Mediterranean facilities in Yugoslavia, for a generation the symbol of independent communism. Tito rejected a request from Brezhnev for closer military cooperation between the two countries, and for naval facilities at Kotor. At present, the nearest base facilities of this sort enjoyed by the Soviet fleet are at Odessa, 650 miles away.

Tito gave overflight rights to the Red Air Force for its resupply of Egypt in 1973—but more out of "non-aligned" loyalty to Egypt than concern for Moscow. The Russians were obliged to make specific requests for each flight. Because the Russian plea to Yugoslavia for naval rights came at a time when Moscow had lost its permanent port facilities at Alexandria, and its anchorage and storage facility at Sollum—also on the Egyptian coast—and was concerned about the future of its rights at Latakia, in Syria, Western analysts brooded darkly on what might happen to Yugoslavia after Tito dies.

But the Yugoslav coast is not Russia's only hope of an eastern Mediterranean outlet. A more likely possibility seemed to be the Greek portion of Cyprus—perhaps Larnaca, just possibly Limassol. Forty per cent of the vote in Greek Cyprus is now Communist, and the current division of the island—splitting off the anti-Communist, anti-Russian Turkish Cypriots—reinforces Moscow's leverage on the uncertain successor governments to that of the late President Makarios.

In late 1978, a flight of six MiG-23s visited Finland, apparently on a sales trip. Finland is a long-standing customer for Soviet arms.

The Soviet Union was also making modest gestures toward the Western European market. Visits between Soviet and French air force units were exchanged in the early seventies; a similar exchange was accepted by the RAF in 1978, when Russian aviation exhibited for the first time at the Farnborough air show.

The Kremlin certainly does more long-term planning in its arms-sales policy than the White House because, unlike the White House, it faces no "Congress" problem. It mostly faces a market already geared to standardization. Any country with some serious Soviet presence in its arms inventory is theoretically capable of going over to Soviet weaponry on a major scale.

Countries whose modern weaponry is almost exclusively standardized on Soviet systems make up an impressive list. In Europe, in addition to the "Warsaw" states, they are Finland and Yugoslavia. In Asia, the list includes China, North Korea, India, Afghanistan, Bangladesh, Burma, Cambodia and Laos. Vietnam's *active* inventory is entirely of Soviet design, and the core of equipment in Indonesia's armed forces is Russian also. In the Arab world, Iraq, Egypt, Syria, Sudan, Algeria, Libya and South Yemen are similarly standardized on Soviet equipment. In Africa, Somalia, Uganda, Guinea, Nigeria, Congo-Brazzaville, Equatorial Guinea, Angola, Mozambique, other former territories of Portuguese Africa, and Tanzania fall into this category. In Latin America, there are only two states so far—Cuba and Peru. Enough Soviet weaponry exists in Austria, Thailand, Lebanon, Chile and Guyana to make Soviet standardization fairly easy. According to German intelligence, countries which may go "Soviet" in arms in the foreseeable future include Mexico, Bolivia, other Latin-American states, some more countries in Africa— including Mauritius, where Russia bases a militarized "trawler" fleet— Iceland and even Turkey.

Faced, before 1978, with a succession of bad harvests, Moscow has even found a practical motive for arms sales—the need for hard currency: Moscow will—like France, Britain and Israel—sell arms to almost anyone who is friendly enough to want to buy, and will use sales by one country to stimulate purchases by neighbors. (For instance, after selling two submarines to Peru in the mid-seventies, Moscow easily picked up orders for two more from Ecuador.)

According to the CIA, Russia's new, overall favorable trade balance with the Third World is the result of military sales. Weapons exports are now half of all Soviet exports to developing countries. Hard-currency clients like Iraq, Algeria and Libya have been particularly courted; deliveries to Algeria have been notably increased since that country came under threat from Morocco because of Algiers' support for the population of former Spanish Sahara—under invasion by Morocco since 1975.

Soviet military advisers are a drain on Soviet arms profits, because their full costs are not passed on to the customers; but they are a necessary part of weapons diplomacy. The CIA believes that the Soviet Union is also paying most of the costs of the Cuban presence in Africa. Cubans, of course, come cheaper than people from Russia and Eastern Europe, whose technicians—once again, according to the CIA—receive average salaries of between $15,000 and $20,000 a year, plus allowances. Cuban technicians, according to Cuban officials, earn about half as much.

In late 1977, as noted in Chapter 3, the Carter administration started talks with Moscow on mutually lowering arms sales abroad; as mentioned earlier in this chapter, Latin America is one focus for this effort; but there seemed little chance of more than a cosmetic success. Russia was seen by the CIA as still badly in need of hard currencies to purchase advanced industrial equipment from the West. Between 1972 and 1977, Moscow spent $3.1 billion on oil machinery in the United States and Europe, and was expected to spend as much again by 1982. Moscow was offering "arms for oil" to Algeria, Iraq, Libya and Syria.

In the New York *Times*, military correspondent Drew Middleton quoted intelligence sources as saying that the Soviet Union was now proposing to improve maintenance and resupply arrangements for purchasers, by providing more technicians along with weapons, notably for aircraft and tank engines, missiles, radar and other electronic equipment. This would reduce spare parts costs—and also spare-parts dependency

on Moscow. But it clearly meant the presence of larger numbers of Soviet citizens, and host countries are usually responsible for the housing
and feeding of Communist technicians.

The Vietnam Stockpile

Perhaps the most interesting source of Communist arms supplies in the
world today is in neither Russia, nor China, nor Czechoslovakia, but in
Vietnam. These are "Communist weapons" made in America. Yet the role
that the huge mountain of weapons left behind there after the Thieu debacle is playing on the arms market remains shrouded thus far in mystery. Officially, few of these arms are for sale—to hear some Pentagon
sources tell it, none of them are for sale at all. Yet the arms make Vietnam, on paper at least, the third most armed nation on earth, after the
two superpowers. Nonetheless, Vietnam seems genuinely reluctant to
sell.

In May 1975, Congressman Robert Sikes of Florida questioned Erich
von Marbod of the State Department about the future of the trove:

> *Sikes:* I am told that the American equipment over there is for sale. They
> apparently have more than they need, free, from Russia and China, and
> they are putting ours on the world market.
> *Marbod:* I don't have any information that—
> *Sikes:* If we could buy that equipment on credit it might be a smart thing
> to do. You haven't explored the possibility?
> *Marbod:* No, sir.
> *Sikes:* Tell us something about what has happened to American equipment
> left in Vietnam . . .
> *Marbod:* We estimate that there are approximately 300 operable craft of
> every description remaining in South Vietnam, the majority of which are
> brown-water navy . . . On my last day there, I met with the Vietnamese
> Navy on their plans to extract their vessels. Many of them could not, of
> course, make it to Subic Bay, a distance of approximately 940 nautical
> miles. They ultimately sailed offshore with the smaller vessels, which were
> scuttled after transferring the people to the larger vessels . . .

Democratic congressman John Flynt of Georgia asked what was left
in Cam Ranh Bay, the giant U.S. naval and air base. At first, Marbod
said that he didn't have an estimate. Sikes pressed him: "Two billion dollars in serviceable equipment?" Marbod agreed: "And facilities, yes, sir.
This is out of a total of $5 billion that remained as of the cease-fire."

Later, Marbod said that half a billion dollars' worth of aircraft and
ships had been saved either by removal or "in the reversal of the pipeline

which we effected during the last days of the conflict." In other words, to get the figure of weaponry saved that high, the Pentagon was counting equipment which *would* have been delivered if the war had continued, but which had in fact not reached Vietnam. (Only a last-minute, "afterthought" evacuation saved about $1 billion of similarly modern equipment being left behind in Thailand, when U.S. forces were ordered to leave the country in 1975.) Marbod said the Bien Hoa base had been destroyed, along with sizable oil supplies, but that about $10 million in oil had been abandoned.

> *Flynt:* What about ammunition?
> *Marbod:* Unfortunately, there is probably around $30 million to $40 million in ammunition in serviceable condition, from military region 1 through military region 4, that would be available to the North Vietnamese.

That the Vietnamese had badly wanted to capture the weapons was sure. Shortly before the fighting ended, the United States thought it had an agreement with the Viet Cong and North Vietnam that there would be a cease-fire, permitting an orderly evacuation. This understanding inspired the title of Frank Snepp's book on the Vietnam debacle, *Decent Interval.* The Communists reneged on the arrangement. The assumption, afterward, in Washington, was that Hanoi saw the stockpile as a source of badly needed foreign exchange; the small arms were expected to turn up in the armories of guerrilla movements. A London source claimed to have reliable information that American surplus lost in Vietnam had turned up among the Kambas—a Tibetan group now living in exile in Nepal but making frequent raids into Chinese-occupied Tibet. This would indicate the determining Soviet influence on Hanoi—which was also aided by China during its war with the United States but has never been particularly pro-Chinese and has even had constant border engagements with China since independence including even, in 1979, a brief war. (The Kambas also received aid from India, Taiwan and the United States.) Viet surplus has been reported, the source said, among the Nagas—an insurgent group in eastern India—as well as in Eritrea, the Sudan, the South Moluccas and among the Filipino Muslim movement, with Libya footing the bill in all four cases. The British source thought overseas Chinese and Thai middlemen in Bangkok were handling the Hanoi surplus.

Shortly after the fall of Saigon, there were reports of naval craft being offered to Singapore for hard currency, and of F-4s being offered to Iran for dollars. Washington sources theorized that arms dealers had started the rumors in order to inform Hanoi that there were waiting markets in

Teheran and Singapore. When some American weaponry from Vietnam turned up in the hands of captured Malaysian Communist forces, Vietnamese Deputy Foreign Minister Phan Hien told a reporter in Manila that Vietnam was simply not selling: Vietnam would keep the stockpile for its own defense. Washington analysts said that if the minister meant anything, he presumably meant defense against China—still quarreling with Hanoi over ownership of two groups of China Sea islands, the Paracels and the Spratlys. Vietnam later released film of some of the captured American weaponry being melted down.

In September, a report from Hong Kong said North Vietnam had invited international arms dealers to visit Hanoi to buy captured American military equipment. The first dealers would be arriving in the following few weeks. About two billion dollars' worth of equipment was said to be on the block. But the report appeared in the *Far Eastern Economic Review*, a journal with reported links to the CIA, and it seems to have been a plant—a "kite-flyer" to see how Hanoi would react.

Although a year later the Ford administration said it was willing to "help" friendly countries buy the mountain of surplus, no more was heard of the proposed auction. The Ford White House said purchasers would be able to get spare parts from the United States for their purchases from Vietnam—or from Laos or Cambodia.

By late 1976, official Washington was still assuming that much of the arms would inevitably appear on the market soon, and was letting it be known that it would be easier for Hanoi to sell to America's friends because they would be assured of parts and maintenance—even training. The purchasers, Ford administration sources said, would have to accept American restrictions on their not selling to third—or rather, fourth—parties. There were vague threats to seize on the high seas any weapons being exported to guerrilla groups.

American arms dealers would be forbidden from dealing in the weapons. This would not inhibit Sam Cummings, who is now a British citizen. As recorded earlier, Cummings told the writer in 1977 that he would be eager to handle some or all of the Vietnam stockpile, but that so far there was no evidence that the Vietnamese were willing to sell. Pentagon sources once again insisted that this was true. Intelligence reports showed that some American M-16s were by then available in Bangkok stores for as little as $50, but these appeared to be guns that had fallen into the hands of local private smugglers.

In November 1976, the Pentagon, under prodding, finally released the inventory of captured weapons, putting the global value at $6 billion, of which a third was said to be immovable equipment, notably at Cam Ranh Bay.

It was an impressive list: 529 fixed-wing aircraft, including 73 F-5s and 113 A-37s, along with 466 helicopters, 550 tanks, 1,200 armored personnel carriers, 1,250 howitzers, 1,648,580 rifles—including 791,000 M-16s—and hundreds of thousands of self-propelled guns, mortars, grenade-launchers, antitank weapons, recoilless rifles, machine guns, pistols and radios. The figure of 300 naval craft had grown to 940, along with 42,000 trucks and 130,000 tons of ammunition.

An analyst said that the number of armored personnel carriers surpassed those in India's armed forces. Vietnam's was now the second Asian navy to China's.

But the mystery of what would happen to all these arms still remained obscure. Weapons have a value which diminishes with each "weapon generation," so that early sales would seem to be desirable, at least from a hard-currency point of view. In late 1977, some Pentagon analysts were inclined to believe the Vietnamese—that they had decided to keep the bonanza and remain, for a while at least, theoretically the third greatest military power in the world. After all, it was reasoned, the power caste in Hanoi is military, and what officers anywhere would seek to reduce their forces and equipment? But meanwhile, little was being said of the U.S.-Vietnam talks in Paris, except that the United States would not give economic aid to its former enemy. But would the United States, perhaps, as Congressman Sikes suggested back in 1975, buy back its armory, thus giving aid of sorts, and removing a fascinating stockpile from Communist control?

9

In the Name of the Game

ALTHOUGH A cursory reading of arms-export figures in recent years may not suggest it, both the Soviet Union and the United States have exercised some restraint in their weapons transfers. The new Carter guidelines are riddled with loopholes through which a Mach-2 interceptor or a self-guiding missile could zoom with impunity, but there probably will be some sort of—rather elastic—"ceiling" on U.S. arms sales in the immediate future; meanwhile, in the Middle East in particular, Soviet weapons diplomacy has been essentially responsive, and cautious. Across the Atlantic, however, cash, not caution, is usually the name of the game.

Congressmen, as noted in an earlier chapter, receive a barrage of lobbying against cutting arms programs, and one of the arms lobbyists' arguments is hard to refute. America's competitors *are* anxious to take over any part of the U.S. overseas arms market which Congress or the White House may deny to American industry. There is, in Europe, little "moral" opposition to governmental arms-peddling abroad: France is even able to concentrate its aerospace industries in Communist- or socialist-dominated areas like Toulouse, the industrial northeast and the Paris blue-collar suburbs.

Europe would have come up from behind as a challenger in the arms race in the late seventies in any case, because of the huge backlog of orders to American armorers; but now the transatlantic challenge is more evident than ever before since World War Two. For a decade, until 1975, as we have seen, the United States held about 50 per cent of the world market in arms, Moscow about 30 per cent, France and Britain about 5 per cent each, with the rest being largely shared by Sweden, Germany, Israel, Italy and Belgium. By 1978, America's 20:1 ratio on arms exports when compared to either of the two leading European suppliers had slipped to 7:1 in Britain's case, less than 5:1 in the case of France.

France is America's prime competitor, and in 1977 it began amalgamating its parastatal corporation Aérospatiale and the semiprivate

Dassault-Bréguet giant, grouping over fifty thousand employees, in order to compete better. French overseas sales reached over $1.9 billion in 1976 and were $2.9 billion in the first nine months of 1977, of which $1.7 billion was for Dassault-Bréguet, maker of the Mirage planes. Dassault reported a 40 per cent increase in revenues in 1976 and a 63.7 per cent increase in profits over 1975. Export sales were 77 per cent of the total—a 77.5 per cent increase over the previous year. In 1977, over 87 per cent of the firm's $2.8 billion order book was for overseas customers. Profits were again up, by about a third. Military sales were 77 per cent of the total.

Aérospatiale, with $600 million of overseas orders in 1976—30 per cent of the French share of the world market—beat its previous annual sales records partly thanks to the U.S. embargo on arms to Turkey, which provided the French firm with a big missile order. Aérospatiale reported a profitable year in its helicopter, tactical missile, space and ballistic missile divisions, but lost on aircraft. The firm registered an overall loss of $132 million for the year. SNECMA, the French nationalized aero-engine firm, made $13,830,000 profits on sales of $538 million, 53 per cent of them overseas—a 66 per cent increase in profits and a 31.7 per cent increase in revenues over 1975. In 1978, French aerospace export deliveries reached $3.1 billion, and fresh orders $4 billion: Total aerospace industry revenues that year reached $5.8 billion. Despite Aérospatiale's difficulties, restraint on the Potomac was clearly paying dividends along the Seine.

And along the Thames. London's export sales went from $250 million in 1966 to an estimated $1.45 billion in 1977, $1.7 billion in 1978. British aerospace exports for January of that year—$268.6 million, compared to $145.2 million in January 1977—were the highest in history for a single month, and included $60.2 million from the United States; but not all these aerospace sales were military. The 1977 total included sales to the United States of $293 million of engines and engine parts and $146 million of aircraft and parts. The most successful company was British Aerospace: One of its subsidiaries, the B.A. Dynamics Group, which makes missiles and guided weapons, alone made $580 million of sales in 1978, and had an order backlog of $1.88 billion, of which 47 per cent was exports. It projected earnings of $625 million in 1979, $676 million in 1980 and $850 million by 1982. BAC announced a 1978 pre-tax profit of $161 million. Overseas orders for British military aircraft and engines and other weapons already mean employment for 80,000 workers and indirectly give work to 100,000 more. Britain nationalized its remaining large private aerospace industries in 1977, but the new Thatcher government announced partial, gradual denationalization in 1979.

Germany, while not considering nationalization, was pondering "consolidation" of Messerschmitt-Bolkow-Blohm with VFW-Fokker, a Dutch-German firm. German overseas weapons sales were expected to reach $1 billion in 1978. So were Israel's. Even Switzerland reported increased sales of antiaircraft artillery, cannons and ammunition to South Africa, Israel, Egypt, Saudi Arabia, Lebanon and Nigeria.

All the economic arguments, and not just the balance of trade, favor France and Britain boosting their weaponry exports. Both countries possess advanced technology for which the R & D could not be solely supported by their own relatively small armed forces. France and Britain must export or buy, and U.S. protectionism encourages Europe to look elsewhere than North America for markets. British arms exports to Germany almost cover the costs of British forces in that country. British Aerospace's highly successful Rapier surface-to-air missile was to have been jointly developed with Iran, for export to third countries. The Iranians were to pay for their $700 million investment in oil, through Shell. Britain will soon not need imported oil, but would have resold the Iranian oil for harder currencies than Iranian rials. Britain, as noted earlier, also made a major sale of Chieftain tanks to Iran. (The Chieftain and Rapier sales, along with a $105 million order for five British ships, a $1.5 billion military-industry complex at Isfahan, and a $160 million tank base and maintenance facility at Dorud, were halted in 1979. In all, Britain's war industry lost about $4.7 billion, two thousand direct jobs and five thousand indirect jobs from the fall of the Shah.)

Britain pays lip service to Carter's self-restraint ideals; but now that Israel and Saudi Arabia are to get the F-15, Britain feels free to sell the Jaguar to Arab countries, and France a whole range of new Mirages—a competing sales drive which probably influenced Carter's decision to sell the F-15 to Saudi Arabia in the first place. Moreover, European diplomats asked in 1978, had not Carter's decision to sell AWACS to Iran not violated his decision not to provide new systems to Third World countries?

France, with no North Sea oil, is even more mercenary than Britain. Just after the 1973 war, it agreed to sell Saudi Arabia Mirages, missiles and 250 tanks in return for 800,000 barrels of oil a day for twenty years—thus stabilizing its purchase price for that crude. Some form of this arrangement is likely to become common in the eighties. Meanwhile, France's main customer in the Middle East seems likely to be Egypt, beginning with a major co-production of Mirages.

France's and Germany's Dassault-Bréguet/Dornier twin-engined Alphajet attack plane/military trainer and Britain's single-engined Hawker-Siddeley Hawk are both competing to be the U. S. Navy's new trainer.

Both are cheaper than their American competitors. But not all the prospective purchasers for European arms are big or oil-rich or oil-subsidized countries. Poorer nations, as noted earlier, are buying more and more, notably in Latin America. In 1977, non-oil-producing Third World countries bought a quarter of the arms involved in global sales—up from 5 per cent in 1974—and Europe had a major share of this trade.

European salesmen point to congressional and Carterian restraints on sales as evidence that the United States may not be a reliable supplier over the long haul. America, they say, may cut back orders, or balk on spare parts or maintenance, because some lobby group has leaned on Congress. This makes the "all-European" plane attractive, even if no European country has the reputation for computerized follow-up services of the United States.

The Paris Air Show of 1977 and the Farnborough Air Show of 1978 were fiestas of eager salesmanship by Western European manufacturers, as well as by the hucksters of Israel and Sweden, and even of Japan, India and the Soviet Union. At the French show, police motorcycle outriders whisked Third World dignitaries through the city traffic to their waiting seats of honor—usually somewhere not far from the mock-up of the new Dassault-Bréguet 2000, significantly named to imply that it will still be around when the century isn't. Now Dassault is developing, with its own funds—plus possibly, soon, financial assistance from Saudi Arabia—a twin-engined Mirage-4000, for export markets. Both the 2000 and the 4000 flew for the first time in 1978.

When the Carter administration reneged on Dr. Kissinger's promise of A-7s to Pakistan, offering A-4s instead, France offered Mirages. When Carter decided against F-18Ls for Iran, French and British aerospace salesmen saw the decision as a gift to their order books. When the White House and the State Department backed and filled on what to do with its new friend, Somalia, the Europeans—and even the privateers—took off for Mogadishu.

Competing with the Mirage-2000 for honors at the Paris display of 1977 was the $11 million Anglo-Italo-German Tornado MRCA (Multirole Combat Aircraft), of which Britain has already ordered 385, Germany 324 and Italy 100. Panavia (British Aerospace, Messerschmitt-Bolkow-Blohm and Aeritalia) and Turbo-Union (Rolls-Royce, Fiat and Motoren-und-Turbinen Union) planned to build 809 Tornados over ten years for earnings of $10 billion, spread among 500 firms with 116,000 workers. Intended to replace some of the F-4s and F-104s in Western Europe's military aviation, the Tornado will be a direct competitor with the F-15 and the F-16. Pilots from Britain, Germany, Italy and foreign-

customer countries will all be trained on the aircraft at Cottesmore, in
England.

Also vying with the Mirage-2000 was Israel's Kfir fighter, a cheaper,
improved model of an earlier Mirage, whose genesis was described in
Chapter 2. Israel also drew buyers for missiles. Other prominently featured aerospace weapons included Britain's Nimrod command and control plane, the Sea Harrier (carrier version of the Harrier), British
Aerospace's Hawk fighter-trainer and the Alphajet. The Soviet Union
canceled its decision to display the Yak-42.

When looking at recent weapons sales and arms diplomacy by European countries, one important factor to bear in mind is the degree to
which mergers have made some of these industries comparable to American firms, and the important growth of American participation in these
theoretically rival concerns.

All France's main aerospace firms have been merged into two, on a geographical basis: Sud-Aviation and Nord-Aviation. SNECMA makes
power plants. Four small and medium French arms firms which have
also merged are Thomson, Houston, Hotchkiss and Brandt. (Some of
these are not all that small: Thomson, in 1978, signed a contract with the
Arab Organization for Industrialization to produce an air-defense surveillance network for Saudi Arabia, worth potentially $1 billion.) Plans
to extend nationalization further—notably by taking . over Dassault-
Bréguet completely—were put back after the socialist-Communist alliance lost the 1978 elections.

The cutthroat arms market forced British firms which had become
world-famous in World War Two to amalgamate or disappear. By 1967,
the Hawker-Siddeley Group brought together—in addition to the two
firms in the title—Blackburn, De Havilland, Avro, Whitworth, Gloster
and Folland. British Aircraft Company (later, British Aircraft *Corporation*—meaning, government-owned—and now British Aerospace)
grouped Vickers, English Electric, Bristol, Vickers-Armstrong, Hunting
and the government. Another important British concentration is International Computers Limited, grouping English Electric Computers, Elliott
Automation and International Computers and Tabulators. All these are
comparable to American mergers of recent decades such as Ling-Temco-
Vought (LTV), Avco, Litton Industries, General Dynamics and McDonnell-Douglas. The 1966 merger of Bristol-Siddeley and Rolls-Royce
created the world's largest producer of aviation engines, with Rolls-
Royce owning half the stock, the others a quarter each. Remaining independent of the British mergers, until nationalization was announced in
1977, were Westland Aircraft (helicopters)—which was 25 per cent

owned by John Brown Shipyards—Bristol Aeronautics and ten smaller manufacturers.

Transnationally in Europe, Nord-Aviation owns 25 per cent of Bolkow, while Fokker of Holland controls 50 per cent of SABCA—a Belgian airframe firm with co-production contracts with Northrop. Marconi owns 29 per cent of Svenska Radio.

Many American firms have used their close contacts with European firms to "brain-drain" away European engineering talent. Jointly produced U.S.-European weapons compete with single-nation or multination European systems such as the Thomson-Brandt air-to-air missiles and air-to-surface missiles, Thomson-CSF surface-to-air missiles, Bofors surface-to-air missiles, British Aerospace Swingfire and Beeswing long-range, mobile antitank missiles, or Rheinmetall guns.

Europe's true sales may be higher than they seem, for except in the United States sales are usually only published, and customers identified, if they are page-one news. Some sales are listed outside the weapons column: For instance, when Britain sells Rapiers mounted on tracked carriers, this appears as a "vehicle" sale in the statistics of London's Board of Trade, even though the missile battery is worth about ten times the value of the vehicle.

European arms sales have traditionally had strong support from the firms' own governments, and now that most European arms industries are nationalized, this is naturally even more the case. British military attachés have always been arms salesmen. The sole function of a "Counselor, Defense Supply" in a British embassy is to hawk weapons. Similarly, the French have added on *attachés d'armament* to their *attachés militaires*. The French embassy in Washington is active in selling to third countries, through their military missions to the United States.

Britain first sought to compete with U.S. "MAAG" sales by sending a supply attaché to Bonn as early as 1955. Britain's equivalent of the ILN was the Defense Sales Organization. The French equivalent was the export section of the DMA, expanded in 1965 into the Direction des Affaires Internationales (DAI). The French were more aggressive than the British. The DAI sent teams overseas to assess potential customer needs. It paid for demonstrations of French weaponry, which were reimbursed by the producer firms only if sales were made; the DAI had its own loans budget. It claimed, however, to spend less than a million dollars a year on promotion.

French parastatal organizations also promoted sales. From 1937 to shortly after World War Two, aircraft sales were the province of the Office Général de l'Air (OGA). In 1950, the Office Français d'Exporta-

tion de Matériel Aéronautique (OFEMA) was set up, with the OGA
continuing under government control. OFEMA and the OGA promoted
and prepared sales and handled after-sales service. The existence of two
organizations made sales to both sides in a conflict possible. OFEMA,
for instance, handled India and Israel while the OGA handled Pakistan
and the Arab countries.

Army weapons were sold by the Société Française de Matériel d'Armements (SOFMA) and naval sales were made by the Société Française
d'Exportation d'Armements Navals (SOFREXAN). In all these cases,
producing firms only had to pay the cost of promoting exports when
sales were actually achieved. By 1970, the Dassault firm, which was already exporting two thirds of its entire production, had an export staff of
only thirty people.

Several Western European governments follow the U.S. example in
guaranteeing arms-purchase export loans. In France, this is the province
of the Compagnie Française d'Assurances pour le Commerce Extérieur;
in Britain, it is the Export Credit Guarantee Department; in Germany,
the Hermes Bank; in Belgium, the Office National du Ducroire; in
Holland, the Ministry of Finance; in Switzerland, the National Bank. In
Sweden the Exportkreditnamnden doesn't normally provide credit for
arms sales, but there have been exceptions. Stanley and Pearton, in their
study, estimated that seven eighths of arms sales to the "developing
world" are covered by credit.

Switzerland sells mostly through small, government-controlled firms.
Sweden sells principally through Forsvarets Fabriksverk (FFV)—National Defense Industries—founded by the government in 1943. Holland
sells through the earlier-mentioned SAI. Italy's arms industry was nationalized through the Istituto per la Ricostruzione Industriale, set up as a
finance bank by Mussolini in 1933: Its two principal holding companies
are Finmeccanica (industrial plants) and Fincantieri (shipyards), which
have acquired majority holdings in most large Italian arms firms. The
IRI has 90 per cent of Fincantieri. It also has 49 per cent of Alfa Romeo
(aircraft engines) and Finmeccanica the other 51 per cent. Oto-Melara,
a similarly held firm, co-produces the American M-60 tank.

If France is the prime example of a country which has used the arms
industry to make a major contribution to its economy, Israel is energetically following suit. As far back as the fifties, the Israelis had made a
mark with the "political" and inexpensive Uzi submachine gun, thousands of which were sold not only in the Third World but in Western
Europe. When Germany resold ten thousand Uzis to Portugal and these
turned up in Angola and Mozambique, the embarrassed Israeli Government—then courting the African states—decided in 1961 to forbid the

sale or resale of its weapons to countries "fighting to preserve colonial rule." But by the seventies, South Africa had become Israel's closest friend in Africa—and closest friend anywhere, after the United States—so that this proviso has been abandoned. Even Israeli nuclear technology, as noted in Chapter 3, was ultimately made available to Pretoria.

Sweden, for neutralist and ideological reasons, has limited its arms trade. Both Germany and Switzerland usually refuse sales to areas of potential conflict. In Germany's case, this followed the 1965 threat by Arab countries to recognize East Germany because Germany was supplying arms to Israel. Under the 1949 COCOM (Coordinating Committee) Agreement, Japan and all the NATO countries except Iceland agreed not to sell strategic goods to Communist countries. In London, the Foreign Office does not authorize sales of weapons that might be used against Britain or its allies for aggressive purposes, or for third-country subversion—but there are exceptions.

America's major Western competitors for arms sales, France and Britain, have been largely unsuccessful in competing with Washington for the German market, but they have often been very successful in Third World countries. Both have been willing to provide pilots to fly sophisticated aircraft until the client-country could train its own. Rebel movements in small southeast Arabian states were put down by RAF crews, seconded by the RAF to local air forces. The British Government saw such assistance as necessary to achieving sales, and the RAF welcomed it as battle training unobtainable elsewhere. The United States was and is reluctant to allow American citizens to fight other people's wars, although the considerable U.S. technical team which was in Iran might well have been obliged to stay and keep the Iranian Air Force in the air if the country had found itself at war.

Purchaser countries anxious not to be too dependent on the credit or favor of one country, especially a major power, sometimes order a mixed basket of weapons—perhaps FN rifles from Belgium, jet aircraft from Italy, Uzi submachine guns from Israel, Swedish missiles and cannons. But this usually makes the package more expensive, and imposes a terrible cost in terms of loss of standardization, and in the problems involved in training Third World technicians in maintaining vastly differing types of equipment.

British Weapons Sales

In arms, the European countries today are like a group of aging actors who, after years of bit parts and commercials, have suddenly decided to

take on the star roles of yore, and who find that none of the old magic
has been forgotten. Britain is a good example. Before 1955, Britain supplied 95 per cent of all military jet aircraft shipped to the Middle East;
by the mid-seventies, the share was 10 per cent; now it is rising again.

Britain's huge slippage was partly due to the curious organization of
the British arms industry. Private firms had to compete with government
ordnance factories and a plethora of parastatal R & D establishments—
the Royal Small Arms Ordnance factories, the Royal Aircraft Establishments, the Royal Radar Establishment, the Armaments and Development Establishment. Each of the three services had its own competing
"Establishment." Some of these units merely designed, while others designed, tested and manufactured. Since all had a captive client in the
Ministry of Defense, their overseas selling effort for a long time was ama-
teurish, while private manufacturers, who were aggressive overseas, had
difficulty acquiring the initial home market to make production possible.
This was unfortunate for British manufacturers, as the continental
market is nearly three times the size of the potential British market,
while the U.S. market is fifteen times as large.

British Aircraft Company, for instance, had difficulty selling its Vigilant antitank missile to Britain's Defense Ministry because several "Establishments" were working on their own antitank missiles. The Vigilant,
which eventually sold to Finland, Kuwait and Saudi Arabia, was typical
of a British specialty—smaller, cheaper, easier-to-maintain missiles.
Other countries—Italy, France, Holland, Germany and Switzerland, for
instance—also sought to undercut U.S. missiles, but this is probably the
field in which the British have done best. Even in the doldrums of their
trade, in the sixties, they sold Bloodhounds to Sweden and Switzerland,
and ship-to-air Seacats to Holland, Germany, Sweden, New Zealand,
Australia, Malaysia, Chile and Brazil.

Already, by the late sixties, the British were seeking to head off American and Soviet sales by promising not to use "spare parts dependency" in
the manner of the superpowers. British contracts sometimes guaranteed
parts under all circumstances—even to both sides in a potential conflict.
Many British suppliers, for this reason, refused to observe the international embargo on arms for Pakistan and India.

Before Vietnam, the British would also push—as Israel does today—
the fact that some of its weapons were "battle-tested." Britain tried and
failed to sell Italy Chieftain tanks—the Italians bought American M-60s
—by pointing to the Chieftain's successes in both the Indian Army and
in Israel, although in neither case did Chieftains actually fight M-60s (it
was Centurions that faced M-48 Pattons).

But Britain did observe the embargo on arms to Mideast contestants until Washington broke its own rules. London held off selling Blood-hounds to Israel at U.S. insistence, but Henry Kuss secretly sold Israel Hawks. Later, when he sold A-4s to Israel, F-104s to Jordan, F-4s to Iran and other jet fighters to Latin America, Britain protested these "breaches"; Britain sold Hawker Hunters to Chile and Canberras to Peru when it learned that Venezuela had been secretly offered F-5s.

Already by the sixties the scent of angry rivalry with U.S. manufac-turers was growing stronger. An earlier English Electric ET-316 Rapier surface-to-air missile was canceled by Britain's Defense Ministry in favor of the U.S. Mauler. EE refused to give up and campaigned in the British press against the Mauler, which it said was too sophisticated for field maintenance by ordinary soldiers, too heavy for two soldiers to carry, and needed a three-second preparation to shoot down a low-flying super-sonic jet—thus making aim difficult. Mauler, they said, was a relatively slow, heat-seeking proximity missile which could only chase a plane, while the Rapier was optically tracked—a direct-hit missile with a Mach-3 speed.

EE carried on research at its own expense. Then, in 1965, Johnson can-celed Mauler after $200 million of R & D. The British Government went back to the Rapier, which went into production in 1967, and urged Washington to buy it too. But the United States turned it down in a re-port which cast doubts on the utility of the optical-tracking system.

The British became more convinced that it was the Rapier's foreignness, not any serious second thoughts about the optical tracking, which was stymieing sales at the Pentagon. When U. S. Army Ordnance developed the Chaparral surface-to-air missile from the Sidewinder, Brit-ain again pointed out that it was proximity-fused (to go off when close to target) and, because of its relatively small warhead, could not destroy a supersonic jet with certainty. The Rapier, they urged, was a direct-hit missile with a delayed fuse (exploding within the target aircraft). The Pentagon then offered to do comparison tests—then quietly forgot about it. Britain's more recent successes with missiles for the U.S. market have been recounted earlier, but its most successful military sale in the United States, in the sixties, was the Hawker Harrier Vertical-and-Short-Takeoff-and-Landing (V-STOL) jet, which was sold, as noted in Chapter 2, to the Marines, with the United States and Britain together now developing an improved version.

Britain complained about the French breaking sales-embargo agree-ments in the Mideast and South Africa, and more recently about Israeli sales to South Africa; but in Latin America, British naval sales have had a similarly mercenary quality in the past, sometimes with amusing re-sults. In 1956, Brazil paid $35 million for a used British carrier reconditioned in Holland. The Brazilian Navy and Air Force quarreled over which service would operate the ship. Ten ministers and admirals resigned over the dispute, which dragged on for nine years. Only in 1965, four presidents later, was it agreed that the Navy would operate the ship and the Air Force its planes. Also in 1956, Britain sold Argentina a carrier so obsolete that its decks were too short for jets. Peru succumbed to British salesmanship and bought two old cruisers, but had only enough technicians to put one of them to sea at a time.

Production was still way down from World War Two, when Britain produced 76,000 major combat aircraft—23,000 Supermarine Spitfires and Seafires, 14,200 Hawker Hurricanes, 11,500 Vickers-Armstrong Wellingtons, 7,800 De Havilland Mosquitos, 7,400 Avro Lancasters, 6,200 Bristol Blenheims, 6,200 Handley-Page Halifaxes. But if numbers were down, prices and potential profits were way up.

In Europe, government subsidies are even more blatant than in the United States. In the sixties, broadly speaking, once a design was approved, the British Government funded 100 per cent of R & D costs, then initially put a levy on sales to recoup part of its investment. The levy produced a disincentive to export—especially since (with R & D taken care of by the taxpayer) all domestic sales were profitable. Now Britain's Defense Sales Organization shares both R & D and profits with the firms and there is no export levy. This is in contrast to France, where a contract from the government obligates the manufacturer to seek export sales—but with the government agreeing to purchase the unsold residue of a production run.

Exactly contrary to one of the 1977 Carter arms-sales guidelines, the British Government will advance loans to develop weapons for which there is no domestic requirement, to be paid back wholly or partially according to the success of an export drive. Britain also sells new weaponry abroad, ahead of domestic procurement. Iran's orders for improved Rapiers paid for development of the British missile as it took place: By 1979, British forces had still not received the weapon. American tanks received Chobham armor before British forces did.

Britain's need to buy sophisticated U.S. weapons like the Polaris missile and—until the deal was canceled—the F-111 led to some American assistance for British sales, the best-known example being the Lightnings-for-Arabia contract mentioned earlier in this book. This originated when King Faisal came to the Saudi throne in 1964, determined to improve Saudi defenses. At the time, Arabia's one squadron of F-86s and its nine B-26 bombers were inadequate to prevent frequent intrusions into Saudi airspace by Nasser's MiGs.

Lockheed, Northrop, BAC and Dassault were all competing for the Arabian deal. The Shah of Iran counseled Faisal to buy one of the American aircraft—meaning either Northrop F-5s or Lockheed F-104s with a Hawk SAM system. Then, in June 1965, Chancellor of the Exchequer James Callaghan canceled Britain's TSR-2 program. The swing-wing plane was to have been the main RAF aircraft of the seventies. Soon London had placed a tentative billion-dollar order for General Dynamics F-111As—which wiped out the budgetary savings of canceling the TSR-2. The offset arrangement was that Britain could compete on even terms with U.S. firms for $325 million of U.S. defense contracts over twelve years, through an exception to the Buy America Act, while America would help Britain secure $400 million of third-country sales. The sale of British Lightnings to Riyadh was thus primarily designed to permit F-111 sales to Britain. Defense Minister Denis Healey said later: "We could not have made the offer, never mind won the contract, without American cooperation."

But the low-range Lightning, designed for British airspace (it sold well in Kuwait), was useless for the immensity of Arabia, which is nine times the size of Britain. The British had to supply technicians and pilots. Arabia paid Britain nearly $300 million for the Lightnings, plus some BAC-167 Provost trainers, radar installations and communications equipment. The Lightning sale not only meant $29.5 million annually over ten years, but a continued sale of parts and maintenance. Because of the short life of highly stressed parts, parts sales can often equal the original sale price of an aircraft over ten years or so, and this proved to be the case with the Lightning. Also involved were sales of ancillary equipment and contracts for training and airfield construction, including housing and medical facilities. The Saudi deal gave a thousand Britons employment in that country for about five years. The British defense specialists John Stanley and Maurice Pearton calculate that Britain netted over $40 million yearly in additional sales to Saudi Arabia for the first four years after the Lightning contract was signed. When the United States was slow in delivering Hawks, Saudi Arabia paid another $20 million for thirty-seven British Thunderbird surface-to-air missile batteries. The Hawks eventually arrived, but combining BAC Lightnings with Hawks made little sense, since Hawks are designed for close-in defense of static areas. Although mobile, they could not be dragged over the huge distances of Saudi Arabia. A more sensible package would have been American F-5s or -104s with suitable, light British missiles. Ironically, as mentioned earlier, Britain later canceled the F-111 order.

Britain's military aviation industry re-entered Mideast markets seriously in 1975, when Egypt's President Sadat was looking for Western arms, a year after Kuwait had ordered its first hundred Centurion tanks. In London, Sadat expressed an interest in buying two hundred Anglo-French Jaguars for about $1.2 billion, with early delivery of between thirty and sixty aircraft, the rest to be co-produced in Egypt. He concluded an agreement to buy $40 million worth of Swingfire antitank missiles—also a co-production arrangement, this time by Arab-British Dynamics, a firm owned 30 per cent by British Aerospace and 70 per cent by the Arab Organization for Industrialization. As related later, major helicopter and missile deals were to follow. Sadat also wanted Chieftain tanks; there was pressure from Washington against this sale, and Egypt agreed to consider a compromise suggested in London—that the British re-engine Egypt's Soviet tanks. But British intelligence reported that, despite purchases in Europe, Egypt would still need substantial American arms in the near future.

In 1977, readers will recall, the United States canceled orders for five hundred Hawker-Siddeley XJ-521 Skyflash air-to-air missiles after Britain decided not to buy AWACS. The American cancellation led to a crash program to develop a U.S. equivalent of the Marconi "inverse monopulse seeker" in the Skyflash: This "seeker" reportedly sees targets against ground clutter better than anything in the U.S. inventory. But later in the year, Skyflash was once more orbiting the market. The Pentagon finally agreed to a "competitive shoot-off" in mid-1978 between an improved Skyflash and the two American prototype versions of monopulse seekers on the AIM-7E and AIM-7F. As a result, the Hawker-Siddeley missile may now go on F-15s and F-14s, after a $100 million radar retrofit for the F-15s.

"If this option is adopted," noted *Aviation Week*, "the present Navy/ Air Force program to develop an advanced monopulse seeker almost certainly would be terminated." Another possibility was that the Skyflash seeker would be adapted to fit the AIM-7F, which has nearly twice the range of the Skyflash. As a fallback position, the British salesmen were trying to ensure that Skyflashes at least went on F-4Es based in Europe, since no radar modification would be needed on Phantoms. Helping the British was the fact that Skyflash was only two years from production, while it was estimated that an American advanced monopulse seeker would require five more years' development.

There are lesser-known successes. A British defense contractor called Racal Electronics exports 99 per cent of some of its communications systems, with the United States among its markets. Avionics is a major field for British exports. The F-16 and some other major U.S. combat aircraft use Britain's Marconi-Elliott HUD (Head-Up Display). This is the fire-control screen in front of the pilot's face, and on which he lines up his targets. The F-14 incorporates this also, along with British ejection seats and other systems. (Grumman's heavy purchasing of British avionics was mentioned in Chapter 6.)

Another British HUD, by the Smith Company, is found in the A-4 and the A-7 as well as in Sweden's Viggen fighter. It has been offered to China and India for upgrading their MiG-21s. Ferranti's COMED (Combined Map Electronic Display) is found in the cockpit of the McDonnell-Douglas F/A-18. Ferranti also exports sophisticated equipment to Denmark and Holland and to European constructors of the Sea Harrier and the Tornado. The Marconi digital inertial navigation attack system for the Jaguar is also under evaluation for the U.S. market, as are its flight deck simulators, while the firm's omnidirectional airspeed system is installed in the Bell Cobra gunship. Plessey Radar has exported $200 million of AR-30 and other ground radars, including airfield-control radars, and tracking radars for the guns and missiles of small ships—notably to Egypt. MEL Equipment, a subsidiary of Phillips, supplies Sea Searcher radars for naval helicopters, while Decca sells aircraft weapon delivery systems.

For a while, there seemed to be more trouble for Britain and Hawker-Siddeley over the high crash rate of the AV-8A Harrier supersonic "jump jet," which was giving some congressmen second thoughts about the Marines' V-STOL beachhead-support aircraft. The Harrier's high crash record was noted in Chapter 2. By late 1977, twenty of the aircraft had been written off. Eight more were resold by the United States to Spain, in 1973, over the objections of Britain's Labour Party, then in opposition.

The Marines mounted a strong lobby campaign to be provided with an advanced Harrier, to be built and partly designed by McDonnell-Douglas in the United States, under license, and fitted with imported Bristol Pegasus engines. The Bristol and McDonnell-Douglas firms lobbied discreetly but hard. In the Senate, it was conservative Republican Jesse Helms, the senator from North Carolina itself—where most of the crashes had occurred—who was primed to argue with his colleagues for the Marines' need of the aircraft. Said Helms: "If the Marines must wait, after an amphibious landing, until a runway can be built, they will not have adequate, responsive close air support during the crucial initial days of a campaign. It is during precisely that time that the fighting is likely to be hardest, and the Marines will have their greatest need for supporting aircraft." Helms also said the Navy itself needed an effective V-STOL aircraft to meet the growing Soviet naval challenge. Senator Jake Garn of Utah read into the Congressional Record *Jane's* report on the impressive Soviet V-STOL, the Ram-G. A coalition of defense experts, congressional air force veterans and congressmen from districts with Harrier contracts seemed to be wearing down Carter administration opposition to the building of so many $5.3 million planes (the tab for the revised version) under British franchise. The decision of the British Navy to fit "ski-jump" ramps for Harriers on five new mini-carriers encouraged the U. S. Navy to expand its own ski-jump testing, a crucial factor in the plane's acceptance. Meanwhile, the British triumphally announced other Harrier sales, including AV-8As for the Australian Navy.

Finally, it was Soviet development of the Ram-G—first seen when photographed aboard the carrier *Kiev* in the Mediterranean—which convinced Defense Secretary Harold Brown that the United States was too far behind in VTOL and V-STOL technology to ditch the Harrier. In June 1977, the Pentagon announced that McDonnell-Douglas would assemble 350 advanced Harriers (AV-8Bs) at a cost of $1.5 billion. The B made its first flight at St. Louis in 1978 and two were delivered to Patuxent naval air station in Maryland in 1979 for testing, along with a British 15° "ski-ramp" for launching. In 1979, even the U. S. Air Force was expressing interest in the plane, and McDonnell-Douglas also offered the largely British-designed, but American-built, plane to the RAF. Encouraged by this co-production deal, Britain announced a new program to produce a STOVL (Short Takeoff, Vertical Landing) aircraft to replace the Harrier. Testing of the proposed AST-403 was scheduled for 1983.

Britain also mounted a sales drive for the three-nation, Mach-2 Tornado, which costs $15.4 million, or $18.3 million in the more sophisticated "air defense" version. With a captive market in Britain, Germany and Italy, London's eyes were initially set on selling 150 to Canada—as the hoped-for winner in the contest to provide the new Canadian fighter —and about 100 to Australia.

The offset package offered by the trinational group to Canada included, along with the manufacture of some components for Tornados ordered in Europe and possibly elsewhere—and final assembly and testing of all the Canadian models—the creation of a giant Canadian training base which would train Canadian, British, German and Italian Tornado pilots in Canada's uncrowded skies. In 1979, Grumman agreed to act as sales representative for the Tornado to the USAF.

Britain is also currently pushing sales of Nimrod, London's equivalent of the AWACS radar control plane, notably in the Middle East and Gulf areas, Japan and West Germany. By late 1977, 49 copies of the Nimrod, an adapted Comet airliner, had been built, with 11 of them adapted for full AWACS-type missions. The Australians, having decided that the

Boeing AWACS was too expensive, were actively choosing between Nimrod and the Grumman E-2C.

By mid-1977, Westland had made 223 sales of Lynx three-engined naval helicopters to 6 nations, including West Germany, Norway, Denmark and Indonesia. In 1978, Eygpt, Saudi Arabia, Qatar and the United Arab Emirates ordered 250 Lynxes for over $700 million. The first 20 were to be built in Britain, with 30 to be assembled at Helwan. Subsequent batches of 50 would be built, 40 in Egypt, 10 in England. The planes will be built over seven years by the Arab-British Helicopter Company, then 70 per cent owned by the four-nation Arab Organization for Industrialization, 30 per cent by Westland, which had 3 members on the 12-member board. The AOI was headed at the time by Ashraf Marwan, a son-in-law of the late President Nasser—later dismissed, over Saudi objections, by Sadat. Some of the Egyptian-built Lynxes will be for export. The 750 engines were to be built by the earlier-mentioned Arab-British Engine Company, a combination of the AOI and Rolls-Royce. Assembly of the first aircraft and engines were expected to begin in 1979. Co-production of 30 to 60 Anglo-French Jaguar long-range strike fighters was also under consideration. In addition, in 1976, Egypt had already ordered 100 Hawk fighters from Britain, along with 9 Vosper/Brooke Marine fast missile-carrying motor torpedo boats. By May 1977, Sadat was reported pushing ahead with the purchase of British antitank missiles and naval hovercraft. The missiles—Swingfires—would be co-produced at Helwan, beginning in 1979, to be mounted on American jeeps whose local co-production was mentioned in Chapter 7. Other British co-production sales included rockets, other ordnance and associated handling equipment.

The Lynx sold to Egypt was also competing with two American aircraft, made by Boeing Vertol and Sikorsky, for the U. S. Navy's light airborne multipurpose system (LAMPS) helicopter program—a competition Sikorsky finally won. But Britain was still looking to other major Mideast sales. British Aerospace won a billion-dollar contract to extend its defense management agreement with Saudi Arabia. Outside Egypt and Saudi Arabia, major orders were placed for British aircraft in 1977 by Libya and Oman, and the Sudan was also seeking military aid from its former colonial power, as well as from the United States, France and China. In 1978, Hawker-Siddeley made a sales and demonstration trip for their Hawk trainer/strike aircraft through Egypt, Saudi Arabia, the United Arab Emirates, Qatar, Oman, Kuwait and Jordan. Sales of the Hawk were also expected in Sweden, Argentina, Brazil, Mexico, Africa and perhaps the United States, where co-production was offered.

Overall, British aerospace sales rose from $2.4 billion in 1972 to $4.6 billion in 1978, with exports up from $950 million to $2.3 billion.

But Britain's single main arms export has been the 50-ton Chieftain tank, produced by Vickers and the Royal Ordnance Factory in Leeds. Until the late seventies, it was the world's largest fighting vehicle. London was angered by the U.S. decision of a decade ago to co-produce a main battle tank with Germany. The British argued that the Chieftain was the best tank in Western forces, was "battle-tested," and that there was no need for an MBT-70. At the time, however, Washington was chiefly concerned with easing German payments problems. Later, after Germany had produced the Leopard, Washington, as noted, chose the Chrysler MBT with some Leopard components.

But while the British muttered darkly about the perfidy of Americans in sabotaging a "defense common market" they had themselves proposed, they did bring off a massive sale of Chieftains to the Shah of Iran; this deal, however, soon ran into heavy weather, long before the Shah did himself.

A contract signed between the Iranian Military Industries Organization (IMIO) and Millbank Technical Service Ordnance (MTSO) in December 1974 called for the construction of Chieftain assembly lines at Isfahan and Bandar Abbas. Iran made an initial payment of $122 million. A year later, however, according to IMIO, MTSO produced cost estimates of $1.2 billion which staggered the Iranians. By 1976, the British were estimating total costs at $1.7 billion and wanted a 40 per cent escalation clause. The Iranians then demanded a turnkey agreement with a fixed price. When the British refused, the original contract was terminated by IMIO, which called the British figures excessive; the British blamed the cost increases partly on changes in customer specifications.

Eventually, the original plan was scaled down, and a figure of $825 million was agreed. Wimpey Construction, part of the British consortium, withdrew two hundred technicians from Iran. But sales of Iranian crude slumped that year, leaving a $2.4 billion deficit in the Iranian budget, so Teheran insisted that MTSO accept payment in oil. British Petroleum (BP), which is 68 per cent owned by the British Government and which was formerly called the Anglo-Iranian Oil Company, was brought into the negotiation. The British, already committed to selling the Rapier missile system to Iran for $700 million in oil—17,000 to 20,000 barrels a day for six years—were reluctant to buy more Iranian crude. Two U.S. oil companies—Ashland and New England Petroleum—had just turned down a $13 billion arms-for-oil deal with Iran. But finally, the British had little choice but to accept the Iranian proposal to save the contract. In 1978, as Iran dissolved into chaos, Britain managed to replace its Rapier co-production deal with a contract whereby Iran would buy the missiles in Britain; but payment would still be in oil. Eventually, both tank and missiles deals collapsed with the overthrow of the regime. In late 1979, Britain sold 250 Chieftains to Jordan, after Hussein had turned down an offer of 300 American M-60s for $300 million. Amman had anticipated problems with Congress over Hussein's rejection of the Camp David "separate peace" between Egypt and Israel. Jordan had, in any event, been refused the latest infrared sights for the M-60s' cannon, although these had been sold to Israel. The British offered infrared sights and early delivery, using tanks ordered by the Shah and canceled by Khomeini. The British purchase was made with part of a $1.25 billion arms grant to Jordan from the Gulf oil states.

To develop its Mideast market, the British have had to be discreet about their sales to Israel; but in March 1977, a car accident near Loch Fyne NATO submarine training depot in Scotland led to discovery of a major contract. The accident caused suspicion among local reporters because two Israelis were killed and two injured, and the address for all four was given as 2 Palace Green, London—the Israeli embassy. At first the Israelis said that Israeli tourists frequently used the embassy as a mailing address. Then a hall porter at a Loch Fyne hotel mentioned that some of the Vickers engineers staying at the place were "behaving funny."

Normally, he said, the Vickers men would "eat anything," but now suddenly some of them were talking in strange accents and refusing to eat bacon for breakfast. Then someone in the hotel overheard two of the "Vickers" people speaking together in a guttural language, soon recognized as Hebrew.

The story that emerged was that, not only had Vickers contracted to build three shallow-draft, 500-ton, twenty-five-crew submarines suitable for guerrilla landings, but they were also training the Israeli navy crews at the base—apparently unbeknown to Britain's NATO partners. It was later learned that a similar service had been performed for submariners sent over by the Chilean junta. With some embarrassment all around, the Israeli contract was respected, and the first of the submarines was tested and delivered in 1977.

An at least equally controversial sale was secretly being pushed by the British embassy in Washington that year: Specifically, Britain sought to sell Jaguar fighter-bombers to China. U.S. permission was necessary because the aircraft have American (Teledyne) engines. With Washington anxious to develop relations with Peking, but concerned about the ups and downs of détente with Moscow, sales to China by an ally would be preferable to sales by any firm subject to congressional scrutiny; but the question of the engines remained a stumbling block.

China also expressed an interest in the Harrier. In November 1977, a delegation headed by Li Chiang, the Foreign Trade Minister, watched a Harrier demonstration in Britain, as part of a three-week tour of European aerospace facilities. Two years before, the Russians had made trade deals with Britain contingent on London refusing to sell Harriers to China, a deal also opposed at the time (along with all U.S. potential arms sales to China) by Japan. But in 1978, British defense sources admitted that London had agreed to sell 345 Harriers to China for $1.5 billion in credit-free cash—80 of them British-made, the rest to be co-produced by Peking—along with "billions of dollars" of other military matériel, including tanks, communications satellite equipment and long-distance telecommunications. These were parts of a proposed $8 billion Anglo-Chinese trade agreement, to be partly financed by a $1.2 billion export credit put together by ten British banks. As London, Paris and Washington competed in rhetorical Sinophilia, a feisty British chief of staff, Marshal of the Royal Air Force Sir Neil Cameron, received the plaudits of a Chinese tank division by proclaiming, during a Chinese tour, that Britain and China should unite against Moscow.

In 1978, China said that it expected to spend $10 billion of its estimated $36 billion 1979 defense budget on Western technology, and Britain, West Germany and France were all looking closely at the Peking market. France hoped to sell more helicopters, and surface-to-air missiles. Sweden was offering Viggen fighters and submarines. During 1978, Chinese defense officials attended military shows and displays in Britain, France, Sweden and Italy.

China was said to be more interested in European than American arms, partly because of the problem of congressional opposition and other uncertainties, partly because of continued U.S. military support of Taiwan. Israeli arms were similarly disqualified for consideration because of Tel Aviv's weapons trade with Taipei. Conversely, Britain and other European armorers were reluctant to supply arms to Taiwan, in order not to be closed out of the Chinese market. In Washington in late 1978, President Carter announced that the United States would not discourage European sales to China, providing systems capable of an offensive against Taiwan or the Soviet Union were not included. COCOM, which Carter was bypassing, theoretically might object, but observers noted that it had not objected to limited sales in the past, and in any case member-countries are not bound by its rulings.

The Chinese were seeking current, not obsolescent equipment, putting them on some sort of par with the Soviet Union, but there were two problems: They could not afford the most expensive systems, nor did they want the sort of training missions—instructors and technicians—which go with sophisticated aircraft and other weapons. Peking remained undecided between squaring off with Moscow on Moscow's terms—which would imply buying and installing complex computers and command-and-control equipment—or remaining inferior in the air and boosting its huge ground forces with more and better conventional weapons. These would presumably include antitank and antiaircraft missiles and surface-to-surface missiles. This would still leave Chinese tanks inferior to Russia's in most modern fire-control guidance and tracking equipment. Above all, the Chinese were thought likely to buy some weapons and associated systems in "singles" or small numbers, then try to pirate them.

Britain remains very interested in other Far East markets. In 1977, London's Defense Sales Organization arranged to send a 16,000-ton support ship, the Lyness, on a cruise through East Asia, as a floating exhibition of missiles and other weaponry. The key port of call was to be Tokyo harbor, but the city's mayor, a prominent pacifist and socialist, objected and informed the press, where an editorial campaign soon made it easy for him to refuse to allow the ship in port. The Lyness called without incident at the Philippines, Thailand and Malaysia.

In 1978, India agreed to buy two hundred Jaguars for a deep-penetration role, at a cost of $2.2 billion over ten years. These are to replace the Indian Air Force's obsolescent Canberras and Hunters. The first forty were to come from Britain; all or most of the rest will be co-produced in India. Indian Defense Minister Jagjivan Ram chose the Jaguar over the French F-1 because of a faster delivery schedule, but held out the prospect of buying a French submarine plant. The Jaguar was finally chosen after the United States refused permission for Sweden to sell Viggen fighter-bombers with U.S. engines to New Delhi. In 1979, London announced the sale of three Harriers to Japan for testing, with twenty-seven more to follow.

Britain's arms embargo on South Africa showed signs of leaking. Seven Westland Wasp "antisubmarine" helicopters—probably intended for antiguerrilla work—were sold to Pretoria in 1977, and Jordan was not discouraged from reselling to South Africa 717 British Tigercat surface-to-air missiles with their launchers, other support and maintenance systems, and forty-one Centurion tanks. Intelligence reports later claimed that the Tigercats and Centurions were smuggled to Rhodesia.

In 1978, Britain sold the first twelve Anglo-French Jaguars to Latin

America when it signed a deal with Ecuador that also included the purchase of ten British Strikemasters. Jaguars were also sold to Oman. Looking to future sales all over the world, Britain and Italy announced that year that they would jointly develop a Westland/Agosta antisubmarine warfare helicopter for the eighties. At the Paris Air Show the following year, Westland displayed a new troop-transport helicopter, the WG-30.

But the prime market for a European defense contractor remained the United States, and late in 1977, a senior Pentagon official announced that in future British contractors and subcontractors would be better able to compete for U.S. contracts because of special relaxations, for Britain, of Defense Department rules on releasing sensitive data. But the official, Robert A. Basil, who was then the assistant director (international programs) in the Directorate of Defense Research and Engineering, said U.S. companies which wanted to bid with a British partner would still have to prove "increased NATO conventional-force effectiveness based upon wider standardization or interoperability."

In 1979, this policy seemed to bear fruit when Pentagon sources said the USAF might buy four squadrons of Tornados, for basing in Germany as ground-attack aircraft. This was after the plane had been flown by an approving Lieutenant General Thomas Stafford, the USAF's vice chief of staff for research and development. Later that year, the USAF said it was considering purchase of $178 million worth of Rapier SAMs. In return, the RAF would help man three USAF bases in Britain. But the Buy America Act was still a barrier to British sales, and the same year Rolls-Royce announced that it would probably build a plant in the United States.

Such factors as standardization and interoperability open up vast if less glamorous markets for components. Around the same time, for instance, the USAF announced that it would modify A-10s with a British bomb dispenser, the Hunting-755, and a German air-to-surface missile, the Strebo. A British firm which plays a key role in component exports is the Dowty Aviation Division of the Dowty Group, one of the few foreign firms accepted as a sole-source contractor for U.S. aircraft. A Dowty official noted in 1977 that when the Harrier sale first went through for the Marines, the U.S. and British governments structured a dual relationship between McDonnell-Douglas and Hawker-Siddeley and between Pratt and Whitney and Rolls-Royce. He added: "They forgot that 30 per cent of the aircraft by value was neither airframe nor engines" and that such subsystems manufacturers as Dowty worked on a different basis from their American equivalents.

British practice, he said, was for the subsystem manufacturer to invest his own capital, do the design and development work and retain the design drawings and other rights. McDonnell-Douglas, assuming that the prime contractor had rights to everything in the aircraft, asked Dowty for its drawings and was refused. Eventually, Dowty accepted the American practice.

Dowty has had considerable success with the North American market. Building on initial work for Fairchild and Grumman, and with a growing need to provide support for British-built aircraft operating in North America, Dowty had established product support sites in New York and Washington in the fifties, later combined into a single site at Dulles Airport. Today the facility employs two hundred, and overhauls virtually all Dowty equipment in the United States. A similar facility exists in Rio de Janeiro for Latin America, and another in Canada. Dowty and Rolls-Royce together are currently competing for a contract to provide the engine for the USAF's proposed new VTOL antisubmarine warfare plane.

In 1977, Dowty announced an unusual $3.4 million contract with the Egyptian Government to overhaul and maintain hydraulic equipment, landing gear, engine subcomponents and electronic equipment for the Egyptian Air Force's MiG-21s, Su-7s and Mi-8 helicopters, and to train Egyptian technicians. This was before Lockheed and General Electric briefly won, then lost to Rolls-Royce, the contract to overhaul the MiG airframe and engines.

French Weapons Sales

The French arms industry does not usually have to send supersalesmen overseas—the French Government does most of their salesmanship for them. But then, most of the French arms firms are government-owned. France's parastatal war industry is geared for export. Already by 1969, arms were 15 per cent of all French exports. About 60 per cent of all French aircraft production was sold abroad, 70 per cent of these orders being military. France was at the time the "free world's" largest exporter of helicopters, and has since become its main exporter of submarines.

France trumpets its aircraft sales to drum up others. The Paris Air Show is the major stage, although few purchasers make a decision to buy at an exhibition. The Republic is, however, curiously secretive about its sales of army equipment, despite the fact that it seems in past years to have made roughly as much selling artillery, armor, mines, shells and flamethrowers as selling aviation, and was the first Western nation to propose selling such equipment to Eastern-bloc countries. When the

United States and Holland withdrew their aid from Sukarno's Indonesia —a former Dutch colony—France stepped in with weapons sales, even including Entac antitank missiles, although the forested country is unsuited for armored warfare. It was France that generated jet fighter sales to Latin America. Because Nigeria was seen as a British sphere of influence, France sold weapons to secessionist Biafra (then later covered its options by secretly selling other arms to Nigeria itself).

De Gaulle saw arms sales as weapons of prestige and influence as well as helpful to the trade balance. In 1966, the Lockheed F-104, the Northrop F-5 and the Mirage III/5 fighter-bomber all began competing for a sale of 106 aircraft to Belgium; all were virtually the same price; then, in 1968, Dassault suddenly dropped its price below cost—on the promise of a French Government subsidy—thus winning the contract. This is, of course, a practice to which the United States also resorted at the height of the cold war. The French deal offset 70 per cent of the $148.8 million program in Belgium, with two Belgian firms handling airframe production and a third the engines. The airframe companies were also promised the tail and rear fuselage construction on the F-1, the planned successor to the Mirage-III.

Israel's 1967 onslaught on Egypt, Jordan and Syria was marvelous publicity for French aircraft, which dominated the Mideast skies. French armor also figured prominently in the war. When Israel had ordered AMX-13 tanks in the early sixties, France was unable to produce them fast enough; but France sold the Israelis the crucial AMX-13 turrets, which the Israelis mounted on old Sherman chassis.

After 1967, de Gaulle was mindful enough of arms-race problems to embargo arms for Israel. The ban, as noted earlier, fell on fifty Mirages already ordered and two thirds paid for. Then, with the United States loosening up on arms deliveries to Israel, France lifted the embargo on Arab countries the following year and offered weapons to Syria, Iraq and Libya in return for mineral rights or oil supplies. France also sold Iraq fifty of the latest Mirages for $700 million.

In late 1968, with Moscow withholding arms deliveries to Syria to pressure Damascus both toward an accommodation with Israel and also a friendship treaty with the Soviet Union, the Syrians sent a military purchasing mission to Paris—but apparently mainly with the idea of bringing counterpressure on Moscow, which then agreed to new transfers. France, however, did bring off its sensational sale of 110 Mirages to Libya.

A French government, even more than a British government, can do more or less what it likes in the field of arms sales or bans. It is not responsive to public opinion in the way Washington is—and was even more high-handed in the days of de Gaulle. Moreover, France was less blamed than the United States for the Israeli blitzkrieg of 1967 because, although the triumphant weaponry was mostly French, it was paid for by American Zionists.

France, then the only major armorer of South Africa, also skillfully avoided condemnation by the Organization of African Unity by (as noted earlier) informing leaders of French-speaking Africa that French economic aid came out of the profits on arms sales to their enemy to the south. All through the sixties, with the United States maintaining a virtually total embargo on arms for South Africa, and Britain an almost total one, both countries were more criticized by Africans than France was, whenever "Western" support for South Africa was discussed. Yet by 1969, with the buildup of South African forces mounting, Paris had sold the Afrikaner republic not only a squadron of Mirage-III fighter-bombers with Matra air-to-air missiles and air-to-surface missiles, but also Alouette and Super-Frélon helicopters, AMX-13 tanks, Panhard armored cars, three Daphné-class submarines, radar, ammunition and napalm, thanks to a $210 million credit at 6.5 per cent. The production of Panhards in South Africa was licensed. Virtually all South Africa's new inventory was clearly designed for internal suppression.

In 1971, France took South African orders for sixteen F-1As with Matra-Magic missiles, for delivery in 1975, and authorized South Africa to co-produce thirty-two more. Fresh orders for Matra-Magics were taken the following year, also for 1975 delivery. In 1974, South Africa took delivery of eighteen more Mirage III/5 fighters with Milan air-to-surface missiles and Matra-Magics, three more Daphné-class submarines, four frigates and a corvette. Exocet air-to-surface missiles for use with the Super-Frélon three-engined gunships were ordered that year, for delivery in 1977. In 1975 came orders for two Agosta-class, 1,200-ton French submarines, a $70 million order completed in 1978; and in 1976, Pretoria ordered the military version of the A-300 Airbus as a tanker-transport to support the Mirages. During this time, South Africa also bought six corvettes from France. France's two-way trade with South Africa surpassed $750 million in 1976, with a $150 million surplus in France's favor; arms were a potent factor in that development. The year before, Canada, at France's urging, supplied Pretoria with three amphibious Canadair AL-215s.

In 1966, the United States had blocked the sale of Mystère-20 executive jets to South Africa because they had General Electric engines and could be converted to military purposes. In similar cases involving U.S. avionics, France had simply retrofitted French products to evade the U.S. ban. In the case of the GE engines, it was not possible, so de Gaulle angrily refused to buy any more U.S. arms, saying his gesture was in protest against the Vietnam War. When the United States ordered some Nord-Aviation AS-12 air-to-ship missiles, France refused to supply—although they clearly had no use in the Vietnam War.

George Ivan Smith of the United Nations has testified that France secretly endorsed arms-production deals in South Africa and Rhodesia in the early sixties. Rhodesia even got the franchise to produce cluster bombs—a terror weapon which was used in Vietnam against forest guerrillas, and by Israel in 1978 against Lebanese villagers. After the settler regime in Rhodesia had rebelled against Britain, France (in connivance with British companies) became its main supplier of oil, thus permitting the regime's army and air force to remain in action. The rebels were also helped by France to evade other UN sanctions.

In the seventies, Rhodesia continued to buy Alouette-III and Puma helicopters to sustain its resistance to London. The Puma deal was particularly mischievous, since the aircraft is co-designed by Westland. But after all, even a Commonwealth country such as New Zealand was selling the rebel regime air force training planes.

After the UN voted a mandatory arms embargo on South Africa in November 1977, France agreed to bar delivery of the two Agosta submarines and two corvettes nearing completion—one of which, the *Good Hope,* already had a South African Navy crew aboard at Lorient. The *Good Hope,* due for delivery four months later, after trials, was transferred to Lorient's inner harbor, behind a drawbridge. But South Africa's co-production rights on Mirages, Alouettes, Pumas, armored cars and AMX tanks continued, with some of the helicopters going to Rhodesia. France was found to be illegally selling to Salisbury some of the American Cessna light aircraft made under license at Reims, and which the settler regime was converting for military spotter duties. Only after angry African crowds had cut short a visit to Africa by French Foreign Minister Louis de Guiringaud did France clamp down on all new sales to southern Africa.

With only one eighth of America's GNP—and while only spending one fifteenth as much on its armed forces—France by the mid-sixties was earning a quarter as much from arms exports. Hit then for a decade by the "Kuss buildup" of U.S. sales, Paris is now once again regaining its eminent position in the arms-export world. But even in 1969, a fairly "bad" year, France could boast that of 850 Mirage-IIIs produced, 500 had been for export. By the end of that decade, Nord-Aviation had exported or accepted orders from twenty-four countries for 301,500 missiles, including 290,000 surface-to-surface missiles, while Sud-Aviation had sold 1,700 Alouette-II and -III helicopters to sixty countries.

Paris, in short, was prepared to sell arms to virtually anyone who could pay, and who was unlikely to go to war with France. The main performer remained the Mirage, although in 1974, a $860 million French sale to Saudi Arabia included 200 AMX-30 tanks, 250 armored cars, and antiaircraft and antitank missiles, as well as 38 Mirage-IIIs; a much smaller order from Iraq had still included 31 Alouette-IIIs with SS-11 antitank missiles, 1,000 automatic mortars, laser range finders for armored cars and 60,000 rounds of artillery ammunition. The following year, experiencing problems with Moscow again, Iraq placed further orders in Paris. A sales organization for Dassault-Bréguet Falcon 20Gs—normally a bizjet aircraft—was set up in Saudi Arabia in 1976, the same year that Falcons were sold to the U. S. Coast Guard.

France sold 25 F-1s, 24 Alphajets and 40 Pumas to Morocco, along with an unspecified number of Matra air-to-air missiles and Crotale surface-to-air missile batteries. In 1977, Syria ordered 15 Super-Frélon helicopters, plus an unspecified number of Gazelles with HOT (wireguided) missiles. Further afield, France has licensed Spain to produce AMX-30 tanks. Spain is also building French submarines, and considering co-production of Puma helicopters. Paris was thus acquiring markets rarely tapped before.

But the main market rising on the horizon was not in Iraq, South Africa, America or Spain but in the pro-Western countries of the Middle East. In January 1975, President Sadat followed up his order for 38 Mirage-III fighters of a few months before (for completed delivery by 1977) with a visit to Paris, during which he ordered 44 F-1s for delivery in 1977 and 1978, at a cost of approximately $5 million each, with an initial order of 100 Matra-Magic air-to-air missiles. (This F-1 purchase was later canceled so that Saudi Arabia could buy available units of the plane, and replaced by planned co-production with France of single-engined Mirage-2000s—the basic fighter of the French Air Force for the eighties.

(In June 1978, after securing congressional approval of the sale of 60 F-15s, Arabia's King Khalid went to Paris to sign what the French press called the "arms deal of the century"—$24 billion of F-1s, Mirage-4000s, helicopters, tanks and a radar network to cover the Red Sea. All of this was for delivery in the eighties and nineties. In 1979, Paris announced it would also build an improved version of the Crotale SAM, the Shahine, for Saudi Arabia.)

Soviet Foreign Minister Andrei Gromyko appeared in Cairo a few days after Sadat's Paris visit and stepped up the Moscow pipeline of spare parts; but Egypt seemed likely to buy more and more British and especially French equipment. This posed problems for Egyptian engineers and mechanics, but fortunately Egypt already had some older Mirages in its inventory. Although some of the $1 billion which Saudi Arabia agreed to spend on Egyptian arms that year was to go for British Hawk trainer/light strike aircraft and the first of the 250 Lynx helicopters, plus some other purchases from Britain, the bulk of the bonanza was to pay the groundwork for the new arms industry in Cairo, mainly geared to French weapons. On the same day that Sadat, in Cairo, was asking visiting U.S. senators for American arms, his Premier, Mandouh Salem, was starting talks in Paris with Premier Raymond Barre on arms co-production and the supply of French nuclear reactors. Six months later, Sadat also agreed to buy French helicopters.

In 1978, France and Germany agreed to co-production in Egypt of 160 Alphajet trainer/attack aircraft and SNECMA/Turbomeca engines to power them. SNECMA and Turbomeca set up the Arab-French Engine Company (AFECO) for AOI in Helwan to make the Larzac engines for the Alphajet and the M53s for the Mirage-2000. Other co-production deals with France included an air-defense radar and command-and-control network, an agreement with Aérospatiale, Matra and Thomson-CSF to build surface-to-air missile systems, including the Matra-Thomson-CSF Crotale and the Aérospatiale/Messerschmitt-Bolkow-Blohm Roland, plus possibly some air-to-air missile systems. Future co-production of as many as 200 of the Mirage-4000 was also discussed. AOI and Thomson-CSF agreed to set up the Arab Electronics Company, with 70 per cent of the ownership going to AOI and 30 per cent to the French firm, to manufacture military electronics in Saudi Arabia. Meanwhile, since the mid-seventies, France had been selling F-1s and helicopters to Kuwait.

France was talking more and more openly of arms sales behind the Curtain. A flight of 6 F-1s accepted an invitation to tour Soviet bases in July 1977, and the Russians sent a similar flight of MiG-23s to tour French bases in 1978. That year, France announced its first $700 million of sales of defense equipment to China—antiaircraft and antitank missiles. Earlier, France had sold China helicopters. In 1979, it made the earlier-mentioned sale to Tass of a sophisticated computer with possible military applications.

The rising graph of French aircraft sales was mentioned at the start of this chapter. Meanwhile, French missile and space sales had risen 124 per cent in 1976, from $234 million in 1975 to $560 million. The main selling items were the Aérospatiale Exocet antiship missiles and the Matra-Magic air-to-air missiles. In 1977, Aérospatiale said 1,000 Exocets had been sold to sixteen navies, including France's, and six more were interested either in the MM-38 ship-to-ship version or the AM-39 air-to-surface version, which was undergoing tests from a Super-Frélon helicopter platform in 1977. Air engine sales accounted for another $284 million, helicopter sales for a further $202 million and avionics for $200 million. The five hundredth Puma helicopter was delivered in 1977, and Aérospatiale signed a co-production agreement on the chopper that year with Indonesia.

Brazil became the first customer outside France and Germany to take delivery of the Franco-German Roland, a short-range, low-altitude, surface-to-air missile, and Aérospatiale signed a contract to set up a helicopter plant in Brazil, with the Brazilian interests having a controlling (55 per cent) share. Both civil and military helicopters will be manufactured.

France and Germany also made an important breakthrough in the United States, when Congress finally gave approval for the U.S. purchase of the Roland-II. Congress had balked when R & D costs for Hughes, the main American contractor, had risen from $130 million to $183 million and finally to $265 million. The whole pre-production phase—technology transfer, manufacture and test—was expected to cost $356 million. American technicians faced the task of dealing with 93,000 metric drawings, along with parts lists and tables which had to be translated. Even the standard wire gauges were different from American usage. Six hundred interchangeable parts with U.S. components had to be devised. The Army countered critics by saying that to develop a purely American system would have cost "from $800 million to $1.2 billion," and would have taken up to ten years. Finally, the go-ahead came for seventeen batteries, at an estimated cost of $1.6 billion to $2 billion, over five years.

Hughes was building the guidance and tracking systems and the proximity fuse at Tucson, Arizona; Boeing, the main subcontractor, was making the fire unit and the rest of the missile, including the warhead and propulsion systems. The U. S. Army was expected to buy 5,000 to 7,000 Rolands, equipping units at the corps level; but Brigadier General Frank P. Rogano, the Roland project manager, said an eight-to-ten-year program, costing $4 billion, was envisaged, bringing Roland to the division level. France and Germany hoped to sell the missile to other interested countries, including Norway, Canada, South Korea, Israel and Taiwan.

Yet another possible customer for the F-1 seemed for a while to be Canada. In March 1977, when the Canadian Government approved expenditure of $2.08 billion for a new fighter to replace Canada's CF-5s, -104s and -101s, France proposed both the F-1 with Matra-Magic missiles and the as yet undeveloped, single-engined Mirage-2000 with Matra-Super long-range missiles. If France had secured the order, it would have meant a major inroad into a traditionally American market.

Brazil ordered 7 more Mirage-IIIs, Argentina a supplementary batch of 4. Fourteen were sold to Sudan, 5 to Gabon. In 1979, 32 Mirage-IIIs and -III/5s were sold to Pakistan, following Washington's denial of A-7s. Dassault-Bréguet anticipated enough orders to keep the III/5 assembly lines going until 1982. A new Dassault strike aircraft, the Super Etendard, was announced, with an initial domestic order of 80 for France's two aircraft carriers. In Canberra, the Mirage-2000 was competing with the Tornado and the Northrop F-18L to be Australia's fighter of the eighties.

During 1977, Dassault took orders for a further 72 F-1s for Iraq, for $560 million, and by 1979 France was announcing a "$1.2 billion to $2.2 billion" sale to Baghdad of naval equipment—ships, helicopters, missiles and radars. Morocco increased its orders for F-1s from 25 to 50, with options on 25 more. Jordan bought 36. Ecuador took 18; Spain, which already had 15, took another 10—and in 1978 announced plans to buy 48 more, while threatening to cancel orders for 72 F-16s. Australia was considering buying 100. In 1978, the Dassault Atlantique was competing with the Lockheed P-3 Orion for a Dutch order for 13 ASW planes.

A half-French missile, the tube-launched, optically tracked, wire-launched HOT antitank projectile, was sold to Peking in 1978. HOT, jointly produced by Aérospatiale and Messerschmitt-Bolkow-Blohm, compares to the American TOW. The sale was announced by Wu Hsiu-chuan, a deputy chief of staff. Later, France announced a seven-year, $13.6 billion trade agreement with China, including the initial $700 million for arms mentioned earlier, and $4.5 billion for two nuclear power stations. French banks opened an initial credit of $6.8 billion.

New French weapons offered at the 1979 Paris Air Show included the Mirage-4000—a prototype was flown in demonstrations—and Aérospatiale's AS-332 Super-Puma and SA-365N troop-transport helicopters. The SA-365N was ordered by the U. S. Coast Guard: Bell, which was competing for the order with its 222C, filed a complaint with the GAO.

France and Germany both came under stronger American pressure because of their proposed nuclear-plant sales to Third World countries. Both the French and German governments and the press in both countries criticized Americans as repentant proliferators reluctant to see other advanced countries make money out of nuclear exports. *Die Welt,* supporting German nuclear sales to Brazil, noted that the United States had sold South Africa the two computers that controlled Pretoria's plutonium plant, and others pointed out that the French sale to South Africa of generators went through only after South Africa had rejected a bid by American firms. But there was clearly worldwide concern about putting nuclear power in the hands of the maverick and unpredictable South Africans. However, the deal cut both ways: In July, France's nuclear authority signed a contract to buy 1,000 tons of South African uranium at below the world price—$27 a pound instead of $40, a saving of $26 million. In 1979, France agreed to replace, by 1981, the Osiris nuclear reactor which it had built for Iraq, and which saboteurs, presumed to be Israeli, had blown up in April: Iraq is France's second largest source of oil, after Saudi Arabia.

German Arms Sales

Deliberate restrictions on the German forces and arms industry following World War Two were lifted slowly; although France is only dependent on the United States for 7 per cent of its military aircraft, Italy 10 per cent and Britain 26 per cent, Germany still buys 65 per cent of its warplanes and missiles in America; but by 1965, Bonn was giving military aid to Greece, Turkey, Sudan, Guinea, Somalia, Madagascar and Portugal, and selling military equipment to Nigeria. Later, Ethiopia, India, Libya, Tanzania and Israel were added to the list, although aid to Israel had to cease following Arab reactions. One curious exception was that, after the 1967 war, Germany offered twenty thousand gas masks to Israel. Until very recent times, however, most of the equipment sold by Germany was obsolescent U.S. matériel.

Germany's best arms exports have been technicians. With no arms industry to employ them at home immediately after the war, many highly skilled and innovative technicians had to look to foreign employers. The best-known were rocket experts like Wernher von Braun and his team, which moved to America. Others were in Eastern Germany at the fall and were drafted into scientific service by the Russians. Willi Messerschmitt moved to Spain. Ferdinand Brandner went to Egypt; Messerschmitt joined him there briefly, and together with Messerschmitt's new employers, Hispano-Aviación, Brandner took over the development of the HA-300 jet fighter at Helwan, outside Cairo. Other German engineers went to work for Israeli Aircraft Industries. Kurt Tank, a former chief designer for Focke-Wulf, took a team to India, where it designed and developed the supersonic HF-24 fighter.

By 1960, Germany was producing its own missiles, but many highly skilled technicians were still out of work. Eugen Sänger, head of the Stuttgart Institute of Jet Propulsion, went to Egypt to help develop an indigenous rocket industry. With him went Wolfgang Pilz, a rocket and propulsion expert who helped von Braun build the V-1—the first modern cruise missile—at Peenemünde. He had worked after the war for the rocket industry in France, designing the Véronique, and later took over from Sänger in Helwan. Germany's brief foray into arms sales to Israel was to cost Pilz and eighty of his associates their jobs in Egypt.

By the time they left, Egypt had three rockets in the development stage: the Al Zafir (Victory), with a 230-mile range, the Al Khir (Conqueror), with a 370-mile range, and the Al Ared (Vanguard), with a 590-mile range. The departure of the Germans meant that none were usable at the time of the Israeli invasion of 1967: Had they been, they might obviously have altered the turn of events, since they were potentially superior to anything in the invader's armory. Nasser seems to have recognized the usefulness of his German experts, since he initially refused to recognize East Germany in hopes of luring them back. A new but less brilliant team, mostly German but including two American scientists, succeeded them.

Germany entered the big time in arms diplomacy again with the Leopard tank, sold in 1967 to Belgium, and to Holland and Norway the following year. The Belgian sale, totaling $91.4 million, was half offset by German Government contracts to Belgian industries for munitions and electronic goods and the overhaul of German armor in Belgian plants, the other half of the cost being offset by co-production in Belgium of Leopard parts and by the import of Belgian luxury goods. When Belgium ordered forty-two more Leopards in 1968, Germany—almost alone among European countries in offering such facilities—again provided 100 per cent offset, thus besting France's offset arrangements to that country for aircraft co-production.

The Dutch order, worth $112.8 million, was 90 per cent offset: 50 per cent by German government purchases of military supplies in Holland, 40 per cent by similar purchases by Kraus Maffei, the manufacturer of the Leopard. The Norwegian deal was the most generous of all: For every three deutsche marks spent by Oslo to buy Leopards, Bonn agreed to buy five deutsche marks' worth of Norwegian goods. Germany's offset arrangements contrast favorably with those of other European countries.

By 1977, the U. S. Army Proving Grounds at Aberdeen, Maryland, was testing the Leopard's smooth-bore 120mm. tank gun for possible use on the new Chrysler tank, against the British rifle-bore 120mm. and the U. S. Army-built American rifle-bore 105mm. gun; but members of Congress were insisting that the choice be made on grounds of efficiency alone, not as a counterbalance to European purchases of U.S. equipment —notably, the proposed sale of AWACS planes to Bonn. A House Armed Services investigations subcommittee noted, however, that "leading members of the German Bundestag" had said that failure to buy the German gun would mean a German refusal of AWACS.

A curiosity of the German gun is that its shells deploy wings to stabilize them in flight. Intense secrecy surrounded the Aberdeen testing, and when this writer visited the Proving Grounds that year he was not even allowed to see the gun fired.

Finally, in 1978, the U. S. Army decided—despite opposition from the House Armed Services Committee—in favor of the German weapon, with installation on U.S. tanks to begin in 1984. Germany agreed to have the guns co-produced in the United States. Army Secretary Clifford Alexander said the British gun was as good, but the German gun was more advanced in development and Germany had more tanks in NATO than Britain. Royalty payments to the gun manufacturer, Rheinmetall—3 per cent on U.S. tanks, 5 per cent on Chrysler MBTs sold abroad—would add about $16,000 to the cost of each Abrams.

According to *Wehrdienst*, an arms-industry magazine, Germany achieved $1 billion of arms exports in 1977. During 1978, Bonn was negotiating a $3.5 billion warship program for Iran, including 6 submarines, and appeared to be challenging Britain for third place in the non-Communist weapons-sales race. Alphajet production was 12 a month—6 for the Luftwaffe, 4 for France, 2 for export—and was planned to go to 15 a month as export orders developed. In 1978, Bonn sold 12 Alphajets to Nigeria for $80 million, replacing Czech L-39s; 24 more were sold to Morocco, 12 to Ivory Coast and 5 to Togo, as well as the order from Egypt for 160. Sweden was even considering purchase. Backed by strong NATO orders—800 Tornados, with 42 per cent of the production work on the 2,000 Rolls-Royce/Turbo-Union engines, Dornier airframes for 500 Alphajets and the engines for these, Milan, HOT and Roland missiles, and a 1978 order for about half the work on 25 more Franco-German Transall transports—German aerospace was pushing ahead with a new, German-designed twin-engined helicopter and with plans for a TKF-90 tactical fighter for the nineties, in cooperation with McDonnell-Douglas and Northrop. France and Britain may also cooperate on this potentially 1,000-aircraft, $20 billion program, which would probably use V-STOL technology. But there was substantial disagreement between the German, U.S., French and British air staffs on what the plane's main missions would be. Germany was also now producing more and more weapons of its own design. In 1979, Boeing took on representation of Messerschmitt-Bolkow-Blohm and was hoping to sell 50,000 Armbrust shoulder-launched SAMs to the United States and Canada for $600 each. MBB said twenty-one other countries had bought or expressed interest in the weapon.

In Zaire, a private German firm, Orbital Transport and Rocket Corporation (OTRAG) negotiated use of an equatorial test range for a new, cut-rate German satellite launcher with possible military applications.

An unusual order in 1977 was for 4 Sportavia-Fournier RF-4 powered gliders for Egypt, which wanted them for electronic intelligence and artillery spotting. By and large, Germany was still cautious about Mideast sales, however. When Syria bought 32 Messerschmitt-Bolkow-Blohm Flamingo trainers in 1977, it obtained them from the Spanish firm franchised to build them; a further 16 were supplied from Switzerland.

Germany was still behind France and Britain in arms sales, but was beginning to overtake thanks largely to the Leopard tank and the Rheinmetall gun. Kraus-Maffei, the manufacturer of the Leopard, even engaged a Washington lobbyist in 1977—William Weitzen of D. G. Aggers International, a firm headed by former senator Charles Goodell of New York. Weitzen filed lobby papers with the Hill expressing an interest in "military authorizations and appropriations [and] foreign purchases."

In late 1978, Messerschmitt-Bolkow-Blohm signed a $100 million agreement with Peking to cooperate in a number of "scientific and technological fields," including aviation, space, high-energy physics and lasers, and the building of a nuclear accelerator.

In 1979, however, Zaire canceled German rocket-development facilities in that country, at the request of the Bonn government—itself under pressure to do so from Moscow. Annulling the agreement with OTRAG, the earlier-mentioned private German company using the Zairian site, was said by the Kinshasa government at the time to involve the loss of $6.2 billion of revenues over the next twenty-five years.

Other European Sales

A highly efficient producer of weapons and other precision machinery, Sweden has, as briefly noted earlier, many well-known arms firms: Bofors makes guns, Bantam makes antitank missiles, other artillery and armored vehicles; Svenska Flygmotor makes jet engines under American and British licenses; Swedish Phillips, Ericsson, Standard Radio and Telefon make air defense, fire-control and radar systems. SAAB, in addition to the J-35 and -35X Draken, also produces the J-105X and the contemporary Viggen fighter. Government and private production share the arms-manufacture field, which embraces missile systems, avionics and naval vessels—submarines, destroyers and patrol boats.

Sweden sells only to countries which it thinks are unlikely to be in-

·volved in war, although there have been numerous exceptions. When Israel attacked Suez in 1956, it used twenty-five P-51 Mustangs from
World War Two which had been sold to Tel Aviv by Sweden, while
Egypt helped defend itself with a 40mm. Bofors antiaircraft gun and
quantities of M-45 Carl Gustav submachine guns, as well as 7.92mm.
Model-42 Ljungmann rifles, manufactured under license in Egypt. Sweden has also sold P-51s and (through Sam Cummings) British Vampires
to the Dominican Republic: Both types of aircraft were subsequently
used in war.

In 1978, Stockholm sold antitank missiles to Argentina and antiaircraft
artillery to the Iranian Navy in spite of legislation prohibiting arms sales
to countries "where human rights are being systematically repressed."
Sweden was hoping to sell 150 Viggens to India, against competition
from the F-1 and the Jaguar.

In earlier years, Sweden transferred quantities of SAAB Safir SK-50s—
a piston-engine attack aircraft—to several small countries, including
Ethiopia. Its T-28 trainer, in an attack version, has sold to Ethiopia,
Laos, Cambodia, Zaire, Argentina, Brazil, Haiti and Mexico. As its industry became more sophisticated, Sweden even began to offer arms to
NATO countries—airborne missiles and military electronics to France, as
well as to Spain and South Africa, and bomb-throwing and rocket-firing
computers to France and Denmark, as well as to Switzerland. Sweden
has developed a revolutionary turretless tank, the Strv-S. But its best-
known military product until recent times was the Mach-2 Draken
(Dragon), in full production since 1969. Sweden has been reluctant to
share production or offset costs, but when the Draken was sold to Denmark in 1968, about 50 per cent was offset. This helped the Draken win
out over the F-5 and the Mirage-V. When the Draken was followed by
the Viggen (Thunderbolt), it was offered to NATO, but lost out to the
F-16 mostly (as mentioned earlier) because of Sweden's neutral politics
—seen as a sign of unreliability as to supply.

SAAB had hoped originally to build 800 Viggens, but after the NATO
refusal the production line was cut back to 175, which raised the cost.
Sweden's difficulties in selling the U.S.-engined plane to India, Taiwan
and Latin America have been mentioned. A Swedish general told the
writer: "We were very disappointed at the U.S. veto on Viggen sales to
India." He said sales to Austria were still a possibility—"but Austria has
financial problems and the order would be small—perhaps twenty aircraft. Australia has decided to stay with American aircraft." The vague
possibility of sales to Peking has been mentioned, but the general—an
expert on military sales—was pessimistic: "SAAB will probably have to
give up developing aircraft of its own and just build U.S. or foreign Eu-

ropean aircraft on license. So sooner or later, we [the Swedish Air Force] will have to buy aircraft from abroad, and this will not be cheaper. American aircraft are overpowered for our purposes. We have no need for a refueling capability, and if we buy an American plane we will have to buy that capability. Then we will have to buy different fueling equipment, different weaponry, and all that will be expensive too." Thus the virtual U.S. veto on major Swedish arms sales will affect the whole concept of Swedish military aviation.

Sweden has stuck sincerely enough in recent years to its policy of not selling to probable users by foreclosing the Mideast market to itself, at great expense. Stanley and Pearton, in their study, say: "One is led therefore to the ironic conclusion that the expense of modern weapons development makes it impossible for a neutral nation to arm itself at a politically acceptable cost without substantial export sales which themselves must eventually compromise its neutrality."

Because Sweden's outlets are limited, its aircraft are in any event more expensive. Whereas the basic F-16 and the Jaguar cost under $8 million, and the subsidized Mirage-2000 under $5 million, the Viggen costs nearly $10 million without the NATO market. Sweden spends 39 per cent of its armed-forces budget on procurement, compared to the Western average of 23 per cent, keeping manpower costs down by having a conscript army.

Sweden's odd situation as a small, neutral, highly independent, sometimes anti-American and even anti-Western nation, producing weapons of major-power quality, and self-righteously accepting self-imposed sales restraints which its seniors in the comity of nations are too greedy to try, arouses a feast of resentments. When small quantities of Swedish arms turn up in an active conflict, this is trumpeted with indignation, as though the Mafia had caught the local patrolman accepting a free ticket to a ball game. Stories of Swedish hypocrisy are leaked relentlessly to defense writers and are sometimes published without evaluation. In 1978, *Newsweek*'s "Periscope" section reported that Stockholm was to receive a "strongly worded message" from the United States because of its decision to put the RBS-70 short-range antiaircraft missile launcher on the "open market." The "message" was part of a quest to "curb international terrorism," and the RBS-70 was described as portable "by one person" and "even more advanced than the U.S. and Soviet models." In reality, the RBS-70 weighs 180 pounds—more than six times the weight of its competitors. It is not shoulder-fired, but erected on an awkward, three-legged stand. It is well behind its U.S., Soviet, British and German competitors, and unsuitable for guerrilla warfare, which is probably why Sweden is trying to unload it.

Switzerland is less independent than Sweden, since it builds its combat aircraft under license and imports most of its armor from France and Britain. Switzerland's home-built armor is mostly the work of Hispano-Suiza, which also makes cannons, antiaircraft rockets, machine guns, other automatic weapons, ammunition rifles and mortar grenades. Switzerland co-produces the Mosquito antitank missile with Italy. Some of the PX-58 tanks, Type-38 tank missiles and Pirate armored personnel carriers produced for the Swiss defense forces are also exported to Germany. The 20mm. Oerlikon cannon is exported, notably to Austria, and is co-produced in Japan. In the United States, it is being tested for use in the Vought A-7.

Behind its lace-curtain, "neutral" facade, Swiss business can be as tough as its competition. A few months before the Biafran war started in July 1967, Lagos approached Switzerland for arms. The Foreign Ministry in Berne forbade the Defense Ministry from selling weapons to a visiting Nigerian Government team because of tension within the country. Yet by August, the Swiss embassy in Lagos was reporting that two Oerlikon-Buhrle employees were instructing Nigerian artillerymen in the use of Oerlikon antiaircraft guns. Clearly, the 20mm. guns had been exported illegally from Switzerland.

The batch included 210 made for Nazi Germany, undelivered by the end of the war and sequestered by the Swiss Government as part of Germany's war debt. Under an agreement with Berne, Oerlikon could sell these government-owned weapons for a 50 per cent commission. Swiss investigators turned up a bill for $1,250,000 for the weapons, but further probing showed that over three years, illegal sales to various countries had reached more than $20 million, or more than total legal arms exports by Switzerland that year (1967). Included in the purchases were 324 antiaircraft guns, 5,500 rockets and 230,000 rounds of heavy ammunition. All had ended up in countries on Switzerland's embargo list, after first going to permitted countries where officials had signed end-use certificates agreeing not to re-export them. About 60 per cent of the traffic had gone to South Africa, which had received heavy 35mm. cannons. In November 1963, the Berne government had actually agreed to the sale of seven Oerlikon antiaircraft batteries and ammunition to Pretoria, saying that southern Africa was not an area of international tension. This raised a storm of protests, and Berne reversed itself. Switzerland, however, is not a UN member.

Switzerland has also sold light arms to Denmark, Chile and Zaire. But because of Switzerland's official "armed neutrality" policy, Swiss arms exports are effectively limited.

The main Swiss arms plants are the federal arsenal—the Waffenfabrik Bern; the privately owned SIG (Schweizerische Industrie Gesellschaft) at Neuhausen, formerly owned by Oerlikon; and Hispano-Suiza—the only one of the three which specializes in large-caliber weapons. Hispano-Suiza is privately owned and has subsidiaries in Britain and Holland. It buys exploitation rights to technological patents from Germany and the United States. Hispano-Suiza builds the Finnish Suomi 9mm. submachine gun under license for the Swiss forces, and has assembled nearly 3 million Luger 9mm. pistols under German license.

The Federal Aircraft Plant and Sulzer AG produced 57 Mirage-IIIs under license; rising costs forced a reduction from the planned figure of 100, as well as the resignation of the chief of the Swiss Air Force. In the fifties, the FAP produced British Vampires under license. Switzerland's air defense system is by Hughes, but incorporates Ferranti and Plessey radars made in Britain. Following the expensive Dassault experience, Switzerland has begun pooling its technology with Sweden. Jointly produced products are to be sold to Austria and Finland.

Italy's arms industry was slow to recover from World War Two, but by the sixties Rome was selling destroyers to Venezuela and Indonesia, Aermacchi jets to Ghana, Singapore, Somalia and other countries, and more advanced models to South Africa—notably forty Aeritalia AM-3C close-support aircraft. South Africa also bought other Italian weapons—helicopters, air-to-surface missiles, armored cars, transport aircraft. Since 1966, Aermacchi's MB-326 attack aircraft has been produced under license in South Africa.

Italy's rank in the world arms market was modest; but just as Krupp had brought in customer capital by allowing the Shah of Iran to buy 25 per cent of the corporation's stock, so Italy's truck and plane maker Fiat, in 1976, sold 9.6 per cent of its stock to Libya for $300 million and a soft loan of just over $100 million. The thought of exploiting U.S. arms-sales restraints was undoubtedly one motive behind a decision, the following year, for Italy's Aermacchi and Brazil's Embraer firm to cooperate in the production of a light, long-range attack aircraft for the eighties to be called the Macchi-340. Fear of the drift of U.S. policy partly dictated the subsequent decision not to buy General Electric TF-34 engines for the planes, but to adapt a Rolls-Royce engine instead. Aermacchi would market the aircraft in Europe, Embraer in Latin America, and they would share out the rest of the world market between them. Italy is of course the junior partner in the trinational consortium, Panavia, which produces the Tornado.

But Italy's principal potential new arms market, in 1979, was China. With Peking making commercial deals with major countries contingent on them agreeing to sell arms, Italy found itself under even heavier Soviet pressure than Britain, France and Germany. Moscow was threatening to withhold oil and gas—the Soviet Union supplies 25 per cent of Italy's natural gas and 7.5 per cent of its oil. Not surprisingly, when China began exporting oil to Western Europe in 1978, Italy was the first country to be offered some. Italian armaments of interest to Peking included the Oto-Melara Otomat ship-to-ship missile, the Selenia Aspile surface-to-air and air-to-air missile, Galileo target-control devices and Agosta helicopters. Rome was talking of initial sales of over $300 million.

Of the junior-league European arms countries, the most enterprising continued to be Belgium, still selling small arms to over sixty countries, including the Mag-58 machine gun in the United States. The Mag-58, and FN hunting guns, may soon be manufactured in Columbia, South Carolina. Belgian arms sales were up from $120 million in 1973 to over $250 million in 1976. The figures seem modest—and constitute only slightly over 1 per cent of Belgium's total exports—but are impressive when the relatively low prices of small arms are taken into account, and when the major role of small arms in those conflicts which actually take place is considered. More people may well be killed in warfare each day with Belgian small arms than with Soviet or U.S. weapons.

Belgium's arms-export earnings are destined to rise further: Fabrique Nationale d'Armes de Guerre (FN) has a contract to build 1,000 engines for the General Dynamics F-16, most of them for export. The country buys 62 per cent of its military aviation in the United States. FN's label is famous across the world: 90 per cent of the parastatal concern's production is exported, and since World War Two FN has sold its weapons to over 130 countries in all 5 continents. They are produced under license in the United States, Canada, Britain, Australia, Argentina, Israel and Austria.

As well as a long shipbuilding tradition, Holland has a venerable arms industry, the Artillerie Inrichtingen, which manufactures American rifles under license, mostly for export. Holland, which buys 75 per cent of its war planes and missiles from America, has also manufactured and exported F-104Gs in the past, as well as British aircraft—Gloster Meteors and Hawker Hunters. Today, it co-produces the Hawk missile and will soon co-produce the F-16.

Turkey's war industry predates that of most European countries, but its first modern plant was for aircraft assembly, set up by Junkers in 1927. A modern small-arms factory made a Turkish copy, called the Kirikkale, of the German Walther pistol. An important early export market was Iraq. When France withdrew from the NATO military structure, an American jet-repair installation was relocated at Eskisehir; but it has only been in recent years that major co-production plans have begun to blossom.

Elsewhere in the European area, both Denmark and Spain export pistols, rifles and machine guns, but no major arms. Denmark's Madsen firm, in particular, has a good small-arms reputation; but Copenhagen, which buys 98 per cent of its air force matériel in the United States, is one of the NATO capitals most dissatisfied with America's failure to buy European arms in quantity.

Overall, Europe is still far behind the United States. Whereas eight American firms can design and produce combat aircraft, only three can do so in Europe—Dassault-Bréguet, British Aerospace and SAAB. The French and British aircraft industries together amount only to one third of America's, while all of the European Community's equals only half. Profits for the European industry are one fifteenth those of the United States. Says Lawrence G. Franko of the RAND Corporation:

> If the United States is serious about multilateral restraint in arms exports, it must bargain with other suppliers about market share, and world market share at that.

Canadian Sales

Canada also co-produces heavily with the United States, with an eye to export, notably in the field of aircraft. Its airplane industry grew during World War Two, mostly for supplying the British Air Force, and since then Canada has kept busy supplying NATO countries. Canada built the F-5 for the RCAF and, in conjunction with Fokker, for the Dutch Air Force. Earlier, the F-86 Saber and the F-104 Starfighter were co-produced in Canada. Canadian-made Sabers were exported to Britain, Italy, Germany, Sweden, Turkey, South Africa and Colombia. Canadian 104s went to Germany, Denmark, Greece, Turkey and Norway. The Orenda division of the (40 per cent U.S.-owned) Canadian subsidiary of

Hawker-Siddeley builds American jet engines under license. Today, Canada is looking more and more toward export markets.

Japanese Sales

A modern Japanese war industry dates from 1890. For half a century, Japan copied Western weapons, predominantly for its own forces. Between 1906 and 1945, it made 10 million Arisaka rifles. In the thirties, as well as building Japanese copies of German U-boats, the Japanese also produced Vickers and Browning aircraft guns. During the war, Japan built 52,000 combat aircraft.

Japanese arms sales abroad are a relatively new phenomenon. In the mid-sixties, Tokyo began selling Kappa-6 rockets to Yugoslavia and Kappa-8 rockets to Indonesia, and since then a small export industry has developed. In 1977, Japan and Australia promised economic and military assistance to the less developed countries of the ASEAN Treaty—Malaysia, the Philippines, Indonesia, Singapore and Thailand. In 1978, the United States authorized Japan to sell three big computers, built under RCA license, to China; the Chinese said they were needed for meteorological work.

Only in the late seventies did Japan think of designing warplanes of its own with an export potential. The main one was to be a V-STOL fighter to replace Japan's F-4s in the nineties; but in 1978, after selling its first six co-produced Boeing-Vertol V-107-1 helicopters to Saudi Arabia, Tokyo announced that it would be exhibiting a twin-engined BK-11 helicopter, largely of Japanese design, at the Paris Air Show of June 1979. This is a joint production of Kawasaki Industries and Germany's Messerschmitt-Bolkow-Blohm.

Sales by Third World Countries

Notable among Third World countries building up their own armaments self-sufficiency has been India, especially since the 1962 clash with China and the fighting with Pakistan over Kashmir in 1965, which led to an American and a theoretical British embargo on arms.

India had several small arms factories under British rule. During World War Two, the plant at Ishapore produced 690,000 Enfield bolt-action rifles; after independence, it manufactured its own weapon, the Ishapore rifle, and the FN 7.62mm. assault rifle—for several years the standard NATO infantry weapon—under license. Under an agreement with the Soviet Union, airframe plants were set up at Nasik, Koraput and Hyderabad to build the MiG-21 Mach-2 interceptor and the Russian Atoll air-to-air missile, while Hindustan Aeronautics made the Folland-Hawker-Siddeley Gnat, a tactical naval fighter. When the United States refused to sell India the F-104, and forbade France and Britain to sell aircraft containing American components, New Delhi concentrated on producing a fighter of its own—the Marut—but with mixed success. Ouragan and Mystère fighters were built under license, along with Vampires, Canberras, Hunters, Sea Hawks, and Bréguet-Alizé antisubmarine aircraft. Now India seems to have overcome its design problems and may well develop an aerospace industry with an export market for its HF-24 all-weather fighter.

In the critical period following 1965, India also expanded its tank and small-arms production, building French AMX-13 and Soviet T-34 tanks under license. Today it builds its own Vijayanta tank, which is available for export. There are naval shipyards in Bombay and Calcutta.

Iran set up arsenals with U.S. and British aid during World War Two, producing machine guns for the Red Army; it had earlier had a co-production arrangement for small arms with Skoda. The phenomenal growth of the Iranian defense industry in recent years has been mostly a reflection of American and European weapons diplomacy; but until the events of 1978 occurred, export production had been planned, notably of helicopters, and this may well be one aspect of the Shah's arms economy which future governments will preserve.

South Africa, as noted, has developed a considerable native arms industry in its bid for weapons self-sufficiency, and is now offering arms for export—notably, locally made FN assault rifles, Macchi MB-326 Impala attack aircraft (co-produced under license at the Atlas Aircraft Corporation plant), and a sophisticated line of French helicopters. Eventually, it is expected to offer French-designed tanks, French- and Israeli-designed missiles, and patrol craft. So far, however, South African weapons exports have been limited to small arms for neighboring countries.

Blacklisted by the United States, Brazil is becoming "the Third World's most advanced arms producer and exporter," according to a RAND Corporation study. Brazil has co-production plants with Oerlikon for antiaircraft artillery, with West Germany for Cobra missiles, with France for helicopters, with Belgium for cannons and automatic weapons, with Britain for surface ships and submarines and with Italy for pistols and the new light attack plane mentioned earlier. In 1978, Brazil was negotiating to co-produce the Leopard tank, the Marder armored car, a range of Messerschmitt-Bolkow-Blohm aircraft, and Zeiss gunsights, and was also hoping to build surface-to-surface and surface-to-air missiles. But the Washington *Post* quoted a Brazilian official as saying that year: "Our main interest is export. By 1980, arms exports are going to be a billion-dollar-a-year item in our balance of trade."

When the Indian subcontinent was divided in 1947, Pakistan found itself with no arms plants at all. Some have been developed in recent years, but the country remains essentially arms-dependent on the United States, and to a lesser degree Western Europe, for its major weaponry. Export of arms is minimal.

A modest war industry grew up in Indonesia immediately after the war of independence ended, in 1950. Its first task was to rebore thousands of captured Dutch Mannlicher 6.5mm. rifles. Then Sukarno standardized his armory on American models until 1959, when he went over to Soviet models. Thereafter, important caches of American, Dutch, British and Japanese weapons were sold on the world market through private dealers.

Many smaller countries with no or little arms industry of their own also engage in weapons diplomacy. In 1978, for instance, Algeria shipped 18 tons of Kalashnikov assault rifles to the Seychelles, whose army and "people's militia" number only a few hundred each. Both South Africa and Rhodesia have been supplied with obsolescent U.S. armor by Jordan, while North Korea, which has supplied advisers to Syria, Madagascar and the Polisario resistance in ex-Spanish Sahara, as well as "100" MiG-23 pilot instructors to Libya, is now reported looking for markets for its own Soviet-style arms.

Israeli Arms Sales

The star of the Third World arms exporters—and about to move into the big time—is Israel. Initially discreet about its weapons-sales program, Israel's armaments industry finally went public in a 1976 *Aviation Week* supplement. This advertised the availability of its Mach-2.2 Kfir fighter—offered at $4.4 million, or about 25 per cent less than the F-16—along with its STOL Arava transport planes, missile boats, the Shafrir air-to-air missile (described as "battle-proven" and with an "overall kill ratio of about 60 per cent"), the Gabriel ship-to-ship missile (billed as the "free world's only combat-proven ShShM"), along with rockets, bombs, numerous automatic weapons and avionics. A senior U.S. official told the writer at the time that prospective Kfir purchasers who inquired about the true availability of the plane's General Electric J-79 engines and classified inertial platform were told by Israeli officials: "Don't worry. If anyone squawks, we'll handle the U. S. Congress." But for once, as it happened, Congress and the lobby did not have the last word.

By seeking to sell to anyone friendly enough to want to buy, Israel raised its 1976 military sales of $340 million (Israeli figure) or $500 million (Pentagon estimate) to nearly a billion dollars in 1977, Defense experts, quoted later by *Aviation Week,* calculated. The calculation does not sound unreasonable: When President Carter later vetoed the sale of twenty-four Kfirs for $150 million "flyaway cost" to Ecuador, the full value of the loss to Israel's revenues was initially put at $300 million for that one deal alone—and ten times as much for forbidding Kfir sales throughout Latin America. Israel, like Germany, was fast overhauling Britain for third place among non-Communist arms sales, and now sells to over forty countries.

Israeli Military Industries (IMI) began exporting its lightweight, easily maintained Uzi submachine gun, named after its designer, Major Uziel Ghalil, in the fifties. Initial sales to Germany and Holland, and to Communist guerrillas in Cuba and Venezuela, made the weapon's reputation, and it is now to be found in Third World armies across the globe. Only in the seventies did Israel begin to push the export of aircraft, missiles and missile boats.

Tel Aviv is particularly prepared to sell to unpopular regimes in Latin America, southern Africa, Asia and elsewhere, offering to be more "reliable" about deliveries and spares than critical Western governments concerned about democracy. Ecuador—which finally bought Nesher (Eagle) fighters (a pre-Kfir adaptation of the Mirage-III with French SNECMA Atar engines)—also bought other weapons beside aircraft, in an arms-for-oil deal. Other rightist regimes in Latin America dealing with Israeli armorers have included Brazil, El Salvador, Chile, Honduras, Guatemala, Nicaragua and Argentina—which has bought Gabriel missiles and, in 1978, thirty-one Neshers. In 1978, Israel rushed a fresh supply of arms to the floundering Somoza regime in Managua. Argentina, Brazil and Chile are virtually excluded from U.S. arms deals under the "human rights" guidelines. South Africa's growing involvement with Israeli arms will be related later.

A German private arms dealer told the writer that Guatemala bought the Ghalil assault rifle from Israel for $350 apiece even though the United States had offered the M-16 for $148—because Washington had refused to sell Guatemala six elderly C-47 transports (possibly requested for mounting an attack on Belize) and the Israelis had pointed to this as evidence that Washington was an unreliable, capricious supplier.

The Shafrir had been sold to eight countries by 1978. One recipient was Chile, which had been refused U.S. Sidewinders as part of a White House policy not to supply infrared guided missiles to Latin America. U.S. sources estimated that a third of the Shafrir production line was already being exported by 1977, along with about 35 per cent of the Israeli arms industry as a whole. By then, 3 million Ghalil rifles had been sold abroad.

Just as Yugoslavia built up its modest arms industry after World War Two by pirating German designs, so Israel has built a larger and better industry by pirating mostly French and American systems—with some of the French systems having earlier been pirated by France from U.S. models. The Shafrir is essentially the Raytheon AIM-9D/G Super-Sidewinder air-to-air missile. The new, "secret" Shafrir-3 is the AIM-9L. The Kfir is an improved Mirage-III/5 with U.S. engines. The Ghalil assault rifle is a pirated version of the Soviet AK-47 Kalashnikov, adapted for NATO-caliber ammunition. The Gabriel ship-to-ship missile is a blend of American and Soviet technology. Israel's high-speed missile boats are derived mostly from British designs. Its avionics mostly use American technology.

Aviation Week quoted "senior [U.S.] officials" in 1976 as concerned that the Israelis could acquire American technology and then swiftly re-export it to other nations, "circumventing the intent of Congress." Israel's burgeoning arms industry was the spur behind the Iranian arms-industry buildup and especially the plans of the AOI—making comparable self-sufficiency to Israel the obvious long-term aim.

Israel's weapons diplomacy is, like the West's, aimed both at acquiring political leverage and earning money. As with France and Britain, money seems to be the main single driving force behind sales promotion. The massive immigration of Israelis in recent years to the United States, Canada, Brazil and elsewhere has weakened the economically depressed country's tax base, making Treasury returns from Israeli arms sales that much more welcome. Foreign sales also reduce procurement costs for Israel's own forces. Israeli Aircraft Industries, which employed four thousand people a decade ago, now gives work to twenty thousand. The Kfir production line alone is an impressive six planes per month: With the Israeli Air Force's own Kfir needs—two hundred—fulfilled in 1979, three hundred of the planes will be made available for export over the next four years or so.

When Israel ordered 250 F-16s, 200 of them to be co-produced in Israel by IAI, the Carter administration forbade co-production, partly because Israel would have competed with the United States and co-production NATO countries in the export of spare parts, a prospect which particularly infuriated Belgium, Holland, Denmark and Norway. But fear of Israeli technological piracy was the principal reason for the U.S. refusal. Israeli Defense Minister Ezer Weizmann told American reporters in 1978 that his government had abandoned hope of reversing that decision, but still hoped to co-produce some of the avionics, and perhaps spare parts for the F-16's and F-15's Pratt and Whitney F-100 engine, with resale rights.

In 1976, the Ford administration had blocked a deal between IAI and United Technologies Inc. (parent firm of Pratt and Whitney) whereby Israel would build components for Pratt and Whitney engines, until Israel agreed to ship total production to the United States. A similar arrangement between UT and IAI for the Israeli production of fuel-control systems, involving classified technology, was passed only on condition that IAI sell their product exclusively to Hamilton Standard, a UT subsidiary; but the fear of the technology being pirated and eventually lost (through intermediaries) to the Soviet Union remained.

When IAI perkily threatened to cancel a purchase of Samsons—rocket-powered decoys for F-4 training—unless some components could be made in Israel, the State Department vetoed co-production and Israel backed down. A similar request for co-production on Hughes data-links for electro-optically guided weapons was also refused by a wary OMC, and "discreet elements" in the keying control were removed before export of the links to Israel.

Both the Pentagon and the State Department vetoed a request by IAI's Taman division to manufacture 25 per cent of the entire production run of Litton inertial precision-guided weapons-control systems for the F-4, along with another whereby Israel would have made armor-piercing shells for 105mm. and 155mm. cannons. Israel was further refused the right to buy indium antimonide, an alloy which would have enabled the Jewish state to duplicate exactly the detection system of the AIM-9L in the Shafrir-3—and then undersell Raytheon on world markets. Limits were put on the number of components Israel could manufacture for the Ford 2-B RPV (Remotely Piloted Vehicle), which has numerous battle-field applications, and for a Hughes communication system for Army command and control.

Overall, in 1977, reporters found especial irritation at the Pentagon that some of the U.S. technology which Israel is selling in competition with the U.S. and its allies was acquired through ten-figure gifts of grant aid made to Israel by a pliant Congress. The AFL-CIO also began to get agitated about the export of jobs and loss of U.S. markets. *Aviation Week*, the voice of the U.S. aerospace industry, said: "There is a growing trend for the Israelis to use product purchases as a lever to obtain concessions from a vendor, particularly where technology is involved, and in some cases to use political leverage."

In 1976, Israel sold Israeli-made U.S. radar warning receivers, radio jamming equipment and other electronic warfare gadgetry to Greece, Turkey and Taiwan, exploiting American embargoes on this equipment for those countries and undercutting U.S. suppliers. Pentagon sources complained that Israel was selling military radio transceivers worldwide in competition with the more expensive American original. Some of the Israeli production went to Arab countries, through middlemen in Germany and Brazil—presumably because it is easier for the Israelis to jam systems they know. (At the 1979 Paris Air Show, Israeli officials actually gave briefings on the Kfir fighter, the Picket shoulder-fired missile and other weapons systems to Egyptian and Saudi military visitors, but presumably not with sales intentions.)

Israel has further angered American officials and unions by trying to impose a boycott on the sale of some American weapons systems by the American manufacturer: This is done by a clause in some Israeli purchase contracts denying the vendor the right to sell the product to any country where Israel does not maintain a diplomatic staff. This was to have been the case with the Litton inertial-guidance system, chosen over competing bids from Lear Siegler (which produces the weapons delivery system for the A-4) and Singer-Kearfott. Following complaints from industry, the U. S. Government has since ruled the Israeli boycott provisions unacceptable.

Near East Report, the organ of the chief Israeli lobbying organization on Capitol Hill, responded to criticisms in 1977 by noting that Israel had repaid, in part, American arms generosity by supplying classified Soviet equipment to the United States. Since Israel was the only American arms client that regularly went to war with sophisticated equipment, no other U.S. arms client could match this. In an editorial, *Near East Report* said: "The giant Galaxy transport planes that brought weapons to Israel during the 1973 war emergency airlift did not return home empty. They carried captured Soviet weapons systems for U.S. military experts to inspect at the Aberdeen testing grounds in Maryland. To this day, most of America's expertise on Soviet conventional weaponry comes from Israel's experience—and cooperation—with the U.S. military." The journal identified some of the systems as being the MiG-21, the Su-7, the Su-11, certain surface-to-air missiles, tanks, armored personnel carriers, antiaircraft artillery and antitank missiles.

CBS, reporting on the Israeli arms-export industry in 1976, claimed that Israel had already sold $250 million worth of Gabriels and Gabriel-IIs. With a 25-mile range, these are thought to be as good as the Soviet Styx missile, and a third, more advanced version is currently under development. The network also said that IAI was offering co-production rights on the Kfir to many countries, and was on the point of selling two squadrons of Kfirs to Austria—as the firm ultimately did, defeating the competition from Sweden's Viggen. In the eighties, Israel will market the (still developmental) Arieh ("lion") attack plane, which will probably have the same Motoren und Turbinen Union engines as the Tornado. Michael Parks, then the respected Mideast correspondent of the Baltimore *Sun*, reported in a censored dispatch from Israel that the Austrians sought twenty-eight Kfirs, including four for training and attrition, for an overall cost with support charges of about $200 million.

Before Carter turned thumbs down on the Israeli plan to sell twenty-four Kfirs to Ecuador, the government had earlier rapped Israel for selling six Super-Mystères re-equipped with Pratt and Whitney engines to Honduras without prior U.S. approval. To compensate Israel for the loss from selling Mirages instead of Kfirs to Ecuador, Mr. Carter added $250 million to Israeli military aid for fiscal 1978, holding the announcement for Premier Menachem Begin's visit to Washington in July 1977. The Israeli lobby in Washington maintained pressure on the White House to reconsider its ban on state-of-the-art weapons for Latin America, and Ecuadorian officials even asked a visiting Rosalynn Carter, in June, to take up the Kfir issue with her husband. But this apparently was a bluff: Israel had already offered Ecuador the earlier-mentioned French-engined Neshers—with the new Kfir equipment added; being used planes, these were cheaper for Ecuador, which was glad to accept.

The United States did give permission for the Kfirs with their General Electric engines to be sold to Austria, and Israel agreed to submit for U.S. approval a list of countries where it hoped to sell the aircraft. (Tel Aviv was informed that no markets in Latin America would be approved.) Pentagon experts were puzzled at Austria's choice of the Kfir, however, since it is not an all-weather fighter and therefore unsuitable for any European country, especially a mountainous one with a bitter winter. A Pentagon source also told the writer that the Austrian Kfirs carried heat-seeking missiles—Austria is forbidden such a system under its peace treaty. But that would be a subject for Soviet, not American, complaint. It was about the time of the Austrian sale that the remarkable, American-born Al Schwimmer resigned as president of IAI, to be succeeded by Gabriel Gidor, a forty-six-year-old Hungarian who had been the Israeli Air Force's head of maintenance before becoming IAI's vice-president in charge of manufacturing.

Of even more concern to Washington than some of Israel's conventional arms sales was Israel's nuclear-weapons program and its possible export role. Thirteen U.S. senators headed by Abraham Ribicoff of Connecticut were refused permission to visit the Dimona nuclear station in November 1976. They sought to examine safeguards in connection with Dr. Kissinger's promise of U.S. nuclear reactors for Israel and Egypt; the Israeli intention seemed to be to get *both* deals canceled. Part of the concern over Israeli nuclear-weapons capacity came from the growing Israeli link with South Africa, another "nuclear-capable" country, following the visit to Israel by South Africa's Premier Balthazar Johannes Vorster that year.

To many outside observers, including many Jewish Americans, the visit came as a shock. Vorster spent two years in the penitentiary during World War Two for Nazi activities and had been an avid exponent of books of Nazi theory in the thirties. But observers in Israel noted a consonance of theories between the Israelis and the Afrikaners: Both were a self-segregating people, believing themselves divinely chosen. Vorster and then-Premier Yitshak Rabin pledged each other mutual support in critical international fora. Jerusalem spokesmen actually talked of a "two outcasts" policy.

By late 1976, Israel's diplomatic, commercial and military ties with South Africa were being expanded rapidly. Between 1972 and 1976, trade between the two countries tripled, and Israeli Government spokesmen said it would triple again by 1978 or 1979. The first two of six missile patrol boats were delivered to a South African naval mission in Israel, along with American-designed but Israeli-built electronic warfare equipment, and huge quantities of machine guns and Uzi submachine guns. The last of the six missile boats was delivered in 1978. South Africa has also purchased undisclosed quantities of Shafrir missiles and is co-producing the Gabriel-II naval missile. It has expressed interest in the Kfir. Israeli volunteers went to join South African forces fighting nationalists in Namibia. Earlier, with U.S. approval, Israel had sent counterinsurgency instructors to help the South African forces in Angola in 1975.

The *Sun's* correspondent Parks reported in 1976:

> The expanding ties between the two countries run even deeper than the multimillion-dollar trade deals and the semisecret arms pacts, with the establishment of a broad network of intergovernmental committees, joint Israeli-South African cooperation and military consultations.

Israel is known to be training South Africans to handle the weapons systems Pretoria is buying. About fifty South African naval officers and sailors are reported to be training at a base near Tel Aviv to operate the 420-ton patrol boats and their sea-to-sea Gabriel missiles, the first of which will be delivered in January [1977] with more to follow.

In addition, senior South African staff officers have begun holding military seminars with Israelis, now that they are effectively barred from participating in such conferences in the United States and Britain.

If South Africa buys the two squadrons of . . . Kfirs, which . . . can be used for both air-superiority fighting and ground attacks, far more extensive working relations are expected between the Israeli and South African military.

The two countries are also cooperating in energy. Pretoria is helping Israel go over from oil to coal for power, by supplying 40,000 tons of coal a month for the Hadera station, thus more than replacing the coal lost by Israel's first Sinai withdrawal. According to a London *Economist* report: "Should there be an oil embargo, South Africa will let Israel have as much coal as it wants. In time of war, the coal convoys will be escorted to their destination by joint South African-Israeli naval forces."

By 1978, Israel was modernizing South Africa's 150 Centurion tanks, notably by installing new armor plate. IAI and two Israeli corporations, Tadiran and Elvit, were selling South Africa complete radar stations, electronic fences, antiguerrilla infiltration alarm systems, communications systems, computers and night-vision devices. Israel was by then also providing Pretoria with 105mm. self-propelled howitzers, air-to-air missiles and antitank missiles.

South Africa supplies Israel not only with coal but with much-needed steel for the Merkava (Chariot) tank, and is helping fund development of a copter-carrying missile vessel. This will have a range of up to 7,000 nautical miles (an odd requirement for an Israeli ship) and carry a crew of sixty. South Africa is to receive the first "four or five" produced, intelligence sources say. Five thousand Israelis have immigrated to South Africa, including some with military-industry skills.

This cooperation did not spring up overnight. As far back as 1967, when de Gaulle clamped his own arms embargo on Israel, it was South Africa that supplied the spare parts for Israel's Mirages. Frequently being paired in UN resolutions condemning racism has helped bring Jerusalem and Pretoria closer together. Also important has been the presence of 120,000 South African Jews, whose annual contributions to Israel of $20 million—nearly $170 per person—have made South African Jewry second only in importance to Israel to American Jewry. South African Jews were active in building the new commercial contacts, which often involved exchanging Israeli weapons for South African raw materials. Many Israelis, including former Foreign Minister Abba Eban, are South African-born.

Parks quoted a Jewish leader from South Africa as saying in Jerusalem: "Israelis have begun to appreciate that Zionism and Afrikanerdom are very close as homeland philosophies." Parks added:

> Jerusalem has already received virtually blanket clearance to sell Pretoria whatever it requires regardless of normal U.S. restrictions prohibiting the transfer of weapons systems and parts without Washington's permission.

The Carter administration soon moved to make it clear that U.S. approval *would* be needed, and would not be given where U.S. components were involved, as with the Kfir. That year—1976—Pretoria announced an increase in its defense budget from $1.5 to $1.87 billion. An "influx" of Israeli nuclear physicists into South Africa was reported by the Washington *Post*. As a gesture of goodwill, a twenty-two-year-old former Israeli tank commander, convicted of raping two South African women, was released after serving only seven months of a six-year sentence and returned to Israel in the company of a visiting Israeli general.

In February 1978, Israel's Finance Minister, Simcha Ehrlich, made an official visit to South Africa. Ostensibly, he was to discuss Israel's unfavorable $28 million trade balance with South Africa, but this modest figure does not take the arms trade into account (or the fact that about half of all South African diamonds pass through Israel for polishing by experts). In April 1978, Israel informed the UN that it would conform with the body's mandatory arms embargo on South Africa; but like France when making a similar assurance, Israel said it would fulfill the huge backlog of orders it had accepted and would "honor" co-production agreements.

In 1978, Israel sold eleven Bell 205A helicopters to a "client in Singapore," after getting approval from a suitably fooled OMC in Washington. The 205As, civilian versions of the troop-carrying Hueys, never got near the Malacca Straits. They soon turned up in Rhodesia, via South Africa, and—militarized—were used in attacks on neighboring Zambia

A third member of the "outcasts" axis—a fourth, if Rhodesia is counted as a nation—appears to be the Kuomintang regime on Taiwan. The New York *Times* reported in 1977 that Taipei was buying Gabriel missiles and seeking Kfirs to replace F-104s and some F-5Es, following Washington's refusal to sell Harpoon missiles and reluctance to sell F-16s in order not to offend Peking. Taiwan's outdated Navy had bought patrol boats from the United States but was reportedly seeking ASW (antisubmarine warfare) technology from Israel. Israeli technicians were later reported at the Taiwanese naval port of Kaohsiung, helping install the Gabriels.

Taiwan had already called on Israeli assistance in 1976. Then, under pressure from Peking, MIT had terminated—six months early—a program for training Taiwanese in designing and building inertial guidance systems. As well as navigating aircraft and ships, such systems are also used for targeting long-range missiles. But the Taiwanese engineers were thought to have acquired enough know-how to build inertial-guidance navigators, since the following year a team at the Chung Shan Institute of Science and Technology near Taipei were reportedly installing, with Israeli assistance, such a system on their locally made Hsiung Feng medium-range surface-to-surface missile.

As with Jerusalem's links to Pretoria, its links to Taipei were not new. Taiwan had bought Shafrirs in 1973, and other arms deals had been bruited since. Discretion was maintained, since Taiwan depends heavily on Saudi Arabia and Kuwait for oil and exports labor to Saudi Arabia. Israel could always respond to critics by pointing out that, if Sino-Soviet relations got any worse, Taiwan might well successfully turn to Moscow for arms. Observers also noted that the United States certainly does not regard the Taipei regime in anything like the same negative light as the regime in Pretoria.

During the Weizmann visit to Washington in 1978, Pinchas Lussman, director general of the Israeli Ministry of Defense, said his government had requested U.S. authorization to sell Kfirs to Taiwan. Taiwan was thought to be seeking at least forty aircraft—two squadrons—and the Kfir was regarded as the front-runner in the sales competition, because it has the same J79 engine as the 104 it would replace. But later that year, under Saudi pressure, Taipei canceled its request for Kfirs, for an estimated loss to Israel of $325 million. The Carter administration then responded favorably to Israel's own request to be able to sell up to sixty of the planes to Taiwan, with a White House spokesman noting that "we understand that Taiwan is no longer interested." Israel said it still hoped to change Taiwan's mind. A sixty-plane deal would be worth about half a billion dollars.

Yet another group of arms customers acquired by Israel in 1976 was the Christian Lebanese forces fighting the Palestinians in Lebanon. In July that year, the Christian port of Jounieh was closed to all other ships for days while the Israeli Navy brought in armor and guns. Christian forces brandished M-16s with their serial numbers and insignia scraped off the stock and leather sling. Earlier, Israeli weapons had reached the Christians through Larnaca, Cyprus and Athens, with the connivance of fanatically anti-Muslim EOKA-B Greek terrorists on Cyprus. The chief Lebanese gunrunners were said to be Catholic ex-President Camille Chamoun and Charbel Cassis, a Maronite monk with an Israeli visa who performs sacerdotal functions for the small Maronite community in Israel. Saudi aid to the Christians—reportedly as much as $200 million—petered off when the Israeli connection began.

Beirut was awash with rumor: that the Israelis were also selling captured Soviet weaponry to confuse the issue; that Israel was acting as a conduit for the CIA; and so on. Perhaps the fullest story of the operation came from Maxim Ghilan, an incredibly well-informed Paris-based Israeli editor and former Stern Gang guerrilla. Writing in his monthly *Israel and Palestine,* Ghilan said that a West German merchant had come to Israel in February or March 1976 to buy Soviet weapons for the Falangist forces. Former Skorzeny lieutenant Gerhard Mertins has denied to the author that he was that man; but Ghilan describes the merchant as being "known for his reactionary, even Nazi politics." The merchant sought Soviet howitzers, carbines, antiaircraft artillery, machine guns and ammunition, both for the Lebanese Falange and for anti-Communist guerrillas in Angola.

Israel, according to Ghilan, refused to sell Soviet arms, or any arms for Angola, but offered NATO weapons if the United States approved. Although Israel's ally South Africa favored the Angolan delivery, Israel apparently sought to signal Moscow that if it would continue to refraim from intervening in Lebanon, Israel would now refrain from aiding the Angolan anti-Communists. Not sending Soviet arms was also intended to avoid embarrassment to the Russians. Ghilan says the United States approved the Israeli sale of NATO weapons and that the German filled three "rather big" freighters with them. Once again according to Ghilan, discreet Arab pressure then persuaded the State Department to forbid any further deliveries. The Israelis then reacted by implementing a naval blockade of the Lebanese coast, abducting two left-wing Lebanese from one ship, the *Hermes,* and six Palestinians aboard an Egyptian freighter, the *Abu Washid.*

During the first week of August 1976, Premier Rabin informed Israeli editors on an unpublishable basis of Israel's operations in Lebanon. Then, apparently, the blockade was stepped up. Israeli frogmen sunk the *Athena* in the port of Tyre. Other arms ships for left-wing forces were intercepted and their cargoes sent to Jounieh "with the full knowledge and connivance of the Syrian naval authorities," Ghilan reported.

Then, in 1978, Israel invaded and occupied southern Lebanon for several months, and was thus able to establish a direct arms channel to its Lebanese allies.

In early 1978, despite pressure from Presidents Carter and Sadat, Israel stepped up its military aid to the Soviet-backed Communist junta in Ethiopia, where it had retained a small team of flight mechanics servicing F-5s—an American plane which the Israeli Air Force itself does not fly. Tel Aviv began sending in cluster bombs, napalm, ammunition and spare parts, and built adaptors to enable the F-5s to use the bombs and napalm canisters. The notion of Israel's supporting a Soviet satellite matched with the fact that Iraq—which supports the Eritrean dissidence in Ethiopia—allowed the Soviet Air Force to refuel at Baghdad during its airlift of weapons to Addis Ababa to help put down both the Somali and Eritrean dissidences.

Poker-faced, Begin told Carter in a telephone conversation that Israel's support of Ethiopia was "historic," going back to "the Queen of Sheba and Solomon." But in February, Defense Minister Moshe Dayan said in Geneva that the reason was that "we want very much to retain good relationships with the countries along the Red Sea." He also noted that Israel had, after all, never supported Somalia—which belongs to the Arab League. Later, Ethiopia expelled the Israeli technicians.

Perhaps the fastest-developing aspect of the Israeli arms industry is avionics, a field which lends itself to less noticeable sales than aircraft, but one that is just as lucrative. Three companies dominate the industry, with 80 per cent of production by value. They are Elta, MBT (both subsidiaries of the government-owned IAI) and Tadiran. Elta, whose plant is at Ashdod, developed the systems for the Gabriel missile. A division of Elta called Tamam produces North American Rockwell inertial systems. Elta itself manufactures airborne tracking radars under license from France's Thomson-CSF. Under director Moshe Orbasse, Elta now also makes systems of its own design, including airborne computers which, it is claimed, consume 25 per cent less power than U.S. computers.

MBT—"Plant B" in Hebrew—also works on the Gabriel systems, including final assembly of the missile, its engines and the warhead, and on the fire-control systems of the Kfir; it has the contract to overhaul Hawk missiles. Situated at Yehud near Tel Aviv, its two thousand employees include about six hundred professional engineers.

Tadiran is the manufacturer of an early-warning RPV (Remotely Piloted Vehicle) with a 14-foot wingspan almost unnoticeable on radar screens. A squadron of six of the pilotless planes with their ground support and radar-analysis equipment was offered to foreign buyers at a Washington show in 1978, for $500,000—about 75 per cent less than American equivalents. The 33-pound payload is said to include the capacity to distinguish between enemy missiles, keeping a battlefield watch for friendly fighters and fighter-bombers.

Other avionics concerns include AEL Israel Ltd., Elbit, and Elron—founded by "Uzi" Ghalil, designer of the Uzi submachine gun. Israeli Electro-Optical Industry Ltd. manufactures HUDs (head-up displays) for fighter cockpits, designed by Britain's Marconi. "El-Op" also produces a pirated "Israeli" version for the Kfir with four modes—two for air-to-surface missiles, one for air-to-air missiles and one for navigation. The firm, founded in the thirties by a German refugee who had been general manager of Zeiss Ikon, also makes gunsight cameras, laser range finders and night-vision devices.

Motorola Israel is a wholly owned subsidiary of the parent company, as is Astronautics C.A. Ltd., which makes cockpit instruments. Motorola produces counterinsurgency warning systems, as does Electronics Corporation of Israel. Some of these have been sold to the settler regimes in South Africa and Rhodesia.

POSTFACE

Major Barbara, Where Are You?

War today is a luxury that only
the weak and poor can afford.
ZBIGNIEW BRZEZINSKI

Miles copeland recalls a lecture given by Nasser's vice-president, Zaharia Mohieddin, at the Egyptian War College. Mohieddin, the leader of a weak country who scurried to the UN in 1967 to try to avoid war in the Middle East, and who was upstaged by Israel's spectacular blitzkrieg on his country, said: "In the game of nations, there are no winners, only losers. The objective of each player is not so much to win as to avoid losing."

As in track athletics, all the players are unequal in ability. It is not only a question of power—planes, missiles, guns—but of different political systems. There is, for instance, a clear advantage in negotiating with a country, like the Soviet Union, in which decisions are taken by few people and can be adhered to. Such countries also have greater negotiating freedom. There is an inherent disadvantage in the way Western countries in general, and the United States in particular, disperse power between the executive and the legislature, and indeed between government and the press, which largely controls the public. This disadvantage is shared both by us and by those who negotiate with us.

In a much-quoted phrase, Alexis de Tocqueville wrote: "I have no hesitation in saying that in the control of a society's foreign affairs, democratic governments do appear decidedly inferior to others." In America, which the itinerant Frenchman had in mind, post-Watergate congressional control of foreign policy has hampered all recent Presidents. The argument *for* greater congressional oversight is that, in open debate, compromise and reason will triumph; but in reality, while trade-offs between different vested interests may make for consensus policy, they do not always make for intelligent policy. Congress and press interreact in an orgy of emotions. As Tocqueville also said: "In politics, the tendency of a democracy to obey its feelings rather than its calculations [is a] weakness." Richard J. Barnet of the Institute of Policy Studies has written of the growing feeling—which he himself does not entirely share—

that "ambitious politicians ready to pander to the prejudices of the mob are . . . given to overreacting and underreacting to foreign crises."

What Congress and the public—and often the daily press—tend to miss, above all, is the "big picture," the interrelationship of a dozen or more international problems. Writing in *Foreign Affairs* back in 1973, Dr. Brzezinski noted that "the politics of interdependence—largely a consequence of America's economic and social intimacy with Western Europe and Japan—are beginning to overshadow the politics of confrontation with the Communist world."

The United States is dependent on imports for twenty-six of the thirty-six main basic raw materials for industry, including the arms industry. The sources are more in the Third World than in Europe or Japan. Brzezinski again: "One may wonder whether the balance-of-power approach provides an adequate response to a world dominated by rapid change." Brzezinski himself sees "safety" in the growing multipolarity—hence his exuberant Sinophilia. Yet at a time when the United States is more and more intimately involved with societies which were never more than exotic pawns in the recent past, post-Vietnam America is increasingly, if not isolationist, at least escapist. This in turn induces skepticism among policymakers. Says Barnet in *The Roots of War:* "The picture of the average American which the national security manager carries around with him in his head . . . is of a private, apathetic fellow, with fundamentally peaceful and decent instincts, who is moved not by reason but by theater."

Brzezinski has talked to reporters of his view of a world dominated by nationalisms and by a new awareness of human rights, in which the "average" person is "young, poor, newly literate, newly liberated, newly urbanized and ripe for [political] mobilization." Human rights are "the genuine historical inevitability of our time," and the current surge of Islamic conservatism from Libya to Pakistan is an overreaction to the crass materialism perceived as permeating the new consumer societies. Even Kissinger, who sees the world in more nineteenth-century terms, told an audience in 1977 that "anticommunism is not enough: There must be a response to legitimate social and economic aspirations."

Today's Americans are less prejudiced about "foreigners" than generations past: But all things are relative, and clearly America's education in world affairs has not kept up with the pace of "rapid change" to which Brzezinski has referred. This is an increasingly socialistic and moralistic world, dominated by exasperatingly self-righteous Third World "strongmen," with Islam—the fastest-growing major faith—markedly more puritan and fundamentalist than the Christianity of the West. How much has

American public opinion kept pace with what these factors involve? How has academia adapted to preparing the next generation for the political market forces with which they must live?

The Kennedy urge to save the world is no longer in fashion. The crusaders of yore have furled their standards. This is not just the result of the Vietnam experience: The world is just too slow at being saved, by America's impatient standards. It is this which has helped push the game of weapons to the fore, for the game is no longer the crude battlefield slugfest understood by Napoleon or Caesar. It involves more poker, and it is tempting to see it therefore as a game in which America, the league leader in computers, should score handily. Yet the game is not only poker, but chess, and the "queens"—the superpowers—cannot be put at risk at all: Moscow refused to fight for Cuba in 1962, because it dared not expose itself to direct confrontation with the United States, and the United States, for the same reason, probably would not willingly fight for South Korea tomorrow. Direct confrontation in Europe is almost unthinkable, while Moscow's Mideast protégés could not be allowed to occupy Israel, just as U.S. forces could not occupy North Vietnam—since such situations could bring about direct U.S.-Soviet confrontation just as much as warfare in Europe.

Hence, the paradox: Governments of past eras were criticized for spending on World War One enough treasure to build a hospital in every city; but at least arms were made to be used. President Johnson noted once that "the cost of acquiring and maintaining one squadron of supersonic aircraft diverts resources that could build and maintain a university." Yet to suggest that sophisticated arms are produced today for the primary purpose of making war would be naive or specious. Today, expenditure on weapons of the sort which major powers deploy is immensely greater than in the past, but with no intention of their being used, only "expended politically," in George Brown's phrase.

Today, a defense writer is tempted to read, not Liddell Hart or Caesar's campaign diaries, but mythology or Machiavelli. We write of Armageddon, while thinking of Minuteman as simply a nuclear-tipped rattling saber. Arms have acquired a political life of their own, manipulating man himself as a sort of misguided missile. Arms are probably less of a threat to peace than to our economies, if we are a poor nation, while disarmament may be a threat to our economies if we are rich. Yet to be prepared to die for what Jimmy Carter would call "our nation" is still an honorable stance, and I cannot die for America unless an armorer gives me an F-15 or a guided-missile destroyer or an M-16 with which to make my willingness apparent; so "beating up" on the armorers is somewhat hypocritical.

But, you say, what about the excess? Okay, you concede, nodding your head—okay for a strong army, etc., and adequate defenses, and even a little left over in case the Marines have to seize the wellheads in the Gulf. But why so much, you ask? Why have the most brilliant advances in science gone to the R & D of armaments? The reason lies in the new role of arms as political weapons. The United States is no more likely to be discouraged by its experience in Iran than Moscow has been by its similar humiliations in Egypt and Indonesia. The role of Western countries in China's current expansion of defense spending—Rolls-Royce aircraft engines, French and British aircraft, U.S. computers, German technology—emphasizes the strangely nonmilitary, almost entirely political role of most arms and arms transfers today. China, after all, still believes that capitalism should be destroyed, and U.S. capitalism most of all. Yet our response is to flick out a brochure of antitank missiles like a humidor of cigars, and say "Have some of mine."

The time has come to try to bring together the raveled skeins of the game of weapons. The subject is genuinely confusing. More reading is involved than for a standard major history—books, countless articles, hundreds of regular periodicals, still more hundreds upon hundreds of newspaper stories; agency, think-tank and congressional reports that arrive, inches thick, each week; reference works; and countless other documents. What is perplexing is how all the skeins intertwine. Which aspects of the order of battle are military, and which are diplomatic, or economic, or just "political"? Are arms industries predominantly industrial—economic—or political, or military? If politics dictate weapons, then weapons dictate politics.

The subject is rife with contradictions. A pious person might spend his life designing "city-busting" warheads with a clear conscience: He can be reasonably sure that they will only be fired across a green baize table in Geneva, where they will—he hopes—win a peaceful victory for America. An informed pacifist in Los Angeles could legitimately write to his congressman opposing the closedown of the local B-1 assembly line, secure in the thought that the B-1 will not increase the chances of war (and might increase the chances for a better SALT agreement—détente, peace-in-our-time), while shutting down the B-1 program unquestionably causes unemployment, therefore real suffering. Viewed "seriously," however, even SALT and MBFR (the Mutual and Balanced Force Reductions talks) are only methods for closing the stable door after the Four Horsemen of the Apocalypse have fled. What has changed is that we are no longer so uncomfortable with the notion of having the

Four Horsemen, now largely reduced to a quartet of bluffers, abroad among us.

Talking of SALT reminds us that the Wimbledon center court of the game of weapons is the nuclear standoff. The name of the game, Mohieddin said, was not so much to win as to avoid losing. Phil Stanford of the Center for Defense Information puts it this way:

> Deterrence, that is, preventing the use of nuclear weapons by either side, is a mutual undertaking. Under the doctrine of deterrence, it is, in fact, to the advantage of both superpowers for the other side to have a nuclear strike force that can survive any conceivable attack and still destroy the attacker. It is crucial that the other side should not feel that its nuclear forces are subject to attack. Otherwise, in a crisis it might get nervous and attack first. Therefore, the more perfect the other side's nuclear weapons are, the safer both sides will be . . .
>
> Bombers are slow, and because of the threat of enemy air defenses, somewhat uncertain. Fixed land-based missiles—ICBMs—take only thirty minutes to strike their targets, but because they can be located by satellite, they are subject to attack by enemy missiles. Only nuclear-missile submarines are both devastating and, when they are hiding in the ocean, virtually invulnerable for all practical purposes. Therefore, it is logical for each side not only to build up its own nuclear submarine force, but to encourage the other side to do the same.

Fred Charles Ikle, the Republican who formerly headed the Arms Control and Disarmament Agency, has put it the other way round in *Foreign Affairs*:

> If we can eliminate the vulnerability of our strategic arms to surprise attack, we will have broken the vicious circle: that they must be ready for prompt launching because they are vulnerable, and that they are vulnerable because they are ready. Furthermore, should the Russians come to agree with us, we could jointly decide to replace the doomsday catapults invented in the fifties with arms that are incapable of being launched swiftly.

We shake our heads. How could we achieve such a high degree of trust in the sanctity of a U.S.-Soviet agreement? Yet the hawks can be equally naive, as many doves have happily noted: For instance, in a 1978 article on doomsday scenarii, former White House science adviser G. B Kistiakowsky said too much attention was being paid to Soviet writings such as those of Marshal Vassily Sokolowsky claiming the Soviet Union could win a nuclear war. "Should he tell his juniors they cannot win a future nuclear war?" Professor Kistiakowsky asks—noting that, in Stalin's time, to have suggested this would have led to Sokolowsky being "stood up against the wall and shot for . . . heresy." A surprise attack, Kistiakowsky claims, is impossible, since if our space sensors were put out of action, this would herald an attack and invite a pre-emptive strategic nuclear strike by the United States.

But concern remains. In 1978, John Kenneth Galbraith noted: "We all know that, at budget time, Soviet power and perfidy show a sharp seasonal increase. None can doubt tension is helpful for the war industry." Current informed predictions, however, are for a slowdown in the Soviet economy; this, and continued, unresolved agricultural problems, would seem to make Soviet adventurism on the grand scale less likely than ever.

But many doves, like most professional diplomats, tend to adulterate their analyses with heavy doses of wishful thinking. Defense secretaries are paid to warn us of the worst. In 1977, Secretary Harold Brown circulated a film, *The Price of Peace and Freedom*, emphasizing the Soviet threat and military buildup, to U.S. military facilities. The film was made by the right-wing American Security Council, with assistance from the AFL-CIO, and the ASC sold the prints to the Pentagon for $25,000. Yet from Room 3E880 in the Pentagon, seated at the desk which once belonged to General Pershing, Brown's fourteen-hour days are mostly spent on lesser crises than on direct confrontation with Moscow. With Bach and Beethoven playing in the background, he peers owlishly at a visitor and says caustically: "Nuclear war is the least likely contingency we face." He agrees with Kissinger that fear of Soviet missile throw-weight—the one clear Soviet advantage in the nuclear standoff—is a "phony issue" (Kissinger's words), and that even SALT is essentially a psychological exercise. "Both sides have more than they need for inflicting unacceptable damage on the other after absorbing a first strike," he notes. If SALT II was intended to "eliminate" the threat of war, would the Russians have agreed to leave out forward systems in Europe?

But are the Russians equally philosophical when they consider the "threat" from the West? The writer asked the late General George Brown if he thought there was any broad-range thinking in the Soviet military, beyond straightforward military planning. Does détente interest them? Said Brown:

> I think that the only thing that is attractive about détente to them is that it might conceivably lead us into a false sense of security. Now, this is the military people I'm talking about. The political leadership, I wouldn't say that about them, because I don't know. But the military guys—I think they are interested in détente only because they think that we will be foolish enough to take it seriously.
>
> I think they must be very proud of the tremendous machine they've built. Four million men under arms, forty thousand tanks. What do we

have—nine or ten thousand? Their Navy has expanded to the point where it is over the oceans of all the world now. Take air lift: The air lift they mounted to Angola was superbly done. It was a first-rate operation. It was the first time we had seen them really reach out. Now we have seen it again in Ethiopia.

I think they must be very proud. They have got a good strong military machine and I don't think they are like we are. I don't know anybody, any senior [American] officer in uniform today, who, contrary to the image we may have, is a bit damn interested in seeing a big military machine in the United States, or who is interested in seeing a retention of forces that really are not needed, the acquisition of expensive weapons that are not required to respond to the threat.

I will admit that we don't have that image because the political cartoonists and others take us on about the B-1 being the generals' toy and all this kind of crap, but in point of fact we have to pay for this stuff too. We are taxpayers like everybody else.

But I think the Russians are different. Maybe I can't judge, because I've never met [Soviet chief of staff Marshal] Ogarkov. I tried to invite him over here, but the message never got to him. It got caught up in Moscow—that's another story.

U.S. evaluation of Soviet defense planning is, as Brown implied, facilitated by the very conservatism of the Soviet state and the Soviet mind. "The best guide to what the Russians will do tomorrow," says Arthur J. Alexander of the RAND Corporation, "is what they did yesterday." This tends to mean that when a weapons system has been decided on, after much bureaucratic consideration, it is extraordinarily difficult to persuade the Russians to drop the program by offering to drop an American program in exchange.

Dismantling the nuclear arsenal implies some belief in détente; and because we believe communism is a mistaken political science, we feel justified in our disbelief in détente itself. Concern with possible nuclear war springs mainly from our distrust of a superpower which is also a ruthless dictatorship. But Harvard professor David Riesman, author of *The Lonely Crowd*, says: "In a bipolar nuclear world, we cannot afford to hold on to a simple, straightforward, universalistic moral standard." The bear and the eagle are not really in the ring, Riesman contends; instead, "Tribalism within nation-states and among nation-states remains the most powerful force at work in the world today."

"Each weapon put up for discard from the nuclear arsenal," says Paul Warnke, who was Ikle's successor, "looks better than ever before . . . [and] harder to give up." The Carter administration has itself reviewed the triad, through a team under the direction of Russell Murray, assistant Defense secretary for program evaluation and analysis, with input from the NSC. Murray's conclusions are cloaked in caveats, but the implications are that land-based ICBMs might be curtailed in a decade's time because of their uncertain "survivability." The objective, Murray thinks, should remain that of ensuring that the Soviet Union, after a holocaust, would take longer than the United States to recover "the status of a twentieth-century military and industrial power." The study also assumed that any future war would continue on a twenty-four-hours-a-day basis from start to finish, which has never been absolutely true of previous conflicts.

Reviewing the "triad" policy is incumbent on every analyst. The so-called Boston Study Group at MIT has advocated retaining "the half of the present military establishment designed for the defense of the United States and its allies in Europe and Japan. Most of the other half should be phased out" over five to ten years. This is the "Fortress America" theory. The BSG would keep strategic submarines but phase out ICBMs, including the M-X mobile missile, and strategic bombers, including cruise missiles, both land- and air-based strategic weapons being seen as too vulnerable (which is of course Phil Stanford's earlier-mentioned argument for their retention). There would be a two-thirds cut in the Marines and in light army divisions for brush-fire warfare. Aircraft carriers would go from thirteen to three, but there would be more antitank weapons systems. And so on.

Earl Ravenal is less radical, but he also wants forces reduced to those needed to defend the United States, and for the triad to become a diad. There should be "no civilian targeting, even if the enemy strikes first and hits cities." There should also be "no first use" of nuclear weapons.

Because all this is a game in which no one's plans are ever likely to be tested, the uncertainty remains. China plays the two barbarian superpowers off against each other, the two superpowers negotiate SALT II and will later try for SALT III, while liberal voices arise in America for unilateral restraints. Says Ravenal: "Getting rid of surplus killing power would not in itself impose strategic stability . . . Genuine unilateral moves would have to make strategic sense in themselves, so that they could be sustained whether or not they were reciprocated by the other nuclear superpower."

Ravenal admits that reliance on Tridents and cruise missiles would complicate verification, but adds: "Verification is not an independent objective of arms control. It is only a tool." Soviet mobile ICBMs would be the equivalent of our submarine-based weapons, with our SLBMs gradually becoming accurate enough to supplant our ICBMs.

But "fiddling with the triad" is still academic. General Alexander Haig has said: "The components of NATO's triad are not mutually competitive. On the contrary, they are mutually essential. None can replace another; nor can improvements in one be considered to lessen the need for confidence—and balance—in the other two."

For what purpose—if Secretary Brown says nuclear warfare is the "least likely contingency"? Wherefore SALT? The Joint Chiefs, as Senator Culver has noted, could kill SALT II simply by saying they found it "adverse to our national-security interests," but they are not doing so: They play the game of weapons as politically as the politicians. It remains for an Edward Kennedy to rock the boat. He asked a caller in 1978: "Why do we sit down and talk about numbers of launchers, bans on systems? Why are we meeting on Saturday morning talking about these issues when we know what each side would do if there was a confrontation?" Is SALT's only nongame rationale a more "practical" use of equity and skills—civilizing the Pentagon's engineers?

The military is paid to be uncertain about our security, and the French note that détente, after all, also means "trigger"; probably nothing has raised military uncertainties more in the late seventies than the apparent Soviet breakthrough in particle-beam technology, implying a nascent capacity to neutralize our entire triad. But if the Russians are as far ahead of the United States in this field as some American experts think, and given the fact that U.S. strategy calls for deterrence through the threat of "punishment"—unacceptable damage—while Soviet policy stresses deterrence by the denial of an American first-strike capability, consider the following formula for peace:

Moscow announces one day that the Soviet Union is invulnerable. It could destroy our land-based and submarine-based strategic missile launchers aimed at Soviet territory, our SAC bases, our SAC bombers in the air, and so on. And it can intercept *all* our missiles. To prove its point, it suggests that a U.S. Trident fire its full load. The United States, convinced that the challenge would not be made if there was the slightest chance of Soviet lasers etc. not exploding all the American ballistic missiles in the stratosphere, and downing all the cruise missiles short of target, accepts that a nuclear checkmate has been achieved. Unless the Soviet Union actually wants to conquer, and occupy, the United States, which no one believes, the hair trigger of a holocaust has been dismantled. Or, if you prefer—it does sound more reassuring—conceive of American technology overtaking Soviet technology in the laser/particle beam areas, and throwing a similar gauntlet on the Kremlin's doorstep.

But to think such thoughts is to alter the rules of the game. The core of the nuclear standoff remains the two triads, ours and theirs, and the only permissible debate is whether all of the triad is needed to deter a Soviet first strike or to win a second strike of our own. The United States has so far retained its land-based ICBMs, not only because they are vulnerable, therefore not destabilizing, but also because land-based missiles could not be *mutually* abandoned: They are the *first* leg of Russia's triad. They have, nonetheless, on both sides, the least chance of survival. SAC is preserved as the ultimate diplomatic threat rather than for real offense: If eleventh-hour diplomacy fails, and the bombers continue on course, they would be literally overtaken in flight by the ICBMs and the SLBMs. So where does the cruise missile fit? Cruise missiles, too, humming subsonically along like a mule train in a blitzkrieg, would also be overtaken by Minuteman and Trident. Moreover, former Air Force Secretary John L. McLucas has saliently pointed out that engaging the Russians in a cruise-missile race would oblige the United States to undertake a huge air-defense system in mainland America unlike anything that exists at present. Is Congress ready?

What goes through the mind of Jimmy Carter as he pays one of his occasional calls at the national security situation room in the White House basement? Here the staff work twelve-hour shifts and six-day weeks, in the calm atmosphere of a fire station that has not yet had a real fire. The room, these days, lacks the excitement of the time when President Johnson paced the gold carpet, looked at the computer terminals and read some of the Top Secret papers from the safes, to try to second-guess the Viet Cong; but this is probably the closest today's President gets to thinking of doomsday scenarii. As Kistiakowsky says, destruction of America's early-warning satellites—with the intention that U.S. ballistic missiles would not be launched before they were destroyed—would probably be the first Soviet move, followed by destruction of communications satellites, leaving the Poseidon and Trident subs "deaf"; then the navigation satellites—so that surviving missiles would land, say, in the center of Paris instead of on the Odessa docks; then as many Soviet missiles as could get through U.S. defenses would go for the ballistic-missile sites themselves, the command-and-communication centers, the nuclear storage depots, the SAC bomber bases, the aircraft carriers, strategic submarine bases and perhaps submarines at sea, if detectability is achieved. To do all this, as noted earlier, Moscow would have to be reasonably confident that its laser and particle-beam defenses could intercept any incoming U.S. missiles.

It is all, fortunately, unlikely. Only a little over 10 per cent of the U.S. defense budget is concerned with the defense of the United States. The main cost is Europe, although it is hard to see how U.S. reinforcements could arrive in that theater in time to affect the outcome of a war.

"Détente is admittedly far from a modern equivalent to (*sic*) the kind of stable peace that characterized most of the nineteenth century," Kissinger has written; but he added that it has made Europe a less likely threat of conflict—perhaps the least likely.

This is just as well. In classified reports made available to the House Armed Services Committee in 1979, a simulated operation called "Nifty Nugget," played on a Pentagon computer in October 1978, showed that any attempt to "rescue" Europe would probably be a disaster. In "Nifty Nugget," the United States lost 600,000 dead and ran out of ammunition—both in three weeks; the report blamed shortages caused by Israeli resupply five years earlier. Because of another shortage—of 3,500 doctors—130,000 casualties had to be flown to the United States *untreated;* 200,000 reservists could not be found; many who were, arrived in Europe without uniforms; 900,000 American civilians were stranded in the war zone; and the computer itself broke down.

Many hawks, however, do see Moscow's civil-defense preparations as indicative of an expectation of nuclear war involving the superpowers. In decrying this view, the doves are virtually unanimous. Herbert Scoville sees the Russian developments as panicky and purely defensive. Dr. Jeremy Stone notes that under SALT I, both superpowers agreed not to place strategic defenses around their cities, thus implicitly putting them at risk. He sees Moscow as principally concerned with the threat from Peking. How real, Dr. Stone asks, is "civil defense"? The survivors of a nuclear attack would have to live in a "famine" ecology in which mammals and birds would have died, while the hole punched in the ozone layer by a nuclear duel would cause sunburn on those who stayed out of doors for long. A westward drive into Europe would be "suicidal" for Moscow. Scoville's reasoning is similar: "The very concept that Soviet leaders would consciously launch a nuclear strike and accept the destruction of their cities, a large part of their industries and a minimum of 20 million casualties in order to destroy the United States, I find incredible. What would they gain by destroying the United States, when they have essentially wiped out their civilization in order to do it?"

The Soviet Union, says Elmo R. Zumwalt, the former chief of naval operations, and a typical hawk, has a long-term aim—the communization of the world. The United States, he implies with some reason, goes for short-term, mostly reactive objectives. But Zumwalt agrees that the Soviet Union seeks domination without direct involvement in war. He too watches what General Haig has called the "ambiguous situations on the flanks"—proxy wars.

Yet, as of 1979, there are 272,000 U.S. personnel attached to NATO, including 224,000 in Germany. Some Soviet writers have even welcomed this presence as containing German militarism. But many see the U.S. commitment of forces to Germany as essentially planning for the last war rather than the "next" one.

However, nuclear holocausts aside, conflict scenarii do exist in Europe. What will happen to Yugoslavia now that Tito has died at the age of eighty-seven? Tito's has been a government of personality rather than of institutions. Yugoslavia has support from the nonaligned movement, but of what value would that be if a Russian-encouraged Croat secession movement swells? Yugoslavia might be saved by détente; but if Moscow behaves aggressively toward Belgrade, it will do so in the knowledge that it will sacrifice détente only temporarily.

A dissatisfied Turkey faces provocations from Greece, and poverty. Neither NATO ally feels adequately supported by the United States, and Turkey least of all. Has the United States any leverage to solve the Cyprus dispute, when this inevitably means a temporary loss of face by Athens? Will Turkey go "nonaligned"? And Greece? As a new member of the European Community, this would be difficult, but should Andreas Papandreou and the socialists come to power, it would not be unthinkable. As the IISS says, over the long run, the Greco-Turkish dispute over Aegean seabed rights could be a "more explosive and contentious issue than Cyprus."

Both Ankara and Athens are courting the Arab countries, especially "oil" capitals. Both have suffered from oil pricing, and are bankrupt— especially Turkey. Ankara formerly received economic help from Iran, and votes with the Arab states on Middle East issues at the UN; but it is still seen as being only modestly a "Muslim" state, despite the current challenge from the right wing to Atatürk's half-century-old commitment to a lay republic.

The Soviet Union is ambiguous on the Cyprus question; the Communist Party is strong in the Greek sector of the island, and may take over power. Russia has a long history of wars with Turkey—thirteen since 1677, not counting innumerable border skirmishes. Yet U.S. hesitancy during the Iranian revolution, and American defection from Taiwan, have induced second thoughts in many of America's "friends." A Turkish general was quoted in *Harper's* magazine in 1979 as saying: "The trouble with having the United States as an ally is that you never know when the Americans are going to stab themselves in the back."

What of the Soviet threat—of winning without war—to the rest of the European Mediterranean through "Eurocommunism"? In a 1977 speech, Kissinger told his audience:

The solidarity of the great industrial democracies has maintained global security for thirty years. Western collective defense provided the shield behind which the United States, Western Europe and Japan developed the institutions of European unity and the progressive world economic system. All these relationships would be severely jeopardized if Communists came to power in allied governments . . .

It is hard to visualize how the present NATO structure could continue with its exchange of highly classified information, its integrated military planning and political consultation, if Communists had a significant share of power.

The participation of Communist parties in West European governments would force a major change in NATO practices, as occurred temporarily with Portugal, which had to exclude itself from classified discussions within the Organization when its own political future was in doubt . . .

NATO may turn by default into a largely German-American alliance.

What *is* NATO's future? It seems safe to assume that, as long as the Warsaw Treaty exists, so will NATO—and vice versa. The existence of military alliances helps the arms industries, which helps employment, and is essential to weapons diplomacy. Client-states around the world buy the NATO and Warsaw Treaty weaponry and thus help the balance of payments and the recycling of petrodollars, while enhancing the influence which suppliers have. Since NATO and Warsaw Treaty weapons are more political than military, so are the alliances themselves. Should World War Three break out, with missiles crossing each other 800 miles above the waves, what would Western and Eastern Europe be doing? This has never been clear. France and Britain have strategic nuclear weapons, but would be hesitant to use them because they have so few. Using them pre-emptively would leave the user comparatively defenseless. Occupation of territory would be meaningless—even dangerous, because of radiation. Thus weapons are not all even "deterrents." Not surprisingly, in late 1979, the European NATO nations decided to give sole control of the decision to fire the new Pershing-2 nuclear missiles in Germany—and the cruise missiles in Britain, Belgium and Holland—to the United States. And small wonder that France, after two hundred years of uninterrupted defeats in war, wanted to beat the Katangese. Perhaps the Russians enjoyed trouncing the Somalis.

Indeed, conceivably the most interesting aspect of the Soviet switch of sides in the Horn, becoming the protector of Ethiopia and throwing Somalia to the West, was Washington's predictable inability to profit from it. Mused the late General George Brown: "I don't think there was any doubt about our not knowing how to react. But I think what was in their (Soviet) minds was just a game—they saw clearly that they would be on the side of the angels, as well as of a Marxist revolution. The 'aggressors' were the Somalis. The Soviets were going to the assistance of the fellow who was attacked. So in the UN and anywhere else, they were in the right. And if we had armed Somalia, we would have been in the wrong."

U.S. commitment to the defense of Europe and Japan is essentially an economic consideration, as is the U.S. interest in protecting the Persian Gulf area. As NATO loses real importance in the defense tableau, Japan becomes more important. Subic Bay in the Philippines, along with Guam, are evidence of the U.S. role as a Pacific power, and the Trident submarine force is to be based at Bangor, Washington, not Charleston or Norfolk. Perhaps, now, Moscow will cultivate Taiwan and the insular nationalists who must eventually come to power there. Perhaps Moscow, which knows that nationalism is a more powerful force than ideology, will even court Israel while continuing to arm Iraq and Syria. The United States, after all, has full relations with Communist Peking, while continuing to supply arms to Taiwan and refusing arms to China, and while encouraging its allies to arm the Communists.

The real nuclear fears come mainly from the spread of atomic technology to the Third World, a development in which the West is more recklessly involved than the Communist powers. As Riesman says, tribalism—in the confrontation states of the Middle East, in the Persian Gulf, on Vietnam's border, between Somalia and Ethiopia, between whites and blacks in southern Africa, between Chinese and Taiwanese, and in a host of other places—is the dominant world force for conflict in our time. If U.S. forces fight again, it is indeed likely to be in the Third World. Some observers, such as Stephen S. Rosenfeld of the Washington *Post*, welcome this, since winning in small countries would be easier. That is where the natural resources are, Rosenfeld points out, and military action in those areas need not escalate to World War Three.

At least one of our NATO allies already has chosen this route. France has intervened in the civil war in Chad and has helped Mauritania in its attempted annexation of the western Sahara. Its forces protect Djibouti from Somalia, and they intervened—with Belgium and Morocco—to prop up the Mobutu dictatorship in Zaire when the perennial Katangese secession movement came back to life again in 1978. Accused of being "NATO's Cubans," the French argued that they were countering "destabilization" by the Russians and Cubans. The United States gave cautious approval by supplying some logistic help.

It says a great deal about NATO today that its current assertiveness should be in minor African tribal wars, and that there should be substantial disagreement within the Alliance even over this. The "might of the West" is thus presently more exercised with Cuba's military assistance to Ethiopia and Angola and to southern African guerrillas (even though Cuba's African aims are those the West also proclaims—self-determination) than with the Soviet "threat" in central Europe, where there has been no attempt to counter the Warsaw Treaty's vast superiority in armor, which is probably mainly intended to contain Czech- or Hungarian-style nationalist—"tribal"—risings.

The conflictual Third World areas are often the natural consumers of last-generation, "Vietnam era" weaponry, now urgently in need of sale as the state-of-the-art arms of the eighties take over in the major league. Even the more sophisticated use of weapons, to threaten and deter rather than to kill, is now a Third World characteristic too, as the Middle East and the Koreas exemplify. Yet "conventional," nonnuclear weapons always carry the implicit threat of use. The risk of war is greatest where the potential battlefield is exclusively "conventional," and the risk of actual war is what perpetuates the Nixon Doctrine—native self-reliance, with weapons made in the U.S.A. But how long will, say, Korea remain "conventional," and how reluctant would Seoul be to use nuclear arms?

In economic terms, the Pacific must be America's first concern. Japan is the United States' main trading partner, and Korea is the tinderbox on Tokyo's doorstep. But the American relationship with South Korea, notes the IISS, "in some respects . . . resembles that of the United States and Israel, which is not based on any vital strategic importance for American security but on the shared experience of a difficult history." The possibility of détente between North and South Korea, raised by limited negotiations between the two sides in 1979, just might change the extent of the U.S. commitment; it is too early to say. In any event, the planned U.S. troop withdrawal from Korea will not save money, if the forces are merely redeployed, because it is cheaper to have U.S. troops in Korea than in the United States; the withdrawal is political.

There are plenty of conflict scenarii in the Indian Ocean area. On the Afric shore, the Horn is already in flames, and in southern Africa the tinderwood is beginning to crackle. Diego Garcia grows, and will soon harbor Trident subs. France lost Diégo-Suarez to Madagascar, but still has Réunion and Mayotte. Quarrels over the 200-mile ocean border could flare up around many islands, especially if oil is found. The United States and Britain have numerous naval facilities in the area, and the Russians have Chittagong and Vishakhapatnam in India, port rights in Mauritius, Madagascar, Aden, Hoseida and Umm Qasr, along with anchorages near Socotra and the Seychelles.

Conflict scenarii, as noted earlier, are even more numerous in the Gulf,

an Indian Ocean cul-de-sac, while farther afield there is Tamil irredentism in Sri Lanka, and there are Communist uprisings in Malaysia
and Thailand. Most importantly, there is the central conflict over Palestine in the Levant. In the United States, policy here is guided by both
domestic and foreign considerations, and derives from Jewish sufferings
under Nazism; Soviet policy is purely related to foreign affairs, and
derives from exploiting the iniquities inflicted on the Palestinians by Jewish colonists. The United States is the link between the two natural adversaries, Israel—seen in Washington as a sort of burdensome dependent, whose affection is bought and assured—and Egypt—seen as a
chosen friend, but only for so long as a powerful moderate remains in
power. Will the historic compromise be a mini-Palestine in the West
Bank and Gaza, federated to Jordan, with the Hashemite kingdom eventually becoming the Republic of Palestine, thus "solving" the problem
once and for all? For the interim period, could there be demilitarized
zones, defense guarantees by the superpowers? Or is another war, or
wars, in the offing first? In the Middle East, it is central to the policies of
both the United States and the Soviet Union that neither side should
clearly win when fighting occurs. To Washington, another Israeli territorial conquest would be disastrous, leaving more problems to solve than
those that exist already, while a threatened conquest of Israel by its
neighbors would raise enormous pressure on Washington to increase still
further the level of arms assistance to Tel Aviv, probably with more
nuclear-capable tactical weapons, which in turn could suscitate World
War Three by injecting the nuclear component.

Counterbalancing the arms won for Israel by the Israeli lobby in the
past have been petrodollar-recycling supplies to Saudi Arabia and especially Iran, with more modest exports to Egypt, Jordan and Syria, supple-
mented by the NATO allies. The supposition has been that Saudi and
Iranian weapons could be transferred—albeit illegally, under the Foreign
Military Sales Act—to the three hard-pressed confrontation states to
avert Israeli territorial gains. But the United States has little control over
Israel or its other friends when conflict starts, and Moscow is equally
hobbled with its protégés.

Israel is not alone in risking a war between the superpowers. Had U.S.
technicians remained in Iran, for instance, they could have found themselves helping to manage a war one day against pro-Soviet Iraq. But if
Israel is not unique in creating this concern, it is the country most often
mentioned as having the itchiest finger on the trigger of regional conflict.
Kissinger, who spent more time in Israel than any other American states-
man in recent times, came well prepared for the issue by the research
work for his first book, *A World Restored*. As though writing on his prob-

lems with Golda Meir and Itzhak Rabin—or Carter's later, with Begin—
Kissinger said then:

> It is characteristic of a policy which bases itself on purely military con-
> siderations to be immoderate in triumph and panicky in adversity . . .
>
> The logic of war is power, and power has no inherent limit. The logic of
> peace is proportion and proportion implies limitation. The success of war
> is victory; the success of peace is stability. The conditions of victory are
> commitment; the condition of stability is self-restraint. The motivation of
> war is extrinsic: the fear of an enemy. The motivation of peace is intrinsic:
> the balance of forces and the acceptance of its legitimacy. A war without
> an enemy is inconceivable; a peace built on the myth of an enemy is an
> armistice. It is the temptation of war to punish; it is the task of policy to
> construct . . .
>
> The greater the suffering, the more the war will be conceived an end in
> itself and the rules of war applied to the peace settlement. The more total
> the commitment, the more "natural" unlimited claims will appear. Suffer-
> ing leads to self-righteousness more than to humility . . . as if only the
> "innocent" could suffer. Each peace settlement is thus confronted with the
> fate of the enemy and with the more fundamental problem whether the
> experience of war has made it impossible to conceive of a world without
> an enemy . . .
>
> Since absolute security for one power means absolute insecurity for all
> others, it is never obtainable as part of a "legitimate" settlement, and can
> be achieved only through conquest . . .
>
> [In] an international settlement . . . were any one power *totally*
> satisfied, all others would have to be *totally* dissatisfied and a revolu-
> tionary situation would ensue. The foundation of a stable order is the *rela-
> tive* security—and therefore the *relative* insecurity—of its members . . .
>
> If a society legitimizes itself by a principle which claims both universal-
> ity and exclusiveness, if its concept of "justice," in short, does not include
> the existence of different principles of legitimacy, relations between it and
> other societies will come to be based on force.

Like Metternich in his time, Kissinger insisted that he was an intermediary between Israel and Egypt and between Israel and Syria, not a mediator, since being a "mediator" would imply a "commitment to fight" for
the conditions of peace which he would impose. On such semantics,
much can depend, when even a brief, shooting war is essentially just part
of an elaborate game.

Besides regional conflicts and cold-war conflicts, what of direct
conflicts between the world's rich industrial "North" and the tropical
"South"? Some see this growing adversary relationship as the chief ex-
pender of ordnance of the future. Rajni Kothari, professor of world order

studies at Columbia University, has been articulate on this point, seeing the greatest threat to peace in the years to come as stemming from the widening gap between the developed and "developing" economies.

Speaking in London in 1977, Kothari said:

> The fulcrum of world power has begun to shift from the East-West to the North-South axis . . .
>
> We have yet to see the worst of racial, intraregional and interstate tension and warfare in these parts of the world, even in those regions which at present appear to be stable and thriving.

Making his predictions well before the earliest signs of the revolution in Iran, Kothari went on:

> The typical response to tensions and conflicts in these regions—often aided by the machinations of superpowers and multinational enterprises—will be a further growth of authoritarian regimes, military coups and the rise of personal dictatorships. This will produce intermittent political chaos and concomitant economic mismanagement, resulting in a further fall in the quality of life and the standard of living . . . and producing shortages, unemployment, malnutrition and hunger on a mass scale . . .
>
> The response of the North to such developments in the South is likely to be to isolate the world of ghettos, and to leave it to stew in its own juice . . .
>
> The nations of the Third World will be obliged to close ranks . . . and apply collective bargaining pressure, to the extent that the *status quo* powers will allow. As such attempts are frustrated, they will resort to trade-unionism in commodity relationships, individual and collective terrorism in interstate relationships and, eventually, warfare in which fairly sophisticated armaments supplied by the Northern powers and indigenously developed through independent access to new technologies will be used to disrupt the tranquillity of the North and the Northern-dominated world at large. At the economic level, this may lead to a repetition of the trade cycle of recession and unemployment in capitalist economies.

Kothari said the watershed was the massive adjustment of oil prices forced by Iran, Nigeria and Venezuela in 1973 and 1974.

> It gave a boost to the Third World as a whole, despite the fact that the immediate impact on a number of Third World countries created serious shortages and balance-of-payments deficits. In spite of these difficulties, a new sense of power emerged in the Third World leadership, and this has been reflected in their collective thinking and in world fora.

Initially, Kothari suggested, the Third Worlders would try to use their majorities in the UN and other world bodies to secure "reform." Then, lack of oil or other commodity power in most Third World countries to alter effectively the distribution of world resources and power within the inflexible framework of existing institutions would

> make some of these countries lose faith in it and return to the path of confrontation. This they can do by turning to a weapon that can prove even more deadly than oil.
>
> This weapon is nuclear power . . .
>
> And what is true of nuclear proliferation is also true of political terrorism, guerrilla warfare and savage acts of violence and destruction in the heart of Northern metropolitan centers . . .
>
> The response of the North is likely to be at once opportunistic and aimed at maintaining the world *status quo*, though this will not be easy.

Kothari foresaw a "phase of disintegration and anarchy" and of collective Third World nationalism "directed at the Northern bastions of power and technology." He went on:

> A whole new brand of nongovernmental and intergovernmental organizations will emerge which, while no match for their far more numerous, organized and resourceful counterparts in the North, will most likely disrupt the tranquillity in which the Northern organizations function and destroy the institutional and moral support that they are able to draw from the present workings of the United Nations system and other international organizations . . .
>
> In such a world, only a world war can bring order, and that too will be an order from which freedom and the finer human values will have disappeared.

Kothari's preventive cure for all this was more "flexible thinking" by the West, with Europe, he thought, taking the lead.

Some see other solutions, such as barring all weapons deliveries to countries newly developing a nuclear-weapons capacity, and stopping deliveries to those who have built nuclear arms since the Non-Proliferation Treaty was signed. How much would this prevent? U.S. nuclear exclusivity ended the Korean War in 1953, but U.S. nuclear superiority did not prevent the rape of Czechoslovakia or Hungary, nor did it conquer North Vietnam, nor prevent Israel from invading Egypt, Syria and Jordan in 1967 and giving the world the "oil embargo."

Even given the notion that preparation for war is more theater than reality, how much of our expensive and sophisticated armory is there solely to please political constituencies? How much of it is "suitable"? This writer has reasoned that the controversial F-16 was chosen, both for the United States and for Europe, for rational reasons, in competition. But the late General Brown noted that "of course, General Dynamics didn't ever see the game that way. They saw it as an opportunity to reach the pot of gold at the end of the rainbow, which is what has turned out. It is going to be a massive program. However, it didn't start that way.

"When we compete things like the XM-1 tank between two manufacturers, General Motors and Chrysler, that competition is run in such a manner that we try to remove all pressures from special-interest groups. Not that there isn't some—it comes from the manufacturers of the bits and pieces just as much as the engine, just as much as the vehicle itself. But the competition is run in such a way that the results can be audited by anybody who is technically competent to do so; the results of measured performance are there to be seen, because we couldn't stand up against the political pressure on the Hill if we haven't done it in a precise manner. And that is true of all weapons systems."

Be that as it may, there is enough evidence that key political figures and key political coalitions can decide for or against parts of the armory; and on the question of "suitability" in a larger sense, Barry M. Blechman and Stephen S. Kaplan, both then of Brookings, had this to say: "If U.S. military forces are acquired and operated solely to meet the needs of the 'worst case'—the big war—they are likely to be inappropriately configured for the needs of the many crises which occur more frequently. Use as a political instrument is an important function of the armed forces: These operations should have commensurate attention in force planning and deployment decisions."

Actually *planning* and designing a *rattling saber?* Robert C. Gray and Robert J. Bresley, in an article in the *Bulletin of the Atomic Scientists,* have said: "Developing a weapon chiefly as a bargaining chip will allow constituencies to build up around that weapon, constituencies that will press for its development." In short, where there's a bang, there's a buck. Such weapons should be kept at the R & D stage, Gray and Bresley argued, since "once tested, such weapons cease to be bargaining chips; they become part of the arsenal."

Of MARV, for instance—the warhead that takes evasive action if targeted by another missile—arms-limitation negotiator Paul Warnke has said: "The threat of deployment might energize diplomacy but the fact of deployment would defeat it."

General Brown, as noted, emphatically denied that any weapon would be designed solely as a "chip," since this would cost it its value. But when the writer suggested that a weapon's lethal effectiveness was just as significant as a bargaining chip as in war, Brown's rejoinder was "Perhaps more so." The bottom line for a skeptic, it seems, is that our order of battle depends more on our scientists than on our military managers. If the technology to install MIRV-ed long-range strategic missiles in submarines had existed a generation ago, the Titan and probably the Minuteman might never have been built. Titan and Minuteman are part of the triad, still, because they are there. The Russians have developed SLBMs because the United States has them, even though *their* first line of "deterrence" remains land-based ICBMs. Nor should the fear of destabilizing systems be taken to assume that these are taboo. If someone invented a method of lobbing toxic gas shells through the windows of the Kremlin from 8,000 miles away, it would be said—with reason—that such a weapon was destabilizing. But it would be researched and developed, and if it worked, we can be sure that it would be built—and deployed, unless the Soviet Union agreed to forgo, say, particle-beam weapon testing. If something as small and cheap as the cruise missile was perfected which, because of some breakthrough in the release of energy through nuclear fission or fusion, had more power than the Titan warhead, this too would be correctly described as destabilizing, but it would be built—because it was there, and it worked—and deployed unless there was an effective trade-off.

Some weapons—say, a new armor-piercing shell—may well be produced to satisfy purely military requirements. But for many others, the military uses are deduced, and the need for those uses is then described to promote the weapon the designer designed.

In short, the order of battle relates only in part to the requirements of the battlefield. We can no more control our weapons, once we have invented them, and brought them to functioning reality, than we can control the children we create, once they have grown up. Arms limitation is a pious and praiseworthy hope, and a possible source of economy, but it is largely whistling in the dark. The superpower peace is not based on disarmament, but on armament. We must reasonably assume that man will build greater and greater weapons, and that although this means that war, if it comes, will be worse than ever before, it also means that superpower war is less likely. In any event, we would seem to have no way of withdrawing from the game of weapons.

The permanent existence of weapons implies the permanent existence of personnel to wield them—you and I. So, by the same token, did Congress abolish the draft to be more militarily effective, to have more "professional" armed forces or to answer another political constituency, the broadest one—to be politically popular? Certainly, it was not to save money, since "regulars" are better-paid than conscripts and gain more salary-raising promotions. Says Senator Culver: "We are concerned about the manpower costs [of the all-volunteer armed forces] because 60 cents out of every [defense] dollar is spent on manpower . . . In the future, the pool of eligible eighteen-year-olds will be substantially reduced; there will be more intense competition from the private sector for those people; and we will need people with higher skills, given the incredible sophistication of the modern military force and the weapons systems. But things are going along really quite well, better than many people expected, though there are critical exceptions, such as the National Guard and Reserve problems."

Hence the talk of a "partial draft" for these reserves. Is this practical? Says Dr. Curtis W. Tarr, a former director of the selective service system who is now a vice-president of Deere and Company: "It is hard to envision the Congress taking action only to bring the reserve forces up to strength." General Maxwell D. Taylor, a former chairman of the Joint Chiefs, has pointed out that "in a public discussion of the all-volunteer force, we do not distinguish between the requirements for a satisfactory or an adequate peacetime force and one that can fight a war. Nearly every one of the good points made about the all-volunteer force applies essentially to the peacetime army. The requirement of our armed forces for trained replacements to conduct sustained operations for an indefinite period simply cannot be met. They are not being met today for the Reserves." Is a force inadequate for war a good peacetime "deterrent"?

Some of these problems or possible errors in the order of battle and even in how we create our armed forces stem from the peculiar way in which our armed forces are managed. Top management is vested in the Joint Chiefs of Staff. Senator Culver has observed on this point: "If the Congress perceives shortcomings in the work of the Chiefs, it is perhaps because their present organizational structure forces them to wear two hats simultaneously. They must advise the President, provide unfettered military advice on defense and security questions to Congress and, at the same time, be advocates for their respective services.

"One consequence of this is that it often results in the various services preparing 'wish lists' and papering over differences. And in order to achieve a watered-down consensus, there must be log-rolling and back-scratching, which result in unrealistic fiscal and budgetary considerations."

General Brown felt the chairman's job was just too overloaded: "There are only twenty-four hours in the day, and this administration [Carter's] requires the presence of the chairman about six to eight times a week for two or more hours in the White House at a meeting of the NSC, or the subcommittee structure thereof. In addition, there are chiefs' meetings, policy council meetings within the Defense Department, NATO meetings, meetings with the Spanish and the Koreans, and so forth. If we add all of the congressional hearings, the poor fellow just meets himself coming and going."

Culver points up another problem: "Our communications have reached such a degree of sophistication and reliability on a global basis that civilian policymakers can get too intimately involved in the actual operation on the ground, and in a way usurp the appropriate function of the field commander, or the one most immediate to the crisis. That can introduce confusion and complication. Besides having no control, there is also the other side—too much control."

This applies even to the peacetime, nonwar, "diplomatic" use of forces. Brown, agreeing with Culver, cited a case in point, during the tree-cutting incident with the North Koreans at Panmunjom: "The then acting Secretary of Defense wasn't satisfied to talk to our commander in Korea. He wanted to talk to the fellow who was handling the rescue. And we had to remind him that he had agreed to the worldwide military command control system, whereby we would only provide communication to the task force commander, not to an individual fellow on a ship or in an airplane or holding a weapon on the ground, even though we have the communications to do that today."

If there are critical problems in the way we create U.S. defenses, what of the way in which the United States contributes to the defense of others? Congressman Lee Hamilton has said that "arms sales have represented a disproportionate part of our total foreign-policy effort, to the detriment of our economic, developmental, political and diplomatic efforts." As this book has shown, arms sales are usually conducted without serious thought of war—to procure political influence and "control" conflictual situations, to outbid the Communists, help the balance of payments, give employment in the constituencies of key political figures, cut unit costs to U.S. forces, save taxpayers' money, or simply to convert the stockpile of obsolescence into equity. Many sales defeat their purpose. As a report by the UN Association of Iowa has put it: "When arms serve the end of dollars and not defense, security has ceased to be the objective." Arms sales to pre-1974 Greece and pre-1979 Iran helped unpopular regimes and made the United States ultimately *less* influential in those countries. Unlike Moscow, the West has no forward-looking policy, destined to buy influence tomorrow—such as supplying arms to southern African guerrillas. We tend to support or tolerate status quos that are not hostile, and go down the tube with them.

Carter's much-quoted campaign statement was that "we cannot be the world's leading champion of peace and the world's leading supplier of weapons of war." Leaving aside the contestable claim to be more committed to peace than, say, Sweden, it is at least curious that no reporter asked Mr. Carter: "Why not?" Today, the President presumably still puts the United States at the top of both leagues, so has had to ask the question "Why not?" of himself.

Leslie H. Gelb, in an article in *Foreign Policy* shortly before he went from the New York *Times* to the State Department, noted the dichotomy between Congress' call for more military self-reliance by friendly countries and congressional opposition to arms sales. The dichotomy is not necessarily dishonest, for there is a genuine dilemma. Is it safer to be the world's policeman, or—Nixon Doctrine fashion—arm others to the teeth to do the job? A Pax Romana or a Pax Britannica worked, in their time, up to a point, but would a Pax Universalis work? This is the basket into which we seem to be putting more and more of our eggs, especially since the Kissinger era. As Gelb puts it, Kissinger was "too preoccupied with *his* purposes in selling rather than in *their* purposes in buying." Should any country, other than a treaty ally, be provided with sufficient weapons to enable it to take independent action beyond its borders without U.S. support? The question is moot in the case of Israel, and the war of 1967 was the result, but what of Iran and South Korea? Before Iran "fell," a senior NSC staffer told the writer: "If you supply a plane which cannot be maintained without U.S. support, then the purchaser cannot really use it without U.S. approval." By this argument, the exuberant sales to the Shah were good, even in retrospect, since American corporations got cash on the barrelhead, petrodollars were recycled and the uncertain regime which has replaced the Shah now has hangars-full of unflyable planes—some of which may now be repurchased, at secondhand prices, by the U. S. Navy.

The Nixon Doctrine did not embrace a purely "Fortress America" concept. Sometimes foreign base rights for U.S. forces have been a rationale for security aid; but—as Gelb has also noticed—the main base-rights countries now place so many restrictions on American use that the whole policy of bases for aid could be usefully reviewed, beginning perhaps with Spain.

But some of Gelb's arguments for restraint lie on sandy soil. He believes that the United States should try to avoid being the sole supplier of any country: "We can say that if France and Great Britain won't provide spare parts and ammunition for their tanks and artillery, we won't for our aircraft." This is a dubious point, for our sales partners are also, and especially, our sales competitors. Bilateral restraints with the Soviet Union would mean that we would have to share similar goals—for instance in southern Africa, the next obvious hot spot, Korea or the Middle

East. This is not an unthinkable concept, but it is not yet the case. Where Gelb is more convincing is where he says, in his article: "While generalizations are tricky, the United States seems to have gotten better leverage from denials or threats to deny sales than by completing sales." This, surely, is part of our human and animal nature: You train a circus dog to jump through a hoop by half starving him until he does.

The hardest "training" to impress on arms clients concerns how they use the arms they acquire. Clients have an uncanny knack of feeling that what they have bought is theirs. As Professor Lincoln Broomfield told the Senate foreign-assistance subcommittee in 1976: "I would have thought one of the overwhelming lessons of three decades of foreign assistance is the absurdity of taking seriously the language contained in the articles of agreement concerning end-use."

Given the general consensus that the Third World, which can afford sophisticated arms the least, is the area most likely to use them, can the arms trade be restrained? President Johnson offered to publicize arms transfers from the United States, and in 1967 he proposed that all powers shipping arms to the Middle East report them to the UN. Recipient countries objected: Since they had little or no production capacity in most cases, and therefore depended almost entirely on arms imports, their entire inventories, they complained, would become known. Earlier still, Thayer had noted:

> A vote in the UN limiting the trade in even the slightest degree would probably show no more than ten nations in favor, at least half of which would be arms-producing nations.

Yet certainly there is an economic argument for doing so. The earlier-mentioned report of the UN Association of Iowa noted that "a person of good educational background trains three years to be an aircraft mechanic at a cost of about $50,000. A single aircraft requires four men for operational maintenance, six men for overhaul and an organization of fifty men for the shop work. Lifetime program costs for such a fighter aircraft may total four times the purchase costs." In addition, as noted earlier, spare parts may equal the cost of the plane over ten or fifteen years.

Such expensive considerations now apply to genuinely poor countries. In their book, Stanley and Pearton wrote:

> It cannot be long before there is a general realization that participation in the arms trade can enable pygmies to conduct power politics as well as giants.

The pygmies naturally welcome this.

Contrary to Jimmy Carter's apparent puzzlement, America is the largest purveyor of lethal instruments partly *because* of its aversion to war and its ambiguous attitude toward its own military. In an article in *Inquiry* magazine, Earl Ravenal has said:

> Beating up on the military . . . serves no useful or honest purpose; in discerning "threats" and asking for resources, they are just doing what we pay them to do. If we want to make large savings . . . we must devise some real alternatives.

The "Fortress America" solution of Ravenal and others would presumably imply *maintaining* the present high level of arms sales to friends and perhaps even *increasing* them—the Nixon Doctrine. Another concomitant of Ravenal's position would be giving up U.S. bases overseas: There are about 250 in all, including 131 serving the Seventh Army and the Seventeenth Air Force in Germany. Some of them, as Gelb implies, probably could be usefully abandoned. Drew Middleton, who is no dove, has argued that Guantánamo in Cuba and the seven Army, three Navy and two Air Force bases in Panama may be counterproductive irritants, while some others—Middleton mentions the Navy's air station at St. George's in Bermuda—are redundant. (He, of course, means: in time of peace.) Even the usefulness of Lajes in the Azores in the resupply of Israel in 1973 has been superseded by new refueling techniques: Israel could now be supplied from the United States direct. Any bases given up would revert to the friendly countries in which they exist, presumably with gifts of equipment and promises of further supplies—more Nixon Doctrine. Would this endanger regional peace?

Admiral T. H. Moorer, when he was chairman of the Joint Chiefs, suggested that the United States should actually create one new major base overseas—in the Middle East. In recent years, this has been quietly urged by Tel Aviv, although Premier Begin once again told an American TV audience in March 1979 that he did not want American soldiers "fighting for Israel." Secretary Brown raised the possibility of a base in Saudi Arabia while visiting that country in 1979, but was apparently turned down. Further U.S. base involvement in foreign countries was, of course, the very development which exuberant arms sales to Iran and other countries were meant to prevent.

Thus, criticizing friendly countries for buying American arms is deceptive, even counterproductive. Stephen S. Rosenfeld, in a 1979 column in the *Post*, said:

> If you want to slow the arms race, you can't expect to get far by shaming people, by saying that they are blind or craven or that their motives for arming are unworthy. Rather, you must provide alternative ways for

helping them protect the legitimate things, their independence or security, for which they armed in the first place. Good diplomacy—the easing of tensions or the settlement of disputes or the solution of grievances—is the best arms-control policy.

Engelbrecht and Hanighen said much the same thing half a century ago:

> The arms industry is plainly a perfectly natural product of our present civilization. More than that, it is an essential element in the chaos and anarchy which characterize our international politics. To eliminate it requires the creation of a world which can get along without war by settling its differences by peaceful means.

There has been some progress. Although some governments today occasionally "push" arms, private dealers now only respond to demand, and that is certainly an asset. The notion of a Zaharoff would be more terrifying today than seventy years ago. Says Dr. Colin S. Gray of the Canadian Institute of International Affairs: "The arms trade is flourishing not because of the nefarious influence of any latter-day merchants of death, but because the use of force is an ever-present reality in the current international system."

Should the West not respond at all to the sometimes spectacular arms transfers carried out by the Russians—for instance, in Ethiopia? This is not meant to be a rhetorical question—maybe we should *not* respond— but clearly the issue is one which justifiably troubles our policymakers. General Brown told the writer:

> The Russians have arms for export on stockpile, apparently, because when they consummate an arrangement, we see deliveries start within weeks, if not days; ours start within years.
>
> We don't have a stockpile from which to draw; neither do the Brits or the French. For the most part, it means orders to manufacturers and you wait the manufacture time.

Brown went on:

> Our government—and this may sound strange because of the recent attention to arms sales in the press, and therefore the public—has not taken an initiative in arms sales in many years, with minor exceptions, for NATO mainly; and there, mostly because we thought we had something in AWACS that gave a capability which would permit NATO to handle a very severe threat, and we know of no other way to handle it—that is, to get early warning and control of low-level attack. And so it was in our interest not only for our own forces over there, but we felt it contributed to the whole alliance.
>
> But we didn't initiate what became the demand for the F-16. It was

NATO and the member-nations in Europe who felt a need to modernize the fighter force, principally to replace the F-104, which was getting obsolete, with a new aircraft . . .

But we didn't go out to sell the F-16. Now, I'm not saying that General Dynamics wouldn't fly across the ocean to try to sell it or any other product that they could get a license to sell, because it's a straight economic venture. But as far as the government goes, we have not pushed arms since Henry Kuss left upstairs.

In short, U.S. arms sales are a genuine response to demand, even if that is not always true of arms sales by our friends, and we impose more restrictions on sales than other Western countries. But arms sales restrictions are often casuistic. Iran was refused the F-18L because it was different from the naval F-18 and would mean selling a Third World country a system not procured by the U.S. forces. But the F-18L is only an adaptation of the F-18, which Iran could have shared with the U. S. Navy if it had wanted. Would the Shah have been refused F-14s if he had wanted their carrier landing gear replaced by something more suitable for a country without carriers? Are human-rights restrictions on sales only applied to "poor" countries? Are they imposed where France, Britain etc. will replace U.S. sales, but not where the client may turn to Moscow? In what way do U.S. human-rights restrictions on sales restrict the offender's armory? Is the Carter administration's whole sales-restraint policy based on the knowledge that Western Europe and Israel are now engaged in the opposite direction—expanding sales enormously?

These questions imply more cynicism than the author intends; but there is clearly less in Jimmy Carter's arms-restraint policies than meets the eye. Few would doubt Carter's sincerity in wishing to have an impact on the dizzy escalation of overkill weaponry around the world. But a popular saw has it that "the trouble with the rat race is that the rats always win"; the same principle apparently applies to the arms race also.

The Oversimplification Problem

Much about "defense" is misunderstood by the general public because it is not what it seems, and much is even more misunderstood because it is not always very well reported. The press oversimplifies defense issues —coverage of the B-1 affair is a good example. William Beecher of the Boston *Globe*, who was formerly in the Defense Department, and Richard Burt of the *Times*, who was with the International Institute of Strategic Studies, are notably better than their daily-newspaper colleagues. But most defense reporters lack a real military background and compare poorly to, say, their colleagues at *Aviation Week*. The press is especially inadequate at covering wars and military strategy, and therefore rarely comprehends a weapons system clearly.

As Peter Braestrup's monumental book *Big Story* shows, the Viet Cong Tet offensive of 1968 was mistaken for a "Cong" victory by most correspondents in Vietnam at the time. In *Army* magazine, Colonel William V. Kennedy has made some telling comparisons between the professional reporting of Hanson W. Baldwin and Braestrup for the *Times* and Margueritte Higgins for the New York *Herald-Tribune*, on the one hand, and the Vietnam dispatches of an inspired generalist, Braestrup's colleague David Halberstam. Says Kennedy:

> Long ago it became obvious that the idea of the universally knowledgeable "general assignment reporter" simply would not work. In one field after another, the press was forced by public criticism and direct economic pressure to accept the idea of specialization.

In the field of the Game of Weapons, most defense reporters seem to lack a synoptic vision of the Game itself. One reason why defense correspondents lack such a synoptic view of defense affairs is that they spend virtually all their time in Washington. They lack a conception not only of how most weapons systems work in practice, but also of the military life, which has changed in many ways since most of them were in uniform. Soldiering, as General Brown pointed out in one of his last conversations, is considerably more organized—"bureaucratic"—than in World War Two and Korea, but young officers and technical noncommissioned officers are considerably more professional and knowledgeable. They handle much more complex equipment. In short, our cartoon- and "M°A°S°H"-induced image of the military is outdated and unsophisticated.

Brown noted one day that eight F-15s had just flown from Langley Field to Hawaii nonstop, then on to Korea for an exercise, then returned without incident. It had not even been mentioned in the papers, because the press took it for granted that eight single-place aircraft could be flown over those immense ocean distances, refueling in flight. This is far from the world of "Hogan's Heroes" or even *The Longest Day*. Brown's point was that major air forces today are no longer made up of swashbucklers of varied intelligence, but of highly capable, technical minds. These minds in turn "impact" on the Game because they understand which weapons system is a bishop and which a knight better than the politicians and most of the congressional aides. We are misunderstanding the Game if we think of modern generals as being cut from the same cloth as the officers in *From Here to Eternity*.

Are we better than the Russians in that regard? Brown could speak only for the Air Force, the most technical branch of the armed forces:

> I would say if we have an advantage—and I think we do—it is in the initiative, the ingenuity of individual air crew. You know, we never see the Soviets sending a flight of four off to do something on their own—they are constantly under ground control. I don't think any Communist air force would send four off to do a job and expect them to come home. And I think it is significant that our Air Force, since World War Two, has never fought under its own radar control. In Korea, we were up north under his radar. In Vietnam, we were under his radar. I don't think an allied air force has flown and fought under its own radar control since the Battle of Britain, and that was a tremendous advantage then—to have somebody tell you where the other fellow is, what vector he is on, what height. And we haven't had that. We have had to rely on our own integral weapon system to do the job—on the initiative and ingenuity of our people.

We could dismiss this as the armchair conversation of an old soldier in the late evening of his warrior life. But it goes to the heart of the enigma —our weapons are immeasurably "better" than ever before because of the minds that created them, the minds of the soldiers, sailors and airmen who give meaning to them as "deterrents" by operating their complexities, and the minds and computers which govern, say, the ultrasophisticated balance of terror which we call "détente," or, perhaps, "peace in the Middle East." Because the United States does not govern the "world," as Alexander or Caesar did, it cannot change the rules of the Game of Weapons, and is at the mercy of its arms clients and of the arms themselves, which American minds often designed. The Soviet Union suffers slightly different, but ultimately similar, inhibitions to those of America. The Game of Weapons is not just military, not just economic, not just political and diplomatic. The role of weapons in politics has been inherent in our human political system since the days when our remote ancestors were nomadic, pillaging warlords. We have come to rely on the weapon almost as we rely on air and water, sex or friendship. We remain rooted in the implications of our assumption that survival stems from strength. The only way we know to preserve the peace is by threatening war. In a world of over 150 ambitious nations, we have become the ultimate contradiction, which Jimmy Carter thought, in his campaign days, was impossible because it was contradictory: Not just Americans, but all of us—Russians, French, British, Israelis, Germans and lesser military nations—are the warlords of a sort of peace. This is a difficult age in which to be a diplomat or a politician, and a hell of a time to be a soldier.

Index

THE
CULTURE OF
NARCISSISM

BY CHRISTOPHER LASCH

'Never has the case against narcissism been made with such an all-embracing sweep'
NEWSWEEK

Freedom from religious superstition has left a gap in our lives which has been replaced by the creed of self-love, maintains Christopher Lasch. Emotional shallowness, fear of intimacy, hypochondria, pseudo-self-insight, promiscuous pansexuality and dread of old age and death are the symptoms of the narcissist whose culture has lost interest in the future. The frantic search for fulfilment – in the new consciousness movements and therapeutic culture; in pseudo-confessional autobiographies; in the replacement of Horatio Alger by the 'Happy Hooker' as the new symbol of success – is the world of the resigned. THE CULTURE OF NARCISSISM points the way to a world where new politics, new discipline and new love are the only hope for a society moving helter-skelter towards total self-absorption.

SOCIOLOGY/PSYCHOLOGY   0 349 12165 6   £1.75

GOOD WORK

BY E. F. SCHUMACHER

WHAT IS THE PURPOSE OF OUR WORK?

When Dr Schumacher took a look at the plight of businesses today and said 'small is beautiful' he spoke to millions and coined a phrase. In GOOD WORK he addresses a question which is central to most of us and one which is all too often ignored by the economic structure of the Western world. Dr Schumacher maintains that the purpose of man's work is threefold: to produce necessary, useful goods and services; to enable us to use and perfect our gifts and skills and, finally, to serve and collaborate with other people in order to liberate ourselves from inbuilt egocentricity. A job in which one finds no personal satisfaction destroys the soul. With sanity and sensitivity the late E. F. Schumacher offers important and thought-provoking alternatives which point the way to mankind's physical and mental liberation.

'Compulsive reading'
TIME OUT

'The message of this set of essays is beguiling; technology is not the inevitable ruler and real alternatives seem possible'
NEW SCIENTIST

ECONOMICS 0 349 13133 3 £1.95

and don't miss
SMALL IS BEAUTIFUL
A GUIDE FOR THE PERPLEXED
also by E. F. Schumacher in Abacus

ALIEN INTELLIGENCE

BY STUART HOLROYD
(Illustrated)

IS THERE ALIEN LIFE ON EARTH?

Bestselling author Stuart Holroyd begins his examination of alternative intelligence with some of its earthly manifestations – the whales, dolphins and chimpanzees who are all capable of abstract thought.

He analyses ESP, ectoplasmic phenomena, out-of-the-body experiences, and the possibilities of alien mind-control, and comes to the startling conclusion that the mind has an independent and immortal psychic existence.

He investigates the claims to intelligence of artificial minds and thinking machines, together with the archetypes of myth and pre-history that hold the clue to alien visitations. These staggering revelations invite the reader to share the author's compelling belief that there is alien life on earth.

COSMOLOGY   0 349 11709 8   £2.50

THE LEAN YEARS

BY RICHARD BARNET

THE LEAN YEARS is the first book to take an overall look at the world's resources – how much we have got, where they are, and who controls them. Richard Barnet, the distinguished economic and political analyst, unravels the scarcity puzzle, exploring the politics of the 'petroleum economy', revealing the role of the giant oil companies and evaluating the energy alternatives to OPEC oil. He examines the changing face of global power and the struggle for food, water and mineral resources which we can expect in the coming lean years, and reports on the role of the multinational corporations in the world employment crisis. In addition, he discusses the politics of a world in transition, the consequences of the growing industrialisation of labour worldwide, and the absurdities of scarcity in a world of plenty. And, finally, he offers positive proposals for reorganising global resource systems to meet the needs of Earth's burgeoning population.

CONSERVATION/ECONOMICS   0 349 10238 4   £2.50

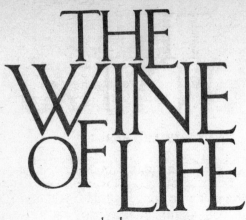

THE WINE OF LIFE

and other essays on
SOCIETIES, ENERGY
& LIVING THINGS

HAROLD J. MOROWITZ

'...a delight to read' CARL SAGAN

Dr Harold J. Morowitz, a distinguished professor of Molecular
Biophysics at Yale University, offers a delightful blend of scientific fact and literary fancy in this collection of essays which has
already been hailed as a contemporary classic. Filled with infectious curiosity and unpretentious wisdom, THE WINE OF
LIFE is the most lively, lucid work of scientific commentary to
appear since Lewis Thomas's LIVES OF A CELL.

'Dr Morowitz' pieces on scientific exposition are some of the
wisest, wittiest, and best informed that I have read . . . I was
deeply impressed' *C. P. Snow*

'A zest for life in general and the scientific life in particular, a
wry slant on human foibles, and a sense of moral purpose flavour
these short essays . . . these are the expressions of a thoughtful,
intelligent man willing to take a stand on important issues'
Kirkus Reviews

SCIENCE   0 349 12386 1   £1.95

PATRICK MARNHAM

DISPATCHES FROM AFRICA

'We fear Africa because when we leave it alone, it works,' says the author of this provocative book. Patrick Marnham shows how outsiders – British, Russian, American, French and Chinese – have repeatedly tried to alter a land they do not understand. The relief workers, scientists, businessmen, tourists and conservationists all roam through Africa wreaking havoc as they go, attempting to mould the continent into their numerous images and ideals. Here are the elephants of Kenya and their predators, the game wardens; the West African outposts and their swollen populations of refugees; the tourists of Africa, who come to enjoy the 'primitive life' by observing a tribe which is desperately trying to flee from them; the citizens of Bamako, building their houses at night only to watch them being bulldozed the next morning; and Gambia, a country of eight barristers and no psychiatrists, where the British Ambassador's grant ignored the inadequate hospitals and instead equipped a new cricket team.

DISPATCHES FROM AFRICA reveals a country beset by illogical boundaries, horribly mismanaged financial aid and comically incompetent government structures. But the true brilliance of the book is its ability to allow still another Africa to seep through. The Africa of powerful ideas and raw energy which, for reasons of politics and ignorance, have gone awry. This Africa is a land of Northern ineptitude superimposed on an inherent native harmony.

'This shrewd, acrid book is an excellent antidote to the usual guff written on Africa' *Sunday Telegraph*

WORLD AFFAIRS   0 349 12280 6   £1.95

WOMEN: PSYCHOLOGY'S PUZZLE

JOANNA BUNKER ROHRBAUGH

WOMEN: PSYCHOLOGY'S PUZZLE is the first attempt to assess the scientific basis of the feminist challenge to male psychology's perception of women.

Avoiding both over-simplification and the polemics frequently found in popular writing on this emotive subject, psychologist Joanna Bunker Rohrbaugh considers whether there is any essential or inherent biological reason why female behaviour or personalities should differ from male.

Clearly distinguishing established fact from popular speculation, Dr Rohrbaugh examines the prevailing myths about female psychology and shows how such myths distort the reality of women's everyday lives. She explores new areas of female experience, previously ignored because they didn't fit the traditional image of 'femininity', including female sexuality, unmarried singles, female workers and women as members of minority groups. Finally, Dr Rohrbaugh looks at the implications of being female in a world where stereotypes determine the place of women in society.

PSYCHOLOGY/NON-FICTION   0 349 12943 6   £2.95

JUST SOME OF THE TITLES ON THE ABACUS LIST: